# Lecture Notes in Computer Science 13371

More information about this series at https://link.springer.com/bookseries/558

Sharon Shoham · Yakir Vizel (Eds.)

# Computer Aided Verification

## 34th International Conference, CAV 2022
## Haifa, Israel, August 7–10, 2022
## Proceedings, Part I

*Editors*
Sharon Shoham
Tel Aviv University
Tel Aviv, Israel

Yakir Vizel
Technion – Israel Institute of Technology
Haifa, Israel

ISSN 0302-9743 ISSN 1611-3349 (electronic)
Lecture Notes in Computer Science
ISBN 978-3-031-13184-4 ISBN 978-3-031-13185-1 (eBook)
https://doi.org/10.1007/978-3-031-13185-1



This Springer imprint is published by the registered company Springer Nature Switzerland AG
The registered company address is: Gewerbestrasse 11, 6330 Cham, Switzerland

# Preface

It was our privilege to serve as the program chairs for CAV 2022, the 34th International Conference on Computer-Aided Verification. CAV 2022 was held during August 7–10, 2022. CAV-affiliated workshops were held on July 31 to August 1 and August 11 to August 12. This year, CAV was held as part of the Federated Logic Conference (FLoC) and was collocated with many other conferences in software/hardware verification and logic for computer science. Due to the easing of COVID-19 travel restrictions, CAV 2022 and the rest of the FLoC were in-person events.

CAV is an annual conference dedicated to the advancement of the theory and practice of computer-aided formal analysis methods for hardware and software systems. The primary focus of CAV is to extend the frontiers of verification techniques by expanding to new domains such as security, quantum computing, and machine learning. This puts CAV at the cutting edge of formal methods research, and this year's program is a reflection of this commitment.

CAV 2022 received a high number of submissions (209). We accepted nine tool papers, two case studies, and 40 regular papers, which amounts to an acceptance rate of roughly 24%. The accepted papers cover a wide spectrum of topics, from theoretical results to applications of formal methods. These papers apply or extend formal methods to a wide range of domains such as smart contracts, concurrency, machine learning, probabilistic techniques, and industrially deployed systems. The program featured a keynote talk by Ziyad Hanna (Cadence Design Systems and University of Oxford), a plenary talk by Aarti Gupta (Princeton University), and invited talks by Arie Gurfinkel (University of Waterloo) and Neha Rungta (Amazon Web Services). Furthermore, we continued the tradition of Logic Lounge, a series of discussions on computer science topics targeting a general audience. In addition to all talks at CAV, the attendees got access to talks at other conferences held as part of FLoC.

In addition to the main conference, CAV 2022 hosted the following workshops: Formal Methods for ML-Enabled Autonomous Systems (FoMLAS), On the Not So Unusual Effectiveness of Logic, Formal Methods Education Online, Democratizing Software Verification (DSV), Verification of Probabilistic Programs (VeriProP), Program Equivalence and Relational Reasoning (PERR), Parallel and Distributed Automated Reasoning, Numerical Software Verification (NSV-XV), Formal Reasoning in Distributed Algorithms (FRIDA), Formal Methods for Blockchains (FMBC), Synthesis (Synt), and Workshop on Open Problems in Learning and Verification of Neural Networks (WOLVERINE).

Organizing a flagship conference like CAV requires a great deal of effort from the community. The Program Committee (PC) for CAV 2022 consisted of 86 members – a committee of this size ensures that each member has a reasonable number of papers to review in the allotted time. In all, the committee members wrote over 800 reviews while investing significant effort to maintain and ensure the high quality of the conference program. We are grateful to the CAV 2022 PC for their outstanding efforts in evaluating the submissions and making sure that each paper got a fair chance. Like recent years in

CAV, we made the artifact evaluation mandatory for tool paper submissions and optional but encouraged for the rest of the accepted papers. The Artifact Evaluation Committee consisted of 79 reviewers who put in significant effort to evaluate each artifact. The goal of this process was to provide constructive feedback to tool developers and help make the research published in CAV more reproducible. The Artifact Evaluation Committee was generally quite impressed by the quality of the artifacts. Among the accepted regular papers, 77% of the authors submitted an artifact, and 58% of these artifacts passed the evaluation. We are very grateful to the Artifact Evaluation Committee for their hard work and dedication in evaluating the submitted artifacts.

CAV 2022 would not have been possible without the tremendous help we received from several individuals, and we would like to thank everyone who helped make CAV 2022 a success. First, we would like to thank Maria A Schett and Daniel Dietsch for chairing the Artifact Evaluation Committee and Hari Govind V K for putting together the proceedings. We also thank Grigory Fedyukovich for chairing the workshop organization and Shachar Itzhaky for managing publicity. We would like to thank the FLoC organizing committee for organizing the Logic Lounge, Mentoring workshop, and arranging student volunteers. We also thank Hana Chockler for handling sponsorship for all conferences in FLoC. We would also like to thank FLoC chair Alexandra Silva and co-chairs Orna Grumberg and Eran Yahav for the support provided. Last but not least, we would like to thank members of the CAV Steering Committee (Aarti Gupta, Daniel Kroening, Kenneth McMillan, and Orna Grumberg) for helping us with several important aspects of organizing CAV 2022.

We hope that you will find the proceedings of CAV 2022 scientifically interesting and thought-provoking!

June 2022

Sharon Shoham
Yakir Vizel

# Organization

## Steering Committee

| | |
|---|---|
| Aarti Gupta | Princeton University, USA |
| Daniel Kroening | Amazon, USA |
| Kenneth McMillan | University of Texas at Austin, USA |
| Orna Grumberg | Technion, Israel |

## Conference Co-chairs

| | |
|---|---|
| Sharon Shoham | Tel Aviv University, Israel |
| Yakir Vizel | Technion, Israel |

## Artifact Evaluation Co-chairs

| | |
|---|---|
| Maria A. Schett | University College London, UK |
| Daniel Dietsch | University of Freiburg, Germany |

## Publicity Chair

| | |
|---|---|
| Shachar Itzhaky | Technion, Israel |

## Workshop Chair

| | |
|---|---|
| Grigory Fedyukovich | Florida State University, USA |

## Proceedings and Talks Chair

| | |
|---|---|
| Hari Govind V. K. | University of Waterloo, Canada |

## Program Committee

| | |
|---|---|
| Aina Niemetz | Stanford, USA |
| Alastair Donaldson | Imperial College London, UK |
| Alessandro Cimatti | FBK, Italy |
| Alexander Ivrii | IBM, Israel |
| Alexander J. Summers | University of British Columbia, Canada |
| Alexander Nadel | Intel, Israel |
| Alexandra Silva | Cornell University, USA |

| | |
|---|---|
| Ana Sokolova | University of Salzburg, Austria |
| Anastasia Mavridou | KBR Inc., NASA Ames Research Center, USA |
| Andreas Podelski | University of Freiburg, Germany |
| Andrei Popescu | University of Sheffield, UK |
| Andrey Rybalchenko | Microsoft Research, UK |
| Anna Lukina | TU Delft, The Netherlands |
| Anna Slobodova | Intel, USA |
| Antoine Miné | Sorbonne Université, France |
| Armin Biere | University of Freiburg, Germany |
| Azalea Raad | Imperial College London, UK |
| Bor-Yuh Evan Chang | University of Colorado Boulder and Amazon, USA |
| Caterina Urban | INRIA, France |
| Corina Pasareanu | CMU/NASA Ames Research Center, USA |
| Dana Drachsler Cohen | Technion, Israel |
| Daniel Kroening | Amazon, USA |
| David Jansen | Institute of Software, Chinese Academy of Sciences, China |
| Deepak D'Souza | Indian Institute of Science, India |
| Dejan Jovanović | Amazon Web Services, USA |
| Derek Dreyer | MPI-SWS, Germany |
| Elizabeth Polgreen | University of Edinburgh, UK |
| Elvira Albert | Complutense University of Madrid, Spain |
| Erika Abraham | RWTH Aachen University, Germany |
| Grigory Fedyukovich | Florida State University, USA |
| Guy Avni | University of Haifa, Israel |
| Guy Katz | Hebrew University of Jerusalem, Israel |
| Hadar Frenkel | CISPA, Germany |
| Hillel Kugler | Bar Ilan University, Israel |
| Hiroshi Unno | University of Tsukuba, Japan |
| Isabel Garcia-Contreras | University of Waterloo, Canada |
| Ivana Cerna | Masaryk University, Czech Republic |
| Jade Alglave | University College London and Arm, UK |
| Jean-Baptiste Jeannin | University of Michigan, USA |
| Joost-Pieter Katoen | RWTH Aachen University, Germany |
| Josh Berdine | Meta, UK |
| Joxan Jaffar | National University of Singapore, Singapore |
| Kenneth L. McMillan | University of Texas at Austin, USA |
| Klaus V. Gleissenthall | Vrije Universiteit Amsterdam, The Netherlands |
| Konstantin Korovin | University of Manchester, UK |
| Krishna Shankaranarayanan | IIT Bombay, India |
| Kuldeep Meel | National University of Singapore, Singapore |

| | |
|---|---|
| Laura Titolo | NIA/NASA LaRC, USA |
| Liana Hadarean | Amazon Web Services, USA |
| Marieke Huisman | University of Twente, The Netherlands |
| Marijana Lazić | TU Munich, Germany |
| Marijn J. H. Heule | CMU, USA |
| Markus Rabe | Google, USA |
| Martina Seidl | Johannes Kepler University Linz, Austria |
| Mingsheng Ying | Chinese Academy of Sciences and Tsinghua University, China |
| Miriam García Soto | IST Austria, Austria |
| Natasha Sharygina | University of Lugano, Switzerland |
| Nikolaj Bjørner | Microsoft Research, USA |
| Nir Piterman | University of Gothenburg, Sweden |
| Oded Padon | VMware Research, USA |
| Parasara Sridhar Duggirala | UNC Chapel Hill, USA |
| Parosh Aziz Abdulla | Uppsala University, Sweden |
| Pavithra Prabhakar | Kansas State University, USA |
| Philippa Gardner | Imperial College London, UK |
| Pierre Ganty | IMDEA Software Institute, Spain |
| Rajeev Joshi | Amazon, USA |
| Rayna Dimitrova | CISPA, Germany |
| Roderick Bloem | Graz University of Technology, Austria |
| Ruben Martins | CMU, USA |
| Rupak Majumdar | MPI-SWS, Germany |
| Ruzica Piskac | Yale University, USA |
| Sébastien Bardin | CEA List, Université Paris-Saclay, France |
| Shuvendu Lahiri | Microsoft Research, USA |
| Sorav Bansal | IIT Delhi and CompilerAI Labs, India |
| Subodh Sharma | IIT Delhi, India |
| Supratik Chakraborty | IIT Bombay, India |
| Swarat Chaudhuri | UT Austin, USA |
| Swen Jacobs | CISPA, Germany |
| Taylor T. Johnson | Vanderbilt University, USA |
| Temesghen Kahsai | Amazon, USA |
| Wei-Ngan Chin | National University of Singapore, Singapore |
| Xavier Rival | INRIA Paris/ENS/PSL, France |
| Xujie Si | McGill University, Canada |
| Yang Liu | Nanyang Technological University, Singapore |
| Yu-Fang Chen | Institute of Information Science, Academia Sinica, Taiwan |
| Yuxin Deng | East China Normal University, China |

## Artifact Evaluation Committee

| | |
|---|---|
| Guy Amir | Hebrew University of Jerusalem, Israel |
| Muqsit Azeem | Technical University of Munich, Germany |
| Kshitij Bansal | Meta, USA |
| Tianshu Bao | Vanderbilt University, USA |
| Fabian Bauer-Marquart | University of Konstanz, Germany |
| Anna Becchi | Fondazione Bruno Kessler, Italy |
| Ranadeep Biswas | Informal Systems, France |
| Christopher Brix | RWTH Aachen University, Germany |
| Marek Chalupa | IST Austria, Austria |
| Kevin Cheang | University of California, Berkeley, USA |
| Lesly-Ann Danie | KU Leuven, Belgium |
| Kinnari Dave | Certified Kernel Tech, LLC, USA |
| Simon Dierl | TU Dortmund, Germany |
| Florian Dorfhuber | Technical University of Munich, Germany |
| Benjamin Farinier | Technische Universität Wien, Austria |
| Parisa Fathololumi | Stevens Institute of Technology, USA |
| Mathias Fleury | University of Freiburg, Germany |
| Luke Geeson | University College London, UK |
| Pablo Gordillo | Complutense University of Madrid, Spain |
| Manish Goyal | University of North Carolina at Chapel Hill, USA |
| Akos Hajdu | Meta Platforms Inc., UK |
| Alejandro Hernández-Cerezo | Complutense University of Madrid, Spain |
| Jana Hofmann | CISPA Helmholtz Center for Information Security, Germany |
| Miguel Isabel | Universidad Complutense de Madrid, Spain |
| Martin Jonáš | Fondazione Bruno Kessler, Italy |
| Samuel Judson | Yale University, USA |
| Sudeep Kanav | LMU Munich, Germany |
| Daniela Kaufmann | Johannes Kepler University Linz, Austria |
| Brian Kempa | Iowa State University, USA |
| Ayrat Khalimov | Université libre de Bruxelles, Belgium |
| Nishant Kheterpal | University of Michigan, USA |
| Edward Kim | University of North Carolina at Chapel Hill, USA |
| John Kolesar | Yale University, USA |
| Bettina Könighofer | Graz University of Technology, Austria |
| Mitja Kulczynski | Kiel University, Germany |
| Thomas Lemberger | LMU Munich, Germany |
| Julien Lepiller | Yale University, USA |
| Sven Linker | Lancaster University in Leipzig, Germany |
| Kirby Linvill | University of Colorado Boulder, USA |
| Y. Cyrus Liu | Stevens Institute of Technology, USA |

| | |
|---|---|
| Tianhan Lu | University of Colorado Boulder, USA |
| Enrico Magnago | Fondazione Bruno Kessler and University of Trento, Italy |
| Tobias Meggendorfer | IST Austria, Austria |
| Fabian Meyer | RWTH Aachen University, Germany |
| Stefanie Mohr | Technical University of Munich, Germany |
| Raphaël Monat | LIP6, Sorbonne Université and CNRS, France |
| Felipe R. Monteiro | Amazon, USA |
| Marcel Moosbrugger | Technische Universität Wien, Austria |
| Marco Muniz | Aalborg University, Denmark |
| Neelanjana Pal | Vanderbilt University, USA |
| Francesco Parolini | Sorbonne University, France |
| Mário Pereira | Universidade NOVA de Lisboa, Portugal |
| João Pereira | ETH Zurich, Switzerland |
| Sumanth Prabhu | Indian Institute of Science and TCS Research, India |
| Cedric Richter | University of Oldenburg, Germany |
| Clara Rodríguez | Complutense University of Madrid, Spain |
| Bob Rubbens | University of Twente, The Netherlands |
| Rubén Rubio | Universidad Complutense de Madrid, Spain |
| Stanly Samuel | Indian Institute of Science, India |
| Daniel Schoepe | Amazon, UK |
| Philipp Schröer | RWTH Aachen University, Germany |
| Joseph Scott | University of Waterloo, Canada |
| Arnab Sharma | University of Oldenburg, Germany |
| Salomon Sickert | Hebrew University of Jerusalem, Israel |
| Yahui Song | National University of Singapore, Singapore |
| Michael Starzinger | University of Salzburg, Austria |
| Martin Tappler | Graz University of Technology, Austria |
| Michael Tautschnig | Queen Mary University of London, UK |
| Mertcan Temel | Intel Corporation, USA |
| Saeid Tizpaz-Niari | University of Texas at El Paso, USA |
| Deivid Vale | Radboud University Nijmegen, The Netherlands |
| Vesal Vojdani | University of Tartu, Estonia |
| Masaki Waga | Kyoto University, Japan |
| Peixin Wang | University of Oxford, UK |
| Tobias Winkler | RWTH Aachen University, Germany |
| Stefan Zetzsche | University College London, UK |
| Xiao-Yi Zhang | National Institute of Informatics, Japan |
| Linpeng Zhang | University College London, UK |
| Đorđe Žikelić | IST Austria, Austria |

## Additional Reviewers

A. R. Balasubramanian
Aaron Gember-Jacobson
Abhishek Rose
Aditya Akella
Alberto Larrauri
Alexander Bork
Alvin George
Ameer Hamza
Andres Noetzli
Anna Becchi
Anna Latour
Antti Hyvarinen
Benedikt Maderbacher
Benno Stein
Bettina Koenighofer
Bruno Blanchet
Chana Weil-Kennedy
Christoph Welzel
Christophe Chareton
Christopher Brix
Chun Tian
Constantin Enea
Daniel Hausmann
Daniel Kocher
Daniel Schoepe
Darius Foo
David Delmas
David MacIver
Dmitriy Traytel
Enrique Martin-Martin
Filip Cano
Francesco Parolini
Frederik Schmitt
Frédéric Recoules
Fu Song
Gadi Aleksandrowicz
Gerco van Heerdt
Grégoire Menguy
Gustavo Petri
Guy Amir
Haggai Landa
Hammad Ahmad
Hanna Lachnitt
Hongfei Fu
Ichiro Hasuo
Ilina Stoilkovska
Ira Fesefeldt
Jens Gutsfeld
Ji Guan
Jiawei Chen
Jip Spel
Jochen Hoenicke
Joshua Moerman
Kedar Namjoshi
Kevin Batz
Konstantin Britikov
Koos van der Linden
Lennard Gäher
Lesly-Ann Daniel
Li Wenhua
Li Zhou
Luca Laurenti
Lukas Armborst
Lukáš Holík
Malte Schledjewski
Martin Blicha
Martin Helfrich
Martin Lange
Masoud Ebrahimi
Mathieu Lehaut
Michael Sammler
Michael Starzinger
Miguel Gómez-Zamalloa
Miguel Isabel
Ming Xu
Noemi Passing
Niklas Metzger
Nishant Kheterpal
Noam Zilberstein
Norine Coenen
Omer Rappoport
Ömer Şakar
Peter Lammich
Prabhat Kumar Jha
Raghu Rajan
Rodrigo Otoni
Romain Demangeon
Ron Rothblum
Roope Kaivola
Sadegh Soudjani
Sepideh Asadi
Shachar Itzhaky
Shaun Azzopardi
Shawn Meier
Shelly Garion
Shubhani
Shyam Lal Karra
Simon Spies
Soline Ducousso
Song Yahui
Spandan Das
Sumanth Prabhu
Teodora Baluta
Thomas Noll
Tim King
Tim Quatmann
Timothy Bourke
Tobias Winkler
Vasileios Klimis
Vedad Hadzic
Vishnu Bondalakunta
Wang Fang
Xing Hong
Yangjia Li
Yash Pote
Yehia Abd Alrahman
Yuan Feng
Zachary Kincaid
Ziv Nevo
Zurab Khasidashvili

# Contents – Part I

## Invited Papers



## Formal Methods for Probabilistic Programs



## Formal Methods for Neural Networks

# Contents – Part II

## Probabilistic Techniques



## Automata and Logic

**Synthesis and Concurrency**

# Invited Papers

# A Billion SMT Queries a Day (Invited Paper)

Neha Rungta(✉)

Amazon Web Services, Seattle, USA
rungta@amazon.com

**Abstract.** Amazon Web Services (AWS) is a cloud computing services provider that has made significant investments in applying formal methods to proving correctness of its internal systems and providing assurance of correctness to their end-users. In this paper, we focus on how we built abstractions and eliminated specifications to scale a verification engine for AWS access policies, ZELKOVA, to be usable by all AWS users. We present milestones from our journey from a thousand SMT invocations daily to an unprecedented billion SMT calls in a span of five years. In this paper, we talk about how the cloud is enabling application of formal methods, key insights into what made this scale of a billion SMT queries daily possible, and present some open scientific challenges for the formal methods community.

**Keywords:** Cloud Computing · Formal Verification · SMT Solving

## 1 Introduction

Amazon Web Services (AWS) has made significant investments in developing and applying formal tools and techniques to prove the correctness of critical internal systems and provide services to AWS users to prove correctness of their own systems [24]. We use and apply a varied set of automated reasoning techniques at AWS. For example, we use (i) bounded model checking [35] to verify memory safety properties of boot code running in AWS data centers and of real-time operating system used in IoT devices [22,25,26], (ii) proof assistants such as EasyCrypt [12] and domain-specific languages such as Cryptol [38] to verify cryptographic protocols [3,4,23], (iii) HOL-Lite [33] to verify the BigNum implementation [2], (iv) P [28] to test key storage components in Amazon S3 [18], and (v) Dafny [37] to verify key authorization and crypto libraries [1]. Automated reasoning capabilities for external AWS users leverage (i) data-flow analysis [17] to prove correct usage of cloud APIs [29,40], (ii) monotonic SAT theories [14] to check properties of network configurations [5,13], and (iii) theories for strings and automaton in SMT solvers [16,39,46] to provide security for access controls [6,19].

This paper describes key milestones in our journey of generating billion SMT queries a day in the context of AWS Identity and Access Management (IAM). IAM is a system for controlling access to resources such as applications, data, and workload in AWS. Resource owners can configure access by writing *policies*


S. Shoham and Y. Vizel (Eds.): CAV 2022, LNCS 13371, pp. 3–18, 2022.
https://doi.org/10.1007/978-3-031-13185-1_1

that describe when to allow and deny user requests that access the resource. These configurations are expressed in the IAM policy language. For example, Amazon Simple Storage Service (S3) is an object storage service that offers data durability, availability, security, and performance. S3 is used widely to store and protect data for a range of applications. A *bucket* is a fundamental container in S3 where users can upload unlimited amounts of data in the form of objects. Amazon S3 supports fine-grained access control to the data based on the needs of the user. Ensuring that only intended users have access to their resource is important for the security of the resource. While the policy language allows for compact specifications of expressive policies, reasoning about the interaction between the semantics of different policy statements can be challenging to manually evaluate, especially in large policies with multiple operators and conditions.

To help AWS users secure their resources, we built ZELKOVA, a policy analysis tool designed to reason about the semantics of AWS access control policies. ZELKOVA translates policies and properties into Satisfiability Modulo Theories (SMT) formulas and uses SMT solvers to prove a variety of security properties such as "*Does the policy grant broad public access?*" [6]. The SMT encoding uses the theory of strings, regular expressions, bit vectors, and integer comparisons. The use of the wildcards $*$ (any number of characters) and ? (exactly one character) in the string constraints makes the decision problem PSPACE-complete. Zelkova uses a portfolio solver, where it invokes multiple solvers in the backend and uses the results from the solver that returns first, in a winner takes all strategy. This allows us to leverage the diversity among solvers and quickly solve queries—a couple hundred milliseconds to tens of seconds. A sample of AWS services that integrate ZELKOVA includes Amazon S3 (object storage), AWS Config (change-based resource auditor), Amazon Macie (security service), AWS Trusted Advisor (compliance to AWS best practices), and Amazon GuardDuty (intelligent threat detection). ZELKOVA drives preventative control features such as Amazon S3 Block Public Access and visibility into who outside an account has access to its resources [19].

ZELKOVA is an automated reasoning tool developed by formal methods experts and requires some degree of expertise in formal methods to use it. We cannot expect all AWS users to be experts in formal methods, have the time to be trained in the use of formal methods tools, or even be experts in the cloud domain. In this paper, we present the three pillars of our solution that enable ZELKOVA to be used by *all AWS users.* Using a combination of techniques such as eliminating specifications, domain-specific abstractions, and advances in SMT solvers we make the power of ZELKOVA available to all AWS users.

## 2 Eliminate Writing Specifications

### End users will not write a specification

ZELKOVA follows a traditional verification approach where it takes as input a policy and a specification, and produces a yes or no answer. We have developers and cloud administrators who author policies to govern access to cloud

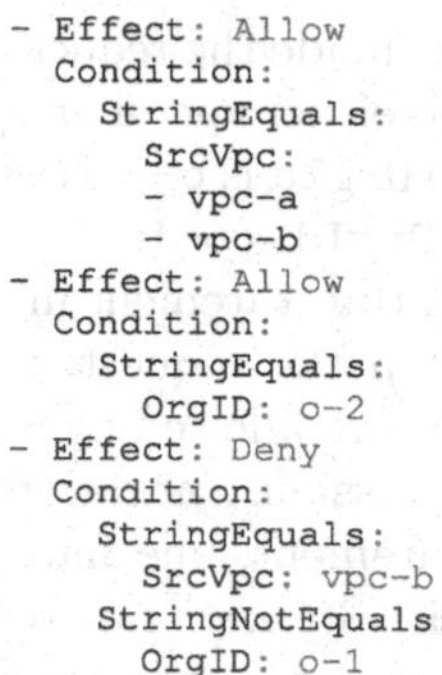
- Effect: Allow
Condition:
StringEquals:
SrcVpc:
- vpc-a
- vpc-b
- Effect: Allow
Condition:
StringEquals:
OrgID: o-2
- Effect: Deny
Condition:
StringEquals:
SrcVpc: vpc-b
StringNotEquals:
OrgID: o-1

**Fig. 1.** An example AWS policy

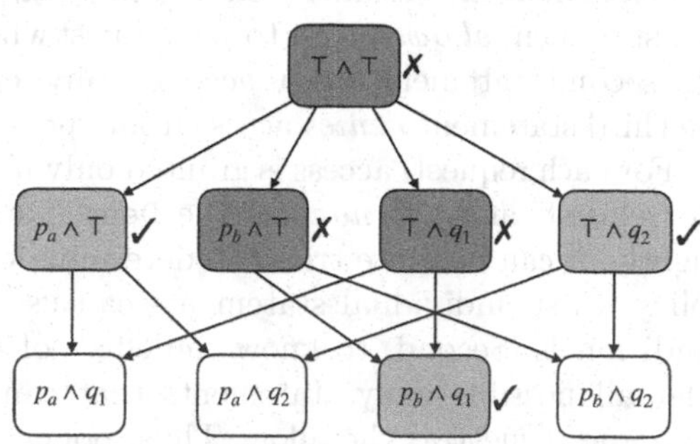
⊤ ∧ ⊤ ✗
$p_a \wedge \top$ ✓
$p_b \wedge \top$ ✗
$\top \wedge q_1$ ✗
$\top \wedge q_2$ ✓
$p_a \wedge q_1$
$p_a \wedge q_2$
$p_b \wedge q_1$ ✓
$p_b \wedge q_2$

**Fig. 2.** Stratified abstraction search tree

resources. We have someone else, a security engineer, who writes a specification of what is considered acceptable. The automated reasoning engine ZELKOVA does the verification and returns a yes or no answer. This approach is effective for a limited number of use cases, but it is hard to scale to all AWS users. The bottleneck to scaling the verification effort is the *human effort required to specify what is acceptable behavior*. The SLAM work had similar a observation about specifications; for use of Static Driver Verifier, they needed to provide the tool as well as the specification [7]. A person has to put in a lot of work upfront to define acceptable behavior and only at the end of the process, they get back an answer—a boolean. It's a single bit of information for all the work they've put in. They have no information about whether they had the right specification or whether they wrote the specification correctly.

To scale our approach to all AWS users, we had to fundamentally rethink our approach and completely remove the bottleneck of having people write a specification. To achieve that, we flipped the rules of the game and made the automated reasoning engine responsible for specification. We had the machine put in the upfront cost. Now it takes as input a policy and returns a detailed set of findings (declarative statements about what is true of the system). These findings are presented to a user, the security engineer, who reviews these findings and makes decisions about whether these findings represent valid risks in the system that should be fixed or are acceptable behaviors of the system. Users are now taking the output of the machine and saying "yes" or "no".

## 2.1 Generating Possible Specifications (Findings)

To remove the bottleneck of specification, we changed the question from is this policy correct? to who has access?. The response to the former is a boolean while the response to the latter is a set of findings. AWS access control policies specify *who* has access to a given resource, via a set of `Allow` and `Deny` statements that grant and prohibit access, respectively. Figure 1 shows a simplified policy specifying access to an AWS resource. This policy specifies conditions on the cloud-based network (known as a VPC) for which the request originated and on the organizational Amazon customer (referred to by an Org ID) who made the request. The first statement *allows* access to any request whose `SrcVpc` is either `vpc-a` *or* `vpc-b`. The second statement *allows* access to any request whose `OrgId` is `o-2`. However, the third statement *denies* access from `vpc-b` *unless* the `OrgId` is `o-1`.

For each request, access is granted only if: (a) *some* `Allow` statement matches the request, and (b) *none* of the `Deny` statements match the request. Consequently, it can be quite tricky to determine what accesses are allowed by a given policy. First, individual statements can use regular expressions, negation, and conditionals. Second, to know the effect of an allow statement, one must consider all possible deny statements that can *overlap* with it, *i.e.*, can refer to the same request as the allow. Thus, policy verification is not *compositional*, in that we cannot determine if a policy is "correct" simply by *locally* checking that each statement is "correct." Instead, we require a *global* verification mechanism, that simultaneously considers all the statements and their subtle interactions, to determine if a policy grants only the intended access.

For the example policy sketch shown in Fig. 1, access can be summarized through a set of three findings, which say that access is granted to a request iff:

- Its `SrcVpc` is `vpc-a`, *or*,
- Its `OrgId` is `o-2`, or,
- Its `SrcVpc` is `vpc-b` *and* its `OrgId` is `o-1`.

The findings are sound as no other requests are granted access. The findings are mostly precise; most of the requests match the conditions that are granted access. The finding "`OrgId` is `o-2`" also includes some requests that are not allowed, *e.g.*, when `SrcVpc` is `vpc-b`. To help understandability of the findings, we sacrifice this precision. Precise findings would need to include negation, and that would add complexity for the users to make decisions. Finally, the findings compactly summarize the policy in three positive statements declaring *who* has access. In principle, the notion of compact findings is similar to abstract counterexamples or minimizing counterexamples [21,30,32]. Since the findings are produced by the machine and already verified to be true, we have a person deciding if they *should be* true. The human is making a judgment call and expressing intent.

We use stratified predicate abstraction for computing the findings. Enumerating all possible requests is computationally *intractable*, and even if it were not, the resulting set of findings is far too large and hence *useless*. We tackle the problem of summarizing the super-astronomical request-space by using *predicate abstraction*. Specifically, we make a syntactic pass over the policy to extract the set of constants that are used to constrain access, and we use those constants to generate a family of predicates whose conjunctions compactly describe partitions of the space of all requests. For example, from the policy in Fig. 1 we would extract the following predicates

$$
\begin{array}{lll}
p_a \doteq \mathsf{SrcVpc} = \mathsf{vpc\text{-}a}, & p_b \doteq \mathsf{SrcVpc} = \mathsf{vpc\text{-}b}, & p_\star \doteq \mathsf{SrcVpc} = \star, \\
q_1 \doteq \mathsf{OrgId} = \mathsf{o\text{-}1}, & q_2 \doteq \mathsf{OrgId} = \mathsf{o\text{-}2}, & q_\star \doteq \mathsf{OrgId} = \star.
\end{array}
$$

The first row has three predicates describing the possible value of the `SrcVpc` of the request: that it equals `vpc-a` or `vpc-b` or some value other than `vpc-a` and `vpc-b`.

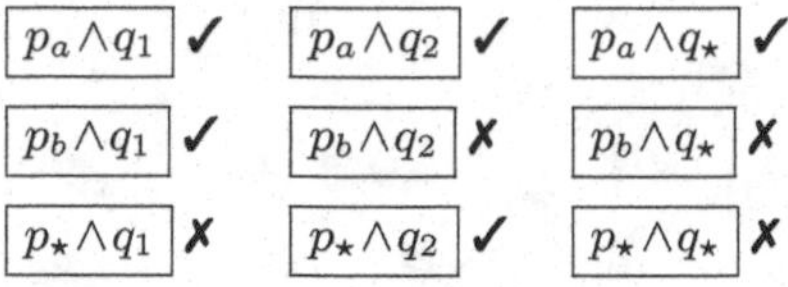


**Fig. 3.** Cubes generated by the predicates $p_a, p_b, p_\star, q_1, q_2, q_\star$ generated from the policy in Fig. 1 and the result of querying ZELKOVA to check if the the requests corresponding to each cube are granted access by the policy.

Similarly, the second row has three predicates describing the value of the `OrgId` of the request: that it equals `o-1` or `o-2` or some value other than `o-1` and `o-2`.

We can compute findings by enumerating all the *cubes* generated by the above predicates and querying ZELKOVA to determine if the policy allows access to the requests described by the cube. The enumeration of cubes is common in SAT solvers and other predicate abstraction based approaches [8,15,36]. The set of all the cubes are shown in Fig. 3. The chief difficulty with enumerating all the cubes *greedily* is that we end up eagerly *splitting-cases* on the values of fields when that may not be required. For example, in Fig. 3, we split cases on the possible value of `OrgId` even though it is irrelevant when `SrcVpc` is `vpc-a`. This observation points the way to a new algorithm where we *lazily* generate the cubes as follows. Our algorithm maintains a *worklist* of minimally refined cubes. At each step, we (1) ask ZELKOVA if the cube allows an access that is not covered by any of its refinements; (2) if so, we add it to the set of findings; and (3) if not, we refine the cube "point-wise" along the values of each field individually and add the results to the worklist. The above process is illustrated in Fig. 2.

The specifications or findings generated by the machine are presented in the context of the access control domain. The developers do not have to learn a new means to specify correctness, think about what they want to be correct of the system, or check the completeness of their specifications. This is a very important lesson that we need to apply across many other applications for formal methods to be successful at scale. The challenge here is the specifics depend on the domain.

## 3 Domain-Specific Abstractions

### It's all about the end user

ZELKOVA was developed by formal methods subject matter experts who learnt domain of AWS access control policies. Once we had the analysis engine, we faced the same challenges all other formal methods tool developers had before us. How do we make it accessible to all users? One hard earned lesson was "eliminating the need for specifications" as discussed in the previous section. But that was only part of the answer. There was a lot more to do. Many more questions to answer—How do we get users to use it? How do we present the results to the

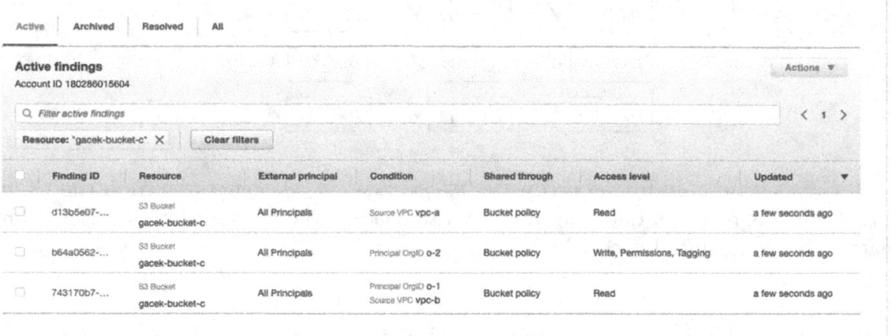

Active | Archived | Resolved | All

**Active findings**
Account ID 180286015604

Filter active findings

Actions

Resource: "gacek-bucket-c" Clear filters

| Finding ID | Resource | External principal | Condition | Shared through | Access level | Updated |
|---|---|---|---|---|---|---|
| d13b5e07-... | S3 Bucket gacek-bucket-c | All Principals | Source VPC vpc-a | Bucket policy | Read | a few seconds ago |
| b64a0562-... | S3 Bucket gacek-bucket-c | All Principals | Principal OrgID o-2 | Bucket policy | Write, Permissions, Tagging | a few seconds ago |
| 743170b7-... | S3 Bucket gacek-bucket-c | All Principals | Principal OrgID o-1 Source VPC vpc-b | Bucket policy | Read | a few seconds ago |

**Fig. 4.** Interface that presents Access Analyzer findings to users.

users? How do the results stay updated? The answer was to design and build domain-specific abstractions. Do one thing and do it really well.

We created a higher level service on top of ZELKOVA called IAM Access Analyzer. We provide a one-click way to enable Access Analyzer for an AWS account or AWS Organization. An account in AWS is a fundamental construct that serves as a container for the user's resources, workloads, and data. Users can create policies to grant access to resources in their account to other users. In Access Analyzer, we use the account as a *zone of trust*. This abstraction lets us say that access to resources by users within their zone of trust is considered safe. But access to resources outside their zone of trust is potentially unsafe.

Once a user enables Access Analyzer, we use stratified predicate abstraction to analyze the policies and generate findings showing which users outside the zone of trust have access to resources. We had to shift from a mode where ZELKOVA can answer "any access query" to ZELKOVA can enumerate "who has access to what". This brings to attention the permissions that could lead to unintended access of data. While this idea seems simple in hindsight, it took us a couple of years to figure out the right abstraction for the domain. It can be used by all AWS users. They did not need to be experts in the area of formal methods or even have deep understanding of how access control in the cloud worked.

Each finding includes details about the resource, the external entity with access to it, and the permissions granted so that the user can take appropriate action. We present example findings in Fig. 4. Note these findings are not presented as SMT-lib formulas but rather in the domain that the user expects—AWS access control constructs. These map to the findings presented in the previous section for Fig. 1. Users can view the details included in the finding to determine whether the access is intentional or a potential risk that the user should resolve.

Most automated reasoning tools are run as a one-off: prove something, and then move on to the next challenge. In the cloud environment this was not the case. Doing the analysis once was not sufficient in our domain. We had to design a means to continuously monitor the environment and changes to access control policies within the zone of trust and update the findings based on that. To that end, Access Analyzer analyzes these policies if a user adds a new policy, or changes an existing policy, and either generates new findings, or removes findings, or updates the existing findings. Access Analyzer also analyzes all policies periodically, to ensure that in a rare case, if a change event to the policy is missed by the system, it is still able to keep the findings updated. The ease of enablement, just-in-time analysis on updates, and periodic analysis across all policies are the key factors in getting us to a billion queries daily.

## 4 SMT Solving at Cloud Scale

**Every query matters**

The use of SMT solving in AWS features and services means that millions of users are relying on the correctness and timeliness of the underlying solvers for the security of their cloud infrastructure. The challenges around correctness and timeliness in solver queries have been well studied in the automated reasoning community, but they have been treated as independent features. Today, we are generating a billion SMT queries every day to support various use cases across a wide variety of AWS services. We have discovered an intricate dependency between correctness and timeliness that manifests at this scale.

### 4.1 Monotonicity in Runtimes Across Solver Versions

Zelkova uses a portfolio solver to discharge its queries. When given a query, Zelkova invokes multiple solvers in the backend and uses the results from the solver that returns first, in a winner takes all strategy [6]. The portfolio approach allows us to leverage the diversity amongst solvers. One of our goals is to leverage the latest advancements in the SMT solver community. SMT solver researchers and developers are fixing issues, making improvements to existing features, adding new theories, adding features such as generation of proofs, and making other performance improvements. Before deploying a new version of the solver within the production environment, we perform extensive offline testing and benchmarking to gain confidence in the correctness of the answers, performance of the queries, and ensure there are no regressions.

While striving for correctness and timeliness, one of the challenges we face is that new solver versions are not monotonically better in their performance than their previous version. A solution that works well in the cloud setting is a massive portfolio, sometimes even containing older versions of the same solver. This presents two issues. One, when we discover a bug in an older version of the solver, we need to patch this old version. This creates an operational burden of maintaining many different versions of the different solvers. Two, when the number of solvers increases, we need to ensure that each solver provides a correct result. Checking the correctness of queries that result in SAT is straightforward, but SMT solvers need to provide proof for the UNSAT queries. The proof generation and checking needs to be timely as well.

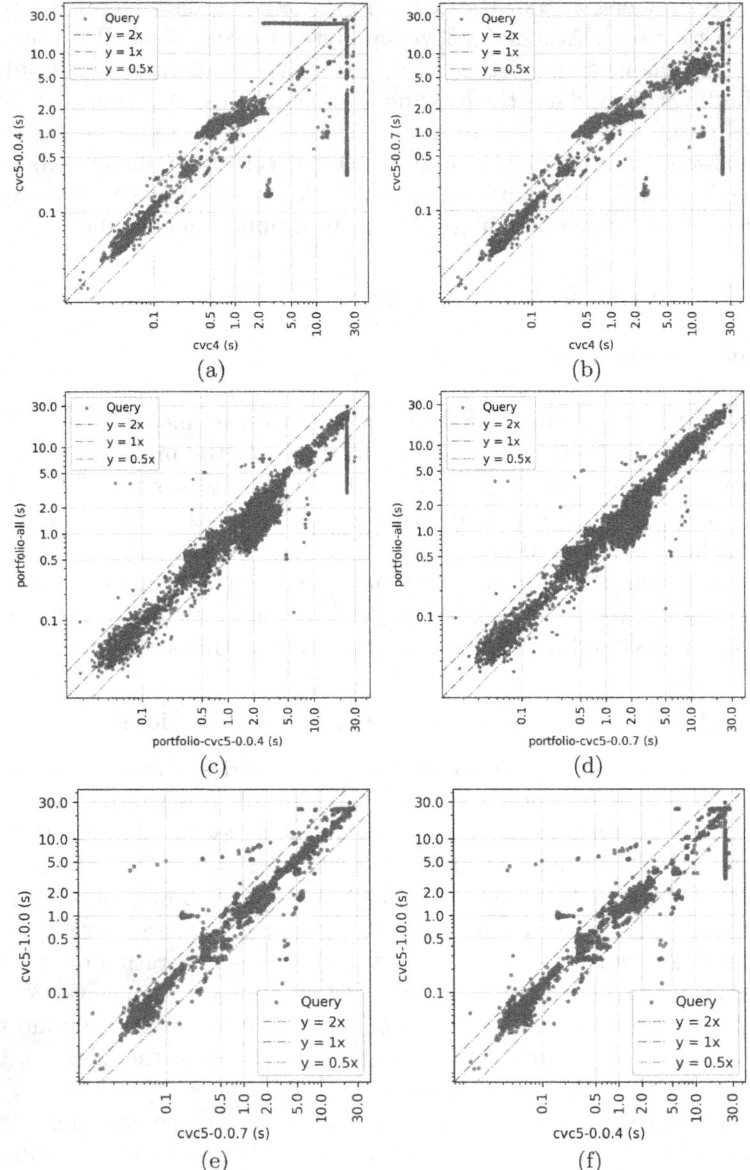


**Fig. 5.** Comparing the runtime for solving SMT queries generated by ZELKOVA by CVC4 and the different cvc5 versions (a) CVC4 vs. cvc5 version 0.0.4, (b) CVC4 vs. cvc5 version 0.0.7. Comparing the runtimes of winner take all in the portfolio solver of ZELKOVA with: (c) a portfolio solver consisting of Z3 sequence string solver, Z3 automata solver, and cvc5 version 0.0.4 (d) a portfolio solver consisting of Z3 sequence string solver, Z3 automata solver, and cvc5 version 0.0.7. Evaluating the performance of the latest cvc5 version 1.0.0 with its older versions (e) cvc5 version 0.0.4 and (f) cvc5 version 0.0.7

In the Zelkova portfolio solver [6], we use CVC4, and our original goal was to replace CVC4 with the then latest version of cvc5 (version 0.0.4)[1]. We wanted to leverage the proof checking capabilities of cvc5 to ensure the correctness of UNSAT queries [11]. To check the timeliness requirements, we ran experiments across our benchmarks, comparing the results of CVC4 to those of cvc5 (version 0.0.4). The results across a representative set of queries are shown in Fig. 5(a). In the graph we have approximately 15,000 SMT queries that are generated by Zelkova; we select a distribution of queries that are solved between 1 s and 30 s, after which the solver process is killed and a timeout is reported. Some queries that are not solved by CVC4 within the time bound of 30 s are now being solved by cvc5 (version 0.0.4), as seen by the points in the graph along the y-axis on the extreme right. However, cvc5 (version 0.0.4) times out on some queries that are solved by CVC4, as seen by the points on the top of the graph.

The results presented in Fig. 5(b) are not surprising given that the problem space is computationally hard, and there is an inherent randomness in search heuristics within SMT solvers. In an evaluation of cvc5, the authors discuss examples where CVC4 outperforms cvc5 [10]. But this poses a challenge for us when we are using the result of these solvers in security controls and services that millions of users rely on. The changes did not meet the timeliness requirement of continuing to solve the queries within 30 s. When a query times out, to be sound, the analysis marks the bucket as public. The impact of a query timing out, that was previously being solved, will lead to the user not being able to access the resource. This is unexpected for the user because there was no change in their configuration.

For example, consider the security checks in the Amazon S3 Block Public Access that block requests based on the results of the analysis. In this context, suppose that there was a bucket marked as "not public" based on the results of a query, and now that same query times out; the bucket will be marked as "public". This will lock down access to the bucket and the intended users will not be able to access it. Even a single regression that leads to loss of access for the user is not an acceptable change. As another example, these security checks are also used by IoT devices. In the case of a smart lock, a time out in the query that was previously being solved could lead to a loss of access to the user's home. The criticality of these use cases combined with the end user expectation is a key challenge in our domain.

We debugged and fixed the issue in cvc5 that was causing certain queries to time out. But even with this fix, CVC4 was 2x faster than cvc5 for many easier problems that took 1 s to solve originally. This slowdown was significant for us because ZELKOVA is called in the request path of security controls such as Amazon S3 Block Public Access. When a user attempts to attach a new access control policy or update an existing one, a synchronous call is made to Zelkova and the corresponding portfolio solvers to determine if the access control policy

[1] Note that while this section talks in detail about the CVC solver, the observations are common across all solvers. We select the results of the CVC solver as a representative because it is a mature solver with an active community.

being attached grants unrestricted public access or not. The bulk of the analysis time is spent in the SMT solvers, so doubling the analysis time for queries can lead to a degraded user experience. Where and how the analysis results are used plays an important role in how we track changes to the timeliness of the solver queries.

Our solution was to *add a new solver to the portfolio rather then replace an existing solver.* We added cvc5 (version 0.0.7) to the existing portfolio of solvers consisting of CVC4, Z3 with the sequence string solver, and a custom Z3-based automata solver. When we started the evaluation of cvc5, we did not plan to add a new version of the CVC solver to the portfolio. We had expected to the latest version of cvc5 to be comparable in timeliness to CVC4. We worked closely with the CVC developers and cvc5 was better on many queries, but it did not meet our timeliness requirements on all queries. This led to our decision to add cvc5 (version 0.0.7) to the Zelkova portfolio solver.

The results of comparing the portfolio solvers of two Z3 solvers, CVC4 and cvc5 (version 0.0.4) with a winner take all and portfolio solver *without* cvc5 (version 0.0.4) is shown in Fig. 5(c). The same configuration now with cvc5 (version 0.0.7) is shown in Fig. 5(d). The results show that the portfolio solving approach that Zelkova takes in the cloud is an effective one.

The cycle now repeats with cvc5 (version 1.0.0), and the same question comes up again. The question we are evaluating yet again is, "do we upgrade the existing cvc5 version with the latest or add yet another version of CVC to the portfolio solver". Some early experiments show that there is no clear answer yet. The results so far comparing the different version of cvc5 shown in Fig. 5(e) and (f) indicate that the latest version of cvc5 is not monotically better in performance than either of its previous versions. We do want to leverage the better proof generating capabilities of cvc5 (version 1.0.0) in order to gain more assurance in the correctness of the UNSAT queries.

### 4.2 Stability of the Solvers

We have spent quite a bit of time defining and implementing the encoding of the AWS access control policies into SMT. We update the encoding as we expand to more use cases or when we support new features in AWS. This is a slow and careful process that requires expertise in understanding AWS and how SMT solvers work. There is a lot of trial and error to figure out what encoding is correct and performant.

To illustrate the importance of the encoding, we present an experiment on solver runtimes with different ordering of clauses for our encoding (Fig. 6). For the same set of problem instances used in Fig. 5, we now use the standard SMT competition shuffler[2] to reorder assertions, terms, and rename variables to study the effect of ordering clauses for our default encoding. In Fig. 6, each point on the x axis corresponds to a single problem instance. For the problem instance, we run it in its original form (default encoding) which is the "base time", and

[2] https://github.com/SMT-COMP/scrambler.

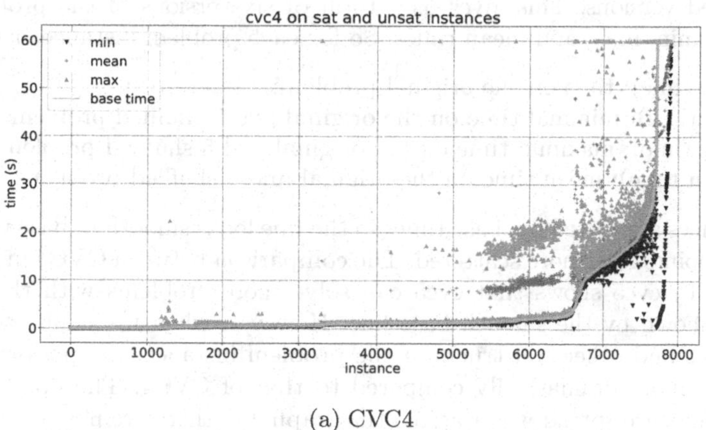


(a) CVC4

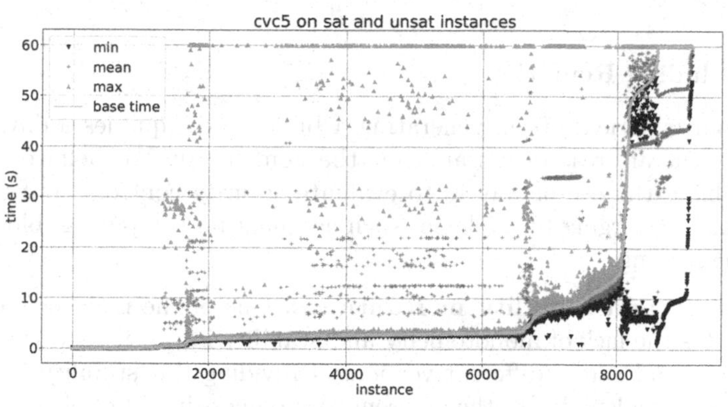


(b) cvc5 version 0.0.7

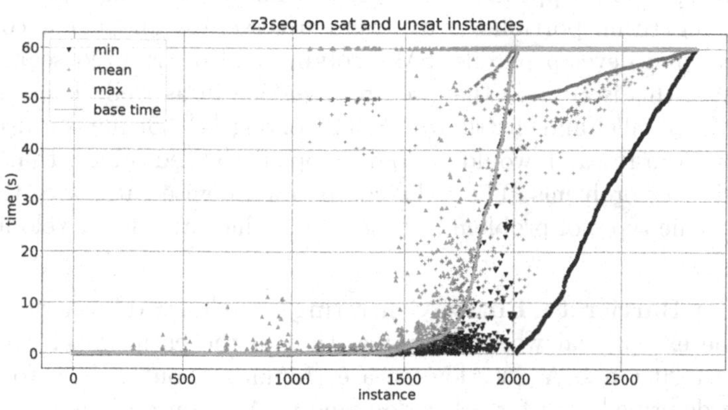


(c) Z3 sequence string solver

**Fig. 6.** Variance in runtimes after shuffling terms in the problem instances.

five shuffled versions. This gives us a total of six versions of the problem; we record the min, max, and mean times. So for each problem instance, $x$ we have:

1. (x, base time): time on the original problem;
2. (x, min time): minimal time on the original and 5 shuffled problems;
3. (x, max time): maximal time on the original and 5 shuffled problems; and
4. (x, mean time): mean time on the original and 5 shuffled problems.

The instances are sorted by 'base time' so the line looks smooth in base time, and the other points look more scattered. The comparison between CVC4 in Fig. 6(a) and Fig. 6(b) cvc5 shows that cvc5 can solve more problems with the default encoding shown by the smooth base line. However, when we shuffle the assertions, terms and other constructs in the problem instance, the performance of cvc5 varies more dramatically compared to that of CVC4. The points for the maximal time are spread wider across the graph and there are now several timeouts in Fig. 6(b).

### 4.3 Concluding Remarks

Based on our experience from generating a billion SMT queries a day, we propose some general areas of research for the community. We believe these are key to enabling the use of solvers to evaluate security controls, and to enable applications in emerging technologies such as quantum computing, blockchains, and bio-engineering.

**Monotonicity and Stability in Runtimes.** One of the main challenges we encountered is the lack of monotonicity and stability in runtimes within a given solver version and across different versions. Providing this stability is a fundamentally hard problem due to the inherent randomness in SMT solver heuristics, search strategies, and configuration flags. One approach would be to incorporate the algorithm portfolio approach [31,34,42] within mainstream SMT solvers. A way enable algorithm portfolio is to leverage serverless and cloud computing environment, and develop parallel SMT solving and distributed search strategies. At AWS, this is an area that we are investing in as well. There has been some work in parallel and distributed SMT solving [41,45] but we need more. Another aspect of research would be to develop specialized solvers that focus on a specific class of problems. The SMT-comp could devise categories that allow room for specific types of problem instances as an incentive for developing these solvers.

**Reduce the Barrier to Entry.** Generating a billion SMT queries day is a result of the exceptional work and innovation of the entire SMT community over the past 20 years. A question we are thinking about is how to replicate the success described here for other domains in Amazon and elsewhere. There is a natural tendency in the formal methods community to target tools for the expert user. This limits their broader use and applicability. If we can find ways to lower the barrier to adoption, we can gain greater traction and improve the security, correctness, availability, and robustness of more systems.

**More Abstractions.** SMT solvers are powerful engines. One potential research direction for the broader community is to provide one or more higher level languages that allows people to specify their problems. We could create different languages based on the domain and take into account the expectations of developers. This would make interacting with a solver a more black-box exercise. The success we have had with SMT in Amazon, can be recreated in other domains if we provide developers the ability to easily encode their problems in a higher level language and use SMT solvers to solve them. It will more easily scale by not requiring a formal methods expert as an intermediary. Developing new abstractions or intermediate representations could be one approach to unlock billions of other SMT queries.

**Proof Generation.** All SMT solvers should be generating proofs to help the end-user gain confidence in the results. There has been some initial work in this area [9,20,27,43,44],but SMT has a long way to catch up with SAT solvers, and for good reason. The proof production is important for us gain greater confidence in the correctness of our answers, though it creates a tension with the timeliness. We need the proof production to be performant and the tools that check the generated proofs to be correct themselves. Continued push on different testing approaches, including fuzzing and property-based testing of SMT solvers, should continue with the same rigor and enthusiasm. Using these fuzz testing and mutation testing based techniques in the development workflow of SMT solvers is something that should become mainstream.

We are working to provide a set of benchmarks that can be leveraged by SMT developers to help further their work, are funding research grants in these areas, and are willing to evaluate new solvers.

## References


1. Encryption SDK Dafny model. https://github.com/aws/aws-encryption-sdk-dafny
2. s2n bignum verification. https://github.com/awslabs/s2n-bignum
3. Almeida, J.B., et al.: A machine-checked proof of security for AWS key management service. In: Proceedings of the 2019 ACM SIGSAC Conference on Computer and Communications Security, pp. 63–78 (2019)
4. Athanasiou, K., Cook, B., Emmi, M., MacCarthaigh, C., Schwartz-Narbonne, D., Tasiran, S.: SideTrail: verifying time-balancing of cryptosystems. In: Piskac, R., Rümmer, P. (eds.) VSTTE 2018. LNCS, vol. 11294, pp. 215–228. Springer, Cham (2018). https://doi.org/10.1007/978-3-030-03592-1_12
5. Backes, J., et al.: Reachability analysis for AWS-based networks. In: Dillig, I., Tasiran, S. (eds.) CAV 2019. LNCS, vol. 11562, pp. 231–241. Springer, Cham (2019). https://doi.org/10.1007/978-3-030-25543-5_14
6. Backes, J., et al.: Semantic-based automated reasoning for AWS access policies using SMT. In: 2018 Formal Methods in Computer Aided Design (FMCAD), pp. 1–9. IEEE (2018)
7. Ball, T., Levin, V., Rajamani, S.K.: A decade of software model checking with slam. Commun. ACM **54**(7), 68–76 (2011)

8. Ball, T., Majumdar, R., Millstein, T., Rajamani, S.K.: Automatic predicate abstraction of c programs. In: Proceedings of the ACM SIGPLAN 2001 Conference on Programming Language Design and Implementation, pp. 203–213 (2001)
9. Barbosa, H.: New techniques for instantiation and proof production in SMT solving. Ph.D. thesis, Université de Lorraine (2017)
10. Barbosa, H., et al.: cvc5: Versatile and industrial-strength SMT solver. In: Fisman, D., Rosu, G. (eds) Tools and Algorithms for the Construction and Analysis of Systems. TACAS 2022. Lecture Notes in Computer Science, vol. 13243. LNCS, pp. 415–442. Springer, Cham (2022). https://doi.org/10.1007/978-3-030-99524-9_24
11. Barrett, C., et al.: cvc5 at the SMT competition 2021
12. Barthe, G., et al.: EasyCrypt: a tutorial. In: Aldini, A., Lopez, J., Martinelli, F. (eds.) FOSAD 2012-2013. LNCS, vol. 8604, pp. 146–166. Springer, Cham (2014). https://doi.org/10.1007/978-3-319-10082-1_6
13. Bayless, S., et al.: Debugging network reachability with blocked paths. In: Silva, A., Leino, K.R.M. (eds.) CAV 2021. LNCS, vol. 12760, pp. 851–862. Springer, Cham (2021). https://doi.org/10.1007/978-3-030-81688-9_39
14. Bayless, S., Bayless, N., Hoos, H., Hu, A.: Sat modulo monotonic theories. In: Proceedings of the AAAI Conference on Artificial Intelligence, vol. 29 (2015)
15. Biere, A., Heule, M., van Maaren, H.: Handbook of Satisfiability, vol. 185. IOS press (2009)
16. Bjørner, N., Ganesh, V., Michel, R., Veanes, M.: An SMT-LIB format for sequences and regular expressions. SMT **12**, 76–86 (2012)
17. Bodden, E.: Inter-procedural data-flow analysis with IFDS/IDE and soot. In: Proceedings of the ACM SIGPLAN International Workshop on State of the Art in Java Program Analysis, pp. 3–8 (2012)
18. Bornholt, J., et al.: Using lightweight formal methods to validate a key-value storage node in Amazon s3. In: Proceedings of the ACM SIGOPS 28th Symposium on Operating Systems Principles, pp. 836–850 (2021)
19. Bouchet, M., et al.: Block public access: trust safety verification of access control policies. In: Proceedings of the 28th ACM Joint Meeting on European Software Engineering Conference and Symposium on the Foundations of Software Engineering, pp. 281–291 (2020)
20. Bouton, T., Caminha B. de Oliveira, D., Déharbe, D., Fontaine, P.: veriT: an open, trustable and efficient SMT-solver. In: Schmidt, R.A. (ed.) CADE 2009. LNCS (LNAI), vol. 5663, pp. 151–156. Springer, Heidelberg (2009). https://doi.org/10.1007/978-3-642-02959-2_12
21. Chaki, S., Groce, A., Strichman, O.: Explaining abstract counterexamples. In: Proceedings of the 12th ACM SIGSOFT twelfth International Symposium on Foundations of Software Engineering, pp. 73–82 (2004)
22. Chong, N., et al.: Code-level model checking in the software development workflow. In: 2020 IEEE/ACM 42nd International Conference on Software Engineering: Software Engineering in Practice (ICSE-SEIP), pp. 11–20. IEEE (2020)
23. Chudnov, A., et al.: Continuous formal verification of Amazon s2n. In: Chockler, H., Weissenbacher, G. (eds.) CAV 2018. LNCS, vol. 10982, pp. 430–446. Springer, Cham (2018). https://doi.org/10.1007/978-3-319-96142-2_26
24. Cook, B.: Formal reasoning about the security of Amazon web services. In: Chockler, H., Weissenbacher, G. (eds.) CAV 2018. LNCS, vol. 10981, pp. 38–47. Springer, Cham (2018). https://doi.org/10.1007/978-3-319-96145-3_3

25. Cook, B., Khazem, K., Kroening, D., Tasiran, S., Tautschnig, M., Tuttle, M.R.: Model checking boot code from AWS data centers. In: Chockler, H., Weissenbacher, G. (eds.) CAV 2018. LNCS, vol. 10982, pp. 467–486. Springer, Cham (2018). https://doi.org/10.1007/978-3-319-96142-2_28
26. Cook, B., Khazem, K., Kroening, D., Tasiran, S., Tautschnig, M., Tuttle, M.R.: Model checking boot code from AWS data centers. Formal Methods Syst. Des. **57**(1), 34–52 (2021)
27. Deharbe, D., Fontaine, P., Paleo, B.W.: Quantifier inference rules for SMT proofs. In: First International Workshop on Proof eXchange for Theorem Proving-PxTP 2011 (2011)
28. Desai, A., Gupta, V., Jackson, E., Qadeer, S., Rajamani, S., Zufferey, D.P.: Safe asynchronous event-driven programming. ACM SIGPLAN Notices **48**(6), 321–332 (2013)
29. Emmi, M., et al.: Rapid: checking API usage for the cloud in the cloud. In: Proceedings of the 29th ACM Joint Meeting on European Software Engineering Conference and Symposium on the Foundations of Software Engineering, pp. 1416–1426 (2021)
30. Gastin, P., Moro, P., Zeitoun, M.: Minimization of counterexamples in SPIN. In: Graf, S., Mounier, L. (eds.) SPIN 2004. Minimization of counterexamples in spin, vol. 2989, pp. 92–108. Springer, Heidelberg (2004). https://doi.org/10.1007/978-3-540-24732-6_7
31. Gomes, C.P., Selman, B.: Algorithm portfolios. Artif. Intell. **126**(1–2), 43–62 (2001)
32. Groce, A., Kroening, D.: Making the most of BMC counterexamples. Electron. Notes Theoret. Comput. Sci. **119**(2), 67–81 (2005)
33. Harrison, J.: HOL light: an overview. In: Berghofer, S., Nipkow, T., Urban, C., Wenzel, M. (eds.) TPHOLs 2009. LNCS, vol. 5674, pp. 60–66. Springer, Heidelberg (2009). https://doi.org/10.1007/978-3-642-03359-9_4
34. Huberman, B.A., Lukose, R.M., Hogg, T.: An economics approach to hard computational problems. Science **275**(5296), 51–54 (1997)
35. Kroening, D., Tautschnig, M.: CBMC – C bounded model checker. In: Ábrahám, E., Havelund, K. (eds.) TACAS 2014. LNCS, vol. 8413, pp. 389–391. Springer, Heidelberg (2014). https://doi.org/10.1007/978-3-642-54862-8_26
36. Lahiri, S.K., Bryant, R.E., Cook, B.: A symbolic approach to predicate abstraction. In: Hunt, W.A., Somenzi, F. (eds.) CAV 2003. LNCS, vol. 2725, pp. 141–153. Springer, Heidelberg (2003). https://doi.org/10.1007/978-3-540-45069-6_15
37. Leino, K.R.M.: Dafny: An automatic program verifier for functional correctness. In: Clarke, E.M., Voronkov, A. (eds.) LPAR 2010. LNCS (LNAI), vol. 6355, pp. 348–370. Springer, Heidelberg (2010). https://doi.org/10.1007/978-3-642-17511-4_20
38. Lewis, J.R., Martin, B.: Cryptol: High assurance, retargetable crypto development and validation. In: IEEE Military Communications Conference, 2003. MILCOM 2003. vol. 2, pp. 820–825. IEEE (2003)
39. Liang, T., et al.: An efficient SMT solver for string constraints. Formal Methods Syst. Des. **48**(3), 206–234 (2016)
40. Luo, L., Schäf, M., Sanchez, D., Bodden, E.: Ide support for cloud-based static analyses. In: Proceedings of the 29th ACM Joint Meeting on European Software Engineering Conference and Symposium on the Foundations of Software Engineering, pp. 1178–1189 (2021)
41. Marescotti, M., Hyvärinen, A.E.J., Sharygina, N.: Clause sharing and partitioning for cloud-based SMT solving. In: Artho, C., Legay, A., Peled, D. (eds.) ATVA 2016. LNCS, vol. 9938, pp. 428–443. Springer, Cham (2016). https://doi.org/10.1007/978-3-319-46520-3_27

42. Rice, J.R.: The algorithm selection problem. In: Advances in Computers, vol. 15, pp. 65–118. Elsevier (1976)
43. Stump, A., Oe, D.: Towards an SMT proof format. In: Proceedings of the Joint Workshops of the 6th International Workshop on Satisfiability Modulo Theories and 1st International Workshop on Bit-Precise Reasoning, pp. 27–32 (2008)
44. Stump, A., Oe, D., Reynolds, A., Hadarean, L., Tinelli, C.: SMT proof checking using a logical framework. Formal Methods Syst. Des. **42**(1), 91–118 (2013)
45. Wintersteiger, C.M., Hamadi, Y., de Moura, L.: A concurrent portfolio approach to SMT solving. In: Bouajjani, A., Maler, O. (eds.) CAV 2009. LNCS, vol. 5643, pp. 715–720. Springer, Heidelberg (2009). https://doi.org/10.1007/978-3-642-02658-4_60
46. Zheng, Y., Zhang, X., Ganesh, V.: Z3-STR: a z3-based string solver for web application analysis. In: Proceedings of the 2013 9th Joint Meeting on Foundations of Software Engineering, pp. 114–124 (2013)

# Program Verification with Constrained Horn Clauses (Invited Paper)

Arie Gurfinkel(✉)

University of Waterloo, Waterloo, Canada
arie.gurfinkel@uwaterloo.ca

**Abstract.** Many problems in program verification, Model Checking, and type inference are naturally expressed as satisfiability of a verification condition expressed in a fragment of First-Order Logic called Constrained Horn Clauses (CHC). This transforms program analysis and verification tasks to the realm of first order satisfiability and into the realm of SMT solvers. In this paper, we give a brief overview of how CHCs capture verification problems for sequential imperative programs, and discuss CHC solving algorithm underlying the SPACER engine of SMT-solver Z3.

## 1 Introduction

First Order Logic (FOL) is a powerful formalism that naturally captures many interesting decision (and optimization) problems. In recent years, there has been a tremendous progress in automated logic reasoning tools, such as Boolean SATisfiability Solvers (SAT) and Satisfiability Modulo Theory (SMT) solvers. This enabled the use of logic and logic satisfiabilty solvers as a universal solution to many problems in Computer Science, in general, and in Program Analysis, in particular. Most new program analysis techniques formalize the desired analysis task in a fragment of FOL, and delegate the analysis to a SAT or an SMT solver. Examples include deductive verification tools such as Dafny [30] and Why3 [13], symbolic execution engines such as KLEE [7], Bounded Model Checking engines such as CBMC [10] and SMACK [9], and many others.

In this paper, we focus on a fragment of FOL called Constrained Horn Clauses (CHC). CHCs arise in many applications of automated verification. They naturally capture such problems as discovery and verification of inductive invariants [4,18]; Model Checking of safety properties of finite- and infinite-state systems [2,23]; safety verification of push-down systems (and their extensions) [4,28]; modular verification of distributed and parameterized systems [17,19,33]; and type inference [35,36], and many others.

Using CHC, developers of program analysis tools can separate the process of developing a proof methodology (also known as generation of Verification Condition (VC)) from the algorithmic details of deciding whether the VC is correct. Such a flexible design simplifies supporting multiple proof methodologies, multiple languages, and multiple verification tasks with a single framework. Today,


S. Shoham and Y. Vizel (Eds.): CAV 2022, LNCS 13371, pp. 19–29, 2022.
https://doi.org/10.1007/978-3-031-13185-1_2

there are multiple effective program verification tools based on the CHC methodology, including a C/C++ verification framework SeaHorn [18], a Java verification framework JayHorn [25], and an Android information flow verification tool HornDroid [8], a Rust verification framework RustHorn [31], Solidity verification tools SmartACE [37] and Solidity Compiler Model Checker [1]. Many more approaches utilize CHC as part of a more general verification solution.

The idea of reducing program verification (and model checking) to FOL satisfiability is well researched. A great example is the use of *Constraint Logic Programming* (CLP) [24] in program verification, or the use of Datalog for pointer analysis [34]. What is unique is the application of SMT-solvers in the decision procedure and lifting of techniques that have been developed in Model Checking and Program Verification communities to the uniform setting of satisfiabilty of CHC formulas. In the rest of this paper, we show how verification problems can be represented in CHCs (Sect. 2), and describe key algorithms behind Spacer [27], a CHC engine of the SMT solver Z3 [32] that is used to solve them (Sect. 3).

## 2 Logic of Constrained Horn Clauses

In this section, we give a brief overview of Constrained Horn Clauses (CHC). We illustrate an application of CHC to verification of a simple imperative program with a loop.

The logic of Constrained Horn Clauses is a fragment of FOL. We assume that the reader is familiar with the basic concepts of FOL, including signatures, theories, and models. For the purpose of this presentation, let $\Sigma$ be some fixed FOL signature and $\mathcal{A}$ be an FOL theory over $\Sigma$. For example, $\Sigma$ is a signature for arithmetic, including constants 0, and 1, and a binary function $\cdot + \cdot$, and $\mathcal{A}$ the theory of Presburger arithmetic. A *Constrained Horn Clause (CHC)* is an FOL sentence of the form:

$$\forall V \cdot (\varphi \wedge p_1(X_1) \wedge \cdots \wedge p_k(X_k) \implies h(X)) \tag{1}$$

where $V$ is the set of all free variables in the body of the sentence, $\{p_i\}_{i=1}^k$ and $h$ are uninterpreted predicate symbols (in the signature), $\{X_i\}_{i=1}^k$ and $X$ are first-order terms, and $p(X)$ stands for application of predicate $p$ to a list of terms $X$.

A CHC in Eq. (1) can be equivalently written as the following clause:

$$(\neg\varphi \vee \neg p_1(X_1) \vee \cdots \vee \neg p_n(X_n) \vee h(X)) \tag{2}$$

where all free variables are implicitly universally quantified. Note that in this case only $h$ appears positively, which explains why these are called *Horn* clauses. We write CHC($\mathcal{A}$) to denote the set of all sentences in FOL modulo theory $\mathcal{A}$ that can be written as a set of Constrained Horn Clauses. A sentence $\Phi$ is in CHC($\mathcal{A}$) if it can be written as a conjunction of clauses of the form of Eq. (1).

```
assume(x <= 0);
while (x < 5) {
    x = x + 1;
}
assert(x < 10);
```

$$\begin{aligned} \forall x \cdot x \leq 0 &\implies \mathit{Inv}(x) \\ \forall x, y \cdot \mathit{Inv}(x) \land x < 5 \land y = x + 1 &\implies \mathit{Inv}(y) \\ \forall x \cdot \mathit{Inv}(x) \land \neg(x < 5) \land \neg(x < 10) &\implies \text{false} \end{aligned}$$

**Fig. 1.** A program and its verification conditions in CHC.

A CHC($\mathcal{A}$) sentence $\Phi$ is satisfiable if there exists a model $\mathcal{M}$ of $\mathcal{A}$ extended with interpretation for all of the uninterpreted predicates in $\Phi$ such that $\mathcal{M}$ satisfies $\Phi$, written $\mathcal{M} \models \Phi$. In practice, we are often interested not in an arbitrary model, but a model that can be described concisely in some target fragment of FOL. We call such models *solutions*. Given an FOL fragment $\mathcal{F}$, an $\mathcal{F}$-solution to a $CHC(\mathcal{A})$ formula $\Phi$ is a model $\mathcal{M}$ such that $\mathcal{M} \models \Phi$ and interpretation of every uninterpreted predicate in $\mathcal{M}$ is definable in $\mathcal{F}$. Most commonly, $\mathcal{F}$ is taken to be either a quantifier free or universally quantified fragment of arithmetic $\mathcal{A}$, often further extended with arrays.

*Example 1.* To illustrate the definitions above consider a C program of a simple counter shown in Fig. 1. The goal is to verify that the assertion at the end of the program holds on every execution. To verify the assertion using the principle of inductive invariants, we need to show that there exists a formula $Inv(x)$ over program variable $x$ such that (a) it is true before the loop, stable at every iteration of the loop, and guarantees the assertion when the loop terminates. Since we are interested in partial correctness, we are not concerned with the case when the loop does not terminate. This principle is naturally encoded as three Constrained Horn Clauses, shown in the in Fig. 1. The uninterpreted predicate *Inv* represents the inductive invariant. The program is correct, hence the CHCs are satisfiable. The satisfying model extends the theory of arithmetic with the following definitions of *Inv*:

$$\mathit{Inv}^{\mathcal{M}} = \{z \mid z \leq 5\} \tag{3}$$

The CHCs also have a *solution* in the quantifier free theory of Linear Integer Arithmetic. In particular, *Inv* can be defined as follows:

$$\mathit{Inv} = \lambda z \cdot z \leq 5 \tag{4}$$

where the notation function with argument $x$ and body $\varphi$.

The CHCs in this example can be expressed as an SMT-LIB script, shown in Fig. 2, and solved by SPACER engine of Z3. Note that the script uses some Z3-specific extensions, including logic `HORN` and several option that disable pre-processing (which is not necessary for such a simple example).

□

*Example 2.* Figure 3 shows a similar program, however, with a function `inc` that abstracts away the increment operation. The corresponding CHCs are also shown

```
(set-logic HORN)
(set-option :fp.xform.inline_linear false)
(set-option :fp.xform.inline_eager false)
(declare-fun Inv ( Int ) Bool)

(assert (forall ((x Int)) (=> (<= x 0) (Inv x))))
(assert (forall ((x Int)) (=> (< x 5) (Inv (+ x 1)))))
(assert (forall ((x Int)) (=> (and (Inv x) (>= x 5) (>= x 10)) false)))
(check-sat)
(get-model)
```

**Fig. 2.** CHCs from Fig. 1 in SMT-LIB format.

```
int inc(int z) { return z + 1; }
assume(x <= 0);
while (x < 5) {
   x = inc(x);
}
assert(x < 10);
```

$$\begin{aligned}\forall z, r \cdot r = z + 1 &\implies \mathit{Inc}(z, r)\\ \forall x \cdot x \leq 0 &\implies \mathit{Inv}(x)\\ \forall x, y \cdot \mathit{Inv}(x) \wedge x < 5 \wedge \mathit{Inc}(y, x) &\implies \mathit{Inv}(y)\\ \forall x \cdot \mathit{Inv}(x) \wedge \neg(x < 5) \wedge \neg(x < 10) &\implies \text{false}\end{aligned}$$

**Fig. 3.** A program with a function and its verification conditions in CHC.

in Fig. 3. There are two unknowns, *Inv* that represents the desired inductive invariant, and *Inc* that represents the summary (i.e., pre- and post-conditions, or an over-approximation) of the function `inc`. Since the program still satisfies the assertion, the CHCs are satisfiable, and have

$$\mathit{Inv}^{\mathcal{M}} = \{z \mid z \leq 5\} = \lambda z \cdot z \leq 5 \tag{5}$$

$$\mathit{Inc}^{\mathcal{M}} = \{(z, r) \mid r = z + 1\} = \lambda z, r \cdot r \leq z + 1 \tag{6}$$

The corresponding SMT-LIB script is shown in Fig. 4. □

*Example 3.* In this last example, consider a set of CHCs shown in Fig. 5. They are similar to CHCs in Fig. 1, with one exception. These CHCs are unsatisfiable. There is no interpretation of *Inv* to satisfy them. This is witnessed by a refutation – a resolution proof – shown in Fig. 6. The corresponding SMT-LIB script in shown in Fig. 7. □

## 3 Solving CHC Modulo Theories

The logic of CHC can be seen as a convenient modelling language. That is, it does not restrict or impose a preference on a decision procedure used to solve the problem. In fact, a variety of solvers and techniques are widely available, including SPACER [28] (that is available as part of Z3), FreqHorn [12], and ELDARICA [22]. There is also an annual competition, CHC-COMP[1], to evaluate state-of-the-art solvers. In the rest of this section, we give a brief overview of the algorithm underlying SPACER.

[1] https://chc-comp.github.io/.

```
(set-logic HORN)
(set-option :fp.xform.inline_linear false)
(set-option :fp.xform.inline_eager false)
(declare-fun Inv ( Int ) Bool)
(declare-fun Inc ( Int Int ) Bool)

(assert (forall ((z Int)) (Inc z (+ z 1))))
(assert (forall ((x Int)) (=> (<= x 0) (Inv x))))
(assert (forall ((x Int) (y Int)) (=> (and (< x 5) (Inc x y)) (Inv y))))
(assert (forall ((x Int)) (=> (and (Inv x) (>= x 5) (>= x 10)) false)))
(check-sat)
(get-model)
```

**Fig. 4.** CHCs from Fig. 3 in SMT-LIB format.

$$\begin{aligned}\forall x \cdot x \leq 0 &\implies \mathit{Inv}(x)\\ \forall x, y \cdot \mathit{Inv}(x) \wedge x < 5 \wedge y = x + 1 &\implies \mathit{Inv}(y)\\ \forall x \cdot \mathit{Inv}(x) \wedge \neg(x \geq 1) &\implies \text{false}\end{aligned}$$

**Fig. 5.** An example of unsatisfiable CHCs.

SPACER is an extension and generalization of SAT-based Model Checking algorithms to CHC modulo SMT-supported theories. On propositional transition systems, SPACER behaves similarly to IC3 [6] and PDR [11], and can be seen as an adaptation of these algorithms. For other first-order theories, SPACER extends Generalized PDR of Hoder and Bjørner [21].

Given a CHC system $\Phi$, SPACER works by iteratively looking for a bounded derivation of false from $\Phi$. It explores $\Phi$ in a top-down (or backwards) direction. Each time SPACER fails to find a derivation of a fixed bound $N$, the reasons for failure are analyzed to derive consequences of $\Phi$ that explain why a derivation of false must have at least $N + 1$ steps. This process is repeated until either (a) false is derived and $\Phi$ is shown to be unsatisfiable, (b) the consequences form a solution to $\Phi$, thus, showing that $\Phi$ satisfiable, or (c) the process continues indefinitely, but continuously ruling out impossibility of longer and longer refutations. Thus, even though the problem is in general undecidable, SPACER always makes progress trying to show that $\Phi$ is unsatisfiable or that there is no short proof of unsatisiability.

SPACER is a procedure for solving linear and non-linear CHCs. For convenience of the presentation, we restrict ourselves to a special case of non-linear CHCs that consists of the following three clauses:

$$\mathit{Init}(X) \Rightarrow P(X) \tag{7}$$

$$P(X) \Rightarrow \mathit{Bad}(X) \tag{8}$$

$$P(X) \wedge P(X^o) \wedge \mathit{Tr}(X, X^o, X') \Rightarrow P(X') \tag{9}$$

$$\dfrac{x=0\;\dfrac{x=0\;\dfrac{\overline{\forall x\cdot x\geq 0 \implies Inv(x)}}{Inv(0)} \qquad \overline{\forall x\cdot Inv(x)\land x<5 \implies Inv(x+1)}}{Inv(1)} \qquad \overline{\forall x\cdot Inv(x)\land x\geq 1 \implies false}}{false}$$

**Fig. 6.** Refutation proof for CHCs in Fig. 5.

```
(set-logic HORN)
(set-option :produce-proofs true)
(set-option :fp.xform.inline_linear false)
(set-option :fp.xform.inline_eager false)
(declare-fun Inv ( Int ) Bool)

(assert (forall ((x Int)) (=> (<= x 0) (Inv x))))
(assert (forall ((x Int)) (=> (< x 5) (Inv (+ x 1)))))
(assert (forall ((x Int)) (=> (and (Inv x) (>= x 5) (>= x 2)) false)))
(check-sat)
(get-proof)
```

**Fig. 7.** CHCs from Fig. 5 in SMT-LIB format.

where, $X$ is a set of free variables, $X' = \{x' \mid x \in X\}$ and $X^o = \{x^o \mid x \in X\}$ are auxiliary free variables, *Init*, *Bad*, and *Tr* are FOL formulas over the free variables (as indicated), and $P$ is an uninterpreted predicate. Recall that all free variables in each clause are implicitly universally quantified. Thus, the only unknown to solve for is the uninterpreted predicate $P$. We call these three clauses a *safety problem*, and write $\langle Init(X), Tr(X, X^o, X'), Bad(X)\rangle$ as a shorthand to represent them. It is not hard to show that satisfiability of arbitrary CHCs is reducible to a safety problem. Thus, this simplification does not lose generality. In practice, SPACER directly supports more complex CHCs with multiple unknown uninterpreted predicates.

Before presenting the algorithm, we need to introduce two concepts from logic: *Craig Interpolation* and *Model Based Projection.*

*Craig Interpolation.* Given two formulas $A[\vec{x}, \vec{z}]$ and $B[\vec{y}, \vec{z}]$ such that $A \land B$ is unsatisfiable, a *Craig interpolant* $I[\vec{z}] = \textsc{Itp}(A[\vec{x}, \vec{z}], B[\vec{y}, \vec{z}])$, is a formula $I[\vec{z}]$ such that $A[\vec{x}, \vec{z}] \Rightarrow I[\vec{z}]$ and $I[\vec{z}] \Rightarrow \neg B[\vec{y}, \vec{z}]$. We further require that the interpolant is a clause. Intuitively, the interpolant $I$ captures the consequences of $A$ that are inconsistent with $B$. If $A$ is a conjunction of literals, the interpolant can be seen as a semantic variant of an UNSAT core.

*Model Based Projection.* Let $\varphi$ be a formula, $U \subseteq Vars(\varphi)$ a subset of variables of $\varphi$, and $P$ a model of $\varphi$. Then, $\psi = \textsc{Mbp}(U, P, \varphi)$ is a model based projection if (a) $\psi$ is a monomial, (b) $Vars(\psi) \subseteq Vars(\varphi) \setminus U$, (c) $P \models \psi$, (d) $\psi \Rightarrow \exists V \cdot \varphi$. Intuitively, an MBP is an under-approximation of existential quantifier elimination, where the choice of the under-approximation is guided by the model.

**Input:** A safety problem $\langle Init(X), Tr(X, X^o, X'), Bad(X)\rangle$.
**Output:** *Unreachable* or *Reachable*
**Data:** A cex queue $Q$, where a cex $c \in Q$ is a pair $\langle m, i\rangle$, $m$ is a cube over state variables, and $i \in \mathbb{N}$. A level $N$. A set of reachable states REACH. A trace $F_0, F_1, \ldots$
**Notation:** $\mathcal{F}(A, B) = Init(X') \vee (A(X) \wedge B(X^o) \wedge Tr)$, and $\mathcal{F}(A) = \mathcal{F}(A, A)$
**Initially:** $Q = \emptyset$, $N = 0$, $F_0 = Init$, $\forall i > 0 \cdot F_i = \emptyset$, REACH $= Init$
**Require:** $Init \rightarrow \neg Bad$
**repeat**

**Unreachable** If there is an $i < N$ s.t. $F_i \subseteq F_{i+1}$ **return** *Unreachable*.

**Reachable** If REACH $\wedge$ *Bad* is satisfiable, **return** *Reachable*.

**Unfold** If $F_N \rightarrow \neg Bad$, then set $N \leftarrow N + 1$ and $Q \leftarrow \emptyset$.

**Candidate** If for some $m$, $m \rightarrow F_N \wedge Bad$, then add $\langle m, N\rangle$ to $Q$.

**Successor** If there is $\langle m, i+1\rangle \in Q$ and a model $M$ s.t. $M \models \psi$, where $\psi = \mathcal{F}(\vee \text{REACH}) \wedge m'$. Then, add $s$ to REACH, where $s' \in \text{MBP}(\{X, X^o\}, \psi)$.

**MustPredecessor** If there is $\langle m, i+1\rangle \in Q$, and a model $M$ s.t. $M \models \psi$, where $\psi = \mathcal{F}(F_i, \vee \text{REACH}) \wedge m'$. Then, add $s$ to $Q$, where $s \in \text{MBP}(\{X^o, X'\}, \psi)$.

**MayPredecessor** If there is $\langle m, i+1\rangle \in Q$ and a model $M$ s.t. $M \models \psi$, where $\psi = \mathcal{F}(F_i) \wedge m'$. Then, add $s$ to $Q$, where $s^o \in \text{MBP}(\{X, X'\}, \psi)$.

**NewLemma** If there is an $\langle m, i+1\rangle \in Q$, s.t. $\mathcal{F}(F_i) \wedge m'$ is unsatisfiable. Then, add $\varphi = \text{ITP}(\mathcal{F}(F_i), m')$ to $F_j$, for all $0 \le j \le i + 1$.

**ReQueue** If $\langle m, i\rangle \in Q$, $0 < i < N$ and $\mathcal{F}(F_{i-1}) \wedge m'$ is unsatisfiable, then add $\langle m, i+1\rangle$ to $Q$.

**Push** For $0 \le i < N$ and a clause $(\varphi \vee \psi) \in F_i$, if $\varphi \notin F_{i+1}$, $\mathcal{F}(\varphi \wedge F_i) \rightarrow \varphi'$, then add $\varphi$ to $F_j$, for all $j \le i + 1$.

**until** $\infty$;

**Algorithm 1:** Rule-based description of SPACER.

We present SPACER [27] as a set of rules shown in Algorithm 1. While the algorithm is sound under any order on application of the rules, it is easy to see that only some orders lead to progress. Since solving CHCs even over LIA is undecidable, we are only concerned with soundness and progress, and do not discuss termination. The algorithm is based on the core principles of IC3 [5], however, it differs significantly in the details. The rules **Unreachable** and **Reachable** detect termination, either by discovering an inductive solution, or by discovering existence of a refutation, respectively. **Unfold** increases the exploration depth, and **Candidate** constructs a new *proof obligation* based on the current depth and the set *Bad* of *bad states*. **Successor** computes additional *reachable states*, that is, an under-approximation of the model of the implicit predicate $P$. Note that it used Model Based Projection to under-approximate forward predicate transformer. The rules **MustPredecessor** and **MayPredecessor** compute a new proof obligation that precedes an existing one. **MustPredecessor** does the computation based on existing reachable states, while **MayPredecessor** makes a guess based on existing over-approximation of $P$. In this case, MBP is used again, but now to under-approximate a backward predicate transformer.

The rule **NewLemma** computes a new over-approximation, called a *lemma*, of what is derivable about $P$ in $i+1$ by blocking a proof obligation. This is very similar to the corresponding step in IC3. Note, however, that interpolation is used to generalize the learned lemma beyond the literals of the proof obligation. **ReQueue** allows pushing blocked proof obligations to higher level, and **Push** allows pushing and inductively generalizing lemmas.

SPACER was introduced in [27]. Extension for convex linear arithmetic (i.e., discovering convex and co-convex solutions) is described in [3]. Support for quantifier free solutions for CHC over the combined theories of arrays and arithmetic is described in [26]. Extension for quantified solutions, which are necessary for establishing interesting properties when arrays are involved is described in [20]. More recently, the interpolation for lemma-generalization has been replaced by more global guidance [14]. This made SPACER competitive with other data-driven approaches that infer new lemmas based on numerical values of blocked counterexamples. Machine Learning-based inductive generalization has been suggested in [29]. The solver has also been extended to support Algebraic Data Types and Recursive Functions [16]. Work on improving support for bit-vectors [15] and experimenting with support for uninterpreted functions is ongoing.

## References


1. Alt, L., Blicha, M., Hyvarinen, A., Sharygina, N.: SolCMC: solidity compiler's model checker. In: Proceedings of CAV 2022 (2022)
2. Beyene, T.A., Popeea, C., Rybalchenko, A.: Efficient CTL verification via horn constraints solving. In: Gallagher, J.P., Rümmer, P. (eds.) Proceedings 3rd Workshop on Horn Clauses for Verification and Synthesis, HCVS@ETAPS 2016, Eindhoven, The Netherlands, 3rd April 2016. EPTCS, vol. 219, pp. 1–14 (2016). https://doi.org/10.4204/EPTCS.219.1
3. Bjørner, N., Gurfinkel, A.: Property directed polyhedral abstraction. In: D'Souza, D., Lal, A., Larsen, K.G. (eds.) VMCAI 2015. LNCS, vol. 8931, pp. 263–281. Springer, Heidelberg (2015). https://doi.org/10.1007/978-3-662-46081-8_15
4. Bjørner, N., Gurfinkel, A., McMillan, K., Rybalchenko, A.: Horn clause solving for program verification. In: Proceedings of a Symposium on Logic in Computer Science celebrating Yuri Gurevich's 75th Birthday (2015)
5. Bradley, A.R.: SAT-based model checking without unrolling. In: Jhala, R., Schmidt, D. (eds.) VMCAI 2011. LNCS, vol. 6538, pp. 70–87. Springer, Heidelberg (2011). https://doi.org/10.1007/978-3-642-18275-4_7
6. Bradley, A.R.: IC3 and beyond: incremental, inductive verification. In: CAV, p. 4 (2012)
7. Cadar, C., Dunbar, D., Engler, D.R.: KLEE: unassisted and automatic generation of high-coverage tests for complex systems programs. In: Draves, R., van Renesse, R. (eds.) 8th USENIX Symposium on Operating Systems Design and Implementation, OSDI 2008, December 8–10, 2008, San Diego, California, USA, Proceedings, pp. 209–224. USENIX Association (2008). http://www.usenix.org/events/osdi08/tech/full_papers/cadar/cadar.pdf

8. Calzavara, S., Grishchenko, I., Maffei, M.: Horndroid: practical and sound static analysis of android applications by SMT solving. CoRR abs/1707.07866 (2017). http://arxiv.org/abs/1707.07866
9. Carter, M., He, S., Whitaker, J., Rakamaric, Z., Emmi, M.: SMACK software verification toolchain. In: Dillon, L.K., Visser, W., Williams, L. (eds.) Proceedings of the 38th International Conference on Software Engineering, ICSE 2016, Austin, TX, USA, May 14–22, 2016 - Companion Volume, pp. 589–592. ACM (2016). https://doi.org/10.1145/2889160.2889163
10. Clarke, E., Kroening, D., Lerda, F.: A tool for checking ANSI-C programs. In: Jensen, K., Podelski, A. (eds.) TACAS 2004. LNCS, vol. 2988, pp. 168–176. Springer, Heidelberg (2004). https://doi.org/10.1007/978-3-540-24730-2_15
11. Eén, N., Mishchenko, A., Brayton, R.K.: Efficient implementation of property directed reachability. In: Bjesse, P., Slobodová, A. (eds.) International Conference on Formal Methods in Computer-Aided Design, FMCAD 2011, Austin, TX, USA, October 30–November 02 2011, pp. 125–134. FMCAD Inc. (2011). http://dl.acm.org/citation.cfm?id=2157675
12. Fedyukovich, G., Prabhu, S., Madhukar, K., Gupta, A.: Solving constrained horn clauses using syntax and data. In: Bjørner, N.S., Gurfinkel, A. (eds.) 2018 Formal Methods in Computer Aided Design, FMCAD 2018, Austin, TX, USA, October 30–November 2 2018, pp. 1–9. IEEE (2018). https://doi.org/10.23919/FMCAD.2018.8603011
13. Filliâtre, J.-C., Paskevich, A.: Why3–where programs meet provers. In: Felleisen, M., Gardner, P. (eds.) ESOP 2013. LNCS, vol. 7792, pp. 125–128. Springer, Heidelberg (2013). https://doi.org/10.1007/978-3-642-37036-6_8
14. Vediramana Krishnan, H.G., Chen, Y.T., Shoham, S., Gurfinkel, A.: Global guidance for local generalization in model checking. In: Lahiri, S.K., Wang, C. (eds.) CAV 2020. LNCS, vol. 12225, pp. 101–125. Springer, Cham (2020). https://doi.org/10.1007/978-3-030-53291-8_7
15. Govind V. K., H., Fedyukovich, G., Gurfinkel, A.: Word level property directed reachability. In: Proceedings of the 39th International Conference on Computer-Aided Design. ICCAD 2020, Association for Computing Machinery, New York, NY, USA (2020). https://doi.org/10.1145/3400302.3415708
16. Govind V. K., H., Shoham, S., Gurfinkel, A.: Solving constrained horn clauses modulo algebraic data types and recursive functions. Proc. ACM Program. Lang. **6**(POPL), 1–29 (2022). https://doi.org/10.1145/3498722
17. Grebenshchikov, S., Lopes, N.P., Popeea, C., Rybalchenko, A.: Synthesizing software verifiers from proof rules. In: Vitek, J., Lin, H., Tip, F. (eds.) ACM SIGPLAN Conference on Programming Language Design and Implementation, PLDI 2012, Beijing, China - 11–16 June 2012, pp. 405–416. ACM (2012). https://doi.org/10.1145/2254064.2254112
18. Gurfinkel, A., Kahsai, T., Komuravelli, A., Navas, J.A.: The SeaHorn Verification Framework. In: Kroening, D., Pasareanu, C.S. (eds.) Computer Aided Verification - 27th International Conference, CAV 2015, San Francisco, CA, USA, July 18–24, 2015, Proceedings, Part I. Lecture Notes in Computer Science, vol. 9206, pp. 343–361. Springer (2015). https://doi.org/10.1007/978-3-319-21690-4⟨errorl=”336” c=”Missing dollar” /¿20, http://dx.doi.org/10.1007/978-3-319-21690-4_20

19. Gurfinkel, A., Shoham, S., Meshman, Y.: SMT-based verification of parameterized systems. In: Zimmermann, T., Cleland-Huang, J., Su, Z. (eds.) Proceedings of the 24th ACM SIGSOFT International Symposium on Foundations of Software Engineering, FSE 2016, Seattle, WA, USA, 13–18 November 2016, pp. 338–348. ACM (2016). https://doi.org/10.1145/2950290.2950330
20. Gurfinkel, A., Shoham, S., Vizel, Y.: Quantifiers on demand. In: Lahiri, S.K., Wang, C. (eds.) ATVA 2018. LNCS, vol. 11138, pp. 248–266. Springer, Cham (2018). https://doi.org/10.1007/978-3-030-01090-4_15
21. Hoder, K., Bjørner, N.: Generalized property directed reachability. In: Cimatti, A., Sebastiani, R. (eds.) SAT 2012. LNCS, vol. 7317, pp. 157–171. Springer, Heidelberg (2012). https://doi.org/10.1007/978-3-642-31612-8_13
22. Hojjat, H., Rümmer, P.: The ELDARICA horn solver. In: Bjørner, N.S., Gurfinkel, A. (eds.) 2018 Formal Methods in Computer Aided Design, FMCAD 2018, Austin, TX, USA, October 30–November 2 2018, pp. 1–7. IEEE (2018). https://doi.org/10.23919/FMCAD.2018.8603013
23. Hojjat, H., Rümmer, P., Subotic, P., Yi, W.: Horn clauses for communicating timed systems. In: Bjørner, N.S., Fioravanti, F., Rybalchenko, A., Senni, V. (eds.) Proceedings First Workshop on Horn Clauses for Verification and Synthesis, HCVS 2014, Vienna, Austria, 17 July 2014. EPTCS, vol. 169, pp. 39–52 (2014). https://doi.org/10.4204/EPTCS.169.6
24. Jaffar, J., Lassez, J.L.: Constraint logic programming. In: POPL, pp. 111–119 (1987)
25. Kahsai, T., Rümmer, P., Sanchez, H., Schäf, M.: JayHorn: a framework for verifying Java programs. In: Chaudhuri, S., Farzan, A. (eds.) CAV 2016. LNCS, vol. 9779, pp. 352–358. Springer, Cham (2016). https://doi.org/10.1007/978-3-319-41528-4_19
26. Komuravelli, A., Bjørner, N., Gurfinkel, A., McMillan, K.L.: Compositional verification of procedural programs using horn clauses over integers and arrays. In: Kaivola, R., Wahl, T. (eds.) Formal Methods in Computer-Aided Design, FMCAD 2015, Austin, Texas, USA, 27–30 September 2015, pp. 89–96. IEEE (2015)
27. Komuravelli, A., Gurfinkel, A., Chaki, S.: SMT-based model checking for recursive programs. In: Biere, A., Bloem, R. (eds.) CAV 2014. LNCS, vol. 8559, pp. 17–34. Springer, Cham (2014). https://doi.org/10.1007/978-3-319-08867-9_2
28. Komuravelli, A., Gurfinkel, A., Chaki, S., Clarke, E.M.: Automatic abstraction in SMT-based unbounded software model checking. In: CAV, pp. 846–862 (2013)
29. Le, N., Si, X., Gurfinkel, A.: Data-driven optimization of inductive generalization. In: Formal Methods in Computer Aided Design, FMCAD 2021, New Haven, CT, USA, 19–22 October 2021, pp. 86–95. IEEE (2021). https://doi.org/10.34727/2021/isbn.978-3-85448-046-4_17
30. Leino, K.R.M.: Developing verified programs with Dafny. In: Brosgol, B., Boleng, J., Taft, S.T. (eds.) Proceedings of the 2012 ACM Conference on High Integrity Language Technology, HILT 2012, 2–6 December 2012, Boston, Massachusetts, USA, pp. 9–10. ACM (2012). https://doi.org/10.1145/2402676.2402682
31. Matsushita, Y., Tsukada, T., Kobayashi, N.: Rusthorn: CHC-based verification for rust programs. ACM Trans. Program. Lang. Syst. **43**(4), 15:1–15:54 (2021). https://doi.org/10.1145/3462205
32. de Moura, L., Bjørner, N.: Z3: an efficient SMT solver. In: Ramakrishnan, C.R., Rehof, J. (eds.) TACAS 2008. LNCS, vol. 4963, pp. 337–340. Springer, Heidelberg (2008). https://doi.org/10.1007/978-3-540-78800-3_24

33. Popeea, C., Rybalchenko, A., Wilhelm, A.: Reduction for compositional verification of multi-threaded programs. In: Formal Methods in Computer-Aided Design, FMCAD 2014, Lausanne, Switzerland, 21–24 October 2014, pp. 187–194. IEEE (2014). https://doi.org/10.1109/FMCAD.2014.6987612
34. Smaragdakis, Y., Balatsouras, G.: Pointer analysis. Found. Trends Program. Lang. **2**(1), 1–69 (2015). https://doi.org/10.1561/2500000014
35. Tan, B., Mariano, B., Lahiri, S.K., Dillig, I., Feng, Y.: SolType: refinement types for arithmetic overflow in solidity. Proc. ACM Program. Lang. **6**(POPL), 1–29 (2022). https://doi.org/10.1145/3498665
36. Toman, J., Siqi, R., Suenaga, K., Igarashi, A., Kobayashi, N.: ConSORT: context- and flow-sensitive ownership refinement types for imperative programs. In: ESOP 2020. LNCS, vol. 12075, pp. 684–714. Springer, Cham (2020). https://doi.org/10.1007/978-3-030-44914-8_25
37. Wesley, S., et al.: Verifying solidity smart contracts via communication abstraction in SmartACE. In: Finkbeiner, B., Wies, T. (eds.) VMCAI 2022. LNCS, vol. 13182, pp. 425–449. Springer, Cham (2022). https://doi.org/10.1007/978-3-030-94583-1_21

# Formal Methods for Probabilistic Programs

# Data-Driven Invariant Learning for Probabilistic Programs

Jialu Bao[1(✉)], Nitesh Trivedi[2], Drashti Pathak[3], Justin Hsu[1], and Subhajit Roy[2]

[1] Cornell University, Ithaca, NY, USA
jb965@cornell.edu, email@justinh.su
[2] Indian Institute of Technology (IIT) Kanpur, Kanpur, India
{nitesht,subhajit}@iitk.ac.in
[3] Amazon, Bengaluru, India

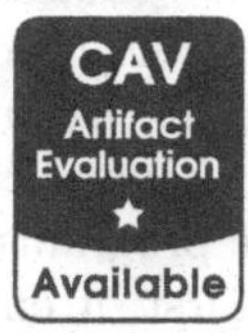


**Abstract.** Morgan and McIver's *weakest pre-expectation* framework is one of the most well-established methods for deductive verification of probabilistic programs. Roughly, the idea is to generalize binary state assertions to real-valued *expectations*, which can measure expected values of probabilistic program quantities. While loop-free programs can be analyzed by mechanically transforming expectations, verifying loops usually requires finding an *invariant expectation*, a difficult task.

We propose a new view of invariant expectation synthesis as a *regression* problem: given an input state, predict the *average* value of the post-expectation in the output distribution. Guided by this perspective, we develop the first *data-driven* invariant synthesis method for probabilistic programs. Unlike prior work on probabilistic invariant inference, our approach can learn piecewise continuous invariants without relying on template expectations. We also develop a data-driven approach to learn *sub-invariants* from data, which can be used to upper- or lower-bound expected values. We implement our approaches and demonstrate their effectiveness on a variety of benchmarks from the probabilistic programming literature.

**Keywords:** Probabilistic programs · Data-driven invariant learning · Weakest pre-expectations

## 1 Introduction

*Probabilistic programs*—standard imperative programs augmented with a sampling command—are a common way to express randomized computations. While the mathematical semantics of such programs is fairly well-understood [25], verification methods remain an active area of research. Existing automated techniques are either limited to specific properties (e.g., [3,9,35,37]), or target simpler computational models [4,15,28].


S. Shoham and Y. Vizel (Eds.): CAV 2022, LNCS 13371, pp. 33–54, 2022.
https://doi.org/10.1007/978-3-031-13185-1_3

*Reasoning About Expectations.* One of the earliest methods for reasoning about probabilistic programs is through *expectations*. Originally proposed by Kozen [26], expectations generalize standard, binary assertions to quantitative, real-valued functions on program states. Morgan and McIver further developed this idea into a powerful framework for reasoning about probabilistic imperative programs, called the *weakest pre-expectation calculus* [30,33].

Concretely, Morgan and McIver defined an operator called the *weakest pre-expectation* (wpe), which takes an expectation $E$ and a program $P$ and produces an expectation $E'$ such that $E'(\sigma)$ is the expected value of $E$ in the output distribution $[\![P]\!]_\sigma$. In this way, the wpe operator can be viewed as a generalization of Dijkstra's weakest pre-conditions calculus [16] to probabilistic programs. For verification purposes, the wpe operator has two key strengths. First, it enables reasoning about probabilities and expected values. Second, when $P$ is a loop-free program, it is possible to transform $\mathsf{wpe}(P, E)$ into a form that does not mention the program $P$ via simple, mechanical manipulations, essentially analyzing the effect of the program on the expectation through syntactically transforming $E$.

However, there is a caveat: the wpe of a loop is defined as a least fixed point, and it is generally difficult to simplify this quantity into a more tractable form. Fortunately, the wpe operator satisfies a *loop rule* that simplifies reasoning about loops: if we can find an expectation $I$ satisfying an *invariant* condition, then we can easily bound the wpe of a loop. Checking the invariant condition involves analyzing just the body of the loop, rather than the entire loop. Thus, finding invariants is a primary bottleneck towards automated reasoning about probabilistic programs.

*Discovering Invariants.* Two recent works have considered how to automatically infer invariant expectations for probabilistic loops. The first is PRINSYS [21]. Using a template with one hole, PRINSYS produces a first-order logical formula describing possible substitutions satisfying the invariant condition. While effective for their benchmark programs, the method's reliance on templates is limiting; furthermore, the user must manually solve a system of logical formulas to find the invariant.

The second work, by Chen et al. [14], focuses on inferring polynomial invariants. By restricting to this class, their method can avoid templates and can apply the Lagrange interpolation theorem to find a polynomial invariant. However, many invariants are not polynomials: for instance, an invariant may combine two polynomials piecewise by branching on a Boolean condition.

*Our Approach: Invariant Learning.* We take a different approach inspired by data-driven invariant learning [17,19]. In these methods, the program is executed with a variety of inputs to produce a set of execution traces. This data is viewed as a training set, and a machine learning algorithm is used to find a classifier describing the invariant. Data-driven techniques reduce the reliance on templates, and can treat the program as a black box—the precise implementation of the program need not be known, as long as the learner can execute the program to gather input and output data. But to extend the data-driven method to the probabilistic setting, there are a few key challenges:

- **Quantitative invariants.** While the logic of expectations resembles the logic of standard assertions, an important difference is that expectations are *quantitative*: they map program states to real numbers, not a binary yes/no. While standard invariant learning is a *classification* task (i.e., predicting a binary label given a program state), our probabilistic invariant learning is closer to a *regression* task (i.e., predicting a number given a program state).
- **Stochastic data.** Standard invariant learning assumes the program behaves like a *function*: a given input state always leads to the same output state. In contrast, a probabilistic program takes an input state to a distribution over outputs. Since we are only able to observe a single draw from the output distribution each time we run the program, execution traces in our setting are inherently *noisy*. Accordingly, we cannot hope to learn an invariant that fits the observed data perfectly, even if the program has an invariant—our learner must be robust to noisy training data.
- **Complex learning objective.** To fit a probabilistic invariant to data, the logical constraints defining an invariant must be converted into a regression problem with a loss function suitable for standard machine learning algorithms and models. While typical regression problems relate the unknown quantity to be learned to known data, the conditions defining invariants are somehow self-referential: they describe how an unknown invariant must be related to itself. This feature makes casting invariant learning as machine learning a difficult task.

*Outline.* After covering preliminaries (Sect. 2), we present our contributions.

- A general method called Exist for learning invariants for probabilistic programs (Sect. 3). Exist executes the program multiple times on a set of input states, and then uses machine learning algorithms to learn models encoding possible invariants. A CEGIS-like loop is used to iteratively expand the dataset after encountering incorrect candidate invariants.
- Concrete instantiations of Exist tailored for handling two problems: learning *exact invariants* (Sect. 4), and learning *sub-invariants* (Sect. 5). Our method for exact invariants learns a *model tree* [34], a generalization of binary decision trees to regression. The constraints for sub-invariants are more difficult to encode as a regression problem, and our method learns a *neural model tree* [41] with a custom loss function. While the models differ, both algorithms leverage off-the-shelf learning algorithms.
- An implementation of Exist and a thorough evaluation on a large set of benchmarks (Sect. 6). Our tool can learn invariants and sub-invariants for examples considered in prior work and new, more difficult versions that are beyond the reach of prior work.

We discuss related work in Sect. 7.

## 2 Preliminaries

*Probabilistic Programs.* We will consider programs written in **pWhile**, a basic probabilistic imperative language with the following grammar:

$$P := \textbf{skip} \mid x \leftarrow e \mid x \xleftarrow{\$} d \mid P \,;\, P \mid \textbf{if}\ e\ \textbf{then}\ P\ \textbf{else}\ P \mid \textbf{while}\ e : P,$$

where $e$ is a boolean or numerical expression. All commands $P$ map memories to distributions over memories [25], and the semantics is entirely standard and can be found in the extended version. We write $[\![P]\!]_\sigma$ for the output distribution of program $P$ from initial state $\sigma$. Since we will be interested in running programs on concrete inputs, *we will assume throughout that all loops are almost surely terminating*; this property can often be established by other methods (e.g., [12, 13, 31]).

*Weakest Pre-expectation Calculus.* Morgan and McIver's *weakest pre-expectation calculus* reasons about probabilistic programs by manipulating *expectations.*

**Definition 1.** *Denote the set of program states by $\Sigma$. Define the set of expectations, $\mathcal{E}$, to be $\{E \mid E : \Sigma \to \mathbb{R}^{\infty}_{\geq 0}\}$. Define $E_1 \leq E_2$ iff $\forall \sigma \in \Sigma : E_1(\sigma) \leq E_2(\sigma)$. The set $\mathcal{E}$ is a complete lattice.*

While expectations are technically mathematical functions from $\Sigma$ to the non-negative extended reals, for formal reasoning it is convenient to work with a more restricted syntax of expectations (see, e.g., [8]). We will often view numeric expressions as expectations. Boolean expressions $b$ can also be converted to expectations; we let $[b]$ be the expectation that maps states where $b$ holds to 1, and other states to 0. As an example of our notation, $[flip = 0] \cdot (x+1)$, $x+1$ are two expectations, and we have $[flip = 0] \cdot (x + 1) \leq x + 1$.

$$\begin{aligned}
\mathsf{wpe}(\textbf{skip}, E) &:= E \\
\mathsf{wpe}(x \leftarrow e, E) &:= E[e/x] \\
\mathsf{wpe}(x \xleftarrow{\$} d, E) &:= \lambda\sigma. \sum_{v \in \mathcal{V}} [\![d]\!]_\sigma(v) \cdot E[v/x] \\
\mathsf{wpe}(P \,;\, Q, E) &:= \mathsf{wpe}(P, \mathsf{wpe}(Q, E)) \\
\mathsf{wpe}(\textbf{if}\ e\ \textbf{then}\ P\ \textbf{else}\ Q, E) &:= [e] \cdot \mathsf{wpe}(P, E) + [\neg e] \cdot \mathsf{wpe}(Q, E) \\
\mathsf{wpe}(\textbf{while}\ e : P, E) &:= \mathsf{lfp}(\lambda X.\ [e] \cdot \mathsf{wpe}(P, X) + [\neg e] \cdot E)
\end{aligned}$$

**Fig. 1.** Morgan and McIver's weakest pre-expectation operator

Now, we are ready to introduce Morgan and McIver's *weakest pre-expectation transformer* wpe. In a nutshell, this operator takes a program $P$ and an expectation $E$ to another expectation $E'$, sometimes called the *pre-expectation.* Formally, wpe is defined in Fig. 1. The case for loops involves the least fixed-point (lfp) of $\Phi^{\mathsf{wpe}}_E := \lambda X.([e] \cdot \mathsf{wpe}(P, X) + [\neg e] \cdot E)$, the *characteristic function* of the loop with respect to $\mathsf{wpe}$ [23]. The characteristic function is monotone on the complete lattice $\mathcal{E}$, so the least fixed-point exists by the Kleene fixed-point theorem.

The key property of the $\mathsf{wpe}$ transformer is that for any program $P$, $\mathsf{wpe}(P, E)(\sigma)$ is the expected value of $E$ over the output distribution $[\![P]\!]_\sigma$.

**Theorem 1 (See, e.g., [23]).** *For any program $P$ and expectation $E \in \mathcal{E}$,* $\mathsf{wpe}(P, E) = \lambda\sigma. \sum_{\sigma' \in \Sigma} E(\sigma') \cdot [\![P]\!]_\sigma(\sigma')$

Intuitively, the weakest pre-expectation calculus provides a syntactic way to compute the expected value of an expression $E$ after running a program $P$, except when the program is a loop. For a loop, the least fixed point definition of $\mathsf{wpe}(\textbf{while } e : P, E)$ is hard to compute.

## 3 Algorithm Overview

In this section, we introduce the two related problems we aim to solve, and a meta-algorithm to tackle both of them. We will see how to instantiate the meta-algorithm's subroutines in Sect. 4 and Sect. 5.

*Problem Statement.* Analogous to when analyzing the weakest pre-conditions of a loop, knowing a loop *invariant* or *sub-invariant* expectation enables one to easily bound the loop's weakest pre-expectations, but a (sub)invariant expectation can be difficult to find. Thus, we aim to develop an algorithm to automatically synthesize invariants and sub-invariants of probabilistic loops. More specifically, our algorithm tackles the following two problems:

1. **Finding exact invariants:** Given a loop $\textbf{while } G : P$ and an expectation $\mathsf{postE}$ as input, we want to find an expectation $I$ such that
$$I = \Phi^{\mathsf{wpe}}_{\mathsf{postE}}(I) := [G] \cdot \mathsf{wpe}(P, I) + [\neg G] \cdot \mathsf{postE}. \tag{1}$$
Such an expectation $I$ is an *exact invariant* of the loop with respect to $\mathsf{postE}$. Since $\mathsf{wpe}(\textbf{while } G : P, \mathsf{postE})$ is a fixed point of $\Phi^{\mathsf{wpe}}_{\mathsf{postE}}$, $\mathsf{wpe}(\textbf{while } G : P, \mathsf{postE})$ has to be an exact invariant of the loop. Furthermore, when $\textbf{while } G : P$ is almost surely terminating and $\mathsf{postE}$ is upper-bounded, the existence of an exact invariant $I$ implies $I = \mathsf{wpe}(\textbf{while } e : P, E)$. (We defer the proof to the extended version.)
2. **Finding sub-invariants:** Given a loop $\textbf{while } G : P$ and expectations $\mathsf{preE}, \mathsf{postE}$, we aim to learn an expectation $I$ such that
$$I \leq \Phi^{\mathsf{wpe}}_{\mathsf{postE}}(I) := [G] \cdot \mathsf{wpe}(P, I) + [\neg G] \cdot \mathsf{postE} \tag{2}$$
$$\mathsf{preE} \leq I. \tag{3}$$
The first inequality says that $I$ is a sub-invariant: on states that satisfy $G$, the value of $I$ lower bounds the expected value of itself after running one loop iteration from initial state, and on states that violate $G$, the value of $I$ lower bounds the value of $\mathsf{postE}$. Any sub-invariant lower-bounds the weakest pre-expectation of the loop, i.e., $I \leq \mathsf{wpe}(\textbf{while } G : P, E)$ [22]. Together with the second inequality $\mathsf{preE} \leq I$, the existence of a sub-invariant $I$ ensures that $\mathsf{preE}$ lower-bounds the weakest pre-expectation.

Note that an exact invariant is a sub-invariant, so one indirect way to solve the second problem is to solve the first problem, and then check $\mathsf{preE} \leq I$. However, we aim to find a more direct approach to solve the second problem because often exact invariants can be complicated and hard to find, while sub-invariants can be simpler and easier to find.

```
EXIST(geo, pexp, N_runs, N_states):
    feat ← getFeatures(geo, pexp)
    states ← sampleStates(feat, N_states)
    data ← sampleTraces(geo, pexp, feat, N_runs, states)
    while not timed out:
        models ← learnInv(feat, data)
        candidates ← extractInv(models)
        for inv in candidates:
            verified, cex ← verifyInv(inv, geo)
            if verified:
                return inv
            else:
                states ← states ∪ cex
                states ← states ∪ sampleStates(feat, N'_states)
        data ← data ∪ sampleTraces(geo, pexp, feat, nruns, states)
```

**Fig. 2.** Algorithm EXIST

*Methods.* We solve both problems with one algorithm, EXIST (short for EXpectation Invariant SynThesis). Our data-driven method resembles Counterexample Guided Inductive Synthesis (CEGIS), but differs in two ways. First, candidates are synthesized by fitting a machine learning model to data consisted of program traces starting from random input states. Our target programs are also probabilistic, introducing a second source of randomness to program traces. Second, our approach seeks high-quality counterexamples—violating the target constraints as much as possible—in order to improve synthesis. For synthesizing invariants and sub-invariants, such counterexamples can be generated by using a computer algebra system to solve an optimization problem.

We present the pseudocode in Fig. 2. EXIST takes a probabilistic program geo, a post-expectation or a pair of pre/post-expectation *pexp*, and hyper-parameters $N_{runs}$ and $N_{states}$. EXIST starts by generating a list of features *feat*, which are numerical expressions formed by program variables used in geo. Next, EXIST samples $N_{states}$ initialization *states* and runs geo from each of those states for $N_{runs}$ trials, and records the value of *feat* on program traces as *data*. Then, EXIST enters a CEGIS loop. In each iteration of the loop, first the learner learnInv trains models to minimize their violation of the required inequalities (e.g., Eqs. (2)

and (3) for learning sub-invariants) on *data*. Next, extractInv translates learned models into a set *candidates* of expectations. For each candidate *inv*, the verifier verifyInv looks for program states that *maximize inv*'s violation of required inequalities. If it cannot find any program state where *inv* violates the inequalities, the verifier returns *inv* as a valid invariant or sub-invariant. Otherwise, it produces a set *cex* of counter-example program states, which are added to the set of initial states. Finally, before entering the next iteration, the algorithm augments *states* with a new batch of $N'_{states}$ initial states, generates trace data from running geo on each of these states for $N_{runs}$ trials, and augments the dataset *data*. This data augmentation ensures that the synthesis algorithm collects more and more initial states, some randomly generated (sampleStates) and some from prior counterexamples (*cex*), guiding the learner towards better candidates. Like other CEGIS-based tools, our method is sound but not complete, i.e., if the algorithm returns an expectation then it is guaranteed to be an exact invariant or sub-invariant, but the algorithm might never return an answer; in practice, we set a timeout.

## 4 Learning Exact Invariants

In this section, we detail how we instantiate EXIST's subroutines to learn an exact invariant $I$ satisfying $I = \Phi^{\mathsf{wpe}}_{\mathsf{postE}}(I)$, given a loop geo and an expectation $pexp = \mathsf{postE}$.

At a high level, we first sample a set of program states *states* using sampleStates. From each program state $s \in states$, sampleTraces executes geo and estimates $\mathsf{wpe}(\mathsf{geo}, \mathsf{postE})(s)$. Next, learnInv trains regression models $M$ to predict the estimated $\mathsf{wpe}(\mathsf{geo}, \mathsf{postE})(s)$ given the value of features evaluated on $s$. Then, extractInv translates the learned models $M$ to an expectation $I$. In an ideal scenario, this $I$ would be equal to $\mathsf{wpe}(\mathsf{geo}, \mathsf{postE})$, which is also always an exact invariant. But since $I$ is learned from stochastic data, it may be noisy. So, we use verifyInv to check whether $I$ satisfies the invariant condition $I = \Phi^{\mathsf{wpe}}_{\mathsf{postE}}(I)$.

The reader may wonder why we took this complicated approach, first estimating the weakest pre-expectation of the loop, and then computing the invariant: If we are able to learn an expression for $\mathsf{wpe}(\mathsf{geo}, \mathsf{postE})$ directly, then why are we interested in the invariant $I$? The answer is that with an invariant $I$, we can also *verify* that our computed value of $\mathsf{wpe}(prog, \mathsf{postE})$ is correct by checking the invariant condition and applying the loop rule. Since our learning process is inherently noisy, this verification step is crucial and motivates why we want to find an invariant.

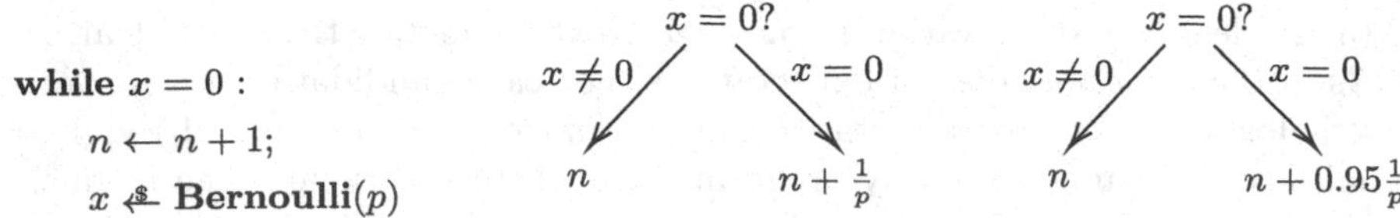


(a) Program: geo (b) Model tree for wpe(geo, $n$) (c) Another model tree

**Fig. 3.** Running example: program and model tree

*A Running Example.* We will illustrate our approach using Fig. 3. The simple program geo repeatedly loops: whenever $x$ becomes non-zero we exit the loop; otherwise we increase $n$ by 1 and draw $x$ from a biased coin-flip distribution ($x$ gets 1 with probability $p$, and 0 otherwise). We aim to learn wpe(geo, $n$), which is $[x \neq 0] \cdot n + [x = 0] \cdot (n + \frac{1}{p})$.

*Our Regression Model.* Before getting into how Exist collects data and trains models, we introduce the class of regression models it uses – *model trees*, a generalization of decision trees to regression tasks [34]. Model trees are naturally suited to expressing piecewise functions of inputs, and are straightforward to train. While our method can in theory generalize to other regression models, our implementation focuses on model trees.

More formally, a model tree $T \in \mathcal{T}$ over features $\mathcal{F}$ is a full binary tree where each internal node is labeled with a predicate $\phi$ over variables from $\mathcal{F}$, and each leaf is labeled with a real-valued model $M \in \mathcal{M} : \mathbb{R}^{\mathcal{F}} \to \mathbb{R}$. Given a feature vector in $x \in \mathbb{R}^{\mathcal{F}}$, a model tree $T$ over $\mathcal{F}$ produces a numerical output $T(x) \in \mathbb{R}$ as follows:

- If $T$ is of the form $\mathsf{Leaf}(M)$, then $T(x) := M(x)$.
- If $T$ is of the form $\mathsf{Node}(\phi, T_L, T_R)$, then $T(x) := T_R(x)$ if the predicate $\phi$ evaluates to true on $x$, and $T(x) := T_L(x)$ otherwise.

Throughout this paper, we consider model trees of the following form as our regression model. First, node predicates $\phi$ are of the form $f \bowtie c$, where $f \in \mathcal{F}$ is a feature, $\bowtie \in \{<, \leq, =, >, \geq\}$ is a comparison, and $c$ is a numeric constant. Second, leaf models on a model tree are either all *linear models* or all products of constant powers of features, which we call *multiplication models*. For example, assuming $n, \frac{1}{p}$ are both features, Fig. 3b and c are two model trees with linear leaf models, and Fig. 3b expresses the weakest pre-expectation wpe(geo, $n$). Formally, the leaf model $M$ on a feature vector $f$ is either

$$M_l(f) = \sum_{i=1}^{|\mathcal{F}|} \alpha_i \cdot f_i \qquad \text{or} \qquad M_m(f) = \prod_{i=1}^{|\mathcal{F}|} f_i^{\alpha_i}$$

with constants $\{\alpha_i\}_i$. Note that multiplication models can also be viewed as linear models on logarithmic values of features because $\log M_m(f) = \sum_{i=1}^{|\mathcal{F}|} \alpha_i \cdot$

$\log(f_i)$. While it is also straightforward to adapt our method to other leaf models, we focus on linear models and multiplication models because of their simplicity and expressiveness. Linear models and multiplication models also complement each other in their expressiveness: encoding expressions like $x + y$ uses simpler features with linear models (it suffices if $\mathcal{F} \ni x, y$, as opposed to needing $\mathcal{F} \ni x+y$ if using multiplicative models), while encoding $\frac{p}{1-p}$ uses simpler features with multiplicative models (it suffices if $\mathcal{F} \ni p, 1-p$, as opposed to needing $\mathcal{F} \ni \frac{p}{1-p}$ if using linear models).

### 4.1 Generate Features (getFeatures)

Given a program, the algorithm first generates a set of features $\mathcal{F}$ that model trees can use to express unknown invariants of the given loop. For example, for geo, $I = [x \neq 0] \cdot n + [x = 0] \cdot (n + \frac{1}{p})$ is an invariant, and to have a model tree (with linear/multiplication leaf models) express $I$, we want $\mathcal{F}$ to include both $n$ and $\frac{1}{p}$, or $n + \frac{1}{p}$ as one feature. $\mathcal{F}$ should include the program variables at a minimum, but it is often useful to have more complex features too. While generating more features increases the expressivity of the models, and richness of the invariants, there is a cost: the more features in $\mathcal{F}$, the more data is needed to train a model.

Starting from the program variables, getFeatures generates two lists of features, $\mathcal{F}_l$ for linear leaf models and $\mathcal{F}_m$ for multiplication leaf models. Intuitively, linear models are more expressive if the feature set $\mathcal{F}$ includes some products of terms, e.g., $n \cdot p^{-1}$, and multiplication models are more expressive if $\mathcal{F}$ includes some sums of terms, e.g., $n + 1$.

### 4.2 Sample Initial States (sampleStates)

Recall that Exist aims to learn an expectation $I$ that is equal to the weakest pre-expectation wpe(**while** $G$ : $P$, postE). A natural idea for sampleTraces is to run the program from all possible initializations multiple times, and record the average value of postE from each initialization. This would give a map close to wpe(**while** $G$ : $P$, postE) if we run enough trials so that the empirical mean is approximately the actual mean. However, this strategy is clearly impractical—many of the programs we consider have infinitely many possible initial states (e.g., programs with integer variables). Thus, sampleStates needs to choose a manageable number of initial states for sampleTraces to use.

In principle, a good choice of initializations should exercise as many parts of the program as possible. For instance, for geo in Fig. 3, if we only try initial states satisfying $x \neq 0$, then it is impossible to learn the term $[x = 0] \cdot (n + \frac{1}{p})$ in wpe(geo, $n$) from data. However, covering the control flow graph may not be enough. Ideally, to learn how the expected value of postE depends on the initial state, we also want data from multiple initial states along each path.

While it is unclear how to choose initializations to ensure optimal coverage, our implementation uses a simpler strategy: sampleStates generates $N_{states}$ states in total, each by sampling the value of every program variable uniformly at random from a space. We assume program variables are typed as booleans, integers, probabilities, or floating point numbers and sample variables of some type from the corresponding space. For boolean variables, the sampling space is simply $\{0, 1\}$; for probability variables, the space includes reals in some interval bounded away from 0 and 1, because probabilities too close to 0 or 1 tend to increase the variance of programs (e.g., making some loops iterate for a very long time); for floating point number and integer variables, the spaces are respectively reals and integers in some bounded range. This strategy, while simple, is already very effective in nearly all of our benchmarks (see Sect. 6), though other strategies are certainly possible (e.g., performing a grid search of initial states from some space).

### 4.3 Sample Training Data (sampleTraces)

We gather training data by running the given program geo on the set of initializations generated by sampleStates. From each program state $s \in \mathit{states}$, the subroutine sampleTraces runs geo for $N_{runs}$ times to get output states $\{s_1, \ldots, s_{N_{runs}}\}$ and produces the following training example:

$$(s_i, v_i) = \left( s_i, \frac{1}{N_{runs}} \sum_{i=1}^{N_{runs}} \mathsf{postE}(s_i) \right).$$

Above, the value $v_i$ is the empirical mean of postE in the output state of running geo from initial state $s_i$; as $N_{runs}$ grows large, this average value approaches the true expected value $\mathsf{wpe}(\mathsf{geo}, \mathsf{postE})(s)$.

### 4.4 Learning a Model Tree (learnInv)

Now that we have the training set $\mathit{data} = \{(s_1, v_1), \ldots, (s_K, v_K)\}$ (where $K = N_{states}$), we want to fit a model tree $T$ to the data. We aim to apply off-the-shelf tools that can learn model trees with customizable leaf models and loss. For each data entry, $v_i$ approximates $\mathsf{wpe}(\mathsf{geo}, \mathsf{postE})(s_i)$, so a natural idea is to train a model tree $T$ that takes the value of features on $s_i$ as input and predicts $v_i$. To achieve that, we want to define the loss to measure the error between predicted values $T(\mathcal{F}_l(s_i))$ (or $T(\mathcal{F}_m(s_i))$) and the target value $v_i$. Without loss of generality, we can assume our invariant $I$ is of the form

$$I = \mathsf{postE} + [G] \cdot I' \tag{4}$$

because $I$ being an invariant means

$$I = [\neg G] \cdot \mathsf{postE} + [G] \cdot \mathsf{wpe}(P, I) = \mathsf{postE} + [G] \cdot (\mathsf{wpe}(P, I) - \mathsf{postE}).$$

In many cases, the expectation $I' = \mathsf{wpe}(P, I) - \mathsf{postE}$ is simpler than $I$: for example, the weakest pre-expectation of geo can be expressed as $n + [x = 0] \cdot (\frac{1}{p})$;

while $I$ is represented by a tree that splits on the predicate $[x = 0]$ and needs both $n, \frac{1}{p}$ as features, the expectation $I' = \frac{1}{p}$ is represented by a single leaf model tree that only needs $p$ as a feature.

Aiming to learn weakest pre-expectations $I$ in the form of Eq. (4), Exist trains model trees $T$ to fit $I'$. More precisely, learnInv trains a model tree $T_l$ with linear leaf models over features $\mathcal{F}_l$ by minimizing the loss

$$err_l(T_l, data) = \left( \sum_{i=1}^{K} (\mathsf{postE}(s_i) + G(s_i) \cdot T_l(\mathcal{F}_l(s_i)) - v_i)^2 \right)^{1/2}, \tag{5}$$

where $\mathsf{postE}(s_i)$ and $G(s_i)$ represents the value of expectation postE and $G$ evaluated on the state $s_i$. This loss measures the sum error between the prediction $\mathsf{postE}(s_i) + G(s_i) \cdot T_l(\mathcal{F}_l(s_i))$ and target $v_i$. Note that when the guard $G$ is false on an initial state $s_i$, the example contributes zero to the loss because $\mathsf{postE}(s_i) + G(s_i) \cdot T_l(\mathcal{F}_l(s_i)) = \mathsf{postE}(s_i) = v_i$; thus, we only need to generate and collect trace data for initial states where the guard $G$ is true.

Analogously, learnInv trains a model tree $T_m$ with multiplication leaf models over features $\mathcal{F}_m$ to minimize the loss $err_m(T_m, data)$, which is the same as $err_l(T_l, data)$ except $T_l(\mathcal{F}_l(s_i))$ is replaced by $T_m(\mathcal{F}_m(s_i))$ for each $i$.

### 4.5 Extracting Expectations from Models (extractInv)

Given the learned model trees $T_l$ and $T_m$, we extract expectations that approximate wpe(geo, postE) in three steps:

1. **Round $T_l$, $T_m$ with different precisions.** Since we obtain the model trees $T_l$ and $T_m$ by learning and the training data is stochastic, the coefficients of features in $T_l$ and $T_m$ may be slightly off. We apply several rounding schemes to generate a list of rounded model trees.
2. **Translate into expectations.** Since we learn model trees, this step is straightforward: for example, $n + \frac{1}{p}$ can be seen as a model tree (with only a leaf) mapping the values of features $n, \frac{1}{p}$ to a number, or an expectation mapping program states where $n, p$ are program variables to a number. We translate each model tree obtained from the previous step to an expectation.
3. **Form the candidate invariant.** Since we train the model trees to fit $I'$ so that $\mathsf{postE} + [G] \cdot I'$ approximates wpe(**while** $G : P$, postE), we construct each candidate invariant $inv \in invs$ by replacing $I'$ in the pattern $\mathsf{postE} + [G] \cdot I'$ by an expectation obtained in the second step.

### 4.6 Verify Extracted Expectations (verifyInv)

Recall that geo is a loop **while** $G : P$, and given a set of candidate invariants $invs$, we want to check if any $inv \in invs$ is a loop invariant, i.e., if $inv$ satisfies

$$inv = [\neg G] \cdot \mathsf{postE} + [G] \cdot \mathsf{wpe}(P, inv). \tag{6}$$

Since the learned model might not predict the expected value for every data point exactly, we must verify whether *inv* satisfies this equality using verifyInv. If not, verifyInv looks for counterexamples that maximize the violation in order to drive the learning process forward in the next iteration. Formally, for every $inv \in invs$, verifyInv queries computer algebra systems to find a set of program states $S$ such that $S$ includes states maximizing the absolute difference of two sides in Eq. (6):

$$S \ni \mathbf{argmax}_s |inv(s) - ([\neg G] \cdot \mathsf{postE} + [G] \cdot wp(P, inv))\,(s)|.$$

If there are no program state where the absolute difference is non-zero, verifyInv returns *inv* as a true invariant. Otherwise, the maximizing states in $S$ are added to the list of counterexamples *cex*; if no candidate in *invs* is verified, verifyInv returns False and the accumulated list of counterexamples *cex*. The next iteration of the CEGIS loop will sample program traces starting from these counterexample initial states, hopefully leading to a learned model with less error.

## 5 Learning Sub-invariants

Next, we instantiate Exist for our second problem: learning sub-invariants. Given a program geo = **while** $G : P$ and a pair of pre- and post- expectations (preE, postE), we want to find a expectation $I$ such that preE $\leq I$, and

$$I \leq \Phi^{\mathsf{wpe}}_{\mathsf{postE}}(I) := [\neg G] \cdot \mathsf{postE} + [G] \cdot \mathsf{wpe}(P, I)$$

Intuitively, $\Phi^{\mathsf{wpe}}_{\mathsf{postE}}(I)$ computes the expected value of the expectation $I$ after one iteration of the loop. We want to train a model $M$ such that $M$ translates to an expectation $I$ whose expected value decrease each iteration, and preE $\leq I$.

The high-level plan is the same as for learning exact invariants: we train a model to minimize a loss defined to capture the sub-invariant requirements. We generate features $\mathcal{F}$ and sample initializations *states* as before. Then, from each $s \in states$, we repeatedly run just the loop body $P$ and record the set of output states in *data*; this departs from our method for exact invariants, which repeatedly runs the entire loop to completion. Given this trace data, for any program state $s \in states$ and expectation $I$, we can compute the empirical mean of $I$'s value after running the loop body $P$ on state $s$. Thus, we can approximate $\mathsf{wpe}(P, I)(s)$ for $s \in states$ and use this estimate to approximate $\Phi^{\mathsf{wpe}}_{\mathsf{postE}}(I)(s)$. We then define a loss to sum up the violation of $I \leq \Phi^{\mathsf{wpe}}_{\mathsf{postE}}(I)$ and preE $\leq I$ on state $s \in states$, estimated based on the collected data.

The main challenge for our approach is that existing model tree learning algorithms do not support our loss function. Roughly speaking, model tree learners typically assume a node's two child subtrees can be learned separately; this is the case when optimizing on the loss we used for exact invariants, but this is *not* the case for the loss for sub-invariants.

To solve this challenge, we first broaden the class of models to neural networks. To produce sub-invariants that can be verified, we still want to learn simple classes of models, such as piecewise functions of numerical expressions. Accordingly, we work with a class of neural architectures that can be translated into model trees, *neural model trees*, adapted from neural decision trees developed by Yang et al. [41]. We defer the technical details of neural model trees to the extended version, but for now, we can treat them as differentiable approximations of standard model trees; since they are differentiable they can be learned with gradient descent, which can support the sub-invariant loss function.

*Outline.* We will discuss changes in sampleTraces, learnInv and verifyInv for learning sub-invariants but omit descriptions of getFeatures, sampleStates, extractInv because EXIST generates features, samples initial states and extracts expectations in the same way as in Sect. 4. To simplify the exposition, we will assume getFeatures generates the same set of features $\mathcal{F} = \mathcal{F}_l = \mathcal{F}_m$ for model trees with linear models and model trees with multiplication models.

### 5.1 Sample Training Data (sampleTraces)

Unlike when sampling data for learning exact invariants, here, sampleTraces runs only one iteration of the given program geo = **while** $G : P$, that is, just $P$, instead of running the whole loop. Intuitively, this difference in data collection is because we aim to directly handle the sub-invariant condition, which encodes a single iteration of the loop. For exact invariants, our approach proceeded indirectly by learning the expected value of postE after running the loop to termination.

From any initialization $s_i \in states$ such that $G$ holds on $s_i$, sampleTraces runs the loop body $P$ for $N_{runs}$ trials, each time restarting from $s_i$, and records the set of output states reached. If executing $P$ from $s_i$ leads to output states $\{s_{i1}, \ldots, s_{iN_{runs}}\}$, then sampleTraces produces the training example:

$$(s_i, S_i) = (s_i, \{s_{i1}, \ldots, s_{iN_{runs}}\}),$$

For initialization $s_i \in states$ such that $G$ is false on $s_i$, sampleTraces simply produces $(s_i, S_i) = (s_i, \emptyset)$ since the loop body is not executed.

### 5.2 Learning a Neural Model Tree (learnInv)

Given the dataset $data = \{(s_1, S_1), \ldots, (s_K, S_K)\}$ (with $K = N_{states}$), we want to learn an expectation $I$ such that $\mathsf{preE} \leq I$ and $I \leq \Phi^{\mathsf{wpe}}_{\mathsf{postE}}(I)$. By case analysis on the guard $G$, the requirement $I \leq \Phi^{\mathsf{wpe}}_{\mathsf{postE}}(I)$ can be split into two constraints:

$$[G] \cdot I \leq [G] \cdot \mathsf{wpe}(P, I) \qquad \text{and} \qquad [\neg G] \cdot I \leq [\neg G] \cdot \mathsf{postE}.$$

If $I = \mathsf{postE} + [G] \cdot I'$, then the second requirement reduces to $[\neg G] \cdot postE \leq [\neg G] \cdot postE$ and is always satisfied. So to simplify the loss and training process, we again aim to learn an expectation $I$ of the form of $\mathsf{postE} + [G] \cdot I'$. Thus, we want to train a model tree $T$ such that $T$ translates into an expectation $I'$, and

$$\mathsf{preE} \leq \mathsf{postE} + [G] \cdot I' \tag{7}$$

$$[G] \cdot (\mathsf{postE} + [G] \cdot I') \leq [G] \cdot \mathsf{wpe}(P, \mathsf{postE} + [G] \cdot I') \tag{8}$$

Then, we define the loss of model tree $T$ on *data* to be

$$err(T, data) := err_1(T, data) + err_2(T, data),$$

where $err_1(T, data)$ captures Eq. (7) and $err_2(T, data)$ captures Eq. (8).

Defining $err_1$ is relatively simple: we sum up the one-sided difference between $\mathsf{preE}(s)$ and $\mathsf{postE}(s) + G(s) \cdot T(\mathcal{F}(s))$ across $s \in states$, where $T$ is the model tree getting trained and $\mathcal{F}(s)$ is the feature vector $\mathcal{F}$ evaluated on $s$. That is,

$$err_1(T, data) := \sum_{i=1}^{K} \max\left(0, \mathsf{preE}(s_i) - \mathsf{postE}(s_i) - G(s_i) \cdot T(\mathcal{F}(s_i))\right). \tag{9}$$

Above, $\mathsf{preE}(s_i)$, $\mathsf{postE}(s_i)$, and $G(s_i)$ are the value of expectations $\mathsf{preE}$, $\mathsf{postE}$, and $G$ evaluated on program state $s_i$.

The term $err_2$ is more involved. Similar to $err_1$, we aim to sum up the one-sided difference between two sides of Eq. (8) across state $s \in states$. On program state $s$ that does not satisfy $G$, both sides are 0; for $s$ that satisfies $G$, we want to evaluate $\mathsf{wpe}(P, \mathsf{postE} + [G] \cdot I')$ on $s$, but we do not have exact access to $\mathsf{wpe}(P, \mathsf{postE} + [G] \cdot I')$ and need to approximate its value on $s$ based on sampled program traces. Recall that $\mathsf{wpe}(P, I)(s)$ is the expected value of $I$ after running program $P$ from $s$, and our dataset contains training examples $(s_i, S_i)$ where $S_i$ is a set of states reached after running $P$ on an initial state $s_i$ satisfying $G$. Thus, we can approximate $[G] \cdot \mathsf{wpe}(P, \mathsf{postE} + G \cdot I')(s_i)$ by

$$G(s_i) \cdot \frac{1}{|S_i|} \cdot \sum_{s \in S_i} \left(\mathsf{postE}(s) + G(s) \cdot I'(s)\right).$$

To avoid division by zero when $s_i$ does not satisfy $G$ and $S_i$ is empty, we evaluate the expression in a short-circuit manner such that when $G(s_i) = 0$, the whole expression is immediately evaluated to zero.

Therefore, we define

$$err_2(T, data) = \sum_{i=1}^{K} \max\Bigg(0, G(s_i) \cdot \mathsf{postE}(s_i) + G(s_i) \cdot T(\mathcal{F}(s_i)) - G(s_i) \cdot \frac{1}{|S_i|} \cdot \sum_{s \in S_i} \left(\mathsf{postE}(s) + G(s) \cdot T(\mathcal{F}(s))\right)\Bigg).$$

Standard model tree learning algorithms do not support this kind of loss function, and since our overall loss $err(T, data)$ is the sum of $err_1(T, data)$ and $err_2(T, data)$, we cannot use standard model tree learning algorithm to optimize $err(T, data)$ either. Fortunately, gradient descent does support this loss function. While gradient descent cannot directly learn model trees, we can use gradient descent to train a *neural* model tree $T$ to minimize $err(T, data)$. The learned neural networks can be converted to model trees, and then converted to expectations as before. (See discussion in the extended version.)

### 5.3 Verify Extracted Expectations (verifyInv)

The verifier verifyInv is very similar to the one in Sect. 4 except here it solves a different optimization problem. For each candidate *inv* in the given list *invs*, it looks for a set $S$ of program states such that $S$ includes

$$\mathbf{argmax}_s \mathsf{preE}(s) - inv(s) \quad \text{and} \quad \mathbf{argmax}_s G(s) \cdot I(s) - [G] \cdot \mathsf{wpe}(P, I)(s).$$

As in our approach for exact invariant learning, the verifier aims to find counterexample states $s$ that violate at least one of these constraints by as large of a margin as possible; these high-quality counterexamples guide data collection in the following iteration of the CEGIS loop. Concretely, the verifier accepts *inv* if it cannot find any program state $s$ where $\mathsf{preE}(s) - inv(s)$ or $G(s) \cdot I(s) - [G] \cdot \mathsf{wpe}(P, I)(s)$ is positive. Otherwise, it adds all states $s \in S$ with strictly positive margin to the set of counterexamples *cex*.

## 6 Evaluations

We implemented our prototype in Python, using sklearn and tensorflow to fit model trees and neural model trees, and Wolfram Alpha to verify and perform counterexample generation. We have evaluated our tool on a set of 18 benchmarks drawn from different sources in prior work [14,21,24]. Our experiments were designed to address the following research questions:

**R1.** Can Exist synthesize exact invariants for a variety of programs?
**R2.** Can Exist synthesize sub-invariants for a variety of programs?

We summarize our findings as follows:

- Exist successfully synthesized and verified exact invariants for 14/18 benchmarks within a timeout of 300 s. Our tool was able to generate these 14 invariants in reasonable time, taking between 1 to 237 s. The sampling phase dominates the time in most cases. We also compare Exist with a tool from prior literature, Mora [7]. We found that Mora can only handle a restrictive set of programs and cannot handle many of our benchmarks. We also discuss how our work compares with a few others in (Sect. 7).
- To evaluate sub-invariant learning, we created multiple problem instances for each benchmark by supplying different pre-expectations. On a total of 34 such problem instances, Exist was able to infer correct invariants in 27 cases, taking between 7 to 102 s.

We present in the extended version the tables of complete experimental results. Because the training data we collect are inherently stochastic, the results produced by our tool are not deterministic.[1] As expected, sometimes different trials on the same benchmarks generate different sub-invariants; while the exact invariant for each benchmark is unique, Exist may also generate semantically equivalent but syntactically different expectations in different trials (e.g. it happens for BiasDir).

[1] The code and data sampled in the trial that produced the tables in this paper can be found at https://github.com/JialuJialu/Exist.

**Table 1.** Exact Invariants generated by EXIST

| Name | postE | Learned Invariant | ST | LT | VT | TT |
|---|---|---|---|---|---|---|
| Bin1 | $n$ | $x + [n < M] \cdot (M \cdot p - n \cdot p)$ | 25.67 | 12.03 | 0.22 | 37.91 |
| Fair | $count$ | $(count + [c1 + c2 == 0] \cdot (p1 + p2)/(p1 + p2 - p1 \cdot p2))$ | 5.78 | 1.62 | 0.30 | 7.69 |
| Gambler | $z$ | $z + [x > 0 \text{ and } y > x] \cdot x \cdot (y - x)$ | 112.02 | 3.52 | 9.97 | 125.51 |
| Geo0 | $z$ | $z + [flip == 0] \cdot (1 - p_1)/p_1$ | 12.01 | 0.85 | 2.65 | 15.51 |
| Sum0 | $x$ | $x + [n > 0] \cdot (0.5 \cdot p \cdot n^2 + 0.5 \cdot p \cdot n)$ | 102.12 | 34.61 | 26.74 | 163.48 |

**Table 2.** Sub-invariants generated by EXIST

| Name | postE | preE | Learned Sub-invariant | ST | LT | VT | TT |
|---|---|---|---|---|---|---|---|
| Gambler | $z$ | $x \cdot (y - x)$ | $z + [x > 0 \text{ and } y > x] \cdot x \cdot (y - x)$ | 7.31 | 28.87 | 8.29 | 44.46 |
| Geo0 | $z$ | $[flip == 0] \cdot (1 - p_1))$ | $z + [flip == 0] \cdot (1 - p_1)$ | 8.70 | 26.13 | 0.19 | 35.02 |
| LinExp | $z$ | $z + [n > 0] \cdot 2$ | $[n > 0] \cdot (n + 1)$ | 53.72 | 30.01 | 0.35 | 84.98 |
| | | $z + [n > 0] \cdot 2 \cdot n$ | $z + [n > 0] \cdot 2 \cdot n$ | 29.18 | 28.61 | 0.68 | 58.48 |
| RevBin | $z$ | $z + [x > 0] \cdot x$ | $z + [x > 0] \cdot x/p$ | 18.17 | 71.15 | 2.17 | 91.55 |
| | | $z$ | $z$ | 15.62 | 18.74 | 0.06 | 34.42 |

*Implementation Details.* For input parameters to EXIST, we use $N_{runs} = 500$ and $N_{states} = 500$. Besides input parameters listed in Fig. 2, we allow the user to supply a list of features as an optional input. In feature generation, getFeatures enumerates expressions made up by program variables and user-supplied features according to a grammar. Also, when incorporating counterexamples $cex$, we make 30 copies of each counterexample to give them more weights in the training. All experiments were conducted on a MacBook Pro 2020 with M1 chip running macOS Monterey Version 12.1.

### 6.1 R1: Evaluation of the Exact Invariant Method

*Efficacy of Invariant Inference.* EXIST was able to infer provably correct invariants in 14/18 benchmarks. Out of 14 successful benchmarks, only 2 of them need user-supplied features ($n \cdot p$ for Bin2 and Sum0). Table 1 shows the post-expectation (postE), the inferred invariant (Learned Invariant), sampling time (ST), learning time (LT), verification time (VT) and the total time (TT) for a few benchmarks. For generating exact invariants, the running time of EXIST is dominated by the sampling time. However, this phase can be parallelized easily.

*Failure Analysis.* EXIST failed to generate invariants for 4/18 benchmarks. For two of them, EXIST was able to generate expectations that are very close to an invariant (DepRV and LinExp); for the third failing benchmarks (Duel), the ground truth invariant is very complicated. For LinExp, while a correct invariant is $z + [n > 0] \cdot 2.625 \cdot n$, EXIST generates expectations like $z + [n > 0] \cdot (2.63 \cdot n - 0.02)$ as candidates. For DepRV, a correct invariant is $x \cdot y + [n > 0] \cdot (0.25 \cdot n^2 + 0.5 \cdot n \cdot x + 0.5 \cdot n \cdot y - 0.25 \cdot n)$, and in our experiment EXIST generates $0.25 \cdot n^2 + 0.5 \cdot n \cdot x + 0.5 \cdot n \cdot y - 0.27 \cdot n - 0.01 \cdot x + 0.12$. In both cases, the ground truth invariants use coefficients with several digits, and since learning from data is inherently stochastic, EXIST cannot generate them consistently. In our experiments, we observe that our CEGIS loop does guide the learner to move closer to the correct invariant in general, but sometimes progress obtained in multiple iterations can be offset by noise in one iteration. For GeoAr, we observe the verifier incorrectly accepted the complicated candidate invariants generated by the learner because Wolfram Alpha was not able to find valid counterexamples for our queries.

*Comparison with Previous Work.* There are few existing tools that can automatically compute expected values after probabilistic loops. We experimented with one such tool, called MORA [7]. (See high-level comparison in Sect. 7.) We managed to encode our benchmarks Geo0, Bin0, Bin2, Geo1, GeoAr, and Mart in their syntax. Among them, MORA fails to infer an invariant for Geo1, GeoAr, and Mart. We also tried to encode our benchmarks Fair, Gambler, Bin1, and RevBin but found MORA's syntax was too restrictive to encode them.

### 6.2 R2: Evaluation of the Sub-invariant Method

*Efficacy of Invariant Inference.* EXIST is able to synthesize sub-invariants for 27/34 benchmarks. As before, Table 2 reports the results for a few benchmarks. Two out of 27 successful benchmarks use user-supplied features – Gambler with pre-expectation $x \cdot (y - x)$ uses $(y - x)$, and Sum0 with pre-expectation $x + [x > 0] \cdot (p \cdot n/2)$ uses $p \cdot n$. Contrary to the case for exact invariants, the learning time dominates. This is not surprising: the sampling time is shorter because we only run one iteration of the loop, but the learning time is longer as we are optimizing a more complicated loss function.

One interesting thing that we found when gathering benchmarks is that for many loops, pre-expectations used by prior work or natural choices of pre-expectations are themselves sub-invariants. Thus, for some instances, the sub-invariants generated by EXIST is the same as the pre-expectation preE given to it as input. However, EXIST is not checking whether the given preE is a sub-invariant: the learner in EXIST does not know about preE besides the value of preE evaluated on program states. Also, we also designed benchmarks where pre-expectations are *not* sub-invariants (BiasDir with preE $= [x \neq y] \cdot x$, DepRV with preE $= x \cdot y + [n > 0] \cdot 1/4 \cdot n^2$, Gambler with preE $= x \cdot (y - x)$, Geo0 with preE $= [flip == 0] \cdot (1 - p1)$), and EXIST is able to generate sub-invariants for 3/4 such benchmarks.

*Failure Analysis.* On program instances where EXIST fails to generate a sub-invariant, we observe two common causes. First, gradient descent seems to get stuck in local minima because the learner returns suboptimal models with relatively low loss. The loss we are training on is very complicated and likely to be highly non-convex, so this is not surprising. Second, we observed inconsistent behavior due to noise in data collection and learning. For instance, for GeoAr with preE $= x + [z \neq 0] \cdot y \cdot (1-p)/p$, EXIST could sometimes find a sub-invariant with supplied feature $(1-p)$, but we could not achieve this result consistently.

*Comparison with Learning Exact Invariants.* The performance of EXIST on learning sub-invariants is less sensitive to the complexity of the ground truth invariants. For example, EXIST is not able to generate an exact invariant for LinExp as its exact invariant is complicated, but EXIST is able to generate sub-invariants for LinExp. However, we also observe that when learning sub-invariants, EXIST returns complicated expectations with high loss more often.

## 7 Related Work

*Invariant Generation for Probabilistic Programs.* There has been a steady line of work on probabilistic invariant generation over the last few years. The PRINSYS system [21] employs a template-based approach to guide the search for probabilistic invariants. PRINSYS is able encode invariants with guard expressions, but the system doesn't produce invariants directly—instead, PRINSYS produces logical formulas encoding the invariant conditions, which must be solved manually.

Chen et al. [14] proposed a counterexample-guided approach to find polynomial invariants, by applying Lagrange interpolation. Unlike PRINSYS, this approach doesn't need templates; however, invariants involving guard expressions—common in our examples—cannot be found, since they are not polynomials. Additionally, Chen et al. [14] uses a weaker notion of invariant, which only needs to be correct on certain initial states; our tool generates invariants that are correct on all initial states. Feng et al. [18] improves on Chen et al. [14] by using *Stengle's Positivstellensatz* to encode invariants constraints as a semidefinite programming problem. Their method can find polynomial sub-invariants that are correct on all initial states. However, their approach cannot synthesize piecewise linear invariants, and their implementation has additional limitations and could not be run on our benchmarks.

There is also a line of work on abstract interpretation for analyzing probabilistic programs; Chakarov and Sankaranarayanan [11] search for linear expectation invariants using a "pre-expectation closed cone domain", while recent work by Wang et al. [40] employs a sophisticated algebraic program analysis approach.

Another line of work applies *martingales* to derive insights of probabilistic programs. Chakarov and Sankaranarayanan [10] showed several applications of martingales in program analysis, and Barthe et al. [5] gave a procedure to generate candidate martingales for a probabilistic program; however, this tool gives no control over which expected value is analyzed—the user can only guess initial expressions and the tool generates valid bounds, which may not be interesting. Our tool allows the user to pick which expected value they want to bound.

Another line of work for automated reasoning uses *moment-based analysis*. Bartocci et al. [6,7] develop the MORA tool, which can find the moments of variables as functions of the iteration for loops that run forever by using ideas from computational algebraic geometry and dynamical systems. This method is highly efficient and is guaranteed to compute moments exactly. However, there are two limitations. First, the moments can give useful insights about the distribution of variables' values after each iteration, but they are fundamentally different from our notion of invariants which allow us to compute the expected value of any given expression *after termination* of a loop. Second, there are important restrictions on the probabilistic programs. For instance, conditional statements are not allowed and the use of symbolic inputs is limited. As a result, most of our benchmarks cannot be handled by MORA.

In a similar vein, Kura et al. [27,39] bound higher *central moments* for running time and other monotonically increasing quantities. Like our work, these works consider probabilistic loops that terminate. However, unlike our work, they are limited to programs with constant size increments.

*Data-Driven Invariant Synthesis.* We are not aware of other data-driven methods for learning probabilistic invariants, but a recent work Abate et al. [1] proves probabilistic termination by learning ranking supermartingales from trace data. Our method for learning sub-invariants (Sect. 5) can be seen as a natural generalization of their approach. However, there are also important differences. First, we are able to learn general sub-invariants, not just ranking supermatingales for proving termination. Second, our approach aims to learn model trees, which lead to simpler and more interpretable sub-invariants. In contrast, Abate, et al. [1] learn ranking functions encoded as two-layer neural networks.

Data-driven inference of invariants for deterministic programs has drawn a lot of attention, starting from DAIKON [17]. ICE learning with decision trees [20] modifies the decision tree learning algorithm to capture *implication counterexamples* to handle inductiveness. HANOI [32] uses counterexample-based inductive synthesis (CEGIS) [38] to build a data-driven invariant inference engine that alternates between weakening and strengthening candidates for synthesis. Recent work uses neural networks to learn invariants [36]. These systems perform classification, while our work uses regression. Data from fuzzing has been used for *almost correct* inductive invariants [29] for programs with closed-box operations.

*Probabilistic Reasoning with Pre-expectations.* Following Morgan and McIver, there are now pre-expectation calculi for domain-specific properties, like expected runtime [23] and probabilistic sensitivity [2]. All of these systems define the pre-expectation for loops as a least fixed-point, and practical reasoning about loops requires finding an invariant of some kind.

**Acknowledgements.** This work is in part supported by National Science Foundation grant #1943130 and #2152831. We thank Ugo Dal Lago, Işil Dillig, IITK PRAISE group, Cornell PL group, and all reviewers for helpful feedback. We also thank Anmol Gupta in IITK for building a prototype verifier using Mathematica.

## References

1. Abate, A., Giacobbe, M., Roy, D.: Learning probabilistic termination proofs. In: Silva, A., Leino, K.R.M. (eds.) CAV 2021. LNCS, vol. 12760, pp. 3–26. Springer, Cham (2021). https://doi.org/10.1007/978-3-030-81688-9_1
2. Aguirre, A., Barthe, G., Hsu, J., Kaminski, B.L., Katoen, J.P., Matheja, C.: A pre-expectation calculus for probabilistic sensitivity. In: POPL (2021). https://doi.org/10.1145/3434333
3. Albarghouthi, A., Hsu, J.: Synthesizing coupling proofs of differential privacy. In: POPL (2018). https://doi.org/10.1145/3158146
4. Baier, C., Clarke, E.M., Hartonas-Garmhausen, V., Kwiatkowska, M., Ryan, M.: Symbolic model checking for probabilistic processes. In: Degano, P., Gorrieri, R., Marchetti-Spaccamela, A. (eds.) ICALP 1997. LNCS, vol. 1256, pp. 430–440. Springer, Heidelberg (1997). https://doi.org/10.1007/3-540-63165-8_199
5. Barthe, G., Espitau, T., Ferrer Fioriti, L.M., Hsu, J.: Synthesizing probabilistic invariants via Doob's decomposition. In: Chaudhuri, S., Farzan, A. (eds.) CAV 2016. LNCS, vol. 9779, pp. 43–61. Springer, Cham (2016). https://doi.org/10.1007/978-3-319-41528-4_3
6. Bartocci, E., Kovács, L., Stankovič, M.: Automatic generation of moment-based invariants for prob-solvable loops. In: Chen, Y.-F., Cheng, C.-H., Esparza, J. (eds.) ATVA 2019. LNCS, vol. 11781, pp. 255–276. Springer, Cham (2019). https://doi.org/10.1007/978-3-030-31784-3_15
7. Bartocci, E., Kovács, L., Stankovič, M.: Mora - automatic generation of moment-based invariants. In: Biere, A., Parker, D. (eds.) TACAS 2020. LNCS, vol. 12078, pp. 492–498. Springer, Cham (2020). https://doi.org/10.1007/978-3-030-45190-5_28
8. Batz, K., Kaminski, B.L., Katoen, J., Matheja, C.: Relatively complete verification of probabilistic programs: an expressive language for expectation-based reasoning. In: POPL (2021). https://doi.org/10.1145/3434320
9. Carbin, M., Misailovic, S., Rinard, M.C.: Verifying quantitative reliability for programs that execute on unreliable hardware. In: OOPSLA (2013). https://doi.org/10.1145/2509136.2509546
10. Chakarov, A., Sankaranarayanan, S.: Probabilistic program analysis with martingales. In: Sharygina, N., Veith, H. (eds.) CAV 2013. LNCS, vol. 8044, pp. 511–526. Springer, Heidelberg (2013). https://doi.org/10.1007/978-3-642-39799-8_34
11. Chakarov, A., Sankaranarayanan, S.: Expectation invariants for probabilistic program loops as fixed points. In: Müller-Olm, M., Seidl, H. (eds.) SAS 2014. LNCS, vol. 8723, pp. 85–100. Springer, Cham (2014). https://doi.org/10.1007/978-3-319-10936-7_6
12. Chatterjee, K., Fu, H., Goharshady, A.K.: Termination analysis of probabilistic programs through Positivstellensatz's. In: Chaudhuri, S., Farzan, A. (eds.) CAV 2016. LNCS, vol. 9779, pp. 3–22. Springer, Cham (2016). ISBN 978-3-319-41528-4. https://doi.org/10.1007/978-3-319-41528-4_1

13. Chatterjee, K., Fu, H., Novotný, P., Hasheminezhad, R.: Algorithmic analysis of qualitative and quantitative termination problems for affine probabilistic programs. In: POPL (2016b). https://doi.org/10.1145/2837614.2837639
14. Chen, Y.-F., Hong, C.-D., Wang, B.-Y., Zhang, L.: Counterexample-guided polynomial loop invariant generation by lagrange interpolation. In: Kroening, D., Păsăreanu, C.S. (eds.) CAV 2015. LNCS, vol. 9206, pp. 658–674. Springer, Cham (2015). https://doi.org/10.1007/978-3-319-21690-4_44
15. Dehnert, C., Junges, S., Katoen, J.-P., Volk, M.: A storm is coming: a modern probabilistic model checker. In: Majumdar, R., Kunčak, V. (eds.) CAV 2017. LNCS, vol. 10427, pp. 592–600. Springer, Cham (2017). https://doi.org/10.1007/978-3-319-63390-9_31
16. Dijkstra, E.W.: Guarded commands, non-determinancy and a calculus for the derivation of programs. In: Language Hierarchies and Interfaces (1975). https://doi.org/10.1007/3-540-07994-7_51
17. Ernst, M.D., et al.: The Daikon system for dynamic detection of likely invariants. Sci. Comput. Program. (2007). https://doi.org/10.1016/j.scico.2007.01.015
18. Feng, Y., Zhang, L., Jansen, D.N., Zhan, N., Xia, B.: Finding polynomial loop invariants for probabilistic programs. In: D'Souza, D., Narayan Kumar, K. (eds.) ATVA 2017. LNCS, vol. 10482, pp. 400–416. Springer, Cham (2017). https://doi.org/10.1007/978-3-319-68167-2_26
19. Flanagan, C., Leino, K.R.M.: Houdini, an annotation assistant for ESC/Java. In: Oliveira, J.N., Zave, P. (eds.) FME 2001. LNCS, vol. 2021, pp. 500–517. Springer, Heidelberg (2001). https://doi.org/10.1007/3-540-45251-6_29
20. Garg, P., Neider, D., Madhusudan, P., Roth, D.: Learning invariants using decision trees and implication counterexamples. In: POPL (2016). https://doi.org/10.1145/2914770.2837664
21. Gretz, F., Katoen, J.-P., McIver, A.: Prinsys—On a quest for probabilistic loop invariants. In: Joshi, K., Siegle, M., Stoelinga, M., D'Argenio, P.R. (eds.) QEST 2013. LNCS, vol. 8054, pp. 193–208. Springer, Heidelberg (2013). https://doi.org/10.1007/978-3-642-40196-1_17
22. Kaminski, B.L.: Advanced weakest precondition calculi for probabilistic programs. Ph.D. thesis, RWTH Aachen University, Germany (2019)
23. Kaminski, B.L., Katoen, J.-P., Matheja, C., Olmedo, F.: Weakest precondition reasoning for expected run–times of probabilistic programs. In: Thiemann, P. (ed.) ESOP 2016. LNCS, vol. 9632, pp. 364–389. Springer, Heidelberg (2016). https://doi.org/10.1007/978-3-662-49498-1_15
24. Kaminski, B.L., Katoen, J.P.: A weakest pre-expectation semantics for mixed-sign expectations. In: LICS (2017). https://doi.org/10.5555/3329995.3330088
25. Kozen, D.: Semantics of probabilistic programs. J. Comput. Syst. Sci. **22**(3) (1981). https://doi.org/10.1016/0022-0000(81)90036-2
26. Kozen, D.: A probabilistic PDL. J. Comput. Syst. Sci. **30**(2) (1985). https://doi.org/10.1016/0022-0000(85)90012-1
27. Kura, S., Urabe, N., Hasuo, I.: Tail probabilities for randomized program runtimes via martingales for higher moments. In: Vojnar, T., Zhang, L. (eds.) TACAS 2019. LNCS, vol. 11428, pp. 135–153. Springer, Cham (2019). https://doi.org/10.1007/978-3-030-17465-1_8
28. Kwiatkowska, M., Norman, G., Parker, D.: PRISM 4.0: verification of probabilistic real-time systems. In: Gopalakrishnan, G., Qadeer, S. (eds.) CAV 2011. LNCS, vol. 6806, pp. 585–591. Springer, Heidelberg (2011). https://doi.org/10.1007/978-3-642-22110-1_47

29. Lahiri, S., Roy, S.: Almost correct invariants: synthesizing inductive invariants by fuzzing proofs. In: ISSTA (2022)
30. McIver, A., Morgan, C.: Abstraction, Refinement, and Proof for Probabilistic Systems. Springer, New York (2005). https://doi.org/10.1007/b138392
31. McIver, A., Morgan, C., Kaminski, B.L., Katoen, J.: A new proof rule for almost-sure termination. In: POPL (2018). https://doi.org/10.1145/3158121
32. Miltner, A., Padhi, S., Millstein, T., Walker, D.: Data-driven inference of representation invariants. In: PLDI 20 (2020). https://doi.org/10.1145/3385412.3385967
33. Morgan, C., McIver, A., Seidel, K.: Probabilistic predicate transformers. In: TOPLAS (1996). https://doi.org/10.1145/229542.229547
34. Quinlan, J.R.: Learning with continuous classes. In: AJCAI, vol. 92 (1992)
35. Roy, S., Hsu, J., Albarghouthi, A.: Learning differentially private mechanisms. In: SP (2021). https://doi.org/10.1109/SP40001.2021.00060
36. Si, X., Dai, H., Raghothaman, M., Naik, M., Song, L.: Learning loop invariants for program verification. In: NeurIPS (2018). https://doi.org/10.5555/3327757.3327873
37. Smith, C., Hsu, J., Albarghouthi, A.: Trace abstraction modulo probability. In: POPL (2019). https://doi.org/10.1145/3290352
38. Solar-Lezama, A.: Program sketching. Int. J. Softw. Tools Technol. Transf. (2013). https://doi.org/10.1007/s10009-012-0249-7
39. Wang, D., Hoffmann, J., Reps, T.: Central moment analysis for cost accumulators in probabilistic programs. In: PLDI (2021), https://doi.org/10.1145/3453483.3454062
40. Wang, D., Hoffmann, J., Reps, T.W.: PMAF: an algebraic framework for static analysis of probabilistic programs. In: PLDI (2018). https://doi.org/10.1145/3192366.3192408
41. Yang, Y., Morillo, I.G., Hospedales, T.M.: Deep neural decision trees. CoRR (2018). http://arxiv.org/abs/1806.06988

# Sound and Complete Certificates for Quantitative Termination Analysis of Probabilistic Programs

Krishnendu Chatterjee[1], Amir Kafshdar Goharshady[2(✉)], Tobias Meggendorfer[1], and Đorđe Žikelić[1]

[1] Institute of Science and Technology Austria (ISTA), Klosterneuburg, Austria
{krishnendu.chatterjee,tobias.meggendorfer,djordje.zikelic}@ist.ac.at

[2] The Hong Kong University of Science and Technology (HKUST), Hong Kong, China
goharshady@cse.ust.hk

**Abstract.** We consider the quantitative problem of obtaining lower-bounds on the probability of termination of a given non-deterministic probabilistic program. Specifically, given a non-termination threshold $p \in [0, 1]$, we aim for certificates proving that the program terminates with probability at least $1 - p$. The basic idea of our approach is to find a terminating stochastic invariant, i.e. a subset $SI$ of program states such that (i) the probability of the program ever leaving $SI$ is no more than $p$, and (ii) almost-surely, the program either leaves $SI$ or terminates.

While stochastic invariants are already well-known, we provide the first proof that the idea above is not only sound, but also complete for quantitative termination analysis. We then introduce a novel sound and complete characterization of stochastic invariants that enables template-based approaches for easy synthesis of quantitative termination certificates, especially in affine or polynomial forms. Finally, by combining this idea with the existing martingale-based methods that are relatively complete for *qualitative* termination analysis, we obtain the first automated, sound, and relatively complete algorithm for *quantitative* termination analysis. Notably, our completeness guarantees for quantitative termination analysis are as strong as the best-known methods for the qualitative variant.

Our prototype implementation demonstrates the effectiveness of our approach on various probabilistic programs. We also demonstrate that our algorithm certifies lower bounds on termination probability for probabilistic programs that are beyond the reach of previous methods.

## 1 Introduction

**Probabilistic Programs.** Probabilistic programs extend classical imperative programs with randomization. They provide an expressive framework for specifying probabilistic models and have been used in machine learning [22,39], network

---

A longer version, including appendices, is available at [12].
Authors are ordered alphabetically.


S. Shoham and Y. Vizel (Eds.): CAV 2022, LNCS 13371, pp. 55–78, 2022.
https://doi.org/10.1007/978-3-031-13185-1_4

analysis [20], robotics [41] and security [4]. Recent years have seen the development of many probabilistic programming languages such as Church [23] and Pyro [6], and their formal analysis is an active topic of research. Probabilistic programs are often extended with non-determinism to allow for either unknown user inputs and interactions with environment or abstraction of parts that are too complex for formal analysis [31].

**Termination.** Termination has attracted the most attention in the literature on formal analysis of probabilistic programs. In non-probabilistic programs, it is a purely qualitative property. In probabilistic programs, it has various extensions:

1. *Qualitative:* The *almost-sure (a.s.) termination* problem asks if the program terminates with probability 1, whereas the *finite termination* problems asks if the expected number of steps until termination is finite.
2. *Quantitative:* The quantitative probabilistic termination problem asks for a tight *lower bound* on the termination probability. More specifically, given a constant $p \in [0, 1]$, it asks whether the program will terminate with probability at least $1 - p$ over all possible resolutions of non-determinism.

**Previous Qualitative Works.** There are many approaches to prove a.s. termination based on weakest pre-expectation calculus [27,31,37], abstract interpretation [34], type systems [5] and martingales [7,9,11,14,25,26,32,35]. This work is closest in spirit to martingale-based approaches. The central concept in these approaches is that of a *ranking supermartingale (RSM)* [7], which is a probabilistic extension of ranking functions. RSMs are a sound and complete proof rule for finite termination [21], which is a stricter notion than a.s. termination. The work of [32] proposed a variant of RSMs that can prove a.s. termination even for programs whose expected runtime is infinite, and lexicographic RSMs were studied in [1,13]. A main advantage of martingale-based approaches is that they can be fully automated for programs with affine/polynomial arithmetic [9,11].

**Previous Quantitative Works.** Quantitative analyses of probabilistic programs are often more challenging. There are only a few works that study the quantitative termination problem: [5,14,40]. The works [14,40] propose martingale-based proof rules for computing lower-bounds on termination probability, while [5] considers functional probabilistic programs and proposes a type system that allows incrementally searching for type derivations to accumulate a lower-bound on termination probability. See Sect. 8 for a detailed comparison.

**Lack of Completeness.** While [5,14,40] all propose sound methods to compute lower-bounds on termination probability, none of them are theoretically complete nor do their algorithms provide relative completeness guarantees. This naturally leaves open whether one can define a complete certificate for proving termination with probability at least $1 - p \in [0, 1]$, i.e. a certificate that a probabilistic program admits if and only if it terminates with probability at least $1 - p$, which allows for automated synthesis. Ideally, such a certificate should also be synthesized automatically by an algorithm with relative completeness guarantees, i.e. an algorithm which is guaranteed to compute such a certificate for a sufficiently general subclass of programs. Note, since the problem of deciding whether a probabilistic program terminates with probability at least $1-p$ is undecidable, one cannot hope for a general complete algorithm so the best one can hope for is relative completeness.

**Our Approach.** We present the first method for the probabilistic termination problem that is complete. Our approach builds on that of [14] and uses stochastic invariants in combination with a.s. reachability certificates in order to compute lower-bounds on the termination probability. A *stochastic invariant* [14] is a tuple $(SI, p)$ consisting of a set $SI$ of program states and an upper-bound $p$ on the probability of a random program run ever leaving $SI$. If one computes a stochastic invariant $(SI, p)$ with the additional property that a random program run would, with probability 1, either terminate or leave $SI$, then since $SI$ is left with probability at most $p$ the program must terminate with probability at least $1-p$. Hence, the combination of stochastic invariants and a.s. reachability certificates provides a sound approach to the probabilistic termination problem.

While this idea was originally proposed in [14], our method for computing stochastic invariants is fundamentally different and leads to completeness. In [14], a stochastic invariant is computed indirectly by computing the set $SI$ together with a *repulsing supermartingale (RepSM)*, which can then be used to compute a probability threshold $p$ for which $(SI, p)$ is a stochastic invariant. It was shown in [40, Section 3] that RepSMs are incomplete for computing stochastic invariants. Moreover, even if a RepSM exists, the resulting probability bound need not be tight and the method of [14] does not allow optimizing the computed bound or guiding computation towards a bound that exceeds some specified probability threshold.

In this work, we propose a novel and orthogonal approach that computes the stochastic invariant and the a.s. termination certificate at the same time and is provably complete for certifying a specified lower bound on termination probability. First, we show that stochastic invariants can be characterized through the novel notion of *stochastic invariant indicators (SI-indicators)*. The characterization is both sound and complete. Furthermore, it allows fully automated computation of stochastic invariants for programs using affine or polynomial arithmetic via a template-based approach that reduces quantitative termination analysis to constraint solving. Second, we prove that stochastic invariants together with an a.s. reachability certificate, when synthesized in tandem, are not only *sound* for probabilistic termination, but also *complete*. Finally, we present the first *relatively complete algorithm* for probabilistic termination. Our algorithm considers polynomial probabilistic programs and *simultaneously* computes a stochastic invariant and an a.s. reachability certificate in the form of an RSM using a template-based approach. Our algorithmic approach is relatively complete.

While we focus on the probabilistic termination problem in which the goal is to *verify* a given lower bound $1-p$ on the termination probability, we note that our method may be straightforwardly adapted to *compute* a lower bound on the termination probability. In particular, we may perform a binary-search on $p$ and search for the smallest value of $p$ for which $1 - p$ can be verified to be a lower bound on the termination probability.

**Contributions.** Our specific contributions in this work are as follows:

1. We present a sound and complete characterization of stochastic invariants through the novel notion of *stochastic invariant indicators* (Sect. 4).
2. We prove that stochastic invariants together with an a.s. reachability certificate are sound and *complete* for proving that a probabilistic program terminates with at least a given probability threshold (Sect. 5).
3. We present a relatively complete algorithm for computing SI-indicators, and hence stochastic invariants over programs with affine or polynomial arithmetic. By combining it with the existing relatively complete algorithms for RSM computation, we obtain the first algorithm for probabilistic termination that provides completeness guarantees (Sect. 6).
4. We implement a prototype of our approach and demonstrate its effectiveness over various benchmarks (Sect. 7). We also show that our approach can handle programs that were beyond the reach of previous methods.

## 2 Overview

Before presenting general theorems and algorithms, we first illustrate our method on the probabilistic program in Fig. 1. The program models a 1-dimensional discrete-time random walk over the real line that starts at $x = 0$ and terminates once a point with $x < 0$ is reached. In every time step, $x$ is incremented by a random value sampled according to the uniform distribution $\mathit{Uniform}([-1, 0.5])$. However, if the stochastic process is in a point with $x \geq 100$, then the value of $x$ might also be incremented by a random value independently sampled from $\mathit{Uniform}([-1, 2])$. The choice on whether the second increment happens is nondeterministic. By a standard random walk argument, the program does not terminate almost-surely.

**Outline of Our Method.** Let $p = 0.01$. To prove this program terminates with probability at least $1 - p = 0.99$, our method computes the following two objects:

1. *Stochastic invariant.* A stochastic invariant is a tuple $(SI, p)$ s.t. $SI$ is a set of program states that a random program run leaves with probability at most $p$.
2. *Termination proof for the stochastic invariant.* A *ranking supermartingale (RSM)* [7] is computed in order to prove that the program will, with probability 1, either terminate or leave the set $SI$. Since $SI$ is left with probability at most $p$, the program must terminate with probability at least $1 - p$.

$$
\begin{array}{ll}
 & x = 0 \\
\ell_{init}: & \textbf{while } x \geq 0 \textbf{ do} \\
\ell_1: & \quad r_1 := \mathit{Uniform}([-1, 0.5]) \\
\ell_2: & \quad x := x + r_1 \\
\ell_3: & \quad \textbf{if } x \geq 100 \textbf{ then} \\
\ell_4: & \quad\quad \textbf{if } \star \textbf{ then} \\
\ell_5: & \quad\quad\quad r_2 := \mathit{Uniform}([-1, 2]) \\
\ell_6: & \quad\quad\quad x := x + r_2 \\
\ell_{out}: &
\end{array}
$$

**Fig. 1.** Our running example.

**Synthesizing SI.** To find a stochastic invariant, our method computes a state function $f$ which assigns a non-negative real value to each reachable program state. We call this function a *stochastic invariant indicator (SI-indicator)*, and it serves the following two purposes: First, exactly those states which are assigned a value strictly less than 1 are considered a part of the stochastic invariant $SI$. Second, the value assigned to each state is an upper-bound on the probability of leaving $SI$ if the program starts from that state. Finally, by requiring that the value of the SI-indicator at the initial state of the program is at most $p$, we ensure a random program run leaves the stochastic invariant with probability at most $p$.

In Sect. 4, we will define SI-indicators in terms of conditions that ensure the properties above and facilitate automated computation. We also show that SI-indicators serve as a *sound and complete* characterization of stochastic invariants, which is one of the core contributions of this work. The significance of completeness of the characterization is that, in order to search for a stochastic invariant with a given probability threshold $p$, one may equivalently search for an SI-indicator with the same probability threshold whose computation can be automated. As we will discuss in Sect. 8, previous approaches to the synthesis of stochastic invariants were neither complete nor provided tight probability bounds. For Fig. 1, we have the following set $SI$ which will be left with probability at most $p = 0.01$ :

$$SI(\ell) = \begin{cases} (x < 99) & \text{if } \ell \in \{\ell_{init}, \ell_1, \ell_2, \ell_3, \ell_{out}\} \\ \text{false} & \text{otherwise.} \end{cases} \tag{1}$$

An SI-indicator for this stochastic invariant is:

$$f(\ell, x, r_1, r_2) = \begin{cases} \frac{x+1}{100} & \text{if } \ell \in \{\ell_{init}, \ell_1, \ell_3, \ell_{out}\} \text{ and } x < 99 \\ \frac{x+1+r_1}{100} & \text{if } \ell = \ell_2 \text{ and } x < 99 \\ 1 & \text{otherwise.} \end{cases} \tag{2}$$

It is easy to check that $(SI, 0.01)$ is a stochastic invariant and that for every state $s = (\ell, x, r_1, r_2)$, the value $f(s)$ is an upper-bound on the probability of eventually leaving $SI$ if program execution starts at $s$. Also, $s \in SI \Leftrightarrow f(s) < 1$.

**Synthesizing a Termination Proof.** To prove that a probabilistic program terminates with probability at least $1-p$, our method searches for a stochastic invariant $(SI, p)$ for which, additionally, a random program run with probability 1 either leaves $SI$ or terminates. This idea is formalized in Theorem 2, which shows that stochastic invariants provide a *sound and complete* certificate for proving that a given probabilistic program terminates with probability at least $1-p$. In order to impose this additional condition, our method simultaneously computes an RSM for the set of states $\neg SI \cup State_{term}$, where $State_{term}$ is the set of all terminal states. RSMs are a classical certificate for proving almost-sure termination or reachability in probabilistic programs. A state function $\eta$ is said to be an RSM for $\neg SI \cup State_{term}$ if it satisfies the following two conditions:

- *Non-negativity.* $\eta(\ell, x, r_1, r_2) \geq 0$ for any reachable state $(\ell, x, r_1, r_2) \in SI$;
- *$\varepsilon$-decrease in expectation.* There exists $\varepsilon > 0$ such that, for any reachable non-terminal state $(\ell, x, r_1, r_2) \in SI$, the value of $\eta$ decreases in expectation by at least $\varepsilon$ after a one-step execution of the program from $(\ell, x, r_1, r_2)$.

The existence of an RSM for $\neg SI \cup State_{term}$ implies that the program will, with probability 1, either terminate or leave $SI$. As $(SI, p)$ is a stochastic invariant, we can readily conclude that the program terminates with probability at least $1-p = 0.99$. An example RSM with $\varepsilon = 0.05$ for our example above is:

$$\eta(\ell, x, r_1, r_2) = \begin{cases} x + 1.1 & \text{if } \ell = \ell_{init} \\ x + 1.05 & \text{if } \ell = \ell_1 \\ x + 1.2 + r_1 & \text{if } \ell = \ell_2 \\ x + 1.15 & \text{if } \ell = \ell_3 \\ x + 1 & \text{if } \ell = \ell_{out} \\ 100 & \text{otherwise.} \end{cases} \tag{3}$$

**Simultaneous Synthesis.** Our method employs a template-based approach and synthesizes the SI and the RSM simultaneously. We assume that our method is provided with an affine/polynomial invariant $I$ which over-approximates the set of all reachable states in the program, which is necessary since the defining conditions of SI-indicators and RSMs are required to hold at all reachable program states. Note that invariant generation is an orthogonal and well-studied problem and can be automated using [10]. For both the SI-indicator and the RSM, our method first fixes a symbolic template affine/polynomial expression for each location in the program. Then, all the defining conditions of SI-indicators and RSMs are encoded as a system of constraints over the symbolic template variables, where reachability of program states is encoded using the invariant $I$, and the synthesis proceeds by solving this system of constraints. We describe our algorithm in Sect. 6, and show that it is *relatively complete* with respect to the provided invariant $I$ and the probability threshold $1-p$. On the other hand, we note that our algorithm can also be adapted to *compute* lower bounds on the termination probability by combining it with a binary search on $p$.

**Completeness vs Relative Completeness.** Our characterization of stochastic invariants using indicator functions is complete. So is our reduction from quantitative termination analysis to the problem of synthesizing an SI-indicator function and a certificate for almost-sure reachability. These are our core theoretical contributions in this work. Nevertheless, as mentioned above, RSMs are complete only for finite termination, not a.s. termination. Moreover, template-based approaches lead to completeness guarantees only for solutions that match the template, e.g. polynomial termination certificates of a bounded degree. Therefore, our end-to-end approach is only relatively complete. These losses of completeness are due to Rice's undecidability theorem and inevitable even in *qualitative* termination analysis. In this work, we successfully provide approaches for *quantitative* termination analysis that are as complete as the best known methods for the qualitative case.

## 3 Preliminaries

We consider imperative arithmetic probabilistic programs with non-determinism. Our programs allow standard programming constructs such as conditional branching, while-loops and variable assignments. They also allow two probabilistic constructs – probabilistic branching which is indicated in the syntax by a command '**if prob**$(p)$ then ... ' with $p \in [0, 1]$ a real constant, and sampling instructions of the form $x := d$ where $d$ is a probability distribution. Sampling instructions may contain both discrete (e.g. Bernoulli, geometric or Poisson) and continuous (e.g. uniform, normal or exponential) distributions. We also allow constructs for (demonic) non-determinism. We have non-deterministic branching which is indicated in the syntax by '**if** $\star$ **then**...', and non-deterministic assignments represented by an instruction of the form $x := \mathbf{ndet}([a, b])$, where $a, b \in \mathbb{R} \cup \{\pm\infty\}$ and $[a, b]$ is a (possibly unbounded) real interval from which the new variable value is chosen non-deterministically. We also allow one or both sides of the interval to be open. The complete syntax of our programs is presented in [12, Appendix A].

**Notation.** We use boldface symbols to denote vectors. For a vector $\mathbf{x}$ of dimension $n$ and $1 \leq i \leq n$, $\mathbf{x}[i]$ denotes the $i$-th component of $\mathbf{x}$. We write $\mathbf{x}[i \leftarrow a]$ to denote an $n$-dimensional vector $\mathbf{y}$ with $\mathbf{y}[i] = a$ and $\mathbf{y}[j] = \mathbf{x}[j]$ for $j \neq i$.

**Program Variables.** Variables in our programs are real-valued. Given a finite set of variables $V$, a *variable valuation* of $V$ is a vector $\mathbf{x} \in \mathbb{R}^{|V|}$.

**Probabilistic Control-Flow Graphs (pCFGs).** We model our programs via probabilistic control-flow graphs (pCFGs) [11,14]. A *probabilistic control-flow graph (pCFG)* is a tuple $\mathcal{C} = (L, V, \ell_{init}, \mathbf{x}_{init}, \mapsto, G, Pr, Up)$, where:

- $L$ is a finite set of *locations*, partitioned into locations of *conditional branching* $L_C$, *probabilistic branching* $L_P$, *non-det branching* $L_N$ and *assignment* $L_A$.
- $V = \{x_1, \ldots, x_{|V|}\}$ is a finite set of *program variables*;
- $\ell_{init}$ is the *initial program location*;

- $\mathbf{x}_{init} \in \mathbb{R}^{|V|}$ is the initial variable valuation;
- $\mapsto \subseteq L \times L$ is a finite set of *transitions*. For each transition $\tau = (\ell, \ell')$, we say that $\ell$ is its *source location* and $\ell'$ its *target location*;
- $G$ is a map assigning to each transition $\tau = (\ell, \ell') \in \mapsto$ with $\ell \in L_C$ a *guard* $G(\tau)$, which is a logical formula over $V$ specifying whether $\tau$ can be executed;
- $Pr$ is a map assigning to each transition $\tau = (\ell, \ell') \in \mapsto$ with $\ell \in L_P$ a *probability* $Pr(\tau) \in [0, 1]$. We require $\sum_{\tau=(\ell,\_)} Pr(\tau) = 1$ for each $\ell \in L_P$;
- $Up$ is a map assigning to each transition $\tau = (\ell, \ell') \in \mapsto$ with $\ell \in L_A$ an *update* $Up(\tau) = (j, u)$ where $j \in \{1, \ldots, |V|\}$ is a *target variable index* and $u$ is an *update element* which can be:
  - the bottom element $u = \bot$, denoting no update;
  - a Borel-measurable expression $u : \mathbb{R}^{|V|} \to \mathbb{R}$, denoting a deterministic variable assignment;
  - a probability distribution $u = d$, denoting that the new variable value is sampled according to $d$;
  - an interval $u = [a, b] \subseteq \mathbb{R} \cup \{\pm\infty\}$, denoting a non-deterministic update. We also allow one or both sides of the interval to be open.

We assume the existence of the special *terminal location* denoted by $\ell_{out}$. We also require that each location has at least one outgoing transition, and that each $\ell \in L_A$ has a unique outgoing transition. For each location $\ell \in L_C$, we assume that the disjunction of guards of all transitions outgoing from $\ell$ is equivalent to *true*, i.e. $\bigvee_{\tau=(l,\_)} G(\tau) \equiv true$. Translation of probabilistic programs to pCFGs that model them is standard, so we omit the details and refer the reader to [11]. The pCFG for the program in Fig. 1 is provided in [12, Appendix B].

**States, Paths and Runs.** A *state* in a pCFG $\mathcal{C}$ is a tuple $(\ell, \mathbf{x})$, where $\ell$ is a location in $\mathcal{C}$ and $\mathbf{x} \in \mathbb{R}^{|V|}$ is a variable valuation of $V$. We say that a transition $\tau = (\ell, \ell')$ is *enabled* at a state $(\ell, \mathbf{x})$ if $\ell \notin L_C$ or if $\ell \in L_C$ and $\mathbf{x} \models G(\tau)$. We say that a state $(\ell', \mathbf{x}')$ is a *successor* of $(\ell, \mathbf{x})$, if there exists an enabled transition $\tau = (\ell, \ell')$ in $\mathcal{C}$ such that $(\ell', \mathbf{x}')$ can be reached from $(\ell, \mathbf{x})$ by executing $\tau$, i.e. we can obtain $\mathbf{x}'$ by applying the updates of $\tau$ to $\mathbf{x}$, if any. A *finite path* in $\mathcal{C}$ is a sequence $(\ell_0, \mathbf{x}_0), (\ell_1, \mathbf{x}_1), \ldots, (\ell_k, \mathbf{x}_k)$ of states with $(\ell_0, \mathbf{x}_0) = (\ell_{init}, \mathbf{x}_{init})$ and with $(\ell_{i+1}, \mathbf{x}_{i+1})$ being a successor of $(\ell_i, \mathbf{x}_i)$ for each $0 \leq i \leq k-1$. A state $(\ell, \mathbf{x})$ is *reachable* in $\mathcal{C}$ if there exists a finite path in $\mathcal{C}$ that ends in $(\ell, \mathbf{x})$. A *run* (or *execution*) in $\mathcal{C}$ is an infinite sequence of states where each finite prefix is a finite path. We use $State_{\mathcal{C}}$, $Fpath_{\mathcal{C}}$, $Run_{\mathcal{C}}$, $Reach_{\mathcal{C}}$ to denote the set of all states, finite paths, runs and reachable states in $\mathcal{C}$, respectively. Finally, we use $State_{term}$ to denote the set $\{(\ell_{out}, \mathbf{x}) \mid \mathbf{x} \in \mathbb{R}^{|V|}\}$ of terminal states.

**Schedulers.** The behavior of a pCFG may be captured by defining a probability space over the set of all runs in the pCFG. For this to be done, however, we need to resolve non-determinism and this is achieved via the standard notion of a scheduler. A *scheduler* in a pCFG $\mathcal{C}$ is a map $\sigma$ which to each finite path $\rho \in Fpath_{\mathcal{C}}$ assigns a probability distribution $\sigma(\rho)$ over successor states of the last state in $\rho$. Since we deal with programs operating over real-valued variables, the set $Fpath_{\mathcal{C}}$ may be uncountable. To that end, we impose an additional *measurability* assumption on schedulers, in order to ensure that the semantics of probabilistc programs with non-determinism is defined in a mathematically sound way. The restriction to measurable schedulers is standard. Hence, we omit the formal definition.

**Semantics of pCFGs.** A pCFG $\mathcal{C}$ with a scheduler $\sigma$ define a stochastic process taking values in the set of states of $\mathcal{C}$, whose trajectories correspond to runs in $\mathcal{C}$. The process starts in the initial state $(\ell_{init}, \mathbf{x}_{init})$ and inductively extends the run, where the next state along the run is chosen either deterministically or is sampled from the probability distribution defined by the current location along the run and by the scheduler $\sigma$. These are the classical operational semantics of Markov decision processes (MDPs), see e.g. [1,27]. A pCFG $\mathcal{C}$ and a scheduler $\sigma$ together determine a probability space $(Run_{\mathcal{C}}, \mathcal{F}_{\mathcal{C}}, \mathbb{P}^{\sigma})$ over the set of all runs in $\mathcal{C}$. For details, see [12, Appendix C]. We denote by $\mathbb{E}^{\sigma}$ the expectation operator on $(Run_{\mathcal{C}}, \mathcal{F}_{\mathcal{C}}, \mathbb{P}^{\sigma})$. We may analogously define a probability space $(Run_{\mathcal{C}(\ell,\mathbf{x})}, \mathcal{F}_{\mathcal{C}(\ell,\mathbf{x})}, \mathbb{P}^{\sigma}_{\mathcal{C}(\ell,\mathbf{x})})$ over the set of all runs in $\mathcal{C}$ that start in some specified state $(\ell, \mathbf{x})$.

**Probabilistic Termination Problem.** We now define the termination problem for probabilistic programs considered in this work. A state $(\ell, \mathbf{x})$ in a pCFG $\mathcal{C}$ is said to be a *terminal state* if $\ell = \ell_{out}$. A run $\rho \in Run_{\mathcal{C}}$ is said to be *terminating* if it reaches some terminal state in $\mathcal{C}$. We use $Term \subseteq Run_{\mathcal{C}}$ to denote the set of all terminating runs in $Run_{\mathcal{C}}$. The *termination probability* of a pCFG $\mathcal{C}$ is defined as $\inf_{\sigma} \mathbb{P}^{\sigma}[Term]$, i.e. the smallest probability of the set of terminating runs in $\mathcal{C}$ with respect to any scheduler in $\mathcal{C}$ (for the proof that $Term$ is measurable, see [40]). We say that $\mathcal{C}$ terminates *almost-surely (a.s.)* if its termination probability is 1. In this work, we consider the Lower Bound on the Probability of Termination (LBPT) problem that, given $p \in [0, 1]$, asks whether $1 - p$ is a lower bound for the termination probability of the given probabilistic program, i.e. whether $\inf_{\sigma} \mathbb{P}^{\sigma}[Term] \geq 1 - p$.

## 4 A Sound and Complete Characterization of SIs

In this section, we recall the notion of stochastic invariants and present our characterization of stochastic invariants through stochastic indicator functions. We fix a pCFG $\mathcal{C} = (L, V, \ell_{init}, \mathbf{x}_{init}, \mapsto, G, Pr, Up)$. A *predicate function* in $\mathcal{C}$ is a map $F$ that to every location $\ell \in L$ assigns a logical formula $F(\ell)$ over program variables. It naturally induces a set of states, which we require to be Borel-measurable for the semantics to be well-defined. By a slight abuse of notation, we identify a predicate function $F$ with this set of states. Furthermore, we use $\neg F$ to denote the negation of a predicate function, i.e. $(\neg F)(\ell) = \neg F(\ell)$. An *invariant* in $\mathcal{C}$ is a predicate function $I$ which additionally over-approximates the set of reachable states in $\mathcal{C}$, i.e. for every $(\ell, \mathbf{x}) \in Reach_{\mathcal{C}}$ we have $\mathbf{x} \models I(\ell)$. *Stochastic invariants* can be viewed as a probabilistic extension of invariants, which a random program run leaves only with a certain probability. See Sect. 2 for an example.

**Definition 1 (Stochastic invariant [14]).** *Let SI a predicate function in $\mathcal{C}$ and $p \in [0,1]$ a probability. The tuple $(SI, p)$ is a* stochastic invariant (SI) *if the probability of a run in $\mathcal{C}$ leaving the set of states defined by SI is at most p under any scheduler. Formally, we require that*

$$\sup_\sigma \mathbb{P}^\sigma\Big[\rho \in Run_{\mathcal{C}} \mid \rho \text{ reaches some } (\ell, \mathbf{x}) \text{ with } \mathbf{x} \not\models SI(\ell)\Big] \leq p.$$

**Key Challenge.** If we find a stochastic invariant $(SI, p)$ for which termination happens almost-surely on runs that do not leave $SI$, we can immediately conclude that the program terminates with probability at least $1-p$ (this idea is formalized in Sect. 5). The key challenge in designing an efficient termination analysis based on this idea is the computation of appropriate stochastic invariants. We present a *sound and complete* characterization of stochastic invariants which allows for their effective automated synthesis through template-based methods.

We characterize stochastic invariants through the novel notion of *stochastic invariant indicators (SI-indicators)*. An SI-indicator is a function that to each state assigns an upper-bound on the probability of violating the stochastic invariant if we start the program in that state. Since the definition of an SI-indicator imposes conditions on its value at reachable states and since computing the exact set of reachable states is in general infeasible, we define SI-indicators with respect to a supporting invariant with the later automation in mind. In order to understand the ideas of this section, one may assume for simplicity that the invariant exactly equals the set of reachable states. A *state-function* in $\mathcal{C}$ is a function $f$ that to each location $\ell \in L$ assigns a Borel-measurable real-valued function over program variables $f(\ell) : \mathbb{R}^{|V|} \to \mathbb{R}$. We use $f(\ell, \mathbf{x})$ and $f(\ell)(\mathbf{x})$ interchangeably.

**Definition 2 (Stochastic invariant indicator).** *A tuple $(f_{SI}, p)$ comprising a state function $f_{SI}$ and probability $p \in [0,1]$ is a* stochastic invariant indicator (SI-indicator) *with respect to an invariant I, if it satisfies the following conditions:*

*($C_1$)* Non-negativity. *For every location $\ell \in L$, we have $\mathbf{x} \models I(\ell) \Rightarrow f_{SI}(\ell, \mathbf{x}) \geq 0$.*

*($C_2$)* Non-increasing expected value. *For every location $\ell \in L$, we have:*

*($C_2^1$) If $\ell \in L_C$, then for any transition $\tau = (\ell, \ell')$ we have $\mathbf{x} \models I(\ell) \wedge G(\tau) \Rightarrow f_{SI}(\ell, \mathbf{x}) \geq f_{SI}(\ell', \mathbf{x})$.*

*($C_2^2$) If $\ell \in L_P$, then $\mathbf{x} \models I(\ell) \Rightarrow f_{SI}(\ell, \mathbf{x}) \geq \sum_{\tau=(\ell,\ell')\in\mapsto} \Pr(\tau) \cdot f_{SI}(\ell', \mathbf{x})$.*

*($C_2^3$) If $\ell \in L_N$, then $\mathbf{x} \models I(\ell) \Rightarrow f_{SI}(\ell, \mathbf{x}) \geq \max_{\tau=(\ell,\ell')\in\mapsto} f_{SI}(\ell', \mathbf{x})$.*

*($C_2^4$) If $\ell \in L_A$ with $\tau = (\ell, \ell')$ the unique outgoing transition from $\ell$, then:*

- *If $Up(\tau) = (j, \bot)$, $\mathbf{x} \models I(\ell) \Rightarrow f(\ell, \mathbf{x}) \geq f(\ell', \mathbf{x})$.*
- *If $Up(\tau) = (j, u)$ with $u : \mathbb{R}^{|V|} \to \mathbb{R}$ an expression, we have $\mathbf{x} \models I(\ell) \Rightarrow f(\ell, \mathbf{x}) \geq f(\ell', \mathbf{x}[x_j \leftarrow u(\mathbf{x}_i)])$.*
- *If $Up(\tau) = (j, u)$ with $u = d$ a distribution, we have $\mathbf{x} \models I(\ell) \Rightarrow f(\ell, \mathbf{x}) \geq \mathbb{E}_{X\sim d}[f(\ell', \mathbf{x}[x_j \leftarrow X])]$.*
- *If $Up(\tau) = (j, u)$ with $u = [a, b]$ an interval, we have $\mathbf{x} \models I(\ell) \Rightarrow f(\ell, \mathbf{x}) \geq \sup_{X\in[a,b]}\{f(\ell', \mathbf{x}[x_j \leftarrow X])\}$.*

*($C_3$)* Initial condition. *We have $f(\ell_{init}, \mathbf{x}_{init}) \leq p$.*

**Intuition.** $(C_1)$ imposes that $f$ is nonnegative at any state contained in the invariant $I$. Next, for any state in $I$, $(C_2)$ imposes that the value of $f$ does not increase in expectation upon a one-step execution of the pCFG under any scheduler. Finally, the condition $(C_3)$ imposes that the initial value of $f$ in $\mathcal{C}$ is at most $p$. Together, the indicator thus intuitively over-approximates the probability of violating $SI$. An example of an SI-indicator for our running example in Fig. 1 is given in (2). The following theorem formalizes the above intuition and is our main result of this section. In essence, we prove that $(SI, p)$ is a stochastic invariant in $\mathcal{C}$ iff there exists an SI-indicator $(f_{SI}, p)$ such that $SI$ contains all states at which $f_{SI}$ is strictly smaller than 1. This implies that, for every stochastic invariant $(SI, p)$, there exists an SI-indicator such that $(SI', p)$ defined via $SI'(\ell) = (\mathbf{x} \models I(\ell) \wedge f_{SI}(\ell, \mathbf{x}) < 1)$ is a stochastic invariant that is at least as tight as $(SI, p)$.

**Theorem 1 (Soundness and Completeness of SI-indicators).** *Let $\mathcal{C}$ be a pCFG, $I$ an invariant in $\mathcal{C}$ and $p \in [0, 1]$. For any SI-indicator $(f_{SI}, p)$ with respect to $I$, the predicate map $SI$ defined as $SI(\ell) = (\mathbf{x} \models I(\ell) \wedge f_{SI}(\ell, \mathbf{x}) < 1)$ yields a stochastic invariant $(SI, p)$ in $\mathcal{C}$. Conversely, for every stochastic invariant $(SI, p)$ in $\mathcal{C}$, there exist an invariant $I_{SI}$ and a state function $f_{SI}$ such that $(f_{SI}, p)$ is an SI-indicator with respect to $I_{SI}$ and for each $\ell \in L$ we have $SI(\ell) \supseteq (\mathbf{x} \models I_{SI}(\ell) \wedge f_{SI}(\ell, \mathbf{x}) < 1)$.*

**Proof Sketch.** Since the proof is technically involved, we present the main ideas here and defer the details to [12, Appendix E]. First, suppose that $I$ is an invariant in $\mathcal{C}$ and that $(f_{SI}, p)$ is an SI-indicator with respect to $I$, and let $SI(\ell) = (\mathbf{x} \models I(\ell) \wedge f_{SI}(\ell, \mathbf{x}) < 1)$ for each $\ell \in L$. We need to show that $(SI, p)$ is a stochastic invariant in $\mathcal{C}$. Let $\sup_\sigma \mathbb{P}^\sigma_{(\ell,\mathbf{x})}[Reach(\neg SI)]$ be a state function that maps each state $(\ell, \mathbf{x})$ to the probability of reaching $\neg SI$ from $(\ell, \mathbf{x})$. We consider a lattice of non-negative semi-analytic state-functions $(\mathcal{L}, \sqsubseteq)$ with the partial order defined via $f \sqsubseteq f'$ if $f(\ell, \mathbf{x}) \leq f'(\ell, \mathbf{x})$ holds for each state $(\ell, \mathbf{x})$ in $I$. See [12, Appendix D] for a review of lattice theory. It follows from a result in [40] that the probability of reaching $\neg SI$ can be characterized as the least fixed point of the *next-time operator* $\mathbb{X}_{\neg SI} : \mathcal{L} \to \mathcal{L}$. Away from $\neg SI$, the operator $\mathbb{X}_{\neg SI}$ simulates a one-step execution of $\mathcal{C}$ and maps $f \in \mathcal{L}$ to its maximal expected value upon one-step execution of $\mathcal{C}$ where the maximum is taken over all schedulers, and at states contained in $\neg SI$ the operator $\mathbb{X}_{\neg SI}$ is equal to 1. It was also shown in [40] that, if a state function $f \in \mathcal{L}$ is a pre-fixed point of $\mathbb{X}_{\neg SI}$, then it satisfies $\sup_\sigma \mathbb{P}^\sigma_{(\ell,\mathbf{x})}[Reach(\neg SI)] \leq f(\ell, \mathbf{x})$ for each $(\ell, \mathbf{x})$ in $I$. Now, by checking the defining properties of pre-fixed points and recalling that $f_{SI}$ satisfies Non-negativity condition $(C_1)$ and Non-increasing expected value condition $(C_2)$ in Definition 2, we can show that $f_{SI}$ is contained in the lattice $\mathcal{L}$ and is a pre-fixed point of $\mathbb{X}_{\neg SI}$. It follows that $\sup_\sigma \mathbb{P}^\sigma_{(\ell_{init},\mathbf{x}_{init})}[Reach(\neg SI)] \leq f_{SI}(\ell_{init}, \mathbf{x}_{init})$. On the other hand, by initial condition $(C_3)$ in Definition 2 we know that $f_{SI}(\ell_{init}, \mathbf{x}_{init}) \leq p$. Hence, we have $\sup_\sigma \mathbb{P}^\sigma_{(\ell_{init},\mathbf{x}_{init})}[Reach(\neg SI)] \leq p$ so $(SI, p)$ is a stochastic invariant.

Conversely, suppose that $(SI, p)$ is a stochastic invariant in $\mathcal{C}$. We show in [12, Appendix E] that, if we define $I_{SI}$ to be the trivial true invariant and define $f_{SI}(\ell, \mathbf{x}) = \sup_\sigma \mathbb{P}^\sigma_{(\ell,\mathbf{x})}[Reach(\neg SI)]$, then $(f_{SI}, p)$ forms an SI-indicator with respect to $I_{SI}$. The claim follows by again using the fact that $f_{SI}$ is the least fixed point of the operator $\mathbb{X}_{\neg SI}$, from which we can conclude that $(f_{SI}, p)$ satisfies conditions $(C_1)$ and $(C_2)$ in Definition 2. On the other hand, the fact that $(SI, p)$ is a stochastic invariant and our choice of $f_{SI}$ imply that $(f_{SI}, p)$ satisfies the initial condition $(C_3)$ in Definition 2. Hence, $(f_{SI}, p)$ forms an SI-indicator with respect to $I_{SI}$. Furthermore, $SI(\ell) \supseteq (\mathbf{x} \models I_{SI}(\ell) \wedge f_{SI}(\ell, \mathbf{x}) < 1)$ follows since $1 > f_{SI}(\ell, \mathbf{x}) = \sup_\sigma \mathbb{P}^\sigma_{(\ell,\mathbf{x})}[Reach(\neg SI)]$ implies that $(\ell, \mathbf{x})$ cannot be contained in $\neg SI$ so $\mathbf{x} \models SI(\ell)$. This concludes the proof. □

Based on the theorem above, in order to compute a stochastic invariant in $\mathcal{C}$ for a given probability threshold $p$, it suffices to synthesize a state function $f_{SI}$ that together with $p$ satisfies all the defining conditions in Definition 2 with respect to some supporting invariant $I$, and then consider a predicate function $SI$ defined via $SI(\ell) = (\mathbf{x} \models I(\ell) \wedge f_{SI}(\ell, \mathbf{x}) < 1)$ for each $\ell \in L$. This will be the guiding principle of our algorithmic approach in Sect. 6.

**Intuition on Characterization.** Stochastic invariants can essentially be thought of as quantitative safety specifications in probabilistic programs – $(SI, p)$ is a stochastic invariant if and only if a random probabilistic program run leaves $SI$ with probability at most $p$. However, what makes their computation hard is that they do not consider probabilities of staying within a specified safe set. Rather, the computation of stochastic invariants requires computing *both* the safe set *and* the certificate that it is left with at most the given probability. Nevertheless, in order to reason about them, we may consider $SI$ as an implicitly defined safe set. Hence, if we impose conditions on a state function $f_{SI}$ to be an upper bound on the reachability probability for the target set of states $(\mathbf{x} \models I(\ell) \wedge f_{SI}(\ell, \mathbf{x}) < 1)$, and in addition impose that $f_{SI}(\ell_{init}, \mathbf{x}_{init}) \leq p$, then these together will entail that $p$ is an upper bound on the probability of ever leaving $SI$ when starting in the initial state. This is the intuitive idea behind our construction of SI-indicators, as well as our soundness and completeness proof. In the proof, we show that conditions $(C_1)$ and $(C_2)$ in Definition 2 indeed entail the necessary conditions to be an upper bound on the reachability probability of the set $(\mathbf{x} \models I(\ell) \wedge f_{SI}(\ell, \mathbf{x}) < 1)$.

## 5 Stochastic Invariants for LBPT

In the previous section, we paved the way for automated synthesis of stochastic invariants by providing a sound and complete characterization in terms of SI-indicators. We now show how stochastic invariants in combination with any a.s. termination certificate for probabilistic programs can be used to compute lower-bounds on the probability of termination. Theorem 2 below states a general result about termination probabilities that is agnostic to the termination certificate, and shows that stochastic invaraints provide a *sound and complete* approach to quantitative termination analysis.

**Theorem 2 (Soundness and Completeness of SIs for Quantitative Termination).** *Let $\mathcal{C} = (L, V, \ell_{init}, \mathbf{x}_{init}, \mapsto, G, Pr, Up)$ be a pCFG and $(SI, p)$ a stochastic invariant in $\mathcal{C}$. Suppose that, with respect to every scheduler, a run in $\mathcal{C}$ almost-surely either terminates or reaches a state in $\neg SI$, i.e.*

$$\inf_{\sigma} \mathbb{P}^{\sigma}\Big[\mathit{Term} \cup \mathit{Reach}(\neg SI)\Big] = 1. \tag{4}$$

*Then $\mathcal{C}$ terminates with probability at least $1 - p$. Conversely, if $\mathcal{C}$ terminates with probability at least $1 - p$, then there exists a stochastic invariant $(SI, p)$ in $\mathcal{C}$ such that, with respect to every scheduler, a run in $\mathcal{C}$ almost-surely either terminates or reaches a state in $\neg SI$.*

**Proof Sketch.** The first part (soundness) follows directly from the definition of $SI$ and (4). The completeness proof is conceptually and technically involved and presented in [12, Appendix H]. In short, the central idea is to construct, for every $n$ greater than a specific threshold $n_0$, a stochastic invariant $(SI_n, p + \frac{1}{n})$ such that a run almost-surely either terminates or exists $SI_n$. Then, we show that $\cap_{n=n_0}^{\infty} SI_n$ is our desired $SI$. To construct each $SI_n$, we consider the infimum termination probability at every state $(\ell, \mathbf{x})$ and call it $r(\ell, \mathbf{x})$. The infimum is taken over all schedulers. We then let $SI_n$ be the set of states $(\ell, \mathbf{x})$ for whom $r(\ell, \mathbf{x})$ is greater than a specific threshold $\alpha$. Intuitively, our stochastic invariant is the set of program states from which the probability of termination is at least $\alpha$, no matter how the non-determinism is resolved. Let us call these states likely-terminating. The intuition is that a random run of the program will terminate or eventually leave the likely-terminating states with high probability. □

**Quantitative to Qualitative Termination.** Theorem 2 provides us with a recipe for computing lower bounds on the probability of termination once we are able to compute stochastic invariants: if $(SI, p)$ is a stochastic invariant in a pCFG $\mathcal{C}$, it suffices to prove that the set of states $\mathit{State}_{term} \cup \neg SI$ is reached almost-surely with respect to any scheduler in $\mathcal{C}$, i.e. the program terminates or violates SI. Note that this is simply a qualitative a.s. termination problem, except that the set of terminal states is now augmented with $\neg SI$. Then, since $(SI, p)$ is a stochastic invariant, it would follow that a terminal state is reached with probability at least $1-p$. Moreover, the theorem shows that this approach is both sound and complete. In other words, proving quantitative termination, i.e. that we reach $\mathit{State}_{term}$ with probability at least $1 - p$ is now reduced to (i) finding a stochastic invariant $(SI, p)$ and (ii) proving that the program $\mathcal{C}'$ obtained by adding $\neg SI$ to the set of terminal states of $\mathcal{C}$ is a.s. terminating. Note that, to preserve completeness, (i) and (ii) should be achieved in tandem, i.e. an approach that first synthesizes and fixes $SI$ and then tries to prove a.s. termination for $\neg SI$ is not complete.

**Ranking Supermartingales.** While our reduction above is agnostic to the type of proof/certificate that is used to establish a.s. termination, in this work we use Ranking Supermartingales (RSMs) [7], which are a standard and classical certificate for proving a.s. termination and reachability. Let $\mathcal{C} = (L, V, \ell_{init}, \mathbf{x}_{init}, \mapsto$

$, G, Pr, Up)$ be a pCFG and $I$ an invariant in $\mathcal{C}$. Note that as in Definition 2, the main purpose of the invariant is to allow for automated synthesis and one can again simply assume it to equal the set of reachable states. An $\varepsilon$-RSM for a subset $T$ of states is a state function that is non-negative in each state in $I$, and whose expected value decreases by at least $\varepsilon > 0$ upon a one-step execution of $\mathcal{C}$ in any state that is not contained in the target set $T$. Thus, intuitively, a program run has an expected tendency to approach the target set $T$ where the distance to $T$ is given by the value of the RSM which is required to be non-negative in all states in $I$. The $\varepsilon$-ranked expected value condition is formally captured via the next-time operator $\mathbb{X}$ (See [12, Appendix E]). An example of an RSM for our running example in Fig. 1 and the target set of states $\neg SI \cup State_{term}$ with $SI$ the stochastic invariant in Eq. (1) is given in Eq. (3).

**Definition 3 (Ranking supermartingales).** *Let $T$ be a predicate function defining a set of target states in $\mathcal{C}$, and let $\varepsilon > 0$. A state function $\eta$ is said to be an* $\varepsilon$-ranking supermartingale ($\varepsilon$-RSM) *for $T$ with respect to the invariant $I$ if it satisfies the following conditions:*

1. Non-negativity. *For each location $\ell \in L$ and $\mathbf{x} \in I(\ell)$, we have $\eta(\ell, \mathbf{x}) \geq 0$.*
2. $\varepsilon$-ranked expected value. *For each location $\ell \in L$ and $\mathbf{x} \models I(\ell) \cap \neg T(\ell)$, we have $\eta(\ell, \mathbf{x}) \geq \mathbb{X}(\eta)(\ell, \mathbf{x}) + \varepsilon$.*

Note that the second condition can be expanded according to location types in the exact same manner as in condition $C_2$ of Definition 2. The only difference is that in Definition 2, the expected value had to be non-increasing, whereas here it has to decrease by $\varepsilon$. It is well-known that the two conditions above entail that $T$ is reached with probability 1 with respect to any scheduler [7,11].

**Theorem 3. (Proof in** [12, **Appendix** I]**).** *Let $\mathcal{C}$ be a pCFG, $I$ an invariant in $\mathcal{C}$ and $T$ a predicate function defining a target set of states. If there exist $\varepsilon > 0$ and an $\varepsilon$-RSM for $T$ with respect to $I$, then $T$ is a.s. reached under any scheduler, i.e.*

$$\inf_{\sigma} \mathbb{P}^{\sigma}_{(\ell_{init}, \mathbf{x}_{init})}\Big[Reach(T)\Big] = 1.$$

The following theorem is an immediate corollary of Theorems 2 and 3.

**Theorem 4.** *Let $\mathcal{C}$ be a pCFG and $I$ be an invariant in $\mathcal{C}$. Suppose that there exist a stochastic invariant $(SI, p)$, an $\varepsilon > 0$ and an $\varepsilon$-RSM $\eta$ for $State_{term} \cup \neg SI$ with respect to $I$. Then $\mathcal{C}$ terminates with probability at least $1 - p$.*

Therefore, in order to prove that $\mathcal{C}$ terminates with probability at least $1 - p$, it suffices to find (i) a stochastic invariant $(SI, p)$ in $\mathcal{C}$, and (ii) an $\varepsilon$-RSM $\eta$ for $State_{term} \cup \neg SI$ with respect to $I$ and some $\varepsilon > 0$. Note that these two tasks are interdependent. We cannot simply choose any stochastic invariant. For instance, the trivial predicate function defined via $SI$ = true always yields a valid stochastic invariant for any $p \in [0, 1]$, but it does not help termination analysis. Instead, we need to compute a stochastic invariant and an RSM for it *simultaneously*.

**Power of Completeness.** We end this section by showing that our approach certifies a tight lower-bound on termination probability for a program that was proven in [40] not to admit any of the previously-existing certificates for lower bounds on termination probability. This shows that our completeness pays off in practice and our approach is able to handle programs that were beyond the reach of previous methods. Consider the program in Fig. 2 annotated by an invariant $I$. We show that our approach certifies that this program terminates with probability at least 0.5. Indeed, consider a stochastic invariant $(SI, 0.5)$ with $SI(\ell) = \text{true}$ if $\ell \neq \ell_3$, and $SI(\ell_3) = \text{false}$, and a state function defined via $\eta(\ell_{init}, x) = -\log(x) + \log(2) + 3$, $\eta(\ell_1, x) = -\log(x) + \log(2) + 2$, $\eta(\ell_2, x) = 1$ and $\eta(\ell_3, x) = \eta(\ell_{out}, x) = 0$ for each $x$. Then one can easily check by inspection that $(SI, 0.5)$ is a stochastic invariant and that $\eta$ is a $(\log(2) - 1)$-RSM for $State_{term} \cup \neg SI$ with respect to $I$. Therefore, it follows by Theorem 4 that the program in Fig. 2 terminates with probability at least 0.5.

## 6 Automated Template-Based Synthesis Algorithm

We now provide template-based relatively complete algorithms for simultaneous and automated synthesis of SI-indicators and RSMs, in order to solve the quantitative termination problem over pCFGs with affine/polynomial arithmetic. Our approach builds upon the ideas of [2,9] for qualitative and non-probabilistic cases.

```
           x = ndet((0,1))
ℓ_init:    while x < 1 do                     {0 < x < 2}
ℓ_1:           x := 2 · x                     {0 < x < 1}
ℓ_2:       if prob(0.5) then                  {1 ≤ x < 2}
ℓ_3:           while true do skip od          {1 ≤ x < 2}
ℓ_out:                                        {1 ≤ x < 2}
```

**Fig. 2.** A program that was shown in [40] not to admit a repulsing supermartingale [14] or a gamma-scaled supermartingale [40], but for which our method can certify the tight lower-bound of 0.5 on the probability of termination.

**Input and Assumptions.** The input to our algorithms consists of a pCFG $\mathcal{C}$ together with a probability $p \in [0, 1]$, an invariant $I$,* and technical variables $\delta$ and $M$, which specify polynomial template sizes used by the algorithm and which will be discussed later. In this section, we limit our focus to affine/polynomial pCFGs, i.e. we assume that all guards $G(\tau)$ in $\mathcal{C}$ and all invariants $I(\ell)$ are conjunctions of affine/polynomial inequalities over program variables. Similarly, we assume that every update function $u : \mathbb{R}^{|V|} \to \mathbb{R}$ used in deterministic variable assignments is an affine/polynomial expression in $\mathbb{R}[V]$.

* We assume an invariant is given as part of the input. Invariant generation is an orthogonal and well-studied problem and can be automated using [10,16].

**Output.** The goal of our algorithms is to synthesize a tuple $(f, \eta, \varepsilon)$ where $f$ is an SI-indicator function, $\eta$ is a corresponding RSM, and $\varepsilon > 0$, such that:

- At every location $\ell$ of $\mathcal{C}$, both $f(\ell)$ and $\eta(\ell)$ are affine/polynomial expressions of fixed degree $\delta$ over the program variables $V$.
- Having $SI(\ell) := \{\mathbf{x} \mid f(\ell, \mathbf{x}) < 1\}$, the pair $(SI, p)$ is a valid stochastic invariant and $\eta$ is an $\varepsilon$-RSM for $State_{term} \cup \neg SI$ with respect to $I$.

As shown in Sects. 4 and 5, such a tuple $w = (f, \eta, \varepsilon)$ serves as a certificate that the probabilistic program modeled by $\mathcal{C}$ terminates with probability at least $1 - p$. We call $w$ a quantitative termination certificate.

**Overview.** Our algorithm is a standard template-based approach similar to [2,9]. We encode the requirements of Definitions 2 and 3 as entailments between affine/polynomial inequalities with unknown coefficients and then apply the classical Farkas' Lemma [17] or Putinar's Positivstellensatz [38] to reduce the synthesis problem to Quadratic Programming (QP). Finally, we solve the resulting QP using a numerical optimizer or an SMT-solver. Our approach consists of the four steps below. Step 3 follows [2] exactly. Hence, we refer to [2] for more details on this step.

**Step 1. Setting Up Templates.** The algorithm sets up symbolic templates with unknown coefficients for $f, \eta$ and $\varepsilon$.

- First, for each location $\ell$ of $\mathcal{C}$, the algorithm sets up a template for $f(\ell)$ which is a polynomial consisting of all possible monomials of degree at most $\delta$ over program variables, each appearing with an unknown coefficient. For example, consider the program in Fig. 1 of Sect. 2. This program has three variables: $x, r_1$ and $r_2$. If $\delta = 1$, i.e. if the goal is to find an affine SI-indicator, at every location $\ell_i$ of the program, the algorithm sets $f(\ell_i, x, r_1, r_2) := \widehat{c_{i,0}} + \widehat{c_{i,1}} \cdot x + \widehat{c_{i,2}} \cdot r_1 + \widehat{c_{i,3}} \cdot r_2$. Similarly, if the desired degree is $\delta = 2$, the algorithm symbolically computes:$f(\ell_i, x, r_1, r_2) := \widehat{c_{i,0}} + \widehat{c_{i,1}} \cdot x + \widehat{c_{i,2}} \cdot r_1 + \widehat{c_{i,3}} \cdot r_2 + \widehat{c_{i,4}} \cdot x^2 + \widehat{c_{i,5}} \cdot x \cdot r_1 + \widehat{c_{i,6}} \cdot x \cdot r_2 + \widehat{c_{i,7}} \cdot r_1^2 + \widehat{c_{i,8}} \cdot r_1 \cdot r_2 + \widehat{c_{i,9}} \cdot r_2^2$. Note that every monomial of degree at most 2 appears in this expression. The goal is to synthesize suitable real values for each unknown coefficient $\widehat{c_{i,j}}$ such that $f$ becomes an SI-indicator. Throughout this section, we use the $\widehat{\cdot}$ notation to denote an unknown coefficient whose value will be synthesized by our algorithm.
- The algorithm creates an unknown variable $\widehat{\varepsilon}$ whose final value will serve as $\varepsilon$.
- Finally, at each location $\ell$ of $\mathcal{C}$, the algorithm sets up a template for $\eta(\ell)$ in the exact same manner as the template for $f(\ell)$. The goal is to synthesize values for $\widehat{\varepsilon}$ and the $\widehat{c}$ variables in this template such that $\eta$ becomes a valid $\widehat{\varepsilon}$-RSM for $State_{term} \cup \neg SI$ with respect to $I$.

**Step 2. Generating Entailment Constraints.** In this step, the algorithm symbolically computes the requirements of Definition 2, i.e. $C_1$–$C_3$, and their analogues in Definition 3 using the templates generated in the previous step.

Note that all of these requirements are entailments between affine/polynomial inequalities over program variables whose coefficients are unknown. In other words, they are of the form $\forall \mathbf{x}\ \ A(\mathbf{x}) \Rightarrow b(\mathbf{x})$ where $A$ is a set of affine/polynomial inequalities over program variables whose coefficients contain the unknown variables $\widehat{c}$ and $\widehat{\varepsilon}$ generated in the previous step and $b$ is a single such inequality. For example, for the program of Fig. 1, the algorithm symbolically computes condition $C_1$ at line $\ell_1$ as follows: $\forall \mathbf{x}\ \ I(\ell_1, \mathbf{x}) \Rightarrow f(\ell_1, \mathbf{x}) \geq 0$. Assuming that the given invariant is $I(\ell_1, \mathbf{x}) := (x \leq 1)$ and an affine (degree 1) template was generated in the previous step, the algorithm expands this to:

$$\forall \mathbf{x}\ \ 1 - \mathbf{x} \geq 0 \Rightarrow \widehat{c_{1,0}} + \widehat{c_{1,1}} \cdot x + \widehat{c_{1,2}} \cdot r_1 + \widehat{c_{1,3}} \cdot r_2 \geq 0. \tag{5}$$

The algorithm generates similar entailment constraints for every location and every requirement in Definitions 2 and 3.

**Step 3. Quantifier Elimination.** At the end of the previous step, we have a system of constraints of the form $\bigwedge_i \left(\forall \mathbf{x}\ \ A_i(\mathbf{x}) \Rightarrow b_i(\mathbf{x})\right)$. In this step, the algorithm sets off to eliminate the universal quantification over $\mathbf{x}$ in every constraint. First, consider the affine case. If $A_i$ is a set of linear inequalities over program variables and $b_i$ is one such linear inequality, then the algorithm attempts to write $b_i$ as a linear combination with non-negative coefficients of the inequalities in $A_i$ and the trivial inequality $1 \geq 0$. For example, it rewrites (5) as $\widehat{\lambda_1} \cdot (1 - x) + \widehat{\lambda_2} = \widehat{c_{1,0}} + \widehat{c_{1,1}} \cdot x + \widehat{c_{1,2}} \cdot r_1 + \widehat{c_{1,3}} \cdot r_2$ where $\widehat{\lambda_i}$'s are new *non-negative* unknown variables for which we need to synthesize non-negative real values. This inequality should hold for all valuations of program variables. Thus, we can equate the corresponding coefficients on both sides and obtain this equivalent system:

$$\begin{aligned} \widehat{\lambda_1} + \widehat{\lambda_2} &= \widehat{c_{1,0}} && \text{(the constant factor)} \\ -\widehat{\lambda_1} &= \widehat{c_{1,1}} && \text{(coefficient of } x\text{)} \\ 0 = \widehat{c_{1,2}} &= \widehat{c_{1,3}} && \text{(coefficients of } r_1 \text{ and } r_2\text{)} \end{aligned} \tag{6}$$

This transformation is clearly sound, but it is also complete due to the well-known Farkas' lemma [17]. Now consider the polynomial case. Again, we write $b_i$ as a combination of the polynomials in $A_i$. The only difference is that instead of having non-negative real coefficients, we use sum-of-square polynomials as our multiplicands. For example, suppose our constraint is

$$\forall \mathbf{x}\ \ g_1(\mathbf{x}) \geq 0 \wedge g_2(\mathbf{x}) \geq 0 \Rightarrow g_3(\mathbf{x}) > 0,$$

where the $g_i$'s are polynomials with unknown coefficients. The algorithm writes

$$g_3(\mathbf{x}) = h_0(\mathbf{x}) + h_1(\mathbf{x}) \cdot g_1(\mathbf{x}) + h_2(\mathbf{x}) \cdot g_2(\mathbf{x}), \tag{7}$$

where each $h_i$ is a sum-of-square polynomial of degree at most $M$. The algorithm sets up a template of degree $M$ for each $h_i$ and adds well-known quadratic constraints that enforce it to be a sum of squares. See [2, Page 22] for details. It then expands (7) and equates the corresponding coefficients of the LHS and RHS as in the linear case. The soundness of this transformation is trivial since each $h_i$ is a sum-of-squares and hence always non-negative. Completeness follows from Putinar's Positivstellensatz [38]. Since the arguments for completeness of this method are exactly the same as the method in [2], we refer the reader to [2] for more details and an extension to entailments between strict polynomial inequalities.

**Step 4. Quadratic Programming.** All of our constraints are converted to Quadratic Programming (QP) over template variables, e.g. see (6). Our algorithm passes this QP instance to an SMT solver or a numerical optimizer. If a solution is found, it plugs in the values obtained for the $\widehat{c}$ and $\widehat{\varepsilon}$ variables back into the template of Step 1 and outputs the resulting termination witness $(f, \eta, \varepsilon)$.

We end this section by noting that our algorithm is sound and relatively complete for synthesizing affine/polynomial quantitative termination certificates.

**Theorem 5 (Soundness and Completeness in the Affine Case).** *Given an affine pCFG $C$, an affine invariant $I$, and a non-termination upper-bound $p \in [0, 1]$, if $C$ admits a quantitative termination certificate $w = (f, \eta, \varepsilon)$ in which both $f$ and $\eta$ are affine expressions at every location, then $w$ corresponds to a solution of the QP instance solved in Step 4 of the algorithm above. Conversely, every such solution, when plugged back into the template of Step 1, leads to an affine quantitative termination certificate showing that $C$ terminates with probability at least $1 - p$ over every scheduler.*

**Theorem 6 (Soundness and Relative Completeness in the Polynomial Case).** *Given a polynomial pCFG $C$, a polynomial invariant $I$ which is a compact subset of $\mathbb{R}^{|V|}$ at every location $\ell$, and a non-termination upper-bound $p \in [0, 1]$, if $C$ admits a quantitative termination certificate $w = (f, \eta, \varepsilon)$ in which both $f$ and $\eta$ are polynomial expressions of degree at most $\delta$ at every location, then there exists an $M \in \mathbb{N}$, for which $w$ corresponds to a solution of the QP instance solved in Step 4 of the algorithm above. Conversely, every such solution, when plugged back into the template of Step 1, leads to a polynomial quantitative termination certificate of degree at most $\delta$ showing that $C$ terminates with probability at least $1 - p$ over every scheduler.*

*Proof.* Step 2 encodes the conditions of an SI-indicator (Definition 2) and RSM (Definition 3). Theorem 4 shows that an SI-indicator together with an RSM is a valid quantitative termination certificate. The transformation in Step 3 is sound and complete as argued in [2, Theorems 4 and 10]**. The affine version relies on Farkas' lemma [17] and is complete with no additional constraints. The polynomial version is based on Putinar's Positivstellensatz [38] and is only complete for large enough $M$, i.e. a high-enough degree for sum-of-square multiplicands. This is why we call our algorithm *relatively* complete. In practice, small values of $M$ are enough to synthesize $w$ and we use $M = 2$ in all of our experiments. □

** We need a more involved transformation for *strict* inequalities. See [2, Theorem 8].

## 7 Experimental Results

**Implementation.** We implemented a prototype of our approach in Python and used SymPy [33] for symbolic computations and the MathSAT5 SMT Solver [15] for solving the final QP instances. We also applied basic optimizations, e.g. checking the validity of each entailment and thus removing tautological constraints.

**Machine and Parameters.** All results were obtained on an Intel Core i9-10885H machine (8 cores, 2.4 GHz, 16 MB Cache) with 32 GB of RAM running Ubuntu 20.04. We always synthesized quadratic termination certificates and set $\delta = M = 2$.

**Benchmarks.** We generated a variety of random walks with complicated behavior, including nested combinations of probabilistic and non-deterministic branching and loops. We also took a number of benchmarks from [14]. Due to space limitations, in Table 1 we only present experimental results on a subset of our benchmark set, together with short descriptions of these benchmarks. Complete evaluation as well as details on all benchmarks are provided in [12, Appendix J].

**Results and Discussion.** Our experimental results are summarized in Table 1, with complete results provided in [12, Appendix J]. In every case, our approach was able to synthesize a certificate that the program terminates with probability at least $1-p$ under any scheduler. Moreover, our runtimes are consistently small and less than 6 s per benchmark. Our approach was able to handle programs that are beyond the reach of previous methods, including those with unbounded differences and unbounded non-deterministic assignments to which approaches such as [14] and [40] are not applicable, as was demonstrated in [40]. This adds experimental confirmation to our theoretical power-of-completeness result at the end of Sect. 5, which showed the wider applicability of our method. Finally, it is noteworthy that the termination probability lower-bounds reported in Table 1 are not tight. There are two reasons for this. First, while our theoretical approach is sound and complete, our algorithm can only synthesize affine/polynomial certificates for quantitative termination, and the best polynomial certificate of a certain degree might not be tight. Second, we rely on an SMT-solver to solve our QP instances. The QP instances often become harder as we decrease $p$, leading to the solver's failure even though the constraints are satisfiable.

## 8 Related Works

**Supermartingale-Based Approaches.** In addition to qualitative and quantitative termination analyses, supermartingales were also used for the formal analysis of other properties in probabilistic programs, such as, liveness and safety properties [3,8,14,42], cost analysis of probabilistic programs [36,43]. While all these works demonstrate the effectiveness of supermartingale-based techniques, below we present a more detailed comparison with other works that consider automated computation of lower bounds on termination probability.

**Table 1.** Summary of our experimental results on a subset of our benchmark set. See [12, Appendix J] for benchmark details and for the results on all benchmarks.

| Benchmark | Short explanation | $p$ | LBPT $1-p$ | Runtime (s) |
|---|---|---|---|---|
| Figure 1 | Our running example | 0.01 | 0.99 | 2.38 |
| Figure 7 | Nested probabilistic and non-deterministic branches leading to infinite loop with maximum probability 0.25 | 0.25 | 0.75 | 1.40 |
| Figure 9 | An a.s. terminating biased random walk with uniformly distributed steps | 0 | 1 | 0.73 |
| Figure 10 | A random walk that starts at $x = 10$ and takes a step of $Uniform(-2, 1)$ each time. Terminates if $x < 0$ and loops forever as soon as $x \geq 100$. | 0.12 | 0.88 | 1.10 |
| Figure 11 | A 2-D random walk starting at $(50, 50)$. In each iteration, $x$ is incremented, while $y$ is increased by $Uniform(-1, 1)$. Terminates when $x > 100$. Loops when $y \leq 0$. | 0.07 | 0.93 | 3.52 |
| Figure 14 | A 3-D random walk. In each iteration, each of $x, y, z$ are incremented with a higher probability than decremented. Terminates when $x + y + z < 0$. | 0.999 | 0.001 | 3.22 |
| Figure 15 | An example with both probabilistic and non-deterministic assignments | 0.51 | 0.49 | 2.73 |
| Figure 16 | A variant of Fig. 15 with unbounded non-determinism in an assignment | 0.51 | 0.49 | 2.70 |
| Figure 17 | A probabilistic branch between an a.s. terminating loop and a loop with small termination probability | 0.4 | 0.6 | 5.17 |
| Figure 18 | A skewed random walk with two barriers, only one of which leads to program termination | 0.51 | 0.49 | 5.26 |
| Figure 19 | Taken from [14] and conceptually similar to Fig. 5 | 0.24 | 0.76 | 0.94 |
| Figure 22 | A more complicated and non-a.s.-terminating random walk taken from [14] | 0.1 | 0.9 | 1.15 |
| Figure 23 | A 2-D variant of Fig. 22, also from [14] | 0.08 | 0.92 | 4.01 |

**Comparison to** [14]**.** The work of [14] introduces stochastic invariants and demonstrates their effectiveness for computing lower bounds on termination probability. However, their approach to computing stochastic invariants is based on repulsing supermartingales (RepSMs), and is orthogonal to ours. RepSMs were shown to be incomplete for computing stochastic invariants [40, Section 3]. Also, a RepSM is required to have *bounded differences*, i.e. the absolute difference of its value is any two successor states needs to be bounded from above by some positive constant. Given that the algorithmic approach of [14] computes linear RepSMs, this implies that the applicability of RepSMs is compromised in practice as well, and is mostly suited to programs in which the quantity that behaves like a RepSM depends only on variables with bounded increments and sampling instructions defined by distributions of bounded support. Our approach does not impose such a restriction, and is the first to provide completeness guarantees.

**Comparison to** [40]**.** The work of [40] introduces $\gamma$-scaled submartingales and proves their effectiveness for computing lower bounds on termination probability. Intuitively, for $\gamma \in (0, 1)$, a state function $f$ is a $\gamma$-scaled submartingale if it is a bounded nonnegative function whose value in each non-terminal state decreases in expected value at least by a factor of $\gamma$ upon a one-step execution of the pCFG. One may think of the second condition as a multiplicative decrease in expected value. However, this condition is too strict and $\gamma$-scaled submartingales are not complete for lower bounds on termination probability [40, Example 6.6].

**Comparison to** [5]. The work of [5] proposes a type system for functional probabilistic programs that allows incrementally searching for type derivations and accumulating a lower bound on termination probability. In the limit, it finds arbitrarily tight lower bounds on termination probability, however it does not provide any completeness or precision guarantees in finite time.

**Other Approaches.** Logical calculi for reasoning about properties of probabilistic programs (including termination) were studied in [18,19,29] and extended to programs with non-determinism in [27,28,31,37]. These works consider proof systems for probabilistic programs based on the weakest pre-expectation calculus. The expressiveness of this calculus allows reasoning about very complex programs, but the proofs typically require human input. In contrast, we aim for a fully automated approach for probabilistic programs with polynomial arithmetic. Connections between martingales and the weakest pre-expectation calculus were studied in [24]. A sound approach for proving almost-sure termination based on abstract interpretation is presented in [34].

**Cores in MDPs.** *Cores* are a conceptually equivalent notion to stochastic invariants introduced in [30] for finite MDPs. [30] presents a sampling-based algorithm for their computation.

## 9 Conclusion

We study the quantitative probabilistic termination problem in probabilistic programs with non-determinism and propose the first relatively complete algorithm for proving termination with at least a given threshold probability. Our approach is based on a sound and complete characterization of stochastic invariants via the novel notion of stochastic invariant indicators, which allows for an effective and relatively complete algorithm for their computation. We then show that stochastic invariants are sound and complete certificates for proving that a program terminates with at least a given threshold probability. Hence, by combining our relatively complete algorithm for stochastic invariant computation with the existing relatively complete algorithm for computing ranking supermartingales, we present the first relatively complete algorithm for probabilistic termination. We have implemented a prototype of our algorithm and demonstrate its effectiveness on a number of probabilistic programs collected from the literature.

**Acknowledgements.** This research was partially supported by the ERC CoG 863818 (ForM-SMArt), the HKUST-Kaisa Joint Research Institute Project Grant HKJRI3A-055, the HKUST Startup Grant R9272 and the European Union's Horizon 2020 research and innovation programme under the Marie Skłodowska-Curie Grant Agreement No. 665385.

## References


1. Agrawal, S., Chatterjee, K., Novotný, P.: Lexicographic ranking supermartingales: an efficient approach to termination of probabilistic programs. In: POPL (2018). https://doi.org/10.1145/3158122
2. Asadi, A., Chatterjee, K., Fu, H., Goharshady, A.K., Mahdavi, M.: Polynomial reachability witnesses via Stellensätze. In: PLDI (2021). https://doi.org/10.1145/3453483.3454076
3. Barthe, G., Espitau, T., Ferrer Fioriti, L.M., Hsu, J.: Synthesizing probabilistic invariants via Doob's decomposition. In: Chaudhuri, S., Farzan, A. (eds.) CAV 2016. LNCS, vol. 9779, pp. 43–61. Springer, Cham (2016). https://doi.org/10.1007/978-3-319-41528-4_3
4. Barthe, G., Gaboardi, M., Grégoire, B., Hsu, J., Strub, P.Y.: Proving differential privacy via probabilistic couplings. In: LICS (2016). http://doi.acm.org/10.1145/2933575.2934554
5. Beutner, R., Ong, L.: On probabilistic termination of functional programs with continuous distributions. In: PLDI (2021). https://doi.org/10.1145/3453483.3454111
6. Bingham, E., et al.: Pyro: Deep universal probabilistic programming. J. Mach. Learn. Res. (2019). http://jmlr.org/papers/v20/18-403.html
7. Chakarov, A., Sankaranarayanan, S.: Probabilistic program analysis with martingales. In: Sharygina, N., Veith, H. (eds.) CAV 2013. LNCS, vol. 8044, pp. 511–526. Springer, Heidelberg (2013). https://doi.org/10.1007/978-3-642-39799-8_34
8. Chakarov, A., Voronin, Y.-L., Sankaranarayanan, S.: Deductive proofs of almost sure persistence and recurrence properties. In: Chechik, M., Raskin, J.-F. (eds.) TACAS 2016. LNCS, vol. 9636, pp. 260–279. Springer, Heidelberg (2016). https://doi.org/10.1007/978-3-662-49674-9_15
9. Chatterjee, K., Fu, H., Goharshady, A.K.: Termination analysis of probabilistic programs through Positivstellensatz's. In: Chaudhuri, S., Farzan, A. (eds.) CAV 2016. LNCS, vol. 9779, pp. 3–22. Springer, Cham (2016). https://doi.org/10.1007/978-3-319-41528-4_1
10. Chatterjee, K., Fu, H., Goharshady, A.K., Goharshady, E.K.: Polynomial invariant generation for non-deterministic recursive programs. In: PLDI (2020). https://doi.org/10.1145/3385412.3385969
11. Chatterjee, K., Fu, H., Novotný, P., Hasheminezhad, R.: Algorithmic analysis of qualitative and quantitative termination problems for affine probabilistic programs. TOPLAS **40**(2), 7:1–7:45 (2018). https://doi.org/10.1145/3174800
12. Chatterjee, K., Goharshady, A., Meggendorfer, T., Žikelić, Đ.: Sound and complete certificates for quantitative termination analysis of probabilistic programs (2022). https://hal.archives-ouvertes.fr/hal-03675086
13. Chatterjee, K., Goharshady, E.K., Novotný, P., Zárevúcky, J., Žikelić, Đ: On lexicographic proof rules for probabilistic termination. In: Huisman, M., Păsăreanu, C., Zhan, N. (eds.) FM 2021. LNCS, vol. 13047, pp. 619–639. Springer, Cham (2021). https://doi.org/10.1007/978-3-030-90870-6_33
14. Chatterjee, K., Novotný, P., Žikelić, Đ.: Stochastic invariants for probabilistic termination. In: POPL (2017). https://doi.org/10.1145/3009837.3009873
15. Cimatti, A., Griggio, A., Schaafsma, B.J., Sebastiani, R.: The MathSAT5 SMT solver. In: Piterman, N., Smolka, S.A. (eds.) TACAS 2013. LNCS, vol. 7795, pp. 93–107. Springer, Heidelberg (2013). https://doi.org/10.1007/978-3-642-36742-7_7

16. Colón, M.A., Sankaranarayanan, S., Sipma, H.B.: Linear invariant generation using non-linear constraint solving. In: Hunt, W.A., Somenzi, F. (eds.) CAV 2003. LNCS, vol. 2725, pp. 420–432. Springer, Heidelberg (2003). https://doi.org/10.1007/978-3-540-45069-6_39
17. Farkas, J.: Theorie der einfachen ungleichungen. J. für die reine und angewandte Mathematik **1902**(124), 1–27 (1902)
18. Feldman, Y.A.: A decidable propositional dynamic logic with explicit probabilities. Inf. Control **63**(1), 11–38 (1984)
19. Feldman, Y.A., Harel, D.: A probabilistic dynamic logic. In: STOC (1982). https://doi.org/10.1145/800070.802191
20. Foster, N., Kozen, D., Mamouras, K., Reitblatt, M., Silva, A.: Probabilistic NetKAT. In: Thiemann, P. (ed.) ESOP 2016. LNCS, vol. 9632, pp. 282–309. Springer, Heidelberg (2016). https://doi.org/10.1007/978-3-662-49498-1_12
21. Fu, H., Chatterjee, K.: Termination of nondeterministic probabilistic programs. In: Enea, C., Piskac, R. (eds.) VMCAI 2019. LNCS, vol. 11388, pp. 468–490. Springer, Cham (2019). https://doi.org/10.1007/978-3-030-11245-5_22
22. Ghahramani, Z.: Probabilistic machine learning and artificial intelligence. Nature **521**(7553), 452–459 (2015). https://doi.org/10.1038/nature14541
23. Goodman, N.D., et al.: Church: a language for generative models. In: UAI (2008)
24. Hark, M., Kaminski, B.L., Giesl, J., Katoen, J.: Aiming low is harder: induction for lower bounds in probabilistic program verification. In: POPL (2020). https://doi.org/10.1145/3371105
25. Huang, M., Fu, H., Chatterjee, K.: New approaches for almost-sure termination of probabilistic programs. In: Ryu, S. (ed.) APLAS 2018. LNCS, vol. 11275, pp. 181–201. Springer, Cham (2018). https://doi.org/10.1007/978-3-030-02768-1_11
26. Huang, M., Fu, H., Chatterjee, K., Goharshady, A.K.: Modular verification for almost-sure termination of probabilistic programs. In: OOPSLA (2019). https://doi.org/10.1145/3360555
27. Kaminski, B.L., Katoen, J., Matheja, C., Olmedo, F.: Weakest precondition reasoning for expected runtimes of randomized algorithms. J. ACM **65**(5), 30:1–30:68 (2018). https://doi.org/10.1145/3208102
28. Katoen, J.-P., McIver, A.K., Meinicke, L.A., Morgan, C.C.: Linear-invariant generation for probabilistic programs: automated support for proof-based methods. In: Cousot, R., Martel, M. (eds.) SAS 2010. LNCS, vol. 6337, pp. 390–406. Springer, Heidelberg (2010). https://doi.org/10.1007/978-3-642-15769-1_24
29. Kozen, D.: Semantics of probabilistic programs. J. Comput. Syst. Sci. **22**(3), 328–350 (1981). https://doi.org/10.1016/0022-0000(81)90036-2
30. Křetínský, J., Meggendorfer, T.: Of cores: a partial-exploration framework for Markov decision processes. LMCS (2020). https://doi.org/10.23638/LMCS-16(4:3)2020
31. McIver, A., Morgan, C.: Abstraction, Refinement and Proof for Probabilistic Systems. Monographs in Computer Science. Springer, New York (2005). https://doi.org/10.1007/b138392
32. McIver, A., Morgan, C., Kaminski, B.L., Katoen, J.: A new proof rule for almost-sure termination. In: POPL (2018). https://doi.org/10.1145/3158121
33. Meurer, A., et al.: SymPy: symbolic computing in Python. PeerJ Comput. Sci. (2017). https://doi.org/10.7717/peerj-cs.103
34. Monniaux, D.: An abstract analysis of the probabilistic termination of programs. In: Cousot, P. (ed.) SAS 2001. LNCS, vol. 2126, pp. 111–126. Springer, Heidelberg (2001). https://doi.org/10.1007/3-540-47764-0_7

35. Moosbrugger, M., Bartocci, E., Katoen, J., Kovács, L.: Automated termination analysis of polynomial probabilistic programs. In: ESOP (2021). https://doi.org/10.1007/978-3-030-72019-3_18
36. Ngo, V.C., Carbonneaux, Q., Hoffmann, J.: Bounded expectations: resource analysis for probabilistic programs. In: PLDI (2018). https://doi.org/10.1145/3192366.3192394
37. Olmedo, F., Kaminski, B.L., Katoen, J.P., Matheja, C.: Reasoning about recursive probabilistic programs. In: LICS (2016). https://doi.org/10.1145/2933575.2935317
38. Putinar, M.: Positive polynomials on compact semi-algebraic sets. Indiana Univ. Math. J. **42**(3), 969–984 (1993)
39. Roy, D., Mansinghka, V., Goodman, N., Tenenbaum, J.: A stochastic programming perspective on nonparametric Bayes. In: ICML (2008)
40. Takisaka, T., Oyabu, Y., Urabe, N., Hasuo, I.: Ranking and repulsing supermartingales for reachability in randomized programs. ACM Trans. Program. Lang. Syst. **43**(2), 5:1–5:46 (2021). https://doi.org/10.1145/3450967
41. Thrun, S.: Probabilistic algorithms in robotics. AI Mag. **21**(4), 93–109 (2000). https://doi.org/10.1609/aimag.v21i4.1534
42. Wang, J., Sun, Y., Fu, H., Chatterjee, K., Goharshady, A.K.: Quantitative analysis of assertion violations in probabilistic programs. In: PLDI (2021). https://doi.org/10.1145/3453483.3454102
43. Wang, P., Fu, H., Goharshady, A.K., Chatterjee, K., Qin, X., Shi, W.: Cost analysis of nondeterministic probabilistic programs. In: PLDI (2019). https://doi.org/10.1145/3314221.3314581

# Does a Program Yield the Right Distribution?

## Verifying Probabilistic Programs via Generating Functions

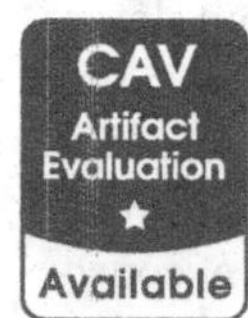

Mingshuai Chen(✉), Joost-Pieter Katoen(✉), Lutz Klinkenberg(✉), and Tobias Winkler(✉)

RWTH Aachen University, Aachen, Germany
{chenms,katoen,lutz.klinkenberg,
tobias.winkler}@cs.rwth-aachen.de

**Abstract.** We study discrete probabilistic programs with potentially unbounded looping behaviors over an infinite state space. We present, to the best of our knowledge, *the first decidability result for the problem of determining whether such a program generates exactly a specified distribution over its outputs* (provided the program terminates almost-surely). The class of distributions that can be specified in our formalism consists of standard distributions (geometric, uniform, etc.) and finite convolutions thereof. Our method relies on representing these (possibly infinite-support) distributions as *probability generating functions* which admit effective arithmetic operations. We have automated our techniques in a tool called Prodigy, which supports automatic invariance checking, compositional reasoning of nested loops, and efficient queries to the output distribution, as demonstrated by experiments.

**Keywords:** Probabilistic programs · Quantitative verification · Program equivalence · Denotational semantics · Generating functions

## 1 Introduction

Probabilistic programs [26,43,48] augment deterministic programs with stochastic behaviors, e.g., random sampling, probabilistic choice, and conditioning (via posterior observations). Probabilistic programs have undergone a recent surge of interest due to prominent applications in a wide range of domains: they steer autonomous robots and self-driving cars [20,54], are key to describe security [6] and quantum [61] mechanisms, intrinsically code up randomized algorithms for solving NP-hard or even deterministically unsolvable problems (in, e.g., distributed computing [2,53]), and are rapidly encroaching on AI as well

This research was funded by the ERC Advanced Project FRAPPANT under grant No. 787914, by the EU's Horizon 2020 research and innovation programme under the Marie Skłodowska-Curie grant No. 101008233, and by the DFG RTG 2236 UnRAVeL.


S. Shoham and Y. Vizel (Eds.): CAV 2022, LNCS 13371, pp. 79–101, 2022.
https://doi.org/10.1007/978-3-031-13185-1_5

as approximate computing [13]. See [5] for recent advancements in probabilistic programming.

The crux of probabilistic programming, à la Hicks' interpretation [30], is to *treat normal-looking programs as if they were probability distributions.* A random-number generator, for instance, is a probabilistic program that produces a uniform distribution across numbers from a range of interest. Such a lift from deterministic program states to possibly infinite-support distributions (over states) renders the verification problem of probabilistic programs notoriously hard [39]. In particular, reasoning about probabilistic loops often amounts to computing quantitative fixed-points which are highly intractable in practice. As a consequence, existing techniques are mostly concerned with approximations, i.e., they strive for verifying or obtaining upper and/or lower bounds on various quantities like assertion-violation probabilities [59], preexpectations [9,28], moments [58], expected runtimes [40], and concentrations [15,16], which reveal only partial information about the probability distribution carried by the program.

In this paper, we address the problem of *how to determine whether a (possibly infinite-state) probabilistic program yields exactly the desired (possibly infinite-support) distribution under all possible inputs.* We highlight two scenarios where encoding the *exact* distribution – other than (bounds on) the above-mentioned quantities – is of particular interest: (I) In many safety- and/or security-critical domains, e.g., cryptography, a slightly perturbed distribution (while many of its probabilistic quantities remain unchanged) may lead to significant attack vulnerabilities or even complete compromise of the cryptographic system, see, e.g., Bleichenbacher's biased-nonces attack [29, Sect. 5.10] against the probabilistic Digital Signature Algorithm. Therefore, the system designer has to impose a complete specification of the anticipated distribution produced by the probabilistic component. (II) In the context of quantitative verification, the user may be interested in multiple properties (of different types, e.g., the aforementioned quantities) of the output distribution carried by a probabilistic program. In absence of the exact distribution, multiple analysis techniques – tailored to different types of properties – have to be applied in order to answer all queries from the user. We further motivate our problem using a concrete example as follows.

*Example 1 (Photorealistic Rendering* [37]*).* Monte Carlo integration algorithms form a well-known class of probabilistic programs which approximate complex integral expressions by sampling [27]. One of its particular use-cases is the photorealistic rendering of virtual scenes by a technique called *Monte Carlo path tracing* (MCPT) [37].

MCPT works as follows: For every pixel of the output image, it shoots $n$ sample rays into the scene and models the light transport behavior to approximate the incoming light at that particular point. Starting from a certain pixel position, MCPT randomly chooses a direction, traces it until a scene object is hit, and then proceeds by either (i) terminating the tracing and evaluating the overall ray, or (ii) continuing the tracing by computing a new direction. In the physical world, the light ray may be reflected arbitrarily often and thus stopping the tracing after a certain amount of bounces would introduce a bias in the

```
while (n > 0) { /* generate n samples */
    running := 1;
    while (running = 1) { /* generate a light ray */
        { running := 0 /* absorb */ } [1/2] { c := c + 1 /* reflect */ } };
    n := n − 1 }
```

**Fig. 1.** Monte Carlo path tracing in a scene with constant reflectivity 1/2.

integral estimation. As a remedy, the decision when to stop the tracing is made in a *Russian roulette* manner by flipping a coin[1] at each intersection point [1].

The program in Fig. 1 is an implementation of a simplified MCPT path generator. The cumulative length of all n rays is stored in the (random) variable c, which is directly proportional to MCPT's expected runtime. The implementation is designed in a way that c *induces a distribution as the sum of* n *independent and identically distributed (i.i.d.) geometric random variables* such that the resulting integral estimation is unbiased. In our framework, we view such an exact output distribution of c as a *specification* and verify – fully automatically – that the implementation in Fig. 1 with nested loops indeed satisfies this specification. ◁

*Approach.* Given a probabilistic loop $L = \texttt{while}\,(\varphi)\,\{P\}$ with guard $\varphi$ and loop-free body $P$, we aim to determine whether $L$ agrees with a specification $S$:

$$L = \texttt{while}\,(\varphi)\,\{P\} \quad \overset{?}{\sim} \quad S\,, \qquad (\star)$$

namely, whether $L$ yields – upon termination – exactly the same distribution as encoded by $S$ under all possible program inputs. This problem is non-trivial: (C1) $L$ may induce an infinite state space and infinite-support distributions, thus making techniques like probabilistic bounded model checking [34] insufficient for verifying the property by means of unfolding the loop $L$. (C2) There is, to the best of our knowledge, a lack of non-trivial characterizations of $L$ and $S$ such that problem $(\star)$ admits a decidability result. (C3) To decide problem $(\star)$ – even for a loop-free program $L$ – one has to account for infinitely or even uncountably many inputs such that $L$ yields the same distribution as encoded by $S$ when being deployed in all possible contexts.

We address challenge (C1) by exploiting the forward denotational semantics of probabilistic programs based on *probability generating function* (PGF) representations of (sub-)distributions [42], which benefits crucially from closed-form (i.e., finite) PGF representations of possibly infinite-support distributions. A probabilistic program $L$ hence acts as a transformer $[\![L]\!](\cdot)$ that transforms an input PGF $g$ into an output PGF $[\![L]\!](g)$ (as an instantiation of Kozen's

[1] The bias of the coin depends on the material's *reflectivity*: a reflecting material such as a mirror requires more light bounces than an absorptive one, e.g., a black surface.

transformer semantics [43]). In particular, we *interpret the specification $S$ as a loop-free probabilistic program $I$*. Such an identification of specifications with programs has two important advantages: (i) we only need a single language to encode programs as well as specifications, and (ii) it enables compositional reasoning in a straightforward manner, in particular, the treatment of nested loops. The problem of checking $L \sim S$ then boils down to checking whether $L$ and $I$ transform every possible input PGF into the same output PGF:

$$\forall g \in \mathsf{PGF}: \quad \underbrace{[\![\texttt{while}\,(\varphi)\,\{P\}]\!]}_{L}(g) \quad \stackrel{?}{=} \quad [\![I]\!](g)\,. \tag{$\dagger$}$$

As $I$ is loop free, problem (†) can be reduced to checking the equivalence of two *loop-free* probabilistic programs (cf. Lemma 2):

$$\forall g \in \mathsf{PGF}: \quad [\![\texttt{if}\,(\varphi)\,\{P\,\text{;}\,I\}\,\texttt{else}\,\{\texttt{skip}\}]\!](g) \quad \stackrel{?}{=} \quad [\![I]\!](g)\,. \tag{$\ddagger$}$$

Now challenge (C3) applies since the universal quantification in problem (‡) requires to determine the equivalence against infinitely many – possibly infinite-support – distributions over program states. We facilitate such an equivalence checking by developing a *second-order PGF* (SOP) semantics for probabilistic programs, which naturally extends the PGF semantics while allowing to reason about infinitely many PGF transformations simultaneously (see Lemma 3).

Finally, to obtain a decidability result (cf. challenge (C2)), we develop the *rectangular discrete probabilistic programming language* (`ReDiP`) – a variant of `pGCL` [46] with syntactic restrictions to rectangular guards – featuring various nice properties, e.g., they inherently support i.i.d. sampling, and in particular, they *preserve closed-form PGF* when acting as PGF transformers. We show that *problem (‡) is decidable for* `ReDiP` *programs $P$ and $I$ if all the distribution statements therein have rational closed-form PGF* (cf. Lemma 4). As a consequence, problem (†) *and thereby* problem ($\star$) *of checking $L \sim S$ are decidable if $L$ terminates almost-surely on all possible inputs $g$* (cf. Theorem 4).

*Demonstration.* We have automated our techniques in a tool called Prodigy. As an example, Prodigy was able to verify, fully automatically in 25 milliseconds, that the implementation of the MCPT path generator with nested loops (in Fig. 1) is indeed equivalent to the loop-free program

$$\texttt{c} \mathrel{+}= \texttt{iid}(\texttt{geometric}(1/2),\, \texttt{n})\,\text{;}\, \texttt{n} := 0$$

which encodes the specification that, upon termination, `c` is distributed as the sum of `n` i.i.d. geometric random variables. With such an output distribution, multiple queries can be efficiently answered by applying standard PGF operations. For example, the expected value and variance of the runtime are $E[\texttt{c}] = n$ and $\mathit{Var}[\texttt{c}] = 2n$, respectively (assuming $\texttt{c} = 0$ initially).

**Contributions.** The main contributions of this paper are:

- The probabilistic programming language `ReDiP` and its forward denotational semantics as PGF transformers. We show that loop-free `ReDiP` programs preserve closed-form PGF.
- The notion of SOP that enables reasoning about infinitely many PGF transformations simultaneously. We show that the problem of determining whether an infinite-state `ReDiP` loop generates – upon termination – exactly a specified distribution is decidable.
- The software tool PRODIGY which supports automatic invariance checking on the source-code level; it allows reasoning about nested `ReDiP` loops in a compositional manner, and supports efficient queries on various quantities including assertion-violation probabilities, expected values, (high-order) moments, precise tail probabilities, as well as concentration bounds.

*Organization.* We introduce generating functions in Sect. 2 and define the `ReDiP` language in Sect. 3. Section 4 presents the PGF semantics. Section 5 establishes our decidability result in reasoning about `ReDiP` loops, with case studies in Sect. 6. After discussing related work in Sect. 7, we conclude the paper in Sect. 8. Further details, e.g., proofs and additional examples, can be found in the full version [18].

## 2 Generating Functions

> *"A generating function is a clothesline on which we hang up a sequence of numbers for display."* — H. S. Wilf, Generatingfunctionology [60]

The method of *generating functions* (GF) is a vital tool in many areas of mathematics. This includes in particular enumerative combinatorics [22,60] and – most relevant for this paper – probability theory [35]. In the latter, the sequences "hanging on the clotheslines" happen to describe probability distributions over the non-negative integers $\mathbb{N}$, e.g., $1/2, 1/4, 1/8, \ldots$ (aka, the geometric distribution).

The most common way to relate an (infinite) *sequence* of numbers to a generating *function* relies on the familiar Taylor series expansion: Given a sequence, for example $1/2, 1/4, 1/8, \ldots$, find a function $x \mapsto f(x)$ whose Taylor series around $x = 0$ uses the numbers in the sequence as coefficients. In our example,

$$\frac{1}{2-x} \;=\; \frac{1}{2} + \frac{1}{4}x + \frac{1}{8}x^2 + \frac{1}{16}x^3 + \frac{1}{32}x^4 + \ldots, \tag{1}$$

for all $|x| < 2$, hence the "clothesline" used for hanging up $1/2, 1/4, 1/8, \ldots$ is the function $1/(2-x)$. Note that the GF is a – from a purely syntactical point of view – *finite* object while the sequence it represents is *infinite*. A key strength of this technique is that many meaningful operations on infinite series can be performed by manipulating an encoding GF (see Table 1 for an overview and examples). In other words, GF provide an *interface* to perform operations on and extract information from infinite sequences in an effective manner.

### 2.1 The Ring of Formal Power Series

Towards our goal of encoding distributions over *program states* (valuations of finitely many integer variables) as generating functions, we need to consider *multivariate* GF, i.e., GF with more than one variable. Such functions represent multidimensional sequences, or *arrays.* Since multidimensional Taylor series quickly become unhandy, we will follow a more *algebraic* approach that is also advocated in [60]: We treat sequences and arrays as elements from an algebraic structure: the *ring of Formal Power Series* (FPS). Recall that a (commutative) *ring* $(A, +, \cdot, 0, 1)$ consists of a non-empty carrier set $A$, associative and commutative binary operations "+" (addition) and "·" (multiplication) such that multiplication distributes over addition, and neutral elements 0 and 1 w.r.t. addition and multiplication, respectively. Further, every $a \in A$ has an additive inverse $-a \in A$. Multiplicative inverses $a^{-1} = 1/a$ need not always exist. Let $k \in \mathbb{N} = \{0, 1, \ldots\}$ be fixed in the remainder.

**Table 1.** GF cheat sheet. $f, g$ and $X, Y$ are arbitrary GF and indeterminates, resp.

| *Operation* | *Effect* | *(Running) example* |
|---|---|---|
| $f^{-1} = 1/f$ | Multiplicative inverse of $f$ (if it exists) | $\frac{1}{1-XY} = 1 + XY + X^2Y^2 + \ldots$ because $(1 - XY)(1 + XY + X^2Y^2 + \ldots) = 1$ |
| $fX$ | Shift in dimension $X$ | $\frac{X}{1-XY} = X + X^2Y + X^3Y^2 + \ldots$ |
| $f[X/0]$ | Drop terms containing $X$ | $\frac{1}{1-0Y} = 1$ |
| $f[X/1]$ | Projection[a] on $Y$ | $\frac{1}{1-1Y} = 1 + Y + Y^2 + \ldots$ |
| $fg$ | Discrete convolution (or Cauchy product) | $\frac{1}{(1-XY)^2} = 1 + 2XY + 3X^2Y^2 + \ldots$ |
| $\partial_X f$ | Formal derivative in $X$ | $\partial_X \frac{1}{1-XY} = \frac{Y}{(1-XY)^2} = Y + 2XY^2 + 3X^2Y^3 + \ldots$ |
| $f + g$ | Coefficient-wise sum | $\frac{1}{1-XY} + \frac{1}{(1-XY)^2} = \frac{2-XY}{(1-XY)^2} = 2{+}3XY{+}4X^2Y^2{+}\ldots$ |
| $af$ | Coefficient-wise scaling | $\frac{7}{(1-XY)^2} = 7 + 14XY + 21X^2Y^2 + \ldots$ |

[a] Projections are not always well-defined, e.g., $\frac{1}{1-X+Y}[X/1] = \frac{1}{Y}$ is ill-defined because $Y$ is not invertible. However, in all situations where we use projection it will be well-defined; in particular, projection is well-defined for PGF.

**Definition 1 (The Ring of FPS).** *A k-dimensional FPS is a k-dim. array* $f\colon \mathbb{N}^k \to \mathbb{R}$. *We denote FPS as* formal sums *as follows: Let* $\mathbf{X}{=}(X_1, \ldots, X_k)$ *be an ordered vector of symbols, called* indeterminates. *The FPS $f$ is written as*

$$f \;=\; \sum\nolimits_{\sigma \in \mathbb{N}^k} f(\sigma)\mathbf{X}^\sigma$$

*where* $\mathbf{X}^\sigma$ *is the* monomial $X_1^{\sigma_1}X_2^{\sigma_2}\cdots X_k^{\sigma_k}$. *The* ring of FPS *is denoted* $\mathbb{R}[[\mathbf{X}]]$ *where the operations are defined as follows: For all* $f, g \in \mathbb{R}[[\mathbf{X}]]$ *and* $\sigma \in \mathbb{N}^k$, $(f + g)(\sigma) = f(\sigma) + g(\sigma)$, *and* $(f \cdot g)(\sigma) = \sum_{\sigma_1+\sigma_2=\sigma} f(\sigma_1)g(\sigma_2)$.

The multiplication $f \cdot g$ is the usual *Cauchy product* of power series (aka discrete convolution); it is well defined because for all $\sigma \in \mathbb{N}^k$ there are just *finitely* many $\sigma_1 + \sigma_2 = \sigma$ in $\mathbb{N}^k$. We write $fg$ instead of $f \cdot g$.

The formal sum notation is standard in the literature and often useful because the arithmetic FPS operations are very similar to how one would do calculations with "real" sums. We stress that the indeterminates $\mathbf{X}$ are merely *labels* for the $k$ dimensions of $f$ and do not have any other particular meaning. In the context of this paper, however, it is natural to identify the indeterminates with the program variables (e.g. indeterminate $X$ refers to variable $\mathtt{x}$, see Sect. 3).

Equation (1) can be interpreted as follows in the ring of FPS: The "sequences" $2 - 1X + 0X^2 + \ldots$ and $1/2 + 1/4X + 1/8X^2 + \ldots$ are (multiplicative) *inverse* elements to each other in $\mathbb{R}[[X]]$, i.e., their product is 1. More generally, we say that an FPS $f$ is *rational* if $f = gh^{-1} = g/h$ where $g$ and $h$ are polynomials, i.e., they have at most finitely many non-zero coefficients; and we call such a representation a *rational closed form*.

A more extensive introduction to FPS can be found in [18, Appx. D].

### 2.2 Probability Generating Functions

We are especially interested in GF that describe probability distributions.

**Definition 2 (PGF).** *A $k$-dimensional FPS $g$ is a* probability generating function *(PGF) if* (i) *for all $\sigma \in \mathbb{N}^k$ we have $g(\sigma) \geq 0$, and* (ii) $\sum_{\sigma \in \mathbb{N}^k} g(\sigma) \leq 1$.

For example, (1) is the PGF of a 1/2-geometric distribution. The PGF of other standard distributions are given in Table 3 further below. Note that Definition 2 also includes *sub-PGF* where the sum in (ii) is strictly less than 1.

## 3 ReDiP: A Probabilistic Programming Language

This section presents our *Rectangular Discrete Probabilistic Programming Language*, or `ReDiP` for short. The word "rectangular" refers to a restriction we impose on the guards of conditionals and loops, see Sect. 3.2. `ReDiP` is a variant of `pGCL` [46] with some extra syntax but also some syntactic restrictions.

### 3.1 Program States and Variables

Every `ReDiP`-program $P$ operates on a finite set of $\mathbb{N}$-valued *program variables* $\mathit{Vars}(P) = \{\mathtt{x}_1, \ldots, \mathtt{x}_k\}$. We do not consider negative or non-integer variables. A *program state* of $P$ is thus a mapping $\sigma\colon \mathit{Vars}(P) \to \mathbb{N}$. As explained in Sect. 1, the key idea is to represent distributions over such program states as PGF. Consequently, we identify a single program state $\sigma$ with the *monomial* $\mathbf{X}^\sigma = X_1^{\sigma(\mathtt{x}_1)} \cdots X_k^{\sigma(\mathtt{x}_k)}$ where $X_1, \ldots, X_k$ are indeterminates representing the program variables $\mathtt{x}_1, \ldots, \mathtt{x}_k$. We will stick to this notation: throughout the whole paper, we typeset program variables as $\mathtt{x}$ and the corresponding FPS indeterminate as $X$. The initial program state on which a given `ReDiP`-program is supposed to operate must always be stated explicitly.

### 3.2 Syntax of ReDiP

The syntax of ReDiP is defined inductively, see the leftmost column of Table 2. Here, x and y are program variables, $n \in \mathbb{N}$ is a constant, $D$ is a *distribution expression* (see Table 3), and $P_1, P_2$ are ReDiP-programs. The general idea of ReDiP is to provide a minimal core language to keep the theory simple. Many other common language constructs such as linear arithmetic updates x := 2y + 3 are expressible in this core language. See [18, Appx. A] for a complete specification.

**Table 2.** Syntax and semantics of ReDiP. $g$ is the input PGF.

| ReDiP-*program* $P$ | *Semantics* $[\![P]\!](g)$ – *see Sect.* 4.2 | *Description* |
|---|---|---|
| x := $n$ | $g[X/1]X^n$ | Assign const. $n \in \mathbb{N}$ to var. x |
| x−− | $(g - g[X/0])X^{-1} + g[X/0]$ | Decr. x ("monus" semantics) |
| x += iid($D$, y) | $g[Y/Y[\![D]\!][T/X]]$ | Incr. x by the sum of y i.i.d. samples from $D$ – see Sect. 3.3 |
| if (x < $n$) {$P_1$} else {$P_2$} | $[\![P_1]\!](g_{x<n}) + [\![P_2]\!](g - g_{x<n})$, where $g_{x<n} = \sum_{i=0}^{n-1} \frac{1}{i!}(\partial^i_X g)[X/0]X^i$ | Conditional branching |
| $P_1 ⨾ P_2$ | $[\![P_2]\!]([\![P_1]\!](g))$ | Sequential composition |
| while (x < $n$) {$P_1$} | $[\mathsf{lfp}\, \Psi_{\mathtt{x}<n,P_1}](g)$, where $\Psi_{\mathtt{x}<n,P_1}(\psi) = \lambda f.\, (f - f_{\mathtt{x}<n}) + \psi([\![P_1]\!](f_{\mathtt{x}<n}))$ | Loop defined as fixed point |

**Table 3.** A non-exhaustive list of common discrete distributions with rational PGF. The parameters $p$, $n$, and $\lambda$ are a probability, a natural, and a non-negative real number, respectively. $T$ is a reserved placeholder indeterminate.

| $D$ | $[\![D]\!]$ | *Description* |
|---|---|---|
| dirac($n$) | $T^n$ | Point mass |
| bernoulli($p$) | $1 - p + pT$ | Bernoulli distribution (coin flip) |
| unif($n$) | $(1 - T^n) / n(1 - T)$ | Discrete uniform distribution on $\{0, \ldots, n-1\}$ |
| geometric($p$) | $(1 - p) / (1 - pT)$ | Geometric distribution (no. trials until first success) |
| binomial($p$, $n$) | $(1 - p + pT)^n$ | Binomial distribution (successes of $n$ yes-no experiments) |
| nbinomial($p$, $n$) | $(1 - p)^n / (1 - pT)^n$ | Negative binomial distribution |

The word "rectangular" in ReDiP emphasizes that our if-guards can only identify *axis-aligned hyper-rectangles*[2] in $\mathbb{N}^k$, but no more general polyhedra. These *rectangular guards* x < $n$ have the fundamental property that they preserve rational PGF. On the other hand, allowing more general guards like x < y breaks this property (see [21] and our comments in [18, Appx. B].

The most intricate feature of ReDiP is the – potentially unbounded – loop while (x < $n$) {$P$}. A program that does not contain loops is called *loop-free*.

[2] More precisely, we can simulate statements like if ($R$) {...} else {...}, where $R$ is a finite Boolean combination of rectangular guards, through appropriate nesting of if () ; note that such an $R$ is indeed a finite union of axis-aligned rectangles in $\mathbb{N}^k$.

### 3.3 The Statement x += iid(*D*, y)

The novel `iid` statement is the heart of the loop-free fragment of `ReDiP` – it subsumes both x := $D$ ("assign a $D$-distributed sample to x") and the standard assignment x := y. We include the assign-increment (+=) version of `iid` in the core fragment of `ReDiP` for technical reasons; the assignment x := iid($D$, y) can be recovered from that as syntactic sugar by simply setting x := 0 beforehand.

Intuitively, the meaning of x += iid($D$, y) is as follows. The right-hand side iid($D$, y) can be seen as a function that takes the current value $v$ of variable y, then draws $v$ i.i.d. samples from distribution $D$, computes the sum of all these samples and finally increments x by the so-obtained value. For example, to perform x := y, we may just write x := iid(dirac(1), y) as this will draw y times the number 1, then sum up these y many 1's to obtain the result y and assign it to x. Similarly, to assign a random sample from a, say, uniform distribution to x, we can execute y := 1 ⨟ x := iid(unif($n$), y).

But `iid` is not only useful for defining standard operations. In fact, taking sums of i.i.d. samples is common in probability theory. The *binomial distribution* with parameters $p \in (0, 1)$ and $n \in \mathbb{N}$, for example, is the defined as the sum of $n$ i.i.d. Bernoulli-$p$-distributed samples and thus

x := binomial($p$, y)    is equivalent to    x := iid(bernoulli($p$), y)

for all constants $p \in (0, 1)$. Similarly, the *negative* $(p, n)$-binomial distribution is the sum of $n$ i.i.d. geometric-$p$-distributed samples. Overall, `iid` renders the loop-free fragment of `ReDiP` *strictly more expressive* than it would be if we had included only x := $D$ and x := y instead. As a consequence, since we use loop-free programs as a specification language (see Sect. 5), `iid` enables us to write more expressive program specifications while retaining decidability.

## 4 Interpreting ReDiP with PGF

In this section, we explain the PGF-based semantics of our language which is given in the second column of Table 2. The overall idea is to view a `ReDiP`-program $P$ as a *distribution transformer* [44,46]. This means that the input to $P$ is a *distribution* over initial program states (inputting a deterministic state is just the special case of a Dirac distribution), and the output is a distribution over final program states. With this interpretation, if one regards distributions as *generalized program states* [33], a probabilistic program is actually *deterministic*: The same input distribution always yields the same output distribution. The goal of our PGF-based semantics is to construct an *interpreter* that executes a `ReDiP`-program statement-by-statement in forward direction, transforming one generalized program state into the next. We stress that these generalized program states, or distributions, can be infinite-support in general. For example, the program x := geometric(0.5) outputs a geometric distribution – which has infinite support – on x.

### 4.1 A Domain for Distribution Transformation

We now define a domain, i.e., an *ordered* structure, where our program's in- and output distributions live. Following the general idea of this paper, we encode them as PGF. Let *Vars* be a fixed finite set of program variables $\mathtt{x}_1, \ldots, \mathtt{x}_k$ and let $\mathbf{X} = (X_1, \ldots, X_k)$ be corresponding formal indeterminates. We let $\mathsf{PGF} = \{g \in \mathbb{R}[[\mathbf{X}]] \mid g \text{ is a PGF}\}$ denote the set of all PGF. Recall that this also includes sub-PGF (Definition 2). Further, we equip $\mathsf{PGF}$ with the pointwise order, i.e., we let $g \sqsubseteq f$ iff $g(\sigma) \leq f(\sigma)$ for all $\sigma \in \mathbb{N}^k$. It is clear that $(\mathsf{PGF}, \sqsubseteq)$ is a partial order that is moreover *$\omega$-complete*, i.e., there exists a least element 0 and all ascending chains $\Gamma = \{g_0 \sqsubseteq g_1 \sqsubseteq \ldots\}$ in $\mathsf{PGF}$ have a least upper bound $\sup \Gamma \in \mathsf{PGF}$. The maxima in $(\mathsf{PGF}, \sqsubseteq)$ are precisely the PGF which are not a sub-PGF.

### 4.2 From Programs to PGF Transformers

Next we explain how distribution transformation works using (P)GF (cf. Table 1). This is in contrast to the PGF semantics from [42] which operates on infinite sums in a non-constructive fashion.

**Definition 3 (The PGF Transformer $[\![P]\!]$).** *Let $P$ be a* `ReDiP`*-program. The* PGF *transformer* $[\![P]\!] \colon \mathsf{PGF} \to \mathsf{PGF}$ *is defined inductively on the structure of $P$ through the second column in Table 2.*

We show in Theorem 2 below that $[\![P]\!]$ is well-defined. For now, we go over the statements in the language `ReDiP` and explain the semantics.

*Sequential Composition.* The semantics of $P_1 ⨾ P_2$ is straightforward and intuitive: First execute $P_1$ on $g$ and then $P_2$ on $[\![P_1]\!](g)$, i.e., $[\![P_1 ⨾ P_2]\!](g) = [\![P_2]\!]([\![P_1]\!](g))$. The fact that our semantics transformer moves *forwards* through the program – as program interpreters usually do – is due to this definition.

*Conditional Branching.* To translate $\mathtt{if}\ (\mathtt{x} < n)\ \{P_1\}\ \mathtt{else}\ \{P_2\}$, we follow the standard procedure which partitions the input distribution according to $\mathtt{x} < n$ and $\mathtt{x} \geq n$, processes the two parts independently and finally recombines the results [44]. We realize the partitioning using the (formal) *Taylor series expansion.* This is feasible because we only allow *rectangular* guards of the form $\mathtt{x} < n$, where $n$ is a constant. Thus, for a given input PGF $g$, the *filtered PGF* $g_{\mathtt{x}<n}$ is obtained through expanding $g$ in its first $n$ terms. The `else` -part is obviously $g_{\mathtt{x} \geq n} = g - g_{\mathtt{x}<n}$. We then evaluate $[\![P_1]\!](g_{\mathtt{x}<n}) + [\![P_2]\!](g_{\mathtt{x} \geq n})$ recursively.

*Assigning a Constant.* Technically, our semantics realizes an assignment $\mathtt{x} := n$ in two steps: It first sets x to 0 and then increments it by $n$. The former is achieved by substituting $X$ for 1 which corresponds to computing the marginal distribution in all variables except $X$. For example,

| | |
|---|---|
| $/\!\!/\!\!/\ 0.5XY^2 + 0.5X^2Y^3$ | $/\!\!/\!\!/\ g$ |
| x := 5 | $P$ |
| $/\!\!/\!\!/\ (0.5Y^2 + 0.5Y^3)X^5$ | $/\!\!/\!\!/\ [\![P]\!](g)$ |
| $/\!\!/\!\!/\ 0.5X^5Y^2 + 0.5X^5Y^3$ | $/\!\!/\!\!/\ \langle$ *reform. of prev. line* $\rangle$ |

where the rightmost four lines explain this annotation style [42]. Note that $0.5Y^2 + 0.5Y^3$ is indeed the marginal of the input distribution in $Y$.

*Decrementing a Variable.* Since our program variables cannot take negative values, we define x-- as max(x−1, 0), i.e., x *monus* (modified minus) 1. Technically, we realize this through `if (x < 1) {skip} else {x--}`, i.e., we apply the decrement only to the portion of the input distribution where $\mathtt{x} \geq 1$. The decrement itself can then be carried out through "multiplication by $X^{-1}$". Note that $X^{-1}$ is not an element of $\mathbb{R}[[X]]$ because $X$ has no inverse. Instead, the operation $gX^{-1}$ is an alias for $\mathit{shift}^{\leftarrow}(g)$ which shifts $g$ "to the left" in dimension $X$. To implement the semantics on top of existing computer algebra software, it is very handy to perform the multiplication by $X^{-1}$ instead. This is justified because for PGF $g$ with $g[X/0] = 0$, $\mathit{shift}^{\leftarrow}(g)$ and $gX^{-1}$ are equal.

*The* `iid` *Statement.* The semantics of `x += iid(D, y)` relies on the fact that

$$T_1 \sim [\![D]\!] \ \ldots\ T_n \sim [\![D]\!] \qquad \text{implies} \qquad \sum\nolimits_{i=1}^{n} T_i \sim [\![D]\!]^n\,, \tag{2}$$

where $X \sim g$ means that r.v. $X$ is distributed according to PGF $g$ (see, e.g., [55, p. 450]). The `iid` statement generalizes this observation further: If $n$ is not a constant but a random (program) variable y with PGF $h(Y)$, then we perform the *substitution* $h[Y/[\![D]\!]]$ (i.e., replace $Y$ by $[\![D]\!]$ in $h$) to obtain the PGF of the sum of y-many i.i.d. samples from $D$. We slightly modify this substitution to $g[Y/Y[\![D]\!][T/X]]$ in order to (i) not alter y, and (ii) account for the increment to x. For example,

$/\!\!/\!\!/\ 0.2 + 0.3Y + 0.5Y^2$

`x += iid(bernoulli(0.5), y)`

$/\!\!/\!\!/\ 0.2 + 0.3Y(0.5 + 0.5X) + 0.5Y^2(0.5 + 0.5X)^2$

$/\!\!/\!\!/\ 0.2 + 0.15Y + 0.125Y^2 + 0.15XY + 0.25XY^2 + 0.125X^2Y^2\ .$

*The* `while`*-Loop.* The fixed point semantics of the while loop is standard [42, 44] and reflects the intuitive *unrolling rule*, namely that `while` $(\varphi)$ $\{P\}$ is equivalent to `if` $(\varphi)$ $\{P⨾$ `while` $(\varphi)$ $\{P\}\}$ `else` `{skip}`. Indeed, the fixed point formula in

Table 2 can be derived using the semantics of `if` discussed above. We revisit this fixed point characterization in Sect. 5.1.

*Properties of* $\llbracket P \rrbracket$. Our PGF semantics has the property that all programs – except while loops – are able to operate on the input PGF in (rational) *closed form*, i.e., they never have to expand the input as an infinite series (which is of course impossible in practice). More formally:

**Theorem 1 (Closed-Form Preservation).** *Let* $P$ *be a* loop-free `ReDiP` *program, and let* $g = h/f \in \mathsf{PGF}$ *be in rational closed form. Then we can compute a rational closed form of* $\llbracket P \rrbracket(g) \in \mathsf{PGF}$ *by applying the transformations in Table 2.*

The proof is by induction over the structure of $P$ noticing that all the necessary operations (substitution, differentiation, etc.) preserve rational closed forms, see [18, Appx. D]. A slight extension of our syntax, e.g., admitting non-rectangular guards, renders that closed forms are not preserved, see [18, Appx. B]. Moreover, $\llbracket P \rrbracket$ has the following *healthiness* [46] properties:

**Theorem 2 (Properties of** $\llbracket P \rrbracket$**).** *The PGF transformer* $\llbracket P \rrbracket$ *is*

- *a well-defined function* $\mathsf{PGF} \to \mathsf{PGF}$ *,*
- continuous, *i.e.,* $\llbracket P \rrbracket(\sup \Gamma) = \sup \llbracket P \rrbracket(\Gamma)$ *for all chains* $\Gamma \subseteq \mathsf{PGF}$ *,*
- linear, *i.e.,* $\llbracket P \rrbracket(\sum_{\sigma \in \mathbb{N}^k} g(\sigma)\mathbf{X}^\sigma) = \sum_{\sigma \in \mathbb{N}^k} g(\sigma) \llbracket P \rrbracket(\mathbf{X}^\sigma)$ *for all* $g \in \mathsf{PGF}$ *.*

### 4.3 Probabilistic Termination

Due to the presence of possibly unbounded `while`-loops, a `ReDiP`-program does not necessarily halt, or may do so only with a certain probability. Our semantics naturally captures the termination probability.

**Definition 4 (AST).** *A* `ReDiP`*-program* $P$ *is called* almost-surely terminating *(AST) for PGF* $g$ *if* $\llbracket P \rrbracket(g)[\mathbf{X}/\mathbf{1}] = g[\mathbf{X}/\mathbf{1}]$*, i.e., if it does not leak probability mass.* $P$ *is called* universally *AST (UAST) if it is AST for all* $g \in \mathsf{PGF}$.

Note that all loop-free `ReDiP`-programs are UAST. In this paper, (U)AST only plays a minor role. Nonetheless, the proof rule below yields a stronger result (cf. Lemma 2) if the program is UAST. There exist various of techniques and tools for proving (U)AST [17,47,50].

## 5 Reasoning About Loops

We now focus on loopy programs $L = \texttt{while}\,(\varphi)\,\{P\}$. Recall from Table 2 that $\llbracket L \rrbracket \colon \mathsf{PGF} \to \mathsf{PGF}$ is defined as the *least fixed point* of a higher order functional

$$\Psi_{\varphi,P} \colon (\mathsf{PGF} \to \mathsf{PGF}) \;\to\; (\mathsf{PGF} \to \mathsf{PGF}).$$

Following [42], we show that $\Psi_{\varphi,P}$ is sufficiently well-behaved to allow reasoning about loops by *fixed point induction.*

### 5.1 Fixed Point Induction

To apply fixed point induction, we need to lift our domain PGF from Sect. 4.1 by one order to (PGF $\rightarrow$ PGF), the domain of *PGF transformers*. This is because the functional $\Psi_{\varphi,P}$ operates on PGF transformers and can thus be seen as a second-order function (this point of view regards PGF as first-order objects). Recall that in contrast to this, the function $[\![P]\!]$ is first-order – it is just a PGF transformer. The order on (PGF $\rightarrow$ PGF) is obtained by lifting the order $\sqsubseteq$ on PGF pointwise (we denote it with the same symbol $\sqsubseteq$). This implies that (PGF $\rightarrow$ PGF) is also an $\omega$-complete partial order. We can then show that $\Psi_{\varphi,P}$ (see Table 2) is a continuous function. With these properties, we obtain the following induction rule for upper bounds on $[\![L]\!]$, cf. [42, Theorem 6]:

**Lemma 1 (Fixed Point Induction for Loops).** *Let* $L = \mathtt{while}\,(\varphi)\,\{P\}$ *be a* ReDiP*-loop. Further, let* $\psi$: PGF $\rightarrow$ PGF *be a PGF transformer. Then*

$$\Psi_{\varphi,P}(\psi) \sqsubseteq \psi \quad \text{implies} \quad [\![L]\!] \sqsubseteq \psi\,.$$

The goal of the rest of the paper is to *apply the rule from* Lemma 1 in *practice*. To this end, we must somehow specify an *invariant* such as $\psi$ by finite means. Since $\psi$ is of type (PGF $\rightarrow$ PGF), we consider $\psi$ as a program $I$ – more specifically, a ReDiP-program – and identify $\psi = [\![I]\!]$. Further, by definition

$$\Psi_{\varphi,P}([\![I]\!]) \;=\; [\![\mathtt{if}\;(\varphi)\,\{P\,⨾\,I\}\,\mathtt{else}\,\{\mathtt{skip}\}]\!],$$

and thus the term $\Psi_{\varphi,P}([\![I]\!])$ is also a PGF-transformer expressible as a ReDiP-program. These observations and Lemma 1 imply the following:

**Lemma 2.** *Let* $L = \mathtt{while}\,(\varphi)\,\{P\}$ *and* $I$ *be* ReDiP*-programs. Then*

$$[\![\mathtt{if}\;(\varphi)\,\{P\,⨾\,I\}\,\mathtt{else}\,\{\mathtt{skip}\}]\!] \sqsubseteq [\![I]\!] \;\text{ implies }\; [\![L]\!] \sqsubseteq [\![I]\!]. \tag{3}$$

*Further, if* $L$ *is UAST (Definition 4), then*

$$[\![\mathtt{if}\;(\varphi)\,\{P\,⨾\,I\}\,\mathtt{else}\,\{\mathtt{skip}\}]\!] \;=\; [\![I]\!] \;\text{ iff }\; [\![L]\!] \;=\; [\![I]\!] \tag{4}$$

Lemma 2 effectively reduces checking whether $\psi$ given as a ReDiP-program $I$ is an invariant of $L$ to checking *equivalence* of $\mathtt{if}\;(\varphi)\,\{P\,⨾\,I\}\,\mathtt{else}\,\{\mathtt{skip}\}$ and $I$ provided $L$ is UAST. If $I$ is loop-free, then the latter two programs are both loop-free and we are left with the task of proving whether they yield the same output distribution for all inputs. We now present a solution to this problem.

### 5.2 Deciding Equivalence of Loop-free Programs

Even in the absence of loops, deciding if two given ReDiP-programs are equivalent is non-trivial as it requires reasoning about infinitely many – possibly infinite-support – distributions on program variables. In this section, we first show that $[\![P_1]\!] = [\![P_2]\!]$ is *decidable* for loop-free ReDiP programs $P_1$ and $P_2$, and then use this result together with Lemma 2 to obtain the main result of this paper.

**SOP: Second-Order PGF.** Our goal is to check if $[\![P_1]\!](g) = [\![P_2]\!](g)$ for *all* $g \in \mathsf{PGF}$. To tackle this, we encode whole *sets* of PGF into a single object – an FPS we call *second-order PGF* (SOP). To define SOP, we need a slightly more flexible view on FPS. Recall from Definition 1 that a $k$-dim. FPS is an array $f : \mathbb{N}^k \to \mathbb{R}$. Such an $f$ can be viewed equivalently as an $l$-dim. array with $(k-l)$-dim. arrays as entries. In the formal sum notation, this is reflected by partitioning $\mathbf{X} = (\mathbf{Y}, \mathbf{Z})$ and viewing $f$ as an FPS in $\mathbf{Y}$ *with coefficients that are FPS in the other indeterminates* $\mathbf{Z}$. For example,

$$\begin{aligned}(1-Y)^{-1}(1-Z)^{-1} &= 1 + Y + Z + Y^2 + YZ + Z^2 + \ldots \\ &= (1-Z)^{-1} + (1-Z)^{-1}Y + (1-Z)^{-1}Y^2 + \ldots\end{aligned}$$

where in the lower line the coefficients $(1-Z)^{-1}$ are considered elements in $\mathbb{R}[[Z]]$.

**Definition 5 (SOP).** *Let* $\mathbf{U}$ *and* $\mathbf{X}$ *be disjoint sets of indeterminates. A formal power series* $f \in \mathbb{R}[[\mathbf{U}, \mathbf{X}]]$ *is a* second-order PGF (SOP) *if*

$$f = \sum\nolimits_{\tau \in \mathbb{N}^{|\mathbf{U}|}} f(\tau)\mathbf{U}^\tau \quad (\textit{with } f(\tau) \in \mathbb{R}[[\mathbf{X}]]) \qquad \text{implies} \qquad \forall \tau \colon f(\tau) \in \mathsf{PGF}.$$

That is, an SOP is simply an FPS whose coefficients are PGF – instead of generating a sequence of probabilities as PGF do, it generates a *sequence of distributions*. An (important) example SOP is

$$f_{dirac} \;=\; (1 - XU)^{-1} \;=\; 1 + XU + X^2U^2 + \ldots \;\in \mathbb{R}[[U, X]], \tag{5}$$

i.e., for all $i \geq 0$, $f_{dirac}(i) = X^i = [\![\texttt{dirac}(i)]\!]$. As a second example consider $f_{binom} = f_{dirac}[X/0.5 + 0.5X]$; it is clear that $f_{binom}(i) = (0.5 + 0.5X)^i = [\![\texttt{binomial}(0.5, i)]\!]$ for all $i \geq 0$. Note that if $\mathbf{U} = \emptyset$, then SOP and PGF coincide. For fixed $\mathbf{X}$ and $\mathbf{U}$, we denote the set of all second-order PGF with $\mathsf{SOP}$.

**SOP Semantics of `ReDiP`.** The appeal of SOP is that, syntactically, they are still formal power series, and some can be represented in closed form just like PGF. Moreover, we can readily extend our PGF transformer $[\![P]\!]$ to an SOP transformer $[\![P]\!] \colon \mathsf{SOP} \to \mathsf{SOP}$. A key insight of this paper is that – without any changes to the rules in Table 2 – applying $[\![P]\!]$ to an SOP is the same as applying $[\![P]\!]$ *simultaneously* to all the PGF it subsumes:

**Theorem 3.** *Let* $P$ *be a* `ReDiP`*-program. The transformer* $[\![P]\!] \colon \mathsf{SOP} \to \mathsf{SOP}$ *is well-defined. Further, if* $f = \sum_{\tau \in \mathbb{N}^{|\mathbf{U}|}} f(\tau)\mathbf{U}^\tau$ *is an SOP, then*

$$[\![P]\!](f) \;=\; \sum\nolimits_{\tau \in \mathbb{N}^{|\mathbf{U}|}} [\![P]\!](f(\tau))\mathbf{U}^\tau \;.$$

**An SOP Transformation for Proving Equivalence.** We now show how to exploit Theorem 3 for equivalence checking. Let $P_1$ and $P_2$ be (loop-free) `ReDiP`-programs; we are interested in proving whether $[\![P_1]\!] = [\![P_2]\!]$. By linearity it holds that $[\![P_1]\!] = [\![P_2]\!]$ iff $[\![P_1]\!](\mathbf{X}^\sigma) = [\![P_2]\!](\mathbf{X}^\sigma)$ for all $\sigma \in \mathbb{N}^k$, i.e., to check equivalence it suffices to consider all (infinitely many) point-mass PGF as inputs.

**Lemma 3 (SOP-Characterisation of Equivalence).** *Let $P_1$ and $P_2$ be* `ReDiP`*-programs with $Vars(P_i) \subseteq \{\mathtt{x}_1, \dots, \mathtt{x}_k\}$ for $i \in \{1, 2\}$. Further, consider a vector $\mathbf{U} = (U_1, \dots, U_k)$ of meta indeterminates, and let $g_{\mathbf{X}}$ be the SOP*

$$g_{\mathbf{X}} = (1 - X_1U_1)^{-1}(1 - X_2U_2)^{-1} \cdots (1 - X_kU_k)^{-1} \in \mathbb{R}[[\mathbf{U}, \mathbf{X}]] .$$

*Then $[\![P_1]\!] = [\![P_2]\!]$ if and only if $[\![P_1]\!](g_{\mathbf{X}}) = [\![P_2]\!](g_{\mathbf{X}})$.*

The proof of Lemma 3 (see [18, Appx. F.5]) relies on Theorem 3 and the fact that the *rational* SOP $g_{\mathbf{X}}$ generates all (multivariate) point-mass PGF; in fact it holds that $g_{\mathbf{X}} = \sum_{\sigma \in \mathbb{N}^k} \mathbf{X}^\sigma \mathbf{U}^\sigma$, i.e., $g_{\mathbf{X}}$ generalizes $f_{dirac}$ from (5). It follows:

**Lemma 4.** *$[\![P_1]\!] = [\![P_2]\!]$ is decidable for loop-free* `ReDiP`*-programs $P_1, P_2$.*

Our main theorem follows immediately from Lemmas 2 and 4:

**Theorem 4.** *Let $L = \mathtt{while}\,(\varphi)\,\{P\}$ be UAST with loop-free body $P$ and $I$ be a loop-free* `ReDiP`*-program. It is decidable whether $[\![L]\!] = [\![I]\!]$.*

*Example 2.* In Fig. 2 we prove that the two UAST programs $L$ and $I$

```
while (n > 0) {                              c += iid(geometric(1/2), n);
    {n := n − 1} [1/2] {c := c + 1}}         n := 0
```

```
/// (1 − NU)^−1 (1 − CV)^−1 = g_{N,C} =: g_0
if (n > 0) {
    /// (1 − CV)^−1 ((1 − NU)^−1 − 1) = g_0 − g_0[N/0] =: g_1
    {n := n − 1
        /// N^−1 (1 − CV)^−1 ((1 − NU)^−1 − 1) = g_1 N^−1 =: g_2
    } [0.5] { c += 1 };
        /// C(1 − CV)^−1 ((1 − NU)^−1 − 1) = g_1 C =: g_3
    /// (2N(1 − CV))^−1 + C(2(1 − CV))^−1)((1 − NU)^−1 − 1) = 0.5g_2 + 0.5g_3 =: g_4
    c += iid(geometric(1/2), n);
    /// (2 − C)(2N(1 − CV))^−1 + C(2(1 − CV))^−1)((2 − C)(2 − C − NU)^−1 − 1)
        = g_4[N/N(2 − C)^−1] =: g_5
    n := 0 }
    /// (1 − CV)^−1 ((2 − C)(2 − C − U)^−1 − 1) = g_5[N/1] = g_6
/// (1 − CV)^−1 (2 − C)(2 − C − U)^−1 = g_6 + g_0[N/0]
```

```
/// (1 − NU)^−1 (1 − CV)^−1
c += iid(geometric(1/2), n);
/// (1 − CV)^−1 (2 − C)(2 − C − NU)^−1
n := 0
/// (1 − CV)^−1 (2 − C)(2 − C − U)^−1
```

**Fig. 2.** Program equivalence follows from the equality of the resulting SOP (Lemma 3).

are equivalent (i.e., $[\![L]\!] = [\![I]\!]$) by showing that $[\![\mathtt{if}\ (\mathtt{n} > 0)\ \{P ⨾ I\}]\!] = [\![I]\!]$ as suggested by Lemma 2. The latter is achieved as in Lemma 3: We run both programs on the input SOP $g_{N,C} = (1 - NU)^{-1}(1 - CV)^{-1}$, where $U, V$ are meta indeterminates corresponding to $N$ and $C$, respectively, and check if the results are equal. Note that $I$ is the loop-free specification from Example 1; thus by transitivity, the loop $L$ is equivalent to the loop in Fig. 1. ◁

## 6 Case Studies

We have implemented our techniques in Python as a prototype called PRODIGY[3]: PRObability DIstributions via GeneratingfunctionologY. By interfacing with different computer algebra systems (CAS), e.g., `Sympy` [49] and `GiNaC` [10,57] – as backends for symbolic computation of PGF and SOP semantics – PRODIGY decides whether a given probabilistic loop agrees with an (invariant) specification encoded as a loop-free `ReDiP` program. Furthermore, it supports efficient queries on various quantities associated with the output distribution.

In what follows, we demonstrate in particular the applicability of our techniques to programs featuring stochastic dependency, parametrization, and nested loops. The examples are all presented in the same way: the iterative program on the left side and its corresponding specification on the right. The presented programs are all UAST, given the parameters are instantiated from a suitable value domain.[4] For each example, we report the time for performing the equivalence check on a 2,4 GHz Intel i5 Quad-Core processor with 16GB RAM running macOS Monterey 12.0.1. Additional examples can be found in [18, Appx. E].

```
while (c > 0) {
    {n := n + 1} [1/2] {m := m + 1};
    c := c − 1;
    tmp := 0
}
```

```
if (c > 0) {
    tmp := binomial(1/2, c);
    m += tmp ; n += c − tmp;
    c := 0 ;
    tmp := 0 }
```

**Fig. 3.** Generating complementary binomial distributions (for n, m) by coin flips. `binomial(1/2, c)` is an alias for `iid(bernoulli(1/2), c)`.

```
while (c = 1 ∧ t ≤ 1) {
    if (t = 0) {
        {c := 0} [a] {t := 1}
    } else {
        {c := 0} [b] {t := 0}
    }
}
```

```
if (c = 1 ∧ t ≤ 1) {
    c := 0
    if (t = 0) {
        t := bernoulli((1−a)b/a+b−ab);
    } else {
        t := bernoulli(b/a+b−ab);
}}
```

**Fig. 4.** A program modeling two dueling cowboys with parametric hit probabilities.

*Example 3 (Complementary Binomial Distributions).* We show that the program in Fig. 3 generates a joint distribution on $\mathtt{n}, \mathtt{m}$ such that both $\mathtt{n}$ and $\mathtt{m}$ are binomially distributed with support $\mathtt{c}$ and are complementary in the sense that $\mathtt{n} + \mathtt{m} = \mathtt{c}$ holds certainly (if $\mathtt{n} = \mathtt{m} = 0$ initially, otherwise the variables

[3] https://github.com/LKlinke/Prodigy.

[4] Parameters of Example 4 have to be instantiated with a probability value in $(0, 1)$.

are incremented by the corresponding amounts). PRODIGY automatically checks that the loop agrees with the specification in 18.3 ms. The resulting distribution can then be analyzed for any given input PGF $g$ by computing $[\![I]\!](g)$, where $I$ is the loop-free program. For example, for input $g = C^{10}$, the distribution as computed by PRODIGY has the *factorized* closed form $(\frac{M+N}{2})^{10}$. The CAS backends exploit such factorized forms to perform algebraic manipulations more efficiently compared to fully expanded forms. For instance, we can evaluate the queries $E[m^3+2mn+n^2] = 235$, or $Pr(m > 7 \wedge n < 3) = 7/128$, almost instantly. ◁

*Example 4 (Dueling Cowboys* [46]*).* The program in Fig. 4 models a duel of two cowboys with *parametric* hit probabilities `a` and `b`. Variable `t` indicates the cowboy who is currently taking his shot, and `c` monitors the state of the duel (`c` = 1: duel is still running, `c` = 0: duel is over). PRODIGY automatically verifies the specification in 11.97 ms. We defer related problems – e.g., *synthesizing* parameter values to meet a parameter-free specification – to future work. ◁

```
while (x > 0) {
    y := 1;
    while (y = 1) {
        {y := 0} [1/2] {x := x + 1}};
    x := x − 1;
    c += 1;
}
```

```
/* inner invariant */
if (y = 1) {
    x += geometric(1/2);
    y := 0;
}
```

```
/* outer invariant */
if (x > 0) {
    c := iid(catalan(1/2), x);
    x := 0;
    y := 0
}
```

**Fig. 5.** Nested loops with invariants for the inner and outer loop.

*Example 5 (Nested Loops).* The inner loop of the program in Fig. 5 modifies `x` which influences the termination behavior of the outer loop. Intuitively, the program models a random walk on $\mathbb{N}$: In every step, the value of the current position `x` changes by some random $\delta \in \{-1, 0, 1, 2, \ldots\}$ such that $\delta + 1$ is geometrically distributed. The example demonstrates how our technique enables *compositional* reasoning. We first provide a loop-free specification for the inner loop, prove its correctness, and then simply *replace* the inner loop by its specification, yielding a program without nested loops. This feature is a key benefit of reusing the loop-free fragment of `ReDiP` as a specification language. Moreover, existing techniques that cannot handle nested loops can profit from it; in fact, we can prove the overall program to be UAST using the rule of [47]. Interestingly, the outer loop has *infinite expected runtime* (for any input distribution where the probability that `x` > 0 is positive). We can prove this by *querying the expected value* of the program variable `c` in the resulting output distribution. The automatically computed result is $\infty$, which indeed proves that the expected runtime of this program is not finite. This example furthermore shows that our technique can be generalized beyond rational functions since the PGF of the `catalan`($p$) distribution is $(1 - \sqrt{1 - 4p(1-p)T})\,/\,2p$, i.e., algebraic but not rational. We leave a formal generalization of the decidability result from Theorem 4 to algebraic functions for future work. PRODIGY verifies this example in 29.17ms. ◁

*Scalability Issue.* It is not difficult to construct programs where PRODIGY poorly scales: its performance depends highly on the number of consecutive probabilistic branches and the size of the constant $n$ in guards (requiring $n$-th order PGF derivation, cf. Table 2).

## 7 Related Work

This section surveys research efforts that are highly related to our approach in terms of semantics, inference, and equivalence checking of probabilistic programs.

*Forward Semantics of Probabilistic Programs.* Kozen established in his seminal work [43] a generic way of giving forward, denotational semantics to probabilistic programs as *distribution transformers.* Klinkenberg et al. [42] instantiated Kozen's semantics as PGF transformers. We refine the PGF semantics substantially such that it enjoys the following crucial properties: (i) our PGF transformers (when restricted to loop-free `ReDiP` programs) preserve closed-form PGF and thus are effectively constructable. In contrast, the existing PGF semantics in [42] operates on infinite sums in a non-constructive fashion; (ii) our PGF semantics naturally extends to SOP, which serves as the key to reason about the exact behavior of unbounded loops (under possibly uncountably many inputs) in a fully automatic manner. The PGF semantics in [42], however, supports only (over-)approximations of looping behaviors and can hardly be automated; and (iii) our PGF semantics is capable of interpreting program constructs like i.i.d. sampling that is of particular interest in practice.

*Backward Semantics of Probabilistic Programs.* Many verification systems for probabilistic programs make use of backward, denotational semantics – most pertinently, the *weakest preexpectation* (WP) calculi [38,46] as a quantitative extension of Dijkstra's weakest preconditions [19]. The WP of a probabilistic program $C$ w.r.t. a postexpectation $g$, denoted by $\mathsf{wp}[\![C]\!](g)(\cdot)$, maps every initial program state $\sigma$ to the expected value of $g$ evaluated in final states reached after executing $C$ on $\sigma$. In contrast to Dijkstra's predicate transformer semantics which admits also strongest postconditions, the counterpart of "strongest postexpectations" does unfortunately not exist [36, Chap. 7], thereby not amenable to forward reasoning. We remark, in particular, that checking program equivalence via WP is difficult, if not impossible, since it amounts to reasoning about uncountably many postexpectations $g$. We refer interested readers to [5, Chaps. 1–4] for more recent advancements in formal semantics of probabilistic programs.

*Probabilistic Inference.* There are a handful of probabilistic systems that employ an alternative forward semantics based on *probability density function* (PDF) representations of distributions, e.g., ($\lambda$)PSI [24,25], AQUA [32], Hakaru [14,52], and the density compiler in [11,12]. These systems are dedicated to probabilistic inference for programs encoding continuous distributions (or joint discrete-continuous distributions). Reasoning about the underlying PDF representations, however, amounts to resolving complex integral expressions in order to answer inference queries, thus confining these techniques either to (semi-)numerical methods [11,12,14,32,52] or exact methods yet limited to bounded looping behaviors [24,25]. Apart from these inference systems, a recently developed language called Dice [31] featuring exact inference for discrete probabilistic programs is also confined to statically bounded loops. The tool Mora [7,8] supports exact inference for various types of Bayesian networks, but relies on a restricted form of intermediate representation known as prob-solvable loops, whose behaviors can be expressed by a system of C-finite recurrences admitting closed-form solutions.

*Equivalence of Probabilistic Programs.* Murawski and Ouaknine [51] showed an EXPTIME decidability result for checking the equivalence of probabilistic programs over *finite* data types by recasting the problem in terms of probabilistic finite automata [23,41,56]. Their techniques have been automated in the equivalence checker APEX [45]. Barthe et al. [4] proved a 2-EXPTIME decidability result for checking equivalence of *straight-line* probabilistic programs (with deterministic inputs and no loops nor recursion) interpreted over all possible extensions of a finite field. Barthe et al. [3] developed a relational Hoare logic for probabilistic programs, which has been extensively used for, amongst others, proving program equivalence with applications in provable security and side-channel analysis.

The decidability result established in this paper is *orthogonal* to the aforementioned results: (i) our decidability for checking $L \sim S$ applies to discrete probabilistic programs $L$ with *unbounded* looping behaviors over a possibly *infinite* state space; the specification $S$ – though, admitting no loops – encodes a possibly *infinite-support* distribution; yet as a compromise, (ii) our decidability result is confined to `ReDiP` programs that necessarily terminate almost-surely on all inputs, and involve only distributions with rational closed-form PGF.

## 8 Conclusion and Future Work

We showed the decidability of – and have presented a fully-automated technique to verifying – whether a (possibly unbounded) probabilistic loop is equivalent to a loop-free specification program. Future directions include determining the complexity of our decision problem; amending the method to continuous distributions using, e.g., *characteristic functions*; extending the notion of probabilistic equivalence to probabilistic refinements; exploring PGF-based counterexample-guided synthesis of quantitative loop invariants (see [18, Appx. F.6] for generating counterexamples); and tackling Bayesian inference.

**Acknowledgments.** The authors thank Philipp Schröer for providing support for his tool PROBABLY ( https://github.com/Philipp15b/Probably) which forms the basis of our implementation.

## References


1. Arvo, J., Kirk, D.B.: Particle transport and image synthesis. In: SIGGRAPH, pp. 63–66. ACM (1990)
2. Aspnes, J., Herlihy, M.: Fast randomized consensus using shared memory. J. Algorithms **11**(3), 441–461 (1990)
3. Barthe, G., Grégoire, B., Béguelin, S.Z.: Formal certification of code-based cryptographic proofs. In: POPL, pp. 90–101. ACM (2009)
4. Barthe, G., Jacomme, C., Kremer, S.: Universal equivalence and majority of probabilistic programs over finite fields. In: LICS, pp. 155–166. ACM (2020)
5. Barthe, G., Katoen, J., Silva, A. (eds.): Foundations of Probabilistic Programming. Cambridge University Press, Cambridge (2020)
6. Barthe, G., Köpf, B., Olmedo, F., Béguelin, S.Z.: Probabilistic relational reasoning for differential privacy. ACM Trans. Program. Lang. Syst. **35**(3), 9:1–9:49 (2013)
7. Bartocci, E., Kovács, L., Stankovič, M.: Analysis of Bayesian networks via prob-solvable loops. In: Pun, V.K.I., Stolz, V., Simao, A. (eds.) ICTAC 2020. LNCS, vol. 12545, pp. 221–241. Springer, Cham (2020). https://doi.org/10.1007/978-3-030-64276-1_12
8. Bartocci, E., Kovács, L., Stankovič, M.: Mora - automatic generation of moment-based invariants. In: TACAS 2020. LNCS, vol. 12078, pp. 492–498. Springer, Cham (2020). https://doi.org/10.1007/978-3-030-45190-5_28
9. Batz, K., Chen, M., Kaminski, B.L., Katoen, J.-P., Matheja, C., Schröer, P.: Latticed $k$-induction with an application to probabilistic programs. In: Silva, A., Leino, K.R.M. (eds.) CAV 2021. LNCS, vol. 12760, pp. 524–549. Springer, Cham (2021). https://doi.org/10.1007/978-3-030-81688-9_25
10. Bauer, C., Frink, A., Kreckel, R.: Introduction to the GiNaC framework for symbolic computation within the C++ programming language. J. Symb. Comput. **33**(1), 1–12 (2002)
11. Bhat, S., Agarwal, A., Vuduc, R.W., Gray, A.G.: A type theory for probability density functions. In: POPL, pp. 545–556. ACM (2012)
12. Bhat, S., Borgström, J., Gordon, A.D., Russo, C.V.: Deriving probability density functions from probabilistic functional programs. Log. Methods Comput. Sci. **13**(2) (2017)
13. Carbin, M., Misailovic, S., Rinard, M.C.: Verifying quantitative reliability for programs that execute on unreliable hardware. Commun. ACM **59**(8), 83–91 (2016)
14. Carette, J., Shan, C.-C.: Simplifying probabilistic programs using computer algebra. In: Gavanelli, M., Reppy, J. (eds.) PADL 2016. LNCS, vol. 9585, pp. 135–152. Springer, Cham (2016). https://doi.org/10.1007/978-3-319-28228-2_9
15. Chakarov, A., Sankaranarayanan, S.: Probabilistic program analysis with martingales. In: Sharygina, N., Veith, H. (eds.) CAV 2013. LNCS, vol. 8044, pp. 511–526. Springer, Heidelberg (2013). https://doi.org/10.1007/978-3-642-39799-8_34
16. Chatterjee, K., Fu, H., Goharshady, A.K.: Termination analysis of probabilistic programs through Positivstellensatz's. In: Chaudhuri, S., Farzan, A. (eds.) CAV 2016. LNCS, vol. 9779, pp. 3–22. Springer, Cham (2016). https://doi.org/10.1007/978-3-319-41528-4_1
17. Chatterjee, K., Fu, H., Novotný, P.: Termination analysis of probabilistic programs with martingales, pp. 221–258. In: Barthe et al. [5] (2020)
18. Chen, M., Katoen, J., Klinkenberg, L., Winkler, T.: Does a program yield the right distribution? Verifying probabilistic programs via generating functions. CoRR abs/2205.01449 (2022)

19. Dijkstra, E.W.: Guarded commands, nondeterminacy and formal derivation of programs. Commun. ACM **18**(8), 453–457 (1975)
20. Evans, O., Stuhlmüller, A., Salvatier, J., Filan, D.: Modeling agents with probabilistic programs. http://agentmodels.org (2017). Accessed 17 Jan 2022
21. Flajolet, P., Pelletier, M., Soria, M.: On Buffon machines and numbers. In: SODA, pp. 172–183. SIAM (2011)
22. Flajolet, P., Sedgewick, R.: Analytic Combinatorics. Cambridge University Press, Cambridge (2009)
23. Forejt, V., Jancar, P., Kiefer, S., Worrell, J.: Language equivalence of probabilistic pushdown automata. Inf. Comput. **237**, 1–11 (2014)
24. Gehr, T., Misailovic, S., Vechev, M.: PSI: exact symbolic inference for probabilistic programs. In: Chaudhuri, S., Farzan, A. (eds.) CAV 2016. LNCS, vol. 9779, pp. 62–83. Springer, Cham (2016). https://doi.org/10.1007/978-3-319-41528-4_4
25. Gehr, T., Steffen, S., Vechev, M.T.: λPSI: exact inference for higher-order probabilistic programs. In: PLDI, pp. 883–897. ACM (2020)
26. Gordon, A.D., Henzinger, T.A., Nori, A.V., Rajamani, S.K.: Probabilistic programming. In: FOSE, pp. 167–181. ACM (2014)
27. Hammersley, J.: Monte Carlo Methods. Springer Science & Business Media (2013)
28. Hark, M., Kaminski, B.L., Giesl, J., Katoen, J.: Aiming low is harder: induction for lower bounds in probabilistic program verification. Proc. ACM Program. Lang. **4**(POPL), 37:1–37:28 (2020)
29. Heninger, N.: RSA, DH and DSA in the wild. In: Bos, J., Stam, M. (eds.) Computational Cryptography: Algorithmic Aspects of Cryptology, pp. 140–181. Cambridge University Press, Cambridge (2021)
30. Hicks, M.: What is probabilistic programming? In: The Programming Languages Enthusiast (2014). http://www.pl-enthusiast.net/2014/09/08. Accessed 09 Dec 2021
31. Holtzen, S., den Broeck, G.V., Millstein, T.D.: Scaling exact inference for discrete probabilistic programs. Proc. ACM Program. Lang. **4**(OOPSLA), 140:1–140:31 (2020)
32. Huang, Z., Dutta, S., Misailovic, S.: AQUA: automated quantized inference for probabilistic programs. In: Hou, Z., Ganesh, V. (eds.) ATVA 2021. LNCS, vol. 12971, pp. 229–246. Springer, Cham (2021). https://doi.org/10.1007/978-3-030-88885-5_16
33. Jacobs, B., Zanasi, F.: The logical essentials of Bayesian reasoning, pp. 295–331. In: Barthe et al. [5] (2020)
34. Jansen, N., Dehnert, C., Kaminski, B.L., Katoen, J.-P., Westhofen, L.: Bounded model checking for probabilistic programs. In: Artho, C., Legay, A., Peled, D. (eds.) ATVA 2016. LNCS, vol. 9938, pp. 68–85. Springer, Cham (2016). https://doi.org/10.1007/978-3-319-46520-3_5
35. Johnson, N., Kotz, S., Kemp, A.: Univariate Discrete Distributions. Wiley, Hoboken (1993)
36. Jones, C.: Probabilistic non-determinism. Ph.D. thesis, University of Edinburgh, UK (1990)
37. Kajiya, J.T.: The rendering equation. In: SIGGRAPH, pp. 143–150. ACM (1986)
38. Kaminski, B.L.: Advanced weakest precondition calculi for probabilistic programs. Ph.D. thesis, RWTH Aachen University, Germany (2019)
39. Kaminski, B.L., Katoen, J.-P., Matheja, C.: On the hardness of analyzing probabilistic programs. Acta Informatica **56**(3), 255–285 (2018). https://doi.org/10.1007/s00236-018-0321-1

40. Kaminski, B.L., Katoen, J., Matheja, C., Olmedo, F.: Weakest precondition reasoning for expected runtimes of randomized algorithms. J. ACM **65**(5), 30:1–30:68 (2018)
41. Kiefer, S., Murawski, A.S., Ouaknine, J., Wachter, B., Worrell, J.: Language equivalence for probabilistic automata. In: Gopalakrishnan, G., Qadeer, S. (eds.) CAV 2011. LNCS, vol. 6806, pp. 526–540. Springer, Heidelberg (2011). https://doi.org/10.1007/978-3-642-22110-1_42
42. Klinkenberg, L., Batz, K., Kaminski, B.L., Katoen, J.-P., Moerman, J., Winkler, T.: Generating functions for probabilistic programs. In: Fernández, M. (ed.) LOPSTR 2020. LNCS, vol. 12561, pp. 231–248. Springer, Cham (2021). https://doi.org/10.1007/978-3-030-68446-4_12
43. Kozen, D.: Semantics of probabilistic programs. J. Comput. Syst. Sci. **22**(3), 328–350 (1981)
44. Kozen, D.: A probabilistic PDL. J. Comput. Syst. Sci. **30**(2), 162–178 (1985)
45. Legay, A., Murawski, A.S., Ouaknine, J., Worrell, J.: on automated verification of probabilistic programs. In: Ramakrishnan, C.R., Rehof, J. (eds.) TACAS 2008. LNCS, vol. 4963, pp. 173–187. Springer, Heidelberg (2008). https://doi.org/10.1007/978-3-540-78800-3_13
46. McIver, A., Morgan, C.: Abstraction, Refinement and Proof For Probabilistic Systems. Monographs in Computer Science. Springer, New York (2005). https://doi.org/10.1007/b138392
47. McIver, A., Morgan, C., Kaminski, B.L., Katoen, J.: A new proof rule for almost-sure termination. PACMPL **2**(POPL), 33:1–33:28 (2018)
48. van de Meent, J., Paige, B., Yang, H., Wood, F.: An introduction to probabilistic programming. CoRR abs/1809.10756 (2018)
49. Meurer, A., et al.: SymPy: symbolic computing in Python. PeerJ Comput. Sci. **3**, e103 (2017)
50. Moosbrugger, M., Bartocci, E., Katoen, J.-P., Kovács, L.: The probabilistic termination tool amber. In: Huisman, M., Păsăreanu, C., Zhan, N. (eds.) FM 2021. LNCS, vol. 13047, pp. 667–675. Springer, Cham (2021). https://doi.org/10.1007/978-3-030-90870-6_36
51. Murawski, A.S., Ouaknine, J.: On probabilistic program equivalence and refinement. In: Abadi, M., de Alfaro, L. (eds.) CONCUR 2005. LNCS, vol. 3653, pp. 156–170. Springer, Heidelberg (2005). https://doi.org/10.1007/11539452_15
52. Narayanan, P., Carette, J., Romano, W., Shan, C., Zinkov, R.: Probabilistic inference by program transformation in Hakaru (system description). In: Kiselyov, O., King, A. (eds.) FLOPS 2016. LNCS, vol. 9613, pp. 62–79. Springer, Cham (2016). https://doi.org/10.1007/978-3-319-29604-3_5
53. Schneider, M.: Self-stabilization. ACM Comput. Surv. **25**(1), 45–67 (1993)
54. Shamsi, S.M., Farina, G.P., Gaboardi, M., Napp, N.: Probabilistic programming languages for modeling autonomous systems. In: MFI, pp. 32–39. IEEE (2020)
55. Tijms, H.C.: A First Course in Stochastic Models. Wiley, Hoboken (2003)
56. Tzeng, W.: A polynomial-time algorithm for the equivalence of probabilistic automata. SIAM J. Comput. **21**(2), 216–227 (1992)
57. Vollinga, J.: GiNaC-symbolic Computation with C++. Nucl. Instrum. Methods Phys. Res. **559**(1), 282–284 (2006)
58. Wang, D., Hoffmann, J., Reps, T.W.: Central moment analysis for cost accumulators in probabilistic programs. In: PLDI, pp. 559–573. ACM (2021)
59. Wang, J., Sun, Y., Fu, H., Chatterjee, K., Goharshady, A.K.: Quantitative analysis of assertion violations in probabilistic programs. In: PLDI, pp. 1171–1186. ACM (2021)

60. Wilf, H.S.: Generating Functionology. CRC Press, Boca Raton (2005)
61. Ying, M.: Floyd-Hoare logic for quantum programs. ACM Trans. Program. Lang. Syst. **33**(6), 19:1–19:49 (2011)

# Abstraction-Refinement for Hierarchical Probabilistic Models

Sebastian Junges[1(✉)] and Matthijs T. J. Spaan[2]

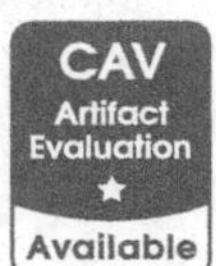


[1] Radboud University, Nijmegen, The Netherlands
sjunges@cs.ru.nl
[2] Delft University of Technology, Delft, The Netherlands

**Abstract.** Markov decision processes are a ubiquitous formalism for modelling systems with non-deterministic and probabilistic behavior. Verification of these models is subject to the famous state space explosion problem. We alleviate this problem by exploiting a hierarchical structure with repetitive parts. This structure not only occurs naturally in robotics, but also in probabilistic programs describing, e.g., network protocols. Such programs often repeatedly call a subroutine with similar behavior. In this paper, we focus on a local case, in which the subroutines have a limited effect on the overall system state. The key ideas to accelerate analysis of such programs are (1) to treat the behavior of the subroutine as uncertain and only remove this uncertainty by a detailed analysis if needed, and (2) to abstract similar subroutines into a parametric template, and then analyse this template. These two ideas are embedded into an abstraction-refinement loop that analyses hierarchical MDPs. A prototypical implementation shows the efficacy of the approach.

## 1 Introduction

Markov Decision Processes (MDPs) are *the* model for sequential decision making under probabilistic uncertainty, and as such are central in modelling of randomized algorithms, distributed systems with lossy channels, or as the underlying formalism in reinforcement learning. A key question in the verification of MDPs is: *What is the maximal probability that some error state is reached?* In this question, one accounts for the probabilistic nature as well as the inherit (potentially adversarial) nondeterminism of the system. Various state-of-the-art probabilistic model checkers, such as Storm [20], Prism [27] and Modest [17] implement a variety of methods that automatically compute such maximal probabilities. Most widespread are variations of value-iteration that iteratively apply a transition function to converge towards the requested probability.

*Hierarchical Structure.* Despite various successes, the state space explosion remains a significant challenge to the model-based analysis of MDPs. To overcome this challenge, some approaches exploit symmetries or the parallel composition of a system. Other approaches exploit that typically not all paths through a system are equally likely and thus aim to find the essential or critical subsystem.


S. Shoham and Y. Vizel (Eds.): CAV 2022, LNCS 13371, pp. 102–123, 2022.
https://doi.org/10.1007/978-3-031-13185-1_6

```
p = 0.5; time = 0; N=3;
repeat N times {
   time += passToken(p);
   if flip(0.5) {p = 0.8p}
   else         {p = 1.25p}
}; return time
```

(a) Repeated invocation of `passToken(p)`

```
passToken(p):
  t = 1;
  while (not flip(p)) {t++};
  t++;
  while (not flip(p)) {t++};
  return t
```

(b) `passToken(p)`: Pass succeed twice.

**Fig. 1.** Simplified example for sending a token over an unreliable channel.

While we exploit related ideas—a detailed comparison is given in the related work, cf. Sect. 7—our approach is fundamentally different and instead exploits a *hierarchical decomposition* natural in many system models. This decomposition is captured naturally by probabilistic programs (over discrete bounded variables) with non-nested subroutines, where some subroutines are called repeatedly with *similar* arguments. Figure 1 shows an example in which we demonstrate our approach in Sect. 2. More generally, we are interested in systems with an overall task that is achieved by a suitable combination of a limited number of sub-tasks. Such a setting occurs naturally, e.g. (i) in robotics, when multiple rooms in a floor need to be inspected, or (ii) in routing, when multiple packets need to be routed sequentially. The underlying problem structure is also exploited in hierarchical planning [5,19,30], where the goal is to find a good but not necessarily optimal policy (and induced value). *We combine insights from hierarchical planning with an abstraction-refinement perspective and then construct an anytime algorithm with strict guarantees on the result.*

*Local Model-Based Analysis.* An adequate operational model for the model-based analysis of hierarchical systems is given by a *hierarchical MDP*, where the state space of a hierarchical MDP can be partitioned into *subMDPs*. Abstractly, one can represent a hierarchical MDP by the collection of subMDPs and a *macro-level MDP* [19] where the probabilities of outgoing transitions at a state are described by a corresponding subMDP, cf. Sect. 3.2. In this paper, we focus on a hierarchical MDPs where the policies that are optimal in (only) a subMDP are optimal (partial) policies in the hierarchical MDP. More intuitively, we can solve the subMDPs individually, i.e., the solution (w.r.t. the fixed measure) for the subMDP is part of the globally optimal solution. While this assumption is restrictive, it is satisfied in various interesting settings. The assumption allows us to analyse subMDPs out-of-context, i.e., we can first analyse the subMDPs and then construct the correct macro-MDP, i.e., extract transition probabilities and rewards from the subMDP analysis. This approach already improves the maximal memory consumption and allows for additional speed ups if the *same* subMDP occurs multiple times.

*Epistemic Uncertainty During Computation.* The key insight to accelerate the outlined approach further is to avoid analysing all subMDPs precisely, while still providing sound guarantees on the obtained results. Therefore, consider that even before analysing the subMDPs we can analyse an uncertain variant of the macro-level MDP where we do not yet know the associated transition probabilities and rewards but instead only know intervals. We may then do two things: First, we can identify the subMDPs which are most critical, i.e., where replacing the interval by a concrete value yields most benefits. Second, and more importantly, we can analyse a set of subMDPs and refine the associated uncertainties, i.e., tighten the associated intervals. To support the analysis of sets of subMDPs, we observe that often, these subMDPs are slight variations. In this paper, we represent them as parameterised instances of a particular templates that we define using parametric MDPs (pMDPs). The resulting intervals can be used to create an (interval-valued version of the) macro-level MDP. Analysing this gives bounds on the expected reward in the hierarchical MDP, and the bounds can be refined by analysing the subMDPs more precisely.

*Contributions.* In a nutshell, we explicitly allow for *uncertainty* during the solving process to speed up the analysis of hierarchical MDPs. Concretely, we contribute a scalable approach to solve hierarchical MDPs with many different subMDPs, in particular when these subMDPs are similar, but not the same. The approach resembles an abstraction-refinement loop where we abstract the hierarchical MDP in two layers and then refine the analysis of the lower layer to get a refined representation of the complete MDP. In every step, we can provide absolute error bounds. Our approach interprets the different subMDPs as a form of uncertainty. The efficient analysis originates from progress made in the analysis of uncertain (or parametric) MDPs, and brings that progress to a novel setting. The empirical evaluation with a prototype called LEVEL-UP shows the efficacy of the approach.

## 2 Overview

We clarify the approach and its applicability with a motivating example that drastically abstracts a token passing process where the channel quality varies [12].

*Setting.* Consider the protocol in Fig. 1a which sends a token $N$ times via a channel. That channel successfully transmits packets with probability $p$, where $p$ varies over time. The subroutine takes $t$ amount of time, depending on $p$. Specifically, in the model, we alternate between accumulating the required time and updating the channel quality for $N$ token transmissions and then return the accumulated time. We aim to compute the expected return value. For the subroutine, we assume that sending a token is repeated until an acknowledgement is received, which is abstractly modelled in Fig. 1b and corresponds to the small Markov chain in Fig. 2a. First, the file must successfully be sent ($s_0 \rightarrow s_1$), then we start sending acknowledgements. The process terminates ($s_1 \rightarrow s_2$) once an acknowledgement is received. The complete protocol from Fig. 1 including the subroutine is reflected by the large Markov chain in Fig. 2b that repeats the small Markov chain (with different probabilities). This model may be analysed with standard tools, but for large $N$ (and larger subroutines), the state space explosion must be alleviated.

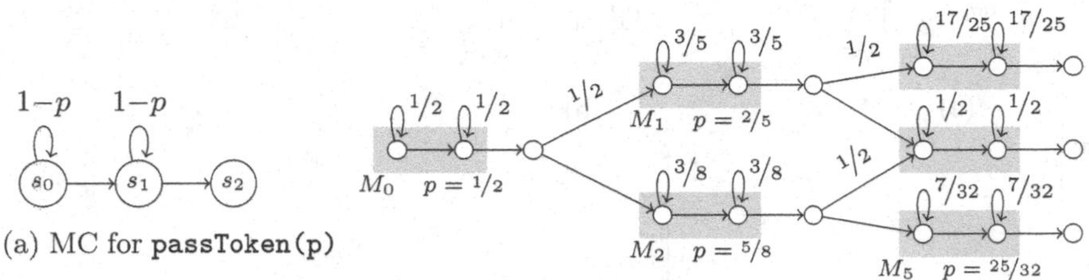


(a) MC for **passToken(p)**

(b) Hierarchical MDP, rewards of 1 at states with loops

**Fig. 2.** Ingredients for hierarchical MDPs with the Example from Fig. 1. Annotations reflect subMDPs within the macro-MDPs in Fig. 3.

*Macro-MDPs and Enumeration.* We thus suggest to abstract the hierarchical model into the macro-level MDP in Fig. 3a. Here, every state corresponds to an invocation of the subprocess. The reward at the states corresponds to the expected reward for the complete subprocess. Thus, naively, one may construct the macro-MDP, analyse all (reachable) subMDPs independently and annotate the macro-MDP states with the appropriate rewards, and finally analyse the macro-MDP to obtain a result of $\approx$12.3. This approach avoids representing the complete hMDP in the memory, but it is still restricted to analysing systems with a limited number of subMDPs.

*Our Approach.* We improve scalability by constructing a parameterized macro-MDP. Reconsider the rewards for Fig. 3a. The values can be computed via the graph in Fig. 3d, where we pick for each value for $p$ (x-axis) and compute the corresponding expected reward $\mathbb{E}$ (y-axis) obtained by analysing the subMDP in Fig. 2a. Intuitively, in our abstraction, we annotate the rewards with lower- and upper bounds rather than exact values. Therefore, we compute bounds on the rewards by selecting an interval for the values $p \in [8/25, 25/32]$, as shown in Fig. 3e. Conceptually, this means that we analyse a set of subMDPs at once, namely all subMDPs with $p \in [8/25, 25/32]$. Annotating the corresponding expected rewards, in this case $[64/25, 25/4]$, then yields the macro-MDP in Fig. 3b. Analysis of this MDP yields that overall expected time is in $[7.68, 18.75]$. We refine these bounds by analysing subsets of the subMDPs. We may split the values for $p$ into two sets $[8/25, 2/5]$ and $[1/2, 25/32]$. Then, we obtain two corresponding intervals on the expected time in the subMDP as shown in Fig. 3f. Model checking the associated macro-MDP, in Fig. 3c, bounds to expected time by $[10.12, 14.25]$. Technically, we realize this reasoning using parameter lifting [33].

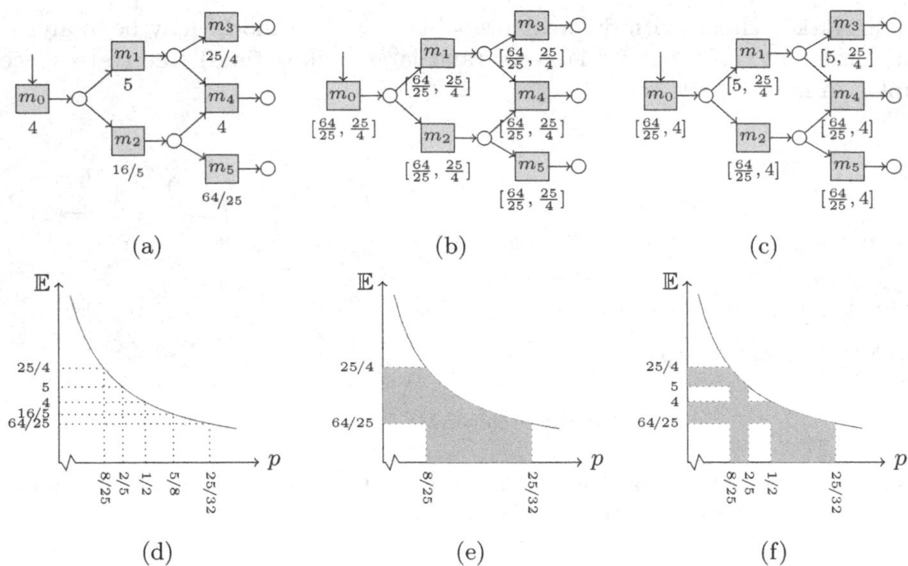


**Fig. 3.** Visualising the computation of expected rewards for the hMDP from Fig. 2b using a macro-MDP and interval-based abstractions.

*Supported Extensions.* For conciseness, this example is necessarily simple. Our approach allows nondeterminism, i.e., action-choices, in the macro-MDP *and* in the subMDPs. The subMDPs may have multiple outgoing transitions, but this must be combined with a restricted type of nondeterminism in the subMDP: If multiple outgoing transitions are present, the macro-MDP has transition probabilities that depend on the subMDPs. We present a useful extension for reachability probabilities, see the discussion at the bottom of Sect. 3.3.

*More Examples.* Key ingredient to models where the approach excels are a repetitive task whose characteristics depend on some global state. Two variations are the expected energy consumption of a robot with slowly degrading components that, e.g., can be improved by maintenance or for job scheduling with periodically changing distribution of tasks (e.g., day vs. night).

## 3 Formal Problem Statement

We formalize MDPs and *hierarchical MDPs* (hMDPs) to pose the problem statement, then identify a subclass of hMDPs which we call *local-policy hMDPs* and restrict our problem on computing optimal expected rewards in local-policy hMDPs. Furthermore, we introduce parametric MDPs as they are key to the abstraction-refinement procedure later in the paper.

### 3.1 Background

**Definition 1 (Parametric MDP).** *A parametric MDP (pMDP) is a tuple* $\mathcal{M} = \langle S_\mathcal{M}, A_\mathcal{M}, \iota_\mathcal{M}, \vec{x}, P_\mathcal{M}, r_\mathcal{M}, T_\mathcal{M}\rangle$ *where* $S_\mathcal{M}$ *is a finite set of* states, $A_\mathcal{M}$ *is a finite set of* actions, $\iota_\mathcal{M} \in S_S$ *is the* initial state, $\vec{x} = \langle x_0, \dots x_n\rangle$ *is a vector of* parameters, $P_\mathcal{M} \colon S_\mathcal{M} \times A_\mathcal{M} \times S_\mathcal{M} \to \mathbb{Q}[\vec{x}]$ *are the* transition probabilities, $r_\mathcal{M} \colon S \to \mathbb{Q}[\vec{x}]$ *the* state rewards, *and* $T_\mathcal{M}$ *is a set of* target states.

We drop the subscripts whenever possible. MDPs are *parametric* if $\vec{x} \neq \langle\rangle$ and *parameter-free* otherwise. We omit parameters for parameter-free MDPs. We recap some standard notions on pMDPs (and MDPs):

For a (parameter) *valuation* $u \in \mathbb{R}^{\vec{x}}$, the *instantiation* $\mathcal{M}[u]$ globally substitutes $P_\mathcal{M}(s,a,s')$ with $P_\mathcal{M}(s,a,s')(u)$ and $r_\mathcal{M}(s)$ with $r_\mathcal{M}(s)(u)$. An assignment $u$ is well-defined, if $\mathcal{M}(u)$ constitutes an MDP, i.e., if $\sum_{s'} P_\mathcal{M}(s,\alpha,s')(u) \in \{0,1\}$ and $r_\mathcal{M}(s)(u) \geq 0$ for each $s \in S$, $\alpha \in A$. We denote the set of all well-defined assignments with $U_\mathcal{M}$. The set $\mathsf{Act}(s)$ denotes the enabled actions at state $s$, $\mathsf{Act}(s) = \{\alpha \mid \sum_{s'} P_\mathcal{M}(s,\alpha,s') \neq 0\ \}$. If $|\mathsf{Act}(s)| = 1$ for every $s \in S$, then the (parametric) MDP is a (parametric) *Markov chain* (MC). A path $\pi$ is an (in)finite sequence of states $s_0 \xrightarrow{\alpha_0} s_1 \dots$, with $s_i \in S$, $\alpha_i \in \mathsf{Act}(s_i)$, $P(s_i, \alpha_i, s_{i+1}) \neq 0$. For finite $\pi$, $\mathsf{last}(\pi)$ denotes the last state of $\pi$. We use $[s \to \Diamond T]$ to denote the set of (finite) paths $T$ only at the end. The reward $r(\pi)$ along a finite path $\pi$ is the sum of the state rewards $r(\pi) := \sum r(s_i)$.

*Specifications.* We consider indefinite horizon expected reward, i.e., the expected accumulated reward until reaching the target states. We refer to [3,32] for a formal treatment and only introduce notation. Therefore, the unique probability measure *Pr* for a set of paths in a parameter-free *Markov chain* $\mathcal{M}$ reaching state $T$ can be defined using the usual cylinder set construction. We define $Pr_\mathcal{M}(s \to \Diamond T)$ as the probability to reach a state in $T$, $\int_{\pi \in [s \to \Diamond T]} Pr(\pi) d\pi$. We then define the expected reward until hitting $T$, $\mathsf{ER}_\mathcal{M}(s \to \Diamond T) = \int_{\pi \in [s \to \Diamond T]} Pr(\pi) \cdot r(\pi) d\pi$. In both definitions, if $s$ is the initial state, we simply write $\dots (\Diamond T)$. For technical conciseness, we make the standard assumption that target states are reached with probability 1, which ensures that the integral exists and is finite. (Arbitrary) reachability probabilities can be nevertheless be modelled using rewards.

*Policies.* In pMDPs, we resolve nondeterminism with policies. In this paper, it suffices to consider *memoryless policies* $\sigma \colon S \to A$. The set of such policies is denoted $\Sigma(\mathcal{M})$. We omit $\mathcal{M}$ if it is clear from the context. It is helpful to also consider *partial* policies $\hat{\sigma} \colon S \nrightarrow A$. For an pMDP $\mathcal{M}$ and a (partial) policy $\hat{\sigma}$, the induced dynamics are described by the *induced pMDP* $\mathcal{M}[\hat{\sigma}]$, defined as $\langle S_\mathcal{M}, A_\mathcal{M}, \iota_\mathcal{M}, \vec{x}, P, r_\mathcal{M}, T_\mathcal{M}\rangle$, where the transition probabilities are given as

$$P(s,\alpha,s') = \begin{cases} P_\mathcal{M}(s,\alpha,s') & \text{if } \hat{\sigma}(s) = \alpha, \\ 0 & \text{otherwise.} \end{cases}$$

If $\sigma$ is total (not partial), then $\mathcal{M}$ is a MC. We define the maximal expected reward $\mathsf{ER}^{\max}_\mathcal{M}(\Diamond T) = \max_{\sigma \in \Sigma} \mathsf{ER}_{\mathcal{M}[\sigma]}(\Diamond T)$, and say that a policy $\sigma$ is optimal, if $\mathsf{ER}^{\max}_\mathcal{M}(\Diamond T) = \mathsf{ER}_{\mathcal{M}[\sigma]}(\Diamond T)$.

*Regions and Parametric Model Checking.* A set of valuations described by is called a (rectangular) *region*, if $R = \{u \mid u^- \leq u \leq u^+\}$ for adequate bounds $u^-, u^+ \in \mathbb{R}^{\vec{x}}$ and using pointwise inequalities, i.e., $R$ is a Cartesian product of intervals of parameter values. We denote this region also with $[[u^-, u^+]]$. For regions, we may compute a lower bound on $\min_{u \in R} \mathsf{ER}^{\max}_{\mathcal{M}[u]}(\lozenge T)$ and an upper bound on $\max_{u \in R} \mathsf{ER}^{\max}_{\mathcal{M}[u]}(\lozenge T)$ via *parameter lifting* [33,36].

### 3.2 Hierarchical MDPs

We concentrate on solving hierarchical MDPs (hMDPs). We assume that hMDPs are parameter-free and that their topology has some additional known structure.

**Definition 2 (Hierarchical MDPs).** *A MDP $\mathcal{M}$ with a partitioning of its states $S_\mathcal{M} = \bigcup \mathbf{S}_i$ is a hierarchical MDP, if for all $i$,*

- *there exists a unique $s^i_\iota \in \mathbf{S}_i$ such that $s^i_\iota = \iota_\mathcal{M}$ or $\mathsf{pred}_\mathcal{M}(s^i_\iota) \not\subseteq \mathbf{S}_i$, and*
- *for all $s \in \mathbf{S}_i \setminus \{s^i_\iota\}$, it holds that $s^i_\iota \neq \iota_\mathcal{M}$ and $\mathsf{pred}_\mathcal{M}(s) \subseteq \mathbf{S}_i$.*

The state $s_\iota$ is called the *entry state*, which we denote $\mathsf{entry}_i$. States with $\mathsf{succ}_\mathcal{M}(s) \cap \mathbf{S}_i = \emptyset$ are called *exit-states.* The set $\mathsf{succ}(i) := \mathsf{succ}_\mathcal{M}(\mathbf{S}_i) \setminus \mathbf{S}_i$ are the *successor states* of the partition $i$. Let $Y = \max_i |\mathsf{succ}(i)|$. By adding auxiliary states, we can assume that $|\mathsf{succ}(i)| = Y$ for all $i$. We call partitions with $|\mathbf{S}_i| = 1$ *trivial.* We use $\mathbb{I} := \{i \mid |\mathbf{S}_i| > 1\}$ to denote the indices of the non-trivial partitions. We remark that every MDP can be considered as an hMDP with only trivial partitions.

> **Problem:** Given a (hierarchical) MDP $\mathcal{M}$ with target states $T$ and $\eta \in [0,1]$, compute bounds $\mathsf{lb}, \mathsf{ub}$ with $\mathsf{lb} \leq \mathsf{ER}^{\max}_\mathcal{M}(\lozenge T) \leq \mathsf{ub}$ and $\eta \cdot \mathsf{ub} \leq \mathsf{lb}$.

The naive solution to this problem is to ignore the hierarchical structure and solve the MDP monolithically. In this paper, we contribute methods that actively exploit the structure of the hierarchical MDPs with $|\mathbb{I}| \gg 1$. We will make an additional assumption on the structure of the hierarchical MDP.

### 3.3 Optimal Local Subpolicies and Beyond

Intuitively, we want to ensure that the optimal policy within the partitions can be computed locally, i.e., on partition without taking into account the complete MDP. Therefore, each partition within the MDP can be considered as an individual MDP. In particular, each $\mathbf{S}_i$ induces a subMDP as follows:

**Definition 3 (subMDP).** *Given a hierarchical MDP $\mathcal{M}$ and partition $\boldsymbol{S}_i$, the corresponding subMDP is an MDP $\mathcal{M}_i := \langle S_i := \boldsymbol{S}_i \cup \mathsf{succ}_\mathcal{M}(\boldsymbol{S}_i) \cup \{\bot\}, A_\mathcal{M} \cup \{\alpha_\bot\}, \iota := \mathsf{entry}_i, P_i, r_i, G_i\rangle$ with $P_i$ defined by*

$$P_i(s, \alpha, s') := \begin{cases} P_\mathcal{M}(s, \alpha, s') & \text{if } s \in \boldsymbol{S}_i \text{ and } \alpha \in A_\mathcal{M}, \\ 1 & \text{else if } s \notin \boldsymbol{S}_i, \alpha = \alpha_\bot, \text{ and } s' = \bot \\ 0 & \text{otherwise.} \end{cases}$$

*$r_i$ is defined as $r_i(s) = r_{\mathcal{M}}(s)$ if $s \in \mathbf{S}_i$, $r_i(s) = 0$ otherwise, and $G_i := \{\bot_i\}$.*

Thus, for every partition of the hierarchical MDP, the corresponding subMDP contains additionally the successor states, and a unique bottom state that is a target state and simplifies our construction later.

Likewise, we can (de)compose memoryless policies for the hierarchical MDP as a union of policies on the individual subMDPs. We do this only for nontrivial partitions. Let $\sigma_i \colon S_i \mapsto A$ denote memoryless policies for $\mathcal{M}_i$ and $\sigma_i'$ the restriction of $\sigma_i$ to $\mathbf{S}_i$, then $(\bigsqcup_{\mathbb{I}} \sigma_i) : S \nrightarrow A$ is the unique partial policy such that

$$(\bigsqcup_{\mathbb{I}} \sigma_i)(s) := \sigma_i'(s) \text{ if } s \in \mathbf{S}_i, i \in \mathbb{I} \quad \text{and} \quad (\bigsqcup_{\mathbb{I}} \sigma_i)(s) := \bot \text{ otherwise.}$$

Intuitively, we want that the union of locally optimal policies, a partial policy, can be completed to a total policy that is optimal.

**Definition 4 (Optimal local subpolicies).** *Given a hierarchical MDP $\mathcal{M}$ with target states $T$ and optimal policies $\sigma_i \in \Sigma(\mathcal{M}_i)$ for all $i \in \mathbb{I}$. The hierarchical MDP has* optimal local subpolicies, *if for $\hat{\sigma} = \bigsqcup_{\mathbb{I}} \sigma_i$ it holds that $\mathsf{ER}^{max}_{\mathcal{M}[\hat{\sigma}]} = \mathsf{ER}^{max}_{\mathcal{M}}$.*

That is, if we collect (locally) optimal policies $\sigma_i$ and apply them to $\mathcal{M}$, we obtain the MDP $\mathcal{M}[(\bigsqcup_{\mathbb{I}} \sigma_i)]$. In that MDP, we can pick an optimal policy, and together with $(\bigsqcup_{\mathbb{I}} \sigma_i)$ this constitutes an optimal and total policy for $\mathcal{M}$.

**Assumption:** The hierarchical MDP has optimal local subpolicies.

Roughly, the idea now becomes that rather than solving one large MDP with $S$ states, we solve $|\mathbb{I}|$ MDPs with $S/|\mathbb{I}|$ states and one MDP with $\mathbb{I}$ states (assuming equally-sized and only nontrivial partitions).

The assumption is restrictive, but not unreasonable: A subroutine may not have any nondeterminism, or a finished task will have no influence on any future task. The following proposition, while obvious, formalizes that:

**Proposition 1 (Sufficient criterion).** *Let $\mathcal{M}$ be a hierarchical MDP. The MDP has optimal local subpolicies, if for each $i \in \mathbb{I}$ either*

- *there is a single successor for the partition, i.e., $|\mathsf{succ}_{\mathcal{M}}(\mathbf{S}_i) \setminus \mathbf{S}_i| = 1$, or*
- *there are no choices, i.e., $|\mathsf{Act}(s)| = 1$ for all $s \in \mathbf{S}_i$,*

**Beyond Optimal Local Subpolicies.** The efficiency of our approach is partly due to the assumption in Definition 4. We observe that adapting this definition allows for a spectrum of specific yet useful cases. In particular, say that our system describes a protocol in which we must optimize the probability to satisfy $N$ tasks all may fail – the subMDPs will have two successor states. Often, it is then easy to see (and model) that a locally optimal policy will aim to satisfy each task and that thus, the locally optimal policy optimizes the probability to reach the corresponding successor state. Then, by adopting the target states in Definition 3 to be the successor state where the task is successful, the notion of an optimal policy—and thus of an optimal local subpolicy—changes. These changes are minimal and everything that follows below is easily adapted to this setting as demonstrated by the prototypical implementation.

## 4 Solving hMDPs with Abstraction-Refinement

In this section, we consider hMDPs with optimal local subpolicies. We step-wise develop a sketch of an anytime algorithm that provides lower and upper bounds on the expected reward in this hMDP. In Sect. 4.1, we introduce an alternative representation of our problem that formalizes the idea of individually computing subMDPs. We then formalize the ideas that allow to construct an anytime algorithm in Sect. 4.2. In Sect. 4.3, we introduce the abstract requirements for analysing sets of subMDPs into the algorithm, and finally, in Sect. 4.4 we introduce a method that realises this using pMDPs.

### 4.1 The Macro-MDP Formulation

We adapt macro-MDPs [5] which summarize the subMDPs by single states.

**Definition 5 (Macro-MDP).** *Let $\mathcal{M}$ be a hMDP with $n$ non-trivial $\boldsymbol{S}_i$ partitions and $S_\mathcal{M}$ partitioned as $S_\mathcal{M} = \bigcup \boldsymbol{S}_i \cup S'$. The* macro-MDP *is defined as $\mu(\mathcal{M}) := \langle S' \cup \{\mathsf{entry}_i \mid 1 \leq i \leq n\}, A_\mathcal{M}, \iota_\mathcal{M}, \emptyset, P, r, T_\mathcal{M}\rangle$ with $P$ and $r$ given by*

$$P(s,\alpha,s') = \begin{cases} \mathsf{Pr}_{\mathcal{M}_i[\sigma_i]}(\lozenge\{s'\}) & \text{if } s \in \boldsymbol{S}_i, \\ P_\mathcal{M}(s,\alpha,s') & \text{otherwise,} \end{cases} \qquad r(s) = \begin{cases} \mathsf{ER}^{\mathsf{max}}_{\mathcal{M}_i}(\lozenge\{\bot\}) & \text{if } s \in \boldsymbol{S}_i, \\ r_\mathcal{M}(s) & \text{otherwise.} \end{cases}$$

*where $\mathcal{M}_i$ is the corresponding subMDP (see Definition 3) and $\sigma_i$ is an arbitrary but fixed optimal policy, i.e., a policy such that $\mathsf{ER}_{\mathcal{M}_i[\sigma_i]}(\lozenge G_i) = \mathsf{ER}^{\mathsf{max}}_{\mathcal{M}_i}(\lozenge G_i)$.*

Intuitively, we replace the transitions within $\mathbf{S}_i$ by a 'big-step semantics' that aggregates the transitions within $\mathbf{S}_i$ by single transitions such that the probability to reach any successor matches the probability to do so within $\mathbf{S}_i$ under a specific –optimal– policy. Likewise, the expected reward matches the expected reward collected in $\mathbf{S}_i$[1].

*Remark 1.* To define a *unique* macro-MDP, we can take the lexicographically smallest policy $\sigma_i$ among the optimal policies. Furthermore, we observe that for the cases covered by Proposition 1, it is not necessary to compute $\sigma_i$ at all: Either there is a single successor—implying $\mathsf{Pr}_{\mathcal{M}_i[\sigma_i]}(\lozenge\{s'\}) = 1$ for any $\sigma_i$—or $|\Sigma(\mathcal{M}_i)| = 1$.

The following theorem formalises that, given the assumptions, taking the big-step semantics is adequate when optimizing for an expected reward.

[1] Due to the additive nature of expected rewards, we can annotate the state with the expected reward even though it may differ over the different paths to an exit of $\mathbf{S}_i$.

**Theorem 1.** *Let $\mathcal{M}$ be a hMDP with optimal local subpolicies and let $\mu(\mathcal{M})$ be the corresponding macro-MDP. Then: $\mathsf{ER}^{max}_{\mu(\mathcal{M})}(\lozenge T) = \mathsf{ER}^{max}_{\mathcal{M}}(\lozenge T)$.*

The important ingredient are the optimal local subpolicies that ensure that we aggregate behavior within the partitions by behavior that agrees with a (globally) optimal policy. We give a proof in the appendix[2].

*Naive Algorithm.* Algorithmically, we first compute $\mathsf{ER}^{max}_{\mathcal{M}_i}(\lozenge T_i)$ and the associated policy $\sigma_i$, then compute the reachability probabilities on the induced Markov chain. We collect these results in a vector $\mathsf{res}_i$, which is helpful to construct the macro-MDP. To clarify further constructions in this paper, we make $\mathsf{res}_i$ explicit. Recall that $|\mathsf{succ}_{\mathcal{M}}(\mathbf{S}_i)| = Y$ for all $i$.

**Definition 6 (Results for subMDP).** *Let $\mathcal{M}_i$ be a subMDP for the partition $\mathbf{S}_i$ of a hMDP $\mathcal{M}$. Let $\mathsf{succ}_{\mathcal{M}}(\mathbf{S}_i)$ be ordered. We define $\mathsf{res}_i \in \mathbb{R}^{Y+1}$ s.t.*

$$\mathsf{res}_i(j) := \mathsf{Pr}_{\mathcal{M}_i[\sigma_i]}(\lozenge\{\mathsf{succ}_{\mathcal{M}}(\mathbf{S}_i)_j\}) \text{ for } 0 \leq j < Y \text{ and } \mathsf{res}_i(Y) := \mathsf{ER}^{max}_{\mathcal{M}_i}(\lozenge G_i),$$

*where $\sigma_i$ is an arbitrary but fixed policy such that $\mathsf{ER}_{\mathcal{M}_i[\sigma_i]}(\lozenge G_i) = \mathsf{ER}^{max}_{\mathcal{M}_i}(\lozenge G_i)$.*

This allows us to reformulate the macro-MDP, in particular, the following two identities do hold:

$$P(s,\alpha,s') = \begin{cases} \mathsf{res}_i(j) & \text{if } s \in \mathbf{S}_i \text{ and} \\ & \quad s' = \mathsf{succ}_{\mathcal{M}}(\mathbf{S}_i)_j \\ P_{\mathcal{M}}(s,\alpha,s') & \text{otherwise,} \end{cases} \qquad r(s) = \begin{cases} \mathsf{res}_i(Y) & \text{if } s \in \mathbf{S}_i, \\ r_{\mathcal{M}}(s) & \text{otherwise.} \end{cases} \tag{1}$$

The identities trivialize that constructing the macro-MDP can be done by precomputing the necessary result-vectors.

> **Enumeration baseline**: With macro-MDPs, we reduce the computation of $\mathsf{ER}^{max}_{\mathcal{M}}(\lozenge T)$ to (1) analysing all subMDPs $\mathcal{M}_i$ and (2) analysing $\mu(\mathcal{M})$.

This rather naive algorithm already limits memory and may exploit similarities between subMDPs during the analysis, e.g., based on the structure discussed in Sect. 4.4. It performs well if the number $|\mathbb{I}|$ of subMDPs is sufficiently small. We are interested in considering methods that allow for larger $\mathbb{I}$ or larger subMDPs. In particular, we want to avoid analysing all subMDPs, all individually.

### 4.2 The Uncertain Macro-MDP Formulation

*Uncertainty Before Computation.* We start introducing a method that allows providing bounds on the expected rewards after individually analysing a subset of the subMDPs. Before computing the individual probabilities in $\mathcal{M}_i$, we are *uncertain* about the probabilities and rewards in the MDP $\mu(\mathcal{M})$. Under this

[2] See: https://doi.org/10.48550/arXiv.2206.02653.

uncertainty, we may not be able to compute $\mathsf{ER}^{\max}_{\mu(\mathcal{M})}(\Diamond T)$ precisely. However, we may solve the problem statement by *bounding* the expected reward. Thus, the goal is to compute values lb, ub s.t.

$$\mathsf{lb} \leq \mathsf{ER}^{\max}_{\mathcal{M}}(\Diamond T) = \mathsf{ER}^{\max}_{\mu(\mathcal{M})}(\Diamond T) \leq \mathsf{ub}. \tag{2}$$

*Uncertain Macro-MDPs.* We capture the a-priori uncertainty about the sub-MDP results in an uncertain macro-MDP, a particularly shaped *parametric* MDP.

**Definition 7 (Uncertain macro-MDP).** *Let $\mathcal{M}$ be a hMDP with $n$ non-trivial $\boldsymbol{S}_i$ partitions and $S_\mathcal{M}$ partitioned as $S_\mathcal{M} = \bigcup \boldsymbol{S}_i \cup S'$. The* uncertain macro-MDP *is defined as $\nu(\mathcal{M}) := \langle S' \cup \{\mathsf{entry}_i \mid 1 \leq i \leq n\}, A_\mathcal{M}, \iota_\mathcal{M}, \vec{x}, P, r, T_\mathcal{M}\rangle$ with parameters $\vec{x} := \{p_{i,j}, q_i \mid 1 \leq i \leq n, 1 \leq j \leq Y\}$ where $Y = |\mathsf{succ}_\mathcal{M}(\boldsymbol{S}_i)|$. $P$ and $r$ given by*

$$P(s,\alpha,s') := \begin{cases} p_{i,j} & \text{if } s \in \boldsymbol{S}_i \text{ and} \\ & s' = \mathsf{succ}_\mathcal{M}(\boldsymbol{S}_i)_j, \\ P_\mathcal{M}(s,\alpha,s') & \text{otherwise,} \end{cases} \quad r(s) := \begin{cases} q_i & \text{if } s \in \boldsymbol{S}_i, \\ r_\mathcal{M}(s) & \text{otherwise.} \end{cases}$$

*Remark 2.* Whenever $\mathcal{M}_i$ and $\mathcal{M}_{i'}$ are isomorphic, we may reduce the parameters and replace each occurrence of $p_{i',j}$ with $p_{i,j}$ and each occurrence of $q_{i'}$ with $q_i$.

The uncertain macro-MDP can be instantiated to coincide with the macro-MDP by setting the parameters accordingly.

**Theorem 2.** *Let $\mathcal{M}$ be a hMDP, $\mu(\mathcal{M})$ the associated unique macro-MDP, and $\nu(\mathcal{M})$ the associated uncertain macro-MDP with parameters $p_{i,j}$ and $q_i$. Let $u^*$ be a parameter valuation with $u^*(p_{i,j}) = \mathsf{res}_i(j)$ and $u^*(q_i) = \mathsf{res}_i(Y)$ for all $i, j$. Then:*

$$\nu(\mathcal{M})[u^*] = \mu(\mathcal{M})$$

*Proof sketch.* The construction of the uncertain macro-MDP and the macro-MDP only differs in the assignment of probabilities. We set $u$ here as in the characterisation in (1) and thus the equality follows. □

*Computing Bounds.* Assume for now that we can derive some (trivial) sound bounds on the results vector for any subMDP $\mathcal{M}_i$[3].

**Definition 8 (Sound bounds on results).** *For $\mathcal{M}_i$, the vectors $\mathsf{lbres}_i$ and $\mathsf{ubres}_i$ are* sound bounds *if the following pointwise inequality holds*

$$\mathsf{lbres}_i \leq \mathsf{res}_i \leq \mathsf{ubres}_i. \tag{3}$$

[3] We discuss our approach in Sect. 4.4, alternatively, one may use bounds from, e.g., [4].

These bounds on properties in the subMDP correspond to bounds on the parameters of the uncertain macro-level MDP $\nu(\mathcal{M})$. Let us formalize this idea.

**Definition 9 (Suitable parameter region).** *Given $u^*$ from Theorem 2. The bounds $u^-, u^+$ are* suitable *if $u^- \leq u^* \leq u^+$. For suitable $u^-, u^+$, the region $[[u^-, u^+]]$ is called* suitable.

Using this notion, sound bounds $\mathsf{lbres}_i$ and $\mathsf{ubres}_i$ thus yield suitable bounds $u^-(x), u^+(x)$ for all $x \in \bigcup_j p_{i,j} \cup \{q_i\}$. Combined, the sound bounds for every $i$ yields a suitable region. Formally:

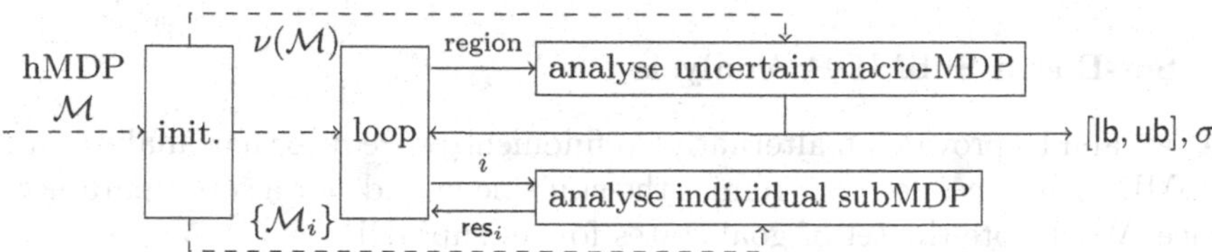


**Fig. 4.** Analysing hMDPs via uncertain macro-MDPs via individual refinement.

**Lemma 1.** *Given sound bounds $\mathsf{lbres}_i$, $\mathsf{ubres}_i$ for each $i$, there exists a trivial mapping $\mathsf{Reg}$ s.t. $\mathsf{Reg}(\mathsf{lbres}_1, \ldots \mathsf{lbres}_n, \mathsf{ubres}_1, \ldots \mathsf{ubres}_n)$ is a suitable region.*

With the suitable region we can apply verification on the parametric MDP.

**Lemma 2.** *Let $R$ be a suitable region. Then:*

$$\min_{u \in R} \mathsf{ER}^{\mathsf{max}}_{\nu(\mathcal{M})[u]}(\lozenge T) \leq \mathsf{ER}^{\mathsf{max}}_{\mathcal{M}}(\lozenge T) \leq \max_{u \in R} \mathsf{ER}^{\mathsf{max}}_{\nu(M)[u]}(\lozenge T).$$

*Proof sketch.* We observe that the inequalities follow from the fact that $u^* \in R$ with $u^*$ as in Theorem 2. By that theorem, $\mathsf{ER}^{\mathsf{max}}_{\nu(\mathcal{M})[u^*]}(\lozenge T) = \mathsf{ER}^{\mathsf{max}}_{\mu(\mathcal{M})}(\lozenge T)$. The statement then follows from Theorem 1. □

From the bounds that we can compute using a suitable region, we then set $\mathsf{lb}$ and $\mathsf{ub}$ for Eq. (2):

$$\mathsf{lb} \leq \min_{u \in R} \mathsf{ER}^{\mathsf{max}}_{\nu(\mathcal{M})[u]}(\lozenge T) \leq \mathsf{ER}^{\mathsf{max}}_{\mathcal{M}}(\lozenge T) \leq \max_{u \in R} \mathsf{ER}^{\mathsf{max}}_{\nu(M)[u]}(\lozenge T) \leq \mathsf{ub}. \qquad (4)$$

Computationally, we may use parameter lifting [33] to find these values.

*Refinement Loop.* The complete anytime algorithm is summarized in Fig. 4. We start with an hMDP $\mathcal{M}$ and extract the uncertain macro-MDP $\nu(\mathcal{M})$ and the subMDPs $\{\mathcal{M}_i\}$[4]. Furthermore we compute (trivial) sound bounds on $\mathsf{lbres}_i \leq \mathsf{res}_i \leq \mathsf{ubres}_i$. This leads to a suitable region $[[u^-, u^+]] = \mathsf{Reg}(\mathsf{lbres}_1, \mathsf{ubres}_1, \ldots)$. Then, we may at any time compute the bounds $\mathsf{lb}, \mathsf{ub}$ on the expected reward

[4] For efficiency, one must implement extraction without first computing an explicit representation of $\mathcal{M}$.

in the hMDP $\mathcal{M}$ by analysing $\nu(\mathcal{M})$ on the region $[[u^-, u^+]]$. To tighten these bounds, we must first refine the suitable region. Therefore, we analyse individual subMDPs $\mathcal{M}_i$ and compute $\mathsf{res}_i$ and thus $u^*(x)$ for $x \in \cup_j p_{i,j} \cup q_i$. This refines the suitable bounds such that $u^-(x) = u^*(x) = u^+(x)$ for $x \in \cup_j p_{i,j} \cup q_i$. We call this refinement *individual refinement*. The new region is suitable and Theorem 2 ensures correctness of the refinement. As we only have finitely many subMDPs, we obtain $\mathsf{lb} = \mathsf{ub}$ after finitely many steps.

**Anytime version of the enumeration baseline.** Individually refine any subset of subMDPs, then analyse the uncertain macro-MDP $\nu(\mathcal{M})$.

### 4.3 Set-Based SubMDP Analysis

Next, we aim to provide an alternative refinement procedure that analyses a set of subMDPs at once, i.e., that refines the suitable bounds for a set of parameters at once. We denote the set of goal states for all subMDPs as $G$[5].

*Adequate Abstractions.* We aim to compute sound bounds on the results for a set of subMDPs such that the bounds are sound for every individual subMDP in this set. We generalize Definition 8 as follows: The (lower and upper) bounds $\mathsf{lbres}_I, \mathsf{ubres}_I$ are *sound*, if they are sound (lower and upper) bounds for every $\mathsf{res}_i$, $i \in I$.

**Lemma 3.** *Let* $\mathsf{lbres}_I$ *satisfy the following inequations using* $0 \leq j < Y$*:*

$$\mathsf{lbres}_I(Y) \leq \min_i \mathsf{ER}^{\mathsf{max}}_{\mathcal{M}_i}(\Diamond G) \qquad \textit{and} \qquad \mathsf{lbres}_I(j) \leq \min_i \min_\sigma \mathsf{Pr}_{\mathcal{M}_i[\sigma]}(\Diamond G). \tag{5}$$

*Then,* $\mathsf{lbres}_I$ *is a sound lower bound.*

*Proof sketch.* We must show $\mathsf{lbres}_I \leq \mathsf{res}_i$ for each $i \in I$. By definition for each $1 \leq j \leq Y$, $\mathsf{lbres}_I(j) \leq \min_{i' \in I} \mathsf{res}_{i'}(j)$ and trivially $\min_{i' \in I} \mathsf{res}_{i'}(j) \leq \mathsf{res}_i(j)$. □

We omit the analogous statement for $\mathsf{ubres}$[6]. In Sect. 4.4, we discuss a particular approach to obtain these bounds, i.e., the right hand sides of the equations in Eq. 5. Here, we update the algorithm sketch to handle this alternative refinement.

*Remark 3.* We cannot compute the optimal policy $\sigma_i$ for the subMDP $\mathcal{M}_i$ in this setting. Thus, we must compute probability bounds for all policies, which may make these bounds weak. Some optimizations are possible as some actions can in fact be excluded. More importantly, however, is that for cases within Proposition 1 the policy $\sigma_i$ is irrelevant.

[5] Formally, we label the goal states and use $G$ to refer to denote those states.

[6] where min becomes max and inequalities flip.

*Updated Algorithm.* We update the loop from Fig. 4: Rather than refining using a single $i$, we refine using a set $I$. Instead of $\mathsf{res}_i$, we use Lemma 3 to compute sound bounds $\mathsf{lbres}_I$, $\mathsf{ubres}_I$ and call this *set-based refinement*. We may set $\mathsf{lbres}_i = \mathsf{lbres}_I$ for each $i \in I$. Then, we can compute a new suitable region via Lemma 1. With the suitable region, we can still utilise Eq. (4) to compute an approximation $[\mathsf{lb}, \mathsf{ub}]$. However, for completeness we must ensure that if $|I| = 1$, the upper and lower bounds coincide, i.e., $\mathsf{lbres}_{\{i\}} = \mathsf{ubres}_{\{i\}}$ for every $i$. That can be ensured by using individual subMDP refinement when $|I| = 1$.

**Idea:** We may improve the anytime algorithm by iteratively considering sets of subMDPs and extract sound bounds.

We now first discuss the set-based analysis of multiple subMDPs $\mathcal{M}_i$. We clarify the realization of the loop box in Sect. 5.

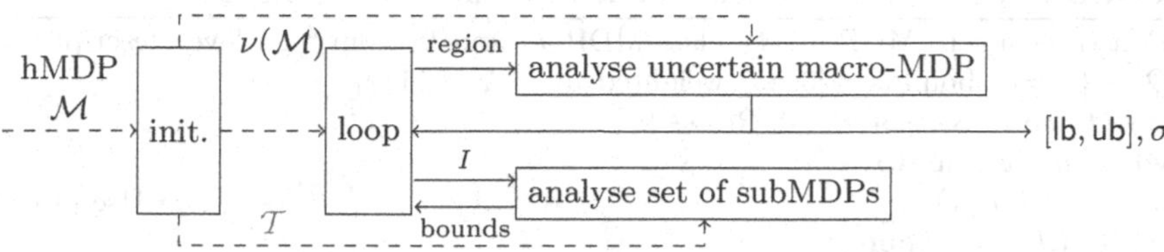


**Fig. 5.** Analysing hMDPs with set-based refinement on templated subMDPs.

### 4.4 Templates for Set-Based subMDP Analysis

We present an instance of set-based subMDP analysis where the subMDPs can be described as instantiations of a parametric MDPs.

*Parametric Templates.* We observe that the subMDPs are often similar, e.g., they define sending a file over a channel, exploring a room, in different conditions. We capture this similarity as follows: Let $\{\mathcal{T}_1, \dots \mathcal{T}_m\}$ define a set of parametric MDPs, where we call each pMDP a *template*. In particular, for a hierarchical MDP $\mathcal{M}$ with partitioning $\mathbf{S}_1, \dots \mathbf{S}_n$ and corresponding subMDPs $\mathcal{M}_1, \dots, \mathcal{M}_n$ a subMDP $\mathcal{M}_i$ is an instantiation of template $\mathcal{T}_j$ and parameter instantiation $v$[7], if $\mathcal{M}_i = \mathcal{T}_j[v]$. For a concise description, this paper considers hMDPs over a single template $\mathcal{T}$ and, for any $I \subseteq \mathbb{I}$, we denote $V_I := \{v_1, \dots, v_n\}$ the finite (multi)set of parameter instantiations for the pMDP $\mathcal{T}$ such that $\mathcal{T}[v_i] = \mathcal{M}_i$.

*Abstractions from Templates.* In terms of the templates, Lemma 3 requires us to bound the expected rewards $\mathsf{ER}^{\mathsf{max}}_{\mathcal{T}[v]}(\lozenge G)$ for all $v \in V_I$. We realize this by defining the smallest region $\mathsf{toRegion}(V_I) \supseteq V_I$. For this region, we obtain expected rewards by computing the minimum maximal reward in $\mathsf{toRegion}(V_I)$. That is:

$$\mathsf{lbres}_I(Y) := \min_{v \in \mathsf{toRegion}(V_I)} \mathsf{ER}^{\mathsf{max}}_{\mathcal{T}[v]}(\lozenge G) \quad \leq \quad \min_i \mathsf{ER}^{\mathsf{max}}_{\mathcal{M}_i}(\lozenge G).$$

[7] We use $v$ instead of $u$ to avoid confusion with the instantiations for pMDP $\nu(\mathcal{M})$.

We handle the probabilities equally while taking into account the quantification over the policies. Following Lemma 3, these bounds are sound. Upper bounds are handled analogously. Computationally, we again use parameter lifting [33] to find these bounds. We can easily refine: Whenever we split $I$ (or equally, $V_I$), we can compute (potentially) smaller regions $\mathsf{toRegion}(V_I)$.

In Fig. 5, we depict our method. In contrast to Fig. 4, we pass the template $\mathcal{T}$ rather than the individual subMDPs. Furthermore, we now compute initial sound bounds via the analysis of the template (i.e., of $V_I$) and must pass the mapping from $I$ to $V_I$ to clarify the shape of the subMDPs.

> **Abstraction-Refinement** on the subMDPs provides increasingly tight suitable regions for the uncertain macro-MDP from the anytime baseline.

**Algorithm 1.** Algorithm for Abstraction-Refinement Procedure

Construct macro-MDP $\nu(\mathcal{M})$, class-MDP $\mathcal{T}$, and $V_{\mathbb{I}}$ from high-level description.<br>
$Q \leftarrow \{\langle I = \mathbb{I}, \text{bounds} = [0, \infty), \text{weightedvals} = \mathbb{I} \to \{1\}\rangle\}$<br>
$\mathsf{lb} \leftarrow 0$; $\mathsf{ub} \leftarrow \infty$; $\#\text{iter} = 0$; $\text{Res} \leftarrow \emptyset$<br>
**while** $\eta \cdot \mathsf{ub} > \mathsf{lb}$ **do**<br>
    $R \leftarrow Q.pop()$ ▷ Use priority<br>
    **if** $R.I = \{i\}$ **then**<br>
        $\text{Res}[i] \leftarrow \mathit{check\_one}(\mathcal{T}[v_i])$ ▷ Computes $\mathsf{res}_i$<br>
    **else**<br>
        $R.\mathit{bounds} \leftarrow \mathit{check\_set}(\mathcal{T}, \mathsf{toRegion}(V_{R.I}))$ ▷ Computes $\mathsf{lbres}_{R.I}, \mathsf{ubres}_{R.I}$<br>
        $Q \leftarrow Q \cup \mathit{split}(R)$ ▷ Split $R.I$, keep bounds and weights<br>
    **end if**<br>
    **if** $\#\text{iter}$ *mod* $k = 1$ or $Q$ is empty **then**<br>
        $R' \leftarrow \mathsf{Reg}(\mathit{extract}(Q, \text{Res}))$ ▷ Compute suitable region via Lem 1<br>
        $\mathsf{lb}, \mathsf{ub} \leftarrow \mathit{check\_set}(\nu(\mathcal{M}), R')$<br>
    **end if**<br>
**end while**

## 5 Implementing the Abstraction-Refinement Loop

Algorithm 1 outlines a basic implementation of the idea sketched in Fig. 5. We detail this implementation and then discuss an essential improvement.

We construct $\nu(\mathcal{M})$, $\mathcal{T}$, and (the implicit) mapping $V : \mathbb{I} \to V_{\mathbb{I}}$ to map subMDPs to instantiations of $\mathcal{T}$ from a suitable high-level representation. We initialize a priority queue with triples that represent sets of template instantiations: $I$ such that $V_I := \{v_i := V(i) \mid i \in I\}$ contains all valuations $v$ such that $\mathcal{T}[v]$ is a subMDP of $\mathcal{M}$. We initially store bounds reflecting $\mathsf{lbres}_I$ and $\mathsf{ubres}_I$ as well as weights for the computation of the priority (see below). Initially, we assume that $\mathsf{lb} = 0$ and $\mathsf{ub} = \infty$, we count the number of iterations in $\#\text{iter}$. Res is map for storing result vectors. The algorithm now refines $\mathsf{lb}$ and $\mathsf{ub}$ until the gap between $\mathsf{lb}$ and $\mathsf{ub}$ is sufficiently small.

The main loop now iteratively refines $\mathsf{lb}, \mathsf{ub}$ by first refining $\mathsf{lbres}_I$ and $\mathsf{ubres}_I$, by splitting $I$ and model checking $\mathcal{T}$ w.r.t. subsequently smaller regions $\mathsf{toRegion}(V_I)$ (l. 5-11): Therefore, we take a set $R$ from the queue. If $R.I = \{i\}$ is a singleton, we compute $\mathsf{lbres}_{R.I} = \mathsf{res}_i = \mathsf{ubres}_{R.I}$ and store this result. Otherwise, we apply model checking to the pMDP $\mathcal{T}$ w.r.t. the region representation of $R.I$. We then split $R.I$, by splitting $I$ into (here) two subsets. For splitting $I$, we use the geometric interpretation of $\mathsf{toRegion}(V_I)$ as a subset of $\mathbb{R}^{|\vec{y}|}$, where we then split along one of the axis into two equally large subsets. Every $k$ (we use $k = 8$) iterations, we analyse the macro-MDP (l. 12-15). From $Q$ and Res we extract the proper bounds $\mathsf{lbres}_i, \mathsf{ubres}_i$ from $Res[i]$ if possible and from $Q$ using $R$.bounds for $R$ such that $i \in R.I$ otherwise. Then via $\mathsf{Reg}(\mathsf{lbres}_1, \mathsf{ubres}_1, \ldots)$ from Lemma 1 we compute a suitable region $R'$. We analyse the uncertain macro-MDP to obtain $\mathsf{lb}$ and $\mathsf{ub}$ in accordance with Eq. (4).

Finally, we discuss the priority function: If we a-priori naively assume that each subMDP contributes an equal amount to the overal minimal expected reward in the hMDP (weights are all one) then the following priority function: $|R.\text{bounds}| \cdot \sum_{v \in I} \text{R.weights}(v)$ computes priorities that correlate with how much computing $\mathsf{res}_i$ for all $i \in I$ would reduce the gap between $\mathsf{lb}$ and $\mathsf{ub}$.

*Termination and Correctness Argument.* Algorithm 1 terminates. We split in such way that $\max_{I \in Q} |I|$ monotonically decreases. Thus, eventually $Q$ is empty and Res contains results for all subMDPs. Then, $R'$ is a point region and checking $\nu(\mathcal{M})$ with this point region ensures that $\mathsf{lb} = \mathsf{ub}$. Correctness follows as $R'$ is always suitable, see Eq. (4).

*Computing Expected Visits.* Based on our empirical evaluation we added one crucial improvement: While the algorithm above assumed that all subMDPs (or states in the macro-MDP) are equally important, that assumption is generally inadequate. Roughly, only states reached by the optimal policy contribute at all (provided the bounds are tight enough that we can identify these states). The reachable states are weighted by the expected number of visits of these states. We compute an approximation of this expected number of visit by computing the currently optimizing policy (a by-product of l. 13) and compute the center of $R'$; this results in a MC for which we can compute the number of expected visits by a standard equation system [32]. Additionally, we update the weights for the regions in the queue based on these new results. We remark that this also makes the priority function more useful.

*Interleaving Individual Refinement.* Furthermore, for a subMDPs for which the expected number of visits is large[8] are individually analysed (and the points are removed from the region in the queue). This optimization reduces the need to split the corresponding regions until we obtain tight bounds.

[8] In our implementation, we define this as subMDPs where the expected number of visits is in the top $1 + 1/16 \cdot \#\text{iter}$ percent, but not more than 150 at a time.

## 6 Experiments

*Implementation.* We implemented LEVEL-UP[9], a prototype on top of the python bindings for Storm [20]. LEVEL-UP analyses hierarchical MDPs by taking two MDPs, each provided as probabilistic program descriptions in the PRISM format: One MDP that encodes the (uncertain) macro-MDP and one that describes the parametric template for the subMDPs. The parameter instance of the subMDP can be deduced as a function of the high-level variable assignment of the macro-MDP states. For technical reasons, the prototype currently provides support for subMDPs with one or two successor states – arguably the setting in which we expect our prototype to perform best. For subMDPs with a single successor state, the uncertain macro-MDP may be represented as an (parameter-free) MDP with interval-valued rewards. For two successors, we include support of the extension of Sect. 3.3 where the successor aims to optimize reaching a fixed successor state.

**Table 1.** Benchmark statistics, runtimes of the approaches, and details for Algorithm 1.

| Name | Inst | $\lvert S_{\mathcal{M}}\rvert$ | $\lvert\mathbb{I}\rvert$ | $\lvert S_{\mu(\mathcal{M})}\rvert$ | $\lvert A_{\mu(\mathcal{M})}\rvert$ | $\lvert S_{\mathcal{T}}\rvert$ | $\lvert A_{\mathcal{T}}\rvert$ | $t_{\text{init}}$ | $t_{\text{enum}}$ | $t_{50}$ | $t_{90}$ | $t_{95}$ | iter. | indrf. | um % | sr % | ir % |
|---|---|---|---|---|---|---|---|---|---|---|---|---|---|---|---|---|---|
| corr | 11,10,50 | $10^7$ | 624 | 255576 | 541704 | 15000 | 65006 | < 1 | 16 | 3 | 9 | **13** | 17 | 14 | 2 | 67 | 2 |
| corr | 11,8,100 | $10^8$ | 624 | 254376 | 539040 | 60000 | 260006 | < 1 | 100 | 10 | 45 | **45** | 9 | 16 | 2 | 80 | 4 |
| corr | 11,8,200 | $10^8$ | 624 | 254376 | 539040 | 240000 | 1040006 | 2 | 689 | 51 | 313 | **568** | 17 | 30 | 0 | 92 | 4 |
| corr | 13,11,50 | $10^7$ | 768 | 1024344 | 2172432 | 15000 | 65006 | 3 | 21 | 8 | **18** | 25 | 17 | 17 | 5 | 36 | 1 |
| corrl | 17,14,75 | $10^8$ | 1056 | 34200 | 83160 | 33750 | 146256 | < 1 | 90 | 4 | 21 | **38** | 17 | 43 | 0 | 84 | 8 |
| corrl | 18,15,75 | $10^8$ | 1128 | 39576 | 96768 | 33750 | 146256 | < 1 | 98 | 4 | 38 | **38** | 17 | 45 | 0 | 84 | 8 |
| corrl | 25,20,75 | $10^8$ | 1632 | 89136 | 224160 | 33750 | 146256 | < 1 | 168 | 5 | 44 | **67** | 25 | 102 | 1 | 80 | 14 |
| mail | 10 | $10^9$ | 173857 | 793971 | 1088152 | 2801 | 3601 | 4 | 552 | 8 | 21 | **48** | 57 | 658 | 29 | 2 | 4 |
| mail | 12 | $10^9$ | 236802 | 1446551 | 2023504 | 2801 | 3601 | 8 | 738 | 16 | 43 | **130** | 97 | 703 | 42 | 1 | 2 |
| netw | 30,50 | $10^8$ | 9801 | 437823 | 437823 | 4026 | 4026 | 1 | 23 | **8** | 33 | 46 | 217 | 150 | 60 | 1 | 1 |
| netw | 30,80 | $10^8$ | 9801 | 437823 | 437823 | 10041 | 10041 | 1 | 62 | 8 | 34 | **48** | 217 | 150 | 59 | 3 | 3 |
| netw | 50,80 | $10^8$ | 9801 | 1025883 | 1025883 | 10041 | 10041 | 2 | 62 | **16** | 94 | 112 | 225 | 150 | 62 | 1 | 1 |
| sdn | 5,12,4,4 | $10^8$ | 23375 | 128386 | 128386 | 13506 | 16855 | < 1 | 62 | 2 | **20** | 112 | 289 | 305 | 2 | 17 | 11 |
| sdn | 5,8,4,4 | $10^8$ | 23375 | 128386 | 128386 | 2802 | 3455 | < 1 | 98 | 1 | 5 | **15** | 281 | 305 | 13 | 17 | 8 |
| sdn | 6,8,4,4 | $10^9$ | 126337 | 408227 | 408227 | 2802 | 3455 | 2 | 519 | 5 | 46 | **394** | 3057 | 305 | 27 | 7 | 0 |

*Setup.* We investigate the scalability and the quality of the approximation over time. Therefore, we run our prototype on an MacBook 2020 M1 with an 8 GB RAM limit. We compare the enumerative baseline from Sect. 4.1 with Algorithm 1. Both exploit the hierarchical nature of the MDP. We qualitatively compare to standard model checking on the flat MDP, see below. We use a collection of benchmarks reflecting networks, job schedulers and robots.

*Results.* We consider instances that we summarize in Table 1. In particular, we give the benchmark name and instance for reference, the approximate number of states in the hierarchical MDP (computed from the macro-MDP and the

[9] The source code and executables, the benchmarks, logfiles and utilities are all available in an archived Docker container: https://doi.org/10.5281/zenodo.6524787.

subMDPs), the number of nontrivial partitions, and the number of states and actions in the (uncertain) macro-MDP and subMDPs, respectively. Then, we give the time to setup the data structures from the high-level representation $t_{\text{init}}$ in seconds. We highlight that a flat representation of all our benchmarks has at least $10^7$, often more, states. As a reference, we present the performance of the enumerative baseline from Sect. 4.1. The performance of this approach is positive as it enables the verification of huge MDPs. A TO indicates >1200 s. To scale to either larger subMDPs or more subMDPs, we use the abstraction-refinement loop. To reflect the anytime nature, we list three run times for terminating when $\eta \cdot \mathsf{ub} \leq \mathsf{lb}$ with $\eta \in \{0.5, 0.9, 0.95\}$ respectively. The largest time faster than the enumerative baseline is highlighted (further to the right is better for the abstraction-refinement). For $\eta = 0.95$, we give details: The number of iterations (iter), the number of individual refinements based on the improvement from Sect. 5, and the fraction of time spent on model checking the uncertain macro-MDPs $\%_{\text{um}}$, the set-refinements $\%_{\text{sr}}$, and the individual refinements $\%_{\text{ir}}$, respectively.

*Discussion.* Before we discuss details of the results, let us clarify that *exploiting the hierarchical structure is essential.* MDPs with $\approx 10^8$ states are at the limit of what fits in around 8GB of memory[10]. Symbolic methods based on MTBDDs easily scale beyond these sizes, but—noting that the subMDPs are all slightly different—the models we consider lack the necessary symmetry that make MTBDDs compact. Thus, support for hierarchical MDPs is a necessary step forward.

Regarding the abstraction-refinement: While a larger study may be necessary, we can start with two standard observations: The abstraction-refinement loop is significantly faster on $\eta \leq 0.9$. As $\eta \rightarrow 1$, coarse abstractions are insufficient. Furthermore, the efficiency of the abstraction-refinement heavily depends on the particular structure. That being said, the approach outperforms the enumerative approach, especially for $\eta = 0.9$, and up to more than an order of magnitude. This happens even if $\mathbb{I}$ is rather small, or if, e.g., $\mathcal{T}$ is small. We furthermore observe that for large $\mathbb{I}$, the bookkeeping in python becomes a bottleneck. We think these observations are promising: we left many options for further optimizations and tweaking towards particular examples on the table. However, for models where most time is spent on model checking the macro-level MDP, the approach is less suitable. We furthermore conjecture that tailored algorithms may exploit some of these dimensions, e.g., when there is the macro-MDP or the subMDPs are indeed MCs or perhaps acyclic, depending on the number of parameters and their influence [36], or based on the relative weight of the uncertain rewards compared to rewards in the macro-MDP.

## 7 Related Work

In the model-free reinforcement learning (RL) setting, hierarchical models are popular. An excellent, recent survey is given in [29]. Our work generalizes the

[10] Assuming 128 byte per state, i.e., 8 doubles and 16 (32-bit) ints, as used in Storm.

solution techniques on hierarchical MDPs that assume that these subMDPs are the same. In RL, this assumption is treated liberally, and the methods provide only weak error bounds. In contrast, our model-based approach provides error-bounds in every step, and the error disappears in finitely many steps.

Hierarchical abstractions are used to analyse large MDPs in [5]. There, the goal is to find a policy that almost optimizes the reward. Rather than preimposing a hierarchy, the algorithm aims to find a hierarchy and define the goal states of the subMDP such that the model admits local policies. Instead, our solution can find the optimal policy and in particular gives strict error bounds at the cost of requiring a high-level model that induces the hierarchy. An symbolic approach for continuous MDP, where the transition probabilities are the result of an associated LP, has recently been discussed in [24]. An hierarchical SCC-decomposition [1] aims to accelerate the process of solving a (given, monolithic) Markov chain. The computation of reward-bounded properties [18] generalizes topological value iteration and their notion of episodes mildly resembles an hierarchical approach but no uncertainty is assumed or used in the approach. The probabilistic model checker PAT [35] analyses a hierarchical probabilistic timed automaton given as a process algebra. The hierarchy is not exploited in the solving process.

While symbolic approaches, often on decision diagrams, exploit the transition system by compressing the data structures, abstractions aim to yield smaller systems that may assess an approximation for the sought-for values. Abstraction-refinement without an imposed hierarchy is explored in [16,21,25]: Refinement amounts to considering a better approximation of the state space. In contrast, we impose the hierarchy, the abstraction amounts to an imprecise analysis of this fixed state space and we refine by analysing the state space more precisely (by means of analysing subMDPs at a greater level of detail). Contract-based abstractions (in probabilistic systems) are used to decompose the analysis of systems given by parallel running subsystems [14,28,38]. Partial exploration and bounded model checking approaches focus on the most critical paths, i.e., the paths where most of the probability mass lies [7,23,26], but these approaches do generally not exploit the hierarchical and repetitive structure. The observation that many parts of the system are not critical allows us to weigh the potential benefit of refining the intervals in various parts of the macro-MDP.

Parametric MDPs are commonly used to model and analyse the effects of uncertainty in the precise transitions [15,23,31]. The methods presented in [13,22] exploit a repetitive structure in parametric MCs to accelerate the construction of closed form solutions and are not applicable to MDPs. Parametric models have been used to support the design of systems [2,8] or their adaption [6,9], to find policies for partially observable systems [11], to analyse Bayesian networks [34], and to speed up the analysis of, e.g., software product lines [10,37]. On top of technical differences, none of these approaches uses a hierarchical decomposition of an MDP or uses the results of the analysis in the analysis of a larger MDP.

## 8 Conclusion

This paper presents a first verification approach that exploits a specific hierarchical structure natural in many models to accelerate analysing the underlying MDP. An essential ingredient is to separate the two levels in the hierarchy. Then, when analysing the (toplevel) macro-MDP, we may consider subMDPs that have not yet been analysed as epistemic uncertainty. Analysis techniques for uncertain (more precise: parametric) MDPs then enable an online approximation loop that incrementally removes uncertainty in a targeted fashion by analysing more and more subMDPs (more) precisely. Three clear directions for future work are to (i) consider an approach where one lifts the restrictions to locally-optimal policies, (ii) investigate the applicability to a richer set of temporal properties and (iii) to allow automatic detection of partitions in, e.g., the Prism language.

## References

1. Ábrahám, E., Jansen, N., Wimmer, R., Katoen, J.-P., Becker, B.: DTMC model checking by SCC reduction. In: QEST, pp. 37–46. IEEE CS (2010)
2. Andriushchenko, R., Češka, M., Junges, S., Katoen, J.-P.: Inductive synthesis for probabilistic programs reaches new horizons. In: TACAS 2021. LNCS, vol. 12651, pp. 191–209. Springer, Cham (2021). https://doi.org/10.1007/978-3-030-72016-2_11
3. Baier, C., Katoen, J.-P.: Principles of Model Checking. MIT Press, Cambridge (2008)
4. Baier, C., Klein, J., Leuschner, L., Parker, D., Wunderlich, S.: Ensuring the reliability of your model checker: interval iteration for markov decision processes. In: Majumdar, R., Kunčak, V. (eds.) CAV 2017. LNCS, vol. 10426, pp. 160–180. Springer, Cham (2017). https://doi.org/10.1007/978-3-319-63387-9_8
5. Barry, J.L., Kaelbling, L.P., Lozano-Pérez, T.: DetH*: approximate hierarchical solution of large Markov decision processes. In IJCAI, pp. 1928–1935. IJCAI/AAAI (2011)
6. Bartocci, E., Grosu, R., Katsaros, P., Ramakrishnan, C.R., Smolka, S.A.: Model repair for probabilistic systems. In: Abdulla, P.A., Leino, K.R.M. (eds.) TACAS 2011. LNCS, vol. 6605, pp. 326–340. Springer, Heidelberg (2011). https://doi.org/10.1007/978-3-642-19835-9_30
7. Brázdil, T., et al.: Verification of Markov decision processes using learning algorithms. In: Cassez, F., Raskin, J.-F. (eds.) ATVA 2014. LNCS, vol. 8837, pp. 98–114. Springer, Cham (2014). https://doi.org/10.1007/978-3-319-11936-6_8
8. Calinescu, R., Ceska, M., Gerasimou, S., Kwiatkowska, M., Paoletti, N.: Efficient synthesis of robust models for stochastic systems. J. Syst. Softw. **143**, 140–158 (2018)
9. Chen, T., Hahn, E.M., Han, T., Kwiatkowska, M.Z., Qu, H., Zhang, L.: Model repair for Markov decision processes. In: TASE, pp. 85–92. IEEE CS (2013)
10. Chrszon, P., Dubslaff, C., Klüppelholz, S., Baier, C.: ProFeat: feature-oriented engineering for family-based probabilistic model checking. Formal Aspects Comput. **30**(1), 45–75 (2018)
11. Cubuktepe, M., Jansen, N., Junges, S., Marandi, A., Suilen, M., Topcu, U.: Robust finite-state controllers for uncertain POMDPs. In: AAAI, pp. 11792–11800. AAAI Press (2021)

12. Dombrowski, C., Junges, S., Katoen, J.-P., Gross, J.: Model-checking assisted protocol design for ultra-reliable low-latency wireless networks. In: SRDS, pp. 307–316. IEEE CS (2016)
13. Fang, X., Calinescu, R., Gerasimou, S., Alhwikem, F.: Fast parametric model checking through model fragmentation. In: ICSE, pp. 835–846. IEEE (2021)
14. Feng, L., Han, T., Kwiatkowska, M., Parker, D.: Learning-based compositional verification for synchronous probabilistic systems. In: Bultan, T., Hsiung, P.-A. (eds.) ATVA 2011. LNCS, vol. 6996, pp. 511–521. Springer, Heidelberg (2011). https://doi.org/10.1007/978-3-642-24372-1_40
15. Hahn, E.M., Hermanns, H., Wachter, B., Zhang, L.: PARAM: a model checker for parametric Markov models. In: Touili, T., Cook, B., Jackson, P. (eds.) CAV 2010. LNCS, vol. 6174, pp. 660–664. Springer, Heidelberg (2010). https://doi.org/10.1007/978-3-642-14295-6_56
16. Hahn, E.M., Hermanns, H., Wachter, B., Zhang, L.: PASS: abstraction refinement for infinite probabilistic models. In: Esparza, J., Majumdar, R. (eds.) TACAS 2010. LNCS, vol. 6015, pp. 353–357. Springer, Heidelberg (2010). https://doi.org/10.1007/978-3-642-12002-2_30
17. Hartmanns, A., Hermanns, H.: The modest toolset: an integrated environment for quantitative modelling and verification. In: Ábrahám, E., Havelund, K. (eds.) TACAS 2014. LNCS, vol. 8413, pp. 593–598. Springer, Heidelberg (2014). https://doi.org/10.1007/978-3-642-54862-8_51
18. Hartmanns, A., Junges, S., Katoen, J.-P., Quatmann, T.: Multi-cost bounded tradeoff analysis in MDP. J. Autom. Reason. **64**(7), 1483–1522 (2020)
19. Hauskrecht, M., Meuleau, N., Kaelbling, L.P., Dean, T.L., Boutilier, C.: Hierarchical solution of Markov decision processes using macro-actions. In: UAI, pp. 220–229. Morgan Kaufmann (1998)
20. Hensel, C., Junges, S., Katoen, J.-P., Quatmann, T., Volk, M.: The probabilistic model checker storm. CoRR, abs/2002.07080 (2020)
21. Hermanns, H., Wachter, B., Zhang, L.: Probabilistic CEGAR. In: Gupta, A., Malik, S. (eds.) CAV 2008. LNCS, vol. 5123, pp. 162–175. Springer, Heidelberg (2008). https://doi.org/10.1007/978-3-540-70545-1_16
22. Jansen, N., et al.: Accelerating parametric probabilistic verification. In: Norman, G., Sanders, W. (eds.) QEST 2014. LNCS, vol. 8657, pp. 404–420. Springer, Cham (2014). https://doi.org/10.1007/978-3-319-10696-0_31
23. Jansen, N., Dehnert, C., Kaminski, B.L., Katoen, J.-P., Westhofen, L.: Bounded model checking for probabilistic programs. In: Artho, C., Legay, A., Peled, D. (eds.) ATVA 2016. LNCS, vol. 9938, pp. 68–85. Springer, Cham (2016). https://doi.org/10.1007/978-3-319-46520-3_5
24. Jeong, J., Jaggi, P., Sanner, S.: Symbolic dynamic programming for continuous state MDPs with linear program transitions. In: IJCAI, pp. 4083–4089. ijcai.org (2021)
25. Kattenbelt, M., Kwiatkowska, M.Z., Norman, G., Parker, D.: A game-based abstraction-refinement framework for Markov decision processes. Formal Methods Syst. Des. **36**(3), 246–280 (2010)
26. Kretínský, J., Meggendorfer, T.: Of cores: a partial-exploration framework for Markov decision processes. Log. Methods Comput. Sci. **16**(4) (2020)
27. Kwiatkowska, M., Norman, G., Parker, D.: PRISM 4.0: verification of probabilistic real-time systems. In: Gopalakrishnan, G., Qadeer, S. (eds.) CAV 2011. LNCS, vol. 6806, pp. 585–591. Springer, Heidelberg (2011). https://doi.org/10.1007/978-3-642-22110-1_47

28. Kwiatkowska, M., Norman, G., Parker, D., Qu, H.: Assume-guarantee verification for probabilistic systems. In: Esparza, J., Majumdar, R. (eds.) TACAS 2010. LNCS, vol. 6015, pp. 23–37. Springer, Heidelberg (2010). https://doi.org/10.1007/978-3-642-12002-2_3
29. Pateria, S., Subagdja, B., Tan, A.-H., Quek, C.: Hierarchical reinforcement learning: a comprehensive survey. ACM Comput. Surv. **54**(5), 109:1–109:35 (2021)
30. Precup, D., Sutton, R.S.: Multi-time models for temporally abstract planning. In: NIPS, pp. 1050–1056. The MIT Press (1997)
31. Puggelli, A., Li, W., Sangiovanni-Vincentelli, A.L., Seshia, S.A.: Polynomial-time verification of PCTL properties of MDPs with convex uncertainties. In: Sharygina, N., Veith, H. (eds.) CAV 2013. LNCS, vol. 8044, pp. 527–542. Springer, Heidelberg (2013). https://doi.org/10.1007/978-3-642-39799-8_35
32. Puterman, M.L.: Markov Decision Processes: Discrete Stochastic Dynamic Programming. Wiley, Hoboken (1995)
33. Quatmann, T., Dehnert, C., Jansen, N., Junges, S., Katoen, J.-P.: Parameter synthesis for Markov models: faster than ever. In: Artho, C., Legay, A., Peled, D. (eds.) ATVA 2016. LNCS, vol. 9938, pp. 50–67. Springer, Cham (2016). https://doi.org/10.1007/978-3-319-46520-3_4
34. Salmani, B., Katoen, J.-P.: Fine-tuning the odds in Bayesian networks. In: Vejnarová, J., Wilson, N. (eds.) ECSQARU 2021. LNCS (LNAI), vol. 12897, pp. 268–283. Springer, Cham (2021). https://doi.org/10.1007/978-3-030-86772-0_20
35. Song, S., Sun, J., Liu, Y., Dong, J.S.: A model checker for hierarchical probabilistic real-time systems. In: Madhusudan, P., Seshia, S.A. (eds.) CAV 2012. LNCS, vol. 7358, pp. 705–711. Springer, Heidelberg (2012). https://doi.org/10.1007/978-3-642-31424-7_53
36. Spel, J., Junges, S., Katoen, J.-P.: Finding provably optimal Markov chains. In: TACAS 2021. LNCS, vol. 12651, pp. 173–190. Springer, Cham (2021). https://doi.org/10.1007/978-3-030-72016-2_10
37. ter Beek, M.H., Legay, A.: Quantitative variability modelling and analysis. Int. J. Softw. Tools Technol. Transfer **21**(6), 607–612 (2019). https://doi.org/10.1007/s10009-019-00535-1
38. Xu, D.N., Gössler, G., Girault, A.: Probabilistic contracts for component-based design. In: Bouajjani, A., Chin, W.-N. (eds.) ATVA 2010. LNCS, vol. 6252, pp. 325–340. Springer, Heidelberg (2010). https://doi.org/10.1007/978-3-642-15643-4_24

# Formal Methods for Neural Networks

# Shared Certificates for Neural Network Verification

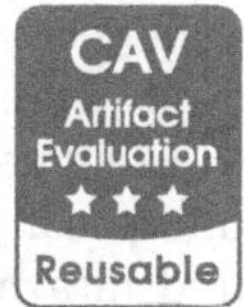

Marc Fischer[1](✉), Christian Sprecher[2], Dimitar Iliev Dimitrov[1], Gagandeep Singh[3], and Martin Vechev[1]

[1] ETH Zurich, Zürich, Switzerland
{marc.fischer,dimitar.iliev.dimitrov,martin.vechev}@inf.ethz.ch
[2] Nostic Solutions AG, Freienbach, Switzerland
christian.sprecher@nostic.ch
[3] University of Illinois at Urbana-Champaign & VMware Research, Champaign, USA
ggnds@illinois.edu

**Abstract.** Existing neural network verifiers compute a proof that each input is handled correctly under a given perturbation by propagating a symbolic abstraction of reachable values at each layer. This process is repeated from scratch independently for each input (e.g., image) and perturbation (e.g., rotation), leading to an expensive overall proof effort when handling an entire dataset. In this work, we introduce a new method for reducing this verification cost without losing precision based on a key insight that abstractions obtained at intermediate layers for different inputs and perturbations can overlap or contain each other. Leveraging our insight, we introduce the general concept of shared certificates, enabling proof effort reuse across multiple inputs to reduce overall verification costs. We perform an extensive experimental evaluation to demonstrate the effectiveness of shared certificates in reducing the verification cost on a range of datasets and attack specifications on image classifiers including the popular patch and geometric perturbations. We release our implementation at https://github.com/eth-sri/proof-sharing.

**Keywords:** Neural Network Verification · Local Verification · Adversarial Robustness

## 1 Introduction

The success of neural networks across a wide range of application domains [21,30] has led to their widespread application and study. Despite this success, neural networks remain vulnerable to adversarial attacks [8,23] which raises concerns over their trustworthiness in safety-critical settings such as autonomous driving and medical devices. To overcome this barrier, formal verification of neural networks has been proposed as a key technology in the literature [39]. As a result,

M. Fischer and C. Sprecher—Equal contribution.
C. Sprecher—Work performed while at ETH Zurich.


S. Shoham and Y. Vizel (Eds.): CAV 2022, LNCS 13371, pp. 127–148, 2022.
https://doi.org/10.1007/978-3-031-13185-1_7

recent years have witnessed a growing interest in verifying critical safety properties of neural networks (e.g., fairness, robustness) [14,17,18,31,32,40,42] specified using pre and post conditions over network inputs and outputs respectively. Conceptually, existing verifiers propagate sets of inputs in the precondition captured in symbolic form (e.g., convex sets) through the network, an expensive process that produces over-approximations of all possible values at intermediate layers. The final abstraction of the output can then be used to check postconditions. The key technical challenge all existing verifiers aim to address is speeding up and scaling the certification process, i.e., faster and more efficient propagation of symbolic shapes while reducing the overapproximation error.

*This Work: Accelerating Certification via Proof Sharing.* In this work, we propose a new, complementary method for accelerating neural network verification based on the key observation that instead of treating each certification attempt in isolation as existing verifiers do, we can reuse proof effort among multiple such attempts, thus obtaining significant overall speed-ups without losing precision. Figure 1 illustrates both, standard verification and the concept of proof sharing.

In standard verification an input region $\mathcal{I}_1(\boldsymbol{x})$ (orange square) is propagated from left to right, obtaining intermediate shapes at each intermediate layer (here the goal is to verify all points in the input region are classified as "cat" by the neural network $N$). We observe that the abstraction obtained for a new region $\mathcal{I}_2(\boldsymbol{x})$ (e.g., blue shapes) can be contained inside existing abstractions from $\mathcal{I}_1(\boldsymbol{x})$, an effect we term *proof subsumption.* This effect can be observed both between abstractions obtained from different specifications (e.g., $\ell_\infty$ and adversarial patches) for the same data point and between proofs for the same property but different, yet semantically similar inputs. Building on this observation, we introduce the notion of proof sharing via templates. Proof sharing works in two steps: first, we leverage abstractions from existing proofs in order to create templates, and second, we augment the verifier with these templates, stopping the expensive propagation at an intermediate layer as soon as the newly generated abstraction is included inside an existing template. Key technical ingredients to the effectiveness of our approach are fast template generation and inclusion checking techniques. We experimentally demonstrate that proof sharing can achieve significant speed-ups in challenging scenarios including proving robustness to adversarial patches [10] and geometric perturbations [3] across different neural network architectures.

*Main Contributions.* Our key contributions are:

- An introduction and formalization of the concept of proof sharing in neural network verification: the idea that some proofs capture others (Sect. 3).
- A general framework leveraging the above concept, enabling proof effort reuse via proof templates (Sect. 4).
- A thorough experimental evaluation involving verification of neural network robustness against challenging adversarial patch and geometric perturbations, demonstrating that our methods can achieve proof match rates of up 95% as well as provide non-trivial end-to-end certification speed-ups (Sect. 5).

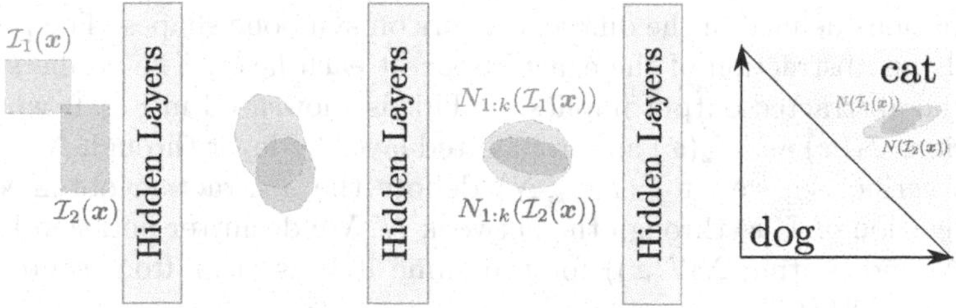


**Fig. 1.** Visualization of neural network verification. The input regions $\mathcal{I}_1(\boldsymbol{x}), \mathcal{I}_2(\boldsymbol{x})$ are propagated layer by layer through a neural network $N$. The high-dimensional convex shapes are visualized in 2d. While initially $\mathcal{I}_1(\boldsymbol{x})$ and $\mathcal{I}_2(\boldsymbol{x})$ only slightly overlap, at layer $k$, $N_{1:k}(\mathcal{I}_2(\boldsymbol{x}))$ is fully contained in $N_{1:k}(\mathcal{I}_1(\boldsymbol{x}))$. (Color figure online)

## 2 Background

Here we formally introduce the necessary background for proof sharing.

*Neural Network.* A neural network $N$ is a function $N : \mathbb{R}^{d_{\text{in}}} \to \mathbb{R}^{d_{\text{out}}}$, commonly built from individual layers $N = N_L \circ N_{L-1} \circ \cdots \circ N_1$. Throughout this text, we consider feed-forward neural networks, where each layer $N_i(\boldsymbol{x}) = \max(\boldsymbol{A}\boldsymbol{x}+\boldsymbol{b}, 0)$ consists of an affine transformation $(\boldsymbol{A}\boldsymbol{x} + \boldsymbol{b})$ as well as a rectified linear unit (ReLU), that applies the max with 0 elementwise. A neural network, classifying inputs into $c$ classes, outputs $d_{\text{out}} := c$ scores, one for each class, and assigns the class with the highest score as the predicted one. While, as is common in the neural network verification literature, we use image classification as a proxy task, many other applications work analogously. Our approach also naturally extends to other types of neural networks, if verifiers exist for these architectures. We discuss the challenges and limitations of such generalizations in Sect. 4.5. In the following, for $k < L$, we let $N_{1:k}$ denote the application of the first $k$ layers and $N_{k+1:L}$ denote the last $L - k$ layers respectively.

*(Local) Neural Network Verification.* Given a set of inputs and a postcondition $\psi$, the goal of neural network verification is to prove that $\psi$ holds over the output of the neural network corresponding to the given set of inputs. In this work, we focus on local verification, proving that $\psi$ holds for the network output for a given region $\mathcal{I}(\boldsymbol{x}) \subseteq \mathbb{R}^{d_{\text{in}}}$ formed around the input $\boldsymbol{x}$. Formally, we state this as:

*Problem 1 (Local neural network verification).* For a region $\mathcal{I}(\boldsymbol{x}) \subseteq \mathbb{R}^{d_{\text{in}}}$, neural network $N$, and postcondition $\psi$, verify that $\forall \boldsymbol{z} \in \mathcal{I}(\boldsymbol{x}).\ N(\boldsymbol{z}) \models \psi$. We write $\mathcal{I}(\boldsymbol{x}) \models \psi$ if $\forall \boldsymbol{z} \in \mathcal{I}(\boldsymbol{x}).\ N(\boldsymbol{z}) \models \psi$.

Here, we restrict ourselves to verifiers based on abstract interpretation [11,14] as they achieve state-of-the-art precision and scalability [31,32]. Further, many other popular verifiers [38,42] can be formulated using abstract interpretation. These verifiers propagate $\mathcal{I}(\boldsymbol{x})$ symbolically through the network $N$ layer-by-layer using abstract transformers, which overapproximate the effect of applying the transformations defined in the different layers on symbolic shapes. The propagation yields an abstraction of the exact shape at each layer. The verifiers finally check if the abstracted output implies $\psi$. This is showcased in Fig. 1, where the input regions $\mathcal{I}_1(\boldsymbol{x})$ and $\mathcal{I}_2(\boldsymbol{x})$ are propagated layer-by-layer through $N$.

For a verifier $V$, we let $V(\mathcal{I}(\boldsymbol{x}), N)$ denote the abstraction obtained after the propagation of $\mathcal{I}(\boldsymbol{x})$ through the network $N$. We declutter notation by overloading $N$ and writing $N(\mathcal{I}(\boldsymbol{x}))$ for the same if $V$ is clear from context, i.e., $V(\mathcal{I}(\boldsymbol{x}), N) = N(\mathcal{I}(\boldsymbol{x}))$.

We consider robustness verification, where the goal is to prove that the network classification does not change within an input region. A common input region is the $\ell_\infty$-bounded additive noise, defined as $\mathcal{I}_\epsilon(\boldsymbol{x}) := \{\boldsymbol{z} \mid \|\boldsymbol{x} - \boldsymbol{z}\|_\infty \leq \epsilon\}$. Here, $\epsilon$ defines the size of the maximal perturbation to $\boldsymbol{x}$. The postcondition $\psi$ denotes classification to the same class as $\boldsymbol{x}$. Throughout this paper, we consider different instantiations for $\mathcal{I}(\boldsymbol{x})$ but assume that $\psi$ denotes classification invariance (although other choices would work analogously). Due to this, we refer to $\mathcal{I}(\boldsymbol{x})$ as input region and specification interchangeably. For example, in Fig. 1, the goal is to verify that all points contained in $N(\mathcal{I}_1(\boldsymbol{x}))$ are classified as "cat".

## 3 Proof Sharing with Templates

Before introducing our framework for proof sharing, we further expand the motivation example discussed in Fig. 1.

### 3.1 Motivation: Proof Subsumption

As stated earlier, we empirically observed that for many input regions $\mathcal{I}_i(\boldsymbol{x})$ and $\mathcal{I}_j(\boldsymbol{x})$, the abstraction corresponding to one region at some intermediate layer $k$ contains that of another. Formally:

**Definition 1 (Proof Subsumption).** *For specifications $\mathcal{I}_i(\boldsymbol{x}), \mathcal{I}_j(\boldsymbol{x})$, we say that the proof of $\mathcal{I}_i(\boldsymbol{x})$ subsumes that of $\mathcal{I}_j(\boldsymbol{x})$ if at some layer $k$, $N_{1:k}(\mathcal{I}_j(\boldsymbol{x})) \subseteq N_{1:k}(\mathcal{I}_i(\boldsymbol{x}))$, which we denote as $\mathcal{I}_j(\boldsymbol{x}) \subseteq_{N,k} \mathcal{I}_i(\boldsymbol{x})$.*

While not formally required, particularly interesting are cases where proof subsumption occurs despite $\mathcal{I}_i(\boldsymbol{x}) \not\subseteq \mathcal{I}_j(\boldsymbol{x})$. This form of proof subsumption is showcased in Fig. 1, where $\mathcal{I}_1(\boldsymbol{x})$ and $\mathcal{I}_2(\boldsymbol{x})$ have only a small overlap, yet $\mathcal{I}_2(\boldsymbol{x}) \subseteq_{N,k} \mathcal{I}_1(\boldsymbol{x})$. For another example, consider a neural network $N$ trained as a hand-written digit classifier for the MNIST dataset [22] (example shown in Fig. 2) and the following two specifications:

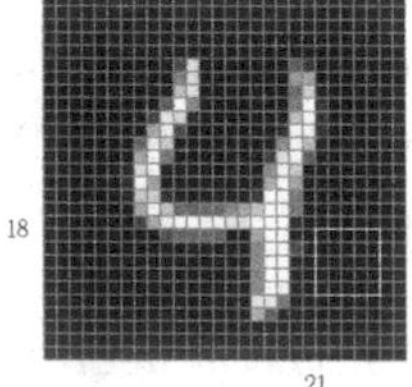


**Fig. 2.** Example of an MNIST image. $\mathcal{I}_{5\times 5}^{18,21}(\boldsymbol{x})$ signifies arbitrary change in the outlined area.

- $\ell_\infty$-bounded perturbations: all the pixels in an input image can arbitrarily be changed independently by a small amount $\mathcal{I}_\epsilon(\boldsymbol{x}) := \{\boldsymbol{z} \mid \|\boldsymbol{x} - \boldsymbol{z}\|_\infty \leq \epsilon\}$,

**Table 1.** Proof subsumption on a robust MNIST classifier with 94 % accuracy. Verif. acc. denotes the percentage of verifiable inputs from the test set for $\ell_\infty$-perturbations ($\mathcal{I}_\epsilon$).

| $\epsilon$ | verif. acc. for $\mathcal{I}_\epsilon$ [%] | $\mathcal{I}^{i,j}_{2\times 2}(\boldsymbol{x}) \subseteq_{N,k} \mathcal{I}_\epsilon(\boldsymbol{x})$ at layer k [%] | | | | |
|---|---|---|---|---|---|---|
| | | 1 | 2 | 3 | 4 | 5 |
| 0.1 | 89.74 | 61.40 | 72.85 | 77.65 | 81.75 | 82.70 |
| 0.2 | 81.40 | 62.85 | 77.05 | 82.40 | 86.05 | 86.60 |

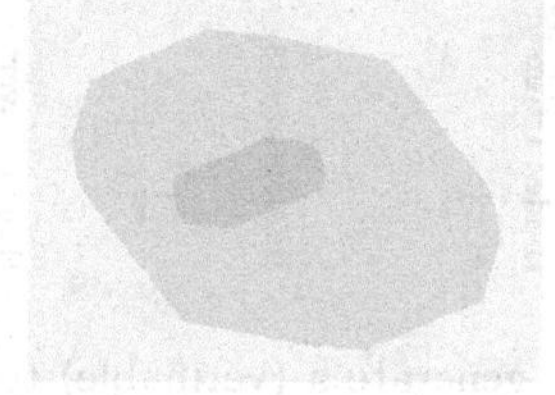

**Fig. 3.** The abstraction obtained for $\mathcal{I}_\epsilon(\boldsymbol{x})$ (blue) contains that for $\mathcal{I}^{i,j}_{2\times 2}(\boldsymbol{x})$ (orange) (projected to $d = 2$). (Color figure online)

- adversarial patches [10]. A $p \times p$ patch inside which the pixel intensity can vary arbitrarily is placed on an image at coordinates $(i, j)$, for which we write $\mathcal{I}^{i,j}_{p\times p}$. We showcase a patch in Fig. 2 and formally define them in Sect. 4.3.

Clearly $\mathcal{I}^{i,j}_{p\times p}(\boldsymbol{x}) \not\subseteq \mathcal{I}_\epsilon(\boldsymbol{x})$ (unless $\epsilon = 1$). In Table 1, we show that for a classifier (5 layers with 100 neurons each) we indeed observe proof subsumption. We report the accuracy, i.e., the rate of correct predictions on the unperturbed test data, as well as the certified accuracy, i.e., the rate of samples $\boldsymbol{x}$ for which the prediction is correct and $\mathcal{I}(\boldsymbol{x}) \models \psi$ is verified, for $\mathcal{I}_\epsilon$ with $\epsilon = 0.1$ and 0.2 over the whole test set. We also show the percentage of $\mathcal{I}^{i,j}_{2\times 2}(\boldsymbol{x})$ contained in $\mathcal{I}_\epsilon(\boldsymbol{x})$ at layer $k$. To this end, we pick 1000 random $\boldsymbol{x}$ for which $\mathcal{I}_\epsilon(\boldsymbol{x})$ is verifiable and sample 2 $(i, j)$ pairs each. We utilize a Box domain verifier and a robustly trained network [24]. Figure 3 shows a patch specification $\mathcal{I}^{i,j}_{2\times 2}(\boldsymbol{x})$ (in orange) contained in the $\ell_\infty$ specification $\mathcal{I}_\epsilon$ (in blue) projected to 2 dimensions via PCA.

*Reasons for Proof Subsumption.* In Table 1, we observe that the rate of proof subsumption increases with larger $\epsilon$ and $k$. These observations give an intuition as to why we observe proof subsumption. First, as input regions pass through the neural network, in each layer the abstractions become more imprecise. While this fundamentally limits verification, it makes the subsumption of abstractions more probable. This effect increases, when increasing $\epsilon$ for $\mathcal{I}_\epsilon$. Second, and more fundamentally, while passing through the layers of a neural network, we observed that semantically similar yet distinct image inputs, e.g., two similar-looking handwritten digits, have activation vectors that grow closer in $\ell_2$ norm as they pass through the layers of the neural network [21,34]. This effect is a consequence of the neural network distilling low-level information (e.g., individual pixel values) into high-level concepts (e.g., the classes of digits). As specifications (and their proofs) correspond to sets of concrete inputs, a similar effect may apply. We conjecture that these two effects drive the observed proof subsumption.

### 3.2 Proof Sharing with Templates

Leveraging this insight, we introduce the idea of proof sharing via templates, showcased in Fig. 4. We use an abstraction obtained from a robustness proof

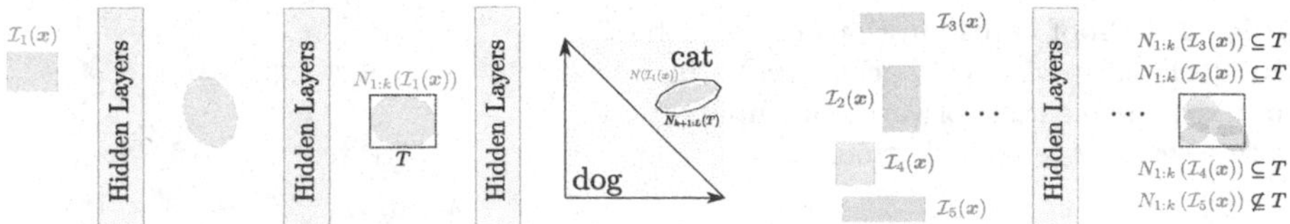


(a) We generate a (verifiable) template $T$ from the abstraction obtained by propagating the orange input.

(b) We shortcut the verification if intermediate abstraction are contained in the $T$.

**Fig. 4.** Conceptualization of proof sharing with templates. In (a) we create a verifiable template $T$ (black-dashed border) from specification $N_{1:k}(\mathcal{I}_1(\boldsymbol{x}))$. When verifying new specifications $\mathcal{I}_2, \ldots, \mathcal{I}_5$, shown in (b), we can shortcut the verification of all but $\mathcal{I}_5$ by subsuming them in $T$.

$N_{1:k}(\mathcal{I}_1(\boldsymbol{x}))$ at layer $k$ to create a template $T$. After ensuring that $T$ is verifiable, it can be used to shortcut the verification of other regions, e.g., of $\mathcal{I}_2(\boldsymbol{x}), \ldots, \mathcal{I}_5(\boldsymbol{x})$. Formally we decompose proof sharing into two sub-problems: (i) the generation of proof templates and (ii) the matching of abstractions corresponding to other properties to these templates. For simplicity, here we only consider templates at a single layer $k$ of the neural network and we show an extension to multiple layers in Sect. 4.3.

Our goal is to construct a template $T$ at layer $k$ that implies the postcondition and captures abstractions at layer $k$ obtained from propagating several $\mathcal{I}_i(\boldsymbol{x})$. As it is challenging to find a single $T$ that captures abstractions corresponding to many input regions, yet remains verifiable, we allow a set of templates $\mathcal{T}$. We state this formally as:

*Problem 2 (Template Generation).* For a given neural network $N$, input $\boldsymbol{x}$ and set of specifications $\mathcal{I}_1, \ldots, \mathcal{I}_r$, layer $k$ and a postcondition $\psi$, find a set of templates $\mathcal{T}$ with $|\mathcal{T}| \leq m$ such that:

$$\begin{aligned} &\arg\max_{\mathcal{T}} \sum_{i=1}^{r} \left[ \bigvee_{T \in \mathcal{T}} N_{1:k}(\mathcal{I}_i(\boldsymbol{x})) \subseteq T \right] \\ &\text{s.t. } \forall\, T \in \mathcal{T}.\, N_{k+1:L}(T) \models \psi. \end{aligned} \tag{1}$$

Intuitively, Eq. (1) aims to find a set $\mathcal{T}$ of templates $T$ at layer $k$, such that the maximal amount (via the sum) of specifications $\mathcal{I}_1, \ldots, \mathcal{I}_r$ is contained in at least one template $T$ (via the disjunction) while ensuring that the individual $T$ are still verifiable (via the constraint on the second line). As neural network verification required by the constraints of Eq. (1), is NP-complete [17], computing an exact solution to Problem 2 is computationally infeasible. Therefore, we compute an approximate solution to Eq. (1). In general, Problem 2 does not necessarily require that the templates $T$ are created from previous proofs. However, building on proof subsumption, as discussed in Sect. 3.1, in Sect. 4 we will infer the templates from previously obtained abstractions.

To leverage proof sharing once the templates $\mathcal{T}$ are obtained, we need to be able to match an abstraction $S = N_{1:k}(\mathcal{I}(\boldsymbol{x}))$ verified using proof transfer to a template in $\mathcal{T}$:

*Problem 3 (Template Matching).* Given a set of templates $\mathcal{T}$ at layer $k$ of a neural network $N$, and a new input region $\mathcal{I}(\boldsymbol{x})$, determine whether there exists a $T \in \mathcal{T}$ such that $S \subseteq T$, where $S = N_{1:k}(\mathcal{I}(\boldsymbol{x}))$.

Together, Problems 2 and 3 outline a general framework for proof sharing, permitting many instantiations. We note that Problems 2 and 3 present an inherent precision vs. speed trade-off: Problem 3 can be solved most efficiently for small values of $m = |\mathcal{T}|$ and simpler representations of $T$ (allowing faster checking of $S \subseteq T$) at the cost of lower proof matching rates. Alternatively, Eq. (1) can be maximized by large $m$ and $T$ represented by complex abstractions, thus attaining high precision but expensive template generation and matching.

*Beyond Proof Sharing on the Same Input.* In this section, we focused on proof sharing for different specifications of the same input $\boldsymbol{x}$. However, we observed that proof sharing is even possible between specifications defined on different inputs $\boldsymbol{x}$ and $\boldsymbol{x}'$. To facilitate the use of templates in this setting, Eq. (1) in Problem 2 can be adapted to consider an input distribution.

## 4 Efficient Verification via Proof Sharing

We now consider an instantiation of proof sharing where we are given an input $\boldsymbol{x}$ and properties $\mathcal{I}_1, \dots, \mathcal{I}_r$ to verify. Our general approach, based on Problems 2 and 3, is shown in Algorithm 1. In this section, we first discuss Algorithm 1 in general. We then describe the possible choices of abstract domains and their implications on the algorithm, followed by a discussion on template generation for two different specific problems. Finally, we conclude the section with a discussion on the conditions for effective proof sharing verification.

In Algorithm 1, we first create the set of templates $\mathcal{T}$ (Line 1, discussed shortly) and subsequently verify $\mathcal{I}_1, \dots, \mathcal{I}_r$ using $\mathcal{T}$. Here, we consider two, potentially identical, verifiers $V_T$ and $V_S$, where $V_T$ is used to create the templates $\mathcal{T}$ and $V_S$ is used to propagate input regions up to the template layer $k$. For each $\mathcal{I}_i$ we propagate it up to layer $k$ (Line 4) to obtain $S = N_{1:k}(\mathcal{I}_i(\boldsymbol{x}))$ and check if we can match it to a template $T_j \in \mathcal{T}$ (Line 6) using an inclusion check. If a match is found, then we conclude that $N(\mathcal{I}_i(\boldsymbol{x})) \models \psi$ and set the verification output $v_i$ to True. If this is not the case (Line 11) we verify $N(\mathcal{I}_i(\boldsymbol{x})) \models \psi$ directly by checking $V_S(S, N_{k+1:L}) \models \psi$. If the template generation fails, we revert to verifying $\mathcal{I}_i$ by applying $V_S$ in the usual way (omitted in Algorithm 1).

*Soundness.* As long as the templates $\mathcal{T}$ are sound, this procedure is sound, i.e. Algorithm 1 only returns $v_i = $ True if $\forall \boldsymbol{z} \in \mathcal{I}_i(\boldsymbol{x})$. $N(z) \models \psi$ holds. Formally:

**Theorem 1.** *Algorithm 1 is sound if* $\forall\, T \in \mathcal{T}$, $z \in T$. $N_{k+1:L}(z) \models \psi$ *and* $V_S$ *is sound.*

**Algorithm 1:** Neural Network Verification Utilizing Proof Templates

**Input:** $\boldsymbol{x}, \mathcal{I}_1, \ldots, \mathcal{I}_r, k, \psi$, verifiers $V_S, V_T$
**Result:** $v_1, \ldots, v_r$ indicating
$v_i := (N(\mathcal{I}_i(\boldsymbol{x})) \models \psi)$

1 $\mathcal{T} \leftarrow$ GEN_TEMPLATES$(\boldsymbol{x}, N, k, \psi, V_S, V_T)$
2 $v_1, \ldots, v_r \leftarrow$ False
3 **for** $i \leftarrow 1$ **to** $r$ **do**
4     $S \leftarrow V_S(\mathcal{I}_i(\boldsymbol{x}), N_{1:k})$
5     **for** $T_j \in \mathcal{T}$ **do**
6         **if** $S \subseteq T_j$ **then**
7             $v_i \leftarrow$ True
8             **break**
9         **end**
10     **end**
11     **if** $\neg v_i$ **then**
12         $v_i \leftarrow (V_S(S, N_{k+1:L}) \models \psi)$
13     **end**
14 **end**
15 **return** $v_1, \ldots, v_r$

This holds by the construction of the algorithm:

*Proof.* For a given $\boldsymbol{x}$ and $\mathcal{I}_i$, Algorithm 1 only claims $v_i$ = True if either the check in (i) Line 6 or (ii) Line 11 succeeds. Since $V_S$ is sound, we know that $\forall \boldsymbol{z} \in \mathcal{I}_i(\boldsymbol{x}).\ N_{1:k}(z) \in S$. Therefore in case (i) by our requirement on $T$ as well as $S \subseteq T$ it follows that $\forall \boldsymbol{z} \in \mathcal{I}_i(\boldsymbol{x}).\ N(z) \models \psi$. In case (ii) we execute Line 12 and the same property holds due to the soundness of $V_S$.

Importantly, Theorem 1 shows that the generation process of $\mathcal{T}$ does not affect the overall soundness as long as the set of templates $\mathcal{T}$ fulfills the condition in Theorem 1. In particular, that means that when solving Problem 2, it suffices to show the side condition ($\forall\ T \in \mathcal{T}.\, N_{k+1:L}(T) \models \psi$) holds, while heuristically approximating the actual optimization criteria. We let $V_T$ denote the verifier used to ensure this property in GEN_TEMPLATES.

*Precision.* We say a verifier $V_1$ is more precise than another verifier $V_2$ on $N$ if out of a set of specifications it can verify some that $V_2$ can not.

**Theorem 2.** *If $V_S(V_S(\mathcal{I}_i(\boldsymbol{x}), N_{1:k}), N_{k+1:L}) = V_S(\mathcal{I}_i(\boldsymbol{x}), N)$, then Algorithm 1 is at least as precise as $V_S$.*

*Proof.* Since, even if the inclusion check in Line 6 fails, due to Line 12 we output $v_i = V_S(V_S(\mathcal{I}_i(\boldsymbol{x}), N_{1:k}), N_{k+1:L}) \models \psi$ (Line 12), which by our requirement equals $v_i = V_S(\mathcal{I}_i(\boldsymbol{x}), N) \models \psi$. Therefore we have at least the precision of $V_S$.

The required property holds for any verifier $V_S$ for which the abstractions of all network layers depends only on the abstractions from previous layers and is fulfilled for all verifiers considered in this paper. For verifiers $V_S$ that do not fulfill the required property, potential losses in precision can be remedied (at the cost of runtime) by using $V_S(\mathcal{I}_i(\boldsymbol{x}), N_{1:L})$ in Line 12. Interestingly, it is even possible to increase the precision of Algorithm 1 over $V_S$ by creating templates $T$ that are verified with a more precise verifier $V_T$. However, in this discussion, we restrict ourselves to speed gains. We believe that obtaining precision gains requires instantiating our framework with a significantly different approach than that taken for improving speed which is the main focus of our work. We leave this as an interesting item for future work.

*Run-Time.* Here, we aim to characterize the run-time of Algorithm 1 as well as its speed-up over conventional verification. For an input $\boldsymbol{x}$, (keeping the other parameters fixed), the expected run time is

$$t_{PS} = t_{\mathcal{T}} + r(t_S + t_{\subseteq} + (1-\rho)t_{\psi}) \tag{2}$$

where $t_{\mathcal{T}}$ is the expected time required to generate the templates at Line 1, $r$ is the number of specifications to be verified, $t_S$ is the expected time to compute $S$ (Line 4), $t_{\subseteq}$ is the time to check $S \subseteq T$ for $T \in \mathcal{T}$ until a match is found (Line 5 to Line 10), $\rho \in [0,1]$ is the rate of specifications where a template is found and $t_{\psi}$ is the time required to check $\psi$ on the network output corresponding to $S$ (Line 12). This time is minimized if the individual expected run times $t_{\mathcal{T}}, t_S, t_{\psi}$ are minimal and $\rho$ is large (i.e., close to 1). Unfortunately, computing the template match rate $\rho$ analytically is challenging and requires global reasoning over the neural network for all valid inputs, which are not clearly defined. However, our empirical analysis (in Sect. 5) shows that $\rho$ is higher when templates are created at later layers (as in Sect. 3.1).

To determine the speed-up compared to a baseline standard verifier, we make the simplifying assumption that there is a single verifier $V = V_S = V_{\mathcal{T}}$ that has expected run-time $\nu$ for each layer. Thus, the expected run-time for the conventional verifier is $t_{BL} = rL\nu$. We have $t_{\mathcal{T}} = \lambda m L \nu$, $t_S = k\nu$, $t_{\psi} = (L-k)\nu$, $t_{\subseteq} = \eta m$ and ultimately $t_{PS} = (m + r(1-\rho))L\nu + r\rho k\nu + r\eta m$ for constants $\lambda \in \mathbb{R}_{>0}$, which indicates the overhead in generating one template over just verifying it, and $\eta \in \mathbb{R}_{>0}$ which denotes the time required to perform an inclusion check for one template. As this phrasing shows, Algorithm 1 has the same asymptotic runtime as the base verifier $V$. Further, this formulation allows us to write our expected speed-up as $\frac{t_{BL}}{t_{PS}} = \frac{r}{\lambda m + \eta r m / L\mu + r\rho k/L + r(1-\rho)}$. This speed-up is maximized when $k$ is small compared to $L$, i.e., templates are placed early in the neural network, the matching rate $\rho$ is close to 1, and $m, \lambda, \eta$ are small, i.e., generation and matching are fast. Unfortunately, these requirements are at odds with each other: as we show in Sect. 5, higher $m$ leads to higher matching rate $\rho$ and $\rho$ is naturally higher for templates later in the neural network (higher $k$). Thus high speed-ups require careful hyper-parameter choices.

To showcase how we can achieve good templates as well as fast matching, we next discuss the choice of the abstract domain to be used in the propagation and the representation of the templates. Then we discuss the template generation procedure and instantiate it for the verification of robustness to adversarial patches and geometric perturbations.

### 4.1 Choice of Abstract Domain

To solve Problems 2 and 3 in a way that minimizes the expected runtime and maximizes the overall precision, the choice of abstract domain is crucial. Here we briefly review common choices of abstract domains for neural network verification and how they are suited to our problem. Geometrically these domains can be thought of as a convex abstraction of the set of vectors representing reachable values at each layer of the neural network. We say that an abstraction $a_1$ is more precise than another abstraction $a_2$, if and only if $a_1 \subseteq a_2$, i.e., all points in $a_1$ occur in $a_2$. Similarly, we say that a domain is more precise than another if it can express all abstractions in the other domain.

The Box (or Interval) domain [14,16,24] abstracts sets in $d$ dimensions as $B = \{\boldsymbol{a} + \text{diag}(\boldsymbol{d})\boldsymbol{e} \mid \boldsymbol{e} \in [-1,1]^d\}$ with center $\boldsymbol{a} \in \mathbb{R}^d$ and width $\boldsymbol{d} \in \mathbb{R}^d_{\geq 0}$. The Zonotope domain [14,15,24,31,40] uses relaxations $Z$ of the form

$$Z = \{\boldsymbol{a} + \boldsymbol{A}\boldsymbol{e} \mid \boldsymbol{e} \in [-1,1]^q\}, \tag{3}$$

parametrized with $\boldsymbol{a} \in \mathbb{R}^d$ and $\boldsymbol{A} \in \mathbb{R}^{d \times q}$.

A third common choice are (restricted) convex Polyhedra $P$ [12,32,42]. Here, we consider $P$ to be in the DeepPoly (DP) domain [32,42]. Generally, Boxes are less precise, i.e. certify fewer properties, than Zonotopes or Polyhedra.

**Table 2.** Feasibility of $S \subseteq T$ for Box $B$, Zonotope $Z$ (with order reduction) and DP Polyhedra $P$.

| | | $T$: $B$ | $Z$ | $\alpha(Z)$ | $P$ |
|---|---|---|---|---|---|
| $S$ | $B$ | ✓ | ✗ | ✓ | (✓) |
| | $Z$ | ✓ | ✗ | ✓ | ✗ |
| | $P$ | ✓ | ✗ | ✓ | (✓) |

For efficient proof sharing, we require a fast inclusion check $S \subseteq T$, which is challenging in our context due to the high dimensionality $d$ of the intermediate neural network layers. While we point the interested reader to [29] for a detailed discussion, we summarize the key results in Table 2. There, ✓ denotes feasibility, i.e. low polynomial runtime (usually $2d$ comparisons, sometimes with an additional matrix multiplication), ✗ denotes infeasibility, e.g. exponential run time. If $T$ is a Box all checks are simple as it suffices to compute the outer bounding box of $S$ and compare the $2d$ constraints. If $T$ is a DP Polyhedra these checks require a linear program (LP) to be solved. While the size of this LP permits a low theoretical time complexity, in case $S$ is a Box or DP Polyhedra, in practice, we consider calling an LP solver too expensive (denoted as (✓)). For Zonotopes these checks are generally infeasible, as they require enumeration of the faces or corners, which is computationally expensive for large $d$ and $P$. While Zonotopes can be encoded as Polyhedra (but not necessarily DP Polyhedra) and the same LP inclusion check as for $P$ could be used, the resulting LP would require exponentially many variables due to the previously mentioned enumeration. However, by placing constraints on the matrix $\boldsymbol{A}$ in Eq. (3) these inclusion checks can be performed efficiently. The mapping of a Zonotope to such a restricted Zonotope is called order reduction via outer-approximation [19,29].

In particular, for a Zonotope $Z$ we consider the order reduction $\alpha_{\text{Box}}$ to its outer bounding box (where $\boldsymbol{A}$ is diagonal) and note that other choices of $\alpha$ are possible (e.g. the reduction to affine transformations of a hyperbox).

For a general Zonotope $Z$ its outer bounding box $Z' = \alpha_{\text{Box}}(Z)$ can be easily obtained. The center of $Z'$ is $\boldsymbol{a}$, the center of Z. The width $\boldsymbol{d} \in \mathbb{R}^d_{\geq 0}$ is given as $d_i = \sum_{j=1}^{q} |A_{i,j}|$. $Z'$ is represented as either a Box or a Zonotope (with

$\boldsymbol{A} = \text{diag}(\boldsymbol{d})$). To check $S \subseteq Z'$ for a general Zontope $S$ it suffices to check $\alpha_{\text{Box}}(S) \subseteq Z'$ which reduces to the simple inclusion check for boxes.

Based on the above discussion we will use the Zonotope domain to represent all abstractions, and use verifiers $V_S = V_T$ that propagate these zonotopes using the state-of-the-art DeepZ transformers [31]. To permit efficient inclusion checks we apply $\alpha_{\text{Box}}$ on the resulting zonotopes to obtain the Box templates $T$, which we treat as a special case of Zonotopes.

### 4.2 Template Generation

We now discuss instantiations for GEN_TEMPLATES in Algorithm 1. Recall from Sect. 3.1 the idea of proof subsumption, i.e. that abstractions for some specification contain abstractions for other specifications. Building on this, we relax the Problem 2 in order to create $m$ templates $T_j$ from intermediate abstractions $N_{1:k}(\hat{\mathcal{I}}_i(\boldsymbol{x}))$ for some $\hat{\mathcal{I}}_1, \ldots, \hat{\mathcal{I}}_m$. Note that $\hat{\mathcal{I}}_j$ are not necessarily directly related to the specifications $\mathcal{I}_1, \ldots, \mathcal{I}_r$ that we want to verify. For a chosen layer $k$, input $\boldsymbol{x}$, number of templates $m$ and verifiers $V_S$ and $V_T$ we optimize

$$\begin{aligned}
&\underset{\hat{\mathcal{I}}_1,\ldots,\hat{\mathcal{I}}_m}{\arg\max} \sum_{i=1}^{r} \left[ \bigvee_{j=1}^{m} V_S(\mathcal{I}_i(\boldsymbol{x}), N_{1:k}) \subseteq T_j \right] \\
&\text{where } T_j = \alpha_{\text{Box}}(V_T(\hat{\mathcal{I}}_j(\boldsymbol{x}), N_{1:k})) \\
&\text{s.t. } V_T(T_j, N_{k+1:L}) \models \psi \text{ for } j \in 1, \ldots, m.
\end{aligned} \tag{4}$$

As originally in Problem 2 (Eq. (1)) we aim to find a set of templates such that the intermediate shapes at layer $k$ for most of the $r$ specifications are covered by at least one template $T$. In contrast to Eq. (1), we tie $T_j$ to the specifications $\hat{\mathcal{I}}_j$. This alone does not make the problem easier to tackle. However, next, we will discuss how to generate application-specific parametric $\hat{\mathcal{I}}_j$ and solve Eq. (4) by optimizing over their parameters, allowing us to solve template generation much more efficiently than in Eq. (1).

### 4.3 Robustness to Adversarial Patches

We now instantiate the above scheme in order to verify the robustness of image classifiers against adversarial patches [10]. Consider an attacker that is allowed to arbitrarily change any $p \times p$ patch of the image, as showcased earlier in Fig. 2. For such a patch over pixel positions $([i, i+p-1] \times [j, j+p-1])$, the corresponding perturbation is

$$\begin{aligned}
&\mathcal{I}^{i,j}_{p\times p}(\boldsymbol{x}) := \{\boldsymbol{z} \in [0,1]^{h\times w} \mid \boldsymbol{z}_{\pi^C_{i,j}} = \boldsymbol{x}_{\pi^C_{i,j}}\} \\
&\text{with } \pi_{i,j} = \left\{(k,l) \mid {\scriptstyle k \in i,\ldots,i+p-1 \atop l \in j,\ldots,j+p-1}\right\}
\end{aligned}$$

where $h$ and $w$ denote the height and width of the input $\boldsymbol{x}$. Here $\pi_{i,j}$ denotes the parts of the image affected by the patch, and $\pi^C_{i,j}$ its complement, i.e., the

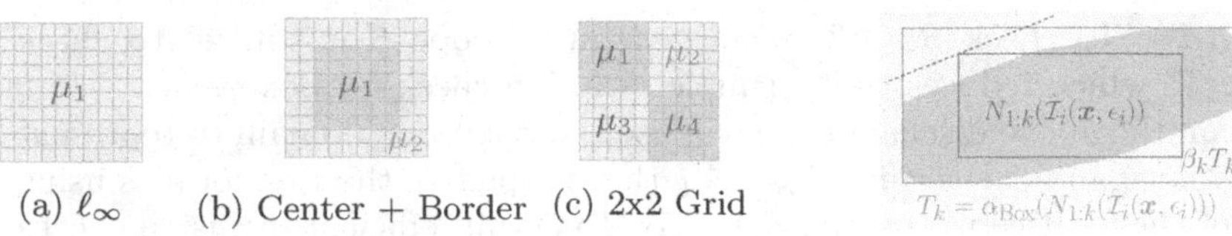


(a) $\ell_\infty$ (b) Center + Border (c) 2x2 Grid

**Fig. 5.** Example splits $\mu$ for $10 \times 10$ pixels.

**Fig. 6.** Example Template. (Color figure online)

unaffected part of the image. To prove robustness for an arbitrarily placed $p \times p$ patch, however, one must consider the perturbation set $\mathcal{I}_{p \times p}(\boldsymbol{x}) := \cup_{i,j} \mathcal{I}^{i,j}_{p \times p}(\boldsymbol{x})$.

To prove robustness for $\mathcal{I}_{p \times p}$, existing approaches [10] separately verify $\mathcal{I}^{i,j}_{p \times p}(\boldsymbol{x})$ for all $i \in \{1, \dots, h-p+1\}, j \in \{1, \dots, w-p+1\}$. For example, with $p = 2$ and a $28 \times 28$ MNIST image, this approach requires 729 individual proofs. Because the different proofs for $\mathcal{I}_{p \times p}$ share similarities, this is an ideal candidate for proof sharing. We utilize Algorithm 1 and check $\wedge_i v_i$ at the end to speed up this process. For template generation, we solve Eq. (4) for $m$ templates with an input perturbation $\hat{\mathcal{I}}_i$ per template.

We empirically found that (recall Table 1) setting $\hat{\mathcal{I}}_i$ to an $\ell_\infty$ region $\mathcal{I}_{\epsilon_i}$ to work particularly well to capture a majority of patch perturbations $\mathcal{I}^{i,j}_{p \times p}$ at intermediate layers. Specifically, we found that setting $\epsilon_i$ to the maximally verifiable value for this input to work particularly well.

To further increase the number of specifications contained in a set of templates $\mathcal{T}$, we use $m$ template perturbations of the form

$$\hat{\mathcal{I}}_i(\boldsymbol{x}) := \{\boldsymbol{z} \mid \|\boldsymbol{x}_{\mu_i} - \boldsymbol{z}_{\mu_i}\|_\infty \leq \epsilon_i \wedge \boldsymbol{x}_{\mu_i^C} = \boldsymbol{z}_{\mu_i^C}\},$$

where $\mu_i$ denotes a subset of pixels of the input image and $\mu_i^C$ its complement and we maximize $\epsilon_i$ in a best-effort manner. In particular, we consider $\mu_1, \dots, \mu_m$, such that they partition the set of pixels in the image (e.g., in Fig. 5).

As noted earlier, this generation procedure needs to be fast, yet obtain $\mathcal{T}$ to which many abstractions match in order to obtain speed-ups. Thus, we consider small $m$, and fixed patterns $\mu_1, \dots, \mu_m$. For each $\hat{\mathcal{I}}_i$, we aim to find the largest $\epsilon_i$ which can still be verified in order to maximize the number of matches. Note that for $m = 1$, this is equivalent to the $\ell_\infty$ input perturbation $\mathcal{I}_\epsilon$ with the maximally verifiable $\epsilon$ for the given image.

Concretely, we can perform binary search over $\epsilon_i$ in order find a large $\epsilon_i$, still satisfying $N_{k+1:L}(\alpha_{\text{Box}}(N_{1:k}(\hat{\mathcal{I}}_i))) \models \psi$. Verification with our chosen DeepZ Zonotopes is not monotonous in $\epsilon_i$ due to the non-monotonic transformers used for non-linearities (e.g., ReLU). This renders the application of binary search a best-effort approximation. As we don't require a formal maximum but rather aim to solve a surrogate for Problem 2, this still works well in practice. Further note that, applying $\alpha_{\text{Box}}$ to templates introduces imprecision, i.e. $V_T$ might not be able to prove properties over templates that it could without the application of $\alpha_{\text{Box}}$. However, Theorem 2 (which only requires properties of $V_S$) still applies.

*Templates at Multiple Layers.* We can extend this approach to obtain templates at multiple layers without a large increase in computational cost. With templates at multiple layers, we first try to match the propagated shape against the earliest template layer and upon failure propagate it further to the next, where we again attempt to match the template. In Algorithm 1, this means repeating the block from Line 4 to Line 10 for each template layer before going on to the check on Line 11.

**Algorithm 2:** Online Template Generation for Patches

**Input:** $\boldsymbol{x}, N, \mu_1, \ldots, \mu_m, K, \psi, V_T$
**Result:** $\mathcal{T}^k$ for $k \in K$
1 $\mathcal{T}^k \leftarrow \{\}$ for $k \in K$
2 **for** $i \leftarrow 1$ **to** $m$ **do**
3 $\quad \hat{\mathcal{I}}_i(\boldsymbol{x}, \epsilon) := \{\boldsymbol{z} \mid \|\boldsymbol{x}_{\mu_i} - \boldsymbol{z}_{\mu_i}\| \leq \epsilon$
4 $\quad\quad \wedge\, \boldsymbol{x}_{\mu_i^C} = \boldsymbol{z}_{\mu_i^C}\}$
5 $\quad f(\epsilon) := V_T(\hat{\mathcal{I}}_i(\boldsymbol{x}, \epsilon), N) \models \psi$
6 $\quad \epsilon_i \leftarrow$ `bin_search`$(\epsilon, f(\epsilon))$
7 $\quad$ **for** $k \in K$ **do**
8 $\quad\quad T_k \leftarrow \alpha_{\text{Box}}(V_T(\hat{\mathcal{I}}_i(\boldsymbol{x}, \epsilon_i), N_{1:k}))$
9 $\quad\quad g(\beta_k) := V_T(\beta T_k, N_{k+1:L}) \models \psi$
10 $\quad\quad \beta_k \leftarrow$ `bin_search`$(\beta, g(\beta))$
11 $\quad\quad \mathcal{T}^k \leftarrow \mathcal{T}^k \cup \{\beta_k T_k\}$
12 $\quad$ **end**
13 **end**
14 **return** $\mathcal{T}^k$ *for* $k \in K$

The full template generation procedure is given in Algorithm 2. First, we perform a binary search over $\epsilon_i$ (Line 6) to find the largest $\epsilon_i$, for which the specification is verifiable. Then for each layer $k$ in the set of layers $K$ at which we are creating templates we create a box $T_k$ from the Zonotope. As this $T_k$ may not be verifiable, due to the imprecision added in $\alpha_{\text{Box}}$, we then perform another binary search for the largest scaling factor $\beta_k$ (Line 10), which is applied to the matrix $\boldsymbol{A}$ in Eq. (3). We denote this operation as $\beta_k T_k$. We show an example for a single layer $k$ in Fig. 6. The blue area outlines the Zonotope found via Line 6, which is verifiable as it is fully on one side of the decision boundary (red, dashed). After applying $\alpha_{\text{Box}}$ (orange), however, is not (crosses the decision boundary). By scaling it with $\beta_k$ the shape is verifiable again (green) and used as a template.

### 4.4 Geometric Robustness

Geometric robustness verification [3,13,28,32] aims to verify the robustness of neural networks against geometric transformations such as image rotations or translations. These transformations typically include an interpolation operation. For example consider rotation $R_\gamma$ of an image by $\gamma \in \Gamma$ degrees for an interval $\Gamma$ (e.g., $\gamma \in [-5, 5]$), for which we consider the specification $\mathcal{I}_\Gamma(\boldsymbol{x}) := \{R_\gamma(\boldsymbol{x}) \mid \gamma \in \Gamma\}$. We note that, unlike $\ell_\infty$ and patch verification, the input regions for geometric transformations are non-linear and have no closed-form solutions. Thus, an overapproximation of the input region must be obtained [3]. For large $\Gamma$, the approximate input region $\mathcal{I}_\Gamma(\boldsymbol{x})$, can be too coarse resulting in imprecise verification. Hence, in order to assert $\psi$ on $\mathcal{I}_\Gamma$, existing state-of-the-art approaches [3], split $\Gamma$ into $r$ smaller ranges $\Gamma_1, \ldots, \Gamma_r$ and then verify the resulting $r$ specifications $(\mathcal{I}_{\Gamma_i}, \psi)$ for $i \in 1, \ldots, r$. These smaller perturbations share similarities facilitating proof sharing. We instantiate our approach similar to Sect. 4.3. A key difference to Sect. 4.3 is that while $\boldsymbol{x} \in \mathcal{I}^{i,j}_{p \times p}(\boldsymbol{x})$ for all $i, j$ in patches, here in general $\boldsymbol{x} \notin \mathcal{I}_{\Gamma_i}(\boldsymbol{x})$ for most $i$. Therefore, the individual perturbations $\mathcal{I}_i(\boldsymbol{x})$ do not overlap. To account for this, we consider $m$ templates and split $\Gamma$ into $m$ equally sized chunks (unrelated to the $r$ splits) obtaining the angles $\gamma_1, \ldots, \gamma_m$ at the center of each chunk. For $m$ templates we then consider the perturbations $\hat{\mathcal{I}}_i := \mathcal{I}_{\epsilon_i}(R_{\gamma_i}(\boldsymbol{x}))$, denoting the $\ell_\infty$ perturbation of size $\epsilon_i$ around the $\gamma_i$ degree rotated $\boldsymbol{x}$. To find the template we employ a procedure analogous to Algorithm 2.

### 4.5 Requirements for Proof Sharing

Now, we discuss the requirements on the neural network $N$ such that proof sharing via templates works well. For simplicity, we discuss simple per-dimension box bounds propagation for $V_S$ and $V_T$. However, similar arguments can be made for more complex relational abstractions such as Zonotopes or Polyhedra.

In order for an abstraction $S$ to match to a template $T$, we need to show interval inclusion for each dimension. For a particular dimension $i$ this can occur in two ways: (i) when both $S$ and $T$ are just a point in that dimension and these points coincide, e.g., $a_i^S = a_i^T$, or (ii) when $a_i^S \pm d_i^S \subseteq a_i^T \pm d_i^T$. While particularly in ReLU networks, the first case can occur after a ReLU layer sets values to zero, we focus our analysis here on the second case as it is more common. In this case, the width of $T$ in that dimension $d_i^T$ must be sufficient to cover $S$. Ignoring case (i) and letting $\text{supp}(T)$ denote the dimensions in which $d_i^T > 0$, we can pose that $\text{supp}(S) \subseteq \text{supp}(T)$ as a necessary condition for inclusion. While it is in general hard to argue about the magnitudes of these values, this approach still provides an intuition. When starting from input specifications $\text{supp}(\mathcal{I}) \nsubseteq \text{supp}(\hat{\mathcal{I}})$, $\text{supp}(S) \subseteq \text{supp}(T)$ can only occur if during propagation through the neural network $N_{1:k}$ the mass in $\text{supp}(\hat{\mathcal{I}})$ can "spread out" sufficiently to cover $\text{supp}(S)$. In the fully connected neural networks that we discuss here, the matrices of linear layers provide this possibility. However, in networks that only read part of the input at a time such as recurrent neural networks, or convolutional neural networks in which only locally neighboring inputs feed into the respective output in the next layer, these connections do not necessarily exist. This makes proof sharing hard until layers later in the neural network, that regionally or globally pool information. As this increases the depth of the layer $k$ at which proof transfer can be applied, this also decreases the potential speed-up of proof transfer. This could be alleviated by different ways of creating templates, which we plan to investigate in the future.

## 5 Experimental Evaluation

We now experimentally evaluate the effectiveness of our algorithms from Sect. 4.

### 5.1 Experimental Setup

We consider the verification of robustness to adversarial patch attacks and geometric transformations in Sect. 5.2 and Sect. 5.3, respectively. We define specifications on the first 100 test set images each from the MNIST [22] and the

**Table 3.** Rate of $\mathcal{I}^{i,j}_{2\times 2}$ matched to templates $\mathcal{T}$ for $\mathcal{I}_{2\times 2}$ patch verification for different combinations of template layers $k$, $7 \times 200$ networks,using $m = 1$ template.

| template at layer $k$ | 1 | 2 | 3 | 4 | 5 | 6 | 7 | patch verif. [%] |
|---|---|---|---|---|---|---|---|---|
| MNIST | 18.6 | 85.6 | 94.1 | 95.2 | 95.5 | 95.7 | 95.7 | 97.0 |
| CIFAR | 0.1 | 27.1 | 33.7 | 34.4 | 34.2 | 34.2 | 34.3 | 42.2 |

**Table 4.** Average verification time in seconds per image for $\mathcal{I}_{2\times 2}$ patches for different combinations of template layers $k$, $7 \times 200$ networks,using $m = 1$ template.

| | | Proof Sharing, template layer $k$ | | | | | | | |
|---|---|---|---|---|---|---|---|---|---|
| | Baseline | 1 | 2 | 3 | 4 | 1+3 | 2+3 | 2+4 | 2+3+4 |
| MNIST | 2.10 | 1.94 | 1.15 | 1.22 | 1.41 | 1.27 | **1.09** | 1.10 | 1.14 |
| CIFAR | 3.27 | 2.98 | 2.53 | 2.32 | 2.47 | 2.35 | 2.49 | **2.42** | 2.55 |

CIFAR-10 dataset [20] ("CIFAR") as with repetitions and parameter variations the overall runtime becomes high. We use DeepZ [31] as the baseline verifier as well as for $V_S$ and $V_T$ [31]. Throughout this section, we evaluate proof sharing for two networks on two common datasets: We use a seven layer neural network with 200 neurons per layer ("$7 \times 200$") and a nine layer network with 500 neurons per layer ("$9 \times 500$") for both the MNIST[22] and CIFAR datasets [20], both utilizing ReLU activations. These architectures are similar to the fully-connected ones used in the ERAN and Mnistfc VNN-Comp categories [2].

For MNIST, we train 100 epochs, enumerating all patch locations for each sample, and for CIFAR we train for 600 with 10 random patch locations, as outlined in [10] with interval training [16,24]. On MNIST the $7 \times 200$ and the $9 \times 500$ achieve a natural accuracy of 98.3% and 95.3% respectively. For CIFAR, these values are 48.8% and 48.1% respectively. Our implementation utilizes PyTorch [25] and is evaluated on Ubuntu 18.04 with an Intel Core i9-9900K CPU and 64 GB RAM. For all timing results, we provide the mean over three runs.

### 5.2 Robustness Against Adversarial Patches

For MNIST, containing $28 \times 28$ images, as outlined in Sect. 4.3, in order to verify inputs to be robust against $2 \times 2$ patch perturbations, 729 individual perturbations must be verified. Only if all are verified, the overall property can be verified for a given image. Similarly, for CIFAR, containing $32 \times 32$ color images, there are 961 individual perturbations (the patch is applied over all color channels).

We now investigate the two main parameters of Algorithm 2: the masks $\mu_1, \ldots, \mu_m$ and the layers $k \in K$. We first study the impact of the layer $k$ used for creating the template. To this end, we consider the $7 \times 200$ networks,

**Table 5.** $\mathcal{I}_{2\times2}$ patch verification with templates at the 2nd & 3rd layer of the $7 \times 200$ networks for different masks.

| Method/Mask | m | patch matched [%] | $t$ [s] |
|---|---|---|---|
| Baseline | - | - | 2.14 |
| L-infinity | 1 | 94.1 | **1.11** |
| Center + Border | 2 | 94.6 | 1.41 |
| $2 \times 2$ Grid | 4 | **95.0** | 3.49 |

**Table 6.** $\mathcal{I}_{2\times2}$ patch verification with templates generated on the second and third layer using the $\ell_\infty$-mask. Verification times are given for the baseline $t^{BL}$ and for applying proof sharing $t^{PS}$ in seconds per image.

| Dataset | Net | verif. acc. [%] | $t^{BL}$ | $t^{PS}$ | patch mat. [%] | patch verif. [%] |
|---|---|---|---|---|---|---|
| MNIST | $7 \times 200$ | 81.0 | 2.10 | **1.10** | 94.1 | 97.0 |
| | $9 \times 500$ | 66.0 | 2.70 | **1.32** | 93.0 | 95.3 |
| CIFAR | $7 \times 200$ | 29.0 | 3.28 | **2.45** | 33.7 | 42.2 |
| | $9 \times 500$ | 28.0 | 5.48 | **4.48** | 34.2 | 46.2 |

use $m = 1$ (covering the whole image; equivalent to $\hat{\mathcal{I}}_\epsilon$). Table 3 shows the corresponding template matching rates, and the overall percentage of individual patches that can be verified "patches verif.". (The overall percentage of images for which $\mathcal{I}_{2\times2}$ is true is reported as "verif." in Table 6.) Table 4 shows the corresponding verification times (including the template generation). We observe that many template matches can already be made at the second or third layer. As creating templates simultaneously at the second and third layer works well for both datasets, we utilize templates at these layers in further experiments.

Next, we investigate the impact of the pixel masks $\mu_1, \ldots, \mu_m$. To this end, we consider three different settings, as showcased in Fig. 5 earlier: (i) the full image ($\ell_\infty$-mask as before; $m = 1$), (ii) "center + border" ($m = 2$), where we consider the $6 \times 6$ center pixel as one group and all others as another, and (iii) the $2 \times 2$ grid ($m = 4$) where we split the image into equally sized quarters.

As we can see in Table 5, for higher $m$ more patches can be matched to the templates, indicating that our optimization procedure is a good approximation to Problem 2, which only considers the number of templates matched. Yet, for $m > 1$ the increase in matching rate $p$ does not offset the additional time in template generation and matching. Thus, $m = 1$ results in a better trade-off. This result highlights the trade-offs discussed throughout Sect. 3 and Sect. 4. Based on this investigation we now, in Table 6, evaluate all networks and datasets using $m = 1$ and template generation at layers 2 and 3. In all cases, we obtain a speed up between 1.2 to $2\times$ over the baseline verifier. Going from $2 \times 2$ to $3 \times 3$ patches speed ups remain around 1.6 and 1.3 for the two datasets respectively.

**Table 7.** Speed-ups achievable in the setting of Table 3. $t^{BL}$ the baseline.

| Layer $k$ | | speedup at layer $k$ 1 | 2 | 3 | 4 |
|---|---|---|---|---|---|
| realized | $t^{BL}/t^{PS}$ | 1.08 | 1.83 | 1.72 | 1.49 |
| optimal | $t^{BL}/(t_T + rt_S + rt_\subseteq)$ | 3.75 | 2.51 | 1.92 | 1.56 |
| optimal, no $\subseteq$ | $t^{BL}/(t_T + rt_S)$ | 4.02 | 2.68 | 2.01 | 1.62 |
| optimal, no gen $\mathcal{T}$., no $\subseteq$ | $t^{BL}/rt_S$ | 4.57 | 2.90 | 2.13 | 1.69 |

*Comparison with Theoretically Achievable Speed-Up.* Finally, we want to determine the maximal possible speed-up with proof sharing and see how much of this potential is realized by our method. To this end we investigate the same setting and network as in Table 3. We let $t^{BL}$ and $t^{PS}$ denote the runtime of the base verifier without and with proof sharing respectively. Similar to the discussion in Sect. 4 we can break down $t^{PS}$ into $t_T$ (template generation time), $t_S$ (time to propagate one input to layer $k$), $t_\subseteq$ (time to perform template matching) and $t_\psi$ (time to verify $S$ if no match). Table 7 shows different ratios of these quantities. For all, we assume a perfect matching rate at layer $k$ and calculate the achievable speed-up for patch verification on MNIST. Comparing the optimal and realized results, we see that at layers 3 and 4 our template generation algorithm, despite only approximately solving Problem 2 achieves near-optimal speed-up. By removing the time for template matching and template generation we can see that, at deeper layers, speeding up $t_\subseteq$ and $t_T$ only yield diminishing returns.

### 5.3 Robustness Against Geometric Perturbations

For the verification of geometric perturbations, we take 100 images from the MNIST dataset and the $7 \times 200$ neural network from Sect. 5.2. In Table 8, we consider an input region with $\pm 2°$ rotation, $\pm 10\%$ contrast and $\pm 1\%$ brightness change, inspired by [3]. To verify this region, similar to existing approaches [3], we choose to split the rotation into $r$ regions, each yielding a Box specification over the input. Here we use $m = 1$, a single template, with the largest verifiable $\epsilon$ found via binary search. We observe that as we increase $r$, the verification rate increases, but also the speed ups. Proof sharing enables significant speed-up between 1.6 to 2.9×.

Finally, we investigate the impact of the number of templates $m$. To this end, we consider a setting with a large parameter space: $\pm 40°$ rotation generated input region with $r = 200$. In Table 9, we evaluate this for $m$ templates obtained from the $\ell_\infty$ input perturbation around $m$ equally spaced rotations, where we apply binary search to find $\epsilon_i$ tailored for each template. Again we observe that $m > 1$ allows more templates matches. However, in this setting the relative increase is much larger than for patches, thus making $m = 3$ faster than $m = 1$.

**Table 8.** ±2° rotation, ±10% contrast and ±1% brightness change split into $r$ perturbations on 100 MNIST images. Verification rate, rate of splits matched and verified along with the run time of Zonotope $t^{BL}$ and proof sharing $t^{PS}$.

| $r$ | verif. [%] | splits verif. [%] | splits matched [%] | $t^{BL}$ | $t^{PT}$ |
|---|---|---|---|---|---|
| 4 | 73.0 | 87.3 | 73.1 | 3.06 | **1.87** |
| 6 | 91.0 | 94.8 | 91.0 | 9.29 | **3.81** |
| 8 | 93.0 | 95.9 | 94.2 | 20.64 | **7.48** |
| 10 | 95.0 | 96.5 | 94.9 | 38.50 | **13.38** |

**Table 9.** ±40° rotation split into 200 perturbations evaluated on MNIST. The verification rate is just 15 %, but 82.1 % of individual splits can be verified.

| Method | $m$ | splits matched [%] | $t$ [s] |
|---|---|---|---|
| Baseline | - | - | 11.79 |
| Proof Sharing | 1 | 38.0 | 9.15 |
| | 2 | 41.1 | 9.21 |
| | 3 | 58.5 | **8.34** |

### 5.4 Discussion

We have shown that proof sharing can achieve speed-ups over conventional execution. While the speed-up analysis (see Sect. 4 and Table 7) put a ceiling on what is achievable in particular settings, we are optimistic that proof sharing can be an important tool for neural network robustness analysis. In particular, as the size of certifiable neural networks continues to grow, the potential for gains via proof sharing is equally growing. Further, the idea of proof effort reuse can enable efficient verification of larger disjunctive specifications such as the patch or geometric examples considered here. Besides the immediately useful speed-ups, the concept of proof sharing is interesting in its own right and can provide insights into the learning mechanisms of neural networks.

## 6 Related Work

Here, we briefly discuss conceptually related work:

*Incremental Model Checking* The field of model checking aims to show whether a formalized model, e.g. of software or hardware, adheres to a specification. As neural network verification can also be cast as model checking, we review incremental model checking techniques which utilize a similar idea to proof sharing: reuse partial previous computations when checking new models or specifications. Proof sharing has been applied for discovering and reusing lemmas when proving theorems for satisfiability [6], Linear Temporal Logic [7], and modal $\mu$-calculus [33].

Similarly, caching solvers [35] for Satisfiability Modulo Theories cache obtained results or even the full models used to obtain the solution, with assignments for all variables, allowing for faster verification of subsequent queries. For program analysis tasks that deal with repeated similar inputs (e.g. individual commits in a software project) can leverage partial results [41], constraints [36] precision information [4,5] from previous runs.

*Proof Sharing Between Networks.* In neural network verification, some approaches abstract the network to achieve speed-ups in verification. These simplifications are constructed in a way that the proof can be adapted for the original neural network [1,43]. Similarly, another family of approaches analyzes the difference between two closely related neural networks by utilizing their structural similarity [26,27]. Such approaches can be used to reuse analysis results between neural network modifications, e.g. fine-tuning [9,37].

In contrast to these works, we do not modify the neural network, but achieve speed-ups rather by only considering the relaxations obtained in the proofs. [37] additionally consider small changes to the input, however, these are much smaller than the difference in specification we consider here.

## 7 Conclusion

We introduced the novel concept of proof sharing in the context of neural network verification. We showed how to instantiate this concept, achieving speed-ups of up to 2 to 3 x for patch verification and geometric verification. We believe that the ideas introduced in this work can serve as a solid foundation for exploring methods that effectively share proofs in neural network verification.

## References

1. Ashok, P., Hashemi, V., Křetínský, J., Mohr, S.: DeepAbstract: neural network abstraction for accelerating verification. In: Hung, D.V., Sokolsky, O. (eds.) ATVA 2020. LNCS, vol. 12302, pp. 92–107. Springer, Cham (2020). https://doi.org/10.1007/978-3-030-59152-6_5
2. Bak, S., Liu, C., Johnson, T.T.: The second international verification of neural networks competition. arXiv preprint abs/2109.00498 (2021)
3. Balunovic, M., Baader, M., Singh, G., Gehr, T., Vechev, M.T.: Certifying geometric robustness of neural networks. In: Neural Information Processing Systems (NIPS) (2019)
4. Beyer, D., Löwe, S., Novikov, E., Stahlbauer, A., Wendler, P.: Precision reuse for efficient regression verification. In: Symposium on the Foundations of Software Engineering (SIGSOFT) (2013)
5. Beyer, D., Wendler, P.: Reuse of verification results - conditional model checking, precision reuse, and verification witnesses. In: Bartocci, E., Ramakrishnan, C.R. (eds.) SPIN 2013. LNCS, vol. 7976, pp. 1–17. Springer, Heidelberg (2013). https://doi.org/10.1007/978-3-642-39176-7_1

6. Bradley, A.R.: SAT-based model checking without unrolling. In: Jhala, R., Schmidt, D. (eds.) VMCAI 2011. LNCS, vol. 6538, pp. 70–87. Springer, Heidelberg (2011). https://doi.org/10.1007/978-3-642-18275-4_7
7. Bradley, A.R., Somenzi, F., Hassan, Z., Zhang, Y.: An incremental approach to model checking progress properties. In: International Conference on Formal Methods in Computer-Aided Design (FMCAD) (2011)
8. Brown, T.B., Mané, D., Roy, A., Abadi, M., Gilmer, J.: Adversarial patch. arXiv preprint abs/1712.09665 (2017)
9. Cheng, C., Yan, R.: Continuous safety verification of neural networks. In: Design, Automation and Test in Europe Conference and Exhibition (2021)
10. Chiang, P., Ni, R., Abdelkader, A., Zhu, C., Studer, C., Goldstein, T.: Certified defenses for adversarial patches. In: Proceedings of International Conference on Learning Representations (ICLR) (2020)
11. Cousot, P., Cousot, R.: Abstract interpretation: A unified lattice model for static analysis of programs by construction or approximation of fixpoints. In: Proceedings of Principles of Programming Languages (POPL) (1977)
12. Cousot, P., Halbwachs, N.: Automatic discovery of linear restraints among variables of a program. In: Proceedings of Principles of Programming Languages (POPL) (1978)
13. Fischer, M., Baader, M., Vechev, M.T.: Certified defense to image transformations via randomized smoothing. In: Neural Information Processing Systems (NIPS) (2020)
14. Gehr, T., Mirman, M., Drachsler-Cohen, D., Tsankov, P., Chaudhuri, S., Vechev, M.T.: AI2: safety and robustness certification of neural networks with abstract interpretation. In: Symposium on Security and Privacy (S&P) (2018)
15. Goubault, E., Putot, S.: A zonotopic framework for functional abstractions. Formal Methods Syst. Des. **47**(3), 302–360 (2016). https://doi.org/10.1007/s10703-015-0238-z
16. Gowal, S., et al.: On the effectiveness of interval bound propagation for training verifiably robust models. arXiv preprint abs/1810.12715 (2018)
17. Katz, G., Barrett, C., Dill, D.L., Julian, K., Kochenderfer, M.J.: Reluplex: an efficient SMT solver for verifying deep neural networks. In: Majumdar, R., Kunčak, V. (eds.) CAV 2017. LNCS, vol. 10426, pp. 97–117. Springer, Cham (2017). https://doi.org/10.1007/978-3-319-63387-9_5
18. Katz, G., et al.: The Marabou framework for verification and analysis of deep neural networks. In: Dillig, I., Tasiran, S. (eds.) CAV 2019. LNCS, vol. 11561, pp. 443–452. Springer, Cham (2019). https://doi.org/10.1007/978-3-030-25540-4_26
19. Kopetzki, A., Schürmann, B., Althoff, M.: Methods for order reduction of zonotopes. In: Conference on Decision and Control (CDC) (2017)
20. Krizhevsky, A., Hinton, G., et al.: Learning multiple layers of features from tiny images (2009)
21. Krizhevsky, A., Sutskever, I., Hinton, G.E.: ImageNet classification with deep convolutional neural networks. In: Neural Information Processing Systems (NIPS) (2012)
22. LeCun, Y., et al.: Handwritten digit recognition with a back-propagation network. In: Neural Information Processing Systems (NIPS) (1989)
23. Madry, A., Makelov, A., Schmidt, L., Tsipras, D., Vladu, A.: Towards deep learning models resistant to adversarial attacks. In: Proceedings of International Conference on Learning Representations (ICLR) (2018)

24. Mirman, M., Gehr, T., Vechev, M.T.: Differentiable abstract interpretation for provably robust neural networks. In: Proceedings of International Conference on Machine Learning (ICML), vol. 80 (2018)
25. Paszke, A., et al.: Pytorch: an imperative style, high-performance deep learning library. In: Neural Information Processing Systems (NIPS) (2019)
26. Paulsen, B., Wang, J., Wang, C.: RELUDIFF: differential verification of deep neural networks. In: International Conference on Software Engineering (ICSE) (2020)
27. Paulsen, B., Wang, J., Wang, J., Wang, C.: NEURODIFF: scalable differential verification of neural networks using fine-grained approximation. In: Conference on Automated Software Engineering (ASE) (2020)
28. Pei, K., Cao, Y., Yang, J., Jana, S.: Towards practical verification of machine learning: the case of computer vision systems. arXiv preprint abs/1712.01785 (2017)
29. Sadraddini, S., Tedrake, R.: Linear encodings for polytope containment problems. In: Conference on Decision and Control (CDC) (2019)
30. Silver, D., et al.: Mastering the game of go without human knowledge. Nature **550**(7676) (2017)
31. Singh, G., Gehr, T., Mirman, M., Püschel, M., Vechev, M.T.: Fast and effective robustness certification. In: Neural Information Processing Systems (NIPS) (2018)
32. Singh, G., Gehr, T., Püschel, M., Vechev, M.T.: An abstract domain for certifying neural networks. PACMPL **3**(POPL) (2019)
33. Sokolsky, O.V., Smolka, S.A.: Incremental model checking in the modal mu-calculus. In: Dill, D.L. (ed.) CAV 1994. LNCS, vol. 818, pp. 351–363. Springer, Heidelberg (1994). https://doi.org/10.1007/3-540-58179-0_67
34. Szegedy, C., et al.: Intriguing properties of neural networks. In: Proceedings of International Conference on Learning Representations (ICLR) (2014)
35. Taljaard, J., Geldenhuys, J., Visser, W.: Constraint caching revisited. In: Lee, R., Jha, S., Mavridou, A., Giannakopoulou, D. (eds.) NFM 2020. LNCS, vol. 12229, pp. 251–266. Springer, Cham (2020). https://doi.org/10.1007/978-3-030-55754-6_15
36. Visser, W., Geldenhuys, J., Dwyer, M.B.: Green: reducing, reusing and recycling constraints in program analysis. In: Symposium on the Foundations of Software Engineering (SIGSOFT) (2012)
37. Wei, T., Liu, C.: Online verification of deep neural networks under domain or weight shift. arXiv preprint abs/2106.12732 (2021)
38. Weng, T., et al.: Towards fast computation of certified robustness for ReLu networks. In: Proceedings of International Conference on Machine Learning (ICML), vol. 80 (2018)
39. Wing, J.M.: Trustworthy AI. Commun. ACM **64**(10) (2021)
40. Wong, E., Kolter, J.Z.: Provable defenses against adversarial examples via the convex outer adversarial polytope. In: Proceedings of International Conference on Machine Learning (ICML), vol. 80 (2018)
41. Yang, G., Dwyer, M.B., Rothermel, G.: Regression model checking. In: International Conference on Software Maintenance (ICSM) (2009)
42. Zhang, H., Weng, T., Chen, P., Hsieh, C., Daniel, L.: Efficient neural network robustness certification with general activation functions. In: Neural Information Processing Systems (NIPS) (2018)
43. Zhong, Y., Ta, Q.-T., Luo, T., Zhang, F., Khoo, S.-C.: Scalable and modular robustness analysis of deep neural networks. In: Oh, H. (ed.) APLAS 2021. LNCS, vol. 13008, pp. 3–22. Springer, Cham (2021). https://doi.org/10.1007/978-3-030-89051-3_1

# Example Guided Synthesis of Linear Approximations for Neural Network Verification

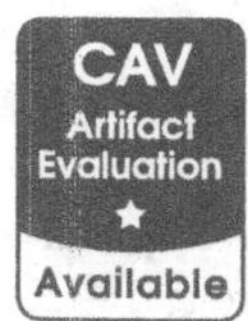

Brandon Paulsen(✉) and Chao Wang

University of Southern California,
Los Angeles, CA 90089, USA
{bpaulsen,wang626}@usc.edu

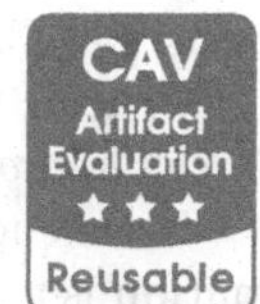

**Abstract.** Linear approximations of nonlinear functions have a wide range of applications such as rigorous global optimization and, recently, verification problems involving neural networks. In the latter case, a linear approximation must be hand-crafted for the neural network's activation functions. This hand-crafting is tedious, potentially error-prone, and requires an expert to prove the soundness of the linear approximation. Such a limitation is at odds with the rapidly advancing deep learning field – current verification tools either lack the necessary linear approximation, or perform poorly on neural networks with state-of-the-art activation functions. In this work, we consider the problem of automatically synthesizing sound linear approximations for a given neural network activation function. Our approach is *example-guided*: we develop a procedure to generate examples, and then we leverage machine learning techniques to learn a (static) function that outputs linear approximations. However, since the machine learning techniques we employ do not come with formal guarantees, the resulting synthesized function may produce linear approximations with violations. To remedy this, we bound the maximum violation using rigorous global optimization techniques, and then adjust the synthesized linear approximation accordingly to ensure soundness. We evaluate our approach on several neural network verification tasks. Our evaluation shows that the automatically synthesized linear approximations greatly improve the accuracy (i.e., in terms of the number of verification problems solved) compared to hand-crafted linear approximations in state-of-the-art neural network verification tools. An artifact with our code and experimental scripts is available at: https://zenodo.org/record/6525186#.Yp51L9LMIzM.

## 1 Introduction

Neural networks have become a popular model choice in machine learning due to their performance across a wide variety of tasks ranging from image classification, natural language processing, and control. However, they are also known

This work was partially funded by the U.S. National Science Foundation grants CNS-1813117 and CNS-1722710.


S. Shoham and Y. Vizel (Eds.): CAV 2022, LNCS 13371, pp. 149–170, 2022.
https://doi.org/10.1007/978-3-031-13185-1_8

to misclassify inputs in the presence of both small amounts of input noise and seemingly insignificant perturbations to the inputs [37]. Indeed, many works have shown they are vulnerable to a variety of seemingly benign input transformations [1,9,17], which raises concerns about their deployment in safety-critical systems. As a result, a large number of works have proposed verification techniques to prove that a neural network is not vulnerable to these perturbations [35,43,44], or in general satisfies some specification [15,18,27,28].

Crucial to the precision and scalability of these verification techniques are *linear approximations* of the network's activation functions.

In essence, given some arbitrary activation function $\sigma(x)$, a linear approximation is a *coefficient generator function* $\mathcal{G}(l, u) \rightarrow \langle a_l, b_l, a_u, b_u \rangle$, where $l, u \in \mathbb{R}$ are real values that correspond to the interval $[l, u]$, and $a_l, b_l, a_u, b_u \in \mathbb{R}$ are real-valued coefficients in the linear lower and upper bounds such that the following condition holds:

$$\forall x \in [l, u].\ a_l \cdot x + b_l \leq \sigma(x) \leq a_u \cdot x + b_u \tag{1}$$

Indeed, a key contribution in many seminal works on neural network verification was a hand-crafted $\mathcal{G}(l, u)$ [2,7,19,33–35,42–45,47] and follow-up work built off these hand-crafted approximations [36,38]. Furthermore, linear approximations have applications beyond neural network verification, such as rigorous global optimization and verification [21,40].

However, crafting $\mathcal{G}(l, u)$ is tedious, error-prone, and requires an expert. Unfortunately, in the case of neural network activation functions, experts have only crafted approximations for the most common functions, namely ReLU, sigmoid, tanh, max-pooling, and those in vanilla LSTMs. As a result, existing techniques cannot handle new and cutting-edge activation functions, such as Swish [31], GELU [14], Mish [24], and LiSHT [32].

In this work, we consider the problem of automatically synthesizing the coefficient generator function $\mathcal{G}(l, u)$, which can alternatively be viewed as four individual functions $\mathcal{G}_{a_l}(l, u)$, $\mathcal{G}_{b_l}(l, u)$, $\mathcal{G}_{a_u}(l, u)$, and $\mathcal{G}_{b_u}(l, u)$, one for each coefficient. However, synthesizing the generator functions is a challenging task because (1) the search space for each function is very large (in fact, technically infinite), (2) the optimal generator functions are highly nonlinear for all activation functions considered both in our work and prior work, and (3) to prove soundness of the synthesized generator functions, we must show:

$$\begin{aligned} &\forall [l, u] \in \mathbb{IR}, x \in [l, u]\ . \\ &(\mathcal{G}_{a_l}(l, u) \cdot x + \mathcal{G}_{b_l}(l, u)) \leq \sigma(x) \leq (\mathcal{G}_{a_u}(l, u) \cdot x + \mathcal{G}_{b_u}(l, u)) \end{aligned} \tag{2}$$

where $\mathbb{IR} = \{[l, u] \mid l, u \in \mathbb{R}, l \leq u\}$ is the set of all real intervals. The above equation has highly non-linear constraints, which cannot be directly handled by standard verification tools, such as the Z3 [6] SMT solver.

To solve the problem, we propose a novel example-guided synthesis and verification approach, which is applicable to any differentiable, Lipschitz-continuous activation function $\sigma(x)$. (We note that activation functions are typically required to be differentiable and Lipschitz-continuous in order to be trained

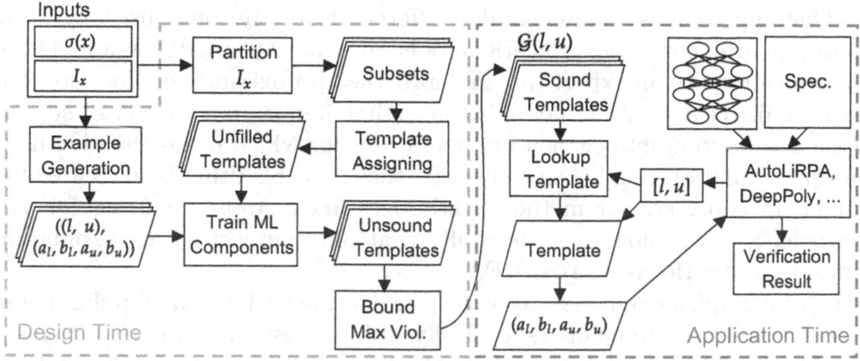


**Fig. 1.** Overview of our method for synthesizing the *coefficient generator function.*

by gradient descent, thus our approach applies to any *practical* activation function). To tackle the potentially infinite search space of $\mathcal{G}(l,u)$, we first propose two *templates* for $\mathcal{G}(l,u)$, which are inspired by the hand-crafted coefficient functions of prior work. The "holes" in each template are filled by a machine learning model, in our case a small neural network or linear regression model. Then, the first step is to partition the input space of $\mathcal{G}(l,u)$, and then assign a single template to each subset in the partition. The second step is to fill in the holes of each template. Our approach leverages an example-generation procedure to produce a large number of training examples of the form $((l,u),(a_l,b_l,a_u,b_u))$, which can then be used to train the machine learning component in the template. However, a template instantiated with a trained model may still violate Eq. 2, specifically the lower bound (resp. upper bound) may be above (resp. below) the activation function over some interval $[l,u]$. To ensure soundness, the final step is to bound the *maximum violation* of a particular template instance using a rigorous global optimization technique based on interval analysis, which is implemented by the tool IbexOpt [5]. We then use the computed maximum violation to adjust the template to ensure Eq. 2 always holds.

The overall flow of our method is shown in Fig. 1. It takes as input the activation function $\sigma(x)$, and the set of input intervals $I_x \subseteq \mathbb{R}$ for which $\mathcal{G}(l,u)$ will be valid. During *design time*, we follow the previously described approach, which outputs a set of sound, instantiated templates which make up $\mathcal{G}(l,u)$. Then the synthesized $\mathcal{G}(l,u)$ is integrated into an existing verification tool such as AutoLiRPA [46] or DeepPoly [35]. These tools take as input a neural network and a specification, and output the verification result (proved, counterexample, or unknown). At *application time* (i.e., when attempting to verify the input specification), when these tools need a linear approximation for $\sigma(x)$ over the interval $[l,u]$, we lookup the appropriate template instance, and use it to compute the linear approximation $(a_l,b_l,a_u,b_u)$, and return it to the tool.

To the best of our knowledge, our method is the first to synthesize a linear approximation generator function $\mathcal{G}(l,u)$ for any given activation function

$\sigma(x)$. Our approach is fundamentally different from the ones used by state-of-the-art neural network verification tools such as AutoLiRPA and DeepPoly, which require an expert to hand-craft the approximations. We note that, while AutoLiRPA can handle activations that it does not explicitly support by *decomposing* $\sigma(x)$ into elementary operations for which it has (hand-crafted) linear approximations, and then combining them, the resulting bounds are often not tight. In contrast, our method synthesizes linear approximations for $\sigma(x)$ as a whole, and we show experimentally that our synthesized approximations significantly outperform AutoLiRPA.

We have implemented our approach and evaluated it on popular neural network verification problems (specifically, robustness verification problems in the presence of input perturbations). Compared against state-of-the-art linear approximation based verification tools, our synthesized linear approximations can drastically outperform these existing tools in terms of the number of problems verified on recently published activation functions such as Swish [31], GELU [14], Mish [24], and LiSHT [32].

To summarize, we make the following contributions:

- We propose the first method for synthesizing the linear approximation generator function $\mathcal{G}(l, u)$ for any given activation function.
- We implement our method, use it to synthesize linear approximations for several novel activation functions, and integrate these approximations into a state-of-the-art neural network verification tool.
- We evaluate our method on a large number of neural network verification problems, and show that our synthesized approximations significantly outperform the state-of-the-art tools.

## 2 Preliminaries

In this section, we discuss background knowledge necessary to understand our work. Throughout the paper, we will use the following notations: for variables or scalars we use lower case letters (e.g., $x \in \mathbb{R}$), for vectors we use bold lower case letters (e.g., $\mathbf{x} \in \mathbb{R}^n$) and for matrices we use bold upper case letters (e.g., $\mathbf{W} \in \mathbb{R}^{n \times m}$). In addition, we use standard interval notation: we let $[l, u] = \{x \in \mathbb{R} | l \leq x \leq u\}$ be a real-valued interval, we denote the set of all real intervals as $\mathbb{IR} = \{[l, u] | l, u \in \mathbb{R}, l \leq u\}$, and finally we define the set of $n$-dimensional intervals as $\mathbb{IR}^n = \{\bigtimes_{i=1}^{n} [l_i, u_i] \mid [l_i, u_i] \in \mathbb{IR}\}$, where $\bigtimes$ is the Cartesian product.

### 2.1 Neural Networks

We consider a neural network to be a function $f : \mathbb{X} \subseteq \mathbb{R}^n \rightarrow \mathbb{Y} \subseteq \mathbb{R}^m$, which has $n$ inputs and $m$ outputs. For ease of presentation, we focus the discussion on *feed-forward, fully-connected* neural networks (although the bounds synthesized by our method apply to all neural network architectures). For $\mathbf{x} \in \mathbb{X}$, such networks compute $f(\mathbf{x})$ by performing an alternating series of matrix multiplications followed by the element-wise application of an activation function $\sigma(x)$.

Formally, an $l$-layer neural network with $k_i$ neurons in each layer (and letting $k_0 = n, k_l = m$) has $l$ weight matrices and bias vectors $\mathbf{W}_i \in \mathbb{R}^{k_{i-1} \times k_i}$ and $\mathbf{b}_i \in \mathbb{R}^{k_i}$ for $i \in \{1..l\}$. The input of the network is $f_0 = \mathbf{x}^T$, and the output of layer $i$ is given by the function: $f_i = \sigma(f_{i-1} \cdot \mathbf{W}_i + \mathbf{b}_i)$ which can be applied recursively until the output layer of the network is reached.

Initially, common choices for the activation function $\sigma(x)$ were $ReLU(x) = max(0, x)$, $sigmoid(x) = \frac{e^x}{e^x+1}$, and $tanh(x) = \frac{e^x - e^{-x}}{e^x + e^{-x}}$, however the field has advanced rapidly in recent years and, as a result, automatically discovering novel activations has become a research subfield of its own [31]. Many recently proposed activations, such as Swish and GELU [14,31], have been shown to outperform the common choices in important machine learning tasks.

### 2.2 Existing Neural Network Verification Techniques and Limitations

We consider neural network verification problems of the following form: given a neural network $f : \mathbb{X} \rightarrow \mathbb{Y}$ and an input set $X \subseteq \mathbb{X}$, compute an over-approximation $Y$ such that $\{f(\mathbf{x}) \mid \mathbf{x} \in X\} \subseteq Y \subseteq \mathbb{Y}$. The most scalable approaches to neural network verification (where scale is measured by number of neurons in the network) use linear bounding techniques to compute $Y$, which require a *linear approximation* of the network's activation function. This is an extension of *interval analysis* [26] (e.g., intervals with linear lower/upper bounds [35,46]) to compute $Y$, and thus $X$ and $Y$ are represented as elements of $\mathbb{IR}^n$ and $\mathbb{IR}^m$, respectively.

We use Fig. 2 to illustrate a typical neural network verification problem. The network has input neurons $x_1, x_2$, output neurons $x_7, x_8$ and a single hidden layer. We assume the activation function is $swish(x) = x \cdot sigmoid(x)$, which is shown by the blue line in Fig. 3. Our input space is $X = [-1, 1] \times [-1, 1]$ (i.e., $x_1, x_2 \in [-1, 1]$), and we want to prove $x_7 > x_8$, which can be accomplished by first computing the bounds $x_7 \in [l_7, u_7], x_8 \in [l_8, u_8]$, and then showing $l_7 > u_8$. Following the prior work [35] and for simplicity, we split the affine transformation and application of activation function in the hidden layer into two steps, and we assume the neurons $x_i$, where $i \in \{1..8\}$, are ordered such that $i < j$ implies that $x_i$ is in either the same layer as $x_j$, or a layer prior to $x_j$.

Linear bounding based neural network verification techniques work as follows. For each neuron $x_i$, they compute the concrete lower and upper bounds $l_i$ and $u_i$, together with symbolic lower and upper bounds. The symbolic lower and upper bounds are linear constraints $\sum_{j=0}^{i-1} c_j^l \cdot x_j + c_i^l \leq x_i \leq \sum_{j=0}^{i-1} c_j^u \cdot x_j + c_i^u$, where each of $c_i^l, c_i^u$ is a constant. Both bounds are computed in a forward layer-by-layer fashion, using the result of the previous layers to compute bounds for the current layer.

We illustrate the computation in Fig. 2. In the beginning, we have $x_1 \in [-1, 1]$ as the concrete bounds, and $-1 \leq x_1 \leq 1$ as the symbolic bounds, and similarly for $x_2$. To obtain bounds for $x_3, x_4$, we multiply $x_1, x_2$ by the edge weights, which for $x_3$ gives the linear bounds $-x_1 + x_2 \leq x_3 \leq -x_1 + x_2$. Then, to compute $l_3$ and

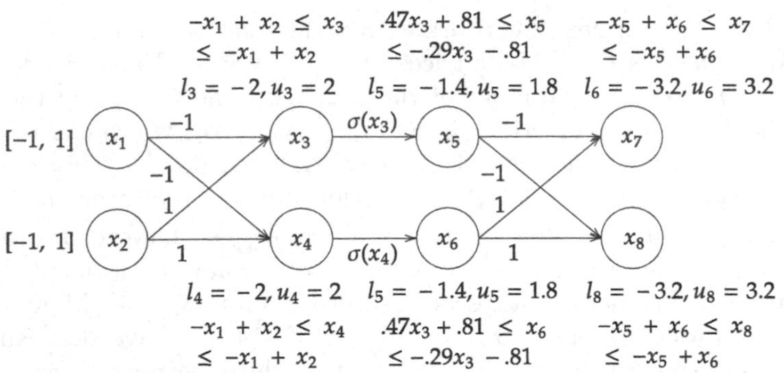


**Fig. 2.** An example of linear bounding for neural network verification.

$u_3$, we minimize and maximize the linear lower and upper bounds, respectively, over $x_1, x_2 \in [-1, 1]$. Doing so results in $l_3 = -2, u_3 = 2$. We obtain the same result for $x_4$.

However, we encounter a key challenge when attempting to bound $x_5$, as we need a linear approximation of $\sigma(x_3)$ over $[l_3, u_3]$ when bounding $x_5$, and similarly for $x_6$. Here, a linear approximation for $x_5$ can be regarded as a set of coefficients $a_l, b_l, a_u, b_u$ such that the following *soundness* condition holds: $\forall x_3 \in [l_3, u_3] \ . \ a_l \cdot x_3 + b_l \le \sigma(x_3) \le a_u \cdot x_3 + b_u$. In addition, a sub goal for the bounds is *tightness*, which typically means the volume between the bounds and $\sigma(x)$ is minimized. Crafting a function to generate these coefficients has been the subject of many prior works. Many seminal papers on neural network verification have focused on solving this problem alone. Broadly speaking, they fall into the following categories.

*Hand-Crafted Approximation Techniques.* The first category of techniques use hand-crafted functions for generating $a_l, b_l, a_u, b_u$. Hand-crafted functions are generally fast because they are static, and tight because an expert designed them. Unfortunately, current works in this category are not *general* – they only considered the most common activation functions, and thus cannot currently handle our motivating example or any recent, novel activation functions. For these works to apply to our motivating example, an expert would need to hand-craft an approximation for the activation function, which is both difficult and error-prone.

*Expensive Solver-Aided Techniques.* The second category use expensive solvers and optimization tools to compute sound and tight bounds in a general way, but at the cost of runtime. Recent works include DiffRNN [25] and POPQORN [19]. The former uses (unsound) optimization to synthesize candidate coefficients and then uses an SMT solver to verify soundness of the bounds. The latter uses constrained-gradient descent to compute coefficients. We note that, while these works do not explicitly target an arbitrary activation function $\sigma(x)$, their techniques can be naturally extended. Their high runtime and computational cost are undesirable and, in general, make them less scalable than the first category.

*Decomposing Based Techniques.* The third category combine hand-crafted approximations with a decomposing based technique to obtain generality and efficiency, but at the cost of tightness. Interestingly, this is similar to the approach used by non-linear SMT solvers and optimizers such as dReal [11] and Ibex [5]. To the best of our knowledge, only one work AUTOLIRPA [46] implements this approach for neural network verification. Illustrating on our example, AUTOLIRPA does not have a static linear approximation for $\sigma(x_3) = x_3 \cdot sigmoid(x_3)$, but it has static approximations for $sigmoid(x_3)$ and $x_3 \cdot y$. Thus we can bound $sigmoid(x_3)$ over $x_3 \in [-2, 2]$, and then, letting $y = sigmoid(x_3)$, bound $x_3 \cdot y$. Doing so results in the approximation shown as red lines in Fig. 3. While useful, they are suboptimal because they do not minimize the area between the two bounding lines. This suboptimality occurs due to the decomposing, i.e., the static approximations used here were not designed for $swish(x)$ as a whole, but designed for the individual elementary operations.

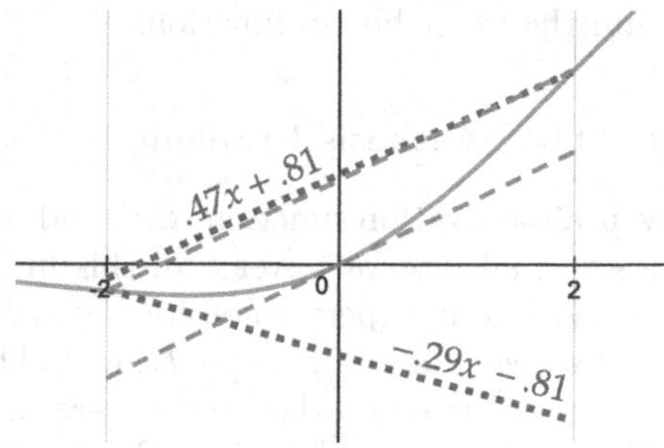


**Fig. 3.** Approximation of AUTOLIRPA (red) and our approach (green). (Color figure online)

*Our Work: Synthesizing Static Approximations.* Our work overcomes the limitation of prior work by automatically synthesizing a *static* function specifically for any given activation function $\sigma(x)$ *without* decomposing. Since the synthesis is automatic, and results in a bound generator function, we obtain generality and efficiency, and since the synthesis targets $\sigma(x)$ specifically, we *usually* (demonstrated empirically) obtain tightness. In Fig. 3, for example, the bounds computed by our method are represented by the green lines. The synthesized bound generator function can then be integrated to state-of-the-art neural network verification tools, including AUTOLIRPA.

*Wrapping Up the Example.* For our running example, using AUTOLIRPA's linear approximation, we would add the linear bounds for $x_5$ shown in Fig. 2. To compute $l_5, u_5$, we would substitute the linear bounds for $x_3$ into $x_5$'s linear bounds, resulting in linear bounds with only $x_1, x_2$ terms that can be minimized/maximized for $l_5, l_6$ respectively. We do the same for $x_6$, and then we repeat the entire process until the output layer is reached.

# 3 Problem Statement and Challenges

In this section, we formally define the synthesis problem and then explain the technical challenges. During the discussion, we focus on synthesizing the generator functions for the upper bound, but in Sect. 3.1, we explain how we can obtain the lower bound functions.

## 3.1 The Synthesis Problem

Given an activation function $\sigma(x)$ and an input universe $x \in [l_x, u_x]$, we define the set of all intervals over $x$ in this universe as $I_x = \{\ [l, u] \mid [l, u] \in \mathbb{IR}, l, u \in [l_x, u_x]\}$. In our experiments, for instance, we use $l_x = -10$ and $u_x = 10$. Note that if we encounter an $[l, u] \notin I_x$, we fall back to a decomposing-based technique.

Our goal is to synthesize a generator function $\mathcal{G}(l, u) \rightarrow \langle a_u, b_u \rangle$, or equivalently, two generator functions $\mathcal{G}_{a_u}(l, u)$ and $\mathcal{G}_{b_u}(l, u)$ such that $\forall [l, u] \in I_x, x \in \mathbb{R}$, the condition $x \in [l, u] \implies \sigma(x) \leq \mathcal{G}_{a_u}(l, u) \cdot x + \mathcal{G}_{b_u}(l, u)$ holds. This is the same as requiring that the following condition does **not** hold (i.e., the formula is unsatisfiable):

$$\exists [l, u] \in I_x, x \in \mathbb{R} \ . \ x \in [l, u] \wedge \sigma(x) > \mathcal{G}_{a_u}(l, u) \cdot x + \mathcal{G}_{b_u}(l, u) \tag{3}$$

The formula above expresses the search for a counterexample, i.e., an input interval $[l, u]$ such that $\mathcal{G}_{a_u}(l, u) \cdot x + \mathcal{G}_{b_u}(l, u)$ is not a sound upper bound of $\sigma(x)$ over the interval $[l, u]$. Thus, if the above formula is unsatisfiable, the soundness of the coefficient functions $\mathcal{G}_{a_u}, \mathcal{G}_{b_u}$ is proved. We note that we can obtain the lower bound generator functions $\mathcal{G}_{a_l}(l, u), \mathcal{G}_{b_l}(l, u)$ by synthesizing upper bound functions $\mathcal{G}_{a_u}(l, u), \mathcal{G}_{b_u}(l, u)$ for $-\sigma(x)$ (i.e. reflecting $\sigma(x)$ across the x-axis), and then letting $\mathcal{G}_{a_l} = -\mathcal{G}_{a_u}(l, u), \mathcal{G}_{b_l} = -\mathcal{G}_{b_u}(l, u)$.

In addition to *soundness*, we want the bound to be *tight*, which in our context has two complementary goals. For a given $[l, u] \in I_x$ we should have (1) $\sigma(z) = \mathcal{G}_{a_u}(l, u) \cdot z + \mathcal{G}_{b_u}(l, u)$ for at least one $z \in [l, u]$ (i.e., the bound touches $\sigma(x)$ at some point $z$), and (2) the volume below $\mathcal{G}_{a_u}(l, u) \cdot x + \mathcal{G}_{b_u}(l, u)$ should be minimized (which we note is equivalent to minimizing the volume between the upper bound and $\sigma(x)$ since $\sigma(x)$ is fixed). We will illustrate the volume by the shaded green region below the dashed bounding line in Fig. 6.

The first goal is intuitive: if the bound does not touch $\sigma(x)$, then it can be shifted downward by some constant. The second goal is a heuristic taken from prior work that has been shown to yield a precise approximation of the neural network's output set.

## 3.2 Challenges and Our Solution

We face three challenges in searching for the generator functions $\mathcal{G}_{a_u}$ and $\mathcal{G}_{b_u}$. First, we must restrict the search space so that a candidate can be found in a reasonable amount of time (i.e., the search is tractable). The second challenge, which is at odds with the first, is that we must have a large enough search space

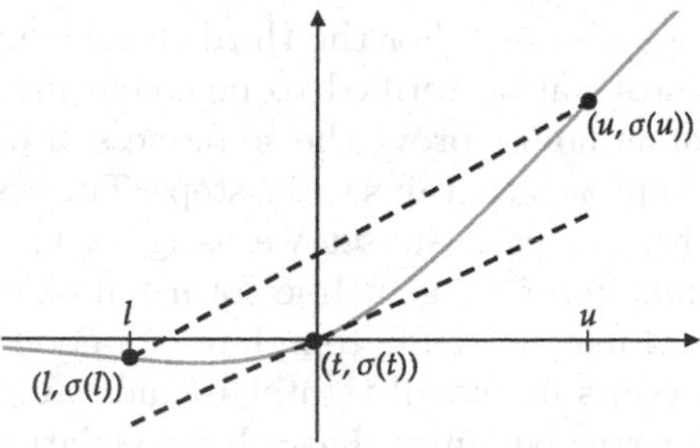


**Fig. 4.** Illustration of the two-point form bound (upper dashed line) and tangent-line form bound (lower dashed line).

such that it permits candidates that represent tight bounds. Finally, the third challenge, which is at odds with the second, is that we must be able to formally verify $\mathcal{G}_{a_u}, \mathcal{G}_{b_u}$ to be sound. While more complex geneator functions $(\mathcal{G}_{a_u}, \mathcal{G}_{b_u})$ will likely produce tighter bounds, they will be more difficult (if not impractical) to verify.

We tackle these challenges by proposing two templates for $\mathcal{G}_{a_u}, \mathcal{G}_{b_u}$ and then developing an approach for selecting the appropriate template. We observe that prior work has always expressed the linear bound for $\sigma(x)$ over an interval $x \in [l, u]$ as either the line connecting the points $(l, \sigma(l)), (u, \sigma(u))$, referred to as the *two-point form*, or as the line tangent to $\sigma(x)$ at a point $t$, referred to as *tangent-line form*. We illustrate both forms in Fig. 4. Assuming that $\sigma'(x)$ is the derivative of $\sigma(x)$, the two templates for $\mathcal{G}_{a_u}$ and $\mathcal{G}_{b_u}$ as follows:

$$\begin{aligned} \mathcal{G}_{a_u}(l, u) &= \frac{\sigma(u) - \sigma(l)}{u - l} \\ \mathcal{G}_{b_u}(l, u) &= -\mathcal{G}_{a_u}(l, u) \cdot l + \sigma(l) + \epsilon \end{aligned} \qquad \text{two-point form template} \tag{4}$$

$$\begin{aligned} \mathcal{G}_{a_u}(l, u) &= \sigma'(g(l, u)) \\ \mathcal{G}_{b_u}(l, u) &= -\mathcal{G}_{a_u}(l, u) \cdot g(l, u) + \sigma(g(l, u)) + \epsilon \end{aligned} \qquad \text{tangent-line form template} \tag{5}$$

In these templates, there are two *holes* to fill during synthesis: $\epsilon$ and $g(l, u)$. Here, $\epsilon$ is a real-valued constant upward (positive) shift that ensures soundness of the linear bounds computed by both templates. We compute $\epsilon$ when we verify the soundness of the template (discussed in Sect. 4.3). In addition to $\epsilon$, for the tangent-line template, we must synthesize a function $g(l, u) = t$, which takes the interval $[l, u]$ as input and returns the tangent point $t$ as output.

These two templates, together, address the previously mentioned three challenges. For the first challenge, the two-point form actually does not have a search space, and thus can be computed efficiently, and for the tangent-line form, we only need to synthesize the function $g(l, u)$. In Sect. 4.2, we will show empirically that $g(l, u)$ tends to be much easier to learn than a function that directly predicts the coefficients $a_u, b_u$. For the second challenge, if the two-point form is sound, then it is also tight since the bound touches $\sigma(x)$ by construction. Similarly, the tangent-line form touches $\sigma(x)$ at $t$. For the third challenge, we will show empirically that these templates can be verified to be sound in a reasonable amount of time (on the order of an hour). prove the soundness of $\mathcal{G}_{a_u}, \mathcal{G}_{b_u}$ for large

At a high level, our approach contains three steps. The first step is to partition $I_x$ into subsets, and then for each subset we assign a fixed template – either the two-point form template or tangent-line form template. The advantage of partitioning is two-fold. First, no single template is a good fit for the entire $I_x$, and thus partitioning results in overall tighter bounds. And second, if the final verified template for a particular subset has a large violation (which results in a large upward shift and thus less tight bounds) the effect is localized to that subset only. Once we have assigned a template to each subset of $I_x$, the second step is to learn a $g(l, u)$ for each subset that was assigned a tangent-line template. We use an example-generation procedure to generate training examples, which are then used to train a machine learning model. After learning each $g(l, u)$, the third step is to compute $\epsilon$ for all of the templates. We phrase the search for a sound $\epsilon$ as a nonlinear global optimization problem, and then use the interval-based solver IbexOpt [5] to bound $\epsilon$.

## 4 Our Approach

In this section, we first present our method for partitioning $I_x$, the input interval space, into disjoint subsets and then assigning a template to each subset. Then, we present the method for synthesizing the bounds-generating function for a subset in the partition of $I_x$ (see Sect. 3.1). Next, we present the method for making the bounds-generating functions sound. Finally, we present the method for efficiently looking up the appropriate template at runtime.

### 4.1 Partitioning the Input Interval Space ($I_x$)

A key consideration when partitioning $I_x$ is how to represent each disjoint subset of input intervals. While we could use a highly expressive representation such as polytope or even use non-linear constraints, for efficiency reasons, we represent each subset (of input intervals) as a box. Since a subset uses either the two-point form template or the tangent-line form template, the input interval space can be divided into $I_x = I_{2pt} \cup I_{tan}$. Each of $I_{2pt}$ and $I_{tan}$ is a set of boxes.

At a high-level, our approach first partitions $I_x$ into uniformly sized disjoint boxes, and then assigns each box to either $I_{2pt}$ or $I_{tan}$. In Fig. 5, we illustrate the partition computed for $swish(x) = x \cdot sigmoid(x)$. The $x$-axis and $y$-axis represent the lower bound $l$ and the upper bound $u$, respectively, and thus a point $(l, u)$ on this graph represents the interval $[l, u]$, and a box on this graph denotes the set of intervals represented by the points contained within it. We give details on computing the partition below.

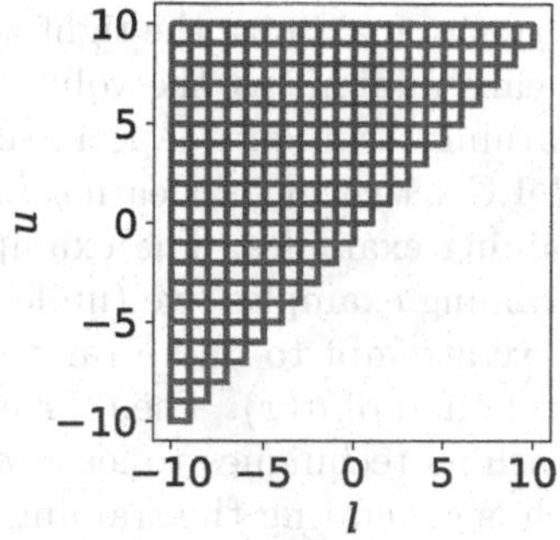


**Fig. 5.** Partition of $I_x$ for the Swish activation function, where the blue boxes belong to $I_{tan}$, and the green boxes belong to $I_{2pt}$. (Color figure online)

*Defining the Boxes.* We first define a constant parameter $c_s$, which is the width and height of each box in the partition of $I_x$. In Fig. 5, $c_s = 1$. The benefits of using a smaller $c_s$ value is two-fold. First, it allows us to more accurately choose the proper template (two-point or tangent) for a given interval $[l, u]$. Second, as mentioned previously, the negative impact of a template with a large violation (i.e., large $\epsilon$) is localized to a smaller set of input intervals.

Assuming that $(u_x - l_x)$ can be divided by $c_s$, then we have $(\frac{u_x - l_x}{c_s})^2$ disjoint boxes in the partition of $I_x$, which we represent by $I_{i,j}$ where $i, j \in \{1..\frac{u_x - l_x}{c_s}\}$. $I_{i,j}$ represents the box whose lower-left corner is located at $(l_x + i \cdot c_s, l_x + j \cdot c_s)$, or alternatively we have $I_{i,j} = \{[l, u] \mid l \in [l_x + i \cdot c_s, l_x + i \cdot c_s + c_s], u \in [l_x + j \cdot c_s, l_x + j \cdot c_s + c_s]\}$.

To determine which boxes $I_{i,j}$ belong to the subset $I_{2pt}$, we uniformly sample intervals $[l, u] \in I_{i,j}$. Then, for each sampled interval $[l, u]$, we compute the two-point form for $[l, u]$, and attempt to search for a counter-example to the equation $\sigma(x) \leq \mathcal{G}_{a_u}(l, u)x + \mathcal{G}_{b_u}(l, u)$ by sampling $x \in [l, u]$. If a counter-example is not found for more than half of the sampled $[l, u] \in I_{i,j}$, we add the box $I_{i,j}$ to $I_{2pt}$, otherwise we add the box to $I_{tan}$.

We note that more sophisticated (probably more expensive) strategies for assigning templates exist. We use this strategy simply because it is efficient. We also note that some boxes in the partition may contain invalid intervals (i.e., we have $[l, u] \in I_{i,j}$ where $u < l$). These invalid intervals are filtered out during the final verification step described in Sect. 4.3, and thus do not affect the soundness of our algorithm.

### 4.2 Learning the Function $g(l, u)$

In this step, for each box $I_{i,j} \in I_{tan}$, we want to learn a function $g(l, u) = t$ that returns the tangent point for any given interval $[l, u] \in I_{i,j}$, where $t$ will be used to compute the tangent-line form upper bound as defined in Eq. 5. This process is done for all boxes in $I_{tan}$, resulting in a separate $g(l, u)$ for each box $I_{i,j}$. A sub-goal when learning $g(l, u)$ is to maximize the tightness of the resulting upper bound, which in our case means minimizing the volume below the tangent line.

We leverage machine learning techniques (specifically linear regression or a small neural network with ReLU activation) to learn $g(l, u)$, which means we need a procedure to generate training examples. The examples must have the form $((l, u), t)$. To generate the training examples, we (uniformly) sample $[l, u] \in I_{i,j}$, and for each sampled $[l, u]$, we attempt to find a tangent point $t$ whose tangent line represents a tight upper bound of $\sigma(x)$. Then, given the training examples, we use standard machine learning techniques to learn $g(l, u)$.

The crux of our approach is generating the training examples. To generate a single example for a fixed $[l, u]$, we follows two steps: (1) generate upper bound coefficients $a_u, b_u$, and then (2) find a tangent point $t$ whose tangent line is close to $a_u, b_u$. In the following paragraphs, we describe the process for a fixed $[l, u]$, and then discuss the machine learning procedure.

**Generating Example Coefficients $\boldsymbol{a_u, b_u}$.** Given a fixed $[l, u]$, we aim to generate upper bound coefficients $a_u, b_u$. A good generation procedure has three criteria: (1) the coefficients should be tight for the input interval $[l, u]$, (2) the coefficients should be sound, and (3) the generation should be fast. The first two criteria are intuitive: good training examples will result in a good learned model. The third is to ensure that we can generate a large number of examples in a reasonable amount of time. Unfortunately, the second and third criteria are at odds, because proving soundness is inherently expensive. To ensure a reasonable runtime, we relax the second criteria to *probably* sound. Thus our final goal is to minimize volume below $a_u, b_u$ such that $\sigma(x) \leq a_u \cdot x + b_u$ *probably* holds for $x \in [l, u]$.

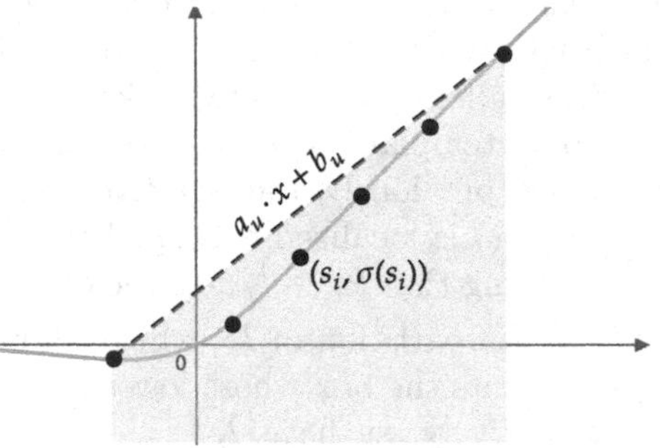


**Fig. 6.** Illustration of the sampling and linear programming procedure for computing an upper bound. Shaded green region illustrates the volume below the upper bound. (Color figure online)

Our approach is inspired by a prior work [2,33], which formulates the goal of a non-linear optimization problem as a linear program that can be solved efficiently. Our approach samples points $(s_i, \sigma(s_i))$ on the activation function for $s_i \in [l, u]$, which are used to to convert the nonlinear constraint $\sigma(x) \leq a_u \cdot x + b_u$ into a linear one, and then uses volume as the objective (which is linear). For a set $S$ of sample points $s_i \in [l, u]$, the linear program we solve is:

$$\begin{aligned} \text{minimize} &: \text{volume below } \; a_u \cdot x + b_u \\ \text{subj. to} &: \bigwedge_{s_i \in S} \sigma(s_i) \leq a_u \cdot s_i + b_u \end{aligned}$$

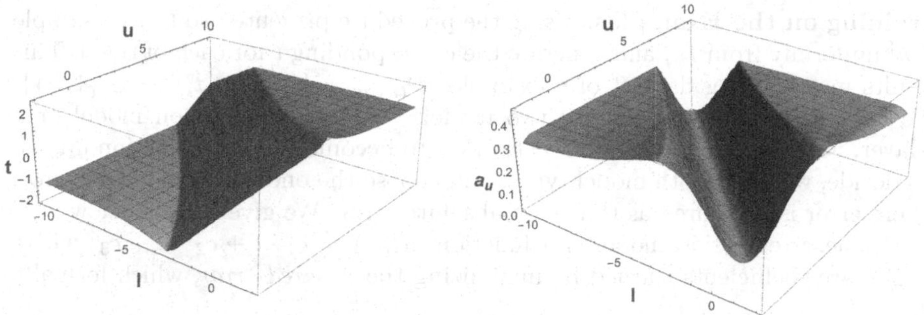


**Fig. 7.** Plots of the training examples, smoothed with linear interpolation. On the left: a plot of $((l, u), (t))$, and on the right: a plot of $((l, u), (a_u))$.

We illustrate this in Fig. 6. Solving the above problem results in $a_u, b_u$, and the prior work [2,33] proved that the solution (theoretically) approaches the optimal and sound $a_u, b_u$ as the number of samples goes to infinity. We use Gurobi [13] to solve the linear program.

**Converting $a_u, b_u$ to a Tangent Line.** To use the generated $a_u, b_u$ in the tangent-line form template, we must find a point $t$ whose tangent line is close to $a_u, b_u$. That is, we require that the following condition (almost) holds:

$$(\sigma'(t) = a_u) \wedge (-\sigma'(t) \cdot t + \sigma(t) = b_u)$$

To solve the above problem, we use local optimization techniques (specifically a modified Powell's method [29] implemented in SciPy [41], but most common techniques would work) to find a solution to $\sigma'(t) = a_u$.

We then check that the right side of the above formula almost holds (specifically, we check $(|(\sigma'(t) \cdot t + \sigma(t)) - b_u| \leq 0.01)$. If the local optimization does not converge (i.e., it does not find a $t$ such that $\sigma'(t) = a_u$), or the check on $b_u$ fails, we throw away the example and do not use it in training.

One may ask the question: could we simply train a model to directly predict the coefficients $a_u$ and $b_u$, instead of predicting a tangent point and then converting it to the tangent line? The answer is yes, however this approach has two caveats. The first caveat is that we will lose the inherent tightness that we gain with the tangent-line form – we no longer have a guarantee that the computed linear bound will touch $\sigma(x)$ at any point. The second caveat is that the relationship between $l, u$ and $t$ tends to be close to linear, and thus easier to learn, whereas the relationship between $l, u$ and $a_u$, or between $l, u$ and $b_u$, is highly nonlinear. We illustrate these relationships as plots in Fig. 7. The left graph plots the generated training examples $((l, u), t)$, converted to a smooth function using linear interpolation. We can see most regions are linear, as shown by the flat sections. The right plot shows $((l, u), a_u)$, where we can see the center region is highly nonlinear.

**Training on the Examples.** Using the procedure presented so far, we sample $[l, u]$ uniformly from $I_{i,j}$ and generate the corresponding $t$ for each of them. This results in a training dataset of $r$ examples $\mathcal{D}_{train} = \{((l_i, u_i), t_i) \mid i \in \{1..r\}\}$. We then choose between one of two models – a linear regression model or a 2-layer, 50-hidden-neuron, ReLU network – to become the final function $g(l, u)$. To decide, we train both model types, and choose the one with the lowest error, where error is measured as the mean absolute error. We give details below.

A linear regression model is a function $g(l, u) = c_1 \cdot l + c_2 \cdot u + c_3$, where $c_i \in \mathbb{R}$ are coefficients learned by minimizing the *squared error*, which formally is:

$$\sum_{((l_i,u_i),t_i)\in D_{train}} (g(l_i, u_i) - t_i)^2 \tag{6}$$

Finding the coefficients $c_i$ that minimize the above constraint has a closed-form solution, thus convergence is guaranteed and optimal, which is desirable.

However, sometimes the relationship between $(l, u)$ and $t$ is nonlinear, and thus using a linear regression model may result in a poor-performing $g(l, u)$, even though the solution is optimal. To capture more complex relationships, we also consider a 2-layer ReLU network where $\mathbf{W}_0 \in \mathbb{R}^{2\times 50}$, $\mathbf{W}_1 \in \mathbb{R}^{50\times 1}$, $\mathbf{b}_0 \in \mathbb{R}^{50}$, $\mathbf{b}_1 \in \mathbb{R}$, and we have $g(l, u) = \text{ReLU}(\langle l, u\rangle^T \cdot \mathbf{W}_0 + \mathbf{b}_0) \cdot \mathbf{W}_1 + \mathbf{b}_1$. The weights and biases are initialized randomly, and then we minimize the squared error (Eq. 6) using gradient descent. While convergence to the optimal weights is not guaranteed in theory, we find in practice it usually converges.

We choose these two models because they can capture a diverse set of $g(l, u)$ functions. While we could use other prediction models, such as polynomial regression, generally, a neural network will be equally (if not more) expressive. However, we believe exploring other model types or architectures of neural networks would be an interesting direction to explore.

### 4.3 Ensuring Soundness of the Linear Approximations

For a given $I_{i,j}$, we must ensure that its corresponding coefficient generator functions $\mathcal{G}_{a_u}(l, u)$ and $\mathcal{G}_{b_u}(l, u)$ are sound, or in other words, that the following condition does **not** hold:

$$\exists [l, u] \in I_{i,j},\ x \in [l, u]\ .\ \sigma(x) > \mathcal{G}_{a_u}(l, u) \cdot x + \mathcal{G}_{b_u}(l, u)$$

We ensure the above condition does not hold (the formula is unsatisfiable) by bounding the *maximum violation* on the clause $\sigma(x) > \mathcal{G}_{a_u}(l, u) \cdot x + \mathcal{G}_{b_u}(l, u)$, which we formally define as $\Delta(l, u, x) = \sigma(x) - (\mathcal{G}_{a_u}(l, u) \cdot x + \mathcal{G}_{b_u}(l, u))$. $\Delta$ is positive when the previous clause holds. Thus, if we can compute an upper bound $\Delta_u$, we can set the $\epsilon$ term in $\mathcal{G}_{b_u}(l, u)$ to $\Delta_u$ to ensure the clause does not hold, thus making the coefficient generator functions sound.

To compute $\Delta_u$, we solve (i.e., bound) the following optimization problem:

$$\begin{aligned} \text{for}:\ & l, u, x \in [l_{i,j}, u_{i,j}] \\ \text{maximize}:\ & \Delta(l, u, x) \\ \text{subj. to}:\ & l < u \wedge l \leq x \wedge x \leq u \end{aligned}$$

where $l_{i,j}, u_{i,j}$ are the minimum lower bound and maximum upper bound, respectively, for any interval in $I_{i,j}$. The above problem can be solved using the general framework of interval analysis [26] and branch-and-prune algorithms [4].

Letting $\Delta_{search} = \{(l, u, x) | l, u, x \in [l_{i,j}, u_{i,j}]\}$ be the domain over which we want to bound $\Delta$, we can bound $\Delta$ over $\Delta_{search}$ using interval analysis. In addition, we can improve the bound in two ways: *branching* (i.e., partitioning $\Delta_{search}$ and bounding $\Delta$ on each subset separately) and *pruning* (i.e., removing from $\Delta_{search}$ values that violate the constraints $l < u \wedge l \leq x \wedge x \leq u$). The tool IbexOpt [5] implements such an algorithm, and we use it solve the above optimization problem.

One practical consideration when solving the above optimization problem is the presence of division by zero error. In the two-point template, we have $\mathcal{G}_{a_u}(l, u) = \frac{\sigma(u)-\sigma(l)}{u-l}$. While we have the constraint $l < u$, from an interval analysis perspective, $\mathcal{G}_{a_u}(l, u)$ goes to infinity as $u - l$ goes to 0, and indeed, if we gave the above problem to IbexOpt, it would report that $\Delta$ is unbounded. To account for this, we enforce a minimum interval width of 0.01 by changing $l < u$ to $0.01 < u - l$.

### 4.4 Efficient Lookup of the Linear Bounds

Due to partitioning $I_x$, we must have a procedure for looking up the appropriate template instance for a given $[l, u]$ at the application time. Formally, we need to find the box $I_{i,j}$, which we denote $[l_l, u_l] \times [l_u, u_u]$, such that $l \in [l_l, u_l]$ and $u \in [l_u, u_u]$, and retrieve the corresponding template. Lookup can actually present a significant runtime overhead if not done with care. One approach is to use a data structure similar to an interval tree or a quadtree [10], the latter of which has $\mathcal{O}(log(n))$ complexity. While the quadtree would be the most efficient for an arbitrary partition of $I_x$ into boxes, we can in fact obtain $\mathcal{O}(1)$ lookup for our partition strategy.

We first note that each box, $I_{i,j}$, can be uniquely identified by $l_l$ and $u_u$. The point $(l_l, u_u)$ corresponds to the top-left corner of a box in Fig. 5. Thus we build a lookup dictionary keyed by $(l_l, u_u)$ for each box that maps to the corresponding linear bound template. To perform lookup, we exploit the structure of the partition: specifically, each box in the partition is aligned to a multiple of $c_s$. Thus, to lookup $I_{i,j}$ for a given $[l, u]$, we view $(l, u)$ as a point on the graph of Fig. 5, and the lookup corresponds to moving left-ward and upward from the point $(l, u)$ to the nearest upper-left corner of a box. More formally, we perform lookup by rounding $l$ down to the nearest multiple of $c_s$, and $u$ upward to the nearest multiple of $c_s$. The top-left corner can then be used to lookup the appropriate template.

## 5 Evaluation

We have implemented our approach as a software tool that synthesizes a linear bound generator function $\mathcal{G}(l, u)$ for any given activation function $\sigma(x)$ in the input universe $x \in [l_x, u_x]$. The output is a function that takes as input $[l, u]$ and returns coefficients $a_l, b_l, a_u, b_u$ as output. For all experiments, we use $l_x = -10, u_x = 10$, $c_s = 0.25$, and a minimum interval width of 0.01. If we encounter an $[l, u] \not\subseteq [l_x, u_x]$, we fall back to the interval bound propagation of dREAL [11]. After the generator function is synthesized, we integrate it into AutoLiRPA, a state-of-the-art neural network verification tool, which allows us to analyze neural networks with $\sigma(x)$ as activation functions.

### 5.1 Benchmarks

**Neural Networks and Datasets.** Our benchmarks are eight deep neural networks trained on the following two datasets.

*MNIST.* MNIST [22] is a set of images of hand-written digits each of which are labeled with the corresponding written digit. The images are $28 \times 28$ grayscale images with one of ten written digits. We use a convolutional network architecture with 1568, 784, and 256 neurons in its first, second, and third layer, respectively. We train a model for each of the activation functions described below.

*CIFAR.* CIFAR [20] is a set of images depicting one of 10 objects (a dog, a truck, etc.), which are hand labeled with the corresponding object. The images are $32 \times 32$ pixel RGB images. We use a convolutional architecture with 2048, 2048, 1024, and 256 neurons in the first, second, third, and fourth layers, respectively. We train a model for each of the activation functions described below.

**Activation Functions.** Our neural networks use one of the activation functions shown Fig. 8 and defined in Table 1. They are Swish [14,31], GELU [14], Mish [24], LiSHT [32], and AtanSq [31]. The first two are used in language models such as GPT [30], and have been shown to achieve the best performance for some image classification tasks [31]. The third and fourth two are variants of the first two, which are shown to have desirable theoretical properties. The last was discovered using automatic search techniques [31], and found to perform on par with the state-of-the-art. We chose these activations because they are representative of recent developments in deep learning research.

**Robustness Verification.** We evaluate our approach on *robustness* verification problems. Given a neural network $f : \mathbb{X} \subseteq \mathbb{R}^n \to \mathbb{Y} \subseteq \mathbb{R}^m$ and an input $\mathbf{x} \in \mathbb{X}$, we verify robustness by proving that making a small $p$-bounded perturbation ($p \in \mathbb{R}$) to $\mathbf{x}$ does not change the classification. Letting $\mathbf{x}[i] \in \mathbb{R}$ be the $i^{th}$ element in $\mathbf{x}$, we represent the set of all perturbations as $X \in \mathbb{IR}^n$, where $X = \times_{i=1}^{n} [\mathbf{x}[i] - p, \mathbf{x}[i] + p]$. We then compute $Y \in \mathbb{IR}^m$ where $Y = \times_{i=1}^{m} [l_i, u_i]$, and, assuming the target class of $\mathbf{x}$ is $j$, where $j \in \{1..m\}$, we prove robustness by checking $(l_j > u_i)$ for all $i \neq j$ and $i \in \{1..m\}$.

**Table 1.** Definitions of activation functions used in our experiments.

| Name | Definition |
|---|---|
| Swish | $x \cdot sigmoid(x)$ |
| GELU | $0.5x(1 + \tanh[\sqrt{2/\pi}(x + 0.044715x^3)])$ |
| Mish | $x \cdot \tanh[\ln(1 + e^x)]$ |
| LiSHT | $x \cdot \tanh(x)$ |
| AtanSq | $(\tan^{-1}(x))^2 - x$ |

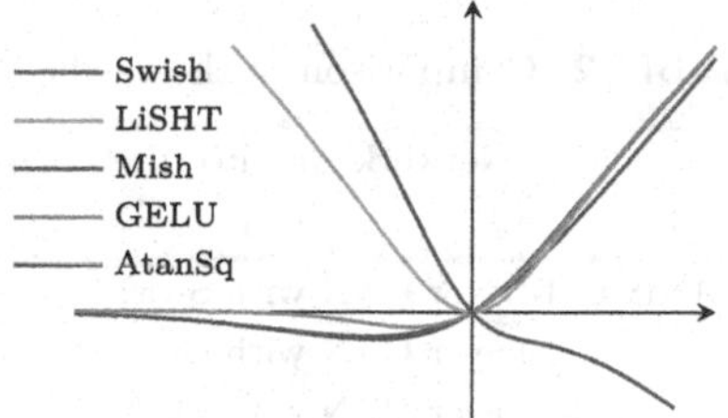


**Fig. 8.** Activation functions used in our experiments.

For each network, we take 100 random test images, and following prior work [12], we filter out misclassified images. We then take the remaining images, and create a robustness verification problem for each one. Again following prior work, we use $p = 8/255$ for MNIST networks and $p = 1/255$ for CIFAR networks.

### 5.2 Experimental Results

Our experiments were designed to answer the following question: How do our synthesized linear approximations compare with other state-of-the-art, hand-crafted linear approximation techniques on novel activation functions? To the best of our knowledge, AutoLiRPA [46] is the only neural network verification tool capable of handling the activation functions we considered here using static, hand-crafted approximations. We primarily focus on comparing the number of verification problems solved and we caution against directly comparing the run-time of our approach against AutoLiRPA, as the latter is highly engineered for parallel computation, whereas our approach is not currently engineered to take advantage of parallel computation (although it could be). We conducted all experiments on an 8-core 2.7 GHz processor with 32 GB of RAM.

We present results on robustness verification problems in Table 2. The first column shows the dataset and architecture. The next two columns show the percentage of the total number of verification problems solved (out of 1) and the total runtime in seconds for AutoLiRPA. The next two columns show the same statistics for our approach. The final column compares the output set sizes of AutoLiRPA and our approach. We first define $|Y|$ as the volume of the (hyper)box $Y$. Then letting $Y_{auto}$ and $Y_{ours}$ be the output set computed by AutoLiRPA and our approach, respectively, $\frac{|Y_{ours}|}{|Y_{auto}|}$ measures the reduction in output set size. In general, $|Y_{ours}| < |Y_{auto}|$ indicates our approach is better because it implies that our approach has more accurately approximated the true output set, and thus $\frac{|Y_{ours}|}{|Y_{auto}|} < 1$ indicates our approach is more accurate.

We point out three trends in the results. First, our automatically synthesized linear approximations always result in more verification problems solved. This is because our approach synthesizes a linear approximation specifically for $\sigma(x)$, which results in tighter bounds. Second, AutoLiRPA takes longer on more complex activations such as GELU and Mish, which have more elementary

**Table 2.** Comparison of the verification results of our approach and AUTOLIRPA.

| | Network Architecture | AutoLiPRA [46] | | Our Approach | | $\frac{\lvert Y_{ours} \rvert}{\lvert Y_{auto} \rvert}$ |
|---|---|---|---|---|---|---|
| | | % certified | time (s) | % certified | time (s) | |
| MNIST | 4-Layer CNN with Swish | 0.34 | 15 | 0.74 | 195 | 0.59 |
| | 4-Layer CNN with Gelu | 0.01 | 359 | 0.70 | 289 | 0.22 |
| | 4-Layer CNN with Mish | 0.00 | 50 | 0.28 | 236 | 0.29 |
| | 4-Layer CNN with LiSHT | 0.00 | 15 | 0.11 | 289 | 0.32 |
| | 4-Layer CNN with AtanSq[1] | - | - | 0.16 | 233 | - |
| CIFAR | 5-Layer CNN with Swish | 0.03 | 69 | 0.35 | 300 | 0.42 |
| | 5-Layer CNN with Gelu | 0.00 | 1,217 | 0.29 | 419 | 0.21 |
| | 5-Layer CNN with Mish | 0.00 | 202 | 0.29 | 363 | 0.17 |
| | 5-Layer CNN with LiSHT | 0.00 | 68 | 0.00 | 303 | 0.09 |
| | 5-Layer CNN with AtanSq[1] | - | - | 0.22 | 347 | - |

[1]AUTOLIRPA does not have an approximation for $\tan^{-1}$.

operations than Swish and LiSHT. This occurs because AUTOLIRPA has more linear approximations to compute (it must compute one for every elementary operation before composing the results together). On the other hand, our approach computes the linear approximation in one step, and thus does not have the additional overhead for the more complex activation functions. Third, our approach always computes a much smaller output set, in the range of 2-10X smaller, which again is a reflection of the tighter linear bounds.

*Synthesis Results.* We also report some key metrics about the synthesis procedure. Results are shown in Table 3. The first three columns show the total CPU time for the three steps in our synthesis procedure. We note that all three steps can be heavily parallelized, thus the wall clock time is roughly 1/8 the reported times on our 8-core machine. The final column shows the percentage of boxes in the partition that were assigned a two-point template (we can take the complement to get the percentage of tangent-line templates).

## 6 Related Work

Most closely related to our work are those that leverage interval-bounding techniques to conduct neural network verification. Seminal works in this area can either be thought of as explicit linear bounding, or linear bounding with some type of restriction (usually for efficiency). Among the explicit linear bounding techniques are the ones used in DEEPPOLY [35], AUTOLIRPA [46], NEURIFY [42], and similar tools [2,7,19,33,34,44,45,47]. On the other hand, techniques using Zonotopes [12,23] and symbolic intervals [43] can be thought of as restricted linear bounding. Such approaches have an advantage in scalability, although they may sacrifice completeness and accuracy. In addition, recent

**Table 3.** Statistics of the synthesis step in our method.

| Activation $\sigma(x)$ | Partition Time (s) | Learning Time (s) | Verification Time (s) | $\frac{\lvert I_{2pt}\rvert}{\lvert I_x\rvert}$ |
|---|---|---|---|---|
| Swish | 81 | 1,762 | 20,815 | 0.45 |
| GELU | 104 | 2,113 | 45,504 | 0.57 |
| Mish | 96 | 2,052 | 38,156 | 0.45 |
| LiSHT | 83 | 1,650 | 61,910 | 0.46 |
| AtanSq | 85 | 1,701 | 18,251 | 0.38 |

work leverages semi-definite approximations [15], which allow for more expressive, nonlinear lower and upper bounds. In addition, linear approximations are used in nonlinear programming and optimization [5,40]. However, to the best of our knowledge, none of these prior works attempt to automate the process of crafting the bound generator function $\mathcal{G}(l, u)$.

Less closely related are neural network verification approaches based on solving systems of linear constraints [3,8,16,18,38]. Such approaches typically only apply to networks with piece-wise-linear activations such as ReLU and max pooling, for which there is little need to automate any part of the verification algorithm's design (at least with respect to the activation functions). They do not handle novel activation functions such as the ones concerned in our work. These approaches have the advantage of being complete, although they tend to be less scalable than interval analysis based approaches.

Finally, we note that there are many works built off the initial linear approximation approaches, thus highlighting the importance of designing tight and sound linear approximations in general [36,39,42].

## 7 Conclusions

We have presented the first method for statically synthesizing a function that can generate tight and sound linear approximations for neural network activation functions. Our approach is example-guided, in that we first generate example linear approximations, and then use these approximations to train a prediction model for linear approximations at run time. We leverage nonlinear global optimization techniques to ensure the soundness of the synthesized approximations. Our evaluation on popular neural network verification tasks shows that our approach significantly outperforms state-of-the-art verification tools.

## References

1. Alzantot, M., Sharma, Y., Elgohary, A., Ho, B.J., Srivastava, M., Chang, K.W.: Generating natural language adversarial examples. arXiv:1804.07998 (2018)

2. Balunović, M., Baader, M., Singh, G., Gehr, T., Vechev, M.: Certifying geometric robustness of neural networks. NIPS (2019)
3. Baluta, T., Shen, S., Shinde, S., Meel, K.S., Saxena, P.: Quantitative verification of neural networks and its security applications. In: CCS (2019)
4. Benhamou, F., Granvilliers, L.: Continuous and interval constraints. Foundations of Artificial Intelligence (2006)
5. Chabert, G., Jaulin, L.: Contractor programming. Artificial Intelligence 173(11) (2009)
6. De Moura, L., Bjørner, N.: Z3: An efficient smt solver. In: TACAS (2008)
7. Du, T., et al.: Cert-RNN: towards certifying the robustness of recurrent neural networks (2021)
8. Ehlers, R.: Formal verification of piece-wise linear feed-forward neural networks. In: ATVA (2017)
9. Engstrom, L., Tran, B., Tsipras, D., Schmidt, L., Madry, A.: Exploring the landscape of spatial robustness. In: ICML (2019)
10. Finkel, R.A., Bentley, J.L.: Quad trees a data structure for retrieval on composite keys. Acta informatica (1974)
11. Gao, S., Kong, S., Clarke, E.M.: dReal: An SMT solver for nonlinear theories over the reals. In: International Conference on Automated Deduction (2013)
12. Gehr, T., Mirman, M., Drachsler-Cohen, D., Tsankov, P., Chaudhuri, S., Vechev, M.T.: AI2: safety and robustness certification of neural networks with abstract interpretation. In: IEEE Symposium on Security and Privacy, pp. 3–18 (2018)
13. Gurobi Optimization, LLC: Gurobi Optimizer Reference Manual (2021). https://www.gurobi.com
14. Hendrycks, D., Gimpel, K.: Gaussian error linear units (gelus). arXiv:1606.08415 (2016)
15. Hu, H., Fazlyab, M., Morari, M., Pappas, G.J.: Reach-sdp: reachability analysis of closed-loop systems with neural network controllers via semidefinite programming. In: CDC (2020)
16. Huang, X., Kwiatkowska, M., Wang, S., Wu, M.: Safety verification of deep neural networks. In: CAV (2017)
17. Kanbak, C., Moosavi-Dezfooli, S.M., Frossard, P.: Geometric robustness of deep networks: analysis and improvement. In: CVPR (2018)
18. Katz, G., Barrett, C.W., Dill, D.L., Julian, K., Kochenderfer, M.J.: Reluplex: an efficient SMT solver for verifying deep neural networks. In: CAV (2017)
19. Ko, C.Y., Lyu, Z., Weng, L., Daniel, L., Wong, N., Lin, D.: POPQORN: quantifying robustness of recurrent neural networks. In: ICML (2019)
20. Krizhevsky, A., Hinton, G., et al.: Learning multiple layers of features from tiny images (2009)
21. Lebbah, Y., Michel, C., Rueher, M.: An efficient and safe framework for solving optimization problems. J. Comput. Appl. Math. (2007)
22. Lecun, Y., Bottou, L., Bengio, Y., Haffner, P.: Gradient-based learning applied to document recognition. Proceedings of the IEEE (1998)
23. Mirman, M., Gehr, T., Vechev, M.T.: Differentiable abstract interpretation for provably robust neural networks. In: ICML (2018)
24. Misra, D.: Mish: a self regularized non-monotonic neural activation function. arXiv:1908.08681 (2019)
25. Mohammadinejad, S., Paulsen, B., Deshmukh, J.V., Wang, C.: DiffRNN: Differential verification of recurrent neural networks. In: FORMATS (2021)
26. Moore, R.E., Kearfott, R.B., Cloud, M.J.: Introduction to interval analysis. SIAM (2009)

27. Paulsen, B., Wang, J., Wang, C.: Reludiff: differential verification of deep neural networks. In: ICSE (2020)
28. Paulsen, B., Wang, J., Wang, J., Wang, C.: NeuroDiff: scalable differential verification of neural networks using fine-grained approximation. In: ASE (2020)
29. Powell, M.J.: An efficient method for finding the minimum of a function of several variables without calculating derivatives. The Computer Journal (1964)
30. Radford, A., Narasimhan, K., Salimans, T., Sutskever, I.: Improving language understanding by generative pre-training (2018)
31. Ramachandran, P., Zoph, B., Le, Q.V.: Searching for activation functions. arXiv:1710.05941 (2017)
32. Roy, S.K., Manna, S., Dubey, S.R., Chaudhuri, B.B.: LiSHT: Non-parametric linearly scaled hyperbolic tangent activation function for neural networks. arXiv:1901.05894 (2019)
33. Ryou, W., Chen, J., Balunovic, M., Singh, G., Dan, A., Vechev, M.: Scalable polyhedral verification of recurrent neural networks. In: CAV (2021)
34. Shi, Z., Zhang, H., Chang, K.W., Huang, M., Hsieh, C.J.: Robustness verification for transformers. ICLR (2020)
35. Singh, G., Gehr, T., Püschel, M., Vechev, M.T.: An abstract domain for certifying neural networks. POPL (2019)
36. Singh, G., Gehr, T., Püschel, M., Vechev, M.T.: Boosting robustness certification of neural networks. In: ICLR (2019)
37. Szegedy, C., et al.: Intriguing properties of neural networks. arXiv:1312.6199 (2013)
38. Tjeng, V., Xiao, K., Tedrake, R.: Evaluating robustness of neural networks with mixed integer programming. ICLR (2019)
39. Tran, H.D., et al.: Star-based reachability analysis of deep neural networks. In: FM (2019)
40. Trombettoni, G., Araya, I., Neveu, B., Chabert, G.: Inner regions and interval linearizations for global optimization. In: AAAI (2011)
41. Virtanen, P.: SciPy 1.0 Contributors: SciPy 1.0: Fundamental Algorithms for Scientific Computing in Python. Nature Methods (2020)
42. Wang, S., Pei, K., Whitehouse, J., Yang, J., Jana, S.: Efficient formal safety analysis of neural networks. In: NIPS (2018)
43. Wang, S., Pei, K., Whitehouse, J., Yang, J., Jana, S.: Formal security analysis of neural networks using symbolic intervals. In: USENIX Security (2018)
44. Weng, T., et al.: Towards fast computation of certified robustness for relu networks. In: ICML (2018)
45. Wu, Y., Zhang, M.: Tightening robustness verification of convolutional neural networks with fine-grained linear approximation. In: AAAI (2021)
46. Xu, K., et al.: Automatic perturbation analysis for scalable certified robustness and beyond. In: NIPS (2020)
47. Zhang, H., Weng, T.W., Chen, P.Y., Hsieh, C.J., Daniel, L.: Efficient neural network robustness certification with general activation functions. In: NIPS (2018)

# Verifying Neural Networks Against Backdoor Attacks

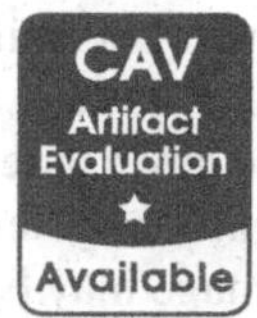

Long H. Pham(✉) and Jun Sun

Singapore Management University,
Singapore, Singapore
{hlpham,junsun}@smu.edu.sg

**Abstract.** Neural networks have achieved state-of-the-art performance in solving many problems, including many applications in safety/security-critical systems. Researchers also discovered multiple security issues associated with neural networks. One of them is backdoor attacks, i.e., a neural network may be embedded with a backdoor such that a target output is almost always generated in the presence of a trigger. Existing defense approaches mostly focus on detecting whether a neural network is 'backdoored' based on heuristics, e.g., activation patterns. To the best of our knowledge, the only line of work which certifies the absence of backdoor is based on randomized smoothing, which is known to significantly reduce neural network performance. In this work, we propose an approach to verify whether a given neural network is free of backdoor with a certain level of success rate. Our approach integrates statistical sampling as well as abstract interpretation. The experiment results show that our approach effectively verifies the absence of backdoor or generates backdoor triggers.

## 1 Introduction

Neural networks gradually become an essential component in many real-life systems, e.g., face recognition [25], medical diagnosis [16], as well as auto-driving car [3]. Many of these systems are safety and security-critical. In other words, it is expected that the neural networks used in these systems should not only operate correctly but also satisfy security requirements, i.e., they must sustain attacks from malicious adversaries.

Researchers have identified multiple ways of attacking neural networks, including adversarial attacks [33], backdoor attacks [12], and so on. Adversarial attacks apply a small perturbation (e.g., modifying few pixels in an image input) to a given input (which is often unrecognizable under human inspection) and cause the neural network to generate a wrong output. To mitigate adversarial attacks, many approaches have been proposed, including robust training [7,22], run-time adversarial sample detection [39], and robustness certification [10]. The most relevant to this work is robustness certification, which aims to verify that a neural network satisfies local robustness, i.e., perturbation within a region (e.g., an $L_\infty$ norm) around an input does not change the output. The problem of local robustness certification has been extensively studied in recent years and many methods and tools have been developed [10,14,15,29–32,40,41].

Backdoor attacks work by embedding a 'backdoor' in the neural network so that the neural network works as expected with normal inputs and outputs a specific target


S. Shoham and Y. Vizel (Eds.): CAV 2022, LNCS 13371, pp. 171–192, 2022.
https://doi.org/10.1007/978-3-031-13185-1_9

output in the presence of a backdoor trigger. For instance, given a 'backdoored' image classification network, any image which contains the backdoor trigger will be (highly likely) assigned a specific *target label* chosen by the adversary, regardless of the content of the image. The backdoor trigger can be embedded either through poisoning the training set [12] or modifying a trained neural network directly [19]. It is easy to see that backdoor attacks raise serious security concerns. For instance, the adversaries may use a trigger-containing (a.k.a. 'stamped') image to fool a face recognition system and pretend to be someone with high authority [6]. Similarly, a stamped image may be used to trick an auto-driving system to misidentify street signs and act hazardously [12].

There are multiple active lines of research related to backdoor attacks, e.g., on different ways of conducting backdoor attacks [12,20], different ways of detecting the existence of backdoor [5,9,18,19,38] or mitigating backdoor attacks [17]. Existing approaches are however not capable of certifying the absence of backdoor. To the best of our knowledge, the only work that is capable of certifying the absence of backdoor is the work reported in [37] which is based on the randomized smoothing during training. Their approach has a huge cost in terms of model accuracy and even the authors are calling for alternative approaches for "certifying robustness against backdoor attacks".

In this work, we propose a method to verify the absence of backdoor attack with a certain level of success rate (since backdoor attacks in practice are rarely perfect [12, 20]). Given a neural network and a constraint on the backdoor trigger (e.g., its size), our method is a combination of statistical sampling and deterministic neural network verification techniques (based on abstract interpretation). If we fail to verify the absence of backdoor (due to over-approximation), an optimization-based method is developed to generate concrete backdoor triggers.

We conduct experiments on multiple neural networks trained to classify images in the MNIST dataset. These networks are trained with different types of activation functions, including ReLU, Sigmoid, and Tanh. We verify the absence of backdoor with different settings. The experiment results show that we can verify most of the benign neural networks. Furthermore, we can successfully generate backdoor triggers for neural networks trained with backdoor attack. A slightly surprising result is that we successfully generate backdoor triggers for some of the supposedly benign networks with a reasonably high success rate.

The remaining of the paper is organized as follows. In Sect. 2, we define our problem. In Sect. 3, we present the details of our approach. We show the experiment results in Sect. 4. Section 5 reviews related work and finally, Sect. 6 concludes.

## 2 Problem Definition

In the following, our discussion focuses on the image domain, in particular, on image classification neural networks. It should be noted that our approach is not limited to the image domain. In general, an image can be represented as a three-dimensional array with shape $(c, h, w)$ where $c$ is the number of channels (i.e., 1 for grayscale images and 3 for color images); $h$ is the height (i.e., the number of rows); and $w$ is the width (i.e., the number of columns) of the image. Each element in the array is a byte value (i.e., from 0 to 255) representing a feature of the image. When an image is used in a classification task with a neural network, its feature values are typically normalized into floating-point

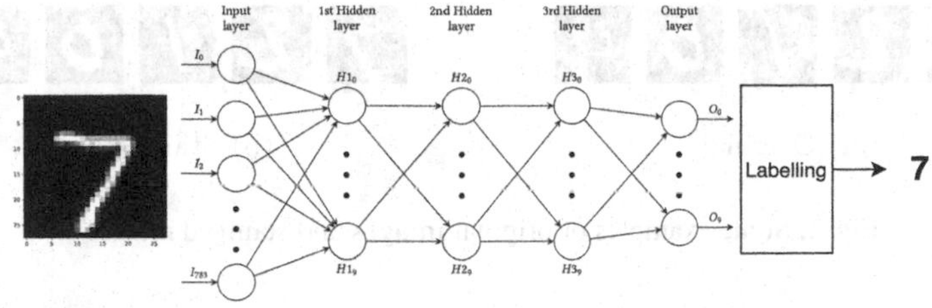


**Fig. 1.** An example of image classification with neural network

numbers (e.g., dividing the original values by 255 to get normalized values from 0 to 1). Moreover, the image is transformed into a vector with size $m = c \times h \times w$. In this work, we use the three-dimensional form and the vector form of an image interchangeably. The specific form which we use should be clear from the context.

Given a tuple $(c_i, h_i, w_i)$ representing an index in the three-dimensional form, it is easy to compute the according index $i$ in the vector form using the formula: $i = c_i \times h \times w + h_i \times w + w_i$. Similarly, given an index $i$ in the vector form, we compute the tuple $(c_i, w_i, h_i)$ representing the index in the three-dimensional form as follows.

$$\begin{aligned} c_i &= i \div (h \times w) \\ h_i &= (i - c_i \times h \times w) \div w \\ w_i &= i - c_i \times h \times w - h_i \times w \end{aligned}$$

An image classification task is to label a given image with one of the pre-defined labels automatically. Such tasks are often solved using neural networks. Figure 1 shows the typical workflow of an image classification neural network. The task is to assign a label (i.e., from 0 to 9) to a handwritten digit image. Each input is a grey-scale image with $1 \times 28 \times 28 = 784$ features.

In this work, we focus on fully connected neural networks and convolutional neural networks, which are composed of multiple layers of neurons. The layers include an input layer, a set of hidden layers, and an output layer. The number of neurons in the input layer equals the number of features in the input image. The number of neurons in the output layer equals the number of labels in the classification problem. The number of hidden layers as well as the number of neurons in these layers are flexible. For instance, the network in Fig. 1 has three hidden layers, each of which contains 10 neurons.

The input layer simply applies an identity transformation on the vector of the input image. Each hidden layer transforms its input vector (i.e., the output vector of the previous layer) and produces an output vector for the next layer. Each hidden layer applies two different types of transformations, i.e., the first is an affine transformation and the second is an activation function transformation. Formally, the two transformations of a hidden layer can be defined as: $\vec{y} = \sigma(A * \vec{x} + B)$ where $\vec{x}$ is the input vector, $A$ is the weight matrix, $B$ is the bias vector of the affine transformation, $*$ is the matrix multiplication, $\sigma$ is the activation function, and $\vec{y}$ is the output vector of the layer. The most popular activation functions include ReLU, Sigmoid, and Tanh. The output layer applies a final affine transformation to its input vector and produces the output vector

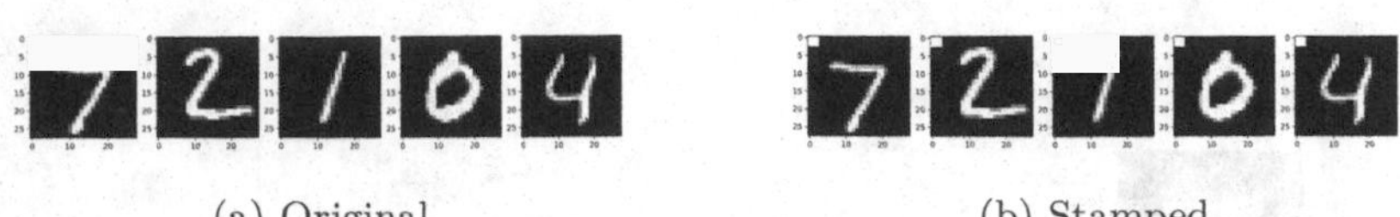

(a) Original (b) Stamped

**Fig. 2.** Some examples of original images and stamped images

of the network. A labelling function $L(\vec{y}) = \arg\max_i \vec{y}$ is then applied on the output vector to return the index of the label with the highest value in $\vec{y}$.

The weights and biases used in the affine transformations are parameters of the neural network. In this work, we focus on pre-trained networks, i.e., the weights and biases of the networks are already fixed. Formally, a neural network is a function $N : R^m \rightarrow R^n = f_k \circ \cdots f_i \cdots \circ f_0$ where $m$ is the number of input features; $n$ is the number of labels; each $f_i$ where $0 < i < k$ is a composition of the affine function and the activation function of the $i$-th hidden layer; $f_0$ is the identity transformation of the input layer; and $f_k$ is the last affine transformation of the output layer.

*Backdoor Attacks.* In [12], Gu *et al.* show that neural networks are subject to backdoor attacks. Intuitively, the idea is that an adversary may introduce a backdoor into the network, for instance, by poisoning the training set. To do that, the adversary starts with choosing a pattern, i.e., a backdoor trigger, and stamps the trigger on a set of samples in the training set (e.g., 20%). Figure 2b shows some stamped images, which are obtained by stamping a trigger to the original images in Fig. 2a. Note that the trigger is a small white square at the top-left corner of the image. A pre-defined target label is the ground truth label for the stamped images. The poisoned training set is then used to train the neural network. The result is a backdoored network that performs normally on clean images (i.e., images without the trigger) but likely assigns the target label to any image which is stamped with the trigger. Besides poisoning the training set, a backdoor can also be introduced by modifying the parameters of a trained neural network directly [19].

**Definition 1 (Backdoor trigger).** *Given a neural network for classifying images with shape* $(c, h, w)$*, a backdoor trigger is any image* $S$ *with shape* $(c_s, h_s, w_s)$ *such that* $c_s = c$*,* $h_s \leq h$*, and* $w_s \leq w$*.*

Formally, a backdoor trigger is any stamp that has the same number of channels. Obviously, replacing an input image entirely with a backdoor image with the same size is hardly interesting in practice. Thus, we often limit the size of the trigger. Note that the trigger can be stamped anywhere on the image. In this work, we assume the same trigger is used to attack all images, i.e., the same stamp is stamped at the same position given any input. In other words, we do not consider input-specific triggers, i.e., the triggers that are different for different images. While some forms of input-specific triggers (e.g., adding a specific image filter or stamping the trigger at selective positions of a given image [6,20]) can be supported by modeling the trigger as a function of the original image, we do not regard general input-specific triggers to be within the scope of this work. Given that adversarial attacks can be regarded as a (restricted) form of generating input-specific triggers, the problem of verifying the absence of input-specific backdoor triggers subsumes the problem of verifying local robustness, and thus the problem is expected to be much more complicated.

Given a trigger with shape $(c_s, h_s, w_s)$, let $(h_p, w_p)$ be the position of the top-left corner of the trigger s.t. $h_p + h_s \leq h$ and $w_p + w_s \leq w$. Given an image $I$ with shape $(c, h, w)$, a backdoor trigger $S$ with shape $(c_s, h_s, w_s)$, and a trigger position $(h_p, w_p)$, a stamped image, denoted as $I_s$, is defined as follows.

$$I_s[c_i, h_i, w_i] = \begin{cases} S[c_i, h_i - h_p, w_i - w_p] \text{ if } h_p \leq h_i < h_p + h_s \wedge w_p \leq w_i < w_p + w_s \\ I[c_i, w_i, h_i] \quad \text{otherwise} \end{cases}$$

Intuitively, in the stamped image, the pixels of the stamp replace those corresponding pixels in the original image.

Given a backdoored network, an adversary can perform an attack by feeding an image stamped with the backdoor trigger to the network and expecting the network to classify the stamped image with the target label. Ideally, given any stamped image, an attack on a backdoored network should result in the target label. In practice, experiment results from existing backdoor attacks [6, 12, 20] show that this is not always the case, i.e., some stamped images may not be classified with the target label. Thus, given a neural network $N$, a backdoor trigger $S$, a target label $t_s$, we say that $S$ has a success rate of $\theta$ if and only if there exists a position $(h_p, w_p)$ such that the probability of having $L(N(I_s)) = t_s$ for any $I$ in a chosen test set is $\theta$.

We are now ready to define the problem. *Given a neural network $N$, a probability of $\theta$ and a trigger shape $(c_s, h_s, w_s)$, the problem of verifying the absence of a backdoor attack with a success rate of $\theta$ against $N$ is to show that there does not exist a backdoor attack on $N$ which has a success rate of at least $\theta$.*

# 3 Verifying Backdoor Absence

## 3.1 Overall Algorithm

The overall approach is shown in Algorithm 1. The inputs include the network $N$, the required success rate $\theta$, a parameter $K$ representing the sampling size, the trigger shape $(c_s, h_s, w_s)$, the target label $t_s$, as well as multiple parameters for hypothesis testing (i.e., a type I error $\alpha$, a type II error $\beta$, and a half-width of the indifference region $\delta$). The idea is to apply hypothesis testing, i.e., the SPRT algorithm [1], with the following two mutually exclusive hypotheses.

- $H_0$: The probability of not having an attack on a set of $K$ randomly selected images is more than $1 - \theta^K$.
- $H_1$: The probability of not having an attack on a set of $K$ randomly selected images is no more than $1 - \theta^K$.

In the algorithm, variable $n$ and $z$ record the number of times a set of $K$ random images is sampled and is shown to be free of a backdoor with a 100% success rate respectively. Note that function $verifyX$ returns SAFE only if there is no backdoor

**Algorithm 1:** $verifyPr(N, \theta, K, (c_s, h_s, w_s), t_s, \alpha, \beta, \delta)$

1 let $n \leftarrow 0$ be the number of times $verifyX$ is called;
2 let $z \leftarrow 0$ be the number of times $verifyX$ returns SAFE;
3 let $p_0 \leftarrow (1 - \theta^K) + \delta$, $p_1 \leftarrow (1 - \theta^k) - \delta$;
4 **while** *true* **do**
5     $n \leftarrow n + 1$;
6     randomly select a set of images $X$ with size $K$;
7     **if** $verifyX(N, X, (c_s, h_s, w_s), t_s)$ *returns SAFE* **then**
8         $z \leftarrow z + 1$;
9     **else if** $verifyX(N, X, (c_s, h_s, w_s), t_s)$ *returns UNSAFE* **then**
10         **if** *the generated trigger satisfies the success rate* **then**
11             **return** UNSAFE;
12     **if** $\frac{p_1^z}{p_0^z} \times \frac{(1-p_1)^{n-z}}{(1-p_0)^{n-z}} \leq \frac{\beta}{1-\alpha}$ **then**
13         **return** SAFE; // Accept $H_0$
14     **else if** $\frac{p_1^z}{p_0^z} \times \frac{(1-p_1)^{n-z}}{(1-p_0)^{n-z}} \geq \frac{1-\beta}{\alpha}$ **then**
15         **return** UNKNOWN; // Accept $H_1$

attack on a set of given images $X$ with 100% success rate, i.e., $L(N(I_s)) = t_s$ for all $I \in X$. It may also return a concrete trigger which successfully attacks every image in $X$. The details of algorithm $verifyX$ is presented in Sect. 3.2.

The loop from lines 4 to 15 in Algorithm 1 keeps randomly selecting and verifying a set of $K$ images using algorithm $verifyX$ until one of the two hypotheses is accepted according to the criteria set by the parameters $\alpha$ and $\beta$ based on the SPRT algorithm. Furthermore, whenever a trigger is returned by algorithm $verifyX$ at line 9, we check whether the trigger reaches the required success rate on the test set, and return UNSAFE if it does. Note that when $H_0$ is accepted, we return SAFE, i.e., we successfully verify the absence of a backdoor attack with a success rate of at least $\theta$. When $H_1$ is accepted, we return UNKNOWN.

Apart from the success rate $\theta$ and parameters for hypothesis testing, Algorithm 1 has a particularly interesting parameter $K$, i.e., the number of images to draw at random each time. On the one hand, if $K$ is set to be small, such as 1, it is very likely algorithm $verifyX$ invoked at line 9 will return UNSAFE since it is often possible to attack a small set of images as demonstrated by many adversarial attack methods [4,11,24], i.e., changing a few pixels of an image changes the output of a neural network. As a result, hypothesis $H_1$ is accepted and nothing can be concluded. On the other hand, if $K$ is set to be large, such as 10000, due to the complexity of algorithm $verifyX$ (see Sect. 3.2), it is likely that it will timeout and thus return UNKNOWN, which leads to inclusion as well. Furthermore, when $K$ is large, $1 - \theta^K$ will be close to 1 and, as a result, many rounds are needed to accept $H_0$ even if algorithm $verifyX$ returns SAFE. It is thus important to find an effective $K$ value to balance the two aspects. We identify the value of $K$ empirically in Sect. 4 and aim to study the problem in the future.

Take as an example the network shown in Fig. 1 which is a feed-forward neural network built with the ReLU activation function and three hidden layers. We aim to verify the absence of a backdoor attack with a success rate of 0.9. We take 10000 images of the MNIST test set to evaluate the success rate of a trigger. We set the parameters in Algorithm 1 as follows: $K = 5$ and $\alpha = \beta = \delta = 0.01$. For the target label 0, after 95 rounds, we have enough evidence to accept the hypothesis $H_0$, which means we have evidence that there is no backdoor attack on the network with the target label 0 and a success rate of at least 0.9. We have similar results for other target labels, although more rounds of tests are required for labels 2, 3, 5, and 8 (i.e., 98 rounds for label 8, 100 rounds for label 3, 117 rounds for label 5, and 188 rounds for label 2).

### 3.2 Verifying Backdoor Absence Against a Set of Images

Next, we present the details of algorithm $verifyX$. The inputs include the neural network $N$, a set of images $X$ with shape $(c, h, w)$, a trigger shape $(c_s, h_s, w_s)$ and a target label $t_s$. The goal is to check whether exists a trigger which successfully attacks every image in $X$. Algorithm $verifyX$ may have three outcomes. One is SAFE, i.e., there is no trigger such that backdoor attack succeeds on all the images in $X$. Another is UNSAFE, i.e., a trigger that can be used to successfully attack all images in $X$ is generated. The last one is UNKNOWN, i.e., we fail to establish either of the above results.

In the following, we describe one concrete realization of the algorithm based on abstract interpretation, as shown in Algorithm 2. At line 1, variable $hasUnknown$ is declared as a flag which is $true$ if and only if we cannot conclude whether there is a successful attack at a certain position. The loop from lines 2 to 15 tries every position for the trigger one by one. Intuitively, variable $\phi$ is the constraint that must be satisfied by a trigger to successfully attack every image in $X$. At line 3, we initialize $\phi$ to be $\phi_{pre}$, which is defined as follows: $\phi_{pre} \equiv \bigwedge_{j \in P(h_p, w_p)} lw_j \leq x_j \leq up_j$ where $j \in P(h_p, w_p)$ denotes that $j$ is an index (of an image pixel) in the trigger, $x_j$ is a variable denoting the value of the $j$-th pixel, $lw_j$ and $up_j$ are the (normalized) minimum (e.g., 0) and maximum (e.g., 1) value of feature $j$ in the image according to the input domain specified by the network $N$. Intuitively, $\phi_{pre}$ requires that the pixels in the trigger must be within its domain.

Given a position, the loop from lines 4 to 10 constructs one constraint $\phi_I$ for each image $I$, which is the constraint that must be satisfied by the trigger to attack $I$. In particular, at line 5, function $attackCondition$ is called to construct the constraint. We present the details of this function in Sect. 3.3. If $\phi_I$ is UNSAT (line 6), attacking image $I$ at position $(h_p, w_p)$ is impossible and we set $\phi$ to be $false$ and break the loop. Otherwise, we conjunct $\phi$ with $\phi_I$.

After collecting one constraint from each image, we solve $\phi$ using a constraint solver. If it is not UNSAT (i.e., SAT or UNKNOWN), function $opTrigger$ is called to generate a trigger which is successful on all images in $X$ (if possible). Note that due to over-approximation, the model returned by the solver might be spurious. The details of function $opTrigger$ is presented in Sect. 3.4. If a trigger is successfully generated, we return UNSAFE (at line 13, together with the trigger); otherwise, we set $hasUnknown$ to be $true$ and continue with the next trigger position. Note that we can return UNKNOWN at line 15 without missing any opportunity for verifying the backdoor absence. We instead continue with the next trigger location hoping a trigger may

**Algorithm 2:** $verifyX(N, X, (c_s, h_s, w_s), t_s)$

```
let hasUnknown ← false;
foreach trigger position (h_p, w_p) do
    let φ ← φ_pre;
    foreach image I ∈ X do
        let φ_I ← attackCondition(N, I, φ_pre, (c_s, h_s, w_s), (h_p, w_p), t_s);
        if φ_I is UNSAT then
            φ ← false;
            break;
        else
            φ ← φ ∧ φ_I;
    if solving φ results in SAT or UNKNOWN then
        if opTrigger(N, X, φ, (c_s, h_s, w_s), (h_p, w_p), t_s) returns a trigger then
            return UNSAFE;
    else
        hasUnknown ← true;
return hasUnknown ? UNKNOWN : SAFE;
```

be generated successfully. After analyzing all trigger positions (and not finding a successful trigger), if $hasUnknown$ is $true$, we return UNKNOWN or otherwise SAFE.

## 3.3 Abstract Interpretation

Function $attackCondition$ returns a constraint that must be satisfied such that the trigger with shape $(c_s, h_s, w_s)$ is successful on the image $I$ at position $(h_p, w_p)$. In this work, for efficiency reasons, it is built based on abstract interpretation techniques [32]. Multiple abstract domains have been proposed to analyze neural networks, such as interval [41], Zonotope [30], and DeepPoly [32]. In this work, we adopt the DeepPoly abstract domain [32], which is shown to balance between precision and efficiency.

In the following, we assume each hidden layer in the network is expanded into two separable layers, one for the affine transformation and the other for the activation function transformation. We use $l$ to denote the number of layers in the expanded network, $n_i$ to denote the number of neurons in layer $i$, and $x^I_{i,j}$ to denote the variable representing the $j$-th neuron in layer $i$ for the image $I$. The constraint $\phi_I$ to be returned by function $attack(N, I, \phi_{pre}, (c_s, h_s, w_s), (h_p, w_p), t_s)$ is a conjunction of three parts.

$$\phi_I \equiv pre_I \wedge \mathcal{A}_\mathcal{I} \wedge post_I$$

where $pre_I$ is the constraint on the input features according to the image $I$, i.e., $pre_I \equiv \phi_{pre} \wedge \left(\bigwedge_{j \in P(h_p, w_p)} x^I_{0,j} = x_j\right) \wedge \left(\bigwedge_{j \notin P(h_p, w_p)} x^I_{0,j} = I[j]\right)$ where $j \notin P(h_p, w_p)$ means that $j$ is not an index (of a pixel) of the trigger; $x^I_{0,j}$ is the variable that represents the input feature $j$ (a.k.a. neuron $j$ at the input layer) of the image $I$ and $I[j]$ is the (normalized) pixel value in the image at index $j$. Intuitively, the constraint $pre_I$ "erases"

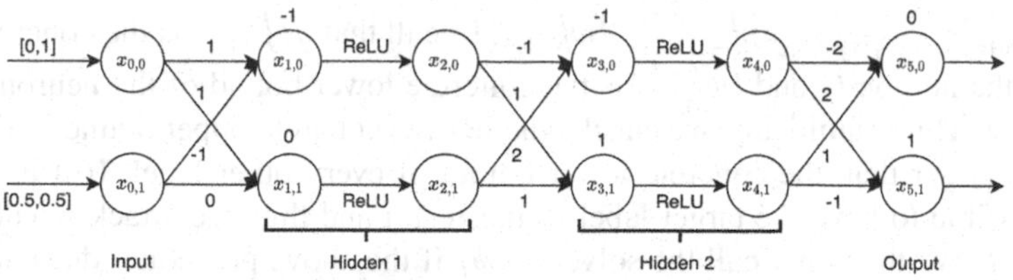


**Fig. 3.** An example of abstract interpretation

the pixels in the trigger, i.e., they can now take any value with their range, while the remaining pixels must have those value from the image. $post_I$ represents the condition for a successful attack. That is, the value of the target label (i.e., $x^I_{l-1,t_s}$) must be greater than the values of any other label, i.e., $post_I \equiv \bigwedge_{0 \leq j < n_{l-1} \wedge j \neq t_s} x^I_{l-1,t_s} > x^I_{l-1,j}$.

More interestingly, $\mathcal{A}_\mathcal{I}$ is a constraint that over-approximates the behavior of the neural network $N$ according to the DeepPoly abstract domain. That is, given the constraint on the input layer $pre_I$, a set of abstract transformers are applied to compute a linear over-approximation of every neuron in the next layer, every neuron in the layer after that, and so on until the output layer. The constraint computed on each neuron $x^I_{i,j}$ is of the form $ge^I_{i,j} \leq x^I_{i,j} \leq le^I_{i,j} \wedge lw^I_{i,j} \leq x^I_{i,j} \leq up^I_{i,j}$ where $ge^I_{i,j}$ and $le^I_{i,j}$ are two linear expressions constituted by variables representing neurons from the previous layer (i.e., layer $i-1$); and $lw^I_{i,j}$ and $up^I_{i,j}$ are the concrete lower bound and upper bound of the neuron. Note that the abstract transformers are different for the activation function layer and affine layer. As the DeepPoly abstract transformers are not our contribution, we skip the details and refer the reader to [32] for details on the abstract transformers, including their soundness (i.e., they always over-approximate).

*Example 1.* Since it is too complicated to show the details of applying abstract interpretation to the neural network shown in Fig. 1, we instead construct a simple example as shown in Fig. 3 to illustrate how it works. There are two features in this artificial image $I$, i.e., $x^I_{0,1}$ has a constant value of 0.5 and $x^I_{0,0}$ is the trigger whose value ranges from 0 to 1. That is, $pre_I \equiv 0 \leq x^I_{0,0} \leq 1 \wedge x^I_{0,1} = 0.5$. After expanding the hidden layers, the network has 6 layers, each of which has 2 neurons. Applying the DeepPoly abstract transformers from the input layer all the way to the output layer, we obtain the abstract states for the last layer. Further, assume that the target label is 0. The constraint $post_I$ is thus as follows: $post_I \equiv x^I_{5,0} > x^I_{5,1}$. Solving the constraints returns SAT with $x^I_{0,0} = 0$. Indeed, with the stamped image $I_s = [0, 0.5]$, the output vector is $[1, 0]$. We thus identified a successful attack on the target label 0.

*Optimization.* Note that at line 6 of Algorithm 2, for each constraint $\phi_I$, we perform a quick check to see if the constraint is satisfiable or not. If $\phi_I$ is UNSAT, we can ignore the remaining images and analyze the next trigger position, which allows us to speed up the process. One naive approach is to call a solver on $\phi_I$, which would incur significant overhead since it could happen many times. To reduce the overhead, we propose a simple procedure to quickly check whether $\phi_I$ is UNSAT based solely on its abstract states at the output layer. That is, we check the satisfiability of the following constraint instead: $\bigwedge_{0 \le j < n_{l-1} \wedge j \ne t_s} up^I_{l-1,t_s} > lw^I_{l-1,j}$. Recall that $up^I_{l-1,t_s}$ is the concrete upper bound of the neuron $t_s$ and $lw^I_{l-1,j}$ is the concrete lower bound of the neuron $j$ at the output layer. Thus, intuitively, we check whether the concrete upper bound of the target label $t_s$ is larger than the concrete lower bound of every other label. If it is UNSAT, it is impossible to have the target label as the result and thus the attack would fail on the image $I$. We then only call the solver on $\phi_I$ if the above procedure does not return UNSAT. Furthermore, the loop in Algorithm 2 can be parallelized straightforwardly, i.e., by using a separate process to verify against a different trigger position. Whenever a trigger is found by any of the processes, the whole algorithm is then interrupted.

### 3.4 Generating Backdoor Triggers

In the following, we present the details of function $opTrigger$, which intuitively aims to generate a trigger $S$ with shape $(c_s, h_s, w_s)$ at position $(h_p, w_p)$ for attacking every image $I$ in $X$ successfully. If the solver applied to solve $\phi$ at line 11 of Algorithm 2 returns a model that satisfies $\phi$, we first check whether the model is indeed a trigger that successfully attacks every image in $X$. Due to over-approximation of abstract interpretation, the model might be a spurious trigger. If it is a real trigger, we return the model. Otherwise, we employ an optimization-based approach to generate a trigger.

Given a network $N$, one image $I$, a target label $t_s$, and a position $(h_p, w_p)$, let $I_s$ is the stamped image generated from $I$ by stamping $I$ with the trigger at the position $(h_p, w_p)$. We generate a backdoor trigger $S$ by minimizing the following loss function.

$$loss(N, I, S, (h_p, w_p), t_s) = \begin{cases} 0 & \text{if } n_s > n_o \\ (n_o - n_s + \epsilon) & \text{otherwise} \end{cases}$$

where $n_s = N(I_s)[t_s]$ is the output value of the target label; $n_o = \max_{j \ne t_s} N(I_s)[j]$ is the maximum value of any label other than the target label; and $\epsilon$ is a small constant (e.g., $10^{-9}$). Note that the trigger $S$ is the only variable in the loss function. Intuitively, the loss function returns 0 if the attack on $I$ by the trigger is successful. Otherwise, it returns a quantitative measure on how far the attack is from being successful on attacking $I$. Given a set of images $X$, the loss function is defined as the sum of the loss for each image $I$ in $X$: $loss(N, X, S, (h_p, w_p), t_s) = \sum_{I \in X} loss(N, I, S, (h_p, w_p), t_s)$. The following optimization problem is then solved to find an attack which successfully attacks all images in $X$: $\arg\min_S loss(N, X, S, (h_p, w_p), t_s)$.

### 3.5 Correctness and Complexity

**Lemma 1.** *Given a neural network $N$, a set of images $X$, a trigger shape $(c_s, h_s, w_s)$, and a target label $t_s$, Algorithm 2 (1) returns SAFE only if there is no backdoor attack which is successful on all images in $X$ with the provided trigger shape and target label; and (2) returns UNSAFE only if there exists a backdoor attack which is successful on all images in $X$ with the provided trigger shape and target label.*

*Proof.* By [32], function $attackCondition$ always returns a constraint which is an over-approximation of the constraint that must be satisfied such that the trigger is successful on image $I$. Furthermore, Algorithm 2 returns SAFE only at line 16, i.e., only if constraints that must be satisfied to attack all images in $X$ at each certain position are UNSAT. Thus, (1) is established. (2) is trivially established since we only return UNSAFE when a trigger that is successful on every provided image is generated. □

The following establishes the soundness of our approach.

**Theorem 1.** *Given a neural network $N$, a success rate $\theta$, a target label $t_s$, a trigger shape $(c_s, h_s, w_s)$, a type I error $\alpha$, a type II error $\beta$, and a half-width of the indifference region $\delta$, Algorithm 1 returns SAFE only if there is sufficient evidence (subject to type I error $\alpha$ and type II error $\beta$) that there is no backdoor attack with a success rate at least $\theta$ with the provided trigger shape and target label at the specified significance level.*

*Proof.* If there is a backdoor attack with a success rate no less than $\theta$, given a set of randomly $K$ selected images, the probability of having an attack is no less than $\theta^K$ (since there is at least one backdoor attack with a success rate no less than $\theta$ and maybe more). Thus, the probability of not having an attack is no more than $1 - \theta^K$. By the correctness of the SPRT algorithm, Algorithm 1 returns SAFE only if there is sufficient evidence that $H_0$ is true, i.e., the probability of not having an attack on a set of $K$ randomly selected images is more than $1 - \theta^K$, implying it is sufficient evidence that there is no backdoor attack with success rate no less than $\theta$. The theorem holds. □

Furthermore, it is trivial to show that Algorithm 1 returns UNSAFE only if there exists a backdoor attack which has a success rate at least $\theta$ with the provided trigger shape and target label.

In the following, we briefly discuss the complexity of our approach. It is straightforward to see that Algorithm 2 always terminates if a timeout is imposed on solving the constraints and the optimization problems. Since we can always set a tight time limit on solving the constraints and the optimization problems, the complexity of the algorithm is determined mainly by the complexity of function $attackCondition$, which in turn is determined by the complexity of abstract interpretation. The complexity of applying abstract interpretation with the DeepPoly abstract domain is $\mathcal{O}(l^2 \times n_{max}^3)$ where $l$ is the number of layers, and $n_{max}$ is the maximum number of neurons in any of the layers. Let $K$ be the number of images in $X$. Note that the number of trigger positions is $\mathcal{O}(h \times w)$, i.e., the size of an image. The best case complexity of Algorithm 2 is $\mathcal{O}(l^2 \times n_{max}^3 \times h \times w)$ and the worst case complexity is $\mathcal{O}(l^2 \times n_{max}^3 \times K \times h \times w)$. We remark that in practice, $l$ typically ranges from 1 to 20; $n_{max}$ is often advised to be no more than the input size (e.g., from dozens to thousands usually); $K$ ranges from a few to hundreds; and $h \times w$ depends on the image resolution (e.g., from hundreds to millions). Thus, in general, Algorithm 2 could be time-consuming in practice and we anticipate further optimization in future work.

The complexity of Algorithm 1 is the complexity of Algorithm 2 times the complexity of the SPRT algorithm. The complexity of the SPRT algorithm is in general hard to quantify and we refer the readers to [1] for a detailed discussion.

### 3.6 Discussion

Our approaches are designed to verify the absence of input-agnostic (i.e., not input-specific) backdoor attacks as presented in Sect. 2. In the following, we briefly review other backdoor attacks and discuss how to extend our approach to support them.

In [12], Gu *et al.* described a backdoor attack which, instead of forcing the network to classify any stamped image with the target label, only alters the label if the original image has a specific ground truth label $t_i$ (e.g., Bob with the trigger will activate the backdoor and be classified as Alice the manager). Our verification approach can be easily adapted to verify the absence of this attack by focusing on images with label $t_i$ in Algorithm 1 and Algorithm 2.

Another attack proposed in [12] works by reducing the performance (e.g., accuracy) of the neural network on the images with a specific ground truth label $t_i$, i.e., given an image with ground truth label $t_i$, the network will classify the stamped image with some label $t_s \neq t_i$. The attack can be similarly handled by focusing on images with ground truth label $t_i$, although due to the disjunction introduced by $t_s \neq t_i$, the constraints are likely to be harder to solve. That is, we can focus on images with ground truth label $t_i$ in Algorithm 2, and define an attack to be successful if $L(N(I_s)) \neq t_i$ is satisfied.

In [19], Liu *et al.* proposed to use backdoor triggers with different shapes (i.e., not just in the form of a square or a rectangle). If the user is aware of the shape of the backdoor trigger, a different trigger can be used as input for Algorithm 1 and Algorithm 2 and the algorithms would work to verify the absence of such backdoor. Alternatively, the users can choose a square-shaped backdoor trigger that is larger enough to cover the actual backdoor trigger, in which case our algorithms would remain to be sound, although it might be inconclusive if the trigger is too big.

Multiple groups [2,20,28,35] proposed the idea of poisoning only those samples in the training data which have the same ground truth label as the target label to improve the stealthiness of the backdoor attack. This type of attack is designed to trick the human inspection on the training data, and so does not affect our verification algorithms.

In this work, we consider a specific type of stamping, i.e., the backdoor trigger replaces the part of the original clean image. Multiple groups [6,19] proposed the use of the blending operation as a way of 'stamping', i.e., the features of the backdoor trigger are blended with the features of the original images with some coefficients $\alpha$. This is a form of input-specific backdoor, the trigger is different for different images. To handle such kind of backdoor attacks, one way is to modify the constraint $pre_I$ according to the blending operation (assuming that $\alpha$ is known). Since the blending operation proposed in [6,19] is linear, we expect this would not introduce additional complexity to our algorithms.

Input-specific triggers, in general, may pose a threat to our approach. First, some input-specific triggers [19,20] cover the whole image, which is likely to make our approach inclusive due to false alarms resulted from over-approximation. Second, it may not be easy to model some of the input-specific triggers in our framework. For instance, Liu *et al.* [20] recently proposed to use reflection to create stamped images that look natural. Modeling the 'stamping' operation for this kind of attack would require us to know where the reflection is in the image, which is highly non-trivial. However, it should also be noted that input-specific triggers are often not as effective as input-agnostic triggers, e.g., the reflection-based attack reported in [20] are hard to reproduce. Furthermore, as discussed in Sect. 2, backdoor attack with input-specific triggers is an attacking method that is more powerful than adversarial attacks, and the problem of verifying the absence of backdoor attack with input-specific triggers is not yet clearly defined.

## 4 Implementation and Evaluation

We have implemented our approach as a self-contained analysis engine in the Socrates framework [26]. We use Gurobi [13] to solve the constraints and use scipy [36] to solve the optimization problems.

We collect a set of 51 neural networks. 45 of them are fully connected ones and are trained on the MNIST training set (i.e., a standard dataset which contains black and white images of digits). These networks have the number of hidden layers ranging from 3 to 5. For each network, the number of neurons in each of its hidden layers ranges from 10 to 50, i.e., 10, 20, 30, 40, or 50. To evaluate our approach on neural networks built with different activation functions, each activation function (i.e., ReLU, Sigmoid, and Tanh) is used in 15 of the neural networks. Among the remaining six networks, three of them are bigger fully connected networks adopted from the benchmarks reported in [32]. They are all built with the ReLU activation function. For convenience, we name the networks in the form of *f_k_n* where $f$ is the name of the activation function, $k$ is the number of hidden layers, and $n$ is the number of neurons in each hidden layer. The remaining three networks are convolutional networks (which are often used in face recognition systems) adopted from [32]. Although they have the same structure, i.e., each of them has two convolutional hidden layers and one fully connected hidden layer, they are trained differently. One is trained in the normal way; one is trained using DiffAI [22], and the last one is trained using projected gradient descent [7]. These training methods are developed to improve the robustness of neural networks against adversarial attacks. Our aim is thus to evaluate whether they help to prevent backdoor attacks as well. We name these networks *conv*, *conv_diffai*, and *conv_pgd*.

We verify the networks against the backdoor trigger with shape $(1, 3, 3)$. All the networks are trained using clean data since we focus on verifying the absence of backdoor attacks. They all have precision of at least 90%, except *Sigmoid_4_10* and *Sigmoid_5_10*, which have precision of 81% and 89% respectively. In the following, we answer multiple research questions. All the experiments are conducted using a machine with 3.1Ghz 16-core CPU and 64GB RAM. All models and experiment details are at [27].

*RQ1: Is our realization of* $verifyX$ *effective?* This question is meaningful as our approach relies on Algorithm $verifyX$. To answer this question, for each network, we select the first 100 images in the test set (i.e., a $K$ of 100 for Algorithm 1, which is more than sufficient) and then apply Algorithm $verifyX$ with these images and each of the labels, i.e., 0 to 9. In total, we have 510 verification tasks. For each network, we run 10 processes in parallel, each of which verifies a separate target. The only exception is the network *ReLU_3_1024*, due to its complexity, we only run five parallel processes (since each process consumes a lot of resources). In each verification process, we filter out those images which are classified wrongly by the network as well as the images which are already classified as the target label.

Figure 4 shows the results. The x-axis show the groups of the networks, e.g., *ReLU_3* means five fully connected networks using the ReLU activation function with three hidden layers; *3 Full* and *3 Conv* mean the three fully connected and the three convolutional networks adapted from [32] respectively. The y-axis shows the number of (network, target) pairs. Note that each group may contain a different number of pairs, i.e., the

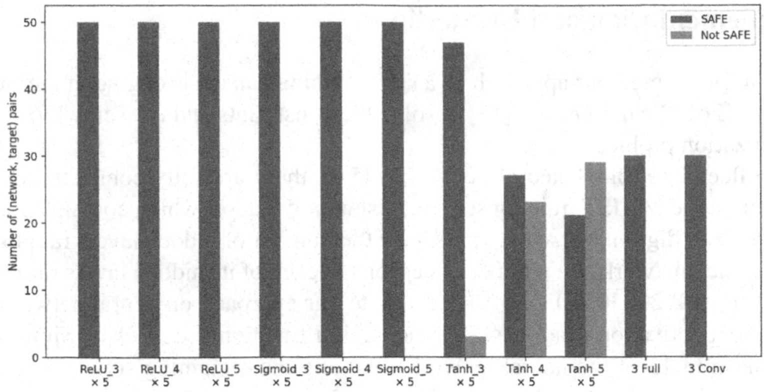


**Fig. 4.** The results of $verifyX$

maximum values for the small network groups are 50, and the maximum values for the last two groups are 30. First, we successfully verify 455 out of 510 verification tasks (i.e., 89%) of them, i.e., the neural network is safe with respect to the selected images. It is encouraging to notice that the verified tasks include all models adopted from [32], which are considerably larger (e.g., with 1024 neurons at each layer) and more complex (i.e., convolutional networks). Second, some networks are not proved to be safe with some target labels. It could be either there is indeed a backdoor trigger that we fail to identify (through optimization), or we fail to verify due to the over-approximation introduced by abstract interpretation. Lastly, with the same structure (i.e., the same number of hidden layers and the same number of neurons in each hidden layer), the networks using the ReLU and Sigmoid activation functions are more often verified to be safe than those using the Tanh activation function. This is most likely due to the difference in the precision of the abstract transformers for these functions.

*RQ2: can we verify the absence of backdoor attacks with a certain level of success rate?* To answer this question, we evaluate our approach on six networks used in RQ1, i.e., *ReLU_3_10*, *ReLU_5_50*, *Sigmoid_3_10*, *Sigmoid_5_50*, *Tanh_3_10*, and *Tanh_5_50*. These networks are chosen to cover a wide range of the number of hidden layers and the number of neurons in each layer, as well as different activation functions. Note that due to the high complexity of Algorithm 1 (which potentially applies Algorithm 2 hundreds of times), running Algorithm 1 on all the networks evaluated in RQ1 requires an overwhelming amount of resources. *Furthermore, since there is no existing work on backdoor verification, we do not have any baseline to compare with.*

Recall that Algorithm 1 has two important parameters $K$ and $\theta$, both of which potentially have a significant impact on the verification result. We thus run each network with four different settings, in which the number of images $K$ is set to be either 5 or 10, and the success rate $\theta$ is either 0.8 or 0.9. In total, with 10 target labels, we have a total of 240 verification tasks for this experiment. Note that some preliminary experiments are conducted before we select these two $K$ values.

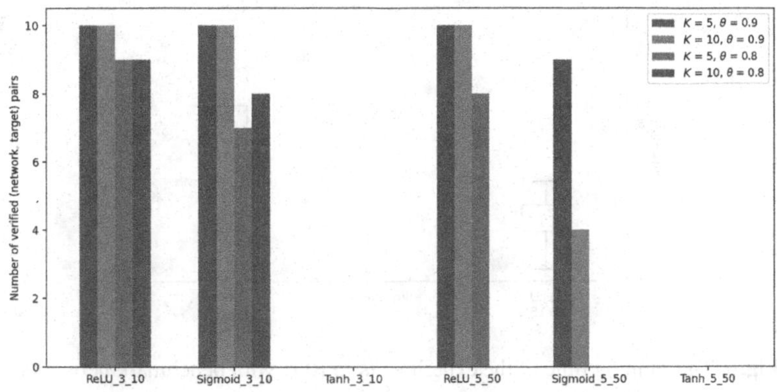


**Fig. 5.** Verification results

We use all the 10000 images in the test set as the image population and randomly choose $K$ images in each round of test. When a trigger is generated, the success rate of the trigger is validated on the images in the test set (after the above-mentioned filtering). Like in RQ1, we run each network with 10 parallel processes, each of which verifies a separate target. As the SPRT algorithm may take a very long time to terminate, we set a timeout for each verification task, i.e., 2 h for those networks with three hidden layers, and 10 h for those networks with five hidden layers.

The results are shown in Fig. 5. The x-axis shows the networks, the y-axis shows the number of verified pairs of network and target label. We have multiple observations based on the experiment results. First, a quick glance shows that with the same structure and hypothesis testing parameters, more networks built with the ReLU activation function are verified than those built with the Sigmoid and Tanh functions. Second, we notice that the best result is achieved with $K = 5$ and $\theta = 0.9$. With these parameter values, we can verify that three networks *ReLU_3_10*, *ReLU_5_50*, and *Sigmoid_3_10* are safe with respect to all the target labels and the network *Sigmoid_5_50* is safe with respect to nine over 10 target labels. If we keep the same success rate as 0.9 and increase the number of images $K$ from 5 to 10, we can see that the number of verified cases in the network *Sigmoid_5_50* decreases. This is because when we increase the number of images that must be attacked successfully together, the probability that we do not have the attack increases, which means we need more rounds of test to confirm the hypothesis $H_0$ and so the verification process for the network *Sigmoid_5_50* times out before reaching the conclusion. We have a similar observation when we keep the number of images $K$ at 5 but decrease the success rate from 0.9 to 0.8. When the success rate decreases, the probability of not having the attack increases, which requires more tests to confirm the hypothesis $H_0$. As a result, for all these four networks, there are multiple verification tasks that time out before reaching the conclusion. However, we notice that there is an exception when we keep the success rate as 0.8 and increase the number of images from 5 to 10. While the number of verified cases for the network *ReLU_5_50* decreases (which can be explained in the same way as above), the number of verified cases for the network *Sigmoid_3_10* increases (and the results for the other two

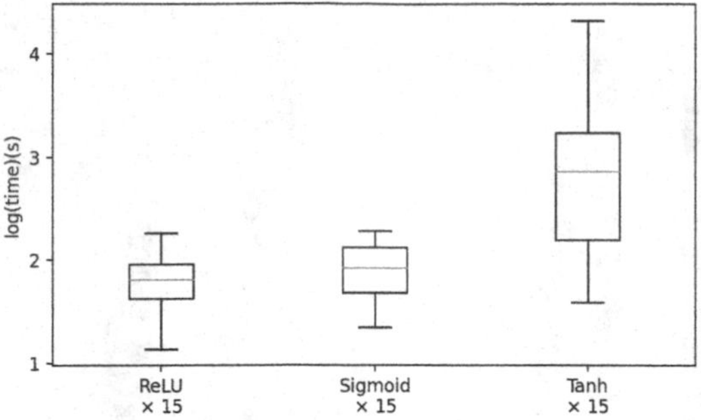


**Fig. 6.** The running time of the experiments in RQ1 with benchmark networks

networks do not change). Our explanation is that when we increase the number of images $K$ to 10, it is easier for the Algorithm 2 to conclude that there is no attack, and so the Algorithm 1 still collects enough evidence to conclude $H_0$. On the other hand, with the number of images is 5, Algorithm 2 may return a lot of UNKNOWN (due to spurious triggers), and so the hypothesis testing in the Algorithm 1 goes back and forth between the two hypotheses $H_0$ and $H_1$ and eventually times out.

A slightly surprising result is obtained for the network *Tanh_3_10*, i.e., our trigger generation process generates two triggers for the target labels 2 and 5 when the success rate is set to be 0.8. This is surprising as these networks are not generated with backdoor attack. This result can be potentially explained by the combination of the relatively low success rate (i.e., 0.8) and the phenomenon known as universal adversarial perturbations [23]. With the returned triggers, the users may want to investigate the network further and potentially improve it with techniques such as robust training [7,22].

*RQ3: Is our approach efficient time-wise?* To answer this question, we collect the wall-clock time to run the experiments in RQ1 and RQ2. For each network, we record the average running time for 10 different target labels. The results for 45 small networks are shown in Fig. 6. The x-axis shows the groups of 15 networks categorized based on their activation functions and the y-axis shows the logarithmic scale of the running time in the form of boxplots (where the box shows the result of 25 percentile to 75 percentile, the bottom and top lines are the minimum and maximum, and the orange line is median). The execution time ranges from 14 s to less than 6 h for these networks. Furthermore, we can see that there is not much difference between the running time of the networks using the ReLU and Sigmoid activation functions. However, the running time of the networks using the Tanh function is one order of magnitude larger than those of the ReLU and Sigmoid networks. The reason is that the Tanh networks have many non-safe cases (as shown in Fig. 4) and, as a result, the verification process needs to check more images at more trigger positions. The running time of those networks adopted from [32] ranges from more than 5 min to less than 4 h, as shown in Table 1. Finally, the running time for each network in RQ2 (i.e., the time required to verify the networks against backdoor attacks) according to different settings is shown in Table 2.

**Table 1.** The running time of the experiments in RQ1 with networks adapted from [32]

| Network | Time | Network | Time |
|---|---|---|---|
| ReLU_3_1024 | 237 m 24s | conv | 194 m 30 s |
| ReLU_5_100 | 5 m 38 s | conv_diffai | 111 m 12 s |
| ReLU_8_200 | 48 m 34s | conv_pgd | 190 m 19 s |

**Table 2.** The running time of the experiments in RQ2

| Network | $K = 5$ $\theta = 0.9$ | $K = 10$ $\theta = 0.9$ | $K = 5$ $\theta = 0.8$ | $K = 10$ $\theta = 0.8$ |
|---|---|---|---|---|
| ReLU_3_10 | 31 m 31 s | 46 m 39 s | 55 m 44 s | 68 m 54 s |
| ReLU_5_50 | 341 m 36 s | 493 m 30 s | 551 m 40 s | 600 m 0 s |
| Sigmoid_3_10 | 46 m 43 s | 59 m 28 s | 92 m 34s | 93 m 21 s |
| Sigmoid_5_50 | 476 m 38 s | 588 m 25 s | 600 m 0s | 600 m 0 s |
| Tanh_3_10 | 114 m 2 s | 105 m 18 s | 50 m 58 s | 26 m 4 s |
| Tanh_5_50 | 600 m 0s | 600 m 0 s | 600 m 0 s | 600 m 0 s |

*RQ4: can our approach generate backdoor triggers?* Being able to generate counterexamples is a part of a useful verification method. We conduct another experiment to evaluate the effectiveness of our backdoor trigger generation approach. We train a new set of 45 networks that have the same structure as those used for answering RQ1. The difference is that this time each network is trained to contain backdoor through data poisoning. In particular, for each network, we randomly extract 20% of the training data, stamp a white square with shape $(1, 3, 3)$ in one corner of the images, assign a random target label, and then train the neural network from scratch with the poisoned training data. While such an attack is shown to be effective [12], it is not guaranteed to be always successful on a randomly selected set of images. Thus, we do the following to make sure that there exists a trigger for a set of selected images. From 10000 images in the test set, we first filter out those images which are classified wrongly or already classified with the target label. The remaining images are collected into a set $X_0$. Next, to make sure that the selected images have a high chance of being attacked successfully, we apply another filter on $X_0$. This time, we stamp each image in $X_0$ with a white square at the same trigger position as we poison the training data. We then keep the image if its stamped version is classified by the network with the target label. The remaining images after the second filter are collected into another set $X$. We apply our approach, in particular, the backdoor trigger generation on $X$, if $|X| \div |X_0| \geq 0.8$, i.e., the backdoor attack has a success rate of 80%.

The results are shown in Fig. 7 in which the y-axis shows the number of networks. The timeout is set to be 120 s. Among the 45 networks, we can see that a trigger is successfully generated for 33 (i.e., 73%) of the networks. A close investigation of these networks shows that the generated trigger is the exact white square that is used to stamp the training data. There are 12 networks for which the trigger is not generated. We

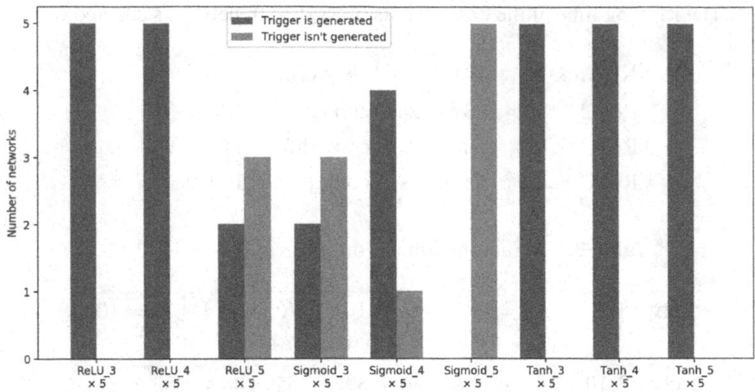


**Fig. 7.** The results of backdoor trigger generation

investigate these networks and see that they are either too biased (i.e., classifying every image with the target label and thus $|X_0| = 0$) or the attack on these networks does not perform well (i.e., $|X| \div |X_0| < 0.8$). In other words, the backdoor attack on these networks failed and, as a result, the generation process does not even begin with these networks. In a nutshell, we successfully generate the trigger for every successful backdoor attack. Finally, note that the running time of the backdoor generation process is reasonable (i.e., on average, 50 s to generate a backdoor trigger for one network) and thus it does not affect the overall performance of our verification algorithm.

## 5 Related Work

The work which is closest to ours is [37] in which Wang *et al.* aim to certify neural networks' robustness against backdoor attack using randomized smoothing. However, there are many noticeable differences between their approach and ours. First, while our work focuses on verifying the absence of backdoor, their work aims to certify the robustness of individual images based on the provided training data and learning algorithm (which can be used to implicitly derive the network). Second, by using random noises to estimate the networks' behaviors, their approach can only obtain very loose results. As shown in their experiments, they can only certify the robustness against backdoor attack with triggers contains two pixels and on a "toy" network with only two layers and two labels, after simplifying the input features by rounding them into 0 or 1. Compare to their approach, our approach can apply to networks used to solve real image classification problems as shown in our experiments.

Our work is closely related to a line of work on verifying neural networks. Existing approaches mostly focus on local robustness property and can be roughly classified into two categories: exact methods and approximation methods. The exact methods aim to model the networks precisely and solve the verification problem using techniques such as mixed-integer linear programming [34] or SMT solving [8,15]. On the one hand, these approaches can guarantee sound and complete results in verifying neural networks. On the other hand, they often have limited scalability and thus are limited to small neural networks. Moreover, these approaches have difficulty in handling activation functions except the ReLU function.

In comparison, the approximation approaches over-approximate neural network behavior to gain better scalability. $AI^2$ [10] is the first work pursuing this direction using the classic abstract interpretation technique. After that, more researchers try to explore different abstract domains for better precision without sacrificing too much scalability [29,30,32]. In general, the approximation approaches are more scalable than the exact methods, and they are capable of handling activation functions such as Sigmoid and Tanh. However, due to the over-approximation, these methods may fail to verify a valid property.

We also notice that it is possible to incorporate abstraction refinement to the approximation methods and gain better precision, for instance, by splitting an abstraction into multiple parts to reduce the imprecision due to over-approximation. There are many works [21,40,41] which fall into this category. We remark that our approach is orthogonal to the development of sophisticated verification techniques for neural networks.

Finally, our approach, especially the part on backdoor trigger generation, is related to many approaches on generating adversarial samples for neural networks. Some representative approaches in this category are FGSM [11], JSMA [24], and C&W [4] which aim to generate adversarial samples to violate the local robustness property, and [42] which aims to violate fairness property.

## 6 Conclusion

In this work, we propose the first approach to formally verify that a neural network is safe from backdoor attacks. We address the problem on how to verify the absence of a backdoor that reaches a certain level of success rate. Our approach is based on abstract interpretation and we provide an implementation based on DeepPoly abstract domain. The experiment results show the potential of our approach. In the future, we intend to extend our approach with more abstract domains as well as improve the performance to verify more real-life networks. Besides that, we also intend to apply our approach to verify the networks designed for other tasks, such as sound or text classification.

**Acknowledgements.** This research is supported by the Ministry of Education, Singapore under its Academic Research Fund Tier 3 (Award ID: MOET32020-0004). Any opinions, findings and conclusions or recommendations expressed in this material are those of the author(s) and do not reflect the views of the Ministry of Education, Singapore. This research is also partly supported by the Starry Night Science Fund of Zhejiang University Shanghai Institute for Advanced Study, Grant No. SN-ZJU-SIAS-001.

## References

1. Agha, G., Palmskog, K.: A survey of statistical model checking. ACM Trans. Model. Comput. Simul. (TOMACS) **28**(1), 1–39 (2018)
2. Barni, M., Kallas, K., Tondi, B.: A new backdoor attack in CNNs by training set corruption without label poisoning. In: ICIP 2019, pp. 101–105. IEEE (2019)

3. Bojarski, M., et al.: End to end learning for self-driving cars. arXiv preprint arXiv:1604.07316 (2016)
4. Carlini, N., Wagner, D.: Towards evaluating the robustness of neural networks. In: S&P 2017, pp. 39–57. IEEE (2017)
5. Chen, B., et al.: Detecting backdoor attacks on deep neural networks by activation clustering. arXiv preprint arXiv:1811.03728 (2018)
6. Chen, X., Liu, C., Li, B., Lu, K., Song, D.: Targeted backdoor attacks on deep learning systems using data poisoning. arXiv preprint arXiv:1712.05526 (2017)
7. Dong, Y., et al.: Boosting adversarial attacks with momentum. In: CVPR 2018, pp. 9185–9193. IEEE (2018)
8. Ehlers, R.: Formal verification of piece-wise linear feed-forward neural networks. In: D'Souza, D., Narayan Kumar, K. (eds.) ATVA 2017. LNCS, vol. 10482, pp. 269–286. Springer, Cham (2017). https://doi.org/10.1007/978-3-319-68167-2_19
9. Gao, Y., Xu, C., Wang, D., Chen, S., Ranasinghe, D.C., Nepal, S.: Strip: a defence against trojan attacks on deep neural networks. In: ACSAC 2019, pp. 113–125. ACM (2019)
10. Gehr, T., Mirman, M., Drachsler-Cohen, D., Tsankov, P., Chaudhuri, S., Vechev, M.: Ai2: Safety and robustness certification of neural networks with abstract interpretation. In: S&P 2018, pp. 3–18. IEEE (2018)
11. Goodfellow, I.J., Shlens, J., Szegedy, C.: Explaining and harnessing adversarial examples. arXiv preprint arXiv:1412.6572 (2014)
12. Gu, T., Dolan-Gavitt, B., Garg, S.: Badnets: Identifying vulnerabilities in the machine learning model supply chain. arXiv preprint arXiv:1708.06733 (2017)
13. Gurobi Optimization, LLC: Gurobi Optimizer Reference Manual (2021). https://www.gurobi.com
14. Huang, X., Kwiatkowska, M., Wang, S., Wu, M.: Safety Verification of Deep Neural Networks. In: Majumdar, R., Kunčak, V. (eds.) CAV 2017. LNCS, vol. 10426, pp. 3–29. Springer, Cham (2017). https://doi.org/10.1007/978-3-319-63387-9_1
15. Katz, G., Barrett, C., Dill, D.L., Julian, K., Kochenderfer, M.J.: Reluplex: An efficient smt solver for verifying deep neural networks. In: CAV 2017, pp. 97–117. Springer (2017)
16. Li, Q., Cai, W., Wang, X., Zhou, Y., Feng, D.D., Chen, M.: Medical image classification with convolutional neural network. In: ICARCV 2014, pp. 844–848. IEEE (2014)
17. Liu, K., Dolan-Gavitt, B., Garg, S.: Fine-pruning: defending against backdooring attacks on deep neural networks. In: Bailey, M., Holz, T., Stamatogiannakis, M., Ioannidis, S. (eds.) RAID 2018. LNCS, vol. 11050, pp. 273–294. Springer, Cham (2018). https://doi.org/10.1007/978-3-030-00470-5_13
18. Liu, Y., Lee, W.C., Tao, G., Ma, S., Aafer, Y., Zhang, X.: Abs: scanning neural networks for back-doors by artificial brain stimulation. In: CCS 2019, pp. 1265–1282. ACM (2019)
19. Liu, Y., Ma, S., Aafer, Y., Lee, W.C., Zhai, J., Wang, W., Zhang, X.: Trojaning attack on neural networks (2017)
20. Liu, Y., Ma, X., Bailey, J., Lu, F.: Reflection backdoor: a natural backdoor attack on deep neural networks. In: Vedaldi, A., Bischof, H., Brox, T., Frahm, J.-M. (eds.) ECCV 2020. LNCS, vol. 12355, pp. 182–199. Springer, Cham (2020). https://doi.org/10.1007/978-3-030-58607-2_11
21. Lu, J., Kumar, M.P.: Neural network branching for neural network verification. arXiv preprint arXiv:1912.01329 (2019)
22. Mirman, M., Gehr, T., Vechev, M.: Differentiable abstract interpretation for provably robust neural networks. In: ICML 2018, pp. 3578–3586. PMLR (2018)
23. Moosavi-Dezfooli, S.M., Fawzi, A., Fawzi, O., Frossard, P.: Universal adversarial perturbations. In: CVPR 2017, pp. 1765–1773. IEEE (2017)
24. Papernot, N., McDaniel, P., Jha, S., Fredrikson, M., Celik, Z.B., Swami, A.: The limitations of deep learning in adversarial settings. In: EuroS&P 2016, pp. 372–387. IEEE (2016)

25. Parkhi, O.M., Vedaldi, A., Zisserman, A.: Deep face recognition (2015)
26. Pham, L.H., Li, J., Sun, J.: Socrates: Towards a unified platform for neural network verification. arXiv preprint arXiv:2007.11206 (2020)
27. Pham, L.H., Sun, J.: Source and Benchmark (2022). https://doi.org/10.6084/m9.figshare.19719742
28. Shafahi, A., Huang, W.R., Najibi, M., Suciu, O., Studer, C., Dumitras, T., Goldstein, T.: Poison frogs! targeted clean-label poisoning attacks on neural networks. arXiv preprint arXiv:1804.00792 (2018)
29. Singh, G., Ganvir, R., Püschel, M., Vechev, M.: Beyond the single neuron convex barrier for neural network certification. In: NeurIPS 2019, pp. 15098–15109 (2019)
30. Singh, G., Gehr, T., Mirman, M., Püschel, M., Vechev, M.: Fast and effective robustness certification. In: NeurIPS 2018, pp. 10802–10813 (2018)
31. Singh, G., Gehr, T., Püschel, M., Vechev, M.: Boosting robustness certification of neural networks. In: International Conference on Learning Representations (2018)
32. Singh, G., Gehr, T., Püschel, M., Vechev, M.: An abstract domain for certifying neural networks. Proceedings of the ACM on Programming Languages **3**, 1–30 (2019)
33. Szegedy, C., Zaremba, W., Sutskever, I., Bruna, J., Erhan, D., Goodfellow, I., Fergus, R.: Intriguing properties of neural networks. arXiv preprint arXiv:1312.6199 (2013)
34. Tjeng, V., Xiao, K., Tedrake, R.: Evaluating robustness of neural networks with mixed integer programming. arXiv preprint arXiv:1711.07356 (2017)
35. Turner, A., Tsipras, D., Madry, A.: Clean-label backdoor attacks (2018)
36. Virtanen, P., et al.: SciPy 1.0 Contributors: SciPy 1.0: Fundamental Algorithms for Scientific Computing in Python. Nature Methods **17**, 261–272 (2020). https://doi.org/10.1038/s41592-019-0686-2
37. Wang, B., Cao, X., Gong, N.Z., et al.: On certifying robustness against backdoor attacks via randomized smoothing. arXiv preprint arXiv:2002.11750 (2020)
38. Wang, B., Yao, Y., Shan, S., Li, H., Viswanath, B., Zheng, H., Zhao, B.Y.: Neural cleanse: Identifying and mitigating backdoor attacks in neural networks. In: S&P 2019, pp. 707–723. IEEE (2019)
39. Wang, J., Dong, G., Sun, J., Wang, X., Zhang, P.: Adversarial sample detection for deep neural network through model mutation testing. In: ICSE 2019, pp. 1245–1256. IEEE/ACM (2019)
40. Wang, S., Pei, K., Whitehouse, J., Yang, J., Jana, S.: Efficient formal safety analysis of neural networks. In: NeurIPS 2018, pp. 6367–6377 (2018)
41. Wang, S., Pei, K., Whitehouse, J., Yang, J., Jana, S.: Formal security analysis of neural networks using symbolic intervals. In: 27th USENIX Security Symposium (USENIX Security 18), pp. 1599–1614 (2018)
42. Zhang, P., et al.: White-box fairness testing through adversarial sampling. In: ICSE 2020, pp. 949–960. IEEE/ACM (2020)

BY

# Trainify: A CEGAR-Driven Training and Verification Framework for Safe Deep Reinforcement Learning

Peng Jin[1], Jiaxu Tian[1], Dapeng Zhi[1], Xuejun Wen[2], and Min Zhang[1,3](✉)

[1] Shanghai Key Laboratory of Trustworthy Computing, ECNU, Shanghai, China
zhangmin@sei.ecnu.edu.cn

[2] Huawei International, Singapore, Singapore

[3] Shanghai Institute of Intelligent Science and Technology, Tongji University, Shanghai, China

CAV Artifact Evaluation ★ Available

**Abstract.** Deep Reinforcement Learning (DRL) has demonstrated its strength in developing intelligent systems. These systems shall be formally guaranteed to be trustworthy when applied to safety-critical domains, which is typically achieved by formal verification performed after training. This *train-then-verify* process has two limits: (i) trained systems are difficult to formally verify due to their continuous and infinite state space and inexplicable AI components (*i.e.*, deep neural networks), and (ii) the *ex post facto* detection of bugs increases both the time- and money-wise cost of training and deployment. In this paper, we propose a novel verification-in-the-loop training framework called Trainify for developing safe DRL systems driven by counterexample-guided abstraction and refinement. Specifically, Trainify trains a DRL system on a finite set of coarsely abstracted but efficiently verifiable state spaces. When verification fails, we refine the abstraction based on returned counterexamples and train again on the finer abstract states. The process is iterated until all predefined properties are verified against the trained system. We demonstrate the effectiveness of our framework on six classic control systems. The experimental results show that our framework yields more reliable DRL systems with provable guarantees without sacrificing system performance such as cumulative reward and robustness than conventional DRL approaches.

**Keywords:** Deep reinforcement learning · Model checking · CEGAR · ACTL

## 1 Introduction

Deep Reinforcement Learning (DRL) has shown its strength in developing intelligent systems for complex control tasks such as autonomous driving [37,40]. Verifiable safety and robustness guarantees are crucial to these safety-critical DRL systems before deploying [23,44]. A typical example is autonomous driving, which is arguably still a long way off due to safety concerns [21,39]. Recently,


S. Shoham and Y. Vizel (Eds.): CAV 2022, LNCS 13371, pp. 193–218, 2022.
https://doi.org/10.1007/978-3-031-13185-1_10

tremendous efforts have been made toward adapting existing and devising new formal methods for DRL systems in order to provide provable safety guarantees [18,25,45,46,51].

Formally verifying DRL systems is still a challenging problem. The challenge arises from DRL systems' three features. First, the state space of a DRL system is usually continuous and infinite [28]. Second, the behavior of a DRL system is non-linear and determined by high-order system dynamics [17]. Last but not least, the controllers, typically deep neural networks (DNN), are almost inexplicable because of their black-box development [20,52]. The three features make it unattainable to verify DRL systems using conventional formal methods, *i.e.*, modeling them as state transition systems and verifying temporal properties using dedicated decision procedures [4]. Most existing approaches have to simplify the problem by abstraction or over-approximation techniques and restrict to specific properties such as safety or reachability [46].

Another common problem with most existing formal verification approaches to DRL systems is that they are applied after the training is concluded. These *train-then-verify* approaches have two limitations. First, verification results may be inconclusive due to abstraction or overestimation. The non-linearity of both system dynamics and deep neural networks makes it difficult to control the overestimation in a reasonable range, resulting in false positives in verification results [50]. Second, the *ex post facto* detection of bugs increases both the time- and money-wise cost of training and deployment. No evidence shows that the iterative training and verification help improve system reliability, as tuning the parameters in neural networks may cause an unpredictable impact on the properties because of the inexplicability [24].

To address the challenges in training and verifying DRL systems, in this paper we propose a novel *verification-in-the-loop* framework for training safe and reliable DRL systems with verifiable guarantees. Provided that a set of properties are predefined for a target DRL system to develop, our framework trains the system and verifies it against the properties in every iteration. To overcome the verification challenges in DRL systems, for the first time, we propose a novel approach in our framework to train the systems on a finite set of *abstract states*, based on the observation that *approximate abstractions can still preserve near-optimal behavior* [1]. These states are the abstractions of the actual states. Training on the finite abstract states allows us to model the AI-embedded systems as finite-state transition systems. We can leverage classic model checking techniques to verify their more complicated temporal properties than safety and reachability.

As system performance may be affected by the abstraction granularity, we employ the idea of the counterexample-guided abstraction and refinement (CEGAR) [8] in model checking along the training process. We start with a coarsely abstracted but efficiently verifiable state space and train and verify DRL systems on the abstract state space. Once verification fails, we refine the abstract state space based on the returned counterexamples and retrain the system on the finer-grained refined state space. The process is repeated until all the properties are verified successfully. We, therefore, call the training and verification framework *CEGAR-driven*, by which we can reach an appropriate abstraction granularity that guarantees both system performance and verification scalability.

Our verification-in-the-loop training framework has four advantages compared with conventional DRL training and verification approaches. Firstly, our approach produces correct-by-construction DRL systems that are verifiably safe with respect to user-defined safety requirements. Secondly, more complicated properties such as safety and liveness can be verified thanks to the dedicated training approach on abstracted state space. Another advantage of the training approach is that it is orthogonal to state-of-the-art DRL algorithms such as Deep Q-Network (DQN) [34] and Deep Deterministic Policy Gradient (DDPG) [32]. Thirdly, our approach provides a flexible mechanism for fine-tuning an appropriate abstraction granularity to balance system performance and verification scalability. Lastly, training on abstract states renders DRL systems to be more robust against adversarial and environmental perturbations because small perturbation to an actual state may not alter the decision of the neural network on the same abstract state.

We implement a prototype tool called TRAINIFY (abbreviated for Train and Verify, available at https://github.com/aptx4869tjx/RL_verification). We perform extensive experiments on six classic control tasks in public benchmarks to evaluate the effectiveness of our framework. For each task, we train two DRL systems under the same settings in our approach and corresponding conventional DRL algorithm, respectively. We compare the two systems in terms of the properties that they shall satisfy and the performance in terms of cumulative reward and robustness. Experimental results show that the systems trained in our approach are more efficient to verify and more reliable than those trained in conventional methods; moreover, their performance is competitive and higher.

In summary, this paper makes the following three major contributions:

1. A novel verification-in-the-loop training framework for developing verifiable and reliable DRL systems with correct-by-construction guarantees.
2. A CEGAR-driven approach for fine-tuning abstraction granularity during training to reach a balance between system performance and verification scalability.
3. A resulting prototype tool called TRAINIFY for training and verifying DRL systems and a thorough evaluation of the proposed approach on public benchmarks.

*Paper Organization.* Section 2 briefly introduces deep reinforcement learning. Section 3 presents the model-checking problem of DRL systems. Section 4 presents our training and verification framework. Section 5 shows six case studies and experimental results. Section 6 mentions some related work, and Sect. 7 concludes the paper.

## 2 Deep Reinforcement Learning (DRL)

DRL is a technique for learning optimal control policies using deep neural networks according to evaluative feedback [31]. An agent in a DRL system interacts with the environment and records its state $s_t$ at each time step $t$. It feeds $s_t$ into a deep neural network to compute an action $a_t$ and transitions to the next state $s_{t+1}$ according to $a_t$ and the system dynamics. The system dynamics describe the non-linear behavior of the agent over time. The agent receives a scalar reward according to reward functions. Some algorithms estimate the distance between the action determined by the network and the expected action in the same state. Then, it updates the parameters in the network according to the estimated distance to maximize the cumulative reward.

***A Running Example.*** Figure 1 shows a classic DRL task of learning a control policy to drive a car to the right hilltop. The car is initially positioned on a track between two mountains. The track is one-dimensional, and thus the car's position is represented as a real number. Velocity is another dimension in the car's state and is represented as a real number too. Thus, the car's state is a pair $(p, v)$ of position $p$ and velocity $v$. An action $a$ is a real number representing the force imposed on the car. The action is computed by a neural network on both $p$ and $v$.

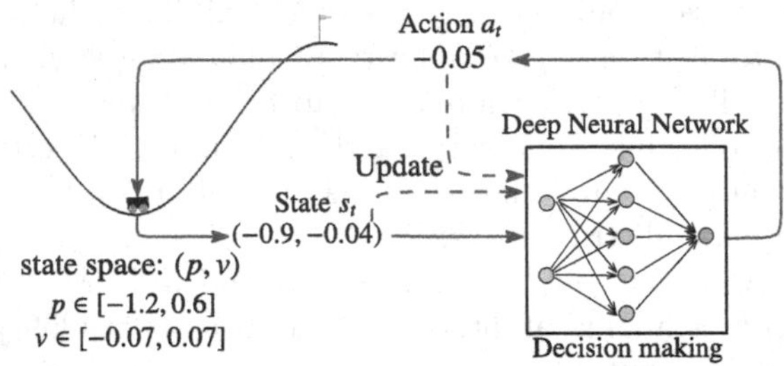


**Fig. 1.** A DRL example of mountain car system.

The sign of $a$ means the direction of the force, *i.e.*, positive for the right and negative for the left, respectively. Given a state $s_t = (p_t, v_t)$ and an action $a_t$ at time step $t$, the system transitions to the next step $s_{t+1} = (p_{t+1}, v_{t+1})$ following the given dynamics:

$$p_{t+1} = p_t + v_t \Delta_t, \quad (1)$$

$$v_{t+1} = v_t + (a_t - m_c \times g \times cos(3p_t))\Delta_t, \quad (2)$$

where $m_c$ denotes the car's mass, $g$ denotes the gravity, and $\Delta_t$ is the unit interval between two consecutive steps. In DRL, time is usually discretized to facilitate implementation. The car is assumed to move in uniform motion during a unit interval.

***Reward Setting.*** The reward function $R$ maps state $s_t$, action $a_t$ and state $s_{t+1}$ to a real number, which represents the rewarded value by applying $a_t$ to $s_t$ to transition to $s_{t+1}$. The purpose of $R$ is to guide the agent to achieve the preset goals by making cumulative reward as great as possible. The definition of $R$ is based on prior knowledge or expert experience before training.

In the Mountain Car example, the controller receives the reward which is defined as $R(\langle p_t, v_t\rangle, a_t, \langle p_{t+1}, v_{t+1}\rangle) = -1.0$ at each time step when $p_{t+1} < 0.45$.

The reward is a negative constant because the goal in this example is to force the car to reach the right hilltop ($p = 0.45$) as quickly as possible. If the corresponding cumulative reward value is larger than another when the car reaches the destination, it means that the car takes fewer steps. A reward function can be a more complex formula than a constant when the reward strategy is related to states and actions.

***Training.*** The essence of DRL training is to update parameters in neural networks so that the networks can compute optimal actions for input states. A deep neural network is a directed graph comprised of an input layer, multiple hidden layers, and an output layer, as shown in Fig. 2. Each layer contains several nodes called *neurons*. They are connected to the neurons on the following layer. Each edge has a weight. The values passed on the edge are multiplied by the weight. A neuron on hidden layers takes the sum of all the incoming values, adds a bias, and feeds the result to its activation function $\sigma$. The output of $\sigma$ is passed to the neurons on the following layer. There are several commonly used activation functions, e.g., ReLU ($\sigma(x) = max(x, 0)$), Sigmoid ($\sigma(x) = \frac{1}{1+e^{-x}}$) and Tanh ($\sigma(x) = \frac{e^x - e^{-x}}{e^x + e^{-x}}$), etc. In DRL, the inputs to a neural network are system states. The outputs are (probably continuous) actions that shall be performed to the present state.

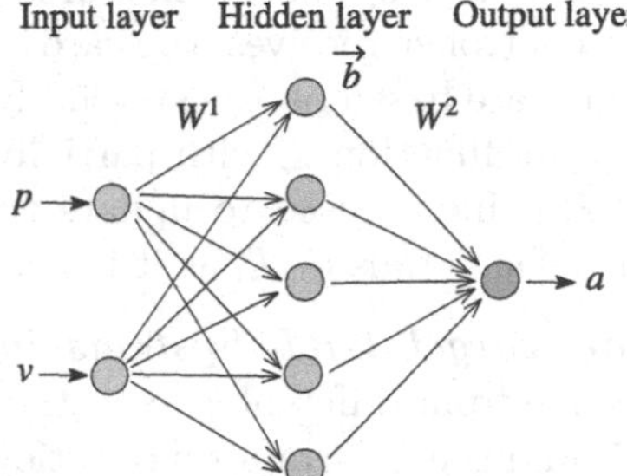


**Fig. 2.** A simple neural network.

During training, agents continuously interact with the environment to obtain trajectories. A trajectory is a 4-tuple, consisting of a state $s$, the action $a$ on $s$, the reward of executing $a$ on $s$, and the successor state after the execution. A predefined loss function uses the collected trajectories to estimate an action value and compute the distance between the estimated value and the one computed by the neural network for the same state. Guided by the distance, the parameters in the network are updated using gradient descent algorithms [12]. The process is repeated until the system reaches a predefined maximal iteration limit or a preset cumulative reward threshold.

**Algorithm 1:** Training for the Mountain Car Task using DQN

**for** *episode* $= 1, \ldots, M$ **do**
  Initialize $s_0 = (p_0, v_0)$
  **for** $t = 0, \ldots, T$ **do**
    $a_t \leftarrow \mathcal{N}(p_t, v_t)$; /* *To determine $a_t$ based on $s_t = (p_t, v_t)$ and $\mathcal{N}$* */
    $(s_{t+1}, -1.0) \leftarrow system(s_t, a_t)$; /* *To execute $a_t$ and transition to the next state $s_{t+1}$* */
    $\mathcal{P} \leftarrow \mathcal{L}(\mathcal{N}, \langle s_i, a_i, -1.0, s_{i+1}\rangle, \ldots, \langle s_j, a_j, -1.0, s_{j+1}\rangle)$; /* *To compute the distance* */
    $\mathcal{N} \leftarrow update(\mathcal{N}, \mathcal{P})$; /* *To update parameters in $\mathcal{N}$ based on $\mathcal{P}$* */

There are several well-established training algorithms, such as Deep Q-Network (DQN) [35] and Deep Deterministic Policy Gradient (DDPG) [32]. Algorithm 1 depicts a high-level process of training the mountain car using DQN. We call the process of training the car to move from the initial position to the destination an *episode*. For each episode, the initial state is firstly determined (Line 2). Then, the controller determines the action to be adopted based on the current state $s_t$ and the neural network $\mathcal{N}$ (Line 4). After performing the action, the controller receives a reward value ($-1.0$ in this case) and transitions to the next state based on the system dynamics (Line 5). A loss is estimated by calling the loss function $\mathcal{L}$ with partially sampled trajectories. The loss is represented by $\mathcal{P}$ (Line 6) used to update the parameters of the network $\mathcal{N}$ (Line 7). We omit the details of $\mathcal{L}$, as it is not the emphasis of our paper.

***The Target DRL Systems in this Work.*** The types of DRL systems are diverse from different perspectives, such as the availability of system dynamics [17] and the determinism of actions. In this work, we assume system dynamics is prior knowledge for training, and the actions are deterministic. That is, a unique action is determined to take on the present state, and its successor state is also uniquely determined by system dynamics.

## 3 Model Checking of DRL Systems

### 3.1 The Model Checking Problem

A trained deterministic DRL system can be represented as a tuple $M = (S, A, f, \pi, S^0, L)$, where $S$ is the state space which is usually infinite, $S^0 \subseteq S$ is the initial state space, $A$ is a set of actions, $f : S \times A \rightarrow S$ is the system dynamics, $\pi : S \rightarrow A$ is a policy function, and $L : S \rightarrow 2^{AP}$ is a state labeling function. In this work, we use $\pi$ to denote the policy that is implemented by the trained deep neural network in the system.

The model $M$ of a DRL system is essentially a Kripke structure [10], which is a 4-tuple $(S, R, S^0, L)$. Given two arbitrary states $s, s'$ in $S$, there is a transition from $s$ to $s'$, denoted by $(s, s') \in R$, if and only if there is an action $a$ in $A$ such that $a = \pi(s)$ and $s' = f(s, a)$. Given that a property is formalized by a formula $\Phi$ in some logic, the model checking problem of the system is to decide whether $M$ satisfies $\Phi$, denoted by $M \models \Phi$.

In this work, we formulate properties in ACTL [4], a segment of CTL where only universal path quantifiers are allowed and negation is restricted to atomic propositions [14,15]. ACTL consists of state formula $\Phi$ and path formula $\varphi$ in the following syntax:

$$\begin{aligned} \Phi &::= \mathit{true} \mid \mathit{false} \mid a \mid \neg a \mid \Phi_1 \wedge \Phi_2 \mid \Phi_1 \vee \Phi_2 \mid A\varphi, \\ \varphi &::= X\Phi \mid \Phi_1 U \Phi_2 \mid \Phi_1 R \Phi_2. \end{aligned}$$

The temporal operators fall into two main categories, *i.e.*, quantifiers over paths and path-specific quantifiers. In ACTL, only the universal path quantifier $A$ is considered. Path-specific quantifiers refer to $X$, $U$ and $R$.

- $A\ \varphi$: Path formula $\varphi$ has to hold on all paths starting from the current state.
- $X\ \Phi$: State formula $\Phi$ has to hold at the next state.
- $\Phi_1\ U\ \Phi_2$: State formula $\Phi_1$ has to hold at least until state formula $\Phi_2$.
- $\Phi_1\ R\ \Phi_2$: Formula $\Phi_2$ has to hold until and including a point where $\Phi_1$ first becomes true. If $\Phi_1$ never becomes true, $\Phi_2$ must hold forever.

Using the above basic temporal operators, we can define another two important path-specific quantifiers $G$ (*globally*) and $F$ (*finally*) with $G\ \Phi = \mathit{false}\ R\ \Phi$ and $F\ \Phi = \mathit{true}\ U\ \Phi$. Intuitively, $G\ \Phi$ means that $\Phi$ has to hold on the entire subsequent path, and $F\ \Phi$ means that $\Phi$ eventually has to hold (somewhere on the subsequent path).

We choose ACTL to formulate system properties or requirements in our framework for two main reasons. Firstly, in our framework, we rely on refinement to the abstract states where system properties are violated. Such states can be obtained as counterexamples returned by model checkers when the system properties defined in ACTL are verified not valid by model checking. Secondly, the verification results of ACTL formulas can be preserved by property-based abstraction [9,11]. Such preservation is vital to ensure the correctness of our verification results because the abstraction is necessary for our framework to guarantee the scalability of the verification algorithm.

### 3.2 Challenges in Model Checking DRL Systems

Unlike the model checking problems for finite-state systems, model checking $M \models \Phi$ for DRL systems is particularly challenging. The challenge arises from the three features of DRL systems, *i.e.*, (i) the infinity and continuity of state space $S$, (ii) the non-linearity of system dynamics $f$, and (iii) the inexplicability of the policy $\pi$ that is encoded as deep neural networks. Usually, the state space of DRL systems is continuous and infinite, and behaviors are non-linear due to high-order system dynamics. Even worse, the actions of states are determined by inexplicable deep neural networks, which means that the transitions between states cannot be defined as straightforwardly as those of traditional software systems.

To build a model $M$ for a DRL system, we have to compute the successor of each state $s$ by applying the neural network $\pi$ on $s$ to compute the action $a$ and then performing $a$ to $s$ according to the system's dynamics $f$. Specifically, the successor of $s$ can be represented as $f(s, \pi(s))$. The non-linearity of both $f$ and $\pi$ and the infinity of $S$ makes the verification problem difficult. Most existing approaches rely on the over-approximation of $f$ and $\pi$ to simplify the problem [16,25,29,46]. However, over-approximation inevitably introduces over-estimation and restricts to only safety properties and reachability analysis in bounded steps.

# 4 The CEGAR-Driven DRL Approach

## 4.1 The Framework

Figure 3 shows the overview of our framework. It consists of three parts, *i.e.*, training, verification and refinement. In the training part, a DRL system is trained on a finite set of abstract states. An actual state is first mapped to its corresponding abstract state, then fed into the neural network to compute a corresponding action. The action is applied to the actual state to drive the system to transition to the next state. The reward is accumulated according to a predefined reward function, and the neural network is updated in the same way as conventional DRL algorithms. In the verification part, we build a Kripke structure on the finite abstract state space based on the trained neural network. Then, we verify the desired properties that are predefined in ACTL formulas $\Phi$. If all the properties are verified valid, we stop training, and a DRL system is developed. If some property is verified not valid, we move to the refinement part. When verification fails, counterexamples are returned. They are the abstract states where the property is violated. We refine these states by subdividing them into fine-grained sub-states and substitute those *bad* states. We resume to train the system on the refined abstract state space and repeat the whole process.

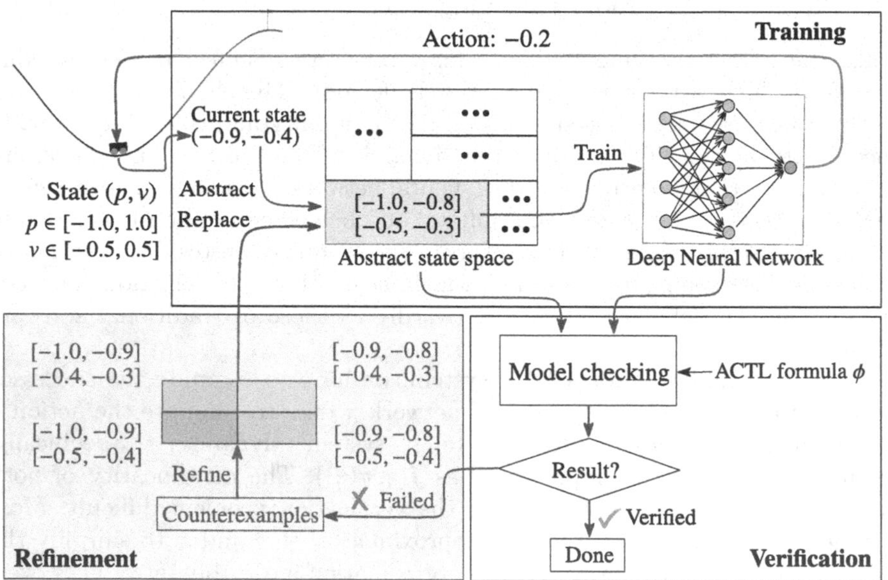


**Fig. 3.** The training, verification and refinement framework for developing DRL systems.

The integration of training, verification and refinement seamlessly constitutes a *verification-in-the-loop* DRL approach, driven by the counterexample-guided abstraction and refinement. We start with a coarse abstraction. After every training episode, we model check the system against all the predefined properties. If all the properties are verified, we stop training and obtain a verified system. Otherwise, counterexamples are returned. The abstract state space is refined for further training. After several iterations, a DRL system is trained with all the predefined properties rigorously verified.

## 4.2 Training on Abstract States

DRL is a process of learning optimal actions on all system states for specific objectives. A trained model partitions the state space into a family of sets such that the same action is taken in the states from a set [38]. Continuous state spaces can be adaptively discretized into finite ones for learning without affecting learning performance [41,42]. Motivated by this observation, we discretize a continuous state space into a finite set of fragments. We call each fragment an abstract state and train the DRL system by feeding abstract states into the deep neural network for decision making.

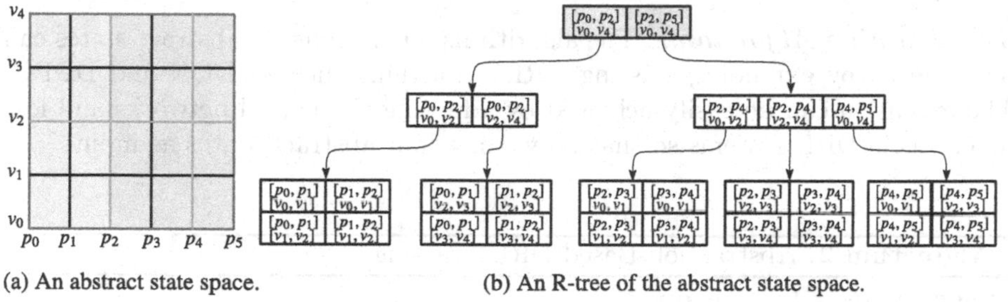


(a) An abstract state space.

(b) An R-tree of the abstract state space.

**Fig. 4.** An example of encoding an abstract state space into an R-tree.

***System State Abstraction.*** Given an $n$-dimension DRL system, a concrete system state $s$ is represented as a vector of $n$ real numbers. Each number has a physical meaning about the system, such as speed and position in the running example. Let $L_i$ and $U_i$ be the lower and upper bounds for the $i$-th dimension value of $S$. Then, the state space $S$ of the control system is $\Pi_{i=1}^{n}[L_i, U_i]$.

Initially, we use interval boxes to discretize $S$. An interval box $I$ is a vector of $n$ intervals, denoted by $(I_1, I_2, \ldots, I_n)$. Each interval $I_i (1 \leq i \leq n)$ represents all the system states, denoted by $S_{I_i}$, where a state $s$ belongs to $S_{I_i}$ if and only if the $i$-th value in $s$ is in $I_i$. An interval box $I$ represents the intersection of all the sets $S_{I_i} (i = 1, \ldots, n)$.

Let $d_i \in \mathbb{R}$ $(0 < d_i \leq U_i - L_i)$ be the diameter by which we subdivide evenly the interval $[L_i, U_i]$ in each dimension $i$ into $(U_i - L_i)/d_i$ unit intervals, and $\mathcal{I}_i = [L_i, U_i]/d_i$ denote the set of all the unit intervals. Then, we obtain the abstract state space $\mathbf{S} = \mathcal{I}_1 \times \ldots \times \mathcal{I}_n$, which is an abstraction of the infinite continuous state space $S$. We call the vector $(d_1, d_2, \ldots, d_n)$ of the $n$ diameters *abstraction granularity* and denote it by $\delta$.

Given a continuous state space $S$ and its corresponding abstract state space $\mathbf{S}$, we call the mapping function from the states in $S$ to the corresponding abstract states in $\mathbf{S}$ a *transformer* $\mathcal{A} : S \rightarrow \mathbf{S}$. The transformer can be encoded as an R-tree, a tree-like data structure devised for efficiently indexing multi-dimensional objects [22]. Figure 4 depicts an example of building an R-tree to index an abstract state space of the continuous space $[v_0, v_4] \times [p_0, p_5]$. A rectangle on a leaf node represents an abstract state, and the one on a non-leaf node represents the minimum bounding rectangle enclosing all the rectangles on its child nodes. There can be multiple rectangles on a single node. R-tree supports intersection search, *i.e.*, searching for the abstract states that intersect with the interval we are querying. Given a concrete state, an R-tree can quickly return its corresponding abstract state. Note that in Fig. 4, we assume state space is discretized evenly for clarity. During training, the size of abstract states becomes diverse after iterative refinement, and the R-tree should be updated correspondingly.

***The Training Algorithms.*** The algorithms for training on abstract states can be achieved by extending existing DRL algorithms such as DQN and DDPG. The extension can be easily achieved by adapting the neural networks and loss functions in DRL systems so that they can admit abstract states as inputs.

**Algorithm 2:** Abstraction-Based DRL Training

**for** *episode* $= 1, \ldots, M$ **do**
  $\mathcal{A} \leftarrow$ ***discretize***$(S, \delta)$; /* *To discretize $S$ by abstraction granularity $\delta$* */
  Initialize $s_0$;
  **for** $t = 0, \ldots, T$ **do**
    $\mathbf{s}_t \leftarrow \mathcal{A}(s_t)$ ; /* *To get abstract state of $s_t$* */
    $a_t \leftarrow \mathcal{N}'(\mathbf{s}_t)$; /* *To determine action $a_t$ based on $\mathbf{s}_t$ and $\mathcal{N}'$* */
    $(s_{t+1}, r_t) \leftarrow$ ***system***$(s_t, a_t)$ ; /* *To execute $a_t$ on $s_t$ and transition to $s_{t+1}$ with reward $r_t$* */
    $\mathcal{P} =$ ***Loss***$(\mathcal{N}', \langle \mathbf{s}_i, a_i, r_i, \mathbf{s}_{i+1}\rangle, \ldots, \langle \mathbf{s}_j, a_j, r_j, \mathbf{s}_{j+1}\rangle)$; /* *To get loss due to $a_t$* */
    $\mathcal{N}' \leftarrow$ ***update***$(\mathcal{N}', \mathcal{P})$; /* *To update parameters in $\mathcal{N}'$ based on $\mathcal{P}$* */

For neural networks, we only need to modify the input layer by doubling the number of neurons on the input layer, denoted by $\mathcal{N}'$. Given an $n$-dimension system, we declare $2n$ neurons. Each pair of neurons read the lower and upper bounds of an interval in an abstract state, respectively. This dedicated structure guarantees that a trained network can produce the same action for all the states that correspond to the same abstract state.

Figure 5 shows an example of adapting the network in the Mountain Car for training it on abstract states. For traditional DRL algorithms, two input neurons are needed in the neural network to take $p$ and $v$ as inputs, respectively. To train on abstract states, four input neurons are needed to take the lower and upper bounds of the position and velocity intervals in abstract states. For instance, let the interval box $(I_p, I_v)$ be the abstract state of $(p, v)$. Then, the lower bounds $\underline{I_p}, \underline{I_v}$ and the upper bounds $\overline{I_p}, \overline{I_v}$ of $p, v$ are input to the four neurons, respectively. Apparently, this adaption guarantees that the neural network always produces the same action on the states that are transformed into the same abstract state.

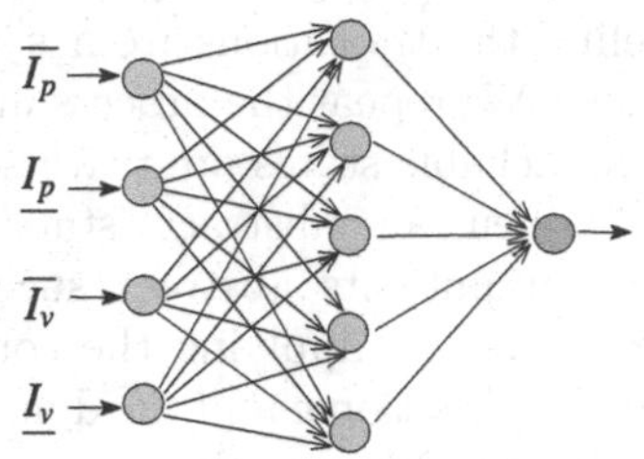


**Fig. 5.** Adapting neural networks for abstract states.

We consider incorporating these two steps to extend Algorithm 1 as an illustrative example. Algorithm 2 depicts the main workflow where the differences are highlighted. The main difference from the traditional training process lies in line 6. Given a concrete state $s = (s_1, \ldots, s_n)$, $\mathcal{A}$ will return the abstract state $\mathbf{s} = ([l_1, u_1], \ldots, [l_n, u_n])$ such that $l_i \leq s_i \leq u_i$ with $i = 1, \ldots, n$, which is also the result fed into neural network. Although the dimension of input states increases, the form of corresponding output actions does not change. Therefore, the loss function can naturally adapt to changes in input states.

### 4.3 Model Checking Trained DRL Systems

A DRL system can be naturally verified using abstract model checking [26]. The actual states of the system are first abstracted in the same way used in training, and then the transitions between abstract states are determined by the corresponding action and dynamics. ACTL formulas are then model checked on the abstract state transition system.

***Building Kripke Structure.*** During the training phase, the actual state space has already been abstracted into a finite set $\mathbf{S}$ of abstract states. Therefore, the main task for abstract model checking is to build a Kripke structure by defining the transition relation on $\mathbf{S}$.

Algorithm 3 depicts the process of building a Kripke structure $\mathcal{K}$ for a trained DRL system. Firstly, $\mathcal{K}$ is initialized on set $\mathbf{S}$ with $R$ being empty. Starting from an initial abstract state $\mathbf{s}^0$, we compute its successors and define the transitions from $\mathbf{s}^0$ to them. We repeat the process until all reachable states are traversed.

---

**Algorithm 3:** Building Kripke Structure

---

**Input:** Initial state $\mathbf{s}^0$, state space $\mathbf{S}$, system dynamics $f$, neural network $\mathcal{N}'$

**Output:** A Kripke Structure $\mathcal{K}$

$\mathcal{K}$ = Initialize_Kripke_Structure()
*Queue* $\leftarrow \{\mathbf{s}^0\}$
**while** *Queue is not empty* **do**
  Fetch $\mathbf{s}$ from *Queue*
  **for** $i = 1, \ldots, n$ **do**
    $[l_i, u_i] \leftarrow g(f(\mathbf{s}, \mathcal{N}'(\mathbf{s})), i)$
  $\{\mathbf{s}^1, \ldots, \mathbf{s}^m\} := h([l_1, u_1], \ldots, [l_n, u_n], \mathbf{S})$
  **for** $j = 1, \ldots, m$ **do**
    $\mathcal{K}$.add_edge($\mathbf{s} \rightarrow \mathbf{s}^j$)
    **if** $\mathbf{s}^j$ *is not traversed* **then**
      Push $\mathbf{s}^j$ into *Queue*
**return** $\mathcal{K}$

---

Given an abstract state $\mathbf{s}$, we compute its abstract successor states by applying the corresponding action $a$ and the dynamics to $\mathbf{s}$. Because the system is trained on abstract states, all the actual states in $\mathbf{s}$ have the same action, *i.e.*, $a = \mathcal{N}'(\mathbf{s})$. Let $f^*(\mathbf{s}, a) = \{f(s, a) | s \in \mathbf{s}\}$ be the set of all the successors of the actual states in $\mathbf{s}$. Due to the non-linearity of $f$ and the infinity of $\mathbf{s}$, we over-approximate the set $f^*(\mathbf{s}, a) = \{f(s, a) | s \in \mathbf{s}\}$ as an interval box. As shown in Fig. 6, the dashed box is an over-approximation of $f^*(\mathbf{s}, a)$. The over-approximation may overlap one or more abstract states, e.g., $\mathbf{s}^1, \ldots, \mathbf{s}^4$ in the example. All the overlapped abstract states are successors of $\mathbf{s}$. In Algorithm 3, function $g$ calculates the interval box and function $h$ determines the overlapped abstract states. Note that the shapes of abstract states may be different because they are refined during training, which is to be detailed in Sect. 4.4.

We use an interval to approximate the $i$-th dimension's values in all the successor states. Then, all the successor states are approximated as a vector of $n$ intervals. We can compute the upper and lower bounds for each $i$ by solving the following two optimization problems, respectively:

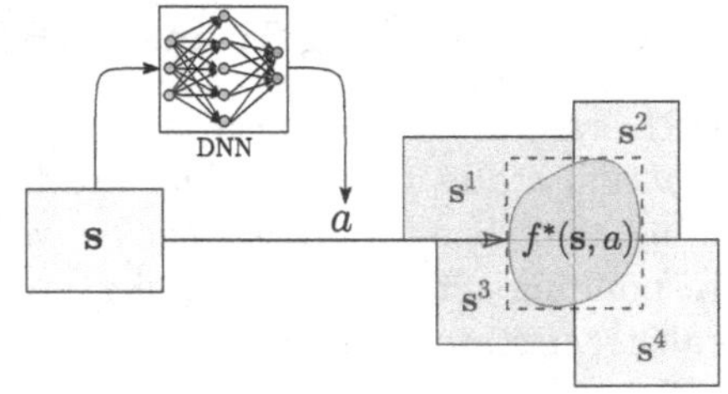


**Fig. 6.** Transitions between abstract states

$$\underset{s \in \mathbf{s}}{\arg\max} \quad v_i \cdot f(s, \mathcal{N}'(\mathbf{s}))$$

$$\underset{s \in \mathbf{s}}{\arg\min} \quad v_i \cdot f(s, \mathcal{N}'(\mathbf{s}))$$

where, $v_i$ is a one-hot vector with the $i$-th element being 1. Because all the states in $\mathbf{s}$ have the same action according to the network, $\mathcal{N}'(\mathbf{s})$ in the above optimization problems can be substituted for a constant, *i.e.*, the action taken by the system on all the states in $\mathbf{s}$. The substitution significantly simplifies the optimization problems; no information of the networks is needed in the simplified problems. The simplified problems can be efficiently solved using off-the-shelf scientific computing tools such as SciPy [48].

We consider an example in the mountain car system. We assume that the current abstract state $\mathbf{s}$ is $([0, 0.2], [0, 0.02])$ and the adopted action is 0.001, which says that the controller accelerates to the right for all states in $\mathbf{s}$. Based on the dynamics defined by Eq. 1, we can compute the upper bounds of both position and velocity in the next step by solving the following two optimization problems:

$$\underset{p_t \in [0,0.2], v_t \in [0,0.02]}{\arg\max} \quad p_t + v_t \tag{$p_{t+1}$}$$

$$\underset{p_t \in [0,0.2], v_t \in [0,0.02]}{\arg\max} \quad v_t + 0.001 - 0.0025\cos(3p_t) \tag{$v_{t+1}$}$$

The lower bounds of $p_{t+1}$ and $v_{t+1}$ are calculated similarly. Then, we obtain an abstract state $\mathbf{s}' = ([0, 0.22], [-0.0035, 0.0165])$, which is an overestimated set of all the actual successors of the states in $\mathbf{s}$. There is a transition from $\mathbf{s}$ to any abstract state $\mathbf{s}'' = ([\underline{p}, \overline{p}], [\underline{v}, \overline{v}])$ in $\mathbf{S}$, if $\mathbf{s}'$ and $\mathbf{s}''$ overlap, *i.e.*, $(0 < \underline{p} < 0.22 \vee 0 < \overline{p} < 0.22) \wedge (-0.0035 < \underline{v} < 0.0165 \vee -0.0035 < \overline{v} < 0.0165)$ is true. Note that the transition from $\mathbf{s}$ to $\mathbf{s}'$ includes all the transitions between the actual states in $\mathbf{s}$ and $\mathbf{s}'$, respectively. It may also include those that do not actually exist due to the overestimation.

There are other approaches for over-approximating the set $f^*(\mathbf{s}, a)$, such as template polyhedrons like rectangle and octagon [2]. Note that there is always a trade-off between the tightness of the polyhedral and the efficiency of computing it. For instance, an octagon can approximate the set more tightly than a rectangle. However, it costs double effort to compute the borders. The tighter an over-approximation is, the more accurate the set of computed successors is, but the more time it costs to compute the approximation.

***Property-Based Abstraction.*** For those high-dimensional DRL systems, the abstract state space may be still too huge to model check directly when the abstraction granularity becomes small after refinement. To improve the model checking scalability, we further abstract the constructed Kripke structure based on the ACTL formula $\Phi$ to be model checked using the abstraction approach in the work [9].

**Definition 1 (State Abstraction).** *Given an abstract state space* $\mathbf{S} = I_1 \times \ldots, \times I_n$ *and an ACTL formula* $\Phi$*, let* $D_\Phi$ *be the set of dimensions that occur in* $\Phi$ *and* $\widehat{\mathbf{S}} = \Pi_{\mathsf{d} \in D_\Phi} I_{\mathsf{d}}$. *Function* $\alpha_\Phi : \mathbf{S} \to \widehat{\mathbf{S}}$ *is an abstract transformer such that for every* $\mathbf{s} \in \mathbf{S}$ *and* $\widehat{\mathbf{s}} \in \widehat{\mathbf{S}}$, $\widehat{\mathbf{s}} = \alpha_\Phi(\mathbf{s})$ *if and only if* $\mathbf{s}[\mathsf{d}] = \widehat{\mathbf{s}}[\mathsf{d}]$ *for all* $\mathsf{d} \in D_\Phi$.

Given a Kripke structure $\mathcal{K} = (\mathbf{S}, R, \mathbf{S}^0, L)$ and an ACTL formula $\Phi$, let $\alpha_\Phi : \mathbf{S} \to \widehat{\mathbf{S}}$ be the abstract transformer, and $\widehat{AP} \subseteq AP$ be all the atomic propositions in $\Phi$. We can construct the following abstract Kripke structure $\widehat{\mathcal{K}} = (\widehat{\mathbf{S}}, \widehat{R}, \widehat{\mathbf{S}}^0, \widehat{L})$ based on $\alpha_\Phi$, where:

- $\widehat{\mathbf{S}} = \Pi_{\mathsf{d} \in D_\Phi} \mathcal{I}_\mathsf{d}$;
- $\widehat{R} = \{(\alpha_\Phi(\mathbf{s}), \alpha_\Phi(\mathbf{s}')) | \mathbf{s}, \mathbf{s}' \in \mathbf{S}.(\mathbf{s}, \mathbf{s}') \in R\}$;
- $\widehat{\mathbf{S}}^0 = \{\alpha_\Phi(\mathbf{s}) \mid \mathbf{s} \in \mathbf{S}^0\}$;
- $\widehat{L} : \widehat{\mathbf{S}} \to 2^{\widehat{AP}}$ such that $\widehat{L}(\widehat{\mathbf{s}}) = L(\mathbf{s}) \cap \widehat{AP}$ where $\mathbf{s} \in \mathbf{S}$ and $\widehat{\mathbf{s}} = \alpha_\Phi(\mathbf{s})$.

We call $\widehat{\mathcal{K}}$ a simulation of $\mathcal{K}$ with respect to $\Phi$. An important property of the simulation is that the property represented by $\Phi$ is preserved by the abstract model $\widehat{\mathcal{K}}$.

**Theorem 1 (Soundness).** *Let $\widehat{\mathcal{K}}$ be a simulation of $\mathcal{K}$ with respect to an ACTL formula $\Phi$, $\widehat{\mathcal{K}} \models \Phi$ implies $\mathcal{K} \models \Phi$.*

The proof of Theorem 1 is straightforward. We omit the proof due to space limit. According to the theorem, we can conclude that $\mathcal{K} \models \Phi$ holds whenever we find a simulation $\widehat{\mathcal{K}}$ of $\mathcal{K}$ and model check that $\widehat{\mathcal{K}} \models \Phi$ holds.

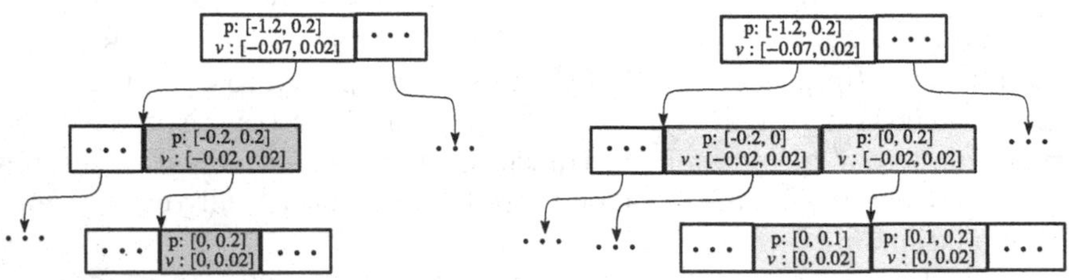


(a) Counterexamples on an R-tree. (b) The R-tree after refinement on the counterexample.

**Fig. 7.** An example of refinements on abstract states where properties are violated.

### 4.4 Counterexample-Guided Refinement

If a formula $\Phi$ is verified not true, our algorithm returns corresponding counterexamples. A counterexample is an abstract state where $\Phi$ is violated. We refine the abstract state into finer ones and substitute them in the abstract state space for further training.

A naïve refinement approach subdivides each dimension of states into two intervals. Assuming that a property is violated on an abstract state $\mathbf{s} = ([l_0, u_0], \ldots, [l_n, u_n])$, we can simply divide each dimension evenly into two intervals $([l_i, (l_i + u_i)/2], [(l_i + u_i)/2, u_i])$, and obtain $2^n$ finer abstract states. Apparently, the refinement may lead to state space explosion, particularly for high-dimensional systems.

In our approach, we only refine the states on the dimensions that are used to define the properties being verified to avoid state explosion. Considering the mountain car example, we assume that the formula is $AF[p \geq 0.45]$, saying that the car will eventually reach the hilltop where $p = 0.45$. Suppose that the property fails and counterexamples are returned. We assume $\mathbf{s} = ([0, 0.2], [0, 0.02])$ is the state where the property is violated, as shown in Fig. 7 (a). We bisect the state into two fine-grained sub-states, $\mathbf{s}^1 = ([0, 0.1], [0, 0.02])$ and $\mathbf{s}^2 = ([0.1, 0.2], [0, 0.02])$. Then, we substitute the two fine-grained states for $\mathbf{s}$ on the R-tree for further training. Figure 7 (b) shows the new R-tree after the substitution.

It is worth mentioning that counterexamples may be false positives. Abstract states may include the actual states that are unreachable in the trained system because of the approximation of system dynamics. Unfortunately, it is difficult to check which states are actually unreachable because we need to know their corresponding initial state to check the reachability of these bad states. However, the corresponding initial state is *enclosed* in an abstract state and cannot be identified due to the abstraction. In our approach, we perform refinement without checking whether the counterexamples are real or not. After refinement, the abstract states become finer-grained. Counterexamples can be discarded by training and verifying on these finer-grained abstract states. The price of such extra refinements is that more iterations of training and verification are conducted, but the benefit is that the performance of the trained systems is better.

## 5 Implementation and Evaluation

### 5.1 Implementation

We implement our framework into a prototype toolkit called TRAINIFY in Python. In the toolkit, we leverage the open-source library *pyModelChecking* [6] as the back-end model checker and the scientific computing tool SciPy [48] as an optimization solver.

### 5.2 Benchmarks and Experimental Settings

We evaluate the effectiveness of our approach on a wide range of classic control tasks from public benchmarks. For each control task, we train two DRL systems using our approach and the corresponding conventional DRL approach, respectively. We compare the two trained systems in terms of their reliability, verifiability and system performance.

***Benchmarks*.** We choose six classic control problems. Three of them are from the DRL training platform Gym [5], including Mountain Car, Pendulum and Cartpole. The other three, *i.e.*, B1, B2 and Tora, are the problems that are widely used for evaluation by state-of-the-art tools [19,25,27,28].

1. **Mountain Car (MC).** The running example in Sect. 2.
2. **Pendulum (PD).** A pendulum that can rotate around an endpoint is delineated. Starting from a random position, the pendulum shall swing up and stay upright.
3. **CartPole (CP).** A pole is attached by an un-actuated joint to a cart. The goal of training is to learn a controller that prevents the pole from falling over by applying a force of $+1$ or $-1$ to the cart.

4. **B1** and **B2**. Two classic nonlinear systems, where agents in both systems aim to arrive at the destination region from the preset initial state space [19].
5. **Tora.** A cart is attached to a wall with a spring. It is free to move on a frictionless surface. Inside the cart, there is an arm free to rotate about an axis. The controller's goal is to stabilize the system at the equilibrium state where all the system variables are equal to 0.

***Training Configurations and Evaluation Metrics.*** We adopt the same system configurations and training parameters for each task, including neural network architecture, system dynamics, time interval, DRL algorithms and the number of training episodes.

We choose three metrics, including the satisfaction of predefined properties, cumulative reward and robustness, to evaluate and compare the reliability, verifiability and performance of the DRL systems trained in our approach and those trained in the conventional DRL approach for the same task. The first metric is about reliability and verifiability. The other two are about performance. The cumulative reward is an important figure to evaluate a trained system's performance because maximizing the cumulative reward is the objective of learning. Robustness is another essential criterion for DRL systems because the systems are expected to be robust against perturbations from both the environment and adversarial attacks. Note that we classify robustness into performance category instead of reliability because we restrict the reliability of DRL systems to the safety and functional requirements.

***Experimental Settings.*** All experiments are conducted on a workstation running Ubuntu 18.04 with a 32-core AMD Ryzen Threadripper CPU @ 3.7 GHz and 128 GB RAM.

### 5.3 Reliability and Verifiability Comparison

We first evaluate the reliability and verifiability of the DRL systems trained in our approach and conventional approach, respectively. For each task, we predefined system properties according to their safety and functional requirements. The functional requirement is usually the objective of control tasks. For instance, the controller's objective to train in the mountain car example is to drive the car to the hilltop. We define an atomic proposition $p > 0.45$ to indicate that the car reaches the hilltop. Then, we can define an ACTL formula $\Phi_1 = AF(p > 0.45)$ to represent the liveness property. Safety requirements in DRL systems usually specify important parameters of the systems that must always be kept in safe ranges. For instance, a safety requirement in the mountain car example is that the car's velocity must be greater than 0.02 when the car moves to a position around 0.2 within a 0.05 deviation. The property can be represented by the ACTL formula $\Phi_2$ as defined in Table 1. The properties of other tasks are formalized similarly. The formulas and the types of properties are shown in the table.

**Table 1.** Expected properties and their definitions in ACTL of the selected control tasks.

| Task | ID | ACTL formula | Type | Meaning |
|---|---|---|---|---|
| MC | $\phi_1$ | $AF(p > 0.45)$ | Liveness | The car always reaches the target finally. |
| | $\phi_2$ | $AG(\|p - 0.2\| < 0.05 \rightarrow v > 0.02)$ | Safety | The car's speed should be greater than 0.02 at the position 0.2 within a 0.05 deviation. |
| PD | $\phi_3$ | $AG(\|\theta\| \leq \frac{\pi}{2})$ | Safety | The pendulum's angle $\theta$ must always be in the preset range $[-\frac{\pi}{2}, \frac{\pi}{2}]$. |
| CP | $\phi_4$ | $AG_{t \leq n}(\|p\| \leq 2.4 \wedge a \leq \|0.21\|)$ | Safety | The cart always stays in the safe region and the pole cannot fall down in $n$ time steps. |
| B1 | $\phi_5$ | $AF(x_1 \in [0, 0.2] \wedge x_2 \in [0.05, 0.3])$ | Liveness | The agent always reaches the target finally. |
| | $\phi_6$ | $AG(\|x_1\| \leq 1.5 \wedge \|x_2\| \leq 1.5)$ | Safety | The agent always stays in the safe region. |
| B2 | $\phi_7$ | $AF(target)$ | Liveness | The agent always reaches the target finally. |
| | $\phi_8$ | $A((\|x_1\| \leq 1.5 \wedge \|x_2\| \leq 1.5)\ U\ target) \vee AG(\|x_1\| \leq 1.5 \wedge \|x_2\| \leq 1.5)$ | Safety | The agent must stay in the safe region until it reaches the target region. |
| Tora | $\phi_9$ | $AG_{t \leq n}(\|x_1\| \leq 1.5 \wedge \|x_3\| \leq 1.5)$ | Safety | The agent can stay in the preset state space with $n$ time steps. |

**Remarks.** *target* is an atomic proposition *i.e.*, $x_1 \in [-0.3, 0.1] \wedge x_2 \in [-0.35, 0.5]$ in B2.

We compare the reliability and verifiability of all the trained DRL systems with respect to their predefined properties using both verification and simulation. The DRL systems trained in our approach can be naturally verified in our framework. For those trained in the conventional DRL approaches, our verification approach is not applicable because we cannot construct abstract Kripke structures for them. The main reason is that we cannot abstract the system states such that there is a unique action on all the actual states represented by the same abstract state. We therefore resort to the state-of-the-art reachability analysis tool Verisig 2.0 [25] to verify them. We also simulate all the trained systems in a fixed number of rounds and detect the occurrences of property violations. The purposes of the simulation are twofold: (i) to partially reflect the reliability of systems; and (ii) to validate the verification results in a bounded number of steps.

Table 2 shows the comparison results. We can observe that all the systems trained in our approach are successfully verified, and the corresponding properties hold on them. No violations are detected by simulation. For those systems trained in conventional DRL algorithms, only 8 out of 16 are successfully verified by Verisig. There are two cases, where Verisig returns **Unknown** when verifying $\phi_7$ for task B2. It means that the verification fails because Verisig 2.0 cannot determine whether the destination region (defined by $x_1 \in [-0.3, 0.1] \wedge x_2 \in [-0.35, 0.5]$) must always be reached when it computes a larger region that overlaps the *target*. The extra part in the larger region may be an overestimation caused by the over-approximation. By simulation, we detect violations to $\phi_7$. The violations can be considered as counterexamples to the property. The other properties such as $\phi_2, \phi_3, \phi_4$, and $\phi_8$ are not supported by Verisig 2.0. Among these unverified properties, we detect there exist violations by simulation for three of them. The violations indicate that the systems trained in conventional DRL approaches may not satisfy expected properties, and existing

**Table 2.** Comparison of the verification and simulation results between the DRL systems trained in our approach and conventional DRL algorithms, respectively.

| Task | Network | | Property | By *Trainify* | | | | By conventional algorithms | | | |
|---|---|---|---|---|---|---|---|---|---|---|---|
| | A.F. | Size | | T.T. | V.R. | V.T. | Vio. | T.T. | V.R. | V.T. | Vio. |
| MC | Sigmoid | 2 × 16 | $\phi_1$ | 306 | ✓ | 26.8 | 0 | 297 | ✓ | 45.5 | 0 |
| | | | $\phi_2$ | 302 | ✓ | 5.9 | 0 | 297 | N/A | – | 0 |
| | Sigmoid | 2 × 200 | $\phi_1$ | 453 | ✓ | 29.1 | 0 | 441 | ✓ | 3709 | 0 |
| | | | $\phi_2$ | 462 | ✓ | 7.1 | 0 | 441 | N/A | – | 0 |
| PD | ReLU | 3 × 128 | $\phi_3$ | 771 | ✓ | 1.2 | 0 | 501 | N/A | – | 0 |
| CP | ReLU | 3 × 64 | $\phi_4$ | 135 | ✓ | 3266 | 0 | 101 | N/A | – | **12** |
| B1 | Tanh | 2 × 20 | $\phi_5$ | 52 | ✓ | 89.0 | 0 | 31 | ✓ | 4.6 | 0 |
| | | | $\phi_6$ | 43 | ✓ | 5.3 | 0 | 31 | ✓ | 4.6 | 0 |
| | Tanh | 2 × 100 | $\phi_5$ | 32 | ✓ | 66 | 0 | 41 | ✓ | 28.2 | 0 |
| | | | $\phi_6$ | 25 | ✓ | 3.8 | 0 | 41 | ✓ | 28.2 | 0 |
| B2 | Tanh | 2 × 20 | $\phi_7$ | 17 | ✓ | 1.2 | 0 | 9 | **Unknown** | 4.8 | **27** |
| | | | $\phi_8$ | 9 | ✓ | 1.3 | 0 | 9 | N/A | - | 0 |
| | Tanh | 2 × 100 | $\phi_7$ | 9 | ✓ | 1.3 | 0 | 11 | **Unknown** | 55.3 | **23** |
| | | | $\phi_8$ | 6 | ✓ | 1.7 | 0 | 11 | N/A | – | 0 |
| Tora | Tanh | 3 × 100 | $\phi_9$ | 402 | ✓ | 1132 | 0 | 217 | ✓ | 1271 | 0 |
| | Tanh | 3 × 200 | $\phi_9$ | 495 | ✓ | 1242 | 0 | 239 | ✓ | 6829 | 0 |

**Remarks. A.F.**: activation function; **T.T.**: average training time per iteration; **V.R.**: verification result; **V.T.**: average verification time per iteration; **Vio.**: the number of violations in simulation; **N/A**: not applicable; **Unknown**: verification fails. Time is recorded in seconds.

state-of-the-art verification tools cannot always verify them or find violations. Our approach can guarantee that the trained systems satisfy the properties. The simulation results show there are indeed no violations.

As for efficiency, on average, our approach costs slightly more time on the training because it takes extra time to look up the corresponding abstract state for an actual state at every training step. But the small-time overhead is worthwhile for the sake of being verifiable. Besides verifiability, another benefit from this extra time cost is that the efficiency of verification in our approach is not affected by the size and type of neural networks because we treat them as blackbox in the verification. On the contrary, the efficiency of verifying the systems that are trained in conventional approaches is restricted by neural networks, as the verification time cost by Verisig 2.0 shows.

Based on the above analysis, we conclude that the reliability of the DRL systems developed in our approach are more trustworthy as their predefined properties are provably satisfied by the systems. Besides, their verification is more amenable and scalable than the systems trained in conventional DRL approaches.

### 5.4 Performance Comparison

We compare the performance of the DRL systems trained in our approach and the conventional approaches in terms of cumulative reward and robustness, respectively.

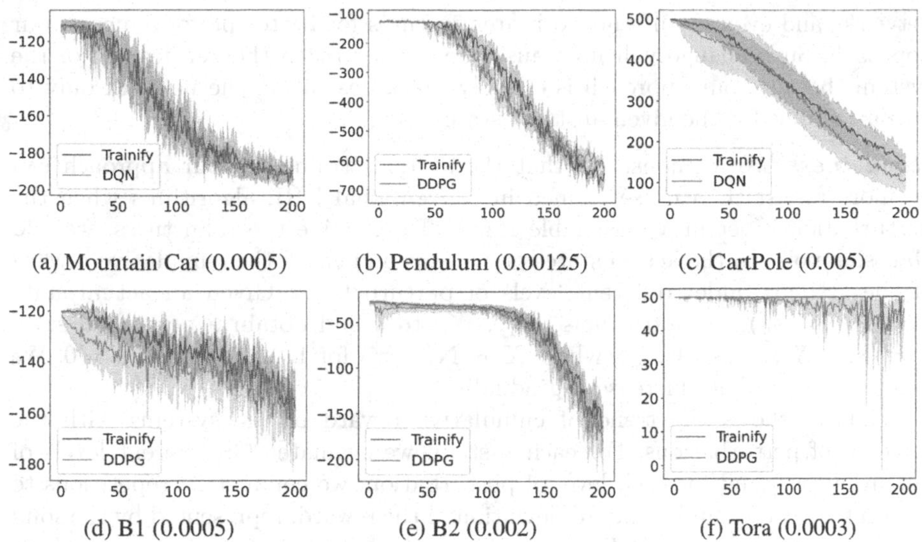


(a) Mountain Car (0.0005) (b) Pendulum (0.00125) (c) CartPole (0.005)

(d) B1 (0.0005) (e) B2 (0.002) (f) Tora (0.0003)

**Fig. 8.** Robustness comparison of the systems trained in our approach (blue) and in conventional approaches (orange). The number in the parentheses is the base of $\sigma$. For example, in Mountain Car, when the abscissa is equal to 50, $\sigma = 50 \times 0.0005 = 0.025$. (Color figure online)

**Table 3.** Comparison of accumulated reward.

| Case | Alg. | Network | | TRAINIFY | Base |
|---|---|---|---|---|---|
| MC | DQN | Sigmoid | $2 \times 16$ | **−112** | **−116** |
| | | Sigmoid | $2 \times 200$ | **−110** | **−111** |
| PD | DDPG | ReLU | $3 \times 128$ | **−131** | **−133** |
| CP | DQN | ReLU | $3 \times 64$ | 500 | 500 |
| B1 | DDPG | Tanh | $2 \times 20$ | −120 | −120 |
| | | Tanh | $2 \times 100$ | **−117** | **−118** |
| B2 | DDPG | Tanh | $2 \times 20$ | −29 | −26 |
| | | Tanh | $2 \times 100$ | −27 | −24 |
| Tora | DDPG | Tanh | $3 \times 100$ | 50 | 50 |
| | | Tanh | $3 \times 200$ | 50 | 50 |

***Cumulative Reward.*** We record the cumulative reward by running each system for 100 episodes in the simulation environment and calculating the averages. A larger reward implies that a system has a better performance. Table 3 shows the cumulative reward of the six DRL systems trained in our approach and conventional approaches, respectively. All the trained systems can achieve almost optimal cumulative reward. Among the ten cases, the systems trained in our approach have better performances in four cases, equivalent in four cases, and lower in the rest two cases. Note that there is a difference, which is due to floating point errors, but it is almost negligible. In this sense, we say that the performance of the systems trained in the two different approaches is comparable.

Another observation from the results is that a system with a bigger neural network produces a larger reward. This characteristic is shared by both our approach and the conventional approaches. Thus, we can increase the size of networks and even modify network architectures for better performance in our approach. Such change will not cause the extra cost to the verification of the systems because our approach is entirely black-box, using the network only to output actions for the given abstract state.

***Robustness.*** We demonstrate that the systems trained in our approach can be more robust than those trained in conventional DRL algorithms when the perturbation is set in a reasonable range. To examine the robustness, we add Gaussian noise to the actual states of systems and check the cumulative reward of the systems under different levels of perturbations. Given an actual state $s = (s_1, \ldots, s_n)$, we add a noise $X_1, ...X_n$ to $s$ and obtain a perturbed state $s' = (s_1 + X_1, \ldots, s_n + X_n)$, where $X_i \sim \mathbf{N}(\mu, \sigma^2)$ for $1 \leq i \leq n$ with $\mu = 0$. We start with $\sigma = 0$ and increase it gradually.

Figure 8 shows the trend of cumulative reward of the systems with the increase of perturbations. For each system, we evaluate 200 different levels of perturbations, and for each level of perturbation, we conduct 20 repetitions to obtain the average and standard deviation of the reward, represented by the solid lines and shadows in Fig. 8. The general trend is that the cumulative reward deteriorate for all the systems that are trained in either of the approaches. The result is reasonable because the actions computed by neural networks are optimal to non-perturbed states but may not be optimal to the perturbed ones, leading to lower reward at some steps. However, we can observe that the decline ratio of the systems trained in our approach (blue) is smaller than the one trained in conventional approaches (orange). When $\sigma = 0$, the accumulated reward of the two systems for the same task is almost the same. With the increase of $\sigma$, the performance declines more slowly for the systems trained in our approach than for those trained in the conventional approaches when $\sigma$ is in a reasonably small range. That is because a perturbed state may belong to the same abstract state as its original state, and thus has the optimal action. In this sense, we say the perturbation is *absorbed* by the abstract state and the neural networks become less sensitive to perturbations. Our additional experiments on these examples show that a larger abstraction granularity produces a more robust system.

## 6 Related Work

Our work has been inspired by several related works, which attempted to integrate formal methods and DRL approaches. We classify them into the following three categories.

***Verification-in-the-Loop Training.*** Verification-in-the-loop training has been proposed for developing reliable AI-powered systems. A pioneering work is that Nilsson *et al.* proposed a correct-by-construction approach for developing Adaptive Cruise Control (ACC) by first formally defining safety properties in Linear Temporal Logic (LTL) and then computing the safe domain where the LTL specification can be enforced [36]. Wang *et al.* proposed a correct-by-construction control learning framework by leveraging verification during training to formally guarantee that the learned controller satisfies the required reach-avoid property [49]. Lin *et al.* proposed an approach for training robust neural networks for general classification problems by fine-tuning the parameters in the networks based on the verification result [33]. Our work is a sequel of these previous works with new features of training on abstract states, counterexample-guided abstraction and refinement, and supporting more complex properties.

***Safe DRL via Formal Methods.*** Most of the existing approaches for formal verification of DRL systems follow the *train-then-verify* style. Bacci and Parker [3] proposed an approach to split an abstract domain into fine-grained ones and compute their successor abstract states separately for probabilistic model checking of DRL systems. The approach can reduce the overestimation and meanwhile construct a transition system upon abstract states, which allows us to verify more complex liveness and probabilistic properties than safety using bounded model checking [29] and probabilistic model checking. A criteria of subdividing an abstract domain is to ensure that all the states in the same sub-domain have the same action. Identifying these sub-domains is computationally expensive because it relies on iterative branching and bounding [3]. Furthermore, these approaches need to compute the output range of the neural networks on the abstract domains, and therefore are restricted to specific types and scales of networks. Besides model checking, reachability analysis [13,16,25,46] has been well studied to ensure the safety of DRL systems. The basic idea is to over-approximate system dynamics and neural networks to compute over-estimated safe regions and check whether they have interactions with unsafe regions. However, large overestimation, limited scalability, and requirements on specific network architectures are the common restrictions of these approaches. Online verification [47] and runtime monitoring [18] in formal methods is another lightweight but effective means to detect potential flaws timely during system execution. Another direction is to synthesize *safe shields* [7,54] and barrier functions [53] to prevent agents from adopting dangerous actions. A strong assumption of these methods is that the valid safe states set is given in advance. However, computing valid safe states set may be computationally intensive, and it is restricted to safety properties.

***Abstraction and State Discretization in DRL.*** Abstraction in DRL has gained more attention in recent years. Abel presented a theory of abstraction for DRL in his dissertation and concluded that learning on abstraction can be more efficient while preserving near-optimal behaviors [1]. Abel's abstraction theory is focused on the systems with finite state space for learning efficiency. Our work demonstrates another advantage of learning on abstraction, *i.e.*, *formal reliability guarantee* to trained systems even with infinite state space.

The state-space abstraction approach in our framework is also inspired by *state space discretization*, a technique for discretizing continuous state space, by which a finer partition of the state-action space is maintained during training for higher payoff estimates [41,42]. Our work shows that, after being integrated with formal verification, state-space discretization is also useful in developing highly reliable DRL systems without loss of performance. In addition, our CEGAR-driven approach provides a flexible mechanism for fine-tuning the granularity of discretization to reach an appropriate balance between system performance and the scale of state space for formal verification.

## 7 Discussion and Conclusion

We have presented a novel verification-in-the-loop framework for training and verifying DRL systems, driven by counterexample-guided abstract and refinement. The framework can be used to train reliable DRL systems with their desired properties on safeties and functionalities formally verified, without compromising system performances. We have implemented a prototype TRAINIFY and evaluated it by training six classic control problems from public benchmarks. The experimental results showed that the systems trained in our approach were more reliable and verifiable than those trained in conventional DRL approaches, while their performances are comparable or even better than the latter.

Our verification-in-the-loop training approach sheds light on a new search direction for developing reliable and verifiable AI-empowered systems. It follows the idea of correctness-by-construction in traditional trustworthy software system development and makes it possible to take system properties (or requirements) into account during the training process. It also reveals that (i) it is not necessary to learn on actual data to build high-performance (e.g., high reward and robust) DRL systems, and (ii) abstraction is an effective means to deal with the challenges in verifying DRL systems and shall be introduced earlier during training, rather than an *ex post facto* method in verification.

Our work would inspire more research in this direction. One important research objective is to investigate appropriate abstractions for the DRL systems with high dimensions. In our current framework, we adopt the simplest interval abstraction that suffices to the systems with low dimensions. It would be interesting to investigate more sophisticated abstractions such as floating-point polyhedra combined with intervals, designed mainly for neural networks [43], to those high-dimensional DRL systems. Another direction is to extend our framework to non-deterministic DRL systems. In the non-deterministic case, a neural network returns both actions and their corresponding probabilities. We can associate probabilities to state transitions and obtain a probabilistic model. The model can be naturally verified using existing probabilistic model checkers such as Prism [30]. Thus, we believe that our approach is also applicable to those systems after a slight extension. It would be another piece of our future work.

**Acknowledgments.** The authors thank all the anonymous reviewers and Katz Guy from the Hebrew University of Jerusalem for their valuable comments on this work. The work has been supported by National Key Research Program (2020AAA0107800), Shanghai Science and Technology Commission (20DZ1100300), Shanghai Trusted Industry Internet Software Collaborative Innovation Center, Shanghai AI Innovation and Development Fund (2020-RGZN-02026), Shenzhen Institute of AI and Robotics for Society (AC01202005020), NSFC-ISF Joint Program (62161146001,3420/21) and NSFC project (61872146).

## References


1. Abel, D.: A theory of abstraction in reinforcement learning. Dissertation, Brown University (2020)
2. Bacci, E., Giacobbe, M., Parker, D.: Verifying reinforcement learning up to infinity. In: IJCAI 2021, Montreal, Canada, pp. 2154–2160. ijcai.org (2021)
3. Bacci, E., Parker, D.: Probabilistic guarantees for safe deep reinforcement learning. In: Bertrand, N., Jansen, N. (eds.) FORMATS 2020. LNCS, vol. 12288, pp. 231–248. Springer, Cham (2020). https://doi.org/10.1007/978-3-030-57628-8_14
4. Baier, C., Katoen, J.P.: Principles of Model Checking. MIT Press, Cambridge (2008)
5. Brockman, G., et al.: OpenAI Gym (2016). arXiv:1606.01540
6. Casagrande, A.: pyModelChecking (2020). https://github.com/albertocasagrande/pyModelChecking
7. Cheng, R., Orosz, G., Murray, R.M., Burdick, J.W.: End-to-end safe reinforcement learning through barrier functions for safety-critical continuous control tasks. In: AAAI 2019, vol. 33, pp. 3387–3395. AAAI Press (2019)
8. Clarke, E., et al.: Abstraction and counterexample-guided refinement in model checking of hybrid systems. Int. J. Found. Comput. Sci. **14**(04), 583–604 (2003)
9. Clarke, E., Grumberg, O., Jha, S., Lu, Y., Veith, H.: Counterexample-guided abstraction refinement. In: Emerson, E.A., Sistla, A.P. (eds.) CAV 2000. LNCS, vol. 1855, pp. 154–169. Springer, Heidelberg (2000). https://doi.org/10.1007/10722167_15
10. Clarke, E.M., Henzinger, T.A., Veith, H., Bloem, R.: Handbook of model checking. Springer, Cham (2018). https://doi.org/10.1007/978-3-319-10575-8
11. Cousot, P.: Abstract interpretation. ACM Comput. Surv. (CSUR) **28**(2), 324–328 (1996)
12. Du, S., Lee, J., Li, H., Wang, L., Zhai, X.: Gradient descent finds global minima of deep neural networks. In: ICML 2019, pp. 1675–1685. PMLR (2019)
13. Dutta, S., Chen, X., Sankaranarayanan, S.: Reachability analysis for neural feedback systems using regressive polynomial rule inference. In: Proceedings of the 22nd ACM International Conference on Hybrid Systems: Computation and Control, pp. 157–168 (2019)
14. Emerson, E.A., Halpern, J.Y.: "sometimes" and "not never" revisited: on branching versus linear time temporal logic. J. ACM (JACM) **33**(1), 151–178 (1986)
15. Emerson, E.A., Sistla, A.P.: Deciding full branching time logic. Inf. Control **61**(3), 175–201 (1984)
16. Fan, J., Huang, C., Chen, X., Li, W., Zhu, Q.: ReachNN*: a tool for reachability analysis of neural-network controlled systems. In: Hung, D.V., Sokolsky, O. (eds.) ATVA 2020. LNCS, vol. 12302, pp. 537–542. Springer, Cham (2020). https://doi.org/10.1007/978-3-030-59152-6_30
17. Faust, A., Ruymgaart, P., Salman, M., Fierro, R., Tapia, L.: Continuous action reinforcement learning for control-affine systems with unknown dynamics. IEEE/CAA J. Automatica Sinica **1**(3), 323–336 (2014)
18. Fulton, N., Platzer, A.: Safe reinforcement learning via formal methods: toward safe control through proof and learning. In: AAAI 2018, pp. 6485–6492. AAAI Press (2018)

19. Gallestey, E., Hokayem, P.: Lecture notes in nonlinear systems and control (2019)
20. Gilpin, L., Bau, D., Yuan, B.Z., et al.: Explaining explanations: an overview of interpretability of machine learning. In: DSAA 2018, pp. 80–89 (2018)
21. Gomes, L.: When will Google's self-driving car really be ready? It depends on where you live and what you mean by "ready.". IEEE Spectr. **53**(5), 13–14 (2016)
22. Guttman, A.: R-trees: A dynamic index structure for spatial searching. In: SIGMOD 1984, pp. 47–57. ACM (1984)
23. Hasanbeig, M., Kroening, D., Abate, A.: Towards verifiable and safe model-free reinforcement learning. In: CEUR Workshop Proceedings (2020)
24. Henderson, P., Islam, R., Bachman, P., Pineau, J., Precup, D., Meger, D.: Deep reinforcement learning that matters. In: AAAI 2018, pp. 3207–3214. AAAI Press (2018)
25. Ivanov, R., Carpenter, T., Weimer, J., Alur, R., Pappas, G., Lee, I.: Verisig 2.0: verification of neural network controllers using Taylor model preconditioning. In: Silva, A., Leino, K.R.M. (eds.) CAV 2021. LNCS, vol. 12759, pp. 249–262. Springer, Cham (2021). https://doi.org/10.1007/978-3-030-81685-8_11
26. Jackson, D.: Abstract model checking of infinite specifications. In: Naftalin, M., Denvir, T., Bertran, M. (eds.) FME 1994. LNCS, vol. 873, pp. 519–531. Springer, Heidelberg (1994). https://doi.org/10.1007/3-540-58555-9_113
27. Jankovic, M., Fontaine, D., KokotoviC, P.V.: Tora example: cascade-and passivity-based control designs. IEEE Trans. Control Syst. Technol. **4**(3), 292–297 (1996)
28. Johnson, T.T., Manzanas Lopez, D., Musau, P., et al.: Arch-comp20 category report: artificial intelligence and neural network control systems (AINNCS) for continuous and hybrid systems plants. EPiC Ser. Comput. **74**, 107–173 (2020)
29. Kazak, Y., Barrett, C., Katz, G., Schapira, M.: Verifying deep-RL-driven systems. In: 2019 Workshop on Network Meets AI & ML, pp. 83–89. ACM (2019)
30. Kwiatkowska, M., Norman, G., Parker, D.: PRISM 4.0: verification of probabilistic real-time systems. In: Gopalakrishnan, G., Qadeer, S. (eds.) CAV 2011. LNCS, vol. 6806, pp. 585–591. Springer, Heidelberg (2011). https://doi.org/10.1007/978-3-642-22110-1_47
31. Li, Y.: Deep reinforcement learning: an overview. arXiv preprint arXiv:1701.07274 (2017)
32. Lillicrap, T.P., Hunt, J.J., Pritzel, A., et al.: Continuous control with deep reinforcement learning. In: ICLR 2016. OpenReview.net (2016)
33. Lin, X., Zhu, H., Samanta, R., Jagannathan, S.: Art: abstraction refinement-guided training for provably correct neural networks. In: FMCAD, pp. 148–157. AAAI Press (2020)
34. Mnih, V., Kavukcuoglu, K., Silver, D., et al.: Playing Atari with deep reinforcement learning. CoRR abs/1312.5602 (2013)
35. Mnih, V., Kavukcuoglu, K., Silver, D., et al.: Human-level control through deep reinforcement learning. Nature **518**(7540), 529–533 (2015)
36. Nilsson, P., Hussien, O., Balkan, A., et al.: Correct-by-construction adaptive cruise control: two approaches. IEEE Trans. Control Syst. Technol. **24**(4), 1294–1307 (2015)
37. Ohn-Bar, E., Trivedi, M.M.: Looking at humans in the age of self-driving and highly automated vehicles. IEEE Trans. Intell. Veh. **1**(1), 90–104 (2016)

38. Pyeatt, L.D., Howe, A.E.: Decision tree function approximation in reinforcement learning. Technical report, ISAS 2011 (2011)
39. Schmidt, L.M., Kontes, G., Plinge, A., Mutschler, C.: Can you trust your autonomous car? interpretable and verifiably safe reinforcement learning. In: 2021 IEEE Intelligent Vehicles Symposium (IV), pp. 171–178. IEEE (2021)
40. Shalev-Shwartz, S., Shammah, S., Shashua, A.: Safe, multi-agent, reinforcement learning for autonomous driving. CoRR abs/1610.03295 (2016). http://arxiv.org/abs/1610.03295
41. Sinclair, S., Wang, T., Jain, G., Banerjee, S., Yu, C.: Adaptive discretization for model-based reinforcement learning. In: NeurIPS 2020. vol. 31, pp. 3858–3871 (2020)
42. Sinclair, S.R., Banerjee, S., Yu, C.L.: Adaptive discretization for episodic reinforcement learning in metric spaces. Proc. ACM Measur. Anal. Comput. Syst. **3**(3), 1–44 (2019)
43. Singh, G., Gehr, T., Püschel, M., Vechev, M.: An abstract domain for certifying neural networks. In: POPL 2019, pp. 1–30. ACM (2019)
44. Srinivasan, K., Eysenbach, B., Ha, S., Tan, J., Finn, C.: Learning to be safe: deep RL with a safety critic. arXiv preprint arXiv:2010.14603 (2020)
45. Stevia, P., Mindom, N., Nikanjam, A., Khomh, F., Mullins, J.: On assessing the safety of reinforcement learning algorithms using formal methods. arXiv preprint arXiv:2111.04865 (2021)
46. Tran, H.D., Cai, F., Diego, M.L., Musau, P., Johnson, T.T., Koutsoukos, X.: Safety verification of cyber-physical systems with reinforcement learning control. ACM Trans. Emb. Comput. Syst. **18**(5s), 1–22 (2019)
47. Van Wesel, P., Goodloe, A.E.: Challenges in the verification of reinforcement learning algorithms. NASA STI Program (2017)
48. Virtanen, P., Gommers, R., Oliphant, T.E., et al.: SciPy 1.0: fundamental algorithms for scientific computing in python. Nat. Meth. **17**, 261–272 (2020)
49. Wang, Y., Huang, C., Wang, Z., Wang, Z., Zhu, Q.: Verification in the loop: correct-by-construction control learning with reach-avoid guarantees. arXiv preprint arXiv:2106.03245 (2021)
50. Xiang, W., Tran, H.D., Johnson, T.T.: Output reachable set estimation and verification for multilayer neural networks. IEEE Trans. Neural Networks Learn. Syst. **29**(11), 5777–5783 (2018)
51. Xiong, Z., Jagannathan, S.: Scalable synthesis of verified controllers in deep reinforcement learning. arXiv preprint arXiv:2104.10219 (2021)
52. Yampolskiy, R.V.: Unexplainability and incomprehensibility of AI. J. Artif. Intell. Conscious. **7**(2), 277–291 (2020)
53. Yang, Z., et al.: An iterative scheme of safe reinforcement learning for nonlinear systems via barrier certificate generation. In: Silva, A., Leino, K.R.M. (eds.) CAV 2021. LNCS, vol. 12759, pp. 467–490. Springer, Cham (2021). https://doi.org/10.1007/978-3-030-81685-8_22
54. Zhu, H., Xiong, Z., Magill, S., Jagannathan, S.: An inductive synthesis framework for verifiable reinforcement learning. In: PLDI 2019. pp. 686–701. ACM (2019)

# Neural Network Robustness as a Verification Property: A Principled Case Study

Marco Casadio[1(✉)], Ekaterina Komendantskaya[1], Matthew L. Daggitt[1], Wen Kokke[2], Guy Katz[3], Guy Amir[3], and Idan Refaeli[3]

[1] Heriot-Watt University, Edinburgh, UK
{mc248,ek19,md2006}@hw.ac.uk
[2] University of Strathclyde, Glasgow, UK
wen.kokke@strath.ac.uk
[3] The Hebrew University of Jerusalem, Jerusalem, Israel
{guykatz,guyam,idan0610}@cs.huji.ac.il

**Abstract.** Neural networks are very successful at detecting patterns in noisy data, and have become the technology of choice in many fields. However, their usefulness is hampered by their susceptibility to *adversarial attacks*. Recently, many methods for measuring and improving a network's robustness to adversarial perturbations have been proposed, and this growing body of research has given rise to numerous explicit or implicit notions of robustness. Connections between these notions are often subtle, and a systematic comparison between them is missing in the literature. In this paper we begin addressing this gap, by setting up general principles for the empirical analysis and evaluation of a network's robustness as a mathematical property—during the network's training phase, its verification, and after its deployment. We then apply these principles and conduct a case study that showcases the practical benefits of our general approach.

**Keywords:** Neural Networks · Adversarial Training · Robustness · Verification

## 1 Introduction

Safety and security are critical for many complex systems that use deep neural networks (DNNs). Unfortunately, due to the opacity of DNNs, these properties are difficult to ensure. Perhaps the most famous instance of this problem is guaranteeing the robustness of DNN-based systems against *adversarial attacks* [5,17]. Intuitively, a neural network is $\epsilon$*-ball robust* around a particular input if, when you move no more than $\epsilon$ away from that input in the input space, the output does not change much; or, alternatively, the classification decision that the network gives does not change. Even highly accurate DNNs will often display only low robustness, and so measuring and improving the adversarial robustness of DNNs has received significant attention by both the machine learning and verification communities [7,8,15].

As a result, neural network verification often follows a *continuous verification cycle* [9], which involves retraining neural networks with a given *verification property* in mind, as Fig. 1 shows. More generally, such training can be regarded as a way to


S. Shoham and Y. Vizel (Eds.): CAV 2022, LNCS 13371, pp. 219–231, 2022.
https://doi.org/10.1007/978-3-031-13185-1_11

impose a formal specification on a DNN; and so, apart from improving its robustness, it may also contribute to the network's explainability, and facilitate its verification. Due to the high level of interest in adversarial robustness, numerous approaches have been proposed for performing such retraining in recent years, each with its own specific details. However it is quite unclear what are the benefits that each approach offers, from a verification point of view.

The primary goal of this case-study paper is to introduce a more holistic methodology, which puts the verification property in the centre of the development cycle, and in turn permits a principled analysis of how this property influences both training and verification practices. In particular, we analyse the verification properties that implicitly or explicitly arise from the most prominent families of training techniques: *data augmentation* [14], *adversarial training* [5,10], *Lipschitz robustness training* [1,12], and *training with logical constraints* [4,20]. We study the effect of each of these properties on verifying the DNN in question.

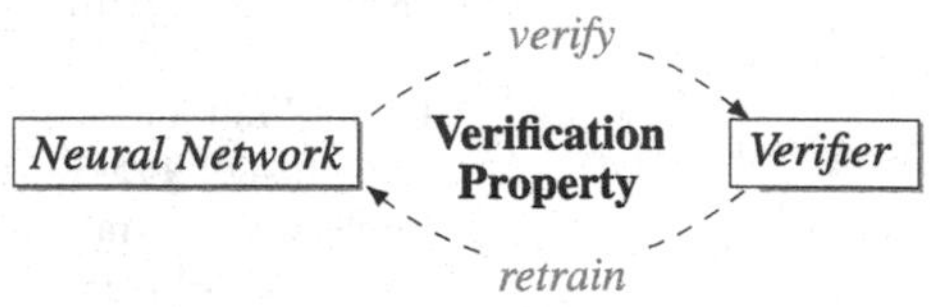


**Fig. 1.** Continuous Verification Cycle

In Sect. 2, we start with the forward direction of the continuous verification cycle, and show how the above training methods give rise to logical properties of *classification robustness* (CR), *strong classification robustness* (SCR), *standard robustness* (SR) and *Lipschitz robustness* (LR). In Sect. 4, we trace the opposite direction of the cycle, i.e. show how and when the verifier failure in proving these properties can be mitigated. However Sect. 3 first gives an auxiliary logical link for making this step. Given a robustness property as a logical formula, we can use it not just in verification, but also in attack or property accuracy measurements. We take property-driven attacks as a valuable tool in our study, both in training and in evaluation. Section 4 makes the underlying assumption that verification requires retraining: it shows that the verifier's success ranges only 0–1.5% for an accurate baseline network. We show how our logical understanding of robustness properties empowers us in property-driven training and in verification. We first give abstract arguments why certain properties are stronger than others or incomparable; and then we use training, attacks and the verifier Marabou to confirm them empirically. Sections 5 and 6 add other general considerations for setting up the continuous verification loop and conclude the paper.

## 2 Existing Training Techniques and Definitions of Robustness

**Data Augmentation** is a straightforward method for improving robustness via training [14]. It is applicable to any transformation of the input (e.g. addition of noise, translation, rotation, scaling) that leaves the output label unchanged. To make the network robust against such a transformation, one augments the dataset with instances sampled via the transformation.

More formally, given a neural network $N : \mathbb{R}^n \rightarrow \mathbb{R}^m$, the goal of data augmentation is to ensure *classification robustness*, which is defined as follows. Given a training dataset input-output pair $(\hat{\mathbf{x}}, \mathbf{y})$ and a distance metric $| \cdot - \cdot |$, for all inputs $\mathbf{x}$ within the $\epsilon$-ball distance of $\hat{\mathbf{x}}$, we say that $N$ is *classification-robust* if class $\mathbf{y}$ has the largest score in output $N(\mathbf{x})$.

**Definition 1 (Classification robustness).**

$$CR(\epsilon, \hat{\mathbf{x}}) \triangleq \forall \mathbf{x} : |\mathbf{x} - \hat{\mathbf{x}}| \leq \epsilon \Rightarrow \arg\max N(\mathbf{x}) = \mathbf{y}$$

In order to apply data augmentation, an engineer needs to specify: **c1.** the value of $\epsilon$, i.e. the admissible range of perturbations; **c2.** the distance metric, which is determined according to the admissible geometric perturbations; and **c3.** the sampling method used to produce the perturbed inputs (e.g., random sampling, adversarial attacks, generative algorithm, prior knowledge of images).

Classification robustness is straightforward, but does not account for the possibility of having "uncertain" images in the dataset, for which a small perturbation ideally should change the class. For datasets that contain a significant number of such images, attempting this kind of training could lead to a significant reduction in accuracy.

**Adversarial training** is a current state-of the-art method to robustify a neural network. Whereas standard training tries to minimise loss between the predicted value, $f(\hat{\mathbf{x}})$, and the true value, $\mathbf{y}$, for each entry $(\hat{\mathbf{x}}, \mathbf{y})$ in the training dataset, adversarial training minimises the loss with respect to the worst-case perturbation of each sample in the training dataset. It therefore replaces the standard training objective $\mathcal{L}(\hat{\mathbf{x}}, \mathbf{y})$ with: $\max_{\forall \mathbf{x}:|\mathbf{x}-\hat{\mathbf{x}}| \leq \epsilon} \mathcal{L}(\mathbf{x}, \mathbf{y})$. Algorithmic solutions to the maximisation problem that find the worst-case perturbation has been the subject of several papers. The earliest suggestion was the Fast Gradient Sign Method (FGSM) algorithm introduced by [5]:

$$\text{FGSM}(\hat{\mathbf{x}}) = \hat{\mathbf{x}} + \epsilon \cdot \text{sign}(\nabla_{\mathbf{x}} \mathcal{L}(\mathbf{x}, \mathbf{y}))$$

However, modern adversarial training methods usual rely on some variant of the Projected Gradient Descent (PGD) algorithm [11] which iterates FGSM:

$$\text{PGD}_0(\hat{\mathbf{x}}) = \hat{\mathbf{x}}; \quad \text{PGD}_{t+1}(\hat{\mathbf{x}}) = \text{PGD}_t(\text{FGSM}(\hat{\mathbf{x}}))$$

It has been empirically observed that neural networks trained using this family of methods exhibit greater robustness at the expense of an increased generalisation error [10,18,21], which is frequently referred to as the *accuracy-robustness trade-off* for neural networks (although this effect has been observed to disappear as the size of the training dataset grows [13]).

In logical terms what is this procedure trying to train for? Let us assume that there's some maximum distance, $\delta$, that it is acceptable for the output to be perturbed given the size of perturbations in the input. This leads us to the following definition, where $|| \cdot - \cdot ||$ is a suitable distance function over the output space:

**Definition 2 (Standard robustness).**

$$SR(\epsilon, \delta, \hat{\mathbf{x}}) \triangleq \forall \mathbf{x} : |\mathbf{x} - \hat{\mathbf{x}}| \leq \epsilon \Rightarrow ||f(\mathbf{x}) - f(\hat{\mathbf{x}})|| \leq \delta$$

We note that, just as with data augmentation, choices **c1–c3** are still there to be made, although the sampling methods are usually given by special-purpose FGSM/PGD heuristics based on computing the loss function gradients.

**Training for Lipschitz Robustness.** More recently, a third competing definition of robustness has been proposed: Lipschitz robustness [2]. Inspired by the well-established concept of Lipschitz continuity, Lipschitz robustness asserts that the distance between the original output and the perturbed output is at most a constant $L$ times the change in the distance between the inputs.

**Definition 3 (Lipschitz robustness).**

$$LR(\epsilon, L, \hat{\mathbf{x}}) \triangleq \forall \mathbf{x} : |\mathbf{x} - \hat{\mathbf{x}}| \leq \epsilon \Rightarrow ||f(\mathbf{x}) - f(\hat{\mathbf{x}})|| \leq L|\mathbf{x} - \hat{\mathbf{x}}|$$

As will be discussed in Sect. 4, this is a stronger requirement than standard robustness. Techniques for training for Lipschitz robustness include formulating it as a semi-definite programming optimisation problem [12] or including a projection step that restricts the weight matrices to those with suitable Lipschitz constants [6].

**Training with Logical Constraints.** Logically, this discussion leads one to ask whether a more general approach to constraint formulation may exist, and several attempts in the literature addressed this research question [4,20], by proposing methods that can translate a first-order logical formula $C$ into a *constraint loss function* $\mathcal{L}_C$. The loss function penalises the network when outputs do not satisfy a given Boolean constraint, and universal quantification is handled by a choice of sampling method. Our standard loss function $\mathcal{L}$ is substituted with:

$$\mathcal{L}^*(\hat{\mathbf{x}}, \mathbf{y}) = \alpha\mathcal{L}(\hat{\mathbf{x}}, \mathbf{y}) + \beta\mathcal{L}_C(\hat{\mathbf{x}}, \mathbf{y}) \tag{1}$$

where weights $\alpha$ and $\beta$ control the balance between the standard and constraint loss.

This method looks deceivingly as a generalisation of previous approaches. However, even given suitable choices for **c1–c3**, classification robustness cannot be modelled via a constraint loss in the DL2 [4] framework, as $argmax$ is not differentiable. Instead, [4] defines an alternative constraint, which we call *strong classification robustness*:

**Definition 4 (Strong classification robustness).**

$$SCR(\epsilon, \eta, \hat{\mathbf{x}}) \triangleq \forall \mathbf{x} : |\mathbf{x} - \hat{\mathbf{x}}| \leq \epsilon \Rightarrow f(\mathbf{x}) \geq \eta$$

which looks only at the prediction of the true class and checks whether it is greater than some value $\eta$ (chosen to be 0.52 in their work).

We note that sometimes, the constraints (and therefore the derived loss functions) refer to the true label $\mathbf{y}$ rather than the current output of the network $f(\hat{\mathbf{x}})$, e.g. $\forall \mathbf{x} : |\mathbf{x} - \hat{\mathbf{x}}| \leq \epsilon \Rightarrow |f(\mathbf{x}) - \mathbf{y}| \leq \delta$. This leads to scenarios where a network that *is* robust around $\hat{\mathbf{x}}$ but gives the wrong prediction, being penalised by $\mathcal{L}_C$ which on paper is designed to maximise robustness. Essentially $\mathcal{L}_C$ is trying to maximise both accuracy and constraint adherence concurrently. Instead, we argue that to preserve the intended semantics of $\alpha$ and $\beta$ it is important to instead compare against the current output of the network. Of course, this does not work for SCR because deriving the most popular class from the output $f(\hat{\mathbf{x}})$ requires the $\arg\max$ operator—the very function that SCR seeks to avoid using. This is another argument why (S)CR should be avoided if possible.

## 3 Robustness in Evaluation, Attack and Verification

Given a particular definition of robustness, a natural question is how to quantify how close a given network is to satisfying it. We argue that there are three different measures that one should be interested in: 1. Does the constraint hold? This is a binary measure, and the answer is either true or false. 2. If the constraint does not hold, how easy is it for an attacker to find a violation? 3. If the constraint does not hold, how often does the average user encounter a violation? Based on these measures, we define three concrete metrics: *constraint satisfaction*, *constraint security*, and *constraint accuracy*.[1]

Let $\mathcal{X}$ be the training dataset, $\mathbb{B}(\hat{\mathbf{x}}, \epsilon) \triangleq \{\mathbf{x} \in \mathbb{R}^n \mid |\mathbf{x} - \hat{\mathbf{x}}| \leq \epsilon\}$ be the $\epsilon$-ball around $\hat{\mathbf{x}}$ and $P$ be the right-hand side of the implication in each of the definitions of robustness. Let $\mathbb{I}_\phi$ be the standard indicator function which is 1 if constraint $\phi(\mathbf{x})$ holds and 0 otherwise. The *constraint satisfaction* metric measures the proportion of the (finite) training dataset for which the constraint holds.

**Definition 5 (Constraint satisfaction).**

$$\mathrm{CSat}(\mathcal{X}) = \frac{1}{|\mathcal{X}|} \sum_{\hat{\mathbf{x}} \in \mathcal{X}} \mathbb{I}_{\forall \mathbf{x} \in \mathbb{B}(\hat{\mathbf{x}}, \epsilon): P(\mathbf{x})}$$

In contrast, *constraint security* measures the proportion of inputs in the dataset such that an attack $A$ is unable to find an adversarial example for constraint $P$. In our experiments we use the PGD attack for $A$, although in general any strong attack can be used.

**Definition 6 (Constraint security).**

$$\mathrm{CSec}(\mathcal{X}) = \frac{1}{|\mathcal{X}|} \sum_{\hat{\mathbf{x}} \in \mathcal{X}} \mathbb{I}_P(A(\hat{\mathbf{x}}))$$

Finally, *constraint accuracy* estimates the probability of a random user coming across a counter-example to the constraint, usually referred as *1 - success rate* in the robustness literature. Let $S(\hat{\mathbf{x}}, n)$ be a set of $n$ elements randomly uniformly sampled from $\mathbb{B}(\hat{\mathbf{x}}, \epsilon)$. Then constraint accuracy is defined as:

**Definition 7 (Constraint accuracy).**

$$\mathrm{CAcc}(\mathcal{X}) = \frac{1}{|\mathcal{X}|} \sum_{\hat{\mathbf{x}} \in \mathcal{X}} \left( \frac{1}{n} \sum_{\mathbf{x} \in S(\hat{\mathbf{x}}, n)} \mathbb{I}_P(\mathbf{x}) \right)$$

Note that there is no relationship between constraint accuracy and constraint security: an attacker may succeed in finding an adversarial example where random sampling fails and vice-versa. Also note the role of sampling in this discussion and compare it to the discussion of the choice **c3** in Sect. 2. Firstly, sampling procedures affect both training and evaluation of networks. But at the same time, their choice is orthogonal

[1] Our naming scheme differs from [4] who use the term *constraint accuracy* to refer to what we term *constraint security*. In our opinion, the term *constraint accuracy* is less appropriate here than the name *constraint security* given the use of an adversarial attack.

to choosing the verification constraint for which we optimise or evaluate. For example, we measure constraint security with respect to the PGD attack, and this determines the way we sample; but having made that choice still leaves us to decide which constraint, SCR, SR, LR, or other we will be measuring as we sample. Constraint satisfaction is different from constraint security and accuracy, in that it must evaluate constraints over infinite domains rather than merely sampling from them.

**Choosing an Evaluation Metric.** It is important to note that for all three evaluation metrics, one still has to make a choice for constraint $P$, namely SR, SCR or LR, as defined in Sect. 2. As constraint security always uses PGD to find input perturbations, the choice of SR, SCR and LR effectively amounts to us making a judgement of what an adversarial perturbation consists of: is it a class change as defined by SCR, or is it a violation of the more nuanced metrics defined by SR and LR? Therefore we will evaluate constraint security on the *SR/SCR/LR constraints* using a *PGD attack*.

For large search spaces in $n$ dimensions, random sampling deployed in constraint accuracy fails to find the trickier adversarial examples, and usually has deceivingly high performance: we found 100% and >98% constraint accuracy for SR and SCR, respectively. We will therefore not discuss these experiments in detail.

## 4 Relative Comparison of Definitions of Robustness

We now compare the strength of the given definitions of robustness using the introduced metrics. For empirical evaluation, we train networks on *FASHION MNIST* (or just *FASHION*) [19] and a modified version of the *GTSRB* [16] datasets consisting, respectively, by $28 \times 28$ and $48 \times 48$ images belonging to 10 classes. The networks consist of two fully connected layers: the first one having 100 neurons and ReLU as activation function, and the last one having 10 neurons on which we apply a clamp function $[-100, 100]$, because the traditional softmax function is not compatible with constraint verification tools such as Marabou. Taking four different robustness properties for which we optimise while training (Baseline, LR, SR, SCR), gives us 8 different networks to train, evaluate and attack. Generally, all trends we observed for the two data sets were the same, and we put matching graphs in [3] whenever we report a result for one of the data sets. Marabou [8] was used for evaluating constraint satisfaction.

### 4.1 Standard and Lipschitz Robustness

Lipschitz robustness is a strictly stronger constraint than standard robustness, in the sense that when a network satisfies $LR(\epsilon, L)$ then it also satisfies $SR(\epsilon, \epsilon L)$. However, the converse does not hold, as standard robustness does not relate the distances between the inputs and the outputs. Consequently, there are $SR(\epsilon, \delta)$ robust models that are not $LR(\epsilon, L)$ robust for any $L$, as for any fixed $L$ one can always make the distance $|\mathbf{x} - \hat{\mathbf{x}}|$ arbitrarily small in order to violate the Lipschitz inequality.

**Table 1.** Constraint satisfaction results for the Classification, Standard and Lipschitz constraints. These values are calculated over the test set and represented as %.

| | FASHION net trained with: | | | | GTSRB net trained with: | | | |
|---|---|---|---|---|---|---|---|---|
| | Baseline | SCR | SR | LR | Baseline | SCR | SR | LR |
| CR satisfaction | 1.5 | 2.0 | 2.0 | 34.0 | 0.5 | 1.0 | 3.0 | 4.5 |
| SR satisfaction | 0.5 | 1.0 | 65.8 | 100.0 | 0.0 | 0.0 | 24.0 | 97.0 |
| LR satisfaction | 0.0 | 0.0 | 0.0 | 0.0 | 0.0 | 0.0 | 0.0 | 0.0 |

**Empirical Significance of the Conclusions for Constraint Security.** Figure 2 shows an empirical evaluation of this general result. If we train two neural networks, one with the SR, and the other with the LR constraint, then the latter always has higher constraint security against both SR and LR attacks than the former. It also confirms that generally, stronger constraints are harder to obtain: whether a network is trained with SR or LR constraints, it is less robust against an LR attack than against any other attack.

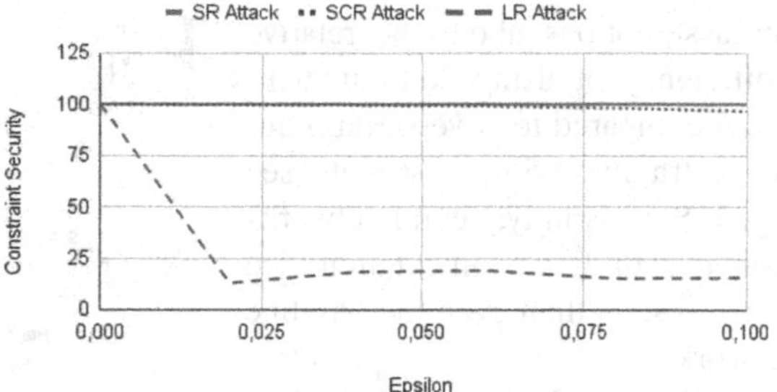




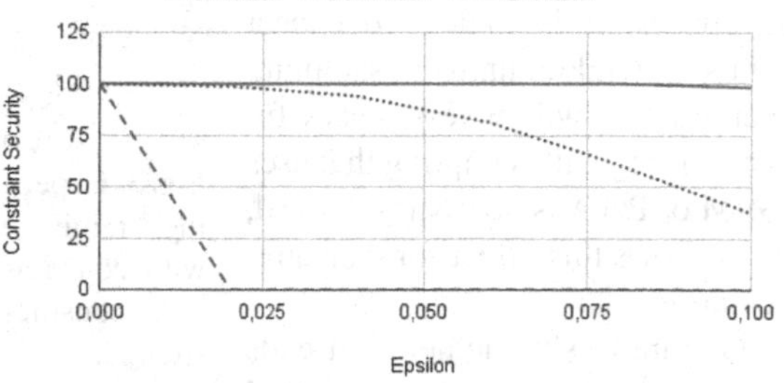


**Fig. 2.** Experiments that show how the two networks trained with LR and SR constraints perform when evaluated against different definitions of robustness underlying the attack; $\epsilon$ measures the attack strength.

**Empirical Significance of the Conclusions for Constraint Satisfaction.** Table 1 shows that LR is very difficult to guarantee as a verification property, indeed none of our networks satisfied this constraint for any image in the data set. At the same time, networks trained with LR satisfy the weaker property SR, for 100% and 97% of images – a huge improvement on the negligible percentage of robust images for the baseline network! Therefore, knowing a verification property or mode of attack, one can tailor the training accordingly, and training with stronger constraint gives better results.

### 4.2 (Strong) Classification Robustness

Strong classification robustness is designed to over-approximate classification robustness whilst providing a logical loss function with a meaningful gradient. We work under the assumption that the last layer of the classification network is a softmax layer, and therefore the output forms a probability distribution. When $\eta > 0.5$ then any network that satisfies $SCR(\epsilon, \eta)$ also satisfies $CR(\epsilon)$. For $\eta \leq 0.5$ this relationship breaks down as the true class may be assigned a probability greater than $\eta$ but may still not be the class with the highest probability. We therefore recommended that one only uses value of $\eta > 0.5$ when using strong classification robustness (for example $\eta = 0.52$ in [4]).

**Empirical Significance of the Conclusions for Constraint Security.** Because the CR constraint cannot be used within a loss function, we use data augmentation when training to emulate its effect. First, we confirm our assumptions about the relative inefficiency of using data augmentation compared to adversarial training or training with constraints, see Fig. 3. Surprisingly, neural networks trained with data augmentation give worse results than even the baseline network.

As previously discussed, random uniform sampling struggles to find adversarial inputs in large searching spaces. It is logical to expect that using random uniform sampling when training will be less successful than training with sampling that uses FGSM or PGD as heuristics. Indeed, Fig. 3 shows this effect for data augmentation.

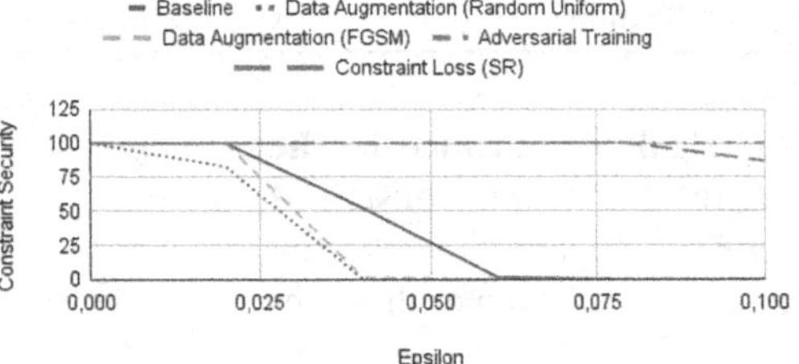


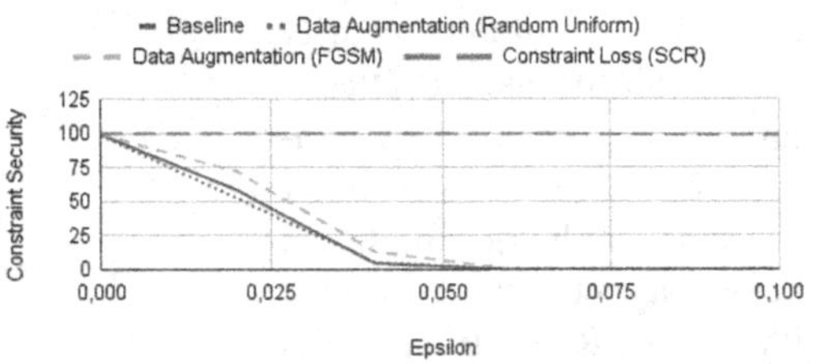


**Fig. 3.** Experiments that show how adversarial training, training with data augmentation, and training with constraint loss affect standard and classification robustness of networks; $\epsilon$ measures the attack strength.

One may ask whether the trends just described would be replicated for more complex architectures of neural networks. In particular, data augmentation is known to require larger networks. By replicating the results with a large, 18-layer convolutional network from [4] (second graph of Fig. 3), we confirm that larger networks handle data augmentation better, and that data augmentation affords improved robustness compared to the baseline. Nevertheless, data augmentation still lags behind all other modes of constraint-driven training, and thus this major trend remains stable across network architectures. The same figure also illustrates our point about the relative strength of SCR compared to CR: a network trained with data augmentation (equivalent to CR) is more prone to SCR attacks than a network trained with the SCR constraint.

**Empirical Significance of the Conclusions for Constraint Satisfaction.** Although Table 1 confirms that training with a stronger property (SCR) does improve the constraint satisfaction of a weaker property (CR), the effect is an order of magnitude smaller than what we observed for LR and SR. Indeed, the table suggests that training with the

LR constraint gives better results for CR constraint satisfaction. This does not contradict, but does not follow from our theoretical analysis.

### 4.3 Standard vs Classification Robustness

Given that LR is stronger than SR and SCR is stronger than CR, the obvious question is whether there is a relationship between these two groups. In short, the answer to this question is no. In particular, although the two sets of definitions agree on whether a network is robust around images with high-confidence, they disagree over whether a network is robust around images with low confidence. We illustrate this with an example, comparing SR against CR. We note that a similar analysis holds for any pairing from the two groups.

The key insight is that standard robustness bounds the drop in confidence that a neural network can exhibit after a perturbation, whereas classification robustness does not. Figure 4a shows two hypothetical images from the MNIST dataset. Our network predicts that Fig. 4a has an 85% chance of being a 7. Now consider adding a small perturbation to the image and consider two different scenarios. In the first scenario the output of the network for class 7 decreases from 85% to 83% and therefore the classification stays the same. In the second scenario the output of the network for class 7 decreases from 85% to 45%, and results in the classification changing from 7 to 9. When considering the two definitions, a small change in the output leads to no change in the classification and a large change in the output leads to a change in classification and so robustness and classification robustness both agree with each other.

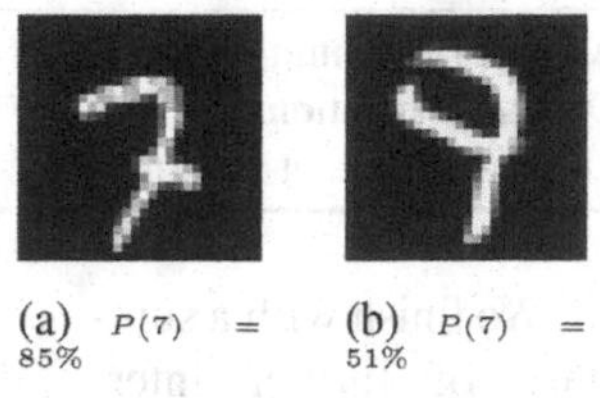

(a) $P(7)$ = 85% (b) $P(7)$ = 51%

**Fig. 4.** Images from the MNIST set

However, now consider Fig. 4b with relatively high uncertainty. In this case the network is (correctly) less sure about the image, only narrowly deciding that it's a 7. Again consider adding a small perturbation. In the first scenario the prediction of the network changes dramatically with the probability of it being a 7 increasing from 51% to 91% but leaves the classification unchanged as 7. In the second scenario the output of the network only changes very slightly, decreasing from 51% to 49% flipping the classification from 7 to 9. Now, the definitions of SR and CR disagree. In the first case, adding a small amount of noise has erroneously massively increased the network's confidence and therefore the SR definition correctly identifies that this is a problem. In contrast CR has no problem with this massive increase in confidence as the chosen output class remains unchanged. Thus, SR and CR agree on low-uncertainty examples, but CR breaks down and gives what we argue are both false positives and false negatives when considering examples with high-uncertainty.

**Empirical Significance of the Conclusions for Constraint Security.** Our empirical study confirms these general conclusions. Figure 2 shows that depending on the properties of the dataset, SR may not guarantee SCR. The results in Fig. 5 tell us that using the SCR constraint for training does not help to increase defences against SR attacks. A similar picture, but in reverse, can be seen when we optimize for SR but attack with SCR. Table 1 confirms these trends for constraint satisfaction.

## 5 Other Properties of Robustness Definitions

**Table 2.** A comparison of the different types of robustness studied in this paper. Top half: general properties. Bottom half: relation to existing machine-learning literature

| Definition | Standard robustness | Lipschitz robustness | Classification robustness | Strong class. robustness |
|---|---|---|---|---|
| Problem domain | General | General | Classification | Classification |
| Interpretability | Medium | Low | High | Medium |
| Globally desirable | ✓ | ✓ | ✗ | ✗ |
| Has loss functions | ✓ | ✓ | ✗ | ✓ |
| Adversarial training | ✓ | ✗ | ✗ | ✗ |
| Data augmentation | ✗ | ✗ | ✓ | ✗ |
| Logical-constraint training [4] | ✓ | ✓ | ✗ | ✓ |

We finish with a summary of further interesting properties of the four robustness definitions. Table 2 shows a summary of all comparison measures considered in the paper.

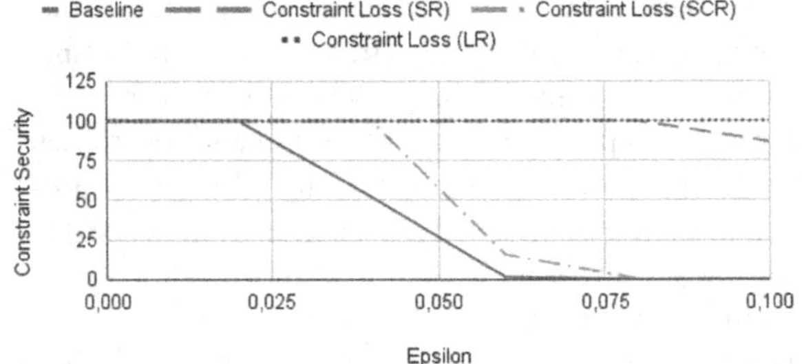


**Fig. 5.** Experiments that show how different choices of a constraint loss affect standard robustness of neural networks.

**Dataset assumptions** concern the distribution of the training data with respect to the data manifold of the true distribution of inputs, and influence evaluation of robustness. For SR and LR it is, at minimum, desirable for the network to be robust over the entire data manifold. In the most domains the shape of the manifold is unknown and therefore it is necessary to approximate it by taking the union of the balls around the inputs in the training dataset. We are not particularly interested about whether the network is robust in regions of the input space that lie off the data manifold, but there is no problem if the network is robust in these regions. Therefore these definitions make no assumptions about the distribution of the training dataset.

This is in contrast to CR and SCR. Rather than requiring that there is only a small change in the output, they require that there is no change to the classification. This is only a desirable constraint when the region being considered does not contain a decision boundary. Consequently when one is training for some form of classification robustness, one is implicitly making the assumption that the training data points lie away from any decision boundaries within the manifold. In practice, most datasets for classification problems assign a single label instead of an entire probability distribution to each input point, and so this assumption is usually valid. However, for datasets that contain input points that may lie close to the decision boundaries, CR and SCR may result in a logically inconsistent specification.

**Interpretability.** One of the key selling points of training with logical constraints is that, by ensuring that the network obeys understandable constraints, it improves the explainability of the neural network. Each of the robustness constraints encode that "small changes to the input only result in small changes to the output", but the interpretability of each definition is also important.

All of the definitions share the relatively interpretable $\epsilon$ parameter, which measures how large a perturbation from the input is acceptable. Despite the other drawbacks discussed so far, CR is inherently the most interpretable as it has no second parameter. In contrast, SR and SCR require extra parameters, $\delta$ and $\eta$ respectively, which measure the allowable deviation in the output. Their addition makes these models less interpretable.

Finally we argue that, although LR is the most desirable constraint, it is also the least interpretable. Its second parameter $L$ measures the allowable change in the output as a proportion of the allowable change in the input. It therefore requires one to not only have an interpretation of distance for both the input and output spaces, but to be able to relate them. In most domains, this relationship simply does not exist. Consider the MNIST dataset, both the commonly used notion of pixel-wise distance used in the input set, although crude, and the distance between the output distributions are both interpretable. However, the relationship between them is not. For example, what does allowing the distance between the output probability distributions being no more than twice the distance between the images actually mean? This therefore highlights a common trade-off between complexity of the constraint and its interpretability.

## 6 Conclusions

These case studies have demonstrated the importance of emancipating the study of desirable properties of neural networks from a concrete training method, and studying these properties in an abstract mathematical way. For example, we have discovered that some robustness properties can be ordered by logical strength and some are incomparable. Where ordering is possible, training for a stronger property helps in verifying a weaker property. Some of the stronger properties, such as Lipschitz robustness, are not yet feasible for the modern DNN solvers, such as Marabou [8]. Moreover, we show that the logical strength of the property may not guarantee other desirable properties, such as interpretability. Some of these findings lead to very concrete recommendations, e.g.: it is best to avoid CR and SCR as they may lead to inconsistencies; when using LR and SR, one should use stronger property (LR) for training in order to be successful in verifying a weaker one (SR). In other cases, the distinctions that we make do not give direct prescriptions, but merely discuss the design choices and trade-offs.

This paper also shows that constraint security, a measure intermediate between constraint accuracy and constraint satisfaction, is a useful tool in the context of tuning the continuous verification loop. It is more efficient to measure and can show more nuanced trends than constraint satisfaction. It can be used to tune training parameters and build hypotheses which we ultimately confirm with constraint satisfaction.

We hope that this study will contribute towards establishing a solid methodology for continuous verification, by setting up some common principles to unite verification and machine learning approaches to DNN robustness.

**Acknowledgement.** Authors acknowledge support of EPSRC grant AISEC EP/T026952/1 and NCSC grant Neural Network Verification: in search of the missing spec.

## References

1. Anil, C., Lucas, J., Grosse, R.: Sorting out Lipschitz function approximation. In: International Conference on Machine Learning, pp. 291–301. PMLR (2019)
2. Balan, R., Singh, M., Zou, D.: Lipschitz properties for deep convolutional networks. Contemp. Math. **706**, 129–151 (2018)
3. Casadio, M., et al.: Neural network robustness as a mathematical property: a principled case study (2021). https://github.com/aisec-private/training-with-constraints
4. Fischer, M., Balunovic, M., Drachsler-Cohen, D., Gehr, T., Zhang, C., Vechev, M.T.: DL2: training and querying neural networks with logic. In: Proceedings of the 36th International Conference Machine Learning, ICML 2019, vol. 97, pp. 1931–1941. PMLR (2019)
5. Goodfellow, I.J., Shlens, J., Szegedy, C.: Explaining and harnessing adversarial examples. In: Bengio, Y., LeCun, Y. (eds.) 3rd International Conference on Learning Representations, ICLR 2015, San Diego, CA, USA, 7–9 May 2015, Conference Track Proceedings (2015)
6. Gouk, H., Frank, E., Pfahringer, B., Cree, M.J.: Regularisation of neural networks by enforcing Lipschitz continuity. Mach. Learn. **110**(2), 393–416 (2020). https://doi.org/10.1007/s10994-020-05929-w
7. Huang, X., Kwiatkowska, M., Wang, S., Wu, M.: Safety verification of deep neural networks. In: Majumdar, R., Kunčak, V. (eds.) CAV 2017. LNCS, vol. 10426, pp. 3–29. Springer, Cham (2017). https://doi.org/10.1007/978-3-319-63387-9_1
8. Katz, G., et al.: The Marabou framework for verification and analysis of deep neural networks. In: Dillig, I., Tasiran, S. (eds.) CAV 2019. LNCS, vol. 11561, pp. 443–452. Springer, Cham (2019). https://doi.org/10.1007/978-3-030-25540-4_26
9. Komendantskaya, E., Kokke, W., Kienitz, D.: Continuous verification of machine learning: a declarative programming approach. In: PPDP 2020: 22nd International Symposium on Principles and Practice of Declarative Programming, Bologna, Italy, 9–10 September 2020, pp. 1:1–1:3. ACM (2020)
10. Madry, A., Makelov, A., Schmidt, L., Tsipras, D., Vladu, A.: Towards deep learning models resistant to adversarial attacks. In: International Conference on Learning Representations (2018)
11. Madry, A., Makelov, A., Schmidt, L., Tsipras, D., Vladu, A.: Towards deep learning models resistant to adversarial attacks (2019)
12. Pauli, P., Koch, A., Berberich, J., Kohler, P., Allgower, F.: Training robust neural networks using Lipschitz bounds. IEEE Control Syst. Lett. (2021)
13. Raghunathan, A., Xie, S.M., Yang, F., Duchi, J.C., Liang, P.: Adversarial training can hurt generalization. arXiv preprint arXiv:1906.06032 (2019)
14. Shorten, C., Khoshgoftaar, T.M.: A survey on image data augmentation for deep learning. J. Big Data **6**, 60 (2019)
15. Singh, G., Gehr, T., Püschel, M., Vechev, M.T.: An abstract domain for certifying neural networks. PACMPL **3**(POPL), 41:1–41:30 (2019). https://doi.org/10.1145/3290354
16. Stallkamp, J., Schlipsing, M., Salmen, J., Igel, C.: The German traffic sign recognition benchmark: a multi-class classification competition. In: IEEE International Joint Conference on Neural Networks, pp. 1453–1460 (2011)

17. Szegedy, C., et al.: Intriguing properties of neural networks. In: 2nd International Conference on Learning Representations, ICLR 2014 (2014)
18. Tsipras, D., Santurkar, S., Engstrom, L., Turner, A., Madry, A.: Robustness may be at odds with accuracy. In: International Conference on Learning Representations (2018)
19. Xiao, H., Rasul, K., Vollgraf, R.: Fashion-MNIST: a novel image dataset for benchmarking machine learning algorithms (2017)
20. Xu, J., Zhang, Z., Friedman, T., Liang, Y., den Broeck, G.V.: A semantic loss function for deep learning with symbolic knowledge. In: Dy, J.G., Krause, A. (eds.) Proceedings of the 35th International Conference on Machine Learning, ICML 2018, Stockholmsmässan, Stockholm, Sweden, 10–15 July 2018. Proceedings of Machine Learning Research, vol. 80, pp. 5498–5507. PMLR (2018)
21. Zhang, H., Yu, Y., Jiao, J., Xing, E., El Ghaoui, L., Jordan, M.: Theoretically principled trade-off between robustness and accuracy. In: International Conference on Machine Learning, pp. 7472–7482. PMLR (2019)

# Software Verification and Model Checking

# The Lattice-Theoretic Essence of Property Directed Reachability Analysis

Mayuko Kori[1,2(✉)], Natsuki Urabe[2], Shin-ya Katsumata[2], Kohei Suenaga[3], and Ichiro Hasuo[1,2]

[1] The Graduate University for Advanced Studies (SOKENDAI), Hayama, Japan
[2] National Institute of Informatics, Tokyo, Japan
{mkori,urabenatsuki,s-katsumata,hasuo}@nii.ac.jp
[3] Kyoto University, Kyoto, Japan
ksuenaga@fos.kuis.kyoto-u.ac.jp

**Abstract.** We present *LT-PDR*, a lattice-theoretic generalization of Bradley's property directed reachability analysis (PDR) algorithm. LT-PDR identifies the essence of PDR to be an ingenious combination of verification and refutation attempts based on the Knaster–Tarski and Kleene theorems. We introduce four concrete instances of LT-PDR, derive their implementation from a generic Haskell implementation of LT-PDR, and experimentally evaluate them. We also present a categorical structural theory that derives these instances.

**Keywords:** Property directed reachability analysis · Model checking · Lattice theory · Fixed point theory · Category theory

## 1 Introduction

*Property directed reachability (PDR)* (also called *IC3*) introduced in [9,13] is a model checking algorithm for proving/disproving safety problems. It has been successfully applied to software and hardware model checking, and later it has been extended in several directions, including *fbPDR* [25,26] that uses both forward and backward predicate transformers and *PrIC3* [6] for the quantitative safety problem for probabilistic systems. See [14] for a concise overview.

The original PDR assumes that systems are given by binary predicates representing transition relations. The PDR algorithm maintains data structures called *frames* and *proof obligations*—these are collections of predicates over states—and updates them. While this logic-based description immediately yields automated tools using SAT/SMT solvers, it limits target systems to qualitative and nondeterministic ones. This limitation was first overcome by PrIC3 [6] whose target is probabilistic systems. This suggests room for further generalization of PDR.

The authors are supported by ERATO HASUO Metamathematics for Systems Design Project (No. JPMJER1603). MK is a JSPS DC fellow and supported by JSPS KAKENHI Grant (No. 22J21742). KS is supported by JST CREST Grant (No. JPMJCR2012) and JSPS KAKENHI Grant (No. 19H04084).


S. Shoham and Y. Vizel (Eds.): CAV 2022, LNCS 13371, pp. 235–256, 2022.
https://doi.org/10.1007/978-3-031-13185-1_12

In this paper, we propose the first lattice theory-based generalization of the PDR algorithm; we call it *LT-PDR*. This makes the PDR algorithm apply to a wider class of safety problems, including qualitative and quantitative. We also derive a new concrete extension of PDR, namely one for Markov reward models.

We implemented the general algorithm LT-PDR in Haskell, in a way that maintains the theoretical abstraction and clarity. Deriving concrete instances for various types of systems is easy (for Kripke structures, probabilistic systems, etc.). We conducted an experimental evaluation, which shows that these easily-obtained instances have at least reasonable performance.

**Preview of the Theoretical Contribution.** We generalize the PDR algorithm so that it operates over an arbitrary complete lattice $L$. This generalization recasts the PDR algorithm to solve a general problem $\mu F \leq^? \alpha$ of over-approximating the least fixed point of an $\omega$-continuous function $F: L \to L$ by a safety property $\alpha$. This lattice-theoretic generalization signifies the relationship between the PDR algorithm and the theory of fixed points. This also allows us to incorporate quantitative predicates suited for probabilistic verification.

More specifically, we reconstruct the original PDR algorithm as a combination of two constituent parts. They are called *positive LT-PDR* and *negative LT-PDR*. Positive LT-PDR comes from a witness-based proof method by the *Knaster–Tarski fixed point theorem*, and aims to *verify* $\mu F \leq^? \alpha$. In contrast, negative LT-PDR comes from the *Kleene fixed point theorem* and aims to *refute* $\mu F \leq^? \alpha$. The two algorithms build up witnesses in an iterative and nondeterministic manner, where nondeterminism accommodates guesses and heuristics. We identify the essence of PDR to be an ingenious combination of these two algorithms, in which intermediate results on one side (positive or negative) give informed guesses on the other side. This is how we formulate LT-PDR in Sect. 3.3.

We discuss several instances of our general theory of PDR. We discuss three concrete settings: Kripke structures (where we obtain two instances of LT-PDR), Markov decision processes (MDPs), and Markov reward models. The two in the first setting essentially subsume many existing PDR algorithms, such as the original PDR [9,13] and Reverse PDR [25,26], and the one for MDPs resembles PrIC3 [6]. The last one (Markov reward models) is a new algorithm that fully exploits the generality of our framework.

In fact, there is another dimension of theoretical generalization: the derivation of the above concrete instances follows a *structural theory of state-based dynamics and predicate transformers*. We formulate the structural theory in the language of *category theory* [3,23]—using especially *coalgebras* [17] and *fibrations* [18]—following works such as [8,15,21,28]. The structural theory tells us which safety problems arise under what conditions; it can therefore suggest that certain safety problems are unlikely to be formulatable, too. The structural theory is important because it builds a mathematical order in the PDR literature, in which theoretical developments tend to be closely tied to implementation and thus theoretical essences are often not very explicit. For example, the theory is useful in classifying a plethora of PDR-like algorithms for Kripke structures (the original, Reverse PDR, fbPDR, etc.). See Sect. 5.1.

We present the above structural theory in Sect. 4 and briefly discuss its use in the derivation of concrete instances in Sect. 5. We note, however, that this categorical theory is not needed for reading and using the other parts of the paper.

There are other works on generalization of PDR [16,24], but our identification of the interplay of Knaster–Tarski and Kleene is new. They do not accommodate probabilistic verification, either. See [22, Appendix A] for further discussions.

**Preliminaries.** Let $(L, \leq)$ be a poset. $(L, \leq)^{\mathrm{op}}$ denotes the opposite poset $(L, \geq)$. Note that if $(L, \leq)$ is a complete lattice then so is $(L, \leq)^{\mathrm{op}}$. An $\omega$-chain (resp. $\omega^{op}$-chain) in $L$ is an $\mathbb{N}$-indexed family of increasing (resp. decreasing) elements in $L$. A monotone function $F : L \to L$ is *$\omega$-continuous* (resp. $\omega^{op}$-continuous) if $F$ preserves existing suprema of $\omega$-chains (resp. infima of $\omega^{\mathrm{op}}$-chains).

## 2 Fixed-points in Complete Lattices

Let $(L, \leq)$ be a complete lattice and $F : L \to L$ be a monotone function. When we analyze fixed points of $F$, pre/postfixed points play important roles.

**Definition 2.1.** *A* prefixed point *of $F$ is an element $x \in L$ satisfying $Fx \leq x$. A* postfixed point *of $F$ is an element $x \in L$ satisfying $x \leq Fx$. We write* $\mathbf{Pre}(F)$ *and* $\mathbf{Post}(F)$ *for the set of prefixed points and postfixed points of $F$, respectively.*

The following results are central in fixed point theory. They allow us to under/over-approximate the least/greatest fixed points.

**Theorem 2.2.** *A monotone endofunction $F$ on a complete lattice $(L, \leq)$ has the least fixed point $\mu F$ and the greatest fixed point $\nu F$. Moreover,*

1. *(Knaster–Tarski [30]) The set of fixed points forms a complete lattice. Furthermore, $\mu F = \bigwedge\{x \in L \mid Fx \leq x\}$ and $\nu F = \bigvee\{x \in L \mid x \leq Fx\}$.*
2. *(Kleene, see e.g. [5]) If $F$ is $\omega$-continuous, $\mu F = \bigvee_{n\in\mathbb{N}} F^n\bot$. Dually, if $F$ is $\omega^{\mathrm{op}}$-continuous, $\nu F = \bigwedge_{n\in\mathbb{N}} F^n\top$.* □

Theorem 2.2.2 is known to hold for arbitrary $\omega$-cpos (complete lattices are their special case). A generalization of Theorem 2.2.2 is the Cousot–Cousot characterization [11], where $F$ is assumed to be monotone (but not necessarily $\omega$-continuous) and we have $\mu F = F^\kappa\bot$ for a sufficiently large, possibly transfinite, ordinal $\kappa$. In this paper, for the algorithmic study of PDR, we assume the $\omega$-continuity of $F$. Note that $\omega$-continuous $F$ on a complete lattice is necessarily monotone.

We call the $\omega$-chain $\bot \leq F\bot \leq \cdots$ *the initial chain of* $F$ and the $\omega^{\mathrm{op}}$-chain $\top \geq F\top \geq \cdots$ *the final chain of* $F$. These appear in Theorem 2.2.2.

Theorem 2.2.1 and 2.2.2 yield the following witness notions for *proving* and *disproving* $\mu F \leq \alpha$, respectively.

**Corollary 2.3.** *Let $(L, \leq)$ be a complete lattice and $F : L \to L$ be $\omega$-continuous.*

1. *(KT) $\mu F \leq \alpha$ if and only if there is $x \in L$ such that $Fx \leq x \leq \alpha$.*
2. *(Kleene) $\mu F \not\leq \alpha$ if and only if there is $n \in \mathbb{N}$ and $x \in L$ such that $x \leq F^n\bot$ and $x \not\leq \alpha$.* □

By Corollary 2.3.1, proving $\mu F \leq \alpha$ is reduced to searching for $x \in L$ such that $Fx \leq x \leq \alpha$. We call such $x$ a *KT (positive) witness*. In contrast, by Corollary 2.3.2, disproving $\mu F \leq \alpha$ is reduced to searching for $n \in \mathbb{N}$ and $x \in L$ such that $x \leq F^n \bot$ and $x \not\leq \alpha$. We call such $x$ a *Kleene (negative) witness*.

**Notation 2.4.** We shall use lowercase (Roman and Greek) letters for elements of $L$ (such as $\alpha, x \in L$), and uppercase letters for (finite or infinite) sequences of $L$ (such as $X \in L^*$ or $L^\omega$). The $i$-th (or $(i-j)$-th when subscripts are started from $j$) element of a sequence $X$ is designated by a subscript: $X_i \in L$.

## 3 Lattice-Theoretic Reconstruction of PDR

Towards the LT-PDR algorithm, we first introduce two simpler algorithms, called positive LT-PDR (Sect. 3.1) and negative LT-PDR (Sect. 3.2). The target problem of the LT-PDR algorithm is the following:

**Definition 3.1 (the LFP-OA problem $\mu F \leq^? \alpha$).** *Let $L$ be a complete lattice, $F : L \to L$ be $\omega$-continuous, and $\alpha \in L$. The* lfp over-approximation (LFP-OA) problem *asks if $\mu F \leq \alpha$ holds; the problem is denoted by $\mu F \leq^? \alpha$.*

*Example 3.2.* Consider a transition system, where $S$ be the set of states, $\iota \subseteq S$ be the set of initial states, $\delta : S \to \mathcal{P}S$ be the transition relation, and $\alpha \subseteq S$ be the set of safe states. Then letting $L := \mathcal{P}S$ and $F := \iota \cup \bigcup_{s \in (-)} \delta(s)$, the lfp over-approximation problem $\mu F \leq^? \alpha$ is the problem whether all reachable states are safe. It is equal to the problem studied by the conventional IC3/PDR [9,13].

Positive LT-PDR iteratively builds a KT witness in a bottom-up manner that positively answers the LFP-OA problem, while negative LT-PDR iteratively builds a Kleene witness for the same LFP-OA problem. We shall present these two algorithms as clear reflections of two proof principles (Corollary 2.3), each of which comes from the fundamental Knaster–Tarski and Kleene theorems.

The two algorithms build up witnesses in an iterative and nondeterministic manner. The nondeterminism is there for accommodating guesses and heuristics. We identify the essence of PDR to be an ingenious combination of these two algorithms, in which intermediate results on one side (positive or negative) give informed guesses on the other side. This way, each of the positive and negative algorithms provides heuristics in resolving the nondeterminism in the execution of the other. This is how we formulate the LT-PDR algorithm in Sect. 3.3.

The dual of LFP-OA problem is called the *gfp-under-approximation problem* (GFP-UA): the GFP-UA problem for a complete lattice $L$, an $\omega^{\mathrm{op}}$-continuous function $F : L \to L$ and $\alpha \in L$ is whether the inequality $\alpha \leq \nu F$ holds or not, and is denoted by $\alpha \leq^? \nu F$. It is evident that the GFP-UA problem for $(L, F, \alpha)$ is equivalent to the LFP-OA problem for $(L^{\mathrm{op}}, F, \alpha)$. This suggests the dual algorithm called LT-OpPDR for GFP-UA problem. See Remark 3.24 later.

### 3.1 Positive LT-PDR: Sequential Positive Witnesses

We introduce the notion of KT$^\omega$ witness—a KT witness (Corollary 2.3) constructed in a sequential manner. Positive LT-PDR searches for a KT$^\omega$ witness by growing its finitary approximations (called KT sequences).

Let $L$ be a complete lattice. We regard each element $x \in L$ as an abstract presentation of a predicate on states. The inequality $x \leq y$ means that the predicate $x$ is stronger than the predicate $y$. We introduce the complete lattice $[n, L]$ of increasing chains of length $n \in \mathbb{N}$, whose elements are $(X_0 \leq \cdots \leq X_{n-1})$ in $L$ equipped with the element-wise order. We similarly introduce the complete lattice $[\omega, L]$ of $\omega$-chains in $L$. We lift $F : L \to L$ to $F^\# : [\omega, L] \to [\omega, L]$ and $F^\#_n : [n, L] \to [n, L]$ (for $n \geq 2$) as follows. Note that the entries are shifted.

$$\begin{aligned} F^\#(X_0 \leq X_1 \leq \cdots) &:= (\bot \leq FX_0 \leq FX_1 \leq \cdots) \\ F^\#_n(X_0 \leq \cdots \leq X_{n-1}) &:= (\bot \leq FX_0 \leq \cdots \leq FX_{n-2}) \end{aligned} \tag{1}$$

**Definition 3.3 (KT$^\omega$ witness).** *Let $L, F, \alpha$ be as in Definition 3.1. Define $\Delta\alpha := (\alpha \leq \alpha \leq \cdots)$. A KT$^\omega$* witness *is $X \in [\omega, L]$ such that $F^\# X \leq X \leq \Delta\alpha$.*

**Theorem 3.4.** *Let $L, F, \alpha$ be as in Definition 3.1. There exists a KT witness (Corollary 2.3) if and only if there exists a KT$^\omega$ witness.* □

Concretely, a KT witness $x$ yields a KT$^\omega$ witness $x \leq x \leq \cdots$; a KT$^\omega$ witness $X$ yields a KT witness $\bigvee_{n\in\omega} X_n$. A full proof (via Galois connections) is in [22].

The initial chain $\bot \leq F\bot \leq \cdots$ is always a KT$^\omega$ witness for $\mu F \leq \alpha$. There are other KT$^\omega$ witnesses whose growth is accelerated by some heuristic guesses—an extreme example is $x \leq x \leq \cdots$ with a KT witness $x$. KT$^\omega$ witnesses embrace the spectrum of such different sequential witnesses for $\mu F \leq \alpha$, those which mix routine constructions (i.e. application of $F$) and heuristic guesses.

**Definition 3.5 (KT sequence).** *Let $L, F, \alpha$ be as in Definition 3.1. A* KT sequence *for $\mu F \leq^? \alpha$ is a finite chain $(X_0 \leq \cdots \leq X_{n-1})$, for $n \geq 2$, satisfying*

1. *$X_{n-2} \leq \alpha$; and*
2. *$X$ is a prefixed point of $F^\#_n$, that is, $FX_i \leq X_{i+1}$ for each $i \in [0, n-2]$.*

*A KT sequence $(X_0 \leq \cdots \leq X_{n-1})$ is* conclusive *if $X_{j+1} \leq X_j$ for some $j$.*

KT sequences are finite by definition. Note that the upper bound $\alpha$ is imposed on all $X_i$ but $X_{n-1}$. This freedom in the choice of $X_{n-1}$ offers room for heuristics, one that is exploited in the combination with negative LT-PDR (Sect. 3.3).

We take KT sequences as finite approximations of KT$^\omega$ witnesses. This view shall be justified by the partial order ($\preceq$) between KT sequences defined below.

**Definition 3.6 (order $\preceq$ between KT sequences).** *We define a partial order relation $\preceq$ on KT sequences as follows: $(X_0, \ldots, X_{n-1}) \preceq (X'_0, \ldots, X'_{m-1})$ if $n \leq m$ and $X_j \geq X'_j$ for each $0 \leq j \leq n-1$.*

The order $X_j \geq X'_j$ represents that $X'_j$ is a stronger predicate (on states) than $X_j$. Therefore $X \preceq X'$ expresses that $X'$ is a longer and stronger/more determined chain than $X$. We obtain KT$^\omega$ witnesses as their $\omega$-superma.

**Theorem 3.7.** *Let $L, F, \alpha$ be as in Definition 3.1. The set of KT sequences, augmented with the set of $KT^{\omega}$ witnesses $\{X \in [\omega, L] \mid F^{\#}X \leq X \leq \Delta\alpha\}$ and ordered by the natural extension of $\preceq$, is an $\omega$-cpo. In this $\omega$-cpo, each $KT^{\omega}$ witness $X$ is represented as the suprema of an $\omega$-chain of KT sequences, namely $X = \bigvee_{n\geq 2} X|_n$ where $X|_n \in [n, L]$ is the length $n$ prefix of $X$.* □

**Proposition 3.8.** *Let $L, F, \alpha$ be as in Definition 3.1. There exists a $KT^{\omega}$ witness if and only if there exists a conclusive KT sequence.*

*Proof.* ($\Rightarrow$): If there exists a $\mathrm{KT}^{\omega}$ witness, $\mu F \leq \alpha$ holds by Corollary 2.3 and Theorem 3.4. Therefore, the "informed guess" ($\mu F \leq \mu F$) gives a conclusive KT sequence. ($\Leftarrow$): When $X$ is a conclusive KT sequence with $X_j = X_{j+1}$, $X_0 \leq \cdots \leq X_j = X_{j+1} = \cdots$ is a $\mathrm{KT}^{\omega}$ witness. □

The proposition above yields the following partial algorithm that aims to answer positively to the LFP-OA problem. It searches for a conclusive KT sequence.

**Definition 3.9 (positive LT-PDR).** *Let $L, F, \alpha$ be as in Definition 3.1.* Positive LT-PDR *is the algorithm shown in Algorithm 1, which says 'True' to the LFP-OA problem $\mu F \leq^{?} \alpha$ if successful.*

The rules are designed by the following principles.

**Valid** is applied when the current $X$ is conclusive.

**Unfold** extends $X$ with $\top$. In fact, we can use any element $x$ satisfying $X_{n-1} \leq x$ and $FX_{n-1} \leq x$ in place of $\top$ (by the application of **Induction** with $x$). The condition $X_{n-1} \leq \alpha$ is checked to ensure that the extended $X$ satisfies the condition in Definition 3.5.1.

**Induction** strengthens $X$, replacing the $j$-th element with its meet with $x$. The first condition $X_k \not\leq x$ ensures that this rule indeed strengthens $X$, and the second condition $F(X_{k-1} \wedge x) \leq x$ ensures that the strengthened $X$ satisfies the condition in Definition 3.5.2, that is, $F_n^{\#}X \leq X$ (see the proof in [22]).

**Theorem 3.10.** *Let $L, F, \alpha$ be as in Definition 3.1. Then positive LT-PDR is sound, i.e. if it outputs 'True' then $\mu F \leq \alpha$ holds.*

*Moreover, assume $\mu F \leq \alpha$ is true. Then positive LT-PDR is weakly terminating (meaning that suitable choices of $x$ when applying* **Induction** *make the algorithm terminate).* □

The last "optimistic termination" is realized by the informed guess $\mu F$ as $x$ in **Induction**. To guarantee the termination of LT-PDR, it suffices to assume that the complete lattice $L$ is well-founded (no infinite decreasing chain exists in $L$) and there is no strictly increasing $\omega$-chain under $\alpha$ in $L$, although we cannot hope for this assumption in every instance (Sect. 5.2, 5.3).

**Lemma 3.11.** *Let $L, F, \alpha$ be as in Definition 3.1. If $\mu F \leq \alpha$, then for any KT sequence $X$, at least one of the three rules in Algorithm 1 is enabled.*

*Moreover, for any KT sequence $X$, let $X'$ be obtained by applying either* ***Unfold*** *or* ***Induction****. Then $X \preceq X'$ and $X \neq X'$.* □

**Input** : An instance ($\mu F \leq^? \alpha$) of the LFP-OA problem in $L$
**Output** : 'True' with a conclusive KT sequence
**Data:** a KT sequence $X = (X_0 \leq \cdots \leq X_{n-1})$
**Initially:** $X := (\bot \leq F\bot)$
**repeat (do one of the following)**

- **Valid** If $X_{j+1} \leq X_j$ for some $j < n-1$, return 'True' with the conclusive KT sequence $X$.
- **Unfold** If $X_{n-1} \leq \alpha$, let $X := (X_0 \leq \cdots \leq X_{n-1} \leq \top)$. ⊤
- **Induction** If some $k \geq 2$ and $x \in L$ satisfy $X_k \not\leq x$ and $F(X_{k-1} \wedge x) \leq x$, let $X := X[X_j := X_j \wedge x]_{2 \leq j \leq k}$.

**until** *any return value is obtained*;

**Algorithm 1:** positive LT-PDR

**Input** : An instance ($\mu F \leq^? \alpha$) of the LFP-OA problem in $L$
**Output** : 'False' with a conclusive Kleene sequence
**Data:** a Kleene sequence $C = (C_0, \ldots, C_{n-1})$
**Initially:** $C := ()$
**repeat (do one of the following)**

- **Candidate** Choose $x \in L$ such that $x \not\leq \alpha$, and let $C := (x)$.
- **Model** If $C_0 = \bot$, return 'False' with the conclusive Kleene sequence $C$.
- **Decide** If there exists $x$ such that $C_0 \leq Fx$, then let $C := (x, C_0, \ldots, C_{n-1})$.

**until** *any return value is obtained*;

**Algorithm 2:** negative LT-PDR

**Input** : An instance ($\mu F \leq^? \alpha$) of the LFP-OA problem in $L$
**Output** : 'True' with a conclusive KT sequence, or 'False' with a conclusive Kleene sequence
**Data:** $(X; C)$ where $X$ is a KT sequence $(X_0 \leq \cdots \leq X_{n-1})$, and $C$ is a Kleene sequence $(C_i, C_{i+1}, \ldots, C_{n-1})$ ($C$ is empty if $n = i$).
**Initially:** $(X; C) := (\bot \leq F\bot;\ ()\,)$
**repeat (do one of the following)**

- **Valid** If $X_{j+1} \leq X_j$ for some $j < n-1$, return 'True' with the conclusive KT sequence $X$.
- **Unfold** If $X_{n-1} \leq \alpha$, let $(X; C) := (X_0 \leq \cdots \leq X_{n-1} \leq \top; ())$.
- **Induction** If some $k \geq 2$ and $x \in L$ satisfy $X_k \not\leq x$ and $F(X_{k-1} \wedge x) \leq x$, let $(X; C) := (X[X_j := X_j \wedge x]_{2 \leq j \leq k}; C)$.
- **Candidate** If $C = ()$ and $X_{n-1} \not\leq \alpha$, choose $x \in L$ such that $x \leq X_{n-1}$ and $x \not\leq \alpha$, and let $(X; C) := (X; (x))$.
- **Model** If $C_1$ is defined, return 'False' with the conclusive Kleene sequence $(\bot, C_1, \ldots, C_{n-1})$.
- **Decide** If $C_i \leq FX_{i-1}$, choose $x \in L$ satisfying $x \leq X_{i-1}$ and $C_i \leq Fx$, and let $(X; C) := (X; (x, C_i, \ldots, C_{n-1}))$.
- **Conflict** If $C_i \not\leq FX_{i-1}$, choose $x \in L$ satisfying $C_i \not\leq x$ and $F(X_{i-1} \wedge x) \leq x$, and let $(X; C) := (X[X_j := X_j \wedge x]_{2 \leq j \leq i}; (C_{i+1}, \ldots, C_{n-1}))$.

**until** *any return value is obtained*;

**Algorithm 3:** LT-PDR

**Theorem 3.12.** *Let $L, F, \alpha$ be as in Definition 3.1. Assume that $\leq$ in $L$ is well-founded and $\mu F \leq \alpha$. Then, any non-terminating run of positive LT-PDR converges to a $KT^\omega$ witness (meaning that it gives a $KT^\omega$ witness in $\omega$-steps). Moreover, if there is no strictly increasing $\omega$-chain bounded by $\alpha$ in $L$, then positive LT-PDR is strongly terminating.* □

### 3.2 Negative PDR: Sequential Negative Witnesses

We next introduce *Kleene sequences* as a lattice-theoretic counterpart of *proof obligations* in the standard PDR. Kleene sequences represent a chain of sufficient conditions to conclude that certain unsafe states are reachable.

**Definition 3.13 (Kleene sequence).** *Let $L, F, \alpha$ be as in Definition 3.1. A* Kleene sequence *for the LFP-OA problem $\mu F \leq^? \alpha$ is a finite sequence $(C_0, \ldots, C_{n-1})$, for $n \geq 0$ ($C$ is empty if $n = 0$), satisfying*

1. *$C_j \leq FC_{j-1}$ for each $1 \leq j \leq n-1$;*
2. *$C_{n-1} \not\leq \alpha$.*

*A Kleene sequence $(C_0, \ldots, C_{n-1})$ is* conclusive *if $C_0 = \bot$. We may use $i$ ($0 \leq i \leq n$) instead of $0$ as the starting index of the Kleene sequence $C$.*

When we have a Kleene sequence $C = (C_0, \ldots, C_{n-1})$, the chain of implications $(C_j \leq F^j \bot) \implies (C_{j+1} \leq F^{j+1} \bot)$ hold for $0 \leq j < n-1$. Therefore when $C$ is conclusive, $C_{n-1}$ is a Kleene witness (Corollary 2.3.2).

**Proposition 3.14.** *Let $L, F, \alpha$ be as in Definition 3.1. There exists a Kleene (negative) witness if and only if there exists a conclusive Kleene sequence.*

*Proof.* ($\Rightarrow$): If there exists a Kleene witness $x$ such that $x \leq F^n \bot$ and $x \not\leq \alpha$, $(\bot, F\bot, \ldots, F^n \bot)$ is a conclusive Kleene sequence. ($\Leftarrow$): Assume there exists a conclusive Kleene sequence $C$. Then $C_{n-1}$ satisfies $C_{n-1} \leq F^{n-1} \bot$ and $C_{n-1} \not\leq \alpha$ because of $C_{n-1} \leq FC_{n-2} \leq \cdots \leq F^{n-1} C_0 = F^{n-1} \bot$ and Definition 3.13.2. □

This proposition suggests the following algorithm to negatively answer to the LFP-OA problem. It searches for a conclusive Kleene sequence. The algorithm updates a Kleene sequence until its first component becomes $\bot$.

**Definition 3.15 (negative LT-PDR).** *Let $L, F, \alpha$ be as in Definition 3.1.* Negative LT-PDR *is the algorithm shown in Algorithm 2, which says 'False' to the LFP-OA problem $\mu F \leq^? \alpha$ if successful.*

The rules are designed by the following principles.

**Candidate** initializes $C$ with only one element $x$. The element $x$ has to be chosen such that $x \not\leq \alpha$ to ensure Definition 3.13.2.

**Model** is applied when the current Kleene sequence $C$ is conclusive.

**Decide** prepends $x$ to $C$. The condition $C_0 \leq Fx$ ensures Definition 3.13.1.

**Theorem 3.16.** *Let $L, F, \alpha$ be as in Definition 3.1.*

1. *Negative LT-PDR is sound, i.e. if it outputs 'False' then $\mu F \not\leq \alpha$.*
2. *Assume $\mu F \not\leq \alpha$ is true. Then negative LT-PDR is weakly terminating (meaning that suitable choices of $x$ when applying rules* ***Candidate*** *and* ***Decide*** *make the algorithm terminate).* □

### 3.3 LT-PDR: Integrating Positive and Negative

We have introduced two simple PDR algorithms, called positive LT-PDR (Sect. 3.1) and negative LT-PDR (Sect. 3.2). They are so simple that they have potential inefficiencies. Specifically, in positive LT-PDR, it is unclear that how we choose $x \in L$ in **Induction**, while in negative LT-PDR, it may easily diverge because the rules **Candidate** and **Decide** may choose $x \in L$ that would not lead to a conclusive Kleene sequence. We resolve these inefficiencies by combining positive LT-PDR and negative LT-PDR. The combined PDR algorithm is called LT-PDR, and it is a lattice-theoretic generalization of conventional PDR.

Note that negative LT-PDR is only weakly terminating. Even worse, it is easy to make it diverge—after a choice of $x$ in **Candidate** or **Decide** such that $x \not\leq \mu F$, no continued execution of the algorithm can lead to a conclusive Kleene sequence. For deciding $\mu F \leq^? \alpha$ efficiently, therefore, it is crucial to detect such useless Kleene sequences.

The core fact that underlies the efficiency of PDR is the following proposition, which says that a KT sequence (in positive LT-PDR) can quickly tell that a Kleene sequence (in negative LT-PDR) is useless. This fact is crucially used for many rules in LT-PDR (Definition 3.20).

**Proposition 3.17.** *Let $C = (C_i, \dots, C_{n-1})$ be a Kleene sequence $(2 \leq n, 0 < i \leq n-1)$ and $X = (X_0 \leq \dots \leq X_{n-1})$ be a KT sequence. Then*

1. *$C_i \not\leq X_i$ implies that $C$ cannot be extended to a conclusive one, that is, there does not exist $C_0, \dots, C_{i-1}$ such that $(C_0, \dots, C_{n-1})$ is conclusive.*
2. *$C_i \not\leq FX_{i-1}$ implies that $C$ cannot be extended to a conclusive one.*
3. *There is no conclusive Kleene sequence with length $n-1$.* □

The proof relies on the following lemmas.

**Lemma 3.18.** *Any KT sequence $(X_0 \leq \dots \leq X_{n-1})$ over-approximates the initial sequence: $F^i\bot \leq X_i$ holds for any $i$ such that $0 \leq i \leq n-1$.* □

**Lemma 3.19.** *Let $C = (C_i, \dots, C_{n-1})$ be a Kleene sequence $(0 < i \leq n-1)$ and $(X_0 \leq \dots \leq X_{n-1})$ be a KT sequence. The following satisfy $1 \Leftrightarrow 2 \Rightarrow 3$.*

1. *The Kleene sequence $C$ can be extended to a conclusive one.*
2. *$C_i \leq F^i\bot$.*
3. *$C_i \leq F^j X_{i-j}$ for each $j$ with $0 \leq j \leq i$.* □

Using the above lattice-theoretic properties, we combine positive and negative LT-PDRs into the following *LT-PDR* algorithm. It is also a lattice-theoretic generalization of the original PDR algorithm. The combination exploits the mutual relationship between KT sequences and Kleene sequences, exhibited as Proposition 3.17, for narrowing down choices in positive and negative LT-PDRs.

**Definition 3.20 (LT-PDR).** *Given a complete lattice $L$, an $\omega$-continuous function $F : L \to L$, and an element $\alpha \in L$,* LT-PDR *is the algorithm shown in Algorithm 3 for the LFP-OA problem $\mu F \leq^? \alpha$.*

The rules are designed by the following principles.

(**Valid**, **Unfold**, and **Induction**): These rules are almost the same as in positive LT-PDR. In **Unfold**, we reset the Kleene sequence because of Proposition 3.17.3. Occurrences of **Unfold** punctuate an execution of the algorithm: between two occurrences of **Unfold**, a main goal (towards a negative conclusion) is to construct a conclusive Kleene sequence with the same length as the $X$.

(**Candidate**, **Model**, and **Decide**): These rules have many similarities to those in negative LT-PDR. Differences are as follows: the **Candidate** and **Decide** rules impose $x \leq X_i$ on the new element $x$ in $(x, C_{i+1}, \ldots, C_{n-1})$ because Proposition 3.17.1 tells us that other choices are useless. In **Model**, we only need to check whether $C_1$ is defined instead of $C_0 = \bot$. Indeed, since $C_1$ is added in **Candidate** or **Decide**, $C_1 \leq X_1 = F\bot$ always holds. Therefore, $2 \Rightarrow 1$ in Lemma 3.19 shows that $(\bot, C_1, \ldots, C_{n-1})$ is conclusive.

(**Conflict**): This new rule emerges from the combination of positive and negative LT-PDRs. This rule is applied when $C_i \not\leq FX_{i-1}$, which confirms that the current $C$ cannot be extended to a conclusive one (Proposition 3.17.2). Therefore, we eliminate $C_i$ from $C$ and strengthen $X$ so that we cannot choose $C_i$ again, that is, so that $C_i \not\leq (X_i \wedge x)$. Let us explain how $X$ is strengthened. The element $x$ has to be chosen so that $C_i \not\leq x$ and $F(X_{i-1} \wedge x) \leq x$. The former dis-inequality ensures the strengthened $X$ satisfies $C_i \not\leq (X_i \wedge x)$, and the latter inequality implies $F(X_{i-1} \wedge x) \leq x$. One can see that **Conflict** is **Induction** with additional condition $C_i \not\leq x$, which enhances so that the search space for $x$ is narrowed down using the Kleene sequence $C$.

Canonical choices of $x \in L$ in **Candidate**, **Decide**, and **Conflict** are $x := X_{n-1}$, $x := X_{i-1}$, and $x := FX_{i-1}$, respectively. However, there can be cleverer choices; e.g. $x := S \setminus (C_i \setminus FX_{i-1})$ in **Conflict** when $L = \mathcal{P}S$.

**Lemma 3.21.** *Each rule of LT-PDR, when applied to a pair of a KT and a Kleene sequence, yields a pair of a KT and a Kleene sequence.* □

**Theorem 3.22 (correctness).** *LT-PDR is sound, i.e. if it outputs 'True' then $\mu F \leq \alpha$ holds, and if it outputs 'False' then $\mu F \not\leq \alpha$ holds.* □

Many existing PDR algorithms ensure termination if the state space is finite. A general principle behind is stated below. Note that it rarely applies to infinitary or quantitative settings, where we would need some abstraction for termination.

**Proposition 3.23 (termination).** *LT-PDR terminates regardless of the order of the rule-applications if the following conditions are satisfied.*

1. ***Valid*** *and* ***Model*** *rules are immediately applied if applicable.*
2. *$(L, \leq)$ is well-founded.*
3. *Either of the following is satisfied: a) $\mu F \leq \alpha$ and $(L, \leq)$ has no strictly increasing $\omega$-chain bounded by $\alpha$, or b) $\mu F \not\leq \alpha$.* □

Cond 1 is natural: it just requires LT-PDR to immediately conclude 'True' or 'False' if it can. Cond. 2–3 are always satisfied when $L$ is finite.

**Table 1.** Categorical modeling of state-based dynamics and predicate transformers

| a transition system as a *coalgebra* [17] in the base category $\mathbb{B}$ of sets and functions | |
|---|---|
| objects $X, Y, \ldots$ in $\mathbb{B}$ | sets (in our examples where $\mathbb{B} = \mathbf{Set}$) |
| an arrow $f: X \to Y$ in $\mathbb{B}$ | a function (in our examples where $\mathbb{B} = \mathbf{Set}$) |
| a functor $G: \mathbb{B} \to \mathbb{B}$ | a transition type $\begin{pmatrix} G = \mathcal{P} \text{ for Kripke structures (§5.1),} \\ G = (\mathcal{D}(-)+1)^{\mathrm{Act}} \text{ for MDPs (§5.2), etc.} \end{pmatrix}$ |
| a *coalgebra* $\delta: S \to GS$ in $\mathbb{B}$ [17] | a transition system (Kripke structure, MDP, etc.) |
| a *fibration* $p: \mathbb{E} \to \mathbb{B}$ [18] that equips sets in $\mathbb{B}$ with *predicates* | |
| the fiber category $\mathbb{E}_S$ over $S$ in $\mathbb{B}$ | the lattice of predicates over a set $S$ |
| the *pullback* functor $l^*: \mathbb{E}_Y \to \mathbb{E}_X$ for $l: X \to Y$ in $\mathbb{B}$ | substitution $P(y) \mapsto P(l(x))$ in predicates $P \in \mathbb{E}_Y$ over $Y$ |
| a *lifting* $\dot{G}: \mathbb{E} \to \mathbb{E}$ of $G$ along $p$ | logical interpretation of the transition type $G$ (specifies e.g. the may vs. must modalities) |
| the *predicate transformer*, whose fixed points are of our interest | |
| the composite $\delta^* \dot{G}: \mathbb{E}_S \to \mathbb{E}_S$ | the predicate transformer associated with the transition system $\delta$ |

Theorem 3.22 and Proposition 3.23 still hold if **Induction** rule is dropped. However, the rule can accelerate the convergence of KT sequences and improve efficiency.

*Remark 3.24 (LT-OpPDR).* The GFP-UA problem $\alpha \leq^? \nu F$ is the dual of LFP-OA, obtained by opposing the order $\leq$ in $L$. We can also dualize the LT-PDR algorithm (Algorithm 3), obtaining what we call the *LT-OpPDR* algorithm for GFP-UA. Moreover, we can express LT-OpPDR as LT-PDR if a suitable *involution* $\neg: L \to L^{\mathrm{op}}$ is present. See [22, Appendix B] for further details; see also Proposition 4.3.

## 4 Structural Theory of PDR by Category Theory

Before we discuss concrete instances of LT-PDR in Sect. 5, we develop a structural theory of transition systems and predicate transformers as a basis of LT-PDR. The theory is formulated in the language of *category theory* [3,17,18,23]. We use category theory because 1) categorical modeling of relevant notions is well established in the community (see e.g. [2,8,17,18,27]), and 2) it gives us the right level of abstraction that accommodates a variety of instances. In particular, qualitative and quantitative settings are described in a uniform manner.

Our structural theory (Sect. 4) serves as a backend, not a frontend. That is,

- the theory in Sect. 4 is important in that it explains how the instances in Sect. 5 arise and why others do not, but
- the instances in Sect. 5 are described in non-categorical terms, so readers who skipped Sect. 4 will have no difficulties following Sect. 5 and using those instances.

### 4.1 Categorical Modeling of Dynamics and Predicate Transformers

Our interests are in instances of the LFP-OA problem $\mu F \leq^? \alpha$ (Definition 3.1) that appear in *model checking*. In this context, 1) the underlying lattice $L$ is that of *predicates* over a state space, and 2) the function $F\colon L \to L$ arises from the dynamic/transition structure, specifically as a *predicate transformer*. The categorical notions in Table 1 model these ideas (state-based dynamics, predicate transformers). This modeling is well-established in the community.

Our introduction of Table 1 here is minimal, due to the limited space. See [22, Appendix C] and the references therein for more details.

A *category* consists of *objects* and *arrows* between them. In Table 1, categories occur twice: 1) a *base category* $\mathbb{B}$ where objects are typically sets and arrows are typically functions; and 2) *fiber categories* $\mathbb{E}_S$, defined for each object $S$ of $\mathbb{B}$, that are identified with the lattices of *predicates*. Specifically, objects $P, Q, \dots$ of $\mathbb{E}_S$ are predicates over $S$, and an arrow $P \to Q$ represents logical implication. A general fact behind the last is that every preorder is a category—see e.g. [3].

**Transition Systems as Coalgebras.** State-based transition systems are modeled as *coalgebras* in the base category $\mathbb{B}$ [17]. We use a *functor* $G\colon \mathbb{B} \to \mathbb{B}$ to represent a transition type. A *G-coalgebra* is an arrow $\delta\colon S \to GS$, where $S$ is a state space and $\delta$ describes the dynamics. For example, a Kripke structure can be identified with a pair $(S, \delta)$ of a set $S$ and a function $\delta\colon S \to \mathcal{P}S$, where $\mathcal{P}S$ denotes the powerset. The powerset construction $\mathcal{P}$ is known to be a functor $\mathcal{P}\colon \mathbf{Set} \to \mathbf{Set}$; therefore Kripke structures are $\mathcal{P}$-coalgebras. For other choices of $G$, $G$-coalgebras become different types of transition systems, such as MDPs (Sect. 5.2) and Markov Reward Models (Sect. 5.3).

**Predicates Form a Fibration.** Fibrations are powerful categorical constructs that can model various indexed entities; see e.g. [18] for its general theory. Our use of them is for organizing the lattices $\mathbb{E}_S$ of *predicates* over a set $S$, indexed by the choice of $S$. For example, $\mathbb{E}_S = 2^S$—the lattice of subsets of $S$—for modeling qualitative predicates. For quantitative reasoning (e.g. for MDPs), we use $\mathbb{E}_S = [0,1]^S$, where $[0,1]$ is the unit interval. This way, qualitative and quantitative reasonings are mathematically unified in the language of fibrations.

A *fibration* is a functor $p\colon \mathbb{E} \to \mathbb{B}$ with suitable properties; it can be thought of as a collection $(\mathbb{E}_S)_{S \in \mathbb{B}}$ of *fiber categories* $\mathbb{E}_S$—indexed by objects $S$ of $\mathbb{B}$—suitably organized as a single category $\mathbb{E}$. Notable in this organization is that we obtain the *pullback* functor $l^*\colon \mathbb{E}_Y \to \mathbb{E}_X$ for each arrow $l\colon X \to Y$ in $\mathbb{B}$. In our examples, $l^*$ is a *substitution* along $l$ in predicates—$l^*$ is the monotone map that carries a predicate $P(y)$ over $Y$ to the predicate $P(l(x))$ over $X$.

In this paper, we restrict to a subclass of fibrations (called $\boldsymbol{CLat}_\wedge$*-fibrations*) in which every fiber category $\mathbb{E}_S$ is a complete lattice, and each pullback functor preserves all meets. We therefore write $P \leq Q$ for arrows in $\mathbb{E}_S$; this represents logical implication, as announced above. Notice that each $f^*$ has a left adjoint (lower adjoint in terms of Galois connection), which exists by Freyd's adjoint functor theorem. The left adjoint is denoted by $f_*$.

We also consider a *lifting* $\dot{G}\colon \mathbb{E} \to \mathbb{E}$ of $G$ along $p$; it is a functor $\dot{G}$ such that $p\dot{G} = Gp$. See the diagram on the right. It specifies the *logical interpretation* of the transition type $G$. For example, for $G = \mathcal{P}$ (the powerset functor) from the above, two choices of $\dot{G}$ are for the *may* and *must* modalities. See e.g. [2, 15, 20, 21].

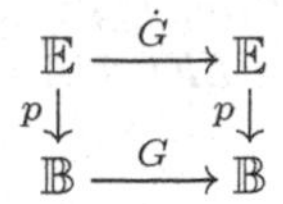

$$\begin{array}{ccc} \mathbb{E} & \xrightarrow{\dot{G}} & \mathbb{E} \\ {\scriptstyle p}\downarrow & & \downarrow{\scriptstyle p} \\ \mathbb{B} & \xrightarrow{G} & \mathbb{B} \end{array}$$

**Categorical Predicate Transformer.** The above constructs allow us to model predicate transformers—$F$ in our examples of the LFP-OA problem $\mu F \leq^? \alpha$—in categorical terms. A *predicate transformer* along a coalgebra $\delta\colon S \to GS$ with respect to the lifting $\dot{G}$ is simply the composite $\mathbb{E}_S \xrightarrow{\dot{G}} \mathbb{E}_{GS} \xrightarrow{\delta^*} \mathbb{E}_S$, where the first $\dot{G}$ is the restriction of $\dot{G}\colon \mathbb{E} \to \mathbb{E}$ to $\mathbb{E}_S$. Intuitively, 1) given a *postcondition* $P$ in $\mathbb{E}_S$, 2) it is first interpreted as the predicate $\dot{G}P$ over $GS$, and then 3) it is pulled back along the dynamics $\delta$ to yield a *precondition* $\delta^*\dot{G}P$. Such (backward) predicate transformers are fundamental in a variety of model checking problems.

### 4.2 Structural Theory of PDR from Transition Systems

We formulate a few general *safety* problems. We show how they are amenable to the LT-PDR (Definition 3.20) and LT-OpPDR (Remark 3.24) algorithms.

**Definition 4.1 (backward safety problem, BSP).** *Let $p$ be a **CLat**$_\wedge$-fibration, $\delta : S \to GS$ be a coalgebra in $\mathbb{B}$, and $\dot{G} : \mathbb{E} \to \mathbb{E}$ be a lifting of $G$ along $p$ such that $\dot{G}_X : \mathbb{E}_X \to \mathbb{E}_{GX}$ is $\omega^{\mathrm{op}}$-continuous for each $X \in \mathbb{B}$. The* backward safety problem *for $(\iota \in \mathbb{E}_S, \delta, \alpha \in \mathbb{E}_S)$ in $(p, G, \dot{G})$ is the GFP-UA problem for $(\mathbb{E}_S, \alpha \wedge \delta^*\dot{G}, \iota)$, that is,*

$$\iota \leq^? \nu x.\, \alpha \wedge \delta^*\dot{G}x. \tag{2}$$

Here, $\iota$ represents the initial states and $\alpha$ represents the safe states. The predicate transformer $x \mapsto \alpha \wedge \delta^*\dot{G}x$ in (2) is the standard one for modeling safety—currently safe ($\alpha$), and the next time $x$ ($\delta^*\dot{G}x$). Its gfp is the safety property; (2) asks if all initial states ($\iota$) satisfy the safety property. Since the backward safety problem is a GFP-UA problem, we can solve it by LT-OpPDR (Remark 3.24).

Additional assumptions allow us to reduce the backward safety problem to LFP-OA problems, which are solvable by LT-PDR, as shown on the right.

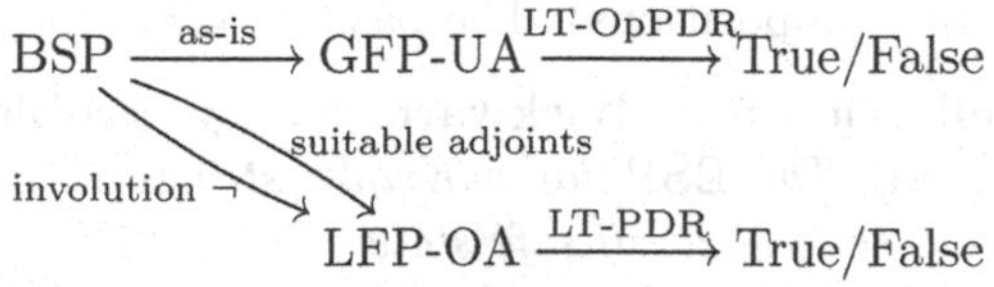

$$\begin{array}{l} \text{BSP} \xrightarrow{\text{as-is}} \text{GFP-UA} \xrightarrow{\text{LT-OpPDR}} \text{True/False} \\ \text{BSP} \xrightarrow{\text{suitable adjoints} \;/\; \text{involution } \neg} \text{LFP-OA} \xrightarrow{\text{LT-PDR}} \text{True/False} \end{array}$$

The first case requires the existence of the *left adjoint* to the predicate transformer $\delta^*\dot{G}_S : \mathbb{E}_S \to \mathbb{E}_S$. Then we can translate BSP to the following LFP-OA problem. It directly asks whether all reachable states are safe.

**Proposition 4.2 (forward safety problem, FSP).** *In the setting of Definition 4.1, assume that each $\dot{G}_X : \mathbb{E}_X \to \mathbb{E}_{GX}$ preserves all meets. Then by* *letting $\dot{H}_S : \mathbb{E}_{GS} \to \mathbb{E}_S$ be the left adjoint of $\dot{G}_S$, the BSP* (2) *is equivalent to the LFP-OA problem for* $(\mathbb{E}_S, \iota \vee \dot{H}_S\delta_*, \alpha)$*:*

$$\mu x.\, \iota \vee \dot{H}_S \delta_* x \;\leq^?\; \alpha. \tag{3}$$

*This problem is called the* forward safety problem *for* $(\iota, \delta, \alpha)$ *in* $(p, G, \dot{G})$. □

The second case assumes that the complete lattice $\mathbb{E}_S$ of predicates admits an involution operator $\neg : \mathbb{E}_S \to \mathbb{E}_S^{\mathrm{op}}$ (cf. [22, Appendix B]).

**Proposition 4.3 (inverse backward safety problem, IBSP).** *In the setting of Definition 4.1, assume further that there is a monotone function $\neg : \mathbb{E}_S \to \mathbb{E}_S^{\mathrm{op}}$ satisfying $\neg \circ \neg = \mathrm{id}$. Then the backward safety problem* (2) *is equivalent to the LFP-OA problem for* $(\mathbb{E}_S, (\neg\alpha) \vee (\neg \circ \delta^* \dot{G} \circ \neg), \neg\iota)$*, that is,*

$$\mu x.\, (\neg\alpha) \vee (\neg \circ \delta^* \dot{G} \circ \neg x) \;\leq^?\; \neg\iota. \tag{4}$$

*We call* (4) *the* inverse backward safety problem *for* $(\iota, \delta, \alpha)$ *in* $(p, G, \dot{G})$*. Here* $(\neg\alpha) \vee (\neg \circ \delta^* \dot{G} \circ \neg(-))$ *is the* inverse backward predicate transformer. □

When both additional assumptions are fulfilled (in Proposition 4.2 and 4.3), we obtain two LT-PDR algorithms to solve BSP. One can even simultaneously run these two algorithms—this is done in fbPDR [25,26]. See also Sect. 5.1.

## 5 Known and New PDR Algorithms as Instances

We present several concrete instances of our LT-PDR algorithms. The one for Markov reward models is new (Sect. 5.3). We also sketch how those instances can be systematically derived by the theory in Sect. 4; details are in [22, Appendix D].

### 5.1 LT-PDRs for Kripke Structures: $\mathrm{PDR}^{\text{F-Kr}}$ and $\mathrm{PDR}^{\text{IB-Kr}}$

In most of the PDR literature, the target system is a Kripke structure that arises from a program's operational semantics. A *Kripke structure* consists of a set $S$ of states and a transition relation $\delta \subseteq S \times S$ (here we ignore initial states and atomic propositions). The basic problem formulation is as follows.

**Definition 5.1 (backward safety problem (BSP) for Kripke structures).** *The* BSP *for a Kripke structure* $(S, \delta)$*, a set* $\iota \in 2^S$ *of initial states, and a set* $\alpha \in 2^S$ *of safe states, is the GFP-UA problem* $\iota \leq^? \nu x.\, \alpha \wedge F'x$*, where* $F' : 2^S \to 2^S$ *is defined by* $F'(A) := \{s \mid \forall s'.\, ((s,s') \in \delta \Rightarrow s' \in A)\}$.

It is clear that the GFP in Definition 5.1 represents the set of states from which all reachable states are in $\alpha$. Therefore the BSP is the usual safety problem.

The above BSP is easily seen to be equivalent to the following problems.

**Proposition 5.2 (forward safety problem (FSP) for Kripke structures).** *The BSP in Definition 5.1 is equivalent to the LFP-OA problem* $\mu x.\, \iota \vee F''x \leq^? \alpha$*, where* $F'' : 2^S \to 2^S$ *is defined by* $F''(A) := \bigcup_{s \in A} \{s' \mid (s,s') \in \delta\}$. □

**Proposition 5.3 (inverse backward safety problem (IBSP) for Kripke structures).** *The BSP in Definition 5.1 is equivalent to the LFP-OA problem* $\mu x. \neg\alpha \vee \neg F'(\neg x) \leq^? \neg\iota$, *where* $\neg\colon 2^S \to 2^S$ *is the complement function* $A \mapsto S \setminus A$. □

**Instances of LT-PDR.** The FSP and IBSP (Propositions 5.2–5.3), being LFP-OA, are amenable to the LT-PDR algorithm (Definition 3.20). Thus we obtain two instances of LT-PDR; we call them ***PDR***$^{\textit{\textbf{F-Kr}}}$ and ***PDR***$^{\textit{\textbf{IB-Kr}}}$. **PDR**$^{\textbf{IB-Kr}}$ is a step-by-step dual to the application of LT-OpPDR to the BSP (Definition 5.1)—see Remark 3.24.

We compare these two instances of LT-PDR with algorithms in the literature. If we impose $|C_i| = 1$ on each element $C_i$ of Kleene sequences, the **PDR**$^{\textbf{F-Kr}}$ instance of LT-PDR coincides with the conventional IC3/PDR [9,13]. In contrast, **PDR**$^{\textbf{IB-Kr}}$ coincides with *Reverse PDR* in [25,26]. The parallel execution of **PDR**$^{\textbf{F-Kr}}$ and **PDR**$^{\textbf{IB-Kr}}$ roughly corresponds to fbPDR [25,26].

**Structural Derivation.** The equivalent problems (Propositions 5.2–5.3) are derived systematically from the categorical theory in Sect. 4.2. Indeed, using a lifting $\dot{\mathcal{P}}\colon 2^S \to 2^{\mathcal{P}S}$ such that $A \mapsto \{A' \mid A' \subseteq A\}$ (the *must modality* □), $F'$ in Definition 5.1 coincides with $\delta^*\dot{\mathcal{P}}$ in (2). The above $\dot{\mathcal{P}}$ preserves meets (cf. the modal axiom $\Box(\varphi \wedge \psi) \cong \Box\varphi \wedge \Box\psi$, see e.g. [7]); thus Proposition 4.2 derives the FSP. Finally, $\neg$ in Proposition 5.3 allows the use of Proposition 4.3. More details are in [22, Appendix D].

### 5.2 LT-PDR for MDPs: PDR$^{\textbf{IB-MDP}}$

The only known PDR-like algorithm for *quantitative* verification is *PrIC3* [6] for Markov decision processes s(MDPs). Here we instantiate LT-PDR for MDPs and compare it with PrIC3.

An *MDP* consists of a set $S$ of states, a set Act of actions and a transition function $\delta$ mapping $s \in S$ and $a \in \mathrm{Act}$ to either $*$ ("the action $a$ is unavailable at $s$") or a probability distribution $\delta(s)(a)$ over $S$.

**Definition 5.4 (IBSP for MDPs).** *The* inverse backward safety problem (IBSP) *for an MDP* $(S, \delta)$, *an initial state* $s_\iota \in S$, *a real number* $\lambda \in [0,1]$, *and a set* $\alpha \subseteq S$ *of safe states, is the LFP-OA problem* $\mu x. F'(x) \leq^? d_{\iota,\lambda}$. *Here* $d_{\iota,\lambda}\colon S \to [0,1]$ *is the predicate such that* $d_{\iota,\lambda}(s_\iota) = \lambda$ *and* $d_{\iota,\lambda}(s) = 1$ *otherwise.* $F'\colon [0,1]^S \to [0,1]^S$ *is defined by* $F'(d)(s) = 1$ *if* $s \notin \alpha$, *and* $F'(d)(s) = \max\{\sum_{s' \in S} d(s') \cdot \delta(s)(a)(s') \mid a \in \mathrm{Act}, \delta(s)(a) \neq *\}$ *if* $s \in \alpha$.

The function $F'$ in Definition 5.4 is a *Bellman operator* for MDPs—it takes the average of $d$ over $\delta(s)(a)$ and takes the maximum over $a$. Therefore the lfp in Definition 5.4 is the maximum reachability probability to $S \setminus \alpha$; the problem asks if it is $\leq \lambda$. In other words, it asks whether the *safety* probability—of staying in $\alpha$ henceforth, under any choices of actions—is $\geq 1 - \lambda$. This problem is the same as in [6].

**Instance of PDR.** The IBSP (Definition 5.4) is LFP-OA and thus amenable to LT-PDR. We call this instance $\boldsymbol{PDR^{IB\text{-}MDP}}$; See [22, Appendix E] for details.

$\mathbf{PDR^{IB\text{-}MDP}}$ shares many essences with PrIC3 [6]. It uses the operator $F'$ in Definition 5.4, which coincides with the one in [6, Def. 2]. PrIC3 maintains *frames*; they coincide with KT sequences in $\mathbf{PDR^{IB\text{-}MDP}}$.

Our Kleene sequences correspond to *obligations* in PrIC3, modulo the following difference. Kleene sequences aim at a negative witness (Sect. 3.2), but they happen to help the positive proof efforts too (Sect. 3.3); obligations in PrIC3 are solely for accelerating the positive proof efforts. Thus, if PrIC3 cannot solve these efforts, we need to check whether obligations yield a negative witness.

**Structural Derivation.** One can derive the IBSP (Definition 5.4) from the categorical theory in Sect. 4.2. Specifically, we first formulate the *BSP* $\neg d_\lambda \leq^? \nu x.\, d_\alpha \wedge \delta^* \dot{G} x$, where $\dot{G}$ is a suitable lifting (of $G$ for MDPs, Table 1) that combines average and minimum, $\neg\colon [0,1]^S \to [0,1]^S$ is defined by $(\neg d)(s) := 1 - d(s)$, and $d_\alpha$ is such that $d_\alpha(s) = 1$ if $s \in \alpha$ and $d_\alpha(s) = 0$ otherwise. Using $\neg\colon [0,1]^S \to [0,1]^S$ in the above as an involution, we apply Proposition 4.3 and obtain the IBSP (Definition 5.4).

Another benefit of the categorical theory is that it can tell us a forward instance of LT-PDR (much like $\mathbf{PDR^{F\text{-}Kr}}$ in Sect. 5.1) is unlikely for MDPs. Indeed, we showed in Proposition 4.2 that $\dot{G}$'s preservation of meets is essential (existence of a left adjoint is equivalent to meet preservation). We can easily show that our $\dot{G}$ for MDPs does not preserve meets. See [22, Appendix G].

### 5.3 LT-PDR for Markov Reward Models: $\mathbf{PDR^{MRM}}$

We present a PDR-like algorithm for *Markov reward models (MRMs)*, which seems to be new, as an instance of LT-PDR. An MRM consists of a set $S$ of states and a transition function $\delta$ that maps $s \in S$ (the current state) and $c \in \mathbb{N}$ (the reward) to a function $\delta(s)(c) : S \to [0,1]$; the last represents the probability distribution of next states.

We solve the following problem. We use $[0,\infty]$-valued predicates—representing accumulated rewards—where $[0,\infty]$ is the set of extended nonnegative reals.

**Definition 5.5 (SP for MRMs).** *The* safety problem (SP) *for an MRM* $(S,\delta)$, *an initial state* $s_\iota \in S$, $\lambda \in [0,\infty]$, *and a set* $\alpha \subseteq S$ *of safe states is* $\mu x.\, F'(x) \leq^? d_{\iota,\lambda}$. *Here* $d_{\iota,\lambda}\colon S \to [0,\infty]$ *maps* $s_\iota$ *to* $\lambda$ *and others to* $\infty$, *and* $F'\colon [0,\infty]^S \to [0,\infty]^S$ *is defined by* $F'(d)(s) = 0$ *if* $s \notin \alpha$, *and* $F'(d)(s) = \sum_{s' \in S, c \in \mathbb{N}} (c + d(s')) \cdot \delta(s)(c)(s')$ *if* $s \in \alpha$.

The function $F'$ accumulates expected reward in $\alpha$. Thus the problem asks if the expected accumulated reward, starting from $s_\iota$ and until leaving $\alpha$, is $\leq \lambda$.

**Instance of PDR.** The SP (Definition 5.5) is LFP-OA thus amenable to LT-PDR. We call this instance $\boldsymbol{PDR^{MRM}}$. It seems new. See [22, Appendix F] for details.

**Structural Derivation.** The function $F'$ in Definition 5.5 can be expressed categorically as $F'(x) = d_\alpha \wedge \delta^* \dot{G}(x)$, where $d_\alpha \colon S \to [0, \infty]$ carries $s \in \alpha$ to $\infty$ and $s \notin \alpha$ to 0, and $\dot{G}$ is a suitable lifting that accumulates expected reward. However, the SP (Definition 5.5) is *not* an instance of the three general safety problems in Sect. 4.2. Consequently, we expect that other instances of LT-PDR than $\mathbf{PDR}^{\mathbf{MRM}}$ (such as $\mathbf{PDR}^{\mathbf{F\text{-}Kr}}$ and $\mathbf{PDR}^{\mathbf{IB\text{-}Kr}}$ in Sect. 5.1) are hard for MRMs.

## 6 Implementation and Evaluation

**Implementation.** `LTPDR` We implemented LT-PDR in Haskell. Exploiting Haskell's language features, it is succinct (~50 lines) and almost a literal translation of Algorithm 3 to Haskell. Its main part is presented in [22, Appendix K]. In particular, using suitable type classes, the code is as abstract and generic as Algorithm 3.

Specifically, our implementation is a Haskell module named `LTPDR`. It has two interfaces, namely the type class `CLat` $\tau$ (the lattice of predicates) and the type `Heuristics` $\tau$ (the definitions of **Candidate**, **Decide**, and **Conflict**). The main function for LT-PDR is `ltPDR` :: `CLat` $\tau \Rightarrow$ `Heuristics` $\tau \to (\tau \to \tau) \to \tau \to$ `IO` (`PDRAnswer` $\tau$) , where the second argument is for a monotone function $F$ of type $\tau \to \tau$ and the last is for the safety predicate $\alpha$.

Obtaining concrete instances is easy by fixing $\tau$ and `Heuristics` $\tau$ . A simple implementation of $\mathbf{PDR}^{\mathbf{F\text{-}Kr}}$ takes 15 lines; a more serious SAT-based one for $\mathbf{PDR}^{\mathbf{F\text{-}Kr}}$ takes ~130 lines; $\mathbf{PDR}^{\mathbf{IB\text{-}MDP}}$ and $\mathbf{PDR}^{\mathbf{MRM}}$ take ~80 lines each.

**Heuristics.** We briefly discuss the heuristics, i.e. how to choose $x \in L$ in **Candidate**, **Decide**, and **Conflict**, used in our experiments. The heuristics of $\mathbf{PDR}^{\mathbf{F\text{-}Kr}}$ is based on the conventional PDR [9]. The heuristics of $\mathbf{PDR}^{\mathbf{IB\text{-}MDP}}$ is based on the idea of representing the smallest possible $x$ greater than some real number $v \in [0,1]$ (e.g. $x$ taken in **Candidate**) as $x = v + \epsilon$, where $\epsilon$ is a symbolic variable. This implies that **Unfold** (or **Valid**, **Model**) is always applied in finite steps, which further guarantees finite-step termination for invalid cases and $\omega$-step termination for valid cases (see [22, Appendix H] for more detail). The heuristics of $\mathbf{PDR}^{\mathbf{MRM}}$ is similar to that of $\mathbf{PDR}^{\mathbf{IB\text{-}MDP}}$.

**Experiment Setting.** We experimentally assessed the performance of instances of `LTPDR`. The settings are as follows: 1.2 GHz Quad-Core Intel Core i7 with 10 GB memory using Docker, for $\mathbf{PDR}^{\mathbf{IB\text{-}MDP}}$; Apple M1 Chip with 16 GB memory for the other. The different setting is because we needed Docker to run PrIC3 [6].

**Experiments with $\mathbf{PDR}^{\mathbf{MRM}}$.** Table 2a shows the results. We observe that $\mathbf{PDR}^{\mathbf{MRM}}$ answered correctly, and that the execution time is reasonable. Further performance analysis (e.g. comparison with [19]) and improvement is future work; the point here, nevertheless, is the fact that we obtained a reasonable MRM model checker by adding ~80 lines to the generic solver `LTPDR`.

**Experiments with $\mathbf{PDR^{IB\text{-}MDP}}$.** Table 2c shows the results. Both PrIC3 and our $\mathbf{PDR^{IB\text{-}MDP}}$ solve a linear programming (LP) problem in **Decide**. PrIC3 uses Z3 for this; $\mathbf{PDR^{IB\text{-}MDP}}$ uses GLPK. PrIC3 represents an MDP symbolically, while $\mathbf{PDR^{IB\text{-}MDP}}$ do so concretely. Symbolic representation in $\mathbf{PDR^{IB\text{-}MDP}}$ is possible—it is future work. PrIC3 can use four different *interpolation generalization* methods, leading to different performance (Table 2c).

We observe that $\mathbf{PDR^{IB\text{-}MDP}}$ outperforms PrIC3 for some benchmarks with smaller state spaces. We believe that the failure of $\mathbf{PDR^{IB\text{-}MDP}}$ in many instances can be attributed to our current choice of a generalization method (it is the closest to the linear one for PrIC3). Table 2c suggests that use of *polynomial* or *hybrid* can enhance the performance.

**Experiments with $\mathbf{PDR^{F\text{-}Kr}}$.** Table 2b shows the results. The benchmarks are mostly from the HWMCC'15 competition [1], except for `latch0.smv`[1] and `counter.smv` (our own).

IC3ref vastly outperforms $\mathbf{PDR^{F\text{-}Kr}}$ in many instances. This is hardly a surprise—IC3ref was developed towards superior performance, while $\mathbf{PDR^{F\text{-}Kr}}$'s emphasis is on its theoretical simplicity and genericity. We nevertheless see that $\mathbf{PDR^{F\text{-}Kr}}$ solves some benchmarks of substantial size, such as `power2bit8.smv`. This demonstrates the practical potential of LT-PDR, especially in view of the following improvement opportunities (we will pursue them as future work): 1) use of well-developed SAT solvers (we currently use `toysolver`[2] for its good interface but we could use Z3); 2) allowing $|C_i| > 1$, a technique discussed in Sect. 5.1 and implemented in IC3ref but not in $\mathbf{PDR^{F\text{-}Kr}}$; and 3) other small improvements, e.g. in our CNF-based handling of propositional formulas.

**Ablation Study.** To assess the value of the key concept of PDR (namely the *positive-negative interplay* between the Knaster–Tarski and Kleene theorems (Sect. 3.3)), we compared $\mathbf{PDR^{F\text{-}Kr}}$ with the instances of positive and negative LT-PDR (Sects. 3.1–3.2) for Kripke structures.

Table 2d shows the results. Note that the value of the positive-negative interplay is already theoretically established; see e.g. Proposition 3.17 (the interplay detects executions that lead to nowhere). This value was also experimentally witnessed: see `power2bit8.smv` and `simpleTrans.smv`, where the one-sided methods made wrong choices and timed out. One-sided methods can be efficient when they get lucky (e.g. in `counter.smv`). LT-PDR may be slower because of the overhead of running two sides, but that is a trade-off for the increased chance of termination.

**Discussion.** We observe that all of the studied instances exhibited at least reasonable performance. We note again that detailed performance analysis and improvement is out of our current scope. Being able to derive these model checkers, with such a small effort as ~100 lines of Haskell code each, demonstrates the value of our abstract theory and its generic Haskell implementation `LTPDR`.

[1] https://github.com/arminbiere/aiger.

[2] https://github.com/msakai/toysolver.

**Table 2.** experimental results for our $\mathbf{PDR^{F\text{-}Kr}}$, $\mathbf{PDR^{IB\text{-}MDP}}$, and $\mathbf{PDR^{MRM}}$

(a) Results with $\mathbf{PDR^{MRM}}$. The MRM is from [4, Example 10.72], whose ground truth expected reward is $\frac{4}{3}$. The benchmarks ask if the expected reward (not known to the solver) is $\leq 1.5$ or $\leq 1.3$.

| Benchmark | Result | Time |
|---|---|---|
| $\text{DieByCoin}^{\leq ? 1.5}$ | True | 6.01 ms |
| $\text{DieByCoin}^{\leq ? 1.3}$ | False | 43.1 µs |

(b) Results with $\mathbf{PDR^{F\text{-}Kr}}$ in comparison with IC3ref, a reference implementation of [9] (https://github.com/arbrad/IC3ref). Both solvers answered correctly. Timeout (TO) is 600 sec.

| Benchmark | $\lvert S\rvert$ | Result | $\mathbf{PDR^{F\text{-}Kr}}$ | IC3ref |
|---|---|---|---|---|
| latch0.smv | $2^3$ | True | 317 µs | 270 µs |
| counter.smv | $2^5$ | False | 1.620 s | 3.27 ms |
| power2bit8.smv | $2^{15}$ | True | 1.516 s | 4.13 ms |
| ndista128.smv | $2^{17}$ | True | TO | 73.1 ms |
| shift1add256.smv | $2^{21}$ | True | TO | 174 ms |

(c) Results with $\mathbf{PDR^{IB\text{-}MDP}}$ (an excerpt of [22, Table 3]). Comparison is against PrIC3 [6] with four different interpolation generalization methods (none, linear, polynomial, hybrid). The benchmarks are from [6]. $|S|$ is the number of states of the benchmark MDP. "GT pr." is for the *ground truth probability*, that is the reachability probability $Pr^{max}(s_\iota \models \diamond(S \setminus \alpha))$ computed outside the solvers under experiments. The solvers were asked whether the GT pr. (which they do not know) is $\leq \lambda$ or not; they all answered correctly. The last five columns show the average execution time in seconds. – is for "did not finish," for out of memory or timeout (600 sec.)

| Benchmark | $\lvert S\rvert$ | GT pr. | $\lambda$ | $\mathbf{PDR^{IB\text{-}MDP}}$ | PrIC3 | | | |
|---|---|---|---|---|---|---|---|---|
| | | | | | none | lin. | pol. | hyb. |
| Grid | $10^2$ | $1.2E^{-3}$ | 0.3 | 0.31 | 1.31 | 19.34 | – | – |
| | | | 0.2 | 0.48 | 1.75 | 24.62 | – | – |
| Grid | $10^3$ | $4.4E^{-10}$ | 0.3 | 122.29 | – | – | – | – |
| | | | 0.2 | 136.46 | – | – | – | – |
| BRP | $10^3$ | 0.035 | 0.1 | – | – | – | – | – |
| | | | 0.01 | 18.52 | 56.55 | 594.89 | – | 722.38 |
| | | | 0.005 | 1.36 | 11.68 | 238.09 | – | – |
| ZeroConf | $10^4$ | 0.5 | 0.9 | – | – | – | 0.58 | 0.51 |
| | | | 0.75 | – | – | – | 0.55 | 0.46 |
| | | | 0.52 | – | – | – | 0.48 | 0.46 |
| | | | 0.45 | $<0.1$ | $<0.1$ | $<0.1$ | $<0.1$ | $<0.1$ |
| Chain | $10^3$ | 0.394 | 0.9 | – | 72.37 | – | 0.91 | 0.70 |
| | | | 0.4 | – | 80.83 | – | 0.93 | – |
| | | | 0.35 | 177.12 | 115.98 | – | – | – |
| | | | 0.3 | 88.27 | 66.89 | 557.68 | – | – |
| DoubleChain | $10^3$ | 0.215 | 0.9 | – | – | – | 1.83 | 1.99 |
| | | | 0.3 | – | – | – | 1.88 | 1.96 |
| | | | 0.216 | – | – | – | 139.76 | – |
| | | | 0.15 | 7.46 | – | – | – | – |

(d) Ablation experiments: LT-PDR ($\mathbf{PDR^{F\text{-}Kr}}$) vs. positive and negative LT-PDRs, implemented for the FSP for Kripke structures. The benchmarks are as in Table 2b, except for a new micro benchmark `simpleTrans.smv`. Timeout (TO) is 600 sec.

| Benchmark | Result | LT-PDR | positive | negative |
|---|---|---|---|---|
| latch0.smv | True | 317 µs | 1.68 ms | TO |
| power2bit8.smv | True | 1.516 s | TO | TO |
| counter.smv | False | 1.620 s | TO | 2.88 µs |
| simpleTrans.smv | False | 295 µs | TO | TO |

## 7 Conclusions and Future Work

We have presented a lattice-theoretic generalization of the PDR algorithm called LT-PDR. This involves the decomposition of the PDR algorithm into positive and negative ones, which are tightly connected to the Knaster–Tarski and Kleene fixed point theorems, respectively. We then combined it with the coalgebraic and fibrational theory for modeling transition systems with predicates. We instantiated it with several transition systems, deriving existing PDR algorithms as well as a new one over Markov reward models. We leave instantiating our LT-PDR and categorical safety problems to derive other PDR-like algorithms, such as PDR for hybrid systems [29], for future work.

We will also work on the combination of our work and the theory of *abstract interpretation* [10,12]. Our current framework axiomatizes what is needed of heuristics, but it does not tell how to realize such heuristics (that differ a lot in different concrete settings). We expect abstract interpretation to provide some general recipes for realizing such heuristics.

## References

1. The 8th competitive event for hardware model checkers (HWMCC 2015) (2015). http://fmv.jku.at/hwmcc15/
2. Aguirre, A., Katsumata, S.: Weakest preconditions in fibrations. Electronic Notes in Theoretical Comput. Sci. **352**, 5–27 (2020). http://www.sciencedirect.com/science/article/pii/S1571066120300487, the 36th Mathematical Foundations of Programming Semantics Conference (2020)
3. Awodey, S.: Category Theory. Oxford Logic Guides. Oxford Univ. Press, Oxford (2006)
4. Baier, C., Katoen, J.: Principles of Model Checking. MIT Press, Cambridge (2008)
5. Baranga, A.: The contraction principle as a particular case of Kleene's fixed point theorem. Discret. Math. **98**(1), 75–79 (1991)
6. Batz, K., Junges, S., Kaminski, B.L., Katoen, J.-P., Matheja, C., Schröer, P.: PrIC3: property directed reachability for MDPs. In: Lahiri, S.K., Wang, C. (eds.) CAV 2020. LNCS, vol. 12225, pp. 512–538. Springer, Cham (2020). https://doi.org/10.1007/978-3-030-53291-8_27
7. Blackburn, P., de Rijke, M., Venema, Y.: Modal Logic. In: Tracts in Theoretical Computer Science No. 53 (2001)
8. Bonchi, F., König, B., Petrisan, D.: Up-to techniques for behavioural metrics via fibrations. In: Schewe, S., Zhang, L. (eds.) 29th International Conference on Concurrency Theory, CONCUR 2018. LIPIcs, vol. 118, pp. 17:1–17:17. Schloss Dagstuhl - Leibniz-Zentrum für Informatik (2018). https://doi.org/10.4230/LIPIcs.CONCUR.2018.17
9. Bradley, A.R.: SAT-based model checking without unrolling. In: Jhala, R., Schmidt, D. (eds.) VMCAI 2011. LNCS, vol. 6538, pp. 70–87. Springer, Heidelberg (2011). https://doi.org/10.1007/978-3-642-18275-4_7
10. Cousot, P., Cousot, R.: Abstract interpretation: a unified lattice model for static analysis of programs by construction or approximation of fixpoints. In: Graham, R.M., Harrison, M.A., Sethi, R. (eds.) Conference Record of the Fourth ACM Symposium on Principles of Programming Languages, pp. 238–252. ACM (1977). https://doi.org/10.1145/512950.512973

11. Cousot, P., Cousot, R.: Constructive versions of Tarski's fixed point theorems. Pacific J. Math. **82**(1), 43–57 (1979). https://doi.org/10.2140/pjm.1979.82.43
12. Cousot, P., Cousot, R.: Systematic design of program analysis frameworks. In: Aho, A.V., Zilles, S.N., Rosen, B.K. (eds.) Conference Record of the Sixth Annual ACM Symposium on Principles of Programming Languages, pp. 269–282. ACM Press (1979). https://doi.org/10.1145/567752.567778
13. Eén, N., Mishchenko, A., Brayton, R.K.: Efficient implementation of property directed reachability. In: Bjesse, P., Slobodová, A. (eds.) International Conference on Formal Methods in Computer-Aided Design, FMCAD 2011, pp. 125–134. FMCAD Inc. (2011). http://dl.acm.org/citation.cfm?id=2157675
14. Gurfinkel, A.: IC3, PDR, and friends (2015). https://arieg.bitbucket.io/pdf/gurfinkel_ssft15.pdf
15. Hermida, C., Jacobs, B.: Structural induction and coinduction in a fibrational setting. Inf. Comput. **145**(2), 107–152 (1998). https://doi.org/10.1006/inco.1998.2725
16. Hoder, K., Bjørner, N.: Generalized property directed reachability. In: Cimatti, A., Sebastiani, R. (eds.) SAT 2012. LNCS, vol. 7317, pp. 157–171. Springer, Heidelberg (2012). https://doi.org/10.1007/978-3-642-31612-8_13
17. Jacobs, B.: Introduction to Coalgebra: Towards Mathematics of States and Observation, Cambridge Tracts in Theoretical Computer Science, vol. 59. Cambridge University Press (2016). https://doi.org/10.1017/CBO9781316823187
18. Jacobs, B.P.: Categorical Logic and Type Theory, Studies in logic and the foundations of mathematics, vol. 141. North-Holland (2001). http://www.elsevierdirect.com/product.jsp?isbn=9780444508539
19. Katoen, J., Khattri, M., Zapreev, I.S.: A Markov reward model checker. In: Second International Conference on the Quantitative Evaluaiton of Systems (QEST 2005), pp. 243–244. IEEE Computer Society (2005). https://doi.org/10.1109/QEST.2005.2
20. Komorida, Y., Katsumata, S., Hu, N., Klin, B., Hasuo, I.: Codensity games for bisimilarity. In: 34th Annual ACM/IEEE Symposium on Logic in Computer Science, LICS 2019, Vancouver, BC, Canada, June 24–27, 2019, pp. 1–13. IEEE (2019). https://doi.org/10.1109/LICS.2019.8785691
21. Kori, M., Hasuo, I., Katsumata, S.: Fibrational initial algebra-final coalgebra coincidence over initial algebras: turning verification witnesses upside down. In: Haddad, S., Varacca, D. (eds.) 32nd International Conference on Concurrency Theory, CONCUR 2021. LIPIcs, vol. 203, pp. 21:1–21:22. Schloss Dagstuhl - Leibniz-Zentrum für Informatik (2021). https://doi.org/10.4230/LIPIcs.CONCUR.2021.21
22. Kori, M., Urabe, N., Katsumata, S.Y., Suenaga, K., Hasuo, I.: The lattice-theoretic essence of propertydirected reachability analysis (2022). https://arxiv.org/abs/2203.14261, a longer version
23. Mac Lane, S.: Categories for the Working Mathematician, 2nd edn. Springer, Heidelberg (1998). https://doi.org/10.1007/978-1-4612-9839-7
24. Rinetzky, N., Shoham, S.: Property directed abstract interpretation. In: Jobstmann, B., Leino, K.R.M. (eds.) VMCAI 2016. LNCS, vol. 9583, pp. 104–123. Springer, Heidelberg (2016). https://doi.org/10.1007/978-3-662-49122-5_5
25. Seufert, T., Scholl, C.: Combining PDR and reverse PDR for hardware model checking. In: Madsen, J., Coskun, A.K. (eds.) 2018 Design, Automation & Test in Europe Conference & Exhibition. DATE 2018, pp. 49–54. IEEE (2018). https://doi.org/10.23919/DATE.2018.8341978

26. Seufert, T., Scholl, C.: fbPDR: In-depth combination of forward and backward analysis in property directed reachability. In: Teich, J., Fummi, F. (eds.) Design, Automation & Test in Europe Conference & Exhibition, DATE 2019. pp. 456–461. IEEE (2019). https://doi.org/10.23919/DATE.2019.8714819
27. Sokolova, A.: Probabilistic systems coalgebraically: a survey. Theor. Comput. Sci. **412**(38), 5095–5110 (2011). https://doi.org/10.1016/j.tcs.2011.05.008
28. Sprunger, D., Katsumata, S., Dubut, J., Hasuo, I.: Fibrational bisimulations and quantitative reasoning. In: Cîrstea, C. (ed.) CMCS 2018. LNCS, vol. 11202, pp. 190–213. Springer, Cham (2018). https://doi.org/10.1007/978-3-030-00389-0_11
29. Suenaga, K., Ishizawa, T.: Generalized property-directed reachability for hybrid systems. In: Beyer, D., Zufferey, D. (eds.) VMCAI 2020. LNCS, vol. 11990, pp. 293–313. Springer, Cham (2020). https://doi.org/10.1007/978-3-030-39322-9_14
30. Tarski, A.: A lattice-theoretical fixpoint theorem and its applications. Pacific J. Math. **5**(2), 285–309 (1955)

# Affine Loop Invariant Generation via Matrix Algebra

Yucheng Ji[1,2], Hongfei Fu[2(✉)], Bin Fang[1], and Haibo Chen[1,2]

[1] OS Kernel Lab, Huawei Technologies, Shanghai, China
{jiyucheng,fangbin11,hb.chen}@huawei.com

[2] Shanghai Jiao Tong University, Shanghai, China
fuhf@cs.sjtu.edu.cn

**Abstract.** Loop invariant generation, which automates the generation of assertions that always hold at the entry of a while loop, has many important applications in program analysis and formal verification. In this work, we target an important category of while loops, namely affine while loops, that are unnested while loops with affine loop guards and variable updates. Such a class of loops widely exists in many programs yet still lacks a general but efficient approach to invariant generation. We propose a novel matrix-algebra approach to automatically synthesizing affine inductive invariants in the form of an affine inequality. The main novelty of our approach is that (i) the approach is general in the sense that it theoretically addresses all the cases of affine invariant generation over an affine while loop, and (ii) it can be efficiently automated through matrix-algebra (such as eigenvalue, matrix inverse) methods.

The details of our approach are as follows. First, for the case where the loop guard is a tautology (i.e., '**true**'), we show that the eigenvalues and their eigenvectors of the matrices derived from the variable updates of the loop body encompass all meaningful affine inductive invariants. Second, for the more general case where the loop guard is a conjunction of affine inequalities, our approach completely addresses the invariant-generation problem by first establishing through matrix inverse the relationship between the invariants and a key parameter in the application of Farkas' lemma, then solving the feasible domain of the key parameter from the inductive conditions, and finally illustrating that a finite number of values suffices for the key parameter w.r.t a tightness condition for the invariants to be generated.

Experimental results show that compared with previous approaches, our approach generates much more accurate affine inductive invariants over affine while loops from existing and new benchmarks within a few seconds, demonstrating the generality and efficiency of our approach.

## 1 Introduction

An *invariant* is a logical assertion at a certain program location that always holds whenever the program executes across that location. Invariants are indispensable parts of program analysis and formal verification, and thus the generation of


S. Shoham and Y. Vizel (Eds.): CAV 2022, LNCS 13371, pp. 257–281, 2022.
https://doi.org/10.1007/978-3-031-13185-1_13

invariants has been key to the proof and analysis of crucial properties like reachability [3,6,15], time complexity [9] and safety [2,32]. To ease program analysis and formal verification, there has been a long thread of research on approaches to automatic generation of invariants, including constraint solving [10,12,27], recurrence analysis [17,24,29,31], abstract interpretation [13,14], logical inference [18,19,38], dynamic analysis [33,39], and machine learning [20,23,44]. To guarantee that an assertion is indeed an invariant, the widely-adopted paradigm is to generate an *inductive invariant* that holds for the first execution and for every periodic execution to the particular program location [12,32]. In this work, we consider an important subclass of invariants called *numerical invariants* which are assertions over the numerical values taken by the program variables, and are closely related to many common vulnerabilities like integer overflow, buffer overflow, division by zero and array out-of-bound. More specifically, we consider *affine* inductive invariants in the form of an affine inequality over program variables, and focus on affine while loops that have affine loop guards (as a conjunction of affine inequalities) and affine updates for the program variables but do not have nested loops.

To automate the generation of affine inductive invariants, we adopt the *constraint-solving* based approach with three steps. First, it establishes a template with unknown parameters for the target invariants. Second, it collects constraints derived from the inductive conditions. Finally, it solves the unknown parameters to get the desired invariants. Prior work in this space [12,37] leverages Farkas' lemma to provide a sound and complete characterization for the inductive conditions and then generates the affine inductive invariants either by the complete approach of quantifier elimination [12] or through several heuristics [37]. Specifically, the StInG invariant generator [40] implements the approach in [37], and the InvGen invariant generator [22] integrates abstract interpretation as well as the approach in [37]. Furthermore, a recent effort [34] leverages eigenvalues and eigenvectors for inferring a restricted class of invariants. Finally, some recent work considers decidable logic fragments that directly verify properties of loops [4,11,28,30]. Compared with other approaches such as machine learning and dynamic analysis, constraint solving has a theoretical guarantee on the correctness and accuracy of the generated invariants, yet typically at the cost of higher runtime complexity.

The novelty of our approach lies in that it completely addresses the constraints derived from Farkas' lemma by matrix methods, thus ensuring both generality and efficiency. In detail, this paper makes the following contributions (due to the page limit, the current paper is abridged. The full version is available at [25]):

- For affine while loops with tautological guard, we prove that the affine inductive invariants are determined by the eigenvalues and eigenvectors of the matrices that describe variable updates in the loop body.
- For affine while loops whose loop guard is a conjunction of affine inequalities, we solve the affine inductive invariants by first deriving through matrix inverse a formula with a key parameter in the application of Farkas' lemma,

then solving the feasible domain of the key parameter from the inductive conditions, and finally showing that it suffices to choose a finite number of values for the key parameter if one imposes a tightness condition on the invariants.
- We generalize our results to affine while loops with non-deterministic updates and to bidirectional affine invariants. A continuity property on the invariants w.r.t. the key parameter is also proved for tackling the numerical issue arising from the computation of eigenvectors. Experimental results on existing benchmarks and new benchmarks arising from linear dynamical systems demonstrate the generality and efficiency of our approach.

### 1.1 Related Work

***Constraint Solving.*** There have been several prior approaches [12,37] using constraint solving for invariant generation based on Farkas' lemma. Compared to the approach in [12] that uses quantifier elimination to solve the constraints from Farkas' lemma, our approach is more efficient since it only involves the matrix computation. Compared with [37] that uses several heuristics, our approach is more general and complete in addressing all the cases in affine invariant generation. While the approach in [34] also uses eigenvectors, it is restricted to the subclass of equality and convergent invariants. In contrast, our approach targets at general affine inductive invariants over affine while loops. Other prior work [4,11,28,30] considers to have a decidable logic for unnested affine while loops with tautological guard but no conditional branches. Compared with them, our approach handles general affine while loops and targets at invariant generation.

***Abstract Interpretation.*** A long thread of research to infer inductive invariants is using *abstract interpretation* [1,7,22,35] framework which constructs sound approximations for program semantics. In a nutshell, it first establishes an abstract domain for the specific form of properties to be generated, and then performs fixed-point computation in the abstract domain. Abstract interpretation generates invariants whose precision depends on the abstract domain and abstract operators, except for rare special cases [21,37].

***Recurrence Analysis.*** Another closely-related technique is *recurrence analysis* [8,17,24,29,31]. The main idea is transforming the problem of invariant generation into a recurrence relation problem and then solve the latter one. The main limitation of recurrence analysis is that it requires the underlying recurrence relation to have a closed-form solution. This requirement, unfortunately, does not hold for the general case of affine inductive invariants over affine while loops.

***Logical Inference.*** Invariants could also be obtained through *logical inference*, such as abductive inference [16], Craig interpolation [18], ICE learning [19,43], random search [38], etc. These approaches, however, cannot provide any theoretical guarantee on the accuracy of the generated numerical invariants. In contrast, our approach essentially addresses this issue.

***Dynamic Analysis.*** *Dynamic analysis* [33,39] has also been exploited to invariant generation. The major process is first to collect the execution traces of a particular program by running it multiple times, and then guess the invariants based on these traces. As indicated in its process, dynamic analysis provides no guarantee on the correctness or accuracy of the inferred invariants, yet still pays the price of running the program at a large amount of time.

***Machine Learning.*** There is a recent trend of applying *machine learning* [20,23,44] to solve the invariant-generation problem. Such approaches first establish a (typically large) training set of data, then use training approaches such as neural networks to generate invariants. Compared to our approach, those approaches require a large training set, while still having no theoretical guarantee on the correctness or accuracy. Specifically, such approaches cannot produce specific numerical values (e.g., eigenvalues) that are required to handle some examples in this work.

## 2 Preliminaries

In this section, we specify the class of affine while loops and define the affine-invariant-generation problem over such loops. Throughout the paper, we use $V = \{x_1, ..., x_n\}$ to denote the set of program variables in an affine while loop; we abuse the notation $V$ so that it also represents the current values (before the execution of the loop body) of the original variables in $V$, and use the primed variables $V' := \{x' \mid x \in V\}$ for the next values (after the execution of the loop body). Furthermore, we denote by $\mathbf{x} = [x_1, ..., x_n]^{\mathrm{T}}$ the vector variable that represents the current values of the program variables, and by $\mathbf{x}' = [x'_1, ..., x'_n]^{\mathrm{T}}$ the vector variable for the next values.

An *affine while loop* is a while loop without nested loops that has affine updates in each assignment statement and possibly multiple conditional branches in the loop body. To formally specify the syntax of it, we first define affine inequalities and assertions, program states and satisfaction relation between them as follows.

***Affine Inequalities and Assertions.*** An *affine inequality* $\phi$ is an inequality of the form $\mathbf{c}^{\mathrm{T}} \cdot \mathbf{y} + d \leq 0$ where $\mathbf{c}$ is a real vector, $\mathbf{y}$ is a vector of real-valued variables and $d$ is a real scalar. An *affine assertion* is a finite conjunction of affine inequalities. An affine assertion is *satisfiable* if it is true under some assignment of real values to its variables. Given an affine assertion $\psi$ over vector variable $\mathbf{x}$, we denote by $\psi'$ the affine assertion obtained by substituting $\mathbf{x}$ in $\psi$ with its next-value variable $\mathbf{x}'$.

***Program States.*** A *program state* $\mathbf{v}$ is a real vector $\mathbf{v} = [v_1, ..., v_n]^{\mathrm{T}}$ such that each $v_i$ is a concrete value for the variable $x_i$ (in the vector variable $\mathbf{x}$). We say that a program state $\mathbf{v}$ satisfies an affine inequality $\phi = \mathbf{c}^{\mathrm{T}} \cdot \mathbf{x} + d \leq 0$, written as $\mathbf{v} \models \phi$, if it holds that $\mathbf{c}^{\mathrm{T}} \cdot \mathbf{v} + d \leq 0$. Likewise, $\mathbf{v}$ satisfies an affine assertion $\psi$ if it satisfies every conjunctive affine inequality in $\psi$. Furthermore, given an affine assertion $\psi$ with both $\mathbf{x}$ and $\mathbf{x}'$, we say that two program states $\mathbf{v}, \mathbf{v}'$ satisfy $\psi$, written as $\mathbf{v}, \mathbf{v}' \models \psi$, if $\psi$ is true when one substitutes $\mathbf{x}$ by $\mathbf{v}$ and $\mathbf{x}'$ by $\mathbf{v}'$.

We then illustrate the syntax of (unnested) affine while loops as follows.

***Affine While Loops.*** We consider affine while loops that take the form:

$$\begin{array}{l} \textbf{initial condition } \theta : \mathbf{R} \cdot \mathbf{x} + \mathbf{f} \le \mathbf{0} \\ \textbf{while } G : \mathbf{P} \cdot \mathbf{x} + \mathbf{q} \le \mathbf{0} \textbf{ do} \\ \quad \textbf{case } \psi_1 : \mathbf{T}_1 \cdot \mathbf{x} - \mathbf{T}'_1 \cdot \mathbf{x}' + \mathbf{b}_1 \le \mathbf{0} \;\; (\tau_1); \\ \qquad \vdots \\ \quad \textbf{case } \psi_k : \mathbf{T}_k \cdot \mathbf{x} - \mathbf{T}'_k \cdot \mathbf{x}' + \mathbf{b}_k \le \mathbf{0} \;\; (\tau_k); \\ \textbf{end} \end{array} \qquad (\dagger)$$

where (i) $\theta$ is an affine assertion that specifies the initial condition for inputs and is given by the real matrix $\mathbf{R}$ and vector $\mathbf{f}$, (ii) $G$ is an affine assertion serving as the loop guard given by the real matrix $\mathbf{P}$ and vector $\mathbf{q}$, and (iii) each $\psi_j$ is an affine assertion that represents a conditional branch, with the relationship between the current-state vector $\mathbf{x}$ and the next-state vector $\mathbf{x}'$ given by the affine assertion $\tau_j := \mathbf{T}_j \cdot \mathbf{x} - \mathbf{T}'_j \cdot \mathbf{x}' + \mathbf{b}_j \le \mathbf{0}$ with transition matrices $\mathbf{T}_j, \mathbf{T}'_j$ and vector $\mathbf{b}_j$. In this work, we always assume that the rows of $\mathbf{R}$ are linearly independent (this condition means that every variable $x_i$ has one independent initial condition attached to it, which holds in most situations such as a fixed initial program state), such that $\mathbf{R}^{\mathrm{T}}$ is left invertible; we denote its left inverse as $(\mathbf{R}^{\mathrm{T}})^{-1}_{\mathrm{L}}$.

The execution of an affine while loop is as follows. First, the loop starts with an arbitrary initial program state $\mathbf{v}^*$ that satisfies the initial condition $\theta$. Then in each loop iteration, the current program state $\mathbf{v}$ is checked against the loop guard $G$. In the case that $\mathbf{v} \models G$, the loop arbitrarily chooses a conditional branch $\psi_j$ satisfying $\mathbf{v} \models \psi_j$, and sets the next program state $\mathbf{v}'$ non-deterministically such that $\mathbf{v}, \mathbf{v}' \models \tau_j$; the next program state $\mathbf{v}'$ is then set as the current program state. Otherwise (i.e., $\mathbf{v} \not\models G$), the loop halts immediately.

Now we define affine inductive invariants over affine while loops. Informally, an affine inductive invariant is an affine inequality satisfying the initiation and consecution conditions which mean that the inequality holds at the start of the loop (initiation) and is preserved under every iteration of the loop body (consecution).

***Affine Inductive Invariants.*** An *affine inductive invariant* for an affine while loop (†) is an affine inequality $\Phi$ that satisfies the initiation and consecution conditions as follows:

- (**Initiation**) $\theta$ implies $\Phi$, i.e., $\mathbf{v} \models \theta$ implies $\mathbf{v} \models \Phi$ for all program states $\mathbf{v}$;
- (**Consecution**) for all program states $\mathbf{v}, \mathbf{v}'$ and every $\psi_j, \tau_j$ $(1 \le j \le k)$ in (†), we have that $(\mathbf{v} \models G \wedge \mathbf{v} \models \Phi \wedge \mathbf{v}, \mathbf{v}' \models \tau_j) \Rightarrow \mathbf{v}' \models \Phi'$.

From the definition above, it can be observed that an affine inductive invariant is an invariant, in the sense that every program state traversed (as a current state at the start or after every loop iteration) in some execution of the underlying affine while loop will satisfy the affine inductive invariant.

From now on, we abbreviate affine while loops as affine loops and affine inductive invariants as affine invariants.

***Problem Statement.*** In this work, we study the problem of automatically generating affine invariants over affine loops. Our aim is to have a complete mathematical characterization on all such invariants and develop efficient algorithms for generating these invariants.

## 3 Affine Invariants via Farkas' Lemma

Affine invariant generation through Farkas' lemma is originally proposed in [12, 37]. Farkas' lemma is a fundamental result in the theory of linear inequalities that leads to a complete characterization for the affine invariants. Since our approach is based on Farkas' lemma, we present a detailed account on the approaches in [12,37], and point out the weakness of each of the approaches.

**Theorem 1 (Farkas' Lemma).** *Consider the following affine assertion $S$ over real-valued variables $y_1, \ldots, y_n$:*

$$S : \begin{bmatrix} a_{11}y_1 + \ldots + a_{1n}y_n + b_1 \le 0 \\ \vdots \\ a_{k1}y_1 + \ldots + a_{kn}y_n + b_k \le 0 \end{bmatrix}$$

*when $S$ is satisfiable, it entails a given affine inequality*

$$\phi : c_1y_1 + \ldots + c_ny_n + d \le 0$$

*if and only if there exist non-negative real numbers $\lambda_0, \ldots, \lambda_k$ such that (i) $c_j = \sum_{i=1}^{k} \lambda_i a_{ij}$ for $1 \le j \le n$ and (ii) $d = (\sum_{i=1}^{k} \lambda_i b_i) - \lambda_0$.*

The application of Farkas' lemma can be visualized by a table form as follows:

$$\begin{array}{c|rl}
\lambda_0 & -1 \le 0 & \\
\lambda_1 & a_{11}y_1 + \ldots + a_{1n}y_n \; +b_1 \le 0 & \multirow{3}{*}{$\left.\right\} (S)$} \\
\vdots & \vdots \qquad\qquad \vdots & \\
\lambda_k & a_{k1}y_1 + \ldots + a_{kn}y_n \; +b_k \le 0 & \\
\hline
 & c_1y_1 + \ldots + c_ny_n \; +d \le 0 & (\phi)
\end{array} \qquad (\ddagger)$$

The intuition of the table form above is that one first multiplies the $\lambda_i$'s on the left to their corresponding affine inequalities (in the same row) on the right, and then sums these affine inequalities together to obtain the affine inequality at the bottom. In this paper, we will call the table form as *Farkas table*.

Given an affine loop as (†), the approaches in [12,37] first establish a template $\Phi : c_1x_1 + \ldots + c_nx_n + d \le 0$ for an affine invariant where $c_1, \ldots, c_n, d$ are the unknown coefficients. Second, they establish constraints for the unknown coefficients from the initiation and consecution conditions for an affine invariant, as follows.

***Initiation.*** By Farkas' lemma, the initiation condition can be solved from the Farkas table (‡) with $S := \theta$ and $\phi := \Phi$:

$$\begin{array}{c|l} \lambda_0^{\mathrm{I}} & \quad -1 \le 0 \\ \boldsymbol{\lambda} & \mathbf{R}\cdot\mathbf{x} + \mathbf{f} \le \mathbf{0}\ (\theta) \\ \hline & \mathbf{c}^{\mathrm{T}}\cdot\mathbf{x} + d \le 0\ (\Phi) \end{array} \qquad (\#)$$

Here we rephrase the affine inequalities in $\theta$ and $\Phi$ with the condensed matrix forms $\mathbf{R}\cdot\mathbf{x}+\mathbf{f}\le\mathbf{0}$ and $\mathbf{c}^{\mathrm{T}}\cdot\mathbf{x}+d\le 0$; we also use $\boldsymbol{\lambda}=[\lambda_1,\ldots,\lambda_k]^{\mathrm{T}}$ to denote the non-negative parameters in the leftmost column of (‡).

***Consecution.*** The consecution condition can be solved by handling each conditional branch (specified by $\tau_j, \psi_j$ in (†)) separately. By Farkas' lemma, we treat each conditional branch by the Farkas table (‡) with $S := \Phi\wedge G\wedge\tau_j$ and $\phi := \Phi'$:

$$\begin{array}{c|l} \mu & \mathbf{c}^{\mathrm{T}}\cdot\mathbf{x} \qquad\qquad\quad + d \le 0\ \ (\Phi) \\ \lambda_0^{\mathrm{C}} & \qquad\qquad\qquad\ \ - 1 \le 0 \\ \boldsymbol{\xi} & \mathbf{P}\cdot\mathbf{x} \qquad\qquad\quad + \mathbf{q} \le \mathbf{0}\ \ (G) \\ \boldsymbol{\eta} & \mathbf{T}_j\cdot\mathbf{x} - \mathbf{T}'_j\cdot\mathbf{x}' + \mathbf{b}_j \le \mathbf{0}\ (\tau_j) \\ \hline & \qquad\quad \mathbf{c}^{\mathrm{T}}\cdot\mathbf{x}' + d \le 0\ \ (\Phi') \end{array} \qquad (*)$$

Note that the Farkas table above contains quadratic constraints as we multiply an unknown non-negative parameter $\mu$ to the unknown invariant $\mathbf{c}^{\mathrm{T}}\cdot\mathbf{x}+d\le 0$ in the table. The Farkas tables for all conditional branches are grouped conjunctively together to represent the whole consecution condition.

The weakness of the approaches presented in [12,37] lies at the treatment of the quadratic constraints from the consecution condition. The approach in [12] addresses the quadratic constraints by quantifier elimination that guarantees the theoretical completeness but typically has high runtime complexity. The approach in [37] solves the quadratic constraints by several heuristics that guess possible values for the key parameter $\mu$ in (∗) which causes non-linearity, hence losing completeness. Our approach considers to address parameter $\mu$ through matrix-based methods (eigenvalues and eigenvectors, matrix inverse, etc.), which is capable of efficiently generating affine invariants (as compared with quantifier elimination in [12]) while still ensuring theoretical completeness (as compared with the heuristics in [37]).

## 4 Single-Branch Affine Loops with Deterministic Updates

For the sake of simplicity, we first consider the affine invariant generation for a simple class of affine loops where there are no conditional branches in the loop body and the updates of the next-value vector $\mathbf{x}'$ are deterministic.

Formally, an affine loop with deterministic updates and a single branch takes the following form:

$$\begin{array}{l}\textbf{initial condition } \theta : \mathbf{R} \cdot \mathbf{x} + \mathbf{f} \leq \mathbf{0} \\ \textbf{while } G \textbf{ do } \mathbf{x}' = \mathbf{T} \cdot \mathbf{x} + \mathbf{b}; \textbf{ end}\end{array}$$

For the loop above, we aim at *non-trivial* affine invariants, i.e., affine invariants $\mathbf{c}^{\mathrm{T}} \cdot \mathbf{x} + d \leq 0$ with $\mathbf{c} \neq \mathbf{0}$. We summarize our results below.

1. When the loop guard is '**true**', there are only finitely many independent non-trivial invariants $\mathbf{c}^{\mathrm{T}} \cdot \mathbf{x} + d \leq 0$ where $\mathbf{c}$ is an eigenvector of the transpose of the transition matrix $\mathbf{T}$.
2. When the loop guard is not a tautology, there can be infinitely many more non-trivial invariants $\mathbf{c}^{\mathrm{T}} \cdot \mathbf{x} + d \leq 0$ with $\mathbf{c}$ given by a direct formula in $\mu$; in this case we derive the *feasible domain* of $\mu$ and select finitely many optimal ones (which we call *tight choices*) among them.

In Sect. 4.1, we first derive the constraints from the initiation (#) and consecution (∗) conditions satisfied by the invariants. Then we solve these constraints for the tautological loop guard case in Sect. 4.2 and the single-constraint loop guard case in Sect. 4.3. Finally we generalize the results to the multi-constraint loop guard case in Sect. 4.4.

### 4.1 Derived Constraints from the Farkas Tables

We first derive the constraints from the Farkas tables as follows:

***Initiation.*** Recall the Farkas table (#) for initiation. We first compare the coefficients of $\mathbf{x}$ above and below the horizontal line in (#), and obtain

$$\boldsymbol{\lambda}^{\mathrm{T}} \cdot \mathbf{R} = \mathbf{c}^{\mathrm{T}} \Rightarrow \mathbf{R}^{\mathrm{T}} \cdot \boldsymbol{\lambda} = \mathbf{c}. \tag{1}$$

Then by comparing the constant terms in (#), we have:

$$-\lambda_0^{\mathrm{I}} + \boldsymbol{\lambda}^{\mathrm{T}} \cdot \mathbf{f} = d \Rightarrow \mathbf{f}^{\mathrm{T}} \cdot \boldsymbol{\lambda} - d = \lambda_0^{\mathrm{I}} \geq 0. \tag{2}$$

Note that $\mathbf{R}^{\mathrm{T}}$ has left inverse $(\mathbf{R}^{\mathrm{T}})_{\mathrm{L}}^{-1}$, thus constraint (1) is equivalent to $\boldsymbol{\lambda} = (\mathbf{R}^{\mathrm{T}})_{\mathrm{L}}^{-1} \cdot \mathbf{c}$. Plugging it into (2) yields

$$\mathbf{f}^{\mathrm{T}} \cdot (\mathbf{R}^{\mathrm{T}})_{\mathrm{L}}^{-1} \cdot \mathbf{c} - d = \lambda_0^{\mathrm{I}} \geq 0. \tag{3}$$

***Consecution.*** The Farkas table (∗) for consecution in the case of single-branch affine loops with deterministic updates is as follows:

$$\begin{array}{r|lll}
\mu & \mathbf{c}^{\mathrm{T}} \cdot \mathbf{x} & & + d \leq 0 \ (\Phi) \\
\lambda_0^{\mathrm{C}} & & & - 1 \leq 0 \\
\boldsymbol{\xi} & \mathbf{P} \cdot \mathbf{x} & & + \mathbf{q} \leq \mathbf{0} \ (G) \\
\boldsymbol{\eta} & \mathbf{T} \cdot \mathbf{x} - & \mathbf{x}' & + \mathbf{b} = \mathbf{0} \ (\tau) \\
\hline
 & & \mathbf{c}^{\mathrm{T}} \cdot \mathbf{x}' & + d \leq 0 \ (\Phi')
\end{array}$$

Here the transition matrix $\mathbf{T}$ is a $n \times n$ square matrix, and $\mathbf{b}$ is a $n$-dimensional vector. Since $\tau$ contains only equalities, the components $\eta_1, ..., \eta_n$ of the vector parameter $\boldsymbol{\eta}$ do not have to be non-negative (while the components $\xi_1, ..., \xi_n$ of $\boldsymbol{\xi}$ and $\mu$ must be non-negative). In this table, by comparing the coefficients of $\mathbf{x}'$ above and below the horizontal line, we easily get $-\boldsymbol{\eta} = \mathbf{c}$. Then we substitute $\boldsymbol{\eta}$ by $-\mathbf{c}$ and compare the coefficients of $\mathbf{x}$ above and below the horizontal line. We get

$$\mu \cdot \mathbf{c}^{\mathrm{T}} + \boldsymbol{\xi}^{\mathrm{T}} \cdot \mathbf{P} - \mathbf{c}^{\mathrm{T}} \cdot \mathbf{T} = \mathbf{0}^{\mathrm{T}} \;\Rightarrow\; \mu \cdot \mathbf{c} - \mathbf{T}^{\mathrm{T}} \cdot \mathbf{c} + \mathbf{P}^{\mathrm{T}} \cdot \boldsymbol{\xi} = \mathbf{0}. \tag{4}$$

We also compare the constant terms and get

$$\mu \cdot d - \lambda_0^{\mathrm{C}} + \boldsymbol{\xi}^{\mathrm{T}} \cdot \mathbf{q} - \mathbf{c}^{\mathrm{T}} \cdot \mathbf{b} = d \;\Rightarrow\; (\mu - 1)d - \mathbf{b}^{\mathrm{T}} \cdot \mathbf{c} + \mathbf{q}^{\mathrm{T}} \cdot \boldsymbol{\xi} = \lambda_0^{\mathrm{C}} \geq 0. \tag{5}$$

The rest of this section is devoted to solving the invariants $\Phi : \mathbf{c}^{\mathrm{T}} \cdot \mathbf{x} + d \leq 0$ which satisfy all constraints (1)–(5).

### 4.2 Loops with Tautological Guard

We first consider the simplest case where the loop guard is '**true**':

$$\begin{array}{l} \textbf{initial condition } \theta : \mathbf{R} \cdot \mathbf{x} + \mathbf{f} \leq \mathbf{0} \\ \textbf{while true do } \mathbf{x}' = \mathbf{T} \cdot \mathbf{x} + \mathbf{b}; \textbf{ end} \end{array} \tag{$\diamond$}$$

In order for completely solving the non-linear constraints, we take three steps:

1. choose the correct $\mu$, thus turn the non-linear constraints into linear ones;
2. use linear algebra method to solve out the vector $\mathbf{c}$;
3. with $\mu$ and $\mathbf{c}$ known, find out the feasible domain of $d$ and determine the optimal value of it. Here 'optimality' is defined by the fact that all invariants with other $d$'s in this domain are implied by the invariant with the 'optimal' $d$.

***Step 1 and Step 2.*** We address the values of $\mu, \mathbf{c}$ by eigenvalues and eigenvectors in the following proposition:

**Proposition 1.** *For any non-trivial invariant* $\mathbf{c}^{\mathrm{T}} \cdot \mathbf{x} + d \leq 0$ *of the loop* ($\diamond$), *we have that* $\mathbf{c}$ *must be an eigenvector of* $\mathbf{T}^{\mathrm{T}}$ *with a non-negative eigenvalue* $\mu$.

*Proof.* Since the loop guard is a tautology, we take the parameter $\boldsymbol{\xi}$ to be $\mathbf{0}$ in (4):

$$\mu \cdot \mathbf{c} - \mathbf{T}^{\mathrm{T}} \cdot \mathbf{c} = \mathbf{0}.$$

It's obvious that $\mu$ must be a non-negative eigenvalue of $\mathbf{T}^{\mathrm{T}}$ and $\mathbf{c}$ is the corresponding eigenvector. □

*Example 1. (Fibonacci numbers).* Consider the sequence $\{s_n\}$ defined by initial condition $s_1 = s_2 = 1$ and recursive formula $s_{n+2} = s_{n+1} + s_n$ for $n \geq 1$. If we use variables $(x_1, x_2)$ to represent $(s_n, s_{n+1})$, then the sequence can be written as a loop:

$$\textbf{initial condition } \theta : \mathbf{R} \cdot \mathbf{x} + \mathbf{f} = \begin{bmatrix} 1 & 0 \\ 0 & 1 \end{bmatrix} \cdot \begin{bmatrix} x_1 \\ x_2 \end{bmatrix} + \begin{bmatrix} -1 \\ -1 \end{bmatrix} = \mathbf{0}$$

$$\textbf{while true do } \begin{bmatrix} x_1' \\ x_2' \end{bmatrix} = \mathbf{T} \cdot \begin{bmatrix} x_1 \\ x_2 \end{bmatrix} + \mathbf{b} = \begin{bmatrix} 0 & 1 \\ 1 & 1 \end{bmatrix} \cdot \begin{bmatrix} x_1 \\ x_2 \end{bmatrix} + \mathbf{0}; \textbf{ end}$$

The eigenvalues of matrix $\mathbf{T}^{\mathrm{T}}$ are $\frac{1-\sqrt{5}}{2}, \frac{1+\sqrt{5}}{2}$; only the second one is non-negative. This eigenvalue $\mu = \frac{1+\sqrt{5}}{2}$ yields eigenvector $\mathbf{c} = [c_1, \frac{1+\sqrt{5}}{2}c_1]^{\mathrm{T}}$, here $c_1$ is a free variable, which could be fixed in the final form of the invariant. □

***Step 3.*** After solving $\mu$ and $\mathbf{c}$, we illustrate the feasible domain of $d$ and its optimal value by the following proposition:

**Proposition 2.** *For any $\mu$ and $\mathbf{c}$ given by Proposition 1, the feasible domain of $d$ is an interval determined by the two conditions below:*

$$d \leq \mathbf{f}^{\mathrm{T}} \cdot (\mathbf{R}^{\mathrm{T}})_{\mathrm{L}}^{-1} \cdot \mathbf{c} \quad \textit{and} \quad (\mu - 1)d \geq \mathbf{b}^{\mathrm{T}} \cdot \mathbf{c}.$$

*If the above conditions have empty solution set, then no affine invariant is available from such $\mu$ and $\mathbf{c}$; otherwise, the optimal value of $d$ falls in one of the two choices:*

$$d = \mathbf{f}^{\mathrm{T}} \cdot (\mathbf{R}^{\mathrm{T}})_{\mathrm{L}}^{-1} \cdot \mathbf{c} \quad \textit{or} \quad (\mu - 1)d = \mathbf{b}^{\mathrm{T}} \cdot \mathbf{c}.$$

*Proof.* Constraint (3) provides one condition for $d$:

$$\mathbf{f}^{\mathrm{T}} \cdot (\mathbf{R}^{\mathrm{T}})_{\mathrm{L}}^{-1} \cdot \mathbf{c} - d = \lambda_0^{\mathrm{I}} \geq 0 \Rightarrow \mathbf{f}^{\mathrm{T}} \cdot (\mathbf{R}^{\mathrm{T}})_{\mathrm{L}}^{-1} \cdot \mathbf{c} \geq d;$$

while constraint (5) with $\boldsymbol{\xi} = \mathbf{0}$ provides the other condition:

$$(\mu - 1)d - \mathbf{b}^{\mathrm{T}} \cdot \mathbf{c} = \lambda_0^{\mathrm{C}} \geq 0 \Rightarrow (\mu - 1)d \geq \mathbf{b}^{\mathrm{T}} \cdot \mathbf{c}.$$

To obtain the strongest inequality $\mathbf{c}^{\mathrm{T}} \cdot \mathbf{x} + d \leq 0$, we need to take $d$ to be either minimal or maximal value, i.e., some boundary point of its interval; thus the invariant with this $d$ would imply all invariants with the same $\mathbf{c}$ and other $d$'s in this interval. The boundary is achieved when one of the two conditions achieves the equality. □

*Example 2 (Fibonacci, Part 2).* We continue with Example 1. Recall that $\mu = \frac{1+\sqrt{5}}{2}$, $\mathbf{c} = [c_1, \frac{1+\sqrt{5}}{2}c_1]^{\mathrm{T}}$; in this case, constraints (3) (5) (with $\boldsymbol{\xi} = \mathbf{0}$) read $-\frac{3+\sqrt{5}}{2}c_1 \geq d$ and $\frac{-1+\sqrt{5}}{2}d \geq 0$, hence yield $0 \leq d \leq -\frac{3+\sqrt{5}}{2}c_1$. The free variable $c_1$ must be negative here, so we choose $c_1 = -2$ and thus $\mathbf{c} = [-2, -1-\sqrt{5}]^{\mathrm{T}}$ and $0 \leq d \leq 3+\sqrt{5}$; there are two boundary values $d = 0$ and $d = 3+\sqrt{5}$, where $d = 3+\sqrt{5}$ leads to the strongest invariant:

$$\mu = (1+\sqrt{5})/2 : \; -2x_1 - (1+\sqrt{5})x_2 + 3 + \sqrt{5} \leq 0.$$ □

### 4.3 Loops with Guard: Single-Constraint Case

Here we study the loops with non-tautological guard. First of all, the eigenvalue method of Sect. 4.2 applies to this case as well; thus for the rest of Sect. 4, we always assume that $\mu$ is not any eigenvalue of $\mathbf{T}$ (and $\mathbf{c}$ is not any eigenvector of $\mathbf{T}^{\mathrm{T}}$ either) and aim for other invariants than the ones from the eigenvectors.

Let us start with the case that the loop guard consists of only one affine inequality:

$$\begin{array}{l}\textbf{initial condition } \theta : \mathbf{R}\cdot\mathbf{x}+\mathbf{f}\le\mathbf{0}\\ \textbf{while } \mathbf{p}^{\mathrm{T}}\cdot\mathbf{x}+q\le 0 \textbf{ do } \mathbf{x}'=\mathbf{T}\cdot\mathbf{x}+\mathbf{b}; \textbf{ end}\end{array} \qquad (\diamond')$$

where $\mathbf{p}$ is a $n$-dimensional real vector and $q$ is a real number.

We again take three steps to compute the invariants; these steps are different from the previous case:

1. we derive a formula to compute $\mathbf{c}$ in terms of $\mu$; so for any non-negative real value $\mu$, we get a corresponding $\mathbf{c}$;
2. however, not all $\mu$'s would produce invariants that satisfy all constraints (1)–(5). We will determine the feasible domain of $\mu$ that does so;
3. we will select finitely many $\mu$'s from its feasible domain which provide *tight invariants*; the meaning of *tightness* will be defined later. For every single $\mu$, we will also determine the feasible domain of $d$ and optimal value of it.

***Step 1.*** We first establish the relationship between $\mu$ and $\mathbf{c}$ through the constraints. The initiation is still (1) (2) (3), while the consecution (4) (5) becomes:

$$\mu\cdot\mathbf{c}-\mathbf{T}^{\mathrm{T}}\cdot\mathbf{c}+\xi\cdot\mathbf{p}=\mathbf{0} \qquad (4')$$

$$(\mu-1)d-\mathbf{b}^{\mathrm{T}}\cdot\mathbf{c}+\xi\cdot q=\lambda_0^{\mathrm{C}}\ge 0 \qquad (5')$$

where the matrix $\mathbf{P}$ in (4) degenerates to vector $\mathbf{p}^{\mathrm{T}}$ and the vectors $\mathbf{q},\boldsymbol{\xi}$ in (5) both have just one component $q,\xi$ here. Note that $\xi$ is a non-negative parameter.

In contrast to Sect. 4.2, we assume that $\mu$ is not any eigenvalue of $\mathbf{T}$, and $\xi\neq 0$. For such $\mu$, we have a new formula to compute $\mathbf{c}$:

**Proposition 3.** *For any non-trivial invariant* $\mathbf{c}^{\mathrm{T}}\cdot\mathbf{x}+d\le 0$ *of the loop* ($\diamond'$), *we have that* $\mathbf{c}$ *is given by*

$$\mathbf{c}=\xi\cdot(\mathbf{T}^{\mathrm{T}}-\mu\cdot\mathbf{I})^{-1}\cdot\mathbf{p} \quad \textit{with} \quad \xi\ge 0 \qquad (6)$$

*when* $\mu$ *is fixed,* $\mathbf{c}$*'s with different* $\xi$*'s are proportional to each other and yield equivalent invariants.*

*Proof.* Since $\mu$ is not any eigenvalue of $\mathbf{T}$, the matrix $\mu\cdot\mathbf{I}-\mathbf{T}^{\mathrm{T}}$ is invertible; thus (4′) is equivalent to

$$(\mu\cdot\mathbf{I}-\mathbf{T}^{\mathrm{T}})\cdot\mathbf{c}=-\xi\cdot\mathbf{p} \;\Rightarrow\; \mathbf{c}=\xi\cdot(\mathbf{T}^{\mathrm{T}}-\mu\cdot\mathbf{I})^{-1}\cdot\mathbf{p}. \qquad \square$$

*Example 3 (Fibonacci, Part 3).* We add a loop guard $x_1 \leq 10$ to Example 1:

$$\textbf{initial condition } \theta : \mathbf{R}\cdot\mathbf{x}+\mathbf{f} = \begin{bmatrix}1&0\\0&1\end{bmatrix}\cdot\begin{bmatrix}x_1\\x_2\end{bmatrix}+\begin{bmatrix}-1\\-1\end{bmatrix}=\mathbf{0}$$

$$\textbf{while } \mathbf{p}^{\mathrm{T}}\cdot\mathbf{x}+q=[1,0]\cdot\begin{bmatrix}x_1\\x_2\end{bmatrix}-10\leq 0 \textbf{ do}$$

$$\begin{bmatrix}x_1'\\x_2'\end{bmatrix}=\mathbf{T}\cdot\begin{bmatrix}x_1\\x_2\end{bmatrix}+\mathbf{b}=\begin{bmatrix}0&1\\1&1\end{bmatrix}\cdot\begin{bmatrix}x_1\\x_2\end{bmatrix}+\mathbf{0};\textbf{ end}$$

and search for more invariants. The formula (6) here reads

$$\begin{bmatrix}c_1\\c_2\end{bmatrix}=\frac{\xi}{\mu^2-\mu-1}\begin{bmatrix}1-\mu&-1\\-1&-\mu\end{bmatrix}\cdot\begin{bmatrix}1\\0\end{bmatrix}=\frac{\xi}{\mu^2-\mu-1}\begin{bmatrix}1-\mu\\-1\end{bmatrix}.$$ □

***Step 2.*** With formula (6) in hand, every non-negative value $\mu$ would give us a vector $\mathbf{c}$; the next step is to find such $\mu$'s that (1) (2) (3) (5′) are all satisfied. We call this set the *feasible domain* of $\mu$.

Notice that (3) and (5′) are two inequalities both containing $d$. When the value of $\mu$ changes, there is a possibility that (3) and (5′) conflict each other, hence make no invariant available. So the feasible domain consists of such $\mu$'s that make the two inequalities compatible with each other:

**Proposition 4.** *For the loop ($\diamond'$), any feasible $\mu$ falls in $[0,1)\cup\big(K\cap[1,+\infty)\big)$, where $K$ is the solution set to the following rational inequality of $\mu$ (which we call 'compatibility condition'):*

$$\mathbf{b}^{\mathrm{T}}\cdot(\mathbf{T}^{\mathrm{T}}-\mu\cdot\mathbf{I})^{-1}\cdot\mathbf{p}-q\leq(\mu-1)\mathbf{f}^{\mathrm{T}}\cdot(\mathbf{R}^{\mathrm{T}})_{\mathrm{L}}^{-1}(\mathbf{T}^{\mathrm{T}}-\mu\cdot\mathbf{I})^{-1}\cdot\mathbf{p}. \tag{7}$$

*Proof.* We multiply $(\mu-1)$ on both sides of (3) and get

$$(\mu-1)\mathbf{f}^{\mathrm{T}}\cdot(\mathbf{R}^{\mathrm{T}})_{\mathrm{L}}^{-1}\cdot\mathbf{c}\leq(\mu-1)d \quad \text{when} \quad 0\leq\mu<1 \tag{3′}$$

$$(\mu-1)\mathbf{f}^{\mathrm{T}}\cdot(\mathbf{R}^{\mathrm{T}})_{\mathrm{L}}^{-1}\cdot\mathbf{c}\geq(\mu-1)d \quad \text{when} \quad \mu\geq 1 \tag{3″}$$

compare them with (5′), we see: (3′) (5′) would not conflict each other because they are both about $(\mu-1)d$ being 'larger' than something. However, (3″) (5′) are two inequalities of opposite directions, they together must satisfy

$$\mathbf{b}^{\mathrm{T}}\cdot\mathbf{c}-\xi\cdot q\leq(\mu-1)d\leq(\mu-1)\mathbf{f}^{\mathrm{T}}\cdot(\mathbf{R}^{\mathrm{T}})_{\mathrm{L}}^{-1}\cdot\mathbf{c}$$

to be compatible. Substitute $\mathbf{c}$ by (6) in the above inequality and cancel out $\xi>0$, we obtain the desired inequality:

$$\mathbf{b}^{\mathrm{T}}\cdot(\mathbf{T}^{\mathrm{T}}-\mu\cdot\mathrm{I})^{-1}\cdot\mathbf{p}-q\leq(\mu-1)\mathbf{f}^{\mathrm{T}}\cdot(\mathbf{R}^{\mathrm{T}})_{\mathrm{L}}^{-1}(\mathbf{T}^{\mathrm{T}}-\mu\cdot\mathbf{I})^{-1}\cdot\mathbf{p}.$$

Every $\mu$ from $[0,1)$ and $K\cap[1,+\infty)$ would lead to non-trivial invariant satisfying all constraints (1) (2) (3) (4′) (5′). □

*Example 4 (Fibonacci, Part 4).* Let us compute the feasible domain of $\mu$ for Example 3. Inequality (5′) is $(\mu-1)d \geq 10\xi$; inequality (3″) is

$$(\mu-1)[-1,-1]\cdot\begin{bmatrix}1 & 0\\ 0 & 1\end{bmatrix}\cdot\mathbf{c} = \frac{\xi(\mu-1)\mu}{\mu^2-\mu-1} \geq (\mu-1)d \ \text{ (when } \mu \geq 1).$$

We combine them to form the compatibility condition (7) as

$$10 \leq \frac{(\mu-1)\mu}{\mu^2-\mu-1} \Rightarrow 0 \leq -\frac{9(\mu-\frac{5}{3})(\mu+\frac{2}{3})}{(\mu-\frac{1-\sqrt{5}}{2})(\mu-\frac{1+\sqrt{5}}{2})} \ \text{ (when } \mu \geq 1).$$

The solution domain of it is $(\frac{1+\sqrt{5}}{2}, \frac{5}{3}]$. Thus by Proposition 4, the feasible domain of $\mu$ is $[0,1) \cup (\frac{1+\sqrt{5}}{2}, \frac{5}{3}]$. □

***Step 3.*** Proposition 4 provides us with a continuum of candidates for $\mu$, thus produces infinitely many legitimate invariants. We want to find a basis consisting of finitely many invariants, such that all invariants are non-negative linear combinations of the basis; however, this idea does not work out, where the reason is explained thoroughly in the full version of this paper [25, Appendix A.1 and A.2]. Instead, we impose a weaker form of optimality called *tightness* coming from the equality cases of constraints (3) (5′):

$$\mathbf{f}^{\mathrm{T}}\cdot(\mathbf{R}^{\mathrm{T}})_{\mathrm{L}}^{-1}\cdot\mathbf{c} - d = \lambda_0^{\mathrm{I}} = 0$$
$$(\mu-1)d - \mathbf{b}^{\mathrm{T}}\cdot\mathbf{c} + \xi\cdot q = \lambda_0^{\mathrm{C}} = 0$$

we call an invariant *tight* and the corresponding $\mu$ as *tight choice* when both equalities are achieved:

- $\lambda_0^{\mathrm{I}} = 0$: The invariant is tight at the initial state, i.e., the invariant reaches equality at the initial state;
- $\lambda_0^{\mathrm{C}} = 0$: The invariant stays as close to being tight as much at later iterations.

The non-tight choices could be kept as back-up for invariant generation. The tight choices are characterized by the following proposition:

**Proposition 5.** *For the loop (◊′), the tight choices of $\mu$ consist of* 0 *and the positive real roots of the following rational equation:*

$$\mathbf{b}^{\mathrm{T}}\cdot(\mathbf{T}^{\mathrm{T}}-\mu\cdot\mathbf{I})^{-1}\cdot\mathbf{p} - q = (\mu-1)\mathbf{f}^{\mathrm{T}}\cdot(\mathbf{R}^{\mathrm{T}})_{\mathrm{L}}^{-1}(\mathbf{T}^{\mathrm{T}}-\mu\cdot\mathbf{I})^{-1}\cdot\mathbf{p}. \quad (8)$$

*Note that these roots are also the boundary points of the intervals in $K$ defined in Proposition 4.*

*Proof.* Recall Proposition 2, constraints (3) (5) form the two boundaries of the domain of $d$, which can not be achieved simultaneously in the case of loops with tautological guard. Nevertheless, in the case of loops with guard, we have an extra freedom on $\mu$ which allows us to set $\lambda_0^{\mathrm{I}} = \lambda_0^{\mathrm{C}} = 0$:

$$\mathbf{f}^{\mathrm{T}}\cdot(\mathbf{R}^{\mathrm{T}})_{\mathrm{L}}^{-1}\cdot\mathbf{c} = d \wedge (\mu-1)d = \mathbf{b}^{\mathrm{T}}\cdot\mathbf{c} - \xi\cdot q$$
$$\Rightarrow \mathbf{b}^{\mathrm{T}}\cdot(\mathbf{T}^{\mathrm{T}}-\mu\cdot\mathbf{I})^{-1}\cdot\mathbf{p} - q = (\mu-1)\mathbf{f}^{\mathrm{T}}\cdot(\mathbf{R}^{\mathrm{T}})_{\mathrm{L}}^{-1}(\mathbf{T}^{\mathrm{T}}-\mu\cdot\mathbf{I})^{-1}\cdot\mathbf{p}.$$

Equation (8) is just the case that (7) achieves the equality, hence is a rational equation of $\mu$ with finite number of roots. These roots are also the boundary points of $K$ since $K$ is the solution domain to (7). Besides the roots of (8), $\mu = 0$ is also a boundary point of the feasible domain; its corresponding invariant reflects the feature of the loop guard itself. Thus we add it into the list of tight choices. □

With $\mu$ determined and $\mathbf{c}$ fixed up to a scaling factor, the last thing remains is to determine the optimal $d$. The strategy here is similar to Proposition 2:

**Proposition 6.** *Suppose $\mu$ is from the feasible domain and $\mathbf{c}$ is given by Proposition 3. Then the optimal value of $d$ is determined by one of the two choices below:*

$$\mathbf{b}^{\mathrm{T}} \cdot \mathbf{c} - \xi \cdot q = (\mu - 1)d \quad \text{or} \quad \mathbf{f}^{\mathrm{T}} \cdot (\mathbf{R}^{\mathrm{T}})_{\mathrm{L}}^{-1} \cdot \mathbf{c} = d.$$

The proof is omitted here and can be found in our full version [25].

*Example 5 (Fibonacci, Part 5).* Remember that

$$\begin{bmatrix} c_1 \\ c_2 \end{bmatrix} = \frac{\xi}{\mu^2 - \mu - 1} \begin{bmatrix} 1-\mu \\ -1 \end{bmatrix} \text{ and the feasible domain of } \mu \text{ is } [0,1) \cup (\frac{1+\sqrt{5}}{2}, \frac{5}{3}].$$

We compute the tight choices of $\mu$ and tight invariants. The equation (8) here is

$$0 = \frac{-9\mu^2 + 9\mu + 10}{\mu^2 - \mu - 1} = -\frac{9(\mu - \frac{5}{3})(\mu + \frac{2}{3})}{(\mu - \frac{1-\sqrt{5}}{2})(\mu - \frac{1+\sqrt{5}}{2})}$$

which has only one positive root $\mu = \frac{5}{3}$. By Proposition 5 and Proposition 6, We get two invariants:

$$\mu = 0: \ -x_1 + x_2 - 10 \leq 0;$$
$$\mu = 5/3: \ -2x_1 - 3x_2 + 5 \leq 0.$$

□

### 4.4 Loops with Guard: Multi-constraint Case

After settling the single-constraint loop guard case, we consider the more general loop guard which contains the conjunction of multiple affine constraints:

$$\begin{array}{l} \textbf{initial condition } \theta : \mathbf{R} \cdot \mathbf{x} + \mathbf{f} \leq \mathbf{0} \\ \textbf{while } \mathbf{P} \cdot \mathbf{x} + \mathbf{q} \leq \mathbf{0} \textbf{ do } \mathbf{x}' = \mathbf{T} \cdot \mathbf{x} + \mathbf{b}; \textbf{ end} \end{array} \qquad (\diamond'')$$

where the loop guard $\mathbf{P} \cdot \mathbf{x} + \mathbf{q} \leq \mathbf{0}$ contains $m$ affine inequalities.

We can easily generalize the results of Sect. 4.3 to this case. First of all, we generalize Proposition 3: one simply needs to modify the formula (6) into

$$\mathbf{c} = (\mathbf{T}^{\mathrm{T}} - \mu \cdot \mathbf{I})^{-1} \mathbf{P}^{\mathrm{T}} \cdot \boldsymbol{\xi} \quad \text{with} \quad \boldsymbol{\xi} \geq \mathbf{0} \qquad (6')$$

here $\boldsymbol{\xi}$ is a free non-negative $m$-dimensional vector parameter. With a fixed $\mu$, we take $\boldsymbol{\xi}$ to traverse all vectors in the standard basis $\{\mathbf{e}_1, ..., \mathbf{e}_m\}$ to get $m$ conjunctive invariants.

Next, we generalize Proposition 4 which describes the feasible domain of $\mu$:

**Proposition 7.** *For the loop* ($\diamond''$)*, the feasible domain of* $\mu$ *is* $[0,1) \cup (\overline{K} \cap [1,+\infty))$*, where* $\overline{K}$ *is the solution set to the following generalized compatibility condition:*

$$\mathbf{b}^{\mathrm{T}} \cdot \mathbf{c} - \mathbf{q}^{\mathrm{T}} \cdot \boldsymbol{\xi} \leq (\mu - 1)d \leq (\mu - 1)\mathbf{f}^{\mathrm{T}} \cdot (\mathbf{R}^{\mathrm{T}})_{\mathrm{L}}^{-1} \cdot \mathbf{c}$$

*substitute* $\mathbf{c}$ *by* ($6'$) *and take* $\boldsymbol{\xi}$ *to traverse all vectors in the standard basis (in order for all constraints in the loop guard to be satisfied by the invariant), we have the above condition completely decoded as* $m$ *conjunctive inequalities:*

$$\begin{aligned} \mathbf{u}(\mu) &:= \mathbf{b}^{\mathrm{T}} \cdot (\mathbf{T}^{\mathrm{T}} - \mu \cdot \mathbf{I})^{-1}\mathbf{P}^{\mathrm{T}} - \mathbf{q}^{\mathrm{T}} \\ &\leq \mathbf{w}(\mu) := (\mu - 1)\mathbf{f}^{\mathrm{T}} \cdot (\mathbf{R}^{\mathrm{T}})_{\mathrm{L}}^{-1}(\mathbf{T}^{\mathrm{T}} - \mu \cdot \mathbf{I})^{-1}\mathbf{P}^{\mathrm{T}} \end{aligned} \tag{7'}$$

*where* $\mathbf{u}(\mu), \mathbf{w}(\mu)$ *are two* $m$*-dimensional vector functions in* $\mu$*. The meaning of* ($7'$) *is that the* $i$*-th component of* $\mathbf{u}(\mu)$ *is no larger than the* $i$*-th component of* $\mathbf{w}(\mu)$ *for all* $1 \leq i \leq m$*; when* $m = 1$*, it goes back to* (7)*.*

At last, we consider the tight choices of $\mu$. The first idea comes up to mind is to repeat Proposition 5: setting $\lambda_0^{\mathrm{I}} = \lambda_0^{\mathrm{C}} = 0$ for arbitary $\boldsymbol{\xi}$ such that the generalized compatibility condition achieves equality, i.e., $\mathbf{u}(\mu) = \mathbf{w}(\mu)$; however, this is the conjunction of $m$ rational equations and probably contains no solution.

Thus we use a different idea: recall that in the single-constraint case, the tight choices are also the (positive) boundary points of $K$ along with 0; so we adopt this property as the definition in the multi-constraint case:

**Definition 1.** *For the loop* ($\diamond''$)*, the tight choices of* $\mu$ *consist of* 0 *and the (positive) boundary points of the domain* $\overline{K}$ *defined in Proposition 7.*

The generalized compatibility condition ($7'$) contains $m$ inequalities; at each (positive) boundary point of $\overline{K}$, at least one inequality achieves equality and all other inequalities are satisfied (equivalently, $\lambda_0^{\mathrm{I}} = \lambda_0^{\mathrm{C}} = 0$ is achieved for at least one non-trivial evaluation of the free vector parameter $\boldsymbol{\xi}$). This is indeed a natural generalization of Proposition 5.

*Example 6.* We consider the loop:

$$\textbf{initial condition } \theta : \mathbf{R} \cdot \mathbf{x} + \mathbf{f} = \begin{bmatrix} 1 & 0 \\ 0 & 1 \end{bmatrix} \cdot \begin{bmatrix} x_1 \\ x_2 \end{bmatrix} + \begin{bmatrix} -1 \\ -1 \end{bmatrix} = \mathbf{0}$$

$$\textbf{while } \mathbf{P} \cdot \mathbf{x} + \mathbf{q} = \begin{bmatrix} 1 & 0 \\ 0 & -1 \end{bmatrix} \cdot \begin{bmatrix} x_1 \\ x_2 \end{bmatrix} + \begin{bmatrix} -10 \\ -5 \end{bmatrix} \leq \mathbf{0} \textbf{ do}$$

$$\begin{bmatrix} x_1' \\ x_2' \end{bmatrix} = \mathbf{T} \cdot \begin{bmatrix} x_1 \\ x_2 \end{bmatrix} + \mathbf{b} = \begin{bmatrix} 1 & 0 \\ 0 & 1 \end{bmatrix} \cdot \begin{bmatrix} x_1 \\ x_2 \end{bmatrix} + \begin{bmatrix} 1 \\ -1 \end{bmatrix}; \textbf{ end}$$

There is one eigenvalue $\mu = 1$ with geometric multiplicity 2; we solve three independent invariants from it:

$$x_1 + x_2 - 2 \leq 0, \; x_1 + x_2 - 2 \geq 0; \; -x_1 + x_2 \leq 0.$$

Next we find out the other invariants from tight $\mu$'s. In this case (7′) read $\frac{11-10\mu}{1-\mu} \le 1 \wedge \frac{6-5\mu}{1-\mu} \le -1$ (when $\mu > 1$). Then $\overline{K} = (1, \frac{10}{9}] \cap (1, \frac{7}{6}] = (1, \frac{10}{9}]$ and the feasible domain of $\mu$ is $[0, 1) \cup (1, \frac{10}{9}]$. The tight choices are $0, \frac{10}{9}$ (taking $\boldsymbol{\xi}$ to be $[1, 0]^{\mathrm{T}}, [0, 1]^{\mathrm{T}}$ respectively yields the two conjunctive invariants for each $\mu$):

$$\mu = 0 : x_1 - 10 \le 0 \ \wedge \ -x_2 - 5 \le 0;$$
$$\mu = 10/9 : \ -x_1 + 1 \le 0 \ \wedge \ x_2 - 1 \le 0. \qquad \square$$

## 5 Generalizations

In this section, we extend our theory developed in Sect. 4 in two directions. For one direction, we consider the invariants $\mathbf{c}^{\mathrm{T}} \cdot \mathbf{x} + d \le 0$ for the affine loops in the general form (†): we will derive the relationship of $\mu$ and $\mathbf{c}$, as well as the feasible domain and tight choices of $\mu$. For the other direction, we stick to the single-branch affine loops with deterministic updates and tautological guard (◇), yet generalize the invariants to bidirectional-inequality form $d_1 \le \mathbf{c}^{\mathrm{T}} \cdot \mathbf{x} \le d_2$; we will apply eigenvalue method to this case for solving the invariants. At the end of the section, we also give a brief discussion on some other possible generalizations.

### 5.1 Affine Loops with Non-deterministic Updates

In Sect. 4, we handled the loops with deterministic updates; here we generalize the results to the non-deterministic case in the form of (†). We focus on the single-branch loops here, because the multi-branch ones can be handled similarly by taking the conjunction of all branches, as illustrated in the full version of this paper [25, Appendix A.3].

**initial condition** $\theta : \mathbf{R} \cdot \mathbf{x} + \mathbf{f} \le \mathbf{0}$
**while** $\mathbf{P} \cdot \mathbf{x} + \mathbf{q} \le \mathbf{0}$ **do** $\mathbf{T} \cdot \mathbf{x} - \mathbf{T}' \cdot \mathbf{x}' + \mathbf{b} \le \mathbf{0}$; **end** (†′)

For this general form, the initiation constraints are still (1) (2) (3), while the consecution constraints from Farkas table (∗) are

$$\mu \cdot \mathbf{c} + \mathbf{P}^{\mathrm{T}} \cdot \boldsymbol{\xi} + \mathbf{T}^{\mathrm{T}} \cdot \boldsymbol{\eta} = \mathbf{0} \tag{9}$$
$$-(\mathbf{T}')^{\mathrm{T}} \cdot \boldsymbol{\eta} = \mathbf{c} \tag{10}$$
$$(\mu - 1)d + \mathbf{q}^{\mathrm{T}} \cdot \boldsymbol{\xi} + \mathbf{b}^{\mathrm{T}} \cdot \boldsymbol{\eta} = \lambda_0^{\mathrm{C}} \ge 0 \tag{11}$$

with $\boldsymbol{\xi}, \boldsymbol{\eta} \ge \mathbf{0}$. The relationship of $\mathbf{c}$ and $\boldsymbol{\eta}$ is given by (10); plugging it into (9) yield

$$\left(\mathbf{T}^{\mathrm{T}} - \mu \cdot (\mathbf{T}')^{\mathrm{T}}\right) \cdot \boldsymbol{\eta} + \mathbf{P}^{\mathrm{T}} \cdot \boldsymbol{\xi} = \mathbf{0}. \tag{9′}$$

Hence for any non-trivial invariant $\mathbf{c}^{\mathrm{T}} \cdot \mathbf{x} + d \le 0$ of this loop (†′), we have $\mathbf{c} = -(\mathbf{T}')^{\mathrm{T}} \cdot \boldsymbol{\eta}$, where $\boldsymbol{\eta}$ is characterized differently in the following three cases:

1. $\mathbf{T}$ and $\mathbf{T}'$ are square matrices and the loop guard is '**true**'. In this case, we take $\boldsymbol{\xi} = \mathbf{0}$ in (9′) and easily see that $\mu$ must be a root of $\det\left(\mathbf{T}^{\mathrm{T}} - \mu \cdot (\mathbf{T}')^{\mathrm{T}}\right) = 0$ and $\boldsymbol{\eta}$ is a kernel vector of the matrix $\mathbf{T}^{\mathrm{T}} - \mu \cdot (\mathbf{T}')^{\mathrm{T}}$.
2. $\mathbf{T}$ and $\mathbf{T}'$ are square matrices and the loop guard is non-tautological. In this case, we set $\mu$ to be values other than the roots of $\det\left(\mathbf{T}^{\mathrm{T}} - \mu \cdot (\mathbf{T}')^{\mathrm{T}}\right) = 0$, thus the inverse matrix $\left(\mathbf{T}^{\mathrm{T}} - \mu \cdot (\mathbf{T}')^{\mathrm{T}}\right)^{-1}$ exists; we multiply it on (9′) and get that $\boldsymbol{\eta}(\mu) = -\left(\mathbf{T}^{\mathrm{T}} - \mu \cdot (\mathbf{T}')^{\mathrm{T}}\right)^{-1}\mathbf{P}^{\mathrm{T}} \cdot \boldsymbol{\xi}$.
3. Neither $\mathbf{T}$ nor $\mathbf{T}'$ is square matrix. In this case, we need to use Gaussian elimination method (with parameters) to solve (9′). By linear algebra, the solution $\boldsymbol{\eta}(\mu)$ would contain 'homogeneous term' (which does not involve $\boldsymbol{\xi}$ but possibly some free variables $\overline{\boldsymbol{\eta}} = [\eta_1, ..., \eta_l]^{\mathrm{T}}$) and 'non-homogeneous term' (which contains $\boldsymbol{\xi}$ linearly). Thus $\boldsymbol{\eta}(\mu)$ could be written in parametric vector form as $\mathbf{M}(\mu) \cdot \overline{\boldsymbol{\eta}} + \mathbf{N}(\mu) \cdot \boldsymbol{\xi}$, where $\mathbf{M}(\mu), \mathbf{N}(\mu)$ are matrix functions only in $\mu$.

For Case 2 and Case 3, we have a continuum of candidates for $\mu$. The feasible domain of $\mu$ is given by $\left([0,1) \cup \left(\widetilde{K} \cap [1,+\infty)\right)\right) \cap J$, where $\widetilde{K}$ is the solution set to the following compatibility condition (obtained by combining constraints (3″) (11)):

$$\mathbf{b}^{\mathrm{T}} \cdot \boldsymbol{\eta}(\mu) + \mathbf{q}^{\mathrm{T}} \cdot \boldsymbol{\xi} \geq (\mu - 1)\mathbf{f}^{\mathrm{T}} \cdot (\mathbf{R}^{\mathrm{T}})_{\mathrm{L}}^{-1}(\mathbf{T}')^{\mathrm{T}} \cdot \boldsymbol{\eta}(\mu)$$

and $J$ is the solution set to constraints $\boldsymbol{\eta}(\mu) \geq \mathbf{0}$. Here both $\overline{\boldsymbol{\eta}}$ and $\boldsymbol{\xi}$ as free non-negative vector parameters are taken to traverse all standard basis vectors, just in the same way as Proposition 7. The tight choices of $\mu$ consists of 0 and the positive boundary points of $\widetilde{K} \cap J$, in the same sense as Definition 1.

### 5.2 An Extension to Bidirectional Affine Invariants

Here we restrict ourselves to single-branch affine loops with deterministic updates and tautological loop guard (◇), but aim for the invariants of bidirectional-inequality form $d_1 \leq \mathbf{c}^{\mathrm{T}} \cdot \mathbf{x} \leq d_2$. This is actually the conjunction of two affine inequalities: $\Phi_1 : -\mathbf{c}^{\mathrm{T}} \cdot \mathbf{x} + d_1 \leq 0 \wedge \Phi_2 : \mathbf{c}^{\mathrm{T}} \cdot \mathbf{x} - d_2 \leq 0$. We have the following proposition:

**Proposition 8.** *For any bidirectional invariant $d_1 \leq \mathbf{c}^{\mathrm{T}} \cdot \mathbf{x} \leq d_2$ of the loop (◇), we have that $\mathbf{c}$ must be an eigenvector of $\mathbf{T}^{\mathrm{T}}$ with a negative eigenvalue.*

*Proof.* We can easily write down the initiation condition: $\theta \models (\Phi_1 \wedge \Phi_2)$ and the corresponding constraints (with $\boldsymbol{\lambda}$, $\widetilde{\boldsymbol{\lambda}}$ being two different vector parameters):

$$\mathbf{R}^{\mathrm{T}} \cdot \boldsymbol{\lambda} = \mathbf{c}, \quad \mathbf{f}^{\mathrm{T}} \cdot \boldsymbol{\lambda} + d_2 = \lambda_0^{\mathrm{I}} \geq 0; \quad \mathbf{R}^{\mathrm{T}} \cdot \widetilde{\boldsymbol{\lambda}} = -\mathbf{c}, \quad \mathbf{f}^{\mathrm{T}} \cdot \widetilde{\boldsymbol{\lambda}} - d_1 = \widetilde{\lambda}_0^{\mathrm{I}} \geq 0.$$

However, there are two possible ways to propose the consecution condition:

$$(\Phi_1 \wedge \tau \models \Phi_1' \text{ and } \Phi_2 \wedge \tau \models \Phi_2') \quad \textbf{or} \quad (\Phi_1 \wedge \tau \models \Phi_2' \text{ and } \Phi_2 \wedge \tau \models \Phi_1')$$

If we choose the first one, there will be nothing different from the things we did in Sect. 4.2. Thus we choose the second one: making the two inequalities induct each other. Hence the Farkas tables are

$$
\begin{array}{r|lllr}
\mu & -\mathbf{c}^{\mathrm{T}}\cdot\mathbf{x} & & & +\, d_1 \leq 0 \ (\varPhi_1) \\
\lambda_0^{\mathrm{C}} & & & & -\, 1 \leq 0 \\
-\mathbf{c} & \mathbf{T}\cdot\mathbf{x} & - & \mathbf{x}' & +\, \mathbf{b} = \mathbf{0} \ \ (\tau) \\
\hline
 & & & & \mathbf{c}^{\mathrm{T}}\cdot\mathbf{x}' - d_2 \leq 0 \ (\varPhi_2')
\end{array}
\qquad
\begin{array}{r|lllr}
\widetilde{\mu} & \mathbf{c}^{\mathrm{T}}\cdot\mathbf{x} & & & -\, d_2 \leq 0 \ (\varPhi_2) \\
\widetilde{\lambda}_0^{\mathrm{C}} & & & & -\, 1 \leq 0 \\
\mathbf{c} & \mathbf{T}\cdot\mathbf{x} & - & \mathbf{x}' & +\, \mathbf{b} = \mathbf{0} \ \ (\tau) \\
\hline
 & & & & -\,\mathbf{c}^{\mathrm{T}}\cdot\mathbf{x}' + d_1 \leq 0 \ (\varPhi_1')
\end{array}
$$

We write out the constraints of consecution:

$$
\begin{gathered}
-\mu\cdot\mathbf{c} = \mathbf{T}^{\mathrm{T}}\cdot\mathbf{c} = -\widetilde{\mu}\cdot\mathbf{c} \\
\mu\cdot d_1 + d_2 - \mathbf{b}^{\mathrm{T}}\cdot\mathbf{c} = \lambda_0^{\mathrm{C}} \geq 0, \quad -\,\widetilde{\mu}\cdot d_2 - d_1 + \mathbf{b}^{\mathrm{T}}\cdot\mathbf{c} = \widetilde{\lambda}_0^{\mathrm{C}} \geq 0
\end{gathered}
\tag{12}
$$

the proposition is verified by (12) since $\mu, \widetilde{\mu} \geq 0$. □

*Example 7 (Fibonacci, Part 6).* Recall that in this example we have a negative eigenvalue $\frac{1-\sqrt{5}}{2}$. It yields the eigenvector $\mathbf{c} = [c_1, \frac{1-\sqrt{5}}{2}c_1]^{\mathrm{T}}$. The other constraints are computed as:

$$
\begin{aligned}
-(3-\sqrt{5})c_1/2 + d_2 = \lambda_0^{\mathrm{I}} \geq 0, &\quad (3-\sqrt{5})c_1/2 - d_1 = \widetilde{\lambda}_0^{\mathrm{I}} \geq 0. \\
-(1-\sqrt{5})d_1/2 + d_2 = \lambda_0^{\mathrm{C}} \geq 0, &\quad (1-\sqrt{5})d_2/2 - d_1 = \widetilde{\lambda}_0^{\mathrm{C}} \geq 0.
\end{aligned}
$$

If we choose $c_1 = 2, \lambda_0^{\mathrm{I}} = 0 = \widetilde{\lambda}_0^{\mathrm{C}}$ (or $c_1 = -2, \widetilde{\lambda}_0^{\mathrm{I}} = 0 = \lambda_0^{\mathrm{C}}$), we get an invariant

$$
\mu = |(1-\sqrt{5})/2| : \ 2(2-\sqrt{5}) \leq 2x_1 + (1-\sqrt{5})x_2 \leq 3 - \sqrt{5}
$$

which reflects the 'golden ratio' property of the Fibonacci numbers. □

*Remark 1.* The generalizations for bidirectional affine invariants to the loops with non-tautological guard or multiple branches are practicable but with some restrictions. The main restriction lies at the point that we need to assume the affine loop guard to also be bidirectional to make our approach for bidirectional affine invariants work. The issue of multiple branches is not critical as the bidirectional invariants can be derived in almost the same way as single-inequality invariants (illustrated in full version [25, Appendix A.3]), with the only difference at the adaption to bidirectional inequalities.

### 5.3 Other Possible Generalizations

***Integer-valued Variables.*** One direction is to transfer some of the results for affine loops over real-valued variables to those over integer-valued variables. Our approach is based on Farkas' lemma which is dedicated to real-valued variables, thus can only provide a sound but not exact treatment for integer-valued variables. An exact treatment for integer-valued variables would require Presburger arithmetics [16], rather than Farkas' lemma.

***Strict-inequality Invariants.*** We handle the non-strict-inequality affine invariants in this work. It's natural to consider the affine invariants of the strict-inequality form. For strict inequalities, we could utilize an extended version of Farkas' lemma in [6, Corollary 1], so that strict inequalities can be generated by either relaxing the non-strict ones obtained from our method or restricting the $\mu$ value to be positive. Since Motzkin transposition theorem is a standard theorem for handling strict inequalities, we believe that Motzkin transposition theorem can also achieve similar results, but may require more tedious manipulations.

## 6 Approximation of Eigenvectors through Continuity

In Sect. 4.2 and Sect. 5.2, we need to solve the characteristic polynomial of the transition matrix to get eigenvalues; while general polynomials with degree $\geq 5$ do not have algebraic solution formula due to Abel-Ruffini theorem. We can develop a number sequence $\{\lambda_i\}$ to approximate the eigenvalue $\lambda$ through root-finding algorithms; however, we cannot approximate the eigenvector of $\lambda$ by solving the kernel of $\mathbf{T}^{\mathrm{T}} - \lambda_i \cdot \mathbf{I}$ since it has trivial kernel. In the case of dimensions $\geq 5$, i.e., when an explicit formula for eigenvalues is unavailable, we introduce an approximation method of the eigenvectors through a continuity property of the invariants:

***Continuity of Invariants w.r.t. $\mu$.*** In Sect. 4, we have shown that for any invariant $\mathbf{c}^{\mathrm{T}} \cdot \mathbf{x} + d \leq 0$ of single-branch affine loops with deterministic updates, the relationship of $\mathbf{c}$ and $\mu$ is given in two ways:

$$\mathbf{c} = \begin{cases} \text{kernel vector of } \mathbf{T}^{\mathrm{T}} - \mu \cdot \mathbf{I} & \text{when } \det(\mathbf{T}^{\mathrm{T}} - \mu \cdot \mathbf{I}) = 0 \\ (\mathbf{T}^{\mathrm{T}} - \mu \cdot \mathbf{I})^{-1} \cdot \mathbf{z} & \text{when } \det(\mathbf{T}^{\mathrm{T}} - \mu \cdot \mathbf{I}) \neq 0 \end{cases}$$

with $\mathbf{z} = \mathbf{P}^{\mathrm{T}} \cdot \boldsymbol{\xi}$. Thus $\mathbf{c} = \mathbf{c}(\mu)$ could be seemed as a vector function in $\mu$ expressed differently at eigenvalues from other points. $\mathbf{c}(\mu)$ is undoubtedly continuous at the points other than eigenvalues, while the following proposition illustrates the continuity property of $\mathbf{c}(\mu)$ at the eigenvalues:

**Proposition 9.** *Suppose $\lambda$ is a real eigenvalue of $\mathbf{T}^{\mathrm{T}}$ with eigenvector $\mathbf{c}(\lambda)$; and $\{\lambda_i\}$ is a sequence lying in the feasible domain of $\mu$ which converges to $\lambda$. If $\lambda$ has geometric multiplicity 1, then the sequence $\{\mathbf{c}(\lambda_i)\}$ converges to $\mathbf{c}(\lambda)$ as well; otherwise, $\{\mathbf{c}(\lambda_i)\}$ converges to $\mathbf{0}$.*

Due to the lack of space, the proof of Proposition 9 is omitted here and available in our full version [25].

***An Algorithmic Approach to Eigenvalue Method in Dimensions $\geq 5$.*** By Proposition 9, if $\lambda$ has geometric multiplicity 1, we can compute $\mathbf{c}(\lambda_i) = (\mathbf{T}^{\mathrm{T}} - \lambda_i \cdot \mathbf{I})^{-1} \cdot \mathbf{z}$ (in the case of tautological loop guard, we just replace $\mathbf{z}$ by any non-zero $n$-dimensional real vector) to approximate the eigenvector $\mathbf{c}(\lambda)$. On the other hand, in the case that $\lambda$ has geometric multiplicity $> 1$, one can adopt Least-squares approximation as presented in [5, Section 8.9]. Though the

Least-squares approximation applies to the cases of eigenvalues with arbitrary geometric multiplicity, our method is much easier to implement and has higher efficiency.

## 7 Experimental Results

***Experiment.*** We implement our automatic invariant-generation algorithm of eigenvalues and tight choices in Python 3.8 and use Sage [42] for matrix manipulation. All results are obtained on an Intel Core i7 (2.00 GHz) machine with 64 GB memory, running Ubuntu 18.04. Our benchmarks are affine loops chosen from some benchmark in the StInG invariant generator [40], some linear dynamical system in [30], some loop programs in [41] and some other linear dynamical systems resulting from well-known linear recurrences such as Fibonacci numbers, Tribonacci numbers, etc.

***Complexity.*** The main bottleneck of our algorithm lies at exactly solving or approximating real roots of univariate polynomials (for computing eigenvalues and boundary points in our algorithmic approach). The rest includes Gaussian elimination with a single parameter (the polynomial-time solvability of which is guaranteed by [26]), matrix inverse and solving eigenvectors with fixed eigenvalues, which can easily be done in polynomial time. The exact solution for degrees less than 5 can be done by directly applying the solution formulas. The approximation of real roots can be carried out through real root isolation and a further divide-and-conquer (or Newton's method) in each obtained interval, which can be completed in polynomial time (see e.g. [36] for the polynomial-time solvability of real root isolation). Thus, our approach runs in polynomial time and is much more efficient than quantifier elimination in [12].

***Results.*** The experimental results are presented in Table 1. In the table, the column 'Loop' specifies the name of the benchmark, 'Dim(ension)' specifies the number of program variables, '$\mu$' specifies the values through eigenvalues of the transition matrices (which we marked with $\mathfrak{e}$) or boundary points of the intervals in the feasible domain, 'Invariants' lists the generated affine invariants from our approach. We compare our approach with the existing generators StInG [40] and InvGen [22], where '$=$', '$>$', '$\gg$' and '$\neq$' means the generated invariants are identical, more accurate, can only be generated in this work, and incomparable, respectively. Table 2 compares the amounts of runtime for our approach and StInG and InvGen respectively, measured in seconds. Note that the runtime of StInG and InvGen are obtained by executing their binary codes on our platform.

***Analysis.*** StInG [40] implements constraint-solving method proposed in [12,37], InvGen [22] integrates both constraint-solving method and abstract interpretation, while our approach uses matrix algebra to refine and upgrade the constraint-solving method. Based on the results in Table 1 and Table 2, we conclude that:

**Table 1.** Experimental Results of Invariants

| Loop | Dim | $\mu$ | Invariants | [40] | [22] |
|---|---|---|---|---|---|
| Fibonacci numbers | 2 | $\lvert(1-\sqrt{5})/2\rvert_e$<br>$(1+\sqrt{5})/2_e$ | $2x_1+(1-\sqrt{5})x_2-3+\sqrt{5}\le 0$<br>$-2x_1-(1-\sqrt{5})x_2+4-2\sqrt{5}\le 0$<br>$-2x_1-(1+\sqrt{5})x_2+3+\sqrt{5}\le 0$<br>$-2x_1-(1+\sqrt{5})x_2\le 0$ | $\gg$ | $\gg$ |
| See-Saw [40] | 2 | $1_e$ | $x_1-2x_2\le 0$<br>$-3x_1+x_2\le 0$ | $=$ | $>$ |
| Example 6.2 [30] | 4 | $\lvert 1-\sqrt{2}\rvert_e$<br>$1+\sqrt{2}_e$ | $w-y-(1-\sqrt{2})x+(1-\sqrt{2})z\le 0$<br>$w-y-(1+\sqrt{2})x+(1+\sqrt{2})z\le 0$ | $>$ | $>$ |
| css2003 [41] | 3 | $0,\ 1_e$ | $i-L^1\le 0$<br>$-i+1\le 0, i+k-1=0$ | $=$ | $=$ |
| afnp2014 [41] | 2 | $0,\ 1_e,\ 1000/999$ | $y-999\le 0$<br>$-y\le 0, x-999y-1\le 0$ | $=$ | $>$ |
| gsv2008 [41] | 2 | $0,\ 1_e,\ 8/7$ | $x-y+2\le 0$<br>$-y\le 0, -x-7y-50\le 0$ | $>$ | $\neq$ |
| cggmp2005 [41] | 2 | $0, 1_e, 4/3$ | $i-j-3\le 0, -i+1\le 0, j-10\le 0$<br>$i+2j-21=0, -i+j-9\le 0$ | $>$ | $>$ |
| Jacobsthal numbers | 2 | $\lvert -1\rvert_e, 2_e$ | $2x_1-x_2-1\le 0, -2x_1+x_2-1\le 0$<br>$-x_1-x_2+2\le 0$ | $\gg$ | $>$ |
| Pell numbers | 2 | $\lvert 1-\sqrt{2}\rvert_e$<br>$1+\sqrt{2}_e$ | $x_1+(1-\sqrt{2})x_2-3+2\sqrt{2}\le 0$<br>$-x_1-(1-\sqrt{2})x_2+7-5\sqrt{2}\le 0$<br>$-x_1-(1+\sqrt{2})x_2+3+2\sqrt{2}\le 0$<br>$-x_1-(1+\sqrt{2})x_2\le 0$ | $\gg$ | $\gg$ |
| Perrin numbers | 3 | $\Delta=\sqrt[3]{\frac{\sqrt{69}+9}{18}}$<br>$\mu=\frac{4}{3}\Delta_e$ | $a=\frac{3\Delta+1/\Delta}{3}, b=1/a+1$<br>$x_1+bx_2+ax_3\ge\frac{2}{3\Delta}+2\Delta+3$ | $\gg$ | $\gg$ |
| Tribonacci numbers | 3 | $\Delta=\sqrt[3]{3\sqrt{33}+19}$<br>$\mu=(5\Delta+1)/3_e$ | $a=\frac{1}{3}(\Delta+\frac{4}{\Delta}+1), b=1/a+1$<br>$x_1+bx_2+ax_3\ge b+a$ | $\gg$ | $\gg$ |

[1] $L$ stands for the variable LARGE_INT in the original program [41]. Note that we modified the loop programs in [41] as affine loops before execution.

**Table 2.** Experimental Results of Execution Time (s)

| Loop | StInG [40] | InvGen [22] | Our Approach |
|---|---|---|---|
| Fibonacci numbers | 0.030 | 0.079 | 0.178 |
| See-Saw [40] | 0.024 | 0.104 | 0.104 |
| Example 6.2 [30] | 0.030 | 0.092 | 0.173 |
| css2003 [41] | 0.019 | 0.111 | 0.193 |
| afnp2014 [41] | 0.025 | 0.076 | 0.193 |
| gsv2008 [41] | 0.027 | 0.092 | 0.207 |
| cggmp2005 [41] | 0.026 | 0.111 | 0.184 |
| Jacobsthal numbers | 0.026 | 0.085 | 0.193 |
| Pell numbers | 0.023 | 0.102 | 0.219 |
| Perrin numbers | 0.031 | 0.129 | 0.250 |
| Tribonacci numbers | 0.029 | 0.115 | 0.262 |

- For the benchmarks with rather simple transition matrices (identity or diagonal matrices), our approach covers or outnumbers the invariants generated by StInG and InvGen.
- For the benchmarks with complicated transition matrices (which are the matrices far away from diagonal ones), especially the ones with irrational eigenvalues, our approach generates adequate accurate invariants while StInG and InvGen generate nothing or only trivial invariants.
- For all benchmarks, the runtime of StInG and InvGen are faster but comparable with our runtime, hence shows the efficiency of our approach.

Summarizing all above, the experimental results demonstrate the wider coverage for the $\mu$ value endowed from our approach, and show the generality and efficiency of our approach.

**Acknowledgements.** This research is partially funded by the National Natural Science Foundation of China (NSFC) under Grant No. 62172271. We sincerely thank the anonymous reviewers for their insightful comments, which helped improve this paper. We also thank Mr. Zhenxiang Huang and Dr. Xin Gao for their pioneering contributions in the experimental part of this work.

## References

1. Adjé, A., Gaubert, S., Goubault, E.: Coupling policy iteration with semi-definite relaxation to compute accurate numerical invariants in static analysis. Log. Methods Comput. Sci. **8**(1) (2012)
2. Albarghouthi, A., Li, Y., Gurfinkel, A., Chechik, M.: UFO: a framework for abstraction- and interpolation-based software verification. In: Madhusudan, P., Seshia, S.A. (eds.) CAV 2012. LNCS, vol. 7358, pp. 672–678. Springer, Heidelberg (2012). https://doi.org/10.1007/978-3-642-31424-7_48
3. Alias, C., Darte, A., Feautrier, P., Gonnord, L.: Multi-dimensional rankings, program termination, and complexity bounds of flowchart programs. In: Cousot, R., Martel, M. (eds.) SAS 2010. LNCS, vol. 6337, pp. 117–133. Springer, Heidelberg (2010). https://doi.org/10.1007/978-3-642-15769-1_8
4. Almagor, S., Karimov, T., Kelmendi, E., Ouaknine, J., Worrell, J.: Deciding $\omega$-regular properties on linear recurrence sequences. Proc. ACM Program. Lang. **5**(POPL), 1–24 (2021)
5. Andrilli, S., Hecker, D.: Chapter 8 - Additional applications. In: Andrilli, S., Hecker, D. (eds.) Elementary Linear Algebra, 5th edn, pp. 513–605. Academic Press, Boston (2016)
6. Asadi, A., Chatterjee, K., Fu, H., Goharshady, A.K., Mahdavi, M.: Polynomial reachability witnesses via Stellensätze. In: PLDI, pp. 772–787. ACM (2021)
7. Bagnara, R., Rodríguez-Carbonell, E., Zaffanella, E.: Generation of basic semi-algebraic invariants using convex polyhedra. In: Hankin, C., Siveroni, I. (eds.) SAS 2005. LNCS, vol. 3672, pp. 19–34. Springer, Heidelberg (2005). https://doi.org/10.1007/11547662_4
8. Breck, J., Cyphert, J., Kincaid, Z., Reps, T.W.: Templates and recurrences: better together. In: PLDI, pp. 688–702. ACM (2020)
9. Chatterjee, K., Fu, H., Goharshady, A.K.: Non-polynomial worst-case analysis of recursive programs. ACM Trans. Program. Lang. Syst. **41**(4), 20:1–20:52 (2019)

10. Chatterjee, K., Fu, H., Goharshady, A.K., Goharshady, E.K.: Polynomial invariant generation for non-deterministic recursive programs. In: PLDI, pp. 672–687. ACM (2020)
11. Chonev, V., Ouaknine, J., Worrell, J.: The polyhedron-hitting problem. In: Indyk, P. (ed.) Proceedings of the Twenty-Sixth Annual ACM-SIAM Symposium on Discrete Algorithms, SODA 2015, San Diego, CA, USA, 4–6 January 2015, pp. 940–956. SIAM (2015)
12. Colón, M.A., Sankaranarayanan, S., Sipma, H.B.: Linear invariant generation using non-linear constraint solving. In: Hunt, W.A., Somenzi, F. (eds.) CAV 2003. LNCS, vol. 2725, pp. 420–432. Springer, Heidelberg (2003). https://doi.org/10.1007/978-3-540-45069-6_39
13. Cousot, P., Cousot, R.: Abstract interpretation: a unified lattice model for static analysis of programs by construction or approximation of fixpoints. In: POPL, pp. 238–252. ACM (1977)
14. Cousot, P., Halbwachs, N.: Automatic discovery of linear restraints among variables of a program. In: POPL, pp. 84–96. ACM Press (1978)
15. David, C., Kesseli, P., Kroening, D., Lewis, M.: Danger invariants. In: Fitzgerald, J., Heitmeyer, C., Gnesi, S., Philippou, A. (eds.) FM 2016. LNCS, vol. 9995, pp. 182–198. Springer, Cham (2016). https://doi.org/10.1007/978-3-319-48989-6_12
16. Dillig, I., Dillig, T., Li, B., McMillan, K.L.: Inductive invariant generation via abductive inference. In: OOPSLA, pp. 443–456. ACM (2013)
17. Farzan, A., Kincaid, Z.: Compositional recurrence analysis. In: 2015 Formal Methods in Computer-Aided Design (FMCAD), pp. 57–64 (2015)
18. Gan, T., Xia, B., Xue, B., Zhan, N., Dai, L.: Nonlinear craig interpolant generation. In: Lahiri, S.K., Wang, C. (eds.) CAV 2020. LNCS, vol. 12224, pp. 415–438. Springer, Cham (2020). https://doi.org/10.1007/978-3-030-53288-8_20
19. Garg, P., Löding, C., Madhusudan, P., Neider, D.: ICE: a robust framework for learning invariants. In: Biere, A., Bloem, R. (eds.) CAV 2014. LNCS, vol. 8559, pp. 69–87. Springer, Cham (2014). https://doi.org/10.1007/978-3-319-08867-9_5
20. Garg, P., Neider, D., Madhusudan, P., Roth, D.: Learning invariants using decision trees and implication counterexamples. In: POPL, pp. 499–512. ACM (2016)
21. Giacobazzi, R., Ranzato, F.: Completeness in abstract interpretation: a domain perspective. In: Johnson, M. (ed.) AMAST 1997. LNCS, vol. 1349, pp. 231–245. Springer, Heidelberg (1997). https://doi.org/10.1007/BFb0000474
22. Gupta, A., Rybalchenko, A.: InvGen: an efficient invariant generator. In: Bouajjani, A., Maler, O. (eds.) CAV 2009. LNCS, vol. 5643, pp. 634–640. Springer, Heidelberg (2009). https://doi.org/10.1007/978-3-642-02658-4_48
23. He, J., Singh, G., Püschel, M., Vechev, M.T.: Learning fast and precise numerical analysis. In: PLDI, pp. 1112–1127. ACM (2020)
24. Humenberger, A., Kovács, L.: Algebra-based synthesis of loops and their invariants (invited paper). In: Henglein, F., Shoham, S., Vizel, Y. (eds.) VMCAI 2021. LNCS, vol. 12597, pp. 17–28. Springer, Cham (2021). https://doi.org/10.1007/978-3-030-67067-2_2
25. Ji, Y., Fu, H., Fang, B., Chen, H.: Affine Loop Invariant Generation via Matrix Algebra, May 2022. https://hal.archives-ouvertes.fr/hal-03494611, preprint
26. Kannan, R.: Solving systems of linear equations over polynomials. Theoret. Comput. Sci. **39**, 69–88 (1985)

27. Kapur, D.: Automatically generating loop invariants using quantifier elimination. In: Deduction and Applications. Dagstuhl Seminar Proceedings, vol. 05431. Internationales Begegnungs- und Forschungszentrum für Informatik (IBFI), Schloss Dagstuhl, Germany (2005)
28. Karimov, T., Lefaucheux, E., Ouaknine, J., Purser, D., Varonka, A., Whiteland, M.A., Worrell, J.: What's decidable about linear loops? Proc. ACM Program. Lang. **6**(POPL) (2022)
29. Kincaid, Z., Breck, J., Boroujeni, A.F., Reps, T.W.: Compositional recurrence analysis revisited. In: PLDI, pp. 248–262. ACM (2017)
30. Kincaid, Z., Breck, J., Cyphert, J., Reps, T.: Closed forms for numerical loops. Proc. ACM Program. Lang. **3**(POPL) (2019)
31. Kincaid, Z., Cyphert, J., Breck, J., Reps, T.W.: Non-linear reasoning for invariant synthesis. Proc. ACM Program. Lang. **2**(POPL), 54:1–54:33 (2018)
32. Manna, Z., Pnueli, A.: Temporal Verification of Reactive Systems: Safety. Springer, New York (2012). https://doi.org/10.1007/978-1-4612-4222-2
33. Nguyen, T., Kapur, D., Weimer, W., Forrest, S.: Using dynamic analysis to discover polynomial and array invariants. In: ICSE. pp. 683–693. IEEE Computer Society (2012)
34. de Oliveira, S., Bensalem, S., Prevosto, V.: Synthesizing invariants by solving solvable loops. In: D'Souza, D., Narayan Kumar, K. (eds.) ATVA 2017. LNCS, vol. 10482, pp. 327–343. Springer, Cham (2017). https://doi.org/10.1007/978-3-319-68167-2_22
35. Rodríguez-Carbonell, E., Kapur, D.: Automatic generation of polynomial invariants of bounded degree using abstract interpretation. Sci. Comput. Program. **64**(1), 54–75 (2007)
36. Sagraloff, M., Mehlhorn, K.: Computing real roots of real polynomials. J. Symb. Comput. **73**, 46–86 (2016)
37. Sankaranarayanan, S., Sipma, H.B., Manna, Z.: Constraint-based linear-relations analysis. In: Giacobazzi, R. (ed.) SAS 2004. LNCS, vol. 3148, pp. 53–68. Springer, Heidelberg (2004). https://doi.org/10.1007/978-3-540-27864-1_7
38. Sharma, R., Aiken, A.: From invariant checking to invariant inference using randomized search. Formal Methods Syst. Des.' **48**(3), 235–256 (2016). https://doi.org/10.1007/s10703-016-0248-5
39. Sharma, R., Gupta, S., Hariharan, B., Aiken, A., Liang, P., Nori, A.V.: A data driven approach for algebraic loop invariants. In: Felleisen, M., Gardner, P. (eds.) ESOP 2013. LNCS, vol. 7792, pp. 574–592. Springer, Heidelberg (2013). https://doi.org/10.1007/978-3-642-37036-6_31
40. Sting: Stanford invariant generator (2004). http://theory.stanford.edu/~srirams/Software/sting.html
41. SV-COMP2021: 11th Competition on Software Verification (2021). https://github.com/sosy-lab/sv-benchmarks
42. The Sage Developers: SageMath, the Sage Mathematics Software System (Version 9.4) (2021). https://www.sagemath.org
43. Xu, R., He, F., Wang, B.: Interval counterexamples for loop invariant learning. In: ESEC/FSE, pp. 111–122. ACM (2020)
44. Yao, J., Ryan, G., Wong, J., Jana, S., Gu, R.: Learning nonlinear loop invariants with gated continuous logic networks. In: PLDI, pp. 106–120. ACM (2020)

BY

# Data-driven Numerical Invariant Synthesis with Automatic Generation of Attributes

Ahmed Bouajjani[1], Wael-Amine Boutglay[1,2](✉), and Peter Habermehl[1]

[1] Université Paris Cité, IRIF, Paris, France
{abou,boutglay,haberm}@irif.fr
[2] Mohammed VI Polytechnic University, Ben Guerir, Morocco

**Abstract.** We propose a data-driven algorithm for numerical invariant synthesis and verification. The algorithm is based on the ICE-DT schema for learning decision trees from samples of positive and negative states and implications corresponding to program transitions. The main issue we address is the discovery of relevant attributes to be used in the learning process of numerical invariants. We define a method for solving this problem guided by the data sample. It is based on the construction of a separator that covers positive states and excludes negative ones, consistent with the implications. The separator is constructed using an abstract domain representation of convex sets. The generalization mechanism of the decision tree learning from the constraints of the separator allows the inference of general invariants, accurate enough for proving the targeted property. We implemented our algorithm and showed its efficiency.

**Keywords:** Invariant synthesis · Data-driven program verification

## 1 Introduction

Invariant synthesis for program safety verification is a highly challenging problem. Many approaches exist for tackling this problem, including abstract interpretation, CEGAR-based symbolic reachability, property-directed reachability (PDR), etc. [3,5,6,8,10,14,17,19]. While those approaches are applicable to large classes of programs, they may have scalability limitations and fail to infer certain types of invariants, such as disjunctive invariants. Emerging data-driven approaches, following the active learning paradigm with various machine learning techniques, have shown their ability to solve efficiently complex instances of the invariant synthesis problem [12,15,16,20,26,30,31]. These approaches are based on the iterative interaction between a *learner* inferring candidate invariants from a *data sample*, i.e., a set of data classified either as positive examples, known to be reachable from the initial states and that therefore must be included in any solution, or negative examples, known to be predecessors of states violating the safety property and that therefore cannot be included in any solution,

This work was supported in part by the french ANR project AdeCoDS.


S. Shoham and Y. Vizel (Eds.): CAV 2022, LNCS 13371, pp. 282–303, 2022.
https://doi.org/10.1007/978-3-031-13185-1_14

and a *teacher* checking the validity of the proposed solutions and providing counterexamples as feedback in case of non-validity. One such data-driven approach is ICE [15] which has shown promising results with its instantiation ICE-DT [16] that uses decision trees for the learning component. ICE is a learning approach tailored for invariant synthesis, where the feedback provided by the teacher can be, in addition to positive and negative examples, implications of the form $p \to q$ expressing the fact that if $p$ is in a solution, then necessarily $q$ should also be included in the solution since there is a transition in the program from $p$ to $q$.

The strength of data-driven approaches is the generalization mechanisms of their learning components, allowing them to find relevant abstractions from a number of examples without exploring the whole state space of the program. In the case of ICE-DT, this is done by a sophisticated construction of decision trees classifying correctly the known positive and negative examples at some point, and taking into account the information provided by the implications. These decision trees, where the tested attributes are predicates on the variables of the program, are interpreted as formulas corresponding to candidate invariants.

However, to apply data-driven methods such as ICE-DT, one needs to have a pool of attributes that are potentially relevant for the construction of the invariant. This is actually a crucial issue. In ICE-DT, as well as in most data-driven methods, finding the predicates involved in the invariant construction is based on systematic enumeration of formulas according to some pre-defined templates or grammars. For instance, in the case of numerical programs, the considered patterns are some special types of linear constraints, and candidate attributes are generated by enumerating all possible values for the coefficients under some fixed bound. While such a brute-force enumeration can be effective in many cases, it represents, in general, an obstacle for both scalability and finding sufficiently accurate inductive invariants in complex cases.

In this paper, we provide an algorithmic method for efficient generation of attributes for data-driven invariant synthesis for numerical programs manipulating integer variables. While enumerative approaches are purely syntactic and do not take into account the data sample, our method is guided by it. We show that this method, when integrated in the ICE-DT schema, leads to a new invariant synthesis algorithm outperforming state-of-the-art methods and tools.

Our method for attributes discovery is based on, given an ICE data sample, computing a *separator* of it as a union of convex sets i.e., (1) it covers all the positive examples, (2) it does not contain any negative example, and (3) it is consistent with the implications (for every $p \to q$ in the sample, if the separator contains $p$, then it should also contain $q$). Then, the set of attributes generated is the set of all constraints defining the separator. However, as for a given sample there might be several possible separators, a question is which separators to consider. Our approach is guided by two requirements: (1) we need to avoid big pools of attributes in order to reduce the complexity of the invariant construction process, and (2) we need to avoid having in the pool constraints that are (visibly) unnecessary, e.g. separating positive examples in a region without any negative ones. Therefore, we consider separators that satisfy the property that, whenever they contain two convex sets, it is impossible to take their convex union (smallest convex set containing the union) without including a negative example.

To represent and manipulate algorithmically convex sets, we consider abstract domains, e.g., intervals, octagons, and polyhedra, as they are defined in the abstract interpretation framework and implemented in tools such as APRON [18]. These domains correspond to particular classes of convex sets, defined by specific types of linear constraints. In these domains, the union operation is naturally over-approximated by the *join* operation that computes the best over-approximation of the union in the considered class of convex sets. Then, constructing separators as explained above can be done by iterative application of the join operation while it does not include negative examples.

Then, this method for generating candidate attributes can be integrated into the ICE-DT schema: in each iteration of ICE loop, given a sample, the learner (1) generates a set of candidate attributes from a separator of the sample, (2) builds a decision tree from these attributes and proposes it as a candidate invariant to the teacher. Then, the teacher (1) checks that the proposed solution is an inductive invariant, and if it is not (2) provides a counterexample to the learner, extending the sample that will be used in the next iteration.

Here a question might be asked: why do we need to construct a decision tree from the constraints of the separator and do not propose directly the formula defining the separator as a candidate invariant to the teacher. The answer is that the decision tree construction is crucial for generalization. Indeed, given a sample, the constructed separator might be too specialized to that sample and does not provide a useful inductive invariant (except for some simple cases). For instance, the constructed separator is a union of *bounded* convex sets (polytopes), while invariants are very often unbounded convex sets (polyhedra). The effect of using decision trees, in this case, is to select the relevant constraints and discard the unnecessary bounds, leading very quickly to an unbounded solution that is general enough to be an inductive invariant. Without this generalization mechanisms, the ICE loop will not terminate in such (quite common) cases.

The integration of our method can be made tighter and more efficient by making the process of building separators incremental along the ICE iterations: at each step, after the extension of the sample by the teacher, instead of constructing a separator of the new sample from scratch, the parts of previously computed separators not affected by the last extension of the sample are reused.

We have implemented our algorithm and carried out experiments on the SyGuS-Comp'19 benchmarks. Our method solves significantly more cases than the tools LoopInvGen [25,26], CVC4 [1,27], and Spacer [19], as well as our implementation of the original ICE-DT [16] algorithm (with template-based enumeration of attributes), with very competitive time performances.

**Related Work.** Many learning-based approaches for the verification of numerical programs have been developed recently. One of the earliest approaches is Daikon [11]. Given a pool of formulas, it computes likely invariants from program executions. Later approaches were developed for the synthesis of sound invariants, for example [30] iteratively generates a set of reachable and bad states and classifies them with a combination of half-spaces computed using SVM. In [29], the problem is reformulated as learning geometric concepts in machine learning. The first instantiation of the ICE framework was based on a constraint solver [15]. Later on, it was instantiated using the decision trees learning algorithm [16]. Both those instantiations require a fixed template for the invariants or the formulas appearing in them. LoopInvGen enumerates predicates on-demand using the approach introduced in [26]. This is extended to a mechanism with hybrid enumeration of several domains or grammars [25]. Continuous logic networks were also used to tackle the problem in CLN2INV [28]. Code2Inv [31], the first approach to introduce general deep learning methods to program verification, uses a graph neural network to capture the program structure and reinforcement learning to guide the search heuristic of a particular domain.

The learning approach of ICE and ICE-DT has been generalized to solve problems given as constrained horn clauses (CHC) in Horn-ICE [12] and HoICE [4]. Outside the ICE framework, [33] proposed a learning approach for solving CHC using decision trees and SVM for the synthesis of candidate predicates from a set of reachable and bad states of the program. The limitation of the non-ICE-based approach is that when the invariant is not inductive, the program has to be rerun, forward and backward, to generate more reachable and bad states.

In more theoretical work, an abstract learning framework for synthesis, introduced in [21], incorporates the principle of CEGIS (counterexample-guided inductive synthesis). A study of overfitting in invariant synthesis was conducted in [25]. ICE was compared with IC3/PDR in terms of complexity in [13]. A generalization of ICE with relative inductiveness [32] can implement IC3/PDR following the paradigm of active learning with a learner and a teacher.

Automatic invariant synthesis and verification has been addressed by many other techniques based on exploring and computing various types of abstract representations of reachable states (e.g., [3,5,6,8,10,14,17,19]). Notice that, although we use abstract domains for representation and manipulation of convex sets, our strategy for exploring the set of potential invariants is different from the ones used typically in abstract interpretation analysis algorithms [8].

## 2 Safety Verification Using Learning of Invariants

This section presents the approach we use for solving the safety verification problem. It is built upon the ICE framework [15] and in particular its instantiation with the learning of decision trees [16]. We first define the verification problem.

### 2.1 Linear Constraints and Safety Verification

Let $X$ be a set of variables. Linear formulas over $X$ are boolean combinations of linear constraints of the form $\sum_{i=1}^{n} a_i x_i \leq b$ where the $x_i$'s are variables in $X$, the $a_i$'s are integer constants, and $b \in \mathbb{Z} \cup \{+\infty\}$. We use linear formulas to reason symbolically about programs with integer variables. Assume we have a program with a set of variables $V$ and let $n = |V|$. A state of the program is a vector of integers in $\mathbb{Z}^n$. Primed versions of these variables are used to encode the transition relation $T$ of the program: for each $v \in V$, we consider a variable $v'$ to represent the value of $v$ after the transition. Let $V'$ be the set of primed variables, and consider linear formulas over $V \cup V'$ to define the relation $T$.

The *safety verification problem* consists in, given a set of safe states *Good*, deciding whether, starting from a set of initial states *Init*, all the reachable states by iterative application of $T$ are in *Good*. Dually, this is equivalent to decide if starting from *Init*, it is possible to reach a state in *Bad* which is the set of unsafe states (the complement of *Good*). Assuming that the sets *Init* and *Good* can be defined using linear formulas, the safety verification problem amounts to find an adequate *inductive invariant* $I$, such that the three following formulas are valid:

$$Init(V) \Rightarrow I(V) \quad (1)$$

$$I(V) \Rightarrow Good(V) \quad (2)$$

$$I(V) \wedge T(V, V') \Rightarrow I(V') \quad (3)$$

We are looking for inductive invariants which can be expressed as a linear formula. In that case, the validity of the three formulas is decidable and can be checked with a standard SMT solver.

### 2.2 The ICE Learning Framework

ICE [15] follows the active learning paradigm to learn adequate inductive invariants of a given program and a given safety property. It consists of an iteratively communicating *learner* and a *teacher* (see Algorithm 1).

**Input** : A transition system and a property: $(Init, T, Good)$
**Output:** An adequate invariant or error
1 initialize ICE-sample $S = (S^+, S^-, S^\rightarrow)$;
2 **while** *true* **do**
3 $\quad J \leftarrow$ LEARN$(S)$;
4 $\quad (success, counterexample) \leftarrow$ IS_INDUCTIVE$(J)$;
5 $\quad$ **if** *success* **then return** $J$ ;
6 $\quad$ **else**
7 $\quad\quad S \leftarrow$ UPDATE$(S, counterexample)$;
8 $\quad\quad$ **if** $contradictory(S)$ **then return** *error*;

**Algorithm 1:** The main loop of ICE.

In each iteration, in line 3, the *learner*, which does not know anything about the program, synthesizes a candidate invariant (as a formula over the program variables) from a *sample* $S$ (containing information about program states) which is enriched during the learning process. Contrary to other learning methods, the sample $S$ not only contains a set of *positive* states $S^+$ which should satisfy the invariant, and a set of *negative* states $S^-$ which should not satisfy the invariant, but it contains also a set of *implications* $S^{\rightarrow}$ of the form $s \rightarrow s'$ meaning that if $s$ satisfies the invariant, then $s'$ should satisfy it as well (because there is a transition from $s$ to $s'$ in the transition relation of the program). Therefore, an ICE-sample $S$ is a triple $(S^+, S^-, S^{\rightarrow})$, where to account for the information contained in implications, it is imposed additionally that

$$\forall s \rightarrow s' \in S^{\rightarrow} : \text{ if } s \in S^+, \text{ then } s' \in S^+, \text{ and if } s' \in S^-, \text{ then } s \in S^- \quad (4)$$

The sample is initially empty (or containing some states whose status, positive or negative, is known). It is assumed that a candidate invariant $J$ proposed by the learner is *consistent* with the sample, i.e. states in $S^+$ satisfy the invariant $J$, the states in $S^-$ falsify it, and for implications $s \rightarrow s' \in S^{\rightarrow}$ it is not the case that $s$ satisfies $J$ but not $s'$. Given a candidate invariant $J$ provided by the *learner* in line 3, the *teacher* who knows the transition relation $T$, checks if $J$ is an inductive invariant in line 4; if yes, the process stops, an invariant has been found; otherwise a counterexample is provided and used in line 7 to update the sample for the next iteration. The teacher checks the three conditions an inductive invariant must satisfy (see Sect. 2.1). If (1) is violated the counterexample is a state $s$ which should be in the invariant because it is in *Init*. Therefore $s$ is added to $S^+$. If (2) is violated the counterexample is a state $s$ which should not be in the invariant because it is not in *Good* and $s$ is added to $S^-$. If (3) is violated the counterexample is an implication $s \rightarrow s'$ where if $s$ is in the invariant, $s'$ should also be in it. Therefore $s \rightarrow s'$ is added to $S^{\rightarrow}$. In all three cases, the sample is updated to satisfy property 4. If this leads to a contradictory sample, i.e. $S^+ \cap S^- \neq \emptyset$, the program is incorrect and an error is returned. Notice that obviously, in general, the loop is not guaranteed to terminate.

### 2.3 ICE-DT: Invariant Learning Using Decision Trees

In [16], the ICE learning framework is instantiated with a learn method, which extends classical decision tree learning algorithms with the handling of implications. In the context of invariant synthesis, *decision trees* are used to classify points from a universe, which is the set of program states. They are binary trees whose inner nodes are labeled by predicates from a set of attributes and whose leaves are either + or −. Attributes are (atomic) formulas over the variables of the program. They can be seen as boolean functions that the decision tree learning algorithm will compose to construct a classifier of the given ICE sample. In our case of numerical programs manipulating integer variables, attributes are linear inequalities. Then, a decision tree can be seen naturally as a quantifier-free formula over program variables.

The main idea of the ICE-DT learner (see Algorithm 2) is as follows. Initially, the learner fixes a set of attributes (possibly empty) which is kept in a global variable and updated in successive executions of LEARN($S$). In line 2, given a sample, the learner checks whether the current set of attributes is sufficient to produce a decision tree corresponding to a formula consistent with the sample. If the check is successful the sample $S$ is changed to $S_{Attr}$ taking

```
  Input  : An ICE sample S = (S+, S-, S→)
  Output: A formula
  Global : Attributes initialized with InitialAttributes
1 Proc LEARN(S)
2   (success, S_Attr) ← SUFFICIENT(Attributes, S);
3   while ¬success do
4     Attributes ← GENERATEATTRIBUTES(Attributes, S);
5     (success, S_Attr) ← SUFFICIENT(Attributes, S);
6   return tree_to_formula(CONSTRUCT-TREE(S_Attr, Attributes))
```

**Algorithm 2:** The ICE-DT learner LEARN($S$) procedure.

into account information gathered during the check (see below for the details of SUFFICIENT(*Attributes*, $S$)). If the check fails new attributes are generated with GENERATEATTRIBUTES(*Attributes*, $S$) until success. Then, a decision tree is constructed in line 6 from the sample $S_{Attr}$ by CONSTRUCT-TREE($S_{Attr}$, *Attributes*) which we present below (Algorithm 3). It is transformed into a formula and returned as a potential invariant. Notice that in the main ICE loop of Algorithm 1 the teacher then checks if this invariant is inductive or not. If not, the original sample $S$ is updated and in the next iteration the learner checks if the attributes are still sufficient for the updated sample. If not, the learner generates new attributes and proceeds with constructing another decision tree and so on.

An important question is how to choose *InitialAttributes* and how to generate new attributes when needed. In [16], the set *InitialAttributes* is for example the set of octagons over program variables with absolute values of constants bounded by $c \in \mathbb{N}$. If these attributes are not sufficient to classify the sample, then new attributes are generated simply by increasing the bound $c$ by 1. We use a different method described in detail in Sect. 4. We now describe how a decision tree can be constructed from an ICE sample and a set of attributes.

**Decision Tree Learning Algorithms.** The well-known standard decision tree learning algorithms like ID3 [23] take as an input a sample containing points marked as positive or negative of some universe and a fixed set *Attributes*. They construct a decision tree by choosing as the root an attribute, splitting the sample in two (one with all points satisfying the attribute and one with the other points) and recursively constructing trees for the two subsamples. At each step the attribute maximizing the information gain computed using the entropy of subsamples is chosen. Intuitively this means that at each step, the attribute which separates the "best" positive and negative points is chosen. In the context of verification, exact classification is needed, and therefore, all points in a leaf must be classified in a way consistent with the sample.

In [16] this idea is extended to handle also implications which is essential for an ICE learner. The basic algorithm to construct a tree (given as Algorithm 3 below) gets as input an ICE sample $S = (S^+, S^-, S^\rightarrow)$ and a set of *Attributes* and produces a decision tree *consistent* with the sample, which means that each point in $S^+$ (resp. $S^-$) is classified as positive (resp. negative) and for each implication $(s, s') \in S^{\rightarrow}$ it is not the case that $s$ is classified as positive and $s'$ as negative. The initial sample $S$ is supposed to be consistent.

```
   Input  : An ICE sample S = (S+, S-, S→) and a set of Attributes.
   Output: A tree
1  Proc CONSTRUCT-TREE(S, Attributes)
2      Set G (partial mapping of end-points of impl. to {POSITIVE, NEGATIVE}) to empty ;
3      Let Unclass be the set of all end-points of implications in S→;
4      Compute the implication closure of G w.r.t. S;
5      return DECISIONTREEICE(⟨S+, S-, Unclass⟩, Attributes);
6  Proc DECISIONTREEICE(Examples = ⟨Pos, Neg, Unclass⟩, Attributes)
7      Move all points of Unclass classified as POSITIVE (resp. NEGATIVE) to Pos (resp. Neg);
8      if Neg = ∅ then
9          Mark all points of Unclass in G as POSITIVE;
10         Compute the implication closure of G w.r.t. S;
11         return Leaf(+);
12     else if Pos = ∅ then
13         Mark all points of Unclass in G as NEGATIVE;
14         Compute the implication closure of G w.r.t. S;
15         return Leaf(−);
16     else
17         a ← CHOOSE(Attributes, Examples);
18         Divide Examples into two: Examples_a with all points satisfying a and
             Examples_¬a the others;
19         T_left ← DECISIONTREEICE(Examples_a, Attributes \ {a});
20         T_right ← DECISIONTREEICE(Examples_¬a, Attributes \ {a});
21         return Tree(a, T_left, T_right);
```

**Algorithm 3:** The ICE-DT decision-tree learning procedures.

The learner is similar to the classical decision tree learning algorithms. However, it has to take care of implications. To this end, the learner also considers the set of points appearing as end-points in the implications but not in $S^+$ and $S^-$. These points are considered in the beginning as unclassified, and the learner will either mark them POSITIVE or NEGATIVE during the construction as follows: if in the construction of the tree a subsample is reached containing only positive (resp. negative) points and unclassified points (lines 8 and 12 resp.), *all* these points are classified as positive (resp. negative). To make sure that implications are still consistent, the *implication closure* with the newly classified points is computed and stored in the global variable $G$, a (partial mapping) of end-points in $S^{\rightarrow}$ to {POSITIVE, NEGATIVE}. The implication closure of $G$ w.r.t. $S$ is defined as: If $G(s) =$ POSITIVE or $s \in S^+$ and $(s, s') \in S^{\rightarrow}$ then also $G(s') =$ POSITIVE. If $G(s') =$ NEGATIVE or $s' \in S^-$ and $(s, s') \in S^{\rightarrow}$ then also $G(s) =$ NEGATIVE.

The set *Attributes* is such that a consistent decision tree will always be found, i.e. the set *Attributes* in line 17 is never empty (see below). An attribute in a node is chosen with CHOOSE(*Attributes*, *Examples*) returning an attribute $a \in$ *Attributes* with the highest *gain* according to *Examples*. We do not give the details of this function. In [16] several gain functions are defined extending the classical gain function based on entropy with the treatment of implications. We use the one which penalizes cutting implications (like ICE-DT-penalty).

**Checking if the Set of Attributes is Sufficient.** Here we show how the function SUFFICIENT(*Attributes*, $S$) of Algorithm 2 is implemented in [16]. Two states $s$ and $s'$ are considered equivalent (denoted by $\equiv_{Attributes}$), if they satisfy the same attributes of *Attributes*. One has to make sure that two equivalent states are never classified in different ways by the tree construction algorithm. This is done by the following procedure: For any two states $s$, $s'$ with $s \equiv_{Attributes} s'$ which appear in the sample (as positive or negative or end-points of the implications) two implications $s \to s'$ and $s' \to s$ are added to $S^{\to}$ of $S$.

Then, the implication closure of the sample is computed starting from an empty mapping $G$ (all end-points are initially unclassified). If during the computation of the implication closure one end-point is classified as both POSITIVE and NEGATIVE, then SUFFICIENT(*Attributes*, $S$) returns $(false, S)$ else it returns $(true, S_{Attr})$ where $S_{Attr}$ is obtained from $S = (S^+, S^-, S^{\to})$ by adding to $S^+$ the end-points of implications classified as POSITIVE and to $S^-$ the end-points classified as NEGATIVE.

In [16] it is shown that this guarantees in general that a tree consistent with the sample will always be constructed regardless of the order in which attributes are chosen. We illustrate now the ICE-DT learner on a simple example.

*Example 1.* Let $S = (S^+, S^-, S^{\to})$ be a sample (illustrated in Fig. 1) with two-dimensional states (variables $x$ and $y$): $S^+ = \{(1,1), (1,4), (3,1), (5,1), (5,4), (6,1), (6,4)\}$, $S^- = \{(4,1), (4,2), (4,3), (4,4)\}$, $S^{\to} = \{(2,2) \to (2,3), (0,2) \to (4,0)\}$. We suppose that $Attributes = \{x \geq 1, x \leq 3, y \geq 1, y \leq 4, x \geq 5, x \leq 6\}$ is given. In Sect. 4 we show how to obtain this set from the sample. The learner first checks that the set *Attributes* is sufficient to construct a formula consistent with $S$. The check succeeds and we have among others that $(2,2)$ and $(2,3)$ and the surrounding positive states on the left are all equivalent w.r.t. $\equiv_{Attributes}$. Therefore after adding implications (which we omit for clarity in the following) and the computation of the implication closure both $(2,2)$ and $(2,3)$ are added to $S^+$. Then, the construction of the tree is started with *Examples* containing 9 positive, 4 negative and 2 unclassified states. Depending on the gain function an attribute is chosen. Here, it is $x \geq 5$, since it separates all the positive states on the right from the rest and does not cut the implication. The set *Examples* is split into the states satisfying $x \geq 5$ and those which don't: $Examples_{x \geq 5}$ and $Examples_{x<5}$. $Examples_{x \geq 5}$ contains only positive states $\{(5,1), (5,4), (6,1), (6,4)\}$ and the branch is finished whereas $Examples_{x<5}$ contains the remaining positive, negative and unclassified states and the construction continues. The attribute $x \leq 3$ is chosen and $Examples_{x<5}$ split in two. $Examples_{x<5 \wedge x \leq 3}$ contains the positive states $\{(1,1), (1,4), (3,1), (2,2), (2,3)\}$ and one unclassified state $(0,2)$. Therefore, the algorithm marks $(0,2)$ as positive and as there is an implication $(0,2) \to (4,0)$, the state $(4,0)$ is marked positive as well and a leaf node is returned. The other branch $Examples_{x<5 \wedge x>3}$ now contains negative states $\{(4,1), (4,2), (4,3), (4,4)\}$ and a positive state $(4,0)$. Therefore another attribute is needed. Finally, the algorithm returns a tree corresponding to the formula $x \geq 5 \vee (x < 5 \wedge x \leq 3) \vee (x < 5 \wedge x > 3 \wedge y < 1)$.

## 3 Linear Formulas as Abstract Objects

Algorithm 2 requires a set of attributes as input. In Sect. 4, we show how to generate these attributes from the sample. For that purpose, we use numerical abstract domains to represent and manipulate algorithmically sets of integer vectors representing program states. We consider standard numerical domains defined in [7,9,22] and implemented in tools such as APRON [18]: Intervals, Octagons, and Polyhedra.

Given a set of $n$ variables $X$ and a linear formula $\varphi$ over $X$, let $[\![\varphi]\!] \subseteq \mathbb{Z}^n$ be the set of all integer points satisfying the formula. Now, a subset of $\mathbb{Z}^n$ is called

- an *interval*, iff it is equal to $[\![\varphi]\!]$ where $\varphi$ is a conjunction of constraints of the form $\alpha \leq x \leq \beta$, where $x \in X$, $\alpha \in \mathbb{Z} \cup \{-\infty\}$ and $\beta \in \mathbb{Z} \cup \{+\infty\}$.
- an *octagon*, iff it is equal to $[\![\varphi]\!]$ where $\varphi$ is a conjunction of constraints of the form $\pm\, x \,\pm\, y \leq \alpha$ where $x, y \in X$ and $\alpha \in \mathbb{Z} \cup \{+\infty\}$.
- a *polyhedra*, iff it is equal to $[\![\varphi]\!]$ where $\varphi$ is a conjunction of linear constraints of the form $\sum_{i=1}^{n} a_i x_i \leq b$ where $X = \{x_1, \ldots, x_n\}$ and for every $i$, $a_i \in \mathbb{Z}$, and $b \in \mathbb{Z} \cup \{+\infty\}$.

Now, we can define several abstract domains as complete lattices $A_X^{type} = \langle D_X^{type}, \sqsubseteq, \sqcup, \sqcap, \bot, \top \rangle$, where *type* is either *int*, *oct* or *poly* and $D_X^{int}$ is the set of intervals, $D_X^{oct}$ is the set of octagons and $D_X^{poly}$ the set of polyhedra.

The relation $\sqsubseteq$ is set inclusion. The binary operation $\sqcup$ (resp. $\sqcap$) is the *join* (resp. *meet*) operation that defines the smallest (resp. greatest) element in $D_X$ that contains (resp. contained in) the union (resp. the intersection) of the two composed elements. Finally $\bot$ (resp. $\top$) corresponds to the empty set (resp. $\mathbb{Z}^n$).

We suppose that we have a function $Form^{type}(d)$ which given an element $d \subseteq \mathbb{Z}^n$ of the lattice provides us a formula $\varphi$ of the corresponding type such that $[\![\varphi]\!] = d$. There are many ways to describe the set $d$ with a formula $\varphi$. Therefore the function $Form^{type}(d)$ depends on the particular implementation of the abstract domains. We furthermore define $Constr^{type}(d)$ to be the set of linear constraints of $Form^{type}(d)$.

We drop the superscript *type* from all preceding definitions, when it is clear from the context or when we define notions for all types.

All singleton subsets of $\mathbb{Z}^n$ are elements of the lattices and for example, if $p = (x = 1, y = 2)$, then, for the domains of Intervals, Octagons, and Polyhedra as implemented in APRON we have: $Constr^{int}(\{p\}) = \{x \leq 1, x \geq 1, y \leq 2, y \geq 2\}$, $Constr^{oct}(\{p\}) = \{x \geq 1, x \leq 1, y - x \geq 1, x + y \geq 3, y \geq 2, y \leq 2, x + y \leq 3, x - y \geq -1\}$ and $Constr^{poly}(\{p\}) = \{x = 1, y = 2\}$.

Notice, that in APRON while equality constraints are used in the Polyhedra domain, these constraints are not explicit in the Interval and Octagon domains.

An important fact about the three domains mentioned above is that, each element of the lattice is the intersection of a convex subset of $\mathbb{Q}^n$ with $\mathbb{Z}^n$. To be able to reason about integer points from *nonconvex* sets, we will use in the next section sets of sets.

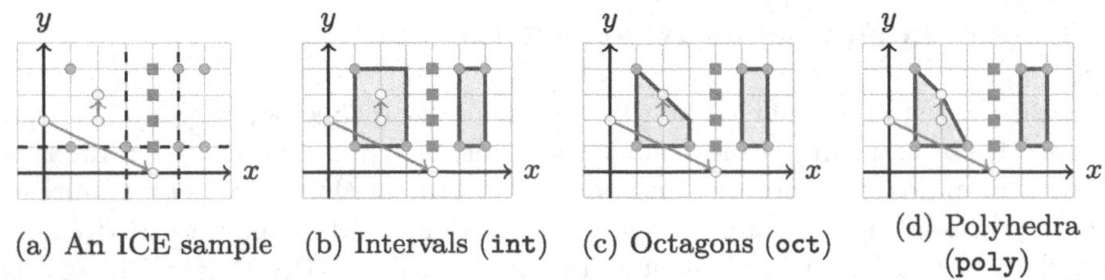


**Fig. 1.** An ICE sample and its separators using different abstract domains.

# 4 Generating Attributes from Sample Separators

We define in this section algorithms for generating a set of attributes that can be used for constructing decision trees representing candidate invariants. Given an ICE sample, these algorithms are based on constructing separators of the two sets of positive and negative states that are consistent with the implications in the sample. These separators are sets of intervals, octagons or polyhedra. The set of all constraints that define these sets are collected as a set of attributes.

## 4.1 Abstract Sample Separators

Let $S = (S^+, S^-, S^\rightarrow)$ be an ICE sample, and let $A_X = \langle D_X, \sqsubseteq, \sqcup, \sqcap, \bot, \top\rangle$ be an abstract domain. Intuitively, a separator has sets containing all positive states, not containing any negative state and is consistent with implications. Formally, an $A_X$-separator of $S$ is a set $\mathbb{S} \in 2^{D_X}$ such that $\forall p \in S^+.\ \exists d \in \mathbb{S}.\ p \in d$ and $\forall p \in S^-.\ \forall d \in \mathbb{S}.\ p \notin d$ and $\forall p \rightarrow q \in S^\rightarrow.\ \forall d \in \mathbb{S}.\ (p \in d \implies (\exists d' \in \mathbb{S}.\ q \in d'))$.

Given a set of positive states $S^+$, we define the basic separator $\mathbb{S}_{basic}$ as $\{\{p\} \mid p \in S^+\}$ where each state is alone in its set. Our method for generating attributes for the learning process is based on computing a special type of separators called *join-maximal*. An $A_X$-separator $\mathbb{S}$ is join-maximal if is not possible to take the join of two of its elements without including a negative state: $\forall d_1, d_2 \in \mathbb{S}.\ d_1 \neq d_2 \implies (\exists n \in S^-.\ n \in d_1 \sqcup d_2)$.

*Example 2.* Let us consider again the ICE sample $S$ given in Example 1. Figure 1 shows the borders of join-maximal $A_X$-separators for $S$ for different abstract domains (Intervals `int`, Octagons `oct`, and Polyhedra `poly`).

*Remark 1.* An ICE sample may have multiple join-maximal separators as Fig. 2 shows for the polyhedra domain. The method presented in the next section computes one of them non-deterministically.

## 4.2 Computing a Join-Maximal Abstract Separator

We present in this section a basic algorithm for computing a join-maximal $A_X$-separator for a given sample $S$. Computing such a separator can be done iteratively starting from $\mathbb{S}_{basic}$, and at each step, choosing two elements $d_1$ and $d_2$

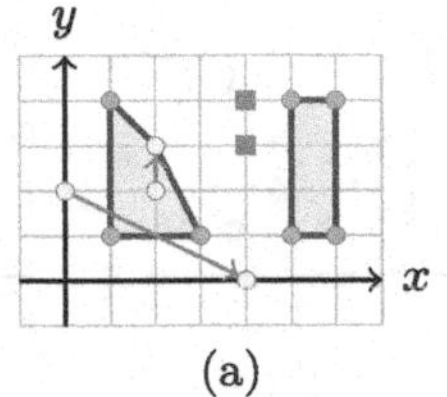

(a)

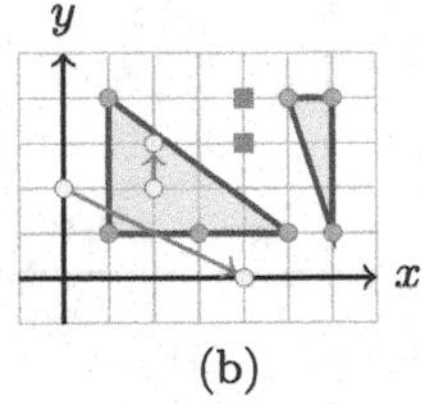

(b)

**Fig. 2.** Different join-maximal separators for a same sample.

in the current separator such that $d_1 \sqcup d_2$ does not contain a negative state in $S^-$ (This can be checked using the meet operation $\sqcap$), and replacing $d_1$ and $d_2$ by $d_1 \sqcup d_2$. Then, if any element of the separator contains the source $p$ of an implication $p \rightarrow q$, which means that $p$ is considered now as a positive state, then since $q$ must also be considered as positive, the element $\{q\}$ must be added to the separator if $q$ is not already in some element of the current separator. When no new join operations (without including negative states) can be done, the obtained set is necessarily a join-maximal $A_X$-separator of $S$. This procedure corresponds to Algorithm 4.

**Input** : An ICE sample $S = (S^+, S^-, S^\rightarrow)$ and an abstract domain $A_X = \langle D_X, \sqsubseteq, \sqcup, \sqcap, \bot, \top \rangle$.
**Output:** $\mathbb{S}$ a join-maximal $A_X$-separator of $S$.
**Proc** CONSTRUCTSEPARATOR($S, A_X$)
  $\mathbb{S} \leftarrow \mathbb{S}_{basic}$ (* $= \{\{s\} \mid s \in S^+\}$ *) ;
  **while** *true* **do**
    **if** $\exists a, b \in \mathbb{S}.\, a \neq b \wedge \forall n \in S^-.\, n \notin a \sqcup b$ **then**
      $\mathbb{S} \leftarrow (\mathbb{S} \setminus \{a, b\}) \cup \{a \sqcup b\}$ ;
      **while** $\exists p \rightarrow q \in S^\rightarrow.\, \exists d \in \mathbb{S}.\, p \in d \wedge \forall d' \in \mathbb{S}.\, q \notin d'$ **do**
        $\mathbb{S} \leftarrow \mathbb{S} \cup \{\{q\}\}$ ;
    **else break;**

**Algorithm 4:** Computing a join-maximal $A_X$-separator.

Notice that instead of starting with the basic separator $\mathbb{S}_{basic}$ defined as above one can start with any separator $\mathbb{S}_{init} \supseteq \mathbb{S}_{basic}$ whose additional sets contain only states which are known to be positive (for example the initial states).

*Example 3.* Consider again the sample $S$ of Example 2. We show how the separators of $S$ in Fig. 1 are constructed using Algorithm 4. The algorithm starts from the basic separator $\mathbb{S}_{basic}$ where every positive state in $S$ is alone (Fig. 3(a)). It picks two elements in that separator, e.g. $\{d_1\}$ and $\{d_2\}$. As their join does not include negative states, $\{d_1\}$ and $\{d_2\}$ are replaced by $j_1 = \{d_1\} \sqcup \{d_2\}$ to get a new separator (Fig. 3(b)). Then, depending on the considered domain, different separators are obtained. For Intervals, the join of $j_1$ and $\{d_3\}$ leads to the separator in Fig. 1(a). Notice that both ends of the implication $(2, 2) \rightarrow (2, 3)$ are included in $j_1 \sqcup \{d_3\}$. In the case of Octagons, the join of $j_1$ and $\{d_3\}$ is the set

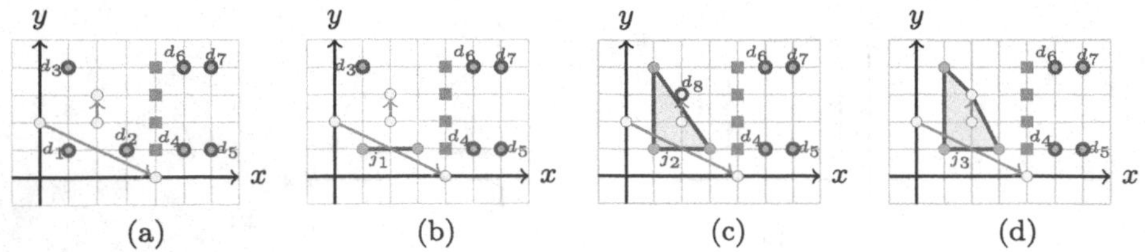


**Fig. 3.** The first iterations of Algorithm 4 on the sample $S$ of Fig. 1

on the left of Fig. 1(b). Again, both ends of the implication $(2, 2) \rightarrow (2, 3)$ are included in $j_1 \sqcup \{d_3\}$. In the case of Polyhedra, $j_2 = j_1 \sqcup \{d_3\}$ is the triangle shown in Fig. 3(c). Since $(2, 2)$ is included in $j_2$ but not $(2, 3)$, the element $\{(2, 3)\}$ is added to the separator, leading to the separator represented in Fig. 3(c). In the next iteration, $j_2$ is joined with $\{d_8\}$ leading to the separator shown in Fig. 3(d). Finally, a similar iteration of join operations leads to the rectangle including the four points, and this leads to the join-maximal separator of Fig. 1.

*Remark 2.* In the best case Algorithm 4 performs $|S^+|$ join and $|S^+|(|S^-|+|S^\rightarrow|)$ meet operations (all pairs of points can be joined and all left end-points of implications are not in the new joined convex sets). In the worst case, it performs $O\big((|S^+| + |S^\rightarrow|)^2\big)$ join and $O\big((|S^+| + |S^\rightarrow|)^2(|S^-| + |S^\rightarrow|)\big)$ meet operations (at most $|S^-| + |S^\rightarrow|$ meets are needed to check if two sets can be joined and implications might add new points to $S^+$). The cost of meet and join depends on the used abstract domain; it is polynomial for intervals and octagons, and exponential for polyhedra, in the number of variables. Algorithm 4 is not designed to compute a join-max separator with a minimal number of convex sets as this would require a potentially exponential number of meet and join operations.

### 4.3 Integrating Separator Computation in ICE-DT

We use the computation of a join-maximal separator to provide an instance of the function GENERATEATTRIBUTES of ICE-DT in Algorithm 2. Given a sample $S$, let $\mathbb{S}$ be the $A_X$-separator of $S$ computed by CONSTRUCTSEPARATOR$(S, A_X)$ defined by Algorithm 4. We consider the set *InitialAttributes* containing all the predicates that constitute the specification (*Init* and *Good*) and those that appear in the programs (as tests in the conditional statements and while loops). Then, we define: GENERATEATTRIBUTES$(S)$ = $\mathit{InitialAttributes} \cup \bigcup_{d \in \mathbb{S}} \mathit{Constr}(d)$

*Remark 3.* Several convex sets of the separator $\mathbb{S}$ might generate the same constraint and the set of attributes generated in this way might contain attributes which partition the state space in the same way (e.g. $x \leq 0$ and $x \geq 1$, equivalent to $x > 0$ over the integers). We keep only one of them. The number of attributes generated is at most linear in the number of positive states in the sample $S$.

```
int j, k, t;
assume(j = 2 ∧ k = 0);
while true do
  | if t = 0 then j ← j + 4 else j ← j + 2; k ← k + 1;
assert(k = 0 ∨ j = 2k + 2);
```

**Fig. 4.** Example program

Notice that our function GENERATEATTRIBUTES(S), contrary to the one used in the original ICE-DT (Algorithm 2), does not expand a set of existing attributes, and therefore it only need the sample $S$ as argument. In fact, with our method for computing attributes, the ICE-DT schema can be simplified: the while loop in Algorithm 2 can be replaced by one single initial test on the condition of success. Indeed, each time the learner is called, it checks whether the set of attributes computed for the previous sample is sufficient to build a separator for the new sample. Only when it is not sufficient that the generation of a separator is performed. Then, the call of the SUFFICIENT function afterward is needed to extend the sample so that the construction of a decision tree can be done (see explanation in Sect. 2.3), but it will necessarily succeed since in our case the set of attributes defines by construction a separator of the sample.

*Example 4.* Consider the program in Fig. 4 whose set of variables is $X = \{j, k, t\}$. We use Polyhedra. First, starting from an empty ICE-sample, regardless of the attributes, the learner proposes *true* as an invariant and $(5, 1, 0)$ is returned as a negative counterexample. Then, it proposes $false$ and $(2, 0, 0)$ is returned as a positive counterexample.

Now, Algorithm 4 is called to compute a separator for $S = (S^+ = \{(2, 0, 0)\}, S^- = \{(5, 1, 0)\}, S^\rightarrow = \emptyset)$. Here, we use initially a separator $\mathbb{S}_{init}$ containing the set of states satisfying the initial condition $j = 2 \wedge k = 0$ denoted by $d_1$ in addition to $d_0$ where $d_0 = \{(2, 0, 0)\}$. Since $d_0 \subseteq d_1$, the algorithm returns the join-maximal separator $\mathbb{S} = \{d_1\}$ with $Constr^{poly}(d_1) = \{j = 2, k = 0\}$.

Using constraints from $\mathbb{S}$ as attributes, the learner constructs the candidate invariant $k = 0$. Then, the teacher provides an implication counterexample $(0, 0, 1) \rightarrow (2, 1, 1)$. Now, without computing another separator (as the one it has is sufficient for the new sample), the learner proposes $j = 2 \wedge k = 0$ as an invariant, and the implication counterexample $(2, 0, 1) \rightarrow (4, 1, 1)$ is returned (and since $(2, 0, 1)$ is an initial state, $(4, 1, 1)$ is also considered positive).

Then, Algorithm 4 is called again to construct a separator for the sample $S = (S^+ = \{(2, 0, 0), (4, 1, 1)\}, S^- = \{(5, 1, 0)\}, S^\rightarrow = \{(0, 0, 1) \rightarrow (2, 1, 1), (2, 0, 1) \rightarrow (4, 1, 1)\})$. Starting from a separator $\mathbb{S}_{init} = \{d_0, d_1, d_2\}$ with $d_2 = \{(4, 1, 1)\}$ it returns the join-maximal separator

$$\mathbb{S} = \{d_3\} \qquad Constr^{poly}(d_3) = \{2k + 2 = j, j \leq 4, j \geq 2\}$$

Based on this separator, the learner proposes $2k+2 = j$, $(2, 0, 0) \rightarrow (6, 0, 0)$ is given as a counterexample (and then, since $(2, 0, 0)$ is in $S^+$, $(6, 0, 0)$ is considered positive). Then, from $\mathbb{S}_{init} = \{d_0, d_1, d_2, d_4\}$ with $d_4 = \{(6, 0, 0)\}$ a new separator $\mathbb{S}$ is constructed

$$\mathbb{S} = \{d_5\} \qquad Constr^{poly}(d_5) = \{j + 2k \leq 6, k \geq 0, j \geq 2k + 2\}$$

leading to a new candidate invariant: $j + 2k \leq 6 \wedge j \geq 2k + 2$. The teacher returns at this point the negative state $(0, -2, 0)$. The attributes of $\mathbb{S}$ are still sufficient to construct a decision tree for the sample. Then, the learner proposes $j + 2k \leq 6 \wedge k \geq 0 \wedge j \geq 2k + 2$, and the teacher returns the counterexample $(3, 0, 1) \rightarrow (5, 1, 1)$ (and since $(5, 1, 1)$ is a negative state, $(3, 0, 1)$ is considered negative). The current sample $S$ is now ($S^+ = \{(2, 0, 0), (4, 1, 1), (6, 0, 0)\}$, $S^- = \{(5, 1, 0), (5, 1, 1), (3, 0, 1), (0, -2, 0)\}$, $S^{\rightarrow} = \{(0, 0, 1) \rightarrow (2, 1, 1),\ (2, 0, 1) \rightarrow (4, 1, 1),\ (2, 0, 0) \rightarrow (6, 0, 0), (3, 0, 1) \rightarrow (5, 1, 1)\}$).

Then, from $\mathbb{S}_{init} = \{d_0, d_1, d_2, d_4\}$, a join-maximal separator is constructed

$$\mathbb{S} = \{d_3, d_4\} \qquad Constr^{poly}(d_4) = \{j = 6, t = 0, k = 0\}$$

Some iterations later, using only the attributes of the last $\mathbb{S}$, the learner generates the inductive invariant $(t = 0 \wedge 2 \leq j \wedge k = 0) \vee (t \neq 0 \wedge 2 \leq j \wedge 2k + 2 = j)$

### 4.4 Computing Separators Incrementally

Algorithm 4 of Sect. 4.2 always starts from the initial separator, regardless of what has been done in the previous iterations of the ICE learning process. Here, we present an incremental approach to exploit the fact that adding a counterexample to the sample may modify the separator only locally allowing parts of separators computed in previous iterations to be reused. The basic idea is to store the history of the separator computation along the ICE iterations, and update it according to the new counterexamples discovered at each step.

**The Algorithm.** We use an abstract stack data structure to represent the history of separators. Along the iterations of the ICE learning algorithm, an increasing sequence of samples $S_i$'s is considered (at each iteration it is enriched by the new counterexample provided by the teacher). Then, at each step $i$, a join-maximal separator $\mathbb{S}_i$ of the sample $S_i$ is computed and stored in the stack. Notice that at a given step $i$, separators of index $j < i$ are not necessarily separators of $S_i$ since they may not cover all positive points of $S_i$. Therefore, we introduce the following notion: a *partial* $A_X$*-separator* of a sample $S$ is a set $\mathbb{S} \in 2^{D_X}$ such that $\forall p \in S^-. \forall d \in \mathbb{S}. p \notin d$.

Now, to compute the separator $\mathbb{S}_i$, we start from one of the partial separators in the stack, the most recent one that is not affected by the last update of the sample. When the sample at step $i$ is extended with positive states, $\mathbb{S}_i$ can be computed directly from $\mathbb{S}_{i-1}$. However, when the sample is extended with negative states, this might require reconsidering several previous steps since some of the elements (convex sets) of their separators might contain states that are (discovered now to be) negative. In that case, we must return to the step of the greatest index $j < i$ (i.e., the last step before $i$) such that $\mathbb{S}_j$ is a partial separator of $S_i$ (i.e., the new knowledge about the negative states does not affect the computed separation at step $j$). By the fact that the sequence of samples is increasing, it is indeed correct to consider the biggest $j < i$ satisfying the property above. Therefore, the separator $\mathbb{S}_i$ is computed starting from $\mathbb{S}_j$ augmented with all the positive states in $S_i^+ \setminus S_j^+$.

This leads to Algorithm 5. We use in its description a stack $P$ supplied with the usual operations: *P.head*() returns the top element of the stack, *P*.pop() removes and returns the top element of the stack, and *P*.push($e$) inserts an element $e$ at the top position of the stack. A refined version of Algorithm 5 is presented in the full paper [2] where the backtracking phase is made more effective: We attach information to each join-created object in order to track its join-predecessors (objects involved in its creation) in the stack.

```
Global  : P = {∅} a stack of partial separators.
Proc constructSeparatorInc(S_i = (S_i^+, S_i^-, S_i^→), A_X)
    // backtracking
    while true do
        if ∃n ∈ S_i^-. ∃d ∈ P.head(). n ∈ d then
            P.pop();
        else break;
    // expansion
    𝕊 ← P.head();
    add ← {p ∈ S_i^+ | ∀d ∈ 𝕊. p ∉ d} ∪ {q | ∃p → q ∈ S_i^→. ∃d' ∈ 𝕊. p ∈ d' ∧ ∀d'' ∈ 𝕊. q ∉ d''};
    while ∃s ∈ add do
        add ← add \ {s};
        if ∃d ∈ 𝕊. ∀n ∈ S_i^-. n ∉ d ⊔ {s} then
            let o = d ⊔ {s};
            𝕊 ← (𝕊 \ {d}) ∪ {o};
            for p → q ∈ S_i^→ s.t. p ∈ o ∧ ∀d' ∈ 𝕊. q ∉ d' do
                add ← add ∪ {q}
        else
            𝕊 ← 𝕊 ∪ {{s}};
            for p → q ∈ S_i^→ s.t. p = s ∧ ∀d' ∈ 𝕊. q ∉ d' do
                add ← add ∪ {q}
    P.push(𝕊);
    return 𝕊;
```

**Algorithm 5:** Incremental computation of an $A_X$-separator of a sample $S$.

**Integration to ICE-DT.** The function constructSeparatorInc can be integrated to the ICE-DT algorithm just as the function constructSeparator in Sect. 4.3, by using it to implement the function *generateAttributes* of the learner. But this time, the learner is more efficient in computing the separator from which the attributes are extracted.

*Example 5.* Consider again the program in Fig. 4 of Example 4. The two first iterations are similar to the ones described in Example 4. Then, the obtained sample is $S = (S^+ = \{(2,0,0)\}, S^- = \{(5,1,0)\}, S^{\rightarrow} = \emptyset)$. Starting from the empty separator, Algorithm 5 computes the separator $\mathbb{S}_1 = \{d_1\}$ where $Constr^{poly}(d_1) = \{j = 2, k = 0\}$. Then, the learner proceeds as in the previous example to get the sample $S = (S^+ = \{(2,0,0),(4,1,1)\}, S^+ = \{(5,1,0)\}, S^{\rightarrow} = \{(0,0,1) \rightarrow (2,1,1), (2,0,1) \rightarrow (4,1,1)\})$. To build a separator of $S$, Algorithm 5 starts from $\mathbb{S}_1$ and produces $\mathbb{S}_2 = \{d_3\}$ where $d_3 = d_1 \sqcup \{(4,1,1)\}$.

| Tool | Solved | | Total |
|---|---|---|---|
| | safe | unsafe | |
| ICE-DT | 111 | 11 | 122 |
| LoopInvGen | 130 | 8 | 138 |
| CVC4 | 129 | - | 129 |
| Spacer | 118 | 18 | 136 |
| NIS(int) | 106 | 17 | 123 |
| NIS(oct) | 122 | 14 | 136 |
| NIS(poly) | 137 | 17 | 154 |
| NIS(VB) | 143 | 17 | 160 |

| | NIS(int) | NIS(oct) | NIS(poly) |
|---|---|---|---|
| NIS(int) | - | 7 | 2 |
| NIS(oct) | 13 | - | 5 |
| NIS(poly) | 31 | 18 | - |

**Fig. 5.** Benchmark results and comparison of NIS wrt. different abstract domains.

Similarly, when the counterexample $(2,0,0) \rightarrow (6,0,0)$ is obtained, the algorithm starts directly from $\mathbb{S}_2$ to produce $\mathbb{S}_3 = \{d_5\}$ where $d_5 = d_3 \sqcup \{(6,0,0)\}$.

After two more iterations, the sample is the same as $S'$ in Example 4. At this point, $\mathbb{S}_3$ cannot be used to construct a separator for $S$ since $d_5$ includes the negative state $(3,0,1)$. Then, the algorithm removes $\mathbb{S}_3$ from the stack. It checks that $\mathbb{S}_2$ is a partial separator of $S$, which is indeed the case. Then, it constructs a new separator $\mathbb{S}_4$ based on $\mathbb{S}_2$ by expanding it with the counterexamples received after the construction of $\mathbb{S}_2$ (the negative state $(0,-2,0)$ and the implications $(2,0,0) \rightarrow (6,0,0)$ and $(3,0,1) \rightarrow (5,1,1)$): $\mathbb{S}_4 = \{d_3, d_6\}$ where $Constr^{poly}(d_6) = \{t = 0, k = 0, j = 6\}$. The rest of the execution proceeds as with Algorithm 4. Here, the advantages of the incremental method are: (1) while positive examples are added the separators are simply expanded, and (2) when a negative example at step 4 is added, only one join operation has to be undone.

## 5 Experiments

We have implemented the prototype tool NIS (Numerical Invariant Synthesizer) using our method for attribute synthesis with the ICE-DT schema. NIS written in C++ is configurable with an abstract domain for the manipulation of abstract objects. It uses Z3 [24] for SMT queries and APRON's [18] abstract domains.

We compare our implementation with ICE-DT[1], LoopInvGen, CVC4, and Spacer[2]. LoopInvGen is a data-driven invariant inference tool based on a syntactic enumeration of candidate predicates [25,26]. It is written in OCaml and uses Z3 as an SMT solver. CVC4 uses an enumerative refutation-based approach [1,27]. It is written in C++ and it includes an SMT solver. Spacer is a PDR-based CHC solver [19], written in C++ and integrated in Z3.

[1] The original ICE-DT tool [16] does not support programs in the SyGuS format. Here we use our own implementation of ICE-DT. It shares with NIS all the components (teacher, decision tree learning algorithm with implications) except that attribute discovery is enumerative.

[2] Spacer does not support programs in the SyGuS format; a wrapper is written in C++ that converts a SyGuS program to a CHC problem and supplies it to Spacer via the Z3 FixedPoint API.

The evaluation was done on 164 linear integer arithmetic (LIA) programs[3] from SyGuS-Comp'19. They have a number of variables ranging from 2 to 10. The experiments were carried out using a timeout of 1800 s (30 min) for each example. They were conducted on a machine with 4 CPUs Intel(R) Xeon(R) 2,13 GHz, 16 cores, and 128 Go RAM running Linux CentOS 7.9.

Figure 5 shows the number of safe and unsafe solved programs by each tool. The instance of our approach using the Polyhedral abstract domain solves 154 programs out of 164, and the virtual best of our approach with the three abstract domains Intervals, Octagons, and Polyhedra, solves 160 programs out of 164. Two of the remaining examples require handling quantifiers, which cannot be done with the current implementation. The two others have not been solved with any of the four tools we considered.

These results show that globally our approach is powerful and is able to solve a significant number of cases that are not solvable by other tools. Interestingly, using different abstract domains leads to incomparable performances: although with polyhedra more cases are solvable, there are some cases that are uniquely solvable with intervals or octagons. Also, while operations on intervals and octagons have a lower complexity than on polyhedra, this is compensated with the fact that polyhedra are more expressive. Indeed, their expressiveness allows in many cases to find quickly invariants for which a less expressive domain requires much more iterations to be learned. Figure 5 shows the number of programs that can be solved using a particular abstract domain but not with another. Polyhedra are globally superior, but the three domains are complementary.

Compared to the other tools, the bottleneck of ICE-DT and also of LoopInvGen is the number of predicates that are generated using enumeration. Our approach avoids the explosion of the size of the attribute pool by guiding their discovery with the data sample, and reducing the size (by replacing objects by their join) of the computed separators from which constraints are extracted. Concerning CVC4, it uses enumerative refutation techniques, which are also subject to an explosion problem. Moreover, CVC4 does not allow to solve the cases of unsafe programs. The performances of Spacer depend on the ability to generalize the set of predecessors computed using the model-based projection and the interpolants used for separation from bad states in the context of IC3/PDR. While this is done efficiently in general, there are cases where this process can lead to fastidious computations while our technique can be much faster using a small number of join operations of positive states.

The scatter plots shown in Fig. 6 compare the execution times of our approach using Polyhedra abstract domain NIS(`poly`) with LoopInvGen, CVC4 and Spacer. (A timeout of 1800 s s is used for each example.) They show that NIS(`poly`) is in general faster than both LoopInvGen and CVC4, and that it has comparable performances in terms of execution time with Spacer. We have

[3] Other programs from SyGuS-Comp'19 have not been taken into account in our evaluations as they are boolean programs with integer variables for encoding nondeterminism or artificial programs augmented with useless variables and statements.

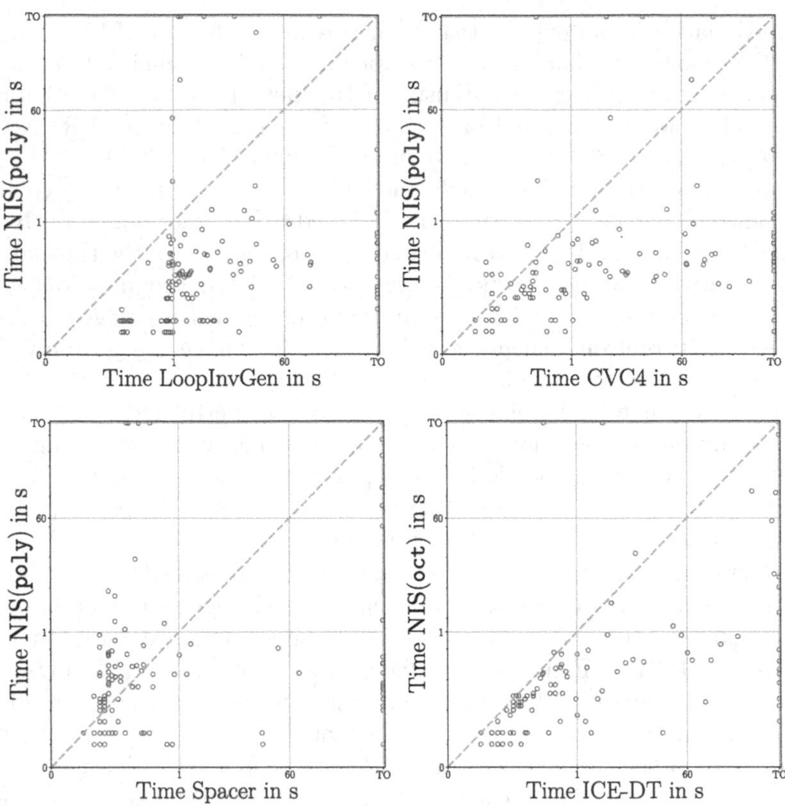


**Fig. 6.** Runtime of NIS(`poly`) vs. LoopInvGen, CVC4, and Spacer, and NIS(`oct`) vs. ICE-DT.

also compared the original ICE-DT, based on enumerative attribute generation using octagonal templates (as in [16]) with NIS(`oct`). The comparison shows that our tool is significantly faster (see the bottom right subfigure of Fig. 6).

## 6 Conclusion

We have defined an efficient method for generating relevant predicates for the learning process of numerical invariants. The approach is guided by the data sample built during the process and is based on constructing a separator of the sample. The construction consists of an iterative application of join operations in numerical abstract domains in order to cover positive states without including negative ones. Our method is tightly integrated to the ICE-DT schema, leading to an efficient data-driven invariant synthesis and verification algorithm.

Future work includes several directions. First, alternative methods for constructing separators should be investigated in order to reduce the size of the pool of attributes along the learning process while increasing their potential relevance.

Another issue to investigate is the control of the counterexamples provided by the teacher since they play an important role in the learning process. In our current implementation, their choice is totally dependent on the SMT solver used for implementing the teacher. Finally, we intend to extend this approach to other types of programs, in particular to programs with other data types, and programs with more general control structures such as procedural programs.

## References


1. Barrett, C., et al.: CVC4. In: Gopalakrishnan, G., Qadeer, S. (eds.) CAV 2011. LNCS, vol. 6806, pp. 171–177. Springer, Heidelberg (2011). https://doi.org/10.1007/978-3-642-22110-1_14
2. Bouajjani, A., Boutglay, W.A., Habermehl, P.: Data-driven numerical invariant synthesis with automatic generation of attributes (2022). https://doi.org/10.48550/ARXIV.2205.14943, https://arxiv.org/abs/2205.14943
3. Bradley, A.R.: SAT-based model checking without unrolling. In: Jhala, R., Schmidt, D. (eds.) VMCAI 2011. LNCS, vol. 6538, pp. 70–87. Springer, Heidelberg (2011). https://doi.org/10.1007/978-3-642-18275-4_7
4. Champion, A., Kobayashi, N., Sato, R.: HoIce: an ICE-based non-linear horn clause solver. In: Ryu, S. (ed.) APLAS 2018. LNCS, vol. 11275, pp. 146–156. Springer, Cham (2018). https://doi.org/10.1007/978-3-030-02768-1_8
5. Clarke, E.M., Grumberg, O., Jha, S., Lu, Y., Veith, H.: Counterexample-guided abstraction refinement for symbolic model checking. J. ACM **50**(5), 752–794 (2003)
6. Colón, M.A., Sankaranarayanan, S., Sipma, H.B.: Linear invariant generation using non-linear constraint solving. In: Hunt, W.A., Somenzi, F. (eds.) CAV 2003. LNCS, vol. 2725, pp. 420–432. Springer, Heidelberg (2003). https://doi.org/10.1007/978-3-540-45069-6_39
7. Cousot, P., Cousot, R.: Static determination of dynamic properties of programs. In: Proceedings of the Second International Symposium on Programming, pp. 106–130. Dunod (1976)
8. Cousot, P., Cousot, R.: Abstract interpretation: a unified lattice model for static analysis of programs by construction or approximation of fixpoints. In: POPL 1977, pp. 238–252. ACM (1977)
9. Cousot, P., Halbwachs, N.: Automatic discovery of linear restraints among variables of a program. In: POPL 1978, pp. 84–96. ACM Press (1978)
10. Eén, N., Mishchenko, A., Brayton, R.K.: Efficient implementation of property directed reachability. In: FMCAD 2011, pp. 125–134. FMCAD Inc. (2011)
11. Ernst, M.D., et al.: The daikon system for dynamic detection of likely invariants. Sci. Comput. Program. **69**(1–3), 35–45 (2007)
12. Ezudheen, P., Neider, D., D'Souza, D., Garg, P., Madhusudan, P.: Horn-ICE learning for synthesizing invariants and contracts. Proc. ACM Program. Lang. **2**(OOPSLA), 131:1-13125 (2018)
13. Feldman, Y.M.Y., Immerman, N., Sagiv, M., Shoham, S.: Complexity and information in invariant inference. Proc. ACM Program. Lang. **4**(POPL), 51–529 (2020)
14. Flanagan, C., Leino, K.R.M.: Houdini, an annotation assistant for ESC/Java. In: Oliveira, J.N., Zave, P. (eds.) FME 2001. LNCS, vol. 2021, pp. 500–517. Springer, Heidelberg (2001). https://doi.org/10.1007/3-540-45251-6_29

15. Garg, P., Löding, C., Madhusudan, P., Neider, D.: ICE: a robust framework for learning invariants. In: Biere, A., Bloem, R. (eds.) CAV 2014. LNCS, vol. 8559, pp. 69–87. Springer, Cham (2014). https://doi.org/10.1007/978-3-319-08867-9_5
16. Garg, P., Neider, D., Madhusudan, P., Roth, D.: Learning invariants using decision trees and implication counterexamples. In: POPL 2016, pp. 499–512. ACM (2016)
17. Hoder, K., Bjørner, N.: Generalized property directed reachability. In: Cimatti, A., Sebastiani, R. (eds.) SAT 2012. LNCS, vol. 7317, pp. 157–171. Springer, Heidelberg (2012). https://doi.org/10.1007/978-3-642-31612-8_13
18. Jeannet, B., Miné, A.: APRON: a library of numerical abstract domains for static analysis. In: Bouajjani, A., Maler, O. (eds.) CAV 2009. LNCS, vol. 5643, pp. 661–667. Springer, Heidelberg (2009). https://doi.org/10.1007/978-3-642-02658-4_52
19. Komuravelli, A., Gurfinkel, A., Chaki, S.: SMT-based model checking for recursive programs. In: Biere, A., Bloem, R. (eds.) CAV 2014. LNCS, vol. 8559, pp. 17–34. Springer, Cham (2014). https://doi.org/10.1007/978-3-319-08867-9_2
20. Li, J., Sun, J., Li, L., Le, Q.L., Lin, S.: Automatic loop-invariant generation and refinement through selective sampling. In: ASE 2017. pp. 782–792. IEEE Computer Society (2017)
21. Löding, C., Madhusudan, P., Neider, D.: Abstract learning frameworks for synthesis. In: Chechik, M., Raskin, J.-F. (eds.) TACAS 2016. LNCS, vol. 9636, pp. 167–185. Springer, Heidelberg (2016). https://doi.org/10.1007/978-3-662-49674-9_10
22. Miné, A.: The octagon abstract domain. High. Order Symb. Comput. **19**(1), 31–100 (2006)
23. Mitchell, T.M.: Machine Learning, International Edition. McGraw-Hill Series in Computer Science, McGraw-Hill (1997)
24. de Moura, L., Bjørner, N.: Z3: an efficient SMT solver. In: Ramakrishnan, C.R., Rehof, J. (eds.) TACAS 2008. LNCS, vol. 4963, pp. 337–340. Springer, Heidelberg (2008). https://doi.org/10.1007/978-3-540-78800-3_24
25. Padhi, S., Millstein, T., Nori, A., Sharma, R.: Overfitting in synthesis: theory and practice. In: Dillig, I., Tasiran, S. (eds.) CAV 2019. LNCS, vol. 11561, pp. 315–334. Springer, Cham (2019). https://doi.org/10.1007/978-3-030-25540-4_17
26. Padhi, S., Sharma, R., Millstein, T.D.: Data-driven precondition inference with learned features. In: PLDI 2016, pp. 42–56. ACM (2016)
27. Reynolds, A., Barbosa, H., Nötzli, A., Barrett, C., Tinelli, C.: CVC4SY: smart and fast term enumeration for syntax-guided synthesis. In: Dillig, I., Tasiran, S. (eds.) CAV 2019. LNCS, vol. 11562, pp. 74–83. Springer, Cham (2019). https://doi.org/10.1007/978-3-030-25543-5_5
28. Ryan, G., Wong, J., Yao, J., Gu, R., Jana, S.: CLN2INV: learning loop invariants with continuous logic networks. In: ICLR 2020. OpenReview.net (2020)
29. Sharma, R., Gupta, S., Hariharan, B., Aiken, A., Nori, A.V.: Verification as learning geometric concepts. In: Logozzo, F., Fähndrich, M. (eds.) SAS 2013. LNCS, vol. 7935, pp. 388–411. Springer, Heidelberg (2013). https://doi.org/10.1007/978-3-642-38856-9_21
30. Sharma, R., Nori, A.V., Aiken, A.: Interpolants as Classifiers. In: Madhusudan, P., Seshia, S.A. (eds.) CAV 2012. LNCS, vol. 7358, pp. 71–87. Springer, Heidelberg (2012). https://doi.org/10.1007/978-3-642-31424-7_11
31. Si, X., Naik, A., Dai, H., Naik, M., Song, L.: Code2Inv: a deep learning framework for program verification. In: Lahiri, S.K., Wang, C. (eds.) CAV 2020. LNCS, vol. 12225, pp. 151–164. Springer, Cham (2020). https://doi.org/10.1007/978-3-030-53291-8_9

32. Vizel, Y., Gurfinkel, A., Shoham, S., Malik, S.: IC3 - flipping the E in ICE. In: Bouajjani, A., Monniaux, D. (eds.) VMCAI 2017. LNCS, vol. 10145, pp. 521–538. Springer, Cham (2017). https://doi.org/10.1007/978-3-319-52234-0_28
33. Zhu, H., Magill, S., Jagannathan, S.: A data-driven CHC solver. In: PLDI 2018. pp. 707–721. ACM (2018)

# Proof-Guided Underapproximation Widening for Bounded Model Checking

Prantik Chatterjee[1(✉)], Jaydeepsinh Meda[2], Akash Lal[3], and Subhajit Roy[1]

[1] Indian Institute of Technology Kanpur, Kanpur, India
prantik@cse.iitk.ac.in, subhajit@iitk.ac.in
[2] Oracle, Bengaluru, India
[3] Microsoft Research, Bengaluru, India
akashl@microsoft.com

**Abstract.** Bounded Model Checking (BMC) is a popularly used strategy for program verification and it has been explored extensively over the past decade. Despite such a long history, BMC still faces scalability challenges as programs continue to grow larger and more complex. One approach that has proven to be effective in verifying large programs is called Counterexample Guided Abstraction Refinement (CEGAR). In this work, we propose a complementary approach to CEGAR for bounded model checking of sequential programs: in contrast to CEGAR, our algorithm gradually widens underapproximations of a program, guided by the proofs of unsatisfiability. We implemented our ideas in a tool called Legion. We compare the performance of Legion against that of Corral, a state-of-the-art verifier from Microsoft, that utilizes the CEGAR strategy. We conduct our experiments on 727 Windows and Linux device driver benchmarks. We find that Legion is able to solve 12% more instances than Corral and that Legion exhibits a complementary behavior to that of Corral. Motivated by this, we also build a portfolio verifier, Legion$^+$, that attempts to draw the best of Legion and Corral. Our portfolio, Legion$^+$, solves 15% more benchmarks than Corral with similar computational resource constraints (i.e. each verifier in the portfolio is run with a time budget that is half of the time budget of Corral). Moreover, it is found to be 2.9× faster than Corral on benchmarks that are solved by both Corral and Legion$^+$.

**Keywords:** Verification · Bounded model checking · Underapproximation widening

## 1 Introduction

Bounded Model Checking (BMC) [11,20,26,33] is a popular option for program verification, primarily due to its ability of side-stepping the necessity of synthesizing complex invariants. BMC harnesses the power of modern SMT solvers to verify a bounded set of behaviors of a program. The user, if interested, may


S. Shoham and Y. Vizel (Eds.): CAV 2022, LNCS 13371, pp. 304–324, 2022.
https://doi.org/10.1007/978-3-031-13185-1_15

re-attempt verification with larger bounds once the program is proven correct with small bounds.

BMC operates by constructing a logical formula that symbolically captures all states reachable by a program under a user-provided bound. A *query*, referred to as the *verification condition (VC)*, is constructed as a conjunction of the program semantics and the negation of the property, which is also expressed as a logical formula. If the verification condition is satisfiable, it implies that some program execution violated the property of interest, thus the program is faulty. If unsatisfiable, the program satisfies the property, i.e. the program is safe under the chosen bound.

However, for large programs, BMC faces scalability challenges as the verification condition for the program tends to grow large, posing difficulties for the SMT solver. Prior work has answered this challenge by using the popular *counterexample-guided abstraction refinement (CEGAR)* strategy: start off with the VC for an *abstraction* of the program, and incrementally refine the abstraction until the program is decided as safe or faulty. The *Stratified Inlining (SI)* [26] algorithm is an instance of this strategy. SI starts off with an abstraction of only the entry procedure of the program, and then incrementally inlines callees, guided by counterexamples. Not surprisingly, the dynamic inlining strategy of SI has been found to be significantly more scalable than algorithms that statically inline all procedures [25]. The SI algorithm is used in practice by the Corral [24] verifier that powers Microsoft's Static Driver Verifier (SDV) [4].

In this work, we propose a new algorithm that uses proofs of unsatisfiability to widen underapproximate models of the program en route to verification of sequential programs. Our algorithm starts off by constructing a partial verification condition for only the program entry procedure and blocks all paths that invoke calls to procedures that have not yet been inlined. This constructs an underapproximation of the original program (because paths are blocked). A satisfiable result on an underapproximation will indicate the presence of a bug. If the VC is unsatisfiable, we examine its *proof of unsatisfiability* in order to guide the inlining of called procedures. The program can be declared safe when the proof of unsatisfiability does not depend on any procedure call that has not been inlined yet. We implemented our ideas in a tool called Legion.

Further, we found that our underapproximation widening algorithm and the abstraction refinement strategy (used by Corral) demonstrate complementary behaviors—many programs that Corral struggles on, yield to the underapproximation based technique, and vice-versa. This observation motivated us to build a portfolio verifier, Legion$^{+}$, that runs both these techniques in parallel. We found that the portfolio is more effective than any of the tools alone (with similar computational resources, i.e. each verifier in the portfolio is run with a time budget that is half of the time budget of Corral). Both Legion and Legion$^{+}$ are available open-source at the *legion* branch of the *corral* repository[1].

Our experiments are conducted on 727 Windows and Linux device driver benchmarks on which Corral struggles, i.e., Corral is unable to solve any of

[1] https://github.com/boogie-org/corral.git (branch: `legion`).

these benchmarks in less than 200 s. We find that LEGION is able to solve 12% more instances than CORRAL with a time budget of 2 h per instance. Further, the portfolio verifier, LEGION$^+$, given half the time budget of CORRAL, solves 15% more benchmarks than CORRAL, and it is found to be 2.9× faster than CORRAL on benchmarks that are solved by both CORRAL and LEGION$^+$.

The primary contributions of this paper are as follows:

- We design a new algorithm, *Underapproximation Widening guided Stratified Inlining*, that uses proof-based artifacts to widen underapproximate models (in contrast to using counterexamples to refine overapproximate models).
- We implemented our ideas in a tool called LEGION for bounded program verification.
- We also design a portfolio verifier, LEGION$^+$, that includes both overapproximation refinement and underapproximation widening to verify a program in an attempt to reap the benefits of both worlds.
- We evaluate both LEGION and LEGION$^+$ on a set of 727 programs from Windows Device Drivers [31] from the SDV test-suite and Linux Device Drivers from SVCOMP [7] benchmarks.

## 2 Background

This section presents background material that we use in the rest of the paper.

A logical formula consists of literals. A literal is either a variable or the negation of a variable. A logical formula expressed in a *Conjunctive Normal Formal* (CNF) is a *conjunction* of clauses where each clause is a *disjunction* of literals. Given a logical formula, a *satisfiability* solver returns whether the formula is *satisfiable* (SAT) or *unsatisfiable* (UNSAT). If a formula is SAT, the solver provides a model in the form of a satisfying assignment of the variables. If a formula is UNSAT, the solver returns an *unsatisfiable core* (unsat core), which is a subset of clauses of the input formula whose conjunction is still UNSAT.

### 2.1 Language Model

We consider a programming language that represents a *passified* form of BOOGIE programs [8]. A program consists of multiple procedures (*Proc*). We assume an *entry-point* procedure called `main` where program execution starts. Each procedure can have any number of local variable declarations followed by a series of basic blocks (*BasicBlock*). We assume that local variables are initially unconstrained. A basic block is labeled by a unique identifier and consists of multiple statements (*Stmt*) followed by a single control statement (*ControlStmt*). A control statement is either a *goto*, which takes a sequence of basic block labels and non-deterministically picks one to jump to, or a *return* that returns control back to the caller. Returning from `main` terminates the program execution. A statement is either an *assume* command or a procedure *call*. The statement (*assume* $\varphi$) allows a feasible execution only if $\varphi$ is satisfiable.

```
procedure main() {
  int x, y, z; bool c;
  L0: assume x == 0;
      assume y == 0;
      goto L1, L2;
  L1: assume c;
      call foo(x,y);
      goto L3;
  L2: assume !c;
      call bar(x,y);
      goto L3;
  L3: assume y != 0
      return; }

procedure foo(int x, int y) {
  bool d;
  L5: goto L6, L7;
  L6: assume d;
      call foo1(x, y);
      goto L8;
  L7: assume !d;
      call foo2(x, y);
      goto L8;
  L8: return; }

procedure foo1(int x, int y) {
  L9: assume y == x + 1;
      return; }

procedure foo2(int x, int y) {
  L10: assume y == x - 1;
       return; }

procedure bar(int x, int y) {
  bool e;
  L11: goto L12, L13;
  L12: assume e;
       call bar1(x, y);
       goto L14;
  L13: assume !e;
       call bar2(x, y);
       goto L14;
  L14: return; }

procedure bar1(int x, int y) {
  L15: assume y == x + 10;
       return; }

procedure bar2(int x, int y) {
  L16: assume y == x - 10;
       return; }
```

**Fig. 1.** A passified program

We leave the set of variable types (*Type*) and expressions (*Expr*) unspecified. In practice, we can use any expression language that can be directly encoded in SMT. Our implementation uses linear arithmetic, fixed-size bit-vectors, uninterpreted functions, and extensional arrays. This combination is sufficient to realistically translate C programs into our language representation [21, 24].

Note that the programs that we consider do not have global variables, return parameters of procedures, or assignments. These restrictions are without loss of generality [23]. Conversion of these additional feature into our language representation is readily available in tools like Boogie. A passified program makes it easy to describe the verification-condition generation process.

Given a program P, we consider the verification question of whether there exists a terminating execution of P. To be precise, we are interested in finding out whether there is any execution of `main` that reaches its *return* statement. If no such execution exists, then P is considered verified, or Safe. Otherwise, we say that P is Unsafe and return the execution trace with concrete variable values along the trace. Note that we consider a bounded version of the verification problem, i.e., we require that P does not contain any loops or recursive procedure calls. All such loops and recursive calls must be unrolled to a pre-determined

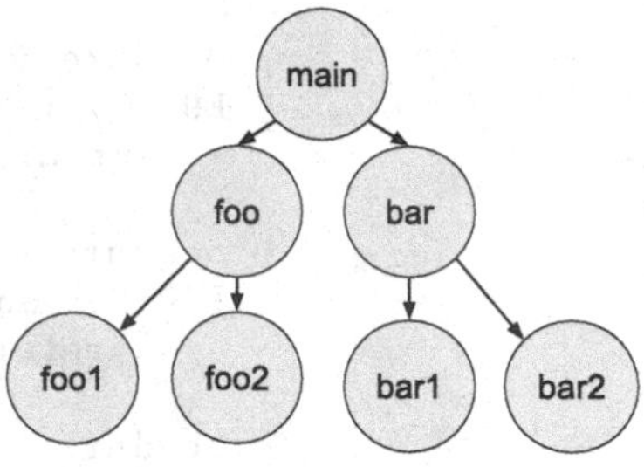


**Fig. 2.** Call graph of the program in Fig. 1.

$$
\begin{array}{ll}
\text{pVC}(\texttt{main}): & \\
& blk_{L0} \\
\wedge & (blk_{L0} \implies x == 0 \wedge y == 0 \\
& \quad \wedge ((blk_{L1} \wedge flow(0) == 1) \vee (blk_{L2} \wedge flow(0) == 2))) \\
\wedge & (blk_{L1} \implies c \wedge blk_{L3} \wedge flow(1) == 3) \\
\wedge & (blk_{L2} \implies \neg c \wedge blk_{L3} \wedge flow(2) == 3) \\
\wedge & (blk_{L3} \implies y \neq 0)
\end{array}
$$

**Fig. 3.** Partial VC of `main()`

depth before proceeding with verification, and thus, the verification problem now becomes decidable (if the expression language of the program is decidable) [23].

### 2.2 VC Generation for a Procedure

Consider a procedure `baz` that does not contain any procedure calls. This section outlines one way of verifying `baz`, i.e., finding out if it has a terminating execution. We use a process called Verification Condition (VC) generation on `baz` to construct a logical formula $\Phi$ and feed it to an SMT solver. If $\Phi$ is UNSAT, then the *return* statement in `baz` is unreachable and `baz` is SAFE. Otherwise, we extract the satisfiable model from the SMT solver, construct the execution trace and return UNSAFE along with the trace. We now outline the VC-generation process.

Suppose that `baz` takes input arguments $\vec{x}$. For each basic block $j$ in `baz`, we define a boolean variable $blk_j$ that is termed as the *control-flow* variable. Let $st_j$ denote the conjunction of all assume statements in basic block $j$. Let $successor(j)$ denote the targets of the *goto* statement in $j$, i.e., all the successor basic blocks in `baz`, to which control may jump non-deterministically from $j$. Let $i_j$ be a unique integer constant representing basic block $j$. We also define an uninterpreted function $flow : \mathbb{Z} \rightarrow \mathbb{Z}$ that records the non-deterministic choice of the successor basic block of $j$. Given the above, we construct a logical formula $\psi_j$ for each basic block $j$ as follows:

$$blk_j \Rightarrow (st_j \wedge \bigvee_{s \in successor(j)} (blk_s \wedge (i_s == flow(i_j))))$$

If basic block $j$ ends with a *return* statement instead of a *goto*, then $\psi_j$ is:

$$blk_j \Rightarrow st_j$$

Assuming the first basic block of `baz`, where procedure execution begin, is labeled $s$, the VC of `baz` is constructed as follows:

$$blk_s \wedge \bigwedge_{l \in basicblocks(p)} \psi_l$$

In Fig. 3, we show the VC of `main` of the program in Fig. 1 as an example, where we ignore the procedure calls in `main` (i.e., treat them as (*assume true*)). We term such a VC (of a procedure where its calls are skipped) as the *partial VC* (pVC) of the procedure.

### 2.3 Static Versus Dynamic Inlining

Given a program `P` with a starting procedure `main`, one simple way to verify `P` would be to construct the VC of `main` by inlining all the procedure calls and check the satisfiability of VC(`main`) with an SMT solver. However, employing such a *static inlining* strategy can cause an exponential blowup in the size of the VC. Hence, we instead make use of *dynamic inlining* algorithm, called Stratified Inlining (SI) [26], that employs a Counterexample Guided Abstraction Refinement (CEGAR) technique [14] to *dynamically* inline procedure VCs. It has been shown that dynamic inlining scales better than static inlining [25]. Dynamic inlining produces more compact VCs during abstraction refinement which leads to significantly faster program verification.

### 2.4 Verification with Stratified Inlining

The working of SI is shown in Algorithm 1. For the sake of simplicity, let us assume that each basic block in `P` may contain only a single procedure call. Every program point, from which a procedure is called, is termed as a callsite. For example, `main` in Fig. 1, has two callsites; `foo` and `bar` which are called from basic blocks `L1`, `L2` and `L3` respectively. A static instance of a callsite is denoted with a pair $(l, c)$ where $l$ denotes the basic block identifier from which a call to the procedure $c$ is made. A dynamic callsite is defined as a stack of static callsites which represents the runtime stack during a program's execution with `main` being present at the bottom of the stack. For example, the dynamic callsite corresponding to the call `foo` from `L1` in `main` is given by [`main`, (`L1`, `foo`)]. The call graph of the program in Fig. 1 is shown in Fig. 2.

**Algorithm 1:** Stratified Inlining (SI) algorithm.

```
   Input: program P with starting procedure main
   Input: An SMT solver S
   Output: Safe, or UnSafe(τ)
1  C ← {[main, s] | s ∈ callsites(main)}
2  S.Assert(pVC(main, [main]))
3  while true do
4      outcome ← OverRefStep(P, C, S)
5      if outcome == Safe ∨ outcome == UnSafe(τ) then
6          return outcome
7      else
8          let NoDecision(_, C′) = outcome
9          C ← C′
```

The SI algorithm takes as input a program P with a starting procedure `main` and an SMT solver $\mathcal{S}$. Initially, we add the dynamic callsites in `main` to a list $C$ (Line 1) and then inline `main`, i.e., assert the pVC of `main` (Line 2). The callsites in $C$ are termed as *open* callsites because they have not yet been inlined. The above steps construct an abstraction of P. The SI algorithm then iteratively calls the OverRefStep routine on this abstraction (Line 4) to perform gradual refinement until we can reach a decision about whether P is Safe or not. Each invocation of OverRefStep can potentially inline more procedures by asserting their partial VC to the solver $\mathcal{S}$. Thus, the state of the solver, as well as the set of open callsites $C$ change across invocations of OverRefStep. We discuss the *Overapproximation Refinement Guided Stratified Inlining* (*OverRefSI*) strategy used by the OverRefStep routine in Sect. 2.5.

### 2.5 Overapproximation Refinement Guided Stratified Inlining

The OverRefStep routine given in Algorithm 2 demonstrates the inner workings of the *OverRefSI* strategy at each verification step. The *OverRefSI* strategy [26] for verifying a program works by iteratively firing overapproximation queries and gradually refining the abstraction of P. If the query returns UNSAT, then we can conclude that P is SAFE with respect to the given property. Otherwise, we extract all the open callsites that appear on the counterexample trace and refine the abstraction of P by inlining these callsites. If the counterexample trace contains no open callsites, then P is UNSAFE and we return the verdict along with the counterexample trace.

The OverRefStep routine takes as input a program P, a set of open callsites $C$ and an SMT solver $\mathcal{S}$. The OverRefStep routine is called iteratively in order to verify the safety of P. We demonstrate the working of *OverRefSI* to verify the pVC of `main` of Fig. 1 in Table 1. At the beginning, the SI algorithm asserts the pVC of `main` to $\mathcal{S}$ and adds [`main`, (`L1`, `foo`)] and [`main`, (`L2`, `bar`)] to the list of open callsites $C$ in step 0.

**Algorithm 2:** OVERREFSTEP(P, $C$, $\mathcal{S}$)

**Input:** procedure P, set of callsites $C$, SMT solver $\mathcal{S}$
**Output:** SAFE, UNSAFE(*trace*), NODECISION($\tau$, C)

1 // *Overapproximate check*
2 **if** $\mathcal{S}$.*Check()* == UNSAT **then**
3     **return** SAFE
4 **else**
5     $\tau \leftarrow$ opencallsites($\mathcal{S}$.Model())
6 **if** $\tau == \emptyset$ **then**
7     **return** UNSAFE($\mathcal{S}$.Model())
8 **else**
9     $C' \leftarrow \emptyset$
10     **forall** $c \in \tau$ **do**
11         $C' \leftarrow$ INLINE(P, $c$)
12     $C \leftarrow (C - \tau) \cup C'$
13     **return** NODECISION($\tau$, $C$)

Next, the SI algorithm calls OVERREFSTEP with P, $C$ and $\mathcal{S}$ as arguments. OVERREFSTEP fires an overapproximation query in Line 2. If the query is unsatisfiable, we return the SAFE verdict. If the query is satisfiable, we get the counterexample trace and extract all the open callsites on the trace in $\tau$ (Line 5). If $\tau$ is empty, i.e., the counterexample trace contains no open callsites, then the trace is not spurious and we can return an UNSAFE verdict with the trace (Line 7). Otherwise, we inline all the callsites in $\tau$ and add all the new callsites that opened up due to the inlinings in $C'$ (Line 11). Inlining a callsite $c$ consists of asserting the partial VC of the procedure that was invoked from $c$.

Subsequently, the inlined callsites are removed from the list of open callsites $C$ and new callsites that opened up due to the inlinings are added to $C$ (Line 12). For example, in step 1 of Table 1, OVERREFSTEP fires an overapproximation query that returns SAT with a counterexample trace that contains the callsite of `foo`, i.e., [`main`, (`L1`,`foo`)]. This callsite is then inlined by asserting the pVC of `foo` to the solver. This opens up the callsites of `foo1` and `foo2`. Since we have not been able to arrive at a decision regarding the safety of P at this step, a verdict of NODECISION is returned along with the list of inlined callsites $\tau$ and the new list of open callsites $C$ (Line 13).

Next, the SI algorithm calls OVERREFSTEP again and in step 2, it fires an overapproximation query again, which returns SAT with the counterexample trace containing the open callsite of `foo1` that we inline by asserting the pVC of `foo1`. The verification process continues in this way by inlining the open callsites on the counterexample trace in every step, which gradually refines the pVC of `main`. Finally, in step 7, the overapproximation query returns UNSAT from which we can conclude that `main` is SAFE.

**Table 1.** Execution of *OverRefSI* on the program of Fig. 1

| Step | Action | Open callsites |
|---|---|---|
| 0 | Assert pVC(`main`) | [`main`, (`L1`,`foo`)]<br>[`main`, (`L2`,`bar`)] |
| 1 | Overapprox check: `SAT`<br>Assert pVC(`foo`) | [`main`, (`L2`,`bar`)]<br>[`main`, (`L1`, `foo`), (`L6`, `foo1`)]<br>[`main`, (`L1`,`foo`), (`L7`, `foo2`)] |
| 2 | Overapprox check: `SAT`<br>Assert pVC(`foo1`) | [`main`, (`L2`,`bar`)]<br>[`main`, (`L1`,`foo`), (`L7`, `foo2`)] |
| 3 | Overapprox check: `SAT`<br>Assert pVC(`foo2`) | [`main`, (`L2`,`bar`)] |
| 4 | Overapprox check: `SAT`<br>Assert pVC(`bar`) | [`main`, (`L2`,`bar`), (`L12`, `bar1`)]<br>[`main`, (`L2`,`bar`), (`L13`, `bar2`)] |
| 5 | Overapprox check: `SAT`<br>Assert pVC(`bar1`) | [`main`, (`L2`,`bar`), (`L13`, `bar2`)] |
| 6 | Overapprox check: `SAT`<br>Assert pVC(`bar2`) | |
| 7 | Overapprox check: `UNSAT`<br>Return Safe | |

## 3 Overview

### 3.1 Underapproximation Widening

We propose a novel algorithm, *Underapproximation Widening Guided Stratified Inlining* (*UnderWidenSI*), that uses proofs of unsatisfiability to guide stratified inlining. *UnderWidenSI* maintains an underapproximated model of the target program and *widens* it until either the program is verified as *safe* or a bug is found.

We illustrate the *UnderWidenSI* strategy in Figs. 4a to 4d. Assume that we are trying to verify whether some required property holds on a program. The space contained by the *yellow* ovals show the reachable program states while the *red* ovals depict error states on which the required property does not hold. The objective of a verification algorithm is to construct a *model* of the program that is precise enough to show that the program can reach an error state or prove that the error states are unreachable. Figures 4a to 4c show a safe program while Fig. 4d depicts an unsafe program.

Consider Fig. 4a: the *UnderWidenSI* algorithm starts off with the partial verification condition of the entry procedure and "blocks" executions though all its open callsites.

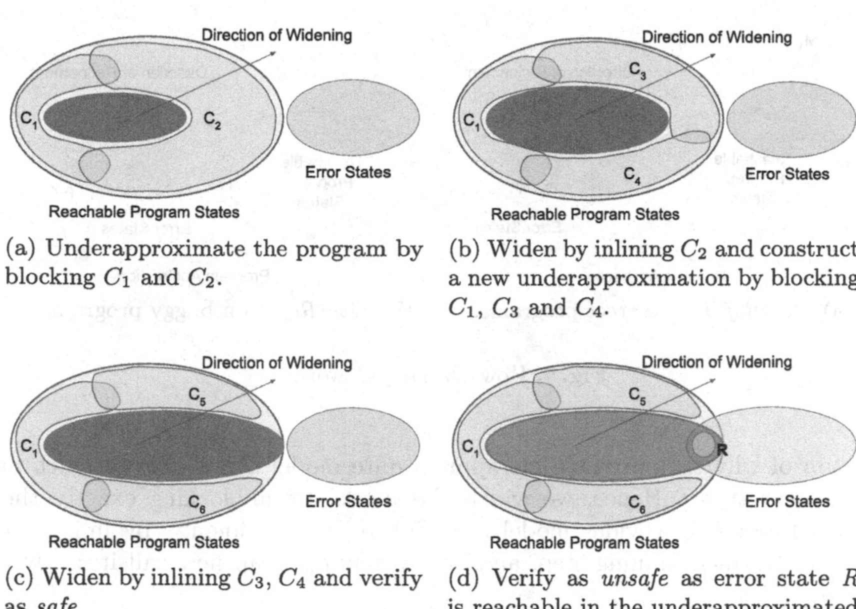


(a) Underapproximate the program by blocking $C_1$ and $C_2$.

(b) Widen by inlining $C_2$ and construct a new underapproximation by blocking $C_1$, $C_3$ and $C_4$.

(c) Widen by inlining $C_3$, $C_4$ and verify as *safe*.

(d) Verify as *unsafe* as error state $R$ is reachable in the underapproximated model.

**Fig. 4.** How *UnderWidenSI* works

**Definition (Blocked callsites).** We use the term, *blocking* a callsite $C$, to imply that all paths that reach $C$ are deemed infeasible. That is, blocking a callsite has the effect of replacing the callsite by (*assume false*).

Essentially, blocking callsites creates underapproximations of the set of feasible program paths. Such underapproximated VCs can be constructed by asserting additional *blocking* clauses corresponding to the control-flow variables of the open callsites. These blocks disallow reachability to certain program states. For example, in Fig. 4a, we construct an underapproximated model of the program by blocking the open callsites $C_1$ and $C_2$. The inner *green* oval depicts the program states that are reachable in the underapproximated model, whereas the outer *gray* regions demonstrate the states that are unreachable due to the blocks on $C_1$ and $C_2$.

If the verification query on this model (conjunction of the underapproximated model and the negation of the property) returns SAT, it implies that an error state in indeed reachable. On the other hand, if the query returns UNSAT (as shown in Fig. 4a), we need to *widen* the model to procure additional reachable executions. We guide this widening operation by extracting the reason for this unsatisfiability from a *minimal unsat core*[2] of the query, that returns the set of block clauses; the callsites corresponding to these blocking clauses constitutes

[2] Although there may exist multiple minimal unsat cores, we found via some preliminary experiments that the choice of the unsat core does not have a significant impact on the overall runtime of our algorithm (on an average).

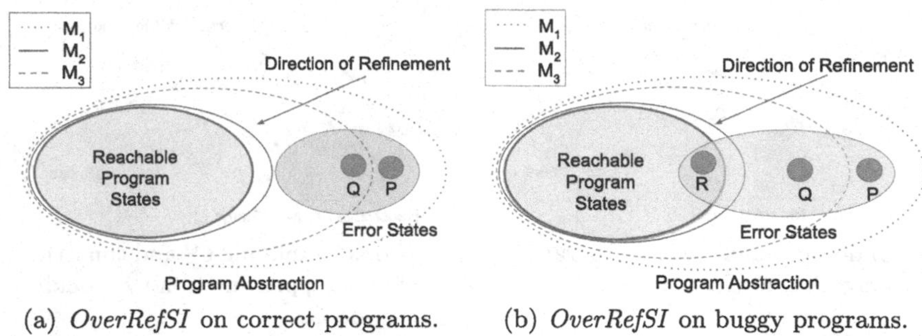


(a) *OverRefSI* on correct programs. (b) *OverRefSI* on buggy programs.

**Fig. 5.** How *OverRefSI* works

a *reason* of why the current underapproximate model is not able to reach any of the error states. Hence, we widen the model by unblocking exactly these callsites leading to a wider model (see Fig. 4b). The widening by inlining $C_2$ causes a stratified inlining step, and hence may open up new callsites, say $C_3$ and $C_4$.

We proceed in the same manner by blocking these open callsites and repeat the query. Finally, (in Fig. 4c) we construct an underapproximated model that still does not intersect with the error states. However, in this case, the unsat core does not contain any blocked clause, as none of the currently blocked callsites would have allowed widening in the direction of the error states.

The unsat core provides a *direction* for widening towards the error states. This also allows us to declare that the program is *safe* without requiring to widen the model to encompass the set of all reachable program states—if the verification query is UNSAT and the unsat core does not contain any blocked clause, then this forms a sufficient condition to declare the program *safe*.

Figure 4d shows how our algorithm proceeds for a faulty program: it incrementally widens the model in the direction of the error states till an error state $R$ is reached. At this point, the *UnderWidenSI* algorithm declares the program as *unsafe*.

Let us now contrast the *UnderWidenSI* strategy with the *OverRefSI* strategy, popularly known as *counterexample-guided abstraction refinement (CEGAR)*, which currently drives the SI algorithm in CORRAL. *OverRefSI* starts off with an overapproximated model of the program: the pVC of the entry procedure with all callsites replaced by non-deterministic updates to its set of modified variables. For example, in Fig. 5a, *OverRefSI* constructs an abstract program/overapproximated model $M_1$ of the program by overapproximating the open callsites. If the resulting verification condition is SAT, it examines the generated counterexample to check if it spurious. If the counterexample is found to be a true bug, it declares the program *unsafe*. If the counterexample is spurious, the model is refined to eliminate this spurious counterexample. For example, in Fig. 5a, we find that there exists an error state/counterexample $P$ within $M_1$, where the property can be violated. Hence, *OverRefSI* refines $M_1$ in Fig. 5a by inlining the overapproximated callsites through which $P$ is reachable. The refinement is done to rule out $P$ as a counterexample, i.e., $P$ becomes unreachable after refinement. We observe in Fig. 5a, that after the first round of refinement, $P$ is no longer reachable in the overapproximated $M_2$, however, we can still find another counterexample $Q$. Hence, the abstraction $M_2$ is refined again. The program is declared *safe* when the model cannot reach any error state. Note that the algorithm can prove the safety of the program without requiring to precisely capture the exact set of reachable program state.

*OverRefSI* and *UnderWidenSI* are complementary: while *OverRefSI* maintains an overapproximated model and refines the model (shrinking the set of reachable states), *UnderWidenSI* maintains an underapproximated model and widens the model (expanding the set of reachable states) incrementally. In terms of the algorithmic details, the *OverRefSI* algorithm in CORRAL uses the models (the counterexamples) to drive refinements, whereas our *UnderWidenSI* algorithm uses the proof (the unsat core) to guide the widenings.

# 4 Algorithms

## 4.1 Underapproximation Widening Guided Stratified Inlining (*UnderWidenSI*)

The UNDERWIDENSTEP routine in Algorithm 3 demonstrates how the *UnderWidenSI* strategy works in each verification step. It takes as input a procedure P, a set of open callsites $C$ and an SMT solver $\mathcal{S}$. The UNDERWIDENSTEP routine is called by the SI algorithm (instead of OVERREFSTEP in Line 4) iteratively in order to verify the safety of P.

In the beginning, we construct an underapproximated pVC of the input procedure P by blocking all calls through the open callsites in $C$ (Line 4). Next, we fire an underapproximation query (Line 5). If the query returns SAT, then we return the verdict UNSAFE with the counterexample trace (Line 6). Otherwise, we get the minimal unsatisfiable core $uc$ and extract all the blocked callsites which appear on $uc$ in $\mu$ (Line 8).

If $\mu$ does not contain any blocked callsites, we deduce that P is SAFE. The proof of the safety of P is captured by $uc$. Hence, we return the verdict that P is SAFE. Otherwise, each of the callsites in $\mu$ are then inlined (Line 15) which constructs a refinement of P. The inlined callsites are then removed from the list of open callsites $C$ and new callsites that opened up due to the inlinings are added to $C$ (Line 16).

When the algorithm is unable to arrive at a decision regarding the safety of P, it returns a verdict of NODECISION along with the list of inlined callsites $\mu$ and the new list of open callsites $C$ (Line 13).

**Example.** We demonstrate the working of *UnderWidenSI* to verify the pVC of `main` of Fig. 1 in Table 2. Initially, we assert the pVC of `main` and add [`main`, (`L1`, `foo`)] and [`main`, (`L2`, `bar`)] to the list of open callsites in step 0.

**Algorithm 3:** UNDERWIDENSTEP(P, $C$, $\mathcal{S}$)

**Input:** procedure P, set of callsites $C$, SMT solver $\mathcal{S}$
**Output:** SAFE, UNSAFE(*trace*), NODECISION($\mu$, C)

```
// Underapproximate check
S.Push()
forall c ∈ C do
    S.Assert(¬ControlVariable(c))
if S.Check() == SAT then
    return UNSAFE(S.Model())
else
    μ ← BlockedCallsites(S.UnsatCore())
S.Pop()
if μ == ∅ then
    return SAFE
else
    C' ← ∅
    forall c ∈ μ do
        C' ← INLINE(P, c)
    C ← (C − μ) ∪ C'
    return NODECISION(μ, C)
```

Replacing each of the open callsites with (*assume false*) statement, i.e., blocking them, constructs an underapproximation of the program. If an SMT solver query on this underapproximation returns SAT, then the program is surely UNSAFE as the satisfiable model can only represent an execution trace that goes through inlined callsites. In that case, we can return the verdict UNSAFE along with an error trace constructed from the model. On the other hand, if the underapproximation check returns UNSAT, then we cannot return a verdict on the safety of the program immediately.

Following this, in step 1 (see Table 2), we push a new frame on the solver and assert $(\neg blk_{L1} \wedge \neg blk_{L2})$ to block executions through the callsites of `foo` and `bar` respectively to construct the underapproximated pVC of `main`. We query the solver with these constraints. Figure 1 shows that if we block executions through basic blocks `L1` and `L2`, the program cannot terminate, i.e., the *return* statement in `L3` is not reachable. Hence, the solver returns UNSAT. The reason for the unsatisfiability is blocking executions through both `L1` and `L2`.

To widen the underapproximated model of the program so that we may reach `L3`, we need to remove the block on at least one of them and inline the respective callsite. The unsat core, in this case, contains the callsite of varbar in basic block `L2`. Therefore, we pop the earlier solver frame containing blocked clauses and assert $(blk_{L2} \implies \text{pVC}(bar))$ in the solver. Inlining `bar`, opens up the callsites $[\texttt{main}, (\texttt{L2}, \texttt{bar}), (\texttt{L12}, \texttt{bar1})]$ and $[\texttt{main}, (\texttt{L2}, \texttt{bar}), (\texttt{L13}, \texttt{bar2})]$.

Next, in step 2, we again construct the underapproximated pVC of `main` by blocking executions through the callsites of `foo`, `bar1` and `bar2`. The solver

**Table 2.** Execution of *UnderWidenSI* on the program of Fig. 1

| Step | Action | Open callsites |
|---|---|---|
| 0 | Assert pVC(main) | [main, (L1,foo)]<br>[main, (L2,bar)] |
| 1 | Underapprox check: UNSAT<br>Assert pVC(bar) | [main, (L1,foo)],<br>[main, (L2,bar), (L12, bar1)]<br>[main, (L2,bar), (L13, bar2)] |
| 2 | Underapprox check: UNSAT<br>Assert pVC(foo)<br>Assert pVC(bar1)<br>Assert pVC(bar2) | [main, (L1,foo), (L6, foo1)]<br>[main, (L1,foo), (L7, foo2)] |
| 3 | Underapprox check: UNSAT<br>Assert pVC(foo1)<br>Assert pVC(foo2) | |
| 4 | Underapprox check: UNSAT<br>Return SAFE | |

query returns UNSAT with *uc* containing the callsites of `foo`, `bar1` and `bar2` which are inlined.

In step 3, the callsites of `foo1` and `foo2` are now open. Blocking both of these callsites and making an underapproximation check returns UNSAT with *uc* containing the callsites of `foo1` and `foo2`. These callsites are now inlined.

In step 4, the underapproximation query returns UNSAT and *uc* contains no blocked callsites. This points to the fact that *uc* contains only inlined callsites, i.e., starting from step 0 if we only inline the callsites in *uc* and leave the remaining callsites overapproximated, we will still get an UNSAT. Therefore, *uc* is the proof of the safety of the program and we return the verdict that the pVC of `main` is safe.

Note that when the underapproximation query returns SAT, then the counterexample trace is constructed on the underapproximated program, i.e., the trace may contain only blocked and inlined callsites. The underapproximated program represents a subset of the paths in the original program, therefore, any counterexample trace present in the underapproximated program is sure to be present in the original program as well. Therefore, if the underapproximated program is unsafe, the original program is unsafe as well.

We have implemented the *UnderWidenSI* algorithm in Legion. We compare the performance of the *UnderWidenSI* algorithm in Legion against that of Corral which uses *OverRefSI*.

### 4.2 Portfolio Technique

The complementary behavior of the *OverRefSI* and the *UnderWidenSI* algorithms motivate us to design a portfolio approach for verifying a program. The portfolio strategy incorporates both the *OverRefSI* algorithm used by CORRAL and the *UnderWidenSI* algorithm implemented in LEGION. We refer to the portfolio verifier as LEGION$^+$. For each program, LEGION$^+$ runs both CORRAL and LEGION in parallel. LEGION$^+$ terminates verification as soon as one of the algorithms finishes verification and reports the outcome. We discuss the performance of LEGION$^+$ against that of CORRAL and LEGION in Sect. 5.

## 5 Experimental Results

We have built a tool, LEGION, that implements our *UnderWidenSI* algorithm. To compare against *OverRefSI*, we use CORRAL [26], a state-of-the-art verifier used at Microsoft [24]. We also build a portfolio solver, LEGION$^+$, that runs both CORRAL and LEGION in parallel. Whenever one of the tools finish verification, LEGION$^+$ terminates the algorithms and reports the outcome.

We compare the performance of CORRAL against LEGION and LEGION$^+$ on a suite of Windows and Linux device driver benchmarks. The Windows device driver benchmarks are obtained by running Static Driver Verifier (SDV) [4] on real windows device drivers that exercise all features of the C language such as arrays, heaps, pointers, loops, recursion etc. SDV compiles these drivers into a suite of BOOGIE [8] programs, each of which is a device driver paired with property (compilation is detailed in [24]). Note that, although the suite of Windows device drivers compiled into BOOGIE programs are available as SDV benchmarks [31], the actual C programs are internal to Microsoft.

Along with this, we also use a set of Linux device drivers that are available as C programs as part of the SVCOMP benchmarks suite [7]. We used SMACK [36] to compile the Linux device drivers into BOOGIE programs. Overall, we elect to use a total of 727 hard programs, on which CORRAL took more than 200 s to verify or times out, from the SDV and SVCOMP benchmarks to run our experiments. We set the timeout for each verification task to 2 h for both CORRAL and LEGION. For all verification tasks, We use an unrolling length of 3 as advised in the benchmarks [31] and used in other works [11].

As LEGION$^+$ uses twice the computational resources compared to CORRAL and LEGION, we halve its time budget to 1 h to make a fair comparison. We also report the performance of LEGION$^+$ with a 2 h time budget (it can be seen as the *virtual best* of CORRAL and LEGION).

The experiments were performed on a machine with AMD EPYC 7452 processor (48 cores) and 384 GB of RAM. Both CORRAL and LEGION uses $Z3$ [15] as the underlying SMT solver. We have used the default setting of a fixed random seed for $Z3$ for all our experiments after verifying the fact that the choice of random seed does not have any significant impact on our results.

### 5.1 Corral Versus Legion

Figure 6 depicts the number of solved instances within the time budget by CORRAL and LEGION. In Fig. 6, a point ($x$, $y$) denotes the number of instances $x$,

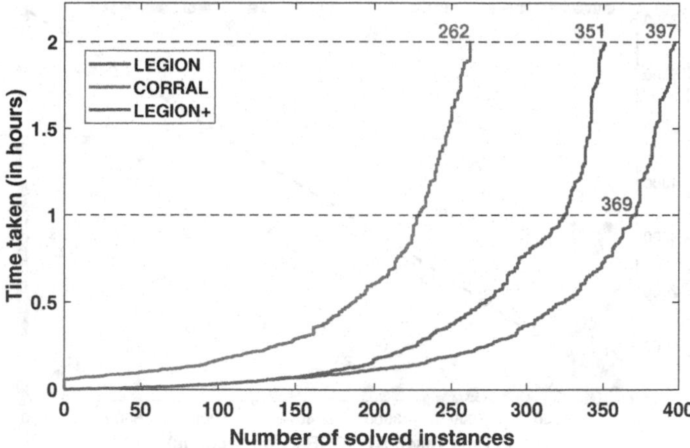


**Fig. 6.** Number of instances solved within time (in hours) for CORRAL vs LEGION vs LEGION$^+$.

**Table 3.** Total time taken by each verifier to solve instances

| Verifier | Solved instances | Total time taken |
|---|---|---|
| CORRAL | 262 | 109 h |
| LEGION | 351 | 112 h |
| LEGION$^+$ | 369 | 71 h |

each of which was solved within time $y$. As we can observe, CORRAL is able to solve 262 out of 727 instances (36%) with a time budget of 2 h per instance, whereas LEGION solves 351 instances (48%) with the same time budget. Both of them fail to solve 330 instances (45%). Out of the 397 instances (55%) that are solved by either CORRAL or LEGION, 46 instances (12%) are solved exclusively by CORRAL, whereas 135 instances (34%) are solved exclusively by LEGION.

The scatter plot of verification times across LEGION and CORRAL is shown in Fig. 7. The spread in the scatter plots demonstrate that these two tools complement each other—the benchmarks on which CORRAL struggles are sometimes handled well by LEGION, and vice-versa. Picking the best of two verifiers solves a total of 397 out of 727 instances (55%). This motivated the design of LEGION$^+$.

### 5.2 Performance of Legion$^+$

As LEGION$^+$ utilizes parallelism, in order to make a fair comparison we halve the time budget for LEGION$^+$ on each verification instance to 1 h. This means that LEGION$^+$ runs both the tools CORRAL and LEGION in parallel but with a time budget of 1 h each.

Figure 6 shows that the portfolio verifier LEGION$^+$ solves 369 out of 727 instances (51%) with a 1 h time budget, whereas CORRAL solves only 262

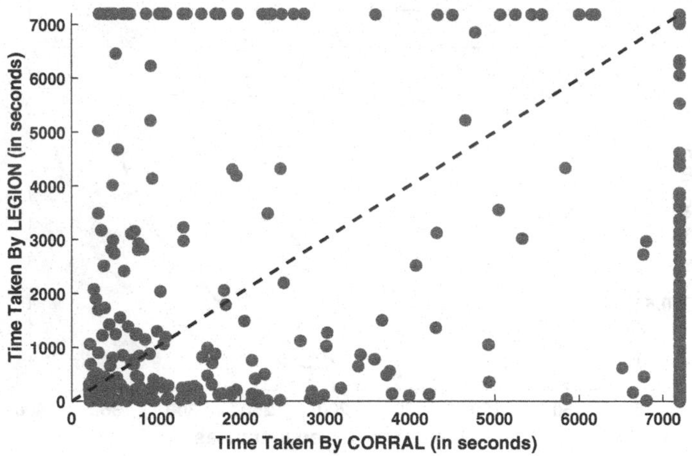


**Fig. 7.** Scatter plot of verification time of CORRAL vs LEGION.

instances (36%) with a total time budget of 2 h. There are only 14 instances that CORRAL solves but LEGION$^{+}$ is unable to solve. Similarly, there are only 17 instances that LEGION solves but LEGION$^{+}$ is unable to solve.

With a 2 h timeout, LEGION$^{+}$ solves 397 instances in total (55%). This is essentially the *virtual best* of CORRAL and LEGION with a 2 h timeout.

Figure 8 shows the total time taken (in hours) by CORRAL, LEGION and LEGION$^{+}$ to verify the instances that were solved by all three of them (total 213 instances). LEGION$^{+}$ is 1.9× faster than LEGION and 2.9× faster than CORRAL.

Across the benchmarks that each of the tools solve individually, CORRAL takes 109 h to solve 262 benchmarks, LEGION takes 112 h to solve 351 benchmarks, whereas LEGION$^{+}$ solves 369 benchmarks within only 71 h (see Table 3).

Note that the benchmarks used in our study are those on which CORRAL took greater than 200 s. On the rest of the benchmarks, clearly LEGION$^{+}$ will perform at least as well as CORRAL. We chose to leave them out to ensure that the experiments run in a reasonable time: there were roughly 14000 of these easy cases. It allowed us to focus on benchmarks where speedup was important.

## 6 Related Work

The high-level idea of using proof-guided abstractions has been long known [3, 30]. Proofs of unsatisfiability have been used to derive abstractions for unbounded model checking in the context of microprocessor verification [30]. Amla et al. have also demonstrated that counterexample based abstraction is complementary to proof based abstraction and they can be combined in a judicious manner to reap the benefits of both the techniques for hardware verification tasks [3]. However, program verification has mostly been dominated by counterexample-guided abstraction refinement (CEGAR) based strategies. Of

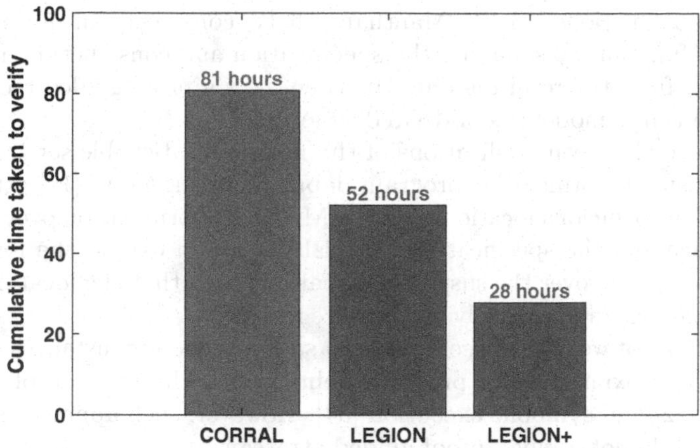


**Fig. 8.** Cumulative time taken (in hours) to verify 213 instances that were solved by all three verifiers.

the few proposals that use proof-guided underapproximation widening strategies, most of them focus on verification of multi-threaded programs [18,35]. These techniques perform underapproximation on the number of thread interleavings allowed, while eagerly inlining all procedures. One technique [18] constrains the number of interleavings to certain bounds, while the other [35] uses dynamically inferred invariants for constructing (potential) underapproximations on interleavings. Note that, these techniques are orthogonal to our approach. Eager inlining is not feasible for our benchmarks, which is precisely the problem that we address. Our proposal shows that proof-guided widening strategies can be effectively employed for verifying large sequential programs. Proof of unsatisfiability from underapproximated models have also been utilized to narrow down the search space for overapproximation refinement in order to decide finite precision bit vector arithmetic with arbitrary bit vector operations [9]. The underapproximation is done on the bit vector variables of a propositional logic formula where some of the bit vector variables are encoded with fewer boolean variables than their width.

Other than using proofs to guide widening heuristics, proof artifacts, like interpolants, have been used to construct annotations [1,2,27–29] that can be useful in constraining future search. Such techniques are orthogonal to underapproximation widening based techniques. However, they can be useful for LEGION and we plan to investigate them in the future.

Underapproximation widening has also been used in program synthesis [37,39,40]. Instead of unleashing the search for the program on the whole search space, such techniques search for the desired program in an underapproximated search space. While prior approaches [37] used a pre-defined widening sequence, later approaches [39,40] use proofs of unsatisfiability to guide the widening sequence. Similar techniques have also been used in the synthesis of boolean functions [16,17]. Manthan [16,17] constructs an initial guess of the boolean function by sampling the specification and constructing a decision-tree classifier from the resulting data. It, then, uses a proof-guided technique to "repair" the learnt model into a desired function.

There have also been applications of the maximal satisfiable set (MAXSAT) on an unsatisfiable formula for program debugging. BugAssist [19] attempts to infer the set of suspicious locations using a MAXSAT formulation over an failing program trace and the specifications. Bavishi et al. [6] extend the formulation to provide a ranking over the suspicious locations such that the locations higher up in the rankings are less likely to cause regressions.

Another line of work is to use fuzzers to sample concrete instances and gradually build approximations of program behavior for the purpose of deductive verification [22] and symbolic execution [34]. However, such approaches use test instances and do not apply a proof-guided strategy.

Legion is inspired by many of the above algorithms and, there is potential of incorporating more of these ideas in Legion in the future.

## 7 Conclusion

Bounded model checking approaches for program verification predominantly focuses on CEGAR based strategies. In this work, we propose a proof-guided underapproximation widening strategy which behaves in a complementary manner to the CEGAR technique. The complementary nature allows us to build a portfolio strategy that takes advantage of both proof-guided underapproximation widening and CEGAR to deliver a significant speed up in verification time over both.

Our current approach only looks at the predicates corresponding to the call-sites to figure out which are most relevant to the proof of unsatisfiability of the underapproximated model. In the future, we aim to extract additional information from the unsat core which would allow us to explore more involved widening strategies. Furthermore, combining the underapproximation techniques that work on the domain of thread interleavings to deal with a large space of sequential behaviors (via lots of procedures) and concurrent behaviors (via lots of interleavings) would be another interesting direction to explore. We also believe that underapproximation widening may yield improvement performance on our distributed bounded model checker, Hydra [11,12]. Another interesting direction that we want to pursue is on combining bounded model checking algorithms (both overapproximation refinement and underapproximation widening) with dynamic analysis [5,13,38] and statistical testing [10,32] based approaches.

**Acknowledgements.** We wish to express our gratitude towards *Microsoft Azure* and *Google Cloud Platform* for providing us with computational resources for the experiments. We are also indebted to the PRAISE group of CSE department, IIT Kanpur and the anonymous reviewers for their helpful suggestions.

## References


1. Albarghouthi, A., Li, Y., Gurfinkel, A., Chechik, M.: Ufo: a framework for abstraction-and interpolation-based software verification. In: CAV (2012)
2. Alt, L., et al.: Hifrog: Smt-based function summarization for software verification. In: TACAS (2017)
3. Amla, N., McMillan, K.L.: A hybrid of counterexample-based and proof-based abstraction. In: FMCAD (2004)
4. Ball, T., Cook, B., Levin, V., Rajamani, S.K.: Slam and static driver verifier: Technology transfer of formal methods inside microsoft. In: International Conference on Integrated Formal Methods (2004)
5. Ball, T., Larus, J.R.: Efficient path profiling. In: Proceedings of the 29th Annual ACM/IEEE International Symposium on Microarchitecture (1996)
6. Bavishi, R., Pandey, A., Roy, S.: To be precise: regression aware debugging. ACM SIGPLAN Notices (2016)
7. Beyer, D.: Automatic verification of C and Java programs: SV-COMP 2019. In: Tools and Algorithms for the Construction and Analysis of Systems - 25 Years of TACAS: TOOLympics, Held as Part of ETAPS 2019, Prague, Czech Republic, 6–11 April, 2019, Proceedings, Part III (2019)
8. Boogie: An intermediate verification language. https://boogie-docs.readthedocs.io/en/latest/. Accessed June 2022
9. Bryant, R.E., Kroening, D., Ouaknine, J., Seshia, S.A., Strichman, O., Brady, B.: Deciding bit-vector arithmetic with abstraction. In: TACAS (2007)
10. Chatterjee, P., Chatterjee, A., Campos, J., Abreu, R., Roy, S.: Diagnosing software faults using multiverse analysis. In: IJCAI (2020). https://doi.org/10.24963/ijcai.2020/226
11. Chatterjee, P., Roy, S., Diep, B.P., Lal, A.: Distributed bounded model checking. In: FMCAD (2020)
12. Chatterjee, P., Roy, S., Diep, B.P., Lal, A.: Distributed bounded model checking. Formal Methods in System Design (2022). https://doi.org/10.1007/s10703-021-00385-1
13. Chouhan, R., Roy, S., Baswana, S.: Pertinent path profiling: tracking interactions among relevant statements. In: CGO (2013). https://doi.org/10.1109/CGO.2013.6494983
14. Clarke, E., Grumberg, O., Jha, S., Lu, Y., Veith, H.: Counterexample-guided abstraction refinement. In: CAV (2000)
15. De Moura, L., Bjørner, N.: Z3: An efficient smt solver. In: TACAS (2008)
16. Golia, P., Roy, S., Meel, K.S.: Manthan: a data-driven approach for boolean function synthesis. In: CAV (2020)
17. Golia, P., Roy, S., Slivovsky, F., Meel, K.S.: Engineering an efficient boolean functional synthesis engine. In: ICCAD (2021)
18. Grumberg, O., Lerda, F., Strichman, O., Theobald, M.: Proof-guided underapproximation-widening for multi-process systems. In: POPL (2005)
19. Jose, M., Majumdar, R.: Cause clue clauses: error localization using maximum satisfiability. ACM SIGPLAN Notices (2011)
20. Kroening, D., Tautschnig, M.: Cbmc-c bounded model checker. In: TACAS (2014)
21. Lahiri, S.K., Qadeer, S.: Back to the future: revisiting precise program verification using smt solvers. In: POPL (2008)
22. Lahiri, S., Roy, S.: Almost correct invariants: synthesizing inductive invariants by fuzzing proofs. In: ISSTA (2022)

23. Lal, A., Qadeer, S.: Reachability modulo theories. In: Reachability Problems - 7th International Workshop, RP (2013)
24. Lal, A., Qadeer, S.: Powering the static driver verifier using Corral. In: FSE (2014)
25. Lal, A., Qadeer, S.: DAG inlining: a decision procedure for reachability-modulo-theories in hierarchical programs. ACM SIGPLAN Notices (2015)
26. Lal, A., Qadeer, S., Lahiri, S.K.: A solver for reachability modulo theories. In: CAV (2012)
27. McMillan, K.L.: Interpolation and SAT-based model checking. In: CAV (2003)
28. McMillan, K.L.: Lazy abstraction with interpolants. In: CAV (2006)
29. McMillan, K.L.: Lazy annotation revisited. In: CAV (2014)
30. McMillan, K.L., Amla, N.: Automatic abstraction without counterexamples. In: TACAS (2003)
31. Microsoft: Static Driver Verifier Benchmarks. https://github.com/boogie-org/sdvbench
32. Modi, V., Roy, S., Aggarwal, S.K.: Exploring program phases for statistical bug localization. In: PASTE (2013). https://doi.org/10.1145/2462029.2462034
33. Morse, J., Ramalho, M., Cordeiro, L., Nicole, D., Fischer, B.: Esbmc 1.22. In: TACAS (2014)
34. Pandey, A., Kotcharlakota, P.R.G., Roy, S.: Deferred concretization in symbolic execution via fuzzing. In: ISSTA (2019). https://doi.org/10.1145/3293882.3330554
35. Prabhu, S., Schrammel, P., Srivas, M., Tautschnig, M., Yeolekar, A.: Concurrent program verification with invariant-guided underapproximation. In: ATVA (2017)
36. Rakamarić, Z., Emmi, M.: SMACK: decoupling source language details from verifier implementations. In: CAV (2014)
37. Roy, S.: From concrete examples to heap manipulating programs. In: SAS (2013). https://doi.org/10.1007/978-3-642-38856-9_9
38. Roy, S., Srikant, Y.N.: Profiling k-iteration paths: A generalization of the ball-larus profiling algorithm. In: CGO (2009). https://doi.org/10.1109/CGO.2009.11
39. Verma, A., Kalita, P.K., Pandey, A., Roy, S.: Interactive debugging of concurrent programs under relaxed memory models. In: CGO (2020)
40. Verma, S., Roy, S.: Synergistic debug-repair of heap manipulations. In: ESEC/FSE (2017)

# SolCMC: Solidity Compiler's Model Checker

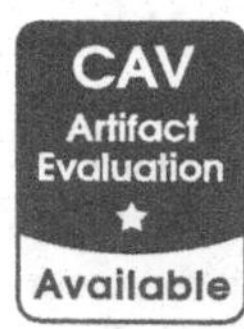


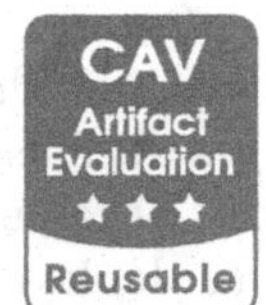


Leonardo Alt[1(✉)], Martin Blicha[2,3],
Antti E. J. Hyvärinen[2], and Natasha Sharygina[2]

[1] Ethereum Foundation, Berlin, Germany
leo@ethereum.org
[2] Università della Svizzera italiana, Lugano, Switzerland
{martin.blicha,antti.hyvaerinen,natasha.sharygina}@usi.ch
[3] Charles University, Prague, Czech Republic

**Abstract.** Formally verifying smart contracts is important due to their immutable nature, usual open source licenses, and high financial incentives for exploits. Since 2019 the Ethereum Foundation's Solidity compiler ships with a model checker. The checker, called SolCMC, has two different reasoning engines and tracks closely the development of the Solidity language. We describe SolCMC's architecture and use from the perspective of developers of both smart contracts and tools for software verification, and show how to analyze nontrivial properties of real life contracts in a fully automated manner.

**Keywords:** Ethereum · Solidity · Symbolic model checking · Constrained Horn clauses · Satisfiability modulo theories

## 1 Introduction

The Ethereum Foundation's compiler for Ethereum platform's most used language Solidity had almost 4 million downloads (3,957,195) over the last 60 days (at the time of submission). Since 2019, this compiler ships with a robust, builtin, easy-to-use, symbolic model checker SolCMC [16], formerly called SMTChecker. SolCMC models a *smart contract*, that is, a program for the Ethereum platform, and its properties as a system of constrained Horn clauses (CHCs) amenable to IC3-style model checking [34]. Since its deployment, SolCMC has increasingly served a dual purpose. On the one hand, smart contract programmers have through it a very visible and easy access to formal verification techniques. On the other hand, perhaps more subtly but no less importantly, the tool serves as a sounding board for developers of Horn solvers. Currently the system interfaces with Spacer [31] and Eldarica [30], making the related techniques available

This work was partially supported by Swiss National Science Foundation grant 200021_185031 and by Czech Science Foundation grant 20-07487S.


S. Shoham and Y. Vizel (Eds.): CAV 2022, LNCS 13371, pp. 325–338, 2022.
https://doi.org/10.1007/978-3-031-13185-1_16

to a large user base. We expect to integrate in SolCMC many other techniques through a similar mechanism. For instance, the tool has a bounded model checking engine for finding bugs by issuing SMT queries to solvers such as z3 [35] and cvc5 [23].

Smart contracts running on the Ethereum platform hold and control billions of dollars through their immutable logic, and therefore bugs can lead to massive losses. There are many recent sophisticated tools that increase the security of the Ethereum contract ecosystem by detecting smart contract bugs before they are deployed. However, new and emerging applications from the diverse user base are driving Solidity development at a fast pace and it is difficult to keep tools synchronized with the language. We believe that in the long run, the best way to ensure that a model checker for Solidity is sustainable is by integrating it directly into the compiler distribution, or the *main repository* of the related language tools, as we have done for SolCMC.

The direct integration of the model checker into the compiler has two main advantages. Firstly, we can model precisely and robustly features that are somewhat specific to Solidity and its applications, such as modeling reentrancy callbacks, and the handling of global storage. This makes the model checker capable of synthesizing new contracts that serve as counterexamples for correctness, and computing inductive invariants for the cases where properties hold. Secondly, the short pipeline between the source code and the model allows the presentation of both counterexamples and invariants as compiler warnings and annotations using a vocabulary that is meaningful for the developer.

The goal of SolCMC is to verify properties of programs with minimal user input. Our system supports writing properties as `assert` statements and can in addition automatically check other structural properties such as popping from an empty array and array accesses that are out of bounds, and the lack of underflows, overflows, divisions by zero, and transfers with insufficient balance. Moreover, common Solidity vulnerabilities such as reentrancy mutability and selfdestruct reachability can be verified using test harnesses that make the assertion-based approach more expressive. Thus, the expressiveness of SolCMC allows efficiently obtaining meaningful results for real life contracts in a way that is in practice fully automated. To demonstrate this we analyze the Beacon Chain Deposit Contract that is the base for Ethereum's proof of stake consensus layer, and the OpenZeppelin implementation of the ERC777 token standard.

An extended version of this tool paper including appendices showing detailed experimental results and other analysis is available online in the accompanying artifact, at https://doi.org/10.5281/zenodo.6512173.

*Related Work.* Proving correctness and finding bugs in smart contracts is useful in different abstraction targets. The technical details of how smart contracts are encoded by SolCMC are presented in [34]. In this tool paper the emphasis is on orthogonal topics: the usage of options, generation of counterexamples in Solidity-like syntax, interfacing with different Horn solvers, and how contract invariants can be obtained. We also demonstrate the tool's capabilities

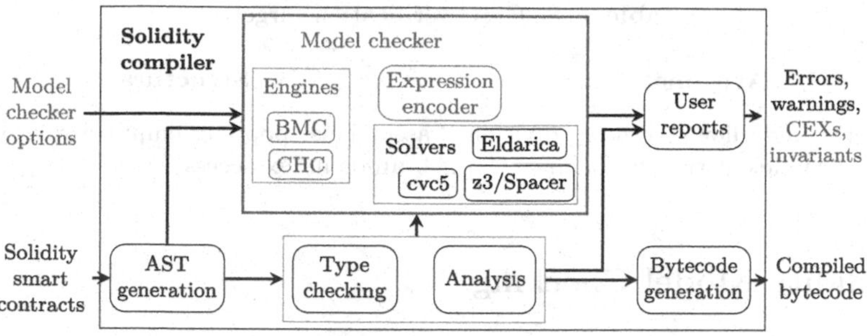


**Fig. 1.** The Solidity compiler stack with the integrated model checker (in green) (Color figure online)

by analysing two important and complex contracts: the Deposit contract and ERC777.

Most current tools either analyse the Solidity high level language, similar to SolCMC, or work directly on Ethereum Virtual Machine (EVM) bytecode.

The tools Solc-verify [28] and Verisol [38] verify Solidity properties in an automated way allowing models with unbounded number of transactions by translating Solidity to Boogie [33]. This gives the tools an advantage in engineering resources, but, compared to SolCMC's direct encoding as CHCs, makes producing counterexamples to the user more difficult. Neither of the two tools produce counterexamples or inductive invariants, and the most recent language versions are not supported. SmartACE [39] relies on translation from Solidity to LLVM-IR. This allows for employing multiple analysis tools, but unlike in SolCMC where we use a direct encoding and tight solver integration, the tools are mostly used as black boxes. EThor [37] also uses Horn clauses but it encodes EVM bytecode, and focuses on specific properties such as reentrancy. The Certora [24] tool relies on invariants to verify EVM bytecode. It is a commercial tool used for smart contract audits and is not publicly available. The $\mathbb{K}$ framework [10] is an assisted theorem prover that provides EVM semantics [29] to analyze EVM bytecode. It is generally able to prove more statements than automated tools, but requires considerable user interaction. HEVM [22] is an implementation of EVM in Haskell that also has a symbolic executor for EVM bytecode. It can prove functional properties but, unlike SolCMC, does not support inductive properties over multiple transactions and loops. HEVM and Echidna [4] also provide fuzzing techniques that help determining whether a candidate assertion is a contract invariant. Slither [14] is a powerful static analyzer that does not provide formal guarantees but can detect many vulnerabilities and dangerous patterns. Act [1] is a declarative specification language for smart contracts that supports three backends: bytecode verification via HEVM, SMT theorems for contract invariants, and a Coq backend that exports Coq definitions of contract state transitions. Finally, the Scribble specification language [13] allows annotating Solidity code and can generate runtime checks for given properties.

**Table 1.** SolCMC verification targets

| Arithmetic | Structural |
|---|---|
| arithmetic underflow/overflow, division by zero, insufficient transfer balance | assertions, popping empty array, out of bounds index access |

## 2 Solidity Model Checking

The high level overview of the compilation process is depicted in Fig. 1, with the model checker module emphasized. When enabled, Solidity model checking becomes another pass over the source code in the normal compilation process that starts after parsing and Abstract Syntax Tree (AST) generation. If there were no errors, the compiler produces the optimized bytecode together with any warnings, such as counterexamples found by the model checker.

This paper concentrates on SolCMC's unbounded model checker based on CHCs. The tool also has a BMC engine that generates SMT queries and links against cvc5 [23] and z3 [35].

### 2.1 The CHC Verification Engine

SolCMC encodes a smart contract as a system of constrained Horn clauses, based on [34]. The checker supports loops, multi-transaction computation paths, contract invariants, tracking contract balances throughout their lifetimes, and precise multi-contract calls. If the analyzed contract calls external functions unsafely, the model checker also synthesizes malicious external actors and represents them as reentrant calls.

The Horn queries are dispatched to a Horn solver. The encoding requires the solver to support nonlinear Horn clauses and at least the SMT theories for Linear Integer Arithmetic (LIA), Arrays, and the tuples subset of Algebraic Datatypes (ADT). Furthermore, nonlinear integer arithmetic and bitwise operations, if present, are encoded in the respective theories NIA and BV. To the best of our knowledge only Spacer [31] and Eldarica [30] satisfy those requirements. SolCMC has a tight integration with Spacer via its C++ API, whereas Eldarica is integrated using the compiler's SMT callback [21], and is currently accessible via solc-js [15], the JavaScript wrapper of the compiler's WebAssembly binary.

The model checker generates verification targets automatically for the conditions listed in Table 1. In particular a smart contract developer can combine *assertions* with *test harnesses* (see, e.g., Sect. 4) to specify complex behavior. The Solidity language has the statements `require` and `assert`, which SolCMC uses to capture developer intent: Conditions inside `require` statements are considered assumptions, and `assert` statements should be true for every execution. The model checker then treats every `assert` as a verification target and attempts to either prove it by finding an invariant, or give a counterexample for its correctness.

### 2.2 Horn Encoding

SolCMC's CHC encoding is based on the imperative encoding of [25], and is presented in detail in [34]. Horn logic is a popular formalism for expressing reachability problems. It is equivalent to the *existential positive fix-point logic* [26], and provides a convenient syntax for the use of existentially quantified predicates that in our encoding represent reachable states and effects of transactions. The Solidity AST first gets transformed into a Control Flow Graph (CFG). CFG nodes have corresponding CHC predicates, and edges are encoded as Horn rules with constraints created from the Single Static Assignment (SSA) form of the statements and expressions of the CFG block. Below we give an overview of the encoding that highlights the critical parts.

The encoding consists of three types of predicates that represent reachable states or possible transitions: *function bodies* ($B_f$) and *summaries* ($S_f$) represent the effect of function calls to $f$; *interfaces* ($I_C$) represent the states a contract $C$ can reach after initialization and each transaction; and *nondeterministic interfaces* ($N_C$) encode the effects the environment may have to a contract $C$. We use the following variables in the encoding: $e$, an integer error flag. Each verification target has a positive unique error id; 0 is reserved for no errors. $a$, the contract address. **abi**, a tuple of Solidity's ABI functions. **cr**, a tuple of Solidity's cryptographic functions: `keccak256`, `sha256`, `ripemd160`, and `ecrecover`. Both **abi** and **cr** are constant in the encoding. They are passed through the rules to ensure consistency everywhere. **tx**, a tuple of the transaction data, e.g., message sender, data, block number, etc. **st**, the blockchain state, a tuple containing the balances and storage for every contract. Balances are represented by an array mapping addresses to their balances. Each contract has a storage tuple that contains the state variables of that contract. **x**, the program state, input, output and local variables in the scope of that node. When necessary, we refer to the state variables as **s**. For **x** and **st** we use primes to denote the effect of rules on these variables.

*Function bodies* encode constructors, deployment procedures, and function summaries. For example, the contract `contract Acc { uint8 x = 0; function acc(uint8 y) external { x += y; } }` gets encoded into the rules

$$e = 0 \wedge \mathbf{st} = \mathbf{st}' \wedge x = x' \wedge y = y' \wedge 0 \leq y' \leq 255 \wedge 0 \leq x' \leq 255 \\ \implies \mathbf{B}_{\mathsf{acc}}(e, a, \mathbf{abi}, \mathbf{cr}, \mathbf{tx}, \mathbf{st}, x, y, \mathbf{st}', x', y')$$

stating that the function can always be called, its execution starts with no error, the initial variables have the current values, and the program variables' types are constrained;

$$\mathbf{B}_{\mathsf{acc}}(e, a, \mathbf{abi}, \mathbf{cr}, \mathbf{tx}, \mathbf{st}, x, y, \mathbf{st}', x', y') \wedge (x' + y' > 255) \\ \implies \mathbf{S}_{\mathsf{acc}}(1, a, \mathbf{abi}, \mathbf{cr}, \mathbf{tx}, \mathbf{st}, x, y, \mathbf{st}', x', y')$$

stating that an overflow in summation is an error, with label 1; and

$$\mathbf{B}_{\mathsf{acc}}(e, a, \mathbf{abi}, \mathbf{cr}, \mathbf{tx}, \mathbf{st}, x, y, \mathbf{st}', x', y') \land (x'' = x' + y) \land (x'' \leq 255) \\ \implies \mathbf{S}_{\mathsf{acc}}(e, a, \mathbf{abi}, \mathbf{cr}, \mathbf{tx}, \mathbf{st}, x, y, \mathbf{st}', x'', y),$$

which exits the function with no error and updates the contract state variable $x$.

*Interface Rules.* The *interface CFG node* is an artificial node that represents the idle state of a contract. This node is crucial to the encoding when modelling transactions, querying error flags, committing state changes, generating counterexamples, and translating inductive contract invariants. It is reachable at the beginning and end of every transaction. Transactions may revert due to invalid inputs or program logic, in which case all state changes are rolled back. The interface node may contain state changes if the transaction did not revert. Each contract `C` has a predicate $\mathbf{I}_{\mathsf{C}}$, whose parameters are $a$, $\mathbf{abi}, \mathbf{cr}$, $\mathbf{st}$ and the state variables $\mathbf{s}$ of the contract. The rules only change $e, \mathbf{st}$ and $\mathbf{s}$, and for better readability we use ellipsis $(\ldots)$ to denote the unchanged parameters. One rule is added per contract linking the deployment procedure to the interface: $\mathbf{D}_{\mathsf{C}}(\ldots) \implies \mathbf{I}_{\mathsf{C}}(\ldots)$. For each external function `f` in the contract `C`, we add the *query rule* and the *update rule*

$$\mathbf{I}_{\mathsf{C}}(\ldots, \mathbf{st}, \mathbf{s}, \ldots) \land \mathbf{S}_{\mathsf{f}}(e, \ldots, \mathbf{st}, \mathbf{s}, \ldots, \mathbf{st}', \mathbf{s}', \ldots) \land e > 0 \implies \mathbf{Err}_{\mathsf{f}}(e)$$

$$\mathbf{I}_{\mathsf{C}}(\ldots, \mathbf{st}, \mathbf{s}, \ldots) \land \mathbf{S}_{\mathsf{f}}(e, \ldots, \mathbf{st}, \mathbf{s}, \ldots, \mathbf{st}', \mathbf{s}', \ldots) \land e = 0 \implies \mathbf{I}_{\mathsf{C}}(\ldots, \mathbf{st}', \mathbf{s}', \ldots).$$

The Horn query given to the solver then asks whether $\mathbf{Err}_{\mathsf{f}}(e)$ is reachable, for each error label $e$. In this modelling, if the property is safe, inductive invariants chosen by the solver as an interpretation for the predicates $\mathbf{I}_{\mathsf{C}}$ represent the invariants for contracts `C`.

*Nondeterministic Interface Rules.* The *nondeterministic interface CFG node* is an artificial node that represents every possible behavior of the contract from an external point of view, in an unbounded number of transactions. This node is essential to model calls that the contract makes to external unknown contracts, as well as reentrancy if present. The predicate that represents this node has the same parameters as the interface predicate, but with the error flag and an extra set of program variables and blockchain state, in order to model possible errors and state changes. For every contract `C` the encoding adds the base case rule $\mathbf{N}_{\mathsf{C}}(0, \ldots, \mathbf{st}, \mathbf{s}, \mathbf{st}, \mathbf{s})$ which performs no state changes. Then for every external function `f` in the contract the encoding adds the inductive rule $\mathbf{N}(0, \ldots, \mathbf{st}, \mathbf{s}, \mathbf{st}', \mathbf{s}') \land \mathbf{S}_{\mathsf{f}}(e, \ldots, \mathbf{st}', \mathbf{s}', \mathbf{st}'', \mathbf{s}'') \implies \mathbf{N}(e, \ldots, \mathbf{st}, \mathbf{s}, \mathbf{st}'', \mathbf{s}'')$. These rules allow us to encode an external call to unknown code using a single constraint $\mathbf{N}(e, \ldots, \mathbf{st}, \mathbf{s}, \mathbf{st}', \mathbf{s}')$ which models every reachable state change in the contract, in any unbounded number of transactions. If a property is unsafe, these rules force the solver to synthesize the behavior of the adversarial contract. Otherwise, the interpretation of such predicate gives us inductive reentrancy properties that are true for every external call to unknown code in the contract.

## 3 User Features

As SolCMC is shipped inside the Solidity compiler, it is available for the users whenever and wherever they interact with the compiler. There are currently three major ways the compiler is used: 1. Interfacing with the WebAssembly release through official JavaScript bindings; 2. Interfacing with a binary release on command line; 3. Using web based IDEs, such as Remix [12]. Option 3 is the most accessible, but currently allows only limited configuration of the model checker through `pragma` statements in source code. Options 1 and 2 both allow extensive configuration, but in addition 1 enables the *SMT callback* feature needed, e.g., for Eldarica. In 2 the options can be provided either on the command line or in JSON [19], whereas 1 accepts only JSON using the JavaScript wrapper [15].

In 1 and 2 several parameters are available to the user for better control when trying to prove complex properties. We list here some examples, using the command line options (without the leading `--`). The JSON descriptions are named similarly. The model checking engine—BMC, CHC or both—is selected with the option `model-checker-engine`. Individual verification targets can be chosen with `model-checker-targets`, and a per-target verification timeout (in ms) can be set with `model-checker-timeout`. By default, all unproved verification targets are given in a single message after execution. More details are available by specifying `model-checker-show-unproved`. Option `model-checker-contracts` provides a way to choose the contracts to verify. Typically the user specifies only the contract they wish to deploy. Inherited and library contracts are included automatically, avoiding verifying every contract as the main one. Some options affect the encoding. For example, integer division and modulo operations can be encoded with the SMT function symbols `div` and `mod` or by SolCMC's own encoding using linear arithmetic and slack variables. Depending on the backend one is often preferred to the other. The default is the latter, the former is set by `model-checker-div-mod-no-slacks`.

Solidity provides the NatSpec [20] format for rich documentation. An annotation `/// @custom:smtchecker abstract-function-nondet` instructs SolCMC to abstract a function nondeterministically. Abstracting functions as an Uninterpreted Function [32] is under development.

*Counterexamples and Inductive Invariants.* When a verification target is disproved, SolCMC provides a readable counterexample describing how to reach the bug. In addition to the line of code where the verification target is breached, the counterexample states the trace of transactions and function calls leading to the failure along with concrete values substituted for the arguments, and the values of the state variables at the point of failure. When necessary, the trace includes also synthesized reentrant calls that trigger the failure.

Similarly, when SolCMC proves a verification target, the user may instrument the checker to provide safe inductive invariants. The invariants can, for instance, be used as an additional proof that the verification target holds. Technically the invariants are interpretations for the predicates in the CHC system and are presented in a human readable Solidity-like syntax. Similarly to counterexamples, the invariants are given also for predicates guaranteeing correctness under reentrancy. The extended version of this paper contains a short example illustrating the counterexamples and inductive invariants. It also presents more complex examples of both features, which were obtained from our experiments with the ERC777 token standard.

# 4 Real World Experiments

In this section we analyse two real world smart contract systems using SolCMC. Both contracts are massively important and highly nontrivial for automated tools due to their use of complex features, loops, and the need to produce nontrivial inductive invariants. While only the main results are stated in this section, we want to emphasize that the results were achieved after an extensive, albeit mechanical, experimentation on the two backend solvers (Spacer and Eldarica) and a range of parameters. To us the fact that they were successfully analysed using an automatic method is a strong proof of the combined power of our encoding approach and the backend solvers.

## 4.1 CHC Solver Options

The options we pass to the underlying CHC solvers Spacer and Eldarica may make the difference between a quick solving and divergences. For Spacer, we use the options `rewriter.pull_cheap_ite=true` which pulls if-then-else terms to the top level when it can be done cheaply, `fp.spacer.q3.use_qgen=true` which enables the quantified lemma generalizer, `fp.spacer.mbqi=false` which disables the model-based quantifier instantiation, and `fp.spacer.ground_pobs=false` which grounds proof obligations using values from a model. For Eldarica, we have found the adjustment of the predicate abstraction to be useful: `-abstract:off` disables abstraction, `-abstract:term` uses term abstraction, and `-abstract:oct` uses the octal abstraction.

## 4.2 Deposit Contract

The Ethereum 2.0 (Eth2) [9] Deposit Contract [2,3] is a smart contract that runs on Ethereum 1.0 collecting deposits from accounts that wish to be validators on Eth2. By the time of submission of this paper more than 9,100,194 ETH were held by the Deposit Contract, the equivalent of tens of billions USD in recent rates. Besides the financial incentive, this contract's functionality is essential to the progress of the protocol. The contract was formally verified before deployment [36] and further proved safe [27] with considerable amount of manual work. Despite having relatively few lines of code (less than 200), the contract remains a challenge for automated tools, because of its use of many complex constructs at the same time, such as ABI encoding functions, loops, dynamic types, and hash functions.

As part of the logic of the `deposit` function, a new entry is created in a Merkle tree for the caller. The contract asserts that such an entry can always be found, expressed as an `assert(false)` in a program location reachable only if such an entry is not found (line 162 in [2]). Using SolCMC this problem can be encoded into a 1.4MB Horn logic file containing 127 rules, which uses the SMT theories for Arrays, ADTs, NIA, and BV. After a syntactical change, Eldarica can show the property safe automatically in 22.4 s, while Spacer times out after 1 h (see the extended version for details). The change is necessary to avoid bit-vector reasoning and consists of replacing the test `if ((size & 1) == 1)` with a semantically equivalent form `if ((size % 2) == 1)` on lines 88 and 153 in [2].

### 4.3 ERC777

ERC777 [6] is a token standard that offers extra features compared to the ERC20 [5] standard. Besides the usual transfer and allowance features, ERC777 mainly adds account operators and transfer hooks which allow smart contracts to react to sending and receiving tokens. This is similar to the native feature of reacting to receiving Ether. In this experiment we analyze the OpenZeppelin implementation [11] of ERC777. This contract is an interesting benchmark for automated tools not only because of its importance, but also because it is a rather large smart contract system with 1200 lines of Solidity code, in 8 files, and it uses complex high level constructs such as assembly blocks, heavy inheritance, strings, arrays, nested mappings, loops, hash functions, and makes external calls to unknown code. The implementation follows the specification precisely, and does not guarantee a basic safety property related to tokens: *The total supply of tokens should not change during a transfer.*

Compared to the usual ERC20 token `transfer` that simply decreases and increases the balances of the two accounts involved in the transfer, the ERC777 `transfer` function may call unknown contracts to notify them that they are sending/receiving tokens. The logic in these external contracts is completely arbitrary and unknown to the token contract. For example, they could make a reentrant call to one of the nine ERC777 token mutable functions from its external interface.

Since the analyzed ERC777 implementation is agnostic on how tokens are initially allocated, no tokens are distributed in the base implementation at deployment. Therefore, to study the property, we write the following test harness [7] that uses the ERC777 token implemented by OpenZeppelin.

```
import "<path>/ERC777.sol";

contract Harness is ERC777 {
 constructor(
    address[] memory defOps_,
    uint amt_
 ) ERC777("ERC777", "E7", defOps_){
    _mint(msg.sender, amt_, "", "");
 }
```

```
  function transfer(address r, uint a)
    public override returns (bool) {
    uint prev = totalSupply();
    bool res = ERC777.transfer(r, a);
    uint post = totalSupply();
    assert(prev == post);
    return res;
  }
}
```

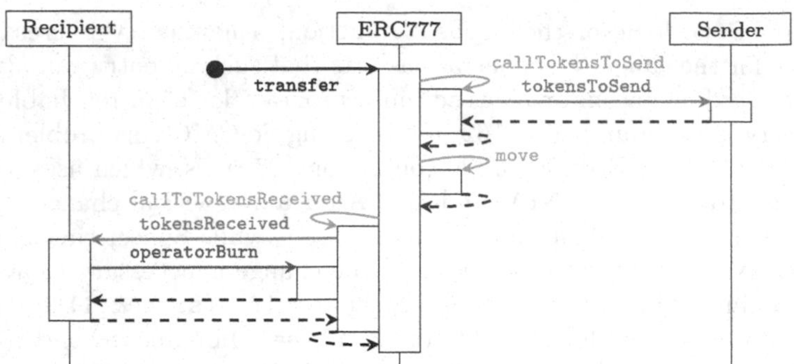


**Fig. 2.** Transaction trace that violates the safety property in `transfer`

First, we allocate `amt_` tokens to the creator of the contract, in order to have tokens circulating. Then, we override the `transfer` function, where our `transfer` function simply wraps the one from the `ERC777` contract, asserting that the property we want to verify is true after the original transfer.

The resulting Horn encoding is 15 MB large and contains 545 rules. The property can be shown unsafe by Eldarica in all its configurations, the quickest taking slightly less than 3 min, including generating the counterexample (see the extended version for details). All Spacer's configurations time out after 1 h. Since the property is unsafe, SolCMC also provides the full transaction trace required to reach the assertion failure. The transaction trace is visualized in Fig. 2 in the form of a sequence diagram, where solid arrows represent function calls and dashed arrows represent the return of the execution control. The full output of the tool can be found in the extended version.

The diagram shows the transaction trace from the call to `transfer` of ERC777 (after our wrapper contract has been created and its `transfer` was called). `transfer` performs 3 internal function calls (in orange): 1) `_callTokensToSend` performs the external call to notify the sender; 2) `_move` moves the tokens from the sender to the recipient; 3) `_callTokensReceived` notifies the recipient. The external calls to unknown code are shown in red. The transaction trace also contains the synthesized behaviour for the recipient (in purple). It is a reentrant call to `operatorBurn` in the ERC777 token contract itself, where some of the tokens of the recipient contract will be burned. At the end of the execution of `transfer`, the assertion is no longer true. The total supply of tokens after the call is not the same as the total supply before the call, as some tokens were burned during the transaction.

Given the number of mutable external functions of ERC777 and their complexity, we consider the discovery of the counterexample to be quite an achievement. We ascribe the success to the combined power of the CHC encoding and the Horn solver.

One way to guarantee that our property holds is to disallow reentrancy throughout the contract using a mutex. After changing the `ERC777` library [8], we ran the tool again on our test harness. Spacer timed out, but Eldarica was able to prove that the restricted system is safe in all its configurations, the fastest one finishing in 26.2 s, including the generation of the inductive invariants for every predicate. SolCMC now reports back the reentrancy property `<errorCode> = 0` given as part of the proof (the property is presented here in a simplified manner, see the extended version for details). The inductive property states that no external call performed by the analyzed contract can lead to an error. This shows that the reentrant path can no longer be taken.

### 4.4 Discussion

While producing the above analysis of the real life contracts, we experimented with two backend solvers Spacer and Eldarica, and a range of parameters for them. This phase (documented in the extended version of this paper) was critical in producing the results, because Eldarica and Spacer excel in different domains and parameter selection has a major impact on both verification success and run time. In both cases above Eldarica performed clearly better than Spacer. This seems to be because Eldarica handles abstract data types better than Spacer. This conclusion is backed by experimental evidence. We ran SolCMC using both Spacer and Eldarica on the SolCMC regression test suite consisting of 1098 solidity files [17] and 3688 Horn queries [18]. The experiment shows that while the solvers give overall similar results, in two categories that make heavy use of ADTs, Eldarica is consistently able to solve more benchmarks than Spacer. For lack of space, the detailed analysis is given in the extended version.

Our encoding uses tuples to encode data that makes sense to be bundled together. Moreover, arrays of tuples are used to emulate Uninterpreted Functions (UFs) to abstract injective functions such as cryptographic primitives. This is necessary due to UFs not being syntactically allowed in predicates of Horn instances. While this increases the complexity of the problem, we have chosen this path to reduce encoding complexity, considering that a pre processing step may be available in the future to flatten such tuples and arrays.

## 5 Conclusions and Future Work

This paper presents the model checker SolCMC that ships with the Ethereum Foundation's compiler for the Solidity language. We believe that the automated and usable tool has the potential to link a high volume of Solidity developers with the community working on tools for formal verification. The tool is stable, and, having been integrated into the compiler, tracks closely the quickly developing language.

We advocate for a *direct encoding approach* where the same AST gets compiled both into EVM bytecode and into a verification model in SMT-LIB2 or the format used in the CHC competition. In our experience this makes it more natural to model features specific to Solidity and Ethereum smart contracts as well as for generating usable counterexamples and inductive invariants in comparison to producing first a language-agnostic intermediate verification representation that is then processed for reasoning engines.

We argue for the ease of use of the tool by showing nontrivial properties of real life contracts. The experiments also identify interesting future development opportunities in the current CHC formalism. We show how the formalism's limitations can be worked around using abstract data types, and discuss their impact on tool efficiency.

## References

1. Act 0.1 released. https://fv.ethereum.org/2021/08/31/act-0.1/. Accessed 21 Feb 2022
2. Deposit Contract deployed on Ethereum mainnet. https://etherscan.io/address/0x00000000219ab540356cbb839cbe05303d7705fa#code. Accessed 21 Jan 2022
3. Deposit Contract specification and source code. https://github.com/ethereum/consensus-specs/blob/master/specs/phase0/deposit-contract.md. Accessed 21 Jan 2022
4. Echidna source code and documentation. https://github.com/crytic/echidna/, Accessed 21 Jan 2022
5. ERC20 documentation. https://eips.ethereum.org/EIPS/eip-20. Accessed 21 Jan 2022
6. ERC777 documentation. https://eips.ethereum.org/EIPS/eip-777. Accessed 21 Jan 2022
7. ERC777 Property Wrapper contract. https://github.com/leonardoalt/openzeppelin-contracts/blob/master/contracts/token/ERC777/ERC777PropertyUnsafe.sol. Accessed 21 Jan 2022
8. ERC777 using a mutex to prevent reentrancy. https://github.com/leonardoalt/openzeppelin-contracts/blob/master/contracts/token/ERC777/ERC777Mutex.sol. Accessed 21 Jan 2022
9. Ethereum Consensus Layer specification. https://github.com/ethereum/consensus-specs. Accessed 21 Jan 2022
10. K framework. https://kframework.org. Accessed 21 Jan 2022
11. Openzeppelin Solidity implementation of the ERC777 standard. https://github.com/OpenZeppelin/openzeppelin-contracts/blob/master/contracts/token/ERC777/ERC777.sol. Accessed 21 Jan 2022
12. Remix IDE. https://remix.ethereum.org. Accessed 21 Jan 2022
13. Scribble documentation. https://docs.scribble.codes/language/introduction. Accessed 21 Jan 2022
14. Slither source code and documentation. https://github.com/crytic/slither. Accessed 21 Jan 2022
15. solc-js documentation. https://github.com/ethereum/solc-js. Accessed 21 Jan 2022
16. SolCMC documentation. https://docs.soliditylang.org/en/latest/smtchecker.html. Accessed 21 Jan 2022
17. SolCMC tests. https://github.com/ethereum/solidity/tree/develop/test/libsolidity/smtCheckerTests. Accessed 21 Jan 2022
18. SolCMC tests' Horn queries. https://github.com/leonardoalt/chc_benchmarks_solidity. Accessed 21 Jan 2022

19. Solidity compiler input and output JSON description. https://docs.soliditylang.org/en/v0.8.11/using-the-compiler.html#compiler-input-and-output-json-description. Accessed 21 Jan 2022
20. Solidity NatSpec Format. https://docs.soliditylang.org/en/v0.8.11/natspec-format.html. Accessed 21 Jan 2022
21. Solidity's SMT callback documentation. https://github.com/ethereum/solc-js#example-usage-with-smtsolver-callback. Accessed 21 Jan 2022
22. Symbolic execution for hevm. https://fv.ethereum.org/2020/07/28/symbolic-hevm-release/. Accessed 21 Jan 2022
23. Barbosa, H., et al.: cvc5: a versatile and industrial-strength SMT solver. In: Proceedings of TACAS 2022. LNCS, vol. 13243, pp. 415–442. Springer (2022). https://doi.org/10.1007/978-3-030-99524-9_24
24. Bernardi, T.P., et al.: WIP: finding bugs automatically in smart contracts with parameterized invariants (2020). https://www.certora.com/pubs/sbc2020.pdf. Accessed 21 Jan 2022
25. Bjørner, N., Gurfinkel, A., McMillan, K., Rybalchenko, A.: Horn clause solvers for program verification. In: Beklemishev, L.D., Blass, A., Dershowitz, N., Finkbeiner, B., Schulte, W. (eds.) Fields of Logic and Computation II. LNCS, vol. 9300, pp. 24–51. Springer, Cham (2015). https://doi.org/10.1007/978-3-319-23534-9_2
26. Blass, A., Gurevich, Y.: Existential fixed-point logic. In: Börger, E. (ed.) Computation Theory and Logic. LNCS, vol. 270, pp. 20–36. Springer, Heidelberg (1987). https://doi.org/10.1007/3-540-18170-9_151
27. Cassez, F.: Verification of the Incremental Merkle Tree Algorithm with Dafny. In: Huisman, M., Păsăreanu, C., Zhan, N. (eds.) FM 2021. LNCS, vol. 13047, pp. 445–462. Springer, Cham (2021). https://doi.org/10.1007/978-3-030-90870-6_24
28. Hajdu, Á., Jovanović, D.: SOLC-VERIFY: a modular verifier for solidity smart contracts. In: Chakraborty, S., Navas, J.A. (eds.) VSTTE 2019. LNCS, vol. 12031, pp. 161–179. Springer, Cham (2020). https://doi.org/10.1007/978-3-030-41600-3_11
29. Hildenbrandt, E., et al.: KEVM: a complete formal semantics of the ethereum virtual machine. In: Proceedings of CSF 2018, pp. 204–217. IEEE Computer Society (2018)
30. Hojjat, H., Rümmer, P.: The ELDARICA Horn solver. In: Proceedings FMCAD 2018, pp. 1–7. IEEE (2018)
31. Komuravelli, A., Gurfinkel, A., Chaki, S.: SMT-based model checking for recursive programs. Formal Methods in System Design **48**(3), 175–205 (2016). https://doi.org/10.1007/s10703-016-0249-4
32. Kroening, D., Strichman, O.: Equality Logic and Uninterpreted Functions. In: Decision Procedures. TTCSAES, pp. 77–95. Springer, Heidelberg (2016). https://doi.org/10.1007/978-3-662-50497-0_4
33. Leino, K.R.M.: This is Boogie 2, June 2008. https://www.microsoft.com/en-us/research/publication/this-is-boogie-2-2/
34. Marescotti, M., Otoni, R., Alt, L., Eugster, P., Hyvärinen, A.E.J., Sharygina, N.: Accurate smart contract verification through direct modelling. In: Margaria, T., Steffen, B. (eds.) ISoLA 2020. LNCS, vol. 12478, pp. 178–194. Springer, Cham (2020). https://doi.org/10.1007/978-3-030-61467-6_12
35. de Moura, L., Bjørner, N.: Z3: an efficient SMT solver. In: Ramakrishnan, C.R., Rehof, J. (eds.) TACAS 2008. LNCS, vol. 4963, pp. 337–340. Springer, Z3: An efficient SMT solver (2008). https://doi.org/10.1007/978-3-540-78800-3_24

36. Park, D., Zhang, Y., Rosu, G.: End-to-end formal verification of ethereum 2.0 deposit smart contract. In: Lahiri, S.K., Wang, C. (eds.) CAV 2020. LNCS, vol. 12224, pp. 151–164. Springer, Cham (2020). https://doi.org/10.1007/978-3-030-53288-8_8
37. Schneidewind, C., Grishchenko, I., Scherer, M., Maffei, M.: EThor: practical and provably sound static analysis of ethereum smart contracts, pp. 621–640. ACM (2020)
38. Wang, Y., Lahiri, S.K., Chen, S., Pan, R., Dillig, I., Born, C., Naseer, I., Ferles, K.: Formal verification of workflow policies for smart contracts in azure blockchain. In: Chakraborty, S., Navas, J.A. (eds.) VSTTE 2019. LNCS, vol. 12031, pp. 87–106. Springer, Cham (2020). https://doi.org/10.1007/978-3-030-41600-3_7
39. Wesley, S., Christakis, M., Navas, J.A., Trefler, R., Wüstholz, V., Gurfinkel, A.: Verifying SOLIDITY smart contracts via communication abstraction in SMARTACE. In: Finkbeiner, B., Wies, T. (eds.) VMCAI 2022. LNCS, vol. 13182, pp. 425–449. Springer, Cham (2022). https://doi.org/10.1007/978-3-030-94583-1_21

# Hyperproperties and Security

# Software Verification of Hyperproperties Beyond $k$-Safety

Raven Beutner[(✉)] and Bernd Finkbeiner

CISPA Helmholtz Center for Information Security, Saarbrücken, Germany
{raven.beutner,finkbeiner}@cispa.de

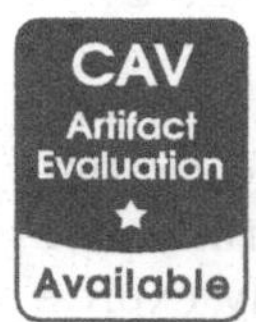


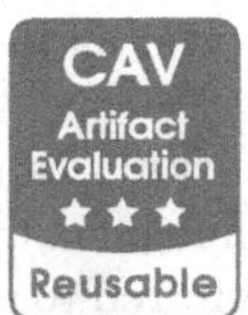


**Abstract.** Temporal hyperproperties are system properties that relate multiple execution traces. For (finite-state) hardware, temporal hyperproperties are supported by model checking algorithms, and tools for general temporal logics like HyperLTL exist. For (infinite-state) software, the analysis of temporal hyperproperties has, so far, been limited to $k$-safety properties, i.e., properties that stipulate the absence of a bad interaction between any $k$ traces. In this paper, we present an automated method for the verification of $\forall^k\exists^l$-safety properties in infinite-state systems. A $\forall^k\exists^l$-safety property stipulates that for any $k$ traces, there *exist* $l$ traces such that the resulting $k+l$ traces do not interact badly. This combination of universal and existential quantification enables us to express many properties beyond $k$-safety, including, for example, generalized non-interference or program refinement. Our method is based on a strategy-based instantiation of existential trace quantification combined with a program reduction, both in the context of a fixed predicate abstraction. Notably, our framework allows for mutual dependence of strategy and reduction.

**Keywords:** Hyperproperties · HyperLTL · Infinite-state systems · Predicate abstraction · Hyperliveness · Verification · Program reduction

## 1 Introduction

Hyperproperties are system properties that relate multiple execution traces of a system [22] and commonly arise, e.g., in information-flow policies [35], the verification of code optimizations [6], and robustness of software [19]. Consequently, many methods for the automated verification of hyperproperties have been developed [27,39–41]. Almost all previous approaches verify a class of hyperproperties called $k$-safety, i.e., properties that stipulate the absence of a bad interaction between any $k$ traces in the system. For example, we can express a simple form of non-interference as a 2-safety property by stating that any *two* traces that agree on the low-security inputs should produce the same observable output.

The vast landscape of hyperproperties does, however, stretch far beyond $k$-safety. The overarching limitation of $k$-safety (or, more generally, of hypersafety [22]) is an implicit *universal* quantification over all executions. By contrast, many


S. Shoham and Y. Vizel (Eds.): CAV 2022, LNCS 13371, pp. 341–362, 2022.
https://doi.org/10.1007/978-3-031-13185-1_17

properties of interest, ranging from applications in information-flow control to robust cleanness, require a combination of universal and existential quantification. For example, consider the reactive program in Fig. 1, where $\star_{\mathbb{N}}$ denotes a nondeterministic choice of a natural number. We assume that $h$, $l$, and $o$ are a high-security input, a low-security input, and a low-security output, respectively. This program violates the simple 2-safety non-interference property given above as the non-determinism influences the output. Nevertheless, the program is "secure" in the sense that an attacker that observes low-security inputs and outputs cannot deduce information about the high-security input. To capture this formally, we use a relaxed notion of non-interference, in the literature often referred to as generalized non-interference (GNI) [35]. We can, informally, express GNI in a temporal logic as follows:

$$\forall \pi. \forall \pi'. \exists \pi''. \Box \left( o_\pi = o_{\pi''} \land l_\pi = l_{\pi''} \land h_{\pi'} = h_{\pi''} \right)$$

This property requires that for any two traces $\pi, \pi'$, there exists some trace $\pi''$ that, globally, agrees with the low-security inputs and outputs on $\pi$ but the high-security inputs on $\pi'$. Phrased differently, any observation on the low-security input-output behavior is compatible with every possible high-security input. The program in Fig. 1 satisfies GNI. Crucially, GNI is no longer a hypersafety property (and, in particular, no $k$-safety property for any $k$) as it requires a combination of universal and *existential* quantification.

### 1.1 Verification Beyond $k$-Safety

Instead, GNI falls in the general class of $\forall^*\exists^*$-safety properties. Concretely, a $\forall^k\exists^l$-safety property (using $k$ universal and $l$ existential quantifiers) stipulates that for any $k$ traces, there exist $l$ traces such that the resulting $k+l$ traces do not interact badly. $k$-safety properties are the *special case* where $l = 0$. We study the verification of such properties in infinite-state systems arising, e.g., in software. In contrast to $k$-safety, where a broad range of methods has been developed [10,27,39–41], no method for the automated verification of *temporal* $\forall^*\exists^*$ properties in infinite-state systems exists (we discuss related approaches in Sect. 8).

**repeat**
  **readInput**$(h, l)$
  **if** $h > l$ **then**
    $o \leftarrow l + \star_{\mathbb{N}}$
  **else**
    $x \leftarrow \star_{\mathbb{N}}$
    **if** $x \geq l$ **then**
      $o \leftarrow x$
    **else**
      $o \leftarrow l$

**Fig. 1.** An example program is depicted.

Our novel verification method is based on a game-based reading of existential quantification *combined* with the search for a program reduction. The game-based reading of existential quantification instantiates existential trace quantification with an explicit strategy and constitutes the first practicable method for the verification of $\forall^*\exists^*$-properties in finite-state systems [23]. Program reductions are a well-established technique to align executions of independent program fragments (such as the individual program copies in a self-composition) to obtain proofs with easier invariants [27,34,39].

So far, both techniques are limited to their respective domain, i.e., the game-based approach has only been applied to finite-state systems and synchronous specifications, and reductions have (mostly) been used for the verification of $k$-safety. We combine both techniques yielding an effective (and first) verification technique for hyperproperties beyond $k$-safety in infinite-state systems arising in software. Notably, our search for reduction and strategy-based instantiation of existential quantification is *mutually dependent*, i.e., a particular strategy might depend on a particular reduction and vice versa.

### 1.2 Contributions and Structure

The starting point of our work is a new temporal logic called *Observation-based HyperLTL* (OHyperLTL for short). Our logic extends the existing hyperlogic HyperLTL [21] with capabilities to reason about asynchronous properties (i.e., properties where the individual traces are traversed at different speeds), and to specify properties using assertions from arbitrary background theories (to reason about the infinite domains encountered in software) (Sect. 4).

To automatically verify $\forall^k\exists^l$ OHyperLTL properties, we combine program reductions with a strategy-based instantiation of existential quantification, both in the context of a fixed predicate abstraction. To facilitate this combination, we first present a game-based approach that automates the search for a reduction. Concretely, we construct an abstract game where a winning strategy for the verifier directly corresponds to a reduction with accompanying proof. As a side product, our game-based interpretation simplifies the search for a reduction in a given predicate abstraction as, e.g., studied by Shemer et al. [39] (Sect. 5).

Our strategic (game-based) view on reductions allows us to combine them with a game-based instantiation of existential quantification. Here, we view the existentially quantified traces as being constructed by a strategy that, iteratively, reacts to the universally quantified traces. As we phrase both the search for a reduction and the search for existentially quantified traces as a game, we can frame the search for both as a combined abstract game. We prove the soundness of our approach, i.e., a winning strategy for the verifier constitutes both a strategy for the existentially quantified traces and accompanying (mutually dependent) reduction. Despite its finite nature, constructing the abstract game is expensive as it involves many SMT queries. We propose an inner refinement loop that determines the winner of the game (without constructing it explicitly) by computing iterative approximations (Sect. 6).

We have implemented our verification approach in a prototype tool called `HyPA` (short for **Hy**perproperty Verification with **P**redicate **A**bstraction) and evaluate `HyPA` on $k$-safety properties (that can already be handled by existing methods) and on $\forall^*\exists^*$-safety benchmarks that cannot be handled by any existing tool (Sect. 7).

*Contributions.* In short, our contributions include the following:

- We propose a temporal hyperlogic that can specify asynchronous hyperproperties in infinite-state systems;

- We propose a game-based interpretation of a reduction (improving and simplifying previous methods for $k$-safety [39]);
- We combine a strategy-based instantiation of existentially quantified traces with the search for a reduction. This yields a flexible (and first) method for the verification of temporal $\forall^*\exists^*$ properties. We propose an iterative method to solve the abstract game that avoids an expensive explicit construction;
- We provide and evaluate a prototype implementation of our method.

## 2 Overview: Reductions and Quantification as a Game

Our verification approach hinges on the observation that we can express both a reduction and existential trace quantification as a game. In this section, we provide an overview of our game-based interpretations. We begin by outlining our game-based reading of a reduction (illustrating this in the simpler case of $k$-safety) in Sect. 2.1 and then extend this to include a game-based interpretation of existential quantification in Sect. 2.2.

### 2.1 Reductions as a Game

Consider the two programs in Fig. 2 and the specification that both programs produce the same output (on initially identical values for $x$). We can formalize this in our logic OHyperLTL (formally defined in Sect. 4) as follows:

$$\forall^{\mathsf{P1}}\pi_1 : (pc = 2).\ \forall^{\mathsf{P2}}\pi_2 : (pc = 2).\ (x_{\pi_1} = x_{\pi_2}) \rightarrow \Box(x_{\pi_1} = x_{\pi_2})$$

The property states that for all traces $\pi_1$ in P1 and $\pi_2$ in P2 the LTL specification $(x_{\pi_1} = x_{\pi_2}) \rightarrow \Box(x_{\pi_1} = x_{\pi_2})$ holds (where $x_\pi$ refers to the value of $x$ on trace $\pi$). Additionally, the observation formula $pc = 2$ marks the positions at which the LTL property is evaluated: We only observe a trace at steps where $pc = 2$ (i.e., where the program counter is at the output position).

The verification of our property involves reasoning about two copies of our system (in this case, one of P1 and one of P2) on *disjoint* state spaces. Consequently, we can interleave the statements of both programs (between two observation points) without affecting the behavior of the individual copies. We refer to each interleaving of both copies as a *reduction*. The choice of a reduction drastically influences the complexity of the needed invariants [27,34,39]. Given an initial abstraction of the system [30,39], we aim to discover a suitable reduction *automatically*. Our first observation is that we can phrase the search for a reduction as a game as follows: In each step, the verifier decides on a *scheduling* (i.e., a non-empty subset $M \subseteq \{1, 2\}$) that indicates which of the copies should take a step (i.e., $i \in M$ iff copy $i$ should make a program step). Afterward, the refuter can choose an abstract successor state compatible with that scheduling, after which the process repeats. This naturally defines a finite-state two-player safety game that we can solve efficiently.[1] If the verifier wins, a winning strategy

[1] The LTL specification is translated to a symbolic safety automaton that moves alongside the game. For sake of readability, we omitted the automaton from the following discussion.

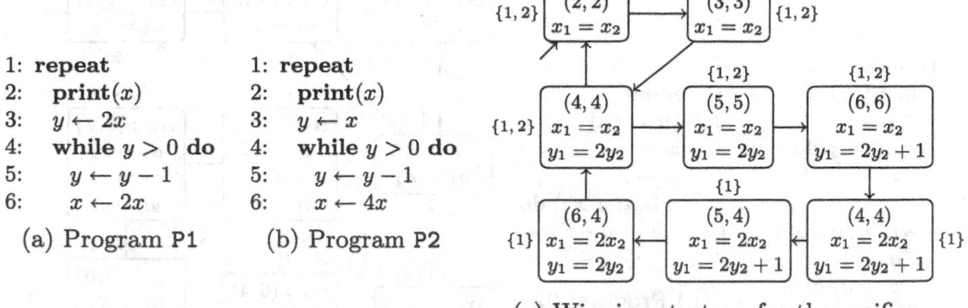

(a) Program P1 (b) Program P2 (c) Winning strategy for the verifier.

**Fig. 2.** Two output-equivalent programs P1 and P2 are depicted in Fig. 2a and 2b. In Fig. 2c a possible winning strategy for the verifier is given. Each abstract state contains the value of the program counter of both copies (given as the pair at the top) and the predicates that hold in that state. For sake of readability we omit the trace variables and write, e.g., $x_1$ for $x_{\pi_1}$. We mark the initial state with an incoming arrow. The outer label at each state gives the scheduling $M \subseteq \{1, 2\}$ chosen by the strategy in that state.

directly corresponds to a reduction and accompanying inductive invariant for the safety property within the given abstraction.

For our example, we give (parts of) a possible winning strategy in Fig. 2c. In each abstract state, the strategy chooses a scheduling (written next to the state), and all abstract states compatible with that scheduling are listed as successors. Note that whenever the program counter is $(2, 2)$ (i.e., both programs are at their output position), it holds that $x_1 = x_2$ (as required). The example strategy schedules in lock-step for the most part (by choosing $M = \{1, 2\}$) but lets P1 take the inner loop *twice*, thereby maintaining the linear invariants $x_1 = x_2$ and $y_1 = 2y_2$. In particular, the resulting reduction is property-based [39] as the scheduling is based on the current (abstract) state. Note that the program cannot be verified with only linear invariants in a sequential or parallel (lock-step) reduction.

### 2.2 Beyond $k$-Safety: Quantification as a Game

We build upon this game-based interpretation of a reduction to move beyond $k$-safety. As a second example, consider the two programs Q1 and Q2 in Fig. 3, where $\star_\tau$ denotes a nondeterministic choice of type $\tau \in \{\mathbb{N}, \mathbb{B}\}$. We wish to check that Q1 refines Q2, i.e., all output behavior of Q1 is also possible in Q2. We can express this in our logic as follows:

$$\forall^{\mathtt{Q1}} \pi_1 : (pc = 2).\ \exists^{\mathtt{Q2}} \pi_2 : (pc = 2).\ \Box(a_{\pi_1} = a_{\pi_2})$$

The property states that for every trace $\pi_1$ in Q1 there *exists* a trace $\pi_2$ in Q2 that outputs the same value. The quantifiers range over infinite traces of variable assignments (with infinite domains), making a direct verification of the

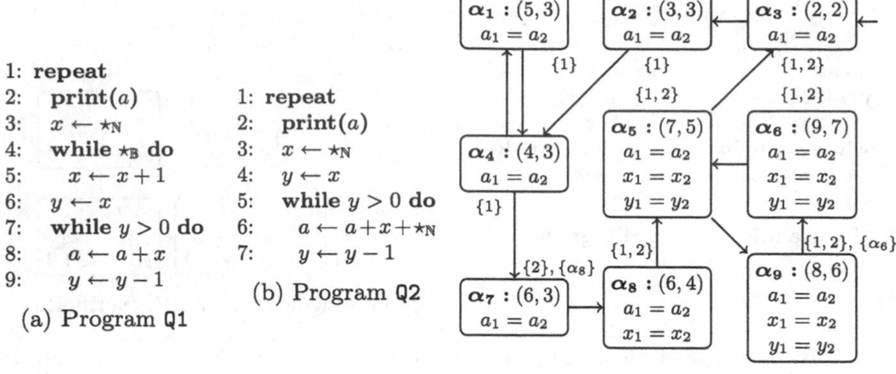


**Fig. 3.** Two programs Q1 and Q2 are given in Fig. 3a and 3b. In Fig. 3c a possible winning strategy for the verifier is depicted. The outer label gives the scheduling $M \subseteq \{1, 2\}$ and, if applicable, the restriction chosen by the witness strategy.

quantifier alternation challenging. In contrast to alternation-free formulas, we cannot reduce the verification to verification on a self composition [8, 28]. Instead, we adopt (yet another) game-based interpretation by viewing the existentially quantified traces as being resolved by a *strategy* (called the witness strategy) [23]. That is, instead of trying to find a witness traces $\pi_2$ in Q2 when given the *entire* trace $\pi_1$, we interpret the $\forall\exists$ property as a game between verifier and refuter. The refuter moves through the state space of Q1 (thereby producing a trace $\pi_1$), and the verifier reacts to each move by choosing a successor in the state space of Q2 (thereby producing a trace $\pi_2$). If the verifier can assure that the resulting traces $\pi_1, \pi_2$ satisfy $\square(a_{\pi_1} = a_{\pi_2})$, the $\forall\exists$ property holds. However, this game-based interpretation fails in many instances. There might exist a witness trace $\pi_2$, but the trace cannot be produced by a witness strategy as it requires knowledge of *future* moves of the refuter. Let us discuss this on the example programs in Fig. 3. A simple (informal) solution to construct a witness trace $\pi_2$ (when given the entire $\pi_1$) would be to guarantee that in Q2:4 (meaning location 4 of Q2) and line Q1:6 the value of $x$ in both programs agrees (i.e., $x_1 = x_2$ holds) and then simply resolve the nondeterminism at Q2:6 with 0. However, to follow this idea, the witness strategy for the verifier, when at Q2:3, would need to know the future value of $x_1$ when Q1 is at location Q1:6.

Our insight in this paper is that we can turn the strategy-based interpretation of the witness trace $\pi_2$ into a useful verification method by *combining* it with a program reduction. As we express both searches strategically, we can phrase the combined search as a combined game. In particular, both the reduction and the witness strategy are controlled by the verifier and can thus *collaborate*. In the resulting game, the verifier chooses a scheduling (as in Sect. 2.1) and, additionally, whenever the existentially quantified copy is scheduled, the verifier also decides on the successor state of that copy. We depict a possible winning strategy in Fig. 3c. This strategy formalizes the interplay of reduction and witness strategy. Initially, the verifier only schedules $\{1\}$ until Q1 has reached program location Q1:6 (at which point the value of $x$ is fixed). Only then does the verifier schedule $\{2\}$, at which point the witness strategy can decide on a successor state for Q2. In our case, the strategy chooses a value for $x$ such that $x_1 = x_2$ holds. As we work in an abstraction of the actual system, we formalize this by restricting the abstract successor states. In particular, in state $\alpha_7$ the verifier schedules $\{2\}$ and simultaneously restricts the successors to $\{\alpha_8\}$ (i.e., the abstract state where $x_1 = x_2$ holds), even though abstract state $[(6,4), a_1 = a_2, x_1 \neq x_2]$ is also a valid successors under scheduling $\{2\}$. We formalize when a restriction is valid in Sect. 6. The resulting strategy is winning and therefore denotes both a reduction *and* witness strategy for the existentially quantified copy. Importantly, both reduction and witness strategy are mutually dependent. Our tool HyPA is able to verify both properties (in Fig. 2 and Fig. 3) in a matter of a few seconds (cf. Sect. 7).

## 3 Preliminaries

We begin by introducing basic preliminaries, including our basic model of computation and background on (finite-state) safety games.

*Symbolic Transition Systems.* We assume some fixed underlying first-order theory. A *symbolic transition system* (STS) is a tuple $\mathcal{T} = (X, \mathit{init}, \mathit{step})$ where $X$ is a finite set of variables (possibly sorted), *init* is a formula over $X$ describing all initial states, and *step* is a formula over $X \uplus X'$ (where $X' := \{x' \mid x \in X\}$ is the set of primed variables) describing the transitions of the system. A concrete state $\mu$ in $\mathcal{T}$ is an assignment to the variables in $X$. We write $\mu'$ for the assignment over $X'$ given by $\mu'(x') := \mu(x)$. A trace in $\mathcal{T}$ is an infinite sequence of assignment $\mu_0\mu_1 \cdots$ such that $\mu_0 \models \mathit{init}$ and for every $i \in \mathbb{N}$, $\mu_i \uplus \mu'_{i+1} \models \mathit{step}$. We write $\mathit{Traces}(\mathcal{T})$ for the set of all traces in $\mathcal{T}$. We can naturally interpret programs as STS by making the program counter explicit.

*Formula Transformations.* For the remainder of this paper, we fix the set of system variables $X$. We also fix a finite set of trace variables $\mathcal{V} = \{\pi_1, \dots, \pi_k\}$. For a trace variable $\pi \in \mathcal{V}$ we define $X_\pi := \{x_\pi \mid x \in X\}$ and write $\vec{X}$ for $X_{\pi_1} \cup \cdots \cup X_{\pi_k}$. For a formula $\theta$ over $X$, we define $\theta_{\langle\pi\rangle}$ as the formula over $X_\pi$ obtained by replacing every variable $x$ with $x_\pi$. Similarly, we define $k$ fresh disjoint copies $\vec{X}' = X'_{\pi_1} \cup \cdots \cup X'_{\pi_k}$ (where $X'_\pi := \{x'_\pi \mid x \in X\}$). For a formula $\theta$ over $\vec{X}$, we define $\theta^{\langle\prime\rangle}$ as the formula over $\vec{X}'$ obtained by replacing every variable $x_\pi$ with $x'_\pi$.

*Safety Games.* A *safety game* is a tuple $\mathcal{G} = (S_{\mathtt{SAFE}}, S_{\mathtt{REACH}}, S_0, T, B)$ where $S = S_{\mathtt{SAFE}} \uplus s_{\mathtt{REACH}}$ is a set of game states, $S_0 \subseteq S$ a set of initial states, $T \subseteq S \times S$ a transition relation, and $B \subseteq S$ a set of bad states. We assume that for every $s \in S$ there exists at least one $s'$ with $(s, s') \in T$. States in $S_{\mathtt{SAFE}}$ are controlled by player SAFE and those in $S_{\mathtt{REACH}}$ by player REACH. A play is an infinite sequence of states $s_0 s_1 \cdots$ such that $s_0 \in S_0$, and $(s_i, s_{i+1}) \in T$ for every $i \in \mathbb{N}$. A positional strategy $\sigma$ for player $p \in \{\mathtt{SAFE}, \mathtt{REACH}\}$ is a function $\sigma : S_p \to S$ such that $(s, \sigma(s)) \in T$ for every $s \in S_p$. A play $s_0 s_1 \cdots$ is compatible with strategy $\sigma$ for player $p$ if $s_{i+1} = \sigma(s_i)$ whenever $s_i \in S_p$. The safety player wins $\mathcal{G}$ if there is a strategy $\sigma$ for SAFE such that all $\sigma$-compatible plays never visit a state in $B$. In particular, SAFE needs to win from *all* initial states.

## 4 Observation-Based HyperLTL

In this section, we present OHyperLTL (short for observation-based HyperLTL). Our logic builds upon HyperLTL [21], which itself extends linear-time temporal logic (LTL) with explicit trace quantification. In OHyperLTL, we include predicates from the background theory (to reason about infinite variable domains) and explicit observations (to express asynchronous properties). Formulas in OHyperLTL are given by the following grammar:[2]

$$\varphi := \forall \pi : \xi . \varphi \mid \exists \pi : \xi . \varphi \mid \phi$$
$$\phi := \theta \mid \neg \phi \mid \phi_1 \wedge \phi_2 \mid \bigcirc \phi \mid \phi_1 \mathcal{U} \phi_2$$

Here $\pi \in \mathcal{V}$ is a trace variable, $\theta$ is a formula over $\vec{X}$, and $\xi$ is a formula over $X$ (called the observation formula). For ease of notation, we assume that all variables in $\mathcal{V}$ occur in the quantifier prefix *exactly* once. We use the standard Boolean connectives $\wedge$, $\rightarrow$, $\leftrightarrow$, and constants $\top, \bot$, as well as the derived LTL operators eventually $\diamondsuit \phi := \top \mathcal{U} \phi$, and globally $\square \phi := \neg \diamondsuit \neg \phi$.

*Semantics.* A trace $t$ is an infinite sequence $\mu_0 \mu_1 \cdots$ of assignments to $X$. For $i \in \mathbb{N}$, we write $t(i)$ to denote the $i$th value in $t$. A trace assignment $\Pi$ is a partial mapping of trace variables in $\mathcal{V}$ to traces. Given a trace assignment $\Pi$ and $i \in \mathbb{N}$, we define $\Pi(i)$ to be the assignment to $\vec{X}$ given by $\Pi(i)(x_\pi) := \Pi(\pi)(i)(x)$, i..e, the value of $x_\pi$ is the value of $x$ on the trace assigned to $\pi$. For the LTL body of an OHyperLTL formula, we define:

$$
\begin{array}{lll}
\Pi, i \models \theta & \text{iff} & \Pi(i) \models \theta \\
\Pi, i \models \neg \phi & \text{iff} & \Pi, i \not\models \phi \\
\Pi, i \models \phi_1 \wedge \phi_2 & \text{iff} & \Pi, i \models \phi_1 \text{ and } \Pi, i \models \phi_2 \\
\Pi, i \models \bigcirc \phi & \text{iff} & \Pi, i+1 \models \phi \\
\Pi, i \models \phi_1 \mathcal{U} \phi_2 & \text{iff} & \exists j \geq i. \Pi, j \models \phi_2 \text{ and } \forall i \leq k < j. \Pi, k \models \phi_1
\end{array}
$$

The distinctive feature of OHyperLTL over HyperLTL are the explicit observations. Given an observation formula $\xi$ and trace $t$, we say that $\xi$ is a *valid*

[2] For the examples in Sect. 2, we additionally annotated quantifiers with an STS if we want to reason about different STSs within the same formula. In the following, we assume that all quantifiers range over traces in the same STS to simplify notation.

*observation on* $t$ (written $valid(t, \xi)$) if there are infinitely many $i \in \mathbb{N}$ such that $t(i) \models \xi$. If $valid(t, \xi)$ holds, we write $(\!|t|\!)_\xi$ for the trace obtained by projecting on those positions $i$ where $t(i) \models \xi$, i.e., $(\!|t|\!)_\xi(i) := t(j)$ where $j$ is the $i$th index that satisfies $\xi$. Given a set of traces $\mathbb{T}$ we resolve trace quantification as follows:

$$\begin{array}{lll} \Pi \models_{\mathbb{T}} \phi & \text{iff} & \Pi, 0 \models \phi \\ \Pi \models_{\mathbb{T}} \forall \pi : \xi . \varphi & \text{iff} & \forall t \in \{t \in \mathbb{T} \mid valid(t, \xi)\}. \Pi[\pi \mapsto (\!|t|\!)_\xi] \models_{\mathbb{T}} \varphi \\ \Pi \models_{\mathbb{T}} \exists \pi : \xi . \varphi & \text{iff} & \exists t \in \{t \in \mathbb{T} \mid valid(t, \xi)\}. \Pi[\pi \mapsto (\!|t|\!)_\xi] \models_{\mathbb{T}} \varphi \end{array}$$

The semantics mostly agrees with that of HyperLTL [21] but projects each trace to the positions where the observation holds. Given an STS $\mathcal{T}$ and OHyperLTL formula $\varphi$, we write $\mathcal{T} \models \varphi$ if $\emptyset \models_{Traces(\mathcal{T})} \varphi$ where $\emptyset$ is the empty assignment.

*The Power of Observations.* The explicit observations in OHyperLTL facilitate the specification of asynchronous hyperproperties, i.e., properties where traces are traversed at different speeds. For the example in Sect. 2.1, the explicit observations allow us to compare the output of both programs even though the actual step at which the output occurs (in a synchronous semantics) differs between both programs (as `P1` takes the inner loop twice as often as `P2`). As the observations are part of the specification, we can model a broad spectrum of properties ranging, e.g., from timing-insensitive properties (by placing observations only at output locations) to timing-sensitive specifications [29] (by placing observations at closer intervals). Functional (opposed to temporal) $k$-safety properties specified by pre-and postcondition [10,39,41] can easily be encoded as $\forall^k$-OHyperLTL properties by placing observations at the start and end of each program. By setting $\xi = \top$, i.e., observing *every* step, we can express synchronous properties. OHyperLTL thus subsumes HyperLTL.

*Finite-State Model Checking.* Many mechanisms used to express asynchronous hyperproperties render finite-state model checking undecidable [9,17,31]. In contrast, the simple mechanism used in OHyperLTL maintains decidable finite-state model checking. Detailed proofs can be found in the full version [15].

**Theorem 1.** *Assume an STS $\mathcal{T}$ with finite variable domains and decidable background theory and an OHyperLTL formula $\varphi$. It is decidable if $\mathcal{T} \models \varphi$.*

*Proof Sketch.* Under the assumptions, we can view $\mathcal{T}$ as an explicit (instead of symbolic) finite-state transition system. Given an observation formula $\xi$ we can effectively compute an explicit finite-state system $\mathcal{T}'$ such that $Traces(\mathcal{T}') = \{(\!|t|\!)_\xi \mid t \in Traces(\mathcal{T}) \wedge valid(t, \xi)\}$. This reduces OHyperLTL model checking on $\mathcal{T}$ to HyperLTL model checking on $\mathcal{T}'$, which is decidable [28]. □

Note that for infinite-state (symbolic) systems, we cannot effectively compute $\mathcal{T}'$ as in the proof of Theorem 1. In fact, there may not even exist a system $\mathcal{T}'$ with the desired property that is expressible in the same background theory.

The finite-state result in Theorem 1 is of little relevance for the present paper. Nevertheless, it indicates that our logic is well suited for verification of infinite-state (software) systems as the (inevitable) undecidability stems from the infinite domains in software programs and not already from the logic itself.

*Safety.* In this paper, we assume that the hyperproperty is temporally safe [12], i.e., the temporal body of any OHyperLTL formula denotes a *safety property.* Note that, as we support quantifier alternation, we can still express hyperliveness properties [22,23]. For example, GNI is both temporally safe and hyperliveness. We model the body of a formula by a symbolic safety automaton [24], which is a tuple $\mathcal{A} = (Q, q_0, \delta, B)$ where $Q$ is a finite set of states, $q_0 \in Q$ the initial state, $B \subseteq Q$ a set of bad-states, and $\delta$ a finite set of automaton edges of the form $(q, \theta, q')$ where $q, q' \in Q$ are states and $\theta$ is a formula over $\vec{X}$. Given a trace $t$ over assignments to $\vec{X}$, a run of $\mathcal{A}$ on $t$ is an infinite sequence of states $q_0 q_1 \cdots$ (starting in $q_0$) such that for every $i$, there exists an edge $(q_i, \theta_i, q_{i+1}) \in \delta$ such that $t(i) \models \theta_i$. A word is accepted by $\mathcal{A}$ if it has *no* run that visits a state in $B$. The automaton is *deterministic* if for every $q \in Q$ and every assignments $\mu$ to $\vec{X}$, there exists exactly one edge $(q, \theta, q') \in \delta$ with $\mu \models \theta$.

## 5 Reductions as a Game

After having defined our temporal logic, we turn our attention to the automatic verification of OHyperLTL formulas on STSs. In this section, we begin by formalizing our game-based interpretation of a reduction. To illustrate this, we consider $\forall^k$ OHyperLTL formulas, which, as the body of the formula is a safety property, always denote $k$-safety properties.

*Predicate Abstraction.* Our search for a reduction is based in the scope of a fixed predicate abstraction [30,33], i.e., we abstract our system by keeping track of the truth value of a few selected predicates that (ideally) identify properties that are relevant to prove the property in question. Let $\mathcal{T} = (X, \mathit{init}, \mathit{step})$ be an STS and let $\varphi = \forall \pi_1 : \xi_1 \ldots \forall \pi_k : \xi_k . \phi$ be the ($k$-safety) OHyperLTL we wish to verify. Let $\mathcal{A}_\phi = (Q_\phi, q_{\phi,0}, \delta_\phi, B_\phi)$ be a deterministic safety automaton for $\phi$. A *relational* predicate $p$ is a formula over $\vec{X}$ that identifies a property of the combined state space of $k$ system copies. Let $\mathcal{P} = \{p_1, \ldots, p_n\}$ be a finite set of relational predicates. We say a formula over $\vec{X}$ is *expressible in* $\mathcal{P}$ if it is equivalent to a boolean combination of the predicates in $\mathcal{P}$. We assume that all edge formulas in the automaton $\mathcal{A}_\phi$, and formulas $\mathit{init}_{\langle \pi_i \rangle}$ and $(\xi_i)_{\langle \pi_i \rangle}$ for $\pi_i \in \mathcal{V}$ are expressible in $\mathcal{P}$. Note that we can always add missing predicates to $\mathcal{P}$.

Given the set of predicates $\mathcal{P}$, the state-space of the abstraction w.r.t. $\mathcal{P}$ is given by $\mathbb{B}^n$, where for each abstract state $\hat{s} \in \mathbb{B}^n$, the $i$th position $\hat{s}[i] \in \mathbb{B}$ tracks whether or not predicate $p_i$ holds. To simplify notation, we write $\mathit{ite}(b, \theta, \theta')$ to be formula $\theta$ if $b = \top$, and $\theta'$ otherwise. For each abstract state $\hat{s} \in \mathbb{B}^n$, we define $[\![\hat{s}]\!] := \bigwedge_{i=1}^n \mathit{ite}(\hat{s}[i], p_i, \neg p_i)$, i.e., $[\![\hat{s}]\!]$ is a formula over $\vec{X}$ that captures all concrete states that are abstracted to $\hat{s}$. To incorporate reductions in our abstraction, we parametrize the abstract transition relation by a *scheduling* $M \subseteq \{\pi_1, \ldots, \pi_k\}$. We lift the *step* formula from $\mathcal{T}$ by defining

$$\mathit{step}_M := \bigwedge_{i=1}^{k} \mathit{ite}\Big(\pi_i \in M, \mathit{step}_{\langle \pi_i \rangle}, \bigwedge_{x \in X} x'_{\pi_i} = x_{\pi_i}\Big).$$

That is all copies in $M$ take a step while all other copies remain unchanged. Given two abstract states $\hat{s}_1, \hat{s}_2$ we say that $\hat{s}_2$ is an *$M$-successor* of $\hat{s}_1$, written $\hat{s}_1 \xrightarrow{M} \hat{s}_2$, if $[\![\hat{s}_1]\!] \wedge [\![\hat{s}_2]\!]^{(\prime)} \wedge step_M$ is satisfiable, i.e., we can transition from $\hat{s}_1$ to $\hat{s}_2$ by only progressing the copies in $M$.

For an abstract state $\hat{s}$, we define $obs(\hat{s}) \in \mathbb{B}^k$ as the boolean vector that indicates which copy (of $\pi_1, \ldots, \pi_k$) is currently at an observation point, i.e., $obs(\hat{s})[i] = \top$ iff $[\![\hat{s}]\!] \wedge (\xi_i)_{\langle \pi_i \rangle}$ is satisfiable. Note that as $(\xi_i)_{\langle \pi_i \rangle}$ is, by assumption, expressible in $\mathcal{P}$, either all or none of the concrete states in $[\![\hat{s}]\!]$ satisfy $(\xi_i)_{\langle \pi_i \rangle}$.

*Game Construction.* Building on the parametrized abstract transition relation, we can construct a (finite-state) safety game where winning strategies for the verifier correspond to valid reductions with accompanying proofs. The nodes in our game have two forms: Either they are of the form $(\hat{s}, q, b)$ where $\hat{s} \in \mathbb{B}^n$ is an abstract state, $q \in Q_\phi$ a state of the safety automaton, and $b \in \mathbb{B}^k$ a boolean vector indicating which copy has moved since the last automaton step; Or of the form $(\hat{s}, q, b, M)$ where $\hat{s}$, $q$, and $b$ are as before and $\emptyset \neq M \subseteq \{\pi_1, \ldots, \pi_k\}$ is a scheduling. The initial states are all states $(\hat{s}, q_{\phi,0}, \top^k)$ where $[\![\hat{s}]\!] \wedge \bigwedge_{i=1}^{k} init_{\langle \pi_i \rangle}$ is satisfiable (recall that $init_{\langle \pi_i \rangle}$ is expressible in $\mathcal{P}$). We mark a state $(\hat{s}, q, b)$ or $(\hat{s}, q, b, M)$ as losing iff $q \in B_\phi$. For automaton state $q \in Q_\phi$ and abstract state $\hat{s}$, we define $\delta_\phi(q, \hat{s})$ as the *unique* state $q'$ such that there is an edge $(q, \theta, q') \in \delta_\phi$ such that $[\![\hat{s}]\!] \wedge \theta$ is satisfiable. Uniqueness follows from the assumption that $\mathcal{A}_\phi$ is deterministic and all edge formulas are expressible in $\mathcal{P}$. The transition relation of our game is given by the following rules:

$$\frac{\forall \pi_i \in M.\, \neg b[i] \vee \neg obs(\hat{s})[i]}{(\hat{s}, q, b) \rightsquigarrow (\hat{s}, q, b, M)}\ \textbf{(1)} \qquad \frac{obs(\hat{s}) = \top^k \quad q' = \delta_\phi(q, \hat{s})}{(\hat{s}, q, \top^k) \rightsquigarrow (\hat{s}, q', \bot^k)}\ \textbf{(2)}$$

$$\frac{\hat{s} \xrightarrow{M} \hat{s}' \quad b' = b[i \mapsto \top]_{\pi_i \in M}}{(\hat{s}, q, b, M) \rightsquigarrow (\hat{s}', q, b')}\ \textbf{(3)}$$

In rule **(1)**, we select any scheduling that schedules only copies that have not reached an observation point or have not moved since the last automaton step. In particular, we cannot schedule any copy that has moved and already reached an observation point. In rule **(2)**, all copies reached an observation point and have moved since the last update (i.e., $b = \top^k$) so we progress the automaton and reset $b$. Lastly, in rule **(3)**, we select an $M$-successor of $\hat{s}$ and update $b$ for all copies that take part in the step. In our game, player `SAFE` takes the role of the verifier, and player `REACH` that of the refuter. It is the safety player's responsibility to select a scheduling in each step, so we assign nodes of the form $(\hat{s}, q, b)$ to `SAFE`. Nodes of the form $(\hat{s}, q, b, M)$ are controlled by `REACH` who can choose an abstract $M$-successor. Let $\mathcal{G}^{\forall}_{(\mathcal{T}, \varphi, \mathcal{P})}$ be the resulting (finite-state) safety game. A winning strategy for `SAFE` in $\mathcal{G}^{\forall}_{(\mathcal{T}, \varphi, \mathcal{P})}$ picks, in each abstract state, a valid scheduling that prevents a visit to a losing state. We can thus show:

**Theorem 2.** *If player `SAFE` wins $\mathcal{G}^{\forall}_{(\mathcal{T}, \varphi, \mathcal{P})}$, then $\mathcal{T} \models \varphi$.*

*Proof Sketch.* Assume $\sigma$ is a winning strategy for SAFE in $\mathcal{G}^{\forall}_{(\mathcal{T},\varphi,\mathcal{P})}$. Let $t_1,\ldots,t_k \in \mathit{Traces}(\mathcal{T})$ be arbitrary. We, iteratively, construct stuttered versions $t'_1,\ldots,t'_k$ of $t_1,\ldots,t_k$ by querying $\sigma$ on abstracted prefixes of $t_1,\ldots,t_k$: Whenever $\sigma$ schedules copy $i$ we take a proper step on $t_i$; otherwise we stutter. By construction of $\mathcal{G}^{\forall}_{(\mathcal{T},\varphi,\mathcal{P})}$ the stuttered traces $t'_1,\ldots,t'_k$ align at observation points. In particular, we have $[\pi_1 \mapsto (\!|t_1|\!)_{\xi_1},\ldots,\pi_k \mapsto (\!|t_k|\!)_{\xi_k}] \models \phi$ iff $[\pi_1 \mapsto (\!|t'_1|\!)_{\xi_1},\ldots,\pi_k \mapsto (\!|t'_k|\!)_{\xi_k}] \models \phi$. Moreover, the sequence of abstract states in $\mathcal{G}^{\forall}_{(\mathcal{T},\varphi,\mathcal{P})}$ forms an abstraction of $t'_1,\ldots,t'_k$ and shows that $\mathcal{A}_\phi$ cannot reach a bad state when reading $(\!|t'_1|\!)_{\xi_1},\ldots,(\!|t'_k|\!)_{\xi_k}$ (as $\sigma$ is winning). This already shows that $[\pi_1 \mapsto (\!|t'_1|\!)_{\xi_1},\ldots,\pi_k \mapsto (\!|t'_k|\!)_{\xi_k}] \models \phi$ and thus $[\pi_1 \mapsto (\!|t_1|\!)_{\xi_1},\ldots,\pi_k \mapsto (\!|t_k|\!)_{\xi_k}] \models \phi$. As this holds for all traces $t_1,\ldots,t_k \in \mathit{Traces}(\mathcal{T})$, we get $\mathcal{T} \models \varphi$ as required. □

*Game Construction and Complexity.* If the background theory is decidable, $\mathcal{G}^{\forall}_{(\mathcal{T},\varphi,\mathcal{P})}$ can be constructed effectively using at most $2^{|\mathcal{P}|+1} \cdot 2^k$ queries to an SMT solver. Checking if SAFE wins $\mathcal{G}^{\forall}_{(\mathcal{T},\varphi,\mathcal{P})}$ can be done with a simple fixpoint computation of the attractor in linear time.

Our game-based method of finding a reduction in a given abstraction is closely related to the notation of a *property-directed self-composition* [39]. The previously only known algorithm for finding such a reduction is based on an optimized enumeration [39], which, in the worst case, requires $\mathcal{O}(2^{|\mathcal{P}|+1} \cdot 2^k)$ many enumerations. Our worst-case complexity thus matches the bounds inferred by [39], but avoids the explicit enumeration of reductions (and the concomitant repeated construction of the abstract state-space) and is, as we believe, conceptually simpler to comprehend. Moreover, our game-based technique is the key stepping stone for extending our method beyond $k$-safety in Sect. 6.

## 6 Verification Beyond $k$-Safety

Building on the game-based interpretation of a reduction, we extend our verification beyond $\forall^*$ properties to support $\forall^*\exists^*$ properties. We accomplish this by *combining* the game-based reading of a reduction (as discussed in the previous section) with a game-based reading of existential quantification. For the remainder of this section, fix an STS $\mathcal{T} = (X, \mathit{init}, \mathit{step})$ and let

$$\varphi = \forall \pi_1 : \xi_1 \ldots \forall \pi_l : \xi_l . \exists \pi_{l+1} : \xi_{l+1} \ldots \exists \pi_k : \xi_k . \phi$$

be the OHyperLTL formula we wish to check, i.e., we universally quantify over $l$ traces followed by an existential quantification over $k - l$ traces. We assume that for every existential quantification $\exists \pi_i : \xi_i$ occurring in $\varphi$, $\mathit{valid}(t, \xi_i)$ holds for every $t \in \mathit{Traces}(\mathcal{T})$ (we discuss this later in Remark 1).

### 6.1 Existential Trace Quantification as a Game

The idea of a game-based verification of $\forall^*\exists^*$ properties is to consider a $\forall^*\exists^*$-property as a game between verifier and refuter [23]. The refuter controls the $l$ universally quantified traces by moving through $l$ copies of the system (thereby producing traces $\pi_1, \ldots, \pi_l$) and the verifier reacts by, incrementally, moving through $k-l$ copies of the system (thereby producing traces $\pi_{l+1}, \ldots, \pi_k$). If the verifier has a strategy that ensures that the resulting traces satisfy $\phi$, $\mathcal{T} \models \varphi$ holds. We call such a strategy for the verifier a *witness strategy*.

We combine this game-based reading of existential quantification with our game-based interpretation of a reduction by, additionally, letting the verifier control the scheduling of the system. When played on the *concrete* state-space of $\mathcal{T}$ the game proceeds in three stages as follows: 1) The verifier selects a valid scheduling $M \subseteq \{\pi_1, \ldots, \pi_k\}$; 2) The refuter selects successor states for all universally quantified copies by fixing an assignment to $X'_{\pi_1}, \ldots, X'_{\pi_l}$ (only moving copies scheduled by $M$); 3) The verifier reacts by choosing successor states for the existentially quantified copies by fixing an assignment to $X'_{\pi_{l+1}}, \ldots, X'_{\pi_k}$ (again, only moving copies scheduled by $M$). Afterward, the process repeats.

As we work within a fixed abstraction of $\mathcal{T}$, the verifier can, however, not choose concrete successor states directly but only work in the precision captured by the abstraction. Following the general scheme of abstract games, we, therefore, underapproximate the moves available to the verifier [2]. Formally, we abstract the three-stage game outlined before (which was played at the level of concrete states) to a simpler abstract game (consisting of only two stages). In the first stage, the verifier selects both a scheduling $M$ and a *restriction* on the set of abstract successor states, i.e., a set of abstract states $A$. In the second stage, the refuter cannot choose any abstract successor state (any $M$-successor in the terminology from Sect. 5), but only successors contained in the restriction $A$. To guarantee the soundness of this approach, we ensure that the verifier can only pick restrictions that are *valid*, i.e., restrictions that underapproximate the possibilities of the verifier on the level of concrete states.

*Game Construction.* We modify our game from Sect. 5 as follows. States are either of the form $(\hat{s}, q, b)$ (as in Sect. 5) or of the form $(\hat{s}, q, b, M, A)$ where $\hat{s}$, $q$, $b$, and $M$ are as in Sect. 5, and $A \subseteq \mathbb{B}^n$ is a subset of abstract states (the restriction). To reflect the restriction, we modify transition rules **(1)** and **(3)**. Rule **(2)** remains unchanged.

$$\frac{\forall \pi_i \in M. \neg b[i] \vee \neg obs(\hat{s})[i] \quad validRes_A^{\hat{s},M}}{(\hat{s}, q, b) \rightsquigarrow (\hat{s}, q, b, M, A)} \,\textbf{(1)} \qquad \frac{\hat{s}' \in A \quad b' = b[i \mapsto \top]_{i \in M}}{(\hat{s}, q, b, M, A) \rightsquigarrow (\hat{s}', q, b')} \,\textbf{(3)}$$

In rule **(1)**, the safety player (who, again, takes the role of the verifier) selects both a scheduling $M$ and a restriction $A$ such that $validRes_A^{\hat{s},M}$ holds (which we define later). The reachability player (who takes the role of the refuter) can, in rule **(3)**, select any successor contained in $A$.

*Valid Restriction.* The above game construction depends on the definition of $validRes_A^{\hat{s},M}$. Intuitively, $A$ is a valid restriction if it underapproximates the possibilities of a witness strategy that can pick concrete successor states for all existentially quantified traces. That is, for every concrete state in $\hat{s}$, a witness strategy (on the level of concrete states) can guarantee a move to a concrete state that is abstracted to an abstract state within $A$. Formally we define $validRes_A^{\hat{s},M}$ as follows:

$$\forall \{X_{\pi_i}\}_{i=1}^{k}. \forall \{X'_{\pi_i}\}_{i=1}^{l}. \ [\![\hat{s}]\!] \wedge \bigwedge_{i=1}^{l} ite\Big(\pi_i \in M, step_{\langle \pi_i \rangle}, \bigwedge_{x \in X} x'_{\pi_i} = x_{\pi_i}\Big)$$
$$\Rightarrow \exists \{X'_{\pi_i}\}_{i=l+1}^{k}. \bigwedge_{i=l+1}^{k} ite\Big(\pi_i \in M, step_{\langle \pi_i \rangle}, \bigwedge_{x \in X} x'_{\pi_i} = x_{\pi_i}\Big) \wedge \bigvee_{\hat{s}' \in A} [\![\hat{s}']\!]^{(')}$$

It expresses that for all concrete states in $[\![\hat{s}]\!]$ (assignments to $\{X_{\pi_i}\}_{i=1}^{k}$) and for all concrete successor states for the universally quantified copies (assignments to $\{X'_{\pi_i}\}_{i=1}^{l}$), there exist successor states for the existentially quantified copies ($\{X'_{\pi_i}\}_{i=l+1}^{k}$) such that one of the abstract states in $A$ is reached.

*Example 1.* With this definition at hand, we can validate the restrictions chosen by the strategy in Fig. 3c. For example, in state $\alpha_7$ the strategy schedules $M = \{2\}$ and restricts the successor states to $\{\alpha_8\}$ even though abstract state $[(6,4), a_1 = a_2, x_1 \neq x_2]$ is also a $\{2\}$-successor of $\alpha_7$. If we spell out $validRes_{\{\alpha_8\}}^{\alpha_7,\{2\}}$ we get

$$\forall X_1 \cup X_2 \cup X'_1. \underbrace{a_1 = a_2}_{[\![\alpha_7]\!]} \wedge \Big(\bigwedge_{z \in X} z'_1 = z_1\Big) \Rightarrow \exists X'_2. \underbrace{a'_2 = a_2 \wedge y'_2 = y_2}_{step_{\langle 2 \rangle}} \wedge \underbrace{(a'_1 = a'_2 \wedge x'_1 = x'_2)}_{[\![\alpha_8]\!]^{(')}}$$

where $X = \{a, x, y\}$. Here we assume that $step := (a' = a \wedge y' = y)$ is the update performed on instruction $x \leftarrow \star_{\mathbb{N}}$ from Q2:3 to Q2:4. The above formula is valid.

*Correctness.* Call the resulting game $\mathcal{G}^{\forall\exists}_{(\mathcal{T},\varphi,\mathcal{P})}$. The game combines the search for a reduction with that of a witness strategy (both within the precision captured by $\mathcal{P}$).[3] We can show:

**Theorem 3.** *If player* SAFE *wins* $\mathcal{G}^{\forall\exists}_{(\mathcal{T},\varphi,\mathcal{P})}$*, then* $\mathcal{T} \models \varphi$.

*Proof Sketch.* Let $\sigma$ be a winning strategy for SAFE in $\mathcal{G}^{\forall\exists}_{(\mathcal{T},\varphi,\mathcal{P})}$. Let $t_1, \ldots, t_l \in Traces(\mathcal{T})$ be arbitrary. We use $\sigma$ to incrementally construct witness traces $t_{l+1}, \ldots, t_k$ by querying $\sigma$. In every abstract state $\hat{s}$, $\sigma$ selects a scheduling $M$ and a restriction $A$ such that $validRes_A^{\hat{s},M}$ holds. We plug the current *concrete* state (reached in our construction of $t_{l+1}, \ldots, t_k$) into the universal quantification of $validRes_A^{\hat{s},M}$ and get (concrete) witnesses for the existential quantification that, by definition of $validRes_A^{\hat{s},M}$, are valid successors for the existentially quantified copies in $\mathcal{T}$. □

*Remark 1.* Recall that we assume that for every existential quantification $\exists \pi_i : \xi_i$ occurring in $\varphi$ and all $t \in Traces(\mathcal{T})$, $valid(t, \xi_i)$ holds. This is important to ensure that the safety player (the verifier) cannot avoid observation points forever. We could drop this assumption by strengthening the winning condition in $\mathcal{G}^{\forall\exists}_{(\mathcal{T},\varphi,\mathcal{P})}$ and explicitly state that, in order to win, SAFE needs to visit observations points on existentially quantified traces infinitely many times.

[3] In particular, $\mathcal{G}^{\forall\exists}_{(\mathcal{T},\varphi,\mathcal{P})}$ (strictly) generalizes the construction of $\mathcal{G}^{\forall}_{(\mathcal{T},\varphi,\mathcal{P})}$ from Sect. 5: If $k = l$ (i.e., the property is a $\forall^*$-property) the unique minimal valid restriction from $\hat{s}, M$ is $\{\hat{s}' \mid \hat{s} \xrightarrow{M} \hat{s}'\}$, i.e., the set of all $M$-successors of $\hat{s}$. The safety player can thus not be more restrictive than allowing *all* $M$-successors (as in $\mathcal{G}^{\forall}_{(\mathcal{T},\varphi,\mathcal{P})}$).

*Clairvoyance vs. Abstraction.* The cooperation between reduction (the ability of the verifier to select schedulings) and witness strategy (the ability to select restrictions on the successor) can be seen as a limited form of prophecy [1,14]. By first scheduling the universal copies, the witness strategy can peek at future moves before committing to a successor state, as we e.g., saw in Fig. 3. The "theoretically optimal" reduction is thus a sequential one that first schedules only the universally quantified traces (until an observation point is reached) and thereby provides maximal information for the witness strategy. However, in the context of a fixed abstraction, this reduction is not always optimal. For example, in Fig. 3 the strategy schedules the loop in lock-step which is crucial for generating a proof with simple (linear) invariants. In particular, Fig. 3 does not admit a witness strategy in the lock-step reduction and does not admit a proof with linear invariants in a sequential reduction. Our verification framework, therefore, strikes a delicate balance between clairvoyance needed by the witness strategy and precision captured in the abstraction, further emphasizing why the searches for reduction and witness strategy need to be mutually dependent.

### 6.2 Constructing and Solving $\mathcal{G}^{\forall\exists}_{(\mathcal{T},\varphi,\mathcal{P})}$

Constructing the game graph of $\mathcal{G}^{\forall\exists}_{(\mathcal{T},\varphi,\mathcal{P})}$ requires the identification of all valid restrictions (of which there are exponentially many in the number of abstract states and thus double exponentially many in the number of predicates) each of which requires to solve a quantified SMT query. We propose a more effective algorithm that solves $\mathcal{G}^{\forall\exists}_{(\mathcal{T},\varphi,\mathcal{P})}$ without constructing it explicitly. Instead, we iteratively refine an abstraction $\tilde{\mathcal{G}}$ of $\mathcal{G}^{\forall\exists}_{(\mathcal{T},\varphi,\mathcal{P})}$. Our method hinges on the following easy observation:

**Algorithm 1.** Iterative solver for $\mathcal{G}^{\forall\exists}_{(\mathcal{T},\varphi,\mathcal{P})}$.

1: **Input:** $\mathcal{T}, \varphi, \mathcal{P}$
2: $\tilde{\mathcal{G}} := \mathit{initialApproximation}(\mathcal{T}, \varphi, \mathcal{P})$
3: **repeat**
4:   **match** $\mathit{Solve}(\tilde{\mathcal{G}})$ **with**
5:     **case** `REACH`($\sigma$): **return** `REACH`
6:     **case** `SAFE`($\sigma$):
7:       **for all** $(\hat{s}, M, A) \in \mathit{Restrictions}(\sigma)$ **do**
8:         **if** $\neg \mathit{validRes}^{\hat{s},M}_{A}$ **then**
9:           **for all** $A' \subseteq A$ **do**
10:             $\tilde{\mathcal{G}} := \mathit{Remove}(\tilde{\mathcal{G}}, (\hat{s}, M, A'))$
11:           **goto** 4
12:       **return** `SAFE`

**Lemma 1.** *For any $\hat{s}$ and $M$, $\{A \mid \mathit{validRes}^{\hat{s},M}_{A}\}$ is upwards closed (w.r.t. $\subseteq$).*

Our initial abstraction consists of all possible restrictions (even those that might be invalid), i.e., we allow all restrictions of the form $(\hat{s}, M, A)$ where $A \subseteq \{\hat{s}' \mid \hat{s} \xrightarrow{M} \hat{s}'\}$.[4] This overapproximates the power of the safety player, i.e., a winning strategy for `SAFE` in $\tilde{\mathcal{G}}$ may not be valid in $\mathcal{G}^{\forall\exists}_{(\mathcal{T},\varphi,\mathcal{P})}$. To remedy this, we propose the following inner refinement loop: If we find a winning strategy $\sigma$ for

[4] Note that $\{\hat{s}' \mid \hat{s} \xrightarrow{M} \hat{s}'\}$ is always a valid restriction. Importantly, we can compute $\{\hat{s}' \mid \hat{s} \xrightarrow{M} \hat{s}'\}$ locally, i.e., by iterating over abstract states opposed to *sets* of abstract states.

`SAFE` in $\tilde{\mathcal{G}}$ we check if all restrictions chosen by $\sigma$ are valid. If this is the case, $\sigma$ is also winning for $\mathcal{G}^{\forall\exists}_{(\mathcal{T},\varphi,\mathcal{P})}$ and we can apply Theorem 3. If we find an invalid restriction $(\hat{s}, M, A)$ used by $\sigma$, we refine $\tilde{\mathcal{G}}$ by removing not only the restriction $(\hat{s}, M, A)$ but *all* $(\hat{s}, M, A')$ with $A' \subseteq A$ (which is justified by Lemma 1). The algorithm is sketched in Algorithm 1. The subroutine *Restrictions*$(\sigma)$ returns all restrictions used by $\sigma$, i.e., all tuples $(\hat{s}, M, A)$ such that $\sigma$ uses an edge $(\hat{s}, q, b) \rightsquigarrow (\hat{s}, q, b, M, A)$ for some $q, b$. *Remove*$(\tilde{\mathcal{G}}, (\hat{s}, M, A'))$ removes from $\tilde{\mathcal{G}}$ all edges of the form $(\hat{s}, q, b) \rightsquigarrow (\hat{s}, q, b, M, A')$ for some $q, b$, and *Solve* solves a finite-state safety game. To improve the algorithm further, in line 4 we always compute a maximal safety strategy, i.e., a strategy that selects maximal restrictions (w.r.t. $\subseteq$) and therefore allows us to eliminate many invalid restrictions from $\tilde{\mathcal{G}}$ simultaneously. For safety games, there always exists such a maximal winning strategy (see e.g. [11]). Note that while $\tilde{\mathcal{G}}$ is large, solving this finite-state game can be done very efficiently. The running time of solving $\mathcal{G}^{\forall\exists}_{(\mathcal{T},\varphi,\mathcal{P})}$ is dominated by the SMT queries of which our refinement loop, in practice, requires very few.

## 7 Implementation and Evaluation

When combining Theorem 3 and our iterative solver from Sect. 6.2 we obtain an algorithm to verify $\forall^*\exists^*$-safety properties within a given abstraction. We have implemented a prototype of our method in a tool we call `HyPA`. We use `Z3` [36] to discharge SMT queries. The input of our tool is provided as an arbitrary STS in the SMTLIB format [5], making it *language independent*. In our programs, we make the program counter explicit, allowing us to track predicates locally [32].

**Table 1.** Evaluation of `HyPA` on $k$-safety instances. We give the size of the abstract game-space (Size), the time taken to compute the abstraction ($t_{abs}$), and the overall time taken by `HyPA` ($t$). Times are given in seconds.

| **Instance** | **Size** | $t_{abs}$ | $t$ |
|---|---|---|---|
| DoubleSquareNI | 819 | 92.3 | 92.8 |
| HalfSquareNI | 1166 | 85.9 | 86.5 |
| SquaresSum | 286 | 29.8 | 29.9 |
| ArrayInsert | 213 | 28.2 | 28.2 |
| Exp1x3 | 112 | 4.5 | 4.5 |
| Fig3 | 268 | 11.9 | 12.0 |
| DoubleSquareNIff | 121 | 9.8 | 9.9 |
| Fig. 2 | 333 | 23.7 | 23.8 |
| CollItem-Symm | 494 | 24.0 | 24.1 |
| Counter-Det | 216 | 10.2 | 10.3 |
| MultEquiv | 757 | 18.9 | 19.0 |

*Evaluation for k-Safety.* As a special case of $\forall^*\exists^*$ properties, `HyPA` is also applicable to $k$-safety verification. We collected an exemplifying suite of programs and $k$-safety properties from the literature [27,39–41] and manually translated them into STS (this can be automated easily). The results are given in Table 1. As done by Shemer et al. [39], we already provide a set of predicates that is sufficient for *some* reduction (but not necessarily the lockstep or sequential one), the search for which is then automated by `HyPA`. Our results show the game-based search for a reduction can verify interesting

**Table 2.** Evaluation of HyPA on $\forall^*\exists^*$-safety verification instances. We give the size and construction time of the initial abstraction (Size and $t_{abs}$). For both the direct (explicit) and lazy (Algorithm 1) solver we give the time to construct (and solve) the game ($t_{solve}$) and the overall time ($t = t_{abs} + t_{solve}$). For the lazy solver we, additionally, give the number of refinement iterations (#Ref). Times are given in seconds. TO indicates a timeout after 5 min.

| | | | Direct | | Lazy | | |
|---|---|---|---|---|---|---|---|
| **Instance** | **Size** | $t_{abs}$ | $t_{solve}$ | $t$ | **#Ref** | $t_{solve}$ | $t$ |
| NonDetAdd | 4568 | 3.5 | TO | TO | 4 | 1.0 | 4.5 |
| CounterSum | 479 | 5.3 | 9.1 | 14.4 | 17 | 0.9 | 6.2 |
| AsynchGNI | 437 | 6.1 | 6.9 | 13.0 | 1 | 0.1 | 6.2 |
| CompilerOpt1 | 354 | 2.4 | 2.3 | 4.7 | 2 | 0.2 | 2.6 |
| CompilerOpt2 | 338 | 2.8 | 2.4 | 5.2 | 2 | 0.2 | 3.0 |
| Refine | 1357 | 6.1 | TO | TO | 4 | 0.7 | 6.8 |
| Refine2 | 1476 | 5.6 | TO | TO | 5 | 0.6 | 6.2 |
| Smaller | 327 | 2.3 | 4.0 | 6.3 | 11 | 0.4 | 2.7 |
| CounterDiff | 959 | 8.5 | 18.3 | 26.8 | 19 | 1.1 | 9.6 |
| Fig. 3 | 3180 | 11.1 | TO | TO | 22 | 2.9 | 14.0 |
| P1 (simple) | 83 | 2.0 | 1.4 | 3.4 | 1 | 0.1 | 2.1 |
| P1 (GNI) | 34793 | 17.0 | TO | TO | 72 | 95.7 | 112.7 |
| P2 (GNI) | 15753 | 10.2 | TO | TO | 7 | 5.1 | 15.3 |
| P3 (GNI) | 1429 | 6.6 | 20.9 | 27.5 | 7 | 0.6 | 7.2 |
| P4 (GNI) | 7505 | 16.5 | TO | TO | 72 | 13.2 | 29.7 |

$k$-safety properties from the literature. We also note that, currently, the vast majority of time is spent on the construction of the abstract system. If we would move to a fixed language, the computation time of the initial abstraction could be reduced by using existing (heavily optimized) abstraction tools [18,32].

*Evaluation Beyond k-Safety.* The main novelty of HyPA lies in its ability to, for the first time, verify temporal properties beyond $k$-safety. As none of the existing tools can verify such properties, we compiled a collection of very small example programs and $\forall^*\exists^*$-safety properties. Additionally, we modified the boolean programs from [13] (where they checked GNI on boolean programs) by including data from infinite domains. The properties we checked range from refinement properties for compiler optimizations, over general refinement of nondeterministic programs, to generalized non-interference. Verification often requires a non-trivial combination of reduction and witness strategy (as the reduction must, e.g., compensate for branches of different lengths). As before, we provide a set of predicates and let HyPA automatically search for a witness strategy with accompanying reduction. We list the results in Table 2. To highlight the effectiveness of our inner refinement loop, we apply both a direct (explicit) construction of $\mathcal{G}^{\forall\exists}_{(\mathcal{T},\varphi,\mathcal{P})}$ and the lazy (iterative) solver in Algorithm 1. Our lazy solver (Algorithm 1) clearly outperforms an explicit construction and is often the only method to solve the game in reasonable time. In particular, we require very few refinement iterations and therefore also few expensive SMT queries. Unsurprisingly, the problem of verifying properties beyond $k$-safety becomes much more challenging (compared to $k$-safety verification) as it involves the *synthesis* of a witness function which is already 2EXPTIME-hard for finite-state systems [23,37]. We emphasize that no other existing tool can verify any of the benchmarks.

## 8 Related Work

*Asynchronous Hyperproperties.* Recently, many logics for the formal specification of asynchronous hyperproperties have been developed [9,13,17,31]. Our logic OHyperLTL is closely related to stuttering HyperLTL (HyperLTL$_S$) [17]. In HyperLTL$_S$ each temporal operator is endowed with a set of temporal formulas $\Gamma$ and steps where the truth values of all formulas in $\Gamma$ remain unchanged are ignored during the operator's evaluation. As for most mechanisms used to design asynchronous hyperlogics [9,17,31], finite-state model checking of HyperLTL$_S$ is undecidable. By contrast, in OHyperLTL, we always observe the trace at a fixed location, which is key for ensuring decidable finite-state model checking.

*$k$-Safety Verification.* The literature on $k$-safety verification is rich. Many approaches verify $k$-safety by using a form of self-composition [8,20,25,28] and often employ reductions to obtain compositions that are easier to verify. Our game-based interpretation of a reduction (Sect. 5) is related to Shemer et al. [39], who study $k$-safety verification within a given predicate abstraction using an enumeration-based solver (see Sect. 5 for a discussion). Farzan and Vandikas [27] present a counterexample-guided refinement loop that simultaneously searches for a reduction and a proof. Sousa and Dillig [40] facilitate reductions at the source-code level in program logic.

*$\forall^*\exists^*$-Verification.* Barthe et al. [7] describe an asymmetric product of the system such that only a subset of the behavior of the second system is preserved, thereby allowing the verification of $\forall^*\exists^*$ properties. Constructing an asymmetric product and verifying its correctness (i.e., showing that the product preserves all behavior of the first, universally quantified, system) is challenging. Unno et al. [41] present a constraint-based approach to verify functional (opposed to temporal) $\forall\exists$ properties in infinite-state systems using an extension of constraint Horn clauses called pfwCHC. The underlying verification approach is orthogonal to ours: pfwCHC allows for a clean separation of the actual verification and verification conditions, whereas our approach combines both. For example, our method can prove the existence of a witness strategy without ever formulating precise constraints on the strategy (which seems challenging). Coenen et

al. [23] introduce the game-based reading of existential quantification to verify temporal $\forall^*\exists^*$ properties in a synchronous and finite-state setting. By contrast, our work constitutes the first verification method for temporal $\forall^*\exists^*$-safety properties in *infinite-state* systems. The key to our method is a careful integration of reductions which is not possible in a synchronous setting. For finite-state systems (where the abstraction is precise) and synchronous specifications (where we observe every step), our method subsumes the one in [23]. Beutner and Finkbeiner [14] use prophecy variables to ensure that the game-based reading of existential quantification is complete in a finite-state setting. Automatically constructing prophecies for infinite-state systems is interesting future work. Pommellet and Touili [38] study the verification of HyperLTL in infinite-state systems arising from pushdown systems. By contrast, we study verification in infinite-state systems that arise from the infinite variables domains used in software.

*Game Solving.* Our game-based interpretations are naturally related to infinite-state game solving [4,16,26,42]. State-of-the-art solvers for infinite-state games unroll the game [26], use necessary subgoals to inductively split a game into subgames [4], encode the game as a constraint system [16], and iteratively refine the controllable predecessor operator [42]. We tried to encode our verification approach directly as an infinite-state linear-arithmetic game. However, existing solvers (which, notably, work *without* a user-provided set of predicates) could not solve the resulting game [4,26]. Our method for encoding the witness strategy using *restrictions* corresponds to hyper-must edges in general abstract games [2, 3]. Our inner refinement loop for solving a game with hyper-must edges without explicitly identifying all edges (Algorithm 1) is thus also applicable in general abstract games.

## 9 Conclusion

In this work, we have presented the first verification method for temporal hyperproperties beyond $k$-safety in infinite-state systems arising in software. Our method is based on a game-based interpretation of reductions and existential quantification and allows for mutual dependence of both. Interesting future directions include the integration of our method in a counter-example guided refinement loop that automatically refines the abstraction and ways to lift the current restriction to temporally safe specifications. Moreover, it is interesting to study if, and to what extent, the numerous other methods developed for $k$-safety verification of infinite-state systems (apart from reductions) are applicable to the vast landscape of hyperproperties that lies beyond $k$-safety.

**Acknowledgments.** This work was partially supported by the DFG in project 389792660 (Center for Perspicuous Systems, TRR 248). R. Beutner carried out this work as a member of the Saarbrücken Graduate School of Computer Science.

## References


1. Abadi, M., Lamport, L.: The existence of refinement mappings. Theor. Comput. Sci. **82**(2), 253–284 (1991). https://doi.org/10.1016/0304-3975(91)90224-P
2. de Alfaro, L., Godefroid, P., Jagadeesan, R.: Three-valued abstractions of games: uncertainty, but with precision. In: IEEE Symposium on Logic in Computer Science, LICS 2004. IEEE (2004). https://doi.org/10.1109/LICS.2004.1319611
3. de Alfaro, L., Roy, P.: Solving games via three-valued abstraction refinement. In: Caires, L., Vasconcelos, V.T. (eds.) CONCUR 2007. LNCS, vol. 4703, pp. 74–89. Springer, Heidelberg (2007). https://doi.org/10.1007/978-3-540-74407-8_6
4. Baier, C., Coenen, N., Finkbeiner, B., Funke, F., Jantsch, S., Siber, J.: Causality-based game solving. In: Silva, A., Leino, K.R.M. (eds.) CAV 2021. LNCS, vol. 12759, pp. 894–917. Springer, Cham (2021). https://doi.org/10.1007/978-3-030-81685-8_42
5. Barrett, C., Stump, A., Tinelli, C., et al.: The SMT-LIB standard: Version 2.0. In: International Workshop on Satisfiability Modulo Theories, vol. 13 (2010)
6. Barrett, C., Fang, Y., Goldberg, B., Hu, Y., Pnueli, A., Zuck, L.: TVOC: a translation validator for optimizing compilers. In: Etessami, K., Rajamani, S.K. (eds.) CAV 2005. LNCS, vol. 3576, pp. 291–295. Springer, Heidelberg (2005). https://doi.org/10.1007/11513988_29
7. Barthe, G., Crespo, J.M., Kunz, C.: Beyond 2-safety: asymmetric product programs for relational program verification. In: Artemov, S., Nerode, A. (eds.) LFCS 2013. LNCS, vol. 7734, pp. 29–43. Springer, Heidelberg (2013). https://doi.org/10.1007/978-3-642-35722-0_3
8. Barthe, G., D'Argenio, P.R., Rezk, T.: Secure information flow by self-composition. Math. Struct. Comput. Sci. **21**(6), 1207–1252 (2011). https://doi.org/10.1017/S0960129511000193
9. Baumeister, J., Coenen, N., Bonakdarpour, B., Finkbeiner, B., Sánchez, C.: A temporal logic for asynchronous hyperproperties. In: Silva, A., Leino, K.R.M. (eds.) CAV 2021. LNCS, vol. 12759, pp. 694–717. Springer, Cham (2021). https://doi.org/10.1007/978-3-030-81685-8_33
10. Benton, N.: Simple relational correctness proofs for static analyses and program transformations. In: ACM Symposium on Principles of Programming Languages, POPL 2004. ACM (2004). https://doi.org/10.1145/964001.964003
11. Bernet, J., Janin, D., Walukiewicz, I.: Permissive strategies: from parity games to safety games. RAIRO Theor. Inf. Appl. **36**(3), 261–275 (2002). https://doi.org/10.1051/ita:2002013
12. Beutner, R., Carral, D., Finkbeiner, B., Hofmann, J., Krötzsch, M.: Deciding hyperproperties combined with functional specifications. In: Annual ACM/IEEE Symposium on Logic in Computer Science, LICS 2022. ACM (2022). https://doi.org/10.1145/3531130.3533369
13. Beutner, R., Finkbeiner, B.: A temporal logic for strategic hyperproperties. In: International Conference on Concurrency Theory, CONCUR 2021. LIPIcs, vol. 203. Schloss Dagstuhl (2021). https://doi.org/10.4230/LIPIcs.CONCUR.2021.24
14. Beutner, R., Finkbeiner, B.: Prophecy variables for hyperproperty verification. In: IEEE Computer Security Foundations Symposium, CSF 2022. IEEE (2022)
15. Beutner, R., Finkbeiner, B.: Software verification of hyperproperties beyond $k$-safety. CoRR (2022). https://doi.org/10.48550/arXiv.2206.03381

16. Beyene, T.A., Chaudhuri, S., Popeea, C., Rybalchenko, A.: A constraint-based approach to solving games on infinite graphs. In: Annual ACM Symposium on Principles of Programming Languages, POPL 2014. ACM (2014). https://doi.org/10.1145/2535838.2535860
17. Bozzelli, L., Peron, A., Sánchez, C.: Asynchronous extensions of HyperLTL. In: Annual ACM/IEEE Symposium on Logic in Computer Science, LICS 2021. IEEE (2021). https://doi.org/10.1109/LICS52264.2021.9470583
18. Chaki, S., Clarke, E.M., Groce, A., Jha, S., Veith, H.: Modular verification of software components in C. IEEE Trans. Softw. Eng. **30**(6), 388–402 (2004). https://doi.org/10.1109/TSE.2004.22
19. Chaudhuri, S., Gulwani, S., Lublinerman, R.: Continuity and robustness of programs. Commun. ACM **55**(8), 107–115 (2012). https://doi.org/10.1145/2240236.2240262
20. Churchill, B.R., Padon, O., Sharma, R., Aiken, A.: Semantic program alignment for equivalence checking. In: ACM SIGPLAN Conference on Programming Language Design and Implementation, PLDI 2019. ACM (2019). https://doi.org/10.1145/3314221.3314596
21. Clarkson, M.R., Finkbeiner, B., Koleini, M., Micinski, K.K., Rabe, M.N., Sánchez, C.: Temporal logics for hyperproperties. In: Abadi, M., Kremer, S. (eds.) POST 2014. LNCS, vol. 8414, pp. 265–284. Springer, Heidelberg (2014). https://doi.org/10.1007/978-3-642-54792-8_15
22. Clarkson, M.R., Schneider, F.B.: Hyperproperties. In: IEEE Computer Security Foundations Symposium, CSF 2008. IEEE (2008). https://doi.org/10.1109/CSF.2008.7
23. Coenen, N., Finkbeiner, B., Sánchez, C., Tentrup, L.: Verifying hyperliveness. In: Dillig, I., Tasiran, S. (eds.) CAV 2019. LNCS, vol. 11561, pp. 121–139. Springer, Cham (2019). https://doi.org/10.1007/978-3-030-25540-4_7
24. D'Antoni, L., Veanes, M.: The power of symbolic automata and transducers. In: Majumdar, R., Kunčak, V. (eds.) CAV 2017. LNCS, vol. 10426, pp. 47–67. Springer, Cham (2017). https://doi.org/10.1007/978-3-319-63387-9_3
25. Eilers, M., Müller, P., Hitz, S.: Modular product programs. ACM Trans. Program. Lang. Syst. **42**(1), 1–37 (2020). https://doi.org/10.1145/3324783
26. Farzan, A., Kincaid, Z.: Strategy synthesis for linear arithmetic games. Proc. ACM Program. Lang. **2**(POPL), 1–30 (2018). https://doi.org/10.1145/3158149
27. Farzan, A., Vandikas, A.: Automated hypersafety verification. In: Dillig, I., Tasiran, S. (eds.) CAV 2019. LNCS, vol. 11561, pp. 200–218. Springer, Cham (2019). https://doi.org/10.1007/978-3-030-25540-4_11
28. Finkbeiner, B., Rabe, M.N., Sánchez, C.: Algorithms for model checking HyperLTL and HyperCTL*. In: Kroening, D., Păsăreanu, C.S. (eds.) CAV 2015. LNCS, vol. 9206, pp. 30–48. Springer, Cham (2015). https://doi.org/10.1007/978-3-319-21690-4_3
29. Ge, Q., Yarom, Y., Cock, D., Heiser, G.: A survey of microarchitectural timing attacks and countermeasures on contemporary hardware. J. Cryptogr. Eng. **8**(1), 1–27 (2016). https://doi.org/10.1007/s13389-016-0141-6
30. Graf, S., Saidi, H.: Construction of abstract state graphs with PVS. In: Grumberg, O. (ed.) CAV 1997. LNCS, vol. 1254, pp. 72–83. Springer, Heidelberg (1997). https://doi.org/10.1007/3-540-63166-6_10
31. Gutsfeld, J.O., Müller-Olm, M., Ohrem, C.: Automata and fixpoints for asynchronous hyperproperties. Proc. ACM Program. Lang. **5**(POPL), 1–29 (2021). https://doi.org/10.1145/3434319

32. Henzinger, T.A., Jhala, R., Majumdar, R., Sutre, G.: Lazy abstraction. In: ACM Symposium on Principles of Programming Languages, POPL 2002. ACM (2002). https://doi.org/10.1145/503272.503279
33. Jhala, R., Podelski, A., Rybalchenko, A.: Predicate abstraction for program verification. In: Handbook of Model Checking, pp. 447–491. Springer, Cham (2018). https://doi.org/10.1007/978-3-319-10575-8_15
34. Lipton, R.J.: Reduction: a method of proving properties of parallel programs. Commun. ACM **18**(12), 717–721 (1975). https://doi.org/10.1145/361227.361234
35. McCullough, D.: Noninterference and the composability of security properties. In: IEEE Symposium on Security and Privacy, SP 1988. IEEE (1988). https://doi.org/10.1109/SECPRI.1988.8110
36. de Moura, L., Bjørner, N.: Z3: an efficient SMT solver. In: Ramakrishnan, C.R., Rehof, J. (eds.) TACAS 2008. LNCS, vol. 4963, pp. 337–340. Springer, Heidelberg (2008). https://doi.org/10.1007/978-3-540-78800-3_24
37. Pnueli, A., Rosner, R.: On the synthesis of a reactive module. In: Annual ACM Symposium on Principles of Programming Languages, POPL 1989. ACM (1989). https://doi.org/10.1145/75277.75293
38. Pommellet, A., Touili, T.: Model-checking HyperLTL for pushdown systems. In: Gallardo, M.M., Merino, P. (eds.) SPIN 2018. LNCS, vol. 10869, pp. 133–152. Springer, Cham (2018). https://doi.org/10.1007/978-3-319-94111-0_8
39. Shemer, R., Gurfinkel, A., Shoham, S., Vizel, Y.: Property directed self composition. In: Dillig, I., Tasiran, S. (eds.) CAV 2019. LNCS, vol. 11561, pp. 161–179. Springer, Cham (2019). https://doi.org/10.1007/978-3-030-25540-4_9
40. Sousa, M., Dillig, I.: Cartesian hoare logic for verifying k-safety properties. In: ACM SIGPLAN Conference on Programming Language Design and Implementation, PLDI 2016. ACM (2016). https://doi.org/10.1145/2908080.2908092
41. Unno, H., Terauchi, T., Koskinen, E.: Constraint-based relational verification. In: Silva, A., Leino, K.R.M. (eds.) CAV 2021. LNCS, vol. 12759, pp. 742–766. Springer, Cham (2021). https://doi.org/10.1007/978-3-030-81685-8_35
42. Walker, A., Ryzhyk, L.: Predicate abstraction for reactive synthesis. In: Formal Methods in Computer-Aided Design, FMCAD 2014. IEEE (2014). https://doi.org/10.1109/FMCAD.2014.6987617

# A Scalable Shannon Entropy Estimator

Priyanka Golia[1,2](✉), Brendan Juba[3], and Kuldeep S. Meel[2]

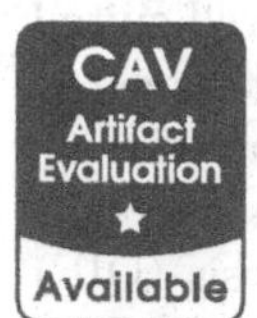

[1] Indian Institute of Technology Kanpur, Kanpur, India
pgolia@cse.iitk.ac.in
[2] National University of Singapore, Singapore, Singapore
[3] Washington University in St. Louis, St. Louis, USA

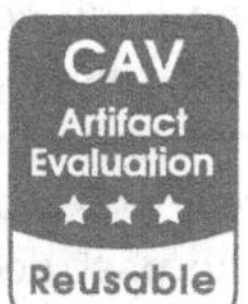

**Abstract.** Quantified information flow (QIF) has emerged as a rigorous approach to quantitatively measure confidentiality; the information-theoretic underpinning of QIF allows the end-users to link the computed quantities with the computational effort required on the part of the adversary to gain access to desired confidential information. In this work, we focus on the estimation of Shannon entropy for a given program $\Pi$. As a first step, we focus on the case wherein a Boolean formula $\varphi(X, Y)$ captures the relationship between inputs $X$ and output $Y$ of $\Pi$. Such formulas $\varphi(X, Y)$ have the property that for every valuation to $X$, there exists exactly one valuation to $Y$ such that $\varphi$ is satisfied. The existing techniques require $\mathcal{O}(2^m)$ model counting queries, where $m = |Y|$.

We propose the first efficient algorithmic technique, called EntropyEstimation to estimate the Shannon entropy of $\varphi$ with PAC-style guarantees, i.e., the computed estimate is guaranteed to lie within a $(1 \pm \varepsilon)$-factor of the ground truth with confidence at least $1 - \delta$. Furthermore, EntropyEstimation makes only $\mathcal{O}(\frac{min(m,n)}{\varepsilon^2})$ counting and sampling queries, where $m = |Y|$, and $n = |X|$, thereby achieving a significant reduction in the number of model counting queries. We demonstrate the practical efficiency of our algorithmic framework via a detailed experimental evaluation. Our evaluation demonstrates that the proposed framework scales to the formulas beyond the reach of the previously known approaches.

## 1 Introduction

Over the past half-century, the cost effectiveness of digital services has led to an unprecedented adoption of technology in virtually all aspects of our modern lives. Such adoption has invariably led to sensitive information being stored in data centers around the world and increasingly complex software accessing the information in order to provide the services that form the backbone of our modern economy and social interactions. At the same time, it is vital that protected information does not leak, as such leakages may have grave financial and societal

---

EntropyEstimation is available open-sourced at https://github.com/meelgroup/entropyestimation. The names of authors are sorted alphabetically and the order does not reflect contribution.


S. Shoham and Y. Vizel (Eds.): CAV 2022, LNCS 13371, pp. 363–384, 2022.
https://doi.org/10.1007/978-3-031-13185-1_18

consequences. Consequently, the detection and prevention of information leakage in software have attracted sustained interest in the security community.

The earliest efforts on information leakage focused on *qualitative* approaches that sought to return a Boolean output of the form "yes" or "no" [11,26,30]. While these qualitative approaches successfully capture situations where part of the code accesses prohibited information, such approaches are not well-suited to situations wherein some information leakage is inevitable. An oft-repeated example of such a situation is a *password checker* wherein every response "incorrect password" does leak information about the *secret password.* As a result, the past decade has seen the rise of quantified information flow analysis (QIF) as a rigorous approach to quantitatively measure confidentiality [7,53,57]. The information-theoretic underpinnings of QIF analyses allow an end-user to link the computed quantities with the probability of an adversary successfully guessing a secret, or the worst-case computational effort required for the adversary to infer the underlying confidential information. Consequently, QIF has been applied in diverse use-cases such as software side-channel detection [40], inferring search-engine queries through auto-complete responses sizes [21], and measuring the tendency of Linux to leak TCP-session sequence numbers [59].

The standard recipe for using the QIF framework is to measure the information leakage from an underlying program $\Pi$ as follows. In a simplified model, a program $\Pi$ maps a set of controllable inputs ($C$) and secret inputs ($I$) to outputs ($O$) observable to an attacker. The attacker is interested in inferring $I$ based on the output $O$. A diverse array of approaches have been proposed to efficiently model $\Pi$, with techniques relying on a combination of symbolic analysis [48], static analysis [24], automata-based techniques [4,5,14], SMT-based techniques [47], and the like. For each, the core underlying technical problem is to determine the leakage of information for a given observation. We often capture this leakage using entropy-theoretic notions, such as Shannon entropy [7,16,48,53] or min-entropy [7,44,48,53]. In this work, we focus on computing Shannon entropy.

In this work, we focus on entropy estimation for programs modeled by Boolean formulas; nevertheless, our techniques are general and can be extended to other models such as automata-based frameworks. Let a formula $\varphi(X,Y)$ capture the relationship between $X$ and $Y$ such that for every valuation to $X$ there is atmost one valuation to $Y$ such that $\varphi$ is satisfied; one can view $X$ as the set of inputs and $Y$ as the set of outputs. Let $m = |Y|$ and $n = |X|$. Let $p$ be a probability distribution over $\{0,1\}^Y$ such that for every assignment to $Y$, $\sigma : Y \mapsto \{0,1\}$, we have $p_\sigma = \frac{|sol(\varphi(Y \mapsto \sigma))|}{2^n}$, where $sol(\varphi(Y \mapsto \sigma))$ denotes the set of solutions of $\varphi(Y \mapsto \sigma)$. Then, the entropy of $\varphi$ is defined as $H_\varphi(Y) = \sum_\sigma p_\sigma \log \frac{1}{p_\sigma}$.

The past decade has witnessed a multitude of entropy estimation techniques with varying guarantees on the quality of their estimates [9,17,35,58]. The problem of computing the entropy of a distribution represented by a given circuit is closely related to the EntropyDifference problem considered by Goldreich and Vadhan [34], and shown to be SZK-complete. We therefore do not expect to obtain polynomial-time algorithms for this problem. The techniques that have been proposed to compute $H(\varphi)$ exactly compute $p_\sigma$ for each $\sigma$. Observe that computing $p_\sigma$ is equivalent to the problem of model counting, which seeks to compute the number of solutions of a given formula. Therefore, the exact techniques require $\mathcal{O}(2^m)$ model-counting queries [13,27,39]; therefore, such techniques often do not scale for large values of $m$. Accordingly, the state of the art often relies on sampling-based techniques that perform well in practice but can only provide lower or upper bounds on the entropy [37,49]. As is often the case, techniques that only guarantee lower or upper bounds can output estimates that can be arbitrarily far from the ground truth. This raises the question: *can we design efficient techniques for approximate estimation, whose estimates have PAC-style* $(\varepsilon, \delta)$ *guarantees? I.e., can we compute an estimate that is guaranteed to lie within a* $(1+\varepsilon)$*-factor of the ground truth for all possible values, with confidence at least* $1-\delta$*?*

The primary contribution of our work is the first efficient algorithmic technique (given in our algorithm EntropyEstimation), to estimate $H_\varphi(Y)$ with PAC-style guarantees for all possible values of $H_\varphi(Y)$. In particular, given a formula $\varphi$, EntropyEstimation returns an estimate that is guaranteed to lie within a $(1 \pm \varepsilon)$-factor of $H_\varphi(Y)$ with confidence at least $1-\delta$. We stress that we obtain such a multiplicative estimate even when $H_\varphi(Y)$ is very small, as in the case of a password-checker as described above. Furthermore, EntropyEstimation makes only $\mathcal{O}(\frac{min(m,n)}{\varepsilon^2})$ counting and sampling queries even though the support of the distribution specified by $\varphi$ can be of the size $\mathcal{O}(2^m)$.

While the primary focus of the work is theoretical, we seek to demonstrate that our techniques can be translated into practically efficient algorithms. As such, we focused on developing a prototype using off-the-shelf samplers and counters. As a first step, we use GANAK [52] for model counting queries and SPUR [3] for sampling queries. Our empirical analysis demonstrates that EntropyEstimation can be translated into practice and achieves significant speedup over baseline.

It is worth mentioning that recent approaches in quantified information leakage focus on programs that can be naturally translated to string and SMT constraints, and therefore, employ model counters for string and SMT constraints. Since counting and sampling are closely related, we hope the algorithmic improvements attained by EntropyEstimation will lead to the development of samplers in the context of SMT and string constraints, and would lead to practical implementation of EntropyEstimation for other domains. We stress again that while we present EntropyEstimation for programs modeled as a Boolean formula, our analysis applies other approaches, such as automata-based approaches, modulo access to the appropriate sampling and counting oracles.

The rest of the paper is organized as follows: we present the notations and preliminaries in Sect. 2. We then discuss related work in Sect. 3. Next, we present an overview of EntropyEstimation including a detailed description of the algorithm and an analysis of its correctness in Sect. 4. We then describe our experimental methodology and discuss our results with respect to the accuracy and scalability of EntropyEstimation in Sect. 5. Finally, we conclude in Sect. 6.

## 2 Preliminaries

We use lower case letters (with subscripts) to denote propositional variables and upper case letters to denote a subset of variables. The formula $\exists Y \varphi(X, Y)$ is existentially quantified in $Y$, where $X = \{x_1, \cdots, x_n\}$ and $Y = \{y_1, \cdots, y_m\}$. For notational clarity, we use $\varphi$ to refer to $\varphi(X, Y)$ when clear from the context. We denote $Vars(\varphi)$ as the set of variables appearing in $\varphi(X, Y)$. A literal is a boolean variable or its negation.

A *satisfying assignment* or solution of a formula $\varphi$ is a mapping $\tau : Vars(\varphi) \rightarrow \{0, 1\}$, on which the formula evaluates to True. For $V \subseteq Vars(\varphi)$, $\tau_{\downarrow V}$ represents the truth values of variables in $V$ in a satisfying assignment $\tau$ of $\varphi$. We denote the set of all the solutions of $\varphi$ as $sol(\varphi)$. For $S \subseteq Vars(\varphi)$, we define $sol(\varphi)_{\downarrow S}$ as the set of solutions of $\varphi$ projected on $S$.

The problem of *model counting* is to compute $|sol(\varphi)|$ for a given formula $\varphi$. Projected model counting is defined analogously using $sol(\varphi)_{\downarrow S}$ instead of $sol(\varphi)$, for a given projection set[1] $S \subseteq Vars(\varphi)$. A *uniform sampler* outputs a solution $y \in sol(\varphi)$ such that $\Pr[y \text{ is output}] = \frac{1}{|sol(\varphi)|}$.

We say that $\varphi$ is a circuit formula if for all assignments $\tau_1, \tau_2 \in sol(\varphi)$, we have $\tau_{1\downarrow X} = \tau_{2\downarrow X} \implies \tau_1 = \tau_2$. It is worth remarking that if $\varphi$ is a circuit formula, then $X$ is an independent support.

For a circuit formula $\varphi(X, Y)$ and for $\sigma : Y \mapsto \{0, 1\}$, we define $p_\sigma = \frac{|sol(\varphi(Y \mapsto \sigma))|}{|sol(\varphi)_{\downarrow X}|}$. Given a circuit formula $\varphi(X, Y)$, we define the entropy of $\varphi$, denoted by $H_\varphi(Y)$ as follows: $H_\varphi(Y) = -\sum_{\sigma \in 2^Y} p_\sigma \log(p_\sigma)$.

## 3 Related Work

The Shannon entropy is a fundamental concept in information theory, and as such have been studied by theoreticians and practitioners alike. While this is the first work, to the best of our knowledge, that provides Probabilistic Approximately Correct (PAC) $(\varepsilon, \delta)$-approximation guarantees for all values of the entropy, while requiring only logarithmically (in the size of the support of distribution) many queries, we survey below prior work relevant to ours.

Goldreich and Vadhan [34] showed that the problem of estimating the entropy for circuit formulas is complete for statistical zero-knowledge. Estimation of the entropy via collision probabilities has been considered in the statistical physics community, but these techniques only provide lower bounds [43,55]. Batu et al. [9] considered entropy estimation in a *black-box* model wherein one is allowed to sample $\sigma \in 2^Y$ with probability proportional to $p_\sigma$ and $p_\sigma$ is revealed along with the sample $\sigma$. Batu et al. showed that any algorithm that can estimate the entropy within a factor of 2 in this model must use $\Omega(2^{m/8})$ samples. Furthermore, Batu et al. proposed a multiplicative approximation scheme assuming a lower bound on $H$—precisely, it required a number of samples that grow linearly with $1/H$; their scheme also gives rise to an additive approximate scheme.

[1] Projection set has been referred to as sampling set in prior work [19,54].

Guha et al. [35] improved Batu et al.'s scheme to obtain $(\epsilon, \delta)$ multiplicative estimates using $\mathcal{O}(\frac{m \log \frac{1}{\delta}}{\epsilon^2 H})$ samples, matching Batu et al.'s lower bound. Note that this grows with $1/H$.

A more restrictive model has been considered wherein we only get access to samples (with the assurance that every $\sigma$ is sampled with probability proportional to $p_\sigma$). Valiant and Valiant [58] obtained an asymptotically optimal algorithm in this setting, which requires $\Theta(\frac{2^m}{\epsilon^2 m})$ samples to obtain an $\epsilon$ additive approximation. Chakraborty et al. [17] considered the problem in a different setting, in which the algorithm is given the ability to sample $\sigma$ from a *conditional distribution*: the algorithm is permitted to specify a set $S$, and obtains $\sigma$ from the distribution conditioned on $\sigma \in S$. We remark that as discussed below, our approach makes use of such conditional samples, by sampling from a modified formula that conjoins the circuit formula to a formula for membership in $S$. In any case, Chakraborty et al. use $\mathcal{O}(\frac{1}{\epsilon^8} m^7 \log \frac{1}{\delta})$ conditional samples to approximately learn the distribution, and can only provide an additive approximation of entropy. A helpful survey of all of these different models and algorithms was recently given by Canonne [15].

In this paper, we rely on the advances in model counting. Theoretical investigations into model counting were initiated by Valiant in his seminal work that defined the complexity class #P and showed that the problem of model counting is #P-complete. From a practical perspective, the earliest work on model counting [12] focused on improving enumeration-based strategies via partial solutions. Subsequently, Bayardo and Pehoushek [10] observed that if a formula can be partitioned into subsets of clauses, also called components, such that each of the subsets is over disjoint sets of variables, then the model count of the formula is the product of the model counts of each of the components. Building on Bayardo and Pehoushek's scheme, Sang et al. [50] showed how conflict-driven clause learning can be combined with component caching, which has been further improved by Thurley [56] and Sharma et al. [52]. Another line of work focuses on compilation-based techniques, wherein the core approach is to compile the input formula into a subset $\mathcal{L}$ in negation normal form, so that counting is tractable for $\mathcal{L}$. The past five years have witnessed a surge of interest in the design of projected model counters [6,18,20,42,45,52]. In this paper, we employ GANAK [52], the state of the art projected model counter; an entry based on GANAK won the projected model counting track at the 2020 model counting competition [31].

Another crucial ingredient for our technique is access to an efficient sampler. Counting and sampling are closely related problems, and therefore, the development of efficient counters spurred the research on the development of samplers. In a remarkable result, Huang and Darwiche [36] showed that the traces of model counters are in d-DNNF (deterministic Decomposable Negation Normal Form [25]), which was observed to support sampling in polynomial time [51]. Achlioptas, Hammoudeh, and Theodoropoulos [3] observed that one can improve the space efficiency by performing an on-the-fly traversal of the underlying trace of a model counter such as SharpSAT [56].

Our work builds on a long line of work in the QIF community that identified a close relationship between quantified information flow and model counting [4, 5, 27, 33, 38, 59]. There are also many symbolic execution based approaches for QIF based on model counting that would require model counting calls that are linear in the size of observable domain, that is, exponential in the number of bits represents the domain [8, 46]. Another closely related line of the work concerns the use of model counting in side-channel analysis [28, 29, 33]. Similarly, there exists sampling based approaches for black-box leakage estimation that either require too many samples, much larger than the product of size of input and output domain [23] to converge or uses ML based approaches that predict the error of the idea classifier for predicting secrets given observable [22]. However, these approaches can not provide PAC guarantees on the estimation. While we focus on the case where the behavior of a program can be modeled with a Boolean formula $\varphi$, the underlying technique is general and can extended to cases where programs (and their abstractions) are modeled using automata [4, 5, 14].

Before concluding our discussion of prior work, we remark that Köpf and Rybalchenko [41] used Batu et al.'s [9] lower bounds to conclude that their scheme could not be improved without usage of structural properties of the program. In this context, our paper continues the direction alluded by Köpf and Rybalchenko and designs the first efficient multiplicative approximation scheme by utilizing white-box access to the program.

## 4 EntropyEstimation: Efficient Estimation of $H(\varphi)$

In this section, we focus on the primary technical contribution of our work: an algorithm, called EntropyEstimation, that takes a circuit formula $\varphi(X, Y)$ and returns an $(\varepsilon, \delta)$ estimate of $H(\varphi)$. We first provide a detailed technical overview of the design of EntropyEstimation in Sect. 4.1, then provide a detailed description of the algorithm, and finally, provide the accompanying technical analysis of the correctness and complexity of EntropyEstimation.

### 4.1 Technical Overview

At a high level, EntropyEstimation uses a median of means estimator, i.e., we first estimate $H(\varphi)$ to within a $(1 \pm \varepsilon)$-factor with probability at least $\frac{5}{6}$ by computing the mean of the underlying estimator and then take the median of many such estimates to boost the probability of correctness to $1 - \delta$.

Let us consider a random variable $S$ over the domain $sol(\varphi)_{\downarrow Y}$ such that $\Pr[S = \sigma] = p_\sigma$ wherein $\sigma \in sol(\varphi)_{\downarrow Y}$ and consider the self-information function $g : sol(\varphi)_{\downarrow Y} \rightarrow [0, \infty)$, given by $g(\sigma) = \log(\frac{1}{p_\sigma})$. Observe that the entropy $H(\varphi) = \mathsf{E}[g(S)]$. Therefore, a simple estimator would be to sample $S$ using our oracle and then estimate the expectation of $g(S)$ by a sample mean. At this point, we observe that given access to a uniform sampler, UnifSample, we can simply first sample $\tau \in sol(\varphi)$ uniformly at random, and then set $S = \tau_{\downarrow Y}$, which gives $\Pr[S = \tau_{\downarrow Y}] = p_{\tau_{\downarrow Y}}$. Furthermore, observe that $g(\sigma)$ can be computed via a query to a model counter. In their seminal work, Batu et al. [9] observed that the variance of $g(S)$, denoted by $\mathsf{variance}[g(S)]$, can be at most $m^2$. The required number of sample queries, based on a straightforward analysis, would be $\Theta\left(\frac{\mathsf{variance}[g(S)]}{\varepsilon^2 \cdot (\mathsf{E}[g(S)])^2}\right) = \Theta\left(\frac{\sum p_\sigma \log^2 \frac{1}{p_\sigma}}{(\sum p_\sigma \log \frac{1}{p_\sigma})^2}\right)$. However, $\mathsf{E}[g(S)] = H(\varphi)$ can be arbitrarily close to 0, and therefore, this does not provide a reasonable upper bound on the required number of samples.

To address the lack of lower bound on $H(\varphi)$, we observe that for $\varphi$ to have $H(\varphi) < 1$, there must exist $\sigma_{high} \in sol(\varphi)_{\downarrow Y}$ such that $p_{(\sigma_{high})} > \frac{1}{2}$. We then observe that given access to a sampler and counter, we can identify such a $\sigma_{high}$ with high probability, thereby allowing us to consider the two cases separately: (A) $H(\varphi) > 1$ and (B) $H(\varphi) < 1$. Now, for case (A), we could use Batu et al.'s bound for $\mathsf{variance}[g(S)]$ [9] and obtain an estimator that would require $\Theta\left(\frac{\mathsf{variance}[g(S)]}{\varepsilon^2 \cdot (\mathsf{E}[g(S)])^2}\right)$ sampling and counting queries. It is worth remarking that the bound $\mathsf{variance}[g(S)] \leq m^2$ is indeed tight as a uniform distribution over $sol(\varphi)_{\downarrow X}$ would achieve the bound. Therefore, we instead focus on the expression $\frac{\mathsf{variance}[g(S)]}{(\mathsf{E}[g(S)])^2}$ and prove that for the case when $\mathsf{E}[g(S)] = H(\varphi) > h$, we can upper bound $\frac{\mathsf{variance}[g(S)]}{(\mathsf{E}[g(S)])^2}$ by $\frac{(1+o(1)) \cdot m}{h \cdot \varepsilon^2}$, thereby reducing the complexity from $m^2$ to $m$ (Observe that we have $H(\varphi) > 1$, that is, we can take $h = 1$).

Now, we return to the case (B) wherein we have identified $\sigma_{high} \in sol(\varphi)_{\downarrow Y}$ with $p_{\sigma_{high}} > \frac{1}{2}$. Let $r = p_{\sigma_{high}}$ and $H_{rem} = \sum_{\sigma \in sol(\varphi)_{\downarrow Y} \setminus \sigma_{high}} p_\sigma \log \frac{1}{p_\sigma}$. Note that $H(\varphi) = r \log \frac{1}{r} + H_{rem}$. Therefore, we focus on estimating $H_{rem}$. To this end, we define a random variable $T$ that takes values in $sol(\varphi)_{\downarrow Y} \setminus \sigma_{high}$ such that $\Pr[T = \sigma] = \frac{p_\sigma}{1-r}$. Using the function $g$ defined above, we have $H_{rem} = (1-r) \cdot \mathsf{E}[g(T)]$. Again, we have two cases, depending on whether $H_{rem} \geq 1$ or not; if it is, then we can bound the ratio $\frac{\mathsf{variance}[g(T)]}{\mathsf{E}[g(T)]^2}$ similarly to case (A). If not, we observe that the denominator is at least 1 for $r \geq 1/2$. And, when $H_{rem}$ is so small, we can upper bound the numerator by $(1 + o(1))m$, giving overall $\frac{\mathsf{variance}[g(T)]}{(\mathsf{E}[g(T)])^2} \leq (1 + o(1)) \cdot \frac{1}{\varepsilon^2} \cdot m$. We can thus estimate $H_{rem}$ using the median of means estimator.

### 4.2 Algorithm Description

Algorithm 1 presents the proposed algorithmic framework EntropyEstimation. EntropyEstimation takes a formula $\varphi(X, Y)$, a tolerance parameter $\varepsilon$, a confidence parameter $\delta$ as input, and returns an estimate $\hat{h}$ of the entropy $H_\varphi(Y)$, that is guaranteed to lie within a $(1 \pm \varepsilon)$-factor of $H_\varphi(Y)$ with confidence at least $1 - \delta$. Algorithm 1 assumes access to following subroutines:

ComputeCount: The subroutine ComputeCount takes a formula $\varphi(X, Y)$ and a projection set $V \subseteq X \cup Y$ as input, and returns a projected model count of $\varphi(X, Y)$ over $V$.

UnifSample: The subroutine UnifSample takes a formula $\varphi(X, Y)$ as an input and returns a uniformly sampled satisfying assignment of $\varphi(X, Y)$.

**Algorithm 1.** EntropyEstimation$(\varphi(X,Y), \varepsilon, \delta)$

1: $m \leftarrow |Y|; n \leftarrow |X|$
2: $z \leftarrow$ ComputeCount$(\varphi(X,Y), X)$
3: **for** $i \in [1, \log(10/\delta)]$ **do**
4: $\quad \tau \leftarrow$ UnifSample$(\varphi)$
5: $\quad r = z^{-1} \cdot$ ComputeCount$(\varphi(X,Y) \wedge (Y \leftrightarrow \tau_{\downarrow Y}), X)$
6: $\quad$ **if** $r > \frac{1}{2}$ **then**
7: $\quad\quad \hat{\varphi} \leftarrow \varphi \wedge (Y \not\leftrightarrow \tau_{\downarrow Y})$
8: $\quad\quad t \leftarrow \frac{6}{\epsilon^2} \cdot \min\left\{\frac{n}{2\log\frac{1}{1-r}}, m + \log(m + \log m + 2.5)\right\}$
9: $\quad\quad \hat{h}_{rem} \leftarrow$ SampleEst$(\hat{\varphi}, z, t, 0.9 \cdot \delta)$
10: $\quad\quad \hat{h} \leftarrow (1-r)\hat{h}_{rem} + r\log(\frac{1}{r})$
11: $\quad\quad$ **return** $\hat{h}$
12: $t \leftarrow \frac{6}{\epsilon^2} \cdot (\min\{n, m + \log(m + \log m + 1.1)\} - 1)$
13: $\hat{h} \leftarrow$ SampleEst$(\varphi, z, t, 0.9 \cdot \delta)$
14: **return** $\hat{h}$

**Algorithm 2.** SampleEst$(\varphi, z, t, \delta)$

1: $C \leftarrow [\,]$
2: $T \leftarrow \frac{9}{2}\log\frac{2}{\delta}$
3: **for** $i \in [1, T]$ **do**
4: $\quad est \leftarrow 0$
5: $\quad$ **for** $j \in [1, t]$ **do**
6: $\quad\quad \tau \leftarrow$ UnifSample$(\varphi)$
7: $\quad\quad r = z^{-1} \cdot$ ComputeCount$(\varphi(X,Y) \wedge (Y \leftrightarrow \tau_{\downarrow Y}), X)$
8: $\quad\quad est \leftarrow est + \log(1/r)$
9: $\quad C.\text{Append}(\frac{est}{t})$
10: **return** Median$(C)$

SampleEst: Algorithm 2 presents the subroutine SampleEst, which also assumes access to the ComputeCount and UnifSample subroutines. SampleEst takes as input a formula $\varphi(X,Y)$; the projected model count of $\varphi(X,Y)$ over $X$, $z$; the number of required samples, $t$; and a confidence parameter $\delta$, and returns a median-of-means estimate of the entropy. Algorithm 2 starts off by computing the value of $T$, the required number of repetitions to ensure at least $1-\delta$ confidence for the estimate. The algorithm has two loops—one outer loop (Lines 3–9), and one inner loop (Lines 5–8). The outer loop runs for $\lceil\frac{9}{2}\log(\frac{2}{\delta})\rceil$ rounds, where in each round, Algorithm 2 updates a list $C$ with the mean estimate, *est*. In the inner loop, in each round, Algorithm 2 updates the value of *est*: Line 6 draws a sample $\tau$ using the UnifSample$(\varphi(X,Y))$ subroutine. At Line 7, value of $r$ is computed as the ratio of the projected model count of $X$ in $\varphi(X,Y) \wedge (Y \leftrightarrow \tau_{\downarrow Y})$ to $z$. To compute the projected model count, Algorithm 2 calls the subroutine ComputeCount on input $(\varphi(X,Y) \wedge (Y \leftrightarrow \tau_{\downarrow Y}), X)$. At line 8, *est* is updated with $\log(\frac{1}{r})$, and at line 9, the final *est* is added to $C$. Finally, at line 10, Algorithm 2 returns the median of $C$.

Returning back to Algorithm 1, it starts by computing the value of $z$ as the projected model count of $\varphi(X,Y)$ over $X$ at line 2. The projected model count is computed by calling the ComputeCount subroutine. Next, Algorithm 1 attempts to determine whether there exists an output $\tau_{high}$ with probability greater than 1/2 or not by iterating over lines 3–11 for $\lceil \log(10/\delta) \rceil$ rounds. Line 4, draws a sample $\tau$ by calling the UnifSample($\varphi(X,Y)$) subroutine. Line 5 computes the value of $r$ by taking the ratio of the projected model count of $\varphi(X,Y) \wedge (Y \leftrightarrow \tau_{\downarrow Y})$ to $z$. Line 6 checks whether the value of $r$ is greater than 1/2 or not, and chooses one of the two paths based on the value of $r$:

1. If the value of $r$ turns out to be greater than 1/2, the formula $\varphi(X,Y)$ is updated to $\varphi(X,Y) \wedge (Y \not\leftrightarrow \tau_{\downarrow Y})$ at line 7. The resulting formula is denoted by $\hat{\varphi}(X,Y)$. Then, the value of required number of samples, $t$, is calculated as per the calculation shown at line 8. At line 9, the subroutine SampleEst is called with $\hat{\varphi}(X,Y)$, $z$, $t$, and $0.9 \times \delta$ as arguments to compute the estimate $\hat{h}_{rem}$. Finally, it computes the estimate $\hat{h}$ at line 10.
2. If the value of $r$ is at most 1/2 in every round, the number of samples we use, $t$, is calculated as per the calculation shown at line 12. At line 13, the subroutine SampleEst is called with $\varphi(X,Y)$, $z$, $t$, and $0.9 \times \delta$ as arguments to compute the estimate $\hat{h}$.

### 4.3 Theoretical Analysis

**Theorem 1.** *Given a circuit formula $\varphi$ with $|Y| \geq 2$, a tolerance parameter $\varepsilon > 0$, and confidence parameter $\delta > 0$, the algorithm* EntropyEstimation *returns $\hat{h}$ such that*

$$\Pr\left[(1-\varepsilon)H_\varphi(Y) \leq \hat{h} \leq (1+\varepsilon)|H_\varphi(Y)|\right] \geq 1-\delta$$

We first analyze the median-of-means estimator computed by SampleEst.

**Lemma 1.** *Given a circuit formula $\varphi$ and $z \in \mathbb{N}$, an accuracy parameter $\varepsilon > 0$, a confidence parameter $\delta > 0$, and a batch size $t \in \mathbb{N}$ for which*

$$\frac{1}{t\epsilon^2} \cdot \left( \frac{\sum_{\sigma \in 2^Y} \frac{|sol(\varphi(Y \mapsto \sigma))|}{|sol(\varphi)_{\downarrow X}|} (\log \frac{z}{|sol(\varphi(Y \mapsto \sigma))|})^2}{\left(\sum_{\sigma \in 2^Y} \frac{|sol(\varphi(Y \mapsto \sigma))|}{|sol(\varphi)_{\downarrow X}|} \log \frac{z}{|sol(\varphi(Y \mapsto \sigma))|}\right)^2} - 1 \right) \leq 1/6$$

*the algorithm* SampleEst *returns an estimate $\hat{h}$ such that with probability $1-\delta$,*

$$\hat{h} \leq (1+\epsilon) \sum_{\sigma \in 2^Y} \frac{|sol(\varphi(Y \mapsto \sigma))|}{|sol(\varphi)_{\downarrow X}|} \log \frac{z}{|sol(\varphi(Y \mapsto \sigma))|} \quad \text{and}$$

$$\hat{h} \geq (1-\epsilon) \sum_{\sigma \in 2^Y} \frac{|sol(\varphi(Y \mapsto \sigma))|}{|sol(\varphi)_{\downarrow X}|} \log \frac{z}{|sol(\varphi(Y \mapsto \sigma))|}.$$

*Proof.* Let $R_{ij}$ be the random value taken by $r$ in the $i$th iteration of the outer loop and $j$th iteration of the inner loop. We observe that $\{R_{ij}\}_{(i,j)}$ are a family of i.i.d. random variables. Let $C_i = \sum_{j=1}^{t} \frac{1}{t} \log \frac{1}{R_{ij}}$ be the value appended to $C$ at the end of the $i$th iteration of the loop. Clearly $\mathsf{E}[C_i] = \mathsf{E}[\log \frac{1}{R_{ij}}]$. Furthermore, we observe that by independence of the $R_{ij}$,

$$\mathsf{variance}[C_i] = \frac{1}{t}\mathsf{variance}[\log \frac{1}{R_{ij}}] = \frac{1}{t}(\mathsf{E}[(\log R_{ij})^2] - \mathsf{E}[\log \frac{1}{R_{ij}}]^2).$$

By Chebyshev's inequality, now,

$$\begin{aligned}\Pr\left[|C_i - \mathsf{E}[\log \frac{1}{R_{ij}}]| > \epsilon\mathsf{E}[\log \frac{1}{R_{ij}}]\right] &< \frac{\mathsf{variance}[C_i]}{\epsilon^2\mathsf{E}[\log \frac{1}{R_{ij}}]^2}\\ &= \frac{\mathsf{E}[(\log R_{ij})^2] - \mathsf{E}[\log \frac{1}{R_{ij}}]^2}{t\cdot\epsilon^2\mathsf{E}[\log \frac{1}{R_{ij}}]^2}\\ &\leq 1/6\end{aligned}$$

by our assumption on $t$.

Let $L_i \in \{0,1\}$ be the indicator random variable for the event that $C_i < \mathsf{E}[\log \frac{1}{R_{ij}}] - \epsilon\mathsf{E}[\log \frac{1}{R_{ij}}]$, and let $H_i \in \{0,1\}$ be the indicator random variable for the event that $C_i > \mathsf{E}[\log \frac{1}{R_{ij}}] + \epsilon\mathsf{E}[\log \frac{1}{R_{ij}}]$. Similarly, since these are disjoint events, $B_i = L_i + H_i$ is also an indicator random variable for the union. So long as $\sum_{i=1}^{T} L_i < T/2$ and $\sum_{i=1}^{T} H_i < T/2$, we note that the value returned by SampleEst is as desired. By the above calculation, $\Pr[L_i = 1] + \Pr[H_i = 1] = \Pr[B_i = 1] < 1/6$, and we note that $\{(B_i, L_i, H_i)\}_i$ are a family of i.i.d. random variables. Observe that by Hoeffding's inequality,

$$\Pr\left[\sum_{i=1}^{T} L_i \geq \frac{T}{6} + \frac{T}{3}\right] \leq \exp(-2T\frac{1}{9}) = \frac{\delta}{2}$$

and similarly $\Pr\left[\sum_{i=1}^{T} H_i \geq \frac{T}{2}\right] \leq \frac{\delta}{2}$. Therefore, by a union bound, the returned value is adequate with probability at least $1-\delta$ overall.

The analysis of SampleEst relied on a bound on the ratio of the first and second "moments" of the self-information in our truncated distribution. Suppose for all assignments $\sigma$ to $Y$, $p_\sigma \leq 1/2$. We observe that then $H_\varphi(Y) \geq \sum_{\sigma\in 2^Y} p_\sigma \cdot 1 = 1$. We also observe that on account of the uniform distribution on $X$, any $\sigma$ in the support of the distribution has $p_\sigma \geq 1/2^{|X|}$. Such bounds allow us to bound the relative variance of the self information:

**Lemma 2.** *Let $\{p_\sigma \in [1/2^{|X|}, 1]\}_{\sigma\in 2^Y}$ be given. Then,*

$$\sum_{\sigma\in 2^Y} p_\sigma(\log p_\sigma)^2 \leq |X| \sum_{\sigma\in 2^Y} p_\sigma \log \frac{1}{p_\sigma}$$

*Proof.* We observe simply that

$$\sum_{\sigma\in 2^Y} p_\sigma(\log p_\sigma)^2 \le \log 2^{|X|} \sum_{\sigma\in 2^Y} p_\sigma \log\frac{1}{p_\sigma} = |X| \sum_{\sigma\in 2^Y} p_\sigma \log\frac{1}{p_\sigma}.$$

**Lemma 3.** *Let $\{p_\sigma \in [0,1]\}_{\sigma\in 2^Y}$ be given with $\sum_{\sigma\in 2^Y} p_\sigma \le 1$ and*

$$H = \sum_{\sigma\in 2^Y} p_\sigma \log\frac{1}{p_\sigma} \ge 1.$$

*Then*

$$\frac{\sum_{\sigma\in 2^Y} p_\sigma(\log p_\sigma)^2}{\left(\sum_{\sigma\in 2^Y} p_\sigma \log\frac{1}{p_\sigma}\right)^2} \le \left(1 + \frac{\log(|Y| + \log|Y| + 1.1)}{|Y|}\right)|Y|.$$

*Similarly, if $H \le 1$ and $|Y| \ge 2$,*

$$\sum_{\sigma\in 2^Y} p_\sigma(\log p_\sigma)^2 \le |Y| + \log(|Y| + \log|Y| + 2.5).$$

Concretely, both cases give a bound that is at most $2|Y|$ for $|Y| \ge 3$; $|Y| = 8$ gives a bound that is less than $1.5 \times |Y|$ in both cases, $|Y| = 64$ gives a bound that is less than $1.1 \times |Y|$, etc.

*Proof.* By induction on the size of the support, denoted as supp and defined as $|\{\sigma \in 2^Y | p_\sigma > 0\}|$, we'll show that when $H \ge 1$, the ratio is at most $\log|\text{supp}| + \log(\log|\text{supp}| + \log\log|\text{supp}| + 1.1)$. The base case is when there are only two elements ($|Y| = 1$), in which case we must have $p_0 = p_1 = 1/2$, and the ratio is uniquely determined to be 1. For the induction step, observe that whenever any subset of the $p_\sigma$ take value 0, this is equivalent to a distribution with smaller support, for which by induction hypothesis, we find the ratio is at most

$$\begin{aligned}\log(|\text{supp}| - 1) &+ \log(\log(|\text{supp}| - 1) + \log\log(|\text{supp}| - 1) + 1.1)\\ &< \log|\text{supp}| + \log(\log|\text{supp}| + \log\log|\text{supp}| + 1.1).\end{aligned}$$

Consider any value of $H_\varphi(Y) = H$. With the entropy fixed, we need only maximize the numerator of the ratio with $H_\varphi(Y) = H$. Indeed, we've already ruled out a ratio of $|\text{supp}(Y)|$ for solutions in which any of the $p_\sigma$ take value 0, and clearly we cannot have any $p_\sigma = 1$, so we only need to consider interior points that are local optima. We use the method of Lagrange multipliers: for some $\lambda$, all $p_\sigma$ must satisfy $\log^2 p_\sigma + 2\log p_\sigma - \lambda(\log p_\sigma - 1) = 0$, which has solutions

$$\log p_\sigma = \frac{\lambda}{2} - 1 \pm \sqrt{(1 - \frac{\lambda}{2})^2 - \lambda} = \frac{\lambda}{2} - 1 \pm \sqrt{1 + \lambda^2/4}.$$

We note that the second derivatives with respect to $p_\sigma$ are equal to $\frac{2\log p_\sigma}{p_\sigma} + \frac{2-\lambda}{p_\sigma}$ which are negative iff $\log p_\sigma < \frac{\lambda}{2} - 1$, hence we attain local maxima only for the solution $\log p_\sigma = \frac{\lambda}{2} - 1 - \sqrt{1 + \lambda^2/4}$. Thus, there is a single $p_\sigma$, which by the entropy constraint, must satisfy $|\text{supp}| p_\sigma \log \frac{1}{p_\sigma} = H$ which we'll show gives

$$p_\sigma = \frac{H}{|\text{supp}|(\log \frac{|\text{supp}|}{H} + \log\log \frac{|\text{supp}|}{H} + \rho)}$$

for some $\rho \leq 1.1$. For $|\text{supp}| = 3$, we know $1 \leq H \leq \log 3$, and we can verify numerically that $\log\left(\frac{\log \frac{3}{H} + \log\log \frac{3}{H} + \rho}{\log \frac{3}{H}}\right) \in (0.42, 0.72)$ for $\rho \in [0, 1]$. Hence, by Brouwer's fixed point theorem, such a choice of $\rho \in [0, 1]$ exists. For $|\text{supp}| \geq 4$, observe that $\frac{|\text{supp}|}{H} \geq 2$, so $\log\left(\frac{\log \frac{|\text{supp}|}{H} + \log\log \frac{|\text{supp}|}{H}}{\log \frac{|\text{supp}|}{H}}\right) > 0$. For $|\text{supp}| = 4$, $\log\left(\frac{\log \frac{4}{H} + \log\log \frac{4}{H} + \rho}{\log \frac{4}{H}}\right) \in [0, 1]$, and similarly for all integer values of $|\text{supp}|$ up to 15, $\log\left(\frac{\log \frac{|\text{supp}|}{H} + \log\log \frac{|\text{supp}|}{H} + 1.1}{\log \frac{|\text{supp}|}{H}}\right) < 1.1$, so we can obtain $\rho \in (0, 1.1)$. Finally, for $|\text{supp}| \geq 16$, we have $\frac{|\text{supp}|}{H} \leq 2^{|\text{supp}|/2H}$, and hence $\frac{\log\log \frac{|\text{supp}|}{H} + \rho}{\log \frac{|\text{supp}|}{H}} \leq 1$, so

$$\begin{aligned}|\text{supp}| \frac{H(\log \frac{|\text{supp}|}{H} + \log(\log \frac{|\text{supp}|}{H} + \log\log \frac{|\text{supp}|}{H} + \rho))}{|\text{supp}|(\log \frac{|\text{supp}|}{H} + \log\log \frac{|\text{supp}|}{H} + \rho)} \\ \leq H \frac{\log \frac{|\text{supp}|}{H} + \log\log \frac{|\text{supp}|}{H} + 1}{\log \frac{|\text{supp}|}{H} + \log\log \frac{|\text{supp}|}{H} + \rho}\end{aligned}$$

Hence it is clear that this gives $H$ for some $\rho \leq 1$. Observe that for such a choice of $\rho$, using the substitution above, the ratio we attain is

$$\begin{aligned}\frac{|\text{supp}| \cdot H}{H^2 \cdot |\text{supp}|(\log \frac{|\text{supp}|}{H} + \log\log \frac{|\text{supp}|}{H} + \rho)} \left(\log \frac{|\text{supp}|(\log \frac{|\text{supp}|}{H} + \log\log \frac{|\text{supp}|}{H} + \rho)}{H}\right)^2 \\ = \frac{1}{H}(\log \frac{|\text{supp}|}{H} + \log(\log \frac{|\text{supp}|}{H} + \log\log \frac{|\text{supp}|}{H} + \rho))\end{aligned}$$

which is monotone in $1/H$, so using the fact that $H \geq 1$, we find it is at most

$$\log|\text{supp}| + \log(\log|\text{supp}| + \log\log|\text{supp}| + \rho)$$

which, recalling $\rho < 1.1$, gives the claimed bound.

For the second part, observe that by the same considerations, for fixed $H$,

$$\sum_{\sigma \in 2^Y} p_\sigma (\log p_\sigma)^2 = H \log \frac{1}{p_\sigma}$$

for the unique choice of $p_\sigma$ for $|Y|$ and $H$ as above, i.e., we will show that for $|Y| \geq 2$, it is

$$H\left(\log \frac{2^{|Y|}}{H} + \log(\log \frac{2^{|Y|}}{H} + \log\log \frac{2^{|Y|}}{H} + \rho)\right)$$

for some $\rho \in (0, 2.5)$. Indeed, we again consider the function

$$f(\rho) = \frac{\log(\log \frac{2^{|Y|}}{H} + \log\log \frac{2^{|Y|}}{H} + \rho)}{\log\log \frac{2^{|Y|}}{H}},$$

and observe that for $2^{|Y|}/H > 2$, $f(0) > 0$. Now, when $|Y| \geq 2$ and $H \leq 1$, $2^{|Y|}/H \geq 4$. We will see that the function $d(\rho) = f(\rho) - \rho$ has no critical points for $2^{|Y|}/H \geq 4$ and $\rho > 0$, and hence its maximum is attained at the boundary, i.e., at $\frac{2^{|Y|}}{H} = 4$, at which point we see that $f(2.5) < 2.5$. So, for such values of $\frac{2^{|Y|}}{H}$, $f(\rho)$ maps $[0, 2.5]$ into $[0, 2.5]$ and hence by Brouwer's fixed point theorem again, for all $|Y| \geq 4$ and $H \geq 1$ some $\rho \in (0, 2.5)$ exists for which $p_\sigma = \log \frac{2^{|Y|}}{H} + \log(\log \frac{2^{|Y|}}{H} + \log\log \frac{2^{|Y|}}{H} + \rho)$ gives $\sum_{p_\sigma \in 2^Y} p_\sigma \log \frac{1}{p_\sigma} = H$.

Indeed, $d'(\rho) = \frac{1}{\ln 2(\log \frac{2^{|Y|}}{H} + \log\log \frac{2^{|Y|}}{H} + \rho)\log\log \frac{2^{|Y|}}{H}} - 1$, which has a singularity at $\rho = -\log\log \frac{2^{|Y|}}{H} - \log\log \frac{2^{|Y|}}{H}$, and otherwise has a critical point at $\rho = \frac{\ln 2}{\log\log \frac{2^{|Y|}}{H}} - \log \frac{2^{|Y|}}{H} - \log\log \frac{2^{|Y|}}{H}$. Since $\log \frac{2^{|Y|}}{H} \geq 2$ and $\log\log \frac{2^{|Y|}}{H} \geq 1$ here, these are both clearly negative.

Now, we'll show that this expression (for $|Y| \geq 2$) is maximized when $H = 1$. Observe first that the expression $H(|Y| + \log \frac{1}{H})$ as a function of $H$ does not have critical points for $H \leq 1$: the derivative is $|Y| + \log \frac{1}{H} - \frac{1}{\ln 2}$, so critical points require $H = 2^{|Y| - (1/\ln 2)} > 1$. Hence we see that this expression is maximized at the boundary, when $H = 1$. Similarly, the rest of the expression,

$$H \log(|Y| + \log \frac{1}{H} + \log(|Y| + \log \frac{1}{H}) + 2.5)$$

viewed as a function of $H$, only has critical points for

$$\log(|Y| + \log \frac{1}{H} + \log(|Y| + \log \frac{1}{H}) + 2.5) = \frac{\frac{1}{\ln 2}(1 + \frac{1}{|Y| + \log \frac{1}{H}})}{|Y| + \log \frac{1}{H} + \log(|Y| + \log \frac{1}{H}) + 2.5}$$

i.e., it requires

$$(|Y| + \log \frac{1}{H} + \log(|Y| + \log \frac{1}{H}) + 2.5)\log(|Y| + \log \frac{1}{H} + \log(|Y| + \log \frac{1}{H}) + 2.5)$$
$$= \frac{1}{\ln 2}(1 + \frac{1}{|Y| + \log \frac{1}{H}}).$$

But, the right-hand side is at most $\frac{3}{2\ln 2} < 3$, while the left-hand side is at least 13. Thus, it also has no critical points, and its maximum is similarly taken at the boundary, $H = 1$. Thus, overall, when $H \leq 1$ and $|Y| \geq 2$ we find

$$\sum_{\sigma \in 2^Y} p_\sigma (\log p_\sigma)^2 \leq |Y| + \log(|Y| + \log |Y| + 2.5).$$

Although the assignment of probability mass used in the bound did not sum to 1, nevertheless this bound is nearly tight. For any $\gamma > 0$, and letting $H = 1 + \Delta$

where $\Delta = \frac{1}{\log^{\gamma}(2^{|Y|}-2)}$, the following solution attains a ratio of $(1-o(1))|Y|^{1-\gamma}$: for any two $\sigma_1^*, \sigma_2^* \in 2^Y$, set $p_{\sigma_i^*} = \frac{1}{2} - \frac{\epsilon}{2}$ and set the rest to $\frac{\epsilon}{2^{|Y|}-2}$, for $\epsilon$ chosen below. To obtain

$$\begin{aligned} H &= 2 \cdot (\frac{1}{2} - \frac{\epsilon}{2}) \log \frac{2}{1-\epsilon} + (2^{|Y|} - 2) \cdot \frac{\epsilon}{2^{|Y|}-2} \log \frac{2^{|Y|}-2}{\epsilon} \\ &= (1-\epsilon)(1 + \log(1 + \frac{\epsilon}{1-\epsilon})) + \epsilon \log \frac{2^{|Y|}-2}{\epsilon} \end{aligned}$$

observe that since $\log(1+x) = \frac{x}{\ln 2} + \Theta(x^2)$, we will need to take

$$\begin{aligned} \epsilon &= \frac{\Delta}{\log(2^{|Y|}-2) + \log\frac{1-\epsilon}{\epsilon} - (1 + \frac{1}{\ln 2}) + \Theta(\epsilon^2)} \\ &= \frac{\Delta}{\log(2^{|Y|}-2) + \log\log(2^{|Y|}-2) + \log\frac{1}{\Delta} - (1+\frac{1}{\ln 2}) - \frac{\epsilon}{\ln 2} + \Theta(\epsilon^2)}. \end{aligned}$$

For such a choice, we indeed obtain the ratio

$$\frac{(1-\epsilon)\log^2 \frac{2}{1-\epsilon} + \epsilon \log^2 \frac{(2^{|Y|}-2)}{\epsilon}}{H^2} \geq (1-o(1))|Y|^{1-\gamma}.$$

Using these bounds, we are finally ready to prove Theorem 1:

*Proof.* We first consider the case where no $\sigma \in sol(\varphi)$ has $p_\sigma > 1/2$; here, the condition in line 6 of EntropyEstimation never passes, so we return the value obtained by SampleEst on line 12. Note that we must have $H_\varphi(Y) \geq 1$ in this case. So, by Lemma 3,

$$\frac{\sum_{\sigma \in 2^Y} p_\sigma (\log p_\sigma)^2}{\left(\sum_{\sigma \in 2^Y} p_\sigma \log \frac{1}{p_\sigma}\right)^2} \leq \min\left\{|X|, \left(1 + \frac{\log(|Y| + \log|Y| + 1.1)}{|Y|}\right)|Y|\right\}$$

and hence, by Lemma 1, using $t \geq \frac{6 \cdot \min\{|X|, |Y| + \log(|Y| + \log|Y| + 1.1)\} - 1)}{\varepsilon^2}$ suffices to ensure that the returned $\hat{h}$ is satisfactory with probability $1-\delta$.

Next, we consider the case where some $\sigma^* \in sol(\varphi)$ has $p_{\sigma^*} > 1/2$. Since the total probability is 1, there can be at most one such $\sigma^*$. So, in the distribution conditioned on $\sigma \neq \sigma^*$, i.e., $\{p'_\sigma\}_{\sigma \in 2^Y}$ that sets $p'_{\sigma^*} = 0$, and $p'_\sigma = \frac{p_\sigma}{1-p_{\sigma^*}}$ otherwise, we now need to show that $t$ satisfies

$$\frac{1}{t\varepsilon^2}\left(\frac{\sum_{\sigma\neq\sigma^*} p'_\sigma (\log\frac{1}{(1-p_{\sigma^*})p'_\sigma})^2}{(\sum_{\sigma\neq\sigma^*} p'_\sigma \log\frac{1}{(1-p_{\sigma^*})p'_\sigma})^2} - 1\right) < \frac{1}{6}$$

to apply Lemma 1. We first rewrite this expression. Letting $H = \sum_{\sigma\neq\sigma^*} p'_\sigma \log\frac{1}{p'_\sigma}$ be the entropy of this conditional distribution,

$$\begin{aligned} \frac{\sum_{\sigma\neq\sigma^*} p'_\sigma (\log\frac{1}{(1-p_{\sigma^*})p'_\sigma})^2}{(\sum_{\sigma\neq\sigma^*} p'_\sigma \log\frac{1}{(1-p_{\sigma^*})p'_\sigma})^2} &= \frac{\sum_{\sigma\neq\sigma^*} p'_\sigma (\log\frac{1}{p'_\sigma})^2 + 2H\log\frac{1}{1-p_{\sigma^*}} + (\log\frac{1}{1-p_{\sigma^*}})^2}{(H + \log\frac{1}{1-p_{\sigma^*}})^2} \\ &= \frac{\sum_{\sigma\neq\sigma^*} p'_\sigma (\log\frac{1}{p'_\sigma})^2 - H^2}{(H + \log\frac{1}{1-p_{\sigma^*}})^2} + 1. \end{aligned}$$

Lemma 2 now gives rather directly that this quantity is at most

$$\frac{H|X| - H^2}{(H + \log\frac{1}{1-p_{\sigma^*}})^2} + 1 < \frac{|X|}{2\log\frac{1}{1-p_{\sigma^*}}} + 1.$$

For the bound in terms of $|Y|$, there are now two cases depending on whether $H$ is greater than 1 or less than 1. When it is greater than 1, the first part of Lemma 3 again gives

$$\frac{\sum_{\sigma \in 2^Y} p'_\sigma (\log p'_\sigma)^2}{H^2} \leq |Y| + \log(|Y| + \log|Y| + 1.1).$$

When $H < 1$, on the other hand, recalling $p_{\sigma^*} > 1/2$ (so $\log\frac{1}{1-p_{\sigma^*}} \geq 1$), the second part of Lemma 3 gives that our expression is less than

$$\frac{|Y| + \log(|Y| + \log|Y| + 2.5)) - H^2}{(H + \log\frac{1}{1-p_{\sigma^*}})^2} < |Y| + \log(|Y| + \log|Y| + 2.5).$$

Thus, by Lemma 1,

$$t \geq \frac{6 \cdot \min\{\frac{|X|}{2\log\frac{1}{1-p_{\sigma^*}}}, |Y| + \log(|Y| + \log|Y| + 2.5)\}}{\varepsilon^2}$$

suffices to obtain $\hat{h}$ such that $\hat{h} \leq (1+\varepsilon)\sum_{\sigma \neq \sigma^*} \frac{p_\sigma}{1-p_{\sigma^*}} \log\frac{1}{p_\sigma}$ and $\hat{h} \geq (1-\varepsilon)\sum_{\sigma \neq \sigma^*} \frac{p_\sigma}{1-p_{\sigma^*}} \log\frac{1}{p_\sigma}$; hence we obtain such a $\hat{h}$ with probability at least $1-0.9 \cdot \delta$ in line 10, if we pass the test on line 6 of Algorithm 1, thus identifying $\sigma^*$. Note that this value is adequate, so we need only guarantee that the test on line 6 passes on one of the iterations with probability at least $1 - 0.1 \cdot \delta$.

To this end, note that each sample($\tau_{\downarrow Y}$) on line 4 is equal to $\sigma^*$ with probability $\frac{|sol(\varphi(Y \mapsto \sigma^*))|}{|sol(\varphi)_{\downarrow X}|} > \frac{1}{2}$ by hypothesis. Since each iteration of the loop is an independent draw, the probability that the condition on line 6 is not met after $\log\frac{10}{\delta}$ draws is less than $(1-\frac{1}{2})^{\log\frac{10}{\delta}} = \frac{\delta}{10}$, as needed.

### 4.4 Beyond Boolean Formulas

We now focus on the case where the relationship between $X$ and $Y$ is modeled by an arbitrary relation $\mathcal{R}$ instead of a Boolean formula $\varphi$. As noted in Sect. 1, program behaviors are often modeled with other representations such as automata [4,5,14]. The automata-based modeling often has $X$ represented as the input to the given automaton $\mathcal{A}$ while every realization of $Y$ corresponds to a state of $\mathcal{A}$. Instead of an explicit description of $\mathcal{A}$, one can rely on a symbolic description of $\mathcal{A}$. Two families of techniques are currently used to estimate the entropy. The first technique is to enumerate the possible *output* states and, for each such state $s$, estimate the number of strings accepted by $\mathcal{A}$ if $s$ was the only accepting state of $\mathcal{A}$. The other technique relies on uniformly sampling a string $\sigma$, noting the final state of $\mathcal{A}$ when run on $\sigma$, and then applying a histogram-based technique to estimate the entropy.

In order to use the algorithm EntropyEstimation one requires access to a sampler and model counter for automata; the past few years have witnessed the design of efficient counters for automata to handle string constraints. In addition, EntropyEstimation requires access to a conditioning routine to implement the substitution step, i.e., $Y \mapsto \tau_{\downarrow Y}$, which is easy to accomplish for automata via marking the corresponding state as a non-accepting state.

## 5 Empirical Evaluation

To evaluate the runtime performance of EntropyEstimation, we implemented a prototype in Python that employs SPUR [3] as a uniform sampler and GANAK [52] as a projected model counter. We experimented with 96 Boolean formulas arising from diverse applications ranging from QIF benchmarks [32], plan recognition [54], bit-blasted versions of SMTLIB benchmarks [52,54], and QBFEval competitions [1,2]. The value of $n = |X|$ varies from 5 to 752 while the value of $m = |Y|$ varies from 9 to 1447.

In all of our experiments, the parameters $\delta$ and $\varepsilon$ were set to 0.09, 0.8 respectively. All of our experiments were conducted on a high-performance computer cluster with each node consisting of a E5-2690 v3 CPU with 24 cores, and 96 GB of RAM with a memory limit set to 4 GB per core. Experiments were run in single-threaded mode on a single core with a timeout of 3000 s.

***Baseline:*** As our baseline, we implemented the following approach to compute the entropy exactly, which is representative of the current state of the art approaches [13,27,39][2]. For each valuation $\sigma \in sol(\varphi)_{\downarrow Y}$, we compute $p_\sigma = \frac{|sol(\varphi(Y \mapsto \sigma))|}{|sol(\varphi)_{\downarrow X}|}$, where $|sol(\varphi(Y \rightarrow \sigma))|$ is the count of satisfying assignments of $\varphi(Y \mapsto \sigma)$, and $|sol(\varphi)_{\downarrow X}|$ represents the projected model count of $\varphi$ over $X$. Then, finally the entropy is computed as $\sum\limits_{\sigma \in 2^Y} p_\sigma \log(\frac{1}{p_\sigma})$.

Our evaluation demonstrates that EntropyEstimation can scale to the formulas beyond the reach of the enumeration-based baseline approach. Within a given timeout of 3000 s, EntropyEstimation is able to estimate the entropy for all the benchmarks, whereas the baseline approach could terminate only for 14 benchmarks. Furthermore, EntropyEstimation estimated the entropy within the allowed tolerance for *all* the benchmarks.

### 5.1 Scalability of EntropyEstimation

Table 1 presents the performance of EntropyEstimation vis-a-vis the baseline approach for 20 benchmarks.[3] Column 1 of Table 1 gives the names of the

[2] We wish to emphasize that none of the previous approaches could provide theoretical guarantees of $(\varepsilon, \delta)$ without enumerating over all possible assignments to $Y$.

[3] The complete analysis for all of the benchmarks is deferred to the technical report https://arxiv.org/pdf/2206.00921.pdf.

**Table 1.** "-" represents that entropy could not be estimated due to timeout. Note that $m = |Y|$ and $n = |X|$.

| Benchmarks | $\|X\|$ | $\|Y\|$ | Baseline | | EntropyEstimation | |
|---|---|---|---|---|---|---|
| | | | Time(s) | count queries | Time(s) | count/sample queries |
| pwd-backdoor | 336 | 64 | - | $1.84\times10^{19}$ | 5.41 | $1.25\times10^{2}$ |
| case31 | 13 | 40 | 201.02 | $1.02\times10^{3}$ | 125.36 | $5.65\times10^{2}$ |
| case23 | 14 | 63 | 420.85 | $2.05\times10^{3}$ | 141.17 | $6.10\times10^{2}$ |
| s1488_15_7 | 14 | 927 | 1037.71 | $3.84\times10^{3}$ | 150.29 | $6.10\times10^{2}$ |
| bug1-fix-4 | 53 | 17 | 373.52 | $1.76\times10^{3}$ | 212.37 | $9.60\times10^{2}$ |
| s832a_15_7 | 23 | 670 | - | $2.65\times10^{6}$ | 247 | $1.04\times10^{3}$ |
| dyn-fix-1 | 40 | 48 | - | $3.30\times10^{4}$ | 252.2 | $1.83\times10^{3}$ |
| s1196a_7_4 | 32 | 676 | - | $4.22\times10^{7}$ | 343.68 | $1.46\times10^{3}$ |
| backdoor-2x16 | 168 | 32 | - | $1.31\times10^{5}$ | 405.7 | $1.70\times10^{3}$ |
| CVE-2007 | 752 | 32 | - | $4.29\times10^{9}$ | 654.54 | $1.70\times10^{3}$ |
| subtraction32 | 65 | 218 | - | $1.84\times10^{19}$ | 860.88 | $3.00\times10^{3}$ |
| case_1_b11_1 | 48 | 292 | - | $2.75\times10^{11}$ | 1164.36 | $2.20\times10^{3}$ |
| s420_15_7-1 | 235 | 116 | - | $3.52\times10^{7}$ | 1187.23 | $5.72\times10^{3}$ |
| case145 | 64 | 155 | - | $7.04\times10^{13}$ | 1243.11 | $2.96\times10^{3}$ |
| floor64-1 | 405 | 161 | - | $2.32\times10^{27}$ | 1764.2 | $7.85\times10^{3}$ |
| s641_7_4 | 54 | 453 | - | $1.74\times10^{12}$ | 1849.84 | $2.48\times10^{3}$ |
| decomp64 | 381 | 191 | - | $6.81\times10^{38}$ | 2239.62 | $9.26\times10^{3}$ |
| squaring2 | 72 | 813 | - | $6.87\times10^{10}$ | 2348.6 | $3.33\times10^{3}$ |
| stmt5_731_730 | 379 | 311 | - | $3.49\times10^{10}$ | 2814.58 | $1.49\times10^{4}$ |

benchmarks, while columns 2 and 3 list the numbers of $X$ and $Y$ variables. Columns 4 and 5 respectively present the time taken, number of samples used by baseline approach, and columns 6 and 7 present the same for EntropyEstimation. The required number of samples for the baseline approach is $|sol(\varphi)_{\downarrow Y}|$.

Table 1 clearly demonstrates that EntropyEstimation outperforms the baseline approach. As shown in Table 1, there are some benchmarks for which the projected model count on $V$ is greater than $10^{30}$, i.e., the baseline approach would need $10^{30}$ valuations to compute the entropy exactly. By contrast, the proposed algorithm EntropyEstimation needed at most $\sim 10^{4}$ samples to estimate the entropy within the given tolerance and confidence. The number of samples required to estimate the entropy is reduced significantly with our proposed approach, making it scalable.

### 5.2 Quality of Estimates

There were only 14 benchmarks out of 96 for which the enumeration-based baseline approach finished within a given timeout of 3000s. Therefore, we compared the entropy estimated by EntropyEstimation with the baseline for those 14 benchmarks only. Figure 1 shows how accurate were the estimates of the entropy by EntropyEstimation. The y-axis represents the observed error, which was calculated as $max(\frac{\text{Estimated}}{\text{Exact}} - 1, \frac{\text{Exact}}{\text{Estimated}} - 1)$, and the x-axis represents the benchmarks ordered in ascending order of observed error; that is, a bar at $x$ represents the observed error for a benchmark—the lower, the better.

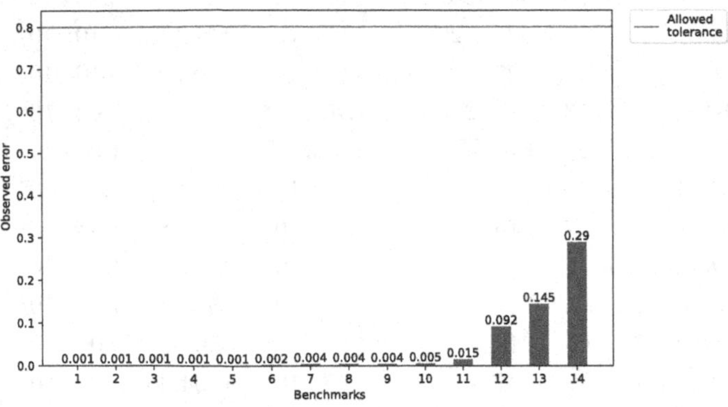


**Fig. 1.** The accuracy of estimated entropy using EntropyEstimation for 14 benchmarks. $\varepsilon = 0.8, \delta = 0.09$. (Color figure online)

The red horizontal line in Fig. 1 indicates the maximum allowed tolerance ($\varepsilon$), which was set to 0.80 in our experiments. We observe that for *all* 14 benchmarks, EntropyEstimation estimated the entropy within the allowed tolerance; in fact, the observed error was greater than 0.1 for just 2 out of the 14 benchmarks, and the maximum error observed was 0.29.

***Alternative Baselines:*** As we discussed earlier, several other algorithms have been proposed for estimating the entropy. For example, Valiant and Valiant's algorithm [58] obtains an $\varepsilon$-additive approximation using $\mathcal{O}(\frac{2^m}{\varepsilon^2 m})$ samples, and Chakraborty et al. [17] compute such approximations using $\mathcal{O}(\frac{m^7}{\varepsilon^8})$ samples. We stress that neither of these is exact, and thus could not be used to assess the accuracy of our method as presented in Fig. 1. Moreover, based on Table 1, we observe that the number of sampling or counting calls that could be computed within the timeout was roughly $2 \times 10^4$, where $m$ ranges between $10^1$–$10^3$. Thus, the method of Chakraborty et al. [17], which would take $10^7$ or more samples on all benchmarks, would not be competitive with our method, which never used $2 \times 10^4$ calls. The method of Valiant and Valiant, on the other hand, would likely allow a few more benchmarks to be estimated (perhaps up to a fifth of the benchmarks). Still, it would not be competitive with our technique except in the smallest benchmarks (for which the baseline required $< 10^6$ samples, about a third of our benchmarks), since we were otherwise more than a factor of $m$ faster than the baseline.

## 6 Conclusion

In this work, we considered estimating the Shannon entropy of a distribution specified by a circuit formula $\varphi(X, Y)$. Prior work relied on $\mathcal{O}(2^m)$ model counting queries and, therefore, could not scale to instances beyond small values of $m$. In contrast, we propose a novel technique, called EntropyEstimation, for estimation of entropy that takes advantage of the access to the formula $\varphi$ via conditioning. EntropyEstimation makes only $\mathcal{O}(\min(m, n))$ model counting and sampling queries, and therefore scales significantly better than the prior approaches.

**Acknowledgments.** This work was supported in part by National Research Foundation Singapore under its NRF Fellowship Programme[NRF-NRFFAI1-2019-0004], Ministry of Education Singapore Tier 2 grant [MOE-T2EP20121-0011], NUS ODPRT grant [R-252-000-685-13], an Amazon Research Award, and NSF awards IIS-1908287, IIS-1939677, and IIS-1942336. We are grateful to the anonymous reviewers for constructive comments to improve the paper. The computational work was performed on resources of the National Supercomputing Centre, Singapore: https://www.nscc.sg.

## References

1. QBF solver evaluation portal 2017. http://www.qbflib.org/qbfeval17.php
2. QBF solver evaluation portal 2018. http://www.qbflib.org/qbfeval18.php
3. Achlioptas, D., Hammoudeh, Z.S., Theodoropoulos, P.: Fast sampling of perfectly uniform satisfying assignments. In: Beyersdorff, O., Wintersteiger, C.M. (eds.) SAT 2018. LNCS, vol. 10929, pp. 135–147. Springer, Cham (2018). https://doi.org/10.1007/978-3-319-94144-8_9
4. Aydin, A., Bang, L., Bultan, T.: Automata-based model counting for string constraints. In: Kroening, D., Păsăreanu, C.S. (eds.) CAV 2015. LNCS, vol. 9206, pp. 255–272. Springer, Cham (2015). https://doi.org/10.1007/978-3-319-21690-4_15
5. Aydin, A., et al.: Parameterized model counting for string and numeric constraints. In: Proceedings of ESEC/FSE, pp. 400–410 (2018)
6. Aziz, R.A., Chu, G., Muise, C., Stuckey, P.: #∃SAT: projected model counting. In: Heule, M., Weaver, S. (eds.) SAT 2015. LNCS, vol. 9340, pp. 121–137. Springer, Cham (2015). https://doi.org/10.1007/978-3-319-24318-4_10
7. Backes, M., Köpf, B., Rybalchenko, A.: Automatic discovery and quantification of information leaks. In: Proceedings of SP (2009)
8. Bang, L., Aydin, A., Phan, Q.S., Păsăreanu, C.S., Bultan, T.: String analysis for side channels with segmented oracles. In: Proceedings of SIGSOFT (2016)
9. Batu, T., Dasgupta, S., Kumar, R., Rubinfeld, R.: The complexity of approximating the entropy. SIAM J. Comput. **35**(1), 132–150 (2005)
10. Bayardo Jr, R.J., Pehoushek, J.D.: Counting models using connected components. In: AAAI/IAAI, pp. 157–162 (2000)
11. Bevier, W.R., Cohen, R.M., Young, W.D.: Connection policies and controlled interference. In: Proceedings of CSF (1995)
12. Birnbaum, E., Lozinskii, E.L.: The good old Davis-Putnam procedure helps counting models. J. Artif. Intell. Res. **10**, 457–477 (1999)
13. Borges, M., Phan, Q.-S., Filieri, A., Păsăreanu, C.S.: Model-counting approaches for nonlinear numerical constraints. In: Barrett, C., Davies, M., Kahsai, T. (eds.) NFM 2017. LNCS, vol. 10227, pp. 131–138. Springer, Cham (2017). https://doi.org/10.1007/978-3-319-57288-8_9

14. Bultan, T.: Quantifying information leakage using model counting constraint solvers. In: Chakraborty, S., Navas, J.A. (eds.) VSTTE 2019. LNCS, vol. 12031, pp. 30–35. Springer, Cham (2020). https://doi.org/10.1007/978-3-030-41600-3_3
15. Canonne, C.L.: A survey on distribution testing: your data is big. But is it blue? Theory Comput. 1–100 (2020)
16. Cernŷ, P., Chatterjee, K., Henzinger, T.A.: The complexity of quantitative information flow problems. In: Proceedings of CSF (2011)
17. Chakraborty, S., Fischer, E., Goldhirsh, Y., Matsliah, A.: On the power of conditional samples in distribution testing. SIAM J. Comput. (2016)
18. Chakraborty, S., Fremont, D.J., Meel, K.S., Seshia, S.A., Vardi, M.Y.: Distribution-aware sampling and weighted model counting for SAT, In: AAAI, pp. 1722–1730. AAAI Press (2014)
19. Chakraborty, S., Meel, K.S., Vardi, M.Y.: Balancing scalability and uniformity in SAT witness generator. In: Proceedings of DAC (2014)
20. Chakraborty, S., Meel, K.S., Vardi, M.Y.: Algorithmic improvements in approximate counting for probabilistic inference: from linear to logarithmic sat calls. In: IJCAI (2016)
21. Chen, S., Wang, R., Wang, X., Zhang, K.: Side-channel leaks in web applications: a reality today, a challenge tomorrow. In: Proceedings of SP (2010)
22. Cherubin, G., Chatzikokolakis, K., Palamidessi, C.: F-BLEAU: fast black-box leakage estimation. In: Proceedings of SP (2019)
23. Chothia, T., Kawamoto, Y., Novakovic, C.: LeakWatch: estimating information leakage from Java programs. In: Kutyłowski, M., Vaidya, J. (eds.) ESORICS 2014. LNCS, vol. 8713, pp. 219–236. Springer, Cham (2014). https://doi.org/10.1007/978-3-319-11212-1_13
24. Clark, D., Hunt, S., Malacaria, P.: A static analysis for quantifying information flow in a simple imperative language. J. Comput. Secur. (2007)
25. Darwiche, A.: On the tractable counting of theory models and its application to truth maintenance and belief revision. J. Appl. Non-Classical Logics **11**(1–2), 11–34 (2001)
26. Denning, D.E.: A lattice model of secure information flow. Commun. ACM (1976)
27. Eiers, W., Saha, S., Brennan, T., Bultan, T.: Subformula caching for model counting and quantitative program analysis. In: 2019 34th IEEE/ACM International Conference on Automated Software Engineering (ASE), pp. 453–464. IEEE (2019)
28. Eldib, H., Wang, C., Schaumont, P.: Formal verification of software countermeasures against side-channel attacks. ACM Trans. Softw. Eng. Methodol. (TOSEM) **24**(2), 1–24 (2014)
29. Eldib, H., Wang, C., Taha, M., Schaumont, P.: QMS: evaluating the side-channel resistance of masked software from source code. In: 2014 51st ACM/EDAC/IEEE Design Automation Conference (DAC), pp. 1–6. IEEE (2014)
30. Ferrari, E., Samarati, P., Bertino, E., Jajodia, S.: Providing flexibility in information flow control for object oriented systems. In: Proceedings of SP (1997)
31. Fichte, J.K., Hecher, M., Hamiti, F.: The model counting competition 2020. arXiv preprint arXiv:2012.01323 (2020). https://arxiv.org/pdf/2012.01323.pdf
32. Fremont, D., Rabe, M., Seshia, S.: Maximum model counting. In: Proceedings of AAAI (2017)
33. Gao, P., Zhang, J., Song, F., Wang, C.: Verifying and quantifying side-channel resistance of masked software implementations. ACM Trans. Softw. Eng. Methodol. (TOSEM) **28**(3), 1–32 (2019)

34. Goldreich, O., Vadhan, S.: Comparing entropies in statistical zero knowledge with applications to the structure of SZK. In: Proceedings of CCC, pp. 54–73. IEEE (1999)
35. Guha, S., McGregor, A., Venkatasubramanian, S.: Sublinear estimation of entropy and information distances. ACM Trans. Algorithms (TALG) **5**(4), 1–16 (2009)
36. Huang, J., Darwiche, A.: The language of search. J. Artif. Intell. Res. **29**, 191–219 (2007)
37. Kadron, İ.B., Rosner, N., Bultan, T.: Feedback-driven side-channel analysis for networked applications. In: Proceedings of SIGSOFT (2020)
38. Kim, S., McCamant, S.: Bit-vector model counting using statistical estimation. In: Beyer, D., Huisman, M. (eds.) TACAS 2018. LNCS, vol. 10805, pp. 133–151. Springer, Cham (2018). https://doi.org/10.1007/978-3-319-89960-2_8
39. Klebanov, V.: Precise quantitative information flow analysis using symbolic model counting. QASA (2012)
40. Köpf, B., Basin, D.: An information-theoretic model for adaptive side-channel attacks. In: Proceedings of CCS (2007)
41. Köpf, B., Rybalchenko, A.: Approximation and randomization for quantitative information-flow analysis. In: Proceedings of CSF, pp. 3–14. IEEE (2010)
42. Lagniez, J.M., Marquis, P.: A recursive algorithm for projected model counting. In: Proceedings of AAAI, vol. 33, pp. 1536–1543 (2019)
43. Ma, S.K.: Calculation of entropy from data of motion. J. Stat. Phys. **26**(2), 221–240 (1981)
44. Meng, Z., Smith, G.: Calculating bounds on information leakage using two-bit patterns. In: Proceedings of PLAS (2011)
45. Möhle, S., Biere, A.: Dualizing projected model counting. In: Proceedings of ICTAI, pp. 702–709. IEEE (2018)
46. Phan, Q.S., Bang, L., Pasareanu, C.S., Malacaria, P., Bultan, T.: Synthesis of adaptive side-channel attacks. In: Proceedings of CSF (2017)
47. Phan, Q.S., Malacaria, P.: Abstract model counting: a novel approach for quantification of information leaks. In: Proceedings of CCS (2014)
48. Phan, Q.S., Malacaria, P., Tkachuk, O., Păsăreanu, C.S.: Symbolic quantitative information flow. Proc. ACM SIGSOFT (2012)
49. Rosner, N., Kadron, I.B., Bang, L., Bultan, T.: Profit: detecting and quantifying side channels in networked applications. In: Proceedings of NDSS (2019)
50. Sang, T., Bacchus, F., Beame, P., Kautz, H.A., Pitassi, T.: Combining component caching and clause learning for effective model counting. SAT 4, 7th (2004)
51. Sharma, S., Gupta, R., Roy, S., Meel, K.S.: Knowledge compilation meets uniform sampling. In: Proceedings of LPAR (2018)
52. Sharma, S., Roy, S., Soos, M., Meel, K.S.: Ganak: a scalable probabilistic exact model counter. In: Proceedings of IJCAI (2019)
53. Smith, G.: On the foundations of quantitative information flow. In: de Alfaro, L. (ed.) FoSSaCS 2009. LNCS, vol. 5504, pp. 288–302. Springer, Heidelberg (2009). https://doi.org/10.1007/978-3-642-00596-1_21
54. Soos, M., Gocht, S., Meel, K.S.: Tinted, detached, and lazy CNF-XOR solving and its applications to counting and sampling. In: Lahiri, S.K., Wang, C. (eds.) CAV 2020. LNCS, vol. 12224, pp. 463–484. Springer, Cham (2020). https://doi.org/10.1007/978-3-030-53288-8_22
55. Strong, S.P., Koberle, R., Van Steveninck, R.R.D.R., Bialek, W.: Entropy and information in neural spike trains. Phys. Rev. Lett. **80**(1), 197 (1998)

56. Thurley, M.: sharpSAT – counting models with advanced component caching and implicit BCP. In: Biere, A., Gomes, C.P. (eds.) SAT 2006. LNCS, vol. 4121, pp. 424–429. Springer, Heidelberg (2006). https://doi.org/10.1007/11814948_38
57. Val, C.G., Enescu, M.A., Bayless, S., Aiello, W., Hu, A.J.: Precisely measuring quantitative information flow: 10k lines of code and beyond. In: Proceedings of EuroS&P, pp. 31–46. IEEE (2016)
58. Valiant, G., Valiant, P.: Estimating the unseen: improved estimators for entropy and other properties. J. ACM **64**(6), 1–41 (2017)
59. Zhou, Z., Qian, Z., Reiter, M.K., Zhang, Y.: Static evaluation of noninterference using approximate model counting. In: Proceedings of SP (2018)

# PoS4MPC: Automated Security Policy Synthesis for Secure Multi-party Computation

Yuxin Fan[1], Fu Song[1,2(✉)], Taolue Chen[3], Liangfeng Zhang[1], and Wanwei Liu[4,5]

[1] School of Information Science and Technology, ShanghaiTech University, Shanghai 201210, China
songfu@shanghaitech.edu.cn
[2] Shanghai Engineering Research Center of Intelligent Vision and Imaging, Shanghai 201210, China
[3] Department of Computer Science, Birkbeck, University of London, London WC1E 7HX, UK
[4] College of Computer Science, National University of Defense Technology, Changsha 410073, China
[5] State Key Laboratory for High Performance Computing, Changsha 410073, China

**Abstract.** Secure multi-party computation (MPC) is a promising technique for privacy-persevering applications. A number of MPC frameworks have been proposed to reduce the burden of designing customized protocols, allowing non-experts to quickly develop and deploy MPC applications. To improve performance, recent MPC frameworks allow users to declare variables secret only for these which are to be protected. However, in practice, it is usually highly non-trivial for non-experts to specify secret variables: declaring too many degrades the performance while declaring too less compromises privacy. To address this problem, in this work we propose an automated security policy synthesis approach to declare as few secret variables as possible but without compromising security. Our approach is a synergistic integration of type inference and symbolic reasoning. The former is able to quickly infer a sound—but sometimes conservative—security policy, whereas the latter allows to identify secret variables in a security policy that can be declassified in a precise manner. Moreover, the results from symbolic reasoning are fed back to type inference to refine the security types even further. We implement our approach in a new tool **PoS4MPC**. Experimental results on five typical MPC applications confirm the efficacy of our approach.

This work is supported by the National Natural Science Foundation of China (NSFC) under Grants No. 62072309, No. 61872340 and No. 61872371, the Open Fund from the State Key Laboratory of High Performance Computing of China (HPCL) (202001-07), an overseas grant from the State Key Laboratory of Novel Software Technology, Nanjing University, and Birkbeck BEI School Project (EFFECT).


S. Shoham and Y. Vizel (Eds.): CAV 2022, LNCS 13371, pp. 385–406, 2022.
https://doi.org/10.1007/978-3-031-13185-1_19

## 1 Introduction

Secure multi-party computation (MPC) is a powerful cryptographic paradigm, allowing mutually distrusting parties to collaboratively compute a public function over their private data without a trusted third party and revealing nothing beyond the result of the computation and their own private data [14,43]. MPC has potential for broader uses in practical applications, e.g., truthful auctions, avoiding satellite collisions [22], private machine learning [41], and data analysis [35]. However, practical deployment of MPC has been limited due to its computational and communication complexity.

To foster applications of MPC, a number of general-purpose MPC frameworks have been proposed, e.g., [9,24,29,34,37,44]. These frameworks provide high-level languages for specifying MPC applications as well as compilers for translating them into executable implementations, thus drastically reduce the burden of designing customized protocols and allow non-experts to quickly develop and deploy MPC applications. To improve performance, many MPC frameworks provide features to declare secret variables so that only these variables are to be protected. However, such frameworks usually do not verify rigorously whether there is information leakage, or, on some occasions, provide only light-weighted checking (via, e.g., information-flow analysis). Even though some frameworks are equipped with formal security guarantees, it is challenging for non-experts to develop an MPC program that simultaneously achieves good performance and formal security guarantees [3,28]. A typical case for an user is to declare all variables secret while ideally one would declare as few secret variables as possible to achieve a good performance without compromising security.

In this work, we propose an automated security policy synthesis approach for MPC. We first formalize the leakage of an MPC application in the ideal-world as a set of private inputs and define the notion of security policy, which assigns each variable a security level. This can bridge the language-level and protocol-level leakages, hence our approach is independent of the specific MPC protocols being used. Based on the leakage characterization, we provide a type system to infer security policies by tracking both control- and data-flow of information from private inputs. While a security policy inferred from the type system formally guarantees that the MPC application will not leak more information than the result of the computation and participants' own private data, it may be too conservative. For instance, some variables could be declassified without compromising security but with improved performance. Therefore, we propose a symbolic reasoning approach to identify secret variables in security policies that can be declassified without compromising security. We also feed back the results from the symbolic reasoning to type inference to refine the security type further.

We implement our approach in a new tool **PoS4MPC** (**Po**licy **S**ynthesis for **MPC**) based on the LLVM Compiler [1] and the KLEE symbolic execution engine [10]. Experimental results on five typical MPC applications show that our approach can generate less restrictive security policies than using the type system solely. We also deploy the generated security policies in two MPC frameworks Obliv-C [44] and MPyC [37]. The results show that, for instance, the security policies generated by our approach can reduce the execution time by 31%–1.56×

```
int demo(int a, int b, int c){
    int r = 1;  int max = a;
    bool c1 = max < b;
    if (c1){ max = b; r = 2;  }
    bool c2 = max < c;
    if (c2){ r = 3; }
    return r; }
```

**Fig. 1.** The richest one of three millionaires

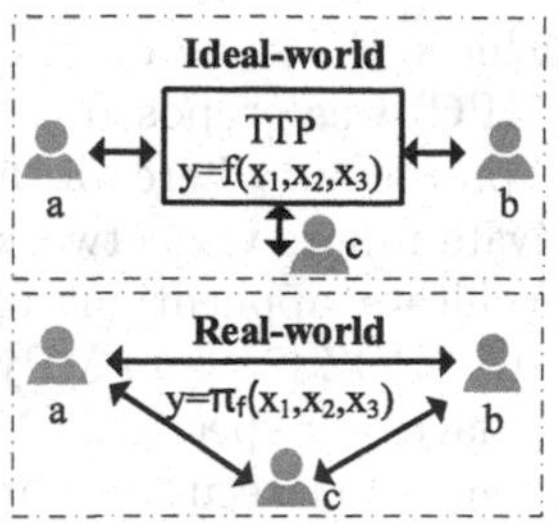


**Fig. 2.** Ideal-world vs. real-world

$10^5$%, the circuit size by 38%–3.61 × $10^5$%, and the communication traffic by 39%–4.17 × $10^5$% in Obliv-C.

To summarize, our main technical contributions are as follows.

- A formalization of information leakage for MPC applications and the notion of security policy to bridge the language-level and protocol-level leakages;
- An automated security policy synthesis approach that is able to generate less restrictive security policies;
- An implementation of our approach for a real-world language and an evaluation on challenging benchmarks from the literature.

**Outline.** Section 2 presents the motivation of this work and overview of our approach. Section 3 gives the background of MPC. Section 4 introduces a simple language on which we formalize the leakage of MPC applications. We propose a type system for inferring security policies in Sect. 5 and a symbolic reasoning approach for declassification in Sect. 6. Implementation details and experimental results are given in Sect. 7. Finally, we discuss related work in Sect. 8 and conclude this paper in Sect. 9.

Missing proofs can be found in the full version of this paper [15].

## 2 Motivation

Figure 1 shows a motivating example that computes the richest among three millionaires. To preserve the privacy, the millionaires can privately send their inputs to a trusted third party (TTP) as shown in Fig. 2 (ideal-world). This reveals the richest millionaire with the least leakage of information. Table 1 shows the leakage for each result $\texttt{r} = 1, 2, 3$, as well as the leakage if the secret branching variables `c1` and `c2` are declassified (i.e., from secret to public).

**Table 1.** Leakage from each result and declassified secret branching variables

| Result | Leakage of Result | Leakage of c1 | Leakage of c2 |
|---|---|---|---|
| $\texttt{r} = 1$ | $\texttt{a} \geq \texttt{b} \land \texttt{a} \geq \texttt{c}$ | $\texttt{a} \geq \texttt{b}$ | $\texttt{a} \geq \texttt{c}$ |
| $\texttt{r} = 2$ | $\texttt{a} < \texttt{b} \land \texttt{b} \geq \texttt{c}$ | $\texttt{a} < \texttt{b}$ | $\texttt{b} \geq \texttt{c}$ |
| $\texttt{r} = 3$ | $\texttt{c} > \max(\texttt{a}, \texttt{b})$ | $\texttt{a} \geq \texttt{b} \lor \texttt{a} < \texttt{b}$ | $\texttt{c} > \max(\texttt{a}, \texttt{b})$ |

To achieve the same functionality without TTP, secure multi-party computation (MPC) was proposed [14,43]. One can implement the computation using an MPC protocol $\pi$ where all the parties collaboratively compute the result over their private inputs via network communications (shown in Fig. 2 (real-world)).

To facilitate applications of MPC, various MPC frameworks, e.g., Obliv-C [44], MP-SPDZ [24] and MPyC [37], have been proposed, which provide high-level languages for specifying MPC applications, as well as compilers for translating them into executable implementations. To improve performance, these frameworks often allow users to declare secret variables so that only the values of secret variables are to be protected. However, in practice, it is usually quite challenging for non-experts to specify secret variables properly: declaring too many secret variables would degrade the performance, whereas declaring too less secret variables risks compromising security and privacy.

In this work, we propose an automated synthesis approach, aiming to declare as few secret variables as possible but without compromising security. To capture privacy, we formalize the leakage of MPC applications in the ideal-world as a set of private inputs. For instance, the leakage of the result $\mathtt{r} = 1$ in the motivating example is the set of inputs such that $\mathtt{a} \geq \mathtt{b} \wedge \mathtt{a} \geq \mathtt{c}$. We introduce the notion of security policy, which assigns each variable a security level, to bridge the language-level and protocol-level leakages, so that our approach is independent of specific MPC protocols being used. The language-level leakage of a security policy is characterized by a set of private inputs with respect to not only the result but also the values of public variables in the intermediate computations.

Based on the leakage characterization, we propose a type system to automatically infer security policies, inspired by the work of proving noninterference of programs [40]. Our type system tracks both control-flow and data-flow of information from the private inputs, and infers a security policy. For instance, all the variables in the motivating example are inferred as secret.

Although a security policy inferred by the type system formally guarantees that the MPC application will not leak more information than that in the ideal-world, it may be too conservative. For instance, declassifying the variable c2 in the example would not compromise security. As shown in Table 1, the leakage caused by declassifying c2 can be deduced from the leakage of the result. In contrast, we cannot declassify c1, as neither $\mathtt{a} \geq \mathtt{b}$ nor $\mathtt{a} < \mathtt{b}$ can be deduced from the leakage $\mathtt{c} > \max(\mathtt{a}, \mathtt{b})$. Once c1 is declassified, the adversary would learn if $\mathtt{a} \geq \mathtt{b}$ or $\mathtt{a} < \mathtt{b}$. This problem is akin to downgrading and declassification of high security levels in information-flow analysis [27], and could be solved via self-composition [39,42] that often require users to write annotations for procedure contracts and loop invariants. In this work, for the sake of efficiency and usability for non-experts, we propose an alternative approach based on symbolic execution. We leverage symbolic execution to finitely represent a potentially infinite set of concrete executions, and propose an automated approach to infer if a secret variable can be declassified by reasoning about pairs of symbolic executions. For instance, in Example 1, our approach is able to identify that c2 can be declassified without compromising security. In general, the experimental results show that our approach is effective and the generated security policies can significantly improve the performance of MPC applications.

## 3 Secure MPC

Fix a set of variables $\mathcal{X}$ over a domain $\mathcal{D}$. We write $\overline{\mathbf{x}}_n \in \mathcal{X}^n$ and $\overline{\mathbf{v}}_n \in \mathcal{D}^n$ for tuples $(x_1, \cdots, x_n)$ and $(v_1, \cdots, v_n)$ respectively. (The subscript $n$ may be dropped when it is clear from the context.)

**MPC in the Ideal-World.** An $n$-party MPC application $f : \mathcal{D}^n \to \mathcal{D}$ is to confidentially compute a given function $f(\overline{\mathbf{x}})$, where each party $\mathsf{P}_\mathsf{i}$ for $1 \leq i \leq n$ sends her private input $v_i \in \mathcal{D}$ to a TTP $\mathsf{T}$ which computes and returns the result $f(\overline{\mathbf{v}})$ to all the parties. In the ideal world, an adversary that controls any of the $n$ parties learns no more than the output $f(\overline{\mathbf{v}})$ and the private inputs of the corrupted (dishonest) parties.

We characterize the leakage of an MPC application $f(\overline{\mathbf{x}})$ by a set of private inputs. Hereafter, we assume, w.l.o.g., the first $k$ parties (i.e., $\mathsf{P}_1, \cdots, \mathsf{P}_\mathsf{k}$) are corrupted by the adversary for some $k \geq 1$. For a given output $v \in \mathcal{D}$, let $\simeq_v^f \subseteq \mathcal{D}^n$ be the set $\{\overline{\mathbf{v}} \in \mathcal{D}^n \mid f(\overline{\mathbf{v}}) = v\}$. Intuitively, $\simeq_v^f$ is the set of the private inputs $\overline{\mathbf{v}} \in \mathcal{D}^n$ under which $f$ is evaluated to $v$. From the result $v$, the adversary is able to learn the set $\simeq_v^f$, but cannot tell which one from $\simeq_v^f$ given $v$. We refer to $\simeq_v^f$ as the indistinguishable space of the private inputs w.r.t. the result $v$. The input domain $\mathcal{D}^n$ is then partitioned into indistinguishable spaces $\{\simeq_v^f\}_{v \in \mathcal{D}}$.

When the adversary controls the parties $\mathsf{P}_1, \cdots, \mathsf{P}_\mathsf{k}$, she will learn the set $\mathsf{Leak}_{\mathtt{iw}}^f(v, \overline{\mathbf{v}}_k) := \{(v_1, \cdots, v_n) \in \mathcal{D}^n \mid \overline{\mathbf{v}}_k = v_1, \cdots, v_k\} \cap \simeq_v^f$, from the result $v$ and the adversary-chosen private inputs $\overline{\mathbf{v}}_k \in \mathcal{D}^k$.

**Definition 1 (Leakage in the ideal-world).** *For an MPC application $f(\overline{\mathbf{x}}_n)$, the leakage of computing $v = f(\overline{\mathbf{v}}_n)$ in the ideal-world is $\mathsf{Leak}_{\mathtt{iw}}^f(v, \overline{\mathbf{v}}_k)$, for the adversary-chosen private inputs $\overline{\mathbf{v}}_k \in \mathcal{D}^k$ and the result $v \in \mathcal{D}$.*

**MPC in the Real-World.** An MPC application in the real-world is implemented using some MPC protocol $\pi$ (denoted by $\pi_f$) by which all the parties collaboratively compute $\pi_f(\overline{\mathbf{x}})$ over their private inputs $\overline{\mathbf{v}}$ without any TTP $\mathsf{T}$. Introduction of MPC protocols can be found in [14].

There are generally two types of adversaries in the real world, i.e., semi-honest and malicious. An adversary is semi-honest (a.k.a. passive) if the corrupted parties run the protocol honestly as specified, but may try to learn private information of other parties by observing the protocol execution (i.e., network messages and program states). An adversary is malicious (a.k.a. active) if the corrupted parties can deviate arbitrarily from the prescribed protocol (e.g., control, manipulate, and inject messages) in an attempt to learn private information of the other parties. In this work, we consider semi-honest adversaries, which are supported by most MPC frameworks and often serve as a basis for MPC in more robust settings with powerful adversaries.

A protocol $\pi$ is (semi-honest) secure if what a (semi-honest) adversary can achieve in the real-world can also be achieved by a corresponding adversary in the ideal-world. Semi-honest security ensures that the corrupted parties learn no more information from executing the protocol than what they can learn from the result and the private inputs of the corrupted parties. Therefore, the leakage of an MPC application $f(\overline{\mathbf{x}})$ in the real-world against the semi-honest adversary can also be characterized using the indistinguishability of private inputs.

**Definition 2.** *An MPC protocol $\pi$ is (semi-honest) secure if for any MPC application $f(\overline{\mathbf{x}}_n)$, adversary-chosen private inputs $\overline{\mathbf{v}}_k \in \mathcal{D}^k$ and result $v \in \mathcal{D}$, the leakage of computing $v = \pi_f(\overline{\mathbf{v}}_n)$ is $\mathsf{Leak}^f_{\mathtt{iw}}(v, \overline{\mathbf{v}}_k)$.*

## 4 Language-Level Leakage Characterization

In this section, we characterize the leakage of MPC applications from the language perspective.

### 4.1 A Language for MPC

We consider a simple language WHILE for implementing MPC applications. The syntax of WHILE programs is defined as follows.

$$\begin{aligned} p ::= & \mathsf{skip} \mid x = e \mid \ p_1; p_2 \mid \mathsf{if}\ x\ \mathsf{then}\ p_1\ \mathsf{else}\ p_2 \mid \mathsf{return}\ x \\ & \mid \mathsf{while}\ x\ \mathsf{do}\ p \mid \mathsf{repeat}\ n\ \mathsf{do}\ p \end{aligned}$$

where $e$ is an expression defined as usual and $n$ is a positive integer.

Despite its simplicity, WHILE suffices to illustrate our approach and our tool supports a real-world language. Note that we introduce two loop constructs. The while loop can only be used with the secret-independent conditions while the repeat loop (with a fixed number $n$ of iterations) can have secret-dependent conditions. The restriction of the while loop is necessary, as the adversary knows when to terminate the loop, so secret information may be leaked if a secret-dependent condition is used [44].

The operational semantics of the WHILE program is defined in a standard way (cf. [15]). In particular, $\mathsf{repeat}\ n\ \mathsf{do}\ p$ means repeating the loop body $p$ for a fixed number $n$ times. A configuration is a tuple $\langle p, \sigma \rangle$, where $p$ denotes a statement and $\sigma : \mathcal{X} \to \mathcal{D}$ denotes a state that maps variables to values. The evaluation of an expression $e$ under a state $\sigma$ is denoted by $\sigma(e)$. A transition from $\langle p, \sigma \rangle$ to $\langle p', \sigma' \rangle$ is denoted by $\langle p, \sigma \rangle \to \langle p', \sigma' \rangle$ and $\to^*$ denotes the transitive closure of $\to$. An execution starting from the configuration $\langle p, \sigma \rangle$ is a sequence of configurations. We write $\langle p, \sigma \rangle \Downarrow \sigma'$ if $\langle p, \sigma \rangle \to^* \langle \mathsf{skip}, \sigma' \rangle$. We assume that each execution ends in a return statement, i.e., all the while loops always terminate. We denote by $\langle p, \sigma \rangle \Downarrow \sigma' : v$ the execution returning value $v$.

### 4.2 Leakage Characterization in Ideal/Real-World

An MPC application $f(\overline{\mathbf{x}})$ is implemented as a WHILE program $p$. An execution of the program $p$ evaluates the computation $f(\overline{\mathbf{x}})$ as if a TTP directly executed the program $p$ on the private inputs. In this setting, the adversary cannot observe any intermediate states of the execution other than the final result.

Let $\mathcal{X}^{\mathtt{in}} = \{x_1, \cdots, x_n\} \subseteq \mathcal{X}$ be the set of private input variables. We denote by $\mathsf{State}_0$ the set of the initial states. Given a tuple of values $\overline{\mathbf{v}}_k \in \mathcal{D}^k$ and a result $v \in \mathcal{D}$, let $\mathsf{Leak}^p_{\mathtt{iw}}(v, \overline{\mathbf{v}}_k)$ denote the set of states $\sigma \in \mathsf{State}_0$ such that $\langle p, \sigma \rangle \Downarrow \sigma' : v$ for some state $\sigma'$ and $\sigma(x_i) = v_i$ for $1 \leq i \leq k$. Intuitively, when the adversary controls the parties $\mathsf{P}_1, \cdots, \mathsf{P}_\mathsf{k}$, she learns the set of states $\mathsf{Leak}^p_{\mathtt{iw}}(v, \overline{\mathbf{v}}_k)$ from the result $v$ and the adversary-chosen private inputs $\overline{\mathbf{v}}_k \in \mathcal{D}^k$. We can reformulate the leakage of an MPC application $f(\overline{\mathbf{x}})$ in the ideal-world (cf. Definition 1) as follows.

**Proposition 1.** *Given an MPC application $f(\overline{\mathbf{x}}_n)$ implemented by a program $p$, $\overline{\mathbf{v}}'_n \in \mathsf{Leak}^f_{\mathtt{iw}}(v, \overline{\mathbf{v}}_k)$ iff there exists a state $\sigma \in \mathsf{Leak}^p_{\mathtt{iw}}(v, \overline{\mathbf{v}}_k)$ such that $\sigma(x_i) = v'_i$ for $1 \leq i \leq n$.*

We use security policies to characterize the leakage of MPC applications in the real-world.

**Security Level.** We consider a lattice of security levels $\mathbb{L} = \{\mathsf{Sec}, \mathsf{Pub}\}$ with $\mathsf{Pub} \sqsubseteq \mathsf{Pub}$, $\mathsf{Pub} \sqsubseteq \mathsf{Sec}$, $\mathsf{Sec} \sqsubseteq \mathsf{Sec}$ and $\mathsf{Sec} \not\sqsubseteq \mathsf{Pub}$. We denote by $\ell_1 \sqcup \ell_2$ the least upper bound of two security levels $\ell_1, \ell_2 \in \mathbb{L}$, namely, $\ell \sqcup \mathsf{Sec} = \mathsf{Sec} \sqcup \ell = \mathsf{Sec}$ for $\ell \in \mathbb{L}$ and $\mathsf{Pub} \sqcup \mathsf{Pub} = \mathsf{Pub}$.

**Definition 3.** *A security policy $\varrho : \mathcal{X} \to \mathbb{L}$ for the MPC application $f(\overline{\mathbf{x}})$ is a function that associates each variable $x \in \mathcal{X}$ with a security level $\ell \in \mathbb{L}$.*

Given a security policy $\varrho$ and a security level $\ell \in \mathbb{L}$, let $\mathcal{X}^\ell := \{x \mid \varrho(x) = \ell\} \subseteq \mathcal{X}$, i.e., the set of variables with the security level $\ell$ under $\varrho$. We lift the order $\sqsubseteq$ to security policies, namely, $\varrho \sqsubseteq \varrho'$ if $\varrho(x) \sqsubseteq \varrho'(x)$ for each $x \in \mathcal{X}$. When executing the program $p$ with a security policy $\varrho$ using an MPC protocol $\pi$, we assume that the adversary can observe the values of the public variables $x \in \mathcal{X}^{\mathsf{Pub}}$, but not that of the secret variables $x \in \mathcal{X}^{\mathsf{Sec}}$.

This is a practical assumption and can be well-supported by the existing approach. For instance, Obliv-C [44] allows developers to define an MPC application in an extension of C language, when compiled and linked, the result will be a concrete garbled circuit protocol $\pi_p$ whose computation does not reveal the values of any oblivious-qualified variables. Thus, all the secret variables specified by the security policy $\varrho$ can be declared as oblivious-qualified variables in Obliv-C, while all the public variables specified by the security policy $\varrho$ are declared without oblivious-qualification. Similarly, MPyC [37] is a Python package for implementing MPC applications that allows programmers to define instances of secret-typed variable classes using Python's class mechanism. When executing MPC applications, instances of secret-typed class variables are protected via Shamir's secret sharing protocol [38]. Thus, all the secret variables specified by the security policy $\varrho$ can be declared as instances of secret-typed variable classes in MPyC, while all the public variables specified by the security policy $\varrho$ are declared as instances of Python's standard classes.

**Leakage Under a Security Policy.** Fix a security policy $\varrho$ for the program $p$. Remark that the values of the secret variables will not be known even at runtime for each party, as they are encrypted. This means that, unlike the secret-independent conditions, the secret-dependent conditions cannot be executed normally, and thus should be removed using, e.g., multiplexers, before transforming into circuits. We define the transformation $\mathcal{T}_\varrho(\cdot,\cdot)$, where $c$ is the selector of a multiplexer.

$$\mathcal{T}_\varrho(c, p_1; p_2) \triangleq \mathcal{T}_\varrho(c, p_1); \mathcal{T}_\varrho(c, p_2) \qquad \mathcal{T}_\varrho(c, \mathsf{return}\ x) \triangleq \mathsf{return}\ x$$

$$\mathcal{T}_\varrho(c, x = e) \triangleq x = x + c \times (e - x) \qquad \mathcal{T}_\varrho(c, \mathsf{skip}) \triangleq \mathsf{skip}$$

$$\mathcal{T}_\varrho(c, \mathsf{if}\ x\ \mathsf{then}\ p_1\ \mathsf{else}\ p_2) \triangleq \begin{cases} \mathsf{if}\ x\ \mathsf{then}\ \mathcal{T}_\varrho(1, p_1)\ \mathsf{else}\ \mathcal{T}_\varrho(1, p_2), & \text{if } c = 1 \wedge \varrho(x) = \mathtt{Pub}; \\ \mathcal{T}_\varrho(c\&x, p_1); \mathcal{T}_\varrho(c\&\neg x, p_2), & \text{otherwise.} \end{cases}$$

$$\mathcal{T}_\varrho(c, \mathsf{while}\ x\ \mathsf{do}\ p) \triangleq \begin{cases} \mathsf{while}\ x\ \mathsf{do}\ \mathcal{T}_\varrho(1, p), & \text{if } c = 1 \wedge \varrho(x) = \mathtt{Pub}; \\ \mathtt{Error}, & \text{otherwise.} \end{cases}$$

$$\mathcal{T}_\varrho(c, \mathsf{repeat}\ n\ \mathsf{do}\ p) \triangleq \mathsf{repeat}\ n\ \mathsf{do}\ \mathcal{T}_\varrho(c, p)$$

Intuitively, $c$ in $\mathcal{T}_\varrho(c,\cdot)$ indicates whether the statement is under some secret-dependent branching statements. Initially, $c = 1$. During the transformation, $c$ will be conjuncted with the branching condition $x$ or $\neg x$ when transforming $\mathsf{if}\ x\ \mathsf{then}\ p_1\ \mathsf{else}\ p_2$ if $x$ is secret or $c \neq 1$. The control flow inside should be protected if $c \neq 1$. If $c = 1$ and the condition variable $x$ is public, the statement needs not be protected. $\mathcal{T}(c, x = e)$ simulates a multiplexer with two different values depending on whether the assignment $x = e$ is in the scope of some secret-dependent conditions. At runtime, the value $e$ is assigned to $x$ if $c$ is 1, otherwise $x$ does not change. $\mathcal{T}_\varrho(c, \mathsf{while}\ x\ \mathsf{do}\ p)$ enforces that the $\mathsf{while}$ loop is used in secret-independent conditions and $x$ is public in the security policy $\varrho$ otherwise throws an error. The other cases are trivial. We denote by $\widehat{p}_\varrho$ the program $\mathcal{T}_\varrho(1, p)$ on which we will define the leakage of $p$ in the real-world.

For every state $\sigma : \mathcal{X} \to \mathcal{D}$, let $\sigma^{\text{Pub}} : \mathcal{X}^{\text{Pub}} \to \mathcal{D}$ denote the state that is the projection of the state $\sigma$ onto the public variables $\mathcal{X}^{\text{Pub}}$. For each execution $\langle \widehat{p}_\varrho, \sigma_1\rangle \Downarrow \sigma_2$, we denote by $\langle \widehat{p}_\varrho, \sigma_1\rangle \Downarrow_\varrho^{\text{Pub}} \sigma_2$ the sequence of configurations where each state $\sigma$ is replaced by the state $\sigma^{\text{Pub}}$.

Recall that the adversary can observe the values of public variables $x \in \mathcal{X}^{\text{Pub}}$ when executing the program $\widehat{p}_\varrho$. Thus, from an execution $\langle \widehat{p}_\varrho, \sigma_1\rangle \Downarrow \sigma_2 : v$, she can observe the sequence $\langle \widehat{p}_\varrho, \sigma_1\rangle \Downarrow_\varrho^{\text{Pub}} \sigma_2$ and the result $v$, written as $\langle \widehat{p}_\varrho, \sigma_1\rangle \Downarrow_\varrho^{\text{Pub}} \sigma_2 : v$. For every state $\sigma \in \mathsf{Leak}_{\mathtt{iw}}^{p}(v, \overline{\mathbf{v}}_k)$, we denote by $\mathsf{Leak}_{\mathtt{rw}}^{p,\varrho}(v, \sigma)$ the set of states $\sigma' \in \mathsf{Leak}_{\mathtt{iw}}^{p}(v, \overline{\mathbf{v}}_k)$ such that $\langle \widehat{p}_\varrho, \sigma'\rangle \Downarrow_\varrho^{\text{Pub}} \sigma_1' : v$ and $\langle \widehat{p}_\varrho, \sigma\rangle \Downarrow_\varrho^{\text{Pub}} \sigma_1 : v$ are identical.

**Definition 4.** *A security policy $\varrho$ is <u>perfect</u> for a given MPC application $f(\overline{\mathbf{x}}_n)$ implemented by the program p, denoted by $\varrho \models_p f(\overline{\mathbf{x}}_n)$, if $\mathcal{T}_\varrho(1, p)$ does not throw any errors, and for adversary-chosen private inputs $\overline{\mathbf{v}}_k \in \mathcal{D}^k$, the result $v \in \mathcal{D}$, and the state $\sigma \in \mathsf{Leak}_{\mathtt{iw}}^{p}(v, \overline{\mathbf{v}}_k)$, we have that*

$$\mathsf{Leak}_{\mathtt{iw}}^{p}(v, \overline{\mathbf{v}}_k) = \mathsf{Leak}_{rw}^{p,\varrho}(v, \sigma).$$

Intuitively, a perfect security policy $\varrho$ ensures that for every state $\sigma \in \mathsf{Leak}_{\mathtt{iw}}^{p}(v, \overline{\mathbf{v}}_k)$, from the observation $\langle \widehat{p}_\varrho, \sigma\rangle \Downarrow_\varrho^{\text{Pub}} \sigma' : v$, the adversary only learns the same set $\mathsf{Leak}_{\mathtt{iw}}^{p}(v, \overline{\mathbf{v}}_k)$ of initial states as that in the ideal-world.

Our goal is to compute a perfect security policy $\varrho$ for every program $p$ that implements the MPC $f(\overline{\mathbf{x}})$. A naive way is to assign the high security level Sec to all the variables $\mathcal{X}$, which may however suffer from a lower performance, as all the intermediate computations have to be performed on encrypted data and conditional statements have to removed. Ideally, a security policy $\varrho$ should not only be perfect but also annotate as few secret variables as possible.

## 5 Type System

In this section, we present a sound type system to automatically infer perfect security policies. We first define noninterference of a program $p$ w.r.t. a security policy $\varrho$, which is shown to entail the perfectness of $\varrho$.

**Definition 5.** *A program $p$ is noninterfering w.r.t. a security policy $\varrho$, written as $\varrho$-noninterfering, if $\mathcal{T}_\varrho(1,p)$ does not throw any errors and $\langle \widehat{p}_\varrho, \sigma_1\rangle \Downarrow_\varrho^{\text{Pub}} \sigma_2 : v$ and $\langle \widehat{p}_\varrho, \sigma_1'\rangle \Downarrow_\varrho^{\text{Pub}} \sigma_2' : v'$ are the same for each pair of states $\sigma_1, \sigma_1' \in \mathsf{State}_0$.*

Intuitively, the $\varrho$-noninterference ensures that for all private inputs of the $n$ parties (without the adversary-chosen private inputs), the adversary observes the same sequence of the configurations from all the executions that return the same value.

The $\varrho$-noninterference of $p$ entails the perfectness of $\varrho$ where the adversary can choose arbitrary private inputs $\overline{\mathbf{v}}_k \in \mathcal{D}^k$ of the corrupted participants $(\mathsf{P}_1, \cdots, \mathsf{P}_\mathsf{k})$ for any $k \geq 1$.

**Proposition 2.** *If $p$ is $\varrho$-noninterfering for a security policy $\varrho$, then $\varrho \models_p f(\overline{\mathbf{x}})$.*

Note that the converse of Proposition 2 does not necessarily hold due to the adversary-chosen private inputs. For instance, suppose $\langle \widehat{p}_\varrho, \sigma_1\rangle \Downarrow_\varrho^{\text{Pub}} \sigma_2 : v$ and $\langle \widehat{p}_\varrho, \sigma_1'\rangle \Downarrow_\varrho^{\text{Pub}} \sigma_2' : v$ are identical for every pair of states $\sigma_1, \sigma_1' \in \mathsf{Leak}_{\mathtt{iw}}^p(v, v_1)$, and $\langle \widehat{p}_\varrho, \sigma_3\rangle \Downarrow_\varrho^{\text{Pub}} \sigma_4 : v$ and $\langle \widehat{p}_\varrho, \sigma_3'\rangle \Downarrow_\varrho^{\text{Pub}} \sigma_4' : v$ are identical for every pair of states $\sigma_3, \sigma_3' \in \mathsf{Leak}_{\mathtt{iw}}^p(v, v_1')$. If $v_1 \neq v_1'$, then $\langle \widehat{p}_\varrho, \sigma_1\rangle \Downarrow_\varrho^{\text{Pub}} \sigma_2 : v$ and $\langle \widehat{p}_\varrho, \sigma_3\rangle \Downarrow_\varrho^{\text{Pub}} \sigma_4 : v$ are different, implying that $p$ is not $\varrho$-noninterfering.

Based on Proposition 2, we present a type system for inferring a perfect security policy $\varrho$ of a given program $p$ such that $p$ is $\varrho$-noninterfering. The typing judgement is in the form of $\mathsf{c} \vdash p : \varrho \Rightarrow \varrho'$, where the type contexts $\varrho, \varrho'$ are security policies, $p$ is the program under typing, and $\mathsf{c}$ is the security level of the current control flow. The typing judgement $\mathsf{c} \vdash p : \varrho \Rightarrow \varrho'$ states that given the security level of the current control flow $\mathsf{c}$ and the type context $\varrho$, the statement $p$ is typable and yields a new updated type context $\varrho'$.

The type inference rules are shown in Fig. 3 which track the security levels of both data- and control-flow of information from private inputs, where $\varrho(e)$ denotes the least upper bound of the security levels $\varrho(x)$ of variables $x$ used in the expression $e$ and $\varrho_1 \sqcup \varrho_2$ is the security policy such that for every variable $x \in \mathcal{X}$, $(\varrho_1 \sqcup \varrho_2)(x) = \varrho_1(x) \sqcup \varrho_2(x)$. $\mathtt{lfp}(\mathsf{c}, n, \varrho, p)$ is $\varrho$ if $n = 0$ or $\varrho' = \varrho$, otherwise $\mathtt{lfp}(\mathsf{c}, n-1, \varrho', p)$, where $\mathsf{c} \vdash p : \varrho \Rightarrow \varrho'$. Note that constants have the security level Pub. Most of those rules are standard.

$$\frac{}{\mathsf{c} \vdash \mathsf{skip} : \varrho \Rightarrow \varrho}[\text{T-SKIP}] \qquad \frac{\varrho' = \varrho[x \mapsto \mathsf{c} \sqcup \varrho(e)]}{\mathsf{c} \vdash x = e : \varrho \Rightarrow \varrho'}[\text{T-ASSIGN}]$$

$$\frac{\mathsf{c} \vdash p_1 : \varrho \Rightarrow \varrho_1 \quad \mathsf{c} \vdash p_2 : \varrho_1 \Rightarrow \varrho_2}{\mathsf{c} \vdash p_1; p_2 : \varrho \Rightarrow \varrho_2}[\text{T-SEQ}] \qquad \frac{\mathsf{c} \sqcup \varrho(x) \vdash p_1 : \varrho \Rightarrow \varrho_1 \quad \mathsf{c} \sqcup \varrho(x) \vdash p_2 : \varrho \Rightarrow \varrho_2 \quad \varrho' = \varrho_1 \sqcup \varrho_2}{\mathsf{c} \vdash \mathsf{if}\ x\ \mathsf{then}\ p_1\ \mathsf{else}\ p_2 : \varrho \Rightarrow \varrho'}[\text{T-IF}]$$

$$\frac{}{\mathsf{c} \vdash \mathsf{return}\ x : \varrho \Rightarrow \varrho}[\text{T-RETURN}] \qquad \frac{\varrho' = \mathbf{lfp}(\mathsf{c}, n, \varrho, p)}{\mathsf{c} \vdash \mathsf{repeat}\ n\ \mathsf{do}\ p : \varrho \Rightarrow \varrho'}[\text{T-REPEAT}]$$

$$\frac{\varrho(x) = \mathsf{Pub} \quad \mathsf{c} = \mathsf{Pub} \quad \varrho' = \mathbf{lfp}(\mathsf{Pub}, -1, \varrho, p)}{\mathsf{c} \vdash \mathsf{while}\ x\ \mathsf{do}\ p : \varrho \Rightarrow \varrho'}[\text{T-WHILE}]$$

**Fig. 3.** Type inference rules

Rule T-ASSIGN disables the data-flow and control-flow of information from the security level $\mathsf{Sec}$ to the security level $\mathsf{Pub}$. To meet this constraint, the security level of the variable $x$ is updated to the least upper bound $\mathsf{c} \sqcup \varrho(e)$ of the security levels of the current control flow $\mathsf{c}$ and variables used in the expression $e$. Rule T-IF passes the security level $\mathsf{c}$ of the current control flow into both branches, preventing from assigning values to public variables in those two branches when $c = \mathsf{Sec}$. Rule T-WHILE requires that the loop condition is public and the loop is used with secret-independent conditions, ensuring that $\mathcal{T}_\varrho(1, p)$ does not throw any errors. Rule T-RETURN does not impose any constraints on $x$, as the return value is observable to the adversary.

Let $\varrho_0 : \mathcal{X} \to \mathbb{L}$ be the mapping such that $\varrho_0(x) = \mathsf{Sec}$ for all $x \in \mathcal{X}^{\mathsf{Sec}}$, $\varrho_0(x) = \mathsf{Pub}$ otherwise. If the typing judgement $\mathsf{Pub} \vdash p : \varrho_0 \Rightarrow \varrho$ is valid, then the values of all the public variables specified by $\varrho$ do not depend on any values of private inputs. Thus, it is straightforward to get that:

**Proposition 3.** *If the typing judgement* $\mathsf{Pub} \vdash p : \varrho_0 \Rightarrow \varrho$ *is valid, then the program* $p$ *is* $\varrho$*-noninterfering.*

From Proposition 2 and Theorem 3, we have

**Corollary 1.** *If* $\mathsf{Pub} \vdash p : \varrho_0 \Rightarrow \varrho$ *is valid, then* $\varrho$ *is perfect, i.e.,* $\varrho \models_p f(\overline{\mathbf{x}})$.

## 6 Degrading Security Levels

The type system allows to infer a security policy $\varrho$ such that the type judgement $\mathsf{Pub} \vdash p : \varrho_0 \Rightarrow \varrho$ is valid, from which we can deduce that $\varrho \models_p f(\overline{\mathbf{x}})$, i.e., $\varrho$ is perfect for the MPC application $f(\overline{\mathbf{x}})$ implemented by the program $p$. However, the security policy $\varrho$ may be too conservative, i.e., some secret variables specified by $\varrho$ can be declassified without compromising the security. In this section, we propose an automated approach to identify these variables. We mainly consider minimizing the number of secret branching variables, viz., the secret variables used in branching conditions, as they usually incur a high computation and communication overhead. W.l.o.g., we assume that for each secret branching variable $x$ there is only one assignment to $x$ and it is used only in one conditional

$$\frac{}{\lceil x = e, \alpha, \phi \rfloor \hookrightarrow \lceil \mathsf{skip}, \alpha[x \mapsto \alpha(e), \phi] \rfloor} \qquad \frac{}{\lceil \mathsf{return}\ x, \alpha, \phi \rfloor \hookrightarrow \lceil \mathsf{skip}, \alpha, \phi \rfloor}$$

$$\frac{\lceil p_1, \alpha_1, \phi_1 \rfloor \hookrightarrow \lceil \mathsf{skip}, \alpha_2, \phi_2 \rfloor \quad \lceil p_2, \alpha_2, \phi_2 \rfloor \hookrightarrow \lceil p_2', \alpha_3, \phi_3 \rfloor}{\lceil p_1; p_2, \alpha_1, \phi_1 \rfloor \hookrightarrow \lceil p_2', \alpha_3, \phi_3 \rfloor} \qquad \frac{\lceil p_1, \alpha_1, \phi_1 \rfloor \hookrightarrow \lceil p_1', \alpha_2, \phi_2 \rfloor \quad p_1' \neq \mathsf{skip}}{\lceil p_1; p_2, \alpha_1, \phi_1 \rfloor \hookrightarrow \lceil p_1'; p_2, \alpha_2, \phi_2 \rfloor}$$

$$\frac{\mathsf{SAT}(\phi') \quad \phi' = \phi \wedge \alpha(x)}{\lceil \mathsf{if}\ x\ \mathsf{then}\ p_1\ \mathsf{else}\ p_2, \alpha, \phi \rfloor \hookrightarrow \lceil p_1, \alpha, \phi' \rfloor} \qquad \frac{\mathsf{SAT}(\phi') \quad \phi' = \phi \wedge \neg\alpha(x)}{\lceil \mathsf{if}\ x\ \mathsf{then}\ p_1\ \mathsf{else}\ p_2, \alpha, \phi \rfloor \hookrightarrow \lceil p_2, \alpha, \phi' \rfloor}$$

$$\frac{\mathsf{SAT}(\phi') \quad \phi' = \phi \wedge \alpha(x) \quad p' = p; \mathsf{while}\ x\ \mathsf{do}\ p}{\lceil \mathsf{while}\ x\ \mathsf{do}\ p, \alpha, \phi \rfloor \hookrightarrow \lceil p', \alpha, \phi' \rfloor} \qquad \frac{\mathsf{SAT}(\phi') \quad \phi' = \phi \wedge \neg\alpha(x) \quad p' = \mathsf{skip}}{\lceil \mathsf{while}\ x\ \mathsf{do}\ p, \alpha, \phi \rfloor \hookrightarrow \lceil p', \alpha, \phi' \rfloor}$$

$$\frac{p' = (n \geq 1)\ ?\ p; \mathsf{repeat}\ n-1\ \mathsf{do}\ p\ :\ \mathsf{skip}}{\lceil \mathsf{repeat}\ n\ \mathsf{do}\ p, \alpha, \phi \rfloor \hookrightarrow \lceil p', \alpha, \phi \rfloor}$$

**Fig. 4.** The symbolic semantics of WHILE programs

statement. (We can rename variables in $p$ if this assumption does not hold, where the named variables have the same security levels as their original names.) With this assumption, whether $x$ can be declassified depends only on the unique conditional statement where it occurs.

Fix a security policy $\varrho$ such that $\varrho \models_p f(\overline{\mathbf{x}})$. Suppose that if $x$ then $p_1$ else $p_2$ is not used with secret-dependent conditions. Let $\varrho'$ be the security policy $\varrho[x \mapsto \mathsf{Pub}]$. It is easy to see that $\mathcal{T}_{\varrho'}(1, p)$ does not raise any errors. Therefore, to declassify $x$, we need to ensure that $\langle \widehat{p}_{\varrho'}, \sigma' \rangle \Downarrow_{\varrho'}^{\mathtt{Pub}} \sigma_1' : v$ and $\langle \widehat{p}_{\varrho'}, \sigma \rangle \Downarrow_{\varrho'}^{\mathtt{Pub}} \sigma_1 : v$ are identical for every adversary-chosen private inputs $\overline{\mathbf{v}}_k \in \mathcal{D}^k$, result $v \in \mathcal{D}$, and states $\sigma, \sigma' \in \mathsf{Leak}_{\mathtt{iw}}^{p}(v, \overline{\mathbf{v}}_k)$. However, as the number of the initial states may be large and even infinite, it is infeasible to check all pairs of executions.

We propose to use symbolic executions to represent the potentially infinite sets of (concrete) executions. Each symbolic execution $t$ is associated with a path condition $\phi$ which denotes the set of initial states satisfying $\phi$, from each of which the execution has the same sequence of statements. Thus, the conjunction $\phi \wedge e = v$, where $e$ is the symbolic return value and $v$ is concrete value, represents the set of initial states from which the executions have the same sequence of statements and returns the same result $v$. It is not difficult to observe that checking whether $x$ in if $x$ then $p_1$ else $p_2$ can be declassified amounts to checking whether for every pair of symbolic executions $t_1$ and $t_2$ that both include if $x$ then $p_1$ else $p_2$, $x$ has the same truth value in $t_1$ and $t_2$ whenever $t_1$ and $t_2$ return the same value. This can be solved by invoking off-the-shelf SMT solvers.

### 6.1 Symbolic Semantics

Let $\mathcal{E}$ denote the set of expressions over the private input variables $\overline{\mathbf{x}}$ and constants. A path condition $\phi \in \mathcal{E}$ is a conjunction of Boolean expressions. A state $\sigma \in \mathsf{State}_0$ satisfies $\phi$, denoted by $\sigma \models \phi$, if $\phi$ evaluates to `True` under $\sigma$. A symbolic state $\alpha$ is a function $\mathcal{X} \to \mathcal{E}$ that maps variables to symbolic expressions. $\alpha(e)$ denotes the symbolic value of the expression $e$ under $\alpha$, obtained from $e$ by replacing each occurrence of variable $x$ by $\alpha(x)$. The initial symbolic state, denoted by $\alpha_0$, is the identity function over the private input variables $\overline{\mathbf{x}}$.

The symbolic semantics of WHILE programs is defined by transitions between symbolic configurations, as shown in Fig. 4, where $\mathsf{SAT}(\phi)$ is $\mathtt{True}$ iff the constraint $\phi$ is satisfiable. A symbolic configuration is a tuple $\lceil p, \alpha, \phi \rfloor$, where $p$ is a statement, $\alpha$ is a symbolic state, and $\phi$ is the path condition that should be satisfied to reach $\lceil p, \alpha, \phi \rfloor$. $\lceil p, \alpha, \phi \rfloor \hookrightarrow \lceil p', \alpha', \phi' \rfloor$ denotes a transition from $\lceil p, \alpha, \phi \rfloor$ to $\lceil p', \alpha', \phi' \rfloor$. The symbolic semantics is almost the same as the operational semantics except that (1) the path conditions are collected and checked for conditional statements and while loops, and (2) the transition may be non-deterministic if both $\phi \wedge \alpha(x)$ and $\phi \wedge \neg\alpha(x)$ are satisfiable.

We denote by $\hookrightarrow^*$ the transitive closure of $\hookrightarrow$, where its path condition is the conjunction of that of each transition. An symbolic execution starting from a symbolic configuration $\lceil p, \alpha, \phi \rfloor$ is a sequence of symbolic configurations, written as $\lceil p, \alpha, \phi \rfloor \Downarrow (\alpha', \phi')$, if $\lceil p, \alpha, \phi \rfloor \hookrightarrow^* \lceil \mathsf{skip}, \alpha', \phi' \rfloor$. Moreover, we denote by $\lceil p, \alpha, \phi \rfloor \Downarrow (\alpha', \phi') : e$ the symbolic execution $\lceil p, \alpha, \phi \rfloor \Downarrow (\alpha', \phi')$ with the symbolic return value $e$. We denote by $\mathtt{SymExe}$ the set of all the symbolic executions $\lceil p, \alpha_0, \mathtt{True} \rfloor \Downarrow (\alpha, \phi) : e$ of the program $p$. Note that $\alpha_0$ is the initial symbolic state. Recall that we assumed all the (concrete) executions always terminate, thus $\mathtt{SymExe}$ is a finite set of finite sequence of symbolic configurations.

### 6.2 Relating Symbolic Executions to Concrete Executions

A symbolic execution $t = \lceil p, \alpha_0, \mathtt{True} \rfloor \Downarrow (\alpha, \phi) : e$ represents the set of (concrete) executions starting from the states $\sigma \in \mathsf{State}_0$ such that $\sigma \models \phi$. Formally, consider $\sigma \in \mathsf{State}_0$ such that $\sigma \models \phi$, by concretizing all the symbolic values of variables $x$ in each symbolic state $\alpha'$ with concrete values $\sigma(\alpha'(x))$ and projecting out all the path conditions, the symbolic execution $t$ is the execution $\langle p, \sigma \rangle \Downarrow \sigma' : \sigma(e)$, written as $\sigma(t)$. For the execution $\langle p, \sigma \rangle \Downarrow \sigma' : v$, there are a unique symbolic execution $t$ such that $\sigma(t) = \langle p, \sigma \rangle \Downarrow \sigma' : v$ and a unique execution $\langle \widehat{p}_\varrho, \sigma \rangle \Downarrow \sigma' : v$ in the program $\widehat{p}_\varrho$. We denote by $\mathsf{RW}_{\varrho,\sigma}(t)$ the execution $\langle \widehat{p}_\varrho, \sigma \rangle \Downarrow_\varrho \sigma' : v$ and denote by $\mathsf{RW}^{\mathsf{Pub}}_{\varrho,\sigma}(t)$ the sequence $\langle \widehat{p}_\varrho, \sigma \rangle \Downarrow^{\mathsf{Pub}}_\varrho \sigma' : v$.

For every adversary-chosen private inputs $\overline{\mathbf{v}}_k \in \mathcal{D}^k$, result $v \in \mathcal{D}$, and initial state $\sigma \in \mathsf{Leak}^p_{\mathtt{iw}}(v, \overline{\mathbf{v}}_k)$, we can reformulate the set $\mathsf{Leak}^{p,\varrho}_{\mathtt{rw}}(v, \sigma)$ as follows. (Recall that $\mathsf{Leak}^{p,\varrho}_{\mathtt{rw}}(v, \sigma)$ is the set of states $\sigma' \in \mathsf{Leak}^p_{\mathtt{iw}}(v, \overline{\mathbf{v}}_k)$ such that $\langle \widehat{p}_\varrho, \sigma' \rangle \Downarrow^{\mathsf{Pub}}_\varrho \sigma'_1 : v$ and $\langle \widehat{p}_\varrho, \sigma \rangle \Downarrow^{\mathsf{Pub}}_\varrho \sigma_1 : v$ are identical.)

**Proposition 4.** *For each state $\sigma' \in \mathsf{Leak}^p_{\mathtt{iw}}(v, \overline{\mathbf{v}}_k)$, $\sigma' \in \mathsf{Leak}_{rw^p,\varrho}(v, \sigma)$ iff for every symbolic execution $t' = \lceil p, \alpha_0, \mathtt{True} \rfloor \Downarrow (\alpha', \phi') : e' \in \mathtt{SymExe}$ such that $\sigma' \models \phi' \wedge e' = v$, $\mathsf{RW}^{\mathsf{Pub}}_{\varrho,\sigma}(t)$ and $\mathsf{RW}^{\mathsf{Pub}}_{\varrho,\sigma'}(t')$ are identical, where $t$ is a symbolic execution $\lceil p, \alpha_0, \mathtt{True} \rfloor \Downarrow (\alpha, \phi) : e$ such that $\sigma \models \phi \wedge e = v$.*

Proposition 4 allows to consider only the symbolic executions $\lceil p, \alpha_0, \mathtt{True} \rfloor \Downarrow (\alpha, \phi) : e \in \mathtt{SymExe}$ such that $\sigma \models \phi \wedge e = v$ when checking if $\varrho$ is perfect or not.

### 6.3 Reasoning About Symbolic Executions

We leverage Proposition 4 to identify secret variables that can be declassified without compromising the security by reasoning about symbolic executions. For each expression $\phi \in \mathcal{E}$, $\mathsf{Primed}(\phi)$ denotes the "primed" expression $\phi$ where each private input variable $x_i$ is replaced by $x'_i$ (i.e., its primed version).

Consider two symbolic executions $t = \lceil p, \alpha_0, \mathtt{True} \rfloor \Downarrow (\alpha, \phi) : e$ and $t' = \lceil p, \alpha_0, \mathtt{True} \rfloor \Downarrow (\alpha', \phi') : e'$. Assume $\mathsf{if}\ x\ \mathsf{then}\ p'\ \mathsf{else}\ p''$ is not used with any secret-dependent conditions. Recall that we assumed $x$ is used only in $\mathsf{if}\ x\ \mathsf{then}\ p'\ \mathsf{else}\ p''$. Then, $t$ and $t'$ execute the same subsequence (say $p_1, \cdots, p_m$) of the statements that are $\mathsf{if}\ x\ \mathsf{then}\ p'\ \mathsf{else}\ p''$. Let $e_1, \cdots, e_m$ (resp. $e'_1, \cdots, e'_m$) be symbolic values of $x$ when executing $p_1, \cdots, p_m$ in the symbolic execution $t$ (resp. $t'$). Define the constraint $\Psi_x(t, t')$ as

$$\Psi_x(t, t') \triangleq (\phi \wedge \mathsf{Primed}(\phi') \wedge e = \mathsf{Primed}(e')) \Rightarrow \Big(\bigwedge_{i=1}^{m} e_i = \mathsf{Primed}(e'_i)\Big)$$

Intuitively, $\Psi_x(t, t')$ asserts that for every pair of states $\sigma, \sigma' \in \mathsf{State}_0$ if $\sigma$ (resp. $\sigma'$ ) satisfies the path condition $\phi$ (resp. $\phi'$), $\sigma(e)$ and $\sigma'(e')$ are identical, then for each $1 \leq i \leq m$, the values of $x$ are the same when executing the conditional statement $p_i$ in both $\mathsf{RW}_{\varrho,\sigma}(t)$ and $\mathsf{RW}_{\varrho,\sigma'}(t')$.

**Proposition 5.** *For each pair of states $\sigma, \sigma' \in \mathsf{Leak}^p_{\mathtt{iw}}(v, \overline{\mathbf{v}}_k)$ such that $\sigma \models \phi \wedge e = v$ and $\sigma' \models \phi' \wedge e' = v$, if $\Psi_x(t, t')$ is valid and $\mathsf{RW}^{\mathrm{Pub}}_{\varrho,\sigma}(t)$ and $\mathsf{RW}^{\mathrm{Pub}}_{\varrho,\sigma'}(t')$ are identical, then $\mathsf{RW}^{\mathrm{Pub}}_{\varrho',\sigma}(t)$ and $\mathsf{RW}^{\mathrm{Pub}}_{\varrho',\sigma'}(t')$ are identical, where $\varrho' = \varrho[x \mapsto \mathrm{Pub}]$.*

Recall that $x$ can be declassified in a perfect security policy $\varrho$ if $\varrho' = \varrho[x \mapsto \mathrm{Pub}]$ is still perfect, namely, $\langle \widehat{p}_{\varrho'}, \sigma' \rangle \Downarrow^{\mathrm{Pub}}_{\varrho'} \sigma'_1 : v$ and $\langle \widehat{p}_{\varrho'}, \sigma \rangle \Downarrow^{\mathrm{Pub}}_{\varrho'} \sigma_1 : v$ are identical for every adversary-chosen private inputs $\overline{\mathbf{v}}_k \in \mathcal{D}^k$, result $v \in \mathcal{D}$, and states $\sigma, \sigma' \in \mathsf{Leak}^p_{\mathtt{iw}}(v, \overline{\mathbf{v}}_k)$. By Proposition 5, if $\Psi_x(t, t')$ is valid for each pair of symbolic executions $t, t' \in \mathtt{SymExe}$, we can deduce that $\varrho'$ is still perfect.

**Theorem 1.** *If $\varrho \models_p f(\overline{\mathbf{x}})$ and $\Psi_x(t, t')$ is valid for each pair of symbolic executions $t, t' \in \mathtt{SymExe}$, then $\varrho[x \mapsto \mathrm{Pub}] \models_p f(\overline{\mathbf{x}})$.*

*Example 1.* Consider two symbolic executions $t$ and $t'$ in the motivating example such that the path condition $\phi$ (resp. $\phi'$) of $t$ (resp. $t'$) is $\mathtt{a} \geq \mathtt{b} \wedge \mathtt{c} > \mathtt{a}$ (resp. $\mathtt{a} < \mathtt{b} \wedge \mathtt{c} > \mathtt{b}$), and both return the result 3. The secret branching variable c2 has the symbolic values $\mathtt{c} > \mathtt{a}$ (resp. $\mathtt{c} > \mathtt{b}$) in $t$ and $t'$, respectively. Then

$$\Psi_{\mathtt{c2}}(t, t') \triangleq (\mathtt{a} \geq \mathtt{b} \wedge \mathtt{c} > \mathtt{a} \wedge \mathtt{a}' < \mathtt{b}' \wedge \mathtt{c}' > \mathtt{b}' \wedge 3 = 3) \Rightarrow ((\mathtt{c} > \mathtt{a}) = (\mathtt{c}' > \mathtt{b}')).$$

Obviously, $\Psi_{\mathtt{c2}}(t, t')$ is valid. We can show that for any other pair $(t, t')$ of symbolic executions, $\Psi_{\mathtt{c2}}(t, t')$ is always valid. Therefore, the secret branching variable c2 can be declassified in any perfect security policy $\varrho$.

In contrast, the secret branching variable c1 has the symbolic value $\mathtt{a} < \mathtt{b}$ in both $t$ and $t'$. Then,

$$\Psi_{\mathtt{c1}}(t, t') \triangleq (\mathtt{a} \geq \mathtt{b} \wedge \mathtt{c} > \mathtt{a} \wedge \mathtt{a}' < \mathtt{b}' \wedge \mathtt{c}' > \mathtt{b}' \wedge 3 = 3) \Rightarrow ((\mathtt{a} < \mathtt{b}) = (\mathtt{a}' < \mathtt{b}')).$$

$\Psi_{\mathtt{c1}}(t, t')$ is not valid, thus the secret branching variable c1 cannot be declassified.

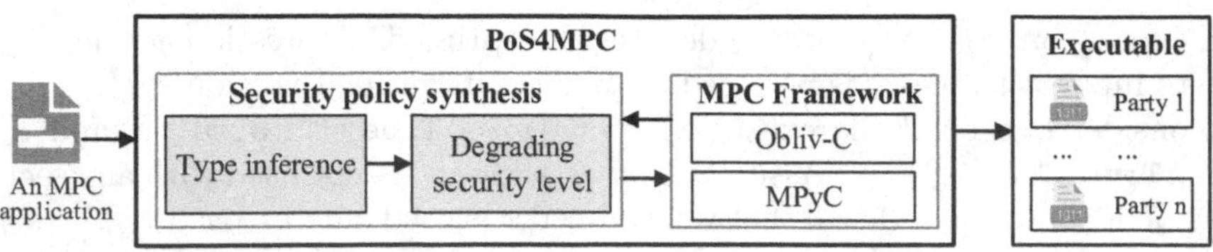


**Fig. 5.** The workflow of our tool **PoS4MPC**

**Refinement.** Theorem 1 allows us to check if the secret branching variable $x$ of a conditional statement $\mathsf{if}\ x\ \mathsf{then}\ p'\ \mathsf{else}\ p''$ that does not used with any secret-dependent conditions can be declassified. After that, if $x$ can be declassified without compromising the security, we feed back the result to the type system before checking the next secret branching variable. This allows us to refine the security level of variables that are updated in branches, namely, the type inference rule T-IF is refined to the following one.

$$\frac{\begin{array}{c}\mathsf{c}' = (\text{can } x \text{ be declassified } ?\ \mathtt{Pub} : \varrho(x)) \\ \mathsf{c} \sqcup \mathsf{c}' \vdash p_1 : \varrho \Rightarrow \varrho_1 \quad \mathsf{c} \sqcup \mathsf{c}' \vdash p_2 : \varrho \Rightarrow \varrho_2 \quad \varrho' = \varrho_1 \sqcup \varrho_2\end{array}}{\mathsf{c} \vdash \mathsf{if}\ x\ \mathsf{then}\ p_1\ \mathsf{else}\ p_2 : \varrho \Rightarrow \varrho'} \ [\text{T-IF}]$$

## 7 Implementation and Evaluation

We have implemented our approach in a tool, named **PoS4MPC**. The workflow of **PoS4MPC** is shown in Fig. 5, The input is an MPC program in C, which is parsed to an intermediate representation (IR) inside the LLVM Compiler [1] where call graph and control flow graphs are constructed at the LLVM IR level. We then perform the type inference which computes the a perfect security policy for the given program. To be accurate, we perform a field-sensitive pointer analysis [6] and our type inference is also field-sensitive. As the next step, we leverage the KLEE symbolic execution engine [10] to explore all the feasible symbolic executions, as well as the symbolic values of the return variable and secret branching variables of each symbolic execution. We fully explore loops since the bounds of loops in MPC are public and decided by user-specified inputs. Based on them, we iteratively check if a secret branching variable is degraded and the result is fed back to the type inference to refine security levels before checking the next secret branching variable. After that, we transform the program into the input of Obliv-C [44] by which the program can be compiled into executable implementations, one for each party. Obliv-C is an extension of C for implementing 2-party MPC applications using Yao's garbled circuit protocol [43]. For experimental purposes, **PoS4MPC** also features the high-level MPC framework MPyC [37], which is a Python package for implementing $n$-party MPC applications ($n \geq 1$) using Shamir's secret sharing protocol [38]. The C program is transformed into Python by a translator.

We also implement an optimization in our tool to alleviate the path explosion problem. Instead of directly checking the validity of $\Psi_x(t, t')$ for each secret

**Table 2.** Number of (secret) branching variables

| Name | LOC | #Branch var | #Other var | #Secret branch var | | #Other secret var | |
|---|---|---|---|---|---|---|---|
| | | | | After TS | After Check | Before refinement | After refinement |
| **QS** | 56 | 4 | 6 | 3 | 0 | 4 | 2 |
| **LinS** | 25 | 1 | 3 | 1 | 0 | 2 | 1 |
| **BinS** | 46 | 2 | 8 | 2 | 1 | 6 | 6 |
| **AlmS** | 73 | 6 | 10 | 6 | 4 | 8 | 8 |
| **PSI** | 34 | 1 | 5 | 1 | 0 | 3 | 1 |

branching variable $x$ and pair of symbolic executions $t$ and $t'$, we first check if the premise $\phi \wedge \mathsf{Primed}(\phi') \wedge e = \mathsf{Primed}(e')$ of $\Psi_x(t,t')$ is satisfiable. We can conclude that $\Psi_x(t,t')$ is valid for any secret branching variable $x$ if the premise $\phi \wedge \mathsf{Primed}(\phi') \wedge e = \mathsf{Primed}(e')$ is unsatisfiable. Furthermore, this yields a sound compositional reasoning approach which allows to split a program into a sequence of function calls. When each pair of the symbolic executions for each function cannot result in the same return value, we can conclude that $\Psi_x(t,t')$ is valid for any secret branching variable $x$ and any pair of symbolic executions $t$ and $t'$ of the entire program. This optimization reduces the evaluation time of symbolic execution of `PSI` (resp. `QS`) from 95.9 s–8.1 h (resp. 504.6 s) to 1.7 s–79.6 s (resp. 11.6 s) in input array size varies from 10 to 100 (resp. 10).

### 7.1 Evaluation Setup

For an evaluation of our approach, we conduct experiments on five typical 2-party MPC applications [2], i.e., quicksort (`QS`) [21], linear search (`LinS`) [13], binary search (`BinS`) [13], almost search (`AlmS`), and private set intersection (`PSI`) [5]. `QS` outputs the list of indices of a given integer array $\bar{\mathtt{a}}$ in its ordered version, where the first half of $\bar{\mathtt{a}}$ is given by one party and the second half of $\bar{\mathtt{a}}$ is given by the another party. `LinS` (resp. `BinS` and `AlmS`) outputs the index of an integer $b$ in an array $\bar{\mathtt{a}}$ if it exists, $-1$ otherwise, where the integer array $\bar{\mathtt{a}}$ is the input from one party and the integer $b$ is the input from the another party. `LinS` always scans the array from the start to the end even though it has found the integer $b$. `BinS` is a standard iterative approach on a sorted array, where the array index is protected via oblivious read access machine [20]. `AlmS` is a variant of `BinS`, where the input array is almost sorted, namely, each element is at either the correct position or the closest neighbour of the correct position. `PSI` outputs the intersection of two integer sets, each of which is an input from one party.

All the experiments were conducted on a desktop with 64-bit Linux Mint 20.1, Intel Core i5-6300HQ CPU, 2.30 GHz and 8 GB RAM. When evaluating MPC applications, the client of each party is executed with a single thread.

### 7.2 Performance of Security Policy Synthesis

**Security Policy**. The results of our approach is shown in Table 2, where column (LOC) shows the number of lines of code, column (#Branch var) shows the number of branching variables while column (#Other var) shows the number

**Table 3.** Execution time of our security policy synthesis approach

| Name | Length | | | | | | | | | | | | | | | | | | | |
|---|---|---|---|---|---|---|---|---|---|---|---|---|---|---|---|---|---|---|---|---|
| | 10 | | 20 | | 30 | | 40 | | 50 | | 60 | | 70 | | 80 | | 90 | | 100 | |
| | SE | Check | SE | Check | SE | Check | SE | Check | SE | Check | SE | Check | SE | Check | SE | Check | SE | Check | SE | Check |
| **QS** | 11.6 | 0.8 | 0.4h | 304.2 | 2.0h | 959.8 | 5.0h | 0.6h | 9.5h | 0.9h | 15.5h | 1.3h | 22.6h | 1.6h | 31.0h | 2.0h | 40.7h | 2.3h | 51.6h | 2.7h |
| **LinS** | 0.4 | 1.0 | 0.6 | 1.0 | 1.0 | 1.0 | 1.4 | 1.0 | 2.0 | 1.1 | 2.6 | 1.1 | 3.4 | 1.2 | 4.2 | 1.2 | 5.2 | 1.3 | 6.2 | 1.4 |
| **BinS** | 0.8 | 1.1 | 2.1 | 4.3 | 3.8 | 10.2 | 6.4 | 20.0 | 9.5 | 34.8 | 13.8 | 54.6 | 19.5 | 80.1 | 25.6 | 103.4 | 34.1 | 151.4 | 42.7 | 204.7 |
| **AlmS** | 1.3 | 0.8 | 4.3 | 3.5 | 7.7 | 10.0 | 14.1 | 18.6 | 20.6 | 32.3 | 28.9 | 51.0 | 40.7 | 77.4 | 55.1 | 110.3 | 74.9 | 148.2 | 94.4 | 200.0 |
| **PSI** | 1.7 | 0.5 | 4.3 | 1.0 | 8.0 | 1.5 | 13.2 | 2.1 | 20.0 | 2.8 | 28.6 | 3.5 | 39.3 | 4.3 | 50.9 | 5.3 | 63.0 | 6.4 | 79.6 | 7.8 |

of other variables, columns (After TS) and (After Check) respectively show the number of secret branching variables after applying the type system and checking if the secret branching variables can be declassified, columns (Before refinement) and (After refinement) respectively show the number of other secret variables before and after refining the type inference by feeding back the results of the symbolic reasoning. (Note that the input variables are excluded in counting.)

We can observe that only few variables (2 for `QS`, 1 for `LinS`, 2 for `BinS`, 2 for `AlmS` and 2 for `PSI`) can be found to be public by solely using the type system. With our symbolic reasoning approach, more secret branching variables can be declassified without compromising the security (3 for `QS`, 1 for `LinS`, 1 for `BinS`, 2 for `AlmS` and 1 for `PSI`). After refining the type inference using results of the symbolic reasoning approach, more secret variables can be declassified (2 for `QS`, 1 for `LinS` and 2 for `PSI`). Overall, our approach annotates 2, 1, 7, 12 and 1 internal variables as secret out of 10, 4, 10, 16 and 6 variables for `QS`, `LinS`, `BinS`, `AlmS` and `PSI`, respectively.

**Execution Time.** The execution time of our approach is shown in Table 3, where columns (SE) and (Check) respectively show the execution time (in second unless indicated by h for hour) of collecting symbolic executions and checking if secret branching variables can be declassified, by varying the size of the input array for each program from 10 to 100 with step 10. We did not report the execution time of our type system, as it is less than 0.1 s for each benchmark.

We can observe that our symbolic reasoning approach is able to check all the secret branching variables in few minutes (up to 294.4 s) except for `QS`. After an in-depth analysis, we found that the number of symbolic executions is exponential in the length of the input array for `QS` and `PSI` while it is linear in the length of the input array for the other benchmarks. Our compositional reasoning approach works very well on `PSI`, otherwise it would take similar execution time as on `QS`. Indeed, a loop of `PSI` is implemented as a sequence of function calls each of which has a fixed number of symbolic executions. Furthermore, each pair of symbolic executions in the called function cannot result in the same return value. Therefore, the number of symbolic executions and the execution time of our symbolic reasoning approach is reduced significantly. However, our compositional reasoning approach does not work on `QS`. Although the number of symbolic executions grows exponentially on `QS`, the execution time of checking if secret branching variables can be declassified is still reduced by our

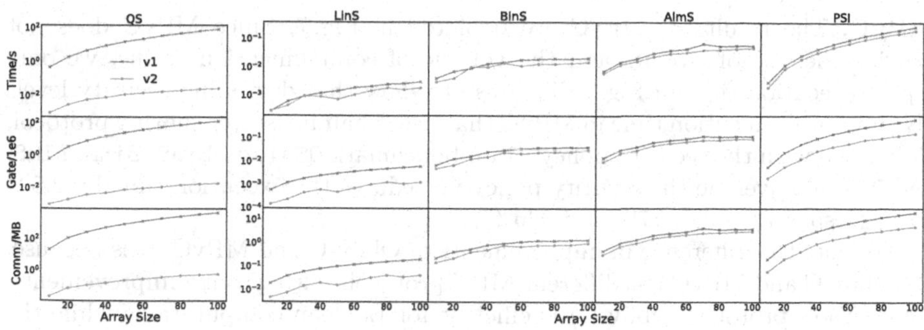


**Fig. 6.** Execution time (Time) in second, the number of gates (Gate) in $10^6$ gates, Communication (Comm.) in MB using Obliv-C

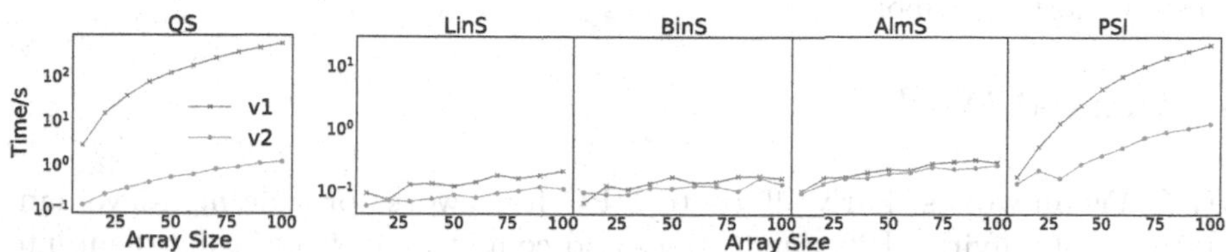


**Fig. 7.** Execution time (Time) in second using MPyC

optimization, which avoids the checking of the constraint $\Psi_x(t, t')$ if its premise $\phi \wedge \mathsf{Primed}(\phi') \wedge e = \mathsf{Primed}(e')$ is unsatisfiable.

### 7.3 Performance Improvement of MPC Applications

To evaluate the performance improvement of the MPC applications, we compare the execution time (in second), the size of the circuits (in $10^6\times$gates), and the volume of communication traffic (in MB) of each benchmark with the security policies v1 and v2, where v1 is obtained by solely applying our type system and v2 is obtained from v1 by degrading security levels and refinement without compromising the security. The measurement results are calculated by $\frac{\text{result of v1}}{\text{result of v2}} - 1$, taking the average of 10 times repetitions in order to minimize the noise.

**Obliv-C.** The results in Obliv-C are depicted in Fig. 6 (note the logarithmic scale of the vertical coordinate), where the size of the random input array for each benchmark varies from 10 to 100 with step size 10. Overall, we can observe that the performance improvement is significant especially on `QS`. In detail, compared with the security policy v1 on `QS` (resp. `LinS`, `BinS`, `AlmS`, and `PSI`), on average the security policy v2 reduces (1) the execution time by $1.56 \times 10^5\%$ (resp. 45%, 38%, 31% and 36%), (2) the size of circuits by $3.61 \times 10^5\%$ (resp. 368%, 52%, 38% and 275%), and (3) the volume of communication traffic by $4.17 \times 10^5\%$ (resp. 367%, 53%, 39% and 274%). This demonstrates the performance improvement of the MPC applications in Obliv-C that uses Yao's garbled circuit protocol.

**MPyC.** The results in MPyC are depicted in Fig. 7. Since MPyC does not provide the size of circuits and the volume of communication traffic, we only report execution time in Fig. 7. The results show that degrading security levels also improves execution time in MPyC that uses Shamir's secret sharing protocol. Compared with the security policy v1 on benchmark `QS` (resp. `LinS`, `BinS`, `AlmS`, and `PSI`), on average the security policy v2 reduces the execution time by $2.5 \times 10^4\%$ (resp. 64%, 23%, 17% and 996%).

We note the difference in improvements of Obliv-C and MPyC. It is because: (1) Obliv-C and MPyC use different MPC protocols with varying improvements, where Yao's protocol (Obliv-C) is efficient for Boolean computations while the secret-sharing protocol (MPyC) is efficient for arithmetic computations; and (2) the proportion of downgrading variables is different where a larger proportion of downgrading variables (in particular branching variables with large branches) boosts performance more.

## 8 Related Work

**MPC Frameworks.** Early efforts to MPC frameworks provide high-level languages for specifying MPC applications and compilers for translating them into executable implementations [8,23,31,32]. For instance, Fairplay complies 2-party MPC programs written in a domain-specific language into Yao's garbled circuits [31]. FairplayMP [8] extends Fairplay to multi-party using a modified version of the BMR protocol [7] with a Java interface. The others are aimed at improving the efficiency of operations in circuits and size of circuits. Mixed MPC protocols were also proposed to improve efficiency [9,26,34], as the efficiency of MPC protocols vary in operations. These frameworks explore the implementation space of operations in specific MPC protocols (e.g., garbled circuits, secret sharing and homomorphic encryption), as well as their conversions. However, all these frameworks either entirely compile an MPC program or compile an MPC program according to user-annotated secret variables to improve performance without formal security guarantees. Our approach improves the performance of MPC applications by declassifying secret variables without compromising security, which is orthogonal to the above optimization work.

**Security of MPC Applications.** Since MPC applications implemented in MPC frameworks are not necessarily secure due to information leakage during execution in the real-world. Therefore, information-flow type systems and data-flow analysis have been adopted in the MPC frameworks, e.g., [24,37,44]. However, they only consider security verification but not automatic generation of security policies as we did in the current paper. Moreover, these approaches cannot identify some variables (e.g., `c2` in our motivating example) that can actually be declassified without compromising security. Kerschbaum [25] proposed to infer public intermediate values by reasoning about epistemic modal logic, with a similar goal to ours for declassifying secret variables. However, it is unclear how efficient this approach is, as the performance of their approach was not reported [25].

Alternatively, self-composition which reduces the security problem to the safety problem on two copies of a program has been adopted by [3], where the safety problem can be solved by safety verification tools. However, safety verification remains challenging and these approaches often require user annotations (e.g., procedure contracts and loop invariants) that are non-trivial for MPC practitioners. Our work is different from them in: (1) they only use the self-composition reduction to verify security instead of automatically generating a security policy; (2) they have to check almost all the program variables which is computational expensive, while we first apply an efficient type system to infer a security policy and then only check if the security branching variables in the security policy can be declassified; and (3) we check if security branching variables can be declassified by reasoning about pairs of symbolic executions which can be seen as a divide-and-conquer approach without annotations, and the results can be fed back to the type system to efficiently refine security levels. We remark that the self-composition reduction could also be used to check if a security branching variable could be declassified.

**Information-Flow Analysis.** A rich body of literature has studied verification of information-flow security and noninterference in programs [12], which requires that confidential data does not flow to outputs. This is too restrictive for programs which allow secret data to flow to some non-secret outputs, e.g., MPC applications, therefore the security notion is extended with declassification (a.k.a. delimited release) later [27]. These security problems are verified by type systems (e.g. [27]) or self-composition (e.g., [39]) or relational reasoning (e.g., [4]). Some of these techniques have been adapted to verify timing side-channel security, e.g., [11,30,42]. However, as the usual notions of security in these settings do not require reasoning about arbitrary leakage, these techniques are not directly applicable to our setting. Different from existing analysis using symbolic execution [33], our approach takes advantage of the public outputs of MPC programs and regards the public outputs as a part of leakage to avoid false positive of the noninterference approach and the quantification of information flow.

Finally, we remark that the leakage model considered in this work is different from the ones used in power side-channel security [16–19,45] and timing side-channel security [11,30,36,42] which leverage side-channel information while ours assumes that the adversary is able to observe all the public information during computation.

## 9 Conclusion

We have formalized the leakage of an MPC application which bridge the language-level and protocol-level leakages via security policies. Based on the formalization, we have presented an approach to automatically synthesize a security policy which can improve the performance of MPC applications while not compromising their privacy. Our approach is essentially a synergistic integration of type inference and symbolic reasoning with security type refinement. We implemented our approach in a tool **PoS4MPC**. The experimental results on five typical MPC applications confirm that our approach can significantly improve the performance of MPC applications.

## References


1. The LLVM compiler infrastructure. https://llvm.org
2. The source code of our benchmarks (2022). https://github.com/SPoS4/PoS4MPC
3. Almeida, J.B., Barbosa, M., Barthe, G., Pacheco, H., Pereira, V., Portela, B.: Enforcing ideal-world leakage bounds in real-world secret sharing MPC frameworks. In: CSF, pp. 132–146 (2018)
4. Amtoft, T., Bandhakavi, S., Banerjee, A.: A logic for information flow in object-oriented programs. In: POPL, pp. 91–102 (2006)
5. Andreea, I.: Private set intersection: past, present and future. In: SECRYPT, pp. 680–685 (2021)
6. Balatsouras, G., Smaragdakis, Y.: Structure-sensitive points-to analysis for C and C++. In: Rival, X. (ed.) SAS 2016. LNCS, vol. 9837, pp. 84–104. Springer, Heidelberg (2016). https://doi.org/10.1007/978-3-662-53413-7_5
7. Beaver, D., Micali, S., Rogaway, P.: The round complexity of secure protocols. In: STOC, pp. 503–513 (1990)
8. Ben-David, A., Nisan, N., Pinkas, B.: FairplayMP: a system for secure multi-party computation. In: CCS, pp. 257–266 (2008)
9. Büscher, N., Demmler, D., Katzenbeisser, S., Kretzmer, D., Schneider, T.: HyCC: compilation of hybrid protocols for practical secure computation. In: CCS, pp. 847–861 (2018)
10. Cadar, C., Dunbar, D., Engler, D.R.: KLEE: unassisted and automatic generation of high-coverage tests for complex systems programs. In: OSDI, pp. 209–224 (2008)
11. Chen, J., Feng, Y., Dillig, I.: Precise detection of side-channel vulnerabilities using quantitative cartesian hoare logic. In: CCS, pp. 875–890 (2017)
12. Denning, D.E., Denning, P.J.: Certification of programs for secure information flow. Commun. ACM **20**(7), 504–513 (1977)
13. Doerner, J.: The absentminded crypto kit. https://bitbucket.org/jackdoerner/absentminded-crypto-kit/
14. Evans, D., Kolesnikov, V., Rosulek, M.: A pragmatic introduction to secure multi-party computation. Found. Trends Priv. Secur. **2**(2–3), 70–246 (2018)
15. Fan, Y., Song, F., Chen, T., Zhang, L., Liu, W.: Pos4mpc: automated security policy synthesis for secure multi-party computation. Technical report, ShanghaiTech University (2022). https://faculty.sist.shanghaitech.edu.cn/faculty/songfu/publications/CAV22full.pdf
16. Gao, P., Xie, H., Song, F., Chen, T.: A hybrid approach to formal verification of higher-order masked arithmetic programs. ACM Trans. Softw. Eng. Methodol. **30**(3), 26:1–26:42 (2021)
17. Gao, P., Xie, H., Sun, P., Zhang, J., Song, F., Chen, T.: Formal verification of masking countermeasures for arithmetic programs. IEEE Trans. Softw. Eng. **48**(3), 973–1000 (2022)
18. Gao, P., Xie, H., Zhang, J., Song, F., Chen, T.: Quantitative verification of masked arithmetic programs against side-channel attacks. In: Vojnar, T., Zhang, L. (eds.) TACAS 2019. LNCS, vol. 11427, pp. 155–173. Springer, Cham (2019). https://doi.org/10.1007/978-3-030-17462-0_9

19. Gao, P., Zhang, J., Song, F., Wang, C.: Verifying and quantifying side-channel resistance of masked software implementations. ACM Trans. Softw. Eng. Methodol. **28**(3), 16:1–16:32 (2019)
20. Goldreich, O., Ostrovsky, R.: Software protection and simulation on oblivious RAMs. J. ACM **43**(3), 431–473 (1996)
21. Hamada, K., Kikuchi, R., Ikarashi, D., Chida, K., Takahashi, K.: Practically efficient multi-party sorting protocols from comparison sort algorithms. In: ICISC, vol. 7839, pp. 202–216 (2012)
22. Hemenway, B., Lu, S., Ostrovsky, R., Welser IV, W.: High-precision secure computation of satellite collision probabilities. In: Zikas, V., De Prisco, R. (eds.) SCN 2016. LNCS, vol. 9841, pp. 169–187. Springer, Cham (2016). https://doi.org/10.1007/978-3-319-44618-9_9
23. Holzer, A., Franz, M., Katzenbeisser, S., Veith, H.: Secure two-party computations in ANSI C. In: CCS, pp. 772–783 (2012)
24. Keller, M.: MP-SPDZ: A versatile framework for multi-party computation. In: CCS, pp. 1575–1590 (2020)
25. Kerschbaum, F.: Automatically optimizing secure computation. In: CCS, pp. 703–714 (2011)
26. Laud, P., Randmets, J.: A domain-specific language for low-level secure multiparty computation protocols. In: CCS, pp. 1492–1503 (2015)
27. Li, P., Zdancewic, S.: Downgrading policies and relaxed noninterference. In: POPL, pp. 158–170 (2005)
28. Lindell, Y.: Secure multiparty computation. Commun. ACM **64**(1), 86–96 (2021)
29. Liu, C., Wang, X.S., Nayak, K., Huang, Y., Shi, E.: ObliVM: a programming framework for secure computation. In: S&P, pp. 359–376 (2015)
30. Malacaria, P., Khouzani, M.H.R., Pasareanu, C.S., Phan, Q., Luckow, K.S.: Symbolic side-channel analysis for probabilistic programs. In: CSF, pp. 313–327 (2018)
31. Malkhi, D., Nisan, N., Pinkas, B., Sella, Y.: Fairplay - secure two-party computation system. In: USENIX Security Symposium, pp. 287–302 (2004)
32. Mood, B., Gupta, D., Carter, H., Butler, K.R.B., Traynor, P.: Frigate: a validated, extensible, and efficient compiler and interpreter for secure computation. In: EuroS&P, pp. 112–127 (2016)
33. Pasareanu, C.S., Kersten, R., Luckow, K.S., Phan, Q.: Chapter six - symbolic execution and recent applications to worst-case execution, load testing, and security analysis. Adv. Comput. **113**, 289–314 (2019)
34. Patra, A., Schneider, T., Suresh, A., Yalame, H.: ABY2.0: improved mixed-protocol secure two-party computation. In: USENIX Security Symposium, pp. 2165–2182 (2021)
35. Poddar, R., Kalra, S., Yanai, A., Deng, R., Popa, R.A., Hellerstein, J.M.: Senate: a maliciously-secure MPC platform for collaborative analytics. In: USENIX Security Symposium, pp. 2129–2146 (2021)
36. Qin, Q., JiYang, J., Song, F., Chen, T., Xing, X.: Preventing timing side-channels via security-aware just-in-time compilation. CoRR abs/2202.13134 (2022)
37. Schoenmakers, B.: MPyC: secure multiparty computation in Python (2020). https://github.com/lschoe/mpyc
38. Shamir, A.: How to share a secret. Commun. ACM **22**(11), 612–613 (1979)
39. Terauchi, T., Aiken, A.: Secure information flow as a safety problem. In: Hankin, C., Siveroni, I. (eds.) SAS 2005. LNCS, vol. 3672, pp. 352–367. Springer, Heidelberg (2005). https://doi.org/10.1007/11547662_24
40. Volpano, D.M., Irvine, C.E., Smith, G.: A sound type system for secure flow analysis. J. Comput. Secur. **4**(2/3), 167–188 (1996)

41. Wagh, S., Gupta, D., Chandran, N.: SecureNN: efficient and private neural network training. IACR Cryptology ePrint Archive, p. 442 (2018)
42. Yang, W., Vizel, Y., Subramanyan, P., Gupta, A., Malik, S.: Lazy self-composition for security verification. In: Chockler, H., Weissenbacher, G. (eds.) CAV 2018. LNCS, vol. 10982, pp. 136–156. Springer, Cham (2018). https://doi.org/10.1007/978-3-319-96142-2_11
43. Yao, A.C.: Protocols for secure computations. In: FOCS, pp. 160–164 (1982)
44. Zahur, S., Evans, D.: Obliv-C: a language for extensible data-oblivious computation. IACR Cryptology ePrint Archive, p. 1153 (2015)
45. Zhang, J., Gao, P., Song, F., Wang, C.: SCInfer: refinement-based verification of software countermeasures against side-channel attacks. In: Chockler, H., Weissenbacher, G. (eds.) CAV 2018. LNCS, vol. 10982, pp. 157–177. Springer, Cham (2018). https://doi.org/10.1007/978-3-319-96142-2_12

# Explaining Hyperproperty Violations

Norine Coenen[1(✉)], Raimund Dachselt[2], Bernd Finkbeiner[1], Hadar Frenkel[1], Christopher Hahn[1], Tom Horak[3], Niklas Metzger[1], and Julian Siber[1]

[1] CISPA Helmholtz Center for Information Security, Saarbrücken, Germany
{norine.coenen,finkbeiner,hadar.frenkel,christopher.hahn, niklas.metzger,julian.siber}@cispa.de

[2] Interactive Media Lab, Technische Universität Dresden, Dresden, Germany
dachselt@acm.org

[3] elevait GmbH & Co. KG, Dresden, Germany
tom.horak@elevait.de

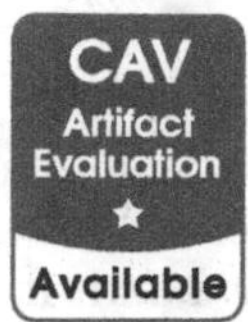

**Abstract.** Hyperproperties relate multiple computation traces to each other. Model checkers for hyperproperties thus return, in case a system model violates the specification, a set of traces as a counterexample. Fixing the erroneous relations between traces in the system that led to the counterexample is a difficult manual effort that highly benefits from additional explanations. In this paper, we present an explanation method for counterexamples to hyperproperties described in the specification logic HyperLTL. We extend Halpern and Pearl's definition of actual causality to sets of traces witnessing the violation of a HyperLTL formula, which allows us to identify the events that caused the violation. We report on the implementation of our method and show that it significantly improves on previous approaches for analyzing counterexamples returned by HyperLTL model checkers.

## 1 Introduction

While model checking algorithms and tools (e.g., [12,17,18,26,47,55]) have, in the past, focused on trace properties, recent failures in security-critical systems, such as Heartbleed [28], Meltdown [59], Spectre [52], or Log4j [1], have triggered the development of model checking algorithms for properties that relate multiple computation traces to each other, i.e., *hyperproperties* [21]. Although the counterexample returned by such a model checker for hyperproperties, which takes the shape of a *set* of traces, may aid in the debugging process, understanding and narrowing down which features are actually responsible for the erroneous

This work was funded by DFG grant 389792660 as part of TRR 248 – CPEC, by the DFG as part of the Germany's Excellence Strategy EXC 2050/1 - Project ID 390696704 - Cluster of Excellence "*Centre for Tactile Internet*" (CeTI) of TU Dresden, by the European Research Council (ERC) Grant OSARES (No. 683300), and by the German Israeli Foundation (GIF) Grant No. I-1513-407./2019.


S. Shoham and Y. Vizel (Eds.): CAV 2022, LNCS 13371, pp. 407–429, 2022.
https://doi.org/10.1007/978-3-031-13185-1_20

relation between the traces in the counterexample requires significantly more manual effort than for trace properties. In this paper, we develop an explanation technique for these more complex counterexamples that identifies the *actual causes* [44–46] of hyperproperty violations.

Existing hyperproperty model checking approaches (e.g., [33,35,49]), take a HyperLTL formula as an input. HyperLTL is a temporal logic extending LTL with explicit trace quantification [20]. For example, observational determinism, which requires that all traces $\pi, \pi'$ agree on their observable outputs $lo$ whenever they agree on their observable inputs $li$, can be formalized in HyperLTL as $\forall \pi. \forall \pi'. \square(li_\pi \leftrightarrow li_{\pi'}) \rightarrow \square(lo_\pi \leftrightarrow lo_{\pi'})$. In case a system model violates observational determinism, the model checker consequently returns a set of two execution traces witnessing the violation.

A first attempt in explaining model checking results of HyperLTL specifications has been made with HyperVis [48], which visualizes a counterexample returned by the model checker MCHyper [35] in a browser application. While the visualizations are already useful to analyze the counterexample at hand, it fails to identify causes for the violation in several security-critical scenarios. This is because HyperVis identifies important atomic propositions that appear in the HyperLTL formula and highlights these in the trace and the formula. For detecting causes, however, this is insufficient: a cause for a violation of observational determinism, for example, could be a branch on the valuation of a secret input $i_s$, which is not even part of the formula (see Sect. 3 for a running example).

Defining what constitutes an actual cause for an effect (a violation) in a given scenario is a precious contribution by Halpern and Pearl [44–46], who refined and formalized earlier approaches based on counterfactual reasoning [58]: Causes are sets of events such that, in the counterfactual world where they do not appear, the effect does not occur either. One of the main insights of Halpern and Pearl's work, however, is that naive counterfactuals are too imprecise. If, for instance, our actual cause preempted another potential cause, the mere absence of the actual cause will not be enough to prevent the effect, which will be still produced by the other cause in the new scenario. Halpern and Pearl's definition therefore allows to carefully control for other possible causes through the notion of *contingencies*. In the modified definition [44], contingencies allow to fix certain features of the counterfactual world to be exactly as they are in the actual world, regardless of the system at hand. Such a contingency effectively modifies the dynamics of the underlying model, and one insight of our work is that defining actual causality for reactive systems also needs to modify the system under a contingency. Notably, most works regarding trace causality [13,39] do not consider contingencies but only counterfactuals, and thus are not able to find true actual causes.

In this paper, we develop the notion of actual causality for effects described by HyperLTL formulas and use the generated causes as explanations for counterexamples returned by a model checker. We show that an implementation of our algorithm is practically feasible and significantly increases the state-of-the-art in explaining and analyzing HyperLTL model checking results.

## 2 Preliminaries

We model a system as a *Moore machine* [62] $T = (S, s_0, AP, \delta, l)$ where $S$ is a finite set of states, $s_0 \in S$ is the initial state, $AP = I \cup O$ is the set of atomic propositions consisting of inputs $I$ and outputs $O$, $\delta : S \times 2^I \to S$ is the transition function determining the successor state for a given state and set of inputs, and $l : S \to 2^O$ is the labeling function mapping each state to a set of outputs. A *trace* $t = t_0 t_1 t_2 \ldots \in (2^{AP})^\omega$ of $T$ is an infinite sequence of sets of atomic propositions with $t_i = A \cup l(s_i)$, where $A \subseteq I$ and $\delta(s_i, A) = s_{i+1}$ for all $i \geq 0$. We usually write $t[n]$ to refer to the set $t_n$ at the $(n+1)$-th position of $t$. With *traces*$(T)$, we denote the set of all traces of $T$. For some sequence of inputs $a = a_0 a_1 a_2 \ldots \in (2^I)^\omega$, the trace $T(a)$ is defined by $T(a)_i = a_i \cup l(s_i)$ and $\delta(s_i, a_i) = s_{i+1}$ for all $i \geq 0$. A trace property $P \subseteq T$ is a set of traces. A hyperproperty $H$ is a lifting of a trace property, i.e., a *set of sets of traces*. A model $T$ satisfies a hyperproperty $H$ if the set of traces of $T$ is an element of the hyperproperty, i.e., *traces*$(T) \in H$.

### 2.1 HyperLTL

HyperLTL is a recently introduced logic for expressing temporal hyperproperties, extending linear-time temporal logic (LTL) [64] with trace quantification:

$$\varphi ::= \forall \pi. \varphi \mid \exists \pi. \varphi \mid \psi$$
$$\psi ::= a_\pi \mid \neg \psi \mid \psi \wedge \psi \mid \bigcirc \psi \mid \psi \mathcal{U} \psi$$

We also consider the usual derived Boolean ($\vee$, $\rightarrow$, $\leftrightarrow$) and temporal operators ($\varphi \mathcal{R} \psi \equiv \neg(\neg\varphi \mathcal{U} \neg\psi)$, $\Diamond \varphi \equiv \mathit{true}\, \mathcal{U} \varphi$, $\Box \varphi \equiv \mathit{false} \mathcal{R} \varphi$). The semantics of HyperLTL formulas is defined with respect to a set of traces $Tr$ and a trace assignment $\Pi : \mathcal{V} \to Tr$ that maps trace variables to traces. To update the trace assignment so that it maps trace variable $\pi$ to trace $t$, we write $\Pi[\pi \mapsto t]$.

$$\begin{array}{ll}
\Pi, i \models_{Tr} a_\pi & \text{iff } a \in \Pi(\pi)[i] \\
\Pi, i \models_{Tr} \neg\varphi & \text{iff } \Pi, i \not\models_{Tr} \varphi \\
\Pi, i \models_{Tr} \varphi \wedge \psi & \text{iff } \Pi, i \models_{Tr} \varphi \text{ and } \Pi, i \models_{Tr} \psi \\
\Pi, i \models_{Tr} \bigcirc \varphi & \text{iff } \Pi, i+1 \models_{Tr} \varphi \\
\Pi, i \models_{Tr} \varphi \mathcal{U} \psi & \text{iff } \exists j \geq i.\, \Pi, j \models_{Tr} \psi \wedge \forall i \leq k < j.\, \Pi, k \models_{Tr} \varphi \\
\Pi, i \models_{Tr} \exists \pi. \varphi & \text{iff there is some } t \in Tr \text{ such that } \Pi[\pi \mapsto t], i \models_{Tr} \varphi \\
\Pi, i \models_{Tr} \forall \pi. \varphi & \text{iff for all } t \in Tr \text{ it holds that } \Pi[\pi \mapsto t], i \models_{Tr} \varphi
\end{array}$$

We explain counterexamples found by MCHyper [24,35], which is a model checker for HyperLTL formulas, building on ABC [12]. MCHyper takes as inputs a hardware circuit, specified in the Aiger format [8], and a HyperLTL formula. MCHyper solves the model checking problem by computing the self-composition [6] of the system. If the system violates the HyperLTL formula, MCHyper returns a counterexample. This counterexample is a set of traces through the original system that together violate the HyperLTL formula. Depending on the type of violation, this counterexample can then be used to debug the circuit or refine the specification iteratively.

### 2.2 Actual Causality

A formal definition of what actually causes an observed effect in a given context has been proposed by Halpern and Pearl [45]. Here, we outline the version later modified by Halpern [44]. Causality is defined with respect to a *causal model* $\mathcal{M} = (\mathcal{S}, \mathcal{F})$, given by a *signature* $\mathcal{S}$ and set of *structural equations* $\mathcal{F}$, which define the dynamics of the system. A signature $\mathcal{S}$ is a tuple $(\mathcal{U}, \mathcal{V}, \mathcal{D})$, where $\mathcal{U}$ and $\mathcal{V}$ are disjoint sets of variables, termed *exogenous* and *endogenous* variables, respectively; and $\mathcal{D}$ defines the *range* of possible values $\mathcal{D}(Y)$ for all variables $Y \in \mathcal{U} \cup \mathcal{V}$. A *context* $\vec{u}$ is an assignment to the variables in $\mathcal{U} \cup \mathcal{V}$ such that the values of the exogenous variables are determined by factors outside of the model, while the value of some endogenous variable $X$ is defined by the associated structural equation $f_X \in \mathcal{F}$. An *effect* $\varphi$ in a causal model is a Boolean formula over assignments to endogenous variables. We say that a context $\vec{u}$ of a model $\mathcal{M}$ satisfies a partial variable assignment $\vec{X} = \vec{x}$ for $\vec{X} \subseteq \mathcal{U} \cup \mathcal{V}$ if the assignments in $\vec{u}$ and in $\vec{x}$ coincide for every variable $X \in \vec{X}$. The extension for Boolean formulas over variable assignments is as expected. For a context $\vec{u}$ and a partial variable assignment $\vec{X} = \vec{x}$, we denote by $(\mathcal{M}, \vec{u})[\vec{X} \leftarrow \vec{x}]$ the context $\vec{u}'$ in which the values of the variables in $\vec{X}$ are set according to $\vec{x}$, and all other values are computed according to the structural equations.

The actual causality framework of Halpern and Pearl aims at defining what events (given as variable assignments) are the cause for the occurrence of an effect in a specific given context. We now provide the formal definition.

**Definition 1** **([44,45]).** *A partial variable assignment $\vec{X} = \vec{x}$ is an* actual cause *of the effect $\varphi$ in $(\mathcal{M}, \vec{u})$ if the following three conditions hold.*

*AC1: $(\mathcal{M}, \vec{u}) \models \vec{X} = \vec{x}$ and $(\mathcal{M}, \vec{u}) \models \varphi$, i.e., both cause and effect are true in the actual world.*
*AC2: There is a set $\vec{W} \subseteq V$ of endogenous variables and an assignment $\vec{x}'$ to the variables in $\vec{X}$ s.t. if $(\mathcal{M}, \vec{u}) \models \vec{W} = \vec{w}$, then $(\mathcal{M}, \vec{u})[\vec{X} \leftarrow \vec{x}', \vec{W} \leftarrow \vec{w}] \models \neg\varphi$.*
*AC3: $\vec{X}$ is minimal, i.e. no subset of $\vec{X}$ satisfies AC1 and AC2.*

Intuitively, AC2 states that in the counterfactual world obtained by intervening on the cause $\vec{X} = \vec{x}$ in the actual world (that is, setting the variables in $\vec{X}$ to $\vec{x}'$), the effect does not appear either. However, intervening on the possible cause might not be enough, for example when that cause preempted another. After intervention, this other cause may produce the effect again, therefore clouding the effect of the intervention. To address this problem, AC2 allows to reset values through the notion of *contingencies*, i.e., the set of variables $\vec{W}$ can be reset to $\vec{w}$, which is (implicitly) universally quantified. However, since the actual world has to model $\vec{W} = \vec{w}$, it is in fact uniquely determined. AC3, lastly, enforces the cause to be minimal by requiring that all variables in $\vec{X}$ are strictly necessary to achieve AC1 and AC2. For an illustration of Halpern and Pearl's actual causality, see Example 1 in Sect. 3.

## 3 Running Example

Consider a security-critical setting with two security levels: a high-security level $h$ and a low-security level $l$. Inputs and outputs labeled as high-security, denoted by $hi$ and $ho$ respectively, are confidential and thus only visible to the user itself, or, e.g., admins. Inputs and outputs labeled as low-security, denoted by $li$ and $lo$ respectively, are public and are considered to be observable by an attacker.

Our system of interest is modeled by the state graph representation shown in Fig. 1, which is treated as a black box by an attacker. The system is run without any low-security inputs, but branches depending on the given high-security inputs. If in one of the first two steps of an execution, a high-security input $hi$ is encountered, the system outputs only the high-security variable $ho$ directly afterwards and in the subsequent steps both outputs, regardless of inputs. If no high-security input is given in the first step, the low-security output $lo$ is enabled and after the second step, again both outputs are enabled, regardless of what input is fed into the system.

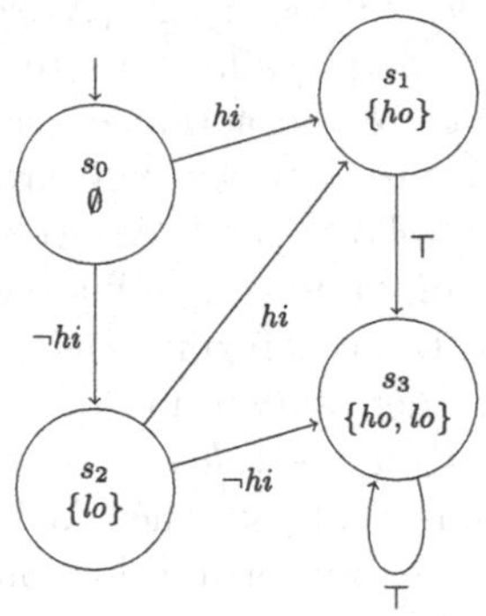


**Fig. 1.** State graph representation of our example system.

A prominent example hyperproperty is *observational determinism* from the introduction which states that any sequence of low-inputs always produces the same low-outputs, regardless of what the high-security level inputs are. $\varphi = \forall \pi . \forall \pi' . \square(li_\pi \leftrightarrow li_{\pi'}) \rightarrow \square(lo_\pi \leftrightarrow lo_{\pi'})$. The formula states that all traces $\pi$ and $\pi'$ must agree in the low-security outputs if they agree in the low-security inputs. Our system at hand does not satisfy observational determinism, because the low-security outputs in the first two steps depend on the present high-security inputs. Running MCHyper, a model checker for HyperLTL, results in the following counterexample: $t_1 = \{\}\{lo\}\{ho, lo\}^\omega$ and $t_2 = \{hi\}\{hi, ho\}\{ho, lo\}^\omega$. With the same low-security input (none) the traces produce different low-security outputs by visiting $s_1$ or $s_2$ on the way to $s_3$.

In this paper, our goal is to explain the violation of a HyperLTL formula on such a counterexample. Following Halpern and Pearl's explanation framework [46], an actual cause that is considered to be possibly true or possibly false constitutes an explanation for the user. We only consider causes over input variables, which can be true and false in any model. Hence, finding an explanation amounts to answering which inputs caused the violation on a specific counterexample. Before we answer this question for HyperLTL and the corresponding counterexamples given by sets of traces (see Sect. 4), we first illustrate Halpern and Pearl's actual causality (see Sect. 2.2) with the above running example.

*Example 1.* Finite executions of a system can be modeled in Halpern and Pearl's causal models. Consider inputs as exogenous variables $\mathcal{U} = \{hi_0, hi_1\}$ and outputs as endogenous variables $\mathcal{V} = \{lo_1, lo_2, ho_1, ho_2\}$. The indices model at which step of the execution the variable appears. We omit the inputs at the third position and the outputs at the first position because they are not relevant for the following exposition. We have that $\mathcal{D}(Y) = \{0,1\}$ for every $Y \in \mathcal{U} \cup \mathcal{V}$. Now, the following manually constructed structural equations encode the transitions: (1) $lo_1 = \neg hi_0$, (2) $ho_1 = hi_0$, (3) $lo_2 = \neg hi_1 \vee \neg lo_1$ and (4) $ho_2 = lo_1 \vee ho_1$. Consider context $\vec{u} = \{hi_0 = 0, hi_1 = 1\}$, effect $\varphi \equiv lo_1 = 1 \vee lo_2 = 1$, and candidate cause $hi_0 = 0$. Because of (1), we have that $(\mathcal{M}, \vec{u}) \models hi_0 = 0$ and $(\mathcal{M}, \vec{u}) \models lo_1 = 1$, hence AC1 is satisfied. Regarding AC2, this example allows us to illustrate the need for contingencies to accurately determine the actual cause: If we only consider intervening on the candidate cause $hi_0 = 0$, we still have $(\mathcal{M}, \vec{u})[hi_0 \leftarrow 1] \models \varphi$, because with $lo_1 = 0$ and (3) it follows that $(\mathcal{M}, \vec{u}) \models lo_2 = 1$. However, in the actual world, the second high input has no influence on the effect. We can control for this by considering the contingency $lo_2 = 0$, which is satisfied in the actual world, but not after the intervention on $hi_0$. Because of this contingency, we then have that $(\mathcal{M}, \vec{u})[hi_0 \leftarrow 1, lo_2 \leftarrow 0] \models \neg\varphi$, and hence, AC2 holds. Because a singleton set automatically satisfies AC3, we can infer that the first high input $hi_0$ was the actual cause for any low output to be enabled in the actual world. Note that, intuitively, the contingency allows us to ignore some of the structural equations by ignoring the value they assign to $lo_2$ in this context. Our definitions in Sect. 4 will allow similar modifications for counterexamples to hyperproperties.

## 4 Causality for Hyperproperty Violations

Our goal in this section is to formally define actual causality for the violation of a hyperproperty described by a general HyperLTL formula $\varphi$, observed in a counterexample to $\varphi$. Such a counterexample is given by a trace assignment to the trace variables appearing in $\varphi$. Note that, for universal quantifiers, the assignment of a single trace to the bounded variable suffices to define a counterexample. For existential quantifiers, this is not the case: to prove that an existential quantifier cannot be instantiated we need to show that no system trace satisfies the formula in its body, i.e., provide a proof for the whole system. In this work, we are interested in explaining violations of hyperproperties, and not proofs of their satisfaction [16]. Hence, we limit ourselves to instantiations of the outermost universal quantifiers of a HyperLTL formula, which can be returned by model checkers like MCHyper [24,35]. Since our goal is to explain counterexamples, restricting ourselves to results returned by existing model checkers is reasonable. Note that MCHyper can still handle formulas of the form $\forall^n \exists^m \varphi$ where $\varphi$ is quantifier free, including interesting information flow policies like generalized noninterference [61]. The returned counterexample then only contains $n$ traces that instantiate the universal quantifiers, the existential quantifiers are not instantiated for the above reason. In the following, we restrict ourselves to formulas and counterexamples of this form.

**Definition 2 (Counterexample).** *Let $T$ be a transition system and denote $Traces(T) := Tr$, and let $\varphi$ be a HyperLTL formula of the form $\forall \pi_1 \ldots \forall \pi_k \psi$,* *where $\psi$ is a HyperLTL formula that does not start with $\forall$. A counterexample to $\varphi$ in $T$ is a partial trace assignment $\Gamma : \{\pi_1, \dots, \pi_k\} \to Tr$ such that $\Gamma, 0 \models_{Tr} \neg\psi$.*

For ease of notation, we sometimes refer to $\Gamma$ simply as the tuple of its instantiations $\Gamma = \langle \Gamma(\pi_1), \dots, \Gamma(\pi_k) \rangle$. In terms of Halpern and Pearl's actual causality as outlined in Sect. 2.2, a counterexample describes the actual world at hand, which we want to explain. As a next step, we need to define an appropriate language to reason about possible causes and contingencies in our counterexample. We will use sets of *events*, i.e., values of atomic propositions at a specific position of a specific trace in the counterexample.

**Definition 3 (Event).** *An event is a tuple $e = \langle l_a, n, t \rangle$ such that $l_a = a$ or $l_a = \neg a$ for some atomic proposition $a \in AP$, $n \in \mathbb{N}$ is a point in time, and $t \in (2^{AP})^\omega$ is a trace of a system $T$. We say that a counterexample $\Gamma = \langle t_1, \dots t_k \rangle$* satisfies *a set of events $\mathcal{C}$, and denote $\Gamma \models \mathcal{C}$, if for every event $\langle l_a, n, t \rangle \in \mathcal{C}$ the two following conditions hold:*

1. *$t = t_i$ for some $i \in \{1, \dots, k\}$, i.e., all events in $\mathcal{C}$ reason about traces in $\Gamma$,*
2. *$l_a = a$ iff $a \in t_i[n]$, i.e., $a$ holds on trace $t_i$ of the counterexample at time $n$.*

We assume that the set $AP$ is a disjoint union of input an output propositions, that is, $AP = I \uplus O$. We say that $\langle l_a, n, t \rangle$ is an *input event* if $a \in I$, and we call it an *output event* if $a \in O$. We denote the set of input events by $IE$ and the set of output events by $OE$. These events have a direct correspondence with the variables appearing in Halpern and Pearl's causal models: we can identify input events with exogenous variables (because their value is determined by factors outside of the system) and output events with endogenous variables.

We define a cause as a set of input events, while an effect is a possibly infinite Boolean formula over $OE$. Note that, similar to [37], every HyperLTL formula can be represented as a first order formula over events, e.g. $\forall\pi\forall\pi' \Box(a_\pi \leftrightarrow a_{\pi'}) = \forall\pi\forall\pi' \bigwedge_{n\in\mathbb{N}}(\langle a, n, \pi \rangle \leftrightarrow \langle a, n, \pi' \rangle)$. For some set of events $\mathcal{S}$, let ${}^{+}\mathcal{S}_\pi^k = \{a \in AP \mid \langle a, k, \pi \rangle \in \mathcal{S}\}$ denote the set of atomic propositions defined positively by $\mathcal{S}$ on trace $\pi$ at position $k$. Dualy, we define ${}^{-}\mathcal{S}_\pi^k = \{a \in AP \mid \langle \neg a, k, \pi \rangle \in \mathcal{S}\}$.

In order to define actual causality for hyperproperties we need to formally define how we obtain the counterfactual executions under some contingency for the case of events on infinite traces. We define a contingency as a set of output events. Mapping Halpern and Pearl's definition to transition systems, contingencies reset outputs in the counterfactual traces back to their value in the original counterexample, which amounts to changing the state of the system, and then following the transition function from the new state. For a given trace of the counterexample, we describe all possible behaviors under *arbitrary* contingencies with the help of a counterfactual automaton. The concrete contingency on a trace is defined by additional input variables. In the following, let $IC = \{o^C \mid o \in O\}$ be a set of auxiliary input variables expressing whether a contingency is invoked at the given step of the execution and $c : O \to IC$ be a function s.t. $c(o) = o^C$.

**Definition 4 (Counterfactual Automaton).** *Let $T = (S, s_0, AP, \delta, l)$ be a system with $S = 2^O$, i.e., every state is uniquely labeled, and there exists a state* *for every combination of outputs. Let* $\pi = \pi_0 \dots \pi_i(\pi_j \dots \pi_n)^\omega \in traces(T)$ *be a trace of* $T$ *in a finite, lasso-shaped representation. The counterfactual automaton* $T_\pi^C = (S \times \{0 \dots n\}, (s_0, 0), (IC \cup I) \cup (O \cup \{0 \dots n\}), \delta^C, l^C)$ *is defined as follows:*

- $\delta^C((s,k), Y) = (s', k')$ *where* $k' = j$ *if* $k = n$, *else* $k' = k + 1$, *and* $l(s') = \{o \in O \mid (o \in \delta(s, Y \cap I) \wedge c(o) \notin Y) \vee (o \in \pi_{k'} \wedge c(o) \in Y)\}$,
- $l^C(s,k) = l(s) \cup \{k\}$.

A counterfactual automaton is effectively a chain of copies of the original system, of the same length as the counterexample. An execution through the counterfactual automaton starts in the first copy corresponding to the first position in the counterexample trace, and then moves through the chain until it eventually loops back from copy $n$ to copy $j$. A transition in the counterfactual automaton can additionally specify setting as a contingency some output variable $o$ if the auxiliary input variable $o^C$ is enabled. In this case, the execution will move to a state in the next automaton of the chain where all the outputs are as usual, except $o$, which will have the same value as in the counterexample $\pi$. Note that, under the assumption that all states of the original system are uniquely labeled and there exists a state for every combination of output variables, the function $\delta^C$ is uniquely determined.[1] A counterfactual automaton for our running example is described in the full version of this paper [22].

Next, we need to define how we intervene on a set of traces with a candidate cause given as a set of input events, and a contingency given as a set of output events. We define an intervention function, which transforms a trace of our original automaton to an input sequence of an counterfactual automaton.

**Definition 5 (Intervention).** *For a cause* $\mathcal{C} \subseteq IE$, *a contingency* $\mathcal{W} \subseteq OE$ *and a trace* $\pi$, *the function intervene* : $(2^{AP})^\omega \times 2^{IE} \times 2^{OE} \to (2^{I \cup IC})^\omega$ *returns a trace such that for all* $k \in \mathbb{N}$ *the following holds:* $intervene(\pi, \mathcal{C}, \mathcal{W})[k] = (\pi[k] \setminus {}^+\mathcal{C}_\pi^k) \cup {}^-\mathcal{C}_\pi^k \cup \{c(o) \mid o \in {}^+\mathcal{W}_\pi^k \cup {}^-\mathcal{W}_\pi^k\}$. *We lift the intervention function to counterexamples given as a tuple* $\Gamma = \langle \pi_1, \dots, \pi_k \rangle$ *as follows:* $intervene(\Gamma, \mathcal{C}, \mathcal{W}) = \langle T_{\pi_1}^C(intervene(\pi_1, \mathcal{C}, \mathcal{W})), \dots, T_{\pi_k}^C(intervene(\pi_k, \mathcal{C}, \mathcal{W}))\rangle$.

Intuitively, the intervention function *flips* all the events that appear in the cause $\Gamma$: If some $a \in I$ appears positively in the candidate cause $\mathcal{C}$, it will appear negatively in the resulting input sequence, and vice-versa. For a contingency $\mathcal{W}$, the intervention function enables their auxiliary input for the counterfactual automaton at the appropriate time point irrespective of their value, as the counterfactual automaton will take care of matching the atomic propositions value to the value in the original counterexample $\Gamma$.

[1] The same reasoning can be applied to arbitrary systems by considering for contingencies largest sets of outputs for which the assumption holds, with the caveat that the counterfactual automaton may model fewer contingencies. Consequently, computed causes may be less precise in case multiple causes appear in the counterexample.

### 4.1 Actual Causality for HyperLTL Violations

We are now ready to formalize what constitutes an actual cause for the violation of a hyperproperty described by a HyperLTL formula.

**Definition 6 (Actual Causality for HyperLTL).** *Let $\Gamma$ be a counterexample to a HyperLTL formula $\varphi$ in a system $T$. The set $\mathcal{C}$ is an actual cause for the violation of $\varphi$ on $\Gamma$ if the following conditions hold.*

**SAT** $\Gamma \vDash \mathcal{C}$.
**CF** *There exists a contingency $\mathcal{W}$ and a non-empty subset $\mathcal{C}' \subseteq \mathcal{C}$ such that: $\Gamma \vDash \mathcal{W}$ and $intervene(\Gamma, \mathcal{C}', \mathcal{W}) \vDash_{traces(T)} \varphi$.*
**MIN** *$\mathcal{C}$ is minimal, i.e., no subset of $\mathcal{C}$ satisfies SAT and CF.*

Unlike in Halpern and Pearl's definition (see Sect. 2.2), the condition SAT requires $\Gamma$ to satisfy only the cause, as we already know that the effect $\neg\varphi$, i.e., the violation of the specification, is satisfied by virtue of $\Gamma$ being a counterexample. CF is the counterfactual condition corresponding to AC2 in Halpern and Pearl's definition, and it states that after intervening on the cause, under a certain contingency, the set of traces satisfies the property. (Note that we use a conjunction of two statements here while Halpern and Pearl use an implication. This is because they implicitly quantify universally over the values of the variables in the set $W$ (which should be as in the actual world) where in our setting the set of contingencies already defines explicit values.) MIN is the minimality criterion directly corresponding to AC3.

*Example 2.* Consider our running example from Sect. 3, i.e., the system from Fig. 1 and the counterexample to observational determinism $\Gamma = \langle t_1, t_2 \rangle$. Let us consider what it means to intervene on the cause $\mathcal{C}_1 = \{\langle hi, 0, t_2 \rangle\}$. Note that we have $\Gamma \vDash \mathcal{C}_1$, hence the condition SAT is satisfied. For CF, let us first consider an intervention without contingencies. This results in $intervene(\Gamma, \mathcal{C}_1, \emptyset) = \langle t_1', t_2' \rangle = \langle t_1, \{\}\{hi, lo\}\{ho\}\{ho, lo\}^\omega \rangle$. However, $intervene(\Gamma, \mathcal{C}_1, \emptyset) \vDash_{traces(T)} \neg\varphi$, because the low outputs of $t_1'$ and $t_2'$ differ at the third position: $lo \in t_1'[2]$ and $lo \notin t_2'[2]$. This is because now the second high input takes effect, which was preempted by the first cause in the actual counterexample. The contingency $\mathcal{W}_2 = \{\langle lo, 2, t_2 \rangle\}\}$ now allows us to control this by *modyfing the state* after taking the second high input as follows: $intervene(\Gamma, \mathcal{C}_2, \mathcal{W}_2)) = \langle t_1'', t_2'' \rangle = \langle t_1, \{\}\{hi, lo\}\{ho, lo\}\{ho, lo\}^\omega \rangle$. Note that $t_2''$ is not a trace of the model depicted in Fig. 1, because there is no transition that explains the step from $t_2''[1]$ to $t_2''[2]$. It is, however, a trace of the counterfactual automaton $T_{t_2}^C$ (see full version [22]), which encodes the set of counterfactual worlds for the trace $t_2$. The fact that we consider executions that are not part of the original system allows us to infer that only the first high input was an actual cause in our running example. Disregarding contingencies, we would need to consider both high inputs as an explanation for the violation of observational determinism, even though the second high input had no influence. Our treatment of contingencies corresponds directly to Halpern and Pearl's causal models, which allow to ignore certain structural equations as outlined in Example 1.

*Remark:* With our definitions, we strictly generalize Halpern and Pearl's actual causality to reactive systems modeled as Moore machines and effects expressed as HyperLTL formulas. Their structural equation models can be encoded in a one-step Moore machine; effect specifying a Boolean combination of primitive events can be encoded in the more expressive logic HyperLTL. Just like for Halpern and Pearl, our actual causes are not unique. While there can exist several different actual causes, the set of all actual causes is always unique. It is also possible that no actual cause exists: If the effect occurs on all system traces, there may be no actual cause on a given individual trace.

### 4.2 Finding Actual Causes with Model Checking

In this section, we consider the relationship between finding an actual cause for the violation of a HyperLTL formula starting with a universal quantifier and model checking of HyperLTL. We show that the problem of finding an actual cause can be reduced to a model checking problem where the generated formula for the model checking problem has one additional quantifier alternation. While there might be a reduction resulting in a more efficient encoding, our current result suggests that causality checking is the harder problem. The key idea of our reduction is to use counterfactual automata (that encode the given counterexample and the possible counterfactual traces) together with the HyperLTL formula described in the proof to ensure the conditions SAT, CF, and MIN on the witnesses for the model checking result.

**Proposition 1.** *We can reduce the problem of finding an actual cause for the violation of an HyperLTL formula starting with a universal quantifier to the HyperLTL model checking problem with one additional quantifier alternation.*

*Proof.* Let $\Gamma = \langle t_1, \dots t_k \rangle$ be a counterexample for the formula $\forall \pi_1 \dots \forall \pi_k . \varphi$ where $\varphi$ is a HyperLTL formula that does not have a universal first quantifier. We provide the proof for the case of $\Gamma = \langle t_1, t_2 \rangle$ for readability reasons, but it can be extended to any natural number $k$. We assume that $t_1, t_2$ have some $\omega$-regular representation, as otherwise the initial problem of computing causality is not well defined. That is, we denote $t_i = u_i(v_i)^\omega$ such that $|u_i \cdot v_i| = n_i$.

In order to find an actual cause, we need to find a pair of traces $t'_1, t'_2$ that are counterfactuals for $t_1, t_2$; satisfy the property $\varphi$; and the changes from $t_1, t_2$ to $t'_1, t'_2$ are minimal with respect to set containment. Changes in inputs between $t_i$ and $t'_i$ in the loop part $v_i$ should reoccur in $t'_i$ repeatedly. Note that the differences between the counterexample $\langle t_1, t_2 \rangle$ and the witness of the model checking problem $\langle t'_1, t'_2 \rangle$ encode the actual cause, i.e. in case of a difference, the cause contains the event that is present on the counterexample. To reason about these changes, we use the counterfactual automaton $T_i^C$ for each $t_i$, which also allows us to search for the contingency $\mathcal{W}$ as part of the input sequence of $T_i^C$. Note that each $T_i^C$ consists of $n_i$ copies, that indicate in which step the automaton is with respect to $t_i$ and its loop $v_i$. For $m > |u_i|$, we label each state $(s_i, m)$ in $T_i^C$ with the additional label $L_{s_m, i}$, to indicate that the system is now in the loop part of $t_i$. In addition, we add to the initial state of $T_i^C$ the label $l_i$, and we add to the initial state of the system $T$ the label $l_{or}$. The formula $\psi^i_{loop}$ below states that the trace $\pi$ begins its run from the initial state of $T_i^C$ (and thus stays in this component through the whole run), and that every time $\pi$ visits a state on the loop, the same input sequence is observed. This way we enforce the periodic input behavior of the traces $t_1, t_2$ on $t'_1, t'_2$.

$$\psi^i_{loop}(\pi) := l_{i,\pi} \wedge \bigwedge_{L_{s_m,i}} \bigvee_{A \subseteq I} \square (L_{s_m,i,\pi} \rightarrow (\bigwedge_{a \in A} a_\pi \wedge \bigwedge_{a \notin A} \neg a_\pi))$$

For a subset of locations $N \subseteq [1, n_i]$ and a subset of input propositions $A \subseteq I$ we define $\psi^i_{diff}[N, A](\pi)$ that states that $\pi$ differs from $t_i$ in at least all events $\langle l_a, m, t_i \rangle$ for $a \in A, m \in N$; and the formula $\psi^i_{eq}[N, A](\pi)$ that states that for all events that are not defined by $A$ and $N$, $\pi$ is equal to $t_i$.

$$\psi^i_{diff}[N, A](\pi) = \bigwedge_{j \in N, a \in A} \bigcirc^j (a_\pi \not\leftrightarrow a_{t_i})$$

$$\psi^i_{eq}[N, A](\pi) = \bigwedge_{j \notin N, a \in I} \bigcirc^j (a_\pi \leftrightarrow a_{t_i}) \wedge \bigwedge_{j \in [1, n_i], a \notin A} \bigcirc^j (a_\pi \leftrightarrow a_{t_i})$$

We now define the formula $\psi^i_{min}$ that states that the set of inputs (and locations) on which trace $\pi$ differs from $t_i$ is not contained in the corresponding set for $\pi'$. We only check locations up until the length $n_i$ of $t_i$.

$$\psi^i_{min}(\pi, \pi') := \bigwedge_{N \subseteq [i, n_i]} \bigwedge_{A \subseteq \mathcal{I}} ((\psi^i_{diff}[N, A](\pi) \wedge \psi^i_{eq}[N, A](\pi)) \rightarrow \neg \psi^i_{eq}[N, A](\pi'))$$

Denote $\varphi := Q_1 \tau_1 \ldots Q_n \tau_n.\ \varphi'(\pi_1, \pi_2)$ where $Q_i \in \{\forall, \exists\}$ and $\tau_i$ are trace variables for $i \in [1, n]$. The formula $\psi_{cause}$ described below states that the two traces $\pi'_1$ and $\pi'_2$ are part of the systems $T_1^C, T_2^C$, and have the same loop structure as $t_1$ and $t_2$, and satisfy $\varphi$. That is, these traces can be obtained by changing the original traces $t_1, t_2$ and avoid the violation.

$$\psi_{cause}(\pi'_1, \pi'_2) := \varphi'(\pi'_1, \pi'_2) \wedge \bigwedge_{i=1,2} \psi^i_{loop}(\pi'_i)$$

Finally, $\psi_{actual}$ described below states that the counterfactuals $\pi'_1, \pi'_2$ correspond to a minimal change in the input events with respect to $t_1, t_2$. All other traces that the formula reasons about start at the initial state of the original system and thus are not affected by the counterfactual changes. We verify $\psi_{actual}$ against the product automaton $T \times T_1^C \times T_2^C$ to find these traces $\pi'_i \in T_i^C$ that witness the presence of a cause, counterfactual and contingency.

$$\psi_{actual} := \exists \pi'_1 \exists \pi'_2.\ \forall \pi''_1 \pi''_2.\ Q_1 \tau_1 \ldots Q_n \tau_n.\ \psi_{cause}(\pi'_1, \pi'_2) \wedge \bigwedge_{i=1,2} (l_{i,\pi'_i} \wedge l_{i,\pi''_i})$$

$$\wedge \bigwedge_{i \in [1,n]} l_{or,\tau_i} \wedge \left( \psi_{cause}(\pi''_1, \pi''_2) \rightarrow \left( \bigwedge_{i=1,2} \psi^i_{min}(\pi'_i, \pi''_i) \right) \right)$$

Then, if there exists two such traces $\pi_1', \pi_2'$ in the system $T \times T_1^C \times T_2^C$, they correspond to a minimal cause for the violation. Otherwise, there are no traces of the counterfactual automata that can be obtained from $t_1, t_2$ using counterfactual reasoning and satisfy the formula $\varphi$. □

We have shown that we can use HyperLTL model checking to find an actual cause for the violation of a HyperLTL formula. The resulting model checking problem has an additional quantifier alternation which suggests that identifying actual causes is a harder problem. Therefore, we restrict ourselves to finding actual causes for violations of universal HyperLTL formulas. This keeps the algorithms we present in the next section practical as we start without any quantifier alternation and need to solve a model checking problem with a single quantifier alternation. While this restriction excludes some interesting formulas, many can be strengthened into this fragment such that we are able to handle close approximations (c.f. [25]). Any additional quantifier alternation from the original formula carries over to an additional quantifier alternation in the resulting model checking problem which in turn leads to an exponential blow-up. The scalability of our approach is thus limited by the complexity of the model checking problem.

## 5 Computing Causes for Counterexamples

In this section, we describe our algorithm for finding actual causes of hyperproperty violations. Our algorithm is implemented on top of MCHyper [35], a model checker for hardware circuits and the alternation-free fragment of HyperLTL. In case of a violation, our analysis enriches the provided counterexample with the actual cause which can explain the reason for the violaiton to the user.

We first provide an overview of our algorithm and then discuss each step in detail. First, we compute an over-approximation of the cause using a satisfiability analysis over transitions taken in the counterexample. This analysis results in a set of events $\tilde{\mathcal{C}}$. As we show in Proposition 2, every actual cause $\mathcal{C}$ for the violation is a subset of $\tilde{\mathcal{C}}$. In addition, in Proposition 3 we show that the set $\tilde{\mathcal{C}}$ satisfies conditions SAT and CF. To ensure MIN, we search for the smallest subset $\mathcal{C} \subseteq \tilde{\mathcal{C}}$ that satisfies SAT and CF. This set $\mathcal{C}$ is then our minimal and therefore actual cause.

To check condition CF, we need to check the counterfactual of each candidate cause $\mathcal{C}$, and potentially also look for contingencies for $\mathcal{C}$. We separate our discussion as follows. We first discuss the calculation of the over-approximation $\tilde{\mathcal{C}}$ (Sect. 5.1), then we present the ActualCause algorithm that identifies a minimal subset of $\tilde{\mathcal{C}}$ that is an actual cause (Sect. 5.2), and finally we discuss in detail the calculation of contingencies (Sect. 5.3). In the following sections, we use a reduction of the universal fragment of HyperLTL to LTL, and the advantages of the linear translation of LTL to alternating automata, as we now briefly outline.

*HyperLTL to LTL.* Let $\varphi$ be a $\forall^n$-HyperLTL formula and $\Gamma$ be the counterexample. We construct an LTL formula $\varphi'$ from $\varphi$ as follows [31]: atomic propositions indexed with different trace variables are treated as different atomic propositions and trace quantifiers are eliminated. For example $\forall\pi,\pi'.a_\pi \wedge a_{\pi'}$ results in the LTL formula $a_\pi \wedge a_{\pi'}$. As for $\Gamma$, we use the same renaming in order to zip all traces into a single trace, for which we assume the finite representation $t'' = u'' \cdot (v'')^\omega$, which is also the structure of the model checker's output. The trace $t''$ is a violation of the formula $\varphi'$, i.e., $t''$ satisfies $\neg\varphi'$. We denote $\bar{\varphi} := \neg\varphi'$. We can then assume, for implementation concerns, that the specification (and its violation) is an LTL formula, and the counterexample is a single trace. After our causal analysis, the translation back to a cause over hyperproperties is straightforward as we maintain all information about the different traces in the counterexample. Note that this translation works due to the synchronous semantics of HyperLTL.

*Finite Trace Model Checking Using Alternating Automata.* In verifying condition CF (that is, in computing counterfactuals and contingencies), we need to apply finite trace model checking, as we want to check if the modified trace in hand still violates the specification $\varphi$, that is, satisfies $\bar{\varphi}$. To this end, we use the linear algorithm of [36], that exploits the linear translation of $\bar{\varphi}$ to an alternating automaton $\mathcal{A}_{\bar{\varphi}}$, and using backwards analysis checks the satisfaction of $\bar{\varphi}$. An alternating automaton [68] generalizes non-deterministic and universal automata, and its transition relation is a Boolean function over the states. The run of alternating automaton is then a *tree run* that captures the conjunctions in the formula. We use the algorithm of [36] as a black box (see App. A.2 in [22] for a formal definition of alternating automata and App. A.3 in [22] for the translation from LTL to alternating automata). For the computation of contingencies we use an additional feature of the algorithm of [36] – the algorithm returns an accepting run tree $\mathcal{T}$ of $\mathcal{A}_{\bar{\varphi}}$ on $t''$, with annotations of nodes that represent atomic subformulas of $\bar{\varphi}$ that take part in the satisfaction of $\bar{\varphi}$. We use this feature also in Sect. 5.1 when calculating the set of candidate causes.

### 5.1 Computing the Set of Candidate Causes

The events that might have been a part of the cause to the violation are in fact all events that appear on the counterexample, or, equivalently, all events that appear in $u''$ and $v''$. Note that due to the finite representation, this is a finite set of events. Yet, not all events in this set can cause the violation. In order to remove events that could not have been a part of the cause, we perform an analysis of the transitions of the system taken during the execution of $t''$. With this analysis we detect which events appearing in the trace locally cause the respective transitions, and thus might be part of the global cause. Events that did not trigger a transition in this specific trace cannot be a part of the cause. Note that causing a transition and being an actual cause are two different notions - actual causality is defined over the behaviour of the system, not on individual traces. We denote the over-approximation of the cause as $\tilde{\mathcal{C}}$. Formally, we represent each transition as a Boolean function over inputs and states. Let $\delta_n$ denote the formula representing the transition of the system taken when reading $t''[n]$, and let $c_{a,n,i}$ be a Boolean variable that corresponds to the event $\langle a_{t_i}, n, t''\rangle$.[2] Denote $\psi_n^t = \bigwedge_{a_{t_i} \in t''[n]} c_{a,n,i} \wedge \bigwedge_{a_{t_i} \notin t''[n]} \neg c_{a,n,i}$, that is, $\psi_n^t$ expresses the exact set of events in $t''[n]$. In order to find events that might trigger the transition $\delta_n$, we check for the *unsatisfiable core* of $\psi_n = (\neg\delta_n) \wedge \psi_n^t$. Intuitively, the unsatisfiable core of $\psi_n$ is the set of events that force the system to take this specific transition. For every $c_{a,n,i}$ (or $\neg c_{a,n,i}$ ) in the unsatisfiable core that is also a part of $\psi_n^t$, we add $\langle a, n, t_i\rangle$ (or $\langle \neg a, n, t_i\rangle$) to $\tilde{\mathcal{C}}$.

We use unsatisfiable cores in order to find input events that are necessary in order to take a transition. However, this might not be enough. There are cases in which inputs that appear in formula $\bar{\varphi}$ are not detected using this method, as they are not essential in order to take a transition; however, they might be considered a part of the actual cause, as negating them can avoid the violation. Therefore, as a second step, we apply the algorithm of [36] on the annotated automaton $\mathcal{A}_{\bar{\varphi}}$ in order to find the specific events that affect the satisfaction of $\bar{\varphi}$, and we add these events to $\tilde{\mathcal{C}}$. Then, the unsatisfiable core approach provides us with inputs that affect the computation and might cause the violation even though they do not appear on the formula itself; while the alternating automaton allows us to find inputs that are not essential for the computation, but might still be a part of the cause as they appear on the formula.

**Proposition 2.** *The set $\tilde{\mathcal{C}}$ is indeed an over-approximation of the cause for the violation. That is, every actual cause $\mathcal{C}$ for the violation is a subset of $\tilde{\mathcal{C}}$.*

*Proof (sketch).* Let $e = \langle l_a, n, t\rangle$ be an event such that $e$ is not in the unsatisfiable core of $\psi_n$ and does not directly affect the satisfaction of $\bar{\varphi}$ according to the alternating automata analysis. That is, the transition corresponding to $\psi_n^t$ is taken regardless of $e$, and thus all future events on $t$ remain the same regardless of the valuation of $e$. In addition, the valuation of the formula $\bar{\varphi}$ is the same regardless of $e$, since: (1) $e$ does not directly affect the satisfaction of $\bar{\varphi}$; (2) $e$ does not affect future events on $t$ (and obviously it does not affect past events). Therefore, every set $\mathcal{C}'$ such that $e \in \mathcal{C}'$ is not minimal, and does not form a cause. Since the above is true for all events $e \notin \tilde{\mathcal{C}}$, it holds that $\mathcal{C} \subseteq \tilde{\mathcal{C}}$ for every actual cause $\mathcal{C}$. □

**Proposition 3.** *The set $\tilde{\mathcal{C}}$ satisfies conditions SAT and CF.*

*Proof.* The condition SAT is satisfied as we add to $\tilde{\mathcal{C}}$ only events that indeed occur on the counterexample trace. For CF, consider that $\tilde{\mathcal{C}}$ is a super-set of the actual cause $\mathcal{C}$, so the same contingency and counterfactual of $\mathcal{C}$ will also apply for $\tilde{\mathcal{C}}$. This is since in order to compute counterfactual we are allowed to flip any subset of the events in $\mathcal{C}$, and any such subset is also a subset of $\tilde{\mathcal{C}}$.

[2] That is, $\neg c_{a,n,i}$ corresponds to the event $\langle \neg a_{t_i}, n, t''\rangle$. Recall that the atomic propositions on the zipped trace $t''$ are annotated with the original trace $t_i$ from $\Gamma$.

**Algorithm 1:** ActualCause($\varphi, \Gamma, \tilde{\mathcal{C}}$)

**Input**: Hyperproperty $\varphi$, counterexample $\Gamma$ violating $\varphi$, and a set of candidate causes $\tilde{\mathcal{C}}$ for which conditions SAT and CF hold.

**Output**: A set of input events $\mathcal{C}$ which is an actual cause for the violation.

```
for i ∈ [1, ..., |C̃| − 1] do
    for C ⊂ C̃ with |C| = i do
        let Γ^f = intervene(Γ, C, ∅);
        if Γ^f ⊨ φ then
            return C;
        else
            W̃ = ComputeContingency(φ, Γ, C);
            if W̃ ≠ ∅ then
                return C;
return C̃;
```

In addition, in computing contingencies, we are allowed to flip any subset of outputs as long as they agree with the counterexample trace, which is independent in $\tilde{\mathcal{C}}$ and $\mathcal{C}$. □

## 5.2 Checking Actual Causality

Due to Proposition 2 we know that in order to find an actual cause, we only need to consider subsets of $\tilde{\mathcal{C}}$ as candidate causes. In addition, since $\tilde{\mathcal{C}}$ satisfies condition SAT, so do all of its subsets. We thus only need to check conditions CF and MIN for subsets of $\tilde{\mathcal{C}}$. Our actual causality computation, presented in Algorithm 1 is as follows. We start with the set $\tilde{\mathcal{C}}$, that satisfies SAT and CF. We then check if there exists a more minimal cause that satisfies CF. This is done by iterating over all subsets $\mathcal{C}'$ of $\tilde{\mathcal{C}}$, ordered by size and starting with the smallest ones, and checking if the counterfactual for the $\mathcal{C}'$ manages to avoid the violation; and if not, if there exists a contingency for this $\mathcal{C}'$. If the answer to one of these questions is yes, then $\mathcal{C}'$ is a minimal cause that satisfies SAT, CF, and MIN, and thus we return $\mathcal{C}'$ as our actual cause. We now elaborate on CF and MIN.

*CF.* As we have mentioned above, checking condition CF is done in two stages – checking for counterfactuals and computing contingencies. We first show that we do not need to consider all possible counterfactuals, but only one counterfactual for each candidate cause.

**Proposition 4.** *In order to check if a candidate cause $\tilde{\mathcal{C}}$ is an actual cause it is enough to test the one counterfactual where all the events in $\tilde{\mathcal{C}}$ are flipped.*

*Proof.* Assume that there is a strict subset $\mathcal{C}$ of $\tilde{\mathcal{C}}$ such that we only need to flip the valuations of events in $\mathcal{C}$ in order to find a counterfactual or contingency, thus $\mathcal{C}$ satisfies CF. Since $\mathcal{C}$ is a more minimal cause than $\tilde{\mathcal{C}}$, we will find it during the minimality check. □

**Algorithm 2:** ComputeContingency($\varphi, \Gamma, \mathcal{C}$)

**Input**: Hyperproperty $\varphi$, a counterexample $\Gamma$ and a potential cause $\mathcal{C}$.
**Output**: a set of output events $\mathcal{W}$ which is a contingency for $\varphi, \Gamma$ and $\mathcal{C}$, or $\emptyset$ if no contingency found.

1 **let** $t''$ be the zipped trace of $\Gamma$, $\varphi'$ be the LTL formula obtained from $\varphi$, and $\bar{\varphi} = \neg\varphi'$;
2 **let** $\mathcal{A}_{\bar{\varphi}}$ be the alternating automaton for $\bar{\varphi}$;
3 **let** $t^f$ be the counterfactual trace obtained from $t''$ by flipping all events in $\mathcal{C}$;
4 **let** $\mathcal{N}$ be the sets of events derived from the annotated run tree of $\mathcal{A}_{\bar{\varphi}}$ on $t^f$;
5 **let** $\mathcal{O}' := \{\langle l_{a_t}, n, t''\rangle \in OE \mid a_t \in t''[n] \leftrightarrow a_t \notin t^f[n]\}$;
6 **for** *every subset* $\mathcal{W}' \subseteq (\mathcal{N} \cap \mathcal{O}')$, *and then for every other subset* $\mathcal{W}' \subseteq \mathcal{O}'$ **do**
7     $t^m := intervene(t'', \mathcal{C}, \mathcal{W}')$;
8     **if** $t^m \vDash \varphi'$ **then**
9         **return** $\mathcal{W}'$;
10 **return** $\emptyset$;

We assume that CF holds for the input set $\tilde{\mathcal{C}}$ and check if it holds for any smaller subset $\mathcal{C} \subset \tilde{\mathcal{C}}$. CF holds for $\mathcal{C}$ if (1) flipping all events in $\mathcal{C}$ is enough to avoid the violation of $\varphi$ or if (2) there exists a non-empty set of contingencies for $\mathcal{C}$ that ensures that $\varphi$ is not violated. The computation of contingencies is described in Algorithm 2. Verifying condition CF involves model checking traces against an LTL formula, as we check in Algorithm 1 (line 3) if the property $\varphi$ is still violated on the counterfactual trace with the empty contingency, and on the counterfactual traces resulting from the different contingency sets we consider in Algorithm 2 (line 7). In both scenarios, we apply finite trace model checking, as described at the beginning of Sect. 5 (as we assume lasso-shaped traces).

*MIN.* To check if $\tilde{\mathcal{C}}$ is minimal, we need to check if there exists a subset of $\tilde{\mathcal{C}}$ that satisfies CF. We check CF for all subsets, starting with the smallest one, and report the first subset that satisfies CF as our actual cause. (Note that we already established that $\tilde{\mathcal{C}}$ and all of its subsets satisfy SAT.)

### 5.3 Computing Contingencies

Recall that the role of contingencies is to eliminate the effect of other possible causes from the counterfactual world, in case these causes did not affect the violation in the actual world. More formally, in computing contingencies we look for a set $\mathcal{W}$ of output events such that changing these outputs from their value in the counterfactual to their value in the counterexample $t''$ results in avoiding the violation. Note that the inputs remain as they are in the counterfactual. We note that the problem of finding contingencies is hard, and in general is equivalent to the problem of model checking. This is since we need to consider all traces that are the result of changing some subset of events (output + time step) from the counterfactual back to the counterexample, and to check if there exists a trace in this set that avoids the violation. Unfortunately, we are unable to avoid an exponential complexity in the size of the original system, in the worst case. However, our experiments show that in practice, most cases do not require the use of contingencies.

Our algorithm for computing contingencies (Algorithm 2) works as follows. Let $t^f$ be the counterfactual trace. As a first step, we use the annotated run tree $\mathcal{T}$ of the alternating automaton $\mathcal{A}_{\bar{\varphi}}$ on $t^f$ to detect output events that appear in $\bar{\varphi}$ and take part in satisfying $\bar{\varphi}$. Subsets of these output events are our first candidates for contingencies as they are directly related to the violation (Algorithm 2 lines 4–9). If we were not able to find a contingency, we continue to check all possible subsets of output events that differ from the original counterexample trace. We test the different outputs by feeding the counterfactual automaton of Definition 4 with additional inputs from the set $I^C$. The resulted trace is then our candidate contingency, which we try to verify against $\varphi$. The number of different input sequences is bounded by the size of the product of the counterfactual automaton and the automaton for $\bar{\varphi}$, and thus the process terminates.

**Theorem 1 (Correctness).** *Our algorithm is sound and complete. That is, let $\Gamma$ be a counterexample with a finite representation to a $\forall^n$-HyperLTL formula $\psi$. Then, our algorithm returns an actual cause for the violation, if such exists.*

*Proof. Soundness.* Since we verify each candidate set of inputs according to the conditions SAT, CF and MIN, it holds that every output of our algorithm is indeed an actual cause. *Completeness.* If there exists a cause, then due to Proposition 2, it is a subset of the finite set $\tilde{\mathcal{C}}$. Since in the worst case we test every subset of $\tilde{\mathcal{C}}$, if there exists a cause we will eventually find it. □

## 6 Implementation and Experiments

We implemented Algorithm 1 and evaluated it on publicly available example instances of HyperVis [48], for which their state graphs were available. In the following, we provide implementation details, report on the running time and show the usefulness of the implementation by comparing to the highlighting output of HyperVis. Our implementation is written in Python and uses py-aiger [69] and Spot [27]. We compute the candidate cause according to Sect. 5.1 with pysat [50], using Glucose 4 [3,66], building on Minisat [66]. We ran experiments on a MacBook Pro with a 3, 3 GHz Dual-Core Intel Core i7 processor and 16 GB RAM[3].

*Experimental Results.* The results of our experimental evaluation can be found in Table 1. We report on the size of the analyzed counterexample $|\Gamma|$, the size of the violated formula $|\varphi|$, how long it took to compute the first, over-approximated cause (see time($\tilde{\mathcal{C}}$)) and state the approximation $\tilde{\mathcal{C}}$ itself, the number of computed minimal causes $\#(\mathcal{C})$ and the time it took to compute all of them (see time($\forall\mathcal{C}$)). The `Running Example` is described in Sect. 3, the instance `Security in & out`

[3] Our prototype implementation and the experimental data are both available at: https://github.com/reactive-systems/explaining-hyperproperty-violations.

**Table 1.** Experimental results of our implementation. Times are given in ms.

| Instance | $\|\Gamma\|$ | $\|\varphi\|$ | time($\tilde{\mathcal{C}}$) | $\tilde{\mathcal{C}}$ | #($\mathcal{C}$) | time($\forall\mathcal{C}$) |
|---|---|---|---|---|---|---|
| `Running example` | 10 | 9 | 19 | $\neg hi^0_{t_1}, hi^0_{t_2}$ | 2 | 55 |
| `Security in & out` | 35 | 19 | 292 | $hi^2_{t_1}, \neg hi^0_{t_1}, \neg hi^3_{t_1}, \neg hi^1_{t_1}$ $hi^2_{t_2}, hi^0_{t_2}, hi^1_{t_2}, hi^3_{t_2}$ | 8 | 798 |
| `Drone example 1` | 24 | 19 | 33 | $bound^2_{t_1}, \neg bound^1_{t_1}, up^1_{t_1}, \neg up^2_{t_1}$ $bound^2_{t_2}, \neg bound^1_{t_2}, \neg up^1_{t_2}$ | 5 | 367 |
| `Drone example 2` | 18 | 36 | 31 | $bound^1_{t_1}, \neg bound^1_{t_2}, up^1_{t_2}$ | 3 | 256 |
| `Asymmetric arbiter '19` | 28 | 35 | 53 | see App. A.4 in [22] | 10 | 490 |
| `Asymmetric arbiter` | 72 | 35 | 70 | see App. A.4 in [22] | 24 | 1480 |

refers to a system which leaks high security input by not satisfying a noninterference property, the `Drone examples` consider a leader-follower drone scenario, and the `Asymmetric Arbiter` instances refer to arbiter implementations that do not satisfy a symmetry constraint. Specifications can be found in the full version of this paper [22].

Our first observation is that the cause candidate $\tilde{\mathcal{C}}$ can be efficiently computed thanks to the iterative computation of unsatisfiable cores (Sect. 5.1). The cause candidate provides a tight over-approximation of possible minimal causes. As expected, the runtime for finding minimal causes increases for larger counterexamples. However, as our experiments show, the overhead is manageable, because we optimize the search for all minimal causes by only considering every subset in $\tilde{\mathcal{C}}$ instead of naively going over every combination of input events (see Proposition 2). Compared to the computationally heavy task of model checking to get a counterexample, our approach incurs little additional cost, which matches our theoretical results (see Proposition 1). During our experiments, we have found that computing the candidate $\tilde{\mathcal{C}}$ first has, additionally to providing a powerful heuristic, another benefit: Even when the computation of minimal causes becomes increasingly expensive, $\tilde{\mathcal{C}}$ can serve as an intermediate result for the user. By filtering for important inputs, such as high security inputs, $\tilde{\mathcal{C}}$ already gives great insight to why the property was violated. In the asymmetric arbiter instance, for example, the input events $\langle \neg tb\_secret, 3, t_0 \rangle$ and $\langle tb\_secret, 3, t_1 \rangle$ of $\tilde{\mathcal{C}}$, which cause the violation, immediately catch the eye (c.f App. A.4 in [22]).

*Comparison to HyperVis.* HyperVis [48] is a tool for visualizing counterexamples returned from the HyperLTL model checker MCHyper [35]. It highlights the events in the trace that it considers responsible for the violation based on the formula and the set of traces, without considering the system model. However, violations of many relevant security policies such as observational determinism are not caused by events whose atomic propositions appear in the formula, as can be seen in our running example (see Sect. 3 and Example 2). When running the highlight function of HyperVis for the counterexample traces $t_1, t_2$ on `Running example`, the output events $\langle lo, 1, t_1 \rangle$ and $\langle \neg lo, 1, t_2 \rangle$ will be highlighted, neglecting the decisive high security input $hi$. Using our method additionally reveals the input events $\langle \neg hi, 0, t_1 \rangle$ and $\langle hi, 0, t_2 \rangle$, i.e., an actual cause (see Table 1). This pattern can be observed throughout all considered instances in our experiments. For instance in the `Asymmetric arbiter` instance mentioned above, the input events causing the violation also do not occur in the formula (see App. A.5 in [22]) and thus HyperVis does not highlight this important cause for the violation.

## 7 Related Work

With the introduction of HyperLTL and HyperCTL* [20], temporal hyperproperties have been studied extensively: satisfiability [29,38,60], model checking [34,35,49], program repair [11], monitoring [2,10,32,67], synthesis [30], and expressiveness studies [23,37,53]. Causal analysis of hyperproperties has been studied theoretically based on counterfactual builders [40] instead of actual causality, as in our work. Explanation methods [4] exist for trace properties [5,39,41,42,70], integrated in several model checkers [14,15,19]. Minimization [54] has been studied, as well as analyzing several system traces together [9,43,65]. There exists work in explaining counterexamples for function block diagrams [51,63]. MODCHK uses a causality analysis [7] returning an over-approximation, while we provide minimal causes. Lastly, there are approaches which define actual causes for the violation of a trace property using Event Order Logic [13,56,57].

## 8 Conclusion

We present an explanation method for counterexamples to hyperproperties described by HyperLTL formulas. We lift Halpern and Pearl's definition of actual causality to effects described by hyperproperties and counterexamples given as sets of traces. Like the definition that inspired us, we allow modifications of the system dynamics in the counterfactual world through contingencies, and define these possible counterfactual behaviors in an automata-theoretic approach. The evaluation of our prototype implementation shows that our method is practically applicable and significantly improves the state-of-the-art in explaining counterexamples returned by a HyperLTL model checker.

## References

1. Log4j vulnerabilities. https://logging.apache.org/log4j/2.x/security.html
2. Agrawal, S., Bonakdarpour, B.: Runtime verification of k-safety hyperproperties in hyperltl. In: CSF 2016. https://doi.org/10.1109/CSF.2016.24
3. Audemard, G., Simon, L.: Predicting learnt clauses quality in modern SAT solvers. In: IJCAI 2009. http://ijcai.org/Proceedings/09/Papers/074.pdf
4. Baier, C., et al.: From verification to causality-based explications. In: ICALP 2021. https://doi.org/10.4230/LIPIcs.ICALP.2021.1

5. Ball, T., Naik, M., Rajamani, S.K.: From symptom to cause: localizing errors in counterexample traces. In: POPL 2003. https://doi.org/10.1145/604131.604140
6. Barthe, G., D'Argenio, P.R., Rezk, T.: Secure information flow by self-composition. Math. Struct. Comput. Sci. **21**(6), 1207–1252 (2011)
7. Beer, I., Ben-David, S., Chockler, H., Orni, A., Trefler, R.: Explaining counterexamples using causality. In: Bouajjani, A., Maler, O. (eds.) CAV 2009. LNCS, vol. 5643, pp. 94–108. Springer, Heidelberg (2009). https://doi.org/10.1007/978-3-642-02658-4_11
8. Biere, A.: The AIGER And-Inverter Graph (AIG) format version 20071012. Technical report 07/1, Inst. f. Form. Model. u. Verifikation, Johannes Kepler University (2007)
9. Bochot, T., Virelizier, P., Waeselynck, H., Wiels, V.: Paths to property violation: a structural approach for analyzing counter-examples. In: HASE 2010. https://doi.org/10.1109/HASE.2010.15
10. Bonakdarpour, B., Finkbeiner, B.: The complexity of monitoring hyperproperties. In: CSF 2018. https://doi.org/10.1109/CSF.2018.00019
11. Bonakdarpour, B., Finkbeiner, B.: Program repair for hyperproperties. In: Chen, Y.-F., Cheng, C.-H., Esparza, J. (eds.) ATVA 2019. LNCS, vol. 11781, pp. 423–441. Springer, Cham (2019). https://doi.org/10.1007/978-3-030-31784-3_25
12. Brayton, R., Mishchenko, A.: ABC: an academic industrial-strength verification tool. In: Touili, T., Cook, B., Jackson, P. (eds.) CAV 2010. LNCS, vol. 6174, pp. 24–40. Springer, Heidelberg (2010). https://doi.org/10.1007/978-3-642-14295-6_5
13. Caltais, G., Guetlein, S.L., Leue, S.: Causality for general LTL-definable properties. In: CREST@ETAPS 2018. https://doi.org/10.4204/EPTCS.286.1
14. Chaki, S., Clarke, E.M., Groce, A., Jha, S., Veith, H.: Modular verification of software components in C. IEEE Trans. Softw. Eng. **30**(6), 388–402 (2004)
15. Chaki, S., Groce, A., Strichman, O.: Explaining abstract counterexamples. In: ACM SIGSOFT Foundations of Software Engineering (2004). https://doi.org/10.1145/1029894.1029908
16. Chockler, H., Halpern, J.Y., Kupferman, O.: What causes a system to satisfy a specification? ACM Trans. Comput. Log. **9**(3), 20:1–20:26 (2008). https://doi.org/10.1145/1352582.1352588
17. Clarke, E.M., Biere, A., Raimi, R., Zhu, Y.: Bounded model checking using satisfiability solving. Formal Methods Syst. Des. **19**(1), 7–34 (2001)
18. Clarke, E.M., Emerson, E.A.: Design and synthesis of synchronization skeletons using branching-time temporal logic. In: Logics of Programs, Workshop, Yorktown Heights, New York, USA, May 1981. https://doi.org/10.1007/BFb0025774
19. Clarke, E., Kroening, D., Lerda, F.: A tool for checking ANSI-C programs. In: Jensen, K., Podelski, A. (eds.) TACAS 2004. LNCS, vol. 2988, pp. 168–176. Springer, Heidelberg (2004). https://doi.org/10.1007/978-3-540-24730-2_15
20. Clarkson, M.R., Finkbeiner, B., Koleini, M., Micinski, K.K., Rabe, M.N., Sánchez, C.: Temporal logics for hyperproperties. In: Abadi, M., Kremer, S. (eds.) POST 2014. LNCS, vol. 8414, pp. 265–284. Springer, Heidelberg (2014). https://doi.org/10.1007/978-3-642-54792-8_15
21. Clarkson, M.R., Schneider, F.B.: Hyperproperties. J. Comput. Secur. **18**(6), 1157–1210 (2010). https://doi.org/10.3233/JCS-2009-0393
22. Coenen, N., et al.: Explaining hyperproperty violations. CoRR (2022). https://doi.org/10.48550/ARXIV.2206.02074, full version with appendix
23. Coenen, N., Finkbeiner, B., Hahn, C., Hofmann, J.: The hierarchy of hyperlogics. In: LICS 2019. https://doi.org/10.1109/LICS.2019.8785713

24. Coenen, N., Finkbeiner, B., Sánchez, C., Tentrup, L.: Verifying hyperliveness. In: Dillig, I., Tasiran, S. (eds.) CAV 2019. LNCS, vol. 11561, pp. 121–139. Springer, Cham (2019). https://doi.org/10.1007/978-3-030-25540-4_7
25. D'Argenio, P.R., Barthe, G., Biewer, S., Finkbeiner, B., Hermanns, H.: Is your software on dope? In: Yang, H. (ed.) ESOP 2017. LNCS, vol. 10201, pp. 83–110. Springer, Heidelberg (2017). https://doi.org/10.1007/978-3-662-54434-1_4
26. Dehnert, C., Junges, S., Katoen, J.-P., Volk, M.: A storm is coming: a modern probabilistic model checker. In: Majumdar, R., Kunčak, V. (eds.) CAV 2017. LNCS, vol. 10427, pp. 592–600. Springer, Cham (2017). https://doi.org/10.1007/978-3-319-63390-9_31
27. Duret-Lutz, A., Lewkowicz, A., Fauchille, A., Michaud, T., Renault, É., Xu, L.: Spot 2.0—a framework for LTL and $\omega$-automata manipulation. In: Artho, C., Legay, A., Peled, D. (eds.) ATVA 2016. LNCS, vol. 9938, pp. 122–129. Springer, Cham (2016). https://doi.org/10.1007/978-3-319-46520-3_8
28. Durumeric, Z., et al.: The matter of heartbleed. In: IMC 2014. https://doi.org/10.1145/2663716.2663755
29. Finkbeiner, B., Hahn, C.: Deciding hyperproperties. In: CONCUR 2016. https://doi.org/10.4230/LIPIcs.CONCUR.2016.13
30. Finkbeiner, B., Hahn, C., Lukert, P., Stenger, M., Tentrup, L.: Synthesis from hyperproperties. Acta Informatica **57**(1-2), 137–163 (2020). https://doi.org/10.1007/s00236-019-00358-2
31. Finkbeiner, B., Hahn, C., Stenger, M., Tentrup, L.: RVHyper: a runtime verification tool for temporal hyperproperties. In: Beyer, D., Huisman, M. (eds.) TACAS 2018. LNCS, vol. 10806, pp. 194–200. Springer, Cham (2018). https://doi.org/10.1007/978-3-319-89963-3_11
32. Finkbeiner, B., Hahn, C., Stenger, M., Tentrup, L.: Monitoring hyperproperties. Formal Methods Syst. Des. **54**(3), 336–363 (2019). https://doi.org/10.1007/s10703-019-00334-z
33. Finkbeiner, B., Hahn, C., Torfah, H.: Model checking quantitative hyperproperties. In: Chockler, H., Weissenbacher, G. (eds.) CAV 2018. LNCS, vol. 10981, pp. 144–163. Springer, Cham (2018). https://doi.org/10.1007/978-3-319-96145-3_8
34. Finkbeiner, B., Müller, C., Seidl, H., Zalinescu, E.: Verifying security policies in multi-agent workflows with loops. In: CCS 2017. https://doi.org/10.1145/3133956.3134080
35. Finkbeiner, B., Rabe, M.N., Sánchez, C.: Algorithms for model checking HyperLTL and HyperCTL*. In: Kroening, D., Păsăreanu, C.S. (eds.) CAV 2015. LNCS, vol. 9206, pp. 30–48. Springer, Cham (2015). https://doi.org/10.1007/978-3-319-21690-4_3
36. Finkbeiner, B., Sipma, H.: Checking finite traces using alternating automata. Formal Methods Syst. Des. **24**(2), 101–127 (2004). https://doi.org/10.1023/B:FORM.0000017718.28096.48
37. Finkbeiner, B., Zimmermann, M.: The first-order logic of hyperproperties. In: STACS 2017. https://doi.org/10.4230/LIPIcs.STACS.2017.30
38. Fortin, M., Kuijer, L.B., Totzke, P., Zimmermann, M.: HyperLTL satisfiability is $\Sigma_1^1$-complete, HyperCTL* satisfiability is $\Sigma_1^2$-complete. In: MFCS 2021. https://doi.org/10.4230/LIPIcs.MFCS.2021.47
39. Gössler, G., Le Métayer, D.: A general trace-based framework of logical causality. In: Fiadeiro, J.L., Liu, Z., Xue, J. (eds.) FACS 2013. LNCS, vol. 8348, pp. 157–173. Springer, Cham (2014). https://doi.org/10.1007/978-3-319-07602-7_11

40. Gössler, G., Stefani, J.: Causality analysis and fault ascription in component-based systems. Theor. Comput. Sci. **837**, 158–180 (2020). https://doi.org/10.1016/j.tcs.2020.06.010
41. Groce, A., Chaki, S., Kroening, D., Strichman, O.: Error explanation with distance metrics. Int. J. Softw. Tools Technol. Transf. **8**(3), 229–247 (2006). https://doi.org/10.1007/s10009-005-0202-0
42. Groce, A., Kroening, D., Lerda, F.: Understanding Counterexamples with explain. In: Alur, R., Peled, D.A. (eds.) CAV 2004. LNCS, vol. 3114, pp. 453–456. Springer, Heidelberg (2004). https://doi.org/10.1007/978-3-540-27813-9_35
43. Groce, A., Visser, W.: What went wrong: explaining counterexamples. In: Ball, T., Rajamani, S.K. (eds.) SPIN 2003. LNCS, vol. 2648, pp. 121–136. Springer, Heidelberg (2003). https://doi.org/10.1007/3-540-44829-2_8
44. Halpern, J.Y.: A modification of the Halpern-Pearl definition of causality. In: IJCAI 2015. http://ijcai.org/Abstract/15/427
45. Halpern, J.Y., Pearl, J.: Causes and explanations: a structural-model approach. Part I: causes. Br. J. Philos. Sci. **56**(4), 843–887 (2005). http://www.jstor.org/stable/3541870
46. Halpern, J.Y., Pearl, J.: Causes and explanations: a structural-model approach. Part II: explanations. Br. J. Philos. Sci. **56**(4), 889–911 (2005). http://www.jstor.org/stable/3541871
47. Holzmann, G.J.: The model checker SPIN. IEEE Trans. Softw. Eng. **23**(5), 279–295 (1997). https://doi.org/10.1109/32.588521
48. Horak, T., et al.: Visual analysis of hyperproperties for understanding model checking results. IEEE Trans. Vis. Comput. Graph. **28**(1), 357–367 (2022). https://doi.org/10.1109/TVCG.2021.3114866
49. Hsu, T.-H., Sánchez, C., Bonakdarpour, B.: Bounded model checking for hyperproperties. In: Groote, J.F., Larsen, K.G. (eds.) TACAS 2021. LNCS, vol. 12651, pp. 94–112. Springer, Cham (2021). https://doi.org/10.1007/978-3-030-72016-2_6
50. Ignatiev, A., Morgado, A., Marques-Silva, J.: PySAT: a Python toolkit for prototyping with SAT oracles. In: Beyersdorff, O., Wintersteiger, C.M. (eds.) SAT 2018. LNCS, vol. 10929, pp. 428–437. Springer, Cham (2018). https://doi.org/10.1007/978-3-319-94144-8_26
51. Jee, E., et al.: FbdVerifier: interactive and visual analysis of counterexample in formal verification of function block diagram. J. Res. Pract. Inf. Technol. **42**(3), 171–188 (2010)
52. Kocher, P., et al.: Spectre attacks: exploiting speculative execution. In: SP 2019. https://doi.org/10.1109/SP.2019.00002
53. Krebs, A., Meier, A., Virtema, J., Zimmermann, M.: Team semantics for the specification and verification of hyperproperties. In: MFCS 2018. https://doi.org/10.4230/LIPIcs.MFCS.2018.10
54. Lahtinen, J., Launiainen, T., Heljanko, K., Ropponen, J.: Model checking methodology for large systems, faults and asynchronous behaviour: SARANA 2011 work report. No. 12 in VTT Tech., VTT Tech. Research Centre of Finland (2012)
55. Larsen, K.G., Pettersson, P., Yi, W.: UPPAAL in a nutshell. Int. J. Softw. Tools Technol. Transf. **1**(1–2) (1997). https://doi.org/10.1007/s100090050010
56. Leitner-Fischer, F., Leue, S.: Causality checking for complex system models. In: Giacobazzi, R., Berdine, J., Mastroeni, I. (eds.) VMCAI 2013. LNCS, vol. 7737, pp. 248–267. Springer, Heidelberg (2013). https://doi.org/10.1007/978-3-642-35873-9_16

57. Leitner-Fischer, F., Leue, S.: Probabilistic fault tree synthesis using causality computation. Int. J. Crit. Comput. Based Syst. **4**(2), 119–143 (2013). https://doi.org/10.1504/IJCCBS.2013.056492
58. Lewis, D.: Causation. J. Philos. **70**(17), 556–567 (1973)
59. Lipp, M., et al.: Meltdown: reading kernel memory from user space. Commun. ACM **63**(6), 46–56 (2020)
60. Mascle, C., Zimmermann, M.: The keys to decidable HyperLTL satisfiability: small models or very simple formulas. In: CSL 2020. https://doi.org/10.4230/LIPIcs.CSL.2020.29
61. McCullough, D.: Noninterference and the composability of security properties. In: Proceedings. 1988 IEEE Symposium on Security and Privacy, pp. 177–186 (1988)
62. Moore, E.F.: Gedanken-experiments on sequential machines. Aut. stud. **34** (1956)
63. Pakonen, A., Buzhinsky, I., Vyatkin, V.: Counterexample visualization and explanation for function block diagrams. In: INDIN 2018. https://doi.org/10.1109/INDIN.2018.8472025
64. Pnueli, A.: The temporal logic of programs. In: FOCS 1977 (1977)
65. Schuppan, V., Biere, A.: Shortest counterexamples for symbolic model checking of LTL with past. In: Halbwachs, N., Zuck, L.D. (eds.) TACAS 2005. LNCS, vol. 3440, pp. 493–509. Springer, Heidelberg (2005). https://doi.org/10.1007/978-3-540-31980-1_32
66. Sörensson, N.: Minisat 2.2 and minisat++ 1.1. SAT Race 2010
67. Stucki, S., Sánchez, C., Schneider, G., Bonakdarpour, B.: Gray-box monitoring of hyperproperties. In: ter Beek, M.H., McIver, A., Oliveira, J.N. (eds.) FM 2019. LNCS, vol. 11800, pp. 406–424. Springer, Cham (2019). https://doi.org/10.1007/978-3-030-30942-8_25
68. Vardi, M.Y.: Alternating automata: unifying truth and validity checking for temporal logics. In: McCune, W. (ed.) CADE 1997. LNCS, vol. 1249, pp. 191–206. Springer, Heidelberg (1997). https://doi.org/10.1007/3-540-63104-6_19
69. Vazquez-C., M., Rabe, M.: py-aiger. https://github.com/mvcisback/py-aiger
70. Wang, C., Yang, Z., Ivančić, F., Gupta, A.: Whodunit? Causal analysis for counterexamples. In: Graf, S., Zhang, W. (eds.) ATVA 2006. LNCS, vol. 4218, pp. 82–95. Springer, Heidelberg (2006). https://doi.org/10.1007/11901914_9

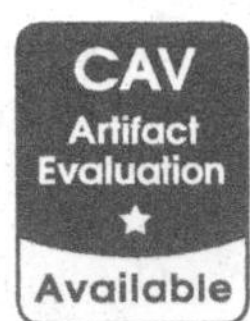


# Distilling Constraints in Zero-Knowledge Protocols

Elvira Albert[1], Marta Bellés-Muñoz[2], Miguel Isabel[1], Clara Rodríguez-Núñez[1](✉), and Albert Rubio[1]

[1] Complutense University of Madrid, Madrid, Spain
clarrodr@ucm.es
[2] Pompeu Fabra University, Barcelona, Spain

**Abstract.** The most widely used *Zero-Knowledge* (ZK) protocols require provers to prove they know a solution to a computational problem expressed as a *Rank-1 Constraint System* (R1CS). An R1CS is essentially a system of non-linear arithmetic constraints over a set of signals, whose security level depends on its non-linear part only, as the linear (additive) constraints can be easily solved by an attacker. Distilling the essential constraints from an R1CS by removing the part that does not contribute to its security is important, not only to reduce costs (time and space) of producing the ZK proofs, but also to reveal to cryptographic programmers the real hardness of their proofs. In this paper, we formulate the problem of distilling constraints from an R1CS as the (hard) problem of simplifying constraints in the realm of non-linearity. To the best of our knowledge, it is the first time that constraint-based techniques developed in the context of formal methods are applied to the challenging problem of analysing and optimizing ZK protocols.

## 1 Introduction

Zero-Knowledge (ZK) protocols [8,15,17,27] enable one party, called prover, to convince another one, called verifier, that a statement is true without revealing any information beyond the veracity of the "statement". In this context, we understand a statement as a relation between an instance, a *public* input known to both prover and verifier, and a *witness*, a *private* input known only to the prover, which belongs to a language $\mathcal{L}$ in the nondeterministic polynomial time (NP) complexity class [5,15]. The most popular, efficient and general-purpose ZK protocols are ZK-SNARKs: ZK Succinct Non-interactive ARguments of Knowledge. While a proof guarantees the existence of a witness in a language $\mathcal{L}$, and *argument of knowledge* proves that, with very high probability, the prover knows a concrete valid witness in $\mathcal{L}$. A ZK-SNARK does not require interaction between the prover and the verifier, and regardless of the size of the statement being proved, the size of the proof is succinct. These appealing properties of ZK-SNARKs have made them become crucial tools in many real-world applications


S. Shoham and Y. Vizel (Eds.): CAV 2022, LNCS 13371, pp. 430–443, 2022.
https://doi.org/10.1007/978-3-031-13185-1_21

with strong privacy issues. A prominent such example is Zcash [4]. ZK protocols are also being used in conjunction with smart contracts, in the so-called *ZK-rollups* for enhancing the scalability of distributed ledgers [18].

Like most ZK systems, ZK-SNARKs operate in the model of *arithmetic circuits*, meaning that the NP language $\mathcal{L}$ is that of satisfiable arithmetic circuits. The gates of an arithmetic circuit consist of additions and multiplications modulo $p$, where $p$ is typically a large prime number of approximately 254 bits [3]. The wires of an arithmetic circuit are called signals, and can carry any value from the prime finite field $\mathbb{F}_p$. In the ZK context, there is usually a set of public inputs known both to the prover and the verifier, and the prover proves that she knows a valid assignment to the rest of signals that satisfies the circuit (i.e., the witness). Most ZK-SNARK protocols draw from a classical algebraic form for encoding circuits and wire assignment called rank-1 constraint system (R1CS). An R1CS encodes a circuit as a set of quadratic constraints over its variables, so that a correct execution of a circuit is equivalent to finding a satisfying variable assignment. This way, a valid witness for an arithmetic circuit translates naturally into a solution of its R1CS representation.

Although ZK protocols guarantee that a malicious verifier cannot extract a witness from a proof, they do not prevent the verifier from attacking the statement directly. Hence, it is important that the prover is aware of the difficulty of the statement being proved. In this regard, it is challenging for cryptographic developers that apply ZK protocols to complex computations to assess the real hardness of the produced computational problem, being hence also difficult to verify and audit the systems. It is partly because a syntactic assessment (e.g. based on counting the number of non-linear constraints) can be inaccurate and misleading. This is the case if the R1CS contains *redundant* constraints, i.e., constraints that can be deduced from others or constraints that follow from linear constraints, since they do not contribute to the hardness of the computational statement. Distilling the relevant constraints is important on one hand for efficiency, to reduce costs (time and space) of producing the ZK proofs, and also because redundancy can mislead developers to believe that the statement is far more complex than it really is. It is clear that when arithmetic circuits are defined over a finite field of small order, the problem can be attacked by brute-force, or if the system consists only of linear constraints, a solution can be found in polynomial time [25]. Moreover, in R1CS-based systems like [17] only multiplication gates add complexity to the statement. Also note that linear constraints induce a way to compute the value of one signal from a linear combination of the others, and hence we can easily extend a witness for the other signals to a witness for all the signals. As a result, the difficulty of finding a solution to a system relies mostly in the number of *non-redundant non-linear constraints.*

*Contributions.* This case study paper applies techniques developed in the context of formal methods to distill constraints from the R1CS systems used by ZK protocols. The main challenges are related, on the one hand, to reasoning with non-linear information in a finite field and, on the other hand, to dealing with very large constraint systems. Briefly, our main contributions are: (1) we present a formal framework to reason on circuit reduction which generalizes the application of different existing optimizations and the reduction strategy in which they are applied, (2) we introduce a concrete new optimization technique based on Gaussian elimination that allows deducing linear constraints from the non-linear constraints, (3) we implement our approach within `circom` [21] (a novel domain-specific language and compiler for defining arithmetic circuits) and also develop an interface for using it on the R1CS generated by `ZoKrates` [12], (4) we experimentally evaluate its performance on multiple real-world circuits (including templates from the `circom` library [22] and from [12], on implementations of different SHA-2 hash functions, on elliptic curve operations, etc.).

## 2 Preliminaries

This section introduces some preliminary notions and notation. We consider $\mathbb{F}_p$ a finite field of prime order $p$. As usual, $\mathbb{F}_p^n$ is a sequence of $n$ values in $\mathbb{F}_p$. We drop $p$ from $\mathbb{F}$ when it is irrelevant. An arithmetic circuit (over the field $\mathbb{F}$) consists of wires (represented by means of signals $s_i \in \mathbb{F}$) connected to gates (represented by *quadratic constraints*). Signals can be public or private. We now define the concepts of quadratic constraints and R1CS over a set of signals.

**Definition 1 (R1CS).** *A* quadratic constraint *over a set of signals* $\{s_1, \ldots, s_n\}$ *is an equation of the form* $Q : A \times B - C = 0$, *where* $A, B, C \in \mathbb{F}[s_1, ..., s_n]$ *are linear polynomials over the variables* $s_1, ..., s_n$, *i.e.,* $A = a_0 + a_1 s_1 + \cdots + a_n s_n$, $B = b_0 + b_1 s_1 + \cdots + b_n s_n$, *and* $C = c_0 + c_1 s_1 + \cdots + c_n s_n$, *where* $a_i, b_i, c_i \in \mathbb{F}$ *for all* $i \in \{0, \ldots, n\}$. *A* rank-1 constraint system (R1CS) *over a set of signals* $T$ *is a collection of quadratic constraints over* $T$.

We say that a quadratic constraint $Q$ is *linear* when $A$ or $B$ only have the constant term, i.e., $a_i = 0 \; \forall i \in \{1, \ldots, n\}$ or $b_i = 0 \; \forall i \in \{1, \ldots, n\}$, and is *non-linear* otherwise. As R1CS systems only contain quadratic constraints, in what follows, we simply call them *constraints*, and specify if they are linear or not where needed. We use the standard notation $S \models c$ to indicate that a constraint $c$ is deducible from a set of constraints $S$ and $|S|$ for the number of constraints.

**Definition 2 (arithmetic circuit and witness).** *An* (arithmetic) circuit *is a tuple* $\mathcal{C} = (U, V, S)$ *where* $U$ *represents the set of public signals,* $V$ *represents the set of private signals, and the R1CS* $S = \{Q_1, \ldots, Q_m\}$ *over the signals* $U \cup V$ *represents the circuit operations. Given an assignment* $u$ *for* $U$, *a* witness *for* $\mathcal{C}$ *is an assignment* $v$ *for* $V$ *s.t.* $u$ *together with* $v$ *are a solution to the R1CS* $S$.

We use the terms *circuit* and, R1CS or just constraint system, indistinctly when the signals used in the circuit are clear. Given a circuit $\mathcal{C}$ and a public assignment for $U$, a ZK protocol is a mechanism that allows a prover to prove to a verifier that she knows a private assignment for $V$ that, together with those for $U$, satisfy the R1CS system describing $\mathcal{C}$. ZK protocols guarantee that the proof will not reveal any information about $V$.

*Example 1.* We consider a circuit $\mathcal{C}_1 = (U, V, S_1)$ over a finite field $\mathbb{F}$, with $U = \{v, w\}$, $V = \{x, y, z\}$, and $S_1$ given by the following constraint system:

$$Q_1 : w \times (y + z) - 4x - 10 = 0, \quad Q_2 : w \times z - w - 3 = 0,$$
$$Q_3 : (x - w + 1) \times v - v + 1 = 0, \; Q_4 : y - z - 2 = 0.$$

This circuit contains 3 non-linear constraints ($Q_1$, $Q_2$, and $Q_3$) and a linear one ($Q_4$). Because of its small size, we can easily solve the system (i.e., give the value of each signal in terms of only one of them) and find the set of solutions:
$W = \{(v, w, x, y, z) \mapsto (1, w, w - 1, 3w^{-1} + 3, 3w^{-1} + 1) \mid w \in \mathbb{F} \setminus \{0\}\}$.

A cryptographic problem can be modeled by different circuits producing the same solutions. This relation among circuits can be formalized as *circuit equivalence*, which is a natural extension of the constraint system equivalence. We say that two circuits $\mathcal{C} = (U, V, S)$ and $\mathcal{C}' = (U, V, S')$ are *equivalent*, written $\mathcal{C} \simeq \mathcal{C}'$, if $S$ and $S'$ have the same set of solutions. Consequently, if $\mathcal{C}$ and $\mathcal{C}'$ are equivalent, they have the same set of solutions and hence of witnesses.

*Example 2.* The circuit $\mathcal{C}_2 = (U, V, S_2)$ with the same sets of public and private signals $U$ and $V$ as $\mathcal{C}_1$, and the R1CS $S_2$ given by the constraints:

$$Q_1' : w \times y - 3w - 3 = 0, \quad Q_2' : y - z - 2 = 0, \quad Q_3' : v - 1 = 0, \quad Q_4' : x - w + 1 = 0,$$

has the same set of solutions (and thus witnesses) as $\mathcal{C}_1$. Hence, $\mathcal{C}_1 \simeq \mathcal{C}_2$.

## 3 A Formal Framework for R1CS Reduction

R1CS optimizations are applied within state-of-the-art compilers like `circom` [21] or `ZoKrates` [12]. Common to such existing compiler optimizations is the application of rules to simplify and eliminate linear constraints and/or to deduce information from them. As our first contribution, we present a formal framework for R1CS reduction based on a rule-based transformation system which is general enough to be a formal basis for developing specific simplification techniques and reduction strategies. In particular, the simplifications already applied in the above compilers are instantiations of our framework.

The notion of reduction that our framework formalizes is key to define the security level of circuits. When two circuits model the same problem, they provide the same level of security. However, an assessment of their security level based on syntactically counting the number of non-linear constraints in the circuits can lead to a wrong understanding/estimation of their security. For instance, circuits $\mathcal{C}_1$ and $\mathcal{C}_2$ (see Examples 1-2) model the same problem, although $\mathcal{C}_2$ needs a single non-linear constraint to define its set of solutions (instead of three as $\mathcal{C}_1$). This happens because some of the non-linear constraints of $\mathcal{C}_1$ are not essential and can be substituted by linear constraints. Besides, we can observe in $\mathcal{C}_2$ that signals $x$ and $z$ are only involved in linear constraints instead of being on non-linear constraints like in $\mathcal{C}_1$. In other words, *having a circuit with more private signals involved in non-linear constraints (e.g.,* $\mathcal{C}_1$*) does not ensure further security if these private* *signals can be deduced from linear combinations of the others.* We build our notion of *circuit reduction* upon this concept.

**Definition 3 (circuit-reduction).** *Let* $\mathcal{C} = (U, V, S)$ *be a circuit with* $U \cup V = \{s_1, \ldots, s_n\}$*, and* $\mathcal{C}' = (U, V', S')$ *another circuit with* $V \subseteq V'$*.*

*(i) We say that* $\mathcal{C}'$ linearly follows *from* $\mathcal{C}$*, denoted by* $\mathcal{C} \models_l \mathcal{C}'$*, if* $\forall s \in V' \setminus V$*,* $\exists \lambda_0^s, \lambda_1^s, \ldots, \lambda_n^s \in \mathbb{F}$*, s.t. given an assignment for* $U$*, every witness* $\phi$ *for* $\mathcal{C}$ *extended with* $s \mapsto \lambda_0^s + \sum_{i=1}^{n} \lambda_i^s * \phi(s_i)$ *is a witness for* $\mathcal{C}'$*.*
*(ii) We say that* $\mathcal{C}'$ reduces *to* $\mathcal{C}$*, written* $\mathcal{C}' \geq \mathcal{C}$*, if* $\mathcal{C} \models_l \mathcal{C}'$*,* $|S'| \geq |S|$ *and every witness of* $\mathcal{C}'$ *restricted to* $V$ *is a witness for* $\mathcal{C}$ *for the same assignment of* $U$*. We say that* $\mathcal{C}'$ strictly reduces *to* $\mathcal{C}$*, written* $\mathcal{C}' > \mathcal{C}$ *if* $|S'| > |S|$ *or* $V \subset V'$*.*

Intuitively, we have that for every signal defined in $V$, the values of the two witnesses match, and for the signals defined in $V' \setminus V$, the value of the witness of $C'$ can be obtained from a linear combination of the values from the assignment for $U$ and $\phi$.

*Example 3.* Let $\mathcal{C}_3$ be $(\{v, w\}, \{y\}, S_3)$ with $S_3 = \{Q_1'' : w \times y - 3w - 3 = 0, Q_2'' : v - 1 = 0\}$. Let us show that $\mathcal{C}_1$ (from Example 1) strictly reduces to $\mathcal{C}_3$. From Example 2, we have that every solution of $\mathcal{C}_1$ restricted to $\{v, w, y\}$ is also a solution of $\mathcal{C}_3$ (since $S_3 \subseteq S_2$ and $\mathcal{C}_2 \simeq \mathcal{C}_1$) and that in every witness $\phi'$ of $\mathcal{C}_2$ we have that $\phi'(x) = \phi'(w) - 1$ and $\phi'(z) = \phi'(y) - 2$. Therefore, taking $\lambda_0^x = -1$, $\lambda_{\text{pos}(w)}^x = 1$, $\lambda_0^z = -2$, $\lambda_{\text{pos}(y)}^z = 1$ (where function $\text{pos}(s_i)$ abstracts the index $i$ of the variable $s_i$ in the set of signals), we have that $\mathcal{C}_3 \models_l \mathcal{C}_1$. Finally, since $\{y\} \subset \{x, y, z\}$ and, given an assignment for $\{v, w\}$, every witness of $\mathcal{C}_1$ restricted to $\{y\}$ is a witness for $\mathcal{C}_3$, and we can conclude.

We now present a set of transformation rules that ensure circuit reducibility. The transformation is based on finding linear consequences of the constraint system to guarantee that the transformed set of constraints linearly follows from the original system. Our transformation rules operate on pairs in $\mathbb{K} \times \mathbb{S}_{\mathbb{L}}$, where $\mathbb{K}$ is the set of arithmetic circuits and $\mathbb{S}_{\mathbb{L}}$ is the set of linear constraint systems. As usual, we use infix notation, writing $(\mathcal{C}, S_L) \Rightarrow (\mathcal{C}', S_L{}')$, and denote respectively by $\Rightarrow^+$ and $\Rightarrow^*$, its transitive and reflexive-transitive closure. Given a circuit $\mathcal{C}$, if $(\mathcal{C}, \emptyset) \Rightarrow^* (\mathcal{C}', S_L)$, then $\mathcal{C}'$ is a reduction for $\mathcal{C}$, and the linear system $S_L$ shows how to prove that $\mathcal{C}' \models_l \mathcal{C}$. In the following, we assume that there exists a total order $<$ among the private signals in $V$ which is used to select a signal among the private signals of a constraint $c$, denoted by $V(c)$.

(REMOVE) $((U, V, S \cup \{c\}), S_L) \Rightarrow ((U, V, S), S_L)$, **if** $S \models c$.
(DEDUCE) $((U, V, S), S_L) \Rightarrow ((U, V, S), S_L \cup \{c\})$, **if** $c$ **linear**, $S \models c$, $c \notin S_L$.
(SIMPLIFY) $((U, V, S), S_L \cup \{s = l\}) \Rightarrow ((U, V \setminus \{s\}, S[s \mapsto l]), S_L[s \mapsto l] \cup \{s = l\})$,
**if** $s \in V$ **and** $\forall x \in V(l)$, $x < s$.

**Fig. 1.** Circuit transformation rules.

The REMOVE rule allows us to remove redundant constraints. The DEDUCE rule is needed to extract from $S$ linear relations among the signals. Finally, the SIMPLIFY rule allows us to safely remove a signal $s$ from $V$ by replacing it by an equivalent linear combination of public and (strictly) smaller private signals in $S$. The fact that we replace a private signal by strictly smaller ones prevents this rule from being applied infinitely many times. When no constraint or private signal can be removed from a circuit (e.g., from $\mathcal{C}_3$) after applying a sequence of reduction rule steps, the circuit is considered *irreducible* and we call it a *normal form*. Note that the linear constraints in $S_L$ with signals not belonging to $U \cup V$ are the ones that track how to obtain the missing signals from the remaining ones.

The three rules from Fig. 1 are terminating and they are contained in the circuit reducibility relation (Definition 3) when projected to the first component (the circuit). Regarding confluence, we have that if $(\mathcal{C}, S_L) \Rightarrow^* (\mathcal{C}_1, S_{L1})$ and $(\mathcal{C}, S_L) \Rightarrow^* (\mathcal{C}_2, S_{L2})$, then we have that $(\mathcal{C}_1, S_{L1}) \Rightarrow^* (\mathcal{C}_1', S_{L1}')$ and $(\mathcal{C}_2, S_{L2}) \Rightarrow^* (\mathcal{C}_2', S_{L2}')$ such that $\mathcal{C}_1'$ and $\mathcal{C}_2'$ are equivalent (see Appendix).

*Example 4.* Let us apply our reduction system to find a normal form of $(\mathcal{C}_1, \emptyset)$ which corresponds to its reduction. At each step we label the arrow with the applied rule and show only the component that is modified from the previous step (we use _ to indicate the value of the component as in the previous step):

$$\begin{aligned}((U,V,S_1),\emptyset) &\overset{\text{DEDUCE}}{\Rightarrow} ((\_,\_,\_),\{L_1 : z = y-2\}) \overset{\text{SIMPLIFY}}{\Rightarrow} (\_,\_ \setminus \{z\}, \_[z \mapsto y-2]),\_) \\ &\overset{\text{REMOVE}}{\Rightarrow} ((\_,\_,\_ \setminus \{0=0\}),\_) \overset{\text{DEDUCE}}{\Rightarrow} ((\_,\_,\_),\_ \cup \{L_2 : x = w-1\}) \\ &\overset{\text{SIMPLIFY}}{\Rightarrow} ((\_,\_ \setminus \{x\}, \_[x \mapsto w-1]),\_) \\ &\overset{\text{REMOVE}}{\Rightarrow} ((\_,\_,\_ \setminus \{Q : w \times (2y-2) - 4w - 6 = 0\}),\_)\end{aligned}$$

Here $(\mathcal{C}_3, \{L_1, L_2\})$ is a normal form of $(\mathcal{C}_1, \emptyset)$ and, as we have already seen in Example 3, $\mathcal{C}_3$ is a reduction for $\mathcal{C}_1$. Note that $\{L_1, L_2\}$ shows how to obtain the values of the removed signals as a linear combination.

## 4 Circuit Reduction Using Constraint Simplification

In this section, we introduce different strategies to apply the transformation rules described in Fig. 1, and also to approximate the deduction relation $S \models c$ in rules REMOVE and DEDUCE. Note that the classical representation of our problem is undecidable, but since we work in a finite field, it becomes decidable. However, as the order of $\mathbb{F}$ is large, it is still impractical and approximation is required.

As an example, let us show how the simplification techniques applied in `ZoKrates` and `circom` fit in our framework. In both languages, besides the removal of tautologies, all simplification steps are made using linear constraints that are part of the set of constraints. In particular, in a first step both languages handle the so-called *redefinitions* (i.e., constraints of the form $x = y$), and in a second step all the remaining linear constraints are eliminated applying the necessary substitutions. In our framework, these simplification steps can be described as a sequence of DEDUCE to obtain the linear constraints that will be applied as substitutions, followed by a sequence of SIMPLIFY, and a sequence of REMOVE to delete the tautologies obtained after the substitutions. The whole sequence can be repeated until no linear constraints are left in the circuit. The specific strategy followed to perform the sequence of DEDUCE steps to obtain the substitutions used to simplify the circuit from its linear constraints has a big impact in the efficiency of the process. For instance, `circom` considers all maximal clusters of linear constraints (sharing signals) in the system and then infers in one go all the substitutions to be applied for every cluster, using a lazy version of Gauss-Jordan elimination. This process can be very expensive when the number of constraints in the R1CS is very large (e.g. hundreds of millions in ZK-Rollups like Hermez [20]).

Similar techniques based on analyzing the linear constraints are applied in other circuit-design languages. However, up to our knowledge, no language uses the non-linear part of the circuit to infer new linear constraints, or to remove redundant constraints, and this constitutes the second main contribution of this work. In the remaining of this section, we present a new approach inspired by techniques used in program analysis and SMT-solving like [9,11], where the non-linear reasoning is reduced to linear-reasoning. We can assume that we have applied first the aforementioned strategies to obtain an R1CS containing only non-linear constraints (or linear constrains with only public signals). Then, in our framework, the problem of inferring new linear constraints from non-linear R1CS can be formalized as a synthesis problem as follows: "*given a circuit* $(U, V, S)$, *where* $U \cup V = \{s_1, \dots, s_n\}$, *our goal is to find a linear expression* $l = c_0 + c_1 s_1 + \dots + c_n s_n$ *with* $c_0, c_1, \dots, c_n \in \mathbb{F}$ *such that* $S \models l = 0$." In order to solve this problem, we follow an efficient approach in which we restrict ourselves to the case where $l = 0$ can be expressed as a linear combination of constraints in $S$, i.e., of the form $\sum \lambda_k * Q_k$ with $Q_k \in S$ and $\lambda_k \in \mathbb{F}$. It is clear that any constraint $l = 0$ obtained using this approach satisfies $S \models l = 0$, but we are only interested in the ones that are linear. In the following two stages, we describe how to obtain linear expressions $l$, and hence, infer the constraints.

**Stage 1.** First, for each constraint $Q_k : A_k \times B_k - C_k = 0$, $k \in \{1, \dots, m\}$, we expand the multiplication $A_k \times B_k$, obtaining the expression $\sum_{1 \le i \le j \le n} Q_k[i,j] * s_i s_j + L_k$, where $Q_k[i,j]$ for $1 \le i \le j \le n$ denotes the coefficient of the monomial $s_i s_j$ in the constraint $Q_k$, and $L_k$ is the linear part of $A_k \times B_k$.

*Example 5.* Let us consider the circuit from Example 4 after applying the first three transformation rules, i.e. after removing the linear constraints. We denote the resulting circuit $C_4 = (U, V_4, S_4)$, where $U \cup V_4 = \{v, w, x, y\}$ and $S_4$ is given by:

$$Q_1 : w \times (2y - 2) - 4x - 10 = 0, \;\; Q_2 : w \times (y - 2) - w - 3 = 0,$$
$$Q_3 : (x - w + 1) \times v - v + 1 = 0.$$

Here, we have for $Q_1$ that $A_1 = w$, $B_1 = 2y - 2$ and $C_1 = 4x + 10$ (recall that we consider $A_1 \times B_1 - C_1 = 0$). Then, we expand the multiplication $A_1 \times B_1 = 2wy - 2w$, so that $L_1 = -2w$ and $Q_1[2,4] = 2$ (for $wy$), where the later is the only non-zero coefficient of a quadratic monomial. Similarly, for $Q_2$ we have

$C_2 = w + 3$, $Q_2[2,4] = 1$ (also for $wy$) and $L_2 = -2w$. Finally, for $Q_3$ we have $C_3 = v - 1$, and $Q_3[1,3] = 1$ (for $vx$) and $Q_3[1,2] = -1$ (for $vw$) and $L_3 = v$.

**Stage 2.** Now, we can model a sufficient condition of linearity using the previous ingredients: if there exist $\lambda_1, \ldots, \lambda_m \in \mathbb{F}$ such that, for every $i, j$ with $1 \leq i \leq j \leq n$, we have that $\sum_{k=1}^{m} \lambda_k * Q_k[i,j] = 0$, then $l = \sum_{k=1}^{m} \lambda_k * (L_k - C_k)$ is linear and $S \models l = 0$. Moreover, assuming that $S$ is consistent, we have that either $l = 0$ is a tautology $0 = 0$ or it is a non-trivial linear constraint. In the first case, any of the constraints $Q_k$ with $\lambda_k \neq 0$ follows from the rest of the constraints and we can apply the REMOVE rule. In the second case, we can apply DEDUCE and later SIMPLIFY if $l$ has at least one private signal. Note that, after applying SIMPLIFY one of the constraints $Q_k$ with $\lambda_k \neq 0$ will follow from the rest, and we will be able to finally apply REMOVE.

*Example 6 (continued).* Following the example, we need to find $\lambda_1, \lambda_2, \lambda_3$ such that (considering only the non-zero coefficients $Q[i,j]$) $2\lambda_1 + \lambda_2 = 0$ (for $Q[2,4]$), $2\lambda_3 = 0$ (for $Q[1,3]$), and $-\lambda_3 = 0$ (for $Q[1,2]$). Since the monomials $vx$ and $vw$ occur only once, the only solution for $\lambda_3$ is 0. Now solving $2\lambda_1 + \lambda_2 = 0$, we get that $\lambda_2 = -2\lambda_1$. Hence, we take the solution $\lambda_1 = 1$ and $\lambda_2 = -2$. With this solution, $l = 1 * (-2w - (4x + 10)) + (-2) * (-2w - (w + 3)) + 0 * (v - (v - 1))$. Hence, we obtain $4w - 4x - 4 = 0$, which is equivalent to $x - w + 1 = 0$ that is the deduced linear constraint used in Example 4 to reduce the original circuit.

To conclude, finding $\lambda_1, \ldots, \lambda_m \in \mathbb{F}$ such that for every $i, j$ with $1 \leq i \leq j \leq n$, then $\sum_{k=1}^{m} \lambda_k * Q_k[i,j] = 0$, is a linear problem that can be solved using Gaussian elimination or similar techniques. Note that we are only interested in solutions with at least one $\lambda_k \neq 0$. Therefore, we can efficiently synthesize new linear constraints or show that some constraint follows from the others using this approach.

Regarding the practical application of our technique, since sometimes we are handling very large sets of non-linear constraints, additional engineering is needed to make it work. For instance, we need to remove those constraints that have a quadratic monomial that appears in no other constraint, and after that, compute maximal clusters sharing the same quadratic monomials. We have observed in our experimental evaluation that, in general, even for large circuits, each cluster remains small. Thanks to this, we obtain rather small independent sets of constraints that can be solved in parallel using Gaussian elimination.

## 5 Experimental Results

This section describes our experimental evaluation on two settings: On one hand (Sect. 5.1), we have implemented them within `circom` [21], a novel domain-specific language and compiler for defining arithmetic circuits, fully written in Rust. The `circom` compiler generates executable code (`WebAssembly` or `C++`) to compute the witness, together with the R1CS, since both are later needed by ZK tools to produce ZK proofs. The implementation is available in a public fork of the compiler [1]; On the other hand (Sect. 5.2), we have decoupled the constraint optimization module from the circom compiler in a new project, which is accessible online [2], in order to be able to use it after other cryptographic-language compilers that produce R1CS, in our case with ZoKrates [12]. ZoKrates is a high-level language that allows the programmer to abstract the technicalities of building arithmetic circuits. The input to our optimizer is the R1CS in the smtlib2 format generated by ZoKrates. The goal of our experiments is two fold: (1) assess the scalability of the approach when applied to real-world circuits used in industry and (2) evaluate its impact on code already highly optimized –such as circom's libraries developed on a low-level language by experienced programmers– and on code automatically compiled from a high-level language such as ZoKrates. In both cases, the optimizations of linear constraints that the compilers include (see Sect. 4) are enabled so that the reduction gains are due only to our optimization. Experimental results have been obtained using an AMD Ryzen Threadripper PRO 3995WX 64-Cores Processor with 512 GB of RAM (Linux Kernel Debian 5.10.70-1).

### 5.1 Results on circom Circomlib

circom is a modular language that allows the definition of parameterizable small circuits called "templates" and has its own library called circomlib [22]. This library is widely used for cryptographic purposes and contains hundreds of templates such as comparators, hash functions, digital signatures, binary and decimal converters, and many more. Our experiments have been performed on the available test cases from circomlib. Many of them have been carefully programmed by experienced cryptographers to avoid unnecessary non-linear constraints and our optimization cannot deduce new linear constraints. Still, we are able to reduce 26% of the total tests (12 out of 46).

Table 1 shows the results for the five circuits that we optimize the most. For each of them, we show: (**#C**) the number of generated constraints, (**#R**) the number of removed constraints, (**G%**) the gains expressed as **#R/#C x 100**, and (**T(s)**) the compilation time. The largest gain is for pointbits_loopback, where circom generates 2.333 constraints and we remove 381 of them, our gain is 16.33% and the compilation time is 13.4s. As explained in Sect. 4, for each linear constraint deduced by our technique, we are always able to remove a non-linear constraint and, in general, also a signal. Note that we sometimes produce new linear constraints in which all the involved signals are public and thus, none of them can be removed. Importantly, in spite of the manual simplifications already made in most of the circuits in circomlib, our techniques detect further redundant constraints in a short time. Such small reductions in templates of circomlib

**Table 1.** Results on circomlib.

| Circuit | #C | #R | G% | T(s) |
|---|---|---|---|---|
| sha256_2_test | 30134 | 32 | 0.11% | 15.6s |
| eddsamimc_test | 5712 | 46 | 0.81% | 1.9s |
| eddsaposeidon_test | 4217 | 46 | 1.09% | 1.7s |
| eddsa_test | 7554 | 556 | 7.36% | 4.8s |
| pointbits_loopback | 2333 | 381 | 16.33% | 13.4s |

can produce larger gains, since they are repeatedly used as subcomponents in industrial circuits.

### 5.2 Results on ZoKrates Stdlib

We have used two kind of circuits from the ZoKrates stdlib for our experimental evaluation: (1) The first four circuits shaXbit are implementations of different SHA-2 hash functions [19], where X indicates the size of the output. SHA-2 hashes are constructed from the repeated use of simple computation units that heavily use bit operations. Bit operations are very inefficient inside arithmetic circuits [13] and, as a result, the number of constraints describing these circuits is very large, see in Table 2. The number of constraints deduced is quite low for this kind of circuits since specialized optimization for bitwise operation is required (other compilers like xJsnark [23] are specialized on this). This also happens in the circom implementation of SHA-256-2 (row 1 of Table 1). However, Poseidon [16] is a recent hash function that was designed taking into account the nature of arithmetic circuits in a prime field $\mathbb{F}$, and as a result, the function can be described with many less constraints. Our approach is able to optimize the current implementation of Poseidon by more than 20%, which represents a very significant reduction. (2) The second kind are the last four circuits: they correspond to the ground for implementing elliptic curve cryptography inside circuits. Our optimizer detects, in a negligible time, that more than 23% of constraints are redundant and can be removed. Verifying if a pair of public/private keys matches (ProofOfOwnership) is fundamental in almost every security situation, hence the optimization of this circuit becomes particularly relevant for saving blockchain space. For this reason, we have parameterized ProofOfOwnership to the number of pairs public/private keys to be verified and we have measured the performance impact (time and memory consumption) of snarkjs setup step of these circuits without simplification (Table 3) and after simplification (Table 4). The results show the effect of our reduction when the constraints are later used by snarkjs to produce ZK proofs.

**Table 2.** Results on stdlib.

| Circuit | #C | #R | G% | T(s) |
|---|---|---|---|---|
| sha256bit | 25730 | 288 | 1.1% | 35.0s |
| sha512bit | 26838 | 544 | 2.0% | 37.8s |
| sha1024bit | 54284 | 1312 | 2.4% | 82.4s |
| sha1536bit | 81730 | 2080 | 2.6% | 128s |
| Poseidon | 3912 | 851 | 21.8% | 0.3s |
| EdwardsAdd | 17 | 4 | 23.6% | 0.07s |
| EdwardsOrderCheck | 56 | 15 | 26.8% | 0.07s |
| EdwardsScalarMult | 9989 | 2304 | 23.1% | 0.2s |
| ProofOfOwnership | 9984 | 2306 | 23.0% | 0.5s |

**Table 3.** Results on different instantiations of `ProofOfOwnership` from `stdlib` without nonlinear simplification. The generated ERROR in last row is an out-of-memory-error.

| Circuit | Generation | | | `snarkjs` | |
|---|---|---|---|---|---|
| | T(s) | #C | Size | T(s) | Memory |
| `ProofOfOwnership-400` | 1m58.1s | 3,902,378 | 582MB | 7m26.8s | 14.4GB |
| `ProofOfOwnership-1000` | 4m54.7s | 9,740,978 | 1.5GB | 37m50.0s | 33.1GB |
| `ProofOfOwnership-1200` | 6m09.6s | 11,687,178 | 1.7GB | 47m15.7s | 36.2GB |
| `ProofOfOwnership-1400` | 6m50.1s | 13,633,378 | 2.0GB | ERROR | ERROR |

**Table 4.** Results on different instantiations of `ProofOfOwnership` from `stdlib` with nonlinear simplification.

| Circuit | Generation | | | `snarkjs` | |
|---|---|---|---|---|---|
| | T(s) | #C | Size | T(s) | Memory |
| `ProofOfOwnership-400` | 3m11.0s | 2,970,072 | 451MB | 5m00.1s | 12.7GB |
| `ProofOfOwnership-1000` | 8m05.1s | 7,413,672 | 1.1GB | 23m40.8s | 24.6GB |
| `ProofOfOwnership-1200` | 9m43.8s | 8,894,872 | 1.4GB | 31m46.8s | 30.7GB |
| `ProofOfOwnership-1400` | 11m06.4s | 10,376,072 | 1.6GB | 38m31.0s | 32.7GB |

The impact of our simplification on the setup step of `snarkjs` is relevant and goes beyond the increase in the compilation time. However, this step is applied only once. We have also measured the impact in performance when generating a ZK-proof for a given witness using `snarkjs` after the setup step. This action that is the one repeated many times when used in a real context. Our experiments show that, e.g., with `ProofOfOwnership-400` we improve from 41 s to 35 s and with `ProofOfOwnership-1000` we improve from 1 m 53 s to 1 m 12 s.

In conclusion, our experiments show that the higher the level of abstraction is, the more redundant constraints the compiler introduces in the R1CS. Our proposed techniques are an efficient and effective solution to enhance the performance in this setting. On the other hand, circuits written in a low-level language by security experts (usually optimized by hand), or circuits using bitwise operations, leave small room for optimization by applying our techniques.

## 6 Related Work and Conclusions

We have proposed the application of (non-linear) constraint reasoning techniques to the new application domain of ZK protocols. Our approach has wide applicability as, in the last few years, much effort has been put in developing new programming languages that enable the generation and verification of ZK proofs and that also focus on the design of arithmetic circuits and the constraint encoding. Among the different solutions, we can distinguish: libraries (`bellman` [7], `libsnark` [29], `snarky` [28]), programming-focused languages (`ZoKrates` [12], xJsnark [23], zinc [24], Leo [10]), and hardware-description languages (circom). As opposed to the initial library approach, both programming and hardware-description languages put focus on the design of arithmetic circuits and the constraint encoding. In this regard, ZoKrates, xJsnark, and the circom compiler implement one simple but powerful R1CS-specific optimization called *linearity reduction*: it consists in substituting the linear constraints to generate a new circuit whose system only consists of non-linear constraints. However, they do not deduce new constraints to detect further redundancies in the system. Linear reduction is a particular case of our reduction rules in which the only linear constraints that can be deduced and added to the linear system are those that follow from linear constraints present in the constraint system. On the other side, the constraint system generated by Leo is only optimized at the level of its intermediate representation not at R1CS-level, as our method works.

Finally, there has been a joint effort towards standardizing and allowing the interoperability between different programs, like CirC [26], an infrastructure for building compilers to logical constraint representation. Currently, CirC only applies the linearity reduction explained above. Recently, an interface called zkInterface [6] has been built to improve the interoperability among several frontends, like ZoKrates and snarky. It provides means to express statements in a high-level language and compile them into an R1CS representation; and several backends that implement ZK protocols like Groth16 [17] and Pinocchio [27] that use the R1CS representation to produce ZK proofs. zkInterface could benefit from our optimization to apply our reduction to every circuit generated by any of the accepted frontends. zkInterface is also written in Rust, then our optimizer could be easily integrated as a new gadget for the tool in the future. Finally, we believe that the techniques presented in this paper can lead us to new reduction schemes to be applied over PlonK [14] constraint systems.

**Acknowledgements.** This research was funded by the Spanish MCIN-AEI-10.13039/501100011033-FEDER “Una manera de hacer Europa” projects RTI2018-094403-B-C31 and RTI2018-094403-B-C33, by the CM project S2018/TCS-4314 co-funded by EIE Funds of the European Union, and by the project RTI2018-102112-B-100 (AEI/FEDER, UE).

## References

1. Albert, E., Bellés-Muñoz, M., Isabel, M., Rodríguez-Núñez, C., Rubio, A.: circom fork including non-linear simplification. GitHub (2022). github.com/clararod9/circom. Accessed 21 Jan 2022
2. Albert, E., Bellés-Muñoz, M., Isabel, M., Rodríguez-Núñez, C., Rubio, A.: An optimizer for non-linear constraints. GitHub (2022). github.com/miguelis/nonlinearoptimizer. Accessed 21 Jan 2022
3. Bellés-Muñoz, M., Whitehat, B., Baylina, J., Daza, V., Tapia, J.L.M.: Twisted edwards elliptic curves for zero-knowledge circuits. Mathematics, 9(23), 2021
4. Sasson, E.B., et al.: Zerocash: decentralized anonymous payments from bitcoin. In: 2014 IEEE Symposium on Security and Privacy, pp. 459–474 (2014)

5. Ben-Sasson, E., Chiesa, A., Genkin, D., Tromer, E., Virza, M.: SNARKs for C: Verifying Program Executions Succinctly and in Zero Knowledge. In: Canetti, R., Garay, J.A. (eds.) CRYPTO 2013. LNCS, vol. 8043, pp. 90–108. Springer, Heidelberg (2013). https://doi.org/10.1007/978-3-642-40084-1_6
6. Benarroch, D., Gurkan, K., Kahat, R., Nicolas, A., Tromer, E.: zkInterface, a standard tool for zero-knowledge interoperability, June 2019. github.com/QED-it/zkinterface/blob/master/zkInterface.pdf. Accessed 15 Jan 2022
7. Bowe, S.: Bellman: zk-snark library. github.com/ebfull/bellman. Accessed 15 Jan 2022
8. Bünz, B., Bootle, J., Boneh, D., Poelstra, A., Wuille, P., Maxwell, G.: Bulletproofs: short proofs for confidential transactions and more. In: 2018 IEEE Symposium on Security and Privacy (SP), pp. 315–334 (2018)
9. Champion, A., Gurfinkel, A., Kahsai, T., Tinelli, C.: CoCoSpec: a mode-aware contract language for reactive systems. In: De Nicola, R., Kühn, E. (eds.) SEFM 2016. LNCS, vol. 9763, pp. 347–366. Springer, Cham (2016). https://doi.org/10.1007/978-3-319-41591-8_24
10. Chin, C., Wu, H., Chu, R., Coglio, A., McCarthy, E., Smith, E.: Leo: a programming language for formally verified, zero-knowledge applications. IACR Cryptology ePrint Archive, Report 2021/651 (2021). ia.cr/2021/651. Accessed 15 Jan 2022
11. Cimatti, A., Griggio, A., Irfan, A., Roveri, M., Sebastiani, R.: Incremental linearization for satisfiability and verification modulo nonlinear arithmetic and transcendental functions. ACM Trans. Comput. Log., **19**(3), 19:1–19:52 (2018)
12. Eberhardt, J., Tai, S.: ZoKrates - scalable privacy-preserving off-chain computations. In: 2018 IEEE International Conference on Internet of Things (iThings) and IEEE Green Computing and Communications (GreenCom) and IEEE Cyber, Physical and Social Computing (CPSCom) and IEEE Smart Data (SmartData), pp. 1084–1091 (2018)
13. Gabizon, A., Williamson, Z.J.: Plookup: a simplified polynomial protocol for lookup. IACR Cryptology ePrint Archive, Report 2020/315 (2020). ia.cr/2020/315. Accessed 15 Dec 2021
14. Gabizon, A., Williamson, Z.J., Ciobotaru, O.: Plonk: permutations over lagrange-bases for oecumenical noninteractive arguments of knowledge. Cryptology ePrint Archive, Paper 2019/953 (2019). eprint.iacr.org/2019/953
15. Goldwasser, S., Micali, S., Rackoff, C.: The knowledge complexity of interactive proof-systems. In: Proceedings of the Seventeenth Annual ACM Symposium on Theory of Computing, STOC '85, pp. 291–304, New York, NY, USA (1985). Association for Computing Machinery
16. Grassi, L., Khovratovich, D., Rechberger, C., Roy, A., Schofnegger, M.: Poseidon: a new hash function for zero-knowledge proof systems. IACR Cryptology ePrint Archive, Report 2019/458, 2019. ia.cr/2019/458. Accessed 15 Dec 2021
17. Groth, J.: On the size of pairing-based non-interactive arguments. In: Fischlin, M., Coron, J.-S. (eds.) EUROCRYPT 2016. LNCS, vol. 9666, pp. 305–326. Springer, Heidelberg (2016). https://doi.org/10.1007/978-3-662-49896-5_11
18. Gudgeon, L., Moreno-Sanchez, P., Roos, S., McCorry, P., Gervais, A.: SoK: layer-two blockchain protocols. In: Bonneau, J., Heninger, N. (eds.) FC 2020. LNCS, vol. 12059, pp. 201–226. Springer, Cham (2020). https://doi.org/10.1007/978-3-030-51280-4_12
19. Handschuh, H.: SHA Family (Secure Hash Algorithm), pp. 565–567. Springer, US, Boston, MA (2005)
20. Hermez Network. Hermez whitepaper, October 2020. hermez.io/hermez-whitepaper.pdf. Accessed 15 Dec 2021

21. Iden3. Circom: Circuit compiler for zero-knowledge proofs. GitHub (2020). ithub.com/iden3/circom. Accessed 21 Jan 2022
22. Iden3. Circomlib: Library of circom templates. GitHub (2020). github.com/iden3/circomlib. Accessed 15 Dec 2021
23. Kosba, A., Papamanthou, C., Shi, E.: xJsnark: a framework for efficient verifiable computation. In: 2018 IEEE Symposium on Security and Privacy (SP), pp. 944–961 (2018)
24. Matter Labs. Zinc v0.2.3. Cryptology ePrint Archive, Report 2019/953 (2019). ia.cr/2020/352. Accessed 15 Dec 2021
25. Nakos, G.C., Turner, P.R., Williams, R.M.: Fraction-free algorithms for linear and polynomial equations. SIGSAM Bull. **31**(3), 11–19 (1997)
26. Ozdemir, A., Brown, F., Wahby, R.S.: Unifying compilers for snarks, smt, and more. IACR Cryptology ePrint Archive, Report 2020/1586, 2020. ia.cr/2020/1586. Accessed 15 Jan 2022
27. Parno, B., Howell, J., Gentry, C., Raykova, M.: Pinocchio: nearly practical verifiable computation. In: Proceedings of the IEEE Symposium on Security and Privacy, pp. 238–252. IEEE, May 2013
28. Protocol, M., Snarky. GitHub (2020). minaprotocol.com/blog/snarky-a-high-level-language-for-verifiable-computation. Accessed 21 Jan 2022
29. Succinct Computational Integrity and Privacy Research (SCIPR) Lab. libsnark: a c++ library for zk-snark proofs. GitHub, First release, June 2014. github.com/scipr-lab/libsnark. Accessed 15 Jan 2022

# Formal Methods for Hardware, Cyber-physical, and Hybrid Systems

# Oblivious Online Monitoring for Safety LTL Specification via Fully Homomorphic Encryption

Ryotaro Banno[1(✉)], Kotaro Matsuoka[1], Naoki Matsumoto[1], Song Bian[2], Masaki Waga[1], and Kohei Suenaga[1]

[1] Kyoto University, Kyoto, Japan
banno@fos.kuis.kyoto-u.ac.jp
[2] Beihang University, Beijing, China

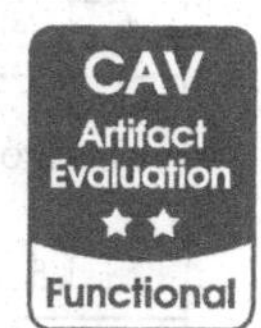


**Abstract.** In many Internet of Things (IoT) applications, data sensed by an IoT device are continuously sent to the server and monitored against a specification. Since the data often contain sensitive information, and the monitored specification is usually proprietary, both must be kept private from the other end. We propose a protocol to conduct *oblivious online monitoring*—online monitoring conducted without revealing the private information of each party to the other—against a safety LTL specification. In our protocol, we first convert a safety LTL formula into a DFA and conduct online monitoring with the DFA. Based on *fully homomorphic encryption (FHE)*, we propose two online algorithms (Reverse and Block) to run a DFA obliviously. We prove the correctness and security of our entire protocol. We also show the scalability of our algorithms theoretically and empirically. Our case study shows that our algorithms are fast enough to monitor blood glucose levels online, demonstrating our protocol's practical relevance.

## 1 Introduction

Internet of Things (IoT) [3] devices enable various service providers to monitor personal data of their users and to provide useful feedback to the users. For example, a smart home system can save lives by raising an alarm when a gas stove is left on to prevent a fire. Such a system is realized by the continuous monitoring of the data from the IoT devices in the house [8,18]. Another application of IoT devices is medical IoT (MIoT) [16]. In MIoT applications, biological information, such as electrocardiograms or blood glucose levels, is monitored, and the user is notified when an abnormality is detected (such as arrhythmia or hyperglycemia).

In many IoT applications, monitoring must be conducted *online*, i.e., a stream of sensed data is continuously monitored, and the violation of the monitoring specification must be reported even before the entire data are obtained. In the smart home and MIoT applications, online monitoring is usually required, as continuous sensing is crucial for the immediate notifications to emergency responders, such as police officers or doctors, for the ongoing abnormal situations.


S. Shoham and Y. Vizel (Eds.): CAV 2022, LNCS 13371, pp. 447–468, 2022.
https://doi.org/10.1007/978-3-031-13185-1_22

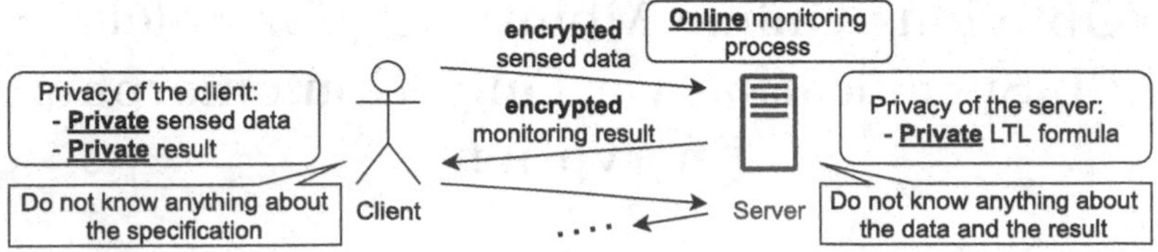


**Fig. 1.** The proposed oblivious online LTL monitoring protocol.

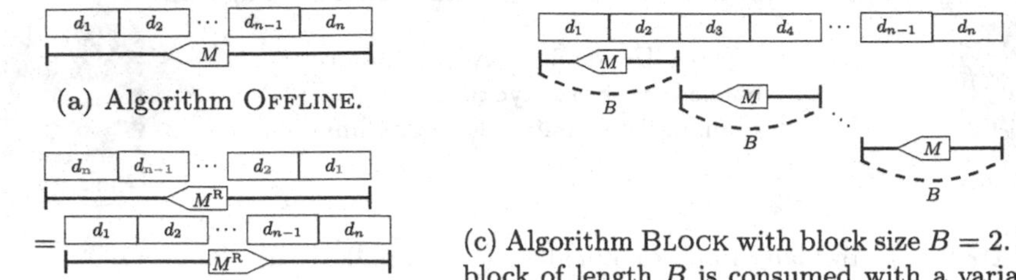

(a) Algorithm Offline.

(b) Algorithm Reverse, where $M^{\mathrm{R}}$ is the reversed DFA of $M$.

(c) Algorithm Block with block size $B = 2$. Each block of length $B$ is consumed with a variant of Offline. The intermediate result at each block is used in the consumption of the next block.

**Fig. 2.** How our algorithms consume the data $d_1, d_2, \ldots, d_n$ with the DFA $M$.

As specifications generally contain proprietary information or sensitive parameters learned from private data (e.g., with specification mining [27]), *the specifications must be kept secret.* One of the approaches for this privacy is to adopt the client-server model to the monitoring system. In such a model, the sensing device sends the collected data to a server, where the server performs the necessary analyses and returns the results to the device. Since the client does not have access to the specification, the server's privacy is preserved.

However, the client-server model does *not* inherently protect the client's privacy from the servers, as the data collected from and results sent back to the users are revealed to the servers in this model; that is to say, a user has to *trust* the server. This trust is problematic if, for example, the server itself intentionally or unintentionally leaks sensitive data of device users to an unauthorized party. Thus, we argue that a monitoring procedure should achieve the following goals:

**Online Monitoring.** The monitored data need not be known beforehand.
**Client's Privacy.** The server shall not know the monitored data and results.
**Server's Privacy.** The client shall not know what property is monitored.

We call a monitoring scheme with these properties *oblivious online monitoring.* By an oblivious online monitoring procedure, 1) a user can get a monitoring result hiding her sensitive data and the result itself from a server, and 2) a server can conduct online monitoring hiding the specification from the user.

*Contribution.* In this paper, we propose a novel protocol (Fig. 1) for oblivious online monitoring against a specification in *linear temporal logic (LTL)* [33]. More precisely, we use a *safety LTL formula* [26] as a specification, which can be translated to a deterministic finite automaton (DFA) [36]. In our protocol, we first convert a safety LTL formula into a DFA and conduct online monitoring with the DFA. For online and oblivious execution of a DFA, we propose two algorithms based on *fully homomorphic encryption* (FHE). FHE allows us to evaluate an arbitrary function over ciphertexts, and there is an FHE-based algorithm to evaluate a DFA obliviously [13]. However, this algorithm is limited to *leveled* homomorphic, i.e., the FHE parameters are dependent on the number of the monitored ciphertexts and thus not applicable to online monitoring.

In this work, we first present a *fully* homomorphic *offline* DFA evaluation algorithm (OFFLINE) by extending the leveled homomorphic algorithm in [13]. Although we can remove the parameter dependence using this method, OFFLINE consumes the ciphertexts from back to front (Fig. 2a). As a result, OFFLINE is still limited to offline usage only. To truly enable online monitoring, we propose two new algorithms based on OFFLINE: REVERSE and BLOCK. In REVERSE, we *reverse* the DFA and apply OFFLINE to the reversed DFA (Fig. 2b). In BLOCK, we split the monitored ciphertexts into fixed-length *blocks* and process each block sequentially with OFFLINE (Fig. 2c). We prove that both of the algorithms have *linear* time complexity and *constant* space complexity to the length of the monitored ciphertexts, which guarantees the scalability of our entire protocol.

On top of our online algorithms, we propose a protocol for oblivious online LTL monitoring. We assume that the client is *malicious*, i.e., the client can deviate arbitrarily from the protocol, while the server is *honest-but-curious*, i.e., the server honestly follows the protocol but tries to learn the client's private data by exploiting the obtained information. We show that the privacy of both parties can be protected under the standard IND-CPA security of FHE schemes with the addition of *shielded randomness leakage* (SRL) security [10,21].

We implemented our algorithms for DFA evaluation in C++20 and evaluated their performance. Our experiment results confirm the scalability of our algorithms. Moreover, through a case study on blood glucose levels monitoring, we also show that our algorithms run fast enough for online monitoring, i.e., our algorithms are faster than the sampling interval of the current commercial devices that samples glucose levels.

Our contributions are summarized as follows:

- We propose two *online* algorithms to run a DFA obliviously.
- We propose the first protocol for oblivious online LTL monitoring.
- We proved the correctness and security of our protocol.
- Our experiments show the scalability and practicality of our algorithms.

*Related Work.* There are various works on DFA execution without revealing the monitored data (See Table 1 for a summary). However, to our knowledge, there is no existing work achieving all of our three goals (i.e., *online monitoring*, *privacy of the client*, and *privacy of the server*) simultaneously. Therefore, none of them is applicable to oblivious online LTL monitoring.

Homomorphic encryption, which we also utilize, has been used to run a DFA obliviously [13,25]. Among different homomorphic encryption schemes, our algorithm is based on the algorithm in [13]. Although these algorithms guarantee the *privacy of the client* and the *privacy of the server*, all of the

**Table 1.** Related work on DFA execution with *privacy of the client*.

| Work | [37] | [20] | [9] | [35] | [31] | [22] | [25] | [13] | [1] | Ours |
|---|---|---|---|---|---|---|---|---|---|---|
| Support online monitoring | ✗ | ✗ | ✗ | ✗ | ✗ | ✗ | ✗ | ✗ | ✓ | ✓ |
| Private the client's monitored data | ✓ | ✓ | ✓ | ✓ | ✓ | ✓ | ✓ | ✓ | ✓ | ✓ |
| Private DFA, except for its number of the states | ✓ | ✓ | ✓ | ✓ | ✓ | ✓ | ✓ | ✓ | ✗ | ✓ |
| Private DFA's number of the states | ✗ | ✗ | ✗ | ✗ | ✗ | ✗ | ✓ | ✓ | ✗ | ✓ |
| Performance report | ✗ | ✓ | ✗ | ✓ | ✓ | ✗ | ✗ | ✗ | ✗ | ✓ |

homomorphic-encryption-based algorithms are limited to offline DFA execution and do not achieve *online monitoring*. We note that the extension of [13] for online DFA execution is one of our technical contributions.

In [1], the authors propose an LTL runtime verification algorithm without revealing the monitored data to the server. They propose both offline and online algorithms to run a DFA converted from a safety LTL formula. The main issue with their online algorithm is that the DFA running on the server must be revealed to the client, and the goal of *privacy of the server* is not satisfied.

*Oblivious DFA evaluation (ODFA)* [9,20,22,31,35,37] is a technique to run a DFA on a server while keeping the DFA secret to the server and the monitored data secret to the client. Although the structure of the DFA is not revealed to the client, the client has to know the number of the states. Consequently, the goal *privacy of the server* is satisfied *only partially*. Moreover, to the best of our knowledge, none of the ODFA-based algorithms support online DFA execution. Therefore, the goal *online monitoring* is not satisfied.

*Organization.* The rest of the paper is organized as follows: In (Sect. 2), we overview LTL monitoring (Sect. 2.1), the FHE scheme we use (Sect. 2.2), and the leveled homomorphic offline algorithm (Sect. 2.3). Then, in Sect. 3, we explain our fully homomorphic offline algorithm (Offline) and two online algorithms (Reverse and Block). We describe the proposed protocol for oblivious online LTL monitoring in Sect. 4. After we discuss our experimental results in Sect. 5, we conclude our paper in Sect. 6.

## 2 Preliminaries

*Notations.* We denote the set of all nonnegative integers by $\mathbb{N}$, the set of all positive integers by $\mathbb{N}^+$, and the set $\{0, 1\}$ by $\mathbb{B}$. Let $X$ be a set. We write $2^X$ for the powerset of $X$. We write $X^*$ for the set of finite sequences of $X$ elements and $X^\omega$ for the set of infinite sequences of $X$ elements. For $u \in X^\omega$, we write $u_i \in X$ for the $i$-th element (0-based) of $u$, $u_{i:j} \in X^*$ for the subsequence $u_i, u_{i+1}, \dots, u_j$ of $u$, and $u_{i:} \in X^\omega$ for the suffix of $u$ starting from its $i$-th element. For $u \in X^*$ and $v \in X^* \cup X^\omega$, we write $u \cdot v$ for the concatenation of $u$ and $v$.

*DFA.* A deterministic finite automaton (DFA) is a 5-tuple $(Q, \Sigma, \delta, q_0, F)$, where $Q$ is a finite set of states, $\Sigma$ is a finite set of alphabet, $\delta\colon Q \times \Sigma \to Q$ is a transition function, $q_0 \in Q$ is an initial state, and $F \subseteq Q$ is a set of final states. If the alphabet of a DFA is $\mathbb{B}$, we call it a *binary* DFA. For a state $q \in Q$ and a word

$w = \sigma_1\sigma_2\dots\sigma_n$ we define $\delta(q, w) := \delta(\dots\delta(\delta(q, \sigma_1), \sigma_2), \dots, \sigma_n)$. For a DFA $M$ and a word $w$, we write $M(w) := 1$ if $M$ accepts $w$; otherwise, $M(w) := 0$. We also abuse the above notations for nondeterministic finite automata (NFAs).

### 2.1 LTL

We use *linear temporal logic (LTL)* [33] to specify the monitored properties. The following BNF defines the syntax of LTL formulae: $\phi, \psi ::= \top \mid p \mid \neg\phi \mid \phi \wedge \psi \mid \mathsf{X}\phi \mid \phi\mathsf{U}\psi$, where $\phi$ and $\psi$ range over LTL formulae and $p$ ranges over a set AP of atomic propositions.

An LTL formula asserts a property of $u \in (2^{\mathrm{AP}})^\omega$. The sequence $u$ expresses an execution trace of a system; $u_i$ is the set of the atomic propositions satisfied at the $i$-th time step. Intuitively, $\top$ represents an always-true proposition; $p$ asserts that $u_0$ contains $p$, and hence $p$ holds at the 0-th step in $u$; $\neg\phi$ is the negation of $\phi$; and $\phi\wedge\psi$ is the conjunction of $\phi$ and $\psi$. The temporal proposition $\mathsf{X}\phi$ expresses that $\phi$ holds from the next step (i.e., $u_{1:}$); $\phi\mathsf{U}\psi$ expresses that $\psi$ holds eventually and $\phi$ continues to hold until then. We write $\bot$ for $\neg\top$; $\phi \vee \psi$ for $\neg(\neg\phi \wedge \neg\psi)$; $\phi \implies \psi$ for $\neg\phi \vee \psi$; $\mathsf{F}\phi$ for $\top\mathsf{U}\phi$; $\mathsf{G}\phi$ for $\neg(\mathsf{F}\neg\phi)$; $\mathsf{G}_{[n,m]}\phi$ for $\overbrace{\mathsf{X}\dots\mathsf{X}}^{n \text{ occurrences of } \mathsf{X}}(\phi\wedge \overbrace{\mathsf{X}(\phi\wedge\mathsf{X}(\cdots\wedge\mathsf{X}\phi))}^{(m-n) \text{ occ. of } \mathsf{X}})$; and $\mathsf{F}_{[n,m]}\phi$ for $\overbrace{\mathsf{X}\dots\mathsf{X}}^{n \text{ occ. of } \mathsf{X}}(\phi\vee\overbrace{\mathsf{X}(\phi\vee\mathsf{X}(\cdots\vee\mathsf{X}\phi))}^{(m-n) \text{ occ. of } \mathsf{X}})$.

We formally define the semantics of LTL below. Let $u \in (2^{\mathrm{AP}})^\omega$, $i \in \mathbb{N}$, and $\phi$ be an LTL formula. We define the relation $u, i \models \phi$ as the least relation that satisfies the following:

$$u, i \models \top \qquad u, i \models p \overset{\text{def}}{\iff} p \in u(i) \qquad u, i \models \neg\phi \overset{\text{def}}{\iff} u, i \not\models \phi$$

$$u, i \models \phi\wedge\psi \overset{\text{def}}{\iff} u, i \models \phi \text{ and } u, i \models \psi \qquad u, i \models \mathsf{X}\phi \overset{\text{def}}{\iff} u, i+1 \models \phi$$

$$u, i \models \phi\mathsf{U}\psi \overset{\text{def}}{\iff} \begin{array}{l}\text{there exists } j \geq i \text{ such that } u, j \models \psi \text{ and,}\\ \text{for any } k,\ i \leq k \leq j \implies u, k \models \phi.\end{array}$$

We write $u \models \phi$ for $u, 0 \models \phi$ and say $u$ *satisfies* $\phi$.

In this paper, we focus on *safety* [26] (i.e., nothing bad happens) fragment of LTL properties. A finite sequence $w \in (2^{\mathrm{AP}})^*$ is a *bad prefix* for an LTL formula $\phi$ if $w \cdot v \not\models \phi$ holds for any $v \in (2^{\mathrm{AP}})^\omega$. For any bad prefix $w$, we cannot extend $w$ to an infinite word that satisfies $\phi$. An LTL formula $\phi$ is a *safety* LTL formula if for any $w \in (2^{\mathrm{AP}})^\omega$ satisfying $w \not\models \phi$, $w$ has a bad prefix for $\phi$.

A *safety monitor* (or simply a *monitor*) is a procedure that takes $w \in (2^{\mathrm{AP}})^\omega$ and a safety LTL formula $\phi$ and generates an alert if $w \not\models \phi$. From the definition of safety LTL, it suffices for a monitor to detect a bad prefix of $\phi$. It is known that, for any safety LTL formula $\phi$, we can construct a DFA $M_\phi$ recognizing the set of the bad prefixes of $\phi$ [36], which can be used as a monitor.

### 2.2 Torus Fully Homomorphic Encryption

Homomorphic encryption (HE) is a form of encryption that enables us to apply operations to encrypted values *without decrypting them.* In particular, a type

**Table 2.** Summary of TFHE ciphertexts, where $N$ is a parameter of TFHE.

| Ciphertext Kind | Notation in this paper | Plaintext Message | Conversion from TRLWE |
|---|---|---|---|
| TLWE | $c$ | a Boolean value $b \in \mathbb{B}$ | SAMPLEEXTRACT (fast) |
| TRLWE | $\mathbf{c}$ | a Boolean vector $v \in \mathbb{B}^N$ | ——— |
| TRGSW | $d$ | a Boolean value $b \in \mathbb{B}$ | SAMPLEEXTRACT and CIRCUITBOOTSTRAPPING (slow) |

of HE, called Fully HE (FHE), allows us to evaluate arbitrary functions over encrypted data [11,19,23,24]. We use an instance of FHE called TFHE [13] in this work. We briefly summarize TFHE below; see [13] for a detailed exposition.

We are concerned with the following two-party secure computation, where the involved parties are a client (called Alice) and a server (called Bob): 1) Alice generates the keys used during computation; 2) Alice encrypts her plaintext messages into ciphertexts with her keys; 3) Alice sends the ciphertexts to Bob; 4) Bob conducts computation over the received ciphertexts and obtains the encrypted result *without decryption*; 5) Bob sends the encrypted results to Alice; 6) Alice decrypts the received results and obtains the results in plaintext.

**Keys.** There are three types of keys in TFHE: *secret key* SK, *public key* PK, and *bootstrapping key* BK. All of them are generated by Alice. PK is used to encrypt plaintext messages into ciphertexts, and SK is used to decrypt ciphertexts into plaintexts. Alice keeps SK private, i.e., the key is known only to herself but not to Bob. In contrast, PK is public and also known to Bob. BK is generated from SK and can be safely shared with Bob without revealing SK. BK allows Bob to evaluate the homomorphic operations (defined later) over the ciphertext.

**Ciphertexts.** Using the public key, Alice can generate three kinds of ciphertexts (Table 2): TLWE (Torus Learning With Errors), TRLWE (Torus Ring Learning With Errors), and TRGSW (Torus Ring Gentry-Sahai-Waters). Homomorphic operations provided by TFHE are defined over each of the specific ciphertexts. We note that different ciphertexts have different data structures, and their conversion can be time-consuming. Table 2 shows one such example.

In TFHE, different types of ciphertexts represent different plaintext messages. A TLWE ciphertext represents a Boolean value. In contrast, TRLWE represents a vector of Boolean values of length $N$, where $N$ is a TFHE parameter. We can regard a TRLWE ciphertext as a vector of TLWE ciphertexts, and the conversion between a TRLWE ciphertext and a TLWE one is relatively easy. A TRGSW ciphertext also represents a Boolean value, but its data structure is quite different from TLWE, and the conversion from TLWE to TRGSW is slow.

TFHE provides different encryption and decryption functions for each type of ciphertext. We write $\mathrm{Enc}(x)$ for a ciphertext of a plaintext $x$; $\mathrm{Dec}(c)$ for the plaintext message for the ciphertext $c$. We abuse these notations for all three types of ciphertexts.

Besides, TFHE supports *trivial samples* of TRLWE. A trivial sample of TRLWE has the same data structure as a TRLWE ciphertext but is *not* encrypted, i.e., anyone can tell the plaintext message represented by the trivial sample. We denote by Trivial($n$) a trivial sample of TRLWE whose plaintext message is $(b_1, b_2, \ldots, b_N)$, where each $b_i$ is the $i$-th bit in the binary representation of $n$.

**Homomorphic Operations.** TFHE provides *homomorphic operations*, i.e., operations over ciphertexts without decryption. Among the operators supported by TFHE [13], we use the following ones.

**CMux**$(d, \mathbf{c}_{\mathbf{true}}, \mathbf{c}_{\mathbf{false}})$ : TRGSW × TRLWE × TRLWE → TRLWE
Given a TRGSW ciphertext $d$ and TRLWE ciphertexts $\mathbf{c}_{\text{true}}, \mathbf{c}_{\text{false}}$, CMux outputs a TRLWE ciphertext $\mathbf{c}_{\text{result}}$ such that $\text{Dec}(\mathbf{c}_{\text{result}}) = \text{Dec}(\mathbf{c}_{\text{true}})$ if $\text{Dec}(d) = 1$, and otherwise, $\text{Dec}(\mathbf{c}_{\text{result}}) = \text{Dec}(\mathbf{c}_{\text{false}})$.

**LookUp**$(\{\mathbf{c}_i\}_{i=1}^{2^n}, \{d_i\}_{i=1}^{n})$ : $(\text{TRLWE})^{2^n} \times (\text{TRGSW})^n \rightarrow$ TRLWE
Given TRLWE ciphertexts $\mathbf{c}_1, \mathbf{c}_2, \ldots, \mathbf{c}_{2^n}$ and TRGSW ciphertexts $d_1, d_2, \ldots,$ $d_n$, LookUp outputs a TRLWE ciphertext $\mathbf{c}$ such that $\text{Dec}(\mathbf{c}) = \text{Dec}(\mathbf{c}_k)$ and $k = \sum_{i=1}^{n} 2^{i-1} \times \text{Dec}(d_i)$.

**SampleExtract**$(k, \mathbf{c})$ : $\mathbb{N}$ × TRLWE → TLWE
Let $\text{Dec}(\mathbf{c}) = (b_1, b_2, \ldots, b_N)$. Given $k < N$ and a TRLWE ciphertext $\mathbf{c}$, SampleExtract outputs a TLWE ciphertext $c$ where $\text{Dec}(c) = b_{k+1}$.

Intuitively, CMux can be regarded as a multiplexer over TRLWE ciphertexts with TRGSW selector input. The operation LookUp regards $\mathbf{c}_1, \mathbf{c}_2, \ldots, \mathbf{c}_{2^n}$ as encrypted entries composing a LookUp Table (LUT) of depth $n$ and $d_1, d_2, \ldots, d_n$ as inputs to the LUT. Its output is the entry selected by the LUT. LookUp is constructed by $2^n - 1$ CMux arranged in a tree of depth $n$. SampleExtract outputs the $k$-th element of $\mathbf{c}$ as TLWE. Notice that all these operations work over ciphertexts without decrypting them.

**Noise and Operations for Noise Reduction.** In generating a TFHE ciphertext, we ensure its security by adding some random numbers called *noise*. An application of a TFHE operation adds noise to its output ciphertext; if the noise in a ciphertext becomes too large, the TFHE ciphertext cannot be correctly decrypted. There is a special type of operation called *bootstrapping*[1] [23], which reduces the noise of a TFHE ciphertext.

**Bootstrapping**$_{\text{BK}}(c)$ : TLWE → TRLWE
Given a bootstrapping key BK and a TLWE ciphertext $c$, Bootstrapping outputs a TRLWE ciphertext $\mathbf{c}$ where $\text{Dec}(\mathbf{c}) = (b_1, b_2, \ldots, b_N)$ and $b_1 = \text{Dec}(c)$. Moreover, the noise of $\mathbf{c}$ becomes a constant that is determined by the parameters of TFHE and is independent of $c$.

**CircuitBootstrapping**$_{\text{BK}}(c)$ : TLWE → TRGSW
Given a bootstrapping key BK and a TLWE ciphertext $c$, CircuitBootstrapping outputs a TRGSW ciphertext $d$ where $\text{Dec}(d) = \text{Dec}(c)$. The noise of $d$ becomes a constant that is determined by the parameters of TFHE and is independent of $c$.

[1] Note that bootstrapping here has nothing to do with bootstrapping in statistics.

**Algorithm 1:** The leveled homomorphic offline algorithm [13].

**Input** : A binary DFA $M = (Q, \Sigma = \mathbb{B}, \delta, q_0, F)$ and TRGSW monitored ciphertexts $d_1, d_2, \dots, d_n$
**Output** : A TLWE ciphertext $c$ satisfying $\mathrm{Dec}(c) = M(\mathrm{Dec}(d_1)\mathrm{Dec}(d_2)\dots\mathrm{Dec}(d_n))$

1 **for** $q \in Q$ **do**
2 | $\mathbf{c}_{n,q} \leftarrow q \in F$ ? TRIVIAL(1) : TRIVIAL(0) // Initialize each $\mathbf{c}_{n,q}$
3 **for** $i = n, n-1, \dots, 1$ **do**
4 | **for** $q \in Q$ *such that q is reachable from* $q_0$ *by* $(i-1)$ *transitions* **do**
5 | | $\mathbf{c}_{i-1,q} \leftarrow \mathrm{CMux}(d_i, \mathbf{c}_{i,\delta(q,1)}, \mathbf{c}_{i,\delta(q,0)})$
6 $c \leftarrow$ SAMPLEEXTRACT$(0, \mathbf{c}_{0,q_0})$
7 **return** $c$

These bootstrapping operations are used to keep the noise of a TFHE ciphertext small enough to be correctly decrypted. BOOTSTRAPPING and CIRCUITBOOTSTRAPPING are almost two and three orders of magnitude slower than CMUX, respectively [13].

**Parameters for TFHE.** There are many parameters for TFHE, such as the length $N$ of the message of a TRLWE ciphertext and the standard deviation of the probability distribution from which a noise is taken. Certain properties of TFHE depend on these parameters. These properties include the security level of TFHE, the number of TFHE operations that can be applied without bootstrapping ensuring correct decryption, and the time and the space complexity of each operation. The complete list of TFHE parameters is presented in the full version [4].

We remark that we need to determine the TFHE parameters *before* performing any TFHE operation. Therefore, we need to know the number of applications of homomorphic operations without bootstrapping *in advance*, i.e., the homomorphic circuit depth must be determined *a priori*.

### 2.3 Leveled Homomorphic Offline Algorithm

Chillotti et al. [13] proposed an *offline* algorithm to evaluate a DFA over TFHE ciphertexts (Algorithm 1). Given a DFA $M$ and TRGSW ciphertexts $d_1, d_2, \dots, d_n$, Algorithm 1 returns a TLWE ciphertext $c$ satisfying $\mathrm{Dec}(c) = M(\mathrm{Dec}(d_1)\mathrm{Dec}(d_2)\dots\mathrm{Dec}(d_n))$. For simplicity, for a state $q$ of $M$, we write $M^i(q)$ for $M(q, \mathrm{Dec}(d_i)\mathrm{Dec}(d_{i+1})\dots\mathrm{Dec}(d_n))$.

In Algorithm 1, we use a TRLWE ciphertext $\mathbf{c}_{i,q}$ whose first element represents $M^{i+1}(q)$, i.e., whether we reach a final state by reading $\mathrm{Dec}(d_{i+1})\mathrm{Dec}(d_{i+2})\dots\mathrm{Dec}(d_n)$ from $q$. We abuse this notation for $i = n$, i.e., the first element of $\mathbf{c}_{n,q}$ represents if $q \in F$. In Lines 1 and 2, we initialize $\mathbf{c}_{n,q}$; For each $q \in Q$, we let $\mathbf{c}_{n,q}$ be TRIVIAL(1) if $q \in F$; otherwise, we let $\mathbf{c}_{n,q}$ be TRIVIAL(0). In Lines 3–5, we construct $\mathbf{c}_{i-1,q}$ inductively by feeding each monitored ciphertext $d_i$ to CMUX from tail to head. Here, $\mathbf{c}_{i-1,q}$ represents $M^i(q)$ because of $M^i(q) = M^{i+1}(\delta(q, \mathrm{Dec}(d_i)))$. We note that for the efficiency, we only construct $\mathbf{c}_{i-1,q}$ for the states reachable from $q_0$ by $i-1$ transitions. In Line 6, we extract the first element of $\mathbf{c}_{0,q_0}$, which represents $M^1(q_0)$, i.e., $M(\mathrm{Dec}(d_1)\mathrm{Dec}(d_2)\dots\mathrm{Dec}(d_n))$.

**Algorithm 2:** Our fully homomorphic offline algorithm (OFFLINE).

```
Input   : A binary DFA M = (Q, Σ = 𝔹, δ, q_0, F), TRGSW monitored ciphertexts
          d_1, d_2, ..., d_n, a bootstrapping key BK, and I_boot ∈ ℕ⁺
Output  : A TLWE ciphertext c satisfying Dec(c) = M(Dec(d_1)Dec(d_2)...Dec(d_n))
for q ∈ Q do
  | c_{n,q} ← q ∈ F ? TRIVIAL(1) : TRIVIAL(0)
for i = n, n − 1, ..., 1 do
  | for q ∈ Q such that q is reachable from q_0 by (i − 1) transitions do
  |   | c_{i−1,q} ← CMUX(d_i, c_{i,δ(q,1)}, c_{i,δ(q,0)})
  | if (n − i + 1) mod I_boot = 0 then
  |   | for q ∈ Q such that reachable from q_0 by (i − 1) transitions do
  |   |   | c_{i−1,q} ← SAMPLEEXTRACT(0, c_{i−1,q})
  |   |   | c_{i−1,q} ← BOOTSTRAPPING_BK(c_{i−1,q})
c ← SAMPLEEXTRACT(0, c_{0,q_0})
return c
```

**Theorem 1 (Correctness [13, Thm. 5.4]).** *Given a binary DFA $M$ and TRGSW ciphertexts $d_1, d_2, \ldots, d_n$, if $c$ in Algorithm 1 can be correctly decrypted, Algorithm 1 outputs $c$ satisfying $Dec(c) = M(Dec(d_1)Dec(d_2)\ldots Dec(d_n))$.* □

**Complexity Analysis.** The time complexity of Algorithm 1 is determined by the number of applications of CMUX, which is $O(n|Q|)$. Its space complexity is $O(|Q|)$ because we can use two sets of $|Q|$ TRLWE ciphertexts alternately for $\mathbf{c}_{2j-1,q}$ and $\mathbf{c}_{2j,q}$ (for $j \in \mathbb{N}^+$).

**Shortcomings of Algorithm 1.** We cannot use Algorithm 1 under an *online* setting due to two reasons. Firstly, Algorithm 1 is a *leveled* homomorphic algorithm, i.e., the maximum length of the ciphertexts that Algorithm 1 can handle is determined by TFHE parameters. This is because Algorithm 1 does not use BOOTSTRAPPING, and if the monitored ciphertexts are too long, the result $c$ cannot be correctly decrypted due to the noise. This is critical in an online setting because we do not know the length $n$ of the monitored ciphertexts in advance, and we cannot determine such parameters appropriately.

Secondly, Algorithm 1 consumes the monitored ciphertext from back to front, i.e., the last ciphertext $d_n$ is used in the beginning, and $d_1$ is used in the end. Thus, we cannot start Algorithm 1 before the last input is given.

## 3 Online Algorithms for Running DFA Obliviously

In this section, we propose two online algorithms that run a DFA obliviously. As a preparation for these online algorithms, we also introduce a fully homomorphic offline algorithm based on Algorithm 1.

### 3.1 Preparation: Fully Homomorphic Offline Algorithm (*OFFLINE*)

As preparation for introducing an algorithm that can run a DFA under an online setting, we enhance Algorithm 1 so that we can monitor a sequence of ciphertexts whose length is unknown *a priori*. Algorithm 2 shows our *fully homomorphic*

**Algorithm 3:** Our first online algorithm (REVERSE).

**Input** : A binary DFA $M$, TRGSW monitored ciphertexts $d_1, d_2, d_3, \dots, d_n$, a bootstrapping key BK, and $I_{\text{boot}} \in \mathbb{N}^+$

**Output** : For every $i \in \{1, 2, \dots, n\}$, a TLWE ciphertext $c_i$ satisfying $\text{Dec}(c_i) = M(\text{Dec}(d_1)\text{Dec}(d_2) \dots \text{Dec}(d_i))$

1 let $M^{\text{R}} = (Q^{\text{R}}, \mathbb{B}, \delta^{\text{R}}, q_0^{\text{R}}, F^{\text{R}})$ be the minimum reversed DFA of $M$<br>
2 **for** $q^{\text{R}} \in Q^{\text{R}}$ **do**<br>
3     $\mathbf{c}_{0,q^{\text{R}}} \leftarrow q^{\text{R}} \in F^{\text{R}}$ ? TRIVIAL(1) : TRIVIAL(0)<br>
4 **for** $i = 1, 2, \dots, n$ **do**<br>
5     **for** $q^{\text{R}} \in Q^{\text{R}}$ **do**<br>
6         $\mathbf{c}_{i,q^{\text{R}}} \leftarrow \text{CMUX}(d_i, \mathbf{c}_{i-1,\delta^{\text{R}}(q^{\text{R}},1)}, \mathbf{c}_{i-1,\delta^{\text{R}}(q^{\text{R}},0)})$<br>
7     **if** $i \bmod I_{\text{boot}} = 0$ **then**<br>
8         **for** $q^{\text{R}} \in Q^{\text{R}}$ **do**<br>
9             $c_{i,q^{\text{R}}} \leftarrow \text{SAMPLEEXTRACT}(0, \mathbf{c}_{i,q^{\text{R}}})$<br>
10             $\mathbf{c}_{i,q^{\text{R}}} \leftarrow \text{BOOTSTRAPPING}_{\text{BK}}(c_{i,q^{\text{R}}})$<br>
11     $c_i \leftarrow \text{SAMPLEEXTRACT}(0, \mathbf{c}_{i,q_0^{\text{R}}})$<br>
12     **output** $c_i$

offline algorithm (OFFLINE), which does not require TFHE parameters to depend on the length of the monitored ciphertexts. The key difference lies in Lines 6–9 (the red lines) of Algorithm 2. Here, for every $I_{\text{boot}}$ consumption of the monitored ciphertexts, we reduce the noise by applying BOOTSTRAPPING to the ciphertext $\mathbf{c}_{i,j}$ representing a state of the DFA. Since the amount of the noise accumulated in $\mathbf{c}_{i,j}$ is determined only by the number of the processed ciphertexts, we can keep the noise levels of $\mathbf{c}_{i,j}$ low and ensure that the monitoring result $c$ is correctly decrypted. Therefore, by using Algorithm 2, we can monitor an arbitrarily long sequence of ciphertexts as long as the interval $I_{\text{boot}}$ is properly chosen according to the TFHE parameters. We note that we still cannot use Algorithm 2 for online monitoring because it consumes the monitored ciphertexts from back to front.

### 3.2 Online Algorithm 1: *REVERSE*

To run a DFA online, we modify OFFLINE so that the monitored ciphertexts are consumed from front to back. Our main idea is illustrated in Fig. 2b: we *reverse* the DFA $M$ beforehand and feed the ciphertexts $d_1, d_2, \dots, d_n$ to the reversed DFA $M^{\text{R}}$ serially from $d_1$ to $d_n$.

Algorithm 3 shows the outline of our first online algorithm (REVERSE) based on the above idea. REVERSE takes the same inputs as OFFLINE: a DFA $M$, TRGSW ciphertexts $d_1, d_2, \dots, d_n$, a bootstrapping key BK, and a positive integer $I_{\text{boot}}$ indicating the interval of bootstrapping. In Line 1, we construct the minimum DFA $M^{\text{R}}$ that satisfies, for any $w = \sigma_1\sigma_2 \dots \sigma_k \in \mathbb{B}^*$, we have $M^{\text{R}}(w) = M(w^R)$, where $w^R = \sigma_k \dots \sigma_1$. We can construct such a DFA by reversing the transitions and by applying the powerset construction and the minimization algorithm.

In the loop from Lines 4-12, the reversed DFA $M^{\text{R}}$ consumes each monitored ciphertext $d_i$, which corresponds to the loop from Lines 3-9 in Algorithm 2. The main difference lies in Line 5 and 8: Algorithm 3 applies CMUX and

**Algorithm 4:** Our second online algorithm (Block).

**Input** : A binary DFA $M = (Q, \Sigma = \mathbb{B}, \delta, q_0, F)$, TRGSW monitored ciphertexts $d_1, d_2, d_3, \ldots, d_n$, a bootstrapping key BK, and $B \in \mathbb{N}^+$
**Output** : For every $i \in \mathbb{N}^+$ $(i \leq \lfloor n/B \rfloor)$, a TLWE ciphertext $c_i$ satisfying $\mathrm{Dec}(c_i) = M(\mathrm{Dec}(d_1)\mathrm{Dec}(d_2)\ldots\mathrm{Dec}(d_{i \times B}))$

$S_1 \leftarrow \{q_0\}$ // $S_i$: the states reachable by $(i-1) \times B$ transitions.
**for** $i = 1, 2, \ldots, \lfloor n/B \rfloor$ **do**
  $S_{i+1} \leftarrow \{q \in Q \mid \exists s_i \in S_i.\, q$ is reachable from $s_i$ by $B$ transitions$\}$ // We denote $S_{i+1} = \{s_1^{i+1}, s_2^{i+1}, \ldots, s_{|S_{i+1}|}^{i+1}\}$
  **for** $q \in Q$ **do**
    **if** $q \in S_{i+1}$ **then**
      $j \leftarrow$ the index of $S_{i+1}$ such that $q = s_j^{i+1}$
      $\mathbf{c}_{B,q}^{T_i} \leftarrow$ Trivial$((j-1) \times 2 + (q \in F\ ?\ 1 : 0))$
  **for** $k = B, B-1, \ldots, 1$ **do**
    **for** $q \in Q$ *such that* $q$ *is reachable from a state in* $S_i$ *by* $(k-1)$ *transitions* **do**
      $\mathbf{c}_{k-1,q}^{T_i} \leftarrow$ CMux$(d_{(i-1)B+k}, \mathbf{c}_{k,\delta(q,1)}^{T_i}, \mathbf{c}_{k,\delta(q,0)}^{T_i})$
  **if** $|S_i| = 1$ **then**
    $\mathbf{c}_{i+1}^{\mathrm{cur}} \leftarrow \mathbf{c}_{0,q}^{T_i}$ where $S_i = \{q\}$
  **else**
    **for** $l = 1, 2, \ldots, \lceil \log_2(|S_i|) \rceil$ **do**
      $c_l \leftarrow$ SampleExtract$(l, \mathbf{c}_i^{\mathrm{cur}})$
      $d'_l \leftarrow$ CircuitBootstrapping$_{\mathrm{BK}}(c_l)$
    $\mathbf{c}_{i+1}^{\mathrm{cur}} \leftarrow$ LookUp$(\{\mathbf{c}_{0,s_1^i}^{T_i}, \mathbf{c}_{0,s_2^i}^{T_i}, \ldots \mathbf{c}_{0,s_{|S_i|}^i}^{T_i}\}, \{d'_1, \ldots, d'_{\lceil \log_2(|S_i|) \rceil}\})$
  $c_i \leftarrow$ SampleExtract$(0, \mathbf{c}_{i+1}^{\mathrm{cur}})$
  **output** $c_i$

Bootstrapping to all the states of $M^{\mathrm{R}}$, while Algorithm 2 only considers the states reachable from the initial state. This is because in online monitoring, we monitor a stream of ciphertexts without knowing the number of the remaining ciphertexts, and all the states of the reversed DFA $M^{\mathrm{R}}$ are potentially reachable from the initial state $q_0^{\mathrm{R}}$ by the reversed remaining ciphertexts $d_n, d_{n-1}, \ldots, d_{i+1}$ because of the minimality of $M^{\mathrm{R}}$.

**Theorem 2.** *Given a binary DFA $M$, TRGSW ciphertexts $d_1, d_2, \ldots, d_n$, a bootstrapping key* BK, *and a positive integer $I_{\mathrm{boot}}$, for each $i \in \{1, 2, \ldots, n\}$, if $c_i$ in Algorithm 3 can be correctly decrypted, Algorithm 3 outputs $c_i$ satisfying $Dec(c_i) = M(Dec(d_1)Dec(d_2)\ldots Dec(d_i))$.*

*Proof (sketch).* SampleExtract and Bootstrapping in Line 9 and 10 do not change the decrypted value of $c_i$. Therefore, $\mathrm{Dec}(c_i) = M^{\mathrm{R}}(\mathrm{Dec}(d_i)\ldots\mathrm{Dec}(d_1))$ for $i \in \{1, 2, \ldots, n\}$ by Theorem 1. As $M^{\mathrm{R}}$ is the reversed DFA of $M$, we have $\mathrm{Dec}(c_i) = M^{\mathrm{R}}(\mathrm{Dec}(d_i)\ldots\mathrm{Dec}(d_1)) = M(\mathrm{Dec}(d_1)\ldots\mathrm{Dec}(d_i))$. □

### 3.3 Online Algorithm 2: *Block*

A problem of Reverse is that the number of the states of the reversed DFA can explode exponentially due to powerset construction (see Sect. 3.4 for the details). Another idea of an online algorithm without reversing a DFA is illustrated in Fig. 2c: we split the monitored ciphertexts into *blocks* of fixed size $B$

and process each block in the same way as Algorithm 2. Intuitively, for each block $d_{1+(i-1)\times B}, d_{2+(i-1)\times B}, \ldots, d_{B+(i-1)\times B}$ of ciphertexts, we compute the function $T_i \colon Q \to Q$ satisfying $T_i(q) = \delta(q, d_{1+(i-1)\times B}, d_{2+(i-1)\times B}, \ldots, d_{B+(i-1)\times B})$ by a variant of OFFLINE, and keep track of the current state of the DFA after reading the current prefix $d_1, d_2, \ldots, d_{B+(i-1)\times B}$.

Algorithm 4 shows the outline of our second online algorithm (BLOCK) based on the above idea. Algorithm 4 takes a DFA $M$, TRGSW ciphertexts $d_1, d_2, \ldots, d_n$, a bootstrapping key BK, and an integer $B$ representing the interval of output. To simplify the presentation, we make the following assumptions, which are relaxed later: 1) $B$ is small, and a trivial TRLWE sample can be correctly decrypted after $B$ applications of CMUX; 2) the size $|Q|$ of the states of the DFA $M$ is smaller than or equal to $2^{N-1}$, where $N$ is the length of TRLWE.

The main loop of the algorithm is sketched on Lines 2–19. In each iteration, we consume the $i$-th block consisting of $B$ ciphertexts, i.e., $d_{(i-1)B+1}, \ldots, d_{(i-1)B+B}$. In Line 3, we compute the set $S_{i+1} = \{s_1^{i+1}, s_2^{i+1}, \ldots, s_{|S_{\mathrm{next}}|}^{i+1}\}$ of the states reachable from $q_0$ by reading a word of length $i \times B$.

In Lines 4–10, for each $q \in Q$, we construct a ciphertext representing $T_i(q)$ by feeding the current block to a variant of OFFLINE. More precisely, we construct a ciphertext $\mathbf{c}_{0,q}^{T_i}$ representing the pair of the Boolean value showing if $T_i(q) \in F$ and the state $T_i(q) \in Q$. The encoding of such a pair in a TRLWE ciphertext is as follows: the first element shows if $T_i(q) \in F$ and the other elements are the binary representation of $j \in \mathbb{N}^+$, where $j$ is such that $s_j^{i+1} = T_i(q)$.

In Lines 11–17, we construct the ciphertext $\mathbf{c}_{i+1}^{\mathrm{cur}}$ representing the state of the DFA $M$ after reading the current prefix $d_1, d_2, \ldots, d_{B+(i-1)\times B}$. If $|S_i| = 1$, since the unique element $q$ of $S_i$ is the only possible state before consuming the current block, the state after reading it is $T(q)$. Therefore, we let $\mathbf{c}_{i+1}^{\mathrm{cur}} = \mathbf{c}_{0,q}^{T_i}$.

Otherwise, we extract the ciphertext representing the state $q$ before consuming the current block, and let $\mathbf{c}_{i+1}^{\mathrm{cur}} = \mathbf{c}_{0,q}^{T_i}$. Since the $\mathbf{c}_i^{\mathrm{cur}}$ (except for the first element) represents $q$ (see Line 7), we extract them by applying SAMPLEEXTRACT (Line 15) and convert them to TRGSW by applying CIRCUITBOOTSTRAPPING (Line 16). Then, we choose $\mathbf{c}_{0,q}^{T_i}$ by applying LOOKUP and set it to $\mathbf{c}_{i+1}^{\mathrm{cur}}$.

The output after consuming the current block, i.e., $M(\mathrm{Dec}(d_1)\mathrm{Dec}(d_2)\ldots\mathrm{Dec}(d_{(i-1)B+B}))$ is stored in the first element of the TRLWE ciphertext $\mathbf{c}_{i+1}^{\mathrm{cur}}$. It is extracted by applying SAMPLEEXTRACT in Line 18 and output in Line19.

**Theorem 3.** *Given a binary DFA $M$, TRGSW ciphertexts $d_1, d_2, \ldots, d_n$, a bootstrapping key* BK, *and a positive integer $B$, for each $i \in \{1, 2, \ldots, \lfloor n/B \rfloor\}$, if $c_i$ in Algorithm 4 can be correctly decrypted, Algorithm 4 outputs a TLWE ciphertext $c_i$ satisfying $Dec(c_i) = M(Dec(d_1)Dec(d_2)\ldots Dec(d_{i\times B}))$.*

*Proof (sketch).* Let $q^i$ be $\delta(q_0, \mathrm{Dec}(d_1)\mathrm{Dec}(d_2)\ldots\mathrm{Dec}(d_{i\times B}))$. It suffices to show that, for each iteration $i$ in Line 2, $\mathrm{Dec}(\mathbf{c}_{i+1}^{\mathrm{cur}})$ represents a pair of the Boolean value showing if $q^i \in F$ and the state $q^i \in Q$ in the above encoding format. This is because $c_i$ represents the first element of $\mathbf{c}_{i+1}^{\mathrm{cur}}$. Algorithm 4 selects $\mathbf{c}_{i+1}^{\mathrm{cur}}$ from $\{\mathbf{c}_{0,q}^{T_i}\}_{q\in S_i}$ in Line 12 or Line 17. By using a slight variant of Theorem 1 in Lines 11–17, we can show that $\mathbf{c}_{0,q}^{T_i}$ represents if $T^i(q) \in F$ and the state $T^i(q)$. Therefore, the proof is completed by showing $\mathrm{Dec}(\mathbf{c}_{i+1}^{\mathrm{cur}}) = \mathrm{Dec}(\mathbf{c}_{0,q^{i-1}}^{T_i})$.

**Table 3.** Complexity of the proposed algorithms with respect to the number $|Q|$ of the states of the DFA and the size $|\phi|$ of the LTL formula. For BLOCK, we show the complexity *before* the relaxation.

| Algorithm | w.r.t. | Number of Applications | | | Space |
|---|---|---|---|---|---|
| | | CMUX | BOOTSTRAPPING | CIRCUITBOOTSTRAPPING | |
| OFFLINE | DFA | $O(n\|Q\|)$ | $O(n\|Q\|/I_{\mathrm{boot}})$ | — | $O(\|Q\|)$ |
| | LTL | $O(n2^{2^{\|\phi\|}})$ | $O(n2^{2^{\|\phi\|}}/I_{\mathrm{boot}})$ | — | $O(2^{2^{\|\phi\|}})$ |
| REVERSE | DFA | $O(n2^{\|Q\|})$ | $O(n2^{\|Q\|}/I_{\mathrm{boot}})$ | — | $O(2^{\|Q\|})$ |
| | LTL | $O(n2^{\|\phi\|})$ | $O(n2^{\|\phi\|}/I_{\mathrm{boot}})$ | — | $O(2^{\|\phi\|})$ |
| BLOCK | DFA | $O(n\|Q\|)$ | — | $O((n \log \|Q\|)/B)$ | $O(\|Q\|)$ |
| | LTL | $O(n2^{2^{\|\phi\|}})$ | — | $O(n2^{\|\phi\|}/B)$ | $O(2^{2^{\|\phi\|}})$ |

We prove $\mathrm{Dec}(\mathbf{c}_{i+1}^{\mathrm{cur}}) = \mathrm{Dec}(\mathbf{c}_{0,q^{i-1}}^{T_i})$ by induction on $i$. If $i = 1$, $|S_i| = 1$ holds, and by $q^{i-1} \in S_i$, we have $\mathrm{Dec}(\mathbf{c}_{i+1}^{\mathrm{cur}}) = \mathrm{Dec}(\mathbf{c}_{0,q^{i-1}}^{T_i})$. If $i > 1$ and $|S_i| = 1$, $\mathrm{Dec}(\mathbf{c}_{i+1}^{\mathrm{cur}}) = \mathrm{Dec}(\mathbf{c}_{0,q^{i-1}}^{T_i})$ holds similarly. If $i > 1$ and $|S_i| > 1$, by induction hypothesis, $\mathrm{Dec}(\mathbf{c}_i^{\mathrm{cur}})$ represents if $T_{i-1}(q^{i-2}) = q^{i-1} \in F$ and the state $q^{i-1}$. By construction in Line 16, $\mathrm{Dec}(d'_l)$ is equal to the $l$-th bit of $(j-1)$, where $j$ is such that $s_j^i = q^{i-1}$. Therefore, the result of the application of LOOKUP in Line 17 is equivalent to $\mathbf{c}_{0,s_j^i}^{T_i} (= \mathbf{c}_{0,q^{i-1}}^{T_i})$, and we have $\mathrm{Dec}(\mathbf{c}_{i+1}^{\mathrm{cur}}) = \mathrm{Dec}(\mathbf{c}_{0,q^{i-1}}^{T_i})$. □

We note that BLOCK generates output for every $B$ monitored ciphertexts while REVERSE generates output for every monitored ciphertext.

We also remark that when $B = 1$, BLOCK consumes every monitored ciphertext from front to back. However, such a setting is slow due to a huge number of CIRCUITBOOTSTRAPPING operations, as pointed out in Sect. 3.4.

**Relaxations of the Assumptions.** When $B$ is too large, $\mathbf{c}_{0,q}^{T_i}$ may not be correctly decrypted. We can relax this restriction by inserting BOOTSTRAPPING just after Line 10, which is much like Algorithm 2. When the size $|Q|$ of the states of the DFA $M$ is larger than $2^{N-1}$, we cannot store the index $j$ of the state using one TRLWE ciphertext (Line 7). We can relax this restriction by using multiple TRLWE ciphertexts for $\mathbf{c}_{0,q}^{T_i}$ and $\mathbf{c}_{i+1}^{\mathrm{cur}}$.

### 3.4 Complexity Analysis

Table 3 summarizes the complexity of our algorithms with respect to both the number $|Q|$ of the states of the DFA and the size $|\phi|$ of the LTL formula. We note that, for BLOCK, we do not relax the above assumptions for simplicity. Notice that the number of applications of the homomorphic operations is linear to the length $n$ of the monitored ciphertext. Moreover, the space complexity is independent of $n$. This shows that our algorithms satisfy the properties essential to good online monitoring; 1) they only store the minimum of data, and 2) they run quickly enough under a real-time setting [5].

The time and the space complexity of Offline and Block are linear to $|Q|$. Moreover, in these algorithms, when the $i$-th monitored ciphertext is consumed, only the states reachable by a word of length $i$ are considered, which often makes the scalability even better. In contrast, the time and the space complexity of Reverse is exponential to $|Q|$. This is because of the worst-case size of the reversed DFA due to the powerset construction. Since the size of the reversed DFA is usually reasonably small, the practical scalability of Reverse is also much better, which is observed through the experiments in Sect. 5.

For Offline and Block, $|Q|$ is *doubly* exponential to $|\phi|$ because we first convert $\phi$ to an NFA (one exponential) and then construct a DFA from the NFA (second exponential). In contrast, for Reverse, it is known that we can construct a reversed DFA for $\phi$ of the size of at most *singly* exponential to $|\phi|$ [15]. Note that, in a practical scenario exemplified in Sect. 5, the size of the DFA constructed from $\phi$ is expected to be much smaller than the worst one.

## 4 Oblivious Online LTL Monitoring

In this section, we formalize the scheme of oblivious online LTL monitoring. We consider a two-party setting with a client and a server and refer to the client and the server as Alice and Bob, respectively. Here, we assume that Alice has private data sequence $w = \sigma_1\sigma_2 \dots \sigma_n$ to be monitored where $\sigma_i \in 2^{\mathrm{AP}}$ for each $i \geq 1$. Meanwhile, Bob has a private LTL formula $\phi$. The purpose of oblivious online LTL monitoring is to let Alice know if $\sigma_1\sigma_2 \dots \sigma_i \models \phi$ for each $i \geq 1$, while keeping the privacy of Alice and Bob.

### 4.1 Threat Model

We assume that Alice is *malicious*, i.e., Alice can deviate arbitrarily from the protocol to try to learn $\phi$. We also assume that Bob is *honest-but-curious*, i.e., Bob correctly follows the protocol, but he tries to learn $w$ from the information he obtains from the protocol execution. We do not assume that Bob is malicious in the present paper; a protocol that is secure against malicious Bob requires more sophisticated primitives such as zero-knowledge proofs and is left as future work.

*Public and Private Data.* We assume that the TFHE parameters, the parameters of our algorithms (e.g., $I_{\mathrm{boot}}$ and $B$), Alice's public key PK, and Alice's bootstrapping key BK are public to both parties. The input $w$ and the monitoring result are private for Alice, and the LTL formula $\phi$ is private for Bob.

### 4.2 Protocol Flow

The protocol flow of oblivious online LTL monitoring is shown in Fig. 3. It takes $\sigma_1, \sigma_2, \dots, \sigma_n$, $\phi$, and $b \in \mathbb{B}$ as its parameters, where $b$ is a flag that indicates the algorithm Bob uses: Reverse ($b = 0$) or Block ($b = 1$). After generating her

**Input** : Alice's private inputs $\sigma_1, \sigma_2, \ldots, \sigma_n \in 2^{\mathrm{AP}}$, Bob's private LTL formula $\phi$, and $b \in \mathbb{B}$
**Output** : For every $i \in \{1, 2, \ldots n\}$, Alice's private output representing $\sigma_1 \sigma_2 \ldots \sigma_i \models \phi$

1 Alice generates her secret key SK.
2 Alice generates her public key PK and bootstrapping key BK from SK.
3 Alice sends PK and BK to Bob.
4 Bob converts $\phi$ to a binary DFA $M = (Q, \Sigma = \mathbb{B}, \delta, q_0, F)$.
5 **for** $i = 1, 2, \ldots, n$ **do**
6     Alice encodes $\sigma_i$ to a sequence $\sigma'_i := (\sigma'^1_i, \sigma'^2_i, \ldots, \sigma'^{|\mathrm{AP}|}_i) \in \mathbb{B}^{|\mathrm{AP}|}$.
7     Alice calculates $d_i := (\mathrm{Enc}(\sigma'^1_i), \mathrm{Enc}(\sigma'^2_i), \ldots \mathrm{Enc}(\sigma'^{|\mathrm{AP}|}_i))$.
8     Alice sends $d_i$ to Bob.
9     Bob feeds the elements of $d_i$ to REVERSE (if $b = 0$) or BLOCK (if $b = 1$).
    // $\sigma'_1 \cdot \sigma'_2 \cdots \sigma'_i$ **refers** $\sigma'^1_1 \ldots \sigma'^{|\mathrm{AP}|}_1 \sigma'^1_2 \ldots \sigma'^{|\mathrm{AP}|}_2 \sigma'^1_3 \ldots \sigma'^{|\mathrm{AP}|}_i$.
10     Bob obtains the output TLWE ciphertext $c$ produced by the algorithm, where $\mathrm{Dec}(c) = M(\sigma'_1 \cdot \sigma'_2 \cdot \cdots \cdot \sigma'_i)$.
11     Bob randomizes $c$ to obtain $c'$ so that $\mathrm{Dec}(c) = \mathrm{Dec}(c')$.
12     Bob sends $c'$ to Alice.
13     Alice calculates $\mathrm{Dec}(c')$ to obtain the result in plaintext.

**Fig. 3.** Protocol of oblivious online LTL monitoring.

secret key and sending the corresponding public and bootstrapping key to Bob (Lines 1–3), Alice encrypts her inputs into ciphertexts and sends the ciphertexts to Bob one by one (Lines 5–8). In contrast, Bob first converts his LTL formula $\phi$ to a binary DFA $M$ (Line 4). Then, Bob serially feeds the received ciphertexts from Alice to REVERSE or BLOCK (Line 9) and returns the encrypted output of the algorithm to Alice (Lines 10–13).

Note that, although the alphabet of a DFA constructed from an LTL formula is $2^{\mathrm{AP}}$ [36], our proposed algorithms require a binary DFA. Thus, in Line 4, we convert the DFA constructed from $\phi$ to a binary DFA $M$ by inserting auxiliary states. Besides, in Line 6, we encode an observation $\sigma_i \in 2^{\mathrm{AP}}$ by a sequence $\sigma'_i := (\sigma'^1_i, \sigma'^2_i, \ldots, \sigma'^{|AP|}_i) \in \mathbb{B}^{|AP|}$ such that $p_j \in \sigma_i$ if and only if $\sigma'^j_i$ is true, where $\mathrm{AP} = \{p_1, \ldots, p_{|\mathrm{AP}|}\}$. We also note that, taking this encoding into account, we need to properly set the parameters for BLOCK to generate an output for each $|\mathrm{AP}|$-size block of Alice's inputs, i.e., $B$ is taken to be equal to $|\mathrm{AP}|$.

Here, we provide brief sketches of the correctness and security analysis of the proposed protocol. See the full version [4] for detailed explanations and proofs.

**Correctness.** We can show that Alice obtains correct results in our protocol directly by Theorem 2 and Theorem 3.

**Security.** Intuitively, after the execution of the protocol described in Fig. 3, Alice should learn $M(\sigma'_1 \cdot \sigma'_2 \cdots \sigma'_i)$ for every $i \in \{1, 2, \ldots, n\}$ but nothing else. Besides, Bob should learn the input size $n$ but nothing else.

*Privacy for Alice.* We observe that Bob only obtains $\mathrm{Enc}(\sigma'^j_i)$ from Alice for each $i \in \{1, 2, \ldots, n\}$ and $j \in \{1, 2, \ldots, |\mathrm{AP}|\}$. Therefore, we need to show that Bob learns nothing from the ciphertexts generated by Alice. Since TFHE provides IND-CPA security [7], we can easily guarantee the client's privacy for Alice.

*Privacy for Bob.* The privacy guarantee for Bob is more complex than that for Alice. Here, Alice obtains $\sigma'_1, \sigma'_2, \ldots, \sigma'_n$ and the results $M(\sigma'_1 \cdot \sigma'_2 \cdots \sigma'_i)$ for every $i \in \{1, 2, \dots, n\}$ in plaintext. In the protocol (Fig. 3), Alice does not obtain $\phi, M$ themselves or their sizes, and it is known that a finite number of checking $M(w)$ cannot uniquely identify $M$ if any additional information (e.g., $|M|$) is not given [2,32]. Thus, it is impossible for Alice to identify $M$ (or $\phi$) from the input/output pairs.

Nonetheless, to fully guarantee the model privacy of Bob, we also need to show that, when Alice inspects the result ciphertext $c'$, it is impossible for Alice to know Bob's specification, i.e., what homomorphic operations were applied by Bob to obtain $c'$. A TLWE ciphertext contains a random nonce and a noise term. By randomizing $c$ properly in Line 11, we ensure that the random nonce of $c'$ is not biased [34]. By assuming SRL security [10,21] over TFHE, we can ensure that there is no information leakage regarding Bob's specifications through the noise bias. A more detailed discussion is in the full version [4].

## 5 Experiments

We experimentally evaluated the proposed algorithms (Reverse and Block) and protocol. We pose the following two research questions:

**RQ1.** Are the proposed algorithms scalable with respect to the size of the monitored ciphertexts and that of the DFA?

**RQ2.** Are the proposed algorithms fast enough in a realistic monitoring scenario?

**RQ3.** Does a standard IoT device have sufficient computational power acting as a client in the proposed protocol?

To answer RQ1, we conducted an experiment with our original benchmark where the length of the monitored ciphertexts and the size of the DFA are configurable (Sect. 5.1). To answer RQ2 and RQ3, we conducted a case study on blood glucose monitoring; we monitored blood glucose data obtained by simglucose[2] against specifications taken from [12,38] (Sect. 5.2). To answer RQ3, we measured the time spent on the encryption of plaintexts, which is the heaviest task for a client during the execution of the online protocol.

We implemented our algorithms in C++20. Our implementation is publicly available[3]. We used Spot [17] to convert a safety LTL formula to a DFA. We also used a Spot's utility program `ltlfilt` to calculate the size of an LTL formula[4]. We used TFHEpp [30] as the TFHE library. We used $N = 1024$ as the size of the message represented by one TRLWE ciphertext, which is a parameter of TFHE. The complete TFHE parameters we used are shown in the full version [4].

For RQ1 and RQ2, we ran experiments on a workstation with Intel Xeon Silver 4216 (3.2 GHz; 32 cores and 64 threads in total), 128 GiB RAM, and Ubuntu 20.04.2 LTS. We ran each instance of the experiment setting five times

[2] https://github.com/jxx123/simglucose.

[3] Our implementation is uploaded to https://doi.org/10.5281/zenodo.6558657..

[4] We desugared a formula by `ltlfilt` with option `--unabbreviate="eFGiMR^W"` and counted the number of the characters.

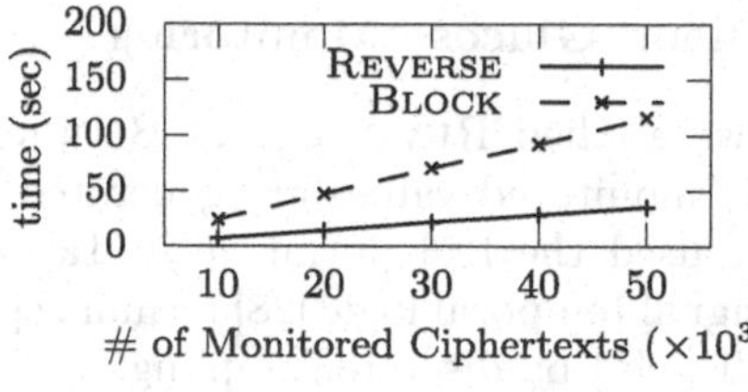


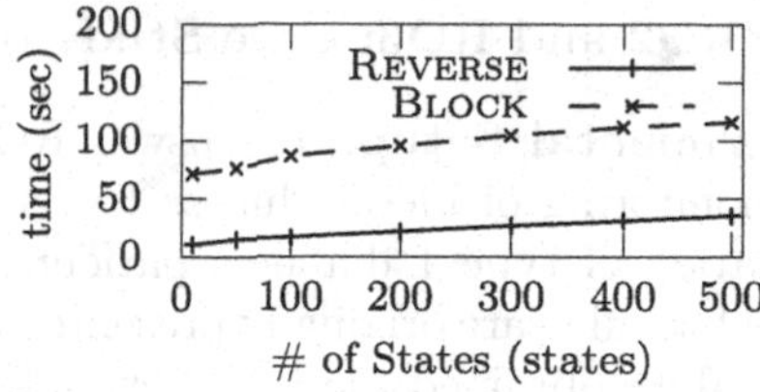


**Fig. 4.** Experimental results of $M_m$. The left figure shows runtimes when the number of states (i.e., $m$) is fixed to 500, while the right one is when the number of monitored ciphertexts (i.e., $n$) is fixed to 50000.

and reported the average. We measured the time to consume all of the monitored ciphertexts in the main loop of each algorithm, i.e., in Lines 4–12 in REVERSE and in Lines 2–19 in BLOCK.

For RQ3, we ran experiments on two single-board computers with and without Advanced Encryption Standard (AES) [14] hardware accelerator. ROCK64 has ARM Cortex A53 CPU cores (1.5 GHz; 4 cores) with AES hardware accelerator and 4 GiB RAM. Raspberry Pi 4 has ARM Cortex A72 CPU cores (1.5 GHz; 4 cores) without AES hardware accelerator and 4 GiB RAM.

### 5.1 RQ1: Scalability

**Experimental Setup.** In the experiments to answer RQ1, we used a simple binary DFA $M_m$, which accepts a word $w$ if and only if the number of the appearance of 1 in $w$ is a multiple of $m$. The number of the states of $M_m$ is $m$.

Our experiments are twofold. In the first experiment, we fixed the DFA size $m$ to 500 and increased the size $n$ of the input word $w$ from 10000 to 50000. In the second experiment, we fixed $n = 50000$ and changed $m$ from 10 to 500. The parameters we used are $I_{\text{boot}} = 30000$ and $B = 150$.

**Results and Discussion.** Figure 4 shows the results of the experiments. In the left plot of Fig. 4, we observe that the runtimes of both algorithms are linear to the length of the monitored ciphertexts. This coincides with the complexity analysis in Sect. 3.4.

In the right plot of Fig. 4, we observe that the runtimes of both algorithms are at most linear to the number of the states. For BLOCK, this coincides with the complexity analysis in Sect. 3.4. In contrast, this is much more efficient than the exponential complexity of REVERSE with respect to $|Q|$. This is because the size of the reversed DFA does not increase.

In both plots of Fig. 4, we observe that REVERSE is faster than BLOCK. Moreover, in the left plot of Fig. 4, the curve of BLOCK is steeper than that of REVERSE. This is because 1) the reversed DFA $M_m^{\text{R}}$ has the same size as $M_m$, 2) CIRCUITBOOTSTRAPPING is about ten times slower than BOOTSTRAPPING, and 3) $I_{\text{boot}}$ is much larger than $B$.

Overall, our experiment results confirm the complexity analysis in Sect. 3.4. Moreover, the practical scalability of REVERSE with respect to the DFA size is much better than the worst case, at least for this benchmark. Therefore, we answer RQ1 affirmatively.

### 5.2 RQ2 and RQ3: Case Study on Blood Glucose Monitoring

**Experimental Setup.** To answer RQ2, we applied Reverse and Block to the monitoring of blood glucose levels. The monitored values are generated by simulation of type 1 diabetes patients. We used the LTL formulae in Table 4. These formulae are originally presented as signal temporal logic [28] formulae [12, 38], and we obtained the LTL formulae in Table 4 by discrete sampling.

To simulate blood glucose levels of type 1 diabetes patients, we adopted simglucose, which is a Python implementation of UVA/Padova Type 1 Diabetes Simulator [29]. We recorded the blood glucose levels every one minute[5] and encoded each of them in nine bits. For $\psi_1, \psi_2, \psi_4$, we used 720 min of the simulated values. For $\phi_1, \phi_4, \phi_5$, we used seven days of the values. The parameters we used are $I_{\mathrm{boot}} = 30000$, $B = 9$.

To answer RQ3, we encrypted plaintexts into TRGSW ciphertexts 1000 times using two single-board computers (ROCK64 and Raspberry Pi 4) and reported the average runtime.

**Results and Discussion (RQ2).** The results of the experiments are shown in Table 5. The result for $\psi_4$ with Reverse is missing because the reversed DFA for $\psi_4$ is too huge, and its construction was aborted due to the memory limit.

Although the size of the reversed DFA was large for $\psi_1$ and $\psi_2$, in all the cases, we observe that both Reverse and Block took at most 24 s to process each blood glucose value on average. This is partly because $|Q|$ and $|Q^R|$ are not so large in comparison with the upper bound described in Sect. 3.4, i.e., doubly or singly exponential to $|\phi|$, respectively. Since each value is recorded every one minute, at least on average, both algorithms finished processing each value before the next measured value arrived, i.e., any congestion did not occur. Therefore, our experiment results confirm that, in a practical scenario of blood glucose monitoring, both of our proposed algorithms are fast enough to be used in the online setting, and we answer RQ2 affirmatively.

We also observe that average runtimes of $\psi_1, \psi_2, \psi_4$ and $\phi_1, \phi_4, \phi_5$ with Block are comparable, although the monitoring DFA of $\psi_1, \psi_2, \psi_4$ are significantly larger than those of $\phi_1, \phi_4, \phi_5$. This is because the numbers of the reachable states during execution are similar among these cases (from 1 up to 27 states). As we mentioned in Sect. 3.4, Block only considers the states reachable by a word of length $i$ when the $i$-th monitored ciphertext is consumed, and thus, it ran much faster even if the monitoring DFA is large.

**Results and Discussion (RQ3).** It took 40.41 and 1470.33 ms on average to encrypt a value of blood glucose (i.e., nine bits) on ROCK64 and Raspberry Pi 4, respectively. Since each value is sampled every one minute, our experiment results confirm that both machines are fast enough to be used in an online setting. Therefore, we answer RQ3 affirmatively.

[5] Current continuous glucose monitors (e.g., Dexcom G4 PLATINUM) record blood glucose levels every few minutes, and our sampling interval is realistic.

**Table 4.** The safety LTL formulae used in our experiments. $\psi_1, \psi_2, \psi_4$ are originally from [12], and $\phi_1$, $\phi_4$, and $\phi_5$ are originally from [38].

| | LTL formula |
|---|---|
| $\psi_1$ | $\mathsf{G}_{[100,700]}(p_8 \lor p_9 \lor (p_4 \land p_7) \lor (p_5 \land p_7) \lor (p_6 \land p_7) \lor (p_2 \land p_3 \land p_7))$ |
| $\psi_2$ | $\mathsf{G}_{[100,700]}(\neg p_9 \lor (\neg p_7 \land \neg p_8) \lor (\neg p_5 \land \neg p_6 \land \neg p_8) \lor (\neg p_4 \land \neg p_6 \land \neg p_8) \lor (\neg p_3 \land \neg p_6 \land \neg p_8) \lor (\neg p_2 \land \neg p_6 \land \neg p_8) \lor (\neg p_1 \land \neg p_6 \land \neg p_8))$ |
| $\psi_4$ | $\mathsf{G}_{[600,700]}((\neg p_8 \land \neg p_9) \lor (\neg p_7 \land \neg p_9) \lor (\neg p_4 \land \neg p_5 \land \neg p_6 \land \neg p_9) \lor (\neg p_1 \land \neg p_2 \land \neg p_3 \land \neg p_5 \land \neg p_6 \land \neg p_9))$ |
| $\phi_1$ | $\mathsf{G}((\neg p_6 \land \neg p_7 \land p_8 \land \neg p_9) \lor (\neg p_5 \land \neg p_7 \land p_8 \land \neg p_9) \lor (\neg p_3 \land \neg p_4 \land \neg p_7 \land p_8 \land \neg p_9) \lor (p_4 \land p_7 \land \neg p_8 \land \neg p_9) \lor (p_5 \land p_7 \land \neg p_8 \land \neg p_9) \lor (p_6 \land p_7 \land \neg p_8 \land \neg p_9) \lor (p_1 \land p_2 \land p_3 \land p_7 \land \neg p_8 \land \neg p_9))$ |
| $\phi_4$ | $\mathsf{G}((\neg p_7 \land \neg p_8 \land \neg p_9) \implies \mathsf{F}_{[0,25]}(p_7 \lor p_8 \lor p_9))$ |
| $\phi_5$ | $\mathsf{G}(p_9 \lor (p_3 \land p_7 \land p_8) \lor (p_4 \land p_7 \land p_8) \lor (p_5 \land p_7 \land p_8) \lor (p_6 \land p_7 \land p_8) \implies \mathsf{F}_{[0,25]}((\neg p_8 \land \neg p_9) \lor (\neg p_7 \land \neg p_9) \lor (\neg p_3 \land \neg p_4 \land \neg p_5 \land \neg p_6 \land \neg p_9)))$ |

**Table 5.** Experimental results of blood glucose monitoring, where $Q$ is the state space of the monitoring DFA and $Q^{\mathrm{R}}$ is the state space of the reversed DFA.

| Formula $\phi$ | $\lvert\phi\rvert$ | $\lvert Q\rvert$ | $\lvert Q^{\mathrm{R}}\rvert$ | # of blood glucose values | Algorithm | Runtime (s) | Mean Runtime (ms/value) |
|---|---|---|---|---|---|---|---|
| $\psi_1$ | 40963 | 10524 | 2712974 | 721 | Reverse | 16021.06 | 22220.62 |
| | | | | | Block | 132.68 | 184.02 |
| $\psi_2$ | 75220 | 11126 | 2885376 | 721 | Reverse | 17035.05 | 23626.97 |
| | | | | | Block | 131.53 | 182.43 |
| $\psi_4$ | 10392 | 7026 | — | 721 | Reverse | — | — |
| | | | | | Block | 35.42 | 49.12 |
| $\phi_1$ | 195 | 21 | 20 | 10081 | Reverse | 22.33 | 2.21 |
| | | | | | Block | 1741.15 | 172.72 |
| $\phi_4$ | 494 | 237 | 237 | 10081 | Reverse | 42.23 | 4.19 |
| | | | | | Block | 2073.45 | 205.68 |
| $\phi_5$ | 1719 | 390 | 390 | 10081 | Reverse | 54.87 | 5.44 |
| | | | | | Block | 2084.50 | 206.78 |

We also observe that encryption on ROCK64 is more than 35 times faster than that on Raspberry Pi 4. This is mainly because of the hardware accelerator for AES, which is used in TFHEpp to generate TRGSW ciphertexts.

## 6 Conclusion

We presented the first oblivious online LTL monitoring protocol up to our knowledge. Our protocol allows online LTL monitoring concealing 1) the client's monitored inputs from the server and 2) the server's LTL specification from the client. We proposed two online algorithms (Reverse and Block) using an FHE scheme called TFHE. In addition to the complexity analysis, we experimentally confirmed the scalability and practicality of our algorithms with an artificial benchmark and a case study on blood glucose level monitoring.

Our immediate future work is to extend our approaches to LTL semantics with multiple values, e.g., $LTL_3$ [6]. Extension to monitoring continuous-time signals, e.g., against an STL [28] formula, is also future work. Another future direction is to conduct a more realistic case study of our framework with actual IoT devices.

**Acknowledgements.** This work was partially supported by JST ACT-X Grant No. JPMJAX200U, JSPS KAKENHI Grant No. 22K17873 and 19H04084, and JST CREST Grant No. JPMJCR19K5, JPMJCR2012, and JPMJCR21M3.

## References

1. Abbas, H.: Private runtime verification: work-in-progress. In: EMSOFT 2019, p. 11. ACM (2019)
2. Angluin, D.: A note on the number of queries needed to identify regular languages. Inf. Control **51**(1), 76–87 (1981)
3. Atzori, L., Iera, A., Morabito, G.: The internet of things: a survey. Comput. Netw. **54**(15), 2787–2805 (2010)
4. Banno, R., Matsuoka, K., Matsumoto, N., Bian, S., Waga, M., Suenaga, K.: Oblivious online monitoring for safety LTL specification via fully homomorphic encryption (extended version). https://www.fos.kuis.kyoto-u.ac.jp/~banno/cav22.pdf
5. Bartocci, E., et al.: Specification-based monitoring of cyber-physical systems: a survey on theory, tools and applications. In: Bartocci, E., Falcone, Y. (eds.) Lectures on Runtime Verification. LNCS, vol. 10457, pp. 135–175. Springer, Cham (2018). https://doi.org/10.1007/978-3-319-75632-5_5
6. Bauer, A., Leucker, M., Schallhart, C.: Runtime verification for LTL and TLTL. ACM Trans. Softw. Eng. Methodol. **20**(4), 14:1–14:64 (2011)
7. Bellare, M., Rogaway, P.: Introduction to Modern Cryptography. UCSD CSE, vol. 207, p. 207 (2005)
8. Bing, K., Fu, L., Zhuo, Y., Yanlei, L.: Design of an internet of things-based smart home system. In: ICICIP 2011, vol. 2, pp. 921–924. IEEE (2011)
9. Blanton, M., Aliasgari, M.: Secure outsourcing of DNA searching via finite automata. In: Foresti, S., Jajodia, S. (eds.) DBSec 2010. LNCS, vol. 6166, pp. 49–64. Springer, Heidelberg (2010). https://doi.org/10.1007/978-3-642-13739-6_4
10. Brakerski, Z., Döttling, N., Garg, S., Malavolta, G.: Factoring and pairings are not necessary for IO: circular-secure LWE suffices. IACR Cryptology ePrint Archive, p. 1024 (2020)
11. Brakerski, Z., Gentry, C., Vaikuntanathan, V.: (leveled) Fully homomorphic encryption without bootstrapping. In: Goldwasser, S. (ed.) ITCS 2012, pp. 309–325. ACM (2012)
12. Cameron, F., Fainekos, G., Maahs, D.M., Sankaranarayanan, S.: Towards a verified artificial pancreas: challenges and solutions for runtime verification. In: Bartocci, E., Majumdar, R. (eds.) RV 2015. LNCS, vol. 9333, pp. 3–17. Springer, Cham (2015). https://doi.org/10.1007/978-3-319-23820-3_1
13. Chillotti, I., Gama, N., Georgieva, M., Izabachène, M.: TFHE: fast fully homomorphic encryption over the torus. J. Cryptol. **33**(1), 34–91 (2020)

14. Daemen, J., Rijmen, V.: AES proposal: Rijndael (1999)
15. De Giacomo, G., Stasio, A.D., Fuggitti, F., Rubin, S.: Pure-past linear temporal and dynamic logic on finite traces. In: Bessiere, C. (ed.) IJCAI 2020, pp. 4959–4965 (2020)
16. Dimitrov, D.V.: Medical internet of things and big data in healthcare. Healthc. Inform. Res. **22**(3), 156–163 (2016)
17. Duret-Lutz, A., Lewkowicz, A., Fauchille, A., Michaud, T., Renault, É., Xu, L.: Spot 2.0—a framework for LTL and $\omega$-automata manipulation. In: Artho, C., Legay, A., Peled, D. (eds.) ATVA 2016. LNCS, vol. 9938, pp. 122–129. Springer, Cham (2016). https://doi.org/10.1007/978-3-319-46520-3_8
18. El-Hokayem, A., Falcone, Y.: Bringing runtime verification home. In: Colombo, C., Leucker, M. (eds.) RV 2018. LNCS, vol. 11237, pp. 222–240. Springer, Cham (2018). https://doi.org/10.1007/978-3-030-03769-7_13
19. Fan, J., Vercauteren, F.: Somewhat practical fully homomorphic encryption. IACR Cryptology ePrint Archive, p. 144 (2012)
20. Frikken, K.B.: Practical private DNA string searching and matching through efficient oblivious automata evaluation. In: Gudes, E., Vaidya, J. (eds.) DBSec 2009. LNCS, vol. 5645, pp. 81–94. Springer, Heidelberg (2009). https://doi.org/10.1007/978-3-642-03007-9_6
21. Gay, R., Pass, R.: Indistinguishability obfuscation from circular security. IACR Cryptology ePrint Archive, p. 1010 (2020)
22. Gennaro, R., Hazay, C., Sorensen, J.S.: Text search protocols with simulation based security. In: Nguyen, P.Q., Pointcheval, D. (eds.) PKC 2010. LNCS, vol. 6056, pp. 332–350. Springer, Heidelberg (2010). https://doi.org/10.1007/978-3-642-13013-7_20
23. Gentry, C.: Fully homomorphic encryption using ideal lattices. In: Mitzenmacher, M. (ed.) STOC 2009, pp. 169–178. ACM (2009)
24. Gentry, C., Sahai, A., Waters, B.: Homomorphic encryption from learning with errors: conceptually-simpler, asymptotically-faster, attribute-based. In: Canetti, R., Garay, J.A. (eds.) CRYPTO 2013. LNCS, vol. 8042, pp. 75–92. Springer, Heidelberg (2013). https://doi.org/10.1007/978-3-642-40041-4_5
25. Ishai, Y., Paskin, A.: Evaluating branching programs on encrypted data. In: Vadhan, S.P. (ed.) TCC 2007. LNCS, vol. 4392, pp. 575–594. Springer, Heidelberg (2007). https://doi.org/10.1007/978-3-540-70936-7_31
26. Kupferman, O., Vardi, M.Y.: Model checking of safety properties. Formal Methods Syst. Des. **19**(3), 291–314 (2001)
27. Lemieux, C., Park, D., Beschastnikh, I.: General LTL specification mining (T). In: Cohen, M.B., Grunske, L., Whalen, M. (eds.) ASE 2015, pp. 81–92. IEEE Computer Society (2015)
28. Maler, O., Nickovic, D.: Monitoring temporal properties of continuous signals. In: Lakhnech, Y., Yovine, S. (eds.) FORMATS/FTRTFT -2004. LNCS, vol. 3253, pp. 152–166. Springer, Heidelberg (2004). https://doi.org/10.1007/978-3-540-30206-3_12
29. Man, C.D., Micheletto, F., Lv, D., Breton, M., Kovatchev, B., Cobelli, C.: The UVA/PADOVA type 1 diabetes simulator: new features. J. Diabetes Sci. Technol. **8**(1), 26–34 (2014)
30. Matsuoka, K., Banno, R., Matsumoto, N., Sato, T., Bian, S.: Virtual secure platform: a five-stage pipeline processor over TFHE. In: Bailey, M., Greenstadt, R. (eds.) USENIX Security 2021, pp. 4007–4024. USENIX Association (2021)

31. Mohassel, P., Niksefat, S., Sadeghian, S., Sadeghiyan, B.: An efficient protocol for oblivious DFA evaluation and applications. In: Dunkelman, O. (ed.) CT-RSA 2012. LNCS, vol. 7178, pp. 398–415. Springer, Heidelberg (2012). https://doi.org/10.1007/978-3-642-27954-6_25
32. Moore, E.F.: Gedanken-experiments on sequential machines. In: Automata Studies. (AM-34), pp. 129–154. Princeton University Press, Princeton (1956)
33. Pnueli, A.: The temporal logic of programs. In: 18th Annual Symposium on Foundations of Computer Science, pp. 46–57. IEEE Computer Society (1977)
34. Regev, O.: On lattices, learning with errors, random linear codes, and cryptography. J. ACM **56**(6), 34:1–34:40 (2009)
35. Sasakawa, H., Harada, H., duVerle, D., Arimura, H., Tsuda, K., Sakuma, J.: Oblivious evaluation of non-deterministic finite automata with application to privacy-preserving virus genome detection. In: Ahn, G., Datta, A. (eds.) WPES 2014, pp. 21–30. ACM (2014)
36. Tabakov, D., Rozier, K.Y., Vardi, M.Y.: Optimized temporal monitors for systemC. Formal Methods Syst. Des. **41**(3), 236–268 (2012)
37. Troncoso-Pastoriza, J.R., Katzenbeisser, S., Celik, M.U.: Privacy preserving error resilient DNA searching through oblivious automata. In: Ning, P., di Vimercati, S.D.C., Syverson, P.F. (eds.) CCS 2007, pp. 519–528. ACM (2007)
38. Young, W., Corbett, J., Gerber, M.S., Patek, S., Feng, L.: DAMON: a data authenticity monitoring system for diabetes management. In: IoTDI 2018, pp. 25–36. IEEE Computer Society (2018)

# Abstraction Modulo Stability for Reverse Engineering

Anna Becchi[1,2(✉)] and Alessandro Cimatti[1]

[1] Fondazione Bruno Kessler, Trento, Italy
{abecchi,cimatti}@fbk.eu
[2] University of Trento, Trento, Italy

**Abstract.** The analysis of legacy systems requires the automated extraction of high-level specifications. We propose a framework, called Abstraction Modulo Stability, for the analysis of transition systems operating in stable states, and responding with run-to-completion transactions to external stimuli. The abstraction captures the effects of external stimuli on the system state, and describes it in the form of a finite state machine. This approach is parametric on a set of predicates of interest and the definition of stability. We consider some possible stability definitions which yield different practically relevant abstractions, and propose a parametric algorithm for abstraction computation. The obtained FSM is extended with guards and effects on a given set of variables of interest. The framework is evaluated in terms of expressivity and adequacy within an industrial project with the Italian Railway Network, on reverse engineering tasks of relay-based interlocking circuits to extract specifications for a computer-based reimplementation.

**Keywords:** Timed Transition Systems · Property extraction · Simulations · Relay-based circuits

## 1 Introduction

The maintenance of legacy systems is known to be a very costly task, and the lack of knowledge hampers the possibility of a reimplementation with more modern technologies. Legacy systems may have been actively operating for decades, but their behavior is known only to a handful of people. It is therefore important to have automated means to reverse-engineer and understand their behavior, for example in the form of state machines or temporal properties.

We focus on understanding systems that exhibit self-stabilizing behaviors, i.e. that are typically in a stable state, and respond to external stimuli by reaching stability in a possibly different state. As an industrially relevant example, consider legacy Railway Interlocking Systems based on Relay technology (RRIS): these are electro-mechanical circuits for the control of railway stations, with thousands of components that respond to the requests of human operators to activate the shunting routes for the movement of the trains. They support a computational model based on "run-to-completion", where a change in a part


S. Shoham and Y. Vizel (Eds.): CAV 2022, LNCS 13371, pp. 469–489, 2022.
https://doi.org/10.1007/978-3-031-13185-1_23

of the circuit (e.g. a switch closing) may change the power in another part of the circuit, and in turn operate other switches, until a stable condition is (hopefully) reached. This is very different in spirit from typical "cycle-based" control implemented in computer-based systems such as SCADA.

In this paper, we tackle the problem of extracting abstract specifications of the possible behaviors of an infinite-state timed transition system. The idea is to understand how the system evolves from a stable state, in response to a given stimulus, to the next stable state. In addition, we are interested in knowing under which conditions the transitions are possible and which are the effects on selected state variables. All this information is presented in the form of an extended finite state machine, which can be seen as a collection of temporal specifications satisfied by the system.

We make the following contributions. First, we propose the general framework of *Abstraction Modulo Stability*, a white-box analysis of self-stabilizing systems with run-to-completion behavior. The set of abstract states is the grid induced by a set of given predicates of interest. The framework is generic and parameterized with respect to the notion of stability. Different notions of stability are possible, depending on several factors: remaining in a region is possible (for some paths) or necessary (for all paths); whether the horizon of persistence in the stable region is unbounded, or lower-bounded on the number of discrete transitions and/or on the actual time. The framework also takes into account the notion of reachability in the concrete space, in order to limit the amount of spurious behaviors in the abstract description. We illustrate the relations holding between the corresponding abstractions, depending on the strength of the selected notion of stability.

Second, we present a practical algorithm to compute stability abstractions. We face two key difficulties. In the general case, one abstract transition is associated to a sequence of concrete transitions, of possibly unbounded length, so that a fix point must be reached. Furthermore, we need to make sure that the sequence is starting from a reachable state. Contrast this with the standard SMT-based computation of predicate abstractions [15], where one transition in the abstract space corresponds to one concrete transition, and reachability is not considered.

Third, we show how to lift to the abstract space other relevant variables from the concrete space, so that each abstract transition is associated with guards and effects. This results in a richer abstraction where the abstract states (typically representing control modes) are complemented by information on the data flow of the additional variables (typically representing the actual control conditions in a given mode).

We experimentally evaluate the approach on several large RRIS implementing the control logic for shunting routes and switch controls. This research is strongly motivated by an ongoing activity on the migration of the Italian Railway Network from relay-based interlocking to computer-based interlocking [3]. Stability abstraction is the chosen formalism to reverse engineer the RRIS, and to automatically provide the actual specifications for computer-based interlocking. We demonstrate the effectiveness of the proposed algorithms, and the crucial role of reachability in terms of precision of the abstractions.

**Related Works.** This work has substantial differences with most of the literature in abstraction. For example, Predicate Abstraction (PA) [11] can be directly embedded within the framework; furthermore, PA does not take into account concrete reachability; finally, an abstract transition is the direct result of a concrete transition, and not, as in our case, of a sequence of concrete transitions.

In [5] the authors propose to analyze abstract transitions between invariant regions with an approximated approach. In comparison, we propose a general framework, parameterized on the notion of stability. Additionally, we propose effective algorithms to construct automata from concrete behaviors only, and that represent symbolically the guards and the effects of the transitions.

The idea of weak bisimilarity [19], proposed for the comparison of observable behaviors of CCS, is based on collapsing sequences of silent, internal actions. The main difference with our approach is that weak bisimilarity is not used to obtain an abstraction for reverse engineering. Furthermore, in Abstraction Modulo Stability, observability is a property of states, and the silent actions are collapsed only when passing through unobservable (i.e., unstable) states.

Somewhat related are the techniques for specification mining, that have been extensively studied, for example in hardware and software. For example, DAIKON [9] extracts candidate invariant specifications from simulations. In our approach, the abstraction directly results in temporal properties that are guaranteed to hold on the system being abstracted. Yet, simulation-based techniques might be useful to bootstrap the computation of Abstraction Modulo Stability.

The work in [1] proposes techniques for the analysis of RRIS, assuming that a description of the stable states is already given. There are two key differences: first, the analysis of transient states is not considered; second, the extraction of a description in terms of stable states is a manual (and thus inefficient and error prone) task. For completeness, we mention the vast literature on the application of formal methods to railways interlocking systems (see e.g. [6,12,13,17,18]). Aside from the similarity in the application domain, these works are not directly related, given their focus on the verification of the control algorithms.

**Structure of the Paper.** In Sect. 2 we present the background notions. In Sect. 3 we present the framework of Abstraction Modulo Stability. In Sect. 4 we present the algorithms for computing abstraction. In Sect. 5 we present the experimental evaluation. In Sect. 6 we draw some conclusions and present the directions of future work.

## 2 Background

We work in the setting of Satisfiability Modulo Theories (SMT) [4], with quantifier-free first order formulae interpreted over the theory of Linear Real

Arithmetic (LRA). We use $P, Q$ to denote sets of Boolean variables, $p, q$ to denote truth assignments, and the standard Boolean connectives $\wedge, \vee, \neg, \rightarrow$ for conjunction, disjunction, negation and implication. $\top$ and $\bot$ define true and false respectively. For a set of variables $V$, let $\Psi_{\mathcal{T}}(V)$ denote the set of first-order formulae over a theory $\mathcal{T}$ with free variables in $V$. When clear from context we omit the subscript. Let $V' \doteq \{v' \mid v \in V\}$. For a formula $\phi \in \Psi(V)$, let $\phi'$ denote $\phi[V/V']$, i.e. the substitution of each variable $v \in V$ with $v'$.

A finite state automaton is a tuple $\mathcal{A} = \langle Q, L, Q_0, R \rangle$ where: $Q$ is a finite set of states; $L$ is the alphabet; $Q_0 \subseteq Q$ is the set of initial states; $R \subseteq (Q \times L \times Q)$ is the labeled transition relation. We also consider automata with transitions annotated by guards and effects expressed as SMT formulae over given sets of variables. For $(q_1, \ell, q_2) \in R$, we write $q_1 \xrightarrow{\ell}_{\mathcal{A}} q_2$. Let $\mathcal{A}_1$ and $\mathcal{A}_2$ be two automata defined on the same set of states $Q$ and on the same alphabet $L$ including a label $\tau$: we say that $\mathcal{A}_1$ weakly simulates $\mathcal{A}_2$, and we write $\mathcal{A}_1 \lesssim \mathcal{A}_2$, if whenever $q \xrightarrow{\ell}_{\mathcal{A}_1} q'$, then $q \xrightarrow{\ell}_{\mathcal{A}_2} \xrightarrow{\tau}^{*}_{\mathcal{A}_2} q'$, where $\xrightarrow{\tau}^{*}$ is a (possibly null) sequence of transitions labeled with $\tau$.

A symbolic timed transition system is a tuple $\mathcal{M} = \langle V, C, \Sigma, \text{Init}, \text{Invar}, \text{Trans} \rangle$, where: $V$ is a finite set of state variables; $C \subseteq V$ is a set of clock variables; $\Sigma$ is a finite set of boolean variables encoding the alphabet; $\text{Init}(V)$, $\text{Invar}(V)$, $\text{Trans}(V, \Sigma, V')$ are SMT formulae describing the initial states, the invariant and the transition relation respectively. The clocks in $C$ are real-valued variables. We restrict the formulae over clock variables to atoms of the form $c \bowtie k$, for $c \in C$, $k \in \mathbb{R}$ and $\bowtie \in \{\leq, <, \geq, >, =\}$. The clock invariants are convex. We allow the other variables in $V$ to be either boolean or real-valued.

A state is an assignment for the $V$ state variables, and let $S$ denote the set of all the interpretations of $V$. We assume a distinguished clock variable $\mathit{time} \in C$ initialized with $\mathit{time} = 0$ in Init, representing the global time.

The system evolves following either a discrete or a timed step. The timed transition entails that there exists $\delta \in \mathbb{R}_+$ such that $c' = c + \delta$ for each clock variable $c \in C$, and $v' = v$ for all the other variables[1]. The discrete transition entails that $\mathit{time}' = \mathit{time}$ and can change the other variables instantaneously.

A valid trace $\pi$ is a sequence of states $(s_0, s_1, \dots)$ that all fulfill the Invar condition, such that $s_0 \models \text{Init}$ and for all $i$, $(s_i, \ell_i, s_{i+1}) \models \text{Trans}(V, \Sigma, V')$ for some $\ell_i$ assignment to $\Sigma$. We denote with $\text{Reach}(\mathcal{M})$ the set of states that are reachable by a valid trace in $\mathcal{M}$. We adopt a hyper-dense semantics: in a trace $\pi$, time is weakly monotonic, i.e. $s_i.\mathit{time} \leq s_{i+1}.\mathit{time}$. We disregard Zeno behaviors, i.e. every finite run is a prefix of a run in which $\mathit{time}$ diverges.

The states in which time cannot elapse, i.e. which are forced to take an instantaneous discrete transition, are called *urgent* states. We assume the existence of a boolean state variable $\mathit{urg} \in V$ which is true in all and only the urgent states. Namely, for every pair of states $(s_i, s_{i+1})$ in a path $\pi$ where $s_i.\mathit{urg}$ is true, then $(s_i.\mathit{time} = s_{i+1}.\mathit{time})$.

[1] We abuse the notation and write $P = Q$ for $P \leftrightarrow Q$ when $P$ and $Q$ are Boolean variables.

We consider CTL+P [16], a branching-time temporal logic with the future and past temporal operators. A history $h = (s_0, ..., s_n)$ for $\mathcal{M}$ is a finite prefix of a trace of $\mathcal{M}$. For a CTL+P formula $\psi$, write $\mathcal{M}, h \models \psi$ meaning that after $h$, $s_n$ satisfies $\psi$ in $\mathcal{M}$. Operators AG$\psi$, $E(\psi_1 \text{ U } \psi_2)$, $H\psi$ are used with their standard interpretations (*in every future $\psi$ will always hold, there exists a future in which $\psi_1$ holds until $\psi_2$, in the current history $\psi$ always held*, respectively).

## 3 The Framework of Abstraction Modulo Stability

### 3.1 Overview

We tackle the problem of abstracting a concrete system in order to mine relevant high-level properties about its behavior.

We are interested in how the system reacts to stimuli: when an action is performed, we want to skip the intermediate steps that are necessary to accomplish an induced effect, and evaluate how stable conditions are connected to each other. The definition of stability is the core filter that defines which states we want to observe when following a run-to-completion process, i.e., the run triggered by a stimulus under the assumption that the inputs remain stationary. In practice, several definitions of stability are necessary, each of them corresponding to a different level of abstraction.

An additional element of the desired abstraction is that relevant properties regard particular evaluations of the system. We consider a defined abstract space which intuitively holds the observable evaluations on the system, on which we will project the concrete states.

In this section we describe a general framework for *Abstraction Modulo Stability*, which is parametric with respect to the abstract domain and the definition of stability. The result will be a finite state system which simulates the original model, by preserving only the stable way-points on the abstract domain, and by skipping the transient (i.e., unstable and unobservable) states.

Finally, we define how the obtained abstract automata can be enriched with guards and effects for each transition.

*Example 1.* Consider as running example the timed transition system $\mathcal{S}$ shown in the right hand side of Fig. 1 which models a tank receiving a constant incoming flow of water, with an automatic safety valve.

$\mathcal{S}$ has a clock variable $c$ which monitors the velocity of filling and emptying processes, and reads an input boolean variable in.flow. The status of this variable is controlled by the environment $\mathcal{E}$, shown in the left hand side of the figure. In the transition relation of $\mathcal{E}$, the variables in $\Sigma$ encode the labels for the stimuli, which are variations of the input variable in.flow. In particular, if $\Sigma = \tau$, then in.flow is unchanged, and we say that the system $\mathcal{S}$ is not receiving any stimulus. $\mathcal{S}$ reacts accordingly to the updated in.flow′. The discrete transitions of $\mathcal{S}$ are labeled with guards and with resetting assignments on the clock variable (in the form *[guards]/resets*). The system starts in the Empty location. A discrete transition reacts to a true in.flow jumping in Filling and resetting $c' := 0$. The invariant $c \leq$

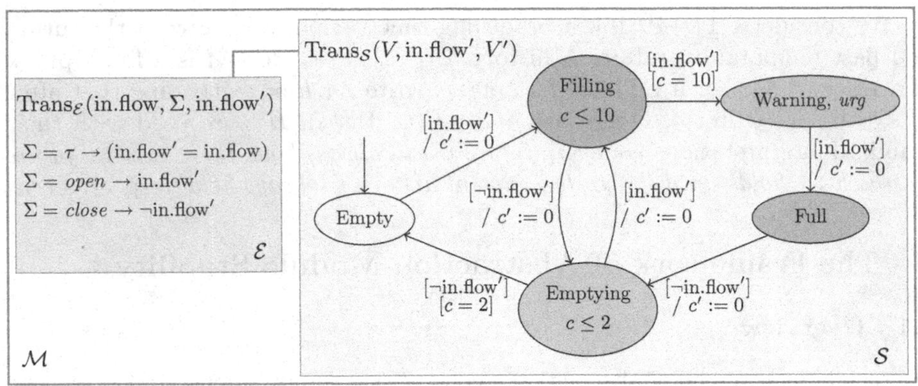


**Fig. 1.** A timed transition system representing a tank of water.

10 of Filling forces the system to transit to a Warning location after 10 time units, corresponding to the time needed to reach a critical level. Warning is urgent: as soon as $\mathcal{S}$ reaches this state, it is forced to take the next discrete transition. The urgency of location Warning models the causality relation between the evaluation on the level of water and the instantaneous opening of a safety valve. Due to the latter, in location Full the system dumps all the incoming water and keeps the level of water stable. If the input is closed, $\mathcal{S}$ transits in Emptying. In this condition, water is discharged faster: after 2 time units the system is again in Empty. Transitions between Filling and Emptying describe the system's reaction to a change of the input while in charging/discharging process.

We consider as predicates of interest exactly the five locations of the system. The stability abstraction of the composed system is meant to represent the stable conditions reached after the triggering events defined by $\Sigma$.

### 3.2 Abstraction Modulo Stability

Consider a symbolic timed transition system $\mathcal{M} = \langle X, C, \Sigma, \text{Init}, \text{Invar}, \text{Trans}\rangle$ whose discrete transitions are labeled by assignments to $\Sigma$ representing stimuli. A stimulus corresponds to a variation of some variables $I \subseteq V$ which we call *input* variables. Namely, we can picture $\mathcal{M}$ as a closed system partitioned into an *environment* $\mathcal{E}$ which changes the variables $I$, and a open system $\mathcal{S}$ which reads the conditions of the updated variables $I$ and reacts accordingly: $\text{Trans}(X, \Sigma, X') = \text{Trans}_\mathcal{E}(I, \Sigma, I') \wedge \text{Trans}_\mathcal{S}(V, I', V')$, with $V = X \setminus I$.

In particular, we assume a distinguished assignment $\tau$ to the labels $\Sigma$, corresponding to the absence of stimuli: $\text{Trans}_\mathcal{E}[\Sigma/\tau] = (I \leftrightarrow I')$. The transition labeled with $\tau$ is the *silent* or *internal* transition. It corresponds to the discrete changes which keep the inputs stationary (i.e., unchanged) and the timed transitions. We write $\mathcal{M}^\tau$ for the restriction of $\mathcal{M}$ which evolves only with the silent transition $\tau$, i.e., under the assumption that no external interrupting action is performed on $\mathcal{S}$, so that $I \leftrightarrow I'$ is entailed by the transition relation. We assume that $\mathcal{M}$ is never blocked waiting for an external action: this makes $\mathcal{M}^\tau$ always responsive to $\tau$ transition. Moreover, we assume that Zeno behaviors are not introduced by this restriction.

We define a framework for abstracting $\mathcal{M}$ parametric on an abstract domain $\Phi$ and a stability definition $\sigma$.

*Abstract Domain.* Between the variables of the system $\mathcal{M}$, consider a set of boolean variables $P \subseteq X$ representing important predicates. The abstract domain $\Phi$ is the domain of the boolean combinations of $P$ variables.

*Stability Definition.* Let $\sigma(X)$ be a CTL+P formula providing a stability criterion.

**Definition 1 ($\sigma$-Stability).** *A concrete state $s$ with history $h = (s_0, \ldots, s)$ is $\sigma$-stable if and only if*

$$\mathcal{M}^\tau, h \models \sigma.$$

Note that the stability is evaluated in $\mathcal{M}^\tau$, i.e. under the assumption that the inputs are stationary: at the reception of an external stimulus, a $\sigma$-stable might move to a new concrete state which does not satisfy $\sigma$. We say that a state $s$ is $\sigma$-stable in a region $p \in \Phi$ if it is $\sigma$-stable and $s \models p$.

The states for which $\mathcal{M}^\tau, (s_0, \ldots, s) \not\models \sigma$, are said *$\sigma$-unstable.* These states might be transient during a convergence process which leads to the next stable state. In the following we will omit the prefix $\sigma$ when clear from context.

**Definition 2 (Abstraction Modulo $\sigma$-Stability).** *Given a concrete system $\mathcal{M} = \langle X, C, \Sigma, \mathrm{Init}, \mathrm{Invar}, \mathrm{Trans}\rangle$, with $P \subseteq X$ boolean variables, the* abstraction modulo $\sigma$-stability *of $\mathcal{M}$ is a finite state automaton $\mathcal{A}_\sigma = \langle \Phi, 2^\Sigma, \mathrm{Init}_\sigma, \mathrm{Trans}_\sigma\rangle$. For each $p_0 \in \Phi$, $p_0 \models \mathrm{Init}_\sigma$ if and only if there exists a state $s_0 \in S$ such that $s_0 \models \mathrm{Init}$, and with $h_0 = (s_0)$*

$$\mathcal{M}^\tau, h_0 \models \mathrm{E}(\neg\sigma \;\mathrm{U}\; (\sigma \wedge p_0)).$$

*For each $p_1, p_2 \in \Phi$, $\ell \in 2^\Sigma$, the triple $(p_1, \ell, p_2) \models \mathrm{Trans}_\sigma$ if and only if there exist states $s_0, s_1, s_2 \in S$ and histories $h_1 = (s_0, \ldots, s_1)$, $h_2 = (s_2)$ such that $(s_1, \ell, s_2) \models \mathrm{Trans}$, and such that*

$$\mathcal{M}^\tau, h_1 \models \sigma \wedge p_1, \qquad \mathcal{M}^\tau, h_2 \models \mathrm{E}(\neg\sigma \;\mathrm{U}\; (\sigma \wedge p_2)).$$

Abstract automaton $\mathcal{A}_\sigma$ simulates with a single abstract transition a run of the concrete system $\mathcal{M}$ that connects two $\sigma$-stable states with a single event and possibly multiple steps of internal $\tau$ transitions. We call such convergence process a *run-to-completion* triggered by the initial event.

Observe that the abstraction is led by the definition of $\sigma$-stability. It preserves only the abstract regions in which there is a $\sigma$-stable state. The transient states are not exposed, hence disregarding also the behaviors of $\mathcal{M}$ in which a new external stimuli interrupts a convergence still in progress. In other words, it represents the effects of stimuli accepted only in stable conditions.

In this way, $\mathcal{A}_\sigma$ satisfies invariant properties that would have been violated in $\sigma$-unstable states, transient along an internal run-to-completion.

*Reachability-Aware Abstraction.* Abstractions modulo stability can be tightened by considering only concrete reachable states in $\mathcal{M}$. In fact, in the setting of reverse engineering, considering unreachable states may result in an abstraction that includes impossible behaviors that have no counterpart in the concrete space. This is done by enforcing that the first state of $h_1$ in Definition 2 to be reachable in $\mathcal{M}$. This is an orthogonal option to the choice of the stability definition $\sigma$.

### 3.3 Instantiating the Framework

The level of abstraction of $\mathcal{A}_\sigma$, i.e., the disregarded behaviors, is directly induced by the chosen definition of $\sigma$. Its adequacy depends on both the application domain and the objective of the analysis. We now explore some possibilities that we consider relevant in practice.

*Predicate Abstraction.* Firstly, we show that the Abstraction Modulo Stability framework is able to cover the known *predicate abstraction* [11,14]. With a trivial stability condition

$$\sigma_1 \doteq \top,$$

every concrete state $s$ is stable and is projected in the abstract region it belongs to ($p = \exists(X \setminus P) \,.\, s$). In this way, all concrete transitions (including the timed ones) are reflected in the corresponding $\mathcal{A}_{\sigma_1}$.

*Non-urgent Abstraction.* Urgent states are the ones in which time cannot elapse, and are forced to transit with a discrete transition. They are usually exploited to decompose a complex action made of multiple steps and to faithfully model the causality along a cyclical chain of events. Unfortunately, by construction, urgent states introduce *transient* conditions which may be physically irrelevant. In practice, in the analysis of the system's behaviors, one may want to disregard the intermediate steps of a complex instantaneous action.

To this aim, we apply the Abstraction Modulo Stability framework and keep only the states in which time can elapse for an (arbitrarily small) time bound $T$.

$$\sigma_2(X) \doteq \neg urg.$$

The obtained abstract automaton $\mathcal{A}_{\sigma_2}$ has transitions that correspond to *instantaneous* run-to-completion processes, skipping urgent states until time is allowed to elapse.

*Example 2.* On the left hand side of Fig. 2 we show the abstraction of the tank system obtained using $\sigma_1$. An abstract transition connects two predicates (recall that in this example predicates correspond to concrete locations) if they are connected in $\mathcal{S}$, by either a discrete or a timed transition.

On the right hand side of Fig. 2 we show the abstraction obtained using $\sigma_2$. With respect to $\mathcal{A}_{\sigma_1}$, here location Warning is missing, since time cannot elapse in it, and an abstract transition connects directly Filling to Full.

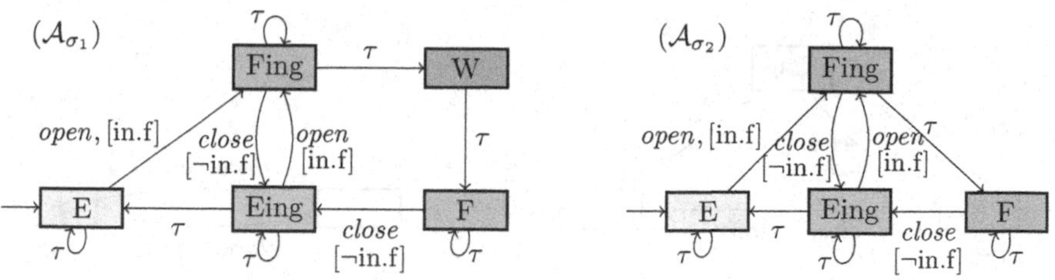


**Fig. 2.** Abstractions modulo $\sigma_1$ and $\sigma_2$ on the tank running example.

*Eq-predicate Abstractions.* Let $Eq(P)$ be a formula expressing implicitly that the interpretations of the abstract predicates are not changing during a transition (either a discrete or a timed step).

We now address the intuitive definition: *"a stable state is associated with behaviors that preserve the abstract predicates for enough time, i.e., if the system is untouched, then the predicates do not change value for a sufficient time interval"*. One can choose to measure the permanence of $s$ in $p \in \Phi$ in terms of number of steps (e.g., at least $K$ concrete steps, with $K \in \mathbb{N}_+$), or in terms of continuous-time (e.g., for at least $T$ time, with $T \in \mathbb{R}_+$), or both.

This intuitive definition can be interpreted both backward and forward. In this paragraph we illustrate the backward perspective.

Consider the doubly bounded definition

$$\sigma_3^{T,K}(X) \doteq \mathrm{H}^{>T,>K} Eq(P),$$

where: $\mathcal{M}^\tau, h \models \sigma_3^{T,K}$, if and only if $h = (s_0 \dots s_i)$, with $i \geq K$ and for some $p \in 2^P$

$$\begin{pmatrix} \forall j \in [(i-K), i] : s_j \models p \ \wedge \\ s_i.time - s_{i-K}.time > T \end{pmatrix}.$$

Such characterization of stability captures the states that have been in the same predicate assignment for at least $K$ steps *and* at least $T$ time has elapsed in such frame. Several variants of this definition are possible, e.g. by using only one bound.

This definition is referred to as *backward* since we consider the history of the system: a stable state has a past trajectory that remained in the same abstract region for enough time/steps. It is practically relevant in contexts where it is useful to highlight the dwell time of the system in a given condition. The only visible behaviors are the ones that were exposed for sufficient time/steps.

It can be easily seen that if a history $h$ satisfies $\sigma_3^{T_2,K}$, then it also satisfies $\sigma_3^{T_1,K}$, with $T_1 \leq T_2$.

Notably, for the instantiations of $\sigma_3$ with $K = 1$, a state is stable if it has just finished a timed transition elapsing at least $T$ time. In the following, we omit the superscript $K$ from $\sigma_3^{T,K}$ when $K = 1$. We have that if a history $h$ satisfies $\sigma_3^T$, then it also satisfies $\sigma_2$. Namely, while every urgent state (i.e., a

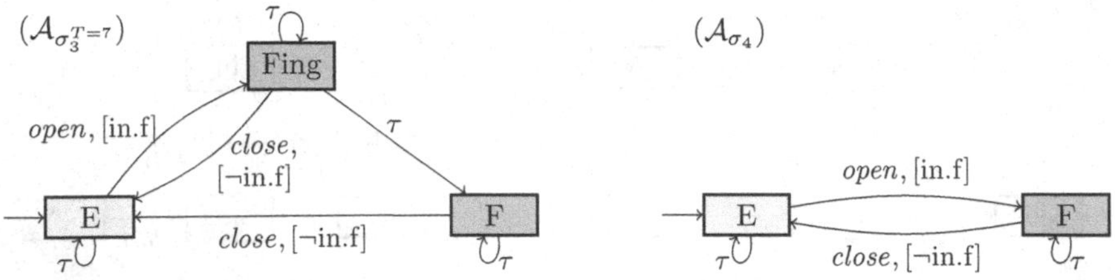


**Fig. 3.** Abstractions modulo $\sigma_3^{T=7}$ and $\sigma_4$ on the tank running example.

transient state for $\sigma_2$) is transient also for $\sigma_3^T$, for $\sigma_3^T$ also become transient the non-urgent states that are accidentally traversed in 0 time, for example because an exiting discrete transition is immediately enabled.

*Future Eq-predicate Abstractions.* In contrast to the backward evaluation of $\sigma_3$, one can think of assessing stability forward, by looking at the future(s)[2] of the state. A possible definition in this perspective would be

$$\sigma_4(X) \doteq \text{AG}Eq(P),$$

asking that, as long as only $\tau$ transitions are taken, the system will never change the evaluation of predicates. Namely, once a state is $\sigma_4$-stable, it can change the predicates only with an external event, and the abstract states in $\mathcal{A}_{\sigma_4}$ are closed under $\tau$ transitions. This is similar in spirit to the notion of $P$-stable abstraction of [5], with the difference that in the latter arbitrary regions are considered.

Within this perspective, alternative definitions can be obtained by interchanging the existential/universal path quantifiers (e.g., $\text{EG}Eq(P)$ characterizes a state for which there exists a future that never changes the predicate evaluations), or by bounding the "globally" operator (e.g., $\text{AG}^{>K}Eq(P)$ captures a state which is guaranteed to expose the same evaluations of predicates in the next $K$ steps). Observe that all these variants would assess $\sigma$-stability of a state *before* it has actually proven to expose the same predicates for enough time/steps.

*Example 3.* On the left hand side of Fig. 2 we show the abstraction obtained with $\sigma_3^{T,K}$ definition, using $T = 7$ and $K = 1$. State Emptying is unstable, since time cannot elapse in it more than $T$ time: namely, from Full, at the reception of the stimulus which opens in.flow, all the $\tau$-paths lead to Empty in less than $T$ time. On the other hand, Fing is kept, since the system may stay in this location for enough time to be considered relevant.

On the right hand side of Fig. 2 we show the abstraction obtained with $\sigma_4$. Here, the stable states are only Empty and Full: the others are abstracted since they are not invariant for the $\tau$ internal transition. Each external event directly leads to the end of a timed process which converges in the next stable state. Note that in this setting, an abstract transition labeled with $\tau$ can only be self loops.

[2] Note that, in contrast to the backward case where the past is unique, in the forward case we adopt a branching time view with multiple futures.

Here, $\mathcal{A}_{\sigma_4}$ corresponds to the $P$-stable abstraction because the chosen abstract domain $\Phi$ is able to express the "minimally stable" regions [5] of $\mathcal{M}$.

Observe that $\mathcal{A}_{\sigma_4}$ would be also obtained by increasing the time bound of $\sigma_3^T$, e.g., with $T = 15$.

As the examples show, different stability definitions induce abstract automata with different numbers of states and transitions. The following proposition states what is the effect on the abstract automata of making stricter the stability definition. Let us write $p_1 \xrightarrow{\ell}_\sigma p_2$ meaning that $(p_1, \ell, p_2) \models \text{Trans}_\sigma$ in $\mathcal{A}_\sigma$.

**Proposition 1.** *Let $\sigma$ and $\sigma'$ be two stability definitions such that every history that is $\sigma$-stable, is also $\sigma'$-stable, and let $\mathcal{A}_\sigma$ and $\mathcal{A}_{\sigma'}$ be the corresponding abstractions modulo stability of the same concrete model $\mathcal{M}$. Then, $\mathcal{A}_\sigma$ weakly simulates $\mathcal{A}_{\sigma'}$.*

*Proof.* By definition, if $p_1 \xrightarrow{\ell}_\sigma p_2$, then there exists $(s_1, \ell, s_2) \models \text{Trans}$ with (1) $\mathcal{M}^\tau, h_1 \models \sigma \wedge p_1$, and (2) $\mathcal{M}^\tau, h_2 \models \text{E}(\neg\sigma \text{ U } (\sigma \wedge p_2)$, with $h_1 = (s_0 \ldots, s_1)$ and $h_2 = (s_2)$. Since every $\sigma$-stable history is also $\sigma'$-stable, from (1) we obtain that $\mathcal{M}^\tau, h_1 \models \sigma' \wedge p_1$, and from (2) we derive

$$\begin{aligned}\mathcal{M}^\tau, h_2 \models \text{EF}(\sigma \wedge p_2) &\implies \mathcal{M}^\tau, h_2 \models \text{EF}(\sigma' \wedge p_2)\\ &\implies \mathcal{M}^\tau, h_2 \models \text{E}(\neg\sigma' \text{ U } (\sigma'\text{EX}(\neg\sigma' \ldots \text{ U } (\sigma' \wedge p_2)\ldots)))\end{aligned}$$

Hence, $p_1 \xrightarrow{\ell}_{\sigma'} \xrightarrow{\tau}{}^{*}_{\sigma'} p_2$ and $\mathcal{A}_\sigma \lesssim \mathcal{A}_{\sigma'}$.

**Corollary 1.** *For every bounds $T_1 \leq T_2 \in \mathbb{R}_+$*

$$\mathcal{A}_{\sigma_3^{T_2}} \lesssim \mathcal{A}_{\sigma_3^{T_1}} \lesssim \mathcal{A}_{\sigma_2} \lesssim \mathcal{A}_{\sigma_1}$$

### 3.4 Extending with Guards and Effects

Abstract transitions in $\mathcal{A}_\sigma$ are labeled with the stimulus that has triggered the abstracted run-to-completion process. Recall that a stimulus $\ell \in 2^\Sigma$ is connected to a (possibly null) variation of the inputs $I$ by $\text{Trans}_\mathcal{E}(I, \Sigma, I')$. A *guard* for an abstract transition $(p_1, \ell, p_2)$ is a formula on $I'$ variables entailed by $\text{Trans}_\mathcal{E}[\Sigma/\ell]$ which describes the configurations of inputs that, starting from $p_1$ with event $\ell$, lead to $p_2$. In order to enrich the description of the *effects* of an abstract transition, we also consider a subset of state variables $O \subseteq V$, called *output* variables. Observe that an abstract transition may be witnessed by multiple concrete paths, each with its own configuration of inputs and outputs. Hence, we can keep track of a precise correlation between guards and effects with a unique relational formula on $I$ and $O$ variables. This formula is obtained as a disjunction of all the configurations of inputs and outputs in the concrete states accomplishing stability in $p_2$ (since the configuration of $I$ set by the stimulus is preserved by $\tau$ along the run-to-completion process).

*Example 4.* The stability abstractions shown in Figs. 2 and 3 are equipped with *guard* constraints, as evaluations on the original input variable in.flow, (shown in square brackets near the label of the stimuli).

## 4 Algorithms for Stability Abstractions

In order to build the abstract automaton structure we have to check whether there exists a (reachable) $\sigma$-stable state in $p_1$, with $(s_1, \ell, s_2) \models$ Trans and $\mathcal{M}^{\tau}, s_2 \models \mathrm{E}(\neg\sigma \ \mathrm{U} \ (\sigma \wedge p_2))$, for every pair $(p_1, p_2) \in \Phi \times \Phi$. Reachability analysis and (C/)LTL model checking for infinite state systems are undecidable problems. The work in [5] computes overapproximations of the regions that are invariant for silent transitions (i.e., addresses an unbounded stability criterion $\mathrm{AG}\phi$), exploiting the abstract interpretation framework. This approach also over-approximates multiple stable targets that may be given by the non-determinism of the concrete system.

Here, instead, we deal precisely with the non-determinism of the underlying concrete system by collecting information about actual, visible consequences of an action, by focusing on *bounded* stability definitions. In fact, we consider stability criteria that do not require fixpoint computations in the concrete system, *and* we under-approximate the reachability analysis fixing a bound for unstable paths. Namely, our algorithm follows an iterative deepening approach, which considers progressively longer unstable run-to-completion paths, seeking for the next stable condition.

Intuitively we search for concrete witnesses for an abstract transition $(p_1, \ell, p_2)$ by searching for a concrete path connecting a concrete $\sigma$-stable state $s_1$ in $p_1$ and a $\sigma$-stable state in $p_2$, with a bounded reachability analysis from $s_1$.

Notice that the algorithm builds a *symbolic* characterization for the stability automaton. In fact, instead of enumerating all $(p_1, p_2) \in \Phi \times \Phi$ and check if they are connected by some concrete path, we incrementally build a formula characterizing all the paths of $\mathcal{M}^{\tau}$ connecting two $\sigma$-stable states. Then, we project such formula on the $P$ variables, hence obtaining symbolically all the abstract transitions having a witness of that length. This intuition is similar to [15] to efficiently compute predicate abstractions.

Moreover, having a formula representing finite paths of $\mathcal{M}^{\tau}$ connecting two $\sigma$-stable states, we can extract guards and effects with a projection on $I$ and $O$ variables. Namely, while checking the existence of an abstract transition, we also synthesize the formula on $I$ and $O$ annotating it.

A significant characteristic of our approach, also with respect to the classical instantiation of predicate abstraction, is that we refine the abstract transitions by forcing the concrete states to be reachable from the initial condition.

In the following we describe the general algorithm for computing abstractions parametric on the stability definition $\sigma$, and then show how the criteria proposed in Sect. 3.3 can be actually passed as parameter.

### 4.1 Symbolic Algorithm for Bounded Stability

Consider the symbolic encoding of automaton $\mathcal{M} = \langle X, C, \Sigma, \mathrm{Init}, \mathrm{Invar}, \mathrm{Trans}\rangle$,[3] and a classification of the variables in $X$ distinguishing $P$ boolean predicates variables, $I$ input variables, $O$ output variables.

[3] For exposition purposes, let Trans entails both Invar and Invar$'$.

We address the computation of the formulae $\text{Init}_\sigma(P)$ and $\text{Trans}_\sigma(P, I, O, P')$, for a stability definition provided as a formula $\sigma(X_0, \ldots, X_n)$ with $n \in \mathbb{N}$.

The algorithm performs a reachability analysis based on two bounds:

- $U \in \mathbb{N}$, as the bound for the length for unstable paths.
- $L \in \mathbb{N}$, with $L \geq n+1$, as the bound for the length of the run witnessing an abstract transition, starting from the initial state, used for the reachability-aware refinement.

**Pseudocode 1.** Reachability-aware symbolic computation of the abstract transition relation $\text{Trans}_\sigma$

```
function EXTRACT-ABSTRACT-TRANS(Init, Trans)
    Trans_σ := ⊥;
    S := new_solver();
    S.ASSERT(Init(X_0));
    for all j ∈ [0, L) do
        S.ASSERT(Trans(X_j, Σ_j, X_{j+1}));
        if j < n + 1 then continue;
        S.PUSH();
        S.ASSERT(σ(X_{j−n}, ..., X_j));                                  ▷ stable slot at j
        for all i ∈ reversed[j − 1 − U, j) do
            if i + 1 < j then
                S.ASSERT(I_{i+1} = I_{i+2} ∧ ¬σ(X_{i+1−n}, ..., X_{i+1}));   ▷ unstable path
            S.PUSH();
            S.ASSERT(σ(X_{i−n}, ..., X_i) ∧ ⋀_{i−n≤h<i} I_h = I_{h+1});     ▷ stable slot at i
            S.ASSERT(¬Trans_σ[P/P_i, I/I_j, O/O_j, P'/P_j]);
            Trans_σ^{(i,j)} ← S.PROJECT-ON(P_i, I_j, O_j, P_j);
            Trans_σ ← Trans_σ ∨ Trans_σ^{(i,j)}[P_i/P, I_j/I, O_j/O, P_j/P'];
            S.POP();
        S.POP();
    return Trans_σ
```

*Computation of* $\text{Trans}_\sigma$. Pseudocode 1 shows the algorithm for extraction of the transition relation $\text{Trans}_\sigma$. It builds a formula

$$\text{Init}(X_0) \wedge \bigwedge_{0 \leq h \leq j} \text{Trans}(X_h, X_{h+1}) \wedge \left( \begin{array}{c} \sigma(X_{i-n}, \ldots, X_i) \wedge \bigwedge_{i-n \leq h < i} I_h = I_{h+1} \wedge \\ \bigwedge_{i<h<j} (I_h = I_{h+1} \wedge \neg\sigma(X_{h-n}, \ldots, X_h)) \wedge \\ \sigma(X_{j-n}, \ldots, X_j) \end{array} \right)$$

for each $i, j$ with $0 \leq j - i \leq U$ and $j < L$. The procedure exploits the incrementality of the SMT solvers which organize assertions in a stack: the push/pop interface allows the addition of layers, in which to insert new formulae with the

ASSERT primitive. In this way, we can progressively build the path and avoid its recomputation for every pair $i, j$. Namely, for each $j < L$, firstly we build the path until $j$ (line 6) and assert $\sigma$-stability in $j$ (line 9). Then we progressively try $i$ going backward (in order to better exploit incrementality), constrain the $I$ variables to be unchanged, and $\sigma$-unstability (lines 11–12).

Function S.PROJECT-ON() (line 16) performs an existential quantification of the formula currently present in the solver stack. We preserve variables $P_i$ and $P_j$, which characterize the two stable states connected by the transition. Variables $I_j$ and $O_j$ are also preserved: in this way, we extract the guards and the effects formulae directly within the building of the abstract transition. Notice that, due to the input stability hypothesis preserved during the unstable path, the input configuration read in $j$ is the same read immediately following the external event in $i + 1$.

Every found contribute $\text{Trans}_\sigma^{(i,j)}$ is then merged in a single $\text{Trans}_\sigma$, after substitution of the variables in $P, I, O, P'$. Observe that an important optimization is to block the negation of the already computed formula $\text{Trans}_\sigma$ (shifted in the current $i$, $j$ indices) before each projection (line 15), in order to avoid recomputing the same transitions.

*Reachability-Awareness.* A reachability-unaware version would drop the first part of the formula characterizing the path from 0 to $i - n$.

The described algorithm is reachability-aware, meaning that every considered stable state is, by construction, reachable from the initial condition Init. This is important to extract actually concretizable behaviors, and is a main difference with respect to the classical predicate abstraction technique: it is well known that mere the projection on the boolean predicates of the single transition relation may introduce several spurious behaviors.

Note that the reachability-aware improvement is based on *concrete* reachability. In contrast, the algorithm of [5], exploits abstract reachability until fixpoint in the abstract automaton, possibly incurring in further overapproximations induced by the use of convergence accelerators.

*Computation of* $\text{Init}_\sigma$*.* The algorithm for the extraction of the initial state $\text{Init}_\sigma$ is similar: it builds a formula

$$\text{Init}(X_0) \wedge \bigwedge_{0 \le h \le i} (\text{Trans}(X_h, X_{h+1}) \wedge I_h = I_{h+1}) \wedge \sigma(X_{i-n}, ..., X_i)$$

for every $i \le U$. $\text{Init}_\sigma$ is the collection of the contributes $\text{Init}_\sigma^{(i)}$, obtained by fixing a stable slot in the last position $i$ and projecting on $P_i$ variables.

### 4.2 Instantiating the Algorithm

The bounded stability definitions presented in Sect. 3 can be unrolled and expressed in the form $\sigma(X_0, \ldots, X_n)$

*Predicate Abstraction.* $\sigma_1(X_0) = \top$ trivially needs only the current variables. Observe that in this case we can use a $U = 1$ bound, since the unstability constraint is always unsatisfiable.

*Non-urgent Abstraction.* Having a classification of urgent conditions, also $\sigma_2(X_0) = \neg urg_0$ can be established looking only at the current variables (it only needs $n = 0$).

*Eq-predicate Abstraction.* More generally, given $K$ and $T$ bounds, we encode that the abstract region has not changed for the last $K$ steps and that at least $T$ time has elapsed using $n = K$ and

$$\sigma_3^{T,K}(X_0 \dots X_K) = \bigwedge_{h<K} (P_h = P_{h+1}) \wedge (time_0 + T < time_K).$$

## 5 Experimental Evaluation

We evaluate the applicability and the adequacy of stability abstractions for the reverse engineering of real-world Relay-based Railway Interlocking Systems.

*Relay-Based Railway Interlocking Systems (RRIS).* RRIS are complex electro-mechanical circuits used for the control stations and train traffic. Such systems receive stimuli from an external environment, including both human operators (e.g., performing actions on buttons) and physical entities (e.g., a train passing on some sensors). In response, they control railway elements, like signaling lights or railway switches. Internally, they use relays to propagate signals: relays are electro-mechanical components which, when activated, change the position of an associated contact after a (possibly null) delay.

The controlling logic implemented by RRIS is hidden by complex legacy internal optimizations performed over the years by numerous electro-mechanical engineers. For this reason, it is hard to understand their high-level behavior and highlight the connections between stimuli and observable railway properties.

The experimental evaluation is based on real-world RRIS schematics that are intended to control level crossing and shunting routes. Using the tool NORMA [2], the considered RRIS have been modeled and automatically converted in timed transition systems in the syntax of Timed NUXMV [7]. The obtained models involve several real-valued variables (modeling voltages and currents in the circuits), changing accordingly to the configuration of the boolean variables (modeling the switches of the circuit). The discrete state changes when an external event updates the position of a switch, or as a consequence of the activation of an internal relay. Hence, these systems react to an external variation with a chain of internal transitions. The duration of the triggered run-to-completion process is important: urgent states are widely used to model the causality relation between the activation of an instantaneous relay and the action performed on the associated switch; timed relays may impose a low delay, so that the internal response is actually very fast and almost non observable.

**Table 1.** Result of the abstraction of `routesN` RRIS benchmarks with different stability definitions.

| | | | | | | | reach. unaware | | | reach. aware | | |
|---|---|---|---|---|---|---|---|---|---|---|---|---|
| test | $X$ | $I$ | $O$ | $P$ | $\Phi$ | $\sigma$ | $\mathcal{A}_\sigma$states | $\mathcal{A}_\sigma$trans | time | $\mathcal{A}_\sigma$states | $\mathcal{A}_\sigma$trans | time |
| `routes01` | 54 | 2 | 1 | 3 | 8 | $\sigma_1$ | 8 | 40 | 01s | 7 | 13 | 26s |
| | | | | | | $\sigma_2$ | 4 | 6 | 20s | 3 | 4 | 3m 09s |
| | | | | | | $\sigma_{3,T=1}$ | 3 | 4 | 15s | 2 | 2 | 1m 57s |
| | | | | | | $\sigma_{3,T=7}$ | 3 | 4 | 15s | 2 | 2 | 1m 57s |
| `routes02` | 90 | 4 | 2 | 6 | 48 | $\sigma_1$ | 48 | 768 | 22s | 11 | 22 | 1m 02s |
| | | | | | | $\sigma_2$ | 7 | 13 | 46s | 6 | 11 | 6m 16s |
| | | | | | | $\sigma_{3,T=1}$ | 5 | 9 | 38s | 4 | 7 | 4m 32s |
| | | | | | | $\sigma_{3,T=7}$ | 5 | 9 | 38s | 4 | 7 | 4m 20s |
| `routes04` | 166 | 8 | 3 | 12 | 4096 | $\sigma_1$ | – | – | TO | 49 | 97 | 3h 7m 03s |
| | | | | | | $\sigma_2$ | 29 | 83 | 1h 42m 29s | 25 | 48 | 2h 56m 46s |
| | | | | | | $\sigma_{3,T=1}$ | 17 | 52 | 1h 41m 17s | 13 | 24 | 2h 42m 04s |
| | | | | | | $\sigma_{3,T=7}$ | 17 | 52 | 1h 41m 10s | 13 | 24 | 2h 41m 55s |

*Abstraction Modulo Stability of RRIS.* The Timed NUXMV model checker was used to convert the models produced by NORMA in untimed transition systems in SMV. The algorithm presented in Sect. 4 has been implemented using the PYSMT library [10] and the MATHSAT5 SMT solver [8]. It requires in input a classification of the variables $X$, selecting the predicates $P$, the inputs $I$ and the outputs $O$, which can be directly provided by railway domain experts. We choose as $P$ the status of some relays or (boolean variables associated with) linear predicates on the electrical variables, representing, as an example, the status of a lamp.

Table 1 and 2 report the number of variables $X$, $P$, $I$, $O$ for each benchmark. Column $\Phi$ reports the size of the resulting abstract domain, obtained by considering all the *consistent* combinations of $P$ predicates (with respect to the invariant of the model).

We show the results of the Abstraction Modulo Stability considering the stability definitions described in Sect. 3.3, using the algorithm of Sect. 4 with bounds $L = 40$ and $U = 15$. All the experiment ran on a 2.4 GHz CPU, with time out (TO) set to 15 h, and memory limit set to 20 GB.

Columns "$\mathcal{A}_\sigma$states" and "$\mathcal{A}_\sigma$trans" hold the number of abstract states and transitions respectively, computed counting the configurations of the predicate variables in the abstract automaton $\mathcal{A}_\sigma$. As stated in Corollary 1, the corresponding abstract automata have progressively less states.

Stability abstractions were used by railway experts from the Italian Railway Network company (RFI) to understand two main families of legacy RRIS.

*Routes.* `routesN` is a RRIS regulating the activation/deactivation of `N` shunting routes concurring for the same resources. The implemented logic takes care of avoiding the simultaneous activation of conflicting routes. In such RRIS the inputs are the switches controlled by a human operator, attempting to enable/disable a route; the outputs are the status of some internal entities that we want to monitor; the predicates are the status of lamps representing whether the routes have been registered.

In the `routes` benchmarks the delays used in the run-to-completion processes are very small, so that in the abstract automata obtained (Table 1) there is no difference between $\sigma_3^{T=1}$ and $\sigma_3^{T=7}$ (i.e., if a state has stayed in the same predicate for 1 time unit, then it can also stay there for 7). These abstract automata clearly highlight what are the consequences of the requests of a human operator with respect to the active/inactive status of the routes involved. As an example, the abstraction `routes02` (a circuit handling two routes) has only 4 stable states which show that the routes are incompatible and one of them has priority on the other, and disregards all the intermediate steps that the concrete system needs to progressively check the availability of the resources. These steps are visible with a less strict stability definition, like $\sigma_1$ or $\sigma_2$.

Table 1 also evaluates the effectiveness of the reachability refinement. When dropping the prefix starting from the initial states of the concrete system, the algorithm would consider several spurious behaviors. Especially in these benchmarks, the resulting abstract automaton would also show the unreachable states (e.g., the ones in which two routes are in conflict), therefore reducing the relevance for the reverse engineering purpose. Moreover, the *reach.unaware* computation may be harder to compute as it has to explore more transitions and more models in the guards and effects formulae.

*Railway Switch.* `r-switch` is a RRIS modeling a railway switch. It has several externally controlled switches and only 4 relevant observations, defining its abstract state. The schema can be instantiated as nominal (N) or faulty (F), by injecting faulty behaviors in some physical components. We consider three versions: `r-switch1` interacts with a free environment, showing a wide number of circuit configurations; `r-switch2` and `r-switch3`, instead, exploit some assumptions on the environment and expose less inputs, and, although using different internal implementations, are supposed to guarantee the same controlling logic.

Table 2 reports the features of the abstract automata obtained for these benchmarks. Here, during a run-to-completion process, some states dwell in the same predicate for a time $1 \leq t \leq 7$, so that are visible in $\sigma_3^{T=1}$ but skipped by $\sigma_3^{T=7}$ when reporting the corresponding abstract transition.

Again, the *reach.unaware* option reports more transitions. The difference is especially evident in the nominal versions, as the faulty concrete system already covers more behaviors. Even when the number of abstract transitions is the same, the *reach.aware* option reports more precise guards and effects, i.e., each annotating formula on $I$ and $O$ has less models.

By looking at the abstract automata, the user could recover what are the triggering reasons that make the system reach certain states (e.g., the ones that are shown in `r-switch1` and not in `r-switch2`). Namely, $\mathcal{A}_\sigma$ could highlight the enabling conditions for certain behaviors, which may apply far from the final observable consequence and were hard to inspect by hand. In this way, the user could also collect what assumptions are needed to avoid certain behaviors (e.g.,

**Table 2.** Result of the abstraction of `r-switch` RRIS benchmarks with different stability definitions.

| | | | | | | | reach. unaware | | | reach. aware | | |
|---|---|---|---|---|---|---|---|---|---|---|---|---|
| test | $X$ | $I$ | $O$ | $P$ | $\Phi$ | $\sigma$ | $\mathcal{A}_\sigma$states | $\mathcal{A}_\sigma$trans | time | $\mathcal{A}_\sigma$states | $\mathcal{A}_\sigma$trans | time |
| r-switch1-N | 128 | 18 | 3 | 4 | 12 | $\sigma_1$ | – | – | TO | 12 | 78 | 8h 12m |
| | | | | | | $\sigma_2$ | 12 | 112 | 4h 12m | 12 | 94 | 2h 42m |
| | | | | | | $\sigma_{3,T=1}$ | 12 | 112 | 7h 47m | 12 | 86 | 2h 30m |
| | | | | | | $\sigma_{3,T=7}$ | 12 | 112 | 7h 24m | 12 | 66 | 2h 07m |
| r-switch1-F | 128 | 18 | 3 | 4 | 12 | $\sigma_1$ | – | – | TO | – | – | TO |
| | | | | | | $\sigma_2$ | – | – | TO | 12 | 112 | 7h 60m |
| | | | | | | $\sigma_{3,T=1}$ | 12 | 112 | 13h 12m | 12 | 112 | 5h 24m |
| | | | | | | $\sigma_{3,T=7}$ | 12 | 112 | 14h 05m | 12 | 112 | 4h 45m |
| r-switch2-N | 127 | 17 | 3 | 4 | 12 | $\sigma_1$ | 12 | 102 | 8h 18m | 12 | 74 | 3h 29m |
| | | | | | | $\sigma_2$ | 10 | 86 | 1h 56m | 10 | 74 | 1h 18m |
| | | | | | | $\sigma_{3,T=1}$ | 10 | 86 | 2h 12m | 10 | 66 | 1h 10m |
| | | | | | | $\sigma_{3,T=7}$ | 10 | 86 | 2h 31m | 10 | 54 | 58m |
| r-switch2-F | 127 | 17 | 3 | 4 | 12 | $\sigma_1$ | – | – | TO | 12 | 90 | 10h 34m |
| | | | | | | $\sigma_2$ | 10 | 86 | 4h 21m | 10 | 86 | 2h 42m |
| | | | | | | $\sigma_{3,T=1}$ | 10 | 86 | 4h 30m | 10 | 86 | 2h 12m |
| | | | | | | $\sigma_{3,T=7}$ | 10 | 86 | 4h 33m | 10 | 86 | 1h 39m |
| r-switch3-N | 121 | 16 | 3 | 4 | 12 | $\sigma_1$ | 12 | 102 | 3h 28m | 12 | 74 | 2h 08m |
| | | | | | | $\sigma_2$ | 10 | 86 | 52m | 10 | 74 | 52m |
| | | | | | | $\sigma_{3,T=1}$ | 10 | 86 | 1h 34m | 10 | 66 | 51m |
| | | | | | | $\sigma_{3,T=7}$ | 10 | 86 | 1h 32m | 10 | 54 | 44m |
| r-switch3-F | 121 | 16 | 3 | 4 | 12 | $\sigma_1$ | – | – | TO | 12 | 90 | 4h 21m |
| | | | | | | $\sigma_2$ | 10 | 86 | 2h 46m | 10 | 86 | 1h 38m |
| | | | | | | $\sigma_{3,T=1}$ | 10 | 86 | 2h 01m | 10 | 86 | 1h 22m |
| | | | | | | $\sigma_{3,T=7}$ | 10 | 86 | 2h 16m | 10 | 86 | 1h 24m |

in understanding what changes were made from `r-switch1` to `r-switch2` or `r-switch3` schemas).

Finally, as expected, `r-switch2` and `r-switch3` have exactly the same abstract automata for every stability definition and nominal/faulty configuration, since they are two different implementations for the same observable properties.

*P-Stable Abstractions.* We also tried the implementation of [5], for approximated $P$-stable abstractions ($\sigma_4$), which uses BDDs and convex polyhedra. On small handcrafted models like the tank system used as running example we could run all the approaches and confirm the output automata described in Sect. 3. Nonetheless, in the analysis of RRIS the approach of [5] turned out to be impractical, and was unable to deal with any of the considered RRIS models, due to the high number of variables.

More importantly, in our case studies, $\sigma_4$ would likely result in abstractions that are too aggressive, hiding states that are practically interesting, such as the ones that emerge from the analysis of run-to-completion processes with non negligible duration.

## 6 Conclusions

In this paper we presented a framework for the reverse engineering of legacy systems. Starting from a symbolic timed transition system, the framework supports the construction of abstractions in the form of state machines with guards and effects over transitions. The abstractions are parameterized on the notion of stability. We propose an SMT-based algorithm for abstraction computation, and we instantiate it over several notions of stability.

The results have been evaluated within an industrial project with the Italian Railway Network, on reverse-engineering tasks of complex relay-based interlocking circuits. The experimental analysis demonstrated that the approach is practical, and able to construct abstractions for complex real-world circuits. Taking reachability into account allowed us to produce tighter, more informative representations of the system under inspection. Railway signaling engineers involved in the project considered the proposed approach adequate in terms of expressiveness and able to provide substantial support in understanding the legacy RRIS.

In the future, we will define an "anytime" version of algorithms, so that the abstraction can be incrementally visualized as the computation proceeds, and leverage parallelization to increase the efficiency. Given the positive feedback from the RFI experts, we plan to integrate the proposed abstraction techniques abstraction within a RRIS modeling front-end, and to apply them on a larger set of interlockings.

## References

1. de Almeida Pereira, D.I.: Analysis and formal specification of relay-based railway interlocking systems. (Analyse et spécification formelle des systèmes d'enclenchement ferroviaire basés sur les relais). Ph.D. thesis, École centrale de Lille, Villeneuve-d'Ascq, France (2020)
2. Amendola, A., et al.: NORMA: a tool for the analysis of relay-based railway interlocking systems. In: Fisman, D., Rosu, G. (eds.) TACAS 2022. LNCS, vol. 13243, pp. 125–142. Springer, Cham (2022). https://doi.org/10.1007/978-3-030-99524-9_7
3. Amendola, A., et al.: A model-based approach to the design, verification and deployment of railway interlocking system. In: Margaria, T., Steffen, B. (eds.) ISoLA 2020. LNCS, vol. 12478, pp. 240–254. Springer, Cham (2020). https://doi.org/10.1007/978-3-030-61467-6_16
4. Barrett, C.W., Sebastiani, R., Seshia, S.A., Tinelli, C.: Satisfiability modulo theories. In: Handbook of Satisfiability, Frontiers in Artificial Intelligence and Applications, vol. 185, pp. 825–885. IOS Press (2009)
5. Becchi, A., Cimatti, A., Zaffanella, E.: Synthesis of P-stable abstractions. In: de Boer, F., Cerone, A. (eds.) SEFM 2020. LNCS, vol. 12310, pp. 214–230. Springer, Cham (2020). https://doi.org/10.1007/978-3-030-58768-0_12
6. ter Beek, M.H., Borälv, A., Fantechi, A., Ferrari, A., Gnesi, S., Löfving, C., Mazzanti, F.: Adopting formal methods in an industrial setting: the railways case. In: ter Beek, M.H., McIver, A., Oliveira, J.N. (eds.) FM 2019. LNCS, vol. 11800, pp. 762–772. Springer, Cham (2019). https://doi.org/10.1007/978-3-030-30942-8_46

7. Cimatti, A., Griggio, A., Magnago, E., Roveri, M., Tonetta, S.: Extending nuXmv with timed transition systems and timed temporal properties. In: Dillig, I., Tasiran, S. (eds.) CAV 2019. LNCS, vol. 11561, pp. 376–386. Springer, Cham (2019). https://doi.org/10.1007/978-3-030-25540-4_21
8. Cimatti, A., Griggio, A., Schaafsma, B.J., Sebastiani, R.: The MathSAT5 SMT solver. In: Piterman, N., Smolka, S.A. (eds.) TACAS 2013. LNCS, vol. 7795, pp. 93–107. Springer, Heidelberg (2013). https://doi.org/10.1007/978-3-642-36742-7_7
9. Ernst, M.D., Perkins, J.H., Guo, P.J., McCamant, S., Pacheco, C., Tschantz, M.S., Xiao, C.: The daikon system for dynamic detection of likely invariants. Sci. Comput. Program. **69**(1–3), 35–45 (2007)
10. Gario, M.E.G., Micheli, A.: PySMT: a solver-agnostic library for fast prototyping of SMT-based algorithms. In: International Workshop on Satisfiability Modulo Theories (SMT) (2015)
11. Graf, S., Saidi, H.: Construction of abstract state graphs with PVS. In: Grumberg, O. (ed.) CAV 1997. LNCS, vol. 1254, pp. 72–83. Springer, Heidelberg (1997). https://doi.org/10.1007/3-540-63166-6_10
12. Haxthausen, A.E., Kjær, A.A., Le Bliguet, M.: Formal development of a tool for automated modelling and verification of relay interlocking systems. In: Butler, M., Schulte, W. (eds.) FM 2011. LNCS, vol. 6664, pp. 118–132. Springer, Heidelberg (2011). https://doi.org/10.1007/978-3-642-21437-0_11
13. Hong, L.V., Haxthausen, A.E., Peleska, J.: Formal modelling and verification of interlocking systems featuring sequential release. Sci. Comput. Program. **133**, 91–115 (2017)
14. Lahiri, S.K., Bryant, R.E., Cook, B.: A symbolic approach to predicate abstraction. In: Hunt, W.A., Somenzi, F. (eds.) CAV 2003. LNCS, vol. 2725, pp. 141–153. Springer, Heidelberg (2003). https://doi.org/10.1007/978-3-540-45069-6_15
15. Lahiri, S.K., Nieuwenhuis, R., Oliveras, A.: SMT techniques for fast predicate abstraction. In: Ball, T., Jones, R.B. (eds.) CAV 2006. LNCS, vol. 4144, pp. 424–437. Springer, Heidelberg (2006). https://doi.org/10.1007/11817963_39
16. Laroussinie, F., Schnoebelen, P.: Specification in CTL+past for verification in CTL. Inf. Comput. **156**(1–2), 236–263 (2000). https://doi.org/10.1006/inco.1999.2817
17. Limbrée, C.: Formal verification of railway interlocking systems. Ph.D. thesis, Catholic University of Louvain, Louvain-la-Neuve, Belgium (2019)
18. Limbrée, C., Cappart, Q., Pecheur, C., Tonetta, S.: Verification of railway interlocking - compositional approach with OCRA. In: Lecomte, T., Pinger, R., Romanovsky, A. (eds.) RSSRail 2016. LNCS, vol. 9707, pp. 134–149. Springer, Cham (2016). https://doi.org/10.1007/978-3-319-33951-1_10
19. Milner, R.: Calculi for synchrony and asynchrony. Theor. Comput. Sci. **25**, 267–310 (1983). https://doi.org/10.1016/0304-3975(83)90114-7

# Reachability of Koopman Linearized Systems Using Random Fourier Feature Observables and Polynomial Zonotope Refinement

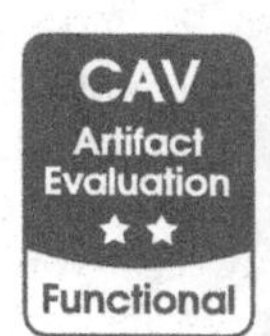


Stanley Bak[1], Sergiy Bogomolov[2], Brandon Hencey[3], Niklas Kochdumper[1(✉)], Ethan Lew[4], and Kostiantyn Potomkin[2]

[1] Department of Computer Science, Stony Brook University, Stony Brook, NY, USA
{stanley.bak,niklas.kochdumper}@stonybrook.edu

[2] School of Computing, Newcastle University, Newcastle Upon Tyne, UK
{sergiy.bogomolov,k.potomkin2}@newcastle.ac.uk

[3] Air Force Research Laboratory, Wright-Patterson Air Force Base, Dayton, OH, USA
brandon.hencey@us.af.mil

[4] Galois Inc., Portland, OR, USA
elew@galois.com

**Abstract.** Koopman operator linearization approximates nonlinear systems of differential equations with higher-dimensional linear systems. For formal verification using reachability analysis, this is an attractive conversion, as highly scalable methods exist to compute reachable sets for linear systems. However, two main challenges are present with this approach, both of which are addressed in this work. First, the approximation must be sufficiently accurate for the result to be meaningful, which is controlled by the choice of *observable functions* during Koopman operator linearization. By using random Fourier features as observable functions, the process becomes more systematic than earlier work, while providing a higher-accuracy approximation. Second, although the higher-dimensional system is linear, simple convex initial sets in the original space can become complex non-convex initial sets in the linear system. We overcome this using a combination of Taylor model arithmetic and polynomial zonotope refinement. Compared with prior work, the result is more efficient, more systematic and more accurate.

**Keywords:** Koopman operator · Reachability analysis · Polynomial zonotopes · Random Fourier features · Formal verification

## 1 Introduction

Despite recent advances, systems described by nonlinear ordinary differential equations are still hard to analyze, control, and verify. On the other hand, a


S. Shoham and Y. Vizel (Eds.): CAV 2022, LNCS 13371, pp. 490–510, 2022.
https://doi.org/10.1007/978-3-031-13185-1_24

powerful body of methods and theories exists for linear systems making analysis, control, and verification much easier, even for high-dimensional systems. The efficiency of techniques related to reachability analysis for linear systems [4,6,15] motivates the use of Koopman operator linearization, where a higher-dimensional linear system approximates the dynamic behavior of a nonlinear system. Koopman operator techniques are also well-suited for data-driven approaches since the Koopman linearized system can be directly created from measurements, bypassing a potentially complex modeling step. The Koopman framework has been successfully applied to many applications, including control [26,28], state estimation [31] and recently, formal verification [5].

The main contribution of this paper is to advance the state-of-the-art in formal verification using reachability analysis on Koopman operator linearized systems. First, we improve the accuracy of the finite Koopman linearization by employing random Fourier features [29]. In contrast with an *ad hoc*, finite-dimensional feature space, random Fourier features leverage the powerful *kernel trick* from machine learning [36,38] to generate a computationally tractable mapping over an infinite-dimensional feature space. Second, we improve speed. Instead of using an SMT solver to reason over non-convex initial sets, we propose combining Taylor models with polynomial zonotope refinement. A comparison on the same nonlinear system benchmarks used in the earlier Koopman verification work [5] demonstrates both the improved accuracy and the improved verification speed.

### 1.1 Related Work

The concept of Koopman operator linearization was originally introduced in 1931 [22]. Instead of investigating the dynamic evolution of the original system state, the Koopman approach considers the evolution of so-called *observable functions* or *observables* defined by nonlinear transformations of the original system state. Since the set of all possible observables defines a vector space, it then holds that the dynamic behavior of every nonlinear system can be equivalently represented by an infinite dimensional linear system. Because it is obviously infeasible to handle infinite dimensions, a finite set of observables is used in practice. Given such a set, the system matrix resulting in the most accurate linear approximation of the original system behavior can be determined using extended dynamic mode decomposition [41].

Many different methods for determining good observables have been proposed: Carleman linearization [7] equivalently represents the dynamic behavior of polynomial systems with an infinite dimensional linear system. The corresponding observables are multi-variate monomials, which are determined by repeatedly computing the time-derivative of the current observables. Terminating this iteration after a certain number of steps yields a finite set of observables. Carleman linearization can be extended to general nonlinear systems by using a Taylor series expansion. A finite set of observables defines an exact linear representation of the original system if the vector space spanned by the observables is closed under the operation of Lie-derivatives [34]. Consequently, a natural approach is to refine an initial set of observables by removing observables that violate the condition [34]. This concept can be extended to obtain polynomial instead of linear representations for the original nonlinear system [35]. Another class of approaches uses neural networks as observables [16,43], where the weights of the network are trained on traces of the real system. Since these approaches usually train the system matrix together with neural networks, they circumvent the subsequent application of dynamic mode decomposition. If one aims to reason about the original system based on the Koopman linearization, some quantification of the approximation error is required. Several approaches derive error bounds for truncated Carleman linearization [3,12,24] considering quadratic systems [24], polynomial systems [12], as well as general nonlinear systems [3].

The main motivation for using the Koopman framework for reachability analysis is that reachable sets for linear systems can be computed efficiently [11,15,23] even for high-dimensional systems [2,4,6], while reachability analysis for nonlinear systems [1,8,27] is often computationally demanding and potentially results in large over-approximations. Another advantage is that the Koopman approach can also be applied to data-driven systems where no model is available. Due to the nonlinear transformation of the initial state defined by the observables, reachability analysis for Koopman operator linearized system represents a special type of reachability problem. To the best of our knowledge only two approaches exist for far: The first approach [13] utilizes the error bounds for quadratic systems [24] to compute an enclosure of the reachable set for weakly nonlinear systems based on a finite Carleman linearization, where interval arithmetic [17] is applied to enclose the image of the initial set through the observables. The second approach [5], which represents the work closest to our method, presents two different verification strategies: 1) Direct encoding of the nonlinear transformation defined by the observables using a SMT solver, and 2) zonotope domain splitting, where the initial set is recursively split into smaller sets until the specification can be verified or falsified.

### 1.2 Overview

In this work we address the two main bottlenecks of formal verification for Koopman operator linearized systems, which are the selection of observables and the computation of the image of the initial set through the nonlinear transformation defined by the observables. In particular, while currently observables often have to be selected manually by the user, we generate observables in a systematic fashion using random Fourier features. As we demonstrate with numerical experiments, these observables yield high-accuracy approximations of the real system behavior. Moreover, while previous approaches either compute very conservative convex enclosures of the image through the observables [13] or have to split the initial set in order to achieve a desired precision [5], we calculate tight non-convex enclosures of the image by combining Taylor model arithmetic with polynomial zonotopes. To conduct collision checks between the resulting non-convex reachable set enclosures and unsafe regions we then use a novel polynomial zonotope refinement strategy, which is significantly faster than the previous SMT solver and zonotope domain splitting approaches [5].

The remainder of the paper is structured as follows: We first recapitulate some preliminary results that are required throughout the paper in Sect. 2. In the main part we then describe the systematic generation of observables using random Fourier features in Sect. 3, before we present our proposed verification algorithm in Sect. 4. Finally, we demonstrate the superior performance of random Fourier feature observables and our verification algorithm in comparison with existing techniques on various benchmark systems in Sect. 5.

### 1.3 Notation

In the remainder of this paper, we will use the following notations: Sets are denoted by calligraphic letters, matrices by uppercase letters, vectors by lowercase letters, and lists by bold uppercase letters. Given a vector $b \in \mathbb{R}^n$, $b_{(i)}$ refers to the $i$-th entry. Given a matrix $A \in \mathbb{R}^{n \times m}$, $A_{(i,\cdot)}$ represents the $i$-th matrix row, $A_{(\cdot,j)}$ the $j$-th column, and $A_{(i,j)}$ the $j$-th entry of matrix row $i$. Given a discrete set of positive integer indices $\mathcal{H} = \{h_1, \dots, h_w\}$ with $1 \leqslant h_i \leqslant m \; \forall i \in \{1, \dots, w\}$, $A_{(\cdot,\mathcal{H})}$ is used for $[A_{(\cdot,h_1)} \; \dots \; A_{(\cdot,h_w)}]$, where $[C \; D]$ denotes the concatenation of two matrices $C$ and $D$. The symbols $\mathbf{0}$ and $\mathbf{1}$ represent matrices of zeros and ones of proper dimension, the empty matrix is denoted by $[\,]$, and $I_n \in \mathbb{R}^{n \times n}$ is the identity matrix. Given an ordered list $\mathbf{L} = (l_1, \dots, l_n)$, $\mathbf{L}_{(i)} = l_i$ refers to the $i$-th entry and $|\mathbf{L}| = n$ denotes the number of elements in the list. Moreover, the concatenation of two lists $\mathbf{L}_1$ and $\mathbf{L}_2$ is denoted by $(\mathbf{L}_1, \mathbf{L}_2)$. The left multiplication of a matrix $M \in \mathbb{R}^{m \times n}$ with a set $\mathcal{S} \subset \mathbb{R}^n$ is defined as $M\mathcal{S} = \{Ms \,|\, s \in \mathcal{S}\}$, and the Cartesian product of two sets is denoted by the $\times$ operator. We further introduce an $n$-dimensional interval as $\mathcal{I} = [l, u], \; \forall i \; l_{(i)} \leqslant u_{(i)}, \; l, u \in \mathbb{R}^n$.

## 2 Preliminaries

Our approach utilizes several existing techniques and concepts, which we shortly recapitulate here. We use the nonlinear system

$$\begin{aligned} \dot{x}_1 &= x_1 \\ \dot{x}_2 &= x_2 - x_1^4 \end{aligned} \tag{1}$$

in combination with the initial set $\mathcal{X}_0 = [-2, 2] \times [0, 4]$ as a running example throughout this section.

### 2.1 Koopman Operator Linearization

First, we describe the general concept of Koopman operator linearization [22]. Given a nonlinear system

$$\frac{\partial x}{\partial t} = f(x) \;\; \text{with} \;\; x \in \mathbb{R}^n, \; f: \mathbb{R}^n \rightarrow \mathbb{R}^n, \tag{2}$$

our goal is to find observables $g_i : \mathbb{R}^n \to \mathbb{R}$ such that the dynamics of the resulting new variables $g_i(x)$ is linear:

$$\frac{\partial g(x)}{\partial t} = A\, g(x) \;\text{ with }\; A \in \mathbb{R}^{m\times m}, \tag{3}$$

where $g(x) = [g_1(x)\; \dots\; g_m(x)]^T$ is the observable function. Since the new variables $g_i(x)$ are functions of the original system state $x$, the linear system (3) defines an equivalent representation of the dynamic behavior of the original system (2). Usually, the number of observables $m$ is significantly larger than the dimension $n$ of the original system.

Let us demonstrate Koopman linearization for our exemplary system in (1). By choosing the observables $g_1(x) = x_1$, $g_2(x) = x_2$, and $g_3(x) = x_1^4$ we obtain the linear system

$$\frac{\partial}{\partial t}\begin{bmatrix} g_1(x) \\ g_2(x) \\ g_3(x) \end{bmatrix} = \begin{bmatrix} 1 & 0 & 0 \\ 0 & 1 & -1 \\ 0 & 0 & 4 \end{bmatrix}\begin{bmatrix} g_1(x) \\ g_2(x) \\ g_3(x) \end{bmatrix}$$

since $\partial g_1(x)/\partial t = \dot{x}_1 = x_1$, $\partial g_2(x)/\partial t = \dot{x}_2 = x_2 - x_1^4 = g_2(x) - g_3(x)$, and $\partial g_3(x)/\partial t = 4\,x_1^3\,\dot{x}_1 = 4\,x_1^4 = 4\,g_3(x)$.

The exact linearization using a finite number of observables demonstrated by the example above is unfortunately only possible for a small number of special systems. In practice one therefore usually aims to instead determine a linear system (3) that approximates the dynamic behavior of the nonlinear system (2) well enough. Given observables $g_i(x)$, the system matrix $A$ resulting in the best approximation can be determined by applying extended dynamic mode decomposition [41] to traces of the original system. Since those traces can also be generated by simulating black-box systems or by measuring the real system behavior, we do not necessarily require a model (2) of the original system. This is one of the biggest advantages of the Koopman framework making it well suited for data-driven approaches. The approach we present in this work verifies Koopman linearized systems using reachability analysis:

**Definition 1.** *(Reachable set) Given an initial set $\mathcal{X}_0 \subset \mathbb{R}^n$, the reachable set for a Koopman linearized system is*

$$\mathcal{R}(t) := \big\{\xi(t, g(x_0)) \;\big|\; x_0 \in \mathcal{X}_0\big\},$$

*where $\xi(t, g(x_0))$ is the solution to (3) at time $t \in \mathbb{R}_{\geqslant 0}$ for the initial state $g(x_0)$.*

Consequently, to compute the reachable set for a Koopman linearized system one first needs to propagate the initial set through the nonlinear transformation defined by the observables, followed by the calculation of the reachable set for the linear system in (3) using a reachability algorithm. This procedure is visualized in Fig. 1. Definition 1 defines the reachable set for the observables $g_i(x)$. However, since safety specifications are typically defined on the original system state $x$ rather than on $g(x)$, we usually require the reachable set for the original state $\mathcal{R}_x(t)$ for verification. This issue can easily be resolved by using the original system state $x$ for the first $n$ observables $g_i(x) = x_{(i)}$, $i = 1, \dots, n$, in which case $\mathcal{R}_x(t)$ can be obtained via projection: $\mathcal{R}_x(t) = [I_n\; \mathbf{0}]\, \mathcal{R}(t)$.

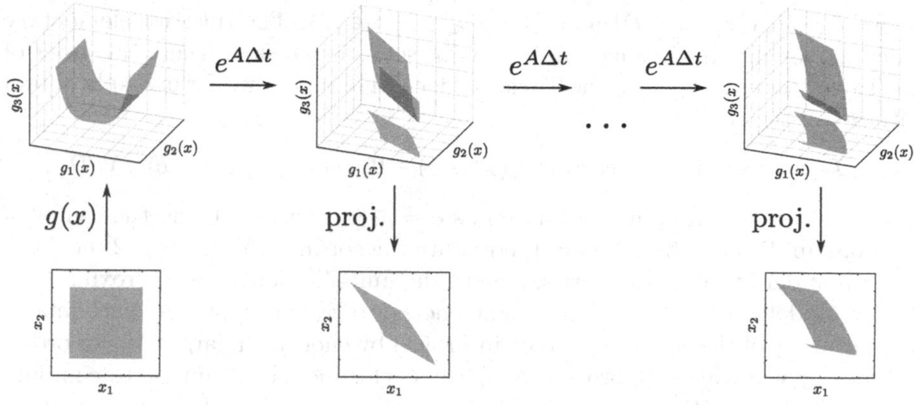


**Fig. 1.** Schematic visualization of reachability analysis for Koopman linearized systems: We first transform the initial set to the higher-dimensional observable space using $g(x)$, then compute the reachable set of the linear system using the matrix exponential $e^{A\Delta t}$ with time-step size $\Delta t$, and finally obtain the reachable set in the original state space via projection.

## 2.2 Taylor Model Arithmetic

Taylor model arithmetic [25] can be utilized to compute tight non-convex enclosures for the image through a nonlinear function. It is based on a set representation called Taylor models:

**Definition 2.** *(Taylor model) Given a polynomial function* $p: \mathbb{R}^s \to \mathbb{R}^n$, *an interval domain* $\mathcal{D} \subset \mathbb{R}^s$, *and an interval remainder* $\mathcal{Y} \subset \mathbb{R}^n$, *a Taylor model* $\mathcal{T}(x)$ *is defined as*

$$\forall x \in \mathcal{D}: \quad \mathcal{T}(x) := \{p(x) + y \mid y \in \mathcal{Y}\}.$$

*The Taylor order* $\kappa \in \mathbb{N}$ *defines an upper bound for the polynomial degree of the polynomial* $p(x)$. *The set defined by a Taylor model is*

$$\{\mathcal{T}(x) \mid x \in \mathcal{D}\} = \{p(x) + y \mid x \in \mathcal{D},\ y \in \mathcal{Y}\}.$$

*For a concise notation we use the shorthand* $\mathcal{T}(x) = \langle p(x), \mathcal{Y}, \mathcal{D}\rangle_T$.

The general concept of Taylor model arithmetic is to define rules on how to perform the arithmetic operations $+$, $-$, $\cdot$, and $/$ as well as elementary functions such as $\sin(x)$ or $\sqrt{x}$ on Taylor models [25, Sec. 2]. Since every nonlinear function represents a composition of arithmetic operations and elementary functions, the image through the function can then be computed by successively evaluating those rules. Given two one-dimensional Taylor models $\mathcal{T}_1(x) = \langle p_1(x), \mathcal{Y}_1, \mathcal{D}\rangle_T$ and $\mathcal{T}_2(x) = \langle p_2(x), \mathcal{Y}_2, \mathcal{D}\rangle_T$ the rules for addition and multiplication are for example given as

$$\begin{aligned}
\mathcal{T}_1(x) + \mathcal{T}_2(x) &:= \big\langle p_1(x) + p_2(x), \mathcal{Y}_1 + \mathcal{Y}_2, \mathcal{D}\big\rangle_T \\
\mathcal{T}_1(x) \cdot \mathcal{T}_2(x) &:= \big\langle p_1(x) \cdot p_2(x), \mathcal{Y}_1 \cdot \mathcal{Y}_2 + \mathcal{I}_1 \cdot \mathcal{Y}_2 + \mathcal{Y}_1 \cdot \mathcal{I}_2, \mathcal{D}\big\rangle_T,
\end{aligned}$$

where $\mathcal{I}_1 = \{p_1(x) \mid x \in \mathcal{D}\}$ and $\mathcal{I}_2 = \{p_2(x) \mid x \in \mathcal{D}\}$. The rules for elementary functions are obtained using a finite Taylor series expansion, where the order of the Taylor series is equal to the Taylor order $\kappa$. For $\sin(x)$ we for example obtain with $\kappa = 2$ the rule

$$\sin\big(\mathcal{T}_1(x)\big) := \big\langle \sin(c) + \cos(c)\,(p_1(x) - c) - 0.5\,\sin(c)\,(p_1(x) - c)^2, \mathcal{Y}, \mathcal{D}\big\rangle_T,$$

where the expansion point $c$ is chosen as $c = p_1(c_d)$ with $c_d$ being the center of the domain $\mathcal{D}$, and the interval $\mathcal{Y}$ computed according to [25, Sec. 2] encloses the remainder of the Taylor series. Due to the finite Taylor series approximation, Taylor model arithmetic yields a tight enclosure rather than the exact image. The accuracy of the enclosure can be improved by choosing a larger Taylor order.

For our verification approach we apply Taylor model arithmetic to compute the image of the initial set through the observable function. The initial set $\mathcal{X}_0 = [-2, 2] \times [0, 4]$ for the exemplary system in (1) can be represented by the Taylor model $\mathcal{T}(x) = \langle x, \varnothing, \mathcal{X}_0\rangle_T$. Applying Taylor model arithmetic to the observable function $g(x)$ defined by the observables $g_1(x) = x_1$, $g_2(x) = x_2$, and $g_3(x) = x_1^4$ then yields the Taylor model

$$\{g(x) \mid x \in \mathcal{X}_0\} \subseteq \left\langle \begin{bmatrix} x_1 \\ x_2 \\ x_1^4 \end{bmatrix}, \varnothing, [-2, 2] \times [0, 4] \right\rangle_T, \tag{4}$$

which represents the exact image in this case since the observables contain polynomial functions only.

### 2.3 Set Representations

In this work we use polynomial zonotopes to represent reachable sets, polytopes to represent unsafe sets, and zonotopes for efficient collision checking. Let us first introduce polytopes, for which we consider the halfspace representation:

**Definition 3.** *(Polytope) Given a matrix $H \in \mathbb{R}^{s\times n}$ and vector $d \in \mathbb{R}^s$, the halfspace representation of a polytope $\mathcal{P} \subset \mathbb{R}^n$ is defined as*

$$\mathcal{P} := \{x \in \mathbb{R}^n \mid H\,x \leqslant d\}.$$

*We use the shorthand $\mathcal{P} = \langle H, d\rangle_P$.*

A halfspace $\mathcal{H} \subset \mathbb{R}^n$ is a special case of a polytope consisting of a single inequality constraint $h^T x \leqslant d$ with $h \in \mathbb{R}^n$, $d \in \mathbb{R}$. We use the shorthand $\mathcal{H} = \langle h, d\rangle_H$. Another special type of polytopes are zonotopes, which can be stored efficiently using so-called generators:

**Definition 4.** *(Zonotope) Given a center vector $c \in \mathbb{R}^n$ and a generator matrix $G \in \mathbb{R}^{n\times p}$, a zonotope $\mathcal{Z} \subset \mathbb{R}^n$ is defined as*

$$\mathcal{Z} := \left\{ c + \sum_{i=1}^{p} \alpha_i\, G_{(\cdot,i)} \;\middle|\; \alpha_i \in [-1, 1] \right\},$$

*where the scalars $\alpha_i$ are called factors. We use the shorthand $\mathcal{Z} = \langle c, G\rangle_Z$.*

Polynomial zonotopes are a novel non-convex set representation that has been originally introduced for reachability analysis of nonlinear systems [1]. We use the sparse representation of polynomial zonotopes [20][1]:

**Definition 5.** *(Polynomial zonotope) Given a constant offset $c \in \mathbb{R}^n$, a generator matrix of dependent generators $G \in \mathbb{R}^{n \times h}$, a generator matrix of independent generators $G_I \in \mathbb{R}^{n \times q}$, and an exponent matrix $E \in \mathbb{N}_0^{p \times h}$, a polynomial zonotope $\mathcal{PZ} \subset \mathbb{R}^n$ is defined as*

$$\mathcal{PZ} := \left\{ c + \sum_{i=1}^{h} \left( \prod_{k=1}^{p} \alpha_k^{E_{(k,i)}} \right) G_{(\cdot,i)} + \sum_{j=1}^{q} \beta_j G_{I(\cdot,j)} \;\middle|\; \alpha_k, \beta_j \in [-1,1] \right\}.$$

*The scalars $\alpha_k$ are called dependent factors since a change in their value affects multiplication with multiple generators. Consequently, the scalars $\beta_j$ are called independent factors because they only affect multiplication with one generator. We use the shorthand $\mathcal{PZ} = \langle c, G, G_I, E \rangle_{PZ}$.*

Using polynomial zonotopes for verification has two main advantages:

1. Due to the similarity with Taylor models the set defined by a Taylor model can be equivalently represented as a polynomial zonotope [20, Prop. 4].
2. Due to the similarity with zonotopes tight enclosing zonotopes can be computed efficiently for polynomial zonotopes [20, Prop. 5].

For verification we therefore convert the Taylor model representing the image of the initial set through the observable function to a polynomial zonotope, for which collision checks with the unsafe sets can be efficiently realized using zonotope enclosures that are iteratively refined by splitting the polynomial zonotope.

The conversion of the Taylor model in (4) corresponding to our running example in (1) yields the following polynomial zonotope

$$\begin{aligned} \left\langle \begin{bmatrix} x_1 \\ x_2 \\ x_1^4 \end{bmatrix}, \varnothing, [-2,2] \times [0,4] \right\rangle_T &= \left\langle \begin{bmatrix} 0 \\ 2 \\ 0 \end{bmatrix}, \begin{bmatrix} 2 & 0 & 0 \\ 0 & 2 & 0 \\ 0 & 0 & 16 \end{bmatrix}, [\,], \begin{bmatrix} 1 & 0 & 4 \\ 0 & 1 & 0 \end{bmatrix} \right\rangle_{PZ} \\ &= \left\{ \begin{bmatrix} 0 \\ 2 \\ 0 \end{bmatrix} + \begin{bmatrix} 2 \\ 0 \\ 0 \end{bmatrix} \alpha_1 + \begin{bmatrix} 0 \\ 2 \\ 0 \end{bmatrix} \alpha_2 + \begin{bmatrix} 0 \\ 0 \\ 16 \end{bmatrix} \alpha_1^4 \;\middle|\; \alpha_1, \alpha_2 \in [-1,1] \right\}, \end{aligned}$$

where the high-level idea of the conversion is to represent the interval domain $\mathcal{D}$ with dependent zonotope factors $\alpha_i \in [-1,1]$.

## 3 Linearization via Fourier Features

We now present the automated generation of observables using random Fourier features [10]. Let us first motivate why Fourier features are a good choice for

[1] In contrast to [20, Def. 1], we explicitly do not integrate the constant offset $c$ in $G$. Moreover, we omit the identifier vector used in the original work [20] for simplicity.

observables. For Koopman linearization, the observables $g(x)$ define a transformation to a high-dimensional space. One commonly used approach to handle such high-dimensional spaces efficiently is the *kernel trick*: In many algorithms the data points $x, y \in \mathbb{R}^n$ only appear in the form of inner products $g(x)^T g(y)$. In this case it suffices to define a kernel function $k(x, y)$ that represents the similarity measure $g(x)^T g(y)$ between data points in the high-dimensional feature space, rather than explicitly defining a transformation $g(x)$ to this space. Kernel functions can also represent more general features that are not vectors and even infinite dimensional features, which motivates their application in the Koopman framework. The kernel trick is mainly applied for machine learning techniques [36], such as regression [38], clustering [18], and classification [39]. However, also the extended dynamic mode decomposition algorithm [41] can be formulated in terms of inner-products [42], so that the kernel trick can be applied for Koopman linearization. Rather than explicitly choosing observables $g(x)$ we can therefore select a kernel function instead, which implicitly defines the observable function $g(x)$ through the kernel's relation to an inner product space. Commonly used kernels are radial basis function kernels, polynomial kernels, and spline kernels.

The kernel trick cannot be applied directly to our reachability technique since we require an explicit formulation of the observables $g(x)$. We therefore first select a kernel function $k(x, y)$, and then determine observables $g(x)$ that yield a good approximation of the kernel function $k(x, y) \approx g(x)^T g(y)$. Random Fourier features are a common technique to approximate kernel functions [10,29]. They are based on Bochner's theorem [33, Sec. 1.4.3], which links a weakly stationary kernel function to a Fourier transform:

$$k(x, y) = \int_{\mathbb{R}^n} e^{j\,\omega^T (x-y)}\, d\mu(\omega) = \mathbb{E}_\omega \left( e^{j\,\omega^T x}\, \overline{e^{j\,\omega^T y}} \right), \tag{5}$$

where the function $\mu : \mathbb{R}^n \to [0, 1]$ defines a probability distribution, $\mathbb{E}_\omega(\cdot)$ denotes the expected value with respect to $\omega$, $j$ is the imaginary unit, and $\overline{a}$ denotes the complex conjugate for a complex number $a \in \mathbb{C}$. The distribution $\mu(\omega)$ associated with a specific kernel can be obtained by taking the inverse Fourier transform of $k(x, y)$ [29]. We can collect $m$ samples from the distribution $\mu(\omega)$ to approximate the expected value in (5), which finally yields

$$k(x, y) = \mathbb{E}_\omega \left( e^{j\,\omega^T x}\, \overline{e^{j\,\omega^T y}} \right) \approx \frac{1}{m} \sum_{i=1}^{m} \underbrace{e^{j\,\omega_i^T x}}_{g_i(x)}\, \underbrace{e^{j\,\omega_i^T y}}_{g_i(y)}.$$

The random Fourier features are the resulting observables $g_i(x)$ that approximate the kernel function. Note that we can omit the constant factor $\frac{1}{m}$ since extended dynamic mode decomposition will automatically scale the observables accordingly. We consider real-valued kernels only, so we use Euler's formula $e^{j\,x} = \cos(x) + j\, \sin(x)$ to simplify the random Fourier features to

$$g_i(x) = \sqrt{2}\, \cos(\omega_i^T x + b_i), \quad i = 1, \ldots, m, \tag{6}$$

where the shift $b_i$ is selected uniformly from the interval $[0, 2\pi]$ and $\omega_i$ is drawn randomly from the probability distribution $\mu(\omega)$ corresponding to the kernel that is used. While this random selection might appear to be a disadvantage at first sight, it is guaranteed that the random Fourier feature approximation converges to the exact kernel function when increasing the number of observables [29]. Moreover, we observed from our numerical experiments that changes in the values for $b_i$ and $\omega_i$ do not significantly influence the accuracy of the resulting linear approximation.

In summary, the random Fourier features presented above represent a systematic method for selecting a finite set of accurate observables, which requires only few hyperparameters. These hyperparameters include the type of kernel that is used, the kernel parameters, and the number of observables. For the numerical experiments in this paper we use a radial basis function kernel

$$k(x, y) = e^{-\frac{\|x-y\|_2^2}{2\,\ell^2}},$$

which contains the lengthscale $\ell$ as the only parameter. The probability distribution $\mu(\omega)$ for this kernel is the multivariate normal distribution with covariance matrix $\ell^2 \cdot I_n$ centered at the origin [29, Fig. 1].

## 4 Verification Using Reachability Analysis

We now present our novel verification algorithm for Koopman linearized systems, which is summarized in Algorithm 1. For simplicity we assume that the specification we aim to verify is described by a single unsafe set $\mathcal{U}$, but the extension to multiple unsafe sets is straightforward. We first apply Taylor model arithmetic (see Sect. 2.2) to compute a tight non-convex enclosure for the image of the initial set $\mathcal{X}_0$ through the observable function $g(x)$ in Line 3. Since it simplifies the computation of the zonotope enclosures required later on, we then convert the resulting Taylor model to a polynomial zonotope in Line 4. This polynomial zonotope is used as the initial set for the computation of the reachable set for the Koopman linearized system as performed in Line 5, for which we can use any reachability algorithm for linear systems. For simplicity we assume here that the obtained reachable sets are exact. In the general case where the exact reachable set cannot be computed one can for example incorporate the error measures from [14] and [40] into the verification algorithm.

The problem we are facing now is that the reachable sets $\mathcal{R}_0, \ldots, \mathcal{R}_{t_F/\Delta t}$ are represented by polynomial zonotopes, a set representation for which exact collision checks with the unsafe set $\mathcal{U}$ are computationally demanding. We resolve this issue by applying a novel polynomial zonotope refinement procedure in lines 6–19, where we recursively split the polynomial zonotopes until we can either verify or falsify the specification using zonotope enclosures of the split sets. In particular, we first enclose each polynomial zonotope in the queue $\mathbf{L}$ with a zonotope in Line 9. For a zonotope $\mathcal{Z} = \langle c, G \rangle_Z$ collision checks with an unsafe set as performed in Line 10 are very efficient: If the unsafe set is a halfspace $\mathcal{U} = \langle h, d \rangle_H$, we have according to [15, Sec. 5.1]

$$(\mathcal{Z} \cap \mathcal{U} \neq \varnothing) \Leftrightarrow \left( h^T c - \sum_{i=1}^{p} |h^T G_{(\cdot,i)})| \leqslant d \right) \tag{7}$$

**Algorithm 1.** Verification of Koopman linearized systems

**Require:** Koopman linearized system $\dot{g}(x) = A\,g(x)$, initial set $\mathcal{X}_0$, final time $t_F$, specification given as an unsafe set $\mathcal{U}$, time step size $\Delta t$, initial Taylor order $\kappa_0$.
**Ensure:** System is safe (res $= \top$) or unsafe (res $= \bot$).

1: res $\leftarrow \bot$, $\kappa \leftarrow \kappa_0$ (initialization)
2: **repeat**
3: $\quad \mathcal{T}(x) \leftarrow \{g(x) \mid x \in \mathcal{X}_0\}$ (comp. using Taylor model arithmetic with order $\kappa$)
4: $\quad \mathcal{PZ} \leftarrow \mathcal{T}(x)$ (convert Taylor model to polynomial zonotope, see [20, Prop. 4])
5: $\quad \mathcal{R}_0, \dots, \mathcal{R}_{t_F/\Delta t} \leftarrow$ reachability analysis of $\dot{g}(x) = A\,g(x)$ for initial set $\mathcal{PZ}$
6: $\quad \mathbf{L} \leftarrow (\mathcal{R}_0, \dots, \mathcal{R}_{t_F/\Delta t})$ (initialize queue of not yet verified sets)
7: $\quad$ **repeat**
8: $\quad\quad \mathcal{PZ} \leftarrow \mathbf{L}_{(1)}, \quad \mathbf{L} \leftarrow (\mathbf{L}_{(2)}, \dots, \mathbf{L}_{(|\mathbf{L}|)})$ (pop first element from queue)
9: $\quad\quad \mathcal{Z} \leftarrow$ zonotope enclosure of $\mathcal{PZ}$ (see [20, Prop. 5])
10: $\quad\quad$ **if** $\mathcal{Z} \cap \mathcal{U} \neq \emptyset$ **then** (check if specification is satisfied, see (7) and (8))
11: $\quad\quad\quad x_0, t \leftarrow$ most critical initial state and corresponding time
12: $\quad\quad\quad$ **if** $[I_n\ \mathbf{0}]\, e^{At} g(x_0) \in \mathcal{U}$ **then**
13: $\quad\quad\quad\quad$ **return** (specification falsified $\Rightarrow$ system is unsafe)
14: $\quad\quad\quad$ **else**
15: $\quad\quad\quad\quad \mathcal{PZ}_1, \mathcal{PZ}_2 \leftarrow$ split $\mathcal{PZ}$ (see Prop. 1 and (11))
16: $\quad\quad\quad\quad \mathbf{L} \leftarrow (\mathbf{L}, \mathcal{PZ}_1, \mathcal{PZ}_2)$ (add new sets to queue)
17: $\quad\quad\quad$ **end if**
18: $\quad\quad$ **end if**
19: $\quad$ **until** $\mathbf{L} = (\,)$ or splitting does not yield any further improvement
20: $\quad \kappa \leftarrow \kappa + 1$ (increase Taylor order)
21: **until** $\mathbf{L} = (\,)$ (queue empty $\Rightarrow$ no intersection with $\mathcal{U}$)
22: res $\leftarrow \top$ (if this line is reached no reach. set intersects $\mathcal{U} \Rightarrow$ system is safe)

For general polytopes $\mathcal{U} = \langle H, d \rangle_P$ collision checks can be realized using linear programming:

$$(\mathcal{Z} \cap \mathcal{U} \neq \emptyset) \Leftrightarrow (\delta = 0), \tag{8}$$

where

$$\delta = \min_{\alpha, x} \|c + G\alpha - x\|_1 \quad \text{s.t.} \quad \alpha \in [-\mathbf{1}, \mathbf{1}],\ Hx \leqslant d. \tag{9}$$

If the specification cannot be verified, we next try to falsfy it in lines 11–13 by extracting the initial point $x_0$ that is expected to violate the specification the most from $\mathcal{Z}$. For a halfspace $\mathcal{U} = \langle h, d \rangle_H$ the vector of zonotope factors $\alpha = [\alpha_1\ \dots\ \alpha_p]^T$ resulting in the largest violation is given as $\alpha = -\text{sign}(h^T G)$, where the signum function is interpreted elementwise. Since the factors $\alpha$ of the zonotope enclosure are related to the dependent factors of the original polynomial zonotope and since polynomial zonotopes preserve dependencies during reachability analysis [21], we can then directly extract the initial point $x_0$ corresponding to $\alpha$ from the polynomial zonotope. For general polytopes we can use the optimal $\alpha$ from the linear program in (9) to estimate the most critical initial point. If we can neither verify nor falsify the specification we have a so called spurious counterexample that arises due to the over-approximation introduced by the zonotope enclosure. We therefore split the polynomial zonotope in

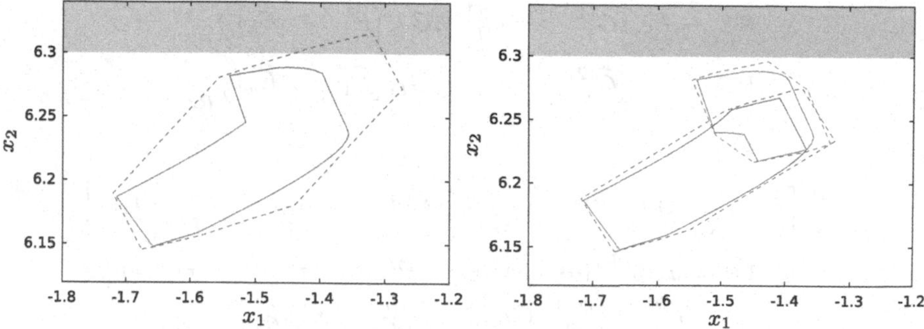


**Fig. 2.** Reachable set for the Roessler system (see Sect. 5.1) at time $t = 2.95$, where polynomial zonotopes are depicted by solid lines, the corresponding zonotope enclosures are depicted by dashed lines, and the unsafe set is shown in orange. While the zonotope enclosure of the original polynomial zonotope is too conservative to verify the specification (left), splitting the polynomial zonotope once reduces the over-approximation enough for verification to succeed (right).

this case in Line 15 since splitting reduces the over-approximation in the zonotope enclosure (see Fig. 2). The split sets are then added to the queue in Line 16, where we use a first-in, first-out scheme for the queue to detect easy falsifications fast before excessively splitting the sets.

One remaining issue we are facing is that Taylor model arithmetic is not exact. Due to the over-approximation in the initial set it can therefore happen that we can neither verify nor falsify the specification by splitting the polynomial zonotope. To solve this issue we embed our whole algorithm into a repeat-until-loop that iteratively increases the order $\kappa$ used for Taylor model arithmetic (see Line 20). Since Taylor model arithmetic converges to the exact result if the order goes to infinity, we obtain a complete algorithm that is guaranteed to terminate. In practice we can often prevent computational expensive iterations of the outer loop by choosing the initial order $\kappa_0$ large enough. It remains to decide when to stop splitting the polynomial zonotopes and increase the Taylor order instead (see Line 19). The simplest method is to just use an upper bound for the number of recursive splits that are performed. A more sophisticated approach is to abort splitting if the distance between the most critical point $[I_n \; \mathbf{0}]\, e^{At} g(x_0)$ and the unsafe set $\mathcal{U}$ is smaller than the over-approximation in the polynomial zonotope $\mathcal{PZ}$, which is given by the independent generators.

Finally, we provide a closed-form expression for splitting a polynomial zonotope since this operation is not specified in the original work [20]:

**Proposition 1.** *(Split) Given a polynomial zonotope* $\mathcal{PZ} = \langle c, G, G_I, E\rangle_{PZ} \subset \mathbb{R}^n$ *and the index* $r \in \{1, \dots, p\}$ *of one dependent factor, the operation* $\texttt{split}(\mathcal{PZ}, r)$ *returns two polynomial zonotopes* $\mathcal{PZ}_1$, $\mathcal{PZ}_2$ *satisfying* $\mathcal{PZ}_1 \cup \mathcal{PZ}_2 = \mathcal{PZ}$*:*

$$\mathcal{PZ}_1 = \Big\langle c, \big[\widehat{G}_1^{(1)} \ \dots \ \widehat{G}_h^{(1)}\big], G_I, \big[\widehat{E}_1 \ \dots \ \widehat{E}_h\big] \Big\rangle_{PZ}$$
$$\mathcal{PZ}_2 = \Big\langle c, \big[\widehat{G}_1^{(2)} \ \dots \ \widehat{G}_h^{(2)}\big], G_I, \big[\widehat{E}_1 \ \dots \ \widehat{E}_h\big] \Big\rangle_{PZ}$$

*with*

$$\widehat{E}_i = \begin{bmatrix} E_{(\{1,\dots,r-1\},i)} & E_{(\{1,\dots,r-1\},i)} & \dots & E_{(\{1,\dots,r-1\},i)} & E_{(\{1,\dots,r-1\},i)} \\ 0 & 1 & \dots & E_{(r,i)} - 1 & E_{(r,i)} \\ E_{(\{r+1,\dots,p\},i)} & E_{(\{r+1,\dots,p\},i)} & \dots & E_{(\{r+1,\dots,p\},i)} & E_{(\{r+1,\dots,p\},i)} \end{bmatrix},$$
$$\widehat{G}_i^{(k)} = \Big[ b_{i,0}^{(k)} \cdot G_{(\cdot,i)} \ \dots \ b_{i,E_{(r,i)}}^{(k)} \cdot G_{(\cdot,i)} \Big],$$
$$b_{i,j}^{(1)} = 0.5^{E_{(r,i)}} \binom{E_{(r,i)}}{j}, \quad b_{i,j}^{(2)} = -0.5^{E_{(r,i)}} \big(2(E_{(r,i)} \bmod 2) - 1\big) \binom{E_{(r,i)}}{j},$$

*where* $x \bmod y$, $x, y \in \mathbb{N}_0$ *is the modulo operation and* $\binom{w}{z}$, $w, z \in \mathbb{N}_0$ *denotes the binomial coefficient. To remove redundancies we subsequently apply the compact operation as defined in [20, Prop. 2] to* $\mathcal{PZ}_1$ *and* $\mathcal{PZ}_2$.

*Proof.* The `split` operation is based on the substitution of the selected dependent factor $\alpha_r$ with two new dependent factors $\alpha_{r,1}$ and $\alpha_{r,2}$:

$$\begin{gathered} \big\{\alpha_r \mid \alpha_r \in [-1,1]\big\} = \big\{0.5(1+\alpha_{r,1}) - 0.5(1+\alpha_{r,2}) \mid \alpha_{r,1}, \alpha_{r,2} \in [-1,1]\big\} \\ \big\{0.5(1+\alpha_{r,1}) \mid \alpha_{r,1} \in [-1,1]\big\} \cup \big\{-0.5(1+\alpha_{r,2}) \mid \alpha_{r,2} \in [-1,1]\big\}. \end{gathered} \tag{10}$$

Inserting this substitution into the definition of polynomial zonotopes in Definition 5 yields

$$\mathcal{PZ} = \bigg\{ c + \sum_{i=1}^{h} \Big( \prod_{k=1}^{p} \alpha_k^{E_{(k,i)}} \Big) G_{(\cdot,i)} + \sum_{j=1}^{q} \beta_j G_{I(\cdot,j)} \ \bigg| \ \alpha_k, \beta_j \in [\text{-}1,1] \bigg\} \overset{(10)}{=}$$

$$\underbrace{\bigg\{ c + \sum_{i=1}^{h} \Big( \prod_{\substack{k=1 \\ k \neq r}}^{p} \alpha_k^{E_{(k,i)}} \Big) \Big( \frac{1+\alpha_{r,1}}{2} \Big)^{E_{(r,i)}} G_{(\cdot,i)} + \sum_{j=1}^{q} \beta_j G_{I(\cdot,j)} \ \bigg| \ \alpha_k, \beta_j, \alpha_{r,1} \in [\text{-}1,1] \bigg\}}_{=\mathcal{PZ}_1}$$

$$\cup \underbrace{\bigg\{ c + \sum_{i=1}^{h} \Big( \prod_{\substack{k=1 \\ k \neq r}}^{p} \alpha_k^{E_{(k,i)}} \Big) \Big( \frac{1+\alpha_{r,2}}{-2} \Big)^{E_{(r,i)}} G_{(\cdot,i)} + \sum_{j=1}^{q} \beta_j G_{I(\cdot,j)} \ \bigg| \ \alpha_k, \beta_j, \alpha_{r,2} \in [\text{-}1,1] \bigg\}}_{=\mathcal{PZ}_2}.$$

Finally, with

$$\Big( \frac{1+\alpha_{r,1}}{2} \Big)^{E_{(r,i)}} = b_{i,0}^{(1)} + b_{i,1}^{(1)} \alpha_{r,1} + b_{i,2}^{(1)} \alpha_{r,1}^2 + \dots + b_{i,E_{(r,i)}}^{(1)} \alpha_{r,1}^{E_{(r,i)}}$$
$$\Big( \frac{1+\alpha_{r,2}}{-2} \Big)^{E_{(r,i)}} = b_{i,0}^{(2)} + b_{i,1}^{(2)} \alpha_{r,2} + b_{i,2}^{(2)} \alpha_{r,2}^2 + \dots + b_{i,E_{(r,i)}}^{(2)} \alpha_{r,2}^{E_{(r,i)}}$$

we obtain the equations above.

The split operation for polynomial zonotopes is not exact, meaning that the resulting sets usually overlap (see Fig. 2). To minimize the size of the overlapping region we split the dependent factor with index $r$ that maximizes the following heuristic:

$$\max_{r \in \{1,\dots,p\}} \sum_{\substack{i=1 \\ E_{(r,i)}>1}}^{h} \left(1 - 0.5^{E_{(r,i)}}\right) \|G_{(\cdot,i)}\|_2, \tag{11}$$

where $G \in \mathbb{R}^{n \times h}$ and $E \in \mathbb{N}_0^{p \times h}$ are the generator and exponent matrix of the polynomial zonotope. Moreover, since the goal of splitting in Algorithm 1 is to verify a certain specification, it is advisable to first project the polynomial zonotope onto the halfspace normal directions of the unsafe set $\mathcal{U}$ before evaluating the heuristic (11) in order to direct the splitting process towards directions that are beneficial for verification.

Note that the polynomial zonotope refinement technique presented in this section is not restricted to verification of Koopman linearized systems, but can equally be applied for collision checks of polynomial zonotopes or Taylor models with halfspaces and polytopes in general. Moreover, by inverting the inequality constraints polynomial zonotope refinement can also be applied to check if a Taylor model or polynomial zonotope is contained in a halfspace or polytope.

## 5 Experimental Results

We now evaluate the performance of random Fourier feature observables and our novel reachability algorithm on various benchmark systems. For this, we compare our approach with the closest method from the literature [5]. Since the algorithms presented there are implemented in Julia, we also implemented our approach in Julia to obtain a fair comparison of the computation time. In our implementation we use the package TaylorModels.jl[2] for Taylor model arithmetic and the package DataDrivenDiffEq.jl[3] for extended dynamic mode decomposition. All computations are carried out on a 3.2 GHz 8-core AMD Ryzen 7 5800H processor with 16 GB memory. We published our implementation together with a repeatability package that reproduces the results shown in this paper as a CodeOcean compute capsule[4].

### 5.1 Benchmarks

Let us first define all benchmarks that we use for the evaluation. Again, we consider the same systems and specifications as in [5] for a fair comparison:

---

[2] https://github.com/JuliaIntervals/TaylorModels.jl.
[3] https://datadriven.sciml.ai/.
[4] https://codeocean.com/capsule/8730054/tree/v1.

**Roessler Attractor:** The dynamic equations for the Roessler attractor [32] are

$$\begin{aligned}\dot{x}_1 &= -x_2 - x_3\\ \dot{x}_2 &= x_1 + 0.2\,x_2\\ \dot{x}_3 &= 0.2 + x_3\,(x_1 - 5.7),\end{aligned}$$

and we consider the initial set $\mathcal{X}_0 = [-0.05, 0.05] \times [-8.45, -8.35] \times [-0.05, 0.05]$, the final time $t_F = 6$, and the unsafe region $x_2 \geqslant 6.375 - 0.025 \cdot i$ parameterized by $i \in [0, 20]$.

**Steam Governor:** The dynamic equations for the steam governor [37] are

$$\begin{aligned}\dot{x}_1 &= x_2\\ \dot{x}_2 &= x_3^2\,\sin(x_1)\,\cos(x_1) - \sin(x_1) - 3\,x_2\\ \dot{x}_3 &= \cos(x_1) - 1,\end{aligned}$$

and we consider the initial set $\mathcal{X}_0 = [0.95, 1.05] \times [-0.05, 0.05] \times [0.95, 1.05]$, the final time $t_F = 3$, and the unsafe set $x_2 \leqslant -0.25 + 0.01 \cdot i$ parameterized by $i \in [0, 10]$.

**Coupled Van-der-Pol Oscillator:** The dynamic equations for the coupled Van-der-Pol oscillator [30] are

$$\begin{aligned}\dot{x}_1 &= x_2 & \dot{x}_3 &= x_4\\ \dot{x}_2 &= (1 - x_1^2)\,x_2 - x_1 + (x_3 - x_1) & \dot{x}_4 &= (1 - x_3^2)\,x_4 - x_3 + (x_1 - x_3),\end{aligned}$$

and we consider the initial set $\mathcal{X}_0 = [-0.025, 0.025] \times [0.475, 0.525] \times [-0.025, 0.025] \times [0.475, 0.525]$, the final time $t_F = 2$, and the unsafe set $x_1 \geqslant 1.25 - 0.05 \cdot i$ parameterized by $i \in [1, 16]$.

**Biological System:** The dynamic equations for the biological system [19] are

$$\begin{aligned}\dot{x}_1 &= -0.4\,x_1 + 5\,x_3\,x_4 & \dot{x}_5 &= -5\,x_5\,x_6 + 5\,x_3\,x_4\\ \dot{x}_2 &= 0.4\,x_1 - x_2 & \dot{x}_6 &= 0.5\,x_7 - 5\,x_5\,x_6\\ \dot{x}_3 &= x_2 - 5\,x_3\,x_4 & \dot{x}_7 &= -0.5\,x_7 + 5\,x_5\,x_6,\\ \dot{x}_4 &= 5\,x_5\,x_6 - 5\,x_3\,x_4 & &\end{aligned}$$

and we consider the initial set $\mathcal{X}_0 = [0.99, 1.01] \times \cdots \times [0.99, 1.01]$, the final time $t_F = 2$, and the unsafe set $x_4 \leqslant 0.883 + 0.002 \cdot i$ parameterized by $i \in [0, 20]$.

### 5.2 Approximation Error

We first investigate the accuracy of the Koopman linearized system with respect to the original nonlinear dynamics, where we compare our random Fourier feature observables with the ad hoc observables from [5]. These ad hoc observables consist of multi-variate polynomials of the system state $x$ up to a fixed order, trigonometric functions of the time $t$, and combinations of these

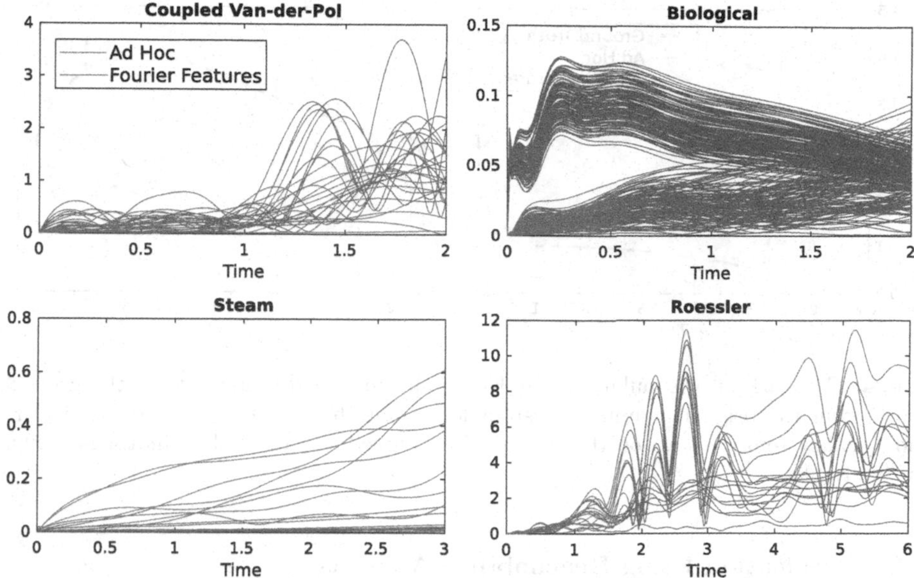


**Fig. 3.** Relative simulation error between Koopman linearized systems and the original nonlinear system in percent.

(*e.g.*, $x_1 x_2 \sin^2(t)\cos(t)$). To obtain the data traces required for extended dynamic mode decomposition we simulate the original nonlinear systems for 500 points sampled from the corresponding initial set, where a Sobol sequence is used for sampling. For the generation of the random Fourier feature observables according to (6) we use the parameter $\ell = 0.3$ and $m = 71$ for the Roessler attractor, $\ell = 1.62$ and $m = 72$ for the steam governor, $\ell = 1.24$ and $m = 132$ for the coupled Van-der-Pol oscillator, and $\ell = 1.81$ and $m = 105$ for the biological system, where $\ell$ is the lengthscale parameter of the kernel and the number of observables $m$ is chosen identical to the one used for the ad hoc observables [5]. As a measure for the accuracy we use the Euclidean distance between simulated trajectories for the original nonlinear system and the Koopman linearized system. The initial points for these trajectories are the center and the vertices of the initial set. According to Fig. 3 random Fourier feature observables are for the steam governor and the Roessler attractor more accurate than than the ad hoc observables used in earlier work [5]. Moreover, while for the short time horizons considered in Fig. 3 it seems that the ad hoc observables are more precise for the coupled Van-der-Pol oscillator and the biological system, over longer time horizons the error of the ad hoc observables is exploding. This is visualized in Fig. 4, where the trajectory corresponding to the ad hoc observables progresses into a completely different direction than the original system, while random Fourier features stay accurate. In this way, random Fourier features are not only a more systematic approach for choosing observables, but also improve the precision of the resulting Koopman linearized system.

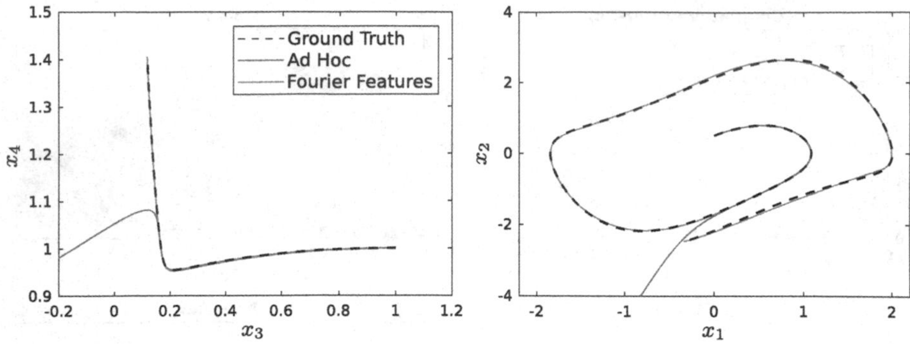


**Fig. 4.** Comparison of simulations for Koopman linearized systems with the ground truth from the original nonlinear system for a time horizon of $t_F = 10$, where the biological system is shown on the left and the coupled Van-der-Pol oscillator is shown on the right.

### 5.3 Verification Using Reachability Analysis

We now compare our novel verification algorithm for Koopman linearized systems with the verification strategies presented in [5]. In particular, we compare to verification of the original nonlinear system using Flow* [9], direct encoding of nonlinear constraints using a SMT solver [5, Sec. 4.1], and zonotope domain splitting [5, Sec. 4.4]. Both approaches from [5] consider discrete-time safety, where the system is considered to be safe if the specification is satisfied at time points $0, \Delta t, 2\Delta t, \ldots, t_F$ with $\Delta t = 0.05$. While our verification algorithm also supports continuous-time safety, we consider discrete-time safety here to obtain a fair comparison. Note that for discrete-time safety the reachable set computation in Line 5 of Algorithm 1 simplifies to $\mathcal{R}_i = [I_n \ \mathbf{0}]\, e^{Ai\Delta t}\, \mathcal{X}_0$, $i = 0, \ldots, t_F/\Delta t$. For the comparison we consider both, the ad hoc observables used in [5] as well as the random Fourier feature observables presented here.

The resulting computation times for verification are summarized in Table 1. For all benchmark instances our novel verification algorithm has the lowest computation time, and is often even magnitudes faster than the other verification approaches. The main reason for this is that with our polynomial refinement strategy we can completely avoid the computational expensive calls to SMT solvers used by the other methods. Moreover, while the computation time for the other approaches often depends on how difficult it is to verify or falsify the specification, our algorithm exhibits roughly equal runtimes for all specifications. The explanation for this is that the polynomial zonotope refinement approach that we use for the collision checks with unsafe sets is very efficient, so that the majority of the runtime is spent on the computation of the image through the observable function using Taylor model arithmetic, a task which is independent from the specification. Interestingly, using random Fourier features instead of ad hoc observables can either prolong or accelerate the verification process, depending on the benchmark instance and verification approach used. However, even if

**Table 1.** Computation time in seconds for verification or falsification of the benchmark systems from Sect. 5.1 using different approaches, where the symbol – indicates that the computation timed-out after 2 h. The parameter $i$ specified in the second column changes the specification, and the third column shows weather the specification can be verified or falsified.

| | $i$ | Safe? | Flow* | Direct Enc. | | Zono. Split. | | Our App. | |
|---|---|---|---|---|---|---|---|---|---|
| | | | | ad hoc | fourier | ad hoc | fourier | ad hoc | fourier |
| Coupled VP | 1 | ✓ | 251 | 788 | 398 | 0.57 | 171 | **0.20** | **3.00** |
| | 8 | × | 497 | 680 | 120 | 53 | 232 | **0.79** | **3.77** |
| | 16 | × | 1665 | 557 | 373 | 18 | 38 | **0.20** | **2.99** |
| Biological | 1 | ✓ | 260 | 470 | – | 0.59 | – | **0.44** | **1.95** |
| | 5 | ✓ | 250 | 426 | – | 49 | – | **0.44** | **1.73** |
| | 10 | ✓ | 238 | 427 | – | 179 | – | **0.46** | **1.76** |
| Steam | 0 | ✓ | 61 | 197 | 149 | 182 | 42 | **0.12** | **0.25** |
| | 5 | × | 285 | 59 | 40 | 37 | 38 | **0.38** | **0.56** |
| | 10 | × | 77 | 29 | 20 | 18 | 27 | **0.12** | **0.26** |
| Roessler | 0 | ✓ | 55 | 181 | 291 | 9.53 | 117 | **0.55** | **0.35** |
| | 10 | × | 78 | 177 | 385 | 5.01 | 241 | **0.22** | **0.75** |
| | 20 | × | 55 | 174 | 158 | 3.5 | 86 | **0.21** | **0.34** |

they prolong the time required for verification in some cases, the usage of random Fourier feature observables can be justified by their superior accuracy demonstrated in Sect. 5.2. Yet another observation is that direct encoding and zonotope domain splitting are not able to verify or falsify the high-dimensional biological model at all if random Fourier feature observables are used. The reason for this is that both of these approaches apply an SMT solver for verification, which do not scale to high-dimensions and are not well-suited for handling the trigonometric functions as well as the high coupling between variables used for random Fourier feature observables. So in summary our proposed verification algorithm outperforms all exiting verification techniques for Koopman linearized systems in terms of runtime. In addition, it handles different types of observables well and scales to high-dimensional systems.

## 6 Conclusion

We presented two major improvements for reachability analysis of Koopman operator linearized systems: First, we use random Fourier features as observable functions, which yields a systematic approach requiring much less user insight than previous methods. Second, we handle the nonlinear transformation of the initial state by combining Taylor model arithmetic with polynomial zonotope refinement. As demonstrated on several nonlinear system benchmarks, the combination of these two techniques is both extremely accurate and extremely fast.

The main trade-off with Koopman linearized systems is that the guarantees are on the system approximation, not the original system. Despite this, we believe the method could still be useful for verification in systems engineering, where the goal is to produce evidence that the system meets its requirements. It could also be effective for finding unsafe counterexamples—falsification—or to analyze systems where only simulation code is provided, or even real-world systems where sensor measurements could be used to create a Koopman linearized model for analysis. As such systems do not have models given with symbolic differential equations, most traditional reachability methods cannot be applied.

**Acknowledgements.** This material is based upon work supported by the Air Force Office of Scientific Research, the DARPA Assured Autonomy program under the United States Air Force, and the Office of Naval Research under award numbers FA9550-19-1-0288, FA9550-21-1-0121, FA9550-22-1-0450, FA2386-17-1-4065, FA8750-19-C-0092, and N00014-22-1-2156. Any opinions, findings, and conclusions or recommendations expressed in this material are those of the author(s) and do not necessarily reflect the views of the United States Air Force, DARPA, or the United States Navy. Distribution Statement A: Approved for Public Release; Distribution is Unlimited. PA: AFRL-2022-1356.

## References

1. Althoff, M.: Reachability analysis of nonlinear systems using conservative polynomialization and non-convex sets. In: Proceedings of the International Conference on Hybrid Systems: Computation and Control, pp. 173–182 (2013)
2. Althoff, M.: Reachability analysis of large linear systems with uncertain inputs in the Krylov subspace. Trans. Autom. Control **65**(2), 477–492 (2019)
3. Amini, A., et al.: Error bounds for Carleman linearization of general nonlinear systems. In: Proceedings of the International Conference on Control and its Applications, pp. 1–8 (2021)
4. Bak, S., et al.: Numerical verification of affine systems with up to a billion dimensions. In: Proceedings of the International Conference on Hybrid Systems: Computation and Control, pp. 23–32 (2019)
5. Bak, S., et al.: Reachability of black-box nonlinear systems after Koopman operator linearization. In: Proceedings of the International Conference on Analysis and Design of Hybrid Systems, pp. 253–258 (2021)
6. Bogomolov, S., et al.: Reach set approximation through decomposition with low-dimensional sets and high-dimensional matrices. In: Proceedings of the International Conference on Hybrid Systems: Computation and Control, pp. 41–50 (2018)
7. Carleman, T.: Application de la théorie des équations intégrales linéaires aux systèmes d'équations différentielles non linéaires. Acta Math. **59**, 63–87 (1932)
8. Chen, X., et al.: Taylor model flowpipe construction for non-linear hybrid systems. In: Proceedings of the Real-Time Systems Symposium, pp. 183–192 (2012)
9. Chen, X., Ábrahám, E., Sankaranarayanan, S.: Flow*: an analyzer for non-linear hybrid systems. In: Sharygina, N., Veith, H. (eds.) CAV 2013. LNCS, vol. 8044, pp. 258–263. Springer, Heidelberg (2013). https://doi.org/10.1007/978-3-642-39799-8_18
10. DeGennaro, A.M., Urban, N.M.: Scalable extended dynamic mode decomposition using random kernel approximation. SIAM J. Sci. Comput. **41**(3), 1482–1499 (2019)

11. Duggirala, P.S., Viswanathan, M.: Parsimonious, simulation based verification of linear systems. In: Proceedings of the International Conference on Computer Aided Verification, pp. 477–494 (2016)
12. Forets, M., Pouly, A.: Explicit error bounds for Carleman linearization. arXiv preprint arXiv:1711.02552 (2017)
13. Forets, M., Schilling, C.: Reachability of weakly nonlinear systems using Carleman linearization. In: Bell, P.C., Totzke, P., Potapov, I. (eds.) RP 2021. LNCS, vol. 13035, pp. 85–99. Springer, Cham (2021). https://doi.org/10.1007/978-3-030-89716-1_6
14. Frehse, G., et al.: SpaceEx: scalable verification of hybrid systems. In: Proceedings of the International Conference on Computer Aided Verification, pp. 379–395 (2011)
15. Girard, A.: Reachability of uncertain linear systems using zonotopes. In: Proceedings of the International Conference on Hybrid Systems: Computation and Control, pp. 291–305 (2005)
16. Han, Y., et al.: Deep learning of Koopman representation for control. In: Proceedings of the International Conference on Decision and Control, pp. 1890–1895 (2020)
17. Jaulin, L., Kieffer, M., Didrit, O., Walter, E.: Interval analysis. In: Applied Interval Analysis, pp. 11–43. Springer (2001)
18. Kim, D.W., et al.: Evaluation of the performance of clustering algorithms in kernel-induced feature space. Pattern Recogn. **38**(4), 607–611 (2005)
19. Klipp, E., et al.: Systems Biology in Practice: Concepts, Implementation and Application. Wiley, Hoboken (2005)
20. Kochdumper, N., Althoff, M.: Sparse polynomial zonotopes: a novel set representation for reachability analysis. Trans. Autom. Control **66**(9), 4043–4058 (2021)
21. Kochdumper, N., et al.: Utilizing dependencies to obtain subsets of reachable sets. In: Proceedings of the International Conference on Hybrid Systems: Computation and Control (2020)
22. Koopman, B.O.: Hamiltonian systems and transformation in Hilbert space. Proc. Natl. Acad. Sci. U.S.A. **17**(5), 315–318 (1931)
23. Kurzhanski, A.B., Varaiya, P.: Ellipsoidal techniques for reachability analysis. In: Proceedings of the International Conference on Hybrid Systems: Computation and Control, pp. 202–214 (2000)
24. Liu, J.P., et al.: Efficient quantum algorithm for dissipative nonlinear differential equations. Proc. Natl. Acad. Sci. U.S.A. **118**(35), e2026805118 (2021)
25. Makino, K., Berz, M.: Taylor models and other validated functional inclusion methods. Int. J. Pure Appl. Math. **4**(4), 379–456 (2003)
26. Mauroy, A., Mezić, I., Susuki, Y. (eds.): The Koopman Operator in Systems and Control. LNCIS, vol. 484. Springer, Cham (2020). https://doi.org/10.1007/978-3-030-35713-9
27. Mitchell, I.M., et al.: A time-dependent Hamilton-Jacobi formulation of reachable sets for continuous dynamic games. Trans. Autom. Control **50**(7), 947–957 (2005)
28. Otto, S.E., Rowley, C.W.: Koopman operators for estimation and control of dynamical systems. Annu. Rev. Control Robot. Auton. Syst. **4**, 59–87 (2021)
29. Rahimi, A., Recht, B.: Random features for large-scale kernel machines. In: Proceedings of the International Conference on Neural Information Processing Systems, pp. 1177–1184 (2007)
30. Rand, R., Holmes, P.: Bifurcation of periodic motions in two weakly coupled Van der Pol oscillators. Int. J. Non-Linear Mech. **15**(4–5), 387–399 (1980)

31. Rauh, A., et al.: Carleman linearization for control and for state and disturbance estimation of nonlinear dynamical processes. In: Proceedings of the International Conference on Methods and Models in Automation and Robotics, pp. 455–460 (2009)
32. Rössler, O.E.: An equation for continuous chaos. Phys. Lett. A **57**(5), 397–398 (1976)
33. Rudin, W.: Fourier Analysis on Groups. Courier Dover Publications, Mineola (2017)
34. Sankaranarayanan, S.: Automatic abstraction of non-linear systems using change of bases transformations. In: Proceedings of the International Conference on Hybrid Systems: Computation and Control, pp. 143–152 (2011)
35. Sankaranarayanan, S.: Change-of-bases abstractions for non-linear hybrid systems. Nonlinear Anal. Hybrid Syst. **19**, 107–133 (2016)
36. Schölkopf, B., Smola, A.J.: Learning with Kernels: Support Vector Machines, Regularization, Optimization, and Beyond. MIT Press, Cambridge (2018)
37. Sotomayor, J., et al.: Bifurcation analysis of the Watt governor system. Comput. Appl. Math. **26**(1), 19–44 (2007)
38. Takeda, H., et al.: Kernel regression for image processing and reconstruction. Trans. Image Process. **16**(2), 349–366 (2007)
39. Tuia, D., et al.: Learning relevant image features with multiple-kernel classification. Trans. Geosci. Remote Sens. **48**(10), 3780–3791 (2010)
40. Wetzlinger, M., et al.: Adaptive parameter tuning for reachability analysis of linear systems. In: Proceedings of the International Conference on Decision and Control, pp. 5145–5152 (2020)
41. Williams, M.O., et al.: A data-driven approximation of the Koopman operator: extending dynamic mode decomposition. J. Nonlinear Sci. **25**(6), 1307–1346 (2015)
42. Williams, M.O., et al.: A kernel-based method for data-driven Koopman spectral analysis. J. Comput. Dyn. **2**(2), 247–265 (2015)
43. Yeung, E., et al.: Learning deep neural network representations for Koopman operators of nonlinear dynamical systems. In: Proceedings of the American Control Conference, pp. 4832–4839 (2019)

# RINO: Robust INner and Outer Approximated Reachability of Neural Networks Controlled Systems

Eric Goubault(✉) and Sylvie Putot

LIX, Ecole Polytechnique, CNRS and Institut Polytechnique de Paris, 91128 Palaiseau, France
{eric.goubault,sylvie.putot}@polytechnique.edu

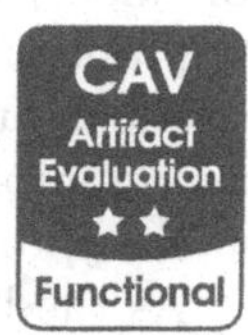


**Abstract.** We present a unified approach, implemented in the RINO tool, for the computation of inner and outer-approximations of reachable sets of discrete-time and continuous-time dynamical systems, possibly controlled by neural networks with differentiable activation functions. RINO combines a zonotopic set representation with generalized mean-value AE extensions to compute under and over-approximations of the robust range of differentiable functions, and applies these techniques to the particular case of learning-enabled dynamical systems. The AE extensions require an efficient and accurate evaluation of the function and its Jacobian with respect to the inputs and initial conditions. For continuous-time systems, possibly controlled by neural networks, the function to evaluate is the solution of the dynamical system. It is over-approximated in RINO using Taylor methods in time coupled with a set-based evaluation with zonotopes. We demonstrate the good performances of RINO compared to state-of-the art tools Verisig 2.0 and ReachNN* on a set of classical benchmark examples of neural network controlled closed loop systems. For generally comparable precision to Verisig 2.0 and higher precision than ReachNN*, RINO is always at least one order of magnitude faster, while also computing the more involved inner-approximations that the other tools do not compute.

**Keywords:** Neural networks verification · Reachability analysis · Robustness · Inner-approximation

## 1 Introduction

Over the last few years, neural networks have emerged as an increasingly classical choice for the control of autonomous systems, in particular due to their properties as universal function approximators. However, their adoption in safety-critical systems, the inherent uncertainties from the dynamic environment, and their sensitivity to adversarial examples make it crucial to establish their safety and robustness. This verification is challenging because of the complex non-linear characteristics of neural networks. Recent works come up with some approaches


S. Shoham and Y. Vizel (Eds.): CAV 2022, LNCS 13371, pp. 511–523, 2022.
https://doi.org/10.1007/978-3-031-13185-1_25

and tools to bound the output uncertainty of neural networks with respect to input perturbations. However, many of them are restricted to the analysis of networks with ReLU activation functions. Moreover, the approaches considering general differentiable activation functions and systems with general non linear dynamics provide over-approximations, which conservatism is difficult to estimate. RINO proposes a scalable and adaptive approach to compute both inner (or under) and outer (or over) approximations for the closed loop reachability problem of neural network controlled systems, with differentiable activation functions. The outer-approximation allows for property verification, while the inner-approximation allows for property refutation. Combined, the inner and outer-approximations allow to assess the conservatism of the approximations.

As the behavior of a neural network controlled closed-loop system relies on the interaction between the continuous dynamics and the neural network controller, a good precision requires to not only compute the output range but also describe the input-output mapping for the controller. In this work, we propose to use a zonotope-based abstraction to compute in a unified way both the reachable sets of neural networks and dynamical systems. This seamless integration of the reachability of neural networks and dynamical systems presents the advantage of a natural propagation of useful correlations through the different components of the closed loop system, resulting in an efficient and precise approach compared to many existing works which rely on external reachability tools.

*Contributions*

- RINO implements all ideas presented in [8–11] for the joint computation of inner and outer approximations of robustly reachable sets of differentiable nonlinear discrete-time or continuous-time systems (without neural networks in the loop), possibly with constant delays. These previous works demonstrated the good scaling properties of our approach on different examples including a full nonlinear quadcoptor flight model but the tool was never presented as such.
- Additionally, we demonstrate here that an application of these ideas to the case of neural networks enabled dynamical systems provides very competitive results for the over-approximation compared to the state of the art (at least similar precision and one order of magnitude faster) while also providing the first approach for inner-approximation of the reachable sets of such systems, which we use to falsify some safety properties.
- Finally, RINO also computes approximations of output ranges that are reachable robustly or adversarially with respect to a subset of inputs: while these robust ranges are mostly used in this work to compute inner-approximations of joint ranges of state variables instead of projections, we believe this sensitivity information can be a useful tool in the future in particular to assess global robustness properties of neural networks.

*Related Work.* The safety verification for DNNs has received considerable attention recently, with several threads of work being developed. We draw below a non exhaustive panorama focusing on available tools for reachability analysis of neural network controlled systems with smooth activation functions.

Different approaches have been proposed to the reachability analysis closed-loop systems with neural network controllers, often by a transformation to a continuous or hybrid system reachability. Sherlock [6] targets both the open-loop and closed-loop problems with ReLU activation functions, in particular using the regressive polynomial rule inference approach [5] for the closed-loop, and Flow* [3] for the reachability of the dynamical system. NNV [24] also targets both the open loop and closed loop verification problems, with various activation functions and set representations such as polyhedra or star sets [23], and different reachability algorithms for dynamical systems relying on CORA [1] and the MPT toolbox [18]. ReachNN [13] and its successor ReachNN* [7] propose a reachability analysis based on Bernstein polynomials for closed-loop systems with general activation functions, also relying on Flow* [3] for the reachability of the dynamical system. Verisig [14] handles NNCS with nonlinear plants controlled by sigmoid-based networks, exploiting the fact that the sigmoid is the solution to a differential equation to transform the neural network into an equivalent hybrid system, which is then fed to Flow*. Verisig 2.0 [15] uses preconditioned Taylor Models to propagate reachable sets in neural networks, and also relies on Flow* for reachability of the hybrid system component.

The very recent works [21] and [12] implemented respectively over JuliaReach and in POLAR are also closely related to our work. In [21], the authors implement a bridge between zonotope abstractions and Taylor model abstractions in order to combine tools analyzing controllers (e.g. using zonotopes like deepZ [22]) with tools analyzing ordinary differential equations (e.g. Flow* [3]). In [12], the authors use a polynomial arithmetic made up of a combination of Berstein polynomials and Taylor models to iteratively overapproximate networks layers, according to whether the activation function is differentiable or not.

## 2 Problem Statement and Background

### 2.1 Robust Reachability of Closed-Loop Dynamical Systems

We consider in this work a closed-loop system consisting of a plant with states $x$, modeled as a discrete-time or continuous-time system with time-varying disturbances $w$ and inputs $u$, where some components of the control inputs can be the output a neural network $h$ taking $x$ as input. For notation's simplicity, we focus on continuous-time systems and define:

$$\begin{cases} \dot{x}(t) = f(x(t), u(t), w(t)) & \text{if } t \geq 0 \\ x(t) = x_0 & \text{if } t = 0 \end{cases} \tag{1}$$

where $f$ is a sufficiently smooth function and at least $\mathcal{C}^1$, and controls $u$ and disturbances $w$ are also supposed to be sufficiently smooth $C^k$ for some $k \geq 0$ stepwise. This allows discontinuous controls and disturbances, where the discontinuities can only appear at discrete times $t_j$.

The neural network $h$ is a fully-connected feedforward NN with differentiable activation functions, defined as the composition $h(x) = h_L \circ h_{L-1} \circ \ldots h_1(x)$ of

$L$ layers where each layer $h_i(x) = \sigma(W_i x + b_i)$ performs a linear transform followed by a sigmoid or hyperbolic tangent activation $\sigma$. We assume the control is decomposed as $u(t) = (u_1(t), u_2(t))$ where $u_2(t)$ is a control input defined in $\mathbb{U}_2$ and $u_1(t)$ is the output of the neural network controller. This controller is executed in a time-triggered fashion with control step $T$, so that $u_1(t) = h(x(t_k))$, for $t \in [t_k, t_k + T)$, where $t_k = kT$ for positive integers $k$. System (1) can then be rewritten as

$$\begin{cases} \dot{x}(t) = f(x(t), h(x(t_k)), u_2(t), w(t)) & \text{if } t \in [t_k, t_k + T),\ t_k = kT, k \geq 0 \\ x(t) = x_0 & \text{if } t = 0 \end{cases} \tag{2}$$

Let $\varphi^f(t; x_0, u_2, w)$ for time $t \in \mathbb{T}$ denote the *time trajectory* of (2) with initial state $x(0) = x_0$, for input signal $u_2$ and disturbance $w$.

We consider the problem of computing inner and outer-approximations of robust reachable sets as introduced in [9], defined here as

$$R^f_{\mathcal{AE}}(t; \mathbb{X}_0, \mathbb{U}_2, \mathbb{W}) = \{x \mid \forall w \in \mathbb{W}, \exists u_2 \in \mathbb{U}_2,\ \exists x_0 \in \mathbb{X}_0,\ x = \varphi^f(t; x_0, u, w)\}$$

Note that this notion of robust reachability extends the classical notions of minimal and maximal reachability [20]. We use the subscript notation $\mathcal{AE}$ to indicate that the reachable set is minimal with respect to the disturbances $w$ (universal quantification $\mathcal{A}$) and maximal with respect to the input $u_2$ (existential quantification indicated by $\mathcal{E}$), and that the universal quantification always precedes the existential quantification.

## 2.2 Mean-Value Inner and Outer-Approximating Robust Extensions

A classical but often overly conservative way to overapproximate the image of a set by a real-valued function $f : \mathbb{R}^m \to \mathbb{R}$ is the natural interval extension $\mathcal{F} : \mathbb{IR}^m \to \mathbb{IR}$, $\mathbb{IR}$ being the set of intervals with real bounds, which consists in replacing real operations by their interval counterparts in the expression of the function.

A generally more accurate extension relies on a linearization by the mean-value theorem. Mean-value extensions can be generalized to compute ranges that are robust to disturbances, identified as a subset of the input components. Let $f$ be a continuously differentiable function from $\mathbb{R}^m$ to $\mathbb{R}$ with input decomposed as $x = (u, w) \in (\mathcal{U}, \mathcal{W}) \subseteq \mathbb{IR}^m$. We define the robust range of function $f$ on $\boldsymbol{x}$, robust with respect to component $w \in \mathcal{W}$, as $R^f_{\mathcal{AE}}(\mathcal{U}, \mathcal{W}) = \{z \mid \forall w \in \mathcal{W}, \exists u \in \mathcal{U},\ z = f(u, w)\}$.

For a continuously differentiable function $f : \mathbb{R}^m \to \mathbb{R}^n$, we note $\nabla f = (\nabla_j f_i)_{ij} = (\frac{\partial f_i}{\partial x_j})_{1 \leq i \leq n, 1 \leq j \leq m}$ its Jacobian matrix. We note $\langle x, y \rangle$ the scalar product of vectors $x$ and $y$, and $|x|$ the absolute value extended componentwise. For a vector of intervals $\mathcal{X} = [\underline{\mathcal{X}}, \overline{\mathcal{X}}]$, we note $c(\mathcal{X}) = (\overline{\mathcal{X}} + \underline{\mathcal{X}})/2.0$ and $r(\mathcal{X}) = (\overline{\mathcal{X}} - \underline{\mathcal{X}})/2.0$ its center and radius defined componentwise.

**Theorem 1. ([8], slightly simplified version of Thm. 2).** *Let $f$ be a continuously differentiable function from $\mathbb{R}^m$ to $\mathbb{R}$ and $\mathcal{X} = \mathcal{U} \times \mathcal{W} \subseteq \mathbb{IR}^m$. Let $\mathcal{F}^0$,*

*$\nabla_w^{\mathcal{X}}$ and $\nabla_u^{\mathcal{X}}$ be vectors of intervals such that $c(\mathcal{X}) \subseteq \mathcal{F}^0$, $\{|\nabla_w f(u,w)|\,, (u,w) \in \mathcal{X}\} \subseteq \nabla_w^{\mathcal{X}}$ and $\{|\nabla_u f(u,w)|\,, (u,w) \in \mathcal{X}\} \subseteq \nabla_u^{\mathcal{X}}$. We have:*

$$[\overline{\mathcal{F}^0} - \langle \underline{\nabla_u^{\mathcal{X}}}, r(\mathcal{U})\rangle + \langle \overline{\nabla_w^{\mathcal{X}}}, r(\mathcal{W})\rangle, \underline{\mathcal{F}^0} + \langle \underline{\nabla_u^{\mathcal{X}}}, r(\mathcal{U})\rangle - \langle \overline{\nabla_w^{\mathcal{X}}}, r(\mathcal{W})\rangle] \subseteq R^f_{\mathcal{AE}}(\mathcal{U},\mathcal{W})$$
$$R^f_{\mathcal{AE}}(\mathcal{U},\mathcal{W}) \subseteq [\underline{\mathcal{F}^0} - \langle \overline{\nabla_u^{\mathcal{X}}}, r(\mathcal{U})\rangle + \langle \underline{\nabla_w^{\mathcal{X}}}, r(\mathcal{W})\rangle, \overline{\mathcal{F}^0} + \langle \overline{\nabla_u^{\mathcal{X}}}, r(\mathcal{U})\rangle - \langle \underline{\nabla_w^{\mathcal{X}}}, r(\mathcal{W})\rangle]$$

Theorem 1 provides inner and outer-approximations of the robust range (or of the classical range when there is no disturbance component $w$) of scalar-valued functions, or of the projections on each component of vector-valued functions, using bounds on the slopes on the input set. The result is useful to compute a projected range that is robustly reachable with respect to the disturbances $w$, or as a brick in computing an under-approximation of the image of a vector-valued function, as stated in Theorem 3 in [8].

Note that the accuracy of the mean-value AE extension can be improved with an evaluation by a quadrature formula ([10], Sect. 4.2). Alternatively, an order 2 Taylor-based extension ([10], Sect. 3) can be used.

### 2.3 Reachability of Neural Network Controlled Closed-Loop Systems

The inner and outer approximations defined in Sect. 2.2 can be computed for $f$ being a simple function, possibly involving a neural network evaluation, or $f$ being the function defined by the iterated values of a discrete systems, or finally $f$ being the solution flow of closed-loop system (2).

In both discrete-time and the continuous-time cases, and whether some neural network controller is present or not, the evaluation of an outer-approximation of the image of the solution and its Jacobian with respect to inputs and disturbances over sets is needed in order to apply Theorem 1.

In our work and implementation, we advocate the use of a unique abstraction by affine forms (or zonotopes for the geometric view of a tuple of variables represented by affine forms) for these sets and these evaluations, including performing reachability of the neural network controller. This abstraction is very convenient and versatile to over-approximate any smooth function, providing a good trade-off between efficiency and precision in most cases (and for more precision, one can consider extensions with e.g. polynomial zonotopes [2]).

For continuous-time systems, we use Taylor expansions in time of the solution on a time grid. To build these Taylor expansions, we evaluate function $f$ and its (Lie) derivatives over affine forms by a combination of automatic differentiation and numerical evaluation by affine arithmetic, as described in e.g. [9]. The neural network is seen as a nonlinear function $h$, composed with $f$ to build function $g$ for which we compute the solution flow. Theorem 1 is applied to this solution flow. We build the abstraction of $h$ and thus $g$ by a simple propagation of affine forms by affine arithmetic in the network: linear transformers are exact, and we propagate affine forms through the activation functions seen as standard nonlinear functions relying on the elementary exponential function, $tanh(x) = 2/(1+e^{-2x}) - 1$ and $sig(x) = 1/(1+e^{-x})$. For differentiating the activation functions, we use $tanh'(x) = 1.0 - tanh(x)^2$ and $sig'(x) = sig(x)(1 - sig(x))$.

## 3 Implementation

As mentioned in the introduction, RINO implements all ideas presented in [8–11] for the joint computation of inner and outer approximations of robustly reachable sets of differentiable nonlinear discrete-time [8,10] or continuous-time systems [8,9], possibly with constant delays [11]. For experiments with systems without neural networks, we refer to the results presented in these works, obtained with a previous version of RINO.

RINO is written in C++. Intervals and zonotopes are used for set representation: the tool relies on the FILIB++ library [19] for interval computations and the aaflib library[1] for affine arithmetic [4]. Ole Stauning's FADBAD++ library[2] is used for automatic differentiation: its implementation with template enables us to easily evaluate the differentiation in the set representation of our choice (affine forms or zonotopes mostly). The tool takes as inputs:

- an open-loop or closed loop system, either discrete time or continuous-time, which for now is hard-coded in C++,
- an optional neural network, provided to the tool in a format directly inspired from the format analyzed by Sherlock [6], which can be used as some inputs of the closed-loop system,
- an optional configuration file to set initial values, input and disturbances ranges, and some parameter of the analysis (such as time step, order of Taylor expansion in time)

It computes inner and outer-approximations of the projection on each component of ranges, as well as joint 2D and 3D inner-approximations (provided as yaml file and Jupyter/python-produced figures). Additionally to the classical ranges, RINO computes approximations of output ranges that are reachable robustly or adversarially with respect to disturbances, specified as a subset of inputs. In the experiments presented herafter, we consider examples only of classical reachability, for which comparisons with existing work are available, but the extension to robust reachability based on our previous work is straightforward.

## 4 Experiments

For space reasons, we focus here on the main novelty which is the extension of this previous work to compute under and over-approximations of (robust) reachable sets of neural network controlled systems (2).

*Choice of Tools and Benchmark Examples.* We compare RINO against ReachNN* and Verisig 2.0 that are the most recent fully-fledged reachability analyzers for neural network based control systems, and for which comparisons with other tools on classical benchmarks are well documented in e.g. [15]. They both improve on previous versions, Verisig and ReachNN, and on state of the art

[1] http://aaflib.sourceforge.net.

[2] http://www.fadbad.com.

tools Sherlock, also based on Flow*, and NNV. As noted in e.g. [15]: "Firstly, note that Verisig takes significantly more time to compute reachable sets (21 times slower in the case of the B5 benchmark). Furthermore, Verisig is unable to verify some properties due to increasing error. Note that NNV is unable to verify any of the properties considered in this paper due to high approximation error.". Remark though that there has been some amelioration to the internal solvers used in NNV which should qualify the latter statement (see e.g. [16]). We do not compare with the implementation in JuliaReach [21] since, first, timings are difficult to compare with an interpreted framework, and second, because it would require mixing several tools together, with many potential combinations. We try to provide elements of comparison with POLAR [12], but in many ways the latter addresses a different problem, with the emphasis on being able to interpret e.g. ReLU activation functions.

**Table 1.** List of benchmarks (see [15])

| Name | Dynamics | Initial set | Horizon | Control step |
|---|---|---|---|---|
| Mountain Car | $\dot{x}_1 = x_2$<br>$\dot{x}_2 = 0.0015u - 0.0025\cos(3x_1)$ | $[-0.5, -0.48]$<br>$[0, 0.001]$ | $T = 75$ | 1 |
| discrete MC (stepsize 1) | $x_1^{n+1} = x_1^n + x_2^n$<br>$x_2^{n+1} = x_2^n + 0.0015u^n$<br>$-0.0025\cos(3x_1^n)$ | $[-0.5, -0.48]$<br>$[0, 0.001]$ | $T = 75$ | 1 |
| TORA | $\dot{x}_1 = x_2$<br>$\dot{x}_2 = -x_1 + 0.1 * \sin(x_3)$<br>$\dot{x}_3 = x_4$<br>$\dot{x}_4 = u$ | $[-0.77, -0.75]$<br>$[-0.45, -0.43]$<br>$[0.51, 0.54]$<br>$[-0.3, -0.28]$ | $T = 5$ | 0.1 |
| ACC | $\dot{x}_1 = x_2,\ \dot{x}_4 = x_5$<br>$\dot{x}_2 = x_3,\ \dot{x}_5 = x_6$<br>$\dot{x}_3 = -4 - 0.0001x_2^2 - 2x_3$<br>$\dot{x}_6 = 2u - 0.0001x_5^2 - 2x_6$ | $x_1 = [90, 91]$<br>$x_2 = [32, 32.05]$<br>$x_4 = [10, 11]$<br>$x_5 = [30, 30.05]$ | $T = 5$ | 0.1 |
| B1 (Ex 1 in [7]) | $\dot{x}_1 = x_2$<br>$\dot{x}_2 = ux_2^2 - x_1$ | $[0.8, 0.9]$<br>$[0.5, 0.6]$ | $T = 7$ | 0.2 |
| B2 (Ex 2 in [7]) | $\dot{x}_1 = x_2 - x_1^3$<br>$\dot{x}_2 = u$ | $[0.7, 0.9]$<br>$[0.7, 0.9]$ | $T = 1.8$ | 0.2 |
| B3 (Ex 3 in [7]) | $\dot{x}_1 = -x_1(0.1 + (x_1 + x_2)^2)$<br>$\dot{x}_2 = (u + x_1)(0.1 + (x_1 + x_2)^2)$ | $[0.8, 0.9]$<br>$[0.4, 0.5]$ | $T = 6$ | 0.1 |
| B4 (Ex 4 in [7]) | $\dot{x}_1 = -x_1 + x_2 - x_3$<br>$\dot{x}_2 = -x_1(x_3 + 1) - x_2$<br>$\dot{x}_3 = -x_1 + u$ | $[0.25, 0.27]$<br>$[0.08, 0.1]$<br>$[0.25, 0.27]$ | $T = 1$ | 0.1 |
| B5 (Ex 5 in [7]) | $\dot{x}_1 = x_3^3 - x_2$<br>$\dot{x}_2 = x_3$<br>$\dot{x}_3 = u$ | $[0.38, 0.4]$<br>$[0.45, 0.47]$<br>$[0.25, 0.27]$ | $T = 2$ | 0.2 |

We use a large subset (7/10) of the examples from Verisig 2.0 [15], which are benchmarks used by most of the tools in the field, through e.g. the ARCH competition [17]. We also consider the same settings in terms of initial sets and the same time horizon. These are recalled in Table 1.

We indicate some of RINO's reachability results on these benchmarks in Table 2, before comparing the tightness and computing times with other tools.

**Table 2.** RINO's results for time step 0.05 (except Mountain Car, step 1.)

| Name | over-approx | under-approx | t (s) | t docker |
|---|---|---|---|---|
| Mountain Car<br>sigmoid (2 × 200) | [−0.78197, −0.64704]<br>[−0.019387, −0.0093975] | ⊥ | 31. | 40.41 |
| Discrete MC<br>sigmoid (2 × 200) | [−0.8711, −0.68326]<br>[−0.026888, −0.01411] | [−0.82466, −0.7297]<br>[−0.023716, −0.017282] | 35 | 19.85 |
| TORA<br>tanh (3 × 20) | [0.022471, 0.04829]<br>[−0.80790, −0.78039]<br>[−0.37201, −0.3433]<br>[0.30682, 0.33235] | [0.029133, 0.041776]<br>[−0.8037, −0.78452]<br>∅<br>∅ | 1.6 | 2.54 |
| ACC<br>tanh | [229.05, 230.29]<br>[22.819, 22.868]<br>[−2.0285, −2.0284]<br>[159.88, 161.02]<br>[29.893, 30.006]<br>[−0.30836, 0.01398] | [229.05, 230.29]<br>[22.819, 22.868]<br>[−2.0285, −2.0284]<br>[160.03, 160.87]<br>∅<br>∅ | 6. | 7.65 |
| B1<br>tanh (3 × 20) | [0.012957, 0.1349]<br>[0.18089, 0.23235] | ∅<br>∅ | 0.7 | 0,92 |
| B1<br>sigmoid (3 × 20) | [0.10155, 0.15331]<br>[0.17188, 0.20041] | [0.12092, 0.13398]<br>∅ | 0.6 | 0.77 |
| B2<br>sigmoid (3 × 20) | [−0.12356, −0.0811]<br>[0.16682, 0.26396] | ⊥ | 0.2 | 0.21 |
| B3<br>tanh | [0.2256, 0.25296]<br>[−0.17777, −0.16092] | [0.23507, 0.24352]<br>∅ | 1.3 | 1.67 |
| B4<br>tanh | [−0.0017942, 0.010039]<br>[−0.03494, −0.02305]<br>[0.064524, 0.070953] | ∅<br>[−0.032405, −0.02557]<br>∅ | 0.1 | 0,098 |
| B5<br>tanh | [−0.42399, −0.38098]<br>[0.16388, 0.17547]<br>[−0.24869, −0.23363] | ⊥ | 2.7 | 3.8 |

*Settings.* All tools, Verisig 2.0 and ReachNN* and RINO, were run without GPU support, under Ubuntu 18.04 docker, on a Mac running Mac OS Big Sur 11.2.3 on a 2.3 GHz Intel Core i9 processor with 16Gb of memory. Verisig 2.0 and ReachNN* were run with the Reproductibility Package of Verisig 2.0 [15].

For fairness of timing results, we also run RINO with docker, and the running ratios given in Table 3 are those using these docker versions. RINO was also run natively on the same Mac. The performance degradation between the two versions of RINO can be estimated from the full data given in Table 2 from none to a 40% increase (with one exception at 80%), and most between 20 and 30%. This is higher than generally observed with docker, but due to the fact that docker on Macintosh is known to perform badly when it comes to IOs, using the underlying file system. Therefore, the performance degrades more when the system is of higher dimension and have more time steps to evaluate, since RINO logs all estimated ranges for all variables in separate files.

*Comparisons Results.* We compare in Table 3 the running times of Verisig 2.0, ReachNN* and RINO, and volumes of their final over-approximations, more precisely the widths of the projections of each component at final time horizon.

The three tools depend on some parameters, in particular integration time steps and order of approximation. RINO does not require tuning the integration time steps and order of Taylor models so much, so we use one fixed time step of 0.05 for all examples. We use for Verisig 2.0 and ReachNN* the settings of the CAV Reproductibility package, that we suppose give good results. Verisig 2.0 and ReachNN* actually perform poorly on the same examples with a fixed time steps of 0.05 s.

We experimented RINO with different time steps. The precision is relatively stable and does not necessarily improve when decreasing the time step. Indeed, as already noted [25], the improvement in approximation by Taylor models on smaller time steps is balanced by the loss of precision due to set-based abstraction being performed more often. Note also that the analysis time does not depend linearly on the time step: the control step, which rules the frequency at which the analysis of the neural net controller has to be performed, is fixed (see Table 1) and does not depend on the integration time step.

Column 2 in Table 3 describes the relative width of the intervals given by Verisig 2.0 for each variable at the final time and for each system, with respect to the one given by RINO. Column 4 is the same, but for ReachNN*. Columns 3 and 5 give the ratio of the analysis time of Verisig 2.0 (respectively ReachNN*), with respect to the analysis time of RINO.

In all cases, RINO is much faster than both Verisig 2.0 and ReachNN*, by factors ranging from 13 to 638.5. Moreover, this includes for RINO the time to compute the inner-approximations that Verisig 2.0 and ReachNN* do not compute. ReachNN* could not analyze TORA because of lack of memory on our platform, and timed out on ACC. Finally, interpolating the timings given in Table 1 of [12], e.g. for B1 (sig), Verisig 2.0 is reported to take 47 s whereas POLAR is reported to take 20 s on their platform. As Verisig 2.0 took 81.33 s on our platform, we can infer that RINO is most certainly much faster, with e.g. 3.62 s for B1, than POLAR.

RINO's precision is of the same order as Verisig 2.0, and always better than ReachNN* by a factor of about 2 to 10. RINO is in fact even substantially more precise than Verisig 2.0 in some cases (B1 and B2 in particular).

*Inner-Approximations.* Let us take example B1 (with sigmoid-based controller), and suppose we have a safety property that the value of $x_1$ should never be bigger than 1. Figure 1a represents in filled blue region the inner-approximation, as plain black lines the bounds of the outer-approximation, and as purple dots values actually reached, obtained by trajectories for sample initial conditions The over-approximation alone does raise a potential alarm with respect to the unsafe zone (in red), only the inner-approximation actually proves that the safety

**Table 3.** Precision and running time comparisons RINO [timestep=0.05] vs Verisig 2.0 [time steps of [15]] vs ReachNN* [time steps of [15]]

| Example | % width Verisig2 over RINO | Ratio time Verisig2/RINO | % width ReachNN* over RINO | Ratio time ReachNN*/RINO |
|---|---|---|---|---|
| TORA (tanh) | 117,6ă% | 38,6 | Mem full | Mem full |
| | 98,4ă% | | | |
| | 106,7ă% | | | |
| | 128,0ă% | | | |
| TORA (sig) | 115,7ă% | 43,4 | Mem full | Mem full |
| | 68,0ă% | | | |
| | 110,1ă% | | | |
| | 133,3ă% | | | |
| ACC (tanh) | 101,9ă% | 500,8 | Time out | Time out |
| | 105,6ă% | | | |
| | 103,3ă% | | | |
| | 110,1ă% | | | |
| | 105,1ă% | | | |
| | 65,8ă% | | | |
| B1 (tanh) | 84,9ă% | 88,8 | 96,7ă% | 85,1 |
| | 287,8ă% | | 245,0ă% | |
| B1 (sig) | 112,1ă% | 105,4 | 227,8ă% | 86,8 |
| | 140,6ă% | | 441,9ă% | |
| B2 (sig) | 263,2ă% | 77,6 | 408,8ă% | 121,9 |
| | 60,4ă% | | 513,7ă% | |
| B3 (tanh) | 99,5ă% | 57,5 | 103,9ă% | 81,9 |
| | 98,5ă% | | 287,3ă% | |
| B3 (sig) | 99,1ă% | 55,2 | 176,8ă% | 76,4 |
| | 98,0ă% | | 1043,9ă% | |
| B4 (tanh) | 105,0ă% | 187,9 | 224,2ă% | 214,6 |
| | 101,6ă% | | 130,6ă% | |
| | 108,7ă% | | 896,0ă% | |
| B4 (sig) | 105,4ă% | 154,4 | 226,9ă% | 173,5 |
| | 101,9ă% | | 132,3ă% | |
| | 107,7ă% | | 908,9ă% | |
| B5 (tanh) | 100,2ă% | 365,3 | 192,6ă% | 8,9 |
| | 99,2ă% | | 826,4ă% | |
| | 100,4ă% | | 635,6ă% | |
| B5 (sig) | 100,2ă% | 360,2 | 192,5ă% | 9,0 |
| | 99,1ă% | | 851,6ă% | |
| | 100,4ă% | | 1437,4ă% | |

property is falsified. We also note on this picture that the over-approximation is very tight, given that samples give almost indistinguishable ranges. Figure 1b represents the inner and outer approximations of joint range $(x_1, x_2)$ as well as estimation by sampling. As shown by the samples, $(x_1, x_2)$ becomes almost a 1D curve after some time, making inner approximation extremely difficult to estimate. Indeed our inner-approximation in orange is fairly precise for the first time steps, and the corresponding inner skewed boxes are rotated to match the curvy, 1D, shape of the samples. The green boxes printed on the picture are the box enclosure of the actually computed outer-approximation. Note that the inner-approximation of the projections on each component can be non-empty while having an empty joint inner range, as some approximation is committed in the joint inner range computation (as a skewed box) from the projected ranges.

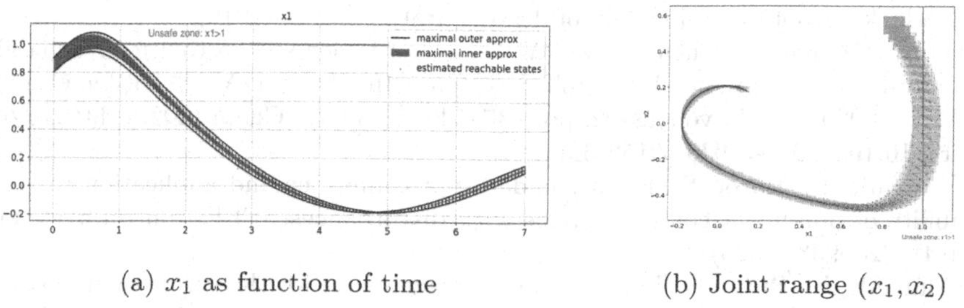


(a) $x_1$ as function of time (b) Joint range $(x_1, x_2)$

**Fig. 1.** B1: inner-approximation, outer-approximation and sampling (purple dots) (Color figure online)

## 5 Conclusion and Future Work

We presented the RINO tool, dedicated to the reachability analysis of dynamical systems, possibly controlled by neural networks. While providing accurate results, RINO is significantly faster than other state-of-the-art tools, which is key in view to address real-life reachability problems, where the systems and neural networks can be of high dimension. Moreover, as far as we are aware, it is the only existing tool to propose inner-approximations of the reachable sets of such systems. We currently handle only differentiable activation functions. We are thinking of some abstractions to handle ReLU activations as well, even though the approach is less natural in that case as it will introduce conservatism. We also plan to improve the accuracy of our current results by further specializing this work to exploit the structure of neural network, such as monotonicity of activation functions. Finally, robustness is a crucial property for neural networks enabled systems, and we plan to explore the possibilities offered by the computation of robust reachable sets.

## References


1. Althoff, M.: An introduction to CORA 2015. In: Proceedings of the Workshop on Applied Verification for Continuous and Hybrid Systems (2015)
2. Althoff, M.: Reachability analysis of nonlinear systems using conservative polynomialization and non-convex sets. In: HSCC 2013, pp. 173–182. Association for Computing Machinery, New York (2013). https://doi.org/10.1145/2461328.2461358
3. Chen, X., Ábrahám, E., Sankaranarayanan, S.: Taylor model flowpipe construction for non-linear hybrid systems. In: 2012 IEEE 33rd Real-Time Systems Symposium, pp. 183–192 (2012)
4. Comba, J., Stolfi, J.: Affine arithmetic and its applications to computer graphics. In: SIBGRAPI (1993)
5. Dutta, S., Chen, X., Sankaranarayanan, S.: Reachability analysis for neural feedback systems using regressive rule inference (2019)
6. Dutta, S., Kushner, T., Jha, S., Sankaranarayanana, S., Shankar, N., Tiwari, A.: Sherlock: a tool for verification of deep neural networks (2019)
7. Fan, J., Huang, C., Chen, X., Li, W., Zhu, Q.: ReachNN*: a tool for reachability analysis of neural-network controlled systems. In: Hung, D.V., Sokolsky, O. (eds.) ATVA 2020. LNCS, vol. 12302, pp. 537–542. Springer, Cham (2020). https://doi.org/10.1007/978-3-030-59152-6_30
8. Goubault, E., Putot, S.: Robust under-approximations and application to reachability of non-linear control systems with disturbances. IEEE Control Syst. Lett. **4**(4), 928–933 (2020)
9. Goubault, E., Putot, S.: Inner and outer reachability for the verification of control systems. In: Proceedings of the 22nd ACM International Conference on Hybrid Systems: Computation and Control, HSCC 2019, Montreal, QC, Canada, 16–18 April 2019, pp. 11–22. ACM (2019)
10. Goubault, E., Putot, S.: Tractable higher-order under-approximating AE extensions for non-linear systems. In: Jungers, R.M., Ozay, N., Abate, A. (eds.) ADHS 2021. IFAC-PapersOnLine, vol. 54, pp. 235–240. Elsevier (2021)
11. Goubault, E., Putot, S., Sahlmann, L.: Inner and outer approximating flowpipes for delay differential equations. In: Chockler, H., Weissenbacher, G. (eds.) CAV 2018. LNCS, vol. 10982, pp. 523–541. Springer, Cham (2018). https://doi.org/10.1007/978-3-319-96142-2_31
12. Huang, C., Fan, J., Chen, X., Li, W., Zhu, Q.: POLAR: a polynomial arithmetic framework for verifying neural-network controlled systems (2021)
13. Huang, C., Fan, J., Li, W., Chen, X., Zhu, Q.: ReachNN: reachability analysis of neural-network controlled systems. ACM Trans. Embed. Comput. Syst. **18**, 1–22 (2019)
14. Ivanov, R., Weimer, J., Alur, R., Pappas, G.J., Lee, I.: Verisig: verifying safety properties of hybrid systems with neural network controllers (2019)
15. Ivanov, R., Carpenter, T., Weimer, J., Alur, R., Pappas, G., Lee, I.: Verisig 2.0: verification of neural network controllers using Taylor model preconditioning. In: Silva, A., Leino, K.R.M. (eds.) CAV 2021. LNCS, vol. 12759, pp. 249–262. Springer, Cham (2021). https://doi.org/10.1007/978-3-030-81685-8_11
16. Johnson, T.T., et al.: ARCH-COMP21 category report: artificial intelligence and neural network control systems (AINNCS) for continuous and hybrid systems plants. In: Frehse, G., Althoff, M. (eds.) 8th International Workshop on Applied Verification of Continuous and Hybrid Systems (ARCH 2021). EPiC Series in Computing, vol. 80, pp. 90–119. EasyChair (2021)

17. Johnson, T.T., et al.: ARCH-COMP20 category report: artificial intelligence and neural network control systems (AINNCS) for continuous and hybrid systems plants. In: ARCH20. 7th International Workshop on Applied Verification of Continuous and Hybrid Systems (ARCH 2020). EPiC Series in Computing, vol. 74, pp. 107–139. EasyChair (2020). https://doi.org/10.29007/9xgv
18. Kvasnica, M., Grieder, P., Baotić, M., Morari, M.: Multi-parametric toolbox (MPT). In: Alur, R., Pappas, G.J. (eds.) HSCC 2004. LNCS, vol. 2993, pp. 448–462. Springer, Heidelberg (2004). https://doi.org/10.1007/978-3-540-24743-2_30
19. Lerch, M., Tischler, G., von Gudenberg, J.W., Hofschuster, W., Kramer, W.: FILIB++, a fast interval library supporting containment computations. ACM Trans. Math. Soft **32**, 299–324 (2006)
20. Mitchell, I.M.: Comparing forward and backward reachability as tools for safety analysis. In: Bemporad, A., Bicchi, A., Buttazzo, G. (eds.) HSCC 2007. LNCS, vol. 4416, pp. 428–443. Springer, Heidelberg (2007). https://doi.org/10.1007/978-3-540-71493-4_34
21. Schilling, C., Forets, M., Guadalupe, S.: Verification of neural-network control systems by integrating Taylor models and zonotopes (2021)
22. Singh, G., Gehr, T., Mirman, M., Püschel, M., Vechev, M.T.: Fast and effective robustness certification. In: Advances in Neural Information Processing Systems, NeurIPS, pp. 10825–10836 (2018)
23. Tran, H.-D., et al.: Star-based reachability analysis of deep neural networks. In: ter Beek, M.H., McIver, A., Oliveira, J.N. (eds.) FM 2019. LNCS, vol. 11800, pp. 670–686. Springer, Cham (2019). https://doi.org/10.1007/978-3-030-30942-8_39
24. Tran, H.-D., et al.: NNV: the neural network verification tool for deep neural networks and learning-enabled cyber-physical systems. In: Lahiri, S.K., Wang, C. (eds.) CAV 2020. LNCS, vol. 12224, pp. 3–17. Springer, Cham (2020). https://doi.org/10.1007/978-3-030-53288-8_1
25. Wetzlinger, M., Kulmburg, A., Althoff, M.: Adaptive parameter tuning for reachability analysis of nonlinear systems. In: Proceedings of the 24th International Conference on Hybrid Systems: Computation and Control. HSCC 2021. Association for Computing Machinery (2021)

# STLmc: Robust STL Model Checking of Hybrid Systems Using SMT

Geunyeol Yu, Jia Lee, and Kyungmin Bae(✉)

Pohang University of Science and Technology,
Pohang, Korea
kmbae@postech.ac.kr

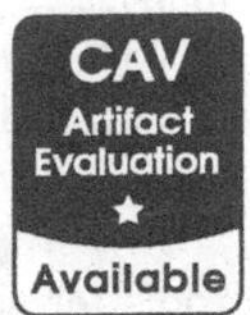


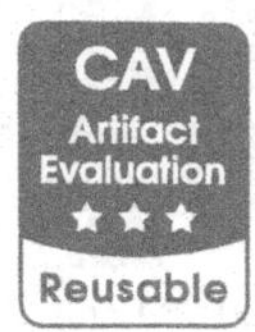


**Abstract.** We present the STLmc model checker for signal temporal logic (STL) properties of hybrid systems. The STLmc tool can perform STL model checking up to a robustness threshold for a wide range of hybrid systems. Our tool utilizes the refutation-complete SMT-based bounded model checking algorithm by reducing the robust STL model checking problem into Boolean STL model checking. If STLmc does not find a counterexample, the system is guaranteed to be correct up to the given bounds and robustness threshold. We demonstrate the effectiveness of STLmc on a number of hybrid system benchmarks.

## 1 Introduction

Signal temporal logic (STL) [31] has emerged as a popular property specification formalism for hybrid systems. STL formulas describe linear-time properties of continuous real-valued signals. Because hybrid systems exhibit both discrete and continuous behaviors, STL provides a convenient and expressive way to specify important requirements of hybrid systems. STL has a vast range of applications on hybrid systems, including automotive systems [26], robotics [24,40], medical systems [36], IoT [7], smart cities [30], etc.

Due to the infinite-state nature of hybrid systems with continuous dynamics, most techniques and tools for analyzing STL properties focus on monitoring and falsification. These techniques analyze concrete samples of signals obtained by simulating hybrid automata to monitor the system's behavior [13,15,32] or find counterexamples [1,37,43], often combined with stochastic optimization. To this end, STL monitoring and falsification use quantitative semantics that defines the *robustness degree* to indicate how well the formula is satisfied. However, these methods cannot be used to guarantee correctness.

Recently, several STL model checking techniques have been proposed for hybrid systems [3,29,35]. In particular, the SMT-based bounded model checking algorithms [3,29] are refutation-complete, i.e., they can guarantee correctness up to given bounds. However, these techniques are based on the Boolean semantics of STL instead of quantitative semantics. This is a limitation for hybrid systems as small perturbations of signals can cause the system to violate the properties *verified* by Boolean STL model checking. Moreover, there exists no tool with a convenient user interface implementing STL model checking techniques.


S. Shoham and Y. Vizel (Eds.): CAV 2022, LNCS 13371, pp. 524–537, 2022.
https://doi.org/10.1007/978-3-031-13185-1_26

This paper presents the STLMC tool for robust STL model checking of hybrid systems. Our tool can verify that, up to given bounds, the robustness degree of an STL formula $\varphi$ is greater than a *robustness threshold* $\epsilon > 0$ for all possible behaviors of the system. We reduce the robust STL model checking problem to Boolean STL model checking using *$\epsilon$-strengthening* (perturbing the problem by $\epsilon$ to make it harder to be true), first proposed in [21] for first-order logic and extended to STL. We then apply the refutation-complete bounded model checking algorithm [3,29] to build the SMT encoding of the resulting Boolean STL model checking problem, which can be solved using SMT solvers.

Apart from the robust STL model checking method, STLMC also implements several techniques to improve the usability and scalability of the tool:

- STLMC implements a generic interface to connect with various SMT solvers, such as Z3 [12], Yices2 [17], and dReal [22]. Since dReal can (approximately) deal with nonlinear ordinary differential equations (ODEs), STLMC can also support hybrid systems with nonlinear ODE dynamics.
- STLMC implements parallelized two-step SMT solving to improve scalability. Instead of directly solving the complex encoding with ODEs, we first obtain a *discrete abstraction* without ODEs and find satisfying scenarios. We then check the *discrete refinements* of such scenarios using dReal in parallel.
- STLMC provides a visualization command to draw counterexample signals and robustness degrees. Such graphs intuitively explain why the robustness degree of the formula is greater than a given threshold, and thus greatly help in analyzing counterexamples and debugging hybrid systems.

We demonstrate the effectiveness of the STLMC tool on a number of hybrid system benchmarks— including linear, polynomial, and ODE dynamics— and nontrivial STL properties. The tool is available at https://stlmc.github.io.

## 2 Background: Robust STL Model Checking

*Hybrid Automata.* Hybrid systems are often formalized as *hybrid automata* [25], defined as a tuple $H = (Q, X, init, inv, jump, flow)$. A set of modes $Q$ specifies discrete states. A set of real-valued variables $X = \{x_1, ...., x_l\}$ gives continuous states. A pair $\langle q, \vec{v} \rangle$ of mode $q \in Q$ and vector $\vec{v} \in \mathbb{R}^l$ constitutes a state of $H$. An initial condition $init(q, \vec{v})$ defines a set of initial states. An invariant condition $inv(q, \vec{v})$ defines a set of valid states. A jump condition $jump(q, \vec{v}, q', \vec{v'})$ defines a discrete transition from $\langle q, \vec{v} \rangle$ to $\langle q', \vec{v'} \rangle$. A flow condition $flow(q, \vec{v}, \vec{v}_t, t)$ defines a continuous evolution of $X$'s values from $\vec{v}$ to $\vec{v}_t$ over time $t$ in mode $q$.

A *signal* $\sigma$ represents a continuous execution of a hybrid automaton $H$, given by a function $[0, \tau) \to Q \times \mathbb{R}^l$ with a time bound $\tau > 0$. A signal $\sigma$ is called a *trajectory* of a hybrid automaton $H$, written $\sigma \in H$, if $\sigma$ describes a valid behavior of $H$: formally, there exists a sequence of times $0 = t_0 < t_1 < ... < \tau$ such that: (i) $\sigma(t_0)$ is an initial state by *init*; (ii) for $i \geq 1$, $H$'s state evolves from $\sigma(t_i)$ according to *flow*, while satisfying *inv*, for each time interval $[t_{i-1}, t_i)$; and (iii) for $i \geq 1$, a discrete transition occurs by *jump* at each time point $t_i$.

*Signal Temporal Logic.* Signal temporal logic (STL) is widely used to specify properties of hybrid systems [31]. The syntax of STL is defined by:

$$\varphi ::= p \mid \neg\varphi \mid \varphi \wedge \varphi \mid \varphi\, \mathbf{U}_I\, \varphi$$

where $p$ denotes state propositions, and $I \subseteq \mathbb{R}_{\geq 0}$ is any interval of nonnegative real numbers. Examples of state propositions include relational expressions of the form $f(\vec{x}) \geq 0$ over variables $X$ with a real-valued function $f : \mathbb{R}^l \to \mathbb{R}$. Other common Boolean and temporal operators can be derived by equivalences: e.g., $\varphi \vee \varphi' \equiv \neg(\neg\varphi \wedge \neg\varphi')$, $\Diamond_I\, \varphi \equiv \top\, \mathbf{U}_I\, \varphi$, $\Box_I\, \varphi \equiv \neg\, \Diamond_I\, \neg\varphi$, etc.

We consider a quantitative semantics of STL based on *robustness degrees* [15]. The semantics of a state proposition $p$ is defined as a function $p : Q \times \mathbb{R}^l \to \overline{\mathbb{R}}$ that assigns to a state the degree to which $p$ is true, where $\overline{\mathbb{R}} = \mathbb{R} \cup \{-\infty, \infty\}$. Specifically, the robustness degree of a state proposition $f(\vec{x}) \geq 0$ is the value of $f(\vec{x})$. E.g., the robustness degree of $x \geq 4$ is the value of $x - 4$ at a given state. The robustness degree of an STL formula can be defined as follows [15], where a time bound $\tau$ of a signal is explicitly taken into account.[1]

**Definition 1.** *Given an STL formula $\varphi$, a signal $\sigma : [0, \tau) \to \mathbb{R}^l$, and a time $t \in [0, \tau)$, the robustness degree $\rho_\tau(\varphi, \sigma, t) \in \overline{\mathbb{R}}$ is defined inductively by:*[2]

$$\begin{aligned}
\rho_\tau(p, \sigma, t) &= p(\sigma(t)) \\
\rho_\tau(\neg\varphi, \sigma, t) &= -\rho_\tau(\varphi, \sigma, t) \\
\rho_\tau(\varphi_1 \wedge \varphi_2, \sigma, t) &= \min(\rho_\tau(\varphi_1, \sigma, t), \rho_\tau(\varphi_2, \sigma, t)) \\
\rho_\tau(\varphi_1\, \mathbf{U}_I\, \varphi_2, \sigma, t) &= \sup\nolimits_{t' \in (t+I) \cap [0,\tau)} \min(\rho_\tau(\varphi_2, \sigma, t'), \inf\nolimits_{t'' \in [t,t']} \rho_\tau(\varphi_1, \sigma, t''))
\end{aligned}$$

The robust STL model checking problem is to determine if the robustness degree of an STL formula $\varphi$ is always greater than a given robustness threshold $\epsilon > 0$ for all possible trajectories of a hybrid automaton $H$.

**Definition 2 (Robust STL Model Checking).** *For a time bound $\tau > 0$, an STL formula $\varphi$ is satisfied at time $t \in [0, \tau)$ on a hybrid automaton $H$ with respect to a robustness threshold $\epsilon > 0$ iff for every trajectory $\sigma \in H$, $\rho_\tau(\varphi, \sigma, t) > \epsilon$.*

*A Running Example.* Consider two rooms interconnected by an open door. The temperature $x_i$ of each room, $i = 0, 1$, changes depending on the heater's mode $q_i \in \{\mathsf{On}, \mathsf{Off}\}$ and the temperature of the other room. The continuous dynamics of $x_i$ can be specified as the following ODEs, where $K_i, h_i, c_i, d_i$ are determined by the size of the room, the heater's power, and the size of the door [2,19,25]:

$$\dot{x}_i = \begin{cases} K_i(h_i - (c_i x_i - d_i x_{1-i})) & (\mathsf{On}) \\ -K_i(c_i x_i - d_i x_{1-i}) & (\mathsf{Off}), \end{cases}$$

[1] C.f., in the Boolean semantics of STL [29,31], the satisfaction of an STL formula is defined as a Boolean value (i.e., true or false).

[2] The Minkowski sum of intervals $I$ and $J$ is denoted by $I + J$. For a singular interval, $\{t\} + I$ is written as $t + I$. We write $\sup_{a \in A} g(a)$ and $\inf_{a \in A} g(a)$ to denote the least upper bound and the greatest lower bound of the set $\{g(a) \mid a \in A\}$, respectively.

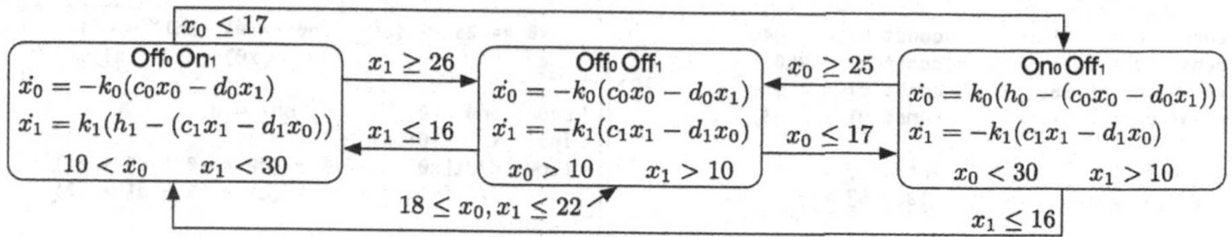


**Fig. 1.** A hybrid automaton for the networked thermostats.

Figure 1 shows a hybrid automaton of our networked thermostat controllers. Initially, both heaters are off and the temperatures are between 18 and 22. The jumps between modes then define a control logic to keep the temperatures within a certain range using only one heater. We are interested in robust model checking of nontrivial STL properties, such as:

$\phi_1$: $\Diamond_{[0,15]}(x_0 \geq 14 \; \mathbf{U}_{[0,\infty)} \; x_1 \leq 19)$: at some moment in the first 15 s, $x_1$ is less than or equal to 19; until then, $x_0$ is greater than or equal to 14.

$\phi_2$: $\Box_{[2,4]}(x_0 - x_1 \geq 4 \rightarrow \Diamond_{[3,10]} \, x_0 - x_1 \leq -3)$: between 2 and 4 s, whenever $x_0 - x_1 \geq 4$, $x_0 - x_1 \leq -3$ holds within 10 s after 3 s.

## 3 The STLMC Model Checker

The STLMC tool can model check STL properties of hybrid automata, given three parameters $\epsilon > 0$ (robustness threshold), $\tau > 0$ (time bound), and $N \in \mathbb{N}$ (discrete bound). STLMC provides an expressive input format to easily specify a wide range of hybrid automata. STLMC also provides a visualization command to give an intuitive description of counterexamples.

### 3.1 Input Format

The input format of STLMC, inspired by dReach [28], consists of five sections: variable declarations, mode definitions, initial conditions, state propositions, and STL properties. Mode and continuous variables define discrete and continuous states of hybrid automata. Mode definitions specify flow, jump, and invariant conditions. STL formulas can also include user-defined state propositions.

Figure 2 shows the input model of the hybrid automaton described in the running example above. Constants are introduced with the `const` keyword. Two mode variables `on0` and `on1` denote the heaters' modes. Continuous variables `x0` and `x1` are declared with domain intervals. There are three "mode blocks" that specify the three modes in Fig. 1 and their invariant, flow, and jump conditions.

In mode blocks, a `mode` component includes a set of logic formulas over mode variables. An `inv` component contains a set of logic formulas over continuous variables. A `flow` component can include ODEs over continuous variables. A `jump` component contains a set of jump conditions of the form *guard* => *reset*, where *guard* and *reset* are logic formulas over mode and continuous variables, and "primed" variables denote states after the jump has occurred.

```
const k0 = 0.015;          const k1 = 0.045;
const h0 = 100;            const h1 = 200;
const c0 = 0.98;           const c1 = 0.97;
const d0 = 0.01;           const d1 = 0.03;

int on0;                   int on1;
[10, 35] x0;               [10, 35] x1;

{ mode: on0 = 0;            on1 = 1;
  inv:  10 < x0; x1 < 30;
  flow: d/dt[x0] = - k0 * (c0 * x0 - d0 * x1);
        d/dt[x1] = k1 * (h1 - (c1 * x1 - d1 * x0));
  jump: x0 <= 17 => (and (on0' = 1) (on1' = 0)
                         (x0' = x0) (x1' = x1));
        x1 >= 26 => (and (on1' = 0) (on0' = on0)
                         (x0' = x0) (x1' = x1));
}
{ mode: on0 = 1;            on1 = 0;
  inv:  x0 < 30; x1 > 10;
  flow: d/dt[x0] = k0 * (h0 - (c0 * x0 - d0 * x1));
        d/dt[x1] = - k1 * (c1 * x1 - d1 * x0);
  jump: x1 <= 16 => (and (on0' = 0) (on1' = 1)
                         (x0' = x0) (x1' = x1));
    x0 >= 25 => (and (on0' = 0) (on1' = on1)
                     (x0' = x0) (x1' = x1));
}
{ mode: on0 = 0;          on1 = 0;
  inv:  x0 > 10; x1 > 10;
  flow: d/dt[x0] = - k0 * (c0 * x0 - d0 * x1);
        d/dt[x1] = - k1 * (c1 * x1 - d1 * x0);
  jump:
    x0 <= 17 => (and (on0' = 1) (on1' = on1)
                     (x0' = x0) (x1' = x1));
    x1 <= 16 => (and (on1' = 1) (on0' = on0)
                     (x0' = x0) (x1' = x1));
}

init: on0 = 0;  18 <= x0;  x0 <= 22;
      on1 = 0;  18 <= x1;  x1 <= 22;

proposition:
  [p1]: x0 - x1 >= 4;      [p2]: x0 - x1 <= -3;

goal:
  [f1]: <>[0,15](x0 >= 14 U[0, inf) x1 <= 19);
  [f2]: [][2, 4](p1 -> <>[3, 10] p2);
```

**Fig. 2.** An input model example

STL properties are declared in the `goal` section, and "named" propositions are declared in the `proposition` section. State propositions are arithmetic and relational expressions over mode and continuous variables. For example, in Fig. 2, the STL formula `f1` contains two state propositions $x_0 \geq 14$ and $x_1 \leq 19$, and the formula `f2` contains the user-defined propositions `p1` and `p2`.

### 3.2 Command Line Options

STLMC provides a command-line interface with various options in Table 1. The options `-two-step` and `-parallel` enable the two-step solving optimization in Sect. 4.3. STLMC supports three SMT solvers to choose from based on continuous dynamics: Z3 [12] and Yices2 [17] can deal with linear and polynomial dynamics (solutions of ODEs are linear functions or polynomials), and dReal [22] can approximately deal with ODE dynamics with Lipschitz-continuous ODEs.

A discrete bound $N$ limits the number of mode changes and *variable points* at which the truth value of some STL subformula changes. This is a distinctive parameter of STL model checking that cannot typically be derived from a time bound $\tau$ or the maximal number of jumps (say, $m$). E.g., for any positive natural number $n \in \mathbb{N}$, consider the function $y(t) = \sin(\frac{\pi}{\tau} \cdot n \cdot t)$; the state proposition $y > 0$ has $n - 1$ variable points even if there is no mode change ($m = 0$).[3]

For the input model in Fig. 2, the following command found a counterexample of the formula `f2` at bound 2 with respect to $\epsilon = 2$ in 15 s using dReal:

[3] This example also hints that STL model checking can be arbitrary complex even for one mode; $\tau$ and $m$ cannot limit such model checking computation, whereas $N$ can limit the computation involving *both* discrete and continuous behaviors.

**Table 1.** Some command line options for STLMC.

| Option | Explanation | Option | Explanation |
|---|---|---|---|
| `-bound`⟨$N$⟩ | a discrete bound | `-two-step` | enable two-step solving |
| `-time-bound`⟨$\tau$⟩ | a time bound | `-parallel` | parallel two-step solving |
| `-threshold`⟨$\epsilon$⟩ | a robustness threshold | `-visualize` | generate visualization data |
| `-solver`⟨Name⟩ | `z3`, `yices`, or `dreal` | `-goal` | goals to be checked |

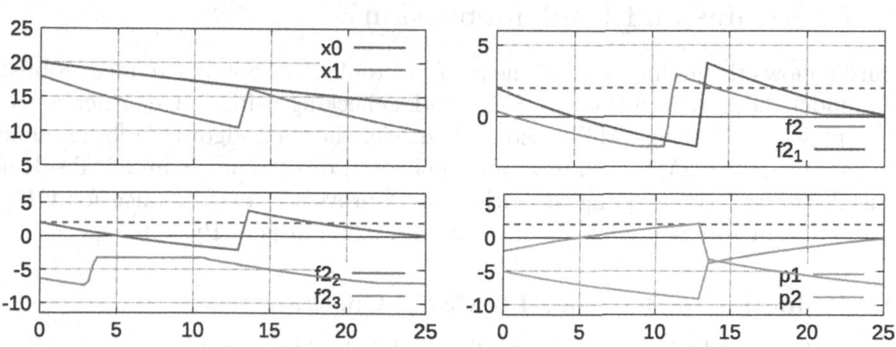


**Fig. 3.** Visualization of a counterexample (horizontal dotted lines denote $\epsilon = 2$).

```
$./stlmc ./therm.model -bound 5 -time-bound 25 -threshold 2 \
        -goal f2 -solver dreal -two-step -parallel -visualize
result: counterexample found at bound 2 (14.70277s)
```

Similarly, the following command verified the formula `f1` up to bounds $N = 5$ and $\tau = 25$ with respect to $\epsilon = 0.5$ in 819 s using dReal:

```
$./stlmc ./therm.model -bound 5 -time-bound 25 -threshold 0.5 \
        -goal f1 -solver dreal -two-step -parallel
result : True (818.73110s)
```

STLMC provides a command to visualize counterexamples for robust STL model checking. It can generate images representing counterexample trajectories and robustness degrees. Figure 3 shows the visualization graphs, showing the values of variables or robustness degrees over time, generated for the formula $\texttt{f2} = \square_{[2,4]}(x_0 - x_1 \geq 4 \rightarrow \lozenge_{[3,10]}(x_0 - x_1 \leq -3))$ with the subformulas:

$$\texttt{f2}_1 = x_0 - x_1 \geq 4 \rightarrow \lozenge_{[3,10]}(x_0 - x_1 \leq -3) \qquad \texttt{f2}_2 = \neg(x_0 - x_1 \geq 4)$$
$$\texttt{f2}_3 = \lozenge_{[3,10]}(x_0 - x_1 \leq -3) \qquad \texttt{p}_1 = x_0 - x_1 \geq 4 \qquad \texttt{p}_2 = x_0 - x_1 \leq -3$$

The robustness degree of `f2` is less than $\epsilon$ at time 0, since the robustness degree of $\texttt{f2}_1$ goes below $\epsilon$ in the interval $[2, 4]$, which is because both the degrees of $\texttt{f2}_2$ and $\texttt{f2}_3$ are less than $\epsilon$ in $[2, 4]$. The robustness degree of $\texttt{f2}_3$ is less than $\epsilon$ in $[2, 4]$, since the robustness degree of $\texttt{p}_2$ is less than $\epsilon$ in $[5, 14] = [2, 4] + [3, 10]$.

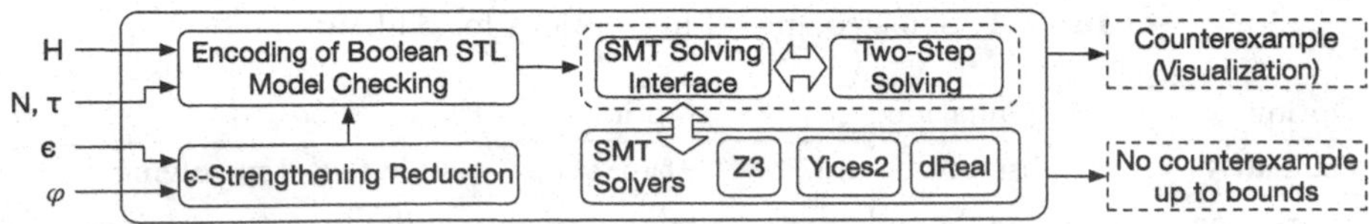


**Fig. 4.** The STLMC architecture

# 4 Algorithms and Implementation

Figure 4 shows the architecture of the STLMC tool. The tool first reduces robust STL model checking into Boolean STL model checking using $\epsilon$-strengthening. It then applies an existing SMT-based STL model checking algorithm [3,29]. The satisfiability of the SMT encoding can be checked directly using an SMT solver or using the two-step solving algorithm to improve the performance for ODE dynamics. Our tool is implemented in around 9,500 lines of Python code.

## 4.1 Reduction to Boolean STL Model Checking

As usual for model checking, robust STL model checking is equivalent to finding a counterexample. Specifically, an STL formula $\varphi$ is not satisfied on a hybrid automata $H$ with respect to a robustness threshold $\epsilon > 0$ iff there exists a counterexample for which the robustness degree of $\neg\varphi$ is greater than or equal to $-\epsilon$. (Formally, $\neg(\forall\sigma \in H.\ \rho_\tau(\varphi, \sigma, t) > \epsilon)$ iff $\exists\sigma \in H.\ \rho_\tau(\neg\varphi, \sigma, t) \geq -\epsilon$.)

Consider a state proposition $x < 0$. Its robust model checking is equivalent to finding a counterexample $\sigma \in H$ with $\rho_\tau(x \geq 0, \sigma, t) \geq -\epsilon$, which is equivalent to $\rho_\tau(x \geq -\epsilon, \sigma, t) \geq 0$. Observe that $x \geq -\epsilon$ is *weaker* than $x \geq 0$ by $\epsilon$. The notion of $\epsilon$-weakening is first introduced in [21] for first-order logic, and we extend the definitions of $\epsilon$-weakening and $\epsilon$-strengthening to STL as follows.

**Definition 3.** *The $\epsilon$-weakening $\varphi^{-\epsilon}$ and $\epsilon$-strengthening $\varphi^{+\epsilon}$ of $\varphi$ are defined as follows: $(p^{-\epsilon})(s) = p(s) - \epsilon$ and $(p^{+\epsilon})(s) = p(s) + \epsilon$ for a state $s$, and:*

$$(\neg\varphi)^{-\epsilon} \equiv \neg(\varphi^{+\epsilon}) \quad (\varphi_1 \wedge \varphi_2)^{-\epsilon} \equiv \varphi_1^{-\epsilon} \wedge \varphi_2^{-\epsilon} \quad (\varphi_1 \mathbf{U}_I \varphi_2)^{-\epsilon} \equiv \varphi_1^{-\epsilon} \mathbf{U}_I \varphi_2^{-\epsilon}$$
$$(\neg\varphi)^{+\epsilon} \equiv \neg(\varphi^{-\epsilon}) \quad (\varphi_1 \wedge \varphi_2)^{+\epsilon} \equiv \varphi_1^{+\epsilon} \wedge \varphi_2^{+\epsilon} \quad (\varphi_1 \mathbf{U}_I \varphi_2)^{+\epsilon} \equiv \varphi_1^{+\epsilon} \mathbf{U}_I \varphi_2^{+\epsilon}$$

Finding a counterexample of $\varphi$ for robust STL model checking can be reduced to finding a counterexample of the $\epsilon$-strengthening $\varphi^{+\epsilon}$ for Boolean STL model checking. The satisfaction of $\varphi$ by the Boolean STL semantics [29,31] is denoted by $\sigma, t \models_\tau \varphi$. We have the following theorem (see our report [42] for details).

**Theorem 1.** *(1) $\exists\sigma \in H.\ \sigma, t \models_\tau \neg(\varphi^{+\epsilon})$ implies $\exists\sigma \in H.\ \rho_\tau(\neg\varphi, \sigma, t) \geq -\epsilon$, and (2) $\forall\sigma \in H.\ \sigma, t \not\models_\tau \neg(\varphi^{+\epsilon})$ implies $\forall\sigma \in H.\ \rho_\tau(\varphi, \sigma, t) \geq \epsilon$.*

As a consequence, a counterexample of $\varphi^{+\epsilon}$ for Boolean STL model checking is also a counterexample of $\varphi$ for robust STL model checking. If there is no counterexample of $\varphi^{+\epsilon}$ for Boolean STL model checking, then $\varphi$ is satisfied on $H$ with respect to any robustness threshold $0 < \epsilon' < \epsilon$. It is worth noting that $\varphi$ may not be satisfied on $H$ with respect to $\epsilon$ itself.

### 4.2 Boolean STL Model Checking Algorithm

For Boolean STL model checking, there exist *refutationally complete* bounded model checking algorithms [3,29] with two bound parameters: $\tau$ for the time domain, and $N$ for the number of mode changes and variable points. A time point $t$ is a variable point if a truth value of $\varphi$'s subformula changes at $t$. The algorithms build an SMT encoding $\Psi^{N,\tau}_{H,\neg\varphi}$ of Boolean STL model checking:

**Theorem 2.** *[3,29] $\Psi^{N,\tau}_{H,\neg\varphi}$ is satisfiable iff there is a counterexample trajectory $\sigma \in H$, with at most $N$ variable points and mode changes, such that $\sigma, t \not\models_\tau \varphi$.*

For hybrid automata with polynomial continuous dynamics, the satisfiability of the encoding $\Psi$ can be precisely determined using standard SMT solvers, including Z3 [12] and Yices2 [17]. For ODE dynamics, the satisfiability of $\Psi$ is undecidable in general, but there exist specialized solvers, such as dReal [22] and iSAT-ODE [18], that can approximately determine the satisfiability.

To support various SMT solvers, the implementation of STLMC utilizes a generic wrapper interface based on the SMT-LIB standard [5]. Therefore, if it follows SMT-LIB, a new SMT solver can be easily integrated with our tool. Moreover, STLMC can also detect the most suitable solver for a given input model; e.g., if the model has ODE dynamics, then the tool chooses dReal.

The encoding $\Psi$ includes universal quantification over time, e.g., because of invariant conditions. Several SMT solvers (including Z3 and Yice2) support these $\exists\forall$-conditions but at high computational costs [27]. For polynomial dynamics, we implement the encoding method [10] to simplify $\exists\forall$-conditions to quantifier-free formulas. For ODE dynamics, dReal natively supports $\exists\forall$-conditions [23].

### 4.3 Two-Step Solving Algorithm

To reduce the complexity of ODE dynamics, we propose a two-step solving algorithm in Algorithm 1, inspired by the lazy SMT solving approach [38]:

1. We obtain the *discrete abstraction* of the encoding $\Psi$ by substituting the flow and invariant conditions with Boolean variables. We then enumerate a satisfying *scenario* $\pi$, a conjunction of literals, where $\pi$ implies $\Psi$.
2. For each scenario $\pi$, we check the satisfiability of its *discrete refinement* with the flow and invariant conditions using dReal. If any refinement is satisfiable, we obtain a counterexample; otherwise, there is no counterexample.

We also implement a simple method to avoid redundant scenarios by minimizing a scenario. A scenario $\pi = l_1 \wedge \cdots \wedge l_m$ is minimal if $(\neg l_i \wedge \bigwedge_{j \neq i} l_j) \rightarrow \Psi$— one literal in $\pi$ is false— is not valid. To minimize a scenario $\pi$, we use a dual propagation approach [33]. Since $\pi$ implies $\Psi$, $\pi \wedge \neg\Psi$ is unsatisfiable. We compute the unsatisfiable core of $\pi \wedge \neg\Psi$ using Z3 to extract a minimal scenario from $\pi$.

We parallelize the two-step solving algorithm by running the satisfiability checking of refinements in parallel. If any of such refinements is satisfied and a counterexample is found, then all other jobs are terminated. If all refinements, checking in parallel, are unsatisfiable, then there is no counterexample. As shown in Sect. 5, it greatly improves the performance for the ODE cases in practice.

**Algorithm 1:** Two-Step SMT Solving Algorithm

**Input**: Hybrid automaton $H$, STL formula $\varphi$, threshold $\epsilon$, bounds $\tau$ and $N$

**for** $k = 1$ **to** $N$ **do**
  $\overline{\Psi} \leftarrow$ abstraction of the encoding $\Psi^{k,\tau}_{H,\neg(\varphi^{+\epsilon})}$ without *flow* and *inv*;
  **while** `checkSat(`$\overline{\Psi}$`)` *is* Sat **do**
    $\pi \leftarrow$ a minimal satisfying scenario;
    $\hat{\pi} \leftarrow$ the refinement of $\pi$ with *flow* and *inv*;
    **if** `checkSat(`$\hat{\pi}$`)` *is* Sat **then**
      **return** `counterexample(`result.*satAssignment*`)`;
    $\overline{\Psi} \leftarrow \overline{\Psi} \wedge \neg\pi$;
**return** True;

## 5 Experimental Evaluation

We evaluate the effectiveness of the STLMC model checker using a number of hybrid system benchmarks and nontrivial STL properties.[4] We use the following models, adapted from existing benchmarks [2,6,19,20,25,34]: load management for two batteries (Bat), two networked water tank systems (Wat), autonomous driving of two cars (Car), a railroad gate (Rail), two networked thermostats (Thm), a spacecraft rendezvous (Space), navigation of a vehicle (Nav), and a filtered oscillator (Oscil). We use a modified model with either linear, polynomial, or ODE dynamics to analyze the effect of different continuous dynamics. For each model, we use three STL formulas with nested temporal operators. More details on the benchmark models can be found in the longer report [42].

We measure the SMT encoding size and execution time for robust STL model checking, up to discrete bound $N = 20$ for linear models, $N = 10$ for polynomial models, and $N = 5$ for ODEs models, with a timeout of 60 min. We use different time bounds $\tau$ and robustness thresholds $\epsilon$ for different models, since $\tau$ and $\epsilon$ depend on each model. As an underlying SMT solver, we use Yices for linear and polynomial models, and dReal for ODE models with a precision $\delta = 0.001$. We run both direct SMT solving (`1-step`) and two-step SMT solving (`2-step`). We use 25 cores for parallelizing the two-phase solving algorithm. We have run all experiments on Intel Xeon 2.8 GHz with 256 GB memory.

The experimental results are summarized in Table 2, where $|\Psi|$ denotes the size of the SMT encoding $\Psi$ (in thousands) as the number of connectives in $\Psi$. For the model checking results, $\top$ indicates that the tool found no counterexample up to bound $N$, and $\bot$ indicates that the tool found a counterexample at bound $k \leq N$. For the algorithms (Alg.), we write one of the results with a better

[4] For reachability properties, STLMC has a similar performance to other SMT-based tools, because STLMC uses the same SMT encoding. Indeed, our previous work [29] shows that the underlying algorithm used for STLMC has comparable performance to other tools for reachability properties. Nonetheless, our companion report [42] also includes some experimental results comparing STLMC with four reachability analysis tools (HyComp [9], SpaceEx [20], Flow* [8], and dReach [28]).

**Table 2.** Robust Bounded Model Checking of STL (Time in seconds)

| Dyn. | Model | $\tau$ | STL formula | $\epsilon$ | $\|\Psi\|$ | Time | Result | k | Alg. | $\#\pi$ |
|---|---|---|---|---|---|---|---|---|---|---|
| Linear (N = 20) | Car | 40 | $(\Diamond_{[3,5]}\, p_1)\, \mathbf{U}_{[2,10]}\, p_2$ | 0.1 | 2.5 | 7.6 | $\bot$ | 5 | 1-step | - |
| | | | $\Box_{[3,10]}(\Diamond_{[5,15]}\, p_1)$ | 0.5 | 10.8 | 559.2 | $\top$ | - | 1-step | - |
| | | | $(\Box_{[2,5]}\, p_1)\, \mathbf{R}_{[0,10)}\, p_2$ | 1.0 | 2.5 | 7.8 | $\bot$ | 5 | 1-step | - |
| | Wat | 20 | $\Box_{[1,3]}(p_1\, \mathbf{R}_{[1,10]}\, p_2)$ | 2.5 | 18.8 | 25.1 | $\top$ | - | 1-step | - |
| | | | $(\Diamond_{[1,10)}\, p_1)\, \mathbf{U}_{[2,5]}\, p_2$ | 0.1 | 1.9 | 4.3 | $\bot$ | 4 | 1-step | - |
| | | | $\Diamond_{[4,10]}(p_1 \to \Box_{[2,5]}\, p_2)$ | 0.01 | 11.2 | 16.3 | $\top$ | - | 1-step | - |
| | Bat | 30 | $\Diamond_{[4,10]}(p_1 \to \Box_{[4,10]}\, p_2)$ | 0.1 | 12.9 | 119.5 | $\top$ | - | 1-step | - |
| | | | $(\Diamond_{[1,5]}\, p_1)\, \mathbf{R}_{[5,20]}\, p_2$ | 3.5 | 2.8 | 6.0 | $\bot$ | 5 | 1-step | - |
| | | | $\Box_{[4,14]}(p_1 \to \Diamond_{[0,10]}\, p_2)$ | 0.1 | 3.8 | 44.6 | $\bot$ | 8 | 1-step | - |
| Poly (N = 10) | Thm | 10 | $(\Box_{[2,10]}\, p_1)\, \mathbf{U}_{[1,4]}\, p_2$ | 0.5 | 2.0 | 4.4 | $\bot$ | 4 | 1-step | - |
| | | | $\Diamond_{[0,5]}(p_1 \to \Box_{[2,5)}\, p_2)$ | 0.1 | 3.9 | 5.0 | $\top$ | - | 1-step | - |
| | | | $\Diamond_{[0,10]}(p_1\, \mathbf{R}_{[2,4]}\, p_2)$ | 1.0 | 5.7 | 6.3 | $\top$ | - | 1-step | - |
| | Car | 15 | $\Box_{[0,4]}(p_1 \to \Diamond_{[2,5]}\, p_2)$ | 0.5 | 2.2 | 5.5 | $\bot$ | 5 | 1-step | - |
| | | | $(\Diamond_{[0,4]}\, p_1)\, \mathbf{U}_{[0,5]}\, p_2$ | 2.0 | 1.7 | 4.7 | $\bot$ | 3 | 1-step | - |
| | | | $\Diamond_{[0,3]}(p_1\, \mathbf{U}_{[0,5]}\, p_2)$ | 0.1 | 7.3 | 7.7 | $\top$ | - | 1-step | - |
| | Rail | 20 | $\Diamond_{[0,5]}(p_1\, \mathbf{U}_{[1,8]}\, p_2)$ | 1.0 | 2.3 | 3.0 | $\bot$ | 5 | 1-step | - |
| | | | $\Diamond_{[0,4]}(p_1 \to \Box_{[2,10]}\, p_2)$ | 5.0 | 3.8 | 3.8 | $\top$ | - | 1-step | - |
| | | | $(\Box_{[0,5)}\, p_1)\, \mathbf{U}_{[2,10]}\, p_2$ | 4.0 | 1.9 | 2.7 | $\bot$ | 4 | 1-step | - |
| ODE (N = 5) | Thm | 25 | $\Diamond_{[0,15]}(p_1\, \mathbf{U}_{[0,\infty)}\, p_2)$ | 0.5 | 1.2 | 818.7 | $\top$ | - | 2-step | 3,580 |
| | | | $\Box_{[2,4]}(p_1 \to \Diamond_{[3,10]}\, p_2)$ | 2.0 | 0.7 | 14.7 | $\bot$ | 2 | 2-step | 91 |
| | | | $\Box_{[0,10]}(p_1\, \mathbf{R}_{[0,\infty)}\, p_2)$ | 2.0 | 1.2 | 161.7 | $\bot$ | 4 | 2-step | 279 |
| | Space | 5 | $\Box_{[0,2]}(p_1 \to \Diamond_{[0,3]}\, p_2)$ | 1.5 | 0.8 | 278.3 | $\bot$ | 2 | 2-step | 79 |
| | | | $\Diamond_{[2,3]}(\Box_{[1,2]}\, p_1)$ | 0.1 | 1.1 | 37.0 | $\bot$ | 3 | 2-step | 138 |
| | | | $\Diamond_{[0,4]}(p_1\, \mathbf{U}_{[0,\infty]}\, p_2)$ | 0.5 | 1.3 | 716.8 | $\top$ | - | 2-step | 2,681 |
| | Oscil | 8 | $\Diamond_{[0,3]}(p_1\, \mathbf{R}_{[0,\infty)}\, p_2)$ | 0.1 | 1.5 | 108.9 | $\top$ | - | 2-step | 326 |
| | | | $\Diamond_{[2,5]}(\Box_{[0,3]}\, p_1)$ | 1.0 | 1.2 | 192.8 | $\bot$ | 3 | 2-step | 601 |
| | | | $(\Box_{[1,3]}\, p_1)\, \mathbf{R}_{[2,5]}\, p_2$ | 0.1 | 1.8 | 112.1 | $\bot$ | 3 | 2-step | 258 |
| | Nav | 10 | $\Diamond_{[2,4]}(p_1 \to \Box_{[1,5]}\, p_2)$ | 3.0 | 1.2 | 399.3 | $\bot$ | 3 | 2-step | 1,388 |
| | | | $\Diamond_{[2,4]}(\Box_{[3,6]}\, p_1)$ | 2.0 | 1.1 | 332.2 | $\bot$ | 3 | 2-step | 1,213 |
| | | | $\Diamond_{[1,5]}(p_1\, \mathbf{R}_{[0,\infty)}\, p_2)$ | 1.0 | 1.4 | 749.6 | $\top$ | - | 2-step | 2,411 |

performance. For the `2-step` case, we also write the number of minimal scenarios generated ($\#\pi$). Actually, two-step SMT solving timed out for all linear and polynomial models, and direct SMT solving timed out for all ODE models.

As shown in Table 2, our tool can perform robust model checking of nontrivial STL formulas for hybrid systems with different continuous dynamics. The cases of ODE models generally take longer than the cases of linear and polynomial models, because of the high computational costs for ODE solving. Nevertheless, our parallelized two-step SMT solving method works well and all model checking analyses are finished before the timeout. In contrast, for linear and polynomial models with a larger discrete bound $N \geq 10$, direct SMT solving is usually effective but the two-step SMT solving method is not. There are too many scenarios, and the scenario generation does not terminate within 60 min. Therefore, the two algorithms implemented in our tool are complementary.

## 6 Related Work

There exist many tools for falsifying STL properties of hybrid systems, including Breach [14], S-talrio [1], and TLTk [11]. STL falsification techniques are based on STL monitoring [13,32], and often use stochastic optimization techniques, such as Ant-Colony Optimization [1], Monte-Carlo tree search [43], deep reinforcement learning [41], and so on. These techniques are often quite useful for finding counterexamples in practice, but, as mentioned, cannot be used to verify STL properties of hybrid systems.

There exist many tools for analyzing reachability properties of hybrid systems based on reachable-set computation, including C2E2 [16], Flow* [8], Hylaa [4], and SpaceEx [20]. They can be used to guarantee the correctness of invariant properties of the form $p \rightarrow \Box_I q$, but cannot verify general STL properties. In contrast, STLMC uses a refutation-complete bounded STL model checking algorithm to verify general STL properties, including complex ones.

Our tool is also related to SMT-based tools for analyzing hybrid systems, including dReach [28], HyComp [9], and HybridSAL [39]. These techniques also focus on analyzing invariant properties of hybrid systems, but some SMT-based tools, such as HyComp, can verify LTL properties of hybrid systems. Unlike STLMC, they cannot deal with general STL properties of hybrid systems.

## 7 Concluding Remarks

We have presented the STLMC tool for robust bounded model checking of STL properties for hybrid systems. STLMC can verify that, up to given bounds, the robustness degree of an STL formula $\varphi$ is always greater than a given robustness threshold for all possible behaviors of a hybrid system. STLMC also provides a convenient user interface with an intuitive counterexample visualization.

Our tool leverages the reduction from robust model checking to Boolean model checking, and utilizes the refutation-complete SMT-based Boolean STL model checking algorithm to guarantee correctness up to given bounds and find subtle counterexamples. STLMC can deal with hybrid systems with (nonlinear) ODEs using dReal. We have shown using various hybrid system benchmarks that STLMC can effectively analyze nontrivial STL properties.

Future work includes extending our tool with other hybrid system analysis methods, such as reachable-set computation, besides SMT-based approaches.

**Acknowledgments.** This work was supported in part by the National Research Foundation of Korea (NRF) grants funded by the Korea government (MSIT) (No. 2021R1A5A1021944 and No. 2019R1C1C1002386).

## References

1. Annpureddy, Y., Liu, C., Fainekos, G., Sankaranarayanan, S.: S-TaLiRo: a tool for temporal logic falsification for hybrid systems. In: Abdulla, P.A., Leino, K.R.M. (eds.) TACAS 2011. LNCS, vol. 6605, pp. 254–257. Springer, Heidelberg (2011). https://doi.org/10.1007/978-3-642-19835-9_21

2. Bae, K., Gao, S.: Modular SMT-based analysis of nonlinear hybrid systems. In: Proceedings FMCAD, pp. 180–187. IEEE (2017)
3. Bae, K., Lee, J.: Bounded model checking of signal temporal logic properties using syntactic separation. Proc. ACM Program. Lang. **3**(POPL), 1–30 (2019). 51
4. Bak, S., Duggirala, P.S.: HYLAA: a tool for computing simulation-equivalent reachability for linear systems. In: Proceedings of the HSCC, pp. 173–178. ACM (2017)
5. Barrett, C., Fontaine, P., Tinelli, C.: The SMT-LIB Standard: Version 2.5. Technical report, Department of Computer Science, University of Iowa (2015). www.SMT-LIB.org
6. Chan, N., Mitra, S.: Verifying safety of an autonomous spacecraft rendezvous mission. In: Proceedings of the ARCH. EPiC Series in Computing, vol. 48. EasyChair (2017)
7. Chen, G., Liu, M., Kong, Z.: Temporal-logic-based semantic fault diagnosis with time-series data from industrial Internet of Things. IEEE Trans. Industr. Electron. **68**(5), 4393–4403 (2020)
8. Chen, X., Ábrahám, E., Sankaranarayanan, S.: Flow*: an analyzer for non-linear hybrid systems. In: Sharygina, N., Veith, H. (eds.) CAV 2013. LNCS, vol. 8044, pp. 258–263. Springer, Heidelberg (2013). https://doi.org/10.1007/978-3-642-39799-8_18
9. Cimatti, A., Griggio, A., Mover, S., Tonetta, S.: HyComp: an SMT-based model checker for hybrid systems. In: Baier, C., Tinelli, C. (eds.) TACAS 2015. LNCS, vol. 9035, pp. 52–67. Springer, Heidelberg (2015). https://doi.org/10.1007/978-3-662-46681-0_4
10. Cimatti, A., Mover, S., Tonetta, S.: A quantifier-free SMT encoding of non-linear hybrid automata. In: Proceedings of the FMCAD, pp. 187–195. IEEE (2012)
11. Cralley, J., Spantidi, O., Hoxha, B., Fainekos, G.: TLTk: a toolbox for parallel robustness computation of temporal logic specifications. In: Deshmukh, J., Ničković, D. (eds.) RV 2020. LNCS, vol. 12399, pp. 404–416. Springer, Cham (2020). https://doi.org/10.1007/978-3-030-60508-7_22
12. de Moura, L., Bjørner, N.: Z3: an efficient SMT solver. In: Ramakrishnan, C.R., Rehof, J. (eds.) TACAS 2008. LNCS, vol. 4963, pp. 337–340. Springer, Heidelberg (2008). https://doi.org/10.1007/978-3-540-78800-3_24
13. Deshmukh, J.V., Donzé, A., Ghosh, S., Jin, X., Juniwal, G., Seshia, S.A.: Robust online monitoring of signal temporal logic. Formal Methods Syst. Des. **51**(1), 5–30 (2017). https://doi.org/10.1007/s10703-017-0286-7
14. Donzé, A.: Breach, a toolbox for verification and parameter synthesis of hybrid systems. In: Touili, T., Cook, B., Jackson, P. (eds.) CAV 2010. LNCS, vol. 6174, pp. 167–170. Springer, Heidelberg (2010). https://doi.org/10.1007/978-3-642-14295-6_17
15. Donzé, A., Ferrère, T., Maler, O.: Efficient robust monitoring for STL. In: Sharygina, N., Veith, H. (eds.) CAV 2013. LNCS, vol. 8044, pp. 264–279. Springer, Heidelberg (2013). https://doi.org/10.1007/978-3-642-39799-8_19
16. Duggirala, P.S., Mitra, S., Viswanathan, M., Potok, M.: C2E2: a verification tool for stateflow models. In: Baier, C., Tinelli, C. (eds.) TACAS 2015. LNCS, vol. 9035, pp. 68–82. Springer, Heidelberg (2015). https://doi.org/10.1007/978-3-662-46681-0_5
17. Dutertre, B.: Yices 2.2. In: Biere, A., Bloem, R. (eds.) CAV 2014. LNCS, vol. 8559, pp. 737–744. Springer, Cham (2014). https://doi.org/10.1007/978-3-319-08867-9_49

18. Eggers, A., Ramdani, N., Nedialkov, N.S., Fränzle, M.: Improving the SAT modulo ODE approach to hybrid systems analysis by combining different enclosure methods. Softw. Syst. Model. **14**(1), 121–148 (2015). https://doi.org/10.1007/s10270-012-0295-3
19. Fehnker, A., Ivančić, F.: Benchmarks for hybrid systems verification. In: Alur, R., Pappas, G.J. (eds.) HSCC 2004. LNCS, vol. 2993, pp. 326–341. Springer, Heidelberg (2004). https://doi.org/10.1007/978-3-540-24743-2_22
20. Frehse, G., Le Guernic, C., Donzé, A., Cotton, S., Ray, R., Lebeltel, O., Ripado, R., Girard, A., Dang, T., Maler, O.: SpaceEx: scalable verification of hybrid systems. In: Gopalakrishnan, G., Qadeer, S. (eds.) CAV 2011. LNCS, vol. 6806, pp. 379–395. Springer, Heidelberg (2011). https://doi.org/10.1007/978-3-642-22110-1_30
21. Gao, S., Avigad, J., Clarke, E.M.: Delta-decidability over the reals. In: 2012 27th Annual IEEE Symposium on Logic in Computer Science, pp. 305–314. IEEE (2012)
22. Gao, S., Kong, S., Clarke, E.M.: dReal: an SMT solver for nonlinear theories over the reals. In: Bonacina, M.P. (ed.) CADE 2013. LNCS (LNAI), vol. 7898, pp. 208–214. Springer, Heidelberg (2013). https://doi.org/10.1007/978-3-642-38574-2_14
23. Gao, S., Kong, S., Clarke, E.M.: Satisfiability modulo ODEs. In: Proceedings of the FMCAD, pp. 105–112. IEEE (2013)
24. Goldman, R.P., Bryce, D., Pelican, M.J.S., Musliner, D.J., Bae, K.: A hybrid architecture for correct-by-construction hybrid planning and control. In: Rayadurgam, S., Tkachuk, O. (eds.) NFM 2016. LNCS, vol. 9690, pp. 388–394. Springer, Cham (2016). https://doi.org/10.1007/978-3-319-40648-0_29
25. Henzinger, T.: The theory of hybrid automata. In: Inan, M.K., Kurshan, R.P. (eds.) Verification of Digital and Hybrid Systems. NATO ASI Series, vol. 170, pp. 265–292. Springer, Heidelberg (2000). https://doi.org/10.1007/978-3-642-59615-5_13
26. Jin, X., Deshmukh, J.V., Kapinski, J., Ueda, K., Butts, K.: Powertrain control verification benchmark. In: Proceedings of the HSCC. ACM (2014)
27. Jovanović, D., de Moura, L.: Solving non-linear arithmetic. In: Gramlich, B., Miller, D., Sattler, U. (eds.) IJCAR 2012. LNCS (LNAI), vol. 7364, pp. 339–354. Springer, Heidelberg (2012). https://doi.org/10.1007/978-3-642-31365-3_27
28. Kong, S., Gao, S., Chen, W., Clarke, E.: dReach: $\delta$-reachability analysis for hybrid systems. In: Baier, C., Tinelli, C. (eds.) TACAS 2015. LNCS, vol. 9035, pp. 200–205. Springer, Heidelberg (2015). https://doi.org/10.1007/978-3-662-46681-0_15
29. Lee, J., Yu, G., Bae, K.: Efficient SMT-based model checking for signal temporal logic. In: Proceedings of the ASE, pp. 343–354. IEEE (2021)
30. Ma, M., Bartocci, E., Lifland, E., Stankovic, J., Feng, L.: SaSTL: spatial aggregation signal temporal logic for runtime monitoring in smart cities. In: Proceedings of the ICCPS, pp. 51–62. IEEE (2020)
31. Maler, O., Nickovic, D.: Monitoring temporal properties of continuous signals. In: Lakhnech, Y., Yovine, S. (eds.) FORMATS/FTRTFT -2004. LNCS, vol. 3253, pp. 152–166. Springer, Heidelberg (2004). https://doi.org/10.1007/978-3-540-30206-3_12
32. Ničković, D., Lebeltel, O., Maler, O., Ferrère, T., Ulus, D.: AMT 2.0: qualitative and quantitative trace analysis with extended signal temporal logic. In: Beyer, D., Huisman, M. (eds.) TACAS 2018. LNCS, vol. 10806, pp. 303–319. Springer, Cham (2018). https://doi.org/10.1007/978-3-319-89963-3_18
33. Niemetz, A., Preiner, M., Biere, A.: Turbo-charging lemmas on demand with don't care reasoning. In: Proceedings of the FMCAD, pp. 179–186. IEEE (2014)

34. Raisch, J., Klein, E., Meder, C., Itigin, A., O'Young, S.: Approximating automata and discrete control for continuous systems — two examples from process control. In: Antsaklis, P., Lemmon, M., Kohn, W., Nerode, A., Sastry, S. (eds.) HS 1997. LNCS, vol. 1567, pp. 279–303. Springer, Heidelberg (1999). https://doi.org/10.1007/3-540-49163-5_16
35. Roehm, H., Oehlerking, J., Heinz, T., Althoff, M.: STL model checking of continuous and hybrid systems. In: Artho, C., Legay, A., Peled, D. (eds.) ATVA 2016. LNCS, vol. 9938, pp. 412–427. Springer, Cham (2016). https://doi.org/10.1007/978-3-319-46520-3_26
36. Roohi, N., Kaur, R., Weimer, J., Sokolsky, O., Lee, I.: Parameter invariant monitoring for signal temporal logic. In: Proceedings of the HSCC, pp. 187–196. ACM (2018)
37. Sankaranarayanan, S., Fainekos, G.: Falsification of temporal properties of hybrid systems using the cross-entropy method. In: Proceedings of the HSCC, pp. 125–134 (2012)
38. Sebastiani, R.: Lazy satisfiability modulo theories. J. Satisfiability Boolean Model. Comput. **3**(3–4), 141–224 (2007)
39. Tiwari, A.: HybridSAL relational abstracter. In: Madhusudan, P., Seshia, S.A. (eds.) CAV 2012. LNCS, vol. 7358, pp. 725–731. Springer, Heidelberg (2012). https://doi.org/10.1007/978-3-642-31424-7_56
40. Xu, Z., Belta, C., Julius, A.: Temporal logic inference with prior information: an application to robot arm movements. IFAC-PapersOnLine **48**(27), 141–146 (2015)
41. Yamagata, Y., Liu, S., Akazaki, T., Duan, Y., Hao, J.: Falsification of cyber-physical systems using deep reinforcement learning. IEEE Trans. Softw. Eng. **47**(12), 2823–2840 (2020)
42. Yu, G., Lee, J., Bae, K.: Robust STL model checking of hybrid systems using SMT (2022). https://stlmc.github.io/assets/files/stlmc-techrep.pdf
43. Zhang, Z., Lyu, D., Arcaini, P., Ma, L., Hasuo, I., Zhao, J.: Effective hybrid system falsification using Monte Carlo tree search guided by QB-robustness. In: Silva, A., Leino, K.R.M. (eds.) CAV 2021. LNCS, vol. 12759, pp. 595–618. Springer, Cham (2021). https://doi.org/10.1007/978-3-030-81685-8_29

# UCLID5: Multi-modal Formal Modeling, Verification, and Synthesis

Elizabeth Polgreen[1,2(✉)], Kevin Cheang[1(✉)], Pranav Gaddamadugu[1], Adwait Godbole[1], Kevin Laeufer[1], Shaokai Lin[1], Yatin A. Manerkar[3], Federico Mora[1], and Sanjit A. Seshia[1]

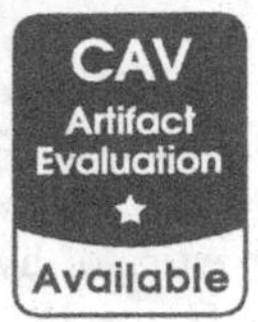


[1] UC Berkeley, Berkeley, USA
elizabeth.polgreen@ed.ac.uk
[2] University of Edinburgh, Edinburgh, UK
[3] University of Michigan, Ann Arbor, USA

**Abstract.** UCLID5 is a tool for the multi-modal formal modeling, verification, and synthesis of systems. It enables one to tackle verification problems for heterogeneous systems such as combinations of hardware and software, or those that have multiple, varied specifications, or systems that require hybrid modes of modeling. A novel aspect of UCLID5 is an emphasis on the use of syntax-guided and inductive synthesis to automate steps in modeling and verification. This tool paper presents new developments in the UCLID5 tool including new language features, integration with new techniques for syntax-guided synthesis and satisfiability solving, support for hyperproperties and combinations of axiomatic and operational modeling, demonstrations on new problem classes, and a robust implementation.

## 1 Overview

Tools for formal modeling and verification are typically specialized for particular domains and for particular methods. For instance, software verification tools like Boogie [4] focuses on modeling sequential software and Floyd-Hoare style reasoning, while hardware verifiers like ABC [5] are specialized for sequential circuits and SAT-based equivalence and model checking. Specialization makes sense when the problems fit well within a homogeneous problem domain with specific verification needs. However, there is an emerging class of problems, such as in security and cyber-physical systems (CPS), where the systems under verification are heterogeneous, or the types of specifications to be verified are varied, or there is not a single type of model that is effective for verification. An example of such a problem is the verification of trusted computing platforms [37] that involve hardware and software components working in tandem, and where the properties to be checked include invariants, refinement checks, and hyperproperties. There is a need for automated formal methods and tools to handle this class of problems.

UCLID5 is a system for *multi-modal* formal modeling, verification, and synthesis that addresses the above need. UCLID5 is multi-modal in three important ways. First, it permits different modes of modeling, using axiomatic and


S. Shoham and Y. Vizel (Eds.): CAV 2022, LNCS 13371, pp. 538–551, 2022.
https://doi.org/10.1007/978-3-031-13185-1_27

operational semantics, or as combinations of concurrent transition systems and procedural code. This enables modeling systems with multiple characteristics. Second, it offers a varied suite of specification modes, including first-order formulas in a combination of logical theories, temporal logic, inline assertions, pre- and post-conditions, system invariants, and hyperproperties. Third, it supports the first two capabilities with a varied suite of verification techniques, including Floyd-Hoare style proofs, k-induction and bounded model checking (BMC), verifying hyperproperties, or using syntax-guided and inductive synthesis to provide more automation in tedious steps of verification, or to automate the modeling process (as proposed in [34]).

The UCLID5 framework was first proposed in 2018 [35], itself a major evolution of the much older UCLID system [6], one of the first satisfiability modulo theories (SMT) based modeling and verification tools. Since that publication [35], which laid out the vision for the tool and described a preliminary implementation, the utility of the tool has been demonstrated on several problem classes (e.g., [7,8,25]), such as for verifying security across the hardware-software interface. The syntax has been extended and state-of-the-art methods for syntax-guided synthesis (SyGuS) have also been integrated into the tool [28], including new capabilities for satisfiability and synthesis modulo oracles [32]. This tool paper presents an overview of the latest version of UCLID5, highlighting novel multi-modal aspects of the tool, as well as the new features supported since 2018 [35]. The paper is structured as follows: in Sect. 2 we give an overview of the UCLID5 tool; in Sect. 3 we detail different multi-modal aspects of the tool, as well as high-lighting new features; and in Sect. 4 we present a case study using UCLID5 to verify a Trusted Abstract Platform. We cover related work in Sect. 5. The new features we highlight are:

1. Fully integrated support for synthesis across all verification modes
2. Support for modeling with external oracles, via satisfiability and synthesis modulo oracles [32]
3. New language features to support combining axiomatic and operational modeling
4. Direct support for hyperproperties
5. Front-end translations from Chisel/FIRRTL to UCLID5, and from RISC-V binaries to UCLID5, referenced in Sect. 6.
6. New case studies: covering models for distributed CPS in Lingua Franca [23], and encodings of $\mu$hb specifications and verification of a Trusted Abstract Platform described in Sects. 3.2 and 4 and in the corresponding artifact [31].

## 2 Overview of UCLID5

In verification mode, UCLID5 reduces the question of whether a model satisfies a given specification to a set of constraints that can be solved by an off-the-shelf SMT solver. In synthesis mode, UCLID5 reduces the problem of finding an interpretation for an uninterpreted function such that the specification is satisfied into a SyGuS problem that can be solved by an off-the-shelf SyGuS solver. In order to do so, UCLID5 performs the following main tasks, as shown in Fig. 1:

*Front End:* UCLID5 takes models written in the UCLID5 language as input. The command-line front-end allows user configuration, including specifying the external SMT-solver/SyGuS-solver to be used, as well as enabling certain utilities such as automatically converting uninterpreted functions to arrays. The parser builds an abstract syntax tree from the model.

*AST Passes:* UCLID5 performs a number of transformations and checks on the abstract syntax tree, including type-checking and inlining of procedures. This intermediate representation supports limited control flow such as if-statements and switch-cases, but loops are not permitted in procedural code and are removed via unrolling (bounded for-loops) or replacement with user-provided invariants (while loops). However, unbounded control flow can be handled by representation as transition systems (where each module consists of a transition system with an initial and a next block, each represented as a separate AST).

*Symbolic Simulator:* The symbolic simulator performs a simulation of the transition system in the model, according to the verification command provided, and produces a set of assertions. For instance, if bounded model checking is used, UCLID5 will symbolically execute the main module a bounded number of times. UCLID5 encodes the violation of each independent verification condition as a separate assertion tree.

*Synth-Lib Interface:* UCLID5 supports both synthesis and verification. The Synth-Lib interface constructs either a verification or a synthesis problem from the assertions generated by the symbolic simulator. The verification problems are passed to the SMT-LIB interface, which converts each assertion in UCLID5's intermediate representation to an assertion in SMT-LIB. Similarly, the synthesis problems are passed to the SyGuS-IF interface, which converts each assertion to an assertion in SyGuS-IF. The verification and synthesis problems are then passed to the appropriate provided external solver and the result is reported back to the user.

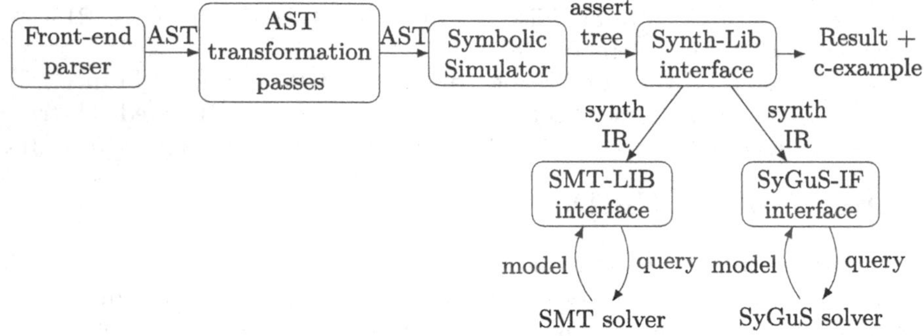


**Fig. 1.** Architecture of UCLID5

**Basic UCLID5 Models.** A simple UCLID5 model that computes the Fibonacci sequence is shown in Fig. 2. UCLID5 models are contained within modules which comprise of 3 parts: a system model represented using combinations of sequential, concurrent, operational and axiomatic modeling, as described in Sects. 3.2; a system specification described in Sect. 3.1; and a proof script that specifies the verification tasks UCLID5 should perform to prove that the system satisfies its specification, using a variety of supported verification and synthesis techniques described in Sect. 3.1.

# 3 Multi-modal Language Features

## 3.1 Multi-modal Verification and Synthesis

**Specification.** UCLID5 supports a variety of different types of specifications. The standard properties supported include inline assertions and assumptions in sequential code, pre-conditions and post-conditions for procedures, and global axioms and invariants (both as propositional predicates, and temporal invariants in Linear Temporal Logic (LTL)).

The latest version of UCLID5 further provides direct support for hyperinvariants and hyperaxioms (for $k$-safety). This new support for direct hyperproperties comprises of two new language constructs: hyperaxiom and hyperinvariant. The former places an assumption on the behavior of the module, if $n$ instances of the module were instantiated, and the latter is an invariant over $n$ instances of the module, which is verified via the usual verification methods. A variable $x$ from the $n^{th}$ instance of the module is reasoned about in the predicate using $x.n$, and the number of modules instantiated is determined by the maximum $n$ in both the invariant and the axiom. For example, `hyperinvariant[2] det_xy: y.1 == y.2` asserts that a 2-safety hyperproperty holds.

**Verification.** To verify these specifications, we implement multiple classic techniques. As a result, once a model is written in UCLID5, the user can deploy a combination of verification techniques, depending on the properties targeted. UCLID5 supports a range of verification techniques including: Bounded Model Checking (for LTL, hyperinvariants and assertion-based properties); induction and k-induction for assertion-based invariants and hyperinvariants; and verification of pre-and post-conditions on procedures and hyperinvariants.

As an exemplar of the utility of multi-modal verification, consider the hyperproperty based models verified by Sahai et al. [33]. These models use both procedure verification and induction to verify k-trace properties.

**Synthesis.** The latest version of UCLID5 integrates program synthesis fully across all the verification modes previously described. Specifically, users are able to declare and use *synthesis functions* anywhere in their models, and UCLID5 will seek to automatically synthesize function bodies for these functions such that the user-selected verification task will pass. In this section, we give an illustrative example of synthesis in UCLID5, we provide the necessary background on program synthesis, and then we formulate the existing verification techniques inside of UCLID5 for synthesis.

```
1 module main {
2
3   // Part 1: System Description.
4   var a, b : integer;
5   init {
6     a, b = 0, 1;
7   }
8   next {
9     a', b' = b, a + b;
10  }
11
12  // Part 2: System Specification.
13  invariant a_le_b: a <= b;
14
15  // Part 3: (NEW) Synthesis Integration
16  synthesis function
17    h(x : integer, y : integer): boolean;
18  invariant hole: h(a, b);
19
20  // Part 4: Proof Script.
21  control {
22    induction;
23    check;
24    print_results;
25  }
26 }
```

**Fig. 2.** UCLID5 Fibonacci model. Part 3 shows the new synthesis syntax, and how to find an auxiliary invariant.

Consider the UCLID5 model in Fig. 2. The user wants to prove by induction that the invariant `a_le_b` at line 13 always holds. Unfortunately, the proof fails because the invariant is not inductive. Without synthesis, the user would need to manually strengthen the invariant until it became inductive. However, the user can ask UCLID5 to automatically do this for them. Figure 2 demonstrates this on lines 16, 17 and 18. Specifically, the user specifies a function to synthesize called `h` at lines 16 and 17, and then uses `h` at line 18 to strengthen the existing set of invariants. Given this input, UCLID5, using e.g. CVC5 [3] as a syntax-guided synthesis engine, will automatically generate the function `h(x, y) = x >= 0`, which completes the inductive proof.

In this example, the function to synthesize represents an inductive invariant. However, functions to synthesize are treated exactly like any interpreted function in UCLID5: the user could have called `h` anywhere in the code. Furthermore, this example uses induction and a global invariant, however, the user could also have used a linear temporal logic (LTL) specification and bounded model checking (BMC). In this sense, our integration is fully flexible and generic. Furthermore, the integration scheme allows us to enable synthesis for any verification procedure in UCLID5, by simply letting users declare and use functions to synthesize and relying on existing SyGuS-IF solvers to carry out the automated reasoning.

### 3.2 Multi-modal Modeling

**Combining Concurrent and Sequential Modeling.** A unique feature of the UCLID5 modeling language is the ability to easily combine sequential and concurrent modeling. This allows a user to easily express models representing sequential programs, including standard control flow, procedure calls, sequential updates, etc., in a sequential model, and to combine these components within a system designed for concurrent modeling based on transition systems. The sequential program modeling is inspired by systems such as Boogie [4] and allows the user to port Boogie models to UCLID5. The concurrent modeling is done by defining transition systems with a set of initial states and a transition relation. Within UCLID5, each module is a transition system. A main module can be defined that triggers when each child module is stepped. For an example of this combination of sequential and concurrent modeling, we refer the reader to the CPU example presented in the original UCLID5 paper [35], which uses concurrent modules to instantiate multiple CPU modules, modeled as transition systems, with sequential code to model the code that executes instructions, and to the case study in Sect. 4.

**Reasoning with External Oracles.** New in the latest version, UCLID5 supports the modeling with *oracle function symbols* [32] in both verification and synthesis. Namely, a user can include "oracle functions" in any UCLID5 model, where an oracle function is a function without a provided implementation, but which is associated to a user-provided external binary that can be queried by the solver. We note that oracle functions (and functions in general) can only be first-order within the UCLID5 modeling language, i.e., functions cannot receive functions as arguments.

This support is useful in cases where some components of the system are difficult or impossible to model, but could be compiled into a binary that the solver can query; or where the model of the system would be challenging for an SMT solver to reason about (for instance, highly non-linear arithmetic), and it may be better to outsource that reasoning to an external binary.

UCLID5 supports oracle function symbols in verification by interfacing with a solver that supports Satisfiability Modulo Theories and Oracles (SMTO) [32], and in synthesis by interfacing with a solver that supports Synthesis Modulo Oracles (SyMO) [32].

Oracle function symbols are declared like functions, with the keyword `oracle`, and an annotation pointing to the binary implementation. For instance `oracle function [isprime] Prime (x: integer): boolean` would indicate to the solver that the binary `isprime` takes an integer as input and returns a boolean. This is translated into the corresponding syntax in SMTO or SyMO, as detailed in [30].

An exemplar of such reasoning in a synthesis file is available in the artifact [31], where we use UCLID5 to synthesize a safe and stabilizing controller for a Linear Time Invariant system, similar to Abate et al. [1].

**Combining Operational and Axiomatic Modeling.** UCLID5 can model a system being verified using an operational (transition system-based) approach, as Fig. 2 shows. However, UCLID5 also supports modeling a system in an *axiomatic* manner, whereby the system is specified as a set of properties over traces. Any execution satisfying the properties is allowed by the system, and any execution violating the properties is disallowed. Axiomatic modeling can provide order-of-magnitude performance improvements over operational models in certain cases [2], and is often well suited to systems with large amounts of non-determinism. We provide an example of fully axiomatic modeling in the artifact [31].

However, uniquely, UCLID5 allows users to specify multi-modal systems using a combination of operational and axiomatic modeling. In such models, some constraints on the execution are enforced by the initial state and transition relation (operational modeling), while others are enforced through axiomatic invariants (axiomatic modeling). This allows the user to choose the mode of modeling most appropriate to each constraint. For example, the ILA-MCM work [39] combined operational ILA (Instruction Level Abstraction) models to describe the functional behavior of processing elements with memory consistency model (MCM) orderings that are more naturally specified axiomatically [2]. (MCM orderings constrain shared-memory communication and synchronization between multiple processing elements.) The combined model, used for System-on-Chip verification, worked by sharing variables (called "facets") between both the models. UCLID5 makes it much easier to perform such a combination.

Figure 3 depicts parts of a UCLID5 model of microarchitectural execution that uses both operational and axiomatic modeling (similar to that from the ILA-MCM work), based on the $\mu$spec specifications of COATCheck [24]. In this model, the steps of instruction execution are driven by the `init` and `next` blocks, i.e., the operational component of the model. Multiple instructions can step at any time (`curTime` denotes the current time in the execution), but they can only take one step per timestep. Meanwhile, axioms such as the `fifoFetch` axiom enforce ordering *between* the execution of multiple instructions. The `fifoFetch` axiom specifically enforces that instructions in program order on the same core must be fetched in program order. (Enforcing this order is tricky using operational modeling alone). The transition rules and axioms operate over the same data structures, ensuring that executions of the final model abide by both sets of constraints.

$\mu$spec models routinely function by grounding quantifiers over a finite set of instructions. Thus, to fully support $\mu$spec axiomatic modeling, we introduce two new language features —namely, *groups* and *finite quantifiers*. A group is a set of objects of a single type. A group can have any number of elements, but it must be finite, and the group is immutable once created. For instance, the group `testInstrs` in Fig. 3 consists of four instructions. Finite quantifiers, meanwhile, are used to quantify over group elements.

This example showcases UCLID5's highly flexible multi-modal modeling capability. Models can be purely operational, purely axiomatic, or a combination of the two. Note that axiomatic modeling relies on the new language features `finite_forall` and `groups`. For a further example of axiomatic and operational multi-modal modeling, we refer the reader to the case study checking reachability properties in reactive embedded systems described in the artifact [31].

```
module main {
    <type declarations>
    var i1, i2, i3, i4 : microop_t;
    <set i1-i4 to be the instructions of a test, like mp>
    group testInstrs : microop_t = {i1, i2, i3, i4};

    //Vars to decide which instrs to step and when.
    var next1, next2, next3, next4 : boolean;
    var curTime : integer;

    init {
        i1.Fetch.nExists = false; i1.Execute.nExists = false;
        <...>
    }
    //Axiom enforcing that instructions are fetched in order.
    axiom fifoFetch :
        finite_forall (i : microop_t) in testInstrs ::
        finite_forall (j : microop_t) in testInstrs ::
        (ProgramOrder(i, j) && NodeExists(j.Fetch)) ==>
            EdgeExists(i.Fetch, j.Fetch);

    procedure stepInst(index : integer)
      returns (instr_next : microop_t)
    {
        //Steps instr@index, unless it has completed.
        case
            (index == 1) : {
                instr_next = i1;
                if(!instr_next.Fetch.nExists) {
                    instr_next.Fetch.nExists = true;
                    instr_next.Fetch.nTime = curTime;
                } else {
                <...>
        esac
    }
    next {
        //Increment the current timestamp and
        //nondeterministically step instructions.
        curTime' = curTime + 1;
        havoc next1, next2, next3, next4;

        if (next1) { call (i1') = stepInst(1); }
        if (next2) { call (i2') = stepInst(2); }
        if (next3) { call (i3') = stepInst(3); }
        if (next4) { call (i4') = stepInst(4); }
    }
}
```

**Fig. 3.** UCLID5 model that incorporates both operational modeling (through the `init` and `next` blocks) and axiomatic modeling (through the `axiom` keyword).

## 4 Case Study: TAP Model

The final case study we wish to describe verifies a model of a trusted execution environment. Trusted execution environments [10,11,17,20] often provide a software interface for users to execute enclaves, using hardware primitives to enforce memory isolation. In contrast to software which requires reasoning about sequential code, hardware modeling uses a paradigm that permits concurrent updates to a system. Moreover, verifying hyperproperties such as integrity requires reasoning about multiple instances of a system which most existing tools are not well suited for. In this section, we present the UCLID5 port[1] of the Trusted

[1] https://github.com/uclid-org/trusted-abstract-platform/.

Abstract Platform (TAP) which was originally[2] written in Boogie and introduced by Subramanyan et al. [37] to model an abstract idealized trusted enclave platform. We demonstrate how UCLID5's multi-model support alleviates the difficulties in modeling the TAP model in existing tools.

```
module tap {
  // State variable declarations
  var tap_enclave_metadata_valid: tap_enclave_metadata_valid_t;
  var tap_enclave_metadata_addr_map: tap_enclave_metadata_addr_map_t;
  ...
  // Enclave operations
  procedure launch(eid: tap_enclave_id_t, ...) { ... }
  ...
  init { ... } // initialize TAP
  next { // step the system
    case
      (tap_current_mode == mode_untrusted) : {
        call (...) = AdversarialStep(...);
      }
      (tap_current_mode == mode_enclave) : {
        call (...) = EnclaveStep(...);
      }
    esac
  }
}

module integrity_proof {
  // Create two instances of the TAP model
  instance tap_1: tap(...);
  instance tap_2: tap(...);
  // Example invariant: Memory that is mapped are equal between the two traces
  invariant equal_mem: (forall (pa : wap_addr_t) ::
    e_excl_map[pa] ==> (tap_1.mem[pa] == tap_2.mem[pa]));
  ...
  init { ... } // initialize proof
  next { // step the system
    next(tap_1); next(tap_2);
  }
  control {
    v = induction;
    check;
  }
}
```

**Fig. 4.** UCLID5 transition system-styled model of TAP and the integrity proof.

**Modeling the TAP and Proving Integrity.** The UCLID5 model of TAP in Fig. 4 demonstrates some of UCLID5's key features: the enclave operations of the TAP model (e.g. `launch`) are implemented as procedures, and a transition relation of the TAP is defined using a next block that either executes an untrusted adversary operation or the trusted enclave, which in turn executes one of the enclave operations atomically. Proving the integrity hyperproperty on the TAP thus only requires two instantiations of the TAP model, specifying the integrity invariants, and defining a next block which steps each of the TAP instances as shown in the `integrity_proof` module. The integrity proof in UCLID5 uses inductive model checking.

[2] https://github.com/0tcb/TAP.

**Results and Statistics of the TAP Modules.** Table 1 shows the approximate size of the TAP model in both Boogie and UCLID5. #pr, #fn, #an, and #ln refer to the number of procedures, functions, annotations, and lines of code respectively. Annotations are the number of loop invariants, assertions, assumptions, pre- and post-conditions that were manually specified. The verification time includes compilation and solving.

**Table 1.** Boogie vs UCLID5 Model Results

| Model/Proof | Size | | | | Verif. |
|---|---|---|---|---|---|
| | #pr | #fn | #an | #ln | Time (s) |
| **Boogie** | | | | | |
| `TAP` | 22 | 25 | 254 | 1840 | 51 |
| `Integrity` | 14 | 11 | 71 | 835 | 346 |
| **UCLID5** | | | | | |
| `TAP` | 53 | 25 | 87 | 2765 | 49 |
| `Integrity` | 2 | 0 | 54 | 293 | 30 |

While the #ln for the TAP model in UCLID5 is higher than that of the model in Boogie due to stylistic differences, the crucial difference is in the integrity proof. The original model in Boogie implements the TAP model and integrity proof as procedures, where the transition of the TAP model is implemented as a while loop. However, this lack of support for modeling transition systems introduces duplicate state variables in a hyperproperty such as integrity, requires context switching and additional procedures for the new variables, which makes the model difficult to maintain and self composition unwieldy. In UCLID5, the proof is no longer implemented as a procedure, but rather, we create instances of the TAP model. We also note that the number of annotations is less in UCLID5 compared to Boogie for the TAP model and proof. Additionally, this model lends itself for more direct verification of hyperproperties.

The verification results are run on a machine with 2.6GHz 6-Core Intel Core i7 and 16GB of RAM running OSX. As shown on the right of Table 1, the verification runtimes between the Boogie and UCLID5 models and proofs are comparable.

## 5 Related Work

There are a multitude of verification and synthesis tools related to UCLID5. In this brief review, we highlight prominent examples and contrast them with UCLID5 along the key language features described in Sect. 3.

UCLID5 allows users to combine sequential and concurrent modeling (see Sect. 3.2). Most existing tools primarily support either sequential, e.g. [4,21,38], or concurrent computation modeling, e.g. [5,9,14,26,27]. Although users of these systems can often overcome the tool's modeling focus by manually including support for different computation paradigms, for example, Dafny can be used to model concurrent systems [22], this is not always straightforward, and limited support for different paradigms can manifest as limitations in downstream applications. For example, the Serval [29] framework, based on Rosette, cannot reason about concurrent code. UCLID5, to the best of our knowledge, is the only verification tool natively supporting modeling with external oracles.

UCLID5 supports different kinds of specifications and verification procedures (see Sect. 3.1). Most existing tools [5,9,21] do not support multi-modal verification at all. Tools that do offer multi-modal verification do not offer the same range of options as UCLID5. For example, [26] does not support linear temporal logic, and [13,27] does not support hyperproperty verification.

Finally, UCLID5 supports a generic integration with program synthesis (see Sect. 3.1), and so related work includes a number of synthesis engines. The SKETCH system [36] synthesizes expressions to fill holes in programs, and has subsequently been applied to program repair [16,19]. UCLID5 is more flexible than this work, and allows users to declare unknown functions even in the verification annotations, as well as supporting multiple verification algorithms and types of properties. Rosette [38] provides support for synthesis and verification, but, unlike UCLID5, the synthesis is limited to bounded specifications of sequential programs and external synthesis engines are not supported. Synthesis algorithms have been used to assist in verification tasks, such as safety and termination of loops [12], and generating invariants [15,40], but none of this work to-date integrates program synthesis fully into an existing verification tool. Before the new synthesis integration, UCLID5 supported synthesis of inductive invariants. The key insight of this work is to generalize the synthesis support, and to unify all synthesis tasks by re-using the verification back-end.

## 6 Software Project

The source code for UCLID5 is made publicly available under a BSD-license[3]. UCLID5 is maintained by the UCLID5 team[4], and we welcome patches from the community. Additional front-ends are available for UCLID5, including translators from Firrtl [18][5], and RISC-V binaries[6] to UCLID5 models. An artifact incuding the code for the case studies in this paper is available [31].

**Acknowledgments.** The UCLID5 project is grateful for the significant contributions by Pramod Subramanyan, one of the original creators of the tool. This work was supported in part by NSF grant 1837132, the DARPA grant FA8750-20-C-0156 (LOGiCS), by the Qualcomm Innovation Fellowship, and by Amazon and Intel.

## References

1. Abate, A., et al.: Automated formal synthesis of provably safe digital controllers for continuous plants. Acta Informatica **57**(1-2), 223–244 (2020)
2. Alglave, J., Maranget, L., Tautschnig, M.: Herding cats: modelling, simulation, testing, and data-mining for weak memory. ACM Trans. Programm. Lang. Syst. (TOPLAS) 36, July 2014

[3] https://github.com/uclid-org/uclid.
[4] https://github.com/uclid-org/uclid/blob/master/CONTRIBUTORS.md.
[5] https://github.com/uclid-org/chiselucl.
[6] https://github.com/uclid-org/riscverifier.

3. Barbosa, H., et al.: CVC5: a versatile and industrial-strength SMT solver. In: TACAS (1), vol. 13243, pp. 415–442. Springer (2022)
4. Barnett, M., Chang, B.-Y.E., DeLine, R., Jacobs, B., Leino, K.R.M.: Boogie: a modular reusable verifier for object-oriented programs. In: de Boer, F.S., Bonsangue, M.M., Graf, S., de Roever, W.-P. (eds.) FMCO 2005. LNCS, vol. 4111, pp. 364–387. Springer, Heidelberg (2006). https://doi.org/10.1007/11804192_17
5. Brayton, R., Mishchenko, A.: ABC: an academic industrial-strength verification tool. In: Touili, T., Cook, B., Jackson, P. (eds.) CAV 2010. LNCS, vol. 6174, pp. 24–40. Springer, Heidelberg (2010). https://doi.org/10.1007/978-3-642-14295-6_5
6. Bryant, R.E., Lahiri, S.K., Seshia, S.A.: Modeling and verifying systems using a logic of counter arithmetic with lambda expressions and uninterpreted functions. In: Brinksma, E., Larsen, K.G. (eds.) CAV 2002. LNCS, vol. 2404, pp. 78–92. Springer, Heidelberg (2002). https://doi.org/10.1007/3-540-45657-0_7
7. Cheang, K., Rasmussen, C., Lee, D., Kohlbrenner, D., Asanović, K., Seshia, S.A.: Verifying RISC-V physical memory protection (2020)
8. Cheang, K., Rasmussen, C., Seshia, S.A., Subramanyan, P.: A formal approach to secure speculation. In: Proceedings of the Computer Security Foundations Symposium (CSF), June 2019
9. Cimatti, A., Roveri, M., Sheridan, D.: Bounded verification of past LTL. In: Hu, A.J., Martin, A.K. (eds.) FMCAD 2004. LNCS, vol. 3312, pp. 245–259. Springer, Heidelberg (2004). https://doi.org/10.1007/978-3-540-30494-4_18
10. Costan, V., Devadas, S.: Intel SGX explained. IACR Cryptol. ePrint Arch. **2016**, 86 (2016)
11. Costan, V., Lebedev, I., Devadas, S.: Sanctum: minimal hardware extensions for strong software isolation. In: 25th USENIX Security Symposium (USENIX Security 16), pp. 857–874. USENIX Association, Austin, TX (2016)
12. David, C., Kroening, D., Lewis, M.: Using program synthesis for program analysis. In: Davis, M., Fehnker, A., McIver, A., Voronkov, A. (eds.) LPAR 2015. LNCS, vol. 9450, pp. 483–498. Springer, Heidelberg (2015). https://doi.org/10.1007/978-3-662-48899-7_34
13. Dill, D.L.: The Murphi verification system. In: CAV (1996)
14. Dutertre, B., Jovanović, D., Navas, J.A.: Verification of fault-tolerant protocols with Sally. In: Dutle, A., Muñoz, C., Narkawicz, A. (eds.) NASA Formal Methods, pp. 113–120. Springer, Cham (2018)
15. Fedyukovich, G., Bodík, R.: Accelerating syntax-guided invariant synthesis. In: Beyer, D., Huisman, M. (eds.) TACAS 2018. LNCS, vol. 10805, pp. 251–269. Springer, Cham (2018). https://doi.org/10.1007/978-3-319-89960-2_14
16. Hua, J., Zhang, M., Wang, K., Khurshid, S.: Towards practical program repair with on-demand candidate generation. In: ICSE, pp. 12–23. ACM (2018)
17. Intel: Intel trust domain extensions (2020). https://www.intel.com/content/www/us/en/developer/articles/technical/intel-trust-domain-extensions.html
18. Izraelevitz, A., et al.: Reusability is FIRRTL ground: Hardware construction languages, compiler frameworks, and transformations. In: 2017 IEEE/ACM International Conference on Computer-Aided Design (ICCAD), pp. 209–216, November 2017
19. Le, X.D., Chu, D., Lo, D., Goues, C.L., Visser, W.: S3: syntax- and semantic-guided repair synthesis via programming by examples. In: ESEC/SIGSOFT FSE, pp. 593–604. ACM (2017)
20. Lee, D., Kohlbrenner, D., Shinde, S., Asanovic, K., Song, D.: Keystone: an open framework for architecting trusted execution environments. In: EuroSys, pp. 38:1–38:16. ACM (2020)

21. Leino, K.R.M.: Dafny: an automatic program verifier for functional correctness. In: Clarke, E.M., Voronkov, A. (eds.) LPAR 2010. LNCS (LNAI), vol. 6355, pp. 348–370. Springer, Heidelberg (2010). https://doi.org/10.1007/978-3-642-17511-4_20
22. Leino, K.R.M.: Modeling concurrency in Dafny. In: Bowen, J.P., Liu, Z., Zhang, Z. (eds.) SETSS 2017. LNCS, vol. 11174, pp. 115–142. Springer, Cham (2018). https://doi.org/10.1007/978-3-030-02928-9_4
23. Lohstroh, M., Menard, C., Bateni, S., Lee, E.A.: Toward a lingua franca for deterministic concurrent systems. ACM Trans. Embed. Comput. Syst. **20**(4), 36:1–36:27 (2021)
24. Lustig, D., Sethi, G., Martonosi, M., Bhattacharjee, A.: Coatcheck: verifying memory ordering at the hardware-os interface. In: ASPLOS, pp. 233–247. ACM (2016)
25. Magyar, A., Biancolin, D., Koenig, J., Seshia, S.A., Bachrach, J., Asanovic, K.: Golden Gate: Bridging the resource-efficiency gap between ASICs and FPGA prototypes. In: Proceedings of the International Conference on Computer-Aided Design (ICCAD), pp. 1–8, November 2019
26. Mann, M., et al.: Pono: a flexible and extensible SMT-based model checker. In: Silva, A., Leino, K.R.M. (eds.) CAV 2021. LNCS, vol. 12760, pp. 461–474. Springer, Cham (2021). https://doi.org/10.1007/978-3-030-81688-9_22
27. McMillan, K.L., Padon, O.: Ivy: a multi-modal verification tool for distributed algorithms. In: Lahiri, S.K., Wang, C. (eds.) CAV 2020. LNCS, vol. 12225, pp. 190–202. Springer, Cham (2020). https://doi.org/10.1007/978-3-030-53291-8_12
28. Mora, F., Cheang, K., Polgreen, E., Seshia, S.A.: Synthesis in UCLID5. CoRR abs/2007.06760 (2020)
29. Nelson, L., Bornholt, J., Gu, R., Baumann, A., Torlak, E., Wang, X.: Scaling symbolic evaluation for automated verification of systems code with serval. In: SOSP, pp. 225–242. ACM (2019)
30. Padhi, S., Polgreen, E., Raghothaman, M., Reynolds, A., Udupa, A.: The SyGuS Language Standard Version 2.1 (2014). https://sygus.org/assets/pdf/SyGuS-IF.pdf
31. Polgreen, E., et al.: UCLID5 artifact. https://doi.org/10.5281/zenodo.6557711. https://doi.org/10.5281/zenodo.6557711
32. Polgreen, E., Reynolds, A., Seshia, S.A.: Satisfiability and synthesis modulo oracles. In: Finkbeiner, B., Wies, T. (eds.) VMCAI 2022. LNCS, vol. 13182, pp. 263–284. Springer, Cham (2022). https://doi.org/10.1007/978-3-030-94583-1_13
33. Sahai, S., Subramanyan, P., Sinha, R.: Verification of quantitative hyperproperties using trace enumeration relations. In: Lahiri, S.K., Wang, C. (eds.) CAV 2020. LNCS, vol. 12224, pp. 201–224. Springer, Cham (2020). https://doi.org/10.1007/978-3-030-53288-8_11
34. Seshia, S.A.: Combining induction, deduction, and structure for verification and synthesis. Proc. IEEE **103**(11), 2036–2051 (2015)
35. Seshia, S.A., Subramanyan, P.: UCLID5: integrating modeling, verification, synthesis and learning. In: MEMOCODE, pp. 1–10. IEEE (2018)
36. Solar-Lezama, A.: The sketching approach to program synthesis. In: Hu, Z. (ed.) APLAS 2009. LNCS, vol. 5904, pp. 4–13. Springer, Heidelberg (2009). https://doi.org/10.1007/978-3-642-10672-9_3
37. Subramanyan, P., Sinha, R., Lebedev, I.A., Devadas, S., Seshia, S.A.: A formal foundation for secure remote execution of enclaves. In: CCS, pp. 2435–2450. ACM (2017)
38. Torlak, E., Bodík, R.: Growing solver-aided languages with rosette. In: Onward!, pp. 135–152. ACM (2013)

39. Zhang, H., Trippel, C., Manerkar, Y.A., Gupta, A., Martonosi, M., Malik, S.: ILA-MCM: integrating memory consistency models with instruction-level abstractions for heterogeneous system-on-chip verification. In: FMCAD, pp. 1–10 (2018)
40. Zhang, H., Yang, W., Fedyukovich, G., Gupta, A., Malik, S.: Synthesizing environment invariants for modular hardware verification. In: Beyer, D., Zufferey, D. (eds.) VMCAI 2020. LNCS, vol. 11990, pp. 202–225. Springer, Cham (2020). https://doi.org/10.1007/978-3-030-39322-9_10

# Author Index

Printed in the United States
by Baker & Taylor Publisher Services

Printed in the United States
by Baker & Taylor Publisher Services